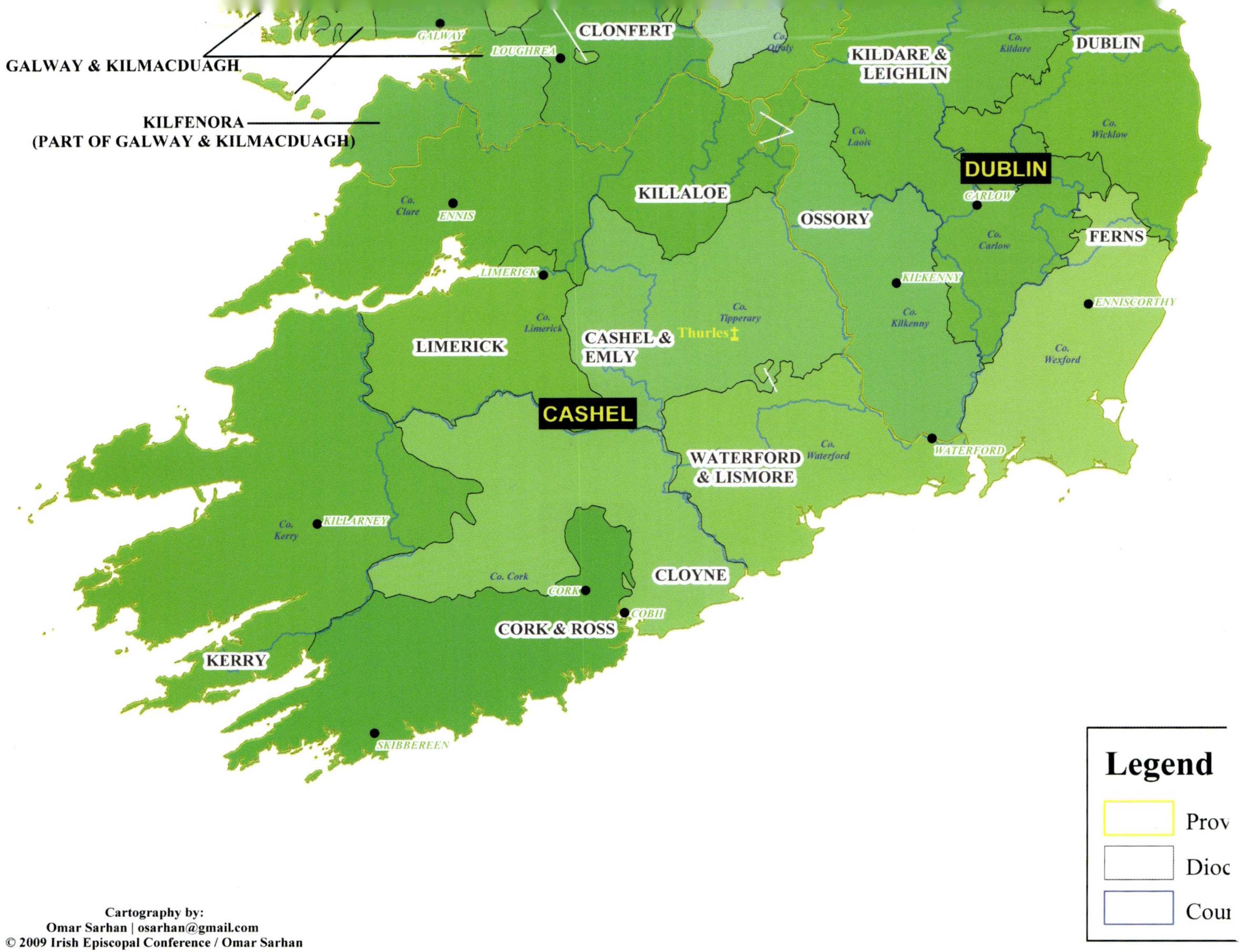

Cartography by:
Omar Sarhan | osarhan@gmail.com

IRISH CATHOLIC DIRECTORY 2022

FRANCIS
BISHOP OF ROME
Vicar of Jesus Christ

Successor of the Prince of the Apostles, Supreme Pontiff of the Universal Church, Primate of Italy, Archbishop and Metropolitan of the Roman Province, Sovereign of the State of the Vatican City.

Servant of the Servants of God, Jorge Mario Bergoglio, born in Buenos Aires, Argentina, on 17 December 1936; ordained priest on 13 December 1969. From 1973 to 1979 he was Argentina's Provincial superior of the Society of Jesus. He was ordained Auxiliary Bishop of Buenos Aires on 27 June 1992; became Archbishop of Buenos Aires in 1998 and created cardinal on 21 February 2001. He was elected pope on 13 March 2013 and inaugurated on 19 March 2013.

IRISH CATHOLIC DIRECTORY 2022

PUBLISHED BY AUTHORITY
FOR THE HIERARCHY OF IRELAND

THE OFFICIAL DIRECTORY OF THE IRISH CATHOLIC CHURCH

This publication has been supported by the generous sponsorship of

VERITAS

Published for the Hierarchy by
Veritas Publications
7–8 Lower Abbey Street
Dublin 1
Ireland
publications@veritas.ie
www.veritas.ie

Copyright © Irish Catholic Bishops' Conference, 2022

The publishers are not responsible for any
errors or omissions.

ISBN 978 1 80097 018 2

Cover design: Colette Dower, Veritas Publications
Design & Typesetting: Colette Dower, Veritas Publications
Printed in Ireland by W & G Baird, Antrim

*Veritas books are printed on paper made from the wood pulp of managed forests.
For every tree felled, at least one tree is planted, thereby renewing natural resources.*

PREFACE

This is the thirty-second edition of the *Irish Catholic Directory*. Information for this edition was collected between August 2021 and November 2021. In general, all information comes from the organisation or community concerned.

Veritas has made every effort to ensure the accuracy and completeness of the information in the *Directory*. However, this information can only be as good as that supplied to us.

We would like to express our gratitude to all the bishops, diocesan secretaries, priests, brothers, sisters and lay people who have over the years supplied information, answered queries, chased details and checked proofs.

We are also indebted to the advertisers and sponsors, without whose support this publication would not be possible.

Finally, it may be appropriate to remind readers that the *Directory* is simply an orderly listing of personnel in the Church and related organisations. Our task is to make this listing as easy to use as possible. The *Directory* is not a statement of Church policy, nor an expression of precedence, and should not be taken as such.

CONTENTS

2021 Review of Pastoral Activities of Irish Episcopal Conference	8
The Roman Curia	13
Apostolic Nunciature	15
The Irish Episcopate	**16**
The Hierarchy	16
The Irish Episcopal Conference	17
Archdioceses and Dioceses of Ireland	**24**
Archdioceses	
Armagh	25
Dublin	39
Cashel and Emly	81
Tuam	91
Dioceses	
Achonry	98
Ardagh and Clonmacnois	102
Clogher	108
Clonfert	114
Cloyne	118
Cork and Ross	129
Derry	138
Down and Connor	149
Dromore	163
Elphin	168
Ferns	174
Galway, Kilmacduagh and Kilfenora	180
Kerry	187
Kildare and Leighlin	199
Killala	207
Killaloe	211
Kilmore	219
Limerick	229
Meath	238
Ossory	247
Raphoe	254
Waterford and Lismore	259
Personal Prelatures	**266**
Religious Orders and Congregations	**267**
Male Religious	267
Communities of Religious Brothers	286
Communities of Religious Sisters	287
Institutes	293
Catholic Education	**294**

Seminaries and Houses of Study	298	Index of Advertisers		330
Retreat and Pastoral Centres	300	Alphabetical List of Clergy in Ireland		331
Permanent Deacons	303			
Marriage Tribunals	304	Parish Index		418
Chaplains	305	General Index		429
The Defence Forces Chaplaincy Service	305			
Britain	306			
Europe	306			
Australia	306			
United States of America	307			
General Information	308			
Obituary List	308			
Ordinations	311			
Irish Council of Churches	312			
Ireland's Cardinals	316			
Statistics	317			
Catholic Archbishops and Bishops of Britain	320			
Forms of Ecclesiastical Address	323			
The Roman Pontiffs	324			
Church of St Columbanus, Ballivor	328			

ALL IRELAND STD DIALLING

All STD numbers in this Directory are listed with both the number and the local area code.

Callers from the Irish Republic to Northern Ireland simply **need to dial 048 followed by the 8-digit local number.**

2021 REVIEW OF PASTORAL ACTIVITIES OF IRISH EPISCOPAL CONFERENCE
(for more information see www.catholicbishops.ie)

JANUARY

On 1 January, Church leaders from across the island published a joint New Year's Message. They highlighted that 2020 served to remind us of our 'interconnectedness', and shared their hopes for a brighter and safer future in 2021.

In his World Day of Peace homily, Archbishop Diarmuid Martin spoke of the ongoing global struggle against Covid-19. He said, 'The defeat of the virus depends on all of us. Every man, woman and child is called to respond with responsibility.'

On 9 January, Bishop Fintan Monahan congratulated Archbishop Eugene M. Nugent, originally from the Diocese of Killaloe, on his appointment as Apostolic Nuncio to Kuwait and Qatar.

Following the publication of the report by the Commission of Inquiry into Mother & Baby Homes, Archbishop Eamon Martin published a statement on 12 January. He said, 'Above all we must continue to find ways of reaching out to those whose personal testimonies are central to this Report.'

Archbishop Michael Neary also issued a statement on the Report of the Commission of Investigation into Mother and Baby Homes, and said 'The Church of Jesus Christ was intended to bring hope and healing, yet it brought harm and hurt for many of these women and children.'

Every January the Holy Land Coordination Group travels to the Holy Land with a focus on prayer, pilgrimage and persuasion. This year, the pandemic prevented the group from travelling. On 21 January, the Holy Land Coordination Group of which Bishop Alan McGuckian SJ and Bishop Noel Treanor are part, issued a statement and said, 'While many of our own countries continue to face severe hardship amid the pandemic, we have a profound responsibility to support our fellow Christians in the Holy Land.'

On 25 January, Archbishop Martin welcomed the World Communications Day message of Pope Francis. He said, 'During these challenging times it is more important than ever that our digital communication is authentic, compassionate and serves to build up rather than knock down or destroy.'

FEBRUARY

On 1 February, Bishop Michael Router welcomed Pope Francis' Message for the World Day of the Sick 2021. He said, 'Pope Francis emphasises that sickness makes us very aware of our own vulnerability, our need for the care and assistance of others and our dependence on God.'

On 2 February, Archbishop Dermot Farrell celebrated a Mass of Thanksgiving on the occasion of his installation as Archbishop of Dublin. He said, 'Today, I stand before you more than aware of my own inadequacies. But you and I also stand before God, the giver of gifts… faith asks us to see life's difficulties as a time of grace.' Following this installation, Bishop Denis Nulty was appointed Apostolic Administrator of Ossory by Pope Francis.

On 3 February, Bishop Alan McGuckian SJ welcomed the First International Day of Human Fraternity. He said, '…there is more that unites us all as human beings, and as believers in God, than that which is too readily focused on as cause for division.'

The same day, Cardinal Mario Grech addressed the Bishops of Ireland in relation to the undertaking of the Synodal Pathway in Ireland. He said, 'On behalf of our dicastery and in my personal capacity as General Secretary, I would like to forcefully reiterate our earnest availability to help and accompany you in this timely synodal experience.'

On 12 February, the Council for Life and the Consultative Group on Bioethics of the Irish Catholic Bishops' Conference made a submission to the Oireachtas Committee on Justice in relation to the Dying with Dignity Bill 2020. Bishops said, 'Assisted suicide reflects a failure of compassion on the part of society. It is a failure to respond to the challenge of caring for terminally ill patients as they approach the end of their lives.'

On 14 February, Archbishop Dermot Farrell spoke at the Memorial Mass on the 40th anniversary of the Stardust fire. During his homily he emphasised, 'The loss of life is always tragic. But the loss of young and innocent life is beyond tragedy.'

On 16 February, Archbishop Eamon Martin launched the #LivingLent campaign, and said that while Ash Wednesday 2021 was mostly without ashes, he encouraged families to pray together, fast and be generous during Lent.

On 19 February, Archbishop Eamon Martin published a message for the Day of Prayer for victims and survivors of abuse. He said, 'I am sorry for the terrible failures and crimes that happened in your Church, and I want to do my best to ensure that no one else suffers in the way that you did.'

A Bilateral Meeting between Taoiseach and Catholic Church leaders was held on 19 February, during which the four Archbishops of Ireland expressed a strong desire that people might gather safely for the important ceremonies of Holy Week and Easter, and requested consideration of an increase in the number of the bereaved who may attend funeral Masses.

On 24 February, Bishops renewed their support of the vaccination programme against Covid-19.

MARCH

In accordance with the public health restrictions to prevent the spread of Covid-19, members of the Irish Catholic Bishops' Conference gathered for their Spring 2021 General Meeting via video-link, instead of the usual location at Saint

Patrick's College, Maynooth. The main talking points at the meeting were: Walking Together – A Synodal Pathway; Trócaire's Lenten Appeal; Covid-19 restrictions in the Republic of Ireland; Covid Vaccination Programme; Saint Patrick's Day and praying for those affected by Covid-19; Pope Francis' year dedicated to the family; Call for submissions for a new lectionary for Ireland; Irish Bishops' Drugs and Alcohol Initiative; Prayers for peace following military coup in Myanmar.

On 11 March, the Bishops issued a statement on the Dying with Dignity Bill, stating 'Dying with Dignity Bill represents a failure of compassion'.

On 16 March, Archbishop Eamon Martin issued his Saint Patrick's Day 2021 message to the people of Ireland at home and abroad. He said, 'I pray that people who are struggling with the pandemic, whose livelihoods have been threatened, or have contracted the virus, that they will find in Saint Patrick the courage and resilience to go on.'

On Saint Patrick's day, the President of Saint Patrick's College, Maynooth, Rev. Prof Michael Mullaney, announced the appointment of Dr Jessie Rogers as the first woman and lay Dean of the Faculty of Theology at the Pontifical University Maynooth.

On 19 March, Archbishop Michael Neary welcomed the 'momentous event' of Pope Francis' formal designation of Knock as an International Eucharistic and Marian Shrine.

On 22 March, Northern Catholic Bishops issued a statement to oppose the introduction of abortion services in Northern Ireland. Bishops said, 'What Westminster seeks to impose, against the clear will of a majority of people here is a law which blatantly undermines the right to life of unborn children and promotes an abhorrent and indefensible prejudice against persons with disabilities, even before they are born.'

On 26 March, Bishop Paul Dempsey published a reflection to mark Pope Francis' 'Amoris Laetitia Family Year'. He said, 'so many people in same sex relationships have enriched the life of the Church and continue to do so in parishes across the world.'

On 28 March, Archbishop Eamon Martin said Mass in memory of the Disappeared for Palm Sunday 2021. In his homily he encouraged anyone with information on the disappeared to share it with the Independent Commision and said, 'Our thoughts and prayers today are especially with the families of Columba McVeigh, Joe Lynskey, Robert Nairac and Lisa Dorian.'

On 31 March, Archbishop Dermot Farrell celebrated the Chrism Mass for 2021. During the Mass he announced, 'I have established a Task Force on a Church for the Dublin of Tomorrow, under the title Building Hope'.

The same day, Bishop Alphonsus Cullinan called for proper consideration for public worship in a statement. He said, 'We must safeguard people's health AND support their spiritual wellbeing.'

In his Easter 2021 Message, also issued on 31 March, Bishop Denis Brennan said, 'This Holy Week and Easter, I invite you to focus primarily upon that opportunity – "to reconcile with God and neighbor" – for this is the ultimate and primary fruit of the life, death and resurrection of Jesus Christ.'

APRIL
On 8 April, Bishops announced the initial submission phase of Synodal Pathway for the Catholic Church in Ireland. Commenting on the Synodal Pathway, Bishop Brendan Leahy of Limerick said, 'It is said that the journey of a thousand miles begins with one step.'

In response to street violence across Belfast, Bishop Noel Treanor issued a statement on 9 April. He said, 'These scenes are deeply concerning for all of us who believe in and have worked together for a shared, brighter future for our society.'

On 9 April, Archbishop Eamon Martin expressed his sympathy to Queen Elizabeth on the death of Prince Philip. He said, 'Her Majesty the Queen, and all the members of the Royal family, are in our prayers on the death of a much loved husband, father, grandfather and great grandfather.'

On 13 April, Church leaders from across the island called for a unified political response to address violence and community tensions. They said, '…we appeal to our political leaders to come together in a unified response to the heartbreaking scenes witnessed on our streets last week and renew their commitment to peace, reconciliation and the protection of the most vulnerable.'

On 14 April, Bishop Brennan stated that the delay in resettling refugee children was 'appalling', and said, 'I call on the Government to act as quickly and decisively as possible in this case to bring these children to safety and shelter.'

On 15 April, a meeting was held between the Church Leaders Group (Ireland) and the Taoiseach. During the meeting, both parties discussed recent incidents of violence on the streets of Northern Ireland and the return of church services in the context of Covid-19.

On 19 April, Bishop Noel Treanor expressed concern over recent attacks on Jewish graves. He said, 'I extend my heartfelt support to all the families and the wider Belfast Jewish community who have been affected and deeply hurt by this incident.'

The same day, Archbishop Eamon Martin met with Minister Stephen Donnelly after the Government's criminalisation of church gatherings. The announcement was made just days after Church leaders met with the Taoiseach to discuss the return of public worship. The Archbishop explained the deep concerns already expressed with regard to the criminalising of leading, and gathering for public worship at this time in Ireland despite the consistent support from the Churches for public health messaging since the beginning of the pandemic.

On 22 April, Bishop Alphonsus Cullinan welcomed Pope Francis' message for vocations to marriage, priesthood or religious life. He said, 'In a world where self-interest stifles a true gift of self, Pope Francis encourages us all to courageously seek God's intended plan for us.'

On 25 April, Father Damian Casey was ordained to the priesthood by Archbishop Dermot Farrell.

On 27 April, Bishop Kevin Doran, President of United Irish Pilgrimages to Lourdes expressed his regret at the closure of Joe Walsh pilgrim tours.

On 28 April, Archbishop Michael Crotty offered prayer following the tragic deaths in Burkina Faso. He said, 'I was very saddened to hear that an Irish national and two Spanish journalists lost their lives while travelling in the East Region of Burkina Faso.'

MAY

On 2 May, Bishop Brendan Leahy welcomed the resumption of public worship, but stated that 'Covid complacency' remains the enemy.

On 5 May, Pope Francis invited Knock Shrine to join a marathon prayer initiative in May to end the pandemic. Archbishop Michael Neary welcomed this invitation and said, 'I commend Pope Francis' wish to involve all the Marian shrines around the world in this initiative, so that they may become vehicles of the prayer of the universal Church.'

On 6 May, the Irish Council for Prisoners Overseas reacted with concern following the publication of the Minister for Justice and Equality's Annual Report on the operation of the Transfer of Sentenced Persons Acts (1995 and 1997). No Irish prisoner was transferred into the State from an overseas prison for the fourth year in a row, and three quarters of those who applied to transfer to an Irish prison were refused last year.

On 9 May, the Diocese of Limerick published a report undertaken within the diocese that found a 'need to honour the dignity of Christian women in ministry'.

To mark World Communications Day, 16 May, Archbishop Eamon Martin paid tribute to all journalists who have given their lives in the search for truth. He said, 'I'm conscious today of the work of brave journalists here in Ireland like Lyra McKee, Veronica Guerin, and Martin O'Hagan who risked and lost their lives while seeking to uncover and report the truth.'

On 31 May, Archbishop Dermot Farrell celebrated an RTÉ televised Mass for Trinity Sunday. During his homily he said, 'Today's feast celebrates the Trinity – Father, Son and Holy Spirit. It is a celebration of how God is, and a call for how we are to be.'

The same day, Bishop Michael Router said Mass at the Armagh Diocesan Pilgrimage to the Basilica of Our Lady Queen of Ireland, Knock. During his homily he spoke of the Towards Healing counselling service, stating that to date, 7,000 survivors of institutional, clerical, and religious abuse and members of their families have availed of the service.

JUNE

On 4 June, Bishop Fintan Monahan prayed for safety on our roads over the June bank holiday weekend ahead of the blessing of the roads ceremony.

On 11 June, Pope Francis appointed Father Ger Nash as the new Bishop of Ferns. Welcoming his successor, Bishop Denis Brennan said, 'I warmly welcome the appointment of Father Ger Nash of the Diocese of Killaloe as my successor as Bishop of Ferns. I know that the people of Ferns, priests, religious, and lay faithful will welcome him too, and make him feel at home in their midst.' Speaking on his appointment, Bishop Nash said, 'I pray that here in Ferns we will turn our faces towards the future set aside for us by God and that we will journey forward together in faith.'

On 16 June, the Summer General Meeting of the Irish Catholic Bishops' Conference, which took place via video-link, concluded. The main topics for discussion were: Bishops express thanks for over 550 submissions received for Synodal Pathway; Safeguarding children in the Catholic Church; Vaccine ethics and equity; Reconfiguration of patronage; Birth Information and Tracing Heads of Bill; Welcome to Pope Francis instituting the Ministry of Catechist; First World Day for Grandparents & the Elderly; Laudato Si' on care for our common home; Prisoner Repatriation; Bishops thank public for generosity to Trócaire; Call on Government to recognise the State of Palestine; Brutality in Myanmar; UN Food Systems Summit.

On 21 June, Bishop John Fleming issued a statement on the announcement of the retirement of Bishop Patrick Rooke. He said, 'I wish him a happy and peaceful retirement and may God continue to bless him, Alison, his wife, and their family in every way.'

On 22 June, Bishop Denis Nulty welcomed Pope Francis' message for the first World Day for Grandparents & the Elderly. He said, 'I would love to see parishes in every diocese across the country celebrating grandparents, elders, not forgetting our older priests and religious, who have given their lives of dedicated service to their families and communities.'

On 24 June, it was announced that the Reek Pilgrimage on Croagh Patrick was to be four days per week in July. A call was extended for priests to attend to help minister the Sacraments for an extended period next month.

On 25 June, the remains of Cardinal Paul Cullen were transferred to the Pro Cathedral crypt.

JULY

On 6 July, Archbishop Dermot Farrell presented the papal honour to Peter Dunn of the *Radharc* Trust. The Archbishop said, 'Since 1996, Peter has worked tirelessly with a steady determination to ensure that the *Radharc* programmes and the essential Christian values they embody should not be forgotten.'

On 15 July, Archbishop Eamon Martin asked for prayers for victims in response to the British government's decision to introduce an amnesty for Troubles-related incidents.

On 21 July, the Funeral Mass of Monaghan U20 Football Captain, Brendan Óg Duffy RIP, was said by Canon Paddy McGinn. During his homily, Canon McGinn said, 'We cannot solve the mystery. All we can do is huddle in grief around the remains of shattered dreams and what might have been.'

The same day, Bishop Brendan Leahy paid tribute to the late Des O'Malley RIP and said that Limerick and Ireland had lost a man and politician of immense courage and decency and a great family man into the bargain.

On 25 July, Archbishop Michael Neary celebrated Mass in Knock for the first World Day for Grandparents. He said, 'The elderly can be wonderful role models for the young as their attitude to God, Jesus, Our Lady and religious values are extremely formative'.

On 26 July, Archbishop Kieran O'Reilly congratulated Limerick Senior Hurling Team on winning third consecutive Munster Title.

On 27 July, Northern Catholic Bishops issued a statement in opposition to the introduction of abortion services. Bishops said, 'Westminster has imposed an unjust law. Christians, and all people of good will, can never ignore the fact that unborn children are human beings worthy of protection'.

On 30 July, Bishop Fintan Gavin congratulated Cork's Olympic winners Emily Hegarty, who won a Bronze medal with her teammates in the Women's Four A Final, and Fintan McCarthy and Paul O'Donovan, who won gold in the Lightweight Men's Double Sculls.

AUGUST

On 7 August, Archbishop Jude Thaddeus Okolo, conferred the Pallium on Archbishop Dermot Farrell as Metropolitan of the Archdiocese of Dublin. During his homily, Archbishop Farrell said, 'The pallium is a sign of the bond we in Dublin share with the successor of Peter'.

On 16 August, the occasion of the dedication of the new altar in the Cathedral of the Assumption, Tuam, Archbishop Michael Neary said, 'This new altar, which will shortly be anointed, incensed and clothed, will each day be reverenced.'

On 18 August, while welcoming Ireland's intervention at the UN Security Council on the crisis in Afghanistan, Bishop Alan McGuckian SJ urged that the processes involved be accelerated and that the acceptance of additional refugees in Ireland should be considered as a policy priority.

On 26 August, an ICPO survey showed that 60% of Irish prisoners abroad experience mental health difficulties, with the biggest concern for Irish prisoners abroad during the pandemic being for their families.

On 30 August, Archbishop Dermot Farrell published a pastoral letter on the climate crisis. He said, 'Faith and science are not opponents; in a truly Christian view, faith and reason – *fides et ratio* – go hand in hand'.

SEPTEMBER

On 2 September, Bishop Donal McKeown paid tribute to the late Mrs Pat Hume RIP. He said, 'It is with great sadness that I have heard of the death of Pat Hume. In her death the city and indeed our country has returned to God an extraordinary person.'

Following feedback from public consultation, on 3 September Bishops progressed preparation of a new edition of the Lectionary.

On 5 September, Bishop Ger Nash was ordained as the new Bishop of Ferns. Speaking at his ordination, Bishop Nash said, 'My hope is that we can work together here in Ferns with the Spirit of God sustaining us to nurture the faith and continue to ensure a place of welcome and hospitality for all.'

On 7 September, the Faculty of Philosophy at Saint Patrick's College, Maynooth was selected to host one of the twelve grants offered by the project *Widening the Horizons in Philosophical Theology*, anchored at the University of Saint Andrews, and funded by a £2m grant from Templeton Religion Trust.

The same day, Bishop Brendan Leahy welcomed the publication of the Vatican preparatory document on Synodality. He said, 'As we embark on our own Synodal Pathway in Ireland, we can look forward to letting ourselves be inspired also by these valuable guiding principles.'

On 8 September, Archbishop Dermot Farrell celebrated Mass for the 160th anniversary of the arrival of the Bon Secours Sisters to Ireland. During his homily he said, 'Since your arrival here it would be impossible to measure your impact on generations of families in the Archdiocese.'

On 11 September, Bishop Michael Router called for an urgent meeting with Minister Frank Feighan to stop the closure of the Family Addiction Support Network. He said, 'It will be devastating for families if FASN is forced to close'.

On 13 September, Bishop Martin Hayes welcomed the 'Healthy Planet and Healthy People – the Catholic Petition' initiative from the Council for Justice and Peace, and stated that change and forthright leadership on climate change 'urgently required'.

On 16 September, Church leaders called on the Government to provide 100% redress for mica and pyrite scandal affected families.

On 21 September, Archbishop Eamon Martin celebrated Mass for the centenary of the Legion of Mary. During his homily he said, 'My dear brothers and sisters in the Legion of Mary here in the Archdiocese of Armagh I congratulate you, thank you and bless you on your 100th anniversary.'

On 24 September, in a joint statement the Church Leaders invited 'prayerful support' for their Service of Reflection and Hope, which took place at Saint Patrick's Church of Ireland Cathedral, Armagh, on 21 October 2021. They said, 'As Church Leaders we have been saddened by the polarised public commentary around our Service of Reflection and Hope. The tone of the public debate has shone a light on the societal wounds we wish to reflect on in this service.'

The same day, Bishop Nulty issued a statement that the Government must honour its commitment to take in refugees and end the desperate system of Direct Provision Centres.

On 27 September, Archbishop Dermot Farrell celebrated Mass to commemorate the 175th Anniversary of the foundation of the Catholic Institute for the Deaf.

On 28 September, Bishop Alphonsus Cullinan ordained Brother John Dineen as a Cistercian Priest.

On 29 September, the Diocese of Dromore launched a Redress Scheme for survivors of clerical sexual abuse. A statement was published, which read, 'The Diocese is committed to doing what it can to help bring healing to the survivors of clerical sexual abuse, and to all those affected by these egregious crimes.'

OCTOBER

On 6 October, Autumn 2021 General Meeting of the Irish Catholic Bishops' Conference concluded in Maynooth. The main topics for discussion were: Bishops' pilgrimage to Knock and Mass in memory of all who died on the island during the Covid 19 pandemic; Housing and homelessness; Bishops call for climate action and support for the 'Healthy Planet, Healthy People' petition ahead of COP15 and COP26; The Synodal Pathway in Ireland; Family Addiction Support Networks; RTÉ to broadcast Mass for World Mission Sunday on 24 October; Trócaire's work to alleviate the humanitarian crisis in East Africa.

On 13 October, nine new students began their studies for the priesthood for Irish dioceses, bringing the total to 64 seminarians currently studying for the priesthood for Irish dioceses.

The same day, Archbishop Dermot Farrell launched the Pastoral Letter, *The Cry of the Earth – The Cry of the Poor*. He said, 'This issue, which is the major challenge confronting our planet, and is now the defining issue of this generation, will not be solved by sound bites or short-term actions.'

On 14 October, Archbishop Dermot Farrell celebrated Mass for the Association of Patrons and Trustees of Catholic Schools. He said, 'Today we remember with gratitude the women and men of religious congregations who established the post-primary schools, at the invitation of the local bishop, for the education and faith formation of the children of the local parish.'

On 15 October, *Let us Journey Together!*, a pastoral message from Archbishop Eamon Martin, Bishop Michael Router and the Synodal Core Group for the Archdiocese of Armagh, was published. It read, 'We encourage you to join us as we respond to Pope Francis' call and set out on a synodal journey in the Archdiocese of Armagh.'

On 18 October, the rebranding of Pope's charity as 'Missio Ireland' ahead of World Mission Sunday took place in Veritas. Speaking at the launch, Father Michael O'Sullivan said, 'Missio Ireland is part of a global network of charities, serving the Church in over 120 countries. Many of these are already known as Missio and, to honour the continued collaboration and union between all the Missio offices, and to harness the energy of the Missio family worldwide, it makes sense to adopt the Missio name.'

On 21 October, the service of Reflection & Hope to mark the Centenary of the partition of Ireland and the formation of Northern Ireland took place in Armagh. During his personal reflection at the event, Archbishop Eamon Martin said, 'When I look back on what happened on this island in 1921, like many others in my community and tradition, I do so with a deep sense of loss; and also sadness. Because for the past 100 years partition has polarised people on this island. It has institutionalised difference, and it remains a symbol of cultural, political and religious division between our communities.'

On 28 October, it was announced that Bishop Martin Hayes would represent the Irish Bishops at the COP26 meetings in Glasgow. He said, 'COP26 will provide an opportunity, in a public way, to renew our care for God's creation which is an integral part of our Christian vocation.'

The same day, Bishop Alphonsus Cullinan ordained Reverend John McEneaney to the priesthood.

NOVEMBER

On 10 November, Pope Francis appointed Bishop Francis Duffy as the new Archbishop of Tuam. Welcoming the appointment, Archbishop Michael Neary said, 'Archbishop Elect Francis, on my own behalf … and faithful of the Archdiocese of Tuam, it is my humble privilege to congratulate you on your appointment as our new Archbishop, and to welcome you warmly to Tuam.' Speaking on the occasion of his appintment, Archbishop Elect Francis Duffy said 'To the parishioners, the priests and religious of this Archdiocese, I say that I really look forward to meeting with you and working with you in the time to come.'

On 14 November, a Mass of Remembrance for the bishops' pilgrimage to Knock was held for all who have died from Covid-19. At the Mass, Archbishop Eamon Martin said 'We pray with Jesus, Mary and Joseph for those who have died during Covid and for all who continue to grieve for them.'

On 20 November, Bishop Tom Deenihan celebrated Mass for the anniversary of Frank Duff RIP. During his homily he said, 'The private Catholic is, by nature, a poor missionary. The Legion of Mary understands this. Indeed, its Raison d'etre is to be the missionary Church…combining prayer and action!'

On 22 November, Archbishop Eamon Martin launched Ireland's digital Advent Calendar. He said, 'During Advent, let us reflect on the eternal message of Christmas, which is, Christ is alive and that He is our hope.'

DECEMBER

On 1 December, the Winter 2021 General Meeting of the Irish Catholic Bishops' Conference, which took place *via* video-link, concluded. The topics for discussion were: Advent 2021; Support from the Bishops' Council for Healthcare for the COVID-19 Vaccine Programme; (i) Universal Synod (ii) Update on Synodal Pathway in the Church in Ireland; Safeguarding children in the Church; Trócaire's 'Christmas Gifts of Love' to support communities in crisis.

On 16 December, Archbishop Eamon Martin and Archbishop John McDowell issued a joint message for Christmas 2021. Archbishops said, 'If the Spirit is saying anything to the Churches this Christmas, might it not be to think about how we… can enter prayerfully and hopefully into that great mystery of the "Word made flesh"?'

On 21 December the Catholic Bishops of Northern Ireland issued a statement on the NI Assembly vote on the Severe Fetal Impairment Abortion. Bishops said, 'the Abortion Law in Northern Ireland will send a message to all citizens that unborn disabled babies, are fundamentally less valued than those who are able-bodied.'

On 24 December, Archbishop Dermot Farrell celebrated the Christmas Vigil Mass in St Mary's Pro-Cathedral, Dublin. During his homily he said, 'I wish that for you and your family this Christmas may be blessed and joyful.'

On 31 December, Archbishop Eamon Martin issued his New Year's message for 2022. He spoke of his hopes for the future and emphasised, 'Governments should see the funding of education and training of our young people not as an expenditure, but as an investment.'

For more information please see www.catholicbishops.ie. See also 'Irish Catholic Bishops' Conference' on Facebook and follow on Twitter @CatholicBishops.

THE ROMAN CURIA

SECRETARIAT OF STATE
Palazzo Apostolico Vaticano,
Città del Vaticano 00120
Tel 66988-3913

Secretary of State:
Cardinal Pietro Parolin

Relations with States
Secretary:
Archbishop Paul Richard Gallagher
Undersecretary:
Mgr Mirosław Stanisław Wachowski

General Affairs
Substitute: Archbishop Edgar Peña Parra
Assessor: Mgr Luigi Roberto Cona
Secretary for Pontifical Representations:
Archbishop Jan Romeo Pawłowski
Head of Protocol: Mgr Joseph Murphy

CONGREGATIONS

Congregation for the Doctrine of the Faith
Prefect: Archbishop Luis Francisco Ladaria Ferrer (SJ)
Secretary: Archbishop Giacomo Morandi
Piazza del S. Uffizio 11, 00193 Roma
Tel 66988-3357/3413

Congregation for the Oriental Churches
Prefect:
Cardinal Leonardo Sandri
Secretary:
Archbishop Giorgio Demetrio Gallaro
Palazzo del Bramante,
Via della Conciliazione, 34, 00193 Roma
Tel 66988-4282

Congregation for Divine Worship and the Discipline of the Sacraments
Prefect: Archbishop Arthur Roche
Secretary:
Archbishop Vittorio Francesco Viola
Palazzo delle Congregazioni,
Piazza Pio XII, 10, 00193 Roma
Tel 66988-4316/4318

Congregation for the Causes of Saints
Prefect: Bishop Marcello Semeraro
Secretary: Archbishop Fabio Fabene
Palazzo delle Congregazioni,
Piazza Pio XII, 10, 00193 Roma
Tel 66988-4247

Congregation for Bishops
Prefect: Cardinal Marc Ouellet (PSS)
Secretary:
Archbishop Ilson de Jesus Montanari
Palazzo della Congregazioni,
Piazza Pio XII, 10, 00193 Roma
Tel 66988-4217

Congregation for the Evangelisation of Peoples
Prefect:
Cardinal Luis Antonio Gokim Tagle
Secretary:
Archbishop Protase Rugambwa
Palazzo di Propaganda Fide, Piazza di Spagna, 48, 00187 Roma
Tel 66987-9299

Congregation for Clergy
Prefect:
Archbishop Lazzaro You Heung-sik
Secretary: Archbishop Andrés Gabriel Ferrada Moreira
Palazzo delle Congregazioni,
Piazza Pio XII, 3, 00193 Roma
Tel 66988-4151

Congregation for the Institutes of Consecrated Life and for Societies of Apostolic Life
Prefect: Cardinal João Bráz de Aviz
Secretary: Archbishop José Rodríguez Carballo (OFM)
Palazzo delle Congregazioni,
Piazza Pio XII, 3, 00193 Roma
Tel 66988-4128

Congregation for Catholic Education (for Educational Institutions)
Prefect: Cardinal Guiseppe Versaldi
Secretary:
Archbishop Angelo Vincenzo Zani
Palazzo della Congregazioni, Piazza Pio XII, 3, 00193 Roma
Tel 66988-4167

TRIBUNALS

Apostolic Penitentiary
Major Penitentiary:
Cardinal Mauro Piacenza
Regent: Mgr Krzysztof Józef Nykiel
Palazzo della Cancelleria,
Piazza della Cancelleria, 1, 00186 Roma
Tel 66988-7526/7523

Supreme Tribunal of the Apostolic Signatura
Prefect: Cardinal Dominique François Joseph Mamberti
Secretary: Bishop Giuseppe Sciacca
Palazzo della Cancelleria,
Piazza della Cancelleria, 1, 00186 Roma
Tel 66988-7520

Tribunal of the Roman Rota
Dean: Mgr Alejandro Arellano Cedillo
Palazzo della Cancelleria,
Piazza della Cancelleria, 1, 00186 Roma
Tel 66988-7502

DICASTERIES

Dicastery for Communication
Prefect: Dr Paulo Ruffini
Secretary: Mgr Lucio Adrián Ruiz
Palazzo Pio, Piassa Pia, 3,
00193 Roma, Italy
Tel 66988-1800

Dicastery for Laity, Family and Life
Prefect: Cardinal Kevin Joseph Farrell
Secretary: Fr Alexandre Awi Mello
Piazza San Callisto 16,
00153 Roma, Italy
Tel 66986-9300/66987-9823

Discastery for Promoting Integral Human Development
President:
Cardinal Peter Kodwo Appiah Turkson
Secretary: Sr Alessandra Smerilli
Piazza San Callisto 16,
00153 Roma, Italy
Tel 066989-2711

PONTIFICAL COUNCILS

Pontifical Council for Promoting Christian Unity
President: Cardinal Kurt Koch
Secretary: Bishop Brian Farrell (LC)
Via dell'Erba, 1, 00193 Roma
Tel 66988-3072/4271

Pontifical Council for Legislative Texts
President:
Archbishop Filippo Iannone
Secretary:
Bishop Juan Ignacio Arrieta Ochoa de Chinchetru
Palazzo delle Congregazioni, Piazza Pio XII, 10, 00193 Roma
Tel 66988-4008

Pontifical Council for Inter-Religious Dialogue
President: Cardinal Miguel Ángel Ayuso Guixot (MCCJ)
Secretary: Mgr Indunil Janakaratne Kodithuwakku Kankanamalage
Via dell'Erba, 1, 00193 Roma
Tel 66988-4321

Pontifical Council for Culture
President:
Cardinal Gianfranco Ravasi
Secretary:
Bishop Paul Tighe
00120 Vatican City State
Tel 66989-3811

Pontifical Council for the Promotion of the New Evangelisation
President:
Archbishop Salvatore Fisichella (Rino)
Via della Conciliazione, 5, 00193 Roma
Tel 66986-9500

OFFICES

Apostolic Camera
Chamberlain of the Holy Roman Church:
Cardinal Kevin Joseph Farrell
Vice-Chamberlain:
Archbishop Ilson de Jesus Montanari
Palazzo Apostolico,
00120 Vatican City State
Tel 66988-3554/2139

Administration of the Patrimony of the Apostolic See
President: Bishop Nunzio Galantino
Secretary: Dr Fabio Gasperini
Palazzo Apostolico,
00120 Vatican City State
Tel 66989-3403

Secretariat for the Economy
Prefect:
Fr Juan Antonio Guerrero Alves (SJ)
Secretary General:
Dr Maximino Caballero Ledo
Palazzo Pio, Piazza Pia, 3,
00193 Roma, Italy
Tel 066988-1098

Council for the Economy
Coordinator: Cardinal Reinhard Marx
Palazzo Apostolico, 00120,
Vatican City State
Tel 66988-1771

Office of the Auditor General
Auditor General:
Dr Alessandro Cassinis Righini

OTHER INSTITUTES OF THE ROMAN CURIA

Prefecture of the Papal Household
Prefect: Archbishop Georg Gänswein
Regent: Mgr Leonardo Sapienza (RCI)
00120 Vatican City State
Tel 66988-3114

Office for the Liturgical Celebrations of the Supreme Pontiff
Master of Papal Liturgical Celebrations:
Mgr Diego Giovanni Ravelli
Palazzo Apostolico, 00120,
Vatican City State
Tel 66988-3253

Press Office of the Holy See
Director: Mr Matteo Bruni
Deputy Director: Dr Cristiane Murray
Via della Conciliazione, 54,
00193 Roma, Italy
Tel 0669-8921

PONTIFICAL COMMISSIONS

Pontifical Commission for Latin America
President: Cardinal Marc Ouellet (PSS)
Secretary: Prof. Rodrigo Guerra López
00120 Vatican City State
Tel 66988-3131/3500

Pontifical Commission for Sacred Archaeology
President: Cardinal Gianfranco Ravasi
Secretary: Mgr Pasquale Iacobone
Via Napoleone III, 1, 00185 Roma
Tel 6446-5610

Pontifical Biblical Commission
President:
Cardinal Luis Francisco Ladaria Ferrer (SJ)
Secretary:
Sr Nuria Calduck-Benages (MHSFN)
Technical Secretary:
Fr Alessandro Belano (FDP)
Palazzo della Congr. per la Dottrina della Fede, Piazza del S. Uffizio, 11, 00193 Roma
Tel 66988-4682

INSTITUTIONS CONNECTED WITH HOLY SEE

L'Osservatore Romano
Director Manager: Prof. Andrea Monda
00120 Vatican City State
Tel 66988-3461

Vatican Apostolic Archives
Archivist: Archbishop José Tolentino Calaça de Mendonça
Prefect: Bishop Sergio Pagano (B)
00120 Vatican City State
Tel 66988-3314

Vatican Apostolic Library
Librarian: Archbishop José Tolentino Calaça de Mendonça
Prefect: Mgr Cesare Pasini
Cortile del Belvedere,
00120 Vatican City State
Tel 66987-9411

APOSTOLIC NUNCIATURE

Address: The Apostolic Nunciature, 183 Navan Road, Dublin D07 CT98
Tel 01-8380577 Fax 01-8380276

Papal Nuncio: His Excellency Archbishop Jude Thaddeus Okolo, Titular Archbishop of Novica
Born 18 December 1956
Ordained priest 2 July 1983
Appointed Titular Archbishop of Novica 2 August 2008
Episcopal Consecration 27 September 2008
Appointed Apostolic Nuncio to Ireland 13 May 2017

Secretary: Very Rev Mgr Francisco Javier Díaz Tenza

THE IRISH EPISCOPATE

THE HIERARCHY

Archbishops

Most Rev Eamon Martin DD
Archbishop of Armagh
Primate of All Ireland
and Apostolic Administrator, Diocese of Dromore
Ara Coeli, Armagh BT61 7QY
Tel 028-37522045 Fax 028-37526182
Email admin@aracoeli.com

Most Rev Dermot Farrell DD
Archbishop of Dublin and Primate of Ireland
Archbishop's House,
Drumcondra, Dublin 9
Tel 01-8373732 Fax 01-8369796

Most Rev Kieran O'Reilly (SMA) DD
Archbishop of Cashel and Emly
Archbishop's House, Thurles,
Co Tipperary
Tel 0504-21512 Fax 0504-22680
Email office@cashel-emly.ie

Most Rev Francis Duffy DD
Archbishop of Tuam
Archbishop's House, Tuam, Co Galway
Tel 093-24166 Fax 093-28070
Email admin@tuamarchdiocese.org

Retired Archbishops

His Eminence Seán Cardinal Brady DCL, DD
Retired Archbishop of Armagh
Ara Coeli, Armagh BT61 7QY

Most Rev Dermot Clifford DD
Retired Archbishop of Cashel and Emly
Archbishop's House, Thurles,
Co Tipperary

Most Rev Diarmuid Martin DD
Retired Archbishop of Dublin and Primate of Ireland
Archbishop's House,
Drumcondra, Dublin 9
Tel 01-8373732 Fax 01-8369796

Most Rev Michael Neary DD
Retired Archbishop of Tuam
Archbishop's House, Tuam, Co Galway
Tel 093-24166 Fax 093-28070
Email admin@tuamarchdiocese.org

Bishops

Most Rev Raymond A. Browne DD
Bishop of Kerry
Bishop's House, Killarney, Co Kerry
Tel 064-6631168 Fax 064-6631364
Email admin@dioceseofkerry.ie

Most Rev William Crean DD
Bishop of Cloyne
Cloyne Diocesan Centre,
Cobh, Co Cork
Tel 021-4811430 Fax 021-4811026
Email info@cloynediocese.ie

Most Rev Alphonsus Cullinan DD
Bishop of Waterford and Lismore
Bishop's House, John's Hill, Waterford
Tel 051-874463 Fax 051-852703
Email info@waterfordlismore.ie

Most Rev Thomas Deenihan DD
Bishop of Meath
Bishop's House, Dublin Road,
Mullingar, Co Westmeath
Tel 044-9348841/9342038
Fax 044-9343020
Email bishop@dioceseofmeath.ie

Most Rev Paul Dempsey DD
Bishop of Achonry
Bishop's House, Ballaghaderreen,
Co Roscommon
Tel 094-986 0034
Email bishop@achonrydiocese.org

Most Rev Kevin Doran DD
Bishop of Elphin
St Mary's, Sligo
Tel 071-9162670/9162769 Fax 071-9162414
Email office@elphindiocese.ie

Most Rev Lawrence Duffy DD
Bishop of Clogher
Bishop's House, Monaghan
Tel 047-81019 Fax 047-84773
Email diocesanoffice@clogherdiocese.ie

Most Rev Michael Duignan DD
Bishop of Clonfert
St Brendan's, Coorheen, Loughrea,
Co Galway
Tel 091-841560 Fax 091-841818
Email office@clonfertdiocese.ie

Most Rev John Fleming DD, DCL
Bishop of Killala
Bishop's House, Ballina, Co Mayo
Tel 096-21518 Fax 096-70344
Email bishop@killaladiocese.org

Most Rev Fintan Gavin DD
Bishop of Cork and Ross
Diocesan Office, Bishop's House,
Redemption Road, Cork
Tel 021-4301717 Fax 021-4301557
Email secretary@corkandross.org

Most Rev Martin Hayes DD
Bishop of Kilmore
Bishop's House, Cullies, Co Cavan
Tel 049-4331496 Fax 049-4361796
Email admin@kilmorediocese.ie

Most Rev Brendan Kelly DD
Bishop of Galway
Diocesan Office,
The Cathedral, Galway
Tel 091-563566 Fax 091-568333
Email info@galwaydiocese.ie

Most Rev Brendan Leahy DD
Bishop of Limerick
Limerick Diocesan Centre, St Munchin's,
Corbally, Limerick
Tel 061-350000
Email office@ldo.ie

Most Rev Alan McGuckian (SJ) DD
Bishop of Raphoe
Ard Adhamhnáin, Letterkenny,
Co Donegal
Tel 074-9121208 Fax 074-9124872
Email diocesanoffice@raphoediocese.ie

Most Rev Donal McKeown DD
Bishop of Derry
Bishop's House, St Eugene's Cathedral
Francis Street, Derry BT48 9AP
Tel 028-71262302 Fax 028-71371960
Email office@derrydiocese.org

Most Rev Fintan Monahan DD
Bishop of Killaloe
Westbourne, Ennis, Co Clare
Tel 065-6828638 Fax 065-6842538
Email office@killaloediocese.ie

Most Rev Ger Nash DD
Bishop of Ferns
Bishop's House, Summerhill, Wexford
Tel 053-9122177 Fax 053-9123436
Email adm@ferns.ie

Most Rev Denis Nulty DD
Bishop of Kildare and Leighlin and
Apostolic Administrator, Diocese of Ossory
Bishop's House, Carlow
Tel 059-9176725 Fax 059-9176850
Email bishop@kandle.ie

Most Rev Michael Router DD
Titular Bishop of Lugmad and
Auxiliary Bishop in Armagh
Annaskeagh, Mount Pleasant,
Dundalk, Co Louth

Most Rev Noël Treanor DD
Bishop of Down and Connor
Lisbreen, 73 Somerton Road,
Belfast, Co Antrim BT15 4DE
Tel 028-90776185 Fax 028-90779377
Email dccuria@downandconnor.org

THE IRISH EPISCOPATE

Retired Bishops

Most Rev Philip Boyce (OCD) DD
Retired Bishop of Raphoe
Columba House, Windyhall,
Letterkenny, Co Donegal

Most Rev Denis Brennan DD
Retired Bishop of Ferns
Bishop's House, Summerhill, Wexford

Most Rev John Buckley DD
Retired Bishop of Cork and Ross
Diocesan Office, Bishop's House,
Redemption Road, Cork

Most Rev Brendan Comiskey DD
Retired Bishop of Ferns
PO Box 40, Summerhill, Wexford

Most Rev Martin Drennan DD
Retired Bishop of Galway
Mount St Mary's, Taylor's Hill, Galway

Most Rev Joseph Duffy DD
Retired Bishop of Clogher
Bishop's House, Monaghan, Co Monaghan

Most Rev Anthony Farquhar DD
Retired Titular Bishop of Ermiana and
Retired Auxiliary Bishop in Down and
Connor
24 Fruithill Park, Belfast BT11 8GE

Most Rev Raymond Field DD
Retired Titular Bishop of Ard Mor and
Auxiliary Bishop in Dublin
3 Castleknock Road,
Blanchardstown, Dublin 15

Most Rev Séamus Freeman (SAC) DD
Retired Bishop of Ossory
Sion House, Kilkenny

Most Rev John Kirby DD
Retired Bishop of Clonfert
St Brendan's, Coorheen, Loughrea,
Co Galway

Most Rev William Lee DD, DCL
Retired Bishop of Waterford and Lismore
Bishop's House, John's Hill, Waterford

Most Rev John McAreavey DD, DCL
Retired Bishop of Dromore
Bishop's House, 44 Armagh Road,
Newry, Co Down BT35 6PN

Most Rev Liam MacDaid DD
Retired Bishop of Clogher
Bishop's House, Monaghan

Most Rev John Magee DD
Retired Bishop of Cloyne
'Cormeen', Convent Hill,
Mitchelstown, Co Cork

Most Rev James Moriarty DD
Retired Bishop of Kildare and Leighlin
Bishop's House, Carlow

Most Rev William Murphy DD
Retired Bishop of Kerry
Bishop's House, Killarney, Co Kerry

Most Rev Donal Murray DD
Retired Bishop of Limerick
Limerick Diocesan Centre, St Munchin's,
Corbally, Limerick

Most Rev Colm O'Reilly DD
Retired Bishop of Ardagh and
Clonmacnois
St Michael's, Longford, Co Longford

Most Rev Leo O'Reilly DD
Retired Bishop of Kilmore
Bishop's House, Cullies, Co Cavan

Most Rev Eamonn Walsh DD, VG
Retired Titular Bishop of Elmham and
Auxiliary Bishop in Dublin
Naomh Brid, Blessington Road,
Tallaght, Dublin 24

Most Rev Patrick J. Walsh DD
Retired Bishop of Down and Connor
6 Waterloo Park North,
Belfast BT15 5HW

Most Rev William Walsh DD
Retired Bishop of Killaloe
Westbourne, Ennis, Co Clare

Most Rev Michael Smith DD, DCL
Retired Bishop of Meath
Bishop's House, Dublin Road,
Mullingar, Co Westmeath

MITRED ABBOTS

Rt Rev Dom Brendan Coffey (OSB),
Abbot
Glenstal Abbey, Murroe, Co Limerick
Tel 061-386103

Rt Rev Dom Michael Ryan (OCSO), Abbot
Bolton Abbey, Moone, Athy, Co Kildare
Tel 059-8624102

Rt Rev Dom Celsus Kelly (OCSO), Abbot
Our Lady of Bethlehem Abbey,
11 Ballymena Road, Portglenone,
Ballymena, Co Antrim BT44 8BL
Tel 028-25821211 Fax 028-25822310

Rt Rev Dom Brendan Freeman (OCSO),
Superior
Mellifont Abbey, Collon, Co Louth
Tel 041-9826103

Br Malachy Thompson (OCSO), Prior
Mount Saint Joseph, Roscrea,
Co Tipperary
Tel 0505-25600

Rt Rev Dom Mark Ephrem Nolan (OSB),
Abbot
Holy Cross Monastery, 119 Kilbroney Road,
Rostrevor, Co Down BT34 3BN
Tel 028-41739979

THE IRISH EPISCOPAL CONFERENCE

President
His Grace Most Rev Eamon Martin
Vice President
His Grace Most Rev Dermot Farrell
Episcopal Secretary
His Grace Most Rev Kieran O'Reilly
Finance Secretary
Most Rev John Fleming
Executive Secretary
Mgr Joseph McGuinness
Columba Centre, Maynooth, Co Kildare
Tel 01-5053000 Fax 01-6292360
Email ex.sec@iecon.ie
Communications Director
Mr Martin Long
Columba Centre, Maynooth, Co Kildare
Tel 01-5053000 Fax 01-6016401
Email mlong@catholicbishops.ie
*Executive Administrator of the
Commissions & Agencies of the Episcopal
Conference:* Mr Harry Casey
Columba Centre, Maynooth, Co Kildare
Tel 01-5053000 Fax 01-6016401
Email harry.casey@iecon.ie

Standing Committee
His Grace Most Rev Eamon Martin; His
Grace Most Rev Dermot Farrell; His Grace
Most Rev Kieran O'Reilly; His Grace Most
Rev Francis Duffy; Most Rev John
Fleming; Most Rev Donal McKeown;
Most Rev Brendan Leahy; Most Rev Noël
Treanor; Most Rev William Crean; Most
Rev Alan McGuckian and Most Rev Denis
Nulty

THE FIVE EPISCOPAL COMMISSIONS OF THE IRISH EPISCOPAL CONFERENCE

*An Episcopal Commission advises or
makes proposals/recommendations to the
Standing Committee and Plenary
Assembly of the Irish Episcopal
Conference. Councils and Agencies assist
the Episcopal Commissions, and the
Episcopal Conference itself, in attaining
their objectives. An Advisory Group/Body/
Committee to a Council of the Irish
Episcopal Conference advises the
relevant Council.*

**Episcopal Commission for Catholic
Education and Formation**
Chaired by Most Rev Brendan Leahy DD

Episcopal Commission for Pastoral Care
Chaired by Most Rev Denis Nulty DD

**Episcopal Commission for Planning,
Communications and Resources**
Chaired by Most Rev John Fleming DD

**Episcopal Commission for Social Issues
and International Affairs**
Chaired by Most Rev Noël Treanor DD

**Episcopal Commission for Worship,
Pastoral Renewal and Faith Development**
Chaired by Most Rev Donal McKeown DD

THE IRISH EPISCOPATE

The Councils and Agencies of the Irish Episcopal Conference are clustered in five Departments corresponding to the five Episcopal Commissions. Details of several bodies which are linked to the Episcopal Conference are placed in square brackets and provided for your information.

COMMISSION FOR CATHOLIC EDUCATION AND FORMATION

Executive Secretary to the Episcopal Commission/Department
Rev Paul Connell PhD
Tel 01-5053014
Email education@iecon.ie

COUNCIL FOR CATECHETICS OF THE IRISH EPISCOPAL CONFERENCE

Members of the Council
Most Rev Brendan Leahy DD *(Chair)*
Most Rev William Crean DD, Ms Maura Hyland, Rt Rev Mgr Dermot A. Lane, Dr Gerry O'Connell, Dr Cora O'Farrell, Ms Hilda Campbell, Fr Edward McGee, Sr Antoinette Dilworth (RSJ), Dr Aiveen Mullaly, Ms Olivia Dolan, Ms Kate Liffey, Dr Daniel O'Connell
National Director & Executive Secretary of the Council for Catechetics
Dr Alexander O'Hara
Columba Centre, Maynooth, Co Kildare
Tel 01-5053000 Fax 01-6016401
Email catechetics@iecon.ie

COUNCIL FOR DOCTRINE OF THE IRISH EPISCOPAL CONFERENCE

Members of the Council
Most Rev Michael Neary DD *(Chair)*;
Most Rev Kevin Doran DD;
The Council for Doctrine works with the Theological Committee and the Bioethics Consultative Group (see Commission for Pastoral Care under Council for Life) on matters relating to faith and morals.
Columba Centre, Maynooth, Co Kildare
Tel 01-5053000

COUNCIL FOR ECUMENISM AND DIALOGUE OF THE IRISH EPISCOPAL CONFERENCE

Members of the Council
Most Rev Lawrence Duffy DD *(Chair)*;
Most Rev Brendan Leahy DD

Advisory Committee on Ecumenism
Secretary: Mr Gary Carville
Clogher Diocesan Office,
Bishop's House, Monaghan
Tel 047-81019

Advises the hierarchy on ecumenical affairs in Ireland and maintains contact with the Pontifical Council for Promoting Christian Unity, Rome. The committee has a membership of approximately 35, including the episcopal members, a priest representative from each diocese, and people chosen for their competence and experience in the ecumenical field.

COUNCIL FOR EDUCATION OF THE IRISH EPISCOPAL CONFERENCE [WITH NORTHERN IRELAND COUNCIL FOR CATHOLIC EDUCATION (NICCE)]

The Council for Education articulates policy and vision for Catholic Education in Ireland, north and south, on behalf of the Episcopal Conference. It has responsibility for the forward planning necessary to ensure the best provision for Catholic Education in the country. It liaises with other Catholic Education Offices, the Department of Education and Skills and the Department of Education, Northern Ireland. The Council advises the Conference on all government legislation as applied to education. It responds to and acts as spokesperson for the Episcopal Conference on issues related to the work of education. It seeks also to develop long-term strategies in education for the Episcopal Conference

Members of the Council for Education
Most Rev Brendan Kelly DD *(Chair)*
Most Rev Donal McKeown DD
Most Rev Thomas Deenihan DD
Most Rev Francis Duffy DD
Rt Rev Mgr Dan O'Connor,
Sr Evelyn Byrne
Mr Seamus Mulconry
Mr John Curtis
Dr Marie Griffin

Executive Secretary
Rev Paul Connell PhD
Council for Education of the IEC,
Columba Centre, Maynooth, Co Kildare
Tel +353-1-5053014
Email education@iecon.ie
Administrative Assistant
Ms Cora Hennelly
Tel +353-1-5053027
Email chennelly@iecon.ie

Northern Ireland Commission for Catholic Education (NICCE)
Until 2005, there was no central body seeking to offer leadership across the Catholic education sector in NI. The 'Maintained' schools (nursery, primary and non-selective post-primary) were managed by CCMS (a statutory body) while the Voluntary Grammar schools had a considerable degree of independence. The Northern Ireland Commission for Catholic Education (NICCE) was set up in 2005 by the Trustees in order to provide co-ordination of the Catholic sector in a time of rapid change. Today, there are 460 Maintained Schools and 29 Voluntary Grammar Schools.

Current Directors of the Northern Ireland Commission for Catholic Education (NICCE)
Most Rev Donal McKeown DD (Chair), Most Rev Eamon Martin DD, Most Rev Noël Treanor DD, Sr Eithne Woulfe (SSL), Mr Dermot McGovern (ERST NI), Monsignor Peter O'Reilly, Dean Kevin Donaghy, Sr Maureen O'Dee (Sister of St Clare), Rev Feidhlimidh Magennis, Rev Timothy Bartlett, Rev Gerard Fox and Sr Brighde Vallely

In attendance
Mr Sean Dogherty
Mr Jim Clarke
Rev Paul Connell
Northern Ireland Commission for Catholic Education (NICCE)
St Eugene's Cathedral, Francis Street, Derry, BT48 9AP
Tel 028-71262302
Email bishop@derrydiocese.org
Website info@catholiceducation-ni.com

The Catholic Education Services Committee (CESC)
The CESC is an education committee established by the Irish Episcopal Conference (IEC) and the Association of Leaders of Missionaries and Religious of Ireland (AMRI). Formally consisting of six Bishops and six Religious nominated by AMRI, it was reconstituted in 2019.

The membership now consists of six Bishops, four Religious nominated by AMRI, two representatives of the six educational Trusts that have Public Juridic Person status (PJPs), and a representative of third level Catholic Education. As such, it is now representative of the entire Catholic Education sector.

CESC aims to support a vibrant Catholic education sector in response to changing social, economic and political conditions in Ireland. It promotes the Catholic education sector nationally and assists providers and practitioners in encouraging people to choose Catholic education at all stages of lifelong learning. The development of a co-ordinated and strategic approach to education across the entire Catholic sector in Ireland is a priority for CESC.

Members of the Catholic Education Services Committee (CESC)
Most Rev Thomas Deenihan DD (Chair), Most Rev Francis Duffy DD, Most Rev Brendan Kelly DD, Most Rev Donal McKeown DD, Most Rev Dermot Farrell DD, Most Rev Fintan Monahan DD, Fr Leonard Moloney (SJ), Fr John Hennebry (OSA), Sr Ella McGuinness (RSM), Sr Aideen Kinlen (RSCJ), Dr Sandra Cullen, Mr Paul Meany and Mr Richard Leonard.
In attendance Dr Marie Criffin (Chair CEP).

Executive Secretaries: Sr Eithne Woulfe;
Rev Paul Connell
Catholic Education Service
Columba Centre, Maynooth, Co Kildare
Tel +353-1-5053014
Email education@iecon.ie

Catholic Education Service Trust (CEST)

The Catholic Education Service is a charity created by Deed of Trust. The Trustees of CEST are four Catholic Bishops who are Ordinaries of Catholic dioceses in Ireland and each representing one of the four ecclesiastical provinces of Ireland (Most Rev Thomas Deenihan DD, Most Rev Fintan Monahan DD, Most Rev Dermot Farrell DD, Most Rev Brendan Kelly DD) and two Religious appointed by AMRI, Rev Leonard Moloney (SJ) and Rev John Hennebry (OSA). The Trustees of the CEST are *ex officio* members of Catholic Education Service Committee (CESC).

Catholic Education Partnership (CEP)

In November 2020, a new structure for the management and trusteeship of Catholic Post-Primary Education came into being. As part of this new structure, two new companies have been established: the Association of Patrons and Trustees of Catholic Schools (APTCS) (see below), and the Catholic Education Partnership (CEP). The CEP replaces the Catholic Schools Partnership (CSP) and will continue its work of providing support for all the partners in Catholic education at first, second and third level in the Republic of Ireland. The CEP going forward will be closely aligned with the Secretariat of Secondary Schools (SSS) which provides support for Boards of Management and Principals in Catholic Post Primary Schools. In addition, it will also be closely aligned with the APTCS which provides support and advice for Patrons and Trustees of Catholic Schools. The activities of the CEP will be supported and funded by CEST.

The Directors of the new CEP Company are:
Most Rev Leo O'Reilly DD, Dr Marie Griffin, Fr Gareth Byrne, Ms Mary Bergin, Mr Declan Lawlor, Dr John McCafferty, Dr Andrew McGrady, Ms Deirdre Matthews, Dr Amalie Meehan, Dom Richard Purcell (OCSO), Mr Jonathan Tiernan and Sr Eithne Woulfe (SSL).

Chair: Dr Marie Griffin
CEO: Ms Gillian McGrath
Company Secretary: Fr Paul Connell
Columba Centre,
Maynooth, Co Kildare
Tel 01-5053100
Email office@catholicschools.ie
Website www.catholicschools.ie

Association of Patrons and Trustees of Catholic Schools (APTCS)

The Association of Patrons and Trustees of Catholic Schools (APTCS) came into being in November 2020. The APTCS is the representative body for the 'Catholic Trustee Voice' in Irish education at primary and post-primary level. Its membership includes members of the Irish Episcopal Conference, representatives of various religious congregations, representatives of the PJP trusts, as well as the trustees of a number of other Catholic schools.

Members of the APTCS Board
Mr Brian Flannery, Mr Paul Meany, Mr Michael Sexton, Ms Sheila McManamly, Ms Clare Ryan, Fr Paul Connell, Mr Gerry Bennett, Mr Edmund Corrigan.

Contact details:
Association of Patrons and Trustees of Catholic Schools (APTCS)
Chairperson: Mr Paul Meany
CEO: Dr Eilis Humphreys
New House, St Patrick's College,
Maynooth, Co Kildare
Tel 01-5053164
Email info@aptcs.ie

Secretariat of Secondary Schools (SSS)

Chair: Ms Deirdre Matthews
General Secretary: Mr John Curtis
Secretariat of Secondary Schools,
Emmet House, Dundrum Road,
Milltown, Dublin 14
Tel +353-1-2838255 Fax +353-1-2695461
Email info@jmb.ie
Website www.jmb.ie

The Secretariat of Secondary Schools is the company which governs the Association of Management of Catholic Secondary Schools (AMCSS). The AMCSS promotes, advises and supports Catholic Voluntary Secondary Schools in Ireland. Founded in the 1960s, it adopted its present structure in 1987. Its membership includes a principal and chairperson of a Board of Management from each of its ten constituent regions. It also includes a representative of the Irish Episcopal Conference and a representative of AMRI (Association of Leaders of Missionaries and Religious of Ireland). The Council cooperates and maintains links with other national and international groups interested in Catholic education. Its Secretariat provides a wide range of educational services and advice to its members. When the Council joins with representatives of the Protestant Voluntary Secondary Schools the Irish School Heads (ISA) it forms the Council of the Joint Managerial Body ((JMB). The JMB is recognised by the Department of Education & Skills as the negotiating body for Voluntary Secondary Schools.

Catholic Primary School Management Association (CPSMA)

Chair: Ms Anne Fay
General Secretary: Mr Seamus Mulconry
New House, St Patrick's College,
Maynooth, Co Kildare
Tel +353-1-6292462/1850-407200
Fax +353-1-6292654
Email info@cpsma.ie
Website www.cpsma.ie

CPSMA represents the boards of management of all Catholic primary schools. Its standing committee has close links with the Episcopal Commission for Education.

COMMISSION FOR PASTORAL CARE

Executive Secretary to the Episcopal Commission/Department
Vacant

COUNCIL FOR MARRIAGE AND THE FAMILY OF THE IRISH EPISCOPAL CONFERENCE

Members of the Council for Marriage and Family of the Irish Episcopal Conference
Most Rev Denis Nulty DD *(Chair)*
Most Rev Dermot Farrell DD
Mr Gerry Mangan, Mrs Breda McDonald,
Very Rev Michael McGinnity,
Ms Patricia Conway, Mr Pat Cunneen,
Mrs Carmel Cunneen,
Rev Mr John Taaffe, Mrs Maire Printer,
Rev Mr Gabriel Corcoran,
Mrs Finola Bruton, Mrs Gemma Rowley,
Mr Francis Cousins, Mrs Madeleine McCully, Mr Tom McCully and
Mr Denis Bradley
Columba Centre, Maynooth, Co Kildare
Tel 01-5053000 Fax 01-6016401
Email columbacentre@iecon.ie

The purpose of the Council for Marriage and the Family is to assist the Bishops in their mission, specifically as it relates to marriage, families and family life.

COUNCIL FOR LIFE

Members of the Council
Most Rev Kevin Doran *(Chair)*
Columba Centre,
Maynooth, Co Kildare
Tel 01-5053000

Consultative Group on Bioethics and Life
Most Rev Kevin Doran *(Chair)*
Secretary: Rev Michael Shortall
St Patrick's College, Maynooth, Co Kildare
Tel 01-7086165

ACCORD

Accord Catholic Marriage Care Service comprises three autonomous companies limited by guarantee: Accord NI, chaired by Archbishop Eamon Martin; Accord Dublin, chaired by Archbishop Dermot Farrell; and Accord Catholic Marriage Care Service CLG, chaired by Mr Gordon Nicholl. Accord has over fifty centres located throughout the 26 dioceses of Ireland. Its ministry is primarily concerned with supporting the Sacrament of Marriage by helping couples as they prepare for sacramental marriage and offering support to them in times of difficulty. Accord's aim is to promote a better understanding of Christian marriage and to help couples initiate, sustain and enrich their commitment to one another and to family life. Accord's core services include Marriage Preparation and Counselling (marriage and relationships) and Schools' Programmes in Relationships and Sexuality Education.

Accord Catholic Marriage Care Service CLG
President: Most Rev Denis Nulty DD
Vice President
Most Rev Michael Router DD
Chairperson
Mr Gordon Nicholl
Executive Director
Mr Tony Shanahan
Central Office: Columba Centre,
Maynooth, Co Kildare
Tel 01-5053112 Fax 01-6016410
Email info@accord.ie
www.accord.ie

ACCORD Dublin Catholic Marriage Care Service CLG
Chairperson
Most Rev Dermot Farrell DD
Diocesan Director: Ms Jennifer Griffin
Holy Cross Diocesan Centre,
Clonliffe Road, Dublin DO3 P2E7
Tel 01-4784400
Emails
marriagepreparation@accorddublin.ie *or*
schoolsprogramme@accorddublin.ie *or*
admin@accorddublin.ie
www.accord.ie and www.accorddublin.ie

Accord Northern Ireland Catholic Marriage Care Service CLG
Chairperson: Most Rev Eamon Martin DD
Regional Director: Ms Deirdre O'Rawe
Cana House, St Mary's Church,
Chapel Lane, Belfast BT11HH
Tel 028-90233002
Email info@accordni.com
www.accord.ie and www.accord-ni.co.uk

COUNCILS FOR EMIGRANTS AND IMMIGRANTS OF THE IRISH EPISCOPAL CONFERENCE

EMIGRANTS (IECE)

The Irish Episcopal Council for Emigrants (IECE) seeks to respond to the needs of Irish emigrants prior to and following departure. It is particularly committed to addressing the needs of our most vulnerable emigrants, especially the elderly Irish emigrant community, the undocumented in the United States and Irish prisoners overseas. Working in conjunction with the host Church, our apostolates and sister organisations, the IECE seeks to respond to the needs of the Irish as an emigrant community.

Members of the Council for Emigrants
Most Rev Paul Dempsey DD *(Chair)*
Most Rev Michael Duignan
Rev Alan Hilliard, Rev Gerry French,
Ms Joanna Joyce, Sr Liz Murphy (RSM)
and Rev John McCarthy
Acting Director of IECE: Mr Harry Casey
Emigrant Officer: Brian Hanley
Administrator: Ms Bernadette Martin
Columba Centre, Maynooth, Co Kildare
Tel 01-5053155 Fax 01-6292363
Email bernie.martin@iecon.ie
emigrants@iecon.ie
Website www.catholicbishops.ie

Irish Council for Prisoners Overseas is an outreach of IECE
The Irish Council for Prisoners Overseas (ICPO) works on behalf of Irish prisoners overseas and their families. Established in 1985, the ICPO promotes social justice and human dignity for Irish people in prisons overseas and for their families. ICPO provides information, support and advocacy to Irish prisoners wherever they are: it makes no distinction in terms of religious faith, the nature of the prison conviction or of a prisoner's status. Casework, family support work, prison visits and policy work comprise core components of this work.

Coordinator: Mr Brian Hanley,
Administrator: Ms Bernadette Martin
Ms Ciara Kirrane, Mr Ian Hanna,
Ms Catherine Kenny and Ms Orla Dick
Volunteers Maynooth: Ms Eileen Boyle,
Ms Joan O'Cléirigh, Sr Anne Sheehy and
Ms Betty Wilson
Staff London: Rev Gerry McFlynn,
Ms Elizabeth Power, Ms Breda Power,
Mr Declan Ganly and Ms Sally Murphy
Volunteers London: Sr Moira Keane and
Ms Sara Thompson
Maynooth Office: Columba Centre,
Maynooth, Co Kildare W23 P6D3
Tel 01-5053156 Fax 01-6292363
Email icpo@iecon.ie
Website www.catholicbishops.ie
www.icpo.ie
London Office: PO Box 75693,
London NW1W 7ZT
Tel 0044-2074824148
Fax 0044-2074824815

[The Irish Chaplaincy
Director: Mr Eddie Gilmore
Tel 0044-207-4825528
Fax 0044-207-4824815
Email prisoners@irishchaplaincy.org.uk
Website www.irishchaplaincy.org.uk]

IMMIGRANTS (IECI)

The Irish Episcopal Council for Immigrants (IECI) develops and fosters initiatives for the pastoral care of immigrants among the dioceses and parishes of Ireland. It identifies immigrant communities within a local setting, recognises their needs and develops pastoral outreach strategies to engage with, support and integrate immigrant communities into dioceses and local parishes.

Most Rev Michael Duignan DD *(Chair)*
Columba Centre,
Maynooth, Co Kildare
Tel 01-5053022
Email gary.carville@iecon.ie

COUNCIL FOR HEALTHCARE

Membership
Most Rev Michael Router DD *(Chair)*;
Most Rev Ray Browne DD;
Fr John Kelly, Sr Helena O'Donoghue RSM, Professor Bernard Walsh,
Fr Pierce Cormac, Dr Keith Holmes,
Sr Dervilla O'Donnell (MMM),
Dr Aoife McGrath

Secretary: Sr Pat O'Donovan (RSM)
c/o Columba Centre,
Maynooth, Co Kildare
Tel 01-5310055
Email pat.odonovan@iecon.ie
www.catholicbishops.ie/healthcare

IRISH BISHOPS' DRUGS INITIATIVE

Chair: Ms Patricia Conway
Vice Chair: Most Rev Michael Router DD
National Coordinator: Mr Darren Butler
Committee Members: Mr David Conway,
Ms Elizabeth Murray, Ms Anne
McDermott Butler and Ms Elizabeth Cullinane
Columba Centre, Maynooth, Co Kildare
Tel 01-5053044/087-7901461
Email ibdi@iecon.ie

The Irish Bishops' Drugs Initiative was established in 1997 as a Church response to the growing problem of drug/alcohol misuse in Ireland. Its vision is to enable parishes to use a pastoral response in partnership with other service providers to respond to the primary and secondary prevention of drug/alcohol harms in parish communities.

OUTREACH TO PRISONERS

Irish Prison Chaplains Team
Episcopal Liaison
Most Rev Martin Hayes DD
National Coordinator of Prison Chaplains
Vacant

There are at present twenty full-time and five part-time chaplains working in Irish prisons. The vision of the chaplaincy is one that affirms the dignity of the person and seeks to be a voice for those deprived of their freedom. It is a vision that urges us to take a prophetic stance on issues of social justice and to continue the exploration of Restorative Justice as a valid alternative to imprisonment.

COMMISSION FOR PLANNING, COMMUNICATIONS AND RESOURCES

Executive Secretary to the Episcopal Commission/Department
Mr Paul Corcoran
Tel 01-5053000
Email paul.corcoran@iecon.ie

COUNCIL FOR COMMUNICATIONS OF THE IRISH EPISCOPAL CONFERENCE

Members of the Council
Archbishop Eamon Martin *(Chair)*
Archbishop Kieran O'Reilly SMA *(ex officio)*
Bishop Alphonsus Cullinan
Mgr Joseph McGuinness
Fr Paul Clayton-Lea *(Intercom)*
Mr Tony Moroney *(Interim Director, Veritas)*
Ms Denise Murphy *(Secretary)*
Fr Bill Kemmy
Ms Petra Conroy
Mr Martin Long *(CCO)*
Veritas Company,
7-8 Lower Abbey Street, Dublin 1
Tel 01-8788177 Fax 01-8786507

Catholic Communications Office
Director: Mr Martin Long
Communications Officer
Ms Brenda Drumm
Communications Office Researcher
Ms Katie Crosby
Editor of **Intercom**: Fr Paul Clayton-Lea
Assistant to Editor of **Intercom**
Mr Oisín Walsh
Columba Centre, Maynooth, Co Kildare
Tel 01-5053000 Fax 01-6016401
Email info@catholicbishops.ie
www.catholicbishops.ie
Twitter: @CatholicBishops
Facebook: Irish Catholic Bishops' Conference
YouTube: Irish Catholic Bishops' Conference
Audioboo:
www.audioboo.fm/IrishCatholicBishops

Veritas Communications
President: Archbishop Dermot Farrell
Bishop Brendan Leahy *(Board Member)*
Deputy Chair: Mr Frank Murphy
Interim Director: Mr Tony Moroney

Veritas advises the Episcopal Commission on Communications on matters related to communications. It has the following divisions:

Veritas Company DAC
7-8 Lower Abbey Street, Dublin 1
Tel 01-8788177 Fax 01-8744913
Email sales@veritas.ie
Unit 309, Blanchardstown Centre,
Dublin 15
Tel 01-8864030 Fax 01-8864031
Email blanchardstownshop@veritas.ie
Carey's Lane, Cork
Tel 021-4251255 Fax 021-4279165
Email corkshop@veritas.ie
20 Shipquay Street,
Derry BT48 6DW
Tel 028-71266888 Fax 028-71365120
Email derryshop@veritas.ie

13 Lower Main Street, Letterkenny,
Co Donegal
Tel 074-9124814 Fax-074-9122716
Email letterkennyshop@veritas.ie
40-41 The Mall, Newry,
Co Down BT34 1AN
Tel 028-30250321
Email newryshop@veritas.ie
Veritas Warehouse,
Unit 8, Orion Business Centre,
Northwest Business Park, Ballycoolin,
Dublin D15 KP74, Ireland
Tel 01-8829680
Email warehouse@veritas.ie

Veritas UK
Contact Veritas Warehouse

Veritas Publications
7-8 Lower Abbey Street, Dublin 1
Tel 01-8788177 Fax 01-8786507
Publishers of general religious books, liturgical texts in Irish and English, and catechetical texts.
Interim Director: Mr Tony Moroney
Managing Editor: Ms Síne Quinn

Intercom *Magazine*
Catholic Communications Office,
Columba Centre, Maynooth, Co Kildare
Tel 01-5053000 Fax 01-6016401
Editor: Rev Paul Clayton-Lea
Assistant to Editor: Mr Oisín Walsh
Email intercom@catholicbishops.ie
Subscriptions: Veritas
Tel 01-8788177 Fax 01-8786507
Email intercomsubscriptions@veritas.ie
Twitter @IntercomJournal

COUNCIL FOR RESEARCH AND DEVELOPMENT OF THE IRISH EPISCOPAL CONFERENCE

Members of the Council
Most Rev Kieran O'Reilly DD *(Chair)*
Prof Darach Turley; Ms Louise McCann;
Ms Ann Morash; Dr Brian Conway

Council for Research and Development
Social Researcher: Vacant
Tel 01-5053000 Fax 01-6016401

The Council co-ordinates and assists in research projects approved or requested by the Episcopal Conference, its Agencies and Commissions.

COUNCIL FOR FINANCE AND GENERAL PURPOSES OF THE IRISH EPISCOPAL CONFERENCE

Episcopal Members of the Council
Most Rev John Fleming DD *(Chair)*
Most Rev Michael Duignan DD
Most Rev Ger Nash DD
Finance Manager: Mr Paul Corcoran
Columba Centre, Maynooth, Co Kildare
Tel 01-5053000 Fax 01-6292360
Email finance@iecon.ie

The Finance and General Purposes Council is composed of three Episcopal members and seven lay persons.

COMMISSION FOR SOCIAL ISSUES AND INTERNATIONAL AFFAIRS

Executive Secretary to the Episcopal Commission/Department
Mr Harry Casey
Tel 01-5053000
Email harry.casey@iecon.ie

COUNCIL FOR EUROPEAN AFFAIRS OF THE IRISH EPISCOPAL CONFERENCE

Members of the Council on European Affairs
Most Rev Noël Treanor DD *(Chair)*
Most Rev Kieran O'Reilly DD

COMECE
19 Square de Meeûs, 1050 Bruxelles,
Belgium
Tel 32-(0)-22350510
Fax 0032-2-2303334
Email comece@comece.eu
Website www.comece.org

COMECE is a Commission of the Episcopal Conferences of the member countries of the European Union, with an office in Brussels.

General Secretary
Fr Manuel Enrique Barrios Prieto
Most Rev Noël Treanor DD is the *Irish Episcopal Conference representative and a Vice-President of COMECE*

COUNCIL FOR JUSTICE AND PEACE OF THE IRISH EPISCOPAL CONFERENCE

Members of the Council
Most Rev Alan McGuckian (SJ) DD *(Chair)*
Most Rev Kevin Doran DD

Research Co-ordinator
Dr Gary Carville
Columba Centre, Maynooth, Co Kildare
Tel 01-5053000 Fax 01-6016401
Email cjp@iecon.ie

The Council's role is to assist the Church in responding to the challenges facing it in the areas of human rights, social justice in Ireland and internationally, peace, including peace education, and world development. Its main activities are in research, education and information.

COUNCIL FOR THE MISSIONS OF THE IRISH EPISCOPAL CONFERENCE

Episcopal Members of the Council
Most Rev Kieran O'Reilly DD *(Chair)*
Most Rev Lawrence Duffy DD

Missio Ireland (Pontifical Mission Societies)
National Director
Fr Michael Kelly (SPS)
64 Lower Rathmines Road, Dublin 6
Tel 01-4972035
Email director@wmi.ie

Co-ordinates the activities of national missionary bodies and acts as a forum for discussion on matters related to national mission policy.

TRÓCAIRE

The Catholic Agency for World Development

Board of Trustees
His Grace Most Rev Eamon Martin DD *(Chair)*
His Grace Most Rev Dermot Farrell DD
His Grace Most Rev Kieran O'Reilly DD
His Grace Most Rev Francis Duffy DD
Most Rev Noël Treanor DD
Most Rev William Crean DD

Executive Committee
Most Rev William Crean DD *(Chair)*
Chief Executive Officer
Caoimhe de Barra
Director of International
Sorcha Fennell
Director of Global Programmes
Finola Finnan

Director of Fundraising and Marketing
Gwen Dempsey
Director of Public Engagement
John Smith
Director of Corporate Services
Dearbhla Fitzsimons
Head of Communications
Miriam Donohoe
Mobile: +353 (0) 872393914
Maynooth, Co Kildare
Tel 01-6293333 Fax 01-6290661
Email info@trocaire.ie
Website http://www.trocaire.org

Offices and Resource Centres:
50 King Street, Belfast BT1 6AD
9 Cook Street, Cork

Trócaire, the Catholic Agency for World Development, was established by the Irish bishops in 1973 to express the Church's concern for the needs and problems of the people of the developing nations. Trócaire's long-term development projects and emergency relief programmes in Africa, Asia, Latin America and the Middle East tackle the injustice of global poverty. In Ireland, hrough its education programmes and campaigning, Trócaire works to raise awareness about development issues and the principles of social justice involved.

COMMISSION FOR WORSHIP, PASTORAL RENEWAL AND FAITH DEVELOPMENT

Executive Secretary to the Episcopal Commission/Department
Rev Neil Xavier O'Donoghue PhD
Tel 01-5053000
Email liturgy@iecon.ie

COUNCIL FOR PASTORAL RENEWAL AND ADULT FAITH DEVELOPMENT OF THE IRISH EPISCOPAL CONFERENCE

Members of the Council
Most Rev Donal McKeown DD *(Chair)*
Most Rev Fintan Gavin DD
Mgr La Flynn
Ms Eileen Kelly
Ms Rosemary Lavelle
Ms Maureen Kelly
Sr Karen Kent
Ms Teresa Geraghty
Mr Seamus McDonald
Ms Anne Murray
Rev Frank McGuinness
Dom Richard Purcell
Rev Dr Gareth Byrne

Executive Staff of the Council
Project Officer: Vacant
Columba Centre,
Maynooth, Co Kildare
Tel 01-5053025

The Council supports ongoing dialogue between the groups and agencies represented by its members. The fruits of these dialogues are brought to the Episcopal Commission for Worship, Pastoral Renewal and Faith Development, from where recommendations are presented to the Episcopal Conference.

On behalf of the Conference, the Council fosters a shared vision as well as pastoral priorities and strategies at national level. Areas for research, reflection and supportive action by the Council include evangelisation, adult faith development, parish development, lay discipleship and ministry, and the young Church.

National Committee of Diocesan Youth Directors (NCDYD)
Most Rev Donal McKeown DD *(Chair)*
St Eugene's Cathedral
Francis Street,
Derry BT48 9AP
Tel 028-71262302 Fax 028-71371960
Email office@derrydiocese.org

COUNCIL FOR LITURGY OF THE IRISH EPISCOPAL CONFERENCE

Episcopal Members of the Council for Liturgy
Most Rev Francis Duffy DD *(Chair)*
Most Rev Brendan Kelly DD
Most Rev Fintan Monahan DD
Secretary
Rev Neil Xavier O'Donoghue PhD
Columba Centre, Maynooth, Co Kildare
Email liturgy@iecon.ie

National Centre for Liturgy
St Patrick's College, Maynooth, Co Kildare
Tel 01-7083478
www.liturgy-ireland.ie

The National Centre, relocated at Maynooth in 1996, offers programmes in liturgical formation and provides an advisory service on liturgical matters. Since 2020, the Centre is a constitutive part of the Maynooth Centre for Mission and Ministries, located within the Faculty of Theology of the Pontifical University.

Advisory Committee on Church Music
Chair: Rev Columba McCann OSB
Secretary: Sr Moira Bergin
National Centre for Liturgy,
St Patrick's College, Maynooth, Co Kildare
Tel 01-7083478
Email moira.bergin@spcm.ie

Advisory Committee on Sacred Art and Architecture
Chair: Mr Brian Quinn
National Centre for Liturgy,
St Patrick's College, Maynooth, Co Kildare
Tel 01-7083478

An Coiste Comhairleach um an Liotúirge i nGaeilge
Cathaoirleach
An Dr Marie Whelton
Rúnaí: An Dr Micheál Ó Cearúil
2 Páirc Ghort na mBláth,
Portobello, An Cuarbhóthar Theas,
Baile Átha Cliath 8
Fón 086-0874814
R-phost cearbhallmp@gmail.com

Schola Cantorum
Director: Mr Gerard Lillis
St Finian's College, Mullingar,
Co Westmeath
Tel 044-9342906/086-2528029
Email schola@stfinianscollege.ie
Website www.scholacantorum.ie

Established by the hierarchy in 1970 to provide specialised training in music for boys and girls within the framework of their general post-primary education.

Scholarships are awarded to students of good general and musical ability.

COUNCIL FOR VOCATIONS OF THE IRISH EPISCOPAL CONFERENCE

Members of the Council
Most Rev Alphonsus Cullinan DD *(Chair)*
Most Rev Lawrence Duffy DD
National Co-ordinator for Vocations
Rev William Purcell
Administrator: Rev Eric Cooney (Deacon)
Tel 01-5053118
Email eric.cooney@vocations.ie
Website www.vocations.ie
Twitter twitter.@nvocations

COUNCIL FOR RELIGIOUS OF THE IRISH EPISCOPAL CONFERENCE

Member of the Council for Religious of the IEC
Most Rev Eamon Martin DD

COUNCIL FOR CLERGY OF THE IRISH EPISCOPAL CONFERENCE

Episcopal Members of the Council
Most Rev Ray Browne DD *(Chair)*
Most Rev Fintan Monahan DD
Most Rev Denis Nulty DD

National Training Authority for the Permanent Diaconate
Most Rev Raymond Browne DD *(Chair)*
Columba Centre, Maynooth, Co Kildare
Tel 01-5053000 Fax 01-6016401

COIMIRCE [NATIONAL BOARD FOR SAFEGUARDING CHILDREN IN THE CATHOLIC CHURCH IN IRELAND

Chief Executive Officer
Ms Teresa Devlin
Director of Training and Support
Mr Niall Moore
Part-time Director of Safeguarding
Mr Peter Kieran
Administrator: Ms Imelda Ashe
Administrator: Ms Ann Cunningham
National Board for Safeguarding Children in the Catholic Church in Ireland
New House, St Patrick's College, Maynooth, Co Kildare
Tel 01-5053124 Fax 01-5053026
Email admin@safeguarding.ie

The National Board for Safeguarding Children in the Catholic Church in Ireland was established in 2008 in order to provide best practice advice and to monitor the safeguarding of children in the Catholic Church.

Over recent years there has been an increasing recognition of the existence of child abuse and growing acceptance of the potential risks to children from others working in positions of trust. Greater attention, therefore, has been paid to how church organisations ensure that the children with whom they are in contact are kept safe from harm.]

ARCHDIOCESES AND DIOCESES OF IRELAND

Ireland is divided into four provinces: Armagh, Dublin, Cashel and Tuam, named from metropolitan sees. The areas covered by each province and diocese are described at the beginning of the entry for each diocese; a map of the ecclesiastical areas is printed on the front endpaper of this directory.

For ease of reference, the four archdioceses appear at the beginning of this section in the traditional order, but the individual dioceses appear in full alphabetical order regardless of province. Thus Achonry, from the Province of Tuam, starts the section, followed by Ardagh and Clonmacnois from the Province of Ardagh and so on.

The provinces and their suffragan sees are as follows:

Province of Armagh
Metropolitan See: Armagh
Suffragan Sees: Dioceses of Ardagh & Clonmacnois, Clogher, Derry, Down & Connor, Dromore, Kilmore, Meath, Raphoe.

The Archbishop of Armagh is Primate of All Ireland.

Province of Dublin
Metropolitan See: Dublin
Suffragan Sees: Dioceses of Ferns, Kildare & Leighlin, Ossory.

The Archbishop of Dublin is Primate of Ireland.

Province of Cashel
Metropolitan See: Cashel
Suffragan Sees: Dioceses of Cloyne, Cork & Ross, Kerry, Killaloe, Limerick, Waterford & Lismore.

Province of Tuam
Metropolitan See: Tuam
Suffragan Sees: Dioceses of Achonry, Clonfert, Elphin, Galway & Kilmacduagh with Kilfenora*, Killala.

*Kilfenora is in the Province of Cashel, but the Bishop of Galway and Kilmacduagh is its Apostolic Administrator.

ARCHDIOCESE OF ARMAGH

PATRONS OF THE ARCHDIOCESE
ST MALACHY, 3 NOVEMBER; ST PATRICK, 17 MARCH;
ST OLIVER PLUNKETT, 1 JULY

SUFFRAGEN SEES: ARDAGH AND CLONMACNOIS, CLOGHER, DERRY,
DOWN AND CONNOR, DROMORE, KILMORE, MEATH, RAPHOE

INCLUDES ALMOST ALL OF COUNTIES ARMAGH AND LOUTH
APPROX HALF OF COUNTY TYRONE
AND PARTS OF COUNTIES DERRY AND MEATH

Most Rev Eamon Martin DD
Archbishop of Armagh;
Primate of All Ireland;
born 30 October 1961;
ordained priest 28 June 1987;
ordained Coadjutor Archbishop
21 April 2013; succeeded as
Archbishop of Armagh
8 September 2014.

Residence: Ara Coeli,
Cathedral Road,
Armagh BT61 7QY
Tel 028-37522045
Fax 028-37526182
Email admin@aracoeli.com
www.armagharchdiocese.org

ST PATRICK'S CATHEDRAL, ARMAGH

The building and decoration of the new St Patrick's Cathedral lasted from St Patrick's Day 1840, when the foundation stone was laid, until its solemn consecration in 1904. The Cathedral had been opened and dedicated in 1873. However, there were occasional intermissions of the work, and one of the longest gaps occurred because of the Great Famine. Primate Crolly, who had initiated the building, became a victim of famine cholera, and, at his own wish, his body was laid to rest under the sanctuary of the unfinished cathedral.

For five years the low outline of the bare walls remained, but with the translation of Dr Paul Cullen to the See of Dublin, work was resumed under Primate Dixon. On Easter Monday 1854, tarpaulins and canvas covers were drawn from wall to wall to allow Mass to be celebrated in the unfinished building.

During the Famine cessation the original architect, Thomas J. Duff, died. The architect to take over from Duff's original perpendicular Gothic design was J. J. McCarthy, destined to become one of the famous architects of the nineteenth century. In his anxiety to achieve a greater degree of classical purity, McCarthy drew up a continuation design in the old fourteenth-century Decorated Gothic. While critics may debate the wisdom of such a radical change when the building had reached a relatively advanced stage, the effect was undoubtedly to create an overall impression of massive grandeur.

The final impetus to complete the building came when Dr McGettigan was appointed (1870) to Armagh, and the solemn dedication took place in 1873.

Cardinal Logue, following Primate McGettigan's death, was to achieve the splendid interior decoration and the addition of the Synod Hall. He travelled to Rome and Carrara in search of precious marble for the reredos, pulpit and altar, and it was he also who achieved the decoration of the interior with mosaic. Under him, stained-glass windows were commissioned from Meyer in Germany. Cardinal Vanutelli represented Pope Pius X at the solemn consecration in 1904. A grand carillon was installed in 1924.

Vatican II's decree on Sacred Liturgy stressed the participation of the laity and hence greater visibility had to be afforded to the congregation. For this reason all the architects who submitted designs based their plans on the removal of the 1904 marble screens, which hindered visibility of the sanctuary from the sides. By raising, enlarging and opening the sanctuary area, the cathedral has, to a large extent, been restored to its original form.

With the removal of the rood screen, a new crucifix had to be placed at the sanctuary, and a specially commissioned 'Cross of Life' by Imogen Stuart was affixed to the right of the sanctuary.

The rededication took place in 1982, and a portion of St Malachy's relics from France, together with a relic of St Oliver Plunkett, was placed in the new altar. And so, the mortal remains of two of Armagh's most celebrated *comharbaí Phádraig* were carried back to the scene of their labours in more troubled times.

The most recent restoration project was completed in 2003 at a cost of £7.5 million, the majority of which was generously funded by parishioners and friends throughout the diocese and beyond.

A unique, but now also an historical feature of the primatial cathedral, are the five Cardinals' Hats. They are no longer conferred on new Cardinals. They were hung here and went deliberately untended so that their decay would represent the end of all earthly glory. The most recently hung (and last to be presented) is that of Cardinal Conway. Beside it are Cardinal Logue's and Cardinal O'Donnell's, while on the opposite side are the hats of Cardinals D'Alton and MacRory.

ARCHDIOCESE OF ARMAGH

His Eminence Cardinal Seán Brady DCL, DD
Archbishop Emeritus of Armagh; born 1939; ordained priest 22 February 1964; ordained Coadjutor Archbishop 19 February 1995; installed Archbishop of Armagh 3 November 1996; created Cardinal 24 November 2007.
Residence: Parochial House, 86 Maydown Road, Tullysaran, Benburb, Co Tyrone BT71 7LN

Most Rev Michael Router DD
Titular Bishop of Lugmad; Auxiliary Bishop of Armagh; born 15 April 1965; ordained priest 25 June 1989; ordained Bishop 21 July 2019
Residence: Annaskeagh, Ravensdale, Dundalk, Co Louth A91 KP64

CHAPTER

Dean: Very Rev Kevin Donaghy PP, VG
Archdeacon: Rt Rev James Carroll
Canons: Rt Rev Mgr Colum Curry PP, VG
Very Rev Eugene Sweeney PP, VG
Very Rev Patrick McDonnell PE
Rt Rev Christopher O'Byrne PE
Rt Rev Raymond Murray PE
Very Rev James Clyne PE, AP
Very Rev Michael Crawley PE
Very Rev Benedict Fee PP, EV
Very Rev Peter Murphy PP
Very Rev Michael C. Toner PP

ADMINISTRATION

Diocesan Secretary
Rev Mr Paul Mallon Deacon

Vicars General
Rt Rev Mgr Colum Curry PP, VG
Very Rev Eugene Sweeney PP, VG
Very Rev Dean Kevin Donaghy PP, VG

Episcopal Vicars
Rt Rev Mgr James Carroll PP, EV
Very Rev Canon Benedict Fee PP, EV
Very Rev Malachy Conlon PP, EV
Very Rev Gerard Campbell PP, EV

Vicars Forane
St John's: Fr Martin McArdle PP
An Ciorcal: Fr Brian Slater CC
The Martyrs: Fr David Moore PP
Cardinal MacRory: Fr Cathal Deveney PP
St Colman's: Canon Benedict Fee PP, EV
Tír Uí Néill: Dean Kevin Donaghy PP, VG
St John Paul II: Fr Michael Woods PP
St Patrick's: Fr John McKeever PP
Cardinal Ó Fiaich: Fr Gerard Tremer PP
Killeavy: Fr Liam McKinney PP
St Brigid's: Fr Emlyn McGinn PP
Peninsula: Fr Malachy Conlon PP, EV
Dún Dealgan: Fr Mark O'Hagan PP
Our Lady Queen of Peace: Fr Gerard Campbell PP, EV
St Cillian's: Canon Peter Murphy PP
St Colmcille's: Fr Patrick Rushe PP
St Oliver's: Canon Eugene Sweeney PP, VG

Chancellor
Very Rev Canon Michael C. Toner PP

Assistant Chancellor
Very Rev John McKeever PP

Diocesan Curia
Mr John McVey
Financial Administrator
Email jmcvey@aracoeli.com
Ara Coeli, Cathedral Road,
Armagh BT61 7QY
Tel 028-37522045 Fax 028-37526182

Diocesan Safeguarding Office
Director and Designated Officer
Mr Aidan Gordon
Email safeguardingdirector@archdioceseofarmagh.com
Tel 028-37525592
Training coordinator and Designated Officer: Mrs Eleanor Kelly
Email ekelly@archdioceseofarmagh.com
Tel 07584-323138
Administrative Staff: Mr Pierce Fox
Email pfox@archdioceseofarmagh.com
Archdiocese of Armagh,
Cathedral Road,
Armagh BT61 7QY
Tel 028-37525592

CATECHETICS EDUCATION

Catholic Primary School Managers' Association
Secretary: Mrs Niamh Black
c/o Parochial House, Top Rath,
Carlingford, Co Louth
Tel 042-9376105
Email armaghedu@gmail.com

Council for Catholic Maintained Schools
Linenhill House, 23 Linenhall Street,
Lisburn BT28 1FJ
Tel 028-92013014

Diocesan Advisers for Religious Education
Primary Schools
Sr Anne Lyng (RSM)
Diocesan Pastoral Office,
Holy Family Parochial House,
Hoey's Lane, Dundalk,
Co Louth A91 K761
Tel 042-9351316
Email annepastoralcentre@gmail.com
Post-Primary Schools
Rev Declan O'Loughlin
Parochial House, 30 Newline,
Killeavy, Newry, Co Down BT35 8TA
Tel 028-30889609
Email decoloughlin@yahoo.co.uk

PASTORAL

ACCORD
Drogheda Chairperson
Ms Eileen Mulcahy
Verona, Cross Lane,
Drogheda, Co Louth
Tel 041-9843860
Email droghedaaccord@gmail.com

Armagh Chairperson
Ms Deirdre O'Rawe
Drumcree Pastoral Centre,
Garvaghy Road, Craigavon
Armagh BT62 1EB
Tel 079-808988399

Dundalk Chairperson
Very Rev Mark O'Hagan PP, VF
St Patrick's, Roden Place,
Dundalk, Co Louth
Tel 042-9331731
Email accorddundalk@eircom.net

Apostolic Work Society
Diocesan President: Ms Jean Hanratty
13 College Street, Armagh BT61 9BT
Tel 028-37522781

Armagh Diocesan Pastoral Office
Diocesan Pastoral Workers
Sr Anne Lyng (RSM)
Email annepastoralcentre@gmail.com
Mrs Sharon Dunne
Email dunnesharon.pastoralcentre@gmail.com
Administrative Staff: Ms Milanda Kelly
Email milanda@parishandfamily.ie
Armagh Diocesan Pastoral Office,
Holy Family Parochial House,
Hoey's Lane, Dundalk,
Co Louth A91 K761
Tel 042-9351316

Armagh Diocesan Pastoral Council
Chairperson: Vacant
Secretary: Mrs Sheila McEneaney
Email sheila.mceneaney@hotmail.com

Charismatic Renewal
Rt Rev Mgr Colum Curry PP, VG

Communications
Diocesan Officer: Mr Martin Long
Catholic Communications Office,
Irish Bishops' Conference,
Columba Centre, Maynooth, Co Kildare
Tel 01-5053010
Email martinlong@catholicbishops.ie

Council of Priests
Chairman: Very Rev Malachy Conlon PP

Ecumenism
Very Rev Pádraig Murphy PE
Very Rev Seán Dooley PP

ARCHDIOCESE OF ARMAGH

Knock Pilgrimage
Director
Very Rev Canon Benedict Fee PP, EV

Legion of Mary
Armagh Curia President
Ms Margaret McManus
73 Newry Road, Armagh BT60 1ES
Tel 077-99867714
Drogheda Curia President
Ms Elizabeth Maloney
Tel 086-3658358
Dundalk Curia President
Ms Katrina Loughran
Tel 087-9903154

Liturgy Commission
Chair: Vacant

LMFM Community Radio
Ven Archdeacon James Carroll PP, EV

Lourdes Pilgrimage
Director: Very Rev Mark O'Hagan PP

Marriage Tribunal
(See Marriage Tribunals section.)

Permanent Diaconate
Director: Rev Brian White CC
6 Circular Road, Dungannon,
Co Tyrone BT71 6BE
Email roadbowler@hotmail.com

Pioneer Total Abstinence Association
Diocesan Director: Ms Mary Livingstone
Tel 028-37551458

Pontifical Mission Societies
Diocesan Director
Rev Barry Matthews CC

SPRED
Co-ordinator: Miss Caoímhe McNeill
14 Annaboe Road, Kilmore,
Co Armagh BT61 8NP
Email caoimhemcneill@gmail.com

Travellers
Co-ordinator: Vacant

Vocations Commission
Vocations Director
Very Rev Peter McAnenly Adm

Youth Commission (ADYC)
Chairperson
Very Rev Thomas McHugh Adm
Director: Vacant
Administrative Staff: Mr Pierce Fox
Archdiocese of Armagh, Cathedral Road,
Armagh BT61 7QY
Tel 028-37523084
Email armaghyouth@yahoo.co.uk

PARISHES

Mensal parishes are listed first. Other parishes follow alphabetically. Historical names are given in parentheses. Church titulars are in italics.

ARMAGH
St Patrick's Cathedral, St Malachy, Irish Street, *St Colmcille's,* Knockaconey
Immaculate Conception, Tullysaran
Email armaghparishoffice@gmail.com
Very Rev Peter McAnenly Adm
Email pmcanenly21@gmail.com
Rev Barry Matthews CC
Email barrymatthews@gmail.com
Rev Emmanuel Fasakin (MSP) CC
Email emmafash725@yahoo.com
Rev Mr Paul Mallon, Permanent Deacon
Email pjmallon@gmail.com
Parochial House, 42 Abbey Street,
Armagh BT61 7DZ
Tel 028-37522802 Fax 028-37522245
Parish Office: Cathedral Gate Lodge,
41a Cathedral Road, Armagh BT61 7QX
Tel 028-37522813

DUNDALK, ST PATRICK'S
St Patrick's, Roden Place
St Nicholas', Church Street
www.stpatricksparishdundalk.org
Email stpatricksparishdundalk@gmail.com
Very Rev Mark O'Hagan PP, VF
Email ohagan.mark2@gmail.com
Rev Maciej Zacharek CC
Email zacharekmaciej8@gmail.com
Rev Michael Darko CC
Email mdarko1937@gmail.com
St Patrick's Presbytery, Roden Place,
Dundalk, Co Louth A91 K2P4
Tel 042-9334648 Fax 042-9336355

DUNDALK, HOLY REDEEMER
Holy Redeemer
www.redeemerparish.ie
Email holyredeemer@eircom.net
Very Rev Michael Sheehan Adm
Email frmichaelpsheehan@gmail.com
Rev Shajan Panachickal Michael CC
Email mckunnel@gmail.com
Ard Easmuinn, Dundalk,
Co Louth A91 W8Y1
Tel 042-9334259 Fax 042-9329073

DUNDALK, ST JOSEPH'S
St Joseph's
Email dundalkoffice@redemptorists.ie
Very Rev Noel Kehoe (CSsR) Adm
Email nkehoe@cssr.ie
Rev Eamon Kavanagh (CSsR) CC
Rev Ryan Holovlasky (CSsR) CC
Email ryanh@cssr.ie
St Joseph's, St Alphonsus Road,
Dundalk, Co Louth A91 F3FC
Tel 042-9334042 Fax 042-9330893

DUNDALK, HOLY FAMILY
Holy Family
Email theholyfamily@eircom.net
Very Rev Derek Ryan (CSsR) Adm
Email dryan@cssr.ie
Rev Richard Delahunty (CSsR) CC
Email richard.delahu@yahoo.ie
Holy Family Parish, Hoey's Lane,
Muirhevnamor, Dundalk,
Co Louth A91 K761
Tel 042-9336301 Fax 042-9336350

DROGHEDA
St Peter's, West Street
Our Lady of Lourdes, Hardman's Gardens
www.saintpetersdrogheda.ie
Email stpetersadmin1@eircom.net
Very Rev Canon Eugene Sweeney PP, VF, VG
Email esweeney64@btconnect.com
Rev Mr David Durrigan, Permanent Deacon
Email ddurrigan@gmx.com
Rev Mr John Taaffe, Permanent Deacon
Email johntaaffe1@gmail.com
Parochial House, 9 Fair Street,
Drogheda, Co Louth A92 T6WY
Tel 041-9838537 Fax 041-9841351
Rev Paul Murphy CC
Email pmurph12@tcd.ie
Rev Desmond Branigan CC
Email desmond.brannigan@gmail.com
Our Lady of Lourdes Presbytery,
Hardman's Gardens,
Drogheda, Co Louth A92 PXF3
Tel 041-9831899
Very Rev Aidan Murphy PE, AP
Email amrev@icloud.com
St Peter's Presbytery, 10 Fair Street,
Drogheda, Co Louth A92 NX3T
Tel 041-9838239

DUNGANNON (DRUMGLASS, KILLYMAN AND TULLYNISKIN)
St Patrick's, Dungannon, *St Malachy's* Edendork, *St Brigid's,* Killyman,
Sacred Heart, Clonmore
www.parishofdungannon.com
Very Rev Kevin Donaghy PP, VF, VG
4 Circular Road, Dungannon,
Co Tyrone BT71 6BE
Tel 028-87722775
Email kdonaghy55@gmail.com
Rev Brian White CC
Email roadbowler@hotmail.com
Very Rev Eamonn McCamley
Email ep2018@btinternet.com
Rev Mr Andrew Hegarty, Permanent Deacon
Email andythegarty@gmail.com
Rev Mr Tony Hughes, Permanent Deacon
Email tonyhughes24@hotmail.com
Parochial House, 6 Circular Road,
Dungannon, Co Tyrone BT71 6BE
Tel 028-87722631
Parish Office: 4 Killyman Road,
Dungannon, Co Tyrone BT71 6DH
Tel/Fax 028-87726893
Email info@parishofdungannon.com

ARCHDIOCESE OF ARMAGH

ARDBOE
Blessed Sacrament, Mullinahoe
Immaculate Conception, Moortown
Very Rev Sean McGuigan PP
Parochial House, 19 Ardboe Road,
Moortown, Cookstown,
Co Tyrone BT80 0HT
Tel 028-86737236
Email seanmcguigan65@gmail.com
Parish Office: 1 Mullanahoe Road,
Ardboe, Dungannon,
Co Tyrone BT71 5AT
Tel 028-86736997
Email ardboeparochial@btinternet.com

ARDEE & COLLON
Nativity of Our Lady, Ardee
St Catherine's, Ballapousta
Mary Immaculate, Collon
Website www.ardeeparish.com
Email ardee.collon@gmail.com
Very Rev Canon Peter Murphy PP, VF
Parochial House, Moorehall,
Ardee, Co Louth A92 PXF3
Tel 041-6850920 Fax 041-6850922
Rev Sean McCartan *(Priest in Residence)*
Parochial House, Ardee Street,
Collon, Co Louth A92 F2P7
Tel 041-9826106
Email seanmccartan@gmail.com

AUGHNACLOY (AGHALOO)
St Mary's, Aughnacloy, St Brigid's, Killens,
St Joseph's, Caledon
Email parishofaghaloo@gmail.com
Very Rev Cathal Deveney PP, VF
Parochial House, 19 Caledon Road,
Aughnacloy, Co Tyrone BT69 6HX
Tel 028-85557212
Email cdeveney@icloud.com
Rev Dermot McCaul (SMA) *(Priest in Residence)*
Parochial House, 56 Minterburn Road,
Lairakeann, Caledon,
Co Tyrone BT68 4XH
Tel 028-37568288
Email mccaulda@hotmail.com

BALLINDERRY
St Patrick's
Very Rev Peter Donnelly PP
Parochial House,
130 Ballinderry Bridge Road, Coagh,
Cookstown, Co Tyrone BT80 0AY
Tel 028-79418244
Email ballinderryparish@outlook.com

BALLYGAWLEY (ERRIGAL KIERAN)
St Matthew's, Garvaghy, St Mary's,
Dunmoyle, Immaculate Conception,
Ballygawley, St Malachy's, Ballymacilroy
Very Rev Michael O'Dwyer PP
Parochial House, 31 Church Street,
Ballygawley, Co Tyrone BT70 2HA
Tel 028-85567096
Email errigalciaran99@gmail.com

BERAGH
Immaculate Conception, Beragh,
St Malachy's, Seskinore,
St Patrick's, Drumduff
Rt Rev Mgr Colum Curry PP, VG
Parochial House, Beragh, Omagh,
Co Tyrone BT79 OSY
Tel 028-80758206
Email columcurry@yahoo.com
Email beraghparochial@btinternet.com

BESSBROOK (KILLEAVY LOWER)
SS Peter and Paul, Bessbrook,
St Malachy, Camlough,
Sacred Heart, Lislea,
Immaculate Conception, Lissummon Road,
Newry, Good Shepherd, Cloughreagh
Very Rev Aidan Dunne PP
Parochial House, 11 Chapel Road,
Bessbrook, Newry, Co Down BT35 7AU
Tel 028-30830206
Email fadunne@gmail.com
Rev Seán Larkin PE, AP
Parochial House, 9 Chapel Road,
Bessbrook, Newry, Co Down BT35 7AU
Tel 028-30830272
Email larkseanj@aol.com
Rev Mr Philip Carder, Deacon
c/o Parochial House, 11 Chapel Road,
Bessbrook, Newry, Co Down BT35 7AU
Tel 028-30830206 Fax 028-30838154
Email philipcarder34@gmail.com

CARLINGFORD AND CLOGHERNY
St Michael's, Carlingford
St Lawrence's, Omeath
www.carlinnparish.com
Very Rev Magnus Ogbonna (MSP) PP
Parochial House, Chapel Hill,
Carlingford, Co Louth A91 FX76
Tel 042-9373111
Email doziemsp@yahoo.com
Rev Christopher McElwee (IC) CC
Parochial House, Omeath,
Co Louth A91 HK76
Tel 042-9375198

CLOGHERHEAD
St Michael's, Clogherhead,
SS Peter and Paul, Walshestown
www.clogherhead.com
Very Rev Martin McVeigh PP
Parochial House, Clogherhead,
Drogheda, Co Louth A92 K97O
Tel 041-9822224
Email clogherheadparish@gmail.com

CLOGHOGUE (KILLEAVY UPPER)
Sacred Heart, Cloghogue, St Joseph's,
Meigh, St Michael's, Killean
Very Rev Richard Naughton PP
Mountain Lodge, 132 Dublin Road,
Newry, Co Down BT35 8QT
Tel 028-30262174 Fax 028-30262174
Very Rev Canon S. James Clyne PE, AP
24 Chapel Road, Killeavy, Newry,
Co Down BT35 8JY
Tel 028-30848222
Email clynesj@gmail.com

CLONOE
St Patrick's, Clonoe, St Columcille's,
Kingsland, St Brigid's, Brockagh
Email clonoeparish@gmail.com
Very Rev Canon Benedict Fee PP, EV, VF
Teac na h'Ard Croise, 3 Cloghog Road,
Clonoe, Coalisland, Co Tyrone BT71 5EH
Tel 028-87749184
Email frbennyfee@hotmail.com
Rev John McCallion CC
Parochial House, 140 Mountjoy Road,
Brocagh, Dungannon,
Co Tyrone BT71 5DY
Tel 028-87738381
Email jmccallion384@gmail.com

COAGH
Our Lady's, Coagh
SS Joseph and Malachy, Drummullan
Very Rev Laurence Boyle PP
Email lorcanboyle@gmail.com
Parochial House, 1 Convent Road,
Cookstown, Co Tyrone BT80 8QA
Tel 028-86763370
Rev Francis Coll CC
Parochial House, Hanover Square,
Coagh, Cookstown, Co Tyrone BT80 0EF
Tel 028-86737212
Email gabrielfcoll@gmail.com

COALISLAND
Holy Family, Coalisland
St Mary & St Joseph, Coalisland,
St Mary's, Stewartstown
Email coalislandparish@yahoo.co.uk
Very Rev Eugene O'Neill PP
Parochial House, 31 Brackaville Road,
Coalisland, Co Tyrone BT71 4NH
Tel 028-87740221 Fax 028-87746449
Email freoneill@btinternet.com
Rev Mr Malachy McElmeel, Permanent Deacon
c/o Parochial House, 31 Brackaville Road,
Coalisland, Co Tyrone BT71 4NH
Tel 028-87740221 Fax 028-87746449
Email malachy.motability@gmail.com

COOKSTOWN (DESERTCREIGHT AND DERRYLORAN)
Holy Trinity, Cookstown, Sacred Heart,
Tullydonnell, St John's, Slatequarry,
St Laurán's, Cookstown
Very Rev Laurence Boyle PP
Email lorcanboyle@gmail.com
Rev Mr Eamon Quinn, Permanent Deacon
Email eamonquinn1@outlook.com
Parochial House, 1 Convent Road,
Cookstown, Co Tyrone BT80 8QA
Parish email cookstownparish@gmail.com
Tel 028-86763370
Rev Brian Slater CC, VF
Email brianslater60@hotmail.com
Parochial House, 3 Convent Road,
Cookstown, Co Tyrone BT80 8QA
Tel 028-86763490

ARCHDIOCESE OF ARMAGH

COOLEY
St James's, Grange
Our Lady, Star of the Sea, Boher
St Anne's, Mullaghbuoy
Very Rev Malachy Conlon PP, VF, EV
Top Rath, Carlingford, Co Louth A91 XW24
Tel 042-9376105 Fax 042-9376075
Email malachycooley@gmail.com

CROSSMAGLEN (CREGGAN UPPER)
St Patrick's, Crossmaglen,
St Brigid's, Glassdrummond,
Sacred Heart, Shelagh
Email uppercreggan@gmail.com
Very Rev Dermot Maloney PP
Parochial House, 9 Newry Road,
Crossmaglen, Newry,
Co Down BT35 9HH
Tel 028-30861208 Fax 028-30860163
Email maloney750@btinternet.com
Very Rev Kevin Cullen PE, AP
Parochial House, 9a Newry Road,
Crossmaglen, Newry,
Co Down BT35 9HH
Tel 028-30868698 Fax 028-30860163
Rev Mr Paul Casey, Permanent Deacon
c/o Parochial House, 9 Newry Road,
Crossmaglen, Newry, Co Down BT35 9HH
Tel 028-30861208
Email paulcasey2121@gmail.com

CULLYHANNA (CREGGAN LOWER)
St Patrick's, Cullyhanna
St Michael's, Newtownhamilton
St Oliver Plunkett's, Dorsey
Email lowercregganparish@hotmail.com
Very Rev Gerard Tremer PP, VF
Parochial House, Tullynavall Road,
Cullyhanna, Newry, Co Down BT35 OPZ
Tel 028-30861235
Email pplowercreggan@gmail.com

DARVER AND DROMISKIN
St Peter's, Dromiskin, St Michael's, Darver
Very Rev Patrick McEnroe PP
Darver, Readypenny, Dundalk,
Co Louth A91 YC60
Tel 042-9379147
Email patmmcenroe@gmail.com

DONAGHMORE
St Patrick's, Donaghmore
St John's, Galbally
Very Rev David Moore Adm
c/o Paochial House, Cavanakeeran Road,
Pomeroy, Co Tyrone BT20 2RD
Tel 028-87757867
Very Rev Gerard McAleer PP
Parochial House, 63 Castlecaulfield Road,
Donaghmore, Dungannon,
Co Tyrone BT70 3HF
Tel 028-87761327
Email gerard0826@icloud.com
Very Rev Patrick Breslan PE, AP
Parochial House, 55 Dermanaught Road,
Galbally, Dungannon,
Co Tyrone BT70 2NR
Tel 028-87758277

DROMINTEE
St Patrick's, Dromintee
Sacred Heart, Jonesboro
Email drominteeparish@btinternet.com
Very Rev Seamus White PP
Email seamuswhite@ymail.com
Parochial House, 40 The Village,
Jonesboro, Newry,
Co Down BT35 8HP
Tel 028-30849345

DUNLEER
St Brigid's, Dunleer,
St Finians', Dromin,
St Kevin's, Philipstown
www.dunleerparish.ie
Very Rev G. Michael Murtagh PP
Parochial House, Old Chapel Lane,
Dunleer, Co Louth A92 W29X
Tel 041-6851278
Email gmichaelmurtagh@gmail.com

EGLISH
St Patrick's
Email parishofeglish@gmail.com
Very Rev Thomas McHugh Adm
Email thomasmch@gmail.com
Very Rev John Heagney PE, AP
Email heagneyjh@aol.com
124 Eglish Road, Dungannon,
Co Tyrone BT70 1LB
Tel 028-37549661

FAUGHART
St Brigid's, Kilcurry,
Most Holy Rosary, Brid-a-Crinn,
St Joseph's, Castletown
Email info@faughartparish.ie
Very Rev Vinod Kurian (IC) PP
Email thennattil@hotmail.com
Rev Oliver Stansfield (IC) CC
Email ostansfield@gmail.com
Parochial House, Kilcurry,
Dundalk, Co Louth, A91 E8N8
Tel 042-9334410/9333235

HAGGARDSTOWN AND BLACKROCK
St Fursey's Haggardstown
St Oliver Plunkett's, Blackrock
Very Rev Pádraig Keenan PP
Parochial House, Chapel Road,
Haggardstown, Dundalk,
Co Louth A91 X0PR
Tel 042-9321621
Email pkballygoley@hotmail.com
Rev Mr Dermot Clarke, Permanent Deacon
c/o Parochial House, Chapel Road,
Haggardstown, Dundalk,
Co Louth A91 X0PR
Tel 042-9321621
Email dkclarke@eircom.net

KEADY (DERRYNOOSE)
St Patrick's, Keady, St Joseph's,
Derrynoose, St Joseph's, Madden
Email info@keadyparish.net
Very Rev John McKeever PP, VF
Assistant Chancellor of the Diocese
Email john_mckeever@yahoo.com
Rev Mr Martin Barlow,
Permanent Deacon
Email martin@thebarlows.biz
Parochial House, 35 St Patrick Street,
Keady, Co Armagh BT60 3TQ
Tel 028-37531246 Fax 028-37530850
Rev Aidan McCann CC
Parochial House, 34 Madden Row,
Keady, Co Armagh, BT60 3RW
Tel 028-37531242
Email aidmccann@gmail.com

KILDRESS
St Joseph's, Killeenan
St Mary's, Dunamore
Very Rev Patrick Hughes PP
Parochial House, 10 Cloughfin Road,
Kildress, Cookstown,
Co Tyrone BT80 9JB
Tel 028-86751206
Email patrickhughes309@btinternet.com

KILKERLEY
Immaculate Conception
Very Rev Gerard Campbell PP, VF, EV
Parochial House, Knockbridge,
Dundalk, Co Louth A91 NA03
Tel 042-9374125
Email gerrycampbell65@gmail.com
Very Rev Brian MacRaois PE, AP
The Holly Tree, Grange,
Knockbridge, Dundalk,
Co Louth A91 VK18
Tel 042-6827409

KILLCLUNEY
St Patrick's, Baile Mhic an Aba,
St Michael's, Cladaí Móra,
St Mary's, Grainseach Mhór
Email cillchluanaparish@gmail.com
Very Rev Gregory Carvill PP
Parochial House,
194 Newtown Hamilton Road,
Ballymacnab, Armagh BT60 2QS
Tel 028-37531641
Email carvillgreg@gmail.com

KILLEESHIL
Assumption, Killeeshil, St Patrick's,
Aughnagar, St Joseph's, Ackenduff
Email killeeshilparish@yahoo.co.uk
Very Rev Patrick Hannigan PP
Parochial House,
65 Tullyallen Road,
Dungannon, Co Tyrone BT70 3AF
Tel 028-87761211 Fax 028-87769211
Email pathannigan494@gmail.com

ARCHDIOCESE OF ARMAGH

KILMORE
Immaculate Conception, Mullavilly,
St Patrick's, Stonebridge
Email parishofkilmore@gmail.com
www.parishofkilmore.com
Very Rev Oliver Brennan PP
Parochial House, 114 Battlehill Road,
Richhill, Co Armagh BT61 8QJ
Tel 028-38871661
Email olivervbrennan@eircom.net

KILSARAN
St Mary's, Kilsaran
St Nicholas, Stabannon
Email kilsaranandstabannonparish@gmail.com
Very Rev Anselm Emechebe (MSP) PP
Parochial House, Kilsaran,
Castlebellingham, Dundalk,
Co Louth A91 A256
Tel 042-9372255 Fax 042-9372255
Email aemechebe@yahoo.com

KNOCKBRIDGE
St Mary's, Knockbridge
www.ourladyqueenofpeacepa.org
Very Rev Gerard Campbell PP, VF, EV
Email gerrycampbell65@gmail.com
Rev Mr Martin Cunningham, Permanent Deacon
Email mtcunningham@gmail.com
Parochial House, Knockbridge,
Dundalk, Co Louth A91 NA03
Tel 042-9374125

LISSAN
St Michael's
Very Rev Patrick Hughes Adm
Parochial House, 10 Cloughfin Road,
Kildress, Cookstown, Co Tyrone BT80 9JB
Tel 028-86751206
Email patrickhughes309@btinternet.com
Rev Seamus McGinley PE, AP
Parochial House, 2 Tullynure Road,
Cookstown, Co Tyrone BT80 9XH
Tel 028-86769921
Email lissanparish2@gmail.com

LORDSHIP (AND BALLYMASCANLON)
St Mary's, Ravensdale
St Mary's, Lordship
Our Lady of the Wayside, Jenkinstown
www.lordship-ballymascanlon.org
Very Rev Stephen Duffy PP
Parochial House, Ravensdale,
Dundalk, Co Louth A91 V523
Tel 042-9371327
Email duffyst@hotmail.co.uk

LOUGHGALL
Our Lady of Peace, Maghery
St Peter's, Collegeland
St Patrick's, Loughgall
St John's, Tartaraghan
Email loughgallsecretary@gmail.com
Very Rev Garrett Campbell PP
Parochial House, 17 Eagralougher Road,
Loughgall, Co Armagh BT61 8LA
Tel 028-38891231 Fax 028-38891827
Email loughgallpp@gmail.com

LOUTH
Our Lady of Immaculate Conception, Louth
Our Lady of the Snows, Stonetown
Very Rev Gerard Campbell Adm
c/o Parochial House, Knockbridge,
Co Louth A91 NA03
Tel 042 9374125
Email gerrycampbell65@gmail.com
Very Rev Sean McArdle (SM) PP
Parochial House, Louth Village,
Dundalk, Co Louth A91 XE42
Tel 042-9374285
Email sbmc@eircom.net

MAGHERAFELT AND ARDTREA NORTH
Assumption, Magherafelt
St John's, Milltown
St Patrick's Castledawson
Email office@magherafeltparish.org
www.magherafeltparish.org
Very Rev John Gates PP
Parochial House, 30 King Street,
Magherafelt, Co Derry BT45 6AS
Tel 028-79632439
Email jgatesbrack@gmail.com
Rev Juan Jesus Gonzalez-Borrallo CC
Parochial House, 12 Aughrim Road,
Magherafelt, Co Derry BT45 6AY
Tel 077-36955013
Email borrallo.juanjesus@gmail.com
Rev Mr Kevin Duffy, Permanent Deacon
Parochial House, 30 King Street,
Magherafelt, Co Derry BT45 6AS
Tel 028-79632439
Email deacon.kevin@yahoo.co.uk

MELL
St Joseph's
Very Rev John McAlinden PP
Parochial House, Slane Road, Mell,
Drogheda, Co Louth A92 WAC4
Tel 041-9838278
Email frjohnmcalinden@gmail.com

MELLIFONT
Our Lady of the Assumption, Tullyallen
Very Rev Seán Dooley PP
Parochial House, Tullyallen,
Drogheda, Co Louth A92 H243
Tel 041-9838520
Email seandooleyfriesian@btconnect.com

MIDDLE KILLEAVY (NEWRY)
St Mary's, Dromalane,
St Malachy's, Carnagat
www.middlekilleavy.com
Email assumptionnewry@gmail.com
Very Rev Liam McKinney PP, VF
'Glenshee', 9 Dublin Road,
Newry, Co Down BT35 8DA
Tel 028-30262376
Tel Parish Office 028-30252459
Email ltpmckinney@yahoo.com
Rev Damien Quigley CC
27 Woodhill, Monaghan Row, Newry,
Co Down BT35 8DP
Tel 028-30269032
Email quigleydamien@gmail.com

MIDDLETOWN (TYNAN)
St John's, Middletown
St Joseph's, Tynan
Very Rev Seán Moore PP
Parochial House,
290 Monaghan Road,
Middletown, Co Armagh BT60 4HS
Tel 028-37568406
middletowntynanparish@hotmail.co.uk

MONASTERBOICE
Immaculate Conception, Tenure,
Nativity of Our Lady, Fieldstown
Email monasterboiceparish2018@gmail.com
Very Rev Patrick Rushe PP, VF
Parochial House, Monasterboice,
Drogheda, Co Louth A92 RT66
Tel 086-8807470
Email patrickrushe@me.com

MONEYMORE (ARDTREA)
SS John and Trea, Moneymore
St Patrick, Loup
Very Rev Martin McArdle PP, VF
Parochial House, 10 Springhill Road,
Moneymore, Magherafelt,
Co Derry BT45 7NG
Tel 028-86748242
Email ardtrea@btconnect.com

MOY (CLONFEACLE)
St John the Baptist, Moy
St Jarlath's, Clonfeacle
www.clonfeacleparish.com
Very Rev Thomas McHugh Adm
75 Clonfeacle Road,
Blackwatertown, Dungannon,
Co Tyrone BT71 7HP
Tel 028-87511215
Email thomasmch@gmail.com

MULLAGHBAWN (FORKHILL)
St Mary's, Mullaghbawn
Our Lady, Queen of Peace, Aughanduff
St Oliver Plunkett, Forkhill
Very Rev Emlyn McGinn PP, VF
Parochial House, 9a Forkhill Road,
Mullaghbawn, Newry,
Co Down BT35 9RA
Tel 028-30888286
Email emlynmcginn@yahoo.com

NEWBRIDGE
St James, Newbridge
Very Rev John Fox PP
Parochial House, 153 Aughrim Road,
Toomebridge, Antrim BT41 3SH
Tel 028-79468277
Email newbridgechurch@gmail.com

ARCHDIOCESE OF ARMAGH

POMEROY
Assumption, Pomeroy,
Immaculate Conception, Altmore
www.pomeroyparish.homestead.com
Very Rev David Moore PP, VF
Parochial House,
9 Cavanakeeran Road,
Pomeroy, Dungannon,
Co Tyrone BT70 2RD
Tel 028-87757867
Email d.moore2323@outlook.com

PORTADOWN (DRUMCREE)
St John the Baptist's, Garvaghy Road
St Patrick's, William Street
www.drumcreeparish.com
Email parishofdrumcree@gmail.com
Very Rev Canon Michael C. Toner PP
Chancellor of the Diocese,
Parochial House, 15 Moy Road,
Portadown, Co Armagh BT62 1QL
Tel 028-38350610
Very Rev Peter Clarke PE, AP
Parochial House,
11 Moy Road, Portadown,
Co Armagh BT62 1QL
Tel 028-38332218
Email petergerardclarke@gmail.com

TALLANSTOWN
St Malachy's, Reaghstown,
St Medoc's, Clonkeen,
SS Peter and Paul, Tallanstown
Very Rev Paul Montague PP
Parochial House, Reaghstown,
Ardee, Co Louth A92 KW68
Tel 041-6855117
Email tallanstownparish@hotmail.com

TANDRAGEE (BALLYMORE AND MULLAGHBRACK)
St James's, Tandragee
St Patrick's, Ballyargan
St Joseph's, Poyntzpass
St James's, Markethill
Very Rev Michael Woods PP, VF
Parochial House, 10 Acton Road,
Poyntzpass, Newry,
Co Down BT35 6TB
Tel 028-38318471
Email admin@parish57.com
Email mjw@mick58.com

TERMONFECHIN
Immaculate Conception, Termonfechin
The Assumption, Sandpit
Email termonfechinparish@gmail.com
Very Rev Paul Byrne PP
Parochial House, Termonfeckin,
Drogheda, Co Louth A92 W4O3
Tel 041-9822121
Email pauldbyrne2012@gmail.com

TERMONMAGUIRC (CARRICKMORE, LOUGHMACRORY & CREGGAN)
St Colmcille's, Carrickmore
St Oliver Plunkett, Creggan
St Mary's, Loughmacrory
Rev Sean O'Neill PP
Parochial House, 1 Rockstown Road,
Carrickmore, Omagh, Co Tyrone BT79 9BE
Tel 028-80761207
Email termonmaguircparish@gmail.com
Very Rev Thomas Mallon PE, AP
Parochial House,
170 Loughmacrory Road,
Loughmacrory, Omagh,
Co Tyrone BT79 9LG
Tel 028-80761230 Fax 028-80761131
Email mallon393@gmail.com

TOGHER
St Columcille, Togher
St Finnian, Dillonstown
St Borchill, Dysart
St Mary's, Drumcar
Rt Rev Mgr James Carroll PP, EV
Parochial House, Big Strand Road,
Clogherhead, Drogheda,
Co Louth A92 T938
Tel 041-9889335
Email jcarlpp73@gmail.com
Very Rev Thomas Daly PE, AP
Parochial House, Boicetown, Togher,
Drogheda, Co Louth A92 C597
Tel 041-6852110
Email macurta6@icloud.com

WHITECROSS (LOUGHILLY)
St Teresa's, Tullyherron
St Malachy's, Ballymoyer
St Brigid's, Carrickananney
St Laurence O'Toole, Belleeks
Parish Email info@parishofloughgilly.com
Very Rev Malachy Murphy PP
Parochial House, 25 Priestbush Road,
Whitecross, Co Armagh BT60 2TP
Tel 028-37507214
Email malomurphy@gmail.com

INSTITUTIONS AND CHAPLAINCY SERVICES

Aiken Military Barracks
27th Infantry Battalion,
Barrack Street, Dundalk, Co Louth
Very Rev Seán McCartan
Tel 042-9332295
Email seancmccartan@gmail.com

Community School
Ardee, Co Louth
Mr Seán Moran
Tel 041-6853313

Our Lady of Lourdes Hospital
Drogheda, Co Louth
Rev Thomas Hogan CSsR
Our Lady of Lourdes Hospital,
Drogheda, Co Louth
Tel 041-9837601
Email tom.hogan1w@gmail.com

St Paul's High School
Bessbrook, Co Armagh
Email drominteeparish@btinternet.com
Very Rev Séamus White PP
Parochial House,
40 The Village, Jonesboro,
Newry, Co Down BT35 8HP
Tel 028-3084945 (H) 028-30830309 (S)
Email seamuswhite@ymail.com

The following hospitals are served by parochial clergy:

Armagh Community Hospital
Armagh
Tel 028-37522802 (Chaplain)

Daisy Hill Hospital
Newry, Co Down
Tel 028-30835000 (Chaplain)

Longstone Special Care Hospital
Armagh
Tel 028-37522802 (Chaplain)

Louth County Hospital
Dundalk, Co Louth
Tel 042-9334648 (Chaplain)

Mid-Ulster Hospital
Magherafelt, Co Derry
Tel 028-79632351

St Brigid's Hospital
Ardee, Co Louth
Tel 041-6850920 (Chaplain)

St Joseph's Hospital
Ardee, Co Louth
Tel 041-6853313 (Chaplain)

St Oliver Plunkett's Hospital
Dundalk, Co Louth
Tel 042-9334259 (Chaplain)

South Tyrone Hospital
Dungannon, Co Tyrone
Tel 028-87722631 (Chaplain)

PRIESTS OF THE DIOCESE ELSEWHERE

Rev John Connolly
c/o Ara Coeli, Armagh BT61 7QY
Rev Patrick Coyle
c/o Ara Coeli, Armagh BT61 7QY
Rev Rory Coyle
c/o Ara Coeli, Armagh BT61 7QY
Email rory_coyle@hotmail.com
Rev Seamus Dobbin
c/o Ara Coeli, Armagh BT61 7QY
Rev Dominic Mallon
13 Richview Heights, Keady,
Co Armagh BT60 3SW
Rev Ryan McAleer
Amerikaans College,
Naamsestraat 100/01.02,
3000 Leuven, Belgium
Email ryankmcaleer@gmail.com

Very Rev Seán McEvoy
St Moninna's Hermitage,
207 Dublin Road, Newry,
Co Down BT35 8RL
Tel 028-30849424

Very Rev John McGoldrick
9999 N Military Trail,
Palm Beach Gardens,
Florida 33410, USA
Tel 001-215-9291326/001-772-2875044
Email minterburn@hotmail.com

Rev Callum Young
On loan to Dromore Diocese

RETIRED PRIESTS

Very Rev John Bradley PE
8 Killymeal Road, Dungannon,
Co Tyrone BT71 6DP
Tel 028-87722183

Very Rev Fergus Breslan PE
Parochial House, 17 Carnmore Drive,
Newry, Co Down BT35 8SB
Tel 028-30269047
Email fr.fergusbreslan@btinternet.com

Very Rev Laurence Caraher PE
The Ravel, School Lane, Tullyallen,
Drogheda, Co Louth
Tel 041-9834293
Email frcaraher@gmail.com

Very Rev Paul Clayton-Lea PE
Woodside, Strand Road, Termonfechin,
Drogheda, Co Louth A92 W7W6
Tel 041-9822631
Email claytonleapaul@gmail.com

Rev Desmond Corrigan
17 Chapel Street, Poyntzpass, Newry,
Co Down BT35 6SY
Tel 028-38318217

Very Rev Canon Michael Crawley PE
Parochial House,
89 Derrynoose Road,
Derrynoose, Co Armagh BT60 3EZ
Tel 028-37531222
Email michaelcrawley89@btinternet.com

Very Rev John Hughes PE
30 Jockey Lane, Moy,
Dungannonn, Co Tyrone BT71 7SR
Tel 028-87784240
Email revhughes135@btinternet

Very Rev Peter Kerr PE
42 Innishatieve Road, Carrickmore,
Omagh, Co Tyrone BT79 9HS
Tel 028-80761837

Very Rev Patrick Larkin PE
Carlingford Nursing Home,
Old Dundalk Road,
Carlingford, Co Louth

Very Rev Patrick J. McCrory PE
Parochial House, Sixemilecross,
Omagh, Co Tyrone BT79 9NF
Tel 028-80758344
Email pjmccrory@icloud.com

Very Rev Canon Patrick McDonnell PE
Our Lady of Lourdes Presbytery,
Hardman's Gardens,
Drogheda, Co Louth
Tel 041-9831899

Very Rev Gerard McGinnity PE
4 Rowan Road, Armagh BT60 3DR

Very Rev Patrick McGuckin PE
79 Reclain Road,
Galbally, Dungannon,
Co Tyrone BT70 2PQ
Tel 028-87759692
Email frpmcguckin@hotmail.com

Very Rev Robert McKenna PE
Parochial House,
28 Newtown Road, Camlough,
Newry, Co Down BT35 7JJ
Tel 028-30830237
Email robert.mckenna3@btinternet.com

Rev Thomas McNulty
Goretti Cottage, Acre Road,
Carlingford, Co Louth A91 PW95
Tel 042-9376577
Email tommymcnulty37@gmail.com

Very Rev Pádraig Murphy PE
Parochial House, Jenkinstown,
Dundalk, Co Louth A91 CC79
Tel 042-9371328
Email pplordship@outlook.com

Rt Rev Mgr Raymond Murray PE
60 Glen Mhacaha, Cathedral Road,
Armagh BT61 8AF
Tel 028-37510821
Email raylmurray@outlook.com

Rt Rev Mgr Christopher O'Byrne PE
3 Grange Court, Magherafelt,
Co Derry BT45 5RU
Tel 028-79631791
Email cobyrne@magherafeltparish.org

Very Rev Owen O'Donnell PE
Parochial House, Dunamore,
Cookstown, Co Tyrone
Tel 028-86751216
Email o.odonnell37@gmail.com

Very Rev Seán F. Quinn PE
Moorehall Lodge, Hale Street,
Ardee, Co Louth
Email sqparish@gmail.com

Very Rev Seán J. Quinn PE
Parochial House,
Dillonstown, Dunleer,
Co Louth A92 HH24
Email sjqdill@gmail.com

Very Rev Séamus Rice PE
4 Ballymacnab Road,
Armagh BT60 2QS
Tel 028-37531620
Email seamusrice@live.co.uk

RELIGIOUS ORDERS AND CONGREGATIONS

PRIESTS

AUGUSTINIANS
St Augustine's Priory, Shop Street,
Drogheda, Co Louth
Tel 041-9838409 Fax 041-9831847
Prior: Rev Colm O'Mahony (OSA)
Email focal@eircom.net

CISTERCIANS
Mellifont Abbey, Collon, Co Louth
Tel 041-9826103 Fax 041-9826713
Email info@mellifontabbey.ie
Superior: Rev Brendan Freeman
Email brbrendan@newmelleray.org

DOMINICANS
St Malachy's Priory, Dundalk, Co Louth
Tel 042-9334179/9333714
Fax 042-9329751
Superior: Rev David Barrins (OP)

JESUITS
Iona, 211 Churchill Park,
Portadown, Co Armagh BT62 1EU
Tel 028-38330366 Fax 028-38338334
Superior: Rev Brendan MacPartlin (SJ)
Email iona@jesuit.ie

MARISTS
Cerdon, Marist Fathers,
St Mary's Road, Dundalk, Co Louth
Tel 042-9334019
Superior: Rev James O'Connell (SM)

St Mary's College, Dundalk, Co Louth
Tel 042-9339984
Principal: Mr Alan Craven

REDEMPTORISTS
St Joseph's, St Alphonsus Road,
Dundalk, Co Louth
Tel 042-9334042/9334762
Fax 042-9330893
Superior: Rev Noel Kehoe (CSsR) PP
Vicar-Superior
Rev Richard Delahunty (CSsR)
Rev Dan Baragry (CSsR) *(Provincial)*

(See also under parishes – Dundalk,
St Joseph's)

ROSMINIANS
See under parishes – Carlingford &
Clogherny and Faughart

SERVITES
Servite Priory, Benburb,
Co Tyrone BT71 7JZ
Tel 028-37548241
Retreat, conference and youth centre
Prior: Rev Bernard Thorne (OSM)

ARCHDIOCESE OF ARMAGH

BROTHERS

DE LA SALLE BROTHERS
De La Salle College, Dundalk, Co Louth
Tel 042-9331179 Fax 042-9330870
Principal: Ms Patricia O'Leary

SAINT JOHN OF GOD BROTHERS
St Mary's Community, Drumcar,
Dunleer, Co Louth A92 X9X4
Tel 041-6851824 Fax 041-6851101
Prior: Br Ronan Lennon (OH)
Community: 3

SAINT JOHN OF GOD NORTH EAST SERVICES
St Mary's, Drumcar, Dunleer, Co Louth
Tel 041-6851211 Fax 041-6851529
Email admin.northeast@sjog.ie
Interim Regional Director: Paula Hand
St Mary's School, Drumcar, Co Louth
Tel 041-6851211
School Principal: Mr Kevin Toale
Residential, day and community services for children and adults with varying degrees of intellectual disability.

SISTERS

CARMELITE SISTERS
Teach Bríd,
7A Coopers Cross, Annagassan Road,
Castlebellinghim, Co Louth
Tel 042-6821550

CONGREGATION OF THE SISTERS OF MERCY
Mill Street, Dundalk, Co Louth A91 C2C4
Tel 042-9334200
Community: 6

Mile End, Avenue Road,
Dundalk, Co Louth A91 X6A0
Tel 042-9330410
Community: 3

Bethany, 34 Point Road,
Dundalk, Co Louth A91 W0C9
Tel 042-9331602

15 Cypress Gardens,
Bay Estate, Dundalk,
Co Louth A91 P0A2
Tel 042-9329315

58 Fairhill Road, Cookstown,
Co Tyrone BT80 8AG
Tel 028-86763363
Community: 5

Sisters of Mercy, 10 Killymeal Road,
Dungannon, Co Tyrone BT71 6DP
Tel 028-87722623

Sisters of Mercy,
90 Church View, Bessbrook,
Newry, Co Down BT35 78T
Tel 028-30837140

115 Oaklawns,
Dundalk, Co Louth A91 K6W7
Tel 042-9334569

No. 8 Central Avenue,
Cookstown, Co Tyrone BT80 8AJ
Tel 028-86764861

Sisters of Mercy, Hale Street,
Ardee, Co Louth A92 NY36
Tel 041-6842001
Community: 8

39 Moorehall Lodge,
Moorehall Village, Ardee, Co Louth
Tel 041-6871406

21 The Village,
Moorehall Lodge, Ardee, Co Louth
Tel 041-6850165

DOMINICAN CONTEMPLATIVE NUNS
Monastery of St Catherine of Siena,
The Twenties, Drogheda,
Co Louth A92 KR84
Tel 041-9838524
Email sienamonastery@gmail.com
www.dominicannuns.ie
Prioress: Sr Mairéad Mullen (OP)
Community: 17

FRANCISCAN MISSIONARIES OF THE DIVINE MOTHERHOOD
No. 1 Fontabranda, Francis Street,
Drogheda, Co Louth A92 V25C
Tel 041-9849189
Community: 1

FRANCISCAN MISSIONARY SISTERS FOR AFRICA
Franciscan Convent, Mount Oliver,
Dundalk, Co Louth (Motherhouse)
Tel 042-9371123 Fax 042-9371159
Email mtofmsa20@gmail.com
Team Leadership
Contact Person
Sr Kathleen Moran (FMSA)
Community: 35

MEDICAL MISSIONARIES OF MARY
Motherhouse, Beechgrove,
Hardman's Gardens,
Drogheda, Co Louth A92 XKX0
Tel 041-9837512 Fax 041-9839219
Email beechgroveadmin@mmm37.org
Leader: Sr Ursula Sharpe

MMM Nursing Facility
Áras Mhuire, Beechgrove,
Hardman's Gardens,
Drogheda, Co Louth A92 HN29
Nursing Tel 041-9842222
Admin Tel 041-9845762
Administration
businessmanager@arasmhuire.com
Pastoral Dept
pastoralcare@arasmhuire.com

Greenbank,
Mell, Drogheda,
Co Louth A92 X54F
Tel 041-9831028
Email mmmgreenbankmell@gmail.com
Community: 5

Area Office, No 13 Ashleigh Heights,
Drogheda, Co Louth A92 RTF4
Tel 041-9830779
Email arealeader@mmmeuarea.ie

No 14 Ashleigh Heights,
Drogheda, Co Louth A92 E6CV
Community: 2

MMM Communications Department,
Beechgrove Hardman's Gardens,
Drogheda, Co Lough A92 XKX0
Email mmmcomm37@gmail.com

MISSIONARIES OF CHARITY
19A Cathedral Road,
Armagh BT61 7QX
Tel 04837-528654
Superior: Sr Gemma Paul (MC)
Community: 4
Hostel for men

PRESENTATION SISTERS
Greenhills,
Drogheda, Co Louth
Tel 041-9831420
Community: 4
School ministry and pastoral

103 Thomas Street,
Portadown,
Co Armagh BT62 3AH
Tel 028-38332220
Community: 2
Cross community work and pastoral ministry

28 Garvaghy Park,
Portadown, Co Armagh BT62 1HB
Tel 028-38335964
Community: 2
Pastoral ministry

SACRED HEART SOCIETY
6 Convent Road,
Armagh BT60 4BJ
Tel 028-37522046 Fax 028-37518764
Education, pastoral work and youth work. Provincial Administration.

Gate Lodge, 4 Convent Road,
Armagh BT60 4BG
Email sr.nora.smyth@googlemail.com
Pastoral work and writing

ST LOUIS SISTERS
Dún Lughaidh, Dundalk, Co Louth
Tel 042-9335786
Community: 8

10 Millstream, Distillery Lane,
Dundalk, Co Louth
Community: 1

Sacred Heart Community,
6 Convent Road, Armagh BT60 4BG
Community: 1

EDUCATIONAL INSTITUTIONS

Redemptoris Mater Archdiocesan Missionary Seminary
De La Salle Terrace, Castletown,
Dundalk, Co Louth A91 C5D6
Tel 042-9336584
Rector: Rev Giuseppe Pollio
Email gpollio24@gmail.com
Director of Studies
Rev Maciej Zacharek CC

Coláiste Rís
Chapel Street, Dundalk, Co Louth
Tel 042-9334336 Fax 042-9338380
Principal: Ms Noilin Ní Dhulaing

St Patrick's Academy
37 Killymeal Road, Dungannon,
Co Tyrone BT71 6DS
Tel 028-87722668
Fax 028-87722745
Principal: Mr Fintan Donnelly

St Patrick's Grammar School
Cathedral Road, Armagh BT61 7QZ
Tel 028-37522018 Fax 028-37525930
Principal: Mr Dominic Clarke

St Joseph's Convent Grammar School
58 Castlecaulfied, Donaghmore,
Co Tyrone BT70 3HE
Tel 028-87761227
Principal: Mrs Geraldine Donnelly

CHARITABLE AND OTHER SOCIETIES

Aras Mhuire
14 Irish Street, Dungannon,
Co Tyrone BT70 1DB
Tel 028-87726852
Oratory and bookshop

Avila Nursing Home
Convent of Mercy, Convent Hill,
Bessbrook, Co Armagh BT35 7AW
Tel 028-30838969

Cuan Mhuire
200 Dublin Road,
Newry, Co Down BT35 8RL
Tel 028-30849010
Alcohol counselling

Family of God Community
The Oratory, Carroll's Village,
Dundalk, Co Louth
Tel 042-9339888

St John of God Community Services CLG
North East Services,
St Mary's, Drumcar, Co Louth
Tel 041-6862600

SOS Prayer
The Oratory, Carroll's Village,
Dundalk, Co Louth
Tel 042-9339888

Allianz

Shop online at www.veritas.ie

The Veritas website features a wide range of resources to meet the needs of parishes, educators, families and individuals.

Visit www.veritas.ie to see how we can help you today.

✳ VERITAS

For Books and Gifts with a Difference · www.veritas.ie

RADIO MARIA
IRELAND
Sanctifying the Airwaves!
MARY FITZPATRICK
hosts
The Immaculate Heart of Mary
Prayer Meeting
WED @ 1PM
only on
RADIO MARIA
DERMOT McGRATH
presents
THE OPEN DOOR OF MUSIC
MON & TUE @ 1PM
only on
RADIO MARIA
Fr. DAVID VARD
presents
VOCATION STORIES
WED @ 2PM
only on
RADIO MARIA
THOMAS ROCHE
presents
CEOL AGUS CRAIC
SAT @ 1PM
only on
RADIO MARIA
Fr. EAMONN McCARTHY
presents
CHATECHESIS
TUE - SAT @ 11.15AM
only on
RADIO MARIA
LIVE ON
PATRICIA KEANE
presents
HEALTH & FAITH MATTERS
TUES @ 2.30PM
only on
RADIO MARIA
MARY STENSON
presents
ALL THINGS LEGION
TUE @ 6.10PM
only on
RADIO MARIA
Fr. JOHN McCARTHY
presents
THE RADIO MARIA BOOK CLUB
THURS @4PM
only on
RADIO MARIA
TARA McDERMOTT
presents
Total Beauty
FRI @ 6.10PM
only on
RADIO MARIA
SAORVIEW
TV Channel 210
Freeview
Download Mobile App
'Radio Maria Ireland'
Online Website
www.radiomaria.ie
Radio Feed via Telephone
Dial: 01-437-3277

IT'S NOT JUST A DROUGHT
Photo: Trócaire
Charity No: 20204842
FOR SARAH,
IT'S A FIGHT FOR SURVIVAL
PLEASE GIVE NOW
TROCAIRE.ORG | 1800 408 408
trōcaire | UNTIL LOVE CONQUERS FEAR

New from Veritas Publications

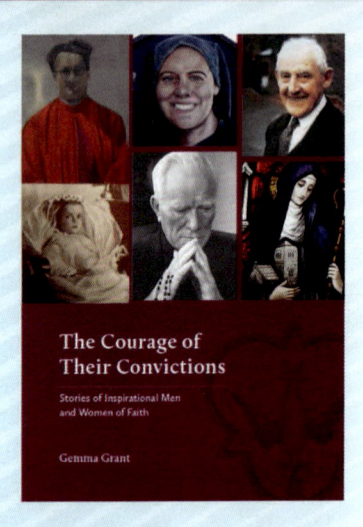

The Courage of their Convictions
Stories of Inspirational Men and Women of Faith

GEMMA GRANT

978 1 80097 007 6
€14.99/£13.50

This fascinating collection details the stories of ordinary, and yet extraordinary, individuals whose unshakable faith and personal courage helped change the lives of millions.

These remarkable stories transport us to places all over the world, including a convent garage in Ohio, where Mother Angelica founded the largest religious television network in the world; inside the walls of the Vatican, where Monsignor Hugh O'Flaherty, 'The Scarlett Pimpernel of the Vatican', evaded the snare of a Gestapo colonel; the depths of the Bolivian jungle where Father Joe Walijewski helped build an entire city; and a church in Dublin where Matt Talbot quietly made his daily pilgrimage.

Common to each of these exceptional men and women, lay and religious alike, was their willingness to take up their cross, no matter what the cost. Their abilities to overcome insurmountable obstacles have made their stories worth telling and their lives worth remembering.

Gemma Grant grew up in Belfast during the Troubles, a harrowing experience that placed an indelible mark on the author. She earned a Degree in History from Trinity College and has travelled extensively, from Rome to Marrakesh to the Dead Sea. Gemma has written for *Ireland's Eye*, and has contributed numerous articles and short stories to *Ireland's Own*, including a series of articles called 'Ireland's Historical Castles'. She has written unpublished works End of the Road: A Belfast Tale and a collection of children's stories. She lives in Dublin with her husband, Ruairí.

Abbey Street & Blanchardstown Centre, Dublin
Cork • Derry • Letterkenny • Newry

VERITAS
www.veritas.ie

ARCHDIOCESE OF DUBLIN

PATRONS OF THE ARCHDIOCESE
ST KEVIN, 3 JUNE; ST LAURENCE O'TOOLE, 14 NOVEMBER

SUFFRAGEN SEES: KILDARE AND LEIGHLIN, FERNS, OSSORY

INCLUDES CITY AND COUNTY OF DUBLIN, NEARLY ALL OF COUNTY WICKLOW AND PORTIONS OF COUNTIES CARLOW, KILDARE, LAOIS AND WEXFORD

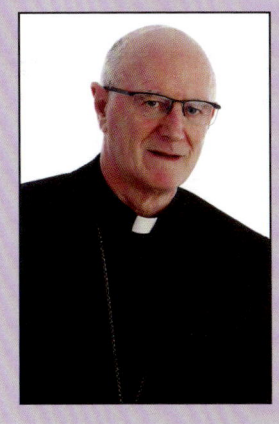

Most Rev Dermot Farrell DD
Born 1954 in Co Westmeath; ordained priest 7 June 1980; appointed as Bishop of Ossory by Pope Francis 3 January 2018; ordained bishop in St Mary's Cathedral, Kilkenny, 11 March 2018; appointed by Pope Francis as Archbishop of Dublin 29 December 2020

Residence: Archbishop's House, Drumcondra, Dublin D09 H4C2
Tel 01-8373732

ST MARYS PRO-CATHEDRAL, DUBLIN

Though Catholic Dublin has not possessed a cathedral since the Reformation, for almost two hundred years now St Mary's Pro-Cathedral has served as the Mother Church of the Dublin arch-diocese. In that time it has won a special place in the hearts of the Dublin people, to whom it is known affectionately as 'The Pro'.

The Pro-Cathedral was born of the vision of Archbishop John Thomas Troy and brought to fruition thanks to the unstinting labours of its second administrator, Archdeacon John Hamilton. The parish of Saint Mary's, straddling the Liffey, was established in 1707 and a chapel dedicated to St Mary was opened in 1729. In 1797 Archbishop Troy successfully petitioned the Holy See to allow him take St Mary's as his *mensal* parish. He thereupon set about raising funds to build a 'dignified, spacious church' in a central location in the parish.

The site chosen was a building on Marlborough Street, opposite Tyrone House. Formerly the town house of the Earl of Annesley, it was purchased for £5,100 and a deposit was paid in 1803. However, it was not until 1814 that designs were publicly invited for the new church. A design of uncertain authorship, marked only with the letter 'P', for a church in the form of a Grecian Doric temple, was chosen as the winner. The only substantial alteration to the design was the erection of a dome.

The foundation stone was laid by Archbishop Troy in 1815. On the feast of St Laurence O'Toole in 1825, Archbishop Murray celebrated High Mass, to mark the dedication of the church to the 'Conception of the Virgin Mary', to a packed congregation, which included Daniel O'Connell. After the dedication, the interior embellishment of the church continued. Highlights included the alto relief representation of the Ascension by John Smyth; the high altar carved by Peter Turnerelli, and the marble statues of Archbishops Murray and Cullen by Thomas Farrell. Stained-glass windows, depicting Our Lady flanked by St Laurence O'Toole and St Kevin, were installed behind the sanctuary in 1886. The high point of liturgical embellishment was the generous benefaction by Edward Martyn, who endowed the Palestrina choir for male voices in 1902.

ARCHDIOCESE OF DUBLIN

Most Rev Diarmuid Martin DD
Archbishop Emeritus of Dublin
c/o Archbishop's House, Drumcondra,
Dublin D09 H4C2

Most Rev Eamonn Walsh DD
Auxiliary Bishop Emeritus;
Residence: Naomh Brid,
Blessington Road, Tallaght, Dublin 24
Tel/Fax 01-4598032

Most Rev Raymond Field DD
Auxiliary Bishop Emeritus;
Residence: 3 Castleknock Road,
Blanchardstown, Dublin 15
Tel/Fax 01-8209191

Vicars General
Very Rev Gareth Byrne VG
Very Rev Ciaran O'Carroll VG
Very Rev Donal Roche VG
Archbishop's House, Dublin 9
Tel 01-8379253

CHAPTER

Dean
Most Rev Eamonn Walsh
Precentor
Very Rev John Canon Flaherty
Chancellor
Very Rev Patrick Canon Fagan PE
Treasurer
Vacant
Archdeacon of Dublin
Ven Archdeacon Peadar Murney
Archdeacon of Glendalough:
Ven Archdeacon Kevin Lyon CC

Prebendaries
Cullen
Very Rev Martin Canon Cosgrove,
(Moderator)
St Mary's Presbytery, Willbrook Road,
Rathfarnham, Dublin 14
Kilmactalway
Very Rev James Canon Fingleton
279 Howth Road, Raheny, Dublin 5
Swords
Very Rev Patrick F. Canon Carroll
124 New Cabra Road, Dublin 7
Yago
Very Rev Damian Canon O'Reilly
Chaplain, St Vincent's University Hospital,
Elm Park, Dublin 4
St Audoen's
Very Rev John Canon McNamara PP
Apt 2, The Presbytery, Dublin Street,
Balbriggan, Co Dublin
Clonmethan
Very Rev Walter Canon Harris PE
151 Clonsilla Road, Blanchardstown,
Dublin 15
Wicklow
Very Rev Liam Canon Belton (Moderator)
Presbytery No 1, St John the Evangelist
Parish, Ballinteer Avenue,
Dublin 16 PY54
Timothan
Very Rev Francis Canon McEvoy Adm
Parochial House, Moyglare Road,
Maynooth, Co Kildare

Malahidert
Very Rev Patrick Canon Shiel
74 Mount Drinan Avenue,
Kinsealy Downs, Swords, Co Dublin
Castleknock
Very Rev Martin Canon Hagan
(Moderator)
186 Clontarf Road, Dublin D03 HK59
Tipper
Rev John Canon Piert *(Team Assistant)*
Our Lady's Manor, Bulloch Harbour,
Dalkey, Co Dublin
Tassagard
Very Rev Padraig Canon Ó Cochlain
Parochial house, Arcklow, Co Wicklow
Dunlavin
Very Rev Liam Canon Rigney
Parochial House, 1 Stanhope Place,
Athy, Co Kildare
Maynooth
Very Rev Sean Canon Smith CC
The Presbytery, Newtownmountkennedy,
Co Wicklow
Howth
Very Rev John Canon Killeen PP
20 Abbey Court, Abbey Road, Blackrock,
Co Dublin
Rathmichael
Very Rev John Canon Delany Adm
Parochial House, St Mary's,
Sandyford Village, Dublin 18
Monmahenock
Very Rev J. Anthony Canon Gaughan PE
56 Newtownpark Avenue,
Blackrock, Co Dublin
Stagonilly
Very Rev Michael Canon Hurley
85 Tymon Crescent, Old Bawn,
Tallaght, Dublin D24 FK0W
Tipperkevin, 1a pars
Very Rev John Canon Fitzgibbon PE
The Presbytery, Chapel Road,
Lusk, Co Dublin
Tipperkevin, 2a pars
Very Rev Anthony Canon Reilly PP
Parochial House, Palmerstown, Dublin 20
Donaghmore, 1a pars
Vacant
Donaghmore, 2a pars
Very Rev Derek Canon Farrell
Parochial House, Garristown, Co Dublin

Deaneries and Vicars Forane
Bray
Very Rev Aquinas Duffy VF
19 Woodlands, Road, Johnstown,
Glenageary, Co Dublin
Tel 01-5672374
Dun Laoghaire
Very Rev Paul Tyrrell PP
St Michael's Parochial House,
4 Eblana Avenue, Dun Laoghaire,
Co Dublin
Te 01-2804969

Wicklow
Very Rev Derek Doyle *(Moderator)* VF
Parochial House, Rathdrum, Co Wicklow
Tel 0404-46229
Donnybrook: Very Rev Fergus O'Connor
(Opus Dei) PP, VF
31 Herbert Avenue,
Merrion Road, Dublin 4
Tel 01-2692001
South City Centre
Very Rev Seán Forde (OCarm) PP, VF
Our Lady of Mount Carmel Parish,
Whitefriar Street Church,
56 Aungier Street, Dublin 2
North City Centre
Very Rev Robert Colclough Adm, VF
Parochial House, Seville Place, Dublin 1
Tel 01-2865457
Cullenswood
Very Rev Paul Taylor Adm, VF
49 Rathgar Road, Dublin 6
South Dublin
Very Rev Philip Bradley Adm, VF
Parochial House, 83 Terenure Road East,
Dublin 6
Tel 01-4905520
Tallaght
Very Rev William O'Shaughnessy CC, VF
70 Maplewood Road, Tallaght, Dublin 24
Tel 01-4590746
Blessington
Very Rev Aidan Kieran Adm, VF
Parochial House,
Castledermot, Co Kildare
Fingal North
Very Rev John Canon McNamara PP
Apt 2, The Presbytery, Dublin Street,
Balbriggan, Co Dublin
Tel 01-8020185
Blanchardstown
Rt Rev Mgr Eoin Thynne Adm, VF
24 The Court, Mulhuddart Wood,
Mulhuddart, Dublin 15
Tel 087-2401432
Maynooth
Very Rev Joseph McDonald PP, VF
Parochial House, Celbridge, Co Kildare
Tel 01-6275874
Fingal South-East
Very Rev Bryan Shortall (OFMCap) PP, VF
Capuchin Parochial Friary,
Clonshaugh Drive, Priorswood, Dublin 17
Tel 01-8474469/8474358
Fingal South-West
Very Rev Richard Sheehy *(Moderator)*, VF
50 Cremore Road, Glasnevin, Dublin 11
Tel 01-5582697
Howth
Very Rev Martin Noone Co-PP, VF
7 Seabury Drive, Malahide,
Co Dublin K36 YN67
Tel 01-8451902

ARCHDIOCESE OF DUBLIN

College of Consultors
Very Rev Gareth Byrne, VG, Moderator of the Diocesan Curia
Very Rev Ciaran O'Carroll PP, VG
Very Rev Donal Roche Adm, VG
Very Rev Paul Coyle, Chancellor
Very Rev Andrew O'Sullivan Adm, Chair of the Council of Priests
Very Rev Joseph Mullan, Moderator, Vice-Chair of the Council of Priests
Very Rev Philip Curran, Moderator
Very Rev Gerry Kane PP

ADMINISTRATION

Moderator of the Curia
Very Rev Gareth Byrne VG
Office of the Moderator,
Archbishop's House, Dublin 9
Tel 01-8379347

Chancellor
Very Rev Paul Coyle
The Chancellery,
Archbishop's House, Dublin 9
Tel 01-8379253 Fax 8571650

Ecclesiastical Censor
Rt Rev Mgr John Dolan
The Chancellery, Archbishop's House, Dublin 9
Tel 01-8379253

Vicar for Clergy
Rt Rev Mgr Eoin Thynne
Archbishop's House, Dublin 9
Tel 01-8379253

Episcopal Vicar for Religious and Extern Priests
Rt Rev Mgr John Dolan
Archbishop's House, Dublin 9
Tel 01-8379253

Diocesan Archivist
Ms Noelle Dowling
Holy Cross Diocesan Centre,
Clonliffe Road, Dublin 3
Tel 01-8379253

General Manager/Financial Administrator
General Manager: Mr Declan McSweeney
Finance Secretariat,
Holy Cross Diocesan Centre,
Clonliffe Road, Dublin 3
Tel 01-8379253 Fax 01-8368393

Archbishop's PA
Ms Mary Irwin
Archbishop's House, Drumcondra, Dublin 9
Tel 01-8373732

Office for Mission and Ministry
Director: Ms Patricia Carroll
Holy Cross Diocesan Centre,
Clonliffe Road, Dublin 3
Tel 01-8373732

Child Safeguarding and Protection Service
Tel 01-8360314 Fax 01-8842599
Email cps@dublindiocese.ie
Website www.cps.dublindiocese.ie
Director: Mr Andrew Fagan
Tel 01-8842590
Priest Delegate: Rev Richard Shannon

Child Safeguarding and Protection Training Co-ordinator
Mr Garry Kehoe
Email garry.kehoe@dublindiocese.ie

Communications Office
Tel 01-8360723 Fax 01-8360793
Email communications@dublindiocese.ie
Website www.dublindiocese.ie

Education Secretariat
Episcopal Vicar for Education
Rt Rev Mgr Dan O'Connor
Tel 01-8379253 Fax 01-8368393
Email dan.oconnor@dublindiocese.ie
Senior Education Specialist
Mr Declan Lawlor
Email declan.lawlor@dublindiocese.ie

Finance Secretariat
Financial Administrator
Mr Declan McSweeney
Email declan.mcsweeney@dublindiocese.ie

DIOCESAN COMMITTEES

Clerical Fund Society
Holy Cross Diocesan Centre,
Clonliffe Road, Dublin 3
Tel 01-8379253
President: The Archbishop of Dublin
Vice-Presidents: The Vicars General

Standing Committee
Chairperson: Very Rev Gareth Byrne VG
Secretary: Ms Ide Finnegan

Commission on Parish Boundaries
c/o Archbishop's House,
Drumcondra, Dublin 9
Tel 01-8379253
Chairperson: Mr Dermot McCarthy

Common Fund Executive Committee
Holy Cross Diocesan Centre,
Clonliffe Road, Dublin 3
Tel 01-8379253
Chairperson: Very Rev Paul Taylor
Secretary: Mr Declan McSweeney

Finance Committee
Holy Cross Diocesan Centre,
Clonliffe Road, Dublin 3
Tel 01-8379253
Chairperson: Mr Michael Duffy
Secretary: Ms Ide Finnegan

CATECHETICS EDUCATION

Diocesan Advisers for Religious Education in Primary Schools
Education Secretariat,
Archbishop's House, Drumcondra, Dublin 9
Tel 01-8379253 Fax 01-8368393
Sr Maureen Matthews,
Sr Anne Neylon DC
All at the Education Secretariat

Diocesan Advisors for Religious Education in Post-Primary Schools
Sr Bernadette Carron DC,
Sr Concepta Foley RSM

LITURGY

Commission for Sacred Art and Architecture & Historic Churches
Chairperson: Edward O'Shea

PASTORAL

ACCORD
Ms Jennifer Griffin (Dublin Director)
Tel 01-4784400
Email admin@dublin.accord.ie

CROSSCARE
Social Support Agency for the Archdiocese of Dublin
Chairperson: Mr Frank O'Connell
Director: Mr Conor Hickey
St Mary's Place, Dorset Street, Dublin 1
Tel 01-8360011

Council of Priests
President: Most Rev Dermot Farrell DD
Chairperson
Very Rev Andrew O'Sullivan Adm

Dublin Roman Catholic Diocesan Hospital Chaplains Association
Chairperson of Committee:
Rev John Kelly
Chaplain, Tallaght Hospital
Tel 01-4142482
Email john.kelly@tuh.ie

Ecumenism
Chairperson and Secretary
Very Rev Kieran McDermott

Knock Diocesan Pilgrimage
Director: Deacon Gerard Reilly

Legion of Mary
Diocesan Chaplain: Vacant

Lourdes Diocesan Pilgrimage
Director: Very Rev Martin Noone
Lourdes Pilgrimage Office,
Holy Cross College, Clonliffe, Dublin 3
Tel 01-8376820

Marriage Tribunal
(See Marriage Tribunals section)

National Chaplaincy for Deaf People
Chaplain: Rev Patrick Boyle
Tel 086-1011415
Website www.ncdp.ie

Permanent Diaconate
Diocesan Director: Very Rev John Gilligan
Assistant Directors
Very Rev Joseph Mullan
Deacon Noel Ryan
Holy Cross Diocesan Centre,
Clonliffe Road, Dublin 3
Tel 01-8087531

Missio Ireland
Diocesan Director
Very Rev Patrick Canon Carroll
Rev John Greene
The Parochial House, St Kevin's Parish,
Laragh, Glendalough, Co Wicklow
Tel 044-45140

ARCHDIOCESE OF DUBLIN

Travellers
Ministry to the Travelling People (Dublin Diocese): Very Rev Paul O'Driscoll PP
Office: St Laurence House,
6 New Cabra Road, Phibsboro, Dublin 7
Tel 01-8388874/087-2573857
Fax 01-8388901
Email partravs@iol.ie

Vocations
Director: Very Rev Seamus McEntee
Holy Cross College, Clonliffe, Dublin 3
Tel 01-8379253

PARISHES

Mensal parishes are listed first. Other parishes follow alphabetically. Church titulars are in italics.

PRO-CATHEDRAL
St Mary's (Immaculate Conception)
Marlborough Street, Dublin 1
Very Rev Kieran McDermott Adm
Rt Rev Mgr Lorcan O'Brien TA
Rev Brendan Staunton (SJ) PC
Parish Sister: Sr Patricia Somers (RSC)
Pro-Cathedral House,
83 Marlborough Street, Dublin 1
Tel 01-8745441
Email procath@dublindiocese.ie
Website www.procathedral.ie

WESTLAND ROW
St Andrew's, Westland Row, Dublin 2
Very Rev Enda Cunningham Adm
47 Westland Row, Dublin 2
Tel 01-8368746
Rev Egidijus Arnasius
48 Westland Row
Tel 01-6761030/087-7477554
Email arnasius@gmail.com
Rev Anthony Hou
Chaplain to the Chinese Community
Rev Deacon Dermot McCarthy
Parish Office: Tel 01-6761270 Fax 01-6763544
Email westlandrow@dublindiocese.ie
Website www.saintandrewsparish.ie

CITY QUAY
Immaculate Heart of Mary, Dublin 2
Rev Pearse Walsh Adm
The Presbytery, City Quay, Dublin 2
Parish Office: Tel 01-6773073
Website jocityquayparish@gmail.com

SEAN MCDERMOTT STREET
Our Lady of Lourdes,
Sean McDermott Street, Dublin 1
Rev Michael Casey (SDB) Adm
Tel 01-8363358
Rev Hugh O'Donnell (SDB) CC
72 Sean McDermott Street,
Dublin 1, D01 K201
Rev Eugen Timpu, Chaplain to Romanian Community
Parish Office: Tel 01-8551259/086-8382631
Email seanmcdermott@dublindiocese.ie

ARDLEA
St John Vianney, Ardlea Road,
Artane, Dublin 5
Very Rev Hugh Hanley (SCJ), *(Moderator)*
Rev Michel Simo Temgo (SCJ) CC
Rev Marian Szalwa (SCJ) PC
Parochial House, St John Vianney,
Ardlea Road, Dublin 5
Tel 01-8474173
Parish Office: Tel 01-8474123
Email ardleaparish@yahoo.com

ARKLOW
(Grouped with the parish of Castletown)
SS Mary and Peter, Arklow, Co Wicklow
Chapel of Ease: St David's, Johnstown,
Co Wicklow
Very Rev Padraig Ó Cochlain *(Moderator)*
Parochial House, Arklow, Co Wicklow
Tel/Fax 0402-32294
Email mfc53@indigo.ie
Very Rev David Brough Co-PP (parishes of Arklow, Castletown, Aughrim & Avoca)
2 St Mary's Terrace, Arcklow, Co Wicklow
Tel 0402-32196
Parish Office: Tel/Fax 0402-31716
Email office@arklowparish.ie
www.arklowparish.ie

ARTANE
Our Lady of Mercy, Brookwood Grove,
Dublin 5
Very Rev Peter O'Reilly Adm
16 Brookwood Grove, Artane, Dublin 5
Rev Brian Durnin CC
12 Brookwood Grove, Artane, Dublin 5
Tel 01-8187996
Parish Office
Tel 01-8314297 Fax 01-8314054
Email ourladyofmercy.church@gmail.com

ASHFORD
Church of the Most Holy Rosary, Co Wicklow
Very Rev Eamonn Crosson Adm
Parochial House, Ashford, Co Wicklow
Tel/Fax 0404-40540
Rev Deacon Jeremy Seligman

ATHY
St Michael's, Co Kildare
Very Rev Canon Liam Rigney PP
Parochial House, 1 Stanhope Place,
Athy, Co Kildare
Tel 059-8631781
Rev Timothy Hannon CC
3 Stanhope Place, Athy
Tel 059-8631698
Very Rev Philip Dennehy PE
4 Stanhope Place, Athy
Tel 059-8631696
Email pdenn@eircom.net
Rev Francis McCarthy CC *(priest of Cashel & Emly diocese)*
Parochial House, Crookstown, Co Kildare
Tel 087-6078143
Ms Natasha Geoghegan, Parish Pastoral Worker
Mr Conor McCann, Parish Pastoral Worker
c/o Parish Office
Email natasha.curran@dublindiocese.ie
Parish Office: Tel 059-8638391
Email athyparishrc@eircom.net
Website www.stmichaelsathy.net

AUGHRIM
The Most Sacred Heart, Co Wicklow
Very Rev Diarmuid Byrne TA
Parochial House, Arklow, Co Wicklow
Tel 0402-32294

AUGHRIM STREET
The Holy Family, Dublin 7
Very Rev Patrick Madden Adm
Parochial House,
34 Aughrim Street, Dublin 7
Tel 01-8386571
Rev Coriolan Muresan CC
Presbytery No 2,
St Joseph's Road, Dublin 7
Rev Deacon Victor Garvin

AVOCA
SS Mary and Patrick, Co Wicklow
Very Rev Padraig Ó Cochlain *(Moderator)*
Parochial House, Arklow, Co Wicklow
Tel 0402-32294
Rev Brian McKittrick Co-PP
Parochial House, Avoca, Co Wicklow
Rev Thomas Coughlan
The Presbytery, Avoca, Co Wicklow
Tel 0402-35204
Parish Offices: Avoca Tel 0402-35156
Email avpar@eircom.net
Templerainey Tel 0402-31943
Email stjoseph@eircom.net

AYRFIELD
St Paul's, Dublin 13
Very Rev Gerard Corcoran *(Moderator)*
Rev Gerard Deegan Co-PP
28 Glentworth Park, Ayrfield, Dublin 13
Tel 01-8674007
Parish Office: Tel 01-8160984
Email parishofficeayrfield@eircom.net
Website www.stpaulsparishayrfield.com

BALALLY
(Grouped with Sandyford)
Church of the Ascension of The Lord,
Dublin 16
Very Rev John Canon Delany *(Moderator)*
Parochial House, St Mary's,
Sandyford, Dublin 18
Tel 01-2956317
Rt Rev Mgr Dermot A. Lane DD, PC
162 Sandyford Road, Dublin 16
Tel 01-2956165
Email dalane@eircom.net
Rev Jim Caffrey CC
The Presbytery, Hawthorns Road,
Dublin 18
Parish Office: Tel 01-2954296
Email parishofbalally@eircom.net
Website www.balallyparish.ie

BALBRIGGAN
SS Peter and Paul, Balbriggan, Co Dublin
Very Rev John Canon McNamara PP, VF
Apt 2, The Presbytery,
Parish of SS Peter & Paul, Dublin Road,
Balbriggan, Co Dublin
Tel 01-8020185
Rev Donal Toal (SMA), CC
Apt 1, Parochial House,
Balbriggan, Co Dublin
Tel 01-8412116

ARCHDIOCESE OF DUBLIN

Rev Anthony Gill (SMA)
Apt 1, Parochial House,
Balbriggan, Co Dublin
Tel 087-369533
Ms Siobhán Tighe, Parish Pastoral Worker
Parish Office: Tel 01-8412116 Fax 01-6904834
Email balbrigganparishoffice@gmail.com

BALDOYLE
(Grouped with Howth/Sutton)
SS Peter and Paul, Dublin 13
Very Rev Cyril Mangan (Moderator)
Rev Gerard Tanham PC
Presbytery No. 1,
Thormanby Road, Howth
Tel 01-8167599
Very Rev Peter O'Connor Co-PP
The Presbytery, Baldoyle, Dublin 13
Tel 01-8322060
Parish Office: Tel 01-8324313
Email info@baldoyleparish.ie
Website www.baldoyleparish.ie

BALLINTEER
Ballinteer parish is now under the Team Ministry of Dundrum/Ballinteer/Meadowbrook
St John the Evangelist, Ballinteer Avenue, Dublin 16
Very Rev Liam Canon Belton (Moderator)
Presbytery No 1, Ballinteer Avenue,
Dublin 16
Tel 01-4944448
Email rmfb@eircom.net
Rev Deacon Noel Ryan
Parish Office: Tel 01-4994203
Email parishoffice@ballinteer.dublindiocese.ie
Website www.ballinteer.dublindiocese.ie

BALLYBODEN
Our Lady of Good Counsel, Dublin 16
Very Rev John Hughes (OSA) PP
Tel 01-4944966
Rev Francis Aherne (OSA) CC
Tel 01-4543356
Rev Dick Lyng (OSA) CC
St Augustine's, Taylor's Lane,
Ballyboden, Dublin 16
Parish Office: Tel 01-4944966
Website www.ballybodenparish.com

BALLYBRACK-KILLINEY
SS Alphonsus and Columba, Co Dublin
Very Rev Tom Dalzell (Moderator)
Parochial House, Church Avenue,
Killiney, Co Dublin
Tel 01-2826404
Rt Rev Mgr Enda Lloyd Co-PP
10 The Oaks, Loughlinstown Drive,
Dun Laoghaire, Co Dublin
Tel 01-2826895
Parish Offices:
St Alphonsus & Columba. Tel 01-2820788
St Stephens Tel 01-2854512
Church of the Apostles Tel 01-2024804
Website www.ballybrack-killiney-parish.org

BALLYFERMOT
Our Lady of the Assumption, Dublin 10
Rev Adrian Egan (CSsR) PP & Coordinator
Rev Seamus Devitt (CSsR) CC
197 Kylemore Road,
Ballyfermot, Dublin 10
Parish Office: Tel 01-6264691
Community: Tel 01-5356977

BALLYFERMOT UPPER
St Matthew, Blackditch Road, Dublin 10
Rev Piaras MacLochlainn Adm
No 2, 148D Presbytery, Blackditch Road,
Dublin 10
Tel 01-6265119
Rev Simon Mundisye PC
Presbytery, Blackditch Road,
Ballyfermot, Dublin 10
Tel 01-6265695
Parish Office:
Tel 01-6265695 Fax 01-6230654
Website www.stmatthewsballyfermot.com

BALLYGALL
(Grouped with Iona Road, Drumcondra, Glasnevin and Ballymun Road)
Our Mother of Divine Grace,
Ballygall Road East, Dublin 11
Very Rev Richard Sheehy (Moderator)
Very Rev Joseph Ryan Co-PP
41 Cremore Heights, St Canice's Road,
Glasnevin, Dublin 11
Tel 01-8573776
Rev Paul St John (SVD) PC
4 Claremount Drive,
Ballygall, Dublin 11
Tel 01-8087553
Very Rev Harry Gaynor Co-PP
112 Ballygall Road East,
Glasnevin, Dublin 11
Tel 01-8342248
Very Rev Gareth Byrne TA
Parish Office: Tel 01-8369291
Email omdgballygallchurch@eircom.net
Website www.ballygallparish.ie

BALLYMORE EUSTACE
Immaculate Conception, Naas, Co Kildare
Very Rev Joe Connolly Adm
Parochial House, Ballymore Eustace,
Naas, Co Kildare
Tel 045-864114
Rev James Prendiville CC
The Presbytery, Hollywood (via Naas),
Co Wicklow
Tel 045-864206
Parish Office: Tel 045-864114
Email hwparishoffice@gmail.com

BALLYMUN, ST PAPPIN'S
Holy Spirit, Silloge Road, Dublin 11
Tel 01-8620586
St Joseph's, Dane Road, Balcurris,
Ballymun. Tel 01-8423865/8165700
Email stpappinspastoralcentre@gmail.com
Church of the Virgin Mary, Shangan
Road, Dublin 9. Tel 01-8421551
Email vmballymun@live.ie
Parish Tel 01-8620586
Email stpappinspastoralcentre@gmail.com
Website www.stpappinsparish.com
Very Rev Declan Blake (Moderator)
Presbytery No. 2,
Shangan Road, Dublin 9
Tel 01-8421486
Very Rev Ciarán Enright Co-PP
30 Willow Park Crescent, Dublin 11
Tel 01-8423865
Rev Rajesh Joseph CC
Presbytery No 2, Shangan Road,
Ballymun, Dublin 9

BALLYMUN ROAD
(Grouped with Iona Road, Drumcondra, Glasnevin and Ballygall)
Our Lady of Victories, Ballymun Road,
Dublin 9
Very Rev Richard Sheehy (Moderator)
Very Rev Frank Reburn Co-PP
137 Ballymun Road, Dublin 11
Tel 01-8376341
Rev Patrick Sweeney TA
13 Home Farm Road, Drumcondra,
Dublin 9
Tel 01-8377402
Very Rev Gareth Byrne TA

BALLYROAN
Ballyroan Parish is now under the Team Ministry of Rathfarnham/Churchtown/Ballyroan
Church of the Holy Spirit, Marian Road,
Dublin 14
Very Rev Michael Murtagh Co-PP
69 Anne Devlin Park,
Ballyroan, Dublin 14
Tel 01-4950444
Rev Deacon Matthew Murphy
Rev Deacon Frank Browne
Parish Office: Tel 01-4947303
Email ballyroanparish@gmail.com
Website www.ballyroanparish.ie

BAWNOGUE
Clondalkin/Rowlagh/Neilstown/Deansrath/Bawnogue Grouping
Church of the Transfiguration,
Bawnogue, Clondalkin, Dublin 22
Very Rev Kieran Coghlan (Moderator)
Very Rev Padraig O'Sullivan Co-PP
Rev Brian Starken (CSSp) Co-PP
Presbytery, Bawnogue, Clondalkin,
Dublin 22
Tel 01-4519810
Ms Christina Malone, Parish Pastoral Worker
Email transfig2000@yahoo.com
www.bawnogueparish.com

BAYSIDE
Church of the Resurrection, Bayside,
Dublin 13
Very Rev Peter Finnerty Adm
Parochial House, Bayside Square North,
Sutton, Dublin 13
Tel 01-8323150
Rev Joe Kelly CC
5 Bayside Square East, Sutton, Dublin 13
Tel 01-8322305
Email gradyjoe1@eircom.net
Rev Christopher Sheridan CC
7 Bayside Square East,
Sutton, Dublin 13
Tel 01-8322964
Parish Office: Tel 01-8323083
Email baysidercchurch@eircom.net
Website www.baysideparish.ie

ARCHDIOCESE OF DUBLIN

BEAUMONT
(Grouped with the parishes of Larkhill, Whitehall, Santry & Kilmore Road West)
Church of Nativity of Our Lord, Dublin 5
Very Rev Robert Smyth Adm
Presbytery, Montrose Park,
Beaumont, Dublin 5
Tel 01-8710013
Rev Dominic Kwikiriza CC
Presbytery 1, Montrose Park,
Beaumont, Dublin 5
Tel 01-8477740
Parish Office:
Tel 01-8477740 Fax 01-8473209

BEECHWOOD AVENUE
Church of the Holy Name, Dublin 6
Very Rev Paul Taylor Adm
49 Rathgar Road, Dublin 6
Tel 01-4971058
Parish Office: Tel 01-4967449
Email info@beechwoodparish.com
Website info@beechwoodparish.com

BERKELEY ROAD
St Joseph's, Dublin 7
Very Rev Paul Churchill PP
The Presbytery,
Berkeley Road, Dublin 7
Tel 01-8306336
Rev Deacon Declan Barry
Parish Office: Tel 01-8302071

BLACKROCK
St John the Baptist, Blackrock, Co Dublin
Very Rev Peter O'Connor Adm
24 Barclay Court, Blackrock, Co Dublin
Tel 01-2832302
Very Rev Edward Conway PC
1 Maretimo Gardens West, Blackrock,
Co Dublin
Tel 01-2882248
Email eddieconway@indigo.ie
Parish Office: Tel 01-2882104
Email saintjohnthebaptist@eircom.net

BLAKESTOWN
Blakestown Parish is now under the Team Ministry of Blakestown/Hartstown/Huntstown/Mountview
St Mary of the Servants, Dublin 15
Very Rev Joseph Coyne *(Moderator)*
36 Ashfield Lawn, Huntstown,
Dublin 15
Tel 01-8216447
Rev George Adzato (SVD)
c/o St Philip the Apostle Church,
No. 2 Presbytery, Mountview,
Blanchardstown, Dublin 14
Rev John Owen (SVD)
The Presbytery Blakestown,
Clonsilla, Dublin 15
Tel 01-8210874
Parish Office: Tel 01-8210874
Email blakestownparish@dublindiocese.ie

BLANCHARDSTOWN
St Brigid's
Very Rev Michael Carey PP
Parochial House,
Blanchardstown, Dublin 15
Tel 01-8213660
Rev Frank Drescher CC
Presbytery, 44 Woodview Grove,
Blanchardstown, Dublin 15
Tel 01-5484038
Rev Deacon Jim Adams
Rev Deacon Michael O'Connor
Ms Mairin Keegan, Parish Pastoral Worker

BLESSINGTON
(Grouped with the parish of Valleymount)
Church of Our Lady
Very Rev Richard Behan PP
The Presbytery, Main Street,
Blessington, Co Wicklow
Tel 045-865442
Our Lady of Mercy, Crosschapel
Archdeacon Kevin Lyon CC
Parochial House, Crosschapel,
Blessington, Co Wicklow
Tel 045-865215
Email lyonk@indigo.ie
St Brigid's Church, Manor Kilbride
Rev Padraic McDermott (CSSp) CC
The Presbytery, Manor Kilbride,
Blessington, Co Wicklow
Tel 01-4582154
Rev Deacon Gerard Malony
Ms Aine Egan, Parish Pastoral Worker
Parish Office: Tel/Fax 045-865327
Email office@blessington.info
Website www.blessington.info

BLUEBELL
Bluebell Parish is now under the Team Ministry of Inchicore (Mary Immaculate & St Michael's) & Bluebell
Our Lady of the Wayside, Dublin 12
Very Rev Leo Philomin (OMI) *(Moderator)*
Very Rev Anthony Clancy (OMI) Co-PP
Oblate Fathers House of Retreat,
Inchicore, Dublin 8
Tel 01-4541117
Parish Office: Tel 01-4501040
Website www.oblateparishesindublin.ie

BOHERNABREENA
St Anne's, Dublin 24
Very Rev James Daly PP
The Parochial House, St Anne's Church,
Bohernabreena, Tallaght, Dublin 24
Rev Michael Canon Hurley PC
85 Tymon Crescent,
Oldbawn, Dublin 24
Tel/Fax 01-4627080
Rev Hilary Etomike PC
Rev Hector Mwale PC
Rev Deacon Padraic O'Sullivan
c/o Parish Office
Parish Office: Tel 01-4626893
Email bohernabreenaparish@eircom.net

BONNYBROOK
St Joseph's, Bonnybrook, Dublin 17
Very Rev Joseph Jones *(Moderator)*
122 Greencastle Road, Dublin 17
Tel 01-8487657
Parish Office: Tel 01-8485262

BOOTERSTOWN
Church of the Assumption
Very Rev Gerry Kane PP
52 Booterstown Avenue,
Blackrock, Co Dublin
Tel 01-2882162
Rev Anastasius Ezenwata PC
Parochial House,
Parish of the Assumption, Booterstown
Parish Office: Tel/Fax 01-2831593
Email info@booterstownparish.ie
Website www.booterstownparish.ie

BRACKENSTOWN
Swords/River Valley/Brackenstown Grouping/St Cronan's
Very Rev Desmond Doyle *(Moderator)*
Very Rev Paul Thornton Co-PP, EV
Parochial House, Brackenstown Road,
Swords, Co Dublin
Tel 01-8401661
Rev Bibin Jacob (CST) CC
Parochial House, Brackenstown Road,
Swords, Co Dublin
Tel 01-8408926
Rev Colin Rothery Co-PP
Rev Deacon Declan Colgan
Ms Niamh Morris, Parish Pastoral Worker
Parish Office: Tel 01-8401188
Email brackenstownparish@gmail.com
www.brackenstown.dublindiocese.ie

BRAY (BALLYWALTRIM)
(Bray grouping: Holy Redeemer/Our Lady Queen of Peace/St Fergal's/St Peter's Little Bray/Enniskerry)
St Fergal's, Bray, Co Wicklow
Very Rev Michael O'Kelly *(Moderator)*
Very Rev Jimmy McPartland Co-PP
St Fergal's, Killarney Road,
Bray, Co Wicklow
Tel 01-2768191
Parish Office: Tel 01-2860980
Fax 01-2768196
Email info@stfergalsbray.ie
Website www.stfergalsbray.ie

BRAY (HOLY REDEEMER)
(Bray grouping: Holy Redeemer/Our Lady Queen of Peace/St Fergal's/St Peter's Little Bray/Enniskerry)
Holy Redeemer, Main Street, Bray, Co Wicklow
Very Rev Michael O'Kelly *(Moderator)*
Cluain Mhuire, Killarney Road,
Bray, Co Wicklow
Tel 01-2862026
Rev James Ayuba PC
Holy Redeemer Parish, Main Street,
Bray, Co Wicklow
Tel 089-9646747
Very Rev John O'Connell PE
17 King Edwards Court, Bray, Co Wicklow
Parish Office: Tel 01-2868413
Email admin@holyredeemerbray.ie
Website www.holyredeemerbray.ie

ARCHDIOCESE OF DUBLIN

BRAY, PUTLAND ROAD
(Bray grouping: Holy Redeemer/Our Lady Queen of Peace/St Fergal's/St Peter's Little Bray/Enniskerry)
Our Lady Queen of Peace
Very Rev Joseph Whelan Co-PP
Parochial House, Putland Road, Bray, Co Wicklow
Tel 01-2865723
Sacristy: 01-2867303
Email secretary@queenofpeace.ie
Parish Office: Tel 01-2745497
Villa Pacis – Parish Centre: 01-2760045
Email villafas1@hotmail.com

BRAY, ST PETER'S
(Bray grouping: Holy Redeemer/Our Lady Queen of Peace/St Fergal's/St Peter's Little Bray/Enniskerry)
St Peter's, Little Bray, Co Wicklow
For clergy: See Bray (Ballywaltrim)
Email stpeterslittlebray1@eircom.net

BROOKFIELD
St Aidan's, Brookfield Road
(Springfield, Jobstown, Brookfield Grouping)
Very Rev Pat McKinley *(Moderator)*
Rev Martin Hughes TA
447 The Oaks, Belgard Heights, Tallaght, Dublin 24
Tel 01-4519399

CABINTEELY
St Brigid's, Dublin 18
Very Rev Aquinas Duffy *(Acting Moderator)*
19 Woodlands Road, Johnstown, Glenageary, Co Dublin
Tel 01-5672374
Rev Arthur O'Neill *(Team Assistant)*
1B Willow Court, Druid Valley, Cabinteely, Dublin 18
Tel 087-2597520
Rev Thomas O'Keeffe
20 Glen Avenue, The Park, Cabinteely
Tel 01-2853643

CABRA
Cabra Parish is now under the Team Ministry of Cabra/Cabra West/Phibsboro
Christ the King, Dublin 7
Very Rev Michael O'Grady PP
No. 3 Presbytery, Dunmanus Court, Cabra West, Dublin 7
Tel 01-8384325
Rev Thomas F. O'Shaughnessy *(Assistant Priest)*
73 Annamoe Road, Dublin 7
Tel 01-8385626
Very Rev Patrick F. Canon Carroll *(retired)*
124 New Cabra Road, Dublin 7
Tel 01-8385244
Email pat47@eircom.net
Rev Deacon Damien Murphy
c/o Parish Office
Parish Office: Tel 01-8680804
Email christthekingchurch@eircom.net

CABRA WEST
Cabra West Parish is now under the Team Ministry of Cabra/Cabra West/Phibsboro
Church of the Most Precious Blood, Dublin 7
Very Rev Michael O'Grady PP
No 3 Presbytery, Dunmanus Court, Cabra West, Dublin 7
Tel 01-8384325
Rev Deacon Damian Murphy
Parish Office: Tel 01-8384418

CASTLEDERMOT
The Assumption, Castledermot, Co Kildare
Very Rev Aidan Kieran Adm, VF
Parochial House, Castledermot, Co Kildare
Tel 059-9144164
Parish Office: Tel/Fax 059-9144888

CASTLEKNOCK
Laurel Lodge/Carpenterstown/Castleknock Grouping
Our Lady Mother of the Church Castleknock, Dublin 15
Very Rev Damian McNeice PP
6 Beechpark Lawn, Castleknock, Dublin 15
Tel 01-6408595
Rev Denis O'Connor (CSsR) CC
32 Auburn Drive, Dublin 15
Tel 01-8214003
Rev Brendan Quinlan CC
The Presbytery, Church Grounds, Laurel Lodge, Castleknock, Dublin 15
Tel 01-8208144

CASTLETOWN
(Grouped with the parish of Arklow)
St Patrick's, Castletown, Co Wexford
Very Rev Padraig Ó Cochlain *(Moderator)*, VF
Parochial House, Arklow, Co Wicklow
Tel 0402-32294
Email mfc53@indigo.ie
Very Rev Eugene McCarney PE
Parochial House, Castletown, Co Wexford
Tel 0402-37112

CELBRIDGE
St Patrick's, Celbridge, Co Kildare
Very Rev Joe McDonald PP
Parochial House, Celbridge, Co Kildare
Tel 01-6275874
Rev Peter Nwigwe PC
12 Coarsemoor Park, Straffan, Co Kildare
Tel 01-6012303
Rev Jacob Shanet PC
c/o 12 Coarsemoor Park, Straffan, Co Kildare
Rev Jonathan Nwanko PC
c/o 12 Coursemoore Park, Straffan, Co Kildare
Rev Deacon John Graham
Parish Office: Tel 01-6288827
Email celbridgeparishoffice@gmail.com

CHAPELIZOD
Nativity of the BVM, Chapelizod, Dublin 20
Rev Sean Mundow
The Presbytery, Chapelizod, Dublin 20
Tel 01-6264645/087-8195073

CHERRY ORCHARD
Most Holy Sacrament
Parish Team
Very Rev Michael Murtagh (CSsR) PP
103 Cherry Orchard Avenue, Dublin 10
Tel 01-6267930

CHURCHTOWN
Churchtown Parish is now under the Team Ministry of Rathfarnham/Churchtown/Ballyroan
The Good Shepherd
Very Rev Brian Edwards Co-PP
23 Oakdown Road, Dublin 14
Tel 01-2981744
Emergencies: Tel 087-2402585
Rev Deacon Matthew Murphy
Rev Deacon Frank Browne
Parish Office: Tel 01-2984642
Email info@goodshepherdchurchtown.ie
Website
www.goodshepherdchurchtown.ie

CLOGHER ROAD
Clogher Parish is now under the Team Ministry of Crumlin/Mourne Road/Clogher Road
St Bernadette's
Very Rev Anthony O'Shaughnessy *(Moderator)*
Very Rev Brian Lawless Co-PP
54 Clogher Road, Dublin 12
Tel 01-4536988
Parish Office: Tel 01-4733109
Sacristy: Tel 01-4535099
Email clogherroadparish@eircom.net
Website www.clogherroad.ie

CLONDALKIN
Clondalkin/Rowlagh/Neilstown/Deansrath/Bawnogue Grouping
Immaculate Conception, Dublin 22
Website
www.clondalkin.dublindiocese.ie
Very Rev Kieran Coghlan *(Moderator)*
St Cecilia's, New Road, Clondalkin, Dublin 22
Tel 01-4592665
Rev Padraig O'Sullivan Co-PP
St Columba Parish House, New Road, Clondalkin, Dublin 22
Tel 01-4640441
Rev Seamus McEntee, Chaplain DCU, St Mary's, New Road, Clondalkin, Dublin 22
Rev Deacon Don Devaney
Ms Christina Malone, Parish Pastoral Worker

Clonburris, Our Lady Queen of the Apostles
Rev Shan O'Cuiv *(Team Assistant)*
c/o The Presbytery, Clonburris, Clondalkin, Dublin 22
Tel 01-4573440
Parish Office: Tel 01-4640706

Knockmitten
Rev Desmond Byrne (CSSp) *(Team Assistant)*
45 Woodford Drive, Monastery Road, Clondalkin, Dublin 22
Tel 01-4592323
Parish Office: Tel 01-4640706

ARCHDIOCESE OF DUBLIN

CLONSKEAGH
(Grouped with Mount Merrion and Kilmacud–Stillorgan)
Immaculate Virgin Mary of the Miraculous Medal, Bird Avenue, Dublin 14
Very Rev Joe Mullan Adm
79 The Rise, Mount Merrion, Co Dublin
Tel 01-2889879
Rev Fergus O'Donoghue (SJ) PC
Gonzaga College, Sandford Road, Dublin 6
Tel 01-4972943
Rev Donie O'Connor (MHM) CC
In residence: Very Rev Maurice O'Shea PE
Parish Office: Tel/Fax 01-2837948
Email parishoffice@clonskeagh.org
Website www.clonskeaghparish.ie

CLONTARF, ST ANTHONY'S
St Anthony, Clontarf, Dublin 3
Very Rev Martin Canon Hogan *(Moderator)*
186 Clontarf Road, Dublin 3
Tel 01-8338575
Very Rev Larry White Co-PP
119 Stiles Road, Clontarf, Dublin 3
Tel 01-8333394/086-4143888
Parish Office: Tel 01-8333459
saintanthonysclontarf@dublindiocese.ie
Website www.stanthonysclontarf.ie

CLONTARF, ST JOHN'S
St John the Baptist, Clontarf Road, Dublin 3
Very Rev Martin Canon Hogan *(Moderator)*
186 Clontarf Road, Dublin 3
Tel 01-8338575
Parish Office: Tel 01-8334606
Email sjtbclontarf@eircom.net
Website stjohnsclontarf.dublindiocese.ie

CONFEY
St Charles Borromeo, Leixlip, Co Kildare
Very Rev Gregory O'Brien PP
Parochial House, Old Hill,
Leixip, Co Kildare
73 Newtown Park, Leixlip, Co Kildare
Tel 01-6244637
Rev Peter Clancy CC
75 Newtown Park, Leixlip, Co Kildare
Tel 01-6243533
Rev Aloysius Zuribo CC
Presbytery No. 1, 4 Old Hill,
Leixlip, Co Kildare
Tel 01-6243718
Parish Office: Tel/Fax 01-6247310
Email confeyparish@gmail.com

COOLOCK
St Brendan's, Coolock Village, Dublin 5
Very Rev Edwin McCallion (SM) PP
Rev John Harrington (SM) TA
Rev Paddy Stanley (SM) PC
Rev Francis Corry (SM) PC
The Presbytery,
Coolock Village, Dublin 5
Tel 01-8477133
Parish Office: Tel 01-8480102/01-8484799
Parish Mobile: 087-2269887
Email malachy@stbrendanscoolock.org
Website www.stbrendanscoolock.org

CORDUFF
St Patrick's, Corduff, Blanchardstown, Dublin 15
Very Rev John O'Connor (SAC) PP
Parochial House, Corduff
Blanchardstown, Dublin 15
Tel 01-8213596
Rev John Regan (SAC) CC
The Presbytery, Corduff,
Blanchardstown, Dublin 15
Tel 01-8215930

CRUMLIN
Crumlin Parish is now under the Team Ministry of Crumlin/Mourne Road/ Clogher Road
St Agnes
Very Rev Anthony O'Shaughnessy *(Moderator)*
41 St Agnes' Road, Crumlin, Dublin 12
Tel 01-5611500
Very Rev Mgr John F. Deasy *(Team Assistant)*
55 St Agnes' Road, Crumlin, Dublin 12
Tel 01-4550955
Rev Thomas Clowe (SDB) *(Team Assistant)*
45 St Teresa's Road, Crumlin,
Dublin D12 XK52
Rev Jimmy Fennell, Permanent Deacon
Parish Office: Tel 01-4555383
Fax 01-4652500
Email info@crumlinparish.ie
Website www.crumlinparish.ie

DALKEY
Assumption of BVM
Very Rev Liam Lacey PP
No 1 Presbytery, Castle Street,
Dalkey, Co Dublin
Tel 01-2857773
Rev Declan Gallagher CC
No 3 Presbytery, Castle Street,
Dalkey, Co Dublin
Tel 01-2859212
Parish Office: Tel 01-2859418
Email office@dalkeyparish.org
Website www.dalkeyparish.org

DARNDALE-BELCAMP
Our Lady Immaculate, Dublin 17
Very Rev Eduardo Nunez Yepez (OMI) PP
The Presbytery, Darndale, Dublin 17
Tel 086-7954706
Rev Michael O'Connor (OMI) CC
The Presbytery, Darndale, Dublin 17
Parish Office: Tel 01-8474547
Email parish@darndaleparish.ie
Website www.darndalebelcamp.ie

DEANSRATH
Clondalkin/Rowlagh/Neilstown/ Deansrath/Bawnogue Grouping
Very Rev Kieran Coghlan *(Moderator)*
Very Rev Padraig O'Sullivan Co-PP
Very Rev Rodrigues Da Silva (CSSp) Co-PP
St Ronan's Presbytery, Deansrath,
Clondalkin, Dublin 22
Tel 01-4570380
Ms Christina Malone, Parish Pastoral Worker
Email stronansdeansrath@hotmail.com

DOLLYMOUNT
St Gabriel's, St Gabriel's Road, Dublin 3
Very Rev Martin Canon Hogan *(Moderator)*
186 Clontarf Road, Dublin 3
Tel 01-8338575
Very Rev Patrick McManus CC
34 Dollymount Grove, Clontarf,
Dublin 3
Tel 01-8057692/087-2371089
Email frpatmcmanus@eircom.net
Parish Office: Tel 01-8333602
Email info@stgabrielsparish.ie

DOLPHIN'S BARN/RIALTO
(Grouped with the parish of Rialto)
Our Lady of Dolours, Dublin 8
Very Rev Fergal MacDonagh *(Moderator)*
18 St Anthony's Road, Rialto, Dublin 8
Tel 01-4534469
Rev Roy George PC
Parish Office: Tel 01-4547271
Email dolphinsbarn@dublindiocese.ie

DOMINICK STREET
St Saviour's, Dublin 1
Very Rev Joseph Dineen (OP) PP
Tel 01-8897610
Rev Cezary Binkiewicz (OP) CC
St Saviour's,
Upper Dorset Street, Dublin 1
Parish Office: Tel 01-8897610
Email stsaviours@eircom.net
Website www.saintsavioursdublin.ie

DONABATE
St Patrick's
Rev Patrick Reilly (OPraem) PP
13 Seaview Park, Portrane, Co Dublin
Tel 01-8436099
Rev Augustine Fokchet PC
St Mary's, Donabate, Co Dublin
Tel 01-8434604
Parish Office: Tel/Fax 01-8434574 (9.30-12.00 noon)
Email stpatricksrcdonabate@gmail.com
Website www.donabateparish.ie

DONAGHMEDE-CLONGRIFFIN-BALGRIFFIN
Church of the Holy Trinity
Very Rev Gerard Corcoran *(Moderator)*
12 Grangemore Grove, Donaghmede,
Dublin D13 A264
Tel 01-8474652
Parish Office: Tel 01-8479822
Email info@holytrinity.ie
Website www.holytrinityparish.ie

DONNYBROOK
Church of the Sacred Heart, Dublin 4
Rt Rev Mgr Ciaran O'Carroll PP, VG
Parochial House,
Stillorgan Road, Dublin 4
Tel 01-2693926
Rev Patrick Sheary (SJ) CC
Jesuit House, Milltown Park,
Sandford Road, Dublin 6
Tel 01-2698411
Rev Kieran O'Mahony (OSA) PC
Presbytery No. 2, Stillorgan Road,
Dublin 4

ARCHDIOCESE OF DUBLIN

Rev John Boyers PC
16 'Wilfield', Sandymount Avenue,
Ballsbridge, Dublin 4
Tel 087-1557887
Parish Office: Tel 01-2693903
Email secretary@donnybrookparish.ie
Website www.donnybrookparish.ie

DONNYCARNEY
Our Lady of Consolation, Dublin 5
Very Rev John Ennis Adm
1 Maypark, Malahide Road, Dublin 5
Tel 01-8313033
Parish Office: Tel 01-8316016 (9 am-12 pm)
Rev Vasyl Kornitsky PC
Chaplain to Ukrainian Community
3 Maypark, Malahide Road, Dublin 5
Tel 01-5164752
Email info@donnycarneyparish.ie
Website www.donnycarneyparish.ie

DONORE AVENUE
St Teresa of the Child Jesus, Dublin 8
Very Rev David Corrigan (SM) PP
Rev John O'Gara (SM) PC
Rev John Hannan (SM) PC
The Presbytery, 78A Donore Avenue,
Dublin 8
Tel 01-4542425
Email donoreavenue@dublindiocese.ie

DRUMCONDRA
(Grouped with Iona Road, Glasnevin,
Ballymun Road and Ballygall)
Corpus Christi, Home Farm Road, Dublin 9
Very Rev Richard Sheehy *(Moderator)*
Rt Rev Mgr Martin O'Shea Co-PP
23 Clare Road, Drumcondra, Dublin 9
Tel 01-8378552
Very Rev Gareth Byrne TA
Parish Office: Tel 01-8360085
Email corpuschristi@eircom.net
Website
www.drumcondra.dublindiocese.ie

DUBLIN AIRPORT see SWORDS

DUNDRUM
(Grouped with Meadow Brook and
Ballinteer)
Holy Cross, Dublin 14
Very Rev Liam Canon Belton *(Moderator)*
Very Rev John Bracken Co-PP
Emmaus, Main Street, Dundrum,
Dublin 14
Tel 01-2983494
Rev Deacon Gabriel Corcoran
Tel 01-4240613
Parish Office: Tel 01-2983494
Email parishofficedundrum@eircom
Website www.holycrossdundrum.org

DUN LAOGHAIRE
St Michael's, Co Dublin
Very Rev Paul Tyrrell PP
St Michael's Parochial House,
4 Eblana Avenue, Dun Laoghaire,
Co Dublin
Tel 01-2801505
Rev Martin Daly CC
'Renvyle', Corrig Avenue,
Dun Laoghaire, Co Dublin
Tel 01-2802100
Parish Office: Tel 01-2804969
Email stmichdl2@eircom.net
Website www.dunlaoghaireparish.ie

DUNLAVIN
St Nicholas of Myra, Dunlavin, Co Wicklow
Rev Douglas Malone Adm
The Presbytery, Dunlavin,
Co Wicklow
Tel 045-401227
Rev Eamonn McCarthy CC
The Presbytery, Donard,
Co Wicklow
Tel 045-404614
Parish Office: Tel 045-401871
Email parish10@eircom.net
Website www.dunlavinparish.ie

EADESTOWN
*The Immaculate Conception,
Naas, Co Kildare*
Very Rev Micheál Comer Adm
The Presbytery, Eadestown,
Naas, Co Kildare
Tel 045-862187
Email eadestownparish@gmail.com

EAST WALL-NORTH STRAND
St Joseph's, Church Road, Dublin 3
Very Rev Richard Shannon Adm
Parochial House, 78 St Mary's Road,
East Wall, Dublin 3
Tel 01-8742320
Rev Deacon Paul F. Kelly
Parish Office: Tel 01-8560980
Email stjosephsparish1941@gmail.com

EDENMORE
(Grouped with the parish of Grange Park)
St Monica's, Dublin 5
Very Rev Patrick Boyle Adm
Rev Ronnie Dunne CC
c/o Parish Office
Tel 086-4513904
Rev Anthony Power CC
35 Grange Park Avenue
Tel 01-8480244
Parish Office: Tel 01-8471497
Email stmonicaedenmore@eircom.net

ENNISKERRY/KILMACANOGUE
(Bray grouping: Holy Redeemer/Our Lady
Queen of Peace/St Fergal's/St Peter's
Little Bray/Enniskerry)
*Immaculate Heart of Mary, Enniskerry,
Co Wicklow*
Very Rev Michael O'Kelly *(Moderator)*
Parochial House, Enniskerry,
Co Wicklow
Tel 01-2863506/087-2660821
Very Rev Bernard Kennedy Co-PP
Parochial House, Enniskerry,
Co Wicklow
Rev Hyacinth Nwakuna (CSSp) CC
The Presbytery,
Kilmacanogue, Co Wicklow
Tel 01-2760030
Parish Office Enniskerry: Tel 01-2760030
(10 am-1 pm, Mon-Fri)
Parish Office Kilmacanogue
Tel 01-2021882 (10 am-1 pm, Mon-Fri)
Email stmochonogs@eircom.net

ESKER-DODDSBORO-ADAMSTOWN
*Esker-Dodsboro-Adamstown Parish is
now under the Team Ministry of Lucan/
Esker-Dodsboro-Adamstown/Lucan South
St Patrick's*
Very Rev Philip Curran *(Moderator)*
Rev John Hassett Co-PP
127 Castlegate Way,
Adamstown, Co Dublin
Tel 01-6812088
Email hassettorama@gmail.com
Parish Office: Tel 01-6281018
Email stpatrickschurchesker@eircom.net
Website www.stpatrickslucan.ie

FAIRVIEW
Church of the Visitation of BVM, Dublin 3
Very Rev Maximilian McKeown (OFM
Conv) PP
Rev Marius Tomulesei (OFM Conv) CC
Rev Aidan Walsh (OFM Conv) CC
Friary of the Visitation,
Fairview Strand, Dublin 3
Tel 01-8376000 Fax 01-8376021
Parish Office: Tel 01-8376000

FINGLAS
St Canice's, Dublin 11
Very Rev Richard Hyland PP
5 The Lawn, Finglas, Dublin 11
Tel 01-8341894
Rev Michael Shiels CC
Tel 01-8341051
The Presbytery 1, St Canice's,
Finglas, Dublin 11
Parish Office: Tel 01-8343110
Fax 01-8646022
Email stcanices2@eircom.net
Website info@stcanicesfinglas.com

FINGLAS WEST
Church of the Annunciation, Dublin 11
Very Rev Éamonn Cahill PP
4 The Lawn, Finglas West, Dublin 11
Tel 01-8341000
Rev John Attoh PC
7 Cardiff Castle Road, Finglas West,
Dublin 11
Tel 01-8343928

FIRHOUSE
Our Lady of Mount Carmel, Dublin 24
Very Rev Peter Reilly Adm
Presbytery 1, Ballycullen Avenue,
Firhouse, Dublin 24
Tel 01-4599855
Parish Office: Tel 01-4524702
Email
ourladyofmountcarmelchurch@eircom.net

FOXROCK
Our Lady of Perpetual Succour
Very Rev Aquinas Duffy *(Acting
Moderator)*
19 Woodlands Road, Johnstown,
Glenageary, Co Dublin
Tel 01-5672374
Very Rev Kieran Dunne Co-PP
Parochial House, Foxrock, Dublin 18
Tel 01-2893229
Parish Office: Tel 01-2893492/01-2898879
Email secretary@foxrockparish.ie
Website www.foxrockparish.ie

ARCHDIOCESE OF DUBLIN

FRANCIS STREET
(Grouped with James' Street and Meath Street)
St Nicholas of Myra, Dublin 8
Very Rev Eugene Taaffe *(Moderator)*
Very Rev Martin Dolan
The Presbytery, Francis Street, Dublin 8
Tel 01-4544861/086-4035318
Parish Office: Tel 01- 4542172
Email rita@francisstreetparish.ie
Website www.francisstreetparish.ie

GARDINER STREET
St Francis Xavier, Dublin 1
Very Rev Richard O'Dwyer (SJ) PP
Rev Niall Leahy (SJ) CC
The Presbytery, Upper Gardiner Street, Dublin 1
Tel 01-8363411
Email sfx@jesuit.ie
Website www.gardinerstparish.ie

GARRISTOWN
(Grouped with Rolestown and The Naul)
Church of the Assumption, Co Dublin
Very Rev Derek Canon Farrell *(Moderator)*
Parochial House, Main Street,
Garristown, Co Dublin A42 PF64
Tel 01-8354138
Parish Office: 01-8354138

GLASNEVIN
(Grouped with Iona Road, Drumcondra, Ballymun Road and Ballygall)
Our Lady of Dolours, Dublin 9
Very Rev Richard Sheehy *(Moderator)*
50 Cremore Road, Glasnevin, Dublin 9
Tel 01-8373455
Very Rev Paul Coyle Co-PP
159 Botanic Road, Glasnevin, Dublin 9
Very Rev Gareth Byrne TA
Parish Office: Tel 01-8379445

GLASTHULE
St Joseph's, Glasthule, Co Dublin
Very Rev William Farrell CC
Parochial House, St Joseph's,
Glasthule, Co Dublin
Tel 01-2801226
Rev Denis Kennedy (CSSp) CC
c/o St Joseph's Pastoral Centre,
Glasthule, Co Dublin
Parish Office: Tel 01-6638604/5
Sacristy: 01-2800182
Email stjosephsglasthule@gmail.com
Website www.glasthuleparish.com

GLENDALOUGH
(Grouped with Rathdrum and Roundwood)
St Kevin's, Co Wicklow
Very Rev Derek Doyle *(Moderator)*
Rev John Greene CC
The Parochial House, St Kevin's Parish,
Laragh, Glendalough, Co Wicklow
Tel 044-45140
Rev Deacon Jeremy Seligman
Parish Office: Tel 0404-45777
Email glendalough2007@eircom.net
Website www.glendalough.dublindiocese.ie

GRANGE PARK
(Grouped with the parish of Edenmore)
St Benedict's, Grange Park View, Dublin 5
Very Rev Patrick Boyle Adm
Rev Ronald Dunne CC
c/o Parish Office
Tel 086-4513904
Rev Tony Power CC
35 Grange Park Avenue
Tel 01-84802441/086-3905205
Email stmonicaedenmore@eircom.net

GREENHILLS
Church of the Holy Spirit, Dublin 12
Very Rev Michael Kilkenny (CSSp) *(Moderator)*
66 Rockfield Avenue, Dublin 12
Tel 01-4558316
Rev Isaac Antwi-Boasiako (CSSp) CC
55 Fernhill Road, Greenhills, Dublin 12
Tel 01-4504040
Parish Office: Tel 01-4509191
Fax 01-4605287
Email greenhillsparish@eircom.net
Website holyspiritparishgreehills.ie

GREYSTONES
Church of the Holy Rosary, Co Wicklow
Very Rev John Daly PP
Parochial House, La Touche Road,
Greystones, Co Wicklow
Tel 01-2874278
Rev Denis Quinn CC
The Presbytery, Kimberley Road,
Greystones, Co Wicklow
Tel 01-2877025
Rev Gerard Tyrrell CC
The Presbytery, Blacklion,
Greystones, Co Wicklow
Tel 01-2819658
Parish Office: Tel 01-2860704
Email office@greystonesparish.com

HADDINGTON ROAD
St Mary's, Dublin 4
Very Rev Fachtna McCarthy Adm
Parochial House, St Mary's,
Haddington Road, Dublin 4
Tel 01-6600075/087-3936327
Rev Pat Claffey (SVD) CC
The Presbytery,
Haddington Road, Dublin 4
Tel 085-7123675
Rev Josip Levakovic CC & Chaplain to the Croatian Community
The Presbytery, Haddington Road, Dublin 4
Tel 01-6600075
Rev Deacon Greg Pepper
Email info@stmaryshaddingtonroad.ie
Website stmaryshaddingtonroad.ie

HALSTON STREET AND ARRAN QUAY
St Michan's, Halston Street, Dublin 7
Very Rev Martin Bennett (OFM Cap) PP
Capuchin Friary, Church Street, Dublin 7
Tel 01-8730599 Fax 01-8730250
Email halstonst@gmail.com
Rev Patrick Flynn (OFM Cap) CC
Capuchin Friary, Church Street, Dublin 7
Tel 01-8730599

HAROLD'S CROSS
Our Lady of the Rosary, Dublin 6W
Very Rev Alex Conlon PP
213B Harold's Cross Road, Dublin 6W
Tel 01-4972816
Parish Office: Tel 01-4965055
Email enquiries@hxparish.ie
Website www.hxparish.ie

HARRINGTON STREET
St Kevin's, Dublin 8
Very Rev Gerard Deighan Adm
Parochial House, Harrington Street, Dublin 8
Tel 01-4751506
Rev William Richardson PC
Rev Michael G. Nevin *(priest in residence)*
The Presbytery, Harrington Street, Dublin 8
Tel 01-4789093

HARTSTOWN
Hartstown Parish is now under the Team Ministry of Blakestown/Hartstown/Huntstown/Mountview
St Ciaran's, Dublin 15
Very Rev Joseph Coyne *(Moderator)*
St Ciaran's, 36 Ashfield Lawn,
Huntstown, Dublin 15
Tel 01-8216447
Rev Deacon Noel McHugh
Parish Office: Tel 01-8249651/01-8204777
Website www.st-ciarans-parish.ie

HOWTH
(Grouped with Balcoyle and Sutton)
Church of the Assumption,
Howth, Co Dublin
Very Rev Cyril Mangan *(Moderator)*
Rev Gerard Tanham PC
Presbytery No 1, Thormanby Road,
Howth, Co Dublin
Tel 01-8232193
Rev Bernard Zong PC
Tel 01-8397398
Email assumptionhowth@eircom.net
Sacristy: Tel 01-8397398
Email assumptionhowth@eircom.net

HUNTSTOWN
Hartstown Parish is now under the Team Ministry of Blakestown/Hartstown/Huntstown/Mountview
Sacred Heart of Jesus, Dublin 15
Very Rev Joseph Coyne *(Moderator)*
36 Ashfield Lawn, Huntstown, Dublin 15
Tel 01-8216447
Rev George Adzato (SVD) Co-PP
Rev John Owen (SVD) PC

INCHICORE, MARY IMMACULATE
Inchicore/Bluebell Grouping
Mary Immaculate, Tyrconnell Road, Dublin 8
Very Rev Leo Philomin (OMI) *(Moderator)*
Very Rev Paul Horrocks (OMI) Co-PP
Oblate Fathers, House of Retreat,
Inchicore, Dublin 8
Tel 01-4541117
Website www.oblateparishesinchicore.ie

ARCHDIOCESE OF DUBLIN

INCHICORE, ST MICHAEL'S
Inchicore/Bluebell Grouping
St Michael's, Emmet Road, Dublin 8
Very Rev Leo Philomin (OMI) *(Moderator)*
Very Rev Dominick Zwierzchowski (OMI) Co-PP
Very Rev Louis McDermott (OMI) Co-PP
Tel 01-4531660
Website www.stmichaelsinchicore.ie

IONA ROAD
(Grouped with Drumcondra, Glasnevin, Ballymun Road and Ballygall)
St Columba's, Dublin 9
Very Rev Richard Sheehy *(Moderator)*
Very Rev Patrick Jones TA
87 Iona Road, Dublin 9
Tel 01-8308257
Very Rev Gareth Byrne TA
Email ionaroadparish@gmail.com
Website www.ionaroadparish.ie

JAMES'S STREET
(Grouped with Meath Street and Francis Street)
St James's Church, Dublin 8
Very Rev Eugene Taaffe *(Moderator)*
The Presbytery,
James's Street, Dublin 8
Tel 01-4531143
Parish Office: Tel 01-4531143
Email jamesstreet@dublindiocese.ie

JOBSTOWN
(Springfield, Jobstown and Bookfield grouping)
St Thomas the Apostle
Very Rev Pat McKinley *(Moderator)*
The Presbytery, Jobstown, Tallaght, Dublin 24
Tel 01-4610971
Email jobstownparish@gmail.com
Rev Deacon Derek Leonard
Ms Saule Cameron, Parish Pastoral Worker
c/o Parish Office

JOHNSTOWN-KILLINEY
Our Lady of Good Counsel, Killiney, Co Dublin
Very Rev John Sinnott Co-PP
56 Auburn Road, Killiney, Co Dublin
Tel 01-2856660/087-8122651
Parish Office: Tel 01-2351416
Email johnstownparish@gmail.com
Website www.johnstownparish.org

KILBARRACK-FOXFIELD
St John the Evangelist, Greendale Road, Kilbarrack, Dublin 5
Very Rev Peter Finnerty Adm
Rev Cathal Price *(retired)*
54 Foxfield St John, Dublin 5
Tel 01-8323683
Rev Finbarr Neylon PC
Parish Office: Tel 01-8390433
Email info@kilbarrackfoxfieldparish.ie
Website www.kilbarrackfoxfieldparish.ie

KILBRIDE AND BARNDARRIG
St Mary's, Barndarrig, Co Wicklow
Very Rev Joseph Doran Adm
The Presbytery, Kilbride, Co Wicklow
Tel 087-2288579
Rev Timothy Murphy PC
St Mary's Barndarrig, Co Wicklow

KILCULLEN
Sacred Heart and St Brigid, Kilcullen
Very Rev Niall Mackey Adm
Parochial House, Kilcullen, Co Kildare
Tel 045-481230
Email mclm@eircom.net
Rev Martin Harte CC
Presbytery, Kilcullen, Co Kildare
Tel 045-481222
Parish Office: Tel 045-480727
Email kilcullenparish@eircom.net
Website www.kilcullenparish.net

KILLESTER
St Brigid's, Howth Road, Dublin 5
Very Rev Liam Ó Cuív Adm
126 Furry Park Road, Dublin 5
Tel 01-8333793
Parish Office: Tel 01-8332974
Website www.killester.dublindiocese.ie

KILLINARDEN
Church of the Sacred Heart, Killinarden, Tallaght, Dublin 24
Very Rev Fintan O'Driscoll (MSC) PP
Rev Con O'Connell (MSC) CC
The Presbytery, Killinarden, Tallaght, Dublin D24 R521
Tel 01-4522251
Email sacredheartparishkillinarden@gmail.com
Website www.sacredheartparishkillinarden.com

KILL-O'-THE-GRANGE
Holy Family, Kill Avenue, Dun Laoghaire, Co Dublin
Very Rev Michael O'Connor Adm
Presbytery No 2, Church Grounds, Kill Avenue, Dun Laoghaire, Co Dublin
Tel 01-2140863
Very Rev John Canon Killeen CC
20 Abbey Court, Monkstown, Co Dublin
Tel 01-2802533
Rev Deacon John O'Neill
Parish Office: Tel 01-2845299

KILMACANOGUE see **ENNISKERRY**

KILMACUD-STILLORGAN
St Laurence, Co Dublin
(Grouped Mount Merrion and Clonskeagh)
Very Rev Joseph Mullan *(Moderator)*
(Kilmacud & Mount Merrion)
79 The Rise, Mount Merrion, Co Dublin
Tel 01-2889879

Rev Paddy O'Byrne CC
Presbytery No. 2, Church Grounds
Tel 01-2882257
Very Rev Brian O'Reilly *(Team Assistant)*
Rev Donie O'Connor (MHM) CC
6 Allen Park Road, Stillorgan,
Co Dublin A94 X261
Tel 089-9796447
Rev Clement Padathiparambil CC
c/o Parish Office
Parish Office: Tel 01-2884009
Email kilmacudparish@eircom.net
Website www.kilmacudparish.com

KILMORE ROAD WEST
St Luke the Evangelist, Dublin 5
Very Rev Gary Darby Co-PP
St Luke's, Kilbarron Road,
Kilmore West, Dublin 5
Tel 01-8486806
Rev Roland Ntambang PC
Parish Office: Tel 01-8488149

KILNAMANAGH-CASTLEVIEW
St Kevin's, Dublin 24
Very Rev Michael Murphy Adm
Presbytery No 1, Treepark Road,
Kilnamanagh, Dublin 24
Tel 01-4523805/086-2408188
Rev Fergus McGlynn *(retired)*
43 Chestnut Grove, Ballymount Road, Dublin 24
Parish Office: Tel 01-4515570

KILQUADE
St Patrick's, Kilquade, Co Wicklow
Very Rev John Daly PP
Parochial House, La Touche Road,
Greystones, Co Wicklow
Tel/Fax 01-2874278
Rev Eamonn Clarke
The Presbytery, Kilcoole, Co Wicklow
Tel 01-2876207
Very Rev Sean Canon Smith CC
The Presbytery,
Newtownmountkennedy, Co Wicklow
Tel 01-2819253
Parish Office: Tel 01-2819658
Email kilquadeparish@eircom.net
Website www.kilquadeparish.com

KIMMAGE MANOR
Church of the Holy Spirit, Kimmage Manor, Whitehall Road, Dublin 12
Very Rev Michael Kilkenny (CSSp) *(Moderator)*
66 Rockfield Avenue, Dublin 12
Rev Isaac Antwi-Boasiako (CSSp) CC
Rev John Mahon (CSSp) CC
Tel 01-4064377
Parish Office: Tel 01-4064377
Email kimmagemanorparish@gmail.com
Website www.kimmagemanorparish.com

KINSEALY
(Grouped with the parishes of Malahide, Yellow Walls & Portmarnock)
St Nicholas of Myra, Malahide Road, Co Dublin
Very Rev Kevin Moore *(Moderator)*
Very Rev Conleth Meehan Co-PP
21 Wheatfield Grove,
Portmarnock, Co Dublin
Tel 01-8461561
Parish Office: Tel 01-8460028

KNOCKLYON
St Colmcille, Idrone Avenue, Dublin 16
PP Appointment pending
Presbytery, Idrone Avenue, Knocklyon,
Dublin 16
Tel 01-4941204
Rev Deacon Michael Giblin
Email knocklyonparish@gmail.com
Website www.knocklyonparish.ie

LARKHILL-WHITEHALL-SANTRY
(Grouped with the parishes of Kilmore Road West & Beaumont)
Holy Child, Thatch Road, Dublin 9
Very Rev Paul Kenny *(Moderator)*
149 Swords Road, Dublin 9
Tel 01-8375274
Very Rev John Jones PC
151 Swords Road, Whitehall, Dublin 9
Tel 01-8374887
Email jj362972@gmail.com
Rev Thomas Kearney PC
137 Shantalla Road,
Whitehall, Dublin 9
Tel 01-8420260
Parish Office: Tel 01-8375274
Email whitehall@dublindiocese.ie
Website www.whitehall@dublindiocese.ie

LAUREL LODGE-CARPENTERSTOWN
St Thomas the Apostle, Laurel Lodge/Carpenterstown, Dublin 15
Very Rev Damian McNeice PP
Rev Brendan Quinlan CC
Presbytery, Church Grounds,
Laurel Lodge, Castleknock, Dublin 15
Tel 01-8208144
Rev Dan Joe O'Mahony (OFM Cap) TA
The Oratory, Blanchardstown Dublin 15
Tel 01-8200915/086-8090633
Email danjoe2006@gmail.com
Parish Office: Tel 01-8208112
Website www.laurellodgeparish.ie

LEIXLIP
Our Lady's Nativity, Co Kildare
Very Rev Gregory O'Brien PP
Parochial House, Old Hill, Leixlip,
Co Kildare
Tel 01-6245597
Rev Aloysius Zuribo CC
No 1 Presbytery, 4 Old Hill,
Leixlip, Co Kildare
Tel 01-6243718
Rev Eladius Leonard Mutunzi PC
Presbytery No 2, 6 Old Hill, Leixlip,
Co Kildare
Parish Office:
Tel 01-6243673/01-6245159
Email leixlip.parish@oln.ie
Website www.oln.ie

LITTLE BRAY see BRAY, ST PETER'S

LOUGHLINSTOWN
(Grouped with Ballybrack-Killiney)
St Columbanus, Dun Laoghaire
Very Rev Tom Dalzell *(Moderator)*
Parochial House, Church Avenue,
Killiney, Co Dublin
Tel 01-2826404
Rt Rev Mgr Enda Lloyd Co-PP
10 The Oaks, Loughlinstown Drive,
Dun Laoghaire, Co Dublin
Tel 01-2826895
Email loughlinstownparish@eircom.net
Website www.loughlinstownparish.ie
Parish Office: Tel 01-2824085

LUCAN
Lucan Parish is now under the Team Ministry of Lucan/Esker-Dodsboro-Adamstown/Lucan South
St Mary's, Lucan, Co Dublin
Very Rev Philip Curran *(Moderator)*
231 Beech Park, Lucan, Co Dublin
Tel 01-2533804
Very Rev Thomas Kennedy Co-PP
14 Roselawn, Lucan, Co Dublin
Tel 01-6280205
Parish Pastoral Worker
Christopher Okereke
Parish Office: Tel 01-6217041
Email parishoffice@stmarysparishlucan.ie
Website www.stmarysparishlucan.ie

LUCAN SOUTH
Lucan South Parish is now under the Team Ministry of Lucan/Esker-Dodsboro-Adamstown/Lucan South
Church of Divine Mercy, Balgaddy
Very Rev Philip Curran *(Moderator)*
Rev Ubaldo Muhindo, Curate in Charge
Rev Pius Faruna PC
Rev Samuel Akughenyi PC
Mr Christopher Okereke, Parish Pastoral Worker
c/o Parish Office, Balgaddy Road, Lucan,
Co Dublin K78 NH05
Parish Office: Tel 01-4572900
Email churchdivinemercy@eircom.net
Website www.lucansouthparish.net

LUSK
St MacCullin's, Lusk, Co Dublin
Very Rev George Begley Adm
Parochial House, Chapel Road,
Lusk, Co Dublin
Tel 01-8949229
Parish Office: Tel 01-8438421
Email luskparish@eircom.net
Website www.luskparish.ie

MALAHIDE
(Grouped with the parishes of Yellow Walls, Kinsealy & Portmarnock)
St Sylvester's, Malahide, Co Dublin
Very Rev Kevin Moore *(Moderator)*
Apartment No. 1, St Sylvester's Church,
Malahide, Co Dublin
Rev Deacon Gerard Reilly
c/o Parish Office
Parish Office: Tel 01-8451244 Fax 01-8168539
Email stsylvesters@eircom.net
Website www.malahideparish.ie

MARINO
St Vincent de Paul, Griffith Avenue, Dublin 9
Very Rev Thomas Noone PP
69 Griffith Avenue, Dublin 9
Tel 01-8332864
Rev Christian Ameh PC
c/o The Sacristy, St Vincent de Paul Church,
Griffith Avenue, Dublin 9
Tel 01-8339756
Parish Office: Tel 01-8332772/087-2506786
Email info@marinoparish.ie
Website www.marinoparish.ie

MARLEY GRANGE
The Divine Word, 25/27 Hermitage Downs, Rathfarnham, Dublin 16
Very Rev Liam Tracey (OSM) PP
Rev Jim Mulherin (OSM) CC
25–27 Hermitage Downs,
Marley Grange, Rathfarnham, Dublin 16
Tel 01-4944295
Parish Office: Tel 01-4944295 Fax 01-4941042
Email divine_word@ireland.com
Website www.marleygrangeparish.ie

MAYNOOTH
St Mary's, Maynooth, Co Kildare
Very Rev Frank Canon McEvoy Adm
Parochial House, Moyglare Road
Tel 01-6286220
Rev Paul Kelly CC
The Presbytery, 18 Straffan Way,
Maynooth, Co Kildare
Tel 087-2463876
Rev Gerhard Osthues (SVD) PC
c/o Parish Office, Maynooth, Co Kildare
Rev Deacon Joe Walsh
Parish Office: Tel 01-5640012/
087-2048898/01-6293885
Email maynoothparishoffice@eircom.net
www.maynoothparish.dublindiocese.ie

MEADOWBROOK
(Grouped with Dundrum and Ballinteer)
St Attracta's Oratory, Dublin 16
Very Rev Liam Canon Belton *(Moderator)*
Presbytery 1,
St John the Evangelist Parish,
Ballinteer Avenue, Dublin 16
Rev Martins Ebuka TA
Rev Moses Daniel Murtala TA
75 Ludford Road, Ballinteer, Dublin 16
Parish Office: Tel 01-2980471
Email info@meadowbrookparish.ie
www.meadowbrookparish.ie

ARCHDIOCESE OF DUBLIN

MEATH STREET AND MERCHANTS QUAY
(Grouped with James' Street and Francis Street)
St Catherine of Alexandria, Dublin 8
Church of the Immaculate Conception
(popularly known as Adam and Eve's)
4 Merchant's Quay, Dublin D08 XY19
Very Rev Eugene Taffe *(Moderator)*
Very Rev Niall Coghlan (OSA) Co-PP
St Catherine's Presbytery, Meath Street, Dublin 8
Tel 01-4543356
Parish Office
Tel 01-4543356 Fax 01-4738303
Email meathst@hotmail.com
Website www.meathstreetparish.ie

MERRION ROAD
Our Lady Queen of Peace, Dublin 4
Very Rev Fergus O'Connor (Opus Dei) PP, VF
Email fc.oconnor@gmail.com
Rev James Hurley CC
Email jpatrickhurley@gmail.com
31 Herbert Ave., Merrion Road, Dublin 4
Tel 01-2692001
Parish Office: Tel 01-2691825
Email info@merrionroadchurch.ie
Website www.merrionroadchurch.ie

MILLTOWN
SS Columbanus and Gall, Dublin 6
Rt Rev Mgr Peter Briscoe Adm
67 Ramleh Park, Milltown, Dublin 6
Tel 01-2196600
Rev Alan Mowbray (SJ) PC
Gonzaga Jesuit Community,
Sandford Road, Dublin 6
Tel 01-4972943
Parish Office: Tel 01-2196740/
01-2680041/087-9500334
Email milltownparishcentre@eircom.net
Website www.milltownparish.ie

MONKSTOWN
St Patrick's, Carrickbrennan Road
Very Rev Kevin Rowan PP
Parochial House, Carrickbrennan Road, Monkstown, Co Dublin
Tel 01-2802130
Rev Deacon Eric Cooney
Parish Office: Tel 01-2807854
Email secretary@monkstownparish.ie
Website www.monkstownparish.ie

MOONE
Church of the Blessed Trinity
Very Rev Liam Canon Rigney PP
Parochial House, 1 Stanhope Place,
Athy, Co Kildare
Tel 059-8631781
Parish Office: Tel 059-8623154
Email stlaurencechurch@gmail.com
Wesbite www.narraghmoreparish.org

MOUNT ARGUS
St Paul of the Cross, Harold's Cross, Dublin 6W
Rev Paul Francis Spencer (CP) PP
Rev Patrick Fitzgerald (CP) CC
St Paul's Retreat,
Mount Argus, Dublin 6W
Email secretary@mountargusparish.ie
Website www.mountargusparish.ie
Parish Office: Tel 01-4992000

MOUNT MERRION
St Therese, Mount Merrion, Co Dublin
Very Rev Joseph Mullan *(Moderator)*
79 The Rise, Mount Merrion, Co Dublin
Tel 01-2889879
Rev Patrick J. O'Byrne CC
188 Lower Kilmacud Road, Kilmacud, Co Dublin
Tel 01-2981955
Rev Brian O'Reilly *(Team Assistant)*
Rev Donie O'Connor (MHM) CC
6 Allen Park Road, Stillorgan, Co Dublin A94 X261
Tel 089-9796447
Parish Office: Tel 01-2881271/01-2783804
Email mountmerrionparishoffice@eircom.net
Website www.mountmerrionparish.ie

MOUNTVIEW
Mountview Road Parish is now under the Team Ministry of Blakestown/Hartstown/Huntstown/Mountview
St Philip the Apostle, Blanchardstown, Dublin 15
Very Rev Joseph Coyne *(Moderator)*
Very Rev George Adzato (SVD) Co-PP
Very Rev John Owen (SVD) PC
No. 2 The Presbytery, Mountview, Blanchardstown, Dublin 15
Tel 01-8216380
Email mountview@dublindiocese.ie
Website www.stphilipsmountview.ie

MOURNE ROAD
Mourne Road Parish is now under the Team Ministry of Crumlin/Mourne Road/Clogher Road
Our Lady of Good Counsel, Dublin 12
Very Rev Anthony O'Shaughnessy *(Moderator)*
Very Rev David Brannigan Co-PP
89 Sperrin Road, Drimnagh, Dublin 12
Tel 01-4652418
Email copp@mourneroad.ie
Rev Dan An Nguyen Co-PP
Parochial House, Sperrin Road, Dublin 12
Parish Office: Tel 01-4556105
Fax 01-4550133
Email mourneroadparish@eircom.net
Website www.mourneroad.ie

MULHUDDART
Rt Rev Mgr Eoin Thynne Adm
24 The Court, Mulhuddart Wood, Mulhuddart, Dublin 15
Rev Adrian F. Crowley CC
4 Summerfield Lawn, Clonsilla Road, Blanchardstown, Dublin 15
Mr Peter Siney, Parish Pastoral Worker
Parish Office: Tel 01-8205480
Email mulhudoffice@gmail.com

NARRAGHMORE
(Grouped with the parish of Moone)
SS Mary and Laurence, Co Kildare
Very Rev Liam Canon Rigney PP
Parochial House, Crookstown,
Athy, Co Kildare
Email stlaurencechurch@gmail.com
Website www.narraghmoreparish.org

NAUL
The Naul Parish is now under the Team Ministry Rolestown/Garristown/The Naul
St Canice's, Damastown, Co Dublin
The Nativity of BVM, Naul
The Assumption of BVM, Ballyboughal
Very Rev Derek Canon Farrell *(Moderator)*
Parochial House, Main Street, Garristown, Co Dublin A42 PF64
Tel 01-8412932
Rev Deacon Declan Colgan

NAVAN ROAD
Our Lady Help of Christians, Dublin 7
Very Rev John O'Brien Adm
Parochial House, 211 Navan Road, Dublin 7
Tel 01-8681436
Rev Patrick O'Byrne CC
194 Navan Road, Dublin 7
Tel 01-8383313
Rev Deacon Eamonn Murray
c/o Parish Office
Parish Office: Tel 01-8380265
Email navanroadparish@eircom.net
Website www.navanroadparish.com

NEILSTOWN
St Peter the Apostle, Dublin 22
(Clondalkin/Rowlagh/Neilstown/Deansrath/Bawnogue Grouping)
Very Rev Kieran Coghlan *(Moderator)*
Very Rev Hugh Kavanagh Co-PP
The Presbytery, Neilstown, Clondalkin, Dublin 22
Tel 01-6263920
Very Rev Padraig O'Sullivan Co-PP
Rev Cherian Thazamhon CC
30 Wheatfield Close, Clondalkin, Dublin 22
(Also Chaplain to Syro-Malakara Community)
Ms Christina Malone, Parish Pastoral Worker
Parish Office:
Tel 01-4573546/085-7199087

NEWCASTLE
(Grouped with the parishes of Saggart, Rathcoole & Brittas)
St Finian's, Co Dublin
Very Rev John Gilligan *(Moderator)*
St Mary's Parochial House,
Saggart, Co Dublin
Tel 087-4103239
Rev Kevin Doherty CC
No 1 The Glebe, Peamount Road,
Newcastle Lyons, Co Dublin
Tel 01-4589230
Rev David Fleming CC
87 Beechwood Lawns,
Rathcoole, Co Dublin
Tel 01-4587187
Rev Deacon Paul Ferris,
c/o Parish Office, Saggart, Co Dublin
Mr Frank Brown, Parish Pastoral Worker

NEWTOWNPARK
The Guardian Angels, Blackrock, Co Dublin
Very Rev Dermot Leycock PP
64 Newtownpark Avenue,
Blackrock, Co Dublin
Tel 01-2784860
Rev William Fortune PC
32 Newtownpark Avenue,
Blackrock, Co Dublin
Tel 01-2100337
Parish Office: Tel 01-2832988
Email newtownparkparish@eircom.net
Website www.newtownparkparish.com

NORTH WALL-SEVILLE PLACE
St Laurence O'Toole's (North Wall), Dublin 1
Very Rev Robert Colclough Adm, VF
Parochial House,
49 Seville Place, Dublin 1
Tel 01-2865457
Parish Office: Tel 01-8744286

NORTH WILLIAM STREET
St Agatha's, Dublin 1
Very Rev Brendan Kealy Adm
Parochial House,
46 North William Street, Dublin 1
Tel 01-8556474
Parish Office: Tel 01-8554078
Email office@stagathasparish.ie
Website www.stagathasparish.ie

OLD BAWN (see TALLAGHT, OLDBAWN)

PALMERSTOWN
St Philomena's, Dublin 20
Very Rev Anthony Canon Reilly PP
Parochial House, Palmerstown, Dublin 20
Tel 01-6266254 Fax 01-6266255
Email reillya48@gmail.com
Parish Office: Tel 01-6260900/01-6266241
Email stphilomenasparish48@gmail.com
Website www.palmerstownparish.com

PHIBSBOROUGH
(Grouped with Cabra and Cabra West)
St Peter's, Dublin 7
Very Rev Eamon Devlin (CM) PP
Email pp@stpetersphibsboro.ie
St Peter's, Phibsboro, Dublin 7
Tel 01-8389708/8102566
Rev Deacon Damian Murphy
Email info@stpetersphibsboro.ie
Website www.stpetersphibsboro.ie

PORTERSTOWN-CLONSILLA
St Mochta's, Porterstown, Dublin 15
Very Rev Paul Ward Adm
St Mochta's, Porterstown, Dublin 15
Tel 01-8213218 Fax 01-8213516
Rev Deacon Timothy Murphy
c/o Parish Office
Website www.stmochtasparish.ie

PORTMARNOCK
(Grouped with the parishes of Malahide, Yellow Walls & Kinsealy)
St Anne's, Portmarnock, Co Dublin
Very Rev Kevin Moore *(Moderator)*
Very Rev John Canon Flaherty Co-PP
St Anne's, Strand Road,
Portmarnock, Co Dublin
Tel/Fax 01-8461081
Rev Deacon Gerard Reilly
Parish Office
Tel 01-8461561 Fax 01-8169802
Email stannes@portmarnockparish.ie
Website www.portmarnockparish.ie

PRIORSWOOD
St Francis of Assisi, Dublin 17
Very Rev Bryan Shortall (OFMCap) PP
Rev Bill Ryan (OFMCap) PC
Clonshaugh Drive, Priorswood, Dublin 17
Parish Office: Tel 01-8474469
Fax 01-8487296
Email priorswoodparish@yahoo.ie
Website www.priorswoodparish.ie

RAHENY
Our Lady Mother of Divine Grace, Howth Road, Dublin 5
Very Rev Michael Cullen Adm
5 St Assam's Road West, Raheny, Dublin 5
Tel 01-8313806
Rev Paul Dunne CC
24 Watermill Road, Raheny, Dublin 5
Tel 01-8313232
Parish Office: Tel 01-8313232
Email oldgraheny@eircom.net

RATHDRUM
SS Mary and Michael, Co Wicklow
Very Rev Derek Doyle *(Moderator)*
Parochial House, Rathdrum, Co Wicklow
Tel 0404-46229
Rev John Greene CC

RATHFARNHAM
(Grouped with Churchtown and Ballyroan)
The Annunciation, Dublin 14
Very Rev Martin Canon Cosgrove *(Moderator)*
St Mary's Presbytery, Willbrook Road,
Rathfarnham, Dublin 14
Tel 01-4954554
Rev Michael Coady Co-PP
St Mary's Presbytery, Willbrook Road,
Rathfarnham, Dublin 14
Tel 01-4932390
Rev Deacon Matthew Murphy
Rev Deacon Frank Browne
Parish Office:
Tel 01-4958695 Fax 01-4958696
Email rathfarnhamparish1@eircom.net

RATHGAR
Church of the Three Patrons, Rathgar Road, Dublin 6
Very Rev Andrew O'Sullivan Adm
52 Lower Rathmines Road,
Dublin D06 AK19
Rev David Larkin (SPS) CC
c/o Parish Office
Parish Office: Tel 01-4972215
Email 3patrons@eircom.net
Website www.rathgarparish.ie

RATHMINES
Mary Immaculate, Refuge of Sinners, Rathmines, Dublin 6
Very Rev Andrew O'Sullivan Adm
52 Lower Rathmines Road, Dublin 6
Tel 01-4969049
Parish Office: Tel 01-4971531
Website www.rathminesparish.ie

RIALTO/DOLPHIN'S BARN
(Grouped with the parish of Dolphin's Barn)
Our Lady of the Holy Rosary of Fatima, Rialto, Dublin 8
Very Rev Fergal MacDonagh *(Moderator)*
18 St Anthony's Road, Rialto, Dublin 8
Tel 01-4534469
Rev Roy George PC
500 South Circular Road, Rialto, Dublin 8
Parish Office: Tel 01-4539020
Website www.rialtoparish.com

RINGSEND
St Patrick's, Dublin 4
Very Rev Ivan Tonge PP
St Patrick's, 2 Cambridge Road, Dublin 4
Tel 087-2726868
Rt Rev Mgr Daniel O'Connor PC
St Mary's, Irishtown Road, Dublin 4
Rev Deacon Thomas Groves
Parish Office: Tel 01-6697429
Email stpatrickschurchringsend@eircom.net
Website www.stpatrickschurchringsend.com

ARCHDIOCESE OF DUBLIN

RIVERMOUNT
St Oliver Plunkett, St Helena's Drive,
Dublin 11
Very Rev Seamus Ahearne (OSA) PP
The Presbytery, 60 Glenties Park,
Finglas South, Dublin 11
Tel 01-8343722/087-6782746
Email seamus.ahearne@gmail.com
Rev Paddy O'Reilly (OSA) CC
Parochial House, St Helena's Drive,
Dublin 11
Tel 01-8343444/086-8279504
Email paddyforeilly@eircom.net

RIVER VALLEY
Swords/River Valley/Brackenstown
Grouping
St Finian's, Swords, Co Dublin
Very Rev Desmond G. Doyle (Moderator)
Tel 01-8447283
Very Rev Colin Rothery Co-PP
5 Lissenhall Park, Seatown Road,
Swords, Co Dublin
Parish Office: Tel 01-8409043
Website www.rivervalley.dublindiocese.ie

ROLESTOWN-OLDTOWN
Rolestown parish is now under the Team
Ministry of Rolestown Garristown/The Naul
St Brigid's, Rolestown, Co Dublin
Very Rev Derek Canon Farrell
(Moderator)
Very Rev John F. Keegan Co-PP
Rolestown, Swords, Co Dublin
Tel 01-8401514
Email parishrolestown@gmail.com

ROUNDWOOD
St Laurence O'Toole, Co Wicklow
Very Rev Derek Doyle (Moderator)
Rev John Greene CC
Rev Deacon Jeremy Seligman
Parish Office: Tel 01-2818384 (mornings)
Email roundwoodparish@eircom.net

ROWLAGH AND QUARRYVALE
Clondalkin/Rowlagh/Neilstown/
Deansrath/Bawnogue Grouping
Immaculate Heart of Mary, Clondalkin,
Dublin 22
Very Rev Kieran Coghlan (Moderator)
Very Rev Hugh Kavanagh Co-PP
Very Rev Padraig O'Sullivan Co-PP
Rev Cherian Thazhamon CC
30 Wheatfield Close,
Clondalkin, Dublin 22
Ms Christina Malone, Parish Pastoral
Worker
Parish Office: Tel/Fax 01-6261010
Email parishofrowlagh@eircom.net
Website
www.rowlaghandquarryvaleparish.com

RUSH
St Maur's, Rush, Co Dublin
Very Rev Kevin Bartley Adm
The Presbytery, Chapel Green,
Rush, Co Dublin
Tel 01-8437208
Rev Clinton Nkem PC
Tel 01-8949464
Email rushparish@dublindiocese.ie
Website www.rushparish.dublindiocese.ie

SAGGART/RATHCOOLE/BRITTAS
(Grouped with the parish of Newcastle)
Nativity of the BVM, Co Dublin
Very Rev John Gilligan (Moderator)
St Mary's Parochial House,
Saggart, Co Dublin
Tel 087-4103239
Rev Kevin Doherty Co-PP
No 1 the Glebe, Peamount Road,
Newcastle Lyons, Co Dublin
Tel 01-4589230
Rev David Fleming CC
87 Beechwood Lawns,
Rathcoole, Co Dublin
Tel 01-4587187
Rev Michael McGowan PC
7 St Patrick's Crescent,
Rathcoole, Co Dublin
Tel 01-4589210
Rev Deacon Paul Ferris
Parish Office, Saggart, Co Dublin
Mr Frank Brown, Parish Pastoral Worker
Tel 01-4589209

SALLYNOGGIN
Our Lady of Victories, Co Dublin
Very Rev Padraig Gleeson Adm
Rev Michael Simpson CC
St Kevin's Presbytery, Pearse Street,
Sallynoggin, Co Dublin
Tel 01-2854667 Fax 01-2847024
Parish Office: Tel 01-2854667
Email sallynogginparish@eircom.net

SANDYFORD
St Mary's, Dublin 18
Very Rev John Canon Delany (Moderator)
Parochial House, St Mary's,
Sandyford Village, Dublin 18
Tel 045-2956317
Very Rev Paul Ludden Co-PP
c/o St Mary's, Sandyford, Dublin 18
Rev Aaron Vinduska (LC) PC
The Presbytery, St Mary's,
Sandyford, Dublin 18
Tel 01-2958933
Rev Jim Caffrey CC
The Presbytery,
Hawthorns Road, Dublin 18
Parish Office: Tel 01-2956414
Email office@sandyfordparish.org
Website www.sandyfordparish.org

SANDYMOUNT
St Mary's Star of the Sea, Dublin 4
Very Rev John McDonagh PP
'Stella Maris', 15 Oswald Road,
Sandymount, Dublin 4
Tel 01-6684265
Rev Cormac McIlraith PC
10 Cranfield Place,
Sandymount, Dublin 4
Tel 01-6686845
Parish Office: Tel 01-6683316
Fax 01-6683894
Email sandymountparish@eircom.net

SHANKILL
St Anne's, Co Dublin
Very Rev Derry Murphy (SAC) PP
St Benin's Parish, Dublin Road,
Shankill, Co Dublin
Tel 01-2824425
Rev Michael O'Dwyer (SAC) CC
Rev Jamie Twohig (SAC) CC
St Benin's, Dublin Road
Tel 01-2824425
Parish Office: Tel 01-2822277
Email st.annes_parishoffice@yahoo.ie

SKERRIES
St Patrick's, Co Dublin
Very Rev Melvyn Mullins PP
42 Strand Street, Skerries,
Co Dublin
Tel 01-8491250
Parish Office: Tel 01-8492145
Email
stpatrickschurchskerries@gmail.com

SPRINGFIELD
St Mark's, Maplewood Road,
Tallaght, Dublin 24
Very Rev Patrick McKinley (Moderator)
68 Maplewood Road, Springfield,
Tallaght, Dublin 24
Rev William O'Shaughnessy CC, VF
70 Maplewood Road,
Tallaght, Dublin 24
Tel 01-4590746
Rev Martin Hughes TA
Youth Evangelisation in Springfield
Group and Tallaght Deanery
Ms Saule Cameron, Parish Pastoral
Worker
Tel 086-3592451
Parish Office: Tel 01-4620777
Email stmarkschurch@eircom.net
Website www.stmarksspringfield.com

SRULEEN
Sacred Heart, St John's Drive, Clondalkin,
Dublin 22
Very Rev Vincent Fallon (SSCC) PP
Rev Michael Ruddy (SSCC) PC
Parish Office: Tel 01-4570032
Website www.sruleenparish.ie

SUTTON
Sutton/Howth/Baldoyle Grouping
St Fintan's, Greenfield Road, Dublin 13
Very Rev Cyril Mangan *(Moderator)*
8 Greenfield Road, Sutton, Dublin 13
Tel 01-8322396
Rev Gerry Tanham PC
Rev Gabriel Flynn TA
Apt 1, The Presbytery, Greenfield Road, Sutton, Dublin 13
Parish Office: Tel 01-8392001
Email office@stfintansparish.ie
Website www.stfintansparish.ie

SWORDS
Swords/River Valley/Brackenstown Grouping
St Colmcille's, Co Dublin
(Dublin Airport Church, Our Lady Queen of Heaven is in this parish)
Very Rev Desmond Doyle *(Moderator)*
Chaplain's Residence,
Dublin Airport, Co Dublin
Very Rev John Collins Co-PP
18 Aspen Road, Kinsealy Court, Swords, Co Dublin
Tel 01-8405948
Very Rev Colin Rothery Co-PP
Parish Office: Tel 01-8407277
Email stcolmcilleschurch@eircom.net
Website www.swordsparish.com

TALLAGHT, DODDER
St Dominic's, Dublin 24
Very Rev Laurence Collins (OP) Adm
Rev Timothy Mulcahy (OP) CC
Presbytery, St Dominic's Road, Tallaght, Dublin 24
Tel 01-4510620 Fax 01-4623223
Parish Office: Tel 01-4510620
Fax 01-4623223
Website www.stdominicsparishtallaght.ie

TALLAGHT, OLDBAWN
St Martin de Porres, Dublin 24
Very Rev James Daly PP
Parochial House,
Bohernabreena, Dublin 24
Rev Michael Canon Hurley PC
The Presbytery, St Martin's, Aylesbury, Dublin 24
Tel 01-4627080
Rev Deacon Padraic O'Sullivan
Parish Office: Tel/Fax 01-4510160
Email stmartinsparish@eircom.net

TALLAGHT, ST MARY'S
St Mary's, Tallaght Village, Dublin 24
Very Rev Donal Roche (OP) Adm
Rev Robert Regula (OP) CC
St Mary's Priory, Tallaght, Dublin 24
Tel 01-4048100 Fax 01-4596784

TALLAGHT, TYMON NORTH
St Aengus's, Castletymon Road, Dublin 24
Very Rev Benedict Moran (OP) PP
Dominican Community,
St Aengus's, Balrothery, Tallaght, Dublin 24
Tel 01-4513757
Email ben.moran25@gmail.com

Rev Pat Lucey (OP) CC
The Presbytery, St Aengus's,
Balrothery, Tallaght, Dublin 24
Tel 01-4528161
Parish Office
Tel 01-4513757 Fax 01-4624038
Email staenguschurch@eircom.net.
Website www.staengusparishtallaght.ie

TEMPLEOGUE
St Pius X, College Drive, Dublin 6W
Very Rev Gerard Moore PP
23 Wainsfort Park,
Terenure, Dublin 6W
Tel 01-4900218
Email frduffy@eircom.net
Rev Deacon Gerard Larkin
Parish Office
Tel 01-4905284/087-9672258
Email info@stpiusx.ie
Website www.stpiusx.ie

TERENURE
St Joseph's, Dublin 6
Very Rev Philip Bradley Adm, VF
Parochial House,
83 Terenure Road East,
Dublin 6
Tel 01-4905520
Parish Office: 01-4921755
Email stjosephterenure@eircom.net

TRAVELLING PEOPLE
Chapel of Ease, St Oliver's Park, Clondalkin, Dublin 22
Very Rev Paul O'Driscoll PP
6 New Cabra Road, Phibsborough, Dublin 7
Parish Office: St Laurence House,
6 New Cabra Road, Phibsborough, Dublin 7
Tel 01-8388874 Fax 01-8388901
Email into@ptrav.ie. www.ptrav.ie
Recommended Websites:
www.exchangehouse.ie
www.paveepoint.ie
www.stpetersphibsborough.com

UNIVERSITY CHURCH
*Our Lady, Seat of Wisdom,
St Stephen's Green, Dublin 2*
Very Rev Enda Cunningham Adm
University Church is in the charge of the Congregation of the Holy Cross, Notre Dame
c/o Parish Office
Parish Office: Tel 01-4759674

VALLEYMOUNT
(Grouped with the parish of Blessington)
*St Joseph's, Valleymount
Our Lady of Mount Carmel, Lacken*
Very Rev Richard Behan PP
The Presbytery, Main Street,
Blessington, Co Wicklow
Tel 045-865442

WALKINSTOWN
Assumption of the BVM, Dublin 12
Very Rev Paul Glennon PP
162 Walkinstown Road, Dublin D12 Y0F1
Tel 01-4501372
Rev John Jacob CC
12 Walkinstown Road, Dublin 12
Tel 01-4502541
Parish Sacristy: Tel 01-4502649

WHITEFRIAR STREET
*Our Lady of Mount Carmel,
Whitefriar Street, Dublin 2*
Very Rev Seán Ford (OCarm) PP, VF
Carmelite Priory,
56 Aungier Street, Dublin 2
Tel 01-4758821
Email whitefriars@eircom.net

WICKLOW
St Patrick's, Wicklow, Co Wicklow
Very Rev Donal Roche Adm, VG
The Abbey, Wicklow, Co Wicklow
Tel 0404-671961 Fax 0404-69971
Rev Patrick O'Rourke CC
The Presbytery, St Patrick's Road,
Wicklow Town, Co Wicklow
Parish Office: Tel 0404-61699
Email parishofficewicklow@eircom.net

WILLINGTON
St Jude the Apostle, Orwell Park, Dublin 6W
Very Rev Brendan Madden PP
2 Rossmore Road,
Templeogue, Dublin 6W
Tel 01-4508432
Parish Office: Tel 01-4600127
Email judesparishoffice@eircom.net

YELLOW WALLS, MALAHIDE
(Grouped with the parishes of Malahide, Kinsealy & Portmarnock)
Sacred Heart Church, Eastuary Road, Malahide, Co Dublin
Very Rev Kevin Moore *(Moderator)*
Very Rev Martin Noone Co-PP
7 Seabury Drive, Malahide,
Co Dublin K36 YN67
Tel 01-8451902
Rev Deacon Gerard Reilly
yellowwallsparish@gmail.com
Website www.yellowwallsparish.ie

INSTITUTIONS AND THEIR CHAPLAINS
COLLEGES

Dublin City University
Chaplains: Rev Seamus McEntee
InterFaith Centre, Dublin 9
Tel 01-7005268 Fax 01-7005663
Rev Paul Hampson
DCU St Patrick's Campus
Drumcondra Road Upper, Dublin 9
Tel 01-8842000

DCU Mater Dei Centre for Catholic Education
DCU St Patrick's Campus
Drumcondra Road Upper, Dublin 9
Director: Dr Cora O'Farrell
Tel 01-7009171

ARCHDIOCESE OF DUBLIN

Institute of Technology
Tallaght, Dublin 24
Tel 01-4042000

National College of Art and Design
100 Thomas Street, Dublin 8
Chaplain: Vacant

National University of Ireland, Maynooth (NUIM)
Tel 01-7086000
Chaplaincy Service,
NUI Maynooth, Co Kildare
Tel 01-7083588
Chaplain: Ciaran Coughlan
Tel 01-7083588
Executive Assistant: Ms Susan Caldwell
Tel 01-7083320
Email chaplaincy@nuim.ie

Trinity College, Dublin 2
Rev Peter Sexton (SJ)
Rev Alan O'Sullivan (OP)
House 27 Trinity College, Dublin 2
Tel 01-8961260

Technological University Dublin
Co-ordinator, Pastoral Care and Chaplaincy Service: Rev Alan Hilliard
Room 254, TU Dublin – Bolton Street, D0l K822
Tel 01-2207085
Email alan.hilliard@tudublin.ie

Technological University Dublin, Bolton Street
Rev. Alan Hilliard
Room 254, TU Dublin – Bolton Street, D0l K822
Tel 01-2207085
Email alan.hilliard@tudublin.ie

Technological University Dublin, Grangegorman
Mr Finbarr O'Leary
Room RD-117, Rathdown House, TU Dublin – Grangegorman, D07 H6K8
Tel 01-2207077
Email finbarr.oleary@tudublin.ie
Fr Ultan Naughton (SSCC)
Room RD-117, Rathdown House, TU Dublin, Grangegorman D07 H6K8
Email ultan.naughton@tudublin.ie

Technological University Dublin, Tallaght
Sr Bernadette Purcell (PBVM)
Room 010, TU Dublin – Tallaght Campus, D24 FKT9
Tel 01-4042615
Email bernadette.purcell@tudublin.ie

Technological University Dublin, Blanchardstown
Sr Susan Jones (CHF)
Room C114, TU Dublin – Blanchardstown Campus, D24 FKT9
Tel 01-2207089
Email susan.jones@tudublin.ie

Technological University Dublin, Grangegorman
Rev Joseph Loftus
Room RD-117, Rathdown House, TU Dublin – Grangegorman, D07 H6K8
Tel 01-2207079
Email joseph.loftus@tudublin.ie

Technological University Dublin, Aungier Street
Sarah Marshall (C of I) and Andrew Somerville (C of I)
Room 4070, TU Dublin – Aungier Street, D02 HW71
Tel 01-2207086
Email sarah.marshall@tudublin.ie/
andrew.somerville@tudublin.ie

Technological University Dublin, Grangegorman
Rev Rob Jones (C of I)
Room RD-117, Rathdown House, TU Dublin – Grangegorman, D07
Tel 01-2205230
Email rob.jones@tudublin.ie

Technological University Dublin
Suzanne Greene, Administrative Assistant to the Pastoral Care and Chaplaincy Service
Room RD-116, Rathdown House, TU Dublin – Grangegorman, D07 H6K8
Tel 01-2207076
Email suzanne.greene@tudublin.ie

University College, Dublin
Chaplains' Room, UCD, Belfield, Dublin 4
Tel 01-7168317
Rev Brendan Ludlow
Head Chaplain: Rev Eamonn Bourke
Chaplains' Residence:
St Stephen's, UCD, Belfield, Dublin 4
Tel 01-7161971

DEFENCE FORCES

Head Chaplain
Rev Séamus Madigan
Rev Paschal Hanrahan (from 1 March 2022)
Administrative Secretary: Sgt Liam Bellew
Tel 01-8042638
Defence Forces Headquarters, McKee Barracks, Blackhorse Avenue, Dublin 7

McKee Barracks
Dublin 7
Tel 086-2256794
Rev Damian Farnon

Cathal Brugha Barracks
Rathmines, Dublin 6
Tel 01-8046484

Casement Aerodrome
Baldonnel, Co Dublin
Tel 01-4037536
Rev Bernard McCay-Morrissey (OP)

International Military Pilgrimage to Lourdes
(Pelerinage Militaire Internationale)
Director: Rev Seamus Madigan
Rev Paschal Hanrahan (from 1 March 2022)
Tel 01-8042637

HOSPITALS

Beaumont Hospital
Beaumont Road, Dublin 9
Tel 01-8377755
Direct Line: 01-8092815/8093229
Rev Eoin Hughes Tel 01-8477573
Rev Suresh Babu Chintagunta (OSCam)
Ms Rosaleen Butterly
Mr Michael Ward
Ms Orla McMahon,
Mr Cathal O'Sullivan
Mr Prakash Varkey

Beaumont Convalescent Home
Tel 8379186
Beaumont Parish

Blackrock Clinic
Blackrock, Co Dublin
Tel 01-2832222
Most Rev Eamonn Walsh, Auxiliary Bishop Emeritus of Dublin

Blackrock Hospice
Sweetman's Avenue, Blackrock, Co Dublin
Tel 01-2064000
Sr Ann Purcell (RSC)
Tel 01-2064024 – direct line

Bloomfield
Donnybrook, Dublin 4
Tel 01-4950021
Carmelite Fathers, Avila, Morehampton Road, Dublin 4
Tel 01-6683091

Bon Secours Hospital
Glasnevin, Dublin 9
Tel 01-8065300
Director of Pastoral Care: Mr Alan Burke
Rev Owen O'Sullivan (OFM Cap),
Ms Ann Martin
Ms Eileen Kavanagh
Ms Julie Long

Cappagh National Orthopaedic Hospital
Cappagh, Dublin 11
Tel 01-8341211
Congregation of the Holy Spirit and Finglas West Parish

Central Mental Hospital
Dundrum
Tel 01-2989266
Ms Mary Monaghan

Cherry Orchard Hospital
Ballyfermot
Tel 01-6264702
Rev Patrick Cully (CSSp) (on behalf of the Holy Spirit Congregation)

Children's Health Ireland at Crumlin (Our Lady's Children's Hospital)
Crumlin, Dublin 12
Tel 01-4096100
Rev John Dunphy
Ms June O'Toole
Ms Deirdre Gallagher
Ms Mary Young

Children's Health Ireland at Temple Street
Temple Street
Tel 01-8784200
Ms Carmel Battigan,
Ms Rachel Cooney

Clonskeagh Hospital
Vergemount, Dublin 6
Tel 01-2697877
Rev Jude Lynch (CSSp) (on behalf of the Holy Spirit Congregation)

Connolly Hospital
Blanchardstown, Dublin 15
Tel 01-8213844
Office (direct line) 01-64656168
Rev Anthony O'Riordan (SVD)
Ms Alison Mannion
Ms Jenny Cuypers

Coombe Women and Infants University Hospital
Dolphin's Barn, Dublin 8
Tel 01-4085200
Ms Catherine Dilworth
Ms Josette Devitt Vassallo

Eye and Ear Hospital (Royal Victoria)
Adelaide Road, Dublin 2
Tel 01-6644600
Jesuit Community, Lower Leeson Street

Hermitage Medical Clinic
Old Lucan Road, Lucan, Co Dublin
Tel 01-6459000
Rev Tomy George Paradiyil (OSCam)

Leopardstown Park Hospital
Tel 01-2955055
Ms Miriam Molan

Mater Hospital
Eccles Street, Dublin 7
Tel 01-8301122/8032000
Direct line 01-8032239/8032411
Rev Vincent Xavier Kakkadampallil (OSCam),
Rev Prince Mathew (OSCam),
Rev Suneesh Mathew (OSCam)
Rev Damian Casey (OFM)
Ms Margaret Sleator

Mater Private Hospital
Dublin 7
Tel 01-8858888
Fr Peter Murphy

National Maternity Hospital
Holles Street, Dublin 2
Tel 01-6373100
Very Rev Enda Cunningham Adm
Ms Helen Miley
Ms Angela Neville-Egan

National Rehabilitation Hospital
Rochestown Avenue,
Dun Laoghaire, Co Dublin
Tel 01-2355000
Rev Michael Kennedy (CSSp)

Newcastle Hospital
Tel 01-2819001
Very Rev Sean Canon Smith CC
The Presbytery, Newtownmountkennedy, Co Wicklow
Tel 01-2819253

Orthopaedic Hospital
Castle Avenue, Clontarf
Tel 01-8332521
Appointment pending

Our Lady's Hospice and Care Services
Harold's Cross
Tel 01-4068700
Rev Kieran Creagh CP

Peamount Hospital
Newcastle, Co Dublin
Tel 01-6010300
Rev Jim Byrnes (CSSp)

Phoenix Care Centre
Grangegorman, North Circular Road, Dublin 7
Tel 01-8276500
Vacant

Rotunda Hospital
Parnell Street, Dublin 1
Tel 01-8730700
Ms Anne Charlton

Royal Hospital Donnybrook
Morehampton Road, Dublin 4
Tel 01-4972844
Appointment Pending

St Bricin's Military Hospital
Infirmary Road, Dublin 8
Tel 01-6776112

St Brigid's
Crooksling
Tel 01-4582133
Very Rev Prior,
St Mary's Priory, Tallaght, Dublin 24
Tel 01-4048100

St Columcille's Hospital
Loughlinstown, Co Dublin
Tel 01-2825800
Mr Jack Michael Byrne

St Francis Hospice, Raheny/Blanchardstown
Tel 01-8327535 (Raheny)
Tel 01-8294000 (Blanchardstown)
Rev Eustace McSweeney (OFMCap),
Rev Michael Duffy (OFMCap)
Capuchin Friary, Raheny, Dublin 5
Tel 01-8313886
Ms Mary Bergin
Sr Maire Brady
Ms Lucy Higgins

St Ita's, Portrane
Tel 01-8436337
Very Rev Patrick Reilly (OPraem) PP

St James's Hospital
James's Street, Dublin 8
Tel 01-4103000
Direct Line 01-4103659
Rev Brian Gough, Rev Jayan Joseph Chamakalayil (MI), Ms Eithne O'Reilly

St John of God Hospital
Stillorgan, Co Dublin
Tel 01-2771400
Rev Hugh Gillan (OH)

St Joseph's Hospital
Clonsilla
Tel 01-8217177
Vacant

St Joseph's Hospital
Springdale Road, Raheny, Dublin 5
Tel 01-8478433
Vacant

St Loman's Hospital
Ballyowen, Palmerstown, Dublin 20
Tel 01-6264077
Vacant

St Luke's Hospital
Highfield Road, Rathgar, Dublin 6
Tel 01-4065000
Fr Michael Commane (OP)

St Mary's Hospital
Phoenix Park, Dublin 20
Tel 01-6250300
Rev Samson Mann (CSSp)

St Michael's Hospital
Lower George's Street, Dun Laoghaire
Tel 01-2806901
Rev Thomas McDonald (CSSp)
Ms Anita Delaney

St Patrick's Hospital
James Street, Dublin 8
Tel 01-2493200
Augustinian Fathers, John's Lane

St Paul's (Autistic Children)
Beaumont
Tel 01-8377673
Beaumont Parish

St Vincent's Hospital
Athy, Co Kildare
Tel 059-8643000
Very Rev Liam Rigney PP
Tel 059-8646022

St Vincent's University Hospital
Elm Park, Dublin 4
Tel 01-2214000
Direct Line 01-2214325
Rev Liam Cuffe
Very Rev Damian Canon O'Reilly
Ms Caoimhe Doherty
Mr Mark Davis
Deacon Matthew Murphy

ARCHDIOCESE OF DUBLIN

St Vincent's Private Hospital
Tel 01-2638000
Sr Mary Helen Anthonythasan

St Vincent's, Fairview
Tel 01-8375101
Sr Angela Burke

Stewart's Hospital, Palmerstown
Tel 01-6264444
Rev Samson Mann (CSSp)

St Colman's, Rathdrum
Tel 0404-46109
Very Rev Derek Doyle
Tel 0404-46229

Tallaght Hospital
Tel 01-4142000
Roman Catholic Bleep: 2725
Director of Pastoral Care: Rev John Kelly
22 Nugent Road, Churchtown,
Dublin 14
Tel 01-4142482
Email john.kelly@tuh.ie
Pastoral Care Team:
Ms Eden Dela Cruz
Mr Gabriel Ogunjobi
Sr Gabrielle Murphy
Ms Amy Guinan
Ms Anne Marie Leahy
Br Stephen Sheilds (OSA)
Tel 01-4142485

PRIESTS ELSEWHERE IN THE DIOCESE

Very Rev Laurence Behan
On Leave
Rev Peter F. Byrne
On Sabbatical
Very Rev Mgr Paul Callan
On Sabbatical
Rev Patrick Desmond
Apostolic Nunciature
The Lodge, Mount Sackville,
Chapelizod, Dublin 20
Tel 01-8214004

PRIESTS WORKING OUTSIDE THE DIOCESE

Rev Ian Evans
Chaplain, England
Rt Rev Mgr John Kennedy (Congregation for the Doctrine of the Faith)
Via del Mascherino 12,
00193 Roma, Italy
Rev Brendan Purcell
St Mary's Cathedral House,
St Mary's Road, Sydney NSW 2000,
Australia
Most Rev Paul Tighe
Bishop of Drivastrum
Adjunct Secretary of the Pontifical Council for Social Communications,
Vatican City

RETIRED PRIESTS

Rev Kilian Brennan
Apartment 3 Seascape,
366 Contarf Road, Dublin 3
Rev Noel Campbell
Ballysmuttan, Manor Kilbride,
Blessington, Co Wicklow
Rev John Carey
Sacred Heart Residence,
Sybil Hill Road, Raheny, Dublin 5
Rev Aidan Carroll
9 Hillcrest Manor,
Templeogue, Dublin 6W
Rev Denis Carroll
Marymount Care Centre,
Westmanstown, Lucan, Co Dublin
Very Rev Canon Patrick Carroll
124 New Cabra Road, Dublin 7
Very Rev Seamus Cassidy
Tavis, Kilmainham Wood,
Kells, Co Meath
Rev Eamonn Clarke
The Presbytery, Beechwood Park,
Kilcoole, Co Wicklow
Rev Michael Collins,
2 Traverslea Woods,
Glenageary Road Lower,
Dun Laoghaire, Co Dublin
Rev Seamus Connell
56 Foxfield St John,
Kilbarrack, Dublin 5
Very Rev Philip Corcoran
542 River Forest Estate,
Leixlip, Co Kildare
Rev Edward Corry
Presbytery No. 2, Treepark Road,
Kilnamanagh, Dublin 24
Rev Thomas Coughlan
The Presytery, Avoca, Co Wicklow
Rev Michael V. Dempsey
The Presbytery, Kilmede,
Narraghmore, Co Kildare
Very Rev Philip Dennehy PE
4 Stanhope Place, Athy, Co Kildare
Rev Patrick Devitt
17 Prospect Lawn, The Park,
Cabinteely, Dublin 18
Very Rev Francis Dooley
45 Westfield, Sion Hill,
Blackrock, Co Dublin
Rev Cornelius Dowling
Our Lady's Manor, Bulloch Harbour,
Dalkey, Co Dublin
Email dowcpb@eircom.net
Rev Edward Downes
Sacred Heart Residence,
Sybil Hill Road, Raheny, Dublin 5
Very Rev Patrick Canon Fagan PE
Our Lady's Manor, Bullock Harbour,
Dalkey, Co Dublin
Rev John Ferris
14 The Coral, The Grange,
Stillorgan, Co Dublin
Most Rev Raymond Field
Auxiliary Bishop Emeritus,
3 Castleknock Road, Blanchardstown,
Dublin 15
Tel 01-8209191
Email rwmfield@gmail.com

Very Rev James Canon Fingleton
279 Howth Road, Raheny, Dublin 5
Very Rev John Canon Fitzgibbon PE
The Presbytery, Chapel Road,
Lusk, Co Dublin
Very Rev Denis Foley
c/o Archbishops House, Dublin 9
Very Rev Paul Freeney PE
Oghill Nursing Home, Oghill,
Monasterevin, Co Kildare
Rev John Galvin
60 Lower Mount Pleasant Avenue,
Rathmines, Dublin 6
Very Rev J. Anthony Canon Gaughan PE
56 Newtownpark Avenue, Blackrock,
Co Dublin
Rev Patrick Gleeson
14 Deerpark Road, Mount Merrion,
Co Dublin A94 Y0C1
Very Rev Edward Griffin
15 Connawood, Bray, Co Wicklow
Very Rev Walter Canon Harris PE
151 Clonsilla Road, Blanchardstown,
Dublin 15
Very Rev Mícheál Hastings
Beneavin Nursing Home,
Glasnevin, Dublin 11
Rev Cecil Johnston
Sacred Hert Residence, Sybil Hill Road,
Raheny, Dublin 5
Rev Peter Kilroy
64 Cherbury Court,
Booterstown, Co Dublin
Very Rev William King
156b Rathgar Road, Dublin 6
Very Rev Paul Lavelle
123 Foxfield Grove,
Kilbarrack, Dublin 5
Rev Denis Laverty
47 Silken Vale, Maynooth, Co Kildare
Very Rev Patrick Littleton
2 Maypark, Donnycarney, Dublin 5
Rev Owen Lynch
c/o Archbishops House, Dublin 9
Very Rev Patrick J. Mangan
Dun Mhuire, 44 Upper Beechwood Avenue,
Ranelagh, Dublin 6
Tel 01-4975180/087-9857264
Most Rev Diarmuid Martin
Archbishop Emeritus
c/o Archbishop's House
Very Rev Val Martin
'Logatryna', Dunlavin, Co Wicklow
Very Rev Eugene McCarney
Parochial House, Castletown,
Gorey, Co Wexford
Rev Peter McCarron
Email petermccarron@eircom.net
Rev Dermod McCarthy
26 Brackens Bush Road,
Killiney, Co Dublin
Rev Padraig McCarthy
14 Blackthorn Court,
Sandyford, Dublin 16
Rev Thomas McCarthy
Ferndene Nursing Home,
Newtown Park, Blackrock, Co Dublin
Very Rev Niall McDermott
The Presbytery, 91 Grange Road,
Baldoyle, Dublin 13

Rev Fergus McGlynn
43 Chestnut Grove,
Ballymount Road, Dublin 24
Rev Thomas McGowan
Beechtree Nursing Home, Murragh,
Oldtown, Co Dublin
Rev Patrick Monahan
Earlsfort, 291A Old Greenfield,
Maynooth, Co Kildare
Rev John F. Moran
192 Navan Road, Dublin 7
Rev Patrick Moran
1 Seapark, Mount Prospect Avenue,
Dublin 3
Very Rev Benedict Mulligan PE
42 Corke Abbey,
Little Bray, Co Wicklow
Very Rev Peadar Canon Murney
25 Thomastown Road,
Dun Laoghaire, Co Dublin
Tel 01-2856660
Rev Eoin Murphy
25 The Haven, Glasnevin, Dublin 9
Very Rev Tim Murphy
Gorey, Co Wexford
Very Rev Liam Murtagh
33 Grace Park Road,
Drumcondra, Dublin 9
Tel 087-2408416
Rev Sean Noone
The Presbytery, Pollathomas, Co Mayo
Very Rev John O'Connell PE
17 King Edward Court,
Bray, Co Wicklow
Very Rev Mgr Donal O'Doherty PE
Orwell Healthcare Home,
112 Orwell Road, Rathgar, Dublin 6
Very Rev Martin O'Farrell
Acorn Nursing Home,
Cashel, Co Tipperary
Very Rev Thomas O'Keeffe
20 Glen Avenue, The Park, Cabinteely,
Dublin 18
Rev Sean O'Rourke
15 Seaview Park, Shankill, Co Dublin
Very Rev Maurice O'Shea PE
64 White Oaks,
Clonskeagh, Dublin 14
Rev Colm O'Siochru
Our Lady's Manor, Bulloch Castle,
Dalkey, Co Dublin
Rev Brian O'Sullivan
The Cottage, Glengara Park,
Glenageary, Dun Laoghaire, Co Dublin
Rev Sean O'Toole
Ballintubber, Claremorris,
Co Mayo F12 VY17
Email seanotoole@eircom.net
Rev John Canon Piert *(Team Assistant)*
Our Lady's Manor, Bulloch Harbour,
Dalkey, Co Dublin
Rev Cathal Price
54 Foxfield St John, Dublin 5
Rev Sean Quigley
Tara Wintrop Nursing Home,
Nevinstown Lane, Pinnockhill,
Swords, Co Dublin
Very Rev Leo Quinlan
'Carrefour', Jarretstown,
Dunboyne, Co Meath

Rev Henry Regan
Presbytery No. 1, Church Grounds,
Kill Avenue, Dun Laoghaire, Co Dublin
Very Rev Seamus Ryan
Milbrea Nursing Home,
Newport, Co Tipperary
Rev Anthony Scully
Presbytery No. 4, Dunmanus Road,
Cabra, Dublin 7
Very Rev Canon Patrick Shiel
74 Mount Drinan Avenue, Kinsealy
Downs, Swords, Co Dublin
Rev Derek Smyth
No 2 Kill Lane, Foxrock, Dublin 18
Rt Rev Mgr Alex Stenson
5 Calderwood Avenue, Drumcondra,
Dublin 9
Very Rev John Stokes
Sacred Heart Residence,
Sybill Hill Road, Raheny, Dublin 5
Rev John M. Ward
1 Chestnut Grove, Ballymount Road,
Dublin 24
Rt Rev Mgr John Wilson
St Mary's, 97 Ballymun Road, Dublin 9
Tel 01-8375440

PERSONAL PRELATURE

OPUS DEI
Harvieston, 22 Cunningham Road,
Dalkey, Co Dublin A96 CX59
Tel 01-2859877 Fax 01-2305059
Vicar for Ireland:
Rev Donncha Ó hAodha

RELIGIOUS ORDERS AND CONGREGATIONS

PRIESTS

AUGUSTINIANS
St Augustine's, Taylor's Lane,
Ballyboden, Dublin 16
Tel 01-4241000 Fax 01-4939915
Email www.augustinians.ie
Provincial: Rev John Hennebry (OSA)
Prior & CC: Rev Francis Aherne (OSA)

St John's Priory,
Thomas Street, Dublin 8
Tel 01-6770393/0415/0601
Fax 01-6713102 (Mission Office)/6770423
(House)
Prior: Rev Padraig A. Daly (OSA)

(See also under parishes – Ballyboden,
Meath Street and Rivermount)

BLESSED SACRAMENT CONGREGATION
Blessed Sacrament Chapel,
20 Bachelors Walk,
Dublin D01 NW14
Tel 01-8724597 Fax 01-8724724
Email sssdublin@eircom.net
Web www.blessedsacramentuki.org
Superior: Rev Darren Maslen (SSS)
Email dunstanmaslen@gmail.com
Provincial: Rev James Campbell (SSS)

CAMILLIANS
St Camillus, South Hill Avenue,
Blackrock, Co Dublin
Tel 01-2882873 Fax 01-2833380
Superior: Rev Denis Sandham

St Camillus,
11 St Vincent Street North, Dublin 7
Tel 01-8300365 (Residence)
Tel 01-8301122 (Mater Hospital)

CAPUCHINS
Provincial Office
12 Halston Street,
Dublin D07 Y2T5
Tel 01-8733205 Fax 01-8730294
Email capcurirl@eircom.net
Provincial Minister
Very Rev Seán Kelly (OFMCap)
Guardian: Br John Wright (OFMCap)

Capuchin Friary, St Mary of the Angels,
137-142 Church Street, Dublin D07 HA22
Tel (Parish) 01-8730925
Tel (Friary) 01-8730599/Fax 01-8730250
Guardian
Rev Richard Hendrick (OFMCap)

Capuchin Friary (Immaculate Heart of
Mary), Station Road, Raheny,
Dublin D05 T9E4
Tel 01-8313886/8312805
Guardian
Rev Seán Donohue (OFMCap)

(See also under parishes – Halston Street
and Priorswood)

CARMELITES (OCARM)
Provincial Office, Gort Muire,
Ballinteer, Dublin D16 EI67
Tel 01-2984014 Fax 01-2987221
Provincial
Very Rev Michael Troy (OCarm)

Whitefriar Street Church,
56 Aungier Street, Dublin D02 R598
Tel 01-4758821 Fax 01-4758825
Email whitefriars@eircom.net
Prior: Rev Simon Nolan (OCarm)
Bursar: Rev Martin Baxter (OCarm)
Parish Priest
Rev Seán MacGiollarnáth (OCarm)

Terenure College,
Terenure, Dublin D6W DK72
Tel 01-4904621 Fax 01-4902403
Email admin@terenurecollege.ie
Prior/Bursar
Rev Éanna Ó hÓbain (OCarm)
Principal (Senior School)
Rev Éanna Ó hÓbáin (OCarm)

(See also under parishes – Whitefriar
Street)

ARCHDIOCESE OF DUBLIN

CARMELITES (OCD)
Avila, Bloomfield Avenue,
Morehampton Road, Dublin 4
Tel 01-6430200 Fax 01-6430281
Email avila@ocd.ie
Prior: Rev Liam Finnerty (OCD)
Provincial: Rev John Grennan (OCD)
Email jtgrennan@hotmail.com
Website www.ocd.ie

St Teresa's,
Clarendon Street, Dublin 2
Tel 01-6718466/6718127
Prior: Rev Jim Noonan (OCD)

CISTERCIANS
Bolton Abbey,
Moone, Co Kildare
Tel 059-8624102/087-9366723
Email boltonabbeymoone@gmail.com
Website www.boltonabbey.ie
Abbot
Rt Rev Dom Michael Ryan (OCSO)

COMBONI MISSIONARIES
8 Clontarf Road,
Dublin 3
Tel/Fax 01-8330051
Email combonimission@eircom.net
Superior
Rev Ruben Padilla Rocha (MCCJ)

CONGREGATION OF THE PRIESTS OF THE SACRED HEART OF JESUS
Fairfield,
66 Inchicore Road, Dublin 8
Tel 01-4538655
Email scjdublin@eircom.net
House of Formation
Superior and Formation Director:
Rev John Kelly (SCJ)

(See also under parishes – Ardlea)

CONGREGATION OF THE SACRED HEARTS OF JESUS AND MARY (SACRED HEARTS COMMUNITY)
Provincialate: Coudrin House,
27 Northbrook Road, Dublin 6
D06 W294
Tel 01-6604898
Email ssccdublin@sacredhearts.ie
Website www.sacredhearts.ie
Provincial: Very Rev Michael Ruddy (SSCC)

Sacred Heart Presbytery,
St John's Drive, Clondalkin,
Dublin D22 W1W6
Tel 01-4570032

(See also under parishes – Sruleen)

DIVINE WORD MISSIONARIES
1 & 3 Pembroke Road,
Dublin 4
Tel 01-6680904
Rector: Rev Liam Dunne (SVD)
Email pembroke@svdireland.com
Provincial: Rev Timothy Lehane (SVD)
Email provincial@svdireland.com
provsec@svdireland.com

133 North Circular Road,
Dublin 7
Tel 01-8386743
Praeses: Rev Anthony O'Riordan (SVD)

Maynooth, Co Kildare
Tel 01-6286391/2 Fax 01-6289184
Rector: Rev Finbarr Tracey (SVD)
Email secretary@svdireland.com

Church of St Philip the Apostle,
Mountview, Dublin 15
Tel 01-9216447

(See also under parishes – Blakestown)

DOMINICANS
Provincial Office, St Mary's,
Tallaght, Dublin D24 X585
Tel 01-4048118
Email provincial@dominicans.ie
Provincial: Very Rev John Harris (OP)

St Mary's Priory, Tallaght, Dublin 24
Tel 01-4048100
Parish 01-4048188
Prior: Very Rev Donal Roche (OP) PP

St Saviour's,
Upper Dorset Street, Dublin 1
Tel 01-8897610 Fax 01-8734003
Email stsaviours@eircom.net
Prior: Very Rev Joseph Dineen (OP) PP

(See also under parishes – Dominick Street and three of the Tallaght parishes)

FRANCISCANS (OFM)
Provincial Office, Franciscan Friary,
4 Merchant's Quay, Dublin D08 XY19
Tel 01-6742500 Fax 01-6742549
Email info@franciscans.ie
Provincial: Rev Aidan McGrath
Email provincial@franciscans.ie

Adam and Eve's, Merchants' Quay,
Dublin D08 XY19
Tel 01-6771128 Fax 01-6771000
Guardian: Br Niall O'Connell (OFM)

Franciscan House of Studies,
Dún Mhuire, Seafield Road,
Killiney, Co Dublin
Tel 01-2826760 Fax 01-2826993
Email dmkilliney@eircom.net
Guardian: Br Stephen O'Kane (OFM)

(See also under parishes – Merchants Quay)

FRANCISCANS: ORDER OF FRIARS MINOR
Conventual (Greyfriars) (OFMConv)
The Friary of the Visitation of the BVM,
Fairview Strand,
Fairview, Dublin 3
Tel 01-8376000 (office)
Tel 01-4825821 (priest)
Guardian: Rev Aidan Walsh (OFM Conv)

(See also under parishes – Fairview)

HOLY SPIRIT CONGREGATION
Holy Spirit Provincialate,
Temple Park,
Richmond Avenue South, Dublin 6
Tel 01-4977230/4975127 Fax 01-4975399
Email communications@spiritanplt.ie
Provincial Leadership Team
Rev Martin Kelly (CSSp) *(Provincial)*
Rev Peter Conaty (CSSp)
Rev Patrick Moran (CSSp)
Rev Colm Reidy (CSSp)
Rev David Conway (CSSp) *(Provincial Bursar)*
Rev Michael Kilkenny (CSSp) *(Provincial Secretary)*

Spiritan Education Trust,
Kimmage Manor, Dublin 12
Tel 01-4997610
www.spiritaneducation.ie
Mr Patrick Kitterick *(Chair)*

Heritage and Archives Centre,
Kimmage Manor, Dublin 12
Manager: vacant
Email archives@spiritan.ie

Holy Spirit Missionary College,
Kimmage Manor,
Whitehall Road, Dublin D12 P5YP
Tel 01-4064300 Fax 01-4920062
Email kimmagereception@spiritan.ie
Community Leader
Rev Colm Reidy (CSSp)

Spiritan House,
213 North Circular Road,
Dublin D07 KH9C
Community Leader
Rev Michael Kilkenny (CSSp)

SPIRASI, Spiritan Asylum Services Initiative, 213 North Circular Road,
Dublin D07 KH9C
Tel 01-8389664
Executive Director: Mr Rory Halpin

Blackrock College,
Blackrock, Co Dublin
Tel 01-2888681 Fax 01-2834267
Email info@blackrockcollege.com
Community Leader
Rev Cormac Ó Brolcháin (CSSp)
Principal: Alan MacGinty

Willow Park
Tel 01-2881651 Fax 01-2783353
Email admin@willowparkschool.ie
Principal Senior School: Mr Alan Rogan
Principal Junior School
Mr James Docherty

St Mary's College, Rathmines, Dublin 6
Tel 01-4995760 Fax 01-4972621
Junior School Tel 01-4995721
Email junsec@stmarys.ie
Senior School Tel 4995700 Fax 01-4972574
Email sensec@stmarys.ie
Community Leader
Rev Patrick Moran (CSSp)
Principal Secondary School
Mr Denis Murphy
Principal Junior School
Ms Judith Keane

St Michael's College,
Ailesbury Road, Dublin 4
Tel 01-2189400 Fax 01-2698862
Email admin@stmc.ie
Principal: Mr Tim Kelleher
Principal Junior School: Ms Lorna Heslin

Duquesne University,
Duquesne in Dublin,
St Michael's College,
1 Ailesbury Road, Ballsbridge, Dublin 4
Tel/Fax 01-2080940
www.duq.edu/ireland
Resident Director: Ms Nora McBurney
Email nora.mcburney@gmail.com

Templeogue College,
Templeville Road, Dublin 6W
Tel 01-4903909 Fax 01-4920903
Principal: Ms Niamh Quinn
Tel 01-4905788
Email info@templeoguecollege.ie

(See also under parishes – Bawnogue/ Deansrath, Greenhills/Kimmage)

JESUITS

Irish Jesuit Provincialate
Milltown Park, Sandford Road, Dublin 6
Tel 01-4987333 Fax 01-4987334
Email curia@jesuit.ie
Provincial: Rev Leonard Moloney (SJ)
Assistant Provincial
Rev Declan Murray (SJ)

Jesuit Centre for Faith and Justice
54/57 Upper Gardiner Street,
Dublin 1
Tel 01-8556814
Email info@jcfj.ie
www.jcfj.ie
Director: Mr Kevin Hargaden

Jesuit Communication Centre
Irish Jesuit Provincialate,
Milltown Park,
Sandford Road, Dublin 6
Tel 01-4987347/01-4987348
Director: Ms Pat Coyle
Email coylep@jesuit.ie

Jesuit Curia Community,
Loyola House, Milltown Park,
Sandford Road, Dublin 6
Tel 01-2180276
Email loyola@jesuit.ie
Rector: Rev Declan Murray (SJ)

Belvedere College SJ, Dublin 1
Tel 01-8586600 Fax 01-8744374
Rector: Rev Patrick Greene (SJ)
Secondary day school
Headmaster: Mr Gerard Foley

Milltown Park,
Sandford Road, Dublin 6
Tel 01-2698411/2698113
Fax 01-2600371
Email milltown@jesuit.ie
Rector: Rev Tom Casey (SJ)

25 Croftwood Park,
Cherry Orchard, Dublin 10
Tel 01-6267413

Gonzaga College SJ,
Sandford Road, Dublin 6
Community Tel 01-4972943
Email gonzaga@s-j.ie
(College) Tel 01-4972931
Fax 01-4967769
Email (College) office@gonzaga.ie
Fax (Community) 01-4960849
Email (Community) gonzaga@jesuit.ie
Rector: Rev John O'Keeffe (SJ)
Headmaster: Mr Damon McCaul

Manresa House,
426 Clontarf Road,
Dollymount, Dublin 3
Tel 01-8331352 Fax 01-8331002
Email manresa@jesuit.ie
Rector: Rev William Reynolds (SJ)

St Ignatius House of Writers,
35 Lower Leeson Street, Dublin 2
Tel 01-6761248 Fax 01-7758598
Superior: Rev Jim Culliton (SJ)
Vice-Superior: Rev Michael Kirwan (SJ)

(See also under parishes – Gardiner Street)

LEGIONARIES OF CHRIST

Leopardstown Road, Foxrock, Dublin 18
Tel 01-2955902
Email ireland@legionaries.org
Superior: Rev Joseph Fazio (LC)

Creidim Centre,
Leopardstown Road,
Dublin D18 FF64
Tel 01-2955902
Email faithandfamilycentre@arcol.org
School Retreats: Email team@clonlost.ie
School retreats, Communion and Confirmation retreats, Children and Adult Catechesis Programmes, Marriage Enrichment days, Spiritual retreats, Courses on the Faith, Spiritual Direction
Director: Rev Aaron Vinduska
Email avinduska@legionaries.org

Dublin Oak Academy
Kilcroney, Bray, Co Wicklow
Tel 01-2863290 Fax 01-2865315
Email secretary@dublinoakacademy.com
Director: Rev Oscar Sanchez (LC)
Chaplain: Rev Joseph Fazio (LC)

Woodlands Academy
Wingfield House,
Bray, Co Wicklow
Tel 01-2866323 Fax 01-2864918
Chaplain: Rev Vincent McMahon (LC)

MARIANISTS

Marianist Community,
13 Coundon Court, Killiney,
Co Dublin A96 K0T9
Tel 01-2858301
Director: Br Gerard McAuley (SM)

St Laurence College,
Loughlinstown, Dublin 18
Tel 01-2826930
Principal: Mr Shane Fitzgerald

MARIST FATHERS

Marist Fathers Chanel,
Finance & Administrative Office,
Coolock Village Dublin D05 KU62
Admnistrator
Rev Declan Marmion (SM)
Tel 01-2698100/086-2597905
Email dmarmion50@gmail.com

Catholic University School,
89 Lower Leeson Street, Dublin 2
Tel 01-6762586
Headmaster: Mr Clive Martin

Chanel College,
Coolock, Dublin 5
Tel 01-8480896/8480655
Superior: Rev Edwin McCallion (SM)
Headmaster: Mr Dara Gill

(See also under parishes – Coolock and Donore Avenue)

ARCHDIOCESE OF DUBLIN

MILL HILL MISSIONARIES
St Joseph's House,
50 Orwell Park, Rathgar,
Dublin D06 C535
Tel 01-4127700 Fax 01-4127781
Email josephmhm@eircom.net
Regional Superior
Rev Philip O'Halloran (MHM)
Tel 089-4385320
Email millhillregional.irl@gmail.com
Rector: Rev Philip O'Halloran (MHM)
Vice Rector: Position vacant
Bursar: Rev Patrick Murray
Email millhill@iol.ie

MISSIONARIES OF AFRICA
Community House, Cypress Grove Road,
Templeogue, Dublin 6W, YV12
Tel 01-4063966
Email pep.irl.del@mafr.org
Community Superior
Rev Michael P. O'Sullivan (White Fathers)
Bursar
Br Karl Kaelin (White Fathers)

Cypress Grove, Templeogue, Dublin 6W
Tel 01-4055263/4055264
Email m.africaprom@yahoo.com
Promotion Director
Rev Neil Loughrey (White Fathers)
Superior
Michael P. O'Sullivan (White Fathers)

MISSIONARIES OF THE SACRED HEART
Provincialate,
65 Terenure Road West,
Dublin D6W P295
Tel 01-4906622 Fax 01-4920148
Provincial Leader
Rev Carl Tranter (MSC)

Woodview House,
Mount Merrion Avenue, Blackrock,
Co Dublin A94 DW95
Tel 01-2881644
Leader: Rev Manus Ferry (MSC)

(See also under parishes – Killinarden)

OBLATES OF MARY IMMACULATE
Provincial Residence,
Oblates of Mary Immaculate House of Retreat, Tyrconnell Road,
Inchicore, Dublin 8
Email provincialoffice@oblates.ie
Provincial: Very Rev Oliver Barry (OMI)

Oblate House of Retreat,
Inchicore, Dublin 8
Tel 01-4534408/4541805 Fax 01-4543466
Superior: Rev William Fitzpatrick (OMI)

170 Merrion Road,
Ballsbridge, Dublin 4
Tel 01-2693658 Fax 01-2600597

Oblate Scholasticate, St Anne's,
Goldenbridge Walk, Inchicore, Dublin 8
Tel 01-4540841/4542955 Fax 01-4731903

(See also under parishes – Bluebell, Darndale and the two Inchicore parishes)

PALLOTTINES
Provincial House, 'Homestead',
Sandyford Road, Dundrum, Dublin 16
Tel 01-2956180
Provincial
Very Rev Liam McClarey (SAC)
Rector: Rev Michael Irwin (SAC)
Director of Formation
Rev John Egan (SAC)
Email motherofdivinelove@gmail.com

(See also under parishes – Corduff and Shankill)

PASSIONISTS
St Paul's Retreat,
Mount Argus, Dublin 6W
Tel 01-4992000 Fax 01-4992001
Email passionistsmtargus@eircom.net
Provincial: Rev James Sweeney (CP)

(See also under parish – Mount Argus)

REDEMPTORISTS
Dún Mhuire
461/463 Griffith Avenue,
Dublin D09 X651
Tel 01-5180196 Fax 01-8369655

(See also under parishes – Ballyfermot and Cherry Orchard)

ROSMINIANS
Clonturk House, Ormond Road,
Drumcondra, Dublin 9, D09 F821
Tel 01-6877014
Provincial: Rev Joseph O'Reilly (IC)
Rector: Rev Matt Gaffney (IC)

SACRED HEART FATHERS
Congregation of the Priests of the Sacred Heart of Jesus
Fairfield, 66 Inchicore Road, Dublin 8
Tel 01-4538655
Email scjdublin@eircom.net
Provincial: Rev John Kelly (SCJ)

St John Vianney, Ardlea Road, Dublin 5
Tel 01-8474123/8474173
Email jvianney@indigo.ie
Rev Hugh Hanley (SCJ) *(Moderator)*

(See also under parishes – Ardlea)

ST COLUMBANS MISSIONARY SOCIETY
House of Studies
St Columban's,
67-68 Castle Dawson, Rathcoffey Road,
Maynooth, Co Kildare
Tel 01-8286036
Contact Person
Rev Hugh MacMahon (SSC)
Email hugh.macmahonssc@columban.ie

ST PATRICK'S MISSIONARY SOCIETY
21 Leeson Park, Dublin 6
Tel 01-4977897 Fax 01-4962812
House Leader: Rev David Larkin (SPS)

SALESIANS
Provincialate: Salesian House,
45 St Teresa's Road, Crumlin,
Dublin 12, D12 XK52
Tel 01-4555787
Email (secretary) office@salesians.ie
Provincial
Very Rev Eunan McDonnell (SDB)
Email provincial@salesiansireland.ie
Provincial Secretary
Rev Lukasz Nawrat (SDB)
Novitiate: Tel 01-4555605
Rector: Rev Martin McCormack (SDB)

Salesian College, Maynooth Road,
Celbridge, Co Kildare, W23 W0XK
Tel 01-6275058/6275060 Fax 01-6272208
Rector: Rev Patrick Hennessey (SDB)
Secondary School Tel 01-6272166/6272200

Don Bosco House, 12 Clontarf Road,
Dublin 3, D03 V3P4
Tel 01-8336009/8337045
Rev Val Collier (SDB) *(Priest-in-charge)*

Rinaldi House, 72 Seán McDermott Street,
Dublin 1, D01 K2O1
Tel 01-8363358 Fax 01-8552320
Rector: Rev Michael Casey (SDB) Adm

(See also under parishes – Crumlin and Seán McDermott Street)

SERVITES
Servite Priory, St Peregrine,
36 Grangewood Estate, Rathfarnham,
Dublin 16
Tel 01-4936755
Prior: Rev Jimmy M. Kelly (OSM)

Prior Provincial
Rev Colm M. McGlynn (OSM)
Email colmmcglynn154@hotmail.com

St Peregrine Ministry – *Director*
Rev Timothy M. Flynn (OSM)

Church of the Divine Word,
Marley Grange, 25-27 Hermitage Downs,
Rathfarnham, Dublin 16
Tel 01-4944295/4941064
Prior: Rev Liam Tracey (OSM) CC

(See also under parish – Marley Grange)

SOCIETY OF AFRICAN MISSIONS
SMA House, 81 Ranelagh Road,
Ranelagh, Dublin D06 WT10
Tel 01-4968162/3 Fax 01-4968164
www.sma.dublin@sma.ie
Superior
Rev Joseph Egan (SMA)

SOCIETY OF ST PAUL
St Paul's House, Moyglare Road,
Maynooth, Co Kildare
Tel 01-6285933 Fax 01-6289330
Email book@stpauls.ie
Rev Alexander Anandam (SSP)
Rev Jose Nunes (SSP)
Rev Thomas Devasia Perumparambil (SSP)
Rev Paul Kottackal Varkey (SSP)

St Paul Book Centre
Moyglare Road, Maynooth,
Co Kildare W23 NX34
Email sspireland@gmail.com
www.stpauls.ie

St Paul's Books and Mass Leaflets
Moyglare Road, Maynooth,
Co Kildare W23 NX34
Email sales@stpauls.ie

SONS OF DIVINE PROVIDENCE
Sarsfield House, Sarsfield Road,
Ballyfermot, Dublin 10
Tel 01-6266233/6266193
Email don-orion@clubi.ie
Rev John Perrotta (FDP)
Email jperrotta16@yahoo.ie

VINCENTIANS
Provincial Office: Sybil Hill, Raheny,
Dublin D05 AE38
Tel 01-8510842 Fax 01-8510846
Email cmdublin@vincentians.ie
Provincial: Very Rev Paschal Scallon (CM)

St Joseph's, 44 Stillorgan Park,
Blackrock, Co Dublin A94 PC62
Tel 01-2886961
Superior: Very Rev Colm McAdam (CM)

St Vincent's College,
Castleknock, Dublin D15 PD95
Tel 01-8213051
Superior: Very Rev Paschal Scallon (CM)

St Paul's,
Raheny, Dublin D05 AE38
Tel 01-8314011/2 Fax 01-8316387
Email rmccm@eircom.net
Tel 01-8318113 (Community)
Superior: Very Rev Michael McCullagh (CM)

(See also under parishes – Phibsboro)

BROTHERS

CHRISTIAN BROTHERS
Province Centre, Marino,
Griffith Avenue, Dublin 9
Tel 01-8073300 Fax 01-8073366
Email cbprov@edmundrice.ie
Province Leader: Br Edmund Garvey
Community Leader: Br Denis Gleeson
Community: 9

St Helen's, York Road,
Dun Laoghaire, Co Dublin
Tel 01-2801214/2841656
Fax 01-2841657
Community Leader: Br Pat Madigan
Community: 7

Christian Brothers' House,
Woodbrook, Bray, Co Wicklow
Tel 01-2821510
Community Leader: Vacant
Community: 3

Christian Brothers; House,
Synge Street, Dublin 8
Tel 01-4751292/4755798 Fax 01-4761015
Community Leader: Br Dermot Ambrose
Community: 7

Christian Brothers' House,
10 Rosmeen Gardens, Dun Laoghaire,
Co Dublin
Tel 01-2844639
Community Leader: Br Pat Payne
Community: 7

Christian Brothers' Residence,
St David's Park, Artane, Dublin 5
Tel 01-8317833
Community Leader: Br Colm Griffey
Community: 4

Oratory of the Resurrection,
Artane, Dublin 5
Tel 01-8317833

St Patrick's, Baldoyle, Dublin 13
Tel 01-8391287
Retirement home for brothers
Community Leader: Br Ferdi Foley
Community: 20

Christian Brothers' Monastery,
St Declan's, Nephin Road, Dublin 7
Tel 01-8389560
Community Leader: Br Pat Bowler
Community: 6

Clareville, 89A Finglas Road,
Finglas, Dublin 11
Tel 01-8309811
Community Leader: Br Tom Connolly
Community: 5

Marino Institute of Education,
Griffith Avenue, Dublin 9
Tel 01-8057700 Fax 01-8335290
President: Teresa O'Doherty

Christian Brothers,
St Joseph's Community,
Marino Institute of Education,
Griffith Avenue, Marino,
Dublin 9
Tel 01-8057790
Community Leader: Br Michael Murray
Community: 5

242 North Circular Road, Dublin 7
Tel 01-8680454
Community Leader: Br Liam Deasy
Community: 4

Edmund Rice House,
North Richmond Street, Dublin 1
Tel 01-8556258 Fax 01-8555243
Community Leader: Br Brendan Prior
Community: 10

Emmaus,
Lissenhall, Swords, Co Dublin
Tel 01-8401399/8402450
Fax 01-8408248
Community Leader: Br Declan Power
Community: 5

Mainistir Aodhain,
Collins Avenue West,
Whitehall, Dublin 9
Tel 01-8379953
Community Leader: Br Des Young
Community: 5

Christian Brothers,
8 Croftwood Grove, Cherry Orchard,
Ballyfermot, Dublin 10
Community: 2
Tel 01-6208920

Lantern Intercultural Centre,
15 Synge Street, Dublin 8
Tel 01-4053868
Co-ordinator: Ms Aine de Baroid
Email bookingslantern@gmail.com

DE LA SALLE BROTHERS
Provincialate,
121 Howth Road,
Dublin D03 XN15
Tel 01-8331815 Fax 01-8339130
Email province@iol.ie
Superior: Br Patrick Collier
Assistant Provincial: Br Ben Hanlon
Community: 3

Beneavin College,
Beneavin Road, Finglas East,
Dublin D11 NH7E
Tel 01-8341410
Principal: Dr Aideen Cassidy

Ard Scoil La Salle,
Raheny Road, Dublin D05 Y132
Tel 01-8480055 Fax 01-8480082
Principal: Mr Colin Mythen

ARCHDIOCESE OF DUBLIN

Benildus House,
160A Upper Kilmacud Road,
Dublin D14 N778
Tel 01-2981110
Superior: Br Patrick Kelliher
Community: 4

Benildus Pastoral Centre,
160A Upper Kilmacud Road,
Dublin D14 N778
Tel 01-2694195 Fax 01-2694168
Director: Mr Eugene Smyth

St Benildus College,
Upper Kilmacud Road,
Dublin A94 X886
Tel 01-2986539 Fax 01-2962710
Principal: Mrs Mary Brohan

St John's Monastery,
Le Fanu Road, Dublin D10 X735
Tel 01-6260867
Superior: Br Lawrence Cahill
Community: 6
Secondary School
Principal: Ms Ann Marie Leonard
Tel/Fax 01-6264943

FRANCISCAN BROTHERS
49 Laurleen Estate,
Stillorgan, Co Dublin
Email franciscanbrs@eircom.net
Contact person: Br Peter Roddy
Tel 087-9970760
Community: 1

MARIST BROTHERS
Marian College, Lansdowne Road,
Ballsbridge, Dublin 4
Tel 01-6683740
Superior: Br Sebastian Davis
Community: 4
Secondary School

Moyle Park College,
Clondalkin, Dublin 22
Tel 01-4577683
Superior: Br Nicholas Smith
Community: 4
Secondary School

PATRICIAN BROTHERS
Patrician College,
35 Cardiffcastle Road,
Finglas West, Dublin 11
Tel 01-8342811
Superior: Br Dermot Dunne (FSP)
Email dermotmdunne@eircom.net
Community: 2

PRESENTATION BROTHERS
Presentation Novitiate,
Glasthule, Co Dublin
Tel 01-2842228
Contact: Br Barry Noel (FPM)
Community: 5

SAINT JOHN OF GOD BROTHERS
St Patrick's Community,
Stillorgan, Co Dublin A94 E244
Tel 01-2771431 Fax 01-2782938
Prior: Br Donatus Forkan (OH)
Community: 9

Lucena Community,
59 Orwell Road, Rathgar,
Dublin D06 W1C0
Prior: Br Finnian Gallagher (OH)
Community: 2

SAINT JOHN OF GOD HOSPITAL
Stillorgan,
Co Dublin A94 7H92
Tel 01-2771400 Fax 01-2881034
Chief Executive: Ms Emma Balmaine
Private psychiatric hospital

St Joseph's Centre,
Crinken Lane, Shankill,
Co Dublin D18 TY00
Tel 01-2823000 Fax 01-2823119
Email stjosephs@sjog.ie
Director of Nursing: Ms Norma Sheehan
Residential and day service for people with dementia

SAINT JOHN OF GOD COMMUNITY SERVICES CLG
Cluain Mhuire,
Community Mental Health Services,
Newtownpark Avenue,
Blackrock, Co Dublin A94 HX01
Tel 01-2172100 Fax 01-2833886
Email cms@sjog.ie
Regional Director: Mr Shane Hill

Saint John of God Lucena Clinic Services,
59 Orwell Road, Rathgar,
Dublin D06 4X93
Tel 01-4923596 Fax 01-4923823
Email admin.lucena@sjog.ie
Regional Director: Mr Shane Hill
St Peter's School,
59 Orwell Road, Rathgar,
Dublin D06 X594
Tel 01-4923596 Fax 01-4907768
School Principal: Ms Helen Heneghan
Child and adolescent psychiatric services

Saint John of God Menni Services,
Block A, Gleann na hEorna,
Springfield, Tallaght,
Dublin D24 AD62
Tel 01-4686400 Fax 01-4686499
Email admin.menni@sjog.ie
Regional Director
Ms Eliza Doyle *(Interim)*
St John of God School,
Islandbridge, Dublin 8
Tel 01-6741534 Fax 01-6741501
School Principal: Ms Marie Ryan
Incorporating day services, residential services (Tel 01-4731474), enterprises (Tel 01-4569320) and community services

Saint John of God Liffey Services,
St Raphael's, Celbridge,
Co Kildare W23 F2P5
Tel 01-6288161 Fax 01-6273614
Email admin.kildare@sjog.ie
Regional Director
Ms Eliza Doyle *(Interim)*
St Raphael's School, Church Road,
Celbridge, Co Kildare W23 F2P5
Tel 01-6288161 Fax 01-6012468
School Principal: Mrs Kathy Waldron
Residential, day centre and community services for children and adults with varying degrees of intellectual disability

Saint John of God,
Carmona Services, Dunmore House,
111 Upper Glenageary Road,
Dun Laoghaire, Co Dublin A96 E223
Tel 01-2852900 Fax 01-2851713
Email admin.carmona@sjog.ie
Regional Director
Mr Desmond North *(Interim)*
St John of God School,
Glenageary Road, Glenageary,
Co Dublin A96 EV66
Tel 01-2852900 Fax 01-2851713
School Principal: Marie Burke
Incorporating residential, day, enterprise and community services for people with intellectual disability.

STEP, 30 Carmanhall Road,
Sandyford Industrial Estate,
Dublin D18 P7X0
Tel 01-2952379 Fax 01-2952371
Email step@sjog.ie
Regional Director
Mr Desmond North *(Interim)*
Training centre and supported employment

City Gate, 30 Carmanhall Road,
Sandyford Industrial Estate,
Dublin D18 P7X0
Tel 01-2952379 Fax 01-2952371
Email citygate@sjog.ie
Regional Director
Mr Desmond North *(Interim)*
Housing Service

St Augustine's School,
Obelisk Park, Carysfort Avenue,
Blackrock, Co Dublin A94 X8K7
Tel 01-2881771 Fax 01-2834117
Email staugustines@sjog.ie
Regional Director
Mr Desmond North *(Interim)*
Principal: Mr David O'Brien
Special National School

Suzanne House, 6 Main Road,
Tallaght, Dublin D24 CC60
Tel 01-4521966 Fax 01-4525504
Director: Ms Eliza Doyle
Email eliza.doyle@sjog.ie
Respite service for children with terminal illness and/or complex nursing needs

SISTERS

BLESSED SACRAMENT SISTERS
91 Seabury Crescent,
Malahide, Co Dublin K36 EY72
Tel 01-8451878
Email annamay@live.ie
Community: 2

BON SECOURS SISTERS (PARIS)
Sisters of Bon Secours,
Sacre Coeur, 1 Beechmount,
Glasnevin Hill, Dublin 9
Tel 01-8065353
Community: 1

Bon Secours Convent,
Glasnevin, Dublin 9
Co-ordinator: Sr Eleanor Hennessy
Tel 01-8375111 Fax 01-8571020
Community: 4
Outreach Ministry

Sisters of Bon Secours,
9 Abbeyvale, 215 Botanic Avenue,
Drumcondra, Dublin 9
Tel 01-8373209
Community: 1
Hospital Ministry

Sisters of Bon Secours,
119 Esker Lawns, Lucan, Co Dublin
Tel 01-6217158
Community: 1
Parish Ministry

BRIGIDINE SISTERS
106 The Edges 1, Beacon South Quarter,
Sandyford, Dublin D18 WY00
Congregational Leader
Sr Catherine O'Connor
Email coconnorcsb07@gmail.com

5 Sycamore Drive,
Dundrum, Dublin 16
Tel 01-2988130
Contact: Sr Theresa Kilmurray
Community: 1
Administration

7 Sycamore Drive, Dublin 16
Tel 01-2966449
Community: 1
Contact: Sr Loretto Ryan
Community Work

15 Gortmore Drive, Rivermount,
Finglas, Dublin 11
Tel 01-8642440
Contact: Sr Imelda Barry
Community: 1
Parish

94 Moyville,
Ballyboden, Dublin 16
Tel 01-7941596
Contact: Sr Anna Hennessy
Community: 1
Education and Parish Ministry

163 Park Drive Avenue, Castleknock,
Dublin 15
Tel 01-8200482
Contact: Sr Kay Mulhall
Community: 1
Retired

18 Maryville Apartments,
Sybil Hill Road, Raheny, Dublin 5
Contact: Sr Elizabeth Cleary
Spiritual Direction

12 Margaret Holme,
Claremont Road,
Sandymount, Dublin 4
Contact: Mairead Brophy

CARMELITES
Carmelite Monastery of the Immaculate
Conception, Roebuck,
Dublin D14 T1H9
Tel 01-2884732
Altar Breads
Email altarbreads@roebuckcarmel.com
www.roebuckcarmel.com
Email carmel@roebuckcarmel.com
Prioress: Sr Teresa Whelan
Community: 9
Contemplatives; altar breads supplied

Star of the Sea Carmelite Monastery,
Seapark, Malahide,
Dublin K36 P586
Tel 01-8454259/087-9643953
Prioress: Sr Rosalie Burke
Email rmebodc@gmail.com
Community: 8
Contemplatives, cards, candles, honey (in
season) and rosettes for First
Communion and Confirmation
www.malahidecarmelites.ie
Contemplative Community

Carmelite Monastery of St Joseph,
Upper Kilmacud Road, Stillorgan,
Blackrock, Co Dublin A94 YY33
Tel 01-2886089
Email contact@kilmacudcarmel.ie
www.kilmacudcarmel.ie
Prioress: Sr Mary Brigeen Wilson
Community: 13
Contemplatives, altar breads

**CARMELITE SISTERS FOR THE AGED AND
INFIRM**
Our Lady's Manor, Bulloch Castle,
Dalkey, Co Dublin
Tel 01-2806993 Fax 01-2844802
Email ourladysmanor1@eircom.net
Superior
Sr Mary Therese Healy (OCarm)
Email smtjhealy57@gmail.com
Administrator
Sr Bernadette Murphy (OCarm)
Community: 6

CHARITY OF NEVERS SISTERS
76 Cherrywood,
Loughlinstown Drive,
Dun Laoghaire, Co Dublin
Contact person: Sr Rosaleen Cullen
Tel 01-4585654/086-8411466
Email rosaleencullen@upcmail.ie

Flat 12 Verschoyle Court,
Dublin 12
Email noradowney60@gmail.com

**CHARITY OF ST PAUL THE APOSTLE
SISTERS**
40 Rockfield Avenue
Perrystown, Dublin D12 N6K5
Tel 01-4556741
Email marylyons2010@gmail.com
Contact: Sr Mary Lyons
Community: 3
Education and parish

51 Orwell Park Rise, Dublin D6W H678
Tel 01-4908856
Contact: Sr Clare Hartley
Email norahartl@yahoo.co.uk
Community: 2
Parish and education

**CLARISSAN MISSIONARY SISTERS OF THE
BLESSED SACRAMENT**
Our Lady of Guadalupe Residence for
Students, 28 Waltersland Road,
Stillorgan, Co Dublin
Tel/Fax 01-2886600
Email misclaridub@hotmail.com
www.guadaluperesidence.com
Superior: Sr Elisa Padilla
Tel 087-0510783
Community: 5

**CONGREGATION OF THE SISTERS OF
MERCY**
'Rachamim', 13/14 Moyle Park,
Convent Road, Clondalkin,
Dublin D22 HR94
Tel 01-4673737 Fax 01-4673749
Email mercy@csm.ie
Website www.sistersofmercy.ie
Congregational Leader
Sr Marie Louise White

Mercy International Centre
64A Lower Baggot Street,
Dublin D02 HD68
Tel 01-6618061
Email director@mercyinternational.ie
Director: Sr Berneice Loch
Heritage tours, school tours, conference
facilities and pilgrimages to the tomb of
Ven. Catherine McAuley
Website www.mercyworld.org

South Central Province

*The Sisters of Mercy minister throughout
the diocese in pastoral and social work,
community development, counselling,
spirituality, education and health care,
answering current needs.*

ARCHDIOCESE OF DUBLIN

1 & 2 Church Crescent,
Athy, Co Kildare R14 KX43
Tel 059-8631361
Community: 7

101 Rockfield Green,
Maynooth, Co Kildare W23 A4P9
Tel 01-6291992
Community: 2

St Anne's, Booterstown,
Co Dublin A94 NW53
Tel 01-2882140
Province Archives
Community: 16

22A Camron Court,
Cork Street, Dublin D08 R3K8
Tel 01-4530498
Community: 2

St Brendan's Drive,
Coolock, Dublin D05 K7F1
Tel 01-8486420
Community: 10

Sisters of Mercy, Convent of Mercy,
Eblana Avenue, Dun Laoghaire,
Co Dublin A96 X657
Tel 01-2360686 Fax 01-2805470
Community: 22

23-26 The Paddocks,
Kilmainham, Dublin D08 N260
Tel 01-4021727
Community: 5

81 Mackintosh Park,
Dun Laoghaire, Co Dublin A96 VIF2
Tel-2851707
Community: 1

13 Emmet Crescent,
Inchicore, Dublin D08 X6X9
Tel 01-4163275
Community: 4

Mater Misericordiae, Eccles Street,
Dublin D07 R2WY
Tel 01-8824550 Fax 01-8309070
Community: 19

9 Leo Street, Dublin D07 V0Y9
Tel 01-8858593
Community: 2

Stella Maris, Convent Lane,
Rush, Co Dublin K56 W965
Tel/Fax 01-8437347
Community: 3

14 Coolatree Close,
Beaumont, Dublin D09 DK29
Tel 01-8377023
Community: 3

63 Kenilworth Park, Harolds Cross,
Dublin D6W E654
Tel 01-4452905
Community: 3

65 Kenilworth Park, Harolds Cross,
Dublin D6W HY57
Tel 01-4929414
Community: 2

90/91 The Park,
Beaumont Woods, Dublin D09 E921
Tel 01-8570741
Community: 2

McAuley House,
Beaumont, Dublin D09 AP9D
Tel 01-8379186 Fax 01-8373503
Community: numbers vary

83/85 Silloge Park,
Ballymun, Dublin D11 AW86
Tel 01-8547611
Community: 2

40 Gilford Road,
Sandymount, Dublin D04 XR61
Tel 01-2601081
Community: 3

Sisters of Mercy, 14 Walnut Avenue,
Courtlands, Drumcondra,
Dublin D09 X5A4
Tel 01-8377602
Community: 4

Sisters of Mercy, 1/2 Charlemont,
Griffith Avenue, Dublin D09 W7X6
Tel 01-8571246
Community: 5

Sisters of Mercy,
25 Cork Street, Dublin D08 RY86
Tel 01-4535262
Community: 4

11 Grangemore Road, Donaghmede,
Dublin D13 H2H9
Tel 01-8482242
Community: 1

CROSS AND PASSION CONGREGATION
Cross and Passion Sisters,
3-5 Carberry Road, Glandore Road,
Dublin 9
Tel 01-8377256
Community: 5
Pastoral ministry

Cross and Passion Convent
22 Griffith Avenue,
Marino, Dublin 9
Tel 01-8336381
Community: 17
Care of elderly

Cross and Passion Convent,
41 Alderwood Green, Springfield,
Tallaght, Dublin 24
Tel 01-4511850
Community: 3
Pastoral ministry, school chaplaincy,
retreat work

Cross and Passion Convent,
13 Clare Road,
Drumcondra, Dublin 9
Tel 01-8375511
Community: 3
Community development, pastoral
ministry

DAUGHTERS OF CHARITY OF ST VINCENT DE PAUL
St Catherine's Provincial House,
Dunardagh, Blackrock,
Co Dublin
Tel 01-2882669/2882896
Local Superior: Sr Marie Fox
Community: 22
Provincial administration and retreats

St Vincent's Centre,
Navan Road, Dublin 7
Tel 01-8684017
Superior: Sr Geraldine Henry
Community: 7
Care, training and education of people
with intellectual disability, mission
development, hospice administration,
parish work

77 Kilbarron Park,
Kilmore West, Dublin 5
Tel 01-8470648
Superior: Sr Mary Connaire
Community: 5
Social and pastoral ministry

3 St Assam's Drive,
Raheny, Dublin 5
Tel 01-8312859
Superior: Sr Maire Brady
Community: 2
House of Residence for Sisters involved
in St Francis Hospice and child and family
services

St Louise's, Drumfinn Road,
Ballyfermot, Dublin 10
Tel 01-6264921
Superior: Sr Helen MacEvilly
Community: 6
Education and parish work

St Joseph's,
Clonsilla, Co Dublin
Tel 01-8217177
Superior: Sr Bernadette Carron
Community: 8
Residential centre for women with
intellectual disability, work for social
justice, diocesan adviser, special schools

St Louise's, Glenmaroon,
Chapelizod, Dublin 20
Tel 01-8999100 Fax 01-8211991
Residential centre for girls with
intellectual disability.

St Michael's School for children with
special needs.
Tel 01-8201859

10 Henrietta Street, Dublin 1
Tel 01-8583063
Superior: Sr Áine O'Brien
Community: 21
House of residence for sisters, catechesis,
parish of the travelling people, Virgo
Potens Office

Daughters of Charity Community
Services,
8/9 Henrietta Street, Dublin 1
Education and Community Services
Tel 01-8874100 Fax 01-8723486

109 Mount Prospect Avenue,
Clontarf, Dublin 3
Tel 01-8338508
Superior: Sr Mary O'Toole
Community: 17
House for retired sisters

7 Belvedere Road,
Dublin 1
Tel 01-8556719
Superior: Sr Brenda Hunter
Community: 3 and 3 sisters in Nursing
Homes attached to this community
House of residence, pastoral care

166 Navan Road, Dublin 7
Tel 01-8383801
Superior: Sr Zoe Killeen
Community: 3
House of residence for sisters involved in
parish work, and pastoral care services
for people with intellectual disability

St Louise's, 16 Dalymount,
Phibsboro, Dublin 7
Tel 01-8680308
Superior: Sr Claire McKiernan
Community: 4
House of residence for sisters involved
in work with pastoral ministry, homeless
people

25 Killarney Street, Dublin 1
Tel 01-8366487
Superior: Sr Angela Burke
Community: 3
House of residence for sisters involved in
day care, prison chaplaincy, work with
refugees, pastoral care

Labouré House,
Dunardagh, Temple Hill,
Blackrock, Co Dublin
Tel 01-2833933
Superior: Sr Christina Quinn
Community: 12
House of residence for sisters, pastoral
care

DAUGHTERS OF THE CROSS OF LIÈGE
Beech Park Convent,
Beechwood Court,
Stillorgan, Co Dublin
Tel 01-2887401/2887315 Fax 01-2881499
Email beechpark1833@gmail.com
Superior: Sr Kathleen McKenna
Community: 8

DAUGHTERS OF THE HEART OF MARY
St Joseph's, 1 Crosthwaite Grove,
Crosthwaite Park South,
Dun Laoghaire, Co Dublin
Superior: Sr Mary Brogan
Tel 01-2801204
Email heartofmary3@gmail.com
St Joseph's Primary School
Principal's Office: Tel 01-2803504

32 Brackenbush Road,
Killiney, Co Dublin
Tel 01-2750917

DAUGHTERS OF THE HOLY SPIRIT
9 Walnut Park,
Drumcondra, Dublin 9
Tel 01-8371825
Community: 2
Contact person: Sr Ita Durnin
Email itadhs@yahoo.co.uk
Pastoral ministry

DAUGHTERS OF MARY AND JOSEPH
65 Iona Road, Glasnevin,
Dublin D09 Y7F4
Tel 01-8305640
Community: 4
Pastoral

37 Bancroft Road,
Tallaght, Dublin 24
Tel 01-4515321
Community: 3
Pastoral

55 Rowan Hamilton Court,
Dublin 7
Tel 01-8380525
Contact person: Sr Peggy McArdle
Community: 1
Community Development

109 Botanic Avenue,
Dublin 9
Community: 1

10 Moynihan Court,
Main Road, Tallaght, Dublin 24

2 Moynihan Court,
Main Road, Tallaght, Dublin 24
Tel 01-4627923

DAUGHTERS OF OUR LADY OF THE SACRED HEART
Provincial House,
14 Rossmore Avenue,
Templeogue, Dublin 6W
Tel 01-4903200 Tel/Fax 01-4903113
Email olshprov@eircom.net
Provincial: Sr Mairead Kelleher
Community: 4

DAUGHTERS OF WISDOM
20 Grace Park Meadows,
Drumcondra,
Dublin D09 X2X5
Tel 01-8316508
Contact: Sr Gráinne Hilton
Community: 2

DISCIPLES OF THE DIVINE MASTER
Divine Master Centre,
Newtownpark Avenue, White's Cross,
Blackrock, Co Dublin A94 V2N8
Tel 01-2114949 (community)
01-2886414 (Liturgical Centre)
Sister-in-Charge: Sr Brid Geraghty
Email dublin@ppdm.org
Community: 6
Contemplative-apostolic Congregation.
Chapel of Adoration with daily
Adoration, open to public. Prayer,
support and intercession for priests.
Website: www.pddm.ie
Liturgical Centre-distributor and
producer of liturgical vestments/altar
linens, high-quality liturgical art,
religious gifts. Promotion of liturgical
formation. Bethany House available for
private retreats. Daily prayer and
support groups.
Website: www.liturgicalcentre.ie

DOMINICAN SISTERS
Congregation Archivist
Sr Mary O'Byrne (OP)

Mary Bellew House,
Dominican Campus,
Cabra, Dublin D07 Y2E7
Tel 01-8299797 Fax 01-8299799
Email marybellewhouse@gmail.com
Community: 5

St Mary's, Rectory Green,
Riverston Abbey, Cabra,
Dublin D07 X5F3
Tel 01-8683041
Email riverstonabbey@gmail.com
Prioress: Sr Teresa Wade (OP)
Community: 8
Varied ministries

St Mary's, Cabra,
Dublin D07 AF8P
Tel 01-8380567 Fax 01-8682050
Email dominicancabra@gmail.com
Prioress: Sr Susie O'Rawe (OP)
Community: 13
Secondary School
Tel 01-8385282 Fax 01-8683003
Primary and secondary schools. Special schools for emotionally disturbed children. Parish work

Dominican Convent,
Sion Hill, Blackrock,
Co Dublin A94 X5N3
Tel 01-2886832/3
Email sionhillconvent@gmail.com
Prioress: Sr Darina Hosey (OP)
Community: 17
Varied ministries
Secondary School. Tel 01-2886791

Dominican Sisters,
St Mary's, 47 Mount Merrion Avenue,
Blackrock, Co Dublin A94 Y94D
Tel 01-2888551
Email 47mtmerrion@gmail.com
Community: 4
Varied ministries

Dominican Convent,
Convent Road,
Dun Laoghaire,
Co Dublin A96 TP02
Tel 01-2801379 Fax 01-2302209
Email domdunlg@gmail.com
Community: 8
Primary School. Tel 01-2809011
Education, varied ministries

Dominican Convent,
204 Griffith Avenue, Dublin 9
Tel 01-8379550 Fax 01-8571802
Email dsisters204@yahoo.ie
Prioress: Sr Catherine Gibson (OP)
Secondary School. Tel 01-8376080
Community: 13
Varied ministries

Veritas House,
Muckross Park,
Marlborough Road,
Donnybrook, Dublin D04 F8E8
Community: 7

Dominican Sisters,
St Catherine's,
2 Heather View Road, Aylesbury,
Tallaght, Dublin D24 EAW8
Tel 01-4523462 Fax 01-4625636
Email domabury2@gmail.com
Community: 2
Education; varied ministries

Dominican Sisters,
1 Avonbeg Road, Tallaght,
Dublin D24 RKH3
Tel 01-4514627
Email ruthpilkington@yahoo.co.uk
Community: 2
Pastoral

Dominican Sisters,
2 Croftwood Crescent,
Cherry Orchard, Ballyfermot,
Dublin D10 XE61
Tel 01-6231127
Email cherrydoms5@gmail.com
Community: 2
Education, varied ministries

Dominican Sisters,
93 Nephin Road,
Cabra, Dublin D07 V0F5
Tel 01-8682054
Email domsis9395@gmail.com
Community: 4
Varied ministries

Dominican Sisters,
Santa Sabina House, Cabra,
Dublin D07 WK25
Tel 01-8682666 Fax 01-8682667
Email santasabina@dominicansisters.com
Community: 25 Nursing Home
Varied ministries

Dominican Sisters,
St Mary's Convent,
Wicklow A67 YX26
Tel 0404-67328 Fax 0404-65054
Email dcw1870@gmail.com
Community: 7
Ecological centre, varied ministries

Dominican Sisters,
62 Ashington Avenue, Navan Road,
Dublin D07 E1X7
Tel 01-8386304
Community: 3
Education and varied ministries

FRANCISCAN MISSIONARIES OF THE DIVINE MOTHERHOOD
Arus Mhuire, 185 Swords Road,
Whitehall, Dublin D09 YW40
Tel 01-8572876
Community: 2

St Francis Convent,
3/4 Fonthill Abbey, Ballyboden Road,
Rathfarnham, Dublin 14
Tel 01-4932537 Fax 01-4954846
Community: 5

FRANCISCAN MISSIONARIES OF MARY
St Francis Convent, The Cloisters,
Mount Tallant Avenue,
Terenure, Dublin 6W
Tel 01-4908549
Email fmmcloisters@eircom.net
Superior: Sr Bernadette Reynolds
Community: 5
House of studies, pastoral work

Assisi, 36 Grange Abbey Drive,
Donaghmede, Dublin 13
Tel 01-8470591
Superior: Sr Mary Dunne
Community: 4
Social, pastoral work

97 St Lawrence Road,
Clontarf, Dublin 3
Tel 01-8332683/8332181
Email fmmclontarf@yahoo.co.uk
Superior: Sr Ann Condon
Community: 4
Pastoral, hospitality for missionary sisters

St Joseph's Convent, Old Road,
Hayestown, Rush, Co Dublin
Tel 01-8439308
Superior: Sr Mary Dornan
Community: 20
Care of elderly sisters

FMM, 4 Muckross Drive,
Perrystown, Dublin 12
Tel 01-4562028
Community: 3
Youth ministry, hospital chaplaincy

FRANCISCAN MISSIONARIES OF ST JOSEPH
St Joseph's, 16 Innismore,
Crumlin Village, Dublin 12
Tel 01-4563445
Regional Leader
Sr Mary Butler
Community Leader
Sr Margaret Lonergan
Community: 3

FRANCISCAN MISSIONARY SISTERS FOR AFRICA
Generalate,
Central Team, 34A Gilford Road,
Sandymount, Dublin 4
Tel 01-2838376 Fax 01-2602049
Email generalate@fmsa.net
Leader: Sr Jeanette Watters (FMSA)
Community: 4

34 Gilford Road,
Sandymount, Dublin 4
Tel 01-2691923
Contact person
Sr Avril Reynolds (FMSA)
Email avrilmreynnolds@gmail.com
Community: 4

142 Raheny Road,
Raheny, Dublin 5
Tel 01-8480852
Email fmsaraheny142@iol.ie
Contact person
Sr Bridgette Cormack (FMSA)
Email bcormack@fmsa.net
Community: 2

FRANCISCAN SISTERS OF THE IMMACULATE CONCEPTION
Franciscan Sisters, 97/99 Riverside Park,
Clonshaugh, Dublin 17
Tel 01-8771778
Contact person: Sr Immaculata Owhotemu
Community: 2
Administration, pastoral ministry, nursing

SISTERS OF ST FRANCIS OF PHILADELPHIA
3 St Andrew Fairway, Lucan, Co Dublin
Contact: Sr Nora McCarthy,
Sr Carmel Earls, Sr Kathleen Kelly

CONGREGATION OF OUR LADY OF CHARITY OF THE GOOD SHEPHERD
Province Administration
63 Lower Sean McDermott Street,
Dublin D01 NX93
Tel 01-8711109
Email province.office@rgs.ie
www.goodshepherdsisters.com
Province Leader: Sr Cait O'Leary

65 Taney Crescent,
Goatstown, Dublin D14 FY62
Tel 01-2960235
Email rgstaney@gmail.com
Community: 2

Beechlawn Complex, High Park,
Grace Park Road, Drumcondra,
Dublin D09 YK82
Nursing Home Tel 01-8369622
Community: 13

Apt 6, Woodview House,
Mount Merrion Avenue,
Blackrock, Co Dublin A94 DW95

HANDMAIDS OF THE SACRED HEART OF JESUS
St Raphaela's, Upper Kilmacud Road,
Stillorgan, Co Dublin A94 TP38
Tel 01-2889963 Fax 01-2889536
Superior: Sr Irene Guia
Email iguiaci@gmail.com
Community: 11
Primary School. Tel 01-2886878
Secondary School. Tel 01-2888730
Students' residence. Tel 01-2887159
Fax 01-2889536

HOLY CHILD JESUS, SOCIETY OF THE
1 Stable Lane, Off Harcourt Street,
Dublin D02 HX83
Tel 01-4754053

21 Grange Park Avenue,
Raheny, Dublin D05 AY65
Tel 01-8488961

HOLY FAITH SISTERS
Generalate, Aylward House,
Glasnevin, Dublin D11 YEF1
Tel 01-8371426
Email admin@hfaith.ie
Congregational Leader
Sr Rosaleen Cunniffe

Regional House,
25 Clare Road,
Drumcondra, Dublin D09 TY76
Tel 01-8572100
Email regional@hfsi.ie
Regional Leader: Sr Evelyn Greene

183 Clontarf Road,
Dublin D03 P3X5
Tel 01-8338331
Community: 5
Varied Apostolates

Star of the Sea,
182 Clontarf Road, Dublin D03 KD63
Tel 01-8338352
Community: 4
Varied Apostolates

The Coombe, Dublin 8
Tel 01-4540244
Email coomconvent@eircom.net
Community: 6
Varied Apostolates

11 Drumcairn Green,
Fettercairn, Tallaght,
Dublin D24 E5X9
Tel 01-4513951
Community: 2
Parish work

12 Finglaswood Road,
Dublin D11 EAX9
Tel 01-8641551
Community: 2
Varied Apostolates

15 Forestwood Avenue,
Ballymun, Dublin D09 EY92
Tel 01-8623482
Community: 1
Varied Apostolates

St Joseph the Artisan Parish,
124 Greencastle Road, Bonnybrook,
Coolock, Dublin 17
Tel 01-5577531
Community 2
Varied Apostolates

13 Wellmount Parade,
Dublin D11 WDE7
Tel 01-8640874
Community: 1
Administration

14 Wellmount Parade,
Dublin D11 F1C8
Tel 01-8645153
Community: 1
Music ministry

Holy Faith Sisters,
144 Cappagh Road, Finglas,
Dublin D11 T3F1
Tel 01-8643205
Community: 1
Varied Apostolates

Glasnevin, Dublin D11 HN8F
Tel 01-8373427/8377967
Pastoral Care Leaders: Sr Rosemary Duffy
and Sr Maureen Ferguson
Community: 23
Varied Apostolates

Margaret Aylward Centre for Faith and Dialogue,
Holy Faith Convent,
Glasnevin, Dublin D11 TC21
Tel 01-7979364/087-6649862
Director: Ms Dympna Mallon

Marian House Nursing Home
Tel 01-8376165
Email marianhouse_hfc@yahoo.ie

Greystones,
Co Wicklow A63 YX40
Tel 01-2874081
Community: 5
Varied Apostolates

Credo, 1 Fairways Grove,
Griffith Road, Dublin D11 E2N6
Tel 01-8348015
Community: 1
Parish ministry

2 Fairways Grove,
Griffith Road, Dublin D11 E2N6
Tel 01-8533772
Community: 1
Holy Faith community service

Haddington Place, Dublin D04 K312
Tel 01-6681124
Community: 7
Varied Apostolates

18 Church Street,
Skerries, Co Dublin K34 X981
Tel 01-8491203
Community: 4
Varied Apostolates

ARCHDIOCESE OF DUBLIN

14 Main Road,
Tallaght, Dublin D24 T2KE
Tel 01-4515904
Community: 2
Faith development

11 Aylward Green,
Finglas, Dublin D11 AV67
Tel 01-8646401
Community: 1
Varied Apostolates

11 Johnstown Park,
Ballygall Road East,
Dublin D11 PF67
Tel 01-864640
Community: 2
Varied Apostolates

178-180 Clontarf Road,
Dublin 3
Community: 9
Varied Apostolates

Joseph's Cottage,
Kippure East, Manor Kilbride,
Co Wicklow W91 AY74
Tel 01-4582923
Community: 1
Varied Apostolates

St Anne's Presbytery,
Kilcarrig Avenue, Fettercairn,
Tallaght, Dublin D24 EN25
Tel 01-4141916
Community: 2
Varied Apostolates

Rosedale Bungalow, Rathdown Road,
Greystones, Co Wicklow A63 V968
Community: 1
Spirituality

20 Seamount, Priory Drive,
Eden Gate, Delgany,
Co Wicklow A63 RC80
Tel 01-2812838
Community 1
Spirituality

SISTERS OF THE HOLY FAMILY OF BORDEAUX
65 Griffith Downs,
Drumcondra, Dublin 9
Tel 01-5477709
Contact : Sr Claire McGrath (Councillor for Ireland)
Email clairemcgrath.hfb@gmail.com

Holy Family of Bordeaux Sisters,
Irishtown, Clane, Co Kildare
Tel 01-6288459
Contact: Sr Bernadette Deegan
Community: 5
Parish work, chaplaincy, adult religious education, literacy and pastoral work

INFANT JESUS SISTERS
Provincial House,
56 St Lawrence Road,
Clontarf, Dublin D03 Y5F2
Tel 01-8338930
Provincial: Sr Kitty Ellard
Email kittyijs@gmail.com
Tel 01-8339577

140 Carrickhill Rise, Portmarnock,
Co Dublin D13 CP74
Tel 01-8461647
Pastoral ministry

16 Ard na Meala, Ballymun,
Dublin D11 P9O2
Tel 01-8426534
Pastoral ministry, youth ministry, social work

7 Ard na Meala, Ballymun,
Dublin D11 YW50
Pastoral ministry

54 Knowth Court, Poppintree,
Ballymun, Dublin D11 PF51
Pastoral ministry

2 Carrig Close, Poppintree,
Ballymun, Dublin D11 T635
Pastoral ministry

1 Eccles Court, Dublin D07 V9K5
Tel 01-8309004
Pastoral ministry

JESUS AND MARY, CONGREGATION OF
Provincialate, 'Errew House',
110 Goatstown Road, Dublin 14
Provincial Offices: Tel 01-2993130
Direct line: Tel 01-2969150
Bursar's Office: Tel 01-2993140
Provincial Superior: Sr Marie O'Halloran
Tel 01-2969150
Email marieohalloran68@gmail.com
Tel 01-2966059
Community: 5

'Errew House',
Our Lady's Grove Community,
110 Goatstown Road, Dublin 14
Community: 5
Convent. Tel 01-2966104
Our Lady's Grove Primary School
Principal: Ms Anne Kernan
Pupils: 480
Jesus & Mary College Secondary School
Principal: Mr Colm Dooley
Tel 01-2951913. Pupils: 360

'Errew House',
110 Goatstown Road, Dublin 14
Tel 01-2993665
Community: 3

LA RETRAITE SISTERS
77 Grove Park, Rathmines, Dublin 6
Tel 01-4911771
Contact: Sr Barbara Stafford
Email barbarastaffordrlr@gmail.com

LA SAINTE UNION DES SACRES COEURS
Teallach Mhuire, 41 Broadway Road,
Blanchardstown, Dublin 15
Tel 01-8214459
Leadership work base – Ireland
Hospitality

9 Tandy's Hill, Lucan, Co Dublin
Tel 01-6218863
Community: 1
Parish work

126 Malahide Road,
Clontarf, Dublin 3
Tel 01-8332778
Community: 3
Pastoral work, literacy

14 Glenshane Grove,
Brookfield, Tallaght, Dublin 24
Tel 01-4527684
Community: 2
Teaching, pastoral work, travellers, counselling

7 Summerfield Close,
Clonsilla Road, Dublin 15
Community: 1
Counselling, education

8 Myross Mews, 181 Strand Road,
Sandymount, Dublin 4
Community: 1
Pastoral

LITTLE COMPANY OF MARY
Provincialate, Cnoc Mhuire,
29 Woodpark, Ballinteer Avenue,
Dublin 16
Tel 01-2987040
Province Leader: Sr Mary Flanagan

40 Braemor Park,
Churchtown, Dublin 14
Tel 01-4991357/4991358/4904795/4904692
Community: 16

14 Heather Lawn,
Marlay Wood, Dublin 16
Tel 01-4942324
Community: 1

16 Heather Lawn,
Marlay Wood, Dublin 16
Tel 01-4947205
Community: 1

Little Company of Mary,
2 Esker Wood Grove,
Lucan, Co Dublin
Tel 01-6210474
Community: 1

Little Company of Mary,
64 Templeroan Avenue, Knocklyon,
Dublin 16
Tel 01-4957130
Community: 1

Little Company of Mary,
45 Priory Way, Whitehall Road,
Dublin 12
Tel 01-4907763
Community: 1

Little Company of Mary,
62 West Priory, Navan Road, Dublin 7
Tel 01-8682312
Community: 1

LITTLE SISTERS OF THE ASSUMPTION
Administration Office,
42 Rathfarnham Road,
Terenure, Dublin 6W
Tel 01-4909850 Fax 01-4925740
Email pernet42r@gmail.com
Co-ordinator: Sr Mary O'Sullivan
Sisters work in family care and with local community development groups

12 Convent Lawns,
Ballyfermot, Dublin 10
Tel 01-6230898
Email conventlawns12@gmail.com

8 Owendore Crescent,
Rathfarnham, Dublin 14
Tel 01-4931147
Email lasair@hotmail.com

Patrickswell Place,
Finglas, Dublin 11
Tel 01-8342592
Email fagefinglas@yahoo.co.uk

Mount Argus,
Assumption Convent,
Mount Argus Road, Dublin 6W
Tel 01-4977038
Email mountarguslsa15@gmail.com

41 Liscarne Court,
Rowlagh,
Clondalkin, Dublin 22
Tel 01-6263077
Email rowlaghlsa@gmail.com

14 Forestwood Avenue,
Santry Avenue, Dublin 9
Email lsaballymun@gmail.com

308 St James Road,
Greenhills, Dublin 12
Tel 01-4089982
Email lsaghills@gmail.com

Apts 196, 198, 199,
Block F Seven Oaks,
Ballyfermot, Dublin 10
Tel 01-6300389
Email sevenoaks.lsa@gmail.com

LITTLE SISTERS OF THE POOR
Sacred Heart Residence,
Sybil Hill Road, Raheny,
Dublin D05 XK58
Tel 01-8332308
Provincial: Sr Anthony Francis (London)
Superior: Sr Jacinta
Email msraheny@lspireland.com
Community: 13
Nursing home for the elderly

Holy Family Residence,
Roebuck Road, Dublin 14
Tel 01-2832455
Superior: Sr Miriam
Email ms.holyfamily@lspireland.com
Community: 12
Nursing home for the elderly

St Brigid's Novitiate,
Roebuck Road, Dublin 14
Tel 01-2832536
Email ms.stbrigids@lspireland.com

LORETO (IBVM)
Provincialate, Loreto House,
Beaufort, Dublin 14
Tel 01-4933827
Email provadmin@loreto.ie
Provincial: Sr Ita Moynihan

Abbey House,
Loreto Terrace, Grange Road,
Rathfarnham, Dublin 14
Tel 01-4932807
Shared Community Leaders
Sr Moira MacManus, Sr Clair Dillon
Community: 25
Primary School, Secondary Day School, pastoral work

Loreto College and Junior School,
53 St Stephen's Green, Dublin 2
Tel 01-6618179/6618181

Loreto Community,
Nos 3, 6, 8, 9 Fort Ostman,
Old County Road, Crumlin, Dublin 12
Community: 4
Co-Leaders
Sr Jane Bailey, Sr Ethel Keegan,
Sr Phil Murphy
Loreto Secondary School. Tel 01-4542380
Senior Primary School. Tel 01-4541669
Junior Primary School. Tel 01-4541746
Loreto Centre Apartments, Crumlin Road
Tel 01-4541078
Community: 7
Personal and community development

Loreto Community,
Bray, Co Wicklow
Tel 01-2862021
Co-Leaders
Sr Mary O'Dwyer, Sr Carmel Swords
Community: 9
Primary and secondary schools; pastoral work

Nos 29/30 The Courtyard
Vevay Crescent
Co-Leaders
Sr Jane Bailey, Sr Ethel Keegan,
Sr Phil Murphy
Community: 2

Loreto Abbey, Dalkey, Co Dublin
Tel 01-2804331/2804416
Email lorcomdalkey@eircom.net
Co-Leaders
Sr Marie Celine Clegg, Sr Mary O'Connor
Community: 10
Primary and secondary schools; pastoral work

Teach Muire, Leslie Avenue,
Dalkey, Co Dublin
Tel 01-2800495
Email lorlesliedalkey@eircom.net
Co-Leaders
Sr Marie Celine Clegg, Sr Mary O'Connor
Community: 6
Educational and pastoral work

Loreto Community,
Balbriggan, Co Dublin
Tel 01-8412796
Team Leaders: Sr Anne Farren,
Sr Patricia Stevens
Community: 16
Secondary school; pastoral work

Loreto Education Trust,
Foxrock, Dublin 18
Tel 01-2899956
Education and offices

Loreto,
13 Carrigmore Place, City West,
Saggart, Co Dublin
Tel/Fax 01-4589918
Also, 15 Carrigmore Place, City West,
Saggart, Co Dublin
Tel 01-4580780

Loreto, 22 Brookdale Drive,
River Valley, Swords, Co Dublin
Co-Leaders
Sr Jane Bailey, Sr Ethel Keegan,
Sr Phil Murphy
Community: 5
Tel 01-8405982
Secondary School, River Valley, Swords
Social and pastoral work

Loreto,
5 Greenville Road, Blackrock,
Co Dublin
Tel 01-2843171
Co-Leaders: Sr Marie Celine Clegg,
Sr Mary O'Connor
Community: 3
Education, social and pastoral work

Loreto, 20 Herberton Park,
Rialto, Dublin 8
Tel 01-4535048
Email lorialto@hotmail.com
Co-Leaders
Sr Jane Bailey, Sr Ethel Keegan,
Sr Phil Murphy
Community: 3
Social and pastoral work

265 Sundrive Road,
Dublin 12
Tel 01-4541509
Co-Leaders
Sr Jane Bailey, Sr Ethel Keegan,
Sr Phil Murphy
Community: 3
Education and pastoral work

7/8/9/10 Stonepark Orchard,
Stonepark Abbey
Tel 01-4952110/4952111/4951444/4950155
Community: 10
Education and pastoral work

175, 176, 178, 184, 185 Prior's Gate,
Greenhills Road, Tallaght, Dublin 24

9, 11, 50, 52 New Bancrost Hall,
Tallaght Main Street, Dublin 24

64, 66, 68 Griffith Hall,
Glandore Road, Dublin 9

10 Loreto, Crescent, Rathfarnham,
Dublin 14

21, 30, 30 The Croft,
Parc na Silla Avenue, Loughlinstown,
Dublin 18

MARIE AUXILIATRICE SISTERS
7 Florence Street,
Portobello, Dublin 8
Tel 01-4537622
Contact Person: Sr Margaret McDermott
Email margaret.mcdermott54@gmail.com
Community: 4
Spiritual direction, social outreach,
counselling

Marie Auxiliatrice Sisters
130 Upper Glenageary Road,
Dun Laoghaire, Co Dublin
Tel 01-2857389
Contact Person: Sr Mary O'Dea
Email maryodea6@gmail.com
Community: 4
Spiritual direction, social outreach,
education

MARIST SISTERS
Provincialate, 51 Kenilworth Square,
Rathgar, Dublin 6
Tel 01-4972196
Email secirlmarists@gmail.com
Leader – Ireland: Sr Miriam McManus
Community: 2

10 Cambridge Terrace,
Dartmouth Square, Dublin 6
Tel 01-6605332
Email maristcam22@gmail.com
Community: 4
Justice, education, social work

Sundrive Road,
Crumlin, Dublin 12
Tel 01-4540778
Email maristsundrive@gmail.com
Community Leader: Sr Ann Wrynn
Community: 10
Primary school
Social work, youth work, adult
education, Marist laity

21 Dunlin House,
Red Court Oak, Seafield Road East,
Clontarf, Dublin 3

MEDICAL MISSIONARIES OF MARY
Congregational Centre,
Rosemount, Rosemount Terrace,
Booterstown, Blackrock,
Co Dublin A94 AH63
Tel 01-2882722 Fax 01-2834626
Email rcsmmm37@gmail.com

3 Danieli Road, Artane,
Dublin D05 KV91
Tel 01-8316469
Community: 1

Réalt na Mara,
11 Rosemount Terrace,
Booterstown, Co Dublin A94 A7P3
Tel 01-2832247
Email mmmrealtnamara@gmail.com
Community: 3

26 Malahide Road,
Artane, Dublin D05 WK53
Tel 01-8310427
Email mmmartane@gmail.com
Community: 3

33 Templeville Drive
Templeogue, Dublin D6W VR62
Tel 01-4991803
Email mmm.templeogue@upcmail.ie
Community: 1

1 The Grange, Laurel Place,
Terenure Road West, Dublin D6W YI90
Tel 01-4925263
Email mmmterenure@gmail.com
Community: 5

2A St Margaret's Avenue,
Raheny, Dublin D05 E0P6
Tel 01-8324221
Email mmmraheny@mmm37.org
Community: 4

MISSIONARIES OF CHARITY
223 South Circular Road, Dublin 8
Tel 01-4540163
Superior: Sr M. Perpetua (MC)
Community 4
Hostel For men

MISSIONARY FRANCISCAN SISTERS OF THE IMMACULATE CONCEPTION
Assisi House, Navan Road, Dublin 7
Tel 01-8682216
Community: 3
Contact: Sr Philomena Conroy

MISSIONARY SISTERS OF THE HOLY ROSARY
Generalate, 23 Cross Avenue,
Blackrock, Co Dublin
Tel 01-2881708/9 Fax 01-2836308
Email mshrgen@indigo.ie
Superior General: Sr Franca Onyibor
Community: 8

Regional Administration,
41 Westpark, Artane, Dublin 5
Tel 01-8510010 Fax 01-8187494
Email mshrreg@eircom.net
Regional Superior: Sr Paula Molloy
Community: 4

Holy Rosary Convent,
Brookville, Westpark, Artane, Dublin 5
Tel 01-8510002
Superior: Sr Maura Garry
House for sisters on leave from mission.
Pastoral, health care
Community: 40

Holy Rosary Convent,
48 Temple Road, Dartry, Dublin 6
Tel 01-4971918/4971094
Superiors: Sr Conchita McDonnell and
Sr Colette McCann
Pastoral, education, care of the elderly
Community: 22

Holy Rosary Sisters,
Glankeen, 9 Richmond Avenue South,
Dartry, Dublin 6
Tel 01-4977277
Pastoral, health care, care of elderly
Community: 7

Holy Rosary Sisters,
2 Grange Abbey Cresent, Baldoyle,
Dublin 13
Tel 01-8476219
Pastoral, health care, education
Community: 3

Holy Rosary Sisters,
72 Grange Park, Baldoyle, Dublin 13
Tel 01-8390291
Regional admin., counselling
Community: 1

MISSIONARY SISTERS OF ST COLUMBAN
St Columban's Convent,
Magheramore, Wicklow
Tel 0404-67348
Email mhreception@mssc.ie
Community Leaders: Sr Anne Ryan/
Sr Margaret Murphy
Community: 55
Motherhouse, congregational nursing
home for sick and retired members

St Agnes Road,
Crumlin, Dublin 12
Tel 01-4555435
Community: 5
Mission awareness

Apt C14, Killarney Court,
Killarney Street, Dublin 1
Tel 01-6577339
Community: 1
Parish ministry, work with migrants

Columban Sisters,
Parish House No. 1,
Holy Spirit Parish, Silloge,
Ballymun, Dublin 11
Tel 01-8423696
Community: 3

Columban Sisters,
5/6 Grange Crescent, off Pottery Road,
Dun Laoghaire, Co Dublin
Tel 01-2853961
Community: 2

Contact Person for above five houses
Sr Nora Wiseman
Columban Sisters,
5/6 Grange Crescent, off Pottery Road,
Dun Laoghaire, Co Dublin
Tel 01-2853961

MISSIONARY SISTERS OF ST PETER CLAVER
81 Bushy Park Road,
Terenure, Dublin D06 V6Y9
Tel 01-4909360
Community: 3
Email missiondublin@stpeterclaver.ie
Dedicated to the Service of the
Missionary Church

MISSIONARY SISTERS SERVANTS OF THE HOLY SPIRIT
143 Philipsburgh Avenue,
Fairview, Dublin D03 HF80
Tel 01-8369383
Email sspsfairview1@gmail.com
Community Leader: Sr Joan Quirke
Community: 5

CONGREGATION OF OUR LADY OF THE MISSIONS
Notre Dame Convent,
Upper Churchtown Road,
Leading to Sweetmount Avenue,
Dublin D14 N8E8
Tel 01-2983306
Community Leader
Sr Elizabeth Hartigan
Tel 0044-(0)-833798969
Email hartiganliz8@gmail.com
Community: 13
Retired sisters

Congregation of Our Lady of the
Missions
5 Griffeen Glen Park,
Griffeen Valley, Lucan South,
Co Dublin K78 XP70
Tel 01-6219088
Community: 1
Retired sister

OUR LADY OF THE CENACLE
Contact: Helen Grealy
Email helenbgrealy@gmail.com
Community: 3

POOR CLARES
St Damian's,
3A Simmonscourt Road,
Ballsbridge, Dublin D04 P8A0
Fax 01-6685464
Email pccdamians@mac.com
Website www.pccdamians.ie
Abbess/Contact: Sr Mary Brigid Haran
Community: 8
Contemplatives
Rosary and Evening Prayer on Sundays at 4 pm
First Fridays, Evening Prayer and
Benediction at 4.30 pm

POOR SERVANTS OF THE MOTHER OF GOD
St Mary's Convent, Manor House,
Raheny, Dublin 5
Tel/Fax 01-8317626

St Mary's Convent, Manor House,
Raheny, Dublin 5
Tel 01-8313652 Fax 01-8313299
Community: 10
Education, pastoral ministry

Maryfield Convent, Chapelizod,
Dublin 20
Tel 01-6264684/6265402
Fax 01-6233673
Community: 17
Home for elderly

216 Tonlegee Road, Dublin 5
Tel 01-8478566
Community: 3
Care of the elderly, pastoral ministry

Croí Mhuire, 120 Lucan Road,
Chapelizod, Dublin 20
Fax/Tel 01-6233734
Community: 2
Elderly and pastoral work

39 Glenayle Road, Dublin 5
Tel 01-8770700
Community: 4
Pastoral Ministry

CONGREGATION OF THE SISTERS OF NAZARETH
Nazareth House,
Malahide Road, Dublin 3
Tel 01-8338205 Fax 01-8330813
Superior: Sr Bridget Broderick
Email srbridget.broderick@
sistersofnazareth.com
Community: 17
Regional Superior: Sr Patricia Enright
Email
srpatricia.enright@sistersofnazareth.com
Tel 01-8338205
Home for elderly. Beds: 120

PRESENTATION SISTERS
Mission House,
Lucan, Co Dublin K78 A6Y5
Tel 01-6280305
Community: 3
Home for missionaries on leave
Mission Office Tel/Fax 01-6282467
Email missionofficelucan@gmail.com

North-East Province:
George's Hill, Dublin 7
Tel 01-8746914
Community: 9
School, safeguarding, adult education,
marriage tribunal, postulator for cause
of Nano Nagle and pastoral ministry

2/3 Castlebridge Estate,
Maynooth, Co Kildare
Tel 01-6289952
Community: 5
Pastoral ministry and province finance

35 Anley Court, Esker Lane, Lucan,
Co Dublin
Tel 01-6289952
Community: 1

36 Anley Court, Esker Lane, Lucan,
Co Dublin
Community: 1
Province leadership and administration

107 Castlegate Way,
Adamstown, Lucan, Co Dublin
Community: 1

69 Fortlawn Drive, Mountview,
Blanchardstown, Dublin 15
Tel 01-8119430
Community: 2
School, prison and pastoral work

27 Wainsfort Drive,
Terenure, Dublin 6W
Tel 01-4929588
Community: 2
Province leadership and administration

Provincialate of NE Province at:
Acorn Centre Warrenmount,
Blackpitts, Dublin 8
Tel 01-4166010 Fax 01-4165787
Email secretary@presprone.com

Presentation Sisters,
Clondalkin, Dublin 22
Tel 01-4592656
Community: 9
School, parish and pastoral work

Presentation Sisters,
Warrenmount, Dublin 8
Tel 01-4113831
Community: 14
Presentation Primary. Tel 01-4539547
Community counselling, education and
prayer ministry and Provincial Leadership

78 Oliver Bond House, Dublin 8
Tel 01-6776702
Community: 1
Community and pastoral work

St Brigid's New Road,
Clondalkin, Dublin 22
Tel 01-4643319
Community: 1
Prison ministry

41 O'Curry Road, Dublin 8
Tel 01-4542806
Community: 3
Education and pastoral work

2 The Weavers,
Meath Place, Dublin 8
Community: 1
Spirituality

27 Mayfield Park,
Watery Lane, Dublin 22
Tel 01-4037316
Community: 1
Education and pastoral work

105 Tyrconnell Place,
Inchicore, Dublin 8
Community: 1
Chaplaincy 3rd Level

42 Temple Hill Apartments,
Terenure Road West, Dublin 6W
Community: 1
Pastoral

9A Kilmahuddrick Walk,
Clondalkin, Dublin 22
Tel 01-4576441
Community: 2
Parish and pastoral work

9B Kilmahuddrick Walk,
Clondalkin, Dublin 22
Community: 1

REDEMPTORISTINES
Monastery of St Alphonsus,
St Alphonsus Road, Dublin D09 HN53
Tel 01-8305723 Fax 01-8309129
Superior: Sr Lucy & Sr Gabrielle
Community: 14
Contemplatives

RELIGIOUS OF CHRISTIAN EDUCATION
Provincial Office,
3 Bushy Park House,
Templeogue Road, Dublin 6W
Tel 01-4901668 Fax 01-4901101
Provincial leader: Sr Rosemary O'Looney

Community Residence,
4/5 Bushy Park House,
Templeogue Road, Dublin 6W
Tel 01-4905516
Superior: Sr Rosemary O'Looney

Our Lady's School,
Templeogue Road, Dublin 6W
Secondary School. Tel 01-4903241
Principal: Ms Marguerite Gorby

RELIGIOUS OF SACRED HEART OF MARY
13/14 Huntstown Wood,
Huntstown, Dublin D15 XT9X
Tel 01-8223566
Community: 2
Spiritual direction, pastoral ministry,
education

70 Upper Drumcondra Road, Dublin 9
Tel 01-8379898
Community: 3 plus 1 attached
Pastoral ministry, prison, refugees

72 Upper Drumcondra Road, Dublin 9
Tel 01-8368331
Community: 1 plus 1 attached
Spiritual direction, ministry in local area

RELIGIOUS SISTERS OF CHARITY
Generalate, Caritas,
15 Gilford Road, Sandymount,
Dublin 4
Tel 01-2697833/2697935

Mary Aikenhead Heritage Centre,
Our Lady's Mount, Harold's Cross,
Dublin 6W
Tel 01-4910041

Office of the Cause,
Sisters of Charity, St Mary's,
Merrion Road, Dublin 4
Tel 086-4680427

Overseas and Development Office,
Sisters of Charity, 15 Gilford Road,
Sandymount, Dublin 4
Tel 01-2605788

Provincialate, Provincial House,
Our Lady's Mount, Harold's Cross,
Dublin D6W W934
Tel 01-4973177

Marmion House, St Mary's,
185 Merrion Road, Dublin D04 P2T8
Tel 01-2027223
Various Apostolic Ministries

St Anne's, 29 Thornville Drive,
Kilbarrack East, Dublin D05 C3V5
Tel 01-8321112/8321114
Various Apostolic Ministries

Stanhope Street Convent,
Manor Street, Dublin D07 T1K2
Tel 01-6779183
Various Apostolic Ministries

Stanhope Lodge,
Stanhope Green, Dublin D07 DH72
Tel 01-6704016
Various Apostolic Ministries

St Monica's,
28/38 Belvedere Place,
Dublin D01 EY21
Tel (Community) 01-8552317
Various Apostolic Ministries

Naomh Bríd Community,
28/38 Belvedere Place,
Dublin D01 EY21
Tel 01-8557647
Various Apostolic Ministries

Our Lady of the Nativity,
Lakelands, Sandymount,
Dublin D04 KP40
Tel 01-2692076/2603362
Various Apostolic Ministries

St Mary's, Donnybrook,
Dublin D04 P7D0
Tel 01-2600315/2600818
Various Apostolic Ministries

Mary Aikenhead House, St Mary's,
Donnybrook, Dublin 4
Tel 01-2693258
Various Apostolic Ministries

Sisters of Charity,
Our Lady's Mount, Harold's Cross,
Dublin D6W W281
Ard Mhuire Community
Tel 01-4961488
Maranatha Community D6W HN76
Tel 01-4961423
Shandon community
Tel 01-4982614

4 Telford House, St Mary's,
Merrion Road, Dublin D04 F9V3
Tel 01-2605495
Various Apostolic Ministries

Stella Maris Convent,
Baily, Co Dublin D13 YK71
Tel 01-8322228 Fax 01-8063469
Various Apostolic Ministries

Our Lady Queen of Ireland,
Walkinstown, Dublin 12
Tel 01-4503491
Various Apostolic Ministries

Sisters of Charity,
St Laurence Place East,
Seville Place, Dublin D01 E5Y9
Tel 01-8744179
Various Apostolic Ministries

Sisters of Charity,
1 Temple Street, Dublin D01 XD99
Tel 01-8745778/8745779

26 Park Avenue,
Sandymount, Dublin 4
Tel 01-2604659
Various Apostolic Ministries

28 Park Avenue,
Sandymount, Dublin 4
Tel 01-2604654
Various Apostolic Ministries

Providence,
St Mary's, Merrion Road,
Dublin D04 H1F2
Tel 01-2693450
Various Apostolic Ministries

Shalom,
St Mary's, Merrion Road,
Dublin D04 A5V0
Tel 01-2602775
Various Apostolic Ministries

SACRED HEART SOCIETY
Provincial Office,
76 Home Farm Road,
Drumcondra, Dublin D09 R903
Tel 01-8375412 Fax 01-8375542
Canonical Leader: Sr Dairne McHenry
Email d.mchenry@rscjirs.org
Executive Officer: Orla O'Hanlon
Email executive@rscjirs.org
Provincial Secretary: Helen Mulholland
Email provsec@rscjirs.org

6 Achill Road, Drumcondra,
Dublin D09 X3K5
Tel 01-8360866
Adult education and pastoral work;
youth and pastoral ministry

37 Church Road,
East Wall, Dublin D03 CP26
Tel 01-2602533
Provincial Administration, Voluntary
work

1 Dunlin House, Redcourt Oaks,
Seafield Road East, Clontarf,
Dublin D03 TX47
Tel 01-8540450
Educational trusteeships and voluntary
work

29 Gilford Pines, Gilford Road,
Sandymount, Dublin D04 DX67
Tel 01-2304094
Historical research

Cedar House Nursing Home,
35 Mount Anville Park,
Dublin D14 F240
Tel 01-2831024/5 Fax 01-2831348
Email cedarhousejim@gmail.com

36 Mount Anville Park,
Dublin D14 X314
Tel 01-2880739
Pastoral ministry and Cedar House

37 Mount Anville Park,
Dublin D14 NX03
38 Mount Anville Park,
Dublin D14 AC98
Tel 01-2880708
Work in parish and community service

96 Mount Anville Wood,
Dublin D14 DD30
Tel 01-2880786
Work in Mount Anville School, spiritual
ministry

201 Lower Kilmacud Road,
Blackrock, Co Dublin A94 FC90
Tel 01-2834832 Fax 01-2104825
Spiritual and parish ministry

Sacred Heart Schools Network Ltd

Mount Anville Primary School,
Lower Kilmacud Road,
Blackrock, Co Dublin A94 E2N7
Pupils: 470
Tel 01-2831138 Fax 01-2836395

Mount Anville Sacred Heart Education
Trust, Mount Anville House,
Mount Anville Road,
Dublin D14 KX80

Mount Anville Secondary School
Mount Anville House,
Mount Anville Road,
Dublin D14 A8P3
Pupils: 679
Tel 01-2885313/4 Fax 01-2832373

Mount Anville Junior and Montessori
School, Mount Anville House,
Mount Anville Road, Dublin D14 A8P3
Pupils: 410
Tel 01-2885313/4 Fax 01-2832373

**SACRED HEARTS OF JESUS AND MARY
(PICPUS) SISTERS**
Delegation House,
11 Northbrook Road,
Ranelagh, Dublin D06 Y962
Tel 01-4974831 (Community)
Community: 4
Contact: Sr Aileen Kennedy (SSCC)
Email aileenkennedysscc@hotmail.com

Aymer House, 11 Northbrook Lane,
Ranelagh, Dublin 6
Tel 01-4975614
Community: 5

SALESIAN SISTERS OF ST JOHN BOSCO
Provincialate,
203 Lower Kilmacud Road,
Stillorgan, Co Dublin
Tel 01-2985188
Provincial Superior: Sr Bridget O'Connell
Convent Tel 01-2985908
Superior: Sr Margaret Sweeney
Community: 6
Parish ministry, provincial administration

38 Morehampton Road,
Donnybrook, Dublin 4
Tel 01-6684643
Community: 3
Mission promotion

ARCHDIOCESE OF DUBLIN

40 Morehampton Road,
Donnybrook, Dublin 4
Tel 01-6680012
Community: 3
Hospital ministry, facilitators' training course for youth retreats, Promotion of Ecology wih young people

91-95 Ashwood Road, Bawnoge,
Clondalkin, Dublin 22
Tel 01-4571792
Contact person: Sr Annette Murtagh
Community: 5
Teaching and related activities

36 Glenties Park,
Finglas South, Dublin 11
Tel 01-8345777
Superior: Sr Elizabeth Lawler
Community: 3
Youth and parish work, mission promotion, Adult Computer Training

28 Hazelwood Crescent,
Greenpark, Clondalkin,
Dublin 22
Tel 01-4123928
Contact person: Sr Catherine Kelly
Community: 4
School chaplaincy, Adult Education

SISTERS OF OUR LADY OF APOSTLES
70b Shellbourne Road,
Ballsbridge, Dublin D04 T021
Tel 01-6685796
Email olasrsdublin@gmail.com
Community: 6

SISTERS OF ST CLARE
St Clare's Convent,
Tel 01-4995100
63 Harold's Cross Road, Dublin 6W
Contact: Sr Anne Kelly
Email annedkelly@yahoo.com
Community: 12
Primary School

Sisters of St Clare, 10 Maple Green,
Laurel Lodge, Dublin 15
Tel 01-8213967
Community: 3

SISTERS OF ST JOHN OF GOD
39 St David's Wood,
Malahide Road,
Artane, Dublin 5
Tel: 01 8329798

SISTERS OF ST JOSEPH OF CHAMBERY
St Joseph's Convent,
Springdale Road,
Raheny, Dublin 5
Tel 01-8478351
Superior: Sr Eileen Silke
Email silkegalway@gmail.com
Regional Superior: Sr Sarah Goss (CSJ)
Email sarahgoss@ymail.com
Community: 9
Care of the sick and pastoral activity

SISTERS OF ST JOSEPH OF CLUNY
Mount Sackville Convent,
Chapelizod, Dublin 20
Tel 01-8213134
Email provirlgb@sjc.ie
Website www.sjc.ie
Provincial Superior: Sr Maeve Guinan
Tel 01-8213134
Superior: Sr Ignatius Davis
Tel 01-8213134
Community: 33
Primary school; secondary day school; nursing home

St Joseph of Cluny Convent,
Ballinclea Road, Killiney, Co Dublin
Tel 01-2851038
Superior: Sr Mary Shiels
Community: 8
Secondary schools

Parslickstown Drive,
Mulhuddart, Dublin 15
Tel 01-8217339
Superior: Sr Rowena Galvin
Community: 3
Pastoral ministry

ST JOSEPH OF THE SACRED HEART SISTERS
St Joseph's Convent,
6 Farmleigh Avenue,
Stillorgan, Co Dublin
Tel 01-2781228
Email farmleigh2017@gmail.com
Sr Eileen Kirby

Sisters of St Joseph of the Sacred Heart,
25 Nutley Square,
Donnybrook, Dublin 4
Tel 01-2602306
Sr Mary Kirrane

Sisters of St Joseph,
11 The Courtyard, Vevay Crescent,
Bray, Co Wicklow
Tel 01-2761288
Sr Briege Buckley

Sisters of St Joseph,
3 Carrigalea, Queens Park,
Monkstown, Co Dublin
Sr Clare Ahern

ST LOUIS SISTERS
St Louis Generalate,
3 Beech Court, Ballinclea Road,
Killiney, Dublin
Tel 01-2350304/2350309 Fax 01-2350345
Institute Leader: Sr Winifred Ojo

St Louis Convent,
Charleville Road, Dublin 6
Tel 01-4975467
Community: 16

7 Grosvenor Road,
Rathgar, Dublin 6
Tel 01-4965485
Community: 5
Varied apostolates

130 Beaufort Downs,
Rathfarnham, Dublin 16
Tel 01-4934194
Community: 2
Varied apostolates

17 Kilclare Crescent, Jobstown,
Tallaght, Dublin 24
Tel 01-4526344
Community: 1
Education

49 Moynihan Court,
Main Road, Tallaght Village,
Dublin 24
Tel 01-4628386
Community: 5
Varied apostolates

8 Grosvenor Road,
Rathgar, Dublin 6
Tel 01-4067861
Community: 2

St Genevieve's Community
1 Charleville Road, Rathmines,
Dublin 6
Tel 01-4914752
Email stgenevievessl@gmail.com
Community: 7

ST PAUL DE CHARTRES SISTERS
6-8 Garville Avenue,
Rathgar, Dublin 6
Tel 01-4972366
Email fabiolapak@gmail.com
Regional Superior: Sr Fabiola Pak
Community: 3
Pastoral care service in Orwell Queen of Peace and Orwell Healthcare

URSULINES
Provincialate, 17 Trimleston Drive,
Booterstown, Co Dublin
Tel 01-2693503
Provincial: Sr Anne Harte Barry
Community: 2

Ursuline Sisters,
3 Cedermount, St Brigid's Church Road,
Stillorgan, Co Dublin
Community: 1
Pastoral ministry

St Ursula's, Sandyford, Dublin 18
Tel 01-2956881
Community: 3
Pastoral ministry

URSULINES OF JESUS
26 The Drive, Seatown Park,
Swords, Co Dublin
Tel 01-8404323
Email ujswords@eircom.net
Contact Person: Sr Mary McLoughney
Email marymcloughney45@gmail.com
Community: 3
Parish ministry, volunteer with Spirasi Befriending service.

EDUCATIONAL INSTITUTIONS

Colaiste Mhuire Marino
President: Teresa O'Doherty
Chaplain: Ms Lily Barry

Marino Institute of Education
Griffith Avenue, Dublin 9
Tel 01-8057700

St Patrick's College
Maynooth, Co Kildare
Tel 01-7083958 Fax 01-7083959
President: Very Rev Michael Mullaney DD
(See Seminaries and Houses of Study section)

EDUCATIONAL TRUSTS

ERST – The Edmund Rice Schools Trust
Meadow Vale, Clonkeen Road,
Blackrock, Co Dublin
Tel 01-2897511 Fax 01-2897540
Email reception@erst.ie
CEO: Gerry Bennett

LE CHÉILE SCHOOLS TRUST
Mobhi Building, Church of Ireland,
Alexandra College,
Upper Rathmines Road, Dublin 6
Tel 01-2375493 Fax 01-6602528
Email admin@lecheiletrust.ie
www.lecheiletrust.ie
Education Officer: Dr Eilís Humphreys
Tel 087-0509227
Email eilis@lecheiletrust.ie
*Faith and Ethos Development
Co-ordinator:* Audrey Doyle

CEIST
Ceist Education Office, Dublin Road,
Kildare Town, Co Kildare
Tel 01-6510350 Fax 01-6510180
Email info@ceist.ie
CEO: Clare Ryan
Tel 01-6510350

DEA – Spiritan Education Trust
Des Places House, Kimmage Manor,
Whitehall Road, Kimmage, Dublin 12
Tel 01-4997610 Fax 01-4997060
Email reception@desplaces.ie

Loreto Education Trust
Springfield Park, Foxrock, Loreto
Education Centre
Tel 01-2899956
Director: Sr Ann O'Donoghue IBVM
Eail info@loretoeducationcentre.ie

CHARITABLE AND OTHER SOCIETIES

Travellers Family Care

Derralossary House
Roundwood, Co Wicklow
Tel 01-2818355
Residential home for girls
Ballyowen Meadows
Tel 01-6235735
Exchange House Youth Service
61 Great Strand Street, Dublin 1
Tel 01-4546488
Training and employment programme and youth work

Hostels

Don Bosco House
57 Lower Drumcondra Road, Dublin 9
Tel 01-8360696
Salesian hostel for homeless boys.
Priest in Charge: Rev V. Collier (SDB)

Homeless Girls' Hostel
Sherrard House,
19 Upper Sherrard Street, Dublin 1
Tel 01-8743742

Iveagh Hostel
Bride Road, Dublin 8
Tel 01-4540182

Morning Star Hostel
Morning Star Avenue,
Brunswick Street, Dublin 7
Tel 01-8723401

Regina Coeli Hostel
Morning Star Avenue,
Brunswick Street, Dublin 7
Tel 01-8723142

St Vincent de Paul Night Shelter
Back Lane, Dublin 8
Tel 01-4542181

Housing

Catholic Housing Aid Society (CHAS)
Fr Scully House,
Middle Gardiner Street, Dublin 1
Tel 01-8741020
Flats for the aged

Threshold
21 Stoneybatter, Dublin 7
Tel 01-6353600/6786090
Website www.threshold.ie

Other

Cuan Mhuire
Athy, Co Kildare
Tel 059-8631493 Fax 059-8638765
Rehabilitation centre for alcoholics and those with allied problems

Irish School of Evangelisation (ISOE)
Co Dublin
Tel 01-2827658
Email isoe@esatclear.ie
www.esatclear.ie/~isoe

Our Lady's Choral Society
(The Archdiocesan Choir)
Director: Rev Paul Ward
Hon Secretary: Tom Gaynor

Society of St Vincent de Paul
Dublin Office,
91-92 Sean McDermott Street, Dublin 1
Tel 01-8550022 Fax 01-8559168

Fear not,
I am with you.

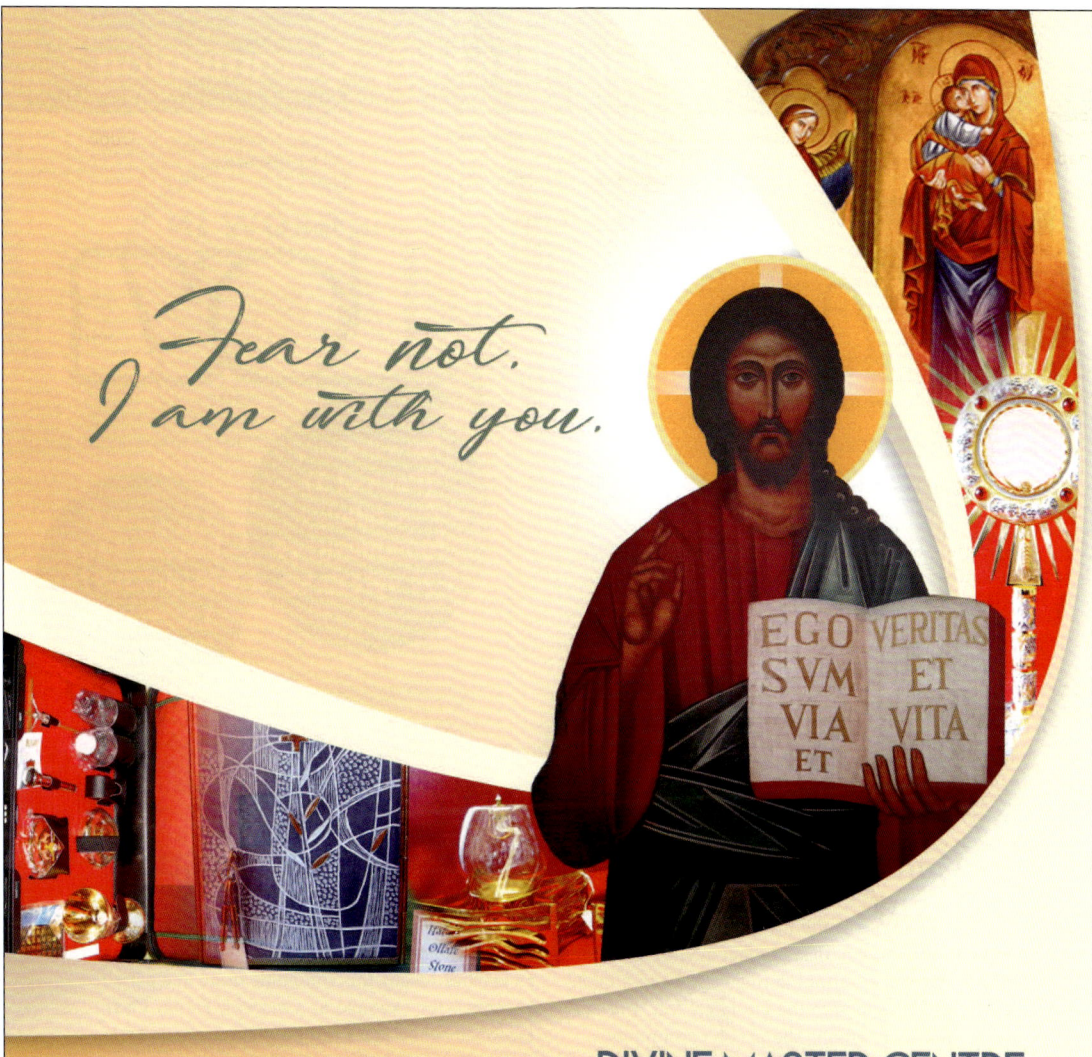

DIVINE MASTER CENTRE
Dedicated as a place of hospitality and welcome
Retreat spaces to rest and encounter the Eucharistic Jesus in the spirit of Bethany

LITURGICAL CENTRE
For liturgical and religious items for homes, churches, chapels, and prayer spaces.
Gift for special religious occasions. Online catalogue: www.liturgical.centre.ie

Ministry of prayer, support and service to priests and those called to serve others in the Church.

ATHLONE
8 Castle Street, Athlone
Co. Westmeath
T: 09064 92278

DUBLIN
Newtownpark Avenue
White's Cross, Blackrock
Co. Dublin A94 VN28
T: 01 2886414 • E: dublin@pddm.org
www.pddm.ie

Parish Resource for First Holy Communion

NEW

Newsletters (Pack of 5)
Code: 2100000058149
€24.99/£22.50

Leader Book
9781847309761
€5.99/£5.40

IN THE PARISH
Connecting Home, School and Parish Communities

The Grow in Love in the Parish programme aims to help parents and guardians to link in with what their child is learning at school during First Communion year. It also links in with the Liturgical Year and builds awareness among the parish community about the preparation for First Communion.

There are three main elements:

1. A series of liturgically based initiatives
These initiatives, which take place during Sunday Mass, help families with young children to be more involved in the celebration of the Eucharist, both in the year of sacramental preparation and beyond, and to be more connected to their parish community.

2. A series of newsletters
The newsletters are designed to run in parallel with the school-based Grow in Love programme, and to reinforce the concepts therein. It is envisaged that they would be distributed on a monthly basis to families. Ideally, this should be done in a parish context – for example, at a monthly Family Mass. However, when that's not possible they can be sent to families directly from the Parish.

3. Speaking notes
Each month, speaking notes are offered for the priest, together with a sample Prayer of the Faithful. The speaking notes draw attention to the key features of the newsletter for that particular month, and the Prayer of the Faithful picks up on the theme for that month.

We hope these newsletters will be a source of information and inspiration to parents/guardians, and will serve to strengthen the engagement of children and their families in the life of the Church.

For further information email: growinlove@veritas.ie

Abbey Street & Blanchardstown Centre, Dublin
Cork • Derry • Letterkenny • Newry

VERITAS
www.veritas.ie

RPD LIMITED

25 Tolka Valley Business Park,
Ballyboggan Road, Glasnevin,
Dublin 11,
Ireland
Tel: +353 (1) 860 3088
Email: hello@rpd.ie

- Collection Envelopes
- Newsletters
- Outdoor Banners
- Pull Up Banners
- Stationery
- Flyers
- Posters
- Badges
- Calendars
- Cards
- Bookmarks
- Brochures
- Memorial Stationery
- QR Code donation systems

and much more

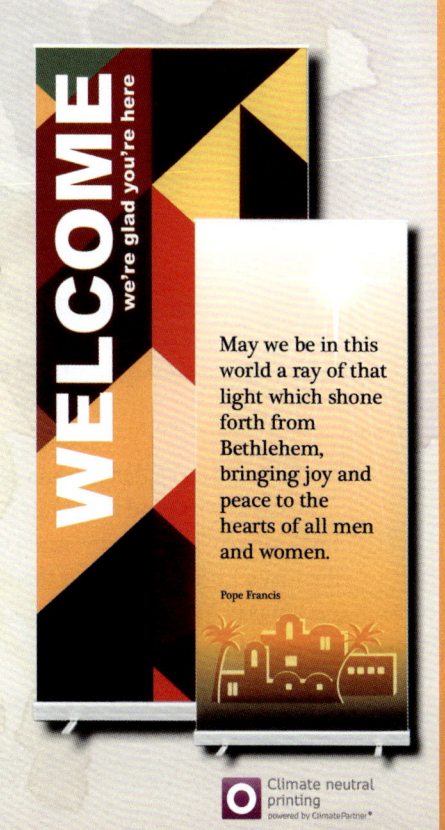

Helping Communities Communicate

WELCOME we're glad you're here

May we be in this world a ray of that light which shone forth from Bethlehem, bringing joy and peace to the hearts of all men and women.

Pope Francis

PRINT IRISH
CLÓBHUAIL IN ÉIRINN

Climate neutral printing
powered by ClimatePartner

New from Veritas Publications

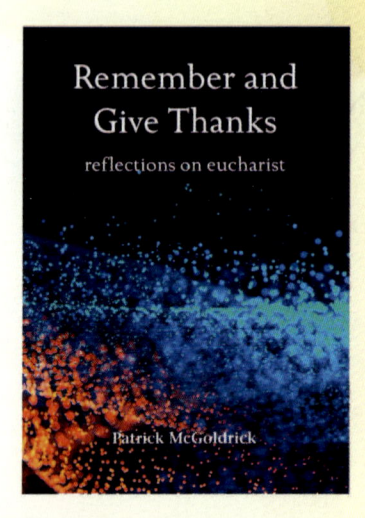

Remember and Give Thanks
reflections on eucharist

PATRICK MCGOLDRICK

978 1 80097 012 0
€17.99/£16.20

Before he died in December 2020, Patrick McGoldrick spent a year writing a collection of reflections on eucharist, drawing on his thirty-six years of studying and teaching liturgy, mostly at Maynooth College, and his twenty-two years as curate in Moville, Co. Donegal.

As the world struggled to come to terms with the Covid-19 pandemic, the author began to write and the result is this insightful collection, which draws on the tradition of Christians over two thousand years gathering to remember the life of the Risen Lord in a spirit of thanksgiving. With words from that tradition and the teachings of Vatican II, with biblical words and the words of the eucharistic prayer to express our eucharistic faith, we remember and give thanks.

Abbey Street & Blanchardstown Centre, Dublin
Cork • Derry • Letterkenny • Newry

VERITAS
www.veritas.ie

ARCHDIOCESE OF CASHEL AND EMLY

PATRON OF THE ARCHDIOCESE
ST AILBE, 12 SEPTEMBER

SUFFRAGEN SEES: CLOYNE, CORK AND ROSS, KERRY, KILLALOE, LIMERICK, WATERFORD AND LISMORE

INCLUDES MOST OF COUNTY TIPPERARY AND PARTS OF COUNTY LIMERICK

Most Rev Kieran O'Reilly (SMA) DD
Archbishop of Cashel and Emly born 1952; ordained priest 17 June 1978; ordained Bishop of Killaloe 29 August 2010; Appointed Archbishop of Cashel and Emly 22 November 2014

Residence: Archbishop's House, Thurles, Co Tipperary E41 NY92
Tel 0504-21512
Email office@cashel-emly.ie
Website www.cashel-emly.ie

The Metropolitan Archdiocese of Cashel and Emly in mid-western Ireland is in the province of Munster. The then separate dioceses of Cashel and Emly were established in 1111 by the Synod of Rathbreasail. Cashel diocese was promoted to the status of a Metropolitan Province in 1152 at the Synod of Kells. Emly diocese was formally joined to Cashel in 1718.

CATHEDRAL OF THE ASSUMPTION, THURLES

The Cathedral of the Assumption stands on the site of earlier chapels. The first church on this site was part of the Carmelite priory, which dates from the early fourteenth century.

Some time before 1730 George Mathew, Catholic proprietor of the Thurles Estate, built a chapel for the Catholics of Thurles beside the ruins of the Carmelite priory. It was known as the Mathew Chapel. In 1810 Archbishop Bray consecrated the new 'Big Chapel', which was more spacious and ornate than its humble predecessor.

Soon after his appointment as archbishop in 1857, Dr Patrick Leahy revealed his plan to replace the Big Chapel with 'a cathedral worthy of the archdiocese'. Building commenced in 1865, and the impressive Romanesque cathedral, with its façade modelled on that of Pisa, was consecrated by Archbishop Croke on 21 June 1879. The architect was J. J. McCarthy. Barry McMullen was the main builder, and J. C. Ashlin was responsible for the enclosing walls, railing and much of the finished work.

The cathedral has many beautiful features, including an impressive rose window, a free-standing baptistry and a magnificent altar. The prize possession of the cathedral is its exquisite tabernacle, the work of Giacomo dello Porta (1537–1602), a pupil of Michelangelo. This tabernacle, which belonged to the Gesú (Jesuit) Church in Rome, was purchased by Archbishop Leahy and transported to Thurles.

The cathedral was extensively renovated and the sanctuary sympathetically remodelled on the occasion of its first centenary in 1979.

The most recent extensive conservation and renewal of the Cathedral, during 2001–2003, has restored the building to its original splendour.

ARCHDIOCESE OF CASHEL AND EMLY

Most Rev Dermot Clifford PhD, DD
Archbishop Emeritus of Cashel and Emly; born 1939; ordained priest 22 February 1964; ordained Coadjutor Archbishop 9 March 1986; installed Archbishop of Cashel and Emly 12 September 1988; acted as Apostolic Administrator of Cloyne, March 2009–January 2013; Retired 22 November 2014
Residence: The Green, Holycross, Thurles, Co Tipperary
Tel 0504-43802

CHAPTER

Dean
Rt Rev Mgr Christy O'Dwyer
Archdeacon
Venerable Eugene Everard
Chancellor: Vacant
Precentor: Vacant
Treasurer: Vacant
Penitentiary
Very Rev Canon Conor Ryan, Hospital
Theologian
Very Rev Canon Liam McNamara,
Prebendaries
Newchapel
Very Rev Canon Thomas J. Ryan, Murroe
Lattin: Vacant
Killennellick: Vacant

ADMINISTRATION

College of Consultors
Rt Rev Mgr Christy O'Dwyer AP, VG
Venerable Archdeacon Eugene Everard PP, VG
Very Rev Nicholas J. Irwin PP
Rev Dr Michael Mullaney CC
Very Rev Joe Egan PP
Very Rev Thomas Fogerty PP

Vicars General
Rt Rev Mgr Christy O'Dwyer AP, VG
Venerable Archdeacon Eugene Everard PP, VG

Vicars Forane
Very Rev Loughlin Brennan
Very Rev Canon Conor Ryan
Very Rev James O'Donnell
Very Rev Canon Thomas F. Breen
Very Rev Canon John O'Neill

Diocesan Finance Committee
Archbishop Kieran O'Reilly
Rt Rev Mgr Christy O'Dwyer
Venerable Archdeacon Eugene Everard
Very Rev Nicholas J. Irwin
Very Rev Thomas Fogerty
Mr Owen Smyth
Mrs Mary Fitzgibbon
Ms Kathleen Burke

Finance Project Manager
Ms Arlene Moore
Archbishop's House, Thurles
Tel 0504-21512

Finance Office
Ms Martha Fitzpatrick
Tel 0504-21512

Diocesan Archivist
Rt Rev Mgr Christy O'Dwyer AP, VG
Moyne, Thurles, Co Tipperary
Tel 0504-34959

Diocesan Secretary/Chancellor
Very Rev Nicholas J. Irwin PP
Archbishop's House,
Thurles, Co Tipperary
Tel 0504-21512

CATECHETICS EDUCATION

Adult Religious Education
Rev Thomas Dunne CC
Ballinree, Boherlahan,
Cashel, Co Tipperary
Tel 083-4854776

Catechetics
Director: Very Rev Pat Coffey PP
Golden, Co Tipperary
Tel 062-72146
Assistant Director
Very Rev Michael Kennedy PP
The Parochial House,
Lattin, Co Tipperary
Tel 087-4147229

Boards of Management of Primary Schools
Education Secretary
Very Rev John O'Keeffe PP
Birdhill, Killaloe, Co Tipperary
Tel 061-379172/087-2421678

St Senan's Education Office
Diocesan Centre,
St Munchin's, Corbally, Limerick
Tel 061-347777

PASTORAL

ACCORD
Accord House, Cathedral Street,
Thurles, Co Tipperary
Tel 0504-22279
Diocesan Director
Very Rev Tomás O'Connell PP
Tel 087-6482544

Adoption Society
Director: Rev Celsus Tierney PP
Holy Cross Abbey, Holy Cross,
Thurles, Co Tipperary
Tel 0504-43118

Communications
Very Rev Joseph Tynan PP
Parochial House, Kilteely, Co Limerick
Tel 061-384213/087-2225445
Email joetynan3@gmail.com

Director of Safeguarding
Ms Cleo Yeats
Tel 087-3553024
Email safeguarding@cashel-emly.ie

Ecumenism
Archbishop's House,
Thurles, Co Tipperary
Tel 0504-21512

Emigrant Commission
Very Rev Loughlin Brennan PP, VF
Liscreagh, Murroe, Co Limerick
Tel 061-386227

Marriage Tribunal
(See Marriage Tribunals section.)

Pastoral Planning and Development
Diocesan Director
Ms Katherine Dullaghan
Assistant: Ms Sadie Moloney
Email pastoral.office@cashel-emly.ie

Pilgrimages
Director: Very Rev James Donnelly PP
Doon, Co Limerick
Tel 061-380165

Pioneer Total Abstinence Association
Diocesan Director
Vacant

Travellers
Chaplain
Very Rev Daniel O'Gorman PP
The Parochial House,
Mullinahone, Co Tipperary
Tel 052-9153152

Trócaire
Diocesan Director
Very Rev Dominic Meehan PP
Templemore, Co Tipperary
Tel 0504-31492

Vocations
Director: Rev Joseph Walsh CC
Thurles, Co Tipperary
Tel 0504-22229
Email vocations@cashel-emly,ie

Missio Ireland
Diocesan Director
Very Rev Celsus Tierney PP
The Parochial House, Holycross,
Thurles, Co Tipperary
Tel 0504-43124

ARCHDIOCESE OF CASHEL AND EMLY

PARISHES

Mensal parishes are listed first. Other parishes follow alphabetically. Church titulars are in italic.

THURLES, CATHEDRAL OF THE ASSUMPTION
Very Rev James Purcell PP
Rev Joseph Walsh CC
Cathedral Presbytery, Thurles,
Co Tipperary
Tel 0504-22229/22779

THURLES, SS JOSEPH AND BRIGID
Rev Vincent Stapleton CC
Bóthar na Naomh Presbytery,
Thurles, Co Tipperary
Tel 0504-22042/22688

ANACARTY
St Brigid's, Anacarty
Immaculate Conception, Donohill
Very Rev James Kennedy PP
Anacarty, Co Tipperary
Tel 062-71104

BALLINA
Our Lady and St Lua, Ballina,
Mary, Mother of the Church, Boher
Very Rev Thomas Lanigan-Ryan PP
Ballina, Killaloe, Co Clare
Tel 061-376178
Very Rev Edmond V. O'Rahelly AP
Main Street, Ballina, Co Clare
Tel 087-2262636

BALLINAHINCH
St Joseph's, Ballinahinch,
Sacred Heart, Killoscully
Very Rev James O'Donoghue PP
Ballinahinch, Birdhill, Limerick
Tel 061-781510

BALLINGARRY
Assumption
Very Rev Gerard Quirke PP
Ballingarry, Thurles, Co Tipperary
Tel 052-9154115

BALLYBRICKEN
St Ailbe's, Ballybricken,
Immaculate Heart of Mary, Bohermore
Very Rev James Walton PP
Ballybricken, Grange, Kilmallock,
Co Limerick
Tel 061-351158

BALLYLANDERS
Assumption of BVM
Very Rev Thomas O. Breen PP
Ballylanders, Kilmallock,
Co Limerick
Tel 062-46705

BANSHA AND KILMOYLER
Annunciation, Our Lady of the Assumption, Kilmoyler
Very Rev Michael Hickey PP
Bansha, Co Tipperary
Tel 062-54132

BOHERLAHAN AND DUALLA
Immaculate Conception, Boherlahan
Our Lady of Fatima, Dualla
Very Rev Joseph Egan PP
Boherlahan, Cashel, Co Tipperary
Tel 0504-41114
Rev Tom Dunne CC
Ballinree, Boherlahan,
Cashel, Co Tipperary
Tel 083-4854776

BORRISOLEIGH
Sacred Heart, Borrisoleigh
Very Rev Gerard Hennessy PP
Parochial House, Borrisoleigh, Thurles,
Co Tipperary
Tel 0504-51935

CAHERCONLISH
Our Lady, Mother of the Church
Arch. O'Hurley Mem., Caherline
Very Rev Roy Donovan PP
Caherconlish, Co Limerick
Tel 061-450730
Very Rev Patrick Currivan AP
Caherconlish, Co Limerick
Tel 061-351248

CAPPAMORE
St Michael's
Very Rev Richard Browne PP
Cappamore, Co Limerick
Tel 061-381288

CAPPAWHITE
Our Lady of Fatima
Very Rev Tadhg Furlong PP
Cappawhite, Co Tipperary
Tel 062-75427

CASHEL
St John the Baptist, Cashel
St Thomas the Apostle, Rosegreen
Very Rev Enda Brady PP
Bohereenglas, Cashel, Co Tipperary
Tel 062-61127
Rt Rev Mgr James Ryan AP
Bohermore, Cashel, Co Tipperary
Tel 062-61353
Very Rev Pat Burns AP
Bohermore, Cashel, Co Tipperary
Tel 087-2036763

CLERIHAN
St Michael's
Very Rev Peter Brennan PP
Parochial House, Clerihan,
Clonmel, Co Tipperary
Tel 087-2362603

CLONOULTY
Church of St John the Baptist, Clonoulty
Church of Jesus Christ Our Saviour, Rossmore
Very Rev Thomas Hearne PP
Parochial House, Clonoulty,
Cashel, Co Tipperary
Tel 052-7462810
Very Rev Matthew McGrath AP
Tel 0504-42494

DOON
St Patrick's
Very Rev James Donnelly PP
Doon, Co Limerick
Tel 061-380165

DRANGAN
Immaculate Conception, Visitation, Cloneen
Very Rev Anthony Lambe PP
Drangan, Thurles, Co Tipperary
Tel 052-9152103

DROM AND INCH
St Mary's, Drom,
St Laurence O'Toole, Inch
Very Rev Martin Murphy PP
Drom, Thurles, Co Tipperary
Tel 0504-51196
Very Rev Thomas Egan *(priest in residence)*
Inch, Bouladuff, Thurles,
Clonmel, Co Tipperary
Tel 086-8199678

EMLY
St Ailbe's
Very Rev Bernie Moloney PP
Emly, Co Tipperary
Tel 062-57111
Very Rev Seamus Rochford AP
Emly, Co Tipperary
Tel 062-57103

FETHARD
Holy Trinity, Fethard
Sacred Heart, Killusty
Very Rev Liam Everard PP
Parochial House, Fethard, Co Tipperary
Tel 052-6131178
Very Rev Canon Thomas F. Breen AP
Fethard, Co Tipperary
Tel 052-6131680

GALBALLY
Christ the King, Galbally
Sacred Heart, Lisvernane
Very Rev Canon John O'Neill PP, VF
Lisvernane, Aherlow,
Co Tipperary
Tel 062-56155
Very Rev Canon Denis Talbot AP
Galbally, Co Limerick
Tel 062-37929

ARCHDIOCESE OF CASHEL AND EMLY

GOLDEN
Blessed Sacrament, Golden
St Patrick's, Kilfeade
Very Rev Patrick Coffey PP
Golden, Co Tipperary
Tel 062-72146

GORTNAHOE
Sacred Heart, Gortnahoe
SS Patrick & Oliver, Glengoole
Very Rev Nicholas J. Irwin PP
Parochial House, Gortnahoe,
Thurles, Co Tipperary
Tel 056-8834855

HOLY CROSS
Holy Cross Abbey, Holy Cross
St Cataldus, Ballycahill
Very Rev Celsus Tierney PP
Parochial House, Holy Cross Abbey,
Thurles, Co Tipperary
Tel 0504-43124
Rev Michael Mullaney CC
Ballycahill, Thurles, Co Tipperary
Tel 0504-26080

HOSPITAL
St John the Baptist, Hospital
Sacred Heart, Herbertstown
Very Rev Canon Conor Ryan PP, VF
Castlefarm, Hospital, Co Limerick
Tel 061-383108
Rev Sean Fennelly *(Chaplain, St John the Baptist Community School)*
Barrisfarm. Hospital, Co Limerick
Tel 061-383565

KILBEHENNY
St Joseph's, Kilbehenny,
St Patrick's, Anglesboro
Very Rev Richard Kelly PP
Kilbehenny, Mitchelstown, Co Cork
Tel 025-24040

KILCOMMON
St Patrick's, Kilcommon
St Joseph's, Hollyford
Our Lady of the Visitation, Rearcross
Very Rev Daniel Woods PP
Kilcommon, Thurles, Co Limerick
Tel 062-78103
Very Rev Patrick O'Gorman AP
Golden, Co Tipperary
Tel 087-6347773

KILLENAULE
St Mary's, Killenaule
St Joseph the Worker, Moyglass
Very Rev James O'Donnell PP
Killenaule, Co Tipperary
Tel 052-9156244

KILTEELY
SS Patrick & Brigid, Kilteely
St Bridget's, Dromkeen
Very Rev Joseph Tynan PP
Kilteely, Co Limerick
Tel 061-384213

KNOCKAINEY
Our Lady, Knockainey
St Patrick's, Patrickswell
Very Rev Edward Cleary PP
Knockainey, Hospital,
Co Limerick
Tel 061-584873

KNOCKAVILLA
Assumption, Knockavilla
St Bridget's, Donaskeigh
Very Rev James Egan PP
Knockavilla, Dundrum,
Co Tipperary
Tel 062-71157

KNOCKLONG
St Joseph's, Knocklong
St Patrick's, Glenbrohane
Very Rev Joe Tynan Adm
Kilteely, Co Limerick
Tel 061-384213

LATTIN AND CULLEN
Assumption, Lattin
St Patrick's, Cullen
Very Rev Michael Kennedy PP
Lattin, Co Tipperary
Tel 087-4147229
Very Rev John Egan AP
Cullen, Co Tipperary
Tel 086-8871961

LOUGHMORE
Nativity of Our Lady, Loughmore
St John the Baptist, Castleiney
Very Rev Dominic Meehan PP
Church Avenue,
Templemore, Co Tipperary
Very Rev Mgr Maurice Dooley AP
Loughmore,
Templemore, Co Tipperary
Tel 0504-31375

MOYCARKEY
St Peter's, Moycarkey
St James's, Two-Mile-Borris
Our Lady & St Kevin, Littleton
Very Rev Thomas Fogarty PP
Ballydavid, Littleton,
Thurles, Co Tipperary
Tel 0504-44317
Very Rev George Bourke AP
Moycarkey,
Thurles, Co Tipperary
Tel 0504-44227

MULLINAHONE
St Michael's
Very Rev Daniel O'Gorman PP
Mullinahone, Co Tipperary
Tel 052-9153152

MURROE AND BOHER
Holy Rosary, Murroe
St Patrick's, Boher
Very Rev Loughlin Brennan PP, VF
Liscreagh, Murroe, Co Limerick
Tel 061-386227
Very Rev Canon Thomas J. Ryan AP
Bohergar, Brittas, Co Limerick
Tel 061-352223

NEW INN
Our Lady Queen, New Inn,
St Bartholomew's, Knockgrafton
Very Rev Robert Fletcher PP
New Inn, Cashel, Co Tipperary
Tel 087-4147229

NEWPORT
Most Holy Redeemer, Newport
Our Lady of the Wayside, Birdhill
Our Lady of Lourdes, Toor
Very Rev John O'Keeffe PP
Birdhill, Killaloe,
Co Tipperary
Tel 061-379172
Very Rev Joseph Delaney AP
Clonbealy, Newport,
Co Tipperary
Tel 061-378126

PALLASGREEN
St John the Baptist, Pallasgreen
St Brigid's, Templebraden
Very Rev Tomás O'Connell PP
Pallasgreen, Co Limerick
Tel 061-384114

SOLOHEAD
Sacred Heart, Oola
Very Rev John Morris PP
Solohead, Co Limerick
Tel 062-47614

TEMPLEMORE
Sacred Heart, Templemore
St Anne's, Clonmore
St James's, Killea
Very Rev Conor Hayes PP
Templemore, Co Tipperary
Tel 0504-31684

ARCHDIOCESE OF CASHEL AND EMLY

TEMPLETUOHY
Sacred Heart, Templetuohy
St Mary's, Moyne
Very Rev Patrick Murphy PP
Templetuohy, Thurles,
Co Tipperary
Tel 0504-53114
Rt Rev Mgr Christy O'Dwyer AP, VG
Moyne, Thurles, Co Tipperary
Tel 0504-34959

TIPPERARY
St Michael's
Ven Archdeacon Eugene Everard PP, VG
St Michael's Street, Tipperary Town
Tel 062-51536
Very Rev John Beaty AP
St Michael's Street, Tipperary Town
Tel 062-80475
Very Rev Canon Liam McNamara AP
Tipperary Town
Tel 062-82664

UPPERCHURCH
Sacred Heart, Upperchurch
St Mary's, Drombane
Very Rev Anthony Ryan PP
Upperchurch, Thurles, Co Tipperary
Tel 0504-54492
Very Rev Donal Cunningham AP
Upperchurch, Thurles, Co Tipperary
Tel 0504-54181

INSTITUTIONS AND THEIR CHAPLAINS

Cashel Community School
Tel 062-61167
Mr Tony Nolan

St John the Baptist Community School, Hospital
Tel 061-383283
Rev Sean Fennelly
Barrisfarm. Hospital, Co Limerick
Tel 061-383565
Email info@johnthebaptist.ie

Colaiste Mhuire Co-Ed, Thurles
Tel 0504-22055
Rev Joe Walsh

MIC (St Patrick's Campus)
Thurles, Co Tipperary
Rev Joe Walsh
Tel 0504-22055

Vocational School, Tipperary Town
Tel 062-51242
Very Rev John Beatty AP

PRIESTS OF THE DIOCESE ELSEWHERE

Rev John Littleton
The Priory Institute,
Tallaght Village, Dublin 24
Tel 01-4048100
Rev Francis McCarthy CC
Parochial House,
Crookstown, Co Kildare

RETIRED PRIESTS

Very Rev Padraig Corbett
Castleiney, Co Tipperary
Rev Daniel J. Ryan
c/o Archbishop's House,
Thurles, Co Tipperary
Rev Seamus Ryan
Cappamore, Co Limerick

RELIGIOUS ORDERS AND CONGREGATIONS

PRIESTS

AUGUSTINIANS
The Abbey,
Fethard, Co Tipperary
Tel 052-31273
Bursar: Rev Gerard Horan (OSA)

BENEDICTINES
Glenstal Abbey,
Murroe, Co Limerick V94 A725
Tel 061-621000 Fax 061-386328
Email monks@glenstal.org
Abbot
Rt Rev Dom Brendan Coffey (OSB)

HOLY SPIRIT CONGREGATION
St Joseph's, Rockwell,
Cashel, Co Tipperary
Tel 062-61444 Fax 062-61661
Email info@rockwellcollege.ie
www.rockwell-college.ie
Principal: Ms Audrey O'Byrne
Secondary Residential and Day School;
Agricultural College

PALLOTTINES
Pallottine College,
Thurles, Co Tipperary
Tel 0504-21202
Rector
Very Rev George Ranahan (SAC)
Vice-Rector
Br Stephen Buckley (SAC)

SISTERS

CONGREGATION OF THE SISTERS OF MERCY
The Sisters of Mercy minister throughout the diocese in pastoral and social work, community development, counselling, spirituality, education and health care, answering current needs.

Sisters of Mercy, 5 Slieve Chormac,
Áras na Rí, Old Road,
Cashel, Co Tipperary E25 Y276
Tel 062-64574
Community: 2

Convent of Mercy, Templemore,
Co Tipperary E41 W025
Tel 0504-31427 Fax 0504-56078
Community: 4

1 Church Street,
Templemore, Co Tipperary E41 YE36
Tel 0504-32019
Community: 2

Sisters of Mercy,
1 Parkview Drive, Thurles,
Co Tipperary E41 V440
Tel 0504-21137
Community: 3

Convent of Mercy,
Tipperary Town E34 FF68
Tel 062-51218 Fax 062-52277
Community: 16

Convent of Mercy,
Knockanrawley,
Tipperary Town E34 YR02
Tel 062-51120
Community: 3

Sisters of Mercy, Clonbealy,
Newport, Co Tipperary V94 H67R
Tel 061-378072
Community: 2

PRESENTATION SISTERS
Presentation Sisters,
Thurles, Co Tipperary
Tel 0504-21250
Community: 22
Education, parish and pastoral area

Presentation Sisters, Hospital,
Co Limerick
Tel 061-383141
Community: 7
Pastoral and prayer ministry

Presentation Sisters,
14 Assumption Terrace, Ballingarry,
Thurles, Co Tipperary
Tel 052-9154118
Community: 1
Community work

Presentation Sisters,
16/17 Greenane Drive, Tipperary
Tel 062-80577
Community: 2
PHN and community/pastoral work

ARCHDIOCESE OF CASHEL AND EMLY

URSULINES
Ursuline Convent,
Thurles, Co Tipperary
Tel 0504-21561
Email srberchmans@uct.ie
Community: 10
Scoil Aingeal Naofa Primary School
Tel 0504-22561 Fax 0504-20763
Email scoilangela@unison.ie
Secondary School
Tel 0504-22147 Fax 0504-22737
Email sec.uct@oceanfree.net
Website www.uct.ie

CHARITABLE AND OTHER SOCIETIES

Community Social Services Centres
Rossa Street, Thurles, Co Tipperary
Tel 0504-22169

St Michael's Street, Tipperary Town
Tel 062-51622

Cashel, Co Tipperary
Tel 062-61395

Peace I leave with you; my peace I give to you

(John 14:27)

The *Prince of Peace*™ Paschal Candle celebrates the glorious message of peace Jesus imparted to his disciples. Striking shades of burgundy, forest green, and gold highlight intricate detailing while the commanding image of a triumphant Jesus Christ reminds us of his eternal promise of heavenly peace.

Part of the Classic Collection of Paschal Candles, each Prince of Peace™ *is finished with a hand-dipped layer of translucent Beeswax, giving the design a beautiful sheen and added durability.*

Cathedral
CANDLE COMPANY
SYRACUSE, NY • SINCE 1897

CathedralCandle.com

New from Veritas Publications

Stolen Moments

JOHN QUINN

978 1 80097 002 1
€16.99/£15.30

Our lives, it may be argued, are but a collection of moments, ranging from the significant to the trivial, from the bright to the dark, from the heartening to the heartbreaking. These moments are often fleeting but it can be rewarding to catch them, hold them and ponder them. Reflecting on them will trigger a variety of emotions that will help give meaning to our lives.

Following the success of his collection *Moments* (2011), John Quinn has assembled this second volume, *Stolen Moments*. The moments collected range from major – the loss of a loved one – to minor – the nuisance of dandelions – and in between embrace an unlikely variety of 'triggers' – a spider's web, the lost art of whistling, a chance remark, a page from a diary, a honeymoon bill. They can all help to nurture and heal, to console and delight. Each retains, in the words of William Wordsworth, a virtue 'whence ... our minds are nourished and invisibly repaired'.
Stolen Moments offers its readers a deep well of nourishment and repair.

John Quinn is a former RTÉ broadcaster who has published several titles with Veritas, including *Walking on the Pastures of Wonder*, *A Little Book of Ledwidge* and, most recently, *Daily Wisdom (Léann an Lae): Irish Proverbs and Sayings for Each Day of the Year* (2020), *A Book of Beginnings* (2019) and *Gratias: A Little Book of Gratitude* (2018).

Abbey Street & Blanchardstown Centre, Dublin
Cork • Derry • Letterkenny • Newry

VERITAS
www.veritas.ie

WE ANSWER YOUR PRAYERS

Health and Safety Advice and Training
First Aid • Fire Training • Risk Assessments • Evacuation • Investigation

Is your parish team at risk?
Have they had Health and Safety training?

For your free Church
Health and Safety check up contact
darren@darrenwhelan.com
01-4301779 • 087-9928031

Darren Whelan
ONLINE & ONSITE TRAINING

VERITAS
www.veritas.ie

For all your parish needs

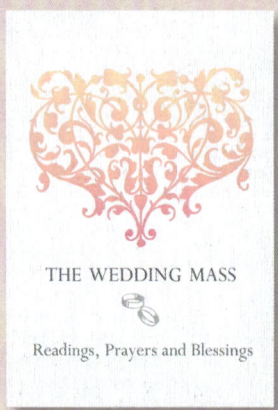

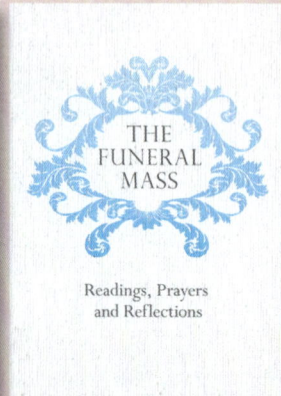

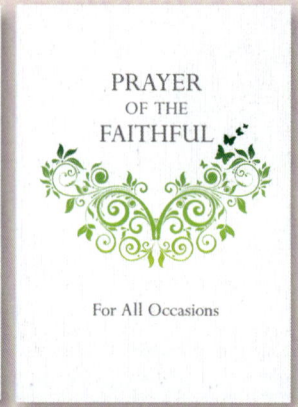

The Wedding Mass: Aids in choosing readings and also includes a selection of intentions for the Prayer of the Faithful, and poignant blessings and reflections.

The Funeral Mass: Aids in choosing the readings for the funeral Mass of a loved one. It also includes a selection of intentions for the Prayer of the Faithful; reflections; as well as hymns and instructions on how to conduct the Rosary.

Prayer of the Faithful: Aids in choosing and composing prayers of intercession for various occasions for the Prayer of the Faithful.

ALSO AVAILABLE IN IRISH!

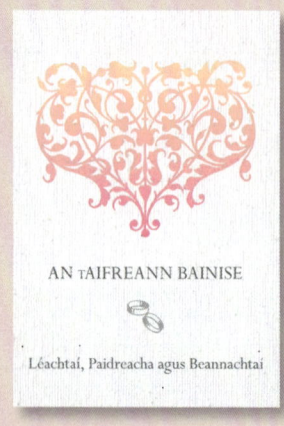

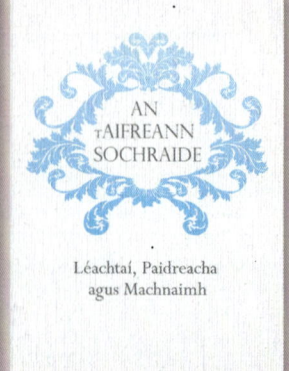

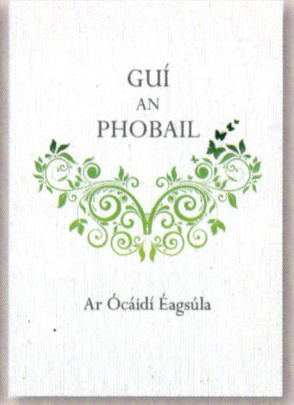

Available from all Veritas stores and online at veritas.ie
Dublin: Abbey Street and Blanchardstown Centre • Cork • Derry • Letterkenny • Newry

ARCHDIOCESE OF TUAM

PATRON OF THE ARCHDIOCESE
ST JARLATH, 6 JUNE

SUFFRAGEN SEES: ACHONRY, CLONFERT, ELPHIN, KILLALA, UNITED DIOCESES OF GALWAY AND KILMACDUAGH

INCLUDES HALF OF COUNTY MAYO, HALF OF COUNTY GALWAY AND PART OF COUNTY ROSCOMMON

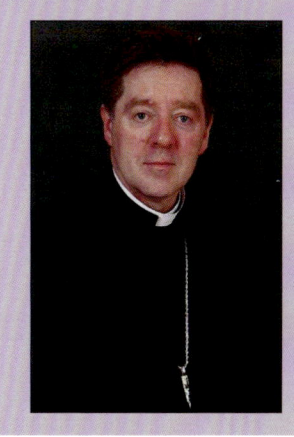

Most Rev Francis Duffy DD
Archbishop of Tuam; born 21 April 1958; ordained priest 20 June 1982; ordained Bishop of Ardagh and Clonmacnois 6 October 2013; appointed Archbishop of Tuam 10 November 2021; installed as Archbishop of Tuam 9 January 2022

Residence: Archbishop's House, Tuam, Co Galway H54 HP57
Tel 093-24166
Email
admin@tuamarchdiocese.org
Twitter Tuamarchdiocese
Facebook Tuam Archdiocese

CATHEDRAL OF THE ASSUMPTION, TUAM

The Cathedral of the Assumption is the metropolitan cathedral of the Western Province.

Archbishop Oliver Kelly (1815–34) laid the foundation stone on 30 April 1827 – before Catholic Emancipation. The cathedral was dedicated on 18 August 1836 by Archbishop John MacHale (1834–81). It cost £14,204.

The cathedral is English-decorated Gothic in style, is cruciform in shape and has a three-stage West Tower. It was designed by architect Dominick Madden. Nineteen windows light the cathedral. It has seating capacity for 1,100 people.

Among the cathedral's notable features are its superbly cut Galway and Mayo limestone, its plaster-vaulted ceiling with heads and bosses, and its cantilevered oak organ loft. Its huge Oriel window has eighty-two compartments, is forty-two feet high and eighteen feet wide; it is the work of Michael O'Connor and was made in Dublin in 1832. Four large windows from the Harry Clarke studio also grace the cathedral. It has a very fine Compton organ with 1,200 pipes, a unique set of early nineteenth-century Stations of the Cross, recently restored, and a seventeenth-century painting of the Assumption by Carlo Maratta.

The sanctuary, as shown below, was completely redesigned by Wejchert Architects in 2020. The altar is of Carrara marble with the reredos combining granite uprights with free-standing oak hardwood screens. The sanctuary floor is of Portuguese granite. The tabernacle and plinth as well as the sanctuary lamp are all retained from the previous sanctuary. Local craftsman Tom O'Dowd designed and executed the ambo. Archbishop Neary dedicated the new Altar on the Feast of the Assumption 2021 in the presence of the Apostolic Nuncio to Ireland, His Excellency Jude Thaddeus Okolo.

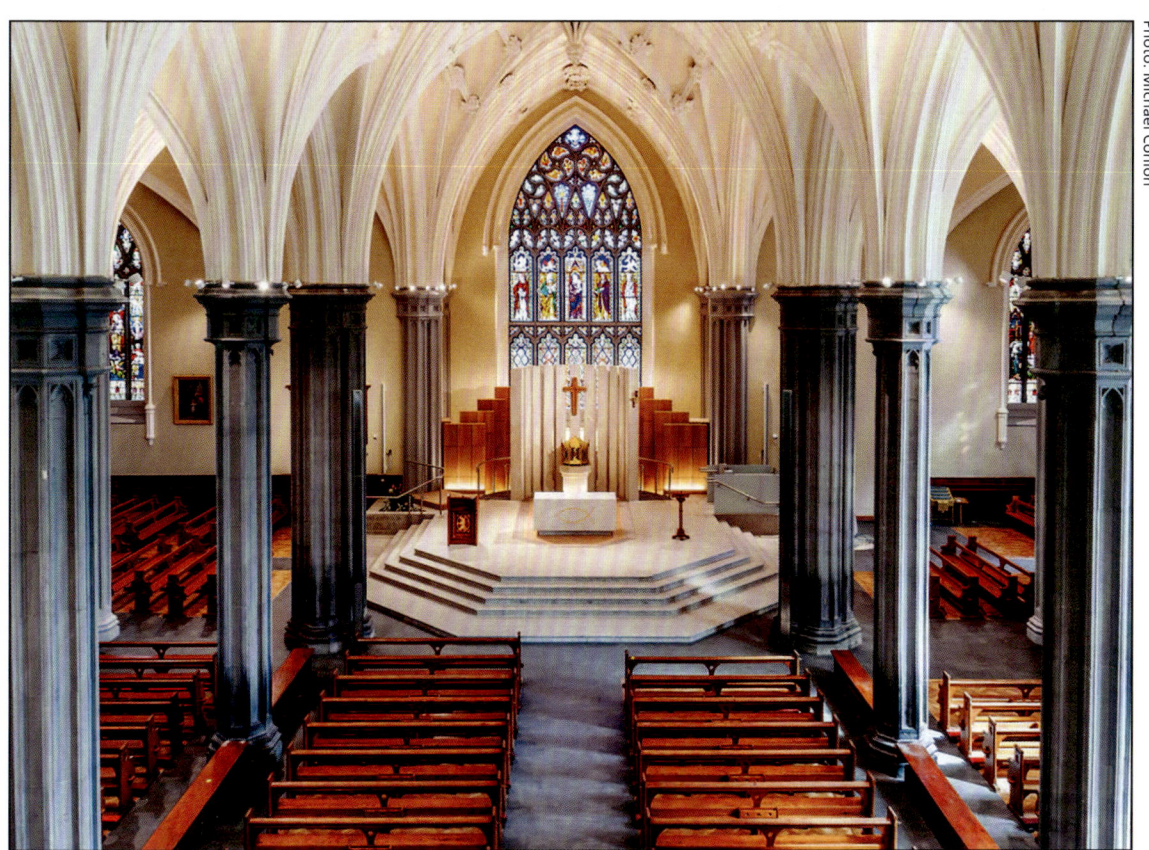

Photo: Michael Conlon

ARCHDIOCESE OF TUAM

Most Rev Michael Neary DD
Retired Archbishop of Tuam;
born 15 April 1946;
ordained priest 20 June 1971; ordained bishop 13 September 1992; installed Archbishop of Tuam 5 March 1995. Retired 9 January 2022.
Residence: Blackfort, Castlebar, Co Mayo

CHAPTER

Dean
Rt Rev Mgr Dermot Moloney PE

Prebendaries
Very Rev Conal Canon Eustace PP, VF
The Parochial House, Castlebar, Co Mayo
Very Rev James Canon Ronayne PP, VF, Clifden
Very Rev Brendan Canon Kilcoyne PP, VF, Athenry
Very Rev James Canon Quinn AP
Taugheen, Claremorris
Very Rev James Canon Walsh AP
Kilmeena, Westport
Very Rev Stephen Canon Farragher, Ballyhaunis
Very Rev Martin Canon O'Connor, Ballindine

Honorary Canons
Very Rev Eamon Canon Concannon PE, Knock
Very Rev John Canon Cosgrove PE, Castlebar
Very Rev Austin Canon Fergus AP, Mayo Abbey
Very Rev John D. Canon Flannery PE, Milltown
Very Rev Anthony Canon King PE, Westport
Very Rev John Canon Garvey PE, Ballinrobe
Very Rev Martin Canon Gleeson PE, Tuam
Very Rev Des Canon Grogan PE, Partry, Claremorris
Very Rev Michael Canon Goaley PE, Glenamaddy
Very Rev Joseph Canon Moloney PE, Tuam
Very Rev Patrick Canon Mooney, Glenamaddy
Very Rev Martin Canon Newell PE, Claran
Very Rev Joseph Canon O'Brien PE, Turloughmore, Co Galway
Very Rev Kieran Canon Waldron PE, Ballyhaunis
Very Rev Des Canon Walsh PE, Claremorris, Co Mayo
Very Rev John Canon Walsh PP, Knock, Co Mayo
Very Rev Enda Canon Howley, College Road, Galway
Very Rev Patrick Canon Mullins, Tuam
Rt Rev John O'Boyle, Galway
Very Rev Joseph Canon Feeney AP, Ballinlough
Very Rev Pádraig Standún PE, Cill Chiaráin

ADMINISTRATION

Vicar General
Vacant

Chancellor
Sr Mary Lyons RSM, JCD
Archbishop's House, Tuam
Tel 093-24166
Email chancellortuam@gmail.com

Data Protection Officer
Mr Malachaí Duddy BL
Email dpo@elphindiocese.ie

Vicars Forane
Very Rev Conal Canon Eustace VF
Very Rev Martin O'Connor VF
Very Rev Brendan Canon Kilcoyne VF
Very Rev James Canon Ronayne VF
Very Rev Michael Molloy VF
Very Rev Charles McDonnell VF
Very Rev Fergal Cunnane VF
Very Rev John Kenny VF

Diocesan Secretary
Rev Francis Mitchell
Archbishop's House, Tuam, Co Galway
Tel 093-24166
Email admin@tuamarchdiocese.org

Council of Priests
Chairperson: Pending election
Secretary: Pending election
Treasurer: Pending election

Communications
Catholic Communications Office
Tel 01-5053017
Email info@catholicbishops.ie

Finance
Ms Catherine Dolan
Diocesan Accountant, Diocesan Resource Centre, Bishop Street, Tuam
Tel 093-52284
Email finance@tuamdiocese.org

CATECHETICS EDUCATION

Post-Primary Education
Director
Sr Margaret Buckley
Email secondaryre@tuamarchdiocese.org
Sisters of the Christian Retreat
Diocesan Resource Centre,
Bishop Street, Tuam, Co Galway
Tel 093-52284

Advisory Council on Catholic Second-level Education
Chairperson: Sr Mary Corr
The Glebe, Tuam, Co Galway

Post-Primary School Retreats and Promotion of Universal Catechism
Director: Rev Benny McHale CC
The Presbytery, New Line,
Athenry, Co Galway
Tel 091-844227

Primary Catechetics
Director: Mr John McDonagh
Diocesan Resource Centre,
Bishop Street, Tuam, Co Galway
Tel 093-52284
Email primarycatechetics@tuamarchdiocese.org

Primary Education
Director
Mrs Rosaleen Crowe-O'Neill *(protem)*
Diocesan Resource Centre,
Bishop Street, Tuam, Co Galway
Tel 093-52284

CPSMA – Diocesan Committee
Chairperson: Mr Frank Burns
Garrafrauns, Dunmore

Safeguarding Office
Director: Maureen Walsh
Diocesan Resource Office
Tel 093-52284
Email safeguarding@tuamarchdiocese.org
Delegates: Rev Francis Mitchell
Archbishop's House, Tuam,
Co Galway H54 HP57
Tel 093-24166 *or*
DLP Official Number 087-4070206
Mrs Mary Trench
Robeen, Hollymount, Co Mayo
Email marytrench@gmail.com
Tel 087-9331679

Diocesan Safeguarding Committee
Chairperson: Ms Maureen Walsh
Designated Liaison Person:
Rev Francis Mitchell
Designated Liaison Person:
Ms Mary Trench

PASTORAL

ACCORD
Diocesan Directors
Rev Conal Eustace PP
Castlebar, Co Mayo Tel 094-9021844
Email eustaceconal@gmail.com
Rev James Ronayne PP
Clifden, Co Galway Tel 095-21251
Email clifdenparish@eircom.net

Archives
Archivist/Historian
Very Rev Kieran Canon Waldron PE
Ballyhaunis
Tel 094-9630246
Email pkwaldron36@gmail.com

ARCHDIOCESE OF TUAM

Catholic Grandparents Association
Contact: Ms Catherine Wiley
Tel 085-8704722
Email info@
catholicgrandparentsassociation.org
www.catholicgrandparentsassociation.org

Diocesan Pastoral Council
Chairperson: Vacant – Pending election
Secretary: Vacant – Pending election

Ecumenism
Contact: Rev Francis Mitchell
Diocesan Office, Tuam, Co Galway
Tel 093-24166
Email admin@tuamarchdiocese.org

Emigrants
Director: Very Rev Gerard Burns PP
The Parochial House,
Clonbur, Co Galway
Email gerburns1956@gmail.com

Family Ministry
www.thefamilycentre.com
Director: Máire Uí Dhomhnaill
The Family Centre, Castle Street,
Castlebar, Co Mayo
Tel 094-9025900
Email info@thefamilycentre.com

GMIT, Castlebar
Castlebar Presbytery Priests
Tel 094-9021844
Mr Daniel Caldwell
Tel 094-9043150

Immigrants
Very Rev Stephen Farragher PP
Ballyhaunis, Co Mayo
Tel 094-9630006
Email stephenfarragher@gmail.com

John Paul II Awards
Ms Trish Gallagher
Diocesan Resource Centre, Tuam
Tel 093-52284
Email youth@tuamarchdiocese.org

L'Arche
National Chaplain
Very Rev Fergal Cunnane PP
Dunmore, Co Galway
Tel 093-38124

Marriage Tribunal
(See Marriage Tribunals section.)

Pilgrimage Director
Mr John McLoughlin
3 Trinity Court, Tuam, Co Galway
Tel 087-7627910
Email latinjohnb@gmail.com

Pioneer Total Abstinence Association
Director: Very Rev Seán Cunningham PP
Parochial House,
Corrandulla, Co Galway
Tel 091-791125
Rev John O'Gorman PP
Lackagh, Turloughmore, Co Galway
Tel 091-797114

Polish Chaplain
Rev Krzysztof Sikora (SVD) PP
The Parochial House,
Roundstone, Co Galway
Tel 095-37123
Email roundstoneparish@gmail.com

Pontifical Mission Societies
Diocesan Director
Very Rev Chris Brennan
Parochial House,
Islandeady, Co Mayo
Tel 087-1962674

Travellers
Chaplain: Very Rev Pat Farragher Adm
Tuam, Co Galway
Tel 093-24250
Email tuamparishoffice@gmail.com

Trócaire
Very Rev Michael Molloy PP
Moore, Ballydangan,
Athlone, Co Roscommon
Tel 090-9673539
Email stmarysmoore@gmail.com

World Youth Day
Ms Trish Gallagher
Tel 093-52284
Email youth@tuamarchdiocese.org

Vocations Committee
Contact: Rev Francis Mitchell
Archbishop's House,
Tuam, Co Galway
Tel 093-24166
Email admin@tuamarchdiocese.org

Youth
Director of Youth Ministry
Ms Trish Gallagher
Diocesan Resource Centre, Bishop Street,
Tuam, Co Galway
Tel 093-52284
Email youth@tuamarchdiocese.org

Youth – Diocesan Youth Council
Chairperson: Vacant
Secretary: Ms Trish Gallagher
www.dyctuam.ie
www.facebook.com/tuamyouthministry

PARISHES

Mensal parishes are listed first. Other parishes follow alphabetically. Historical names are in parentheses.

TUAM (CATHEDRAL OF THE ASSUMPTION)
www.tuamparish.com
Email tuamparishoffice@gmail.com
Very Rev Pat Farragher Adm
Rev Seán Flynn CC
Tuam, Co Galway
Tel 093-24250

WESTPORT (AUGHAVAL)
www.westportparish.ie
Email office@westportparish.ie
Very Rev Charlie McDonnell Adm
Rev Henry O'Connell CC
Westport, Co Mayo
Tel 098-28871

ABBEYKNOCKMOY
Very Rev Ronnie Boyle PP
Parochial House, Chapel Field,
Abbeyknockmoy, Tuam, Co Galway
Tel 093-43510

ACHILL
Email achillparish@gmail.com
Very Rev John Murray PP
Achill Sound, Achill, Co Mayo
Tel 098-45288
Rev Nelson Joseph CC
Achill Sound, Achill, Co Mayo
Tel 098-45109

AGHAMORE
Rev Jerald David Adm
Aghamore, Ballyhaunis, Co Mayo
Tel 094-9367024

ARAN ISLANDS
Very Rev Máirtín Ó Conaire PP
Kilronan, Aran Islands, Co Galway
Tel 099-61221
Email aranislesparish@gmail.com

ATHENRY
www.athenryparish.ie
Very Rev Brendan Canon Kilcoyne PP, VF
Tel 091-844076
Email athenryparish@gmail.com
Rev Benny McHale CC
Tel 091-844169

AUGHAGOWER
Very Rev Britus Kadavunkal Francis Adm
Aughagower, Westport, Co Mayo
Tel 098-25057

BALLA AND MANULLA
Very Rev Denis Carney PP
Balla, Co Mayo
Tel 094-9365025
Email stcronansballa@eircom.net

ARCHDIOCESE OF TUAM

BALLINDINE (KILVINE)
Very Rev Martin Canon O'Connor PP, VF
Ballindine, Co Mayo
Tel 094-9364423
Email kilvine@eircom.net

BALLINLOUGH (KILTULLAGH)
Very Rev Stephen Canon Farragher PP
Very Rev Joseph Canon Feeney AP
Email frjoefeeney@gmail.com
Parochial House, Ballinlough,
Co Roscommon F45 R208
Tel 094-9640155

BALLINROBE
Very Rev Michael Gormally PP
Ballinrobe, Co Mayo
Tel 094-9541085/9541784
Email stmarysbrobe@gmail.com

BALLYHAUNIS (ANNAGH)
Very Rev Stephen Canon Farragher PP
Ballyhaunis, Co Mayo
Tel 094-9630006
Email stephenfarragher@gmail.com

BEKAN
www.bekan-parish.ie
Very Rev Brendan McGuinness PP
Bekan, Claremorris, Co Mayo
Tel 094-9380203
Email brendanmcguinness@eircom.net

BURRISCARRA AND BALLINTUBBER
www.ballintubberabbey.ie
Email info@ballintubberabbey.ie
Very Rev Michael Farragher PP
Carnacon, Claremorris, Co Mayo
Tel 094-9360205

CAHERLISTRANE (DONAGHPATRICK AND KILCOONA)
PP Vacant

CARNA (MOYRUS)
Very Rev Shane Sullivan PP
Carna, Co Galway
Tel 095-32232

CARRAROE (KILEEN)
Very Rev Hugh Loftus PP
Carraroe, Co Galway
Tel 091-595452
Email paroisteanchillin@gmail.com

CASTLEBAR (AGLISH, BALLYHEANE AND BREAGHWY)
Email castlebarparishsecretary@gmail.com
Very Rev Conal Canon Eustace PP, VF
Tel 094-9021274
Rev Dixy Faber CC
Rev Shane Costello CC
Tel 094-9021844
Castlebar, Co Mayo

Parish Co-ordinator: Mrs Mary Connell
The Monastery, Castlebar, Co Mayo
Tel 094-9028473

CLARE ISLAND/INISHTURK
Pastoral Care
Ver Rev John Kenny PP and priests of Westport Deanery
Tel 098-28871

CLAREMORRIS (KILCOLMAN)
Email stcolmansparishchurch@gmail.com
Very Rev Peter Gannon PP
The Presbytery, Claremorris, Co Mayo
Tel 094-9362477

CLIFDEN (OMEY AND BALLINDOON)
Very Rev James Canon Ronayne PP, VF
Clifden, Co Galway
Tel 095-21251
Email clifdenparish@gmail.com

CLONBUR (ROSS)
Very Rev Gerry Burns PP
The Parochial House,
Clonbur, via Claremorris, Co Galway
Tel 094-9546304
Email gerburns1956@gmail.com

CONG AND NEALE
Very Rev Declan Carroll PP
Cong, Co Mayo
Tel 094-9546030
Email congcrossneale@gmail.com

CORRANDULLA (ANNAGHDOWN)
Very Rev Seán Cunningham PP
Corrandulla, Co Galway
Tel 091-791125
Email newsletter@carrandullachurch.com
Rev Oliver McNamara CC
Annaghdown, Co Galway
Tel 091-791142

CROSSBOYNE AND TAUGHEEN
Email crossboyneparish@gmail.com
For Administration
Very Rev Martin Canon O'Connor PP, VF
Ballindine
For Pastoral Services
Very Rev James Canon Quinn AP
Taugheen, Claremorris, Co Mayo
Tel 094-9362500
Email frjquinn@gmail.com

CUMMER (KILMOYLAN AND CUMMER)
Very Rev Ciarán Blake PP
Cummer, Tuam, Co Galway
Tel 093-41427
Email belclare.corofin@gmail.com

DUNMORE
Email newsletter@dunmoreparish.ie
Very Rev Fergal Cunnane PP, VF
Dunmore, Co Galway
Tel 093-38124

GLENAMADDY (BOYOUNAGH)
www.glenamaddychurch.ie
Email glenamaddychurch@gmail.com
Very Rev Eugene O'Boyle PP
Glenamaddy, Co Galway
Tel 094-9659962

HEADFORD (KILLURSA AND KILLOWER)
Email info@headfordchurch.com
Very Rev Raymond Flaherty PP
Headford, Co Galway
Tel 093-35448

INISHBOFIN
Email office@ballinakillparish.com
Very Rev Anthaiah Pudota Adm
Letterfrack, Co Galway
Tel 095-41053

ISLANDEADY
www.islandeady.ie
Very Rev Chris Brennan (SMA) Adm
Islandeady, Castlebar, Co Mayo
Tel 094-9024125
Email parishig2017@gmail.com

KEELOGUES
Very Rev Peter Suttle (CSSp) Adm
Parochial House, Parke,
Castlebar, Co Mayo
Tel 094-9031314

KILCONLY AND KILBANNON
Email kilconlykilbannon@gmail.com
Very Rev Frank Conlisk (SPS) Adm
Parochial House, Milltown,
Tuam, Co Galway
Tel 089-2064773

KILKERRIN AND CLONBERNE
Email kilkerrinclonberneparish@gmail.com
Very Rev Thomas Commins PP
Kilkerrin, Ballinasloe, Co Galway
Tel 094-9659212

KILLERERIN
Email kilererinparish@gmail.com
Very Rev Jarlath Heraty PP
Killererin, Barnderg, Tuam, Co Galway
Tel 093-49222

KILMAINE
Very Rev Michael Gormally PP
Parochial House, Ballinrobe, Co Mayo
Tel 094-9541085
Email stmarysbrobe@gmail.com

KILMEEN
Very Rev Iomar Daniels PP
Killoran, Ballinasloe, Co Galway
Tel 091-841758
Email idaniels@garbally.ie

KILMEENA
For Pastoral Services
Very Rev James Walsh AP
Kilmeena, Westport, Co Mayo
Tel 098-41270
For Administration
Very Rev Charlie McDonnell, Westport

ARCHDIOCESE OF TUAM

KNOCK
Very Rev Richard Gibbons PP
The Presbytery, Knock Shrine,
Knock, Co Mayo
Tel 094-9388100
Email frgibbons@knock-shrine.ie

LACKAGH
email lackaghparish@gmail.com
Very Rev John O'Gorman PP
Turloughmore, Co Galway
Tel 091-797114
Rev Bernard Shaughnessy *(in residence)*
Coolarne, Turloughmore, Co Galway
Tel 091-797626

LEENANE (KILBRIDE)
Very Rev Kieran Burke PP
Leenane, Co Galway
Tel 095-42251
Email rathfran@gmail.com

LETTERFRACK (BALLINAKILL)
Email office@ballinakillparish.com
Very Rev Anthaiah Pudota Adm
The Parochial House, Letterfrack,
Connemara, Co Galway
Tel 095-41053

LOUISBURGH (KILGEEVER)
Email louisburghparish@icloud.com
Very Rev Martin Long PP
Louisburgh, Co Mayo
Tel 098-66198

MAYO ABBEY (MAYO AND ROSSLEA)
For Pastoral Services
Very Rev Austin Canon Fergus AP
Mayo Abbey, Claremorris, Co Mayo
Tel 094-9365086
For Administration
Very Rev Denis Carney PP
Balla
Email stcronansballa@eircom.net

MENLOUGH (KILLASCOBE)
Email killascobeparish@gmail.com
Very Rev Karl Burns PP
Mountbellew, Ballinasloe, Co Galway
Tel 090-9679235

MILLTOWN (ADDERGOLE AND LISKEEVEY)
Email kilconlykilbannon@gmail.com
Very Rev Frank Conlisk (SPS) Adm
Parochial House, Milltown,
Tuam, Co Galway
Tel 089-2064773

MOORE
Very Rev Michael Molloy PP, VF
Ballydangan, Athlone, Co Roscommon
Tel 090-9673539
Email stmarysmoore@gmail.com

MOYLOUGH AND MOUNTBELLEW
Very Rev Karl Burns PP
Mountbellew, Ballinasloe, Co Galway
Tel 090-9679235
Email karlburns07@gmail.com

NEWPORT (BURRISHOOLE)
Email burrishooleparish@gmail.com
Very Rev Tod Nolan PP
Newport, Co Mayo
Tel 098-41123

PARKE (TURLOUGH)
Very Rev Peter Suttle (CSSp), Adm
Parochial House, Parke,
Castlebar, Co Mayo
Tel 094-9031314

PARTRY (BALLYOVEY)
Very Rev John Kenny PP, VF
Partry, Claremorris, Co Mayo
Tel 094-9543013
Email frjohnkenny@yahoo.ie

ROBEEN
Very Rev Michael Murphy PP
Robeen, Hollymount, Co Mayo
Tel 094-9540026
Email michaelmurphypp@gmail.com

ROUNDFORT (KILCOMMON)
Very Rev Michael Murphy PP
Roundfort, Hollymount, Co Mayo
Tel 094-9540934
Email michaelmurphypp@gmail.com

ROUNDSTONE
Email roundstoneparish@gmail.com
Very Rev Krzystof Sikora (SVD) PP
Roundstone, Co Galway
Tel 095-37123

SPIDDAL/KNOCK
Very Rev Hughie Loftus PP
Rev Clement McManus AP
Knock, Inverin, Co Galway
Tel 091-593122

WILLIAMSTOWN (TEMPLETOHER)
For Administration & Pastoral Services
Very Rev Eugene O'Boyle PP
Parochial House,
Williamstown, Co Galway
Tel 094-9659962

PRIESTS OF THE DIOCESE ELSEWHERE

Rev Éamon Conway
Mary Immaculate College,
University of Limerick,
South Circular Road, Limerick
Rev Thomas Gallagher
Cloughmore, Achill, Co Mayo
Very Rev Gerard Needham
Louisburgh, Co Mayo
Very Rev James O'Grady
Headford, Co Galway
Rev Gerard Quirke
Priestly Society of St Peter
Rev Bernard, Shaughnessy
The Parochial House, Coolarne,
Athenry, Co Galway H65 X796
Tel 091-797626
Rev Michael Whelan
c/o Archbishop's House

RETIRED PRIESTS

Very Rev Pádraig Audley PE
Leitir Mealláin, Co na Gaillimhe
Rev James Buggy
Castlebar, Co Mayo
Very Rev Colm Burke PE
Queen of Peace Nursing Home,
Knock, Co Mayo
Very Rev Éamonn Canon Concannon PE
Ballyhowley, Knock, Co Mayo
Very Rev John Canon Cosgrove PE
Claremorris, Co Mayo
Very Rev Séamus Cunnane PE
Grove House, Tuam, Co Galway
Very Rev Patrick Donnellan PE
25 Drisín, Knocknacarra, Galway
Very Rev Frank Fahey
Ballintubber, Claremorris, Co Mayo
Very Rev John D., Canon Flannery PE
Cartron, Milltown, Co Galway
Very Rev John Canon Garvey PE
Clonbur Road, Ballinrobe, Co Mayo
Very Rev Patrick Gill
Louisburgh, Co Mayo
Very Rev Martin Canon Gleeson PE
Tuam, Co Galway
Very Rev Michael Canon Goaley PE
Glenamaddy, Co Galway
Very Rev Des Canon Grogan PE
Partry, Claremorris, Co Mayo
Very Rev Enda Canon Howley
College Road, Galway
Very Rev Christopher Kilkelly PE
c/o Archbishop's House,
Tuam, Co Galway
Very Rev Anthony King PE
Westport, Co Mayo
Very Rev John McCarthy PE
Carrowmore Meadows, Knock, Co Mayo
Rt Rev Mgr Dermot Moloney PE
5 Gold Cave Crescent, Tuam, Co Galway
Tel 093-52946
Very Rev Joseph Canon Moloney PE
Grove House, Tuam, Co Galway
Very Rev Patrick Mooney
Glenamaddy, Co Galway
Very Rev Patrick Canon Mullins PE
Tuam, Co Galway
Rev Anthony Neville
Moycullen, Co Galway
Very Rev Martin Canon Newell PE
Claran, Ower PO, Co Galway
Rt Rev John O'Boyle
Dalysfort Road, Salthill, Galway
Very Rev Joseph Canon O'Brien
Lakcaghmore, Turloughmore, Co Galway
Rev Éamon Ó Conghaile
Ard Thiar, Carna, Co na Gaillimhe
Rev Michael O'Malley
c/o Archbishop's House,
Tuam, Co Galway
Very Rev Pádraig Canon Standún
Cill Chiaráin
Very Rev Kieran Waldron PE
Devlis, Ballyhaunis, Co Mayo
Very Rev Desmond Canon Walsh PE
Claremorris, Co Mayo
Very Rev John Walsh
Knock, Co Mayo

ARCHDIOCESE OF TUAM

RELIGIOUS ORDERS AND CONGREGATIONS

PRIESTS

MILL HILL MISSIONARIES
St James Apartments
Knock Shrine, Knock, Co Mayo
Rev Denis Hartnett (MHM)
Rev Gerald Doyle (MHM)

ST PATRICK'S MISSIONARY SOCIETY (KILTEGAN FATHERS)
Main Street, Knock, Co Mayo
Tel 094-9388661
House Leader
Rev Gary Howley (SPS)

BROTHERS

ALEXIAN BOTHERS
Regional Residence
Churchfield, Knock, Co Mayo
Tel 094-9376996
Email cellerbruders@gmail.com
Community Leader
Br Dermot O'Leary (CFA)
Regional Leader: Br Barry Butler (CFA)
Community: 3

DE LA SALLE BROTHERS
St Gerald's College,
Castlebar, Co Mayo
Tel 094-9021383 Fax 094-9026157
Headmaster: Mr Sean Burke

FRANCISCAN BROTHERS
Franciscan Brothers Generalate
Newtown, Mountbellew, Co Galway
Tel 090-9679295 Fax 090-9679687
Email franciscanbrs@eircom.net
Minister General: Br Tony Dolan

Corrandulla, Co Galway
Tel 091-791127
Local Minister: Br Alan Farrell
Community: 4

Clifden, Co Galway
Tel 095-21195
Local Minister: Br James Mungovan
Community: 3

Franciscan Brothers, Newtown,
Mountbellew, Co Galway
Tel 090-9679906
Contact Person: Br William Martyn
Community: 5

SISTERS

BENEDICTINE NUNS
Kylemore Abbey, Kylemore,
Connemara, Co Galway H91 VR90
Tel 095-52011
Email info@kylemoreabbey.ie
Abbess: Sr Máire Hickey (OSB)
Email patricia@kylemoreabbey.ie
Community: 10
Daily Liturgy: Morning Prayer – 7.15 am weekdays; 8.30 am Sundays and Feasts. Mass or Midday Prayer – 12.15 pm weekdays; 11.30 am Sundays and Feasts. Vespers – 6.00 pm in the Monastic Church. Mondays 5.00 pm. Visitors welcome. Visitor Destination, Abbey, Gothic Church, Craft Shop, Restaurant, Pottery Studio, Monastic Church and 6-acre Victorian Walled Garden open to visitors. Soap and chocolate manufacturing by the Benedictine Community.
Global Centre Catholic University of Notre Dame, Indiana
Website www.kylemoreabbey.com

CARMELITES
Carmelite Monastery,
Tranquilla, Knock,
Claremorris,
Co Mayo F12 AH64
Email tranquilla.knock@gmail.com
Prioress: Sr Claire
Community: 19
Hidden life of prayer in the service of the Church

CHRISTIAN RETREAT SISTERS
'The Demesne',
Mountbellew, Ballinasloe,
Co Galway H53 RH61
Tel 090-9679311
Contact: Sr Assumpta Collins
Community: 3

Holy Rosary College Coeducational Secondary School
Tel 090-9679222
Pupils: 733
Catechetical and pastoral ministry

CONGREGATION OF THE SISTERS OF MERCY
Sisters of Mercy, The Glebe,
Tuam, Co Galway H54 CC43
Tel 093-25045
Community: 2

Teach Mhuire, The Lawn,
Castlebar, Co Mayo F23 YV12
Tel 094-9022141 Fax 094-9025266
Community: 2

Ard Bhride, The Lawn,
Castlebar, Co Mayo F23 W571
Tel 094-9286410 Fax 094-9286404
Community: 30

Pontoon Road,
Castlebar, Co Mayo F23 YX85
Tel 094-9025463 Fax 094-9026695
Community: 3

Chapel Street,
Castlebar, Co Mayo F23 FK52
Tel 094-9021734
Community: 1

6 Riverdale Court,
Castlebar, Co Mayo F23 VW98
Tel/Fax 094-9023622
Community: 2

Manor Court, Westport Road,
Castlebar, Co Mayo
Community: 4

1 Clareville,
Claremorris, Co Mayo F12 T622
Tel 094-9372654
Community: 1

Sisters of Mercy,
16, 28, 38, 39 St Jarlath's Court,
The Glebe, Tuam, Co Galway
Community: 4

7 Spencer Manor,
Castlebar, Co Mayo F23 XT21
Tel 094-9035240
Community: 1

7 Liosdubh Court, Newport Road,
Castlebar, Co Mayo F23 AX08
Tel 094-9035240
Community: 1

5 Manor Quarter,
Knock, Co Mayo F12 Y735
Community: 1

52 Carrowmore, Meadows,
Knock, Co Mayo F12 PH22
Community: 1

31 Carrowmore, Meadows,
Knock, Co Mayo F12 F596
Community: 1

50 An Sruthán, Turlough Road,
Castlebar, Co Mayo F23 DX80
Community: 1

Fern Hill (11, 14, 15, 16),
Knockranny, Westport, Co Mayo
Community: 4

35 Gilmartin Road,
Tuam, Co Galway H54 XV38
Community: 1

New Street,
Ballinrobe, Co Mayo F31 NP94
Community: 1

Sisters of Mercy, Church View, Dalton Street, Claremorris, Co Mayo
Tel 094-9373757
Community: 4

DAUGHTERS OF CHARITY OF ST VINCENT DE PAUL
St Louise's, Carramore, Claremorris,
Knock, Co Mayo F12 WC61
Tel 094-9376828
Superior: Sr Carmel Ryan
Community: 4
Evangelisation, pastoral care

ARCHDIOCESE OF TUAM

FRANCISCAN SISTERS OF LITTLEHAMPTON
Eden, Knock, Claremorris,
Co Mayo FT12 YC83
Leader: Sr Anastasia McGonagle
Email anastasia.mcgonagle@yahoo.co.uk
Sr Benignus Kearney
Registered charity 232931
Community: 2

HOLY FAMILY SISTERS (ST EMILIE DE RODAT)
61 Carrowmore Meadows,
Knock, Co Mayo
Tel 094-9375288
Contact: Sr Josephine Harney
Community: 4

LA SAINTE UNION DES SACRES COEURS
57 Carrowmore Meadows,
Kiltimagh Road, Knock, Co Mayo
Community: 1
Pastoral

13 Glencarra, Kiltimagh Road,
Knock, Co Mayo
Community: 1
Pastoral

13 Carrowmore Drive, Knock, Co Mayo
Community: 1
Pastoral

POOR SERVANTS OF THE MOTHER OF GOD
SMG Sisters, Main Street,
Knock, Co Mayo
Community: 3
Pastoral Ministry

PRESENTATION SISTERS
Presentation Convent,
St Joseph's, Tuam, Co Galway
Tel 093-24111 Fax 093-25584
Community: 20
Community and pastoral ministry

Presentation Convent,
Athenry, Co Galway
Tel 091-844077
Community: 11
School and pastoral ministry

SISTERS OF OUR LADY OF APOSTLES
52 Elm Park, Claremorris,
Co Mayo F12 T0A9
Tel 094-9373569
Community: 1

SACRED HEART SISTERS OF JESUS AND MARY
Fatima House, Carramore North,
Knock, Co Mayo F12 FK49
Tel 094-9388719
Community: 4

ST JOSEPH OF THE SACRED HEART SISTERS
14 Glencara, Kiltimagh Road,
Knock, Co Mayo
Sr Elizabeth McGoldrick

ST LOUIS SISTERS
17 Manor Quarter, Cavanagh Road,
Knock, Co Mayo
Community: 4
Prayer ministry

Brook Lodge, Ballyhaunis Road,
Knock, Co Mayo
Community: 3
Kiltimagh Community School: 730

EDUCATIONAL INSTITUTIONS

St Colman's College
Claremorris, Co Mayo
Tel 094-9371442
Principal: Roy Hession
Chaplain: Very Rev Peter Gannon PP
Claremorris

St Jarlath's College
Tuam, Co Galway
Tel 093-24342
www.jarlaths.ie
President: Mr John Kelly
Tel 093-24248
Email presidentsjc@jarlaths.ie
Chaplain: Rev Francis Mitchell
Email admin@tuamarchdiocese.org
Tel 093-24166

CHARITABLE AND OTHER SOCIETIES

ACCORD
Tuam Parish Centre, Dublin Road,
Tuam, Co Galway
Tel 094-9022214
Contact: Very Rev Conal Canon Eustace

Apostolic Work Society
Branches at:
Abbeyknockmoy, Athenry, Achill,
Ballinrobe, Ballyhaunis, Barnaderg, Balla,
Belcarra, Brickens, Bekan, Castlebar,
Claremorris, Carnacon, Claran, Clifden,
Clonberne, Cortoon, Corofin,
Caherlistrane, Dunmore, Glenamaddy,
Headford, Kilkerrin, Knock, Kilconly,
Lavally, Leenane, Louisburgh, Monivea,
Mountbellew, Moylough, Newport,
Tooreen, Westport, Robeen, Roundfort,
Tuam, Tiernaul

Cenacolo Community
Our Lady of Knock,
Aughaboy, Knock, Co Mayo
Contact: Frank Walsh
Tel 087-9096007
Jean Ward
Tel 087-2687040
Email cenacolocommunityireland@yahoo.ie

Society of St Vincent de Paul
Conferences at: Castlebar, Tuam,
Athenry, Westport, Dunmore,
Claremorris, Ballyhaunis, Ballinrobe,
Ballinlough, Headford, Monivea.

DIOCESE OF ACHONRY

PATRONS OF THE DIOCESE
ST NATHY, 9 AUGUST; ST ATTRACTA, 12 AUGUST

INCLUDES PARTS OF COUNTIES MAYO, ROSCOMMON AND SLIGO

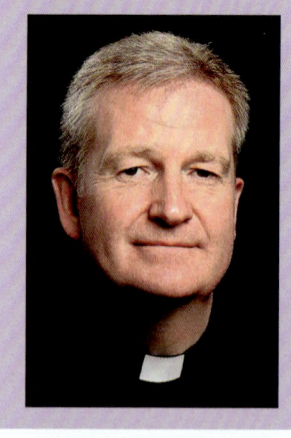

Most Rev Paul Dempsey DD
Bishop of Achonry;
born 20 April 1971;
ordained priest 6 July 1997;
ordained Bishop of Achonry
30 August 2020

Residence: Bishop's House,
Convent Road, Ballaghaderreen,
Co Roscommon F45 H004
Tel 094-9860034
Email
bishop@achonrydiocese.org
Website www.achonrydiocese.org

CATHEDRAL OF THE ANNUNCIATION AND ST NATHY, BALLAGHADERREEN

The building of the cathedral was begun in 1855 by Bishop Durcan. The architects were Messrs Hadfield & Goldie of Sheffield, while the Clerk of Works was Mr Charles Barker. It was completed in 1860.

The style is simple Gothic, known as Early English, of the Gothic Revival. The original intention was to have the roof fan-vaulted in wood and plaster, but it was abandoned owing to cost, and was finished in open timbers. The plan for a spire also had to be abandoned. This, however, was built in 1905 by Bishop Lyster, and a carillon of bells was installed.

The organ was built with continental pipes by Chestnutt of Waterford in 1925. The sanctuary was reconstructed to conform to the liturgical reforms of Vatican II in 1972. The baptistry in the left-hand Side Chapel was donated by Lydia Viscountess Dillon in memory of Charles Henry Viscount Dillon who died on 18 November 1865. The Apostles' Creed is carved on the baptistry lid.

There are commemorative plaques to former bishops of Achonry in the left-hand side Chapel: Bishops McNicholas, Durcan, Lyster and Morrisroe.

The window in the Lady Chapel has the inscription: 'This window to the Glory of God and Honour of the Blessed Virgin Mary was erected by united subscription of the Bishop, Clergy and 19 inhabitants of the Parish and neighbourhood to commemorate their respect and esteem for Charles Strickland and his wife Maria of Loughglynn and their zealous assistance in the erection of the Cathedral Church in 1860.' Charles Strickland was agent for Lord Dillon and was associated with the building of the neighbouring town of Charlestown and its church.

DIOCESE OF ACHONRY

ADMINISTRATION

Vicar General
Very Rev Dermot Meehan
Parochial House, Swinford, Co Mayo
Tel 094-9251790

College of Consultors
Very Rev Dermot Meehan
Very Rev Vincent Sherlock
Very Rev Michael Quinn
Very Rev Gerard Davey
Rev Martin Henry
Very Rev Thomas Towey
Very Rev Padraig Costello

Finance Committee
Chairman: Pending

Vicars Forane
Very Rev Dermot Meehan PP, VG
Swinford
Very Rev James McDonagh PP, VF
Ballymote
Very Rev Padraig Costello PP, VF
Foxford

Church Building Advisory Commission
Rt Rev Mgr Thomas Johnston PP
Charlestown, Co Mayo
Very Rev Joseph Caulfield PP
Gurteen, Co Sligo
Mr John Halligan
Charlestown, Co Mayo

Diocesan Secretary and Communications Officer
Very Rev Vincent Sherlock PP
Parochial House, Tubbercurry,
Co Sligo F91 HN34
Tel 071-9185049
Email vsherlock@achonrydiocese.org

Chancellor
Very Rev Vincent Sherlock PP
Parochial House, Tubbercurry,
Co Sligo F91 HN34
Tel 071-9185049
Email vsherlock@achonrydiocese.org

Episcopal Vicar for Pastoral Renewal and Development
Dr Eugene Duffy
Convent Road, Ballaghaderreen,
Co Roscommon
Tel 087-9621410

CATECHETICS EDUCATION

Primary Education
Secretary: Rev Martin Henry
St Nathy's College,
Ballaghaderreen, Co Roscommon
Tel 094-9861728
Email mhenry@achonrydiocese.org

Religious Education in Schools
Diocesan Religious Adviser
Primary: Sr Mary Richardson
Marist Convent, Tubbercurry, Co Sligo
Tel 071-9185018
Email eskerglas@gmail.com
Ms Marian Maloney
Drum, Knock, Co Mayo
Tel 087-2112555
Email marianmaloney@eircom.net
Post-Primary: Rev Gerry Davey Adm
Carracastle, Ballaghaderreen, Co Mayo
Tel 094-9254301

LITURGY

Chairperson
Very Rev Dermot Meehan PP, VG
Swinford, Co Mayo
Tel 094-9251790
Secretary
Very Rev Thomas Towey PP
Ballisodare, Co Sligo
Tel 071-9167467

PASTORAL

ACCORD
Director
Very Rev Joseph Caulfield PP
Gurteen, Co Sligo
Tel 071-9182551

Council of Priests
Chairman
Very Rev Michael Quinn
Secretary
Very Rev Gerard Davey

Ecumenism
Director: Very Rev John Durkan PP
Killasser, Swinford, Co Mayo
Tel 094-9024761

Emigrants
Director
Very Rev Vincent Sherlock PP
Parochial House, Tubbercurry,
Co Sligo F91 HN34
Tel 071-9185049
Email vsherlock@achonrydiocese.org

Marriage Tribunal
(See Marriage Tribunals section)

Pastoral Centre
Rt Rev Mgr Thomas Johnston PP
St Nathy's Pastoral Centre,
Charlestown, Co Mayo
Tel 094-9254315

Pilgrimage Director
Very Rev John Maloney Adm
Attymass, Ballina, Co Mayo
Tel 096-29990

Pioneer Total Abstinence Association
Spiritual Director
Very Rev Joseph Gavigan PP
Parochial House, Kilmovee,
Ballaghaderreen, Co Roscommon
Tel 094-9649137

Pontifical Mission Society
Diocesan Director
Very Rev Peter Gallagher PP
Lavagh, Ballymote, Co Sligo
Tel 071-9184002

Travellers
Chaplain
Very Rev Patrick Canon Peyton PP
Collooney, Co Sligo
Tel 071-9167235

Trócaire
Very Rev Gerard Davey Adm
Carracastle,
Ballaghaderreen,
Co Mayo F45 W822
Tel 094-9254301

Vocations
Director: Very Rev Paul Kivlehan Adm
Ballaghaderreen, Co Roscommon
Tel 094-9860011

Youth
Very Rev Paul Kivlehan Adm
Ballaghaderreen, Co Roscommon
Tel 094-9860011

PARISHES

The mensal parish is listed first. Other parishes follow alphabetically. Historical names are in parentheses. Church titulars are in italics.

BALLAGHADERREEN (CASTLEMORE AND KILCOLMAN)
Cathedral of The Annunciation & St Nathy
St Aidan, Monasteraden
SS John the Baptist & Colman, Derrinacartha
Sacred Heart, Brusna
Very Rev Paul Kivlehan Adm
The Presbytery, Ballaghaderreen,
Co Roscommon
Tel 094-9860011 Fax 094-9860350

ACHONRY
SS Nathy and Brigid, Achonry, Ballymote
Sacred Heart, Mullinabreena, Ballymote
Very Rev Peter Gallagher PP
Lavagh, Ballymote, Co Sligo
Tel 071-9184002

ATTYMASS
St Joseph's
Very Rev John Maloney Adm
Attymass, Ballina, Co Mayo
Tel 096-29990

DIOCESE OF ACHONRY

BALLISODARE
St Brigid
Very Rev Thomas Towey PP
Ballisodare, Co Sligo
Tel 071-9167467

BALLYMOTE (EMLEFAD AND KILMORGAN)
Immaculate Conception, Ballymote
St Joseph's, Doo
Very Rev James McDonagh PP, VF
Ballymote, Co Sligo
Tel 071-9191790

BOHOLA
Immaculate Conception & St Joseph
Very Rev Stephen O'Mahony PP
Bohola, Claremorris, Co Mayo
Tel 094-9384115

BONNICONLON (KILGARVAN)
Immaculate Heart of Mary
Very Rev John Geelan PP
Parochial House, Bonniconlon,
Ballina, Co Mayo
Tel 096-45016

BUNNINADDEN (KILSHALVEY, KILTURRA AND CLOONOGHILL)
Sacred Heart, Bunninadden
Immaculate Heart of Mary, Killavil
Very Rev Michael Reilly PP
Bunninadden,
Ballymote, Co Sligo
Tel 071-9183232
Fax 071-9189167

CARRACASTLE
St James', Carracastle
St Joseph's, Rooskey
Very Rev Gerard Davey Adm
Carracastle, Ballaghaderreen,
Co Mayo
Tel 094-9254301

CHARLESTOWN (KILBEAGH)
St James', Charlestown
St Patrick's, Bushfield
Rt Rev Mgr Thomas Johnston PP
Charlestown, Co Mayo
Tel 094-9254315

COLLOONEY (KILVARNET)
Assumption, Collooney
SS Fechin & Lassara, Ballinacarrow
Very Rev Patrick Canon Peyton PP
Tel 071-9167235
Very Rev James Canon Finan CC
Tel 071-9167109
Collooney, Co Sligo

COOLANEY (KILLORAN)
Church of the Sacred Heart & St Joseph, Coolaney
Very Rev Patrick Holleran PP
Coolaney, Co Sligo
Tel 071-9167745

CURRY
Immaculate Conception, Curry
St Patrick's, Moylough
Very Rev Leo Henry PP
Curry, Ballymote, Co Sligo
Tel 087-6306938

FOXFORD (TOOMORE)
St Michael's, Foxford
Assumption, Toomore
Attymachugh
Very Rev Padraig Costello PP, VF
Foxford, Co Mayo
Tel 094-9256131

GURTEEN (KILFREE AND KILLARAGHT)
St Patrick's, Gurteen
St Joseph's, Cloonloo
St Attracta's, Killaraght
Very Rev Joseph Caulfield PP
Gurteen, Ballymote, Co Sligo
Tel 071-9182551 Fax 071-9182762

KEASH (DRUMRAT)
St Kevin, Keash
Our Lady of the Rosary, Culfadda
Very Rev Gabriel Murphy PP
Keash, Ballymote, Co Sligo
Tel 086-3429686

KILLASSER
All Saints, Killasser
St Thomas', Callow
Very Rev John Durkan PP
Killasser, Swinford, Co Mayo
Tel 094-9024761

KILMOVEE
Immaculate Conception, Kilmovee
St Joseph's, Urlaur
St Celsus, Kilkelly
St Patrick's, Glann
Very Rev Joseph Gavigan PP
Parochial House, Kilmovee,
Ballaghaderreen, Co Mayo
Tel 094-9649137

KILTIMAGH (KILLEDAN)
Holy Family, Souls in Purgatory & St Aidan
Very Rev Michael Quinn PP
Tel 094-9381198
Rev Patrick Lynch *(priest in residence)*
Tel 094-9381492
Kiltimagh, Co Mayo

STRAIDE (TEMPLEMORE)
SS Peter & Paul
Very Rev Martin Convey PhD, PP
Straide, Foxford, Co Mayo
Tel 094-9031029

SWINFORD (KILCONDUFF AND MEELICK)
Our Lady Help of Christians, Swinford
St Luke's, Meelick
St Joseph's, Midfield
Very Rev Dermot Meehan PP, VG
Swinford, Co Mayo
Tel 094-9251790

TOURLESTRANE (KILMACTIGUE)
St Attracta's, Tourlestrane
Our Lady of the Rosary, Kilmactigue
Sacred Heart, Loch Talt
Very Rev John Glynn PP
Tourlestrane, Ballymote, Co Sligo
Tel 071-9181105

TUBBERCURRY (CLOONACOOL)
St John the Evangelist, Tubbercurry
St Michael's, Cloonacool
Very Rev Vincent Sherlock PP
Parochial House, Tubbercurry,
Co Sligo F91 HN34
Tel 071-9185049
Email vsherlock@achonrydiocese.org

PRIESTS OF THE DIOCESE IN OTHER MINISTRIES

Rev Seamus Collery
St Attracta's Community School,
Tubbercurry, Co Sligo
Tel 071-9120814
Dr Eugene Duffy
Convent Road, Ballaghaderreen,
Co Roscommon
Tel 087-9621410
Rev Martin Henry
St Nathy's College,
Ballaghaderreen, Co Roscommon
Tel 094-9861728
Rev Tomás Surlis DD
St Patrick's College, Maynooth,
Co Kildare
Tel 01-7084700

RETIRED PRIESTS

Very Rev Farrell Cawley PE
Ballinacarrow, Co Sligo
Tel 086-0864347
Rt Rev Mgr John Doherty PE
(priest in residence)
Charlestown, Co Mayo
Tel 094-9255793
Very Rev Martin Jennings PE
4 St Mary's House, Shantalla, Galway
Tel 087-9476115
Very Rev Pat Lynch PE
(Priest in residence)
Kiltimagh, Co Mayo
Tel 094-9381492
Very Rev Tom Mulligan PE
Árd Aoibhinn, Madogue,
Swinford, Co Mayo
Tel 083-8997039
Very Rev Dan O'Mahony PE
Magheraboy, Kilmovee,
Ballaghaderreen, Co Mayo
Te 087-2401625

DIOCESE OF ACHONRY

RELIGIOUS ORDERS AND CONGREGATIONS

SISTERS

CONGREGATION OF THE SISTERS OF MERCY
Convent of Mercy,
Collooney, Co Sligo F91 Y386
Tel/Fax 071-9167153
Community: 3

21 Dun na Rí, Rathscanlon,
Swinford, Co Mayo F12 VK74
Community: 1

An Cheathrú Mhór, Cill Lasrach,
Swinford, Co Mayo
Community: 1

Belgarrow, Sisters of Mercy,
Foxford, Co Mayo F26 PW74
Tel 094-9256573
Community: 2

Apt B5, Cormullen,
Foxford, Co Mayo F26 K721
Community: 1

7 Brabazon Heights,
Swinford, Co Mayo F12 X456
Community: 1

Apt A7, Cormullen,
Foxford, Co Mayo F26 H9E4
Community: 1

48 Marren Park,
Ballymote, Co Sligo F56 VF63
Community: 1

MARIST SISTERS
Marist Convent,
Tubbercurry, Co Sligo
Tel 071-9185018
Email ms3tub@gmail.com
Community Leader: Sr Kathleen Gilligan
Community: 15
Parish ministry, Marist laity

Marist Convent,
Charlestown, Co Mayo
Tel 094-9254133
Email maristch@eircom.net
Community: 2
Parish ministry, Marist laity

SISTERS OF ST JOSEPH OF THE APPARITION
St Joseph's Convent,
Dun Bríd, Ballymote, Co Sligo
Tel 071-9183973
Email stjsligo@eircom.net
Contact: Sr Teresa Cooney
Community: 7
Members: 775
Missionary Congregation

ST JOSEPH OF THE SACRED HEART SISTERS
Sisters of St Joseph of Sacred Heart,
Killasser, Swinford, Co Mayo
Tel 094-9251265
Sr Margaret Maloney

EDUCATIONAL INSTITUTIONS

St Nathy's College
Ballaghaderreen,
Co Roscommon
Tel 094-9860010 Fax 094-9860891
Email info@stnathys.com
Principal: Rev Martin Henry
Chaplain: Appointment pending

St Joseph Secondary School
Foxford, Co Mayo
Tel 094-9256145 Fax 094-9256126
Email info@stjosephsfoxford.ie
Principal: Eileen O'Brien
Chaplain: Very Rev Padraig Costello PP

CHARITABLE AND OTHER SOCIETIES

Hope House
Foxford, Co Mayo
Tel 094-9256888 Fax 094-9256865
Counsellors: Sr Attracta Canny,
Sr Dolores Duggan
Treatment centre for addiction problems

Fr Patrick Peyton Centre
Attymass, Co Mayo
Tel 096-45374 Fax 096-45376
Chaplain: Fr Steve Gibson CSC

Society of St Vincent de Paul
Contact: Mr John McDonnell
Tel 087-9227552

DIOCESE OF ARDAGH AND CLONMACNOIS

PATRON OF THE DIOCESE
ST MEL, 7 FEBRUARY

INCLUDES NEARLY ALL OF COUNTY LONGFORD,
THE GREATER PART OF COUNTY LEITRIM
AND PARTS OF COUNTIES CAVAN, OFFALY, ROSCOMMON,
SLIGO AND WESTMEATH

SEDE VACANTE

Residence: St Michael's,
Ballinalee Road,
Longford N39 Y4X5
Tel 043-3346432
Fax 043-3346833
Email info@ardaghdiocese.org

ST MEL'S CATHEDRAL, LONGFORD

On 19 May 1840, Bishop William O'Higgins laid the foundation stone of a new cathedral for the Diocese of Ardagh and Clonmacnois. The foundation stone was taken from the original Cathedral of St Mel at Ardagh. The preacher at that ceremony was the Archbishop of Tuam, Archbishop John MacHale. Four other bishops, one hundred and twenty priests and an estimated forty thousand people were present.

The architect of the cathedral was Mr John Benjamin Keane. The magnificent portico was not included in the original design. This was the work of another architect, Mr George Ashlin, and was not erected until 1883. Without any doubt Bishop O'Higgins influenced the original design, which reflected some of his own life experience, having been educated in Paris, Rome and having lived for a time in Vienna. The cathedral owes something in its design to the Madeleine in Paris, and the Pantheon and the Basilica of St John Lateran in Rome. Certainly something of the Lateran is to be seen in the attempt that was made to incorporate the bishop's house at the rear of the sanctuary.

Raising the money necessary to build the cathedral was an enormous challenge in poverty-stricken Ireland in the 1840s. Bishop O'Higgins travelled the length and breadth of the diocese and his appeals for help went well beyond the diocesan boundaries. He received great help, especially from the Dioceses of Elphin, Tuam and Meath, and contributions came from as far away as Belfast. A priest of the diocese toured North America and Canada to raise funds there.

By 1846 the walls, pillars and entire masonry were completed and the roof was the next stage in the building programme. Then the potato blight came and the Great Hunger. Work had to be suspended. Bishop O'Higgins would never see the great cathedral completed. He died in 1853.

Bishop John Kilduff, successor of Bishop O'Higgins, resumed work on the cathedral. It was opened for worship in September 1856. Though the work was not complete, it was a time of great rejoicing. Present on that special day were Archbishop Dixon of Armagh and Archbishop Cullen of Dublin, and fourteen other bishops.

It was Bishop Bartholomew Woodlock who commissioned the erection of the impressive portico, with its huge Ionic columns. He was still bishop of the diocese in 1893 when the cathedral was consecrated on 19 May.

Since 1893 much additional work has been done. Bishop Hoare, successor of Bishop Woodlock, added a pipe organ and bell chimes. Later still, two beautiful stained-glass windows, the work of the Harry Clarke Studios in Dublin, were installed in the transepts. In the 1970s a major restyling of the sanctuary was undertaken.

On Christmas Morning 2009 St Mel's Cathedral was badly damaged by fire. A major restoration project was immediately undertaken. St Mel's Cathedral was rededicated on Sunday, 17 May 2015.

DIOCESE OF ARDAGH AND CLONMACNOIS

Most Rev Colm O'Reilly DD
Retired Bishop of Ardagh and Clonmacnois; born 11 January 1935; ordained priest 19 June 1960; ordained Bishop of Ardagh and Clonmacnois 10 April 1983; retired 6 October 2013
Residence: Deanscurragh, Longford
Tel 043-3347831

DIOCESAN TRUSTEES

Rev Tom Healy (Secretary)
Mgr Bernard Noonan
Rev Michael Bannon
Rev Bernard Hogan
Rev Peter Burke
Rev Liam Murray
Rev Pat Murphy
Rev Gerard O'Brien

ADMINISTRATION

Vicar General
Mgr Bernard Noonan PP, VG

Diocesan Chancellor
Rev Michael Bannon PP
Gowna, Co Cavan
Tel 043-6683120

College of Consultors
Mgr Bernard Noonan PP, VG
Rev Michael Bannon
Rev Mark Bennett
Rev Vincent Connaughton
Rev Tom Cox
Rev Frank Garvey
Rev Pat Murphy
Rev Liam Murray

Vicars Forane
Mgr Bernard Noonan PP, VG
Rev Francis Garvey PP, VF
Rev Simon Cadam PP, VF
Rev Bernard Hogan PP, VF

Financial Administrator
Rev Thomas Healy PP
Diocesan Office, St Michael's, Longford
Tel 043-3346432

Finance Committee
Chairman: Most Rev Francis Duffy
Members
Mgr Bernard Noonan
Mr Frank Gearty
Mr Michael Glennon
Rev Thomas Healy
Mr Brian Loughran
Mr Tom Mulligan

Diocesan Archivist
Rev Tom Murray PP
Parochial House, Ballinalee, Co Longford
Tel 043-3323110

Diocesan Secretary
Rev Thomas Healy
Diocesan Office, St Michael's, Longford
Tel 043-3346432
Email diocesansec@ardaghdiocese.org

CATECHETICS EDUCATION

Pastoral Renewal and Faith Development
Rev James MacKiernan Adm
Diocesan Office, St Michael's, Longford
Tel 043-3346432

Religious Education in Schools
Diocesan Advisers
Primary: Mr Colm Harte
Mrs Margaret Kelly
Post-Primary: Fr Turlough Baxter
Diocesan Office,
St Michael's, Longford
Tel 043-3346432

Education Secretary (Primary)
Secretary: Mrs Eileen Ward
Diocesan Office,
St Michael's, Longford
Tel 043-3346432

LITURGY

Church Music
Director: Rev Turlough Baxter Adm
Parochial House, Killashee,
Co Longford
Tel 043-3345546

Liturgy Commission
Secretary: Rev Turlough Baxter Adm
Parochial House, Killashee,
Co Longford
Tel 043-3345546

Sacred Art and Architecture Commission
Secretary: Rev Sean Casey PP
Killoe, Co Longford
Tel 043-3323119

PASTORAL

ACCORD
Director: Rev Patrick Murphy Adm
St Mary's, Athlone, Co Westmeath
Tel 090-6472088

Communications
Diocesan Communications Officer
Rev Tom Cox Adm
Shannonbridge, Athlone, Co Offaly
Tel 090-9674125

Council of Priests
Chairman: Vacant
Secretary: Vacant

Ecumenism
Rev Tony Gilhooly
The Presbytery, Longford
Tel 043-3346465

Marriage Tribunal
(See Marriage Tribunals section.)

Pilgrimage (Lourdes)
Director
Mgr Bernard Noonan PP, VG
Moate, Co Westmeath
Tel 090-6481180

Pioneer Total Abstinence Association
Diocesan Director
Rev Michael Campbell PP
Abbeylara, Co Longford
Tel 043-6686270

Pontifical Mission Societies
Diocesan Director
Rev P.J. Hughes
Parochial House, Mullahoran,
Kilcogy, Co Cavan
Tel 043-6683141

Safeguarding Children Diocesan Committee
Mr Sean Leydon,
Mrs Roisin O'Doherty,
Mr Liam Faughnan,
Sr Una Purcell,
Rev Liam Murray,
Rev Michael Bannon,
Philomena Lynch,
Mr Thomas Dennigan
Ms Clare McLoughlin

Trócaire
Diocesan Director
Rev Bernard Hogan PP, VF
Drumlish, Co Longford
Tel 043-3324132

Vocations
Director: Rev Seamus O'Rourke CC
Curate's Residence, Dublin Road,
Carrick-on-Shannon, Co Leitrim
Tel 071-9620054

DIOCESE OF ARDAGH AND CLONMACNOIS

PARISHES

Mensal parishes are listed first. Other parishes follow alphabetically. Historical names are given in parentheses. Church titulars are in italics.

LONGFORD (TEMPLEMICHAEL, BALLYMACORMACK)
St Mel's Cathedral; St Anne's, Curry; St Michael's, Shroid
Rev James MacKiernan Adm
Rev Michael McGrath CC
Rev Tony Gilhooly CC
Rev Joseph Ukut (MSP) CC
The Presbytery, Longford
Tel 043-3346465

ATHLONE
St Mary's, Athlone
Our Lady Queen of Peace, Coosan
Rev Patrick Murphy Adm
Rev Padraig Kelliher CC
Rev John Eze (MSP) CC
St Mary's, Athlone, Co Westmeath
Tel 090-6472088

ABBEYLARA
St Bernard's, Abbeylara
St Mary's, Carra
Rev Michael Campbell PP
Carra, Granard, Co Longford
Tel 043-6686270

ANNADUFF
Immaculate Conception, Annaduff
Immaculate Conception, Drumsna
Rev John Wall PP
Annaduff, Carrick-on-Shannon,
Co Leitrim
Tel 071-9624093

ARDAGH AND MOYDOW
St Brigid's, Ardagh; Our Lady's, Moydow
Rev Vincent Connaughton PP
Ardagh, Co Longford
Tel 043-6675006

AUGHAVAS AND CLOONE
St Joseph's, Aughavas
St Stephen's, Rossan
St Mary's, Cloone
Rev Peter Tiernan PP
Cloone, Co Leitrim
Tel 071-9636016

BALLINAHOWN, BOHER AND PULLOUGH (LEMANAGHAN)
St Colmcille's, Ballinahown
St Manchain's, Ballycumber
St Mary's, Pullough
Rev Brendan O'Sullivan PP
Ballinahown, Athlone, Co Westmeath
Tel 090-6430124
Rev Reji Kurian (in residence)
Boher, Ballycumber, Co Offaly
Tel 057-9336119

BALLYMAHON (SHRULE)
St Matthew's, Ballymahon
Rev Liam Murray PP
Ballymahon, Co Longford
Tel 090-6432253

BORNACOOLA
St Michael's, Bornacoola
St Joseph's, Clonturk
Rev Gerard O'Brien PP
Bornacoola, Carrick-on-Shannon,
Co Leitrim
Tel 071-9638229

CARRICKEDMOND AND ABBEYSHRULE
(Taghshiney, Taghshinod & Abbeyshrule)
Sacred Heart, Carrickedmond
Our Lady of Lourdes, Abbeyshrule
Rev Charles Healy PP
Carrickedmond, Colehill,
Co Longford
Tel 044-9357442

CARRICK-FINEA (DRUMLUMMAN SOUTH AND BALLYMACHUGH)
St Mary's, Carrick
St Mary's, Ballynarry
Rev Gerard Brady PP
Carrick, Finea, Mullingar,
Co Westmeath
Tel 043-6681129

CARRICK-ON-SHANNON (KILTOGHERT)
St Mary of the Assumption
Carrick-on-Shannon
Sacred Heart, Jamestown
St Patrick's, Gowel
St Joseph's, Leitrim
Rev Francis Garvey PP, VF
Carrick-on-Shannon, Co Leitrim
Tel 071-9620118
Rev Seamus O'Rourke CC
Tel 071-9620054
Rev Mark Bennett CC
Tel 071-9620347
St Mary's, Carrick-on-Shannon,
Co Leitrim

CLOGHAN AND BANAGHER (GALLEN AND REYNAGH)
St Mary's, Cloghan
St Rynagh's Banagher
Rev Pat Kiernan PP
Banagher, Co Offaly
Tel 057-9151338

CLONBRONEY
St James, Clonbroney
Holy Trinity, Ballinalee
Rev Tom Murray PP
Ballinalee, Co Longford
Tel 043-3323110

CLOONE (CLOONE-CONMAICNE)
St Mary's, Cloone
See Aughavas & Cloone

COLMCILLE
St Colmcille's, Aughnacliffe
St Joseph's, Purth
Rev Seamus McKeon PP
Aughnacliffe, Co Longford
Tel 043-6684118

DROMARD
St Mary's, Legga; St Mary's, Moyne
Rev Patrick Lennon PP
Dromard, Moyne, Co Longford
Tel 049-4335248

DRUMLISH
St Mary's, Drumlish
St Patrick's, Ballinamuck
Rev Bernard Hogan PP, VF
Drumlish, Co Longford
Tel 043-3324132

DRUMSHANBO (MURHAUN)
St Patrick's, Drumshanbo
Rev Francis Murray PP
Drumshanbo, Co Leitrim
Tel 071-9641010

EDGEWORTHSTOWN (MOSTRIM)
St Mary of the Immaculate Conception
Rev Thomas Healy PP
St Mary's, Edgeworthstown,
Co Longford
Tel 043-6671046

FENAGH
St Mary's, Foxfield
See Mohill Parish

FERBANE HIGH STREET AND BOORA (TISARAN AND FUITHRE)
Immaculate Conception, Ferbane
SS Patrick and Saran, Belmont
St Oliver Plunkett, Boora
Rev Peter Burke PP
Tel 090-6454380
Rev Michael Morris (SPS) CC
Tel 090-6454309
Ferbane, Co Offaly

GORTLETTERAGH
St Mary's, Gortletteragh
St Thomas', Fairglass
St Joseph's, Cornageetha
Rev John Quinn PP
Gortletteragh,
Carrick-on-Shannon, Co Leitrim
Tel 071-9631074

GRANARD
St Mary's
Rev Simon Cadam PP, VF
St Mary's, Granard, Co Longford
Tel 043-6686550

KEADUE, ARIGNA AND BALLYFARNON (KILRONAN)
Nativity of the Blessed Virgin, Keadue
Immaculate Conception, Arigna
St Patrick's, Ballyfarnon
Rev Cathal Faughnan PP
Keadue, Boyle, Co Roscommon
Tel 071-9647212

KILCOMMOC (KENAGH)
St Dominic's
Rev Thomas Barden PP
Kenagh, Co Longford
Tel 043-3322127

KILLASHEE
St Patrick's, Killashee
St Brendan's, Clondra
Rev Turlough Baxter Adm
Parochial House, Killashee,
Co Longford
Tel 043-3345546

KILLENUMMERY AND BALLINTOGHER (KILLENUMMERY AND KILLERY)
St Mary's, Killenummery
St Michael's, Killavoggy
St Teresa's, Ballintogher
Rev Patsy McDermott PP
Killenummery, Dromahair,
via Sligo, Co Leitrim
Tel 071-9164125

KILLOE
St Mary's, Ennybegs
St Oliver Plunkett's, Cullyfad
Rev Sean Casey PP
Ennybegs, Longford
Tel 043-3323119

KILTUBRID
St Brigid's, Drumcong
St Joseph's, Rantogue
Rev Tomás Flynn PP
Drumcong, Carrick-on-Shannon,
Co Leitrim
Tel 071-9642021

LANESBORO (RATHCLINE)
St Mary's, Lanesboro
Rev Sergiusz Rudczenko
Lanesboro, Co Longford
Tel 043-3321166

LEGAN AND BALLYCLOGHAN (KILGLASS AND RATHREAGH)
Nativity of the Blessed Virgin Mary, Lenamore
St Ann's, Ballycloghan
Rev Charles Healy PP
Carrickedmond, Co Longford
Tel 044-9357442

LOUGH GOWNA AND MULLINALAGHTA (SCRABBY AND COLMCILLE EAST)
Holy Family, Lough Gowna
St Columba's, Mullinalaghta
Rev Michael Bannon PP
Gowna, Co Cavan
Tel 043-6683120

MOATE AND MOUNT TEMPLE (KILCLEAGH AND BALLYLOUGHLOE)
St Patrick's, Moate; St Ciaran's, Castledaly
Corpus Christi, Mount Temple
Mgr Bernard Noonan PP, VG
Tel 090-6481180
Rev Liam Farrell CC
Tel 090-6481189
Moate, Co Westmeath
Rev Joe McGrath CC
Mount Temple, Moate,
Co Westmeath
Tel 090-6481239

MOHILL (MOHILL-MANACHAIN)
St Patrick's, Mohill
St Joseph's, Gorvagh
St Mary's, Eslin Bridge
St Mary's, Foxfield
Rev Nigel Charles PP
Tel 071-9631024
Rev Sean Burke CC
Tel 071-9631097
Mohill, Co Leitrim

MULLAHORAN AND LOUGHDUFF (DRUMLUMMAN NORTH)
Our Lady of Lourdes, Mullahoran
St Joseph's, Loughduff
Rev P.J. Hughes PP
Mullahoran, Kilcogy via Longford,
Co Cavan
Tel 043-6683141

NEWTOWNCASHEL (CASHEL)
The Blessed Virgin
Rev Merlyn Kenny PP
Newtowncashel, Co Longford
Tel 043-3325112

NEWTOWNFORBES (CLONGUISH)
St Mary's
Rev Ciaran McGovern PP
Newtownforbes, Co Longford
Tel 043-3346805

RATHOWEN (RATHASPIC, RUSSAGH & STREETE)
St Mary's, Rathowen
Rev Pierre Pepper Adm
Parochial House,
Boherquill, Lismacaffrey,
Mullingar, Co Westmeath
Tel 043-6685847

SHANNONBRIDGE (CLONMACNOIS)
St Ciaran's, Shannonbridge
St Ciaran's, Clonfanlough
Rev Tom Cox Adm
Shannonbridge, Athlone, Co Offaly
Tel 090-9674125

STREETE AND RATHOWEN
St Mary's
See Rathown (Rathaspic and Rossagh)
Rev Pierre Pepper Adm
Parochial House,
Boherquill, Lismacaffrey,
Mullingar, Co Westmeath
Tel 043-6685847

PRIESTS OF THE DIOCESE ELSEWHERE

Rev Colman Carrigy
Clonee, Killoe, Co Longford
Rev Liam Cuffe
Chaplaincy, St Vincent's Hospital, Dublin 4
Rev Aidan Ryan
Spiritual Director, Irish College, Rome
Rev Declan Shannon
Chaplain, Custume Barracks,
Athlone, Co Westmeath
Rev Christy Stapleton
St Michael's, Longford
Rev Hugh Turbitt
St Michael's, Longford

RETIRED PRIESTS

Rev Peter Beglan PE
The Presbytery,
Edgeworthstown, Co Longford
Rev Peter Brady PE
Lenamore, Co Longford
Rev Brian Brennan PE
Hollybrook, Drumanure,
Abbeyshrule, Co Longford
Tel 044-9357521
Rev Eamonn Corkery PE
Aughnacliffe, Co Longford N39 T2P1
Rev Owen Devaney PE
Treanlawn, Killoe, Co Longford N39 T9F3
Mgr Patrick Earley PE
Parochial House,
Rathowen, Co Westmeath
Tel 043-6676044
Rev PJ Fitzpatrick
6 St Ciaran Park, Tullamore Road,
Shannonbridge, Co Offaly
Rev Francis Gray PE
'Shalom' Tamlaght Beg, Mohill, Co Leitrim
Rev Francis O'Hanlon PE
St James' Apartment, Knock, Co Mayo
Rev Michael Reilly
Park Place, Colehill, Co Longford
Rev Michael Scanlon PE
Parochial House, Cloghan, Co Offaly

DIOCESE OF ARDAGH AND CLONMACNOIS

RELIGIOUS ORDERS AND CONGREGATIONS

PRIESTS

FRANCISCANS
Franciscan Friary,
Athlone, Co Westmeath
Tel 090-6472095 Fax 090-6424713
Email athlonefriary@eircom.net
Guardian: Rev Gabriel Kinahan (OFM)
Vicar: Rev Seamus Donohue (OFM)

MARIST FATHERS (SOCIETY OF MARY)
Rev Tim Kenny (SM)
Innis Ree Nursing Home,
Ballyleague, Lanesboro,
Co Longford

BROTHERS

MARIST BROTHERS
Champagnat House, Athlone,
Co Westmeath
Tel 090-6476032
Superior: Br P.J. McGowan
Community: 3

Marist College,
Athlone, Co Westmeath
Tel 090-6474491
Secondary pupils: 510

SISTERS

CONGREGATION OF THE SISTERS OF MERCY
Sisters of Mercy,
Shalom, Edgeworthstown,
Co Longford N39 TW44
Tel 043-71852 Fax 043-72989
Community: 4

Upper Main Street,
Ballymahon, Co Longford N39 XTD1
Tel 090-6432532
Community: 3

7 Mill Street,
Drumlish, Co Longford N39 X500
Tel 043-29585
Community: 1

Sisters of Mercy, 61 Cnoc na Greine,
Granard, Co Longford N39 XD57
Tel 043-6686563
Community: 1

Shannagh Grove,
Mohill, Co Leitrim N41 X067
Tel 071-9631064
Community: 2

19 Midara Gardens,
Longford N39 W8C2
Tel/Fax 043-3346702
Community: 1

Sisters of Mercy,
The Lodge,
Drumshanbo, Co Leitrim N41 CF64
Tel 071-9641308
Community: 2

19 Cara Court,
Carrick-on-Shannon,
Co Leitrim N41 HP08
Tel 071-9622582
Community: 1

29 Cluain Doire,
Newtownforbes,
Co Longford N39 AN25
Community: 1

107 Mostrim Oaks,
Edgeworthstown,
Co Longford N39 KN12
Community: 1

Apr 1, Boderg House,
Harbour Road, Tarmonbarry,
Co Roscommon N39 YE63
Tel 043-3326027
Community: 1

7 Oaklands Grove,
Oaklands, Ballinalee Road,
Longford N39 X4T1
Community: 1

10 St Mary's Terrace, Dublin Road,
Longford N39 C6C4
Community: 1

108 Mostrim Oaks,
Edgeworthstown,
Co Longford N39 RH67
Community: 1

Convent of Mercy, St Joseph's Road,
Longford N39 C4E4
Community: 20

Sisters of Mercy,
8 St Patrick's Terrace,
Major Well Road, Longford N39 P6Y9
Community: 1

Sisters of Mercy,
10 St Patrick's Terrace,
Longford N39 R9Y7
Community: 1

Rose Cottage,
Ardagh Road, Feraghfad,
Longford N39 P9D3
Community: 1

Sisters of Mercy,
St Joseph's Way, Dublin Road,
Longford N39 C4E4
Community: 6

7 Ard Michael, Ballinalee Road,
Longford N39 T6T3
Community: 1

LA SAINTE UNION DES SACRES COEURS
11 Retreat Park, Athlone,
Co Westmeath
Community: 2
Pastoral

Secondary School (day)
Pupils: 650
Principal: Mr Noel Casey
Tel 090-6474777/6475524
Fax 090-6476356
Email bower@iol.ie

Banagher, Co Offaly
Tel 0509-51319
Email lsu1@eircom.net
Community: 7
Teaching, Parish care of the Sick and Frail Elderly

11 Sonas Care Home,
Cloghanboy, Ballymahon Road,
Athlone, Co Westmeath
Community: 3

MARIST SISTERS
Marist Convent
Carrick-on-Shannon, Co Leitrim
Tel 071-9620010
Email carrickmarist@gmail.com
Co-ordinator: Sr Elizabeth Gilmartin
Community: 9

7 Summerhill Grove,
Carrick-on-Shannon, Co Leitrim
Tel 071-9621396
Community: 2

CONGREGATION OF OUR LADY OF THE MISSIONS SISTERS
Ratharney, Abbeyshrule,
Co Longford N39 RX29
Tel 044-9357827
Community: 1 retired sister
Parish ministry

POOR CLARES
Poor Clare Monastery of Perpetual Adoration, Drumshanbo,
Co Leitrim
Abbess: Mother Jemma Hayag
Community: 6
Contemplatives
Perpetual adoration of the Blessed Sacrament
Fax 071-9640789

ST JOSEPH OF CLUNY SISTERS
St Joseph's Convent,
Main Street, Ferbane,
Co Offaly
Tel 090-6454324
Email stjf@eircom.net
Superior: Sr Benedict Behan
Community: 3
Pastoral Ministry

EDUCATIONAL INSTITUTIONS

St Mel's College, Longford
Tel 043-3346469
Principal: Mr Declan Rowley

Athlone Institute of Technology
Athlone, Co Westmeath
Chaplain: Rev Seamus Casey
Tel 090-6424400
Res: 11 Auburn Heights, Athlone,
Co Westmeath
Tel 090-6478318

DIOCESE OF CLOGHER

PATRON OF THE DIOCESE
ST MACARTAN, 24 MARCH

INCLUDES COUNTY MONAGHAN, MOST OF COUNTY FERMANAGH
AND PORTIONS OF COUNTIES TYRONE, DONEGAL, LOUTH AND CAVAN

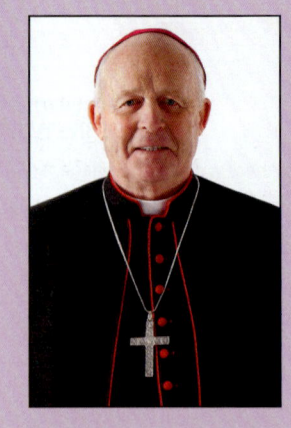

Most Rev Lawrence Duffy DD
Bishop of Clogher;
born 27 November 1951;
ordained priest 13 June 1976
ordained Bishop of Clogher 10 February 2019

Residence: Bishop's House,
Monaghan H18 PN35
Tel 047-81019
Email diocesanoffice
@clogherdiocese.ie
Website www.clogherdiocese.ie

ST MACARTAN'S CATHEDRAL, MONAGHAN

On Sunday, 3 January 1858, at a meeting of the Catholic inhabitants of the parish and vicinity of Monaghan, with the Bishop of Clogher, Dr Charles MacNally, presiding, it was formally resolved that a new Catholic church at Monaghan was urgently required. An eight-acre site was purchased by the bishop from Humphrey Jones of Clontibret for £800, and an architect, James Joseph McCarthy of Dublin, was employed to draw a design.

The style is French Gothic of the fourteenth century. In June 1861 the foundation stone was laid, and the work got underway the following year. Dr MacNally died in 1864, and work resumed under his successor, Dr James Donnelly, in 1865. The architect died in 1882 and was succeeded by William Hague, a Cavan man, who was responsible for the design of the spire and the gate-lodge. The work was completed in 1892, and the cathedral was solemnly dedicated on 21 August of that year.

Under the direction of Bishop Joseph Duffy, a radical rearrangement and refurbishing of the interior of the cathedral was begun in 1982 to meet the requirements of the revised liturgy. The artist responsible for the general scheme was Michael Biggs of Dublin, in consultation with local architect Gerald MacCann. The altar is carved from a single piece of granite from south County Dublin. The sanctuary steps are in solid Travertine marble. The sanctuary crucifix is by Richard Enda King; the cross is of Irish oak and the figure of Christ is cast in bronze. The Lady Chapel has a bronze Pietà by Nell Murphy, and the lettering of the Magnificat is by Michael Biggs. The tabernacle, made of silver-plated sheet bronze and mounted on a granite pillar, has the form of a tent and was designed and made by Richard Enda King. In the chapel of the Holy Oils the aumbry was designed by Michael Biggs, while the miniature bronze gates were executed by Martin Leonard. The five great tapestries on the east walls of the cathedral are a striking feature of the renovation; they were designed by Frances Biggs and woven by Terry Dunne, both of Dublin.

DIOCESE OF CLOGHER

Most Rev Liam S. MacDaid DD
Retired Bishop of Clogher;
born 19 July 1945; ordained priest 15 June 1969; ordained Bishop of Clogher 25 July 2010; retired 1 October 2016
Residence: Drumhirk, Dublin Road, Monaghan H18 YE30
Tel 047-82208

Most Rev Joseph Duffy DD
Bishop Emeritus
born 3 February 1934; ordained priest 22 June 1958; ordained Bishop of Clogher 2 September 1979
Residence: Doire na gCraobh, Monaghan
Tel 047-62725

CHAPTER

Dean: Rt Rev Mgr Peter O'Reilly
Archdeacon
Rt Rev Mgr Shane McCaughey
Members
Rt Rev Mgr Joseph McGuinness
Very Rev Ramon Munster
Very Rev Patrick McHugh
Very Rev Patrick MacEntee
Very Rev Michael Daly
Very Rev Owen J. McEneaney
Very Rev Patrick McGinn
Very Rev Jimmy McPhillips
Very Rev Noel McGahan

ADMINISTRATION

Vicars General
Rt Rev Mgr Peter O'Reilly
Rt Rev Mgr Shane McCaughey

Chancellor
Rt Rev Mgr Shane McCaughey
Diocesan Office, Bishop's House,
Monaghan H18 PN35
Tel 047-81019
Email diocesanoffice@clogherdiocese.ie
frshane@clogherdiocese.ie

Council of Administration
Bishop Lawrence Duffy
Bishop Liam S. MacDaid
Bishop Joseph Duffy
Rt Rev Mgr Peter O'Reilly
Rt Rev Mgr Joseph McGuinness
Rt Rev Mgr Shane McCaughey

Finance Committee
Members: Bishop Lawrence Duffy
Rt Rev Mgr Joseph McGuinness,
Rt Rev Mgr Shane McCaughey,
Rt Rev Mgr Peter O'Reilly
Mr Eamon McArdle, Mr Michael Duffy,
Mr Cormac Meehan, Mr Martin McVicar,
Mr Fintan Timoney
Ms Caitriona Lonergan
Mr Tom McGrade
Financial Administrator
Mrs Aileen Hughes
Bishop's House, Monaghan H18 PN35
Tel 047-81019
Email diocesanoffice@clogherdiocese.ie

Diocesan Secretary
Rt Rev Mgr Shane McCaughey
Diocesan Office, Bishop's House,
Monaghan H18 PN35
Tel 047-81019
Email diocesanoffice@clogherdiocese.ie
frshane@clogherdiocese.ie

Diocesan Archivist
Dr Gary Carville
Diocesan Office, Bishop's House,
Monaghan H18 PN35
Tel 047-81019
Email gary@clogherdiocese.ie

Communications
Director of Communications
Dr Gary Carville. Tel 087-1767226
Diocesan Office, Bishop's House,
Monaghan H18 PN35
Tel 047-81019
Email gary@clogherdiocese.ie

CATECHETICS EDUCATION

Adult Faith Development
Diocesan Adviser
Very Rev Canon Macartan McQuaid
Mullanarockan, Tydavnet,
Co Monaghan H18 YV20
Tel 087-2454705
Email macqua743@gmail.com

Catholic Primary School Managers' Association (RI)
Diocesan Council Secretary
Very Rev Canon Michael Daly PP
Broomfield, Castleblayney,
Co Monaghan A75 A344
Tel 042-9743617
Email dalyml@sky.com

Religious Education
Diocesan Advisers
Primary
Very Rev John Flanagan PP
Ballyoisin Emyvale,
Monaghan H18 F207
Tel 047-87152
Email truaghp@gmail.com
Post-Primary (NI)
Mrs Eileen Gallagher
St Michael's College,
Enniskillen, Co Fermanagh BT74 6DE
(Friday 9.00am-5.00pm)
Tel 028-66328210
Email eccgallagher@yahoo.co.uk
Post-Primary (ROI)
Ms Claudine Marron
Tel 086-3529498
Email claudinesh@eircom.net

LITURGY

Diocesan Liturgy Commission
Chairman: Rev Deacon Martin Donnelly
St Michael's Parish Centre,
28 Church Street, Enniskillen,
Co Fermanagh BT74 7EJ
Tel 028-66322075
Email deacon@st-michaels.net
Secretary: Dr Gary Carville,
Tel 047-81019/087-1767226
Email gary@clogherdiocese.ie

PASTORAL

ACCORD
Diocesan Directors
Very Rev John Chester PP
Roslea, Co Fermanagh BT92 7QY
Tel 028-67751227
Email parishofroslea@gmail.com
Rt Rev Mgr Peter O'Reilly PP, VG
1 Darling Street, Enniskillen,
Co Fermanagh BT74 7DP
Tel 028-66322075
Email pp@st-michaels.net

Council of Priests
Chairman: Very Rev Canon Michael Daly
Broomfield, Castleblayney,
Co Monaghan A75 A344
Tel 042-9743617
Email dalyml@sky.com
Secretary: Rev Owen Gorman
Shantonagh, Castleblayney,
Co Monaghan A75 NN12
Tel 042-9745015
Email fr.owengorman@gmail.com

Ecumenism
Director: Rt Rev Mgr Peter O'Reilly PP, VG
1 Darling Street, Enniskillen,
Co Fermanagh BT74 7DP
Tel 028-663226275
Email pp@st-michaels.net

Emigrants
Director: Vacant

Lourdes Pilgrimage
Director: Mr Brian Armitage
6 Drumhaw Avenue, Lisnaskea,
Co Fermanagh BT92 0LY
Tel 028-67721964
Secretary: Mr Jonn Heuston
Gave, Mackagh, Crom Road,
Lisnaskea, Co Fermanagh
Tel 028-67724320
Email john.cdp@btconnect.com
Spiritual Director
Very Rev Canon Noel McGahan PP
Clogher, Co Tyrone BT76 0TQ
Tel 028-85549604

Marriage Tribunal
Clogher Office of Armagh Regional Marriage Tribunal
Mr Kevin Slowey
Ros Erne House, 8 Darling Street,
Enniskillen, Co Fermanagh BT74 7DP
Tel 028-66327222
Email tribunalcloghermt@gmail.com

Pioneer Total Abstinence Association
Director: Rev Sean Mulligan CC
Parochial House, 25 Lisdergan Road,
Fintona, Co Tyrone BT78 2NR
Tel 028-82841907

Pontifical Mission Societies
Diocesan Director: Very Rev Brian Early PE
St Dympna's, Tydavnet,
Co Monaghan H18 Y190
Tel 047-79434
Email pbbearly64@gmail.com

DIOCESE OF CLOGHER

Safeguarding
Director/Co-ordinator: Ms Martha Smyth
Ros Erne House, 8 Darling Street,
Enniskillen, Co Fermanagh BT74 7EW
Tel 0044-7775507445
Email
safeguardingdirector@clogherdiocese.ie
Designated Liaison Persons
Ms Martha Smyth
Ros Erne House, 8 Darling Street,
Enniskillen, Co Fermanagh BT74 7EW
Tel 0044-7775507445
Email
safeguardingdirector@clogherdiocese.ie
Mr Brendan Kelly
Safeguarding Office,
St Macartan's College, Mullaghmurphy
Monaghan H18 YX03
Tel 087-3874742
Email dlp1@clogherdiocese.ie
Ms Anne Molloy
Dunene Avenue, Kesh Road, Irvinestown,
Co Fermanagh
Tel 078-79413855
Email amolloy164@live.co.uk
Vetting Officer: Ms Geraldine McKenna
Safeguarding Office,
St Macartan's College,
Monaghan H18 YX03
Tel 087-3874742
Email vetting@clogherdiocese.ie

Suicide Awareness and Prevention
Resource Person
Very Rev Cathal Deery PP
15 Knockmore Road, Drumary,
Derrygonnelly,
Co Fermanagh BT93 6GA
Tel 028-68641207
Email cdeery1966@gmail.com

Synodality Contact Person
Very Rev Canon Patrick McHugh
5 Killynoogan Road, Kesh,
Co Fermanagh BT93 8DF
Email pg3mchugh@gmail.com

Travellers
Chaplain: Rev Michael Jordan CC
Parochial House, Killanny,
Carrickmacross, Co Monaghan A81 PX31
Tel 042-9378105
Email michaelgjordan@aol.com

Vocations
Director and Chairman of Vocations
Rev Raymond Donnelly CC
4 Darling Street, Enniskillen,
Co Fermanagh BT74 7DP
Tel 028-66322075
Email parishcentre@st-michaels.net

Youth Ministry Co-ordinator
Chairperson: Rev Leo Creelman CC
St Joseph's Presbytery, Park Street,
Monaghan H18 C588
Tel 047-81220
Co-ordinator: Mr James McLoughlin
Office: Clogher don Óige,
St Macartan's College,
Monaghan H18 YX03
Tel 047-72784
Email james@clogherdiocese.org
Website www.clogherdonoige.com

PARISHES

The mensal parish is listed first. Other parishes follow alphabetically. In each case the postal name is given first, except where inappropriate, and the official name in parentheses. Church titulars are in italics.

MONAGHAN
St Macartan's Cathedral, St Joseph's,
St Michael's
Email
parishoffice@stjosephsmonaghan.com
Very Rev Canon Patrick McGinn Adm
Rev Leo Crelman CC
St Joseph's Presbytery, Park Street,
Monaghan H18 C588
Tel 047-81220 Fax 047-84004

AUGHNAMULLEN EAST
Sacred Heart, Lough Egish
St Mary's, Carrickatee
Very Rev Adrian Walshe PP
Parochial House, Beech Corner,
Castleblayney, Co Monaghan A75 KR96
Tel 042-9740027
Rev Owen Gorman (OCDS) CC
(Priest in residence)
Shantonagh, Castleblayney,
Co Monaghan A75 NN12
Tel 042-9745015
Email parishaughnamulleneast@yahoo.com

BALLYBAY (TULLYCORBET)
St Patrick's, Ballybay
Holy Rosary, Tullycorbet
Our Lady of Knock, Ballintra
Very Rev Canon Owen J. McEneaney PP
Parochial House, St Patrick's, Ballybay,
Co Monaghan A75 K299
Tel/Fax 042-9741032
Email contact@tullycorbetparish.com

BELLEEK-GARRISON (INIS MUIGHE SAMH)
Our Lady, Queen of Peace, Garrison
St John the Baptist, Toura
St Joseph's, Cashelnadrea
St Patrick's, Belleek
St Michael's, Mulleek
Very Rev Tiernach Beggan PP
6 Boa Island, Belleek, Enniskillen,
Co Fermanagh BT93 3AE
Tel 028-68658229
Email belleekgarrison@btinternet.com
Rev John Kearns CC
Loughside Road, Garrison, Enniskillen,
Co Fermanagh BT93 4AE
Tel 028-68658238
Email kearnzie11578@hotmail.com

BROOKEBORO (AGHAVEA-AGHINTAINE)
St Mary's, Brookeboro
St Joseph's, Coonian
St Mary's, Fivemiletown
Very Rev Brendan Gallagher PP
146 Ballagh Road, Fivemiletown,
Co Tyrone, BT75 OQP
Tel 028-89521291
Email aghaveaaughintaine@gmail.com
Very Rev Canon Laurence Dawson PE
25 Teiges Hill, Brookeborough,
Co Fermanagh BT94 4EZ
Tel 028-89531770
Email dawson829@btinternet.com

BUNDORAN (MAGH ENE)
Our Lady, Star of the Sea, Bundoran
St Joseph's, The Rock, Ballyshannon
Very Rev Canon Ramon Munster PP
Parochial House, Church Road,
Bundoran, Co Donegal F94 AK80
Tel 071-9841290 Fax 071-9841596
Email ppbundoran@gmail.com
Very Rev Canon Michael McGourty PE
(Priest in residence)
Lisnarick Road, Irvinestown, Co Fermanagh
Email mmcgourtylive@co.uk

CARRICKMACROSS (MACHAIRE ROIS)
St Joseph's, Carrickmacross
St Michael's, Corduff
St John the Evangelist, Raferagh
Rt Rev Mgr Shane McCaughey PP, VG
St Joseph's, Carrickmacross,
Co Monaghan A81 F688
Tel 042-9664367
Email
stjosephscarrickmacross@outlook.com
Rev Kevin Connolly CC
St Joseph's, Carrickmacross,
Co Monaghan A81 WP68
Tel 042-9661231

CASTLEBLAYNEY (MUCKNO)
St Mary's, Castleblayney
St Patrick's, Oram
Very Rev Adrian Walshe PP
Teach na Sagart, Castleblayney,
Co Monaghan A75 KR96
Tel 042-9740027
Rev Stephen Duffy CC
Teach na Sagart, Castleblayney,
Co Monaghan A75 PF98
Tel 042-9740637
Email mucknoparish@gmail.com

CLEENISH (ARNEY)
St Mary's, Arney
St Patrick's, Holywell
St Joseph's, Mullaghdun
Very Rev Séamus Quinn PP
Belcoo East, Belcoo,
Co Fermanagh BT93 5FL
Tel/Fax 028-66386225
Email ocoinne@gmail.com
Very Rev Canon John Finnegan PE
Arney, Enniskillen,
Co Fermanagh BT92 2AB
Tel 028-66348217
Email cleenishparish@gmail.com

CLOGHER
St Patrick's, St Macartan's
Very Rev Canon Noel McGahan PP
25 Augher Road, Clogher,
Co Tyrone BT76 0AD
Tel 028-85549604
Email noelmcgahan@gmail.com
Very Rev Canon Laurence Dawson PE
25 Teiges Hill, Brookeborough,
Co Fermanagh BT94 4EZ
Tel 028-89531770
Email dawson829@btinternet.com

CLONES
Sacred Heart, Clones
St Macartan's, Aghadrumsee
St Alphonsus, Connons
Very Rev James Moore PP
Parochial House, Clonkeencole,
Clones, Co Monaghan H23 V895
Tel 047-51048
Email info@clonesparish.ie

DIOCESE OF CLOGHER

Rt Rev Mgr Richard Mohan PE
34 Lacky Road, Drumsword, Roslea,
Co Fermanagh BT92 7NQ
Tel 028-67751374

CLONTIBRET
St Michael's, Annyalla
St Mary's, Clontibret
All Saints, Doohamlet
Very Rev Adrian Walshe PP
Teach na Sagart, Castleblayney,
Co Monaghan A75 KR96
Tel 042-9740027
Email clontibretparish@gmail.com
Very Rev Paudge McDonnell PE
Parochial House, Annyalla, Castleblayney,
Co Monaghan A75 PX20
Tel 042-9740121
Very Rev Canon Philip Connolly PE
Parochial House, Doohamlet,
Castleblayney, Co Monaghan A75 PX09
Tel 042-9741239
Email fr.p.connolly@gmail.com

CORCAGHAN (KILMORE AND DRUMSNAT)
St Michael's, Corcaghan
St Mary's, Threemilehouse
Very Rev Canon Patrick McGinn PP
St Joseph's Presbytery, Park Street,
Co Monaghan H18 C588
Tel 047-81220
Very Rev Canon Macartan McQuaid
(priest in residence)
Parochial House, Threemilehouse,
Co Monaghan H18 E290
Tel 047-81501
Email parishofkilmoreanddrumsnatt@gmail.com
Very Rev Thomas Coffey PE
Parochial House, Corcaghan,
Co Monaghan H18 H673
Tel 042-9744806

DERRYGONNELLY (BOTHA)
St Patrick's, Derrygonnelly
Sacred Heart, Boho
Immaculate Conception, Monea
Email office@bothaparish.com
Very Rev Cathal Deery PP
15 Knockmore Road,
Drumary, Derrygonnelly,
Co Fermanagh BT93 6GA
Tel 028-68641207
Email fr.cathal@bothaparish.com
cdeery1966@gmail.com

DONAGH
St Mary's, Glennan
St Patrick's, Corracrin
Very Rev Hubert Martin PP
Parochial House, Glennan, Glaslough,
Co Monaghan H18 FV10
Tel 047-88120
Email donaghparishoffice@gmail.com

DONAGHMOYNE
St Lastra's, Donaghmoyne
St Patrick's, Broomfield
St Mary's, Lisdoonan
Very Rev Canon Michael Daly PP
Broomfield, Castleblayney,
Co Monaghan A75 A344
Tel 042-9743617
Email dalyml@sky.com
Rev Seán Nolan PE
Parochial House, Donaghmoyne,
Co Monaghan A81 WP63
Tel 042-9661586

DROMORE
St Davog's
Very Rev Canon Patrick MacEntee PP
35A Esker Road, Dromore,
Co Tyrone BT78 3LE
Tel 028-82898641
Email p.macentee1@gmail.com
Very Rev Denis Dolan PE
Shanmullagh, Dromore,
Co Tyrone BT78 3DZ
Tel 028-82898641

EDERNEY (CÚL MÁINE)
St Joseph's, Ederney
St Patrick's, Montiagh
Very Rev Frank McManus PP
19 Ardvarney Road, Ederney,
Enniskillen, Co Fermanagh BT93 0EG
Tel 028-68631315
Email culmaine@gmail.com

ENNISKILLEN
St Michael's, Enniskillen
St Mary's, Lisbellaw
Rt Rev Mgr Peter O'Reilly PP, VG
1 Darling Street, Enniskillen,
Co Fermanagh BT74 7DP
Tel 028-66322075
Email pp@st-michaels.net
Rev Raymond Donnelly CC
4 Darling Street, Enniskillen,
Co Fermanagh BT74 7DP
Tel 028-66322075 Fax 028-66322248
Email parishcentre@st-michaels.net
Rev Joseph McVeigh (priest in residence)
4 Darling Street, Enniskillen,
Co Fermanagh BT74 7EW
Tel 028-66322075
Rev Martin Donnelly (Permanent Deacon)
2 The Everglades,
Enniskillen, Co Fermanagh BT74 6FE
Email deacon@st-michaels.net

ERRIGAL TRUAGH
Holy Family, Ballyoisin
St Patrick's, Clara
Sacred Heart, Carrickroe
Very Rev John Flanagan PP
Ballyoisin, Emyvale,
Co Monaghan H18 F207
Tel/Fax 047-87152
Email truaghp@gmail.com

ESKRA
St Patrick's
Very Rev Canon Noel McGahan PP
25 Augher Road, Clogher,
Co Tyrone BT76 0AD
Tel 028-85549604
Email noelmcgahan@gmail.com
Very Rev Terence Connolly PE
178 Newtownsaville Road,
Omagh, Co Tyrone BT78 2RJ
Tel 028-82841306

FINTONA (DONACAVEY)
St Laurence's
Very Rev Canon Patrick MacEntee PP
35A Esker Road, Dromore,
Co Tyrone BT78 3LE
Tel 028-82898641
Email p.macentee1@gmail.com
Rev Sean Mulligan CC
Parochial House, 25 Lisdergan Road,
Fintona, Co Tyrone BT78 2NR
Tel 028-82841907
Email pastoralcentrefintona@gmail.com

INNISKEEN
Mary, Mother of Mercy
Very Rev Martin Treanor PP
Parochial House, Inniskeen, Dundalk,
Co Louth A91 WN32
Tel 042-9378105
Email inniskeenchurch@gmail.com
Rev Noel Conlon (in residence)
Inniskeen, Dundalk, Co Louth
Tel 042-9378678

IRVINESTOWN (DEVENISH)
Sacred Heart, Irvinestown
St Molaise, Whitehill
Very Rev Kevin Duffy PP
42 Church Street, Burfits Hill,
Irvinestown, Co Fermanagh BT94 1EN
Tel 028-68621856
Email devenishparish19@outlook.com

KILLANNY
St Enda's
Very Rev Martin Treanor PP
Parochial House, Inniskeen, Dundalk,
Co Louth A91 WN32
Tel 042-9378105
Email killannyparish@hotmail.com
Rev Michael Jordan CC (priest in residence)
Parochial House, Killanny,
Carrickmacross, Co Monaghan A81 PX31
Tel 042-9661452
email michaelgjordan@aol.com

KILLEEVAN (CURRIN, KILLEEVAN AND AGHABOG)
St Livinus', Killeevan, St Mary's, Ture
Immaculate Conception, Scotshouse
St Mary's, Latnamard
Ver Rev James Moore PP
Parochial House, Clonkeencole, Clones,
Co Monaghan H23 V895
Tel 047-51048
Email frjimmoore@gmail.com
Very Rev Peter Corrigan PE
Shanco, Newbliss,
Co Monaghan H18 K303
Tel 047-54011
Email pocorragin@yahoo.com
Rev John F. McKenna CC
Scotshouse, Clones,
Co Monaghan H23 YT10
Tel 047-56016
Email jmckenna420@live.ie

LATTON (AUGHNAMULLEN WEST)
St Mary's, Latton, St Patrick's, Bawn
Very Rev Canon Owen J. McEneaney PP
Parochial House, St Patrick's, Ballybay,
Co Monaghan A754 K299
Tel 042-9741032
Email contact@tullycorbetparish.com
Very Rev Thomas Quigley PE
Parochial House, Latton, Castleblayney,
Co Monaghan A75 E953
Tel 042-9742212
Email aughnamullenwestparish@gmail.com

LISNASKEA (AGHALURCHER)
Holy Cross, Lisnaskea
St Mary's, Maguiresbridge
Email fermanaghparishes@gmail.com
Very Rev Canon Jimmy McPhillips PP
10 Knocks Road, Lisnaskea,
Co Fermanagh BT92 0GA
Tel 028-67721342
Email jimmymcp1@gmail.com

DIOCESE OF CLOGHER

MAGHERACLOONE
St Patrick's (The Rock Chapel), Carrickasedge
SS Peter and Paul, Drumgossatt
Rt Rev Mgr Shane McCaughey PP, VG
St Joseph's, Carrickmacross,
Co Monaghan A81 F688
Tel 042-9664367
Rev Philip Crowe (CSSp) CC
Drumgossatt, Carrickmacross, Co Monaghan
Tel 042-9661388
Email magheraclooneparish@gmail.com

NEWTOWNBUTLER (GALLOON)
St Mary's, Newtownbutler
St Patrick's, Donagh, Lisnaskea
Very Rev Canon Jimmy McPhillips PP
10 Knocks Road, Lisnaskea,
Co Fermanagh BT92 0GA
Email jimmymcp1@gmail.com
Very Rev Michael King PE
21 Wattlebridge Road, Drumquilla,
Newtownbutler, Co Fermanagh BT92 8JP
Tel 028-67738229
Email galloonparish@gmail.com
Rev Kevin Malcolmson CC
3 Landbrock Road, Drumquilla,
Newtownbutler, Co Fermanagh BT92 8JJ
Tel 028-67738244
Email frkevinm@gmail.com

PETTIGO
St Mary's, Pettigo
St Joseph's, Lettercran
Rt Rev Mgr Laurence Flynn Adm
Priest's House, Main Street,
Pettigo, Co Donegal F94 FYN7
Tel 071-9861666
Lough Derg (See Charitable Societies)
Tel/Fax 071-9861518
Email pettigoparish@loughderg.org

ROCKCORRY (EMATRIS)
Holy Trinity, St Mary's, Corrawacan
Very Rev Canon Owen J. McEneaney PP
Parochial House, St Patrick's,
Ballybay, Co Monaghan A75 K299
Tel 042-9741032
Email contact@tullycorbetparish.ie
Rev Jerry White (SSCC) CC
Sacred Hearts Community, Tanagh,
Cootehill, Co Cavan H16 CA22
Tel 049-5552188

ROSLEA
St Tierney's, Roslea
St Mary's, Magherarney
Very Rev John Chester PP
4a Monaghan Road, Roslea, Enniskillen,
Co Fermanagh BT92 7QY
Tel 028-67751227
Rt Rev Mgr Vincent Connolly PE
Magherarney, Smithborough,
Co Monaghan H18 H297
Tel 047-57011
Email parishofroslea@gmail.com

TEMPO (POBAL)
Immaculate Conception, Tempo
St Joseph's, Cradien
Rt Rev Mgr Peter O'Reilly PP, VG
1 Darling Street, Enniskillen,
Co Fermanagh BT74 7DP
Tel 028-66322075
Email pp@st-michaels.net

Very Rev John Halton PE
26 Cullion Road, Tempo, Enniskillen,
Co Fermanagh BT94 3LY
Tel 028-89541344
Email johnhalton19@btinternet.com

TRILLICK (KILSKEERY)
St Macartan's, Trillick
St Mary's, Coa
Very Rev Pádraig McKenna PP
Parochial House, Millbank,
Trillick, Co Tyrone
Tel 028-89561982
Email parishoffice@kilskerryparish.co.uk
Very Rev Canon John McKenna PE
Email john.mckenna35@btinternet.com
Trillick, Omagh, Co Tyrone BT78 3RD
Tel 028-89561350

TYDAVNET
St Dympna's, Tydavnet
St Mary's, Urbleshanny
St Joseph's, Knockatallon
Email tydavnetparishoffice@gmail.com
Very Rev Stephen Joyce PP
Parochial House, Stracrunnion,
Scotstown, Co Monaghan H18 X620
Tel 047-89204
Email stephen.joyce@icloud.com
Very Rev Brian Early PE
Parochial House, St Dympna's,
Tydavnet, Co Monaghan H18 Y190
Tel 047-79434
Email pbbearly64@gmail.com

TYHOLLAND
St Patrick's
Very Rev Canon Paddy McGinn Adm
St Joseph's Presbytery, Park Street,
Monaghan H18 C588
Tel 047-81220
Email parishoffice@stjosephsmonaghan.com

INSTITUTIONS AND THEIR CHAPLAINS

Daughters of Our Lady of the Sacred Heart Convent
Ballybay, Co Monaghan A75 K193
Tel 042-9741141

Finner Army Camp
Ballyshannon, Co Donegal F94 C985
Rev Jeremiah (Jerry) Carroll CF
Email jerryzulu@gmail.com
Tel 071-9842294

Monaghan General Hospital
Priests of Monaghan parish
Tel 047-81220 Fax 047-84004

St Davnet's Hospital, Monaghan
Priests of Monaghan parish
Tel 047-81220 Fax 047-84004

St Mary's Hospital
Castleblayney, Co Monaghan
Priests of Castleblayney parish
Tel 042-9740027

South West Acute Hospital, Enniskillen
Priests of Enniskillen Parish
Tel 028-66322075 Fax 028-66322248

PRIESTS OF THE DIOCESE ELSEWHERE

Rev Dr Patrick Connolly
Theology Department,
Mary Immaculate College,
South Circular Road, Limerick V94 VN26
Tel 061-204575 Fax 061-313632
Email patrick.connolly@mic.ul.ie
Rt Rev Mgr Joseph McGuinness
Executive Secretary to the Irish Episcopal Conference
Columba Centre, Maynooth,
Co Kildare W23 P6D3
Tel 01-5053000
Rev Alan Ward
18 Drumlin Heights, Enniskillen,
Co Fermanagh BT74 7NR

Study Leave/contact addresses
Rev Benedict Hughes
Chaplaincy Centre, NUI Galway,
University Road, Galway H91 TK33
Tel 091-495055
Email ben.hughes@nuigalway.ie

RETIRED PRIESTS

Most Rev Liam S. MacDaid DD
Bishop Emeritus
Drumhirk, Dublin Road,
Monaghan H18 YE30
Tel 047-82208
Most Rev Joseph Duffy DD
Bishop Emeritus
Doire na gCraobh, Monaghan
Tel 047-62725
Very Rev Canon Patrick Marron
St Anne's Nursing Home, Clones Road,
Ballybay, Co Monaghan A75 K193
Very Rev Lorcan Lynch
St Anne's Nursing Home,
Clones Road, Ballybay,
Co Monaghan A75 K193
Very Rev Canon Brian McCluskey PE
Apt 2, 2 Danesfort Park North,
Stranhillis Road, Belfast BT9 5RB
Tel 028-90683544
Rev Brendan McCague
Castleross Nursing Home,
Castleross Village, Carrickmacross,
Co Monaghan A81 X242
Rt Rev Mgr Gerard McSorley
St Anne's Nursing Home, Clones Road,
Ballybay, Co Monaghan A75 K193
Very Rev Canon Joseph Mullin PE
c/o 10 Knocks Road, Lisnaskea,
Co Fermanagh BT92 0JA

RELIGIOUS ORDERS AND CONGREGATIONS

PRIESTS

CONGREGATION OF THE SACRED HEARTS OF JESUS AND MARY (SACRED HEARTS COMMUNITY)
Cootehill, Co Cavan H16 CA22
Tel 049-5552188
Rev Jerry White
Email jerrysscc@gmail.com

(See also under Rockcorry parish)

DIOCESE OF CLOGHER

PASSIONISTS
St Gabriel's Retreat, The Graan,
Enniskillen, Co Fermanagh BT7 45PB
Tel 028-66322272 Fax 028-66325201
Superior: Rev Charles Cross (CP)
Email charlescrosscp@gmail.com

SISTERS

CONGREGATION OF THE SISTERS OF MERCY
Northern Province, Provincial House,
74 Main Street, Clogher,
Co Tyrone BT76 0AA
Tel 028-85548127 Fax 028-85549459
Provincial Leader: Sr Rose Marie Conlan

11 Castlehill Gardens, Augher,
Co Tyrone BT77 0HA
Tel 028-85548157

St Brigid's, 2 Ballagh Road, Clogher,
Co Tyrone BT76 0HE
Tel 028-85548015

Convent of Mercy, 6 Belmore Street,
Enniskillen, Co Fermanagh
Tel 028-66322561
Community: 14

6 Gorminish Park, Garrison,
Co Fermanagh BT93 4GP
Tel 028-68659742

No. 16 The Grange,
Presentation Walk, Monaghan
Tel 047-84569

Buíochas,
29 The Commons, Bellanaleck,
Enniskillen, Co Fermanagh BT92 2BD
Tel 028-66349722

St Faber's, 8 Castlecourt, Monea,
Co Fermanagh BT93 7AR
Tel 028-66341197

73 Scaffog Avenue, Sligo Road,
Enniskillen, Co Fermanagh BT74 7JJ
Tel 028-66327474

7 Friar's Park, Drumlyon, Enniskillen,
Co Fermanagh BT74 5NR
Tel 028-66320224

No 19 The Sidings,
Breandrum, Enniskillen,
Co Fermanagh BT74 6GZ
Tel 028-66326836

27 Ashbourne Manor, Charterhill,
Enniskillen, Co Fermanagh BT74 4BB
Tel 028-66426904

The Lodge, Glor na Mara, West End,
Bundoran, Co Donegal F94 NY72
Tel 071-9841818

Glor na Mara, West End,
Bundoran, Co Donegal F94 NY72
Tel 071-9833899

2 Marina View,
Dinglei Coush, Bundoran,
Co Donegal F94 WSR6
Tel 071-9829832

Ennis View,
4A Hollyhill Road, Enniskillen,
Co Fermanagh BT74 6DD

9 Roscarrig,
119 Sligo Road, Enniskillen,
Co Fermanagh BT74 7AZ

DAUGHTERS OF OUR LADY OF THE SACRED HEART
Ballybay, Co Monaghan
Tel 042-9741068
Email olshballybay@eircom.net
Superior: Sr Mary Mallin
Community: 6
St Joseph's Nursing Home
Superior: Sr Kathleen McQuillan
Tel 042-9741141. Beds: 31
Community: 5

ST LOUIS SISTERS
St Louis Convent, Louisville, Monaghan
Community: 16
Varied apostolates

5 Lakeview, Monaghan
Tel 047-84122
Community: 1

173 Mullaghmatt, Monaghan
Tel 047-84110
Community: 1
Varied apostolates

Rowan Tree Court,
24 Mullach Glas Close, Monaghan
Tel 047-38685
Community: 1

Iona House, Farney Street
Carrickmacross, Co Monaghan
Tel 042-9663326
Community: 5
Varied apostolates

4 Lakeview, Monaghan
Tel 047-84719
Community: 1

Drummond Radraic,
Dundalk Road, Carrickmacross,
Co Monaghan
Tel 042-9661827
Community: 1

PRESENTATION SISTERS
14 Laragh Lee, Ballycassidy,
Ballinamallard, Enniskillen,
Co Fermanagh
Community: 1

EDUCATIONAL INSTITUTIONS

St Macartan's College
Monaghan, Co Monaghan H18 X704
Tel 047-81642/83365/83367
Fax 047-83341
Email admin@stmacartanscollege.ie
President
Rt Rev Mgr Shane McCaughey BD
Principal
Mr Raymond McHugh BA, HDipEd, MSc

St Michael's College
Enniskillen, Co Fermanagh BT74 6DE
Tel 028-66322935
Fax 028-66325128
Email office@saintmichaels.org.uk
Principal: Mr Mark Henry

CHARITABLE AND OTHER SOCIETIES

ACCORD
St Macartan's College,
Monaghan H18 YX03
Tel 047-83359
(10am-1pm Mon-Fri)

Ros Erne House,
8 Darling Street, Enniskillen,
Co Fermanagh BT74 7EW
Tel 028-66325696
(9am-5pm Mon-Fri)

Lough Derg, St Patrick's Purgatory
Pettigo, Co Donegal F94 K725
Tel 071-9861518 Fax 071-9861525
Email info@loughderg.org
Prior: Rt Rev Mgr Laurence Flynn
Pilgrimage season, 1 June-15 August.
No advance booking or notice required.
Pilgrims arrive daily before 3 pm, having fasted from midnight, and remain on the island for two complete days of prayer and penance.
One-day retreats before and after main pilgrimage season.
School retreats also offered.
Tel for details and reservations.

DIOCESE OF CLONFERT

PATRON OF THE DIOCESE
ST BRENDAN, 16 MAY

INCLUDES PORTIONS OF COUNTIES GALWAY, OFFALY AND ROSCOMMON

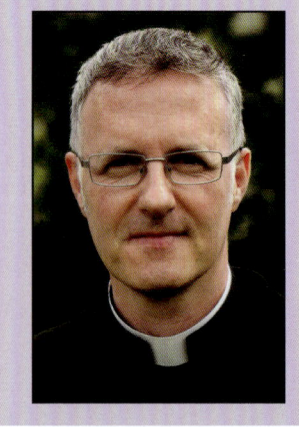

Most Rev Michael Duignan SThD
Bishop of Clonfert;
born 15 July 1970
ordained priest 17 July 1994
ordained Bishop of Clonfert
13 October 2019

Residence: Coorheen,
Loughrea, Co Galway
H62 TD82
Tel 091-841560
Email office@clonfertdiocese.ie

ST BRENDAN'S CATHEDRAL, LOUGHREA

St Brendan's Cathedral stands at the western extremity of the Diocese of Clonfert on the main highway from Dublin to Galway. The foundation stone of the cathedral was laid on 10 October 1897, and the fabric was completed in 1902. Plans were drawn by the Dublin architect William Byrne for a building in the neo-Gothic style, having a nave and an aspidal sanctuary, lean-to aisles and shallow transepts, with a graceful spire at the western end. Its dimensions were determined by the needs of the parish of Loughrea. While not impressive, its proportions are good, and despite a departure from the original plan by curtailment of the sanctuary, the overall effect is pleasing. The simplicity of the exterior, however, hardly prepares the visitor for the riches within.

It was due to two fortuitous circumstances that St Brendan's became a veritable treasure house of the Celtic Revival in sculpture, stained glass, woodcarving, metalwork and textiles.

The first circumstance was that the building of a Catholic cathedral was delayed for various reasons until close to the turn of the last century. The Irish Literary Renaissance was by then well advanced. When the building was completed in 1902, the Arts and Crafts movement was having effect.

The second circumstance was that of Edward Martyn's birth at the home of his maternal grandfather, James Smyth, in the parish of Loughrea. Martyn was an ascetic man and devoted his time and fortune to the development of every phase of the Irish revival, the Gaelic League, Sinn Féin, the Irish Literary Theatre, Irish music, church music and church art. With innate business acumen, he insured by personal donation and the financial support of the Smyth family that the new cathedral would reflect his views. The bishop, Dr John Healy, who was sensitive to the prevailing trend, accepted the challenge and assigned the project to the supervision of a young curate in the parish, Fr Jeremiah O'Donovan, who was himself actively engaged in propaganda for Revival.

John Hughes was the foremost sculptor in the country at the time, and Bishop Healy commissioned him to do the modelling and carving. His work is found in the bronze figure of Christ on the reredos of the high altar and in the magnificent marble statue of the Virgin and Child. Michael Shortall, a student of Hughes in the Metropolitan School of Art, did the carvings on the corbels and executed the statue of St Brendan on the wall of the tower. His connection with the cathedral continued over twenty years, and he was responsible for carvings of incidents from the life and voyage of St Brendan carved on the capitals of the pillars.

The Yeats sisters, Lily and Elizabeth, along with their friend Evelyn Gleeson, set up the Dun Emer guild. They embroidered twenty-four banners of Irish saints for use in the cathedral. Jack B. Yeats and his wife Mary designed these banners. With an economy of detail and richness of colour, they almost achieve the effect of stained glass. Mass vestments, embroidered with silk on poplin, also came from the same studio.

More than anything else, St Brendan's is famous for its stained glass. Martyn was particularly concerned about the quality of stained glass then available in Ireland. He was eager to set up an Irish stained-glass industry. He succeeded in having Alfred E. Childe appointed to the Metropolitan School of Art, and he later persuaded Sarah Purser to open a co-operative studio, where young artists could be trained in the technique of stained glass. This new studio, An Túr Gloinne, opened in January 1903, with Childe as manager, and so began the work of the Loughrea stained-glass windows. Over the next forty years, Childe, Purser and Michael Healy executed almost all the stained-glass windows in the cathedral, and it is these windows that have given St Brendan's its place in the Irish Artistic Revival.

DIOCESE OF CLONFERT

Most Rev John Kirby DD
Retired Bishop of Clonfert;
born October 1938; ordained priest 23 June 1963; ordained Bishop of Clonfert 9 April 1988
Residence: Cappataggle, Ballinasloe, Co Galway H53 X206
Tel 091-843017

ADMINISTRATION

Vicar General
Rt Rev Mgr Cathal Geraghty PP, VG
Cathedral of St Brendan, Barrack Street, Loughrea, Co Galway H62 YE09
Tel 091-841212

Chancellor
Very Rev Michael Byrnes PP, JV
Parochial House, Dunkellin Tec, Portumna, Co Galway H53 F584
Tel 090-9741092

Diocesan Secretary
Ms Marcella Fallon
Coorheen, Loughrea, Co Galway H62 TD82
Tel 091-841560
Email office@clonfertdiocese.ie

Diocesan Communications Officer
Rt Rev Mgr Cathal Geraghty PP, VG
Cathedral of St Brendan, Barrack Street, Loughrea, Co Galway H62 YE09
Tel 091-841212

College of Consultors
Mgr Cathal Geraghty PP, Vicar General
Very Rev Michael Byrnes PP JV, Chancellor
Very Rev Niall Foley PP, VF
Very Rev Iomar Daniels PP, EV
Very Rev John Garvey PP
Very Rev Ciarán Kitching PP

Diocesan Council of Priests
Mgr Cathal Geraghty PP, Vicar General
Very Rev Michael Byrnes PP, JV, Chancellor
Very Rev Niall Foley PP,
Very Rev Seamus Bohan PP
Very Rev Iomar Daniels PP, EV
Very Rev Declan Mc Inerney PP
Very Rev Benny Flanagan PE
Very Rev John Garvey PP
Very Rev Ciarán Kitching PP
Very Rev Mícheál Mc Laifeartaigh (OCD)

Diocesan Finance Committe
Most Rev Michael Duignan SThD,DD
Rt Rev Mgr Cathal Geraghty PP
Very Rev Martin McNamara PP
Mr Gerard McInerney
Mr Terry Doyle
Mr Patrick McDonagh
Mr Sean O'Dwyer
Ms Marcella Fallon
Rev Declan McInerney

Clergy Wellbeing Committee
Chairperson: Very Rev Kieran Kitching PP
Parochial House, Killimor, Ballinasloe, Co Galway H53 R8C4
Tel 090-9676151

Master of Ceremonies and Chairperson of the Diocesan Liturgical Committee
Very Rev Michael Byrnes PP, JV
Parochial House, Dunkellin Tec, Portumna, Co Galway H53 F584
Tel 090-9741092

CATECHETICS AND EDUCATION

Diocesan Education Secretariat
Chairperson
Rt Rev Mgr Cathal Geraghty PP, VG
Cathedral of St Brendan, Barrack Street, Loughrea, Co Galway H62 YE09
Tel 091-841212

Catholic Primary School Managers' Association
Secretary: Mr Eamon Lally
Gortnahorna, Clontuskert, Ballinasloe, Co Galway
Tel 090-9643250

Sacramental Preparation
Chairperson of the Diocesan Committee for Preparation and Celebration of the Sacraments of Initiation
Very Rev Kieran O'Rourke PP
Parochial House, Looscaun, Woodford, Co Galway H62 AK18
Tel 090-9749100

Life-Long Religious Education
Very Rev John Garvey PP
Parochial House, Ballinasloe, Co Galway H53 EC98
Tel 090-9643916

PASTORAL

Diocesan Committee for Parish Restructuring and Renewal
Chairperson: Rev Iomar Daniels PP, EV
Parochial House, Leitrim, Loughrea, Co Galway H62 RP40
Tel 091-841758

Co-ordinator for Safeguarding Children
Ms Isabella Mulkern
Coorheen, Loughrea, Co Galway H62 TD82
Tel 091-841560

Co-ordinator for Safeguarding of Vulnerable Persons
Ms Isabella Mulkern
Coorheen, Loughrea, Co Galway H62 TD82
Tel 091-841560

Youth Ministry
Chairperson of the Dicoesan Committee for Ministry to Young People
Very Rev Declan McInerney PP
Parochial House, Eyrecourt, Ballinasloe, Co Galway H53 KX85
Tel 090-9675113

Marriage and Family Life
Chairperson of the Diocesan Committee for Marriage, Family Life and Life-Long Religious Education and Directory of ACCORD: Very Rev John Garvey PP
Parochial House, Ballinasloe, Co Galway H53 EC98
Tel 090-9643916

Vocations
Director of Vocations and Chairperson of the Diocesan Committee for Vocations:
Rev Aidan Costello CC
Cathedral of St Brendan, Barrack Street, Loughrea, Co Galway H62 YE09

Pilgrimages
Director: Very Rev Pat Conroy PP
Parochial House, Ballinakill, Loughrea, Co Galway H62 AW68
Tel 090-9745021

Trócaire and Pontifical Mission Societies
Director: Very Rev Brendan Lawless PP
Carrabane, Athenry, Co Galway H65 EP04
Tel 091-841103

Ecumenism and Interreligious Dialogue
Chairperson of the Diocesan Committee for Ecumenism and Interreligious Dialogue: Very Rev Raymond Sweeney PP
Parochial House, Ballymacward, Ballainasloe, Co Galway H53 P2W0
Tel 090-9687614

Charitable Outreach
Chairperson of the Diocesan Committee for Charitable Outreach
Very Rev Seamus Bohan PP
Parochial House, Tynagh, Loughrea, Co Galway H62 DH32
Tel 090-9745113

Legion of Mary
Director: Very Rev Patrick Conroy PP
Parochial House, Ballinakill, Loughrea, Co Galway H62 AW68
Tel 090-9745021

PARISHES

Mensal parishes are listed first. Other parishes follow alphabetically. Historical names are given in parentheses. Church titulars are in italics.

LOUGHREA, ST BRENDAN'S CATHEDRAL
Rt Rev Mgr Cathal Geraghty PP
Rev Aidan Costello CC
Rev Charles Nyameh
The Presbytery, Loughrea, Co Galway H62 YE09
Tel 091-841212

BALLINASLOE, CREAGH AND KILCLOONEY
St Michael's, Ballinasloe
Our Lady of Lourdes, Creagh
Very Rev John Garvey PP
Rev Bernard Costello Adm
Very Rev Colm Allman
St Michael's Presbytery, Ballinasloe, Co Galway H53 EC98
Tel 090-9643916

AUGHRIM AND KILCONNELL
St Catherine's, Aughrim
Sacred Heart, Kilconnell
Very Rev Gerard Geraghty PP
Aughrim, Ballinasloe,
Co Galway H53 PY13
Tel 090-9673724

DIOCESE OF CLONFERT

BALLINAKILL AND DERRYBRIEN
St Joseph's, Ballinakill
St Patrick's, Derrybrien
Very Rev Pat Conroy PP
Ballinakill, Loughrea,
Co Galway H62 AW68
Tel 090-9745021

BALLYMACWARD AND GURTEEN (BALLYMACWARD AND CLONKEENKERRIL)
SS Peter and Paul
St Michael's
Very Rev Raymond Sweeney PP
Ballymacward, Ballinasloe,
Co Galway H53 P2W0
Tel 090-9687614

CAPPATAGLE AND KILRICKLE (KILLALAGHTAN AND KILRICKLE)
St Michael's, Cappatagle
Our Lady of Lourdes, Kilrickle
Most Rev John Kirby PP
Cappataggle, Ballinasloe,
Co Galway H53 X206
Tel 091-843017

CLONTUSKERT
St Augustine's
Very Rev Michael Finneran PP, VF
Clontuskert, Ballinasloe,
Co Galway H53 CV99
Tel 090-9642256

CLOSTOKEN AND KILCONIERAN (KILCONICKNY, KILCONIERAN AND LICKERRIG)
Holy Family, Immaculate Conception
Very Rev Brendan Lawless PP
Carrabane, Athenry,
Co Galway H65 EP04
Tel 091-841103

DUNIRY AND ABBEY (DUNIRY AND KILNELEHAN)
Holy Family
Assumption
Very Rev Seamus Bohan, Moderator
Tynagh, Loughrea, Co Galway
Tel 090-9745113

EYRECOURT, CLONFERT AND MEELICK (CLONFERT, DONANAGHTA AND MEELICK)
St Brendan's, St Francis
Very Rev Declan McInerney PP
Eyrecourt, Ballinasloe,
Co Galway H53 KX85
Tel 090-9675113

FAHY AND QUANSBORO (FAHY AND KILQUAIN)
Consoler of the Afflicted, Christ the King
Very Rev Michael Byrnes (Moderator)
Portumna

FOHENAGH AND KILLURE (FOHENAGH AND KILGERRILL)
St Patrick's
St Teresa's
Very Rev Christy McCormack PP
Fohenagh, Ahascragh,
Ballinasloe, Co Galway H53 KO37
Tel 090-9688623

KILLIMOR AND TIRANASCRAGH (KILLIMORBOLOGUE AND TIRANASCRAGH)
St Joseph's
Immaculate Conception
Very Rev Ciaran Kitching PP
Killimor, Ballinasloe,
Co Galway H53 R8C4
Tel 090-9676151

KILNADEEMA AND AILLE (KILNADEEMA AND KILTESKILL)
St Dympna's, St Mary's, Aille, Loughrea
Rt Rev Mgr Cathal Geraghty (Moderator)
Cathedral of St Brendan, Barrack Street,
Loughrea, Co Galway H62 YE09
Tel 091-841212

KILTULLAGH, KILLIMORDALY AND CLOONCAGH
SS Peter & Paul, Kiltulla,
St Mary's, Cloncagh,
St Iomar's, Killimordaly
Very Rev Martin McNamara PP
Kiltulla, Athenry, Co Galway H65 DYM0
Tel 091-848021

LAWRENCETOWN AND KILTORMER (KILTORMER AND OGHILL)
St Mary's, St Patrick's
Very Rev Bernard Costello (Moderator)
13 Garbally Oaks, Ballinasloe,
Co Galway H53 KW27
Tel 087-2396208

LEITRIM AND BALLYDUGGAN (KILCOOLEY AND LEITRIM)
St Andrew's, St Jarlath's, Ballyduggan
Very Rev Iomar Daniels PP
St Andrew's Church, Leitrim,
Loughrea, Co Galway H62 RP40
Tel 091-841758

LUSMAGH
St Cronan's
Very Rev Michael Kennedy PP
Lusmagh, Banagher,
Co Offaly R42 WP40
Tel 0509-51358

MULLAGH AND KILLORAN (ABBEYGORMICAN AND KILLORAN)
St Brendan's
Our Lady of the Assumption
Very Rev Niall Foley PP
Mullagh, Loughrea,
Co Galway H62 AR27
Tel 091-843119

NEW INN AND BULLAUN (BULLAUN, GRANGE AND KILLAAN)
St Killian's, New Inn
St Patrick's, Bullaun
Very Rev Pat Kenny PP
St Killian Church, New Inn,
Ballinasloe, Co Galway H53 P6C0
Tel 090-9675819

PORTUMNA (KILMALINOGUE AND LICKMOLASSEY)
St Brigid's, SS Peter & Paul, Ascension
Very Rev Michael Byrnes PP, JV
Dunkellin Terrace,
Portumna, Co Galway H53 F584
Tel 090-9741092

TAGHMACONNELL
St Ronan's
Very Rev Sean Neylon PP
Taghmaconnell,
Ballinasloe, Co Galway H53 RT28
Tel 090-9683929

TYNAGH AND KILLEEN
St Lawrence's, Sacred Heart
Very Rev Seamus Bohan PP
Tynagh, Loughrea,
Co Galway H62 DH32
Tel 090-9745113

WOODFORD AND LOOSCAUN
St John the Baptist, St Brendan's
Very Rev Kieran O'Rourke PP
Looscaun, Woodford,
Co Galway H62 AK18
Tel 090-9749100

INSTITUTIONS AND THEIR CHAPLAINS

Emmanuel House of Providence
Clonfert, Ballinasloe, Co Galway
Director: Mr Eddie Stones
Chaplain and Episcopal Delegate
Very Rev Michael Kennedy
Tel 057-9151552

Diocesan Family Life Centre (Ballinasloe)
Brackernagh, Ballinasloe, Co Galway
Chairperson Management Board
Very Rev John Garvey PP
St Michael's, Ballinasloe,
Co Galway H53 EC98
Tel 090-9643916

Portiuncula Hospital
Ballinasloe, Co Galway
Tel 090-9648200
Rev Bernard Costello

St Brendan's
Community Nursing Unit
Loughrea, Co Galway
Tel 091-871200
Rt Rev Mgr Cathal Geraghty PP
Tel 091-841212

DIOCESE OF CLONFERT

RETIRED PRIESTS

Rev P. J. Bracken
Portumna Retirement Village,
Portumna, Co Galway
Rev Joe Clarke
Foxhall, Gurlymadden,
Loughrea, Co Galway
Rev Sean Egan
Kilrickle Loughrea, Co Galway H62 PO27
Rev Benny Flanagan
14 Kilgarve Gardens, Creagh,
Ballinasloe, Co Galway
Rev Cathal Stanley
Dominic Street, Portumna,
Co Galway H53 EC66
Tel 090-9759182
Rev Sean Slattery
18 The Orchard, Limerick V94 F97N
Rev John Naughton
Clonfert Avenue, Portumna,
Co Galway H53 WC82

RELIGIOUS ORDERS AND CONGREGATIONS

PRIESTS

CARMELITES (OCD)
The Abbey,
Loughrea, Co Galway
Tel 091-841209 Fax 091-842343
Prior
Rev Mícheál MacLaifeartaigh (OCD)

REDEMPTORISTS
St Patrick's, Esker,
Athenry, Co Galway
Tel 091-844007
Outside office hours 086-8440619
Fax 091-845698
Superior: Rev Brendan Callanan (CSsR)
Vicar Superior: Rev Patrick O'Keeffe (CSsR)

SISTERS

CONGREGATION OF THE SISTERS OF MERCY
Convent of Mercy,
Loughrea, Co Galway H62 NP59
Tel 091-841354 Fax 091-847271
Community: 4

Sisters of Mercy, Lake Road,
Loughrea, Co Galway H62 D592
Tel/Fax 091-847715
Community: 5

Mount Pleasant,
Ballinasloe, Co Galway H53 XP74
Tel 090-9631695
Community: 2

7 Woodview, The Pines,
Ballinasloe, Co Galway H53 H319
Tel 090-9644055
Community: 1

17 Hawthorn Crescent,
Ballinasloe, Co Galway H53 XR86
Tel 090-9644171
Community: 2

An Gairdín,
Portumna, Co Galway H53 E891
Tel 090-9741689
Community: 2

St Brendan's Convent of Mercy,
Eyrecourt, Co Galway H53 V0Y7
Tel 090-9675123
Community: 1

Sisters of Mercy, Bark Hill,
Woodford, Co Galway H62 WN40
Community: 1

5 College Crescent,
The Pines, Ballinasloe,
Co Galway H53 AX82
Community: 1

75 Danesfort Drive, Caheronaun,
Loughrea, Co Galway H62 PR86
Community: 1

Kilgarve, Creagh,
Ballinasloe, Co Galway H53 F2H0
Community: 2

Sisters of Mercy, 1 Church Street,
Ballinasloe, Co Galway
Community: 1

FRANCISCAN MISSIONARIES OF THE DIVINE MOTHERHOOD
Franciscan Convent, Garbally Drive,
Ballinasloe, Co Galway H53 RF84
Tel 090-9642314/9648548
Country Leader: Pending
Community: 26

La Verna, Brackernagh,
Ballinasloe, Co Galway H53 EV97
Tel 090-9643679
Community: 2

St Clare's, Brackernagh,
Ballinasloe, Co Galway H53 E642
Tel 090-9643986 Fax 090-9631757
Community: 2

San Damiano, Ard Mhuire, Ballinasloe,
Co Galway H53 HN28
Community: 3

Assisi, 7 Ard Muire, Ballinasloe,
Co Galway H53 YY18
Community: 2

EDUCATIONAL INSTITUTIONS

St Joseph's College
Garbally Park, Ballinasloe, Co Galway
Tel 090-9642504/9642254
President
Very Rev Colm Allman BA, HDE
Principal
Mr Paul Walsh MA, HDE

Portumna Community School
Portumna, Co Galway
Tel 090-9741053
Principal: Mr Shane McClearn
Chaplain: Ms Brid Dunne

St Raphael's College
Convent of Mercy,
Loughrea, Co Galway
Tel 091-841062
Chaplain: Very Rev Pat Kenny PP

Mercy College
Woodford, Co Galway
Tel 090-9749076
Chaplain: Very Rev Kieran O'Rourke PP

Ardscoil Mhuire
Mackney, Ballinasloe, Co Galway
Chaplain: Very Rev John Garvey PP

St Brigid's College
Loughrea, Co Galway
Tel 091-841919
Chaplain: Very Rev Iomar Daniels PP, EV

St Killian's College
New Inn Ballinasloe
Chaplain: Very Rev Pat Kenny PP

DIOCESE OF CLOYNE

Patron of the Diocese
St Colman, 24 November

Covers most of County Cork

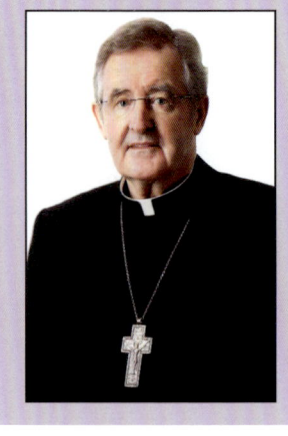

Most Rev William Crean DD
Bishop of Cloyne;
born 16 December 1951;
ordained priest 20 June 1976;
ordained Bishop of Cloyne
27 January 2013

Residence: Cloyne Diocesan
Centre, Cobh, Co Cork
Tel 021-4811430
Fax 021-4811026
Email info@cloynediocese.ie
website: www.cloynediocese.ie

ST COLMAN'S CATHEDRAL, COBH

St Colman's Cathedral, overlooking Cobh, enshrines within its walls the traditions of thirteen centuries of the Diocese of Cloyne.

Built in the form of a Latin cross, its exterior is of Dalkey granite, with dressings of Mallow limestone. The style of architecture is French Gothic. The architects were Pugin (the Younger), Ashlin and Coleman.

The cathedral took forty-seven years to build (1868–1915). The total cost was £235,000. Of this, £90,000 was raised by the people of Cobh, with the remainder coming from the diocese and from collections in America and Australia.

The spire was completed in 1915 and the famous carillon and the clock were installed in 1916. The carillon – the largest in Britain and Ireland – has forty-nine bells and is tuned to the accuracy of a single vibration. This unusual instrument covers a range of four octaves and is played from a console located in the belfry, consisting of a keyboard and pedalboard. Inside, the cathedral has all the hallmarks of Gothic grandeur: the massive marble pillars, the beautiful arches, the capitals with their delicate carving of foliage, the shamrock design on the Bath Stone, and mellow, delicate lighting.

The carved panels over the nave arches give a history of the Church in Ireland from the time of St Patrick. The stained-glass windows in the northern aisle depict the parables of Christ, while those in the southern aisle depict the miracles of Christ. Overhead, in the clerestory, are forty-six windows, each having the patron of one of the forty-six parishes of the diocese. The high altar and its surround was designed by Ashlin. The pulpit is of Austrian oak. Towards the rear of the cathedral is the magnificent rose window, which depicts St John's vision of the throne of God. The organ was built by Telford and Telford, and has a total of 2,468 pipes.

DIOCESE OF CLOYNE

Most Rev John Magee DD
Retired Bishop of Cloyne;
born 24 September 1936;
ordained priest 17 March 1962;
ordained Bishop of Cloyne 17 March 1987;
retired 24 March 2010
Residence: 'Carnmeen', Convent Hill,
Mitchelstown, Co Cork
Tel 025-41887

CHAPTER

Dean: Rt Rev Mgr Eamonn Goold PE
Midleton
Archdeacon: Venerable Gerard Casey PE, Mallow
Chancellor: Very Rev Seán Cotter PE
Charleville
Prebendaries
Aghulter: Vacant
Ballyhea: Rt Rev Mgr Denis O'Callaghan PE, Mallow
Cahirulton: Vacant
Coole: Vacant
Cooline: Very Rev Patrick Twomey PE
Kildorrery
Glanworth: Very Rev Colman O'Donovan PE, Inniscarra
Inniscarra: Rt Rev Mgr James O'Brien PP, Ballyhea
Kilmaclenine: Rt Rev Mgr James O'Donnell AP, Macroom
Killenemer: Very Rev Michael Fitzgerald PE, Mitchelstown
Subulter: Very Rev John Terry PE
Kanturk
Brigown: Very Rev Mgr Denis Reidy PE, Carrigtwohill
Kilmacdonogh: Vacant
Donoughmore: Very Rev Donal Roberts PP, VF, Macroom
Laken: Vacant
Honorary Canons
Very Rev Thomas Browne PE, Youghal
Very Rev Donal Leahy PP, Kilworth
Very Rev Denis Kelleher PP, Aghada
Very Rev David Herlihy PE, Youghal
Very Rev Donal O'Mahony PP, Charleville
Rt Rev Mgr Anthony O'Brien PP, VG, Mallow
Very Rev Michael Leamy PP, VF, Mitchelstown
Rt Rev Mgr Jim Killeen PP, VG, Midleton
Very Rev Tobias Bluitt PP, VF, Kanturk
Very Rev William Bermingham PP, Youghal

ADMINISTRATION

College of Consultors
Secretary: Very Rev Gerard Condon PP
Ballygriffin, Killavullen, Co Cork
Tel 022-46578

Vicars General
Rt Rev Mgr Anthony O'Brien PP, VG
Mallow, Co Cork
Tel 022-20391
Rt Rev Mgr Jim Killeen PP, VG
Midleton, Co Cork
Tel 021-4631750

Episcopal Vicar for the Gaeltacht
Vacant

Financial Administrator
Rt Rev Mgr Eamonn Goold PE
Midleton
Tel 021-4633659
Accountants: Messrs Deloitte & Touche
6 Lapp's Quay, Cork

Diocesan Administration
Diocesan Secretary for Primary Education
Mr Dan Leo
Tel 086-8162370
Diocesan Education Commission
Chairperson
Rt Rev Mgr Jim Killeen PP, VG
Midleton, Co Cork
Diocesan Secretary for Canonical Affairs
Very Rev William O'Donovan PP
Conna, Co Cork
Tel 058-59138

Religious Education
Co-ordinator of Mission and Ministry:
Rev James Moore *(protem)*
Cloyne Diocesan Centre, Cobh, Co Cork
Tel 086-8694744
Sr Emmanuel Leonard
5 Ashgrove, Cluain Ard, Cobh, Co Cork
Tel 021-4815305
Diocesan Advisers
Very Rev Gerard Condon PP
Ballygriffin, Killavullen, Co Cork
Tel 022-46578
Sr Claire Fox
Darchno, Castleredmond,
Midleton, Co Cork
Tel 021-4631912

Diocesan Secretary
Rev James Moore
Cloyne Diocesan Centre, Cobh, Co Cork
Tel 021-4811430

Administrative Secretary
Mrs Eileen Greaney
Cloyne Diocesan Centre, Cobh, Co Cork
Tel 021-4811430
Email info@cloynediocese.ie

Curator of the Diocesan Archives
Rt Rev Mgr Jim Killeen PP, VG
Midleton, Co Cork
Tel 021-4631750

LITURGY

Diocesan Master of Ceremonies
Rev Andrew Carvill
Mallow, Co Cork
Tel 022-51606
Church Music
Director: Very Rev Gerard Coleman PP
Castlelyons, Co Cork
Tel 025-36372

PASTORAL

Accord Catholic Marriage Care Service CLG
Diocesan Director
Very Rev Canon Michael Leamy PP, VF
Mitchelstown, Co Cork
Tel 025-41765

Communications
Diocesan Director
Rev James Moore
Cloyne Diocesan Centre,
Cobh, Co Cork
Tel 021-4811430

Diocesan Youth Services
Chairman: Vacant
Director: Mr Brian Williams
Mallow Community Youth Centre,
New Road, Mallow, Co Cork
Tel 022-53526

Ecumenism
Secretary: Rev Seán Corkery
Mallow, Co Cork
Tel 086-2420240

Immigrant Apostolate
Diocesan Director
Rev Andrew Carvill CC
Mallow, Co Cork
Tel 022-51606

Marriage Tribunal
(See also Marriage Tribunals section)
Cork Regional Marriage Tribunal:
Officialis:
Very Rev Richard Keane VJ

Perpetual Eucharistic Adoration
Diocesan Directors
Rev John Keane CC
53 Ros Álainn, Gurteenroe,
Macroom, Co Cork
Tel 089-7078770
Rev Patrick O'Donoghue CC
Mitchelstown, Co Cork
Tel 025-84077

Pilgrimage Director
Very Rev Canon Tobias Bluitt PP, VF
Kanturk, Co Cork
Tel 029-50192
Assistant Director
Very Rev Canon Donal O'Mahony PP
Charleville, Co Cork
Tel 063-81319

DIOCESE OF CLOYNE

Pioneer Total Abstinence Association
Diocesan Director
Very Rev Chris Donlon PP
Ladysbridge, Co Cork
Tel 021-4667173

Pontifical Mission Societies
Diocesan Director
Very Rev Micheál Leader PP
Ballyclough, Mallow, Co Cork
Tel 022-27650

Prayer Groups
Co-ordinator
Rev John Keane CC
53 Ros Álainn, Gurteenroe,
Macroom, Co Cork
Tel 089-7078770

Safeguarding
Designated Liaison Person (DLP)
Very Rev Patrick Winkle
Cloyne Diocesan Office,
Cobh, Co Cork
Tel 086-0368999
Email dlp@cloynediocese.ie

Deputy Designated Liaison Person
Mr Ger Crowley
Tel 086-0368999
Safeguarding Office, Cloyne Diocesan
Safeguarding Children Office,
Mallow Community Youth Centre,
New Road, Mallow, Co Cork
Tel 022-21009
Email safeguardingchildrenoffice@
cloynediocese.ie
www.safeguardingchildrencloyne.ie

Cloyne Diocesan Safeguarding Children committee (CDSCC)
Chairperson: Mr Willie Keane
Contact through the Safeguarding Office

Safeguarding Children Training Coordinator and Garda Vetting Authorised Liaison Person
Ms Rosarie O'Riordan

Safeguarding Vulnerable Adults
Designated Liaison Person (DLP)
Very Rev Patrick Winkle
Cloyne Diocesan Office,
Cobh, Co Cork
Tel 086-0368999
Email dlp@cloynediocese.ie

Travellers
Chaplain: Vacant

Trócaire
Very Rev Eugene Baker
Buttevant, Co Cork
Tel 086-8031876

Vicar for Religious
Very Rev Canon Sean Cotter PE
Love Lane, Charleville, Co Cork

Vocations
Director: Very Rev Brian Boyle Adm
Ravenswood, Fermoy, Co Cork
Tel 025-34467
Assistant Director: Rev Damien Lynch CC
Berrings, Co Cork
Tel 021-7332155

PARISHES

Mensal parishes are listed first. Other parishes follow alphabetically. Historical names are given in parentheses.

COBH, ST COLMAN'S CATHEDRAL
Sacred Heart, Rushbrooke
Sacred Heart, Ballymore
Very Rev Tom McDermott Adm
Cobh, Co Cork
Tel 021-4815934
Very Rev Liam Kelleher PE
Cobh, Co Cork
Tel 087-8516984
Rev James Moore *(in residence)*
Rushbrooke, Cobh, Co Cork
Tel 086-8694744
Very Rev Aquin Casey CC
Cobh, Co Cork
Tel 021-4908657
Rev Paul Bennett CC
Cobh, Co Cork
Tel 021-4908317

FERMOY
St Patrick's
Very Rev Brian Boyle Adm
Ravenswood, Fermoy, Co Cork
Tel 025-34467
Rev Eamon Roche CC
Monument Hill, Fermoy, Co Cork
Tel 025-32963

AGHABULLOGUE
St John's, Aghabullogue
St Patrick's, Coachford
St Olan's, Rylane
Very Rev Peadar Murphy PP
Aghabullogue, Co Cork
Tel 021-7334035

AGHADA
St Erasmus, Aghada
Church of the Mother of God, Saleen
St Mary's, Ballinrostig
Very Rev Daniel Murphy PP
Church Road, Aghada, Co Cork
Tel 086-0224682

AGHINAGH
St John the Baptist, Bealnamorrive,
Rusheen, Ballinagree
Very Rev Canon Donal Roberts Adm
Macroom, Co Cork
Tel 026-21068

BALLYCLOUGH
St John the Baptist, Ballyclough, Kilbrin
Very Rev Mícheál Leader PP
Ballyclough, Mallow, Co Cork
Tel 022-27650

BALLYHEA
St Mary's
Rt Rev Mgr James O'Brien PP
Ballyhea, Co Cork
Tel 063-81470

BALLYMACODA AND LADYSBRIDGE
St Mary's, Ladysbridge
St Peter in Chains, Ballymacoda
Very Rev Chris Donlon PP
Ladysbridge, Co Cork
Tel 021-4667173

BALLYVOURNEY
St Gobnait, Ballyvourney
Séipéal Ghobnatan, Cúil Aodha
Very Rev John McCarthy PP
Tel 086-8212101

BANTEER (CLONMEEN)
St Fursey's, Banteer
St Nicholas', Kilcorney
St Joseph's, Lyre
Very Rev William Winter PP
Banteer, Co Cork
Tel 029-56010

BLARNEY
Immaculate Conception, Blarney
St Patrick's, Whitechurch
St Mary's, Waterloo
Very Rev Michael Fitzgerald PP
Blarney, Co Cork
Tel 021-4385105
Rev Gabriel Burke CC
5 Lavallin Drive, Whitechurch, Co Cork
Tel 021-4200184

BUTTEVANT
St Mary's, Buttevant
St Mary's, Lisgriffin
Very Rev Eugene Baker PP
Buttevant, Co Cork
Tel 086-8031876

CARRIGTWOHILL
St Mary's
Very Rev Patrick Winkle PP
Carrigtwohill, Co Cork
Tel 021-4882439

CASTLELYONS
St Nicholas', Castlelyons
St Mary's, Coolagown
Very Rev Gerard Coleman PP
Tel/Fax 025-36372
Rev Marek Pecak *(in residence)*
Tel 087-1410470
Castlelyons, Fermoy, Co Cork

CASTLEMAGNER
St Mary's
Very Rev Canon Tobias Bluitt Adm
Kanturk, Co Cork
Tel 029-50192

DIOCESE OF CLOYNE

CASTLETOWNROCHE
Immaculate Conception, Castletownroche
Nativity of Our Lady, Ballyhooly
Very Rev Robin Morrissey PP
Castletownroche, Co Cork
Tel 087-6727925
Very Rev Donal Broderick PE
Ballyhooly, Co Cork
Tel 025-39148

CHARLEVILLE
Holy Cross
Very Rev Canon Donal O'Mahony PP
Tel/Fax 063-81319
Rev Anthony Sheehan AP
Tel 063-32320
Charleville, Co Cork

CHURCHTOWN (LISCARROLL)
St Nicholas', Churchtown
St Joseph's, Liscarroll
Very Rev Eugene Baker Adm
Buttevant, Co Cork
Tel 086-8031876

CILL NA MARTRA
St Lachtaín's, Kilnamartyra
Renaniree Church
Very Rev Joseph O'Mahony Adm
Sandy Hill, Macroom, Co Cork
Tel 026-41092

CLONDROHID
St Abina's, Clondrohid
St John the Baptist, Carriganimma
Very Rev Joseph Rohan PP
Clondrohid, Macroom, Co Cork
Tel 026-31915

CLOYNE
St Colman's, Cloyne
Star of the Sea, Ballycotton
Immaculate Conception, Shanagarry
St Colmcille's, Churchtown South
Very Rev Patrick Linehan PP
Cloyne, Midleton, Co Cork
Tel 021-4652597
Very Rev Michael Dorgan PE, CC
Ballycotton, Co Cork
Tel 083-8230854

CONNA
St Catherine's, Conna
St Catherine's, Ballynoe
St Mary's, Glengoura
Very Rev William O'Donovan PP
Conna, Mallow, Co Cork
Tel 058-59138

DONERAILE
The Nativity of the Blessed Virgin Mary, Doneraile
Christ the King, Shanballymore
St Joseph the Worker, Hazelwood
Very Rev Aidan Crowley PP
Tel 086-0434911
Doneraile, Co Cork
Ven Archdeacon Gerard Casey PE
The Presbytery, Croke Park,
Doneraile, Co Cork
Tel 022-72789

DONOUGHMORE
St Lachteen's, Stuake
St Joseph's, Fornaught
Very Rev Jeremiah O'Riordan PP
Donoughmore, Co Cork
Tel 021-7337023
Very Rev Mortimer Downing PE
Stuake, Donoughmore, Co Cork
Tel 021-7437815

GLANTANE
St Peter the Apostle, Dromahane
St John the Evangelist, Glantane
St Columba, Bweeng
Very Rev Gerard Coleman PP
Dromahane, Mallow, Co Cork
Tel 087-9580420

GLANWORTH AND BALLINDANGAN
Holy Cross, Glanworth
Immaculate Conception, Ballindangan
Holy Family, Curraghagulla
Very Rev Michael Corkery PP
Glanworth, Co Cork
Tel 025-38123
Very Rev Dan Gould PE
Ballindangan, Mitchelstown, Co Cork

GRENAGH
St Lachteen's, Grenagh
St Joseph's, Courtbrack
Very Rev Micheál Ó Loingsigh PP
Grenagh, Co Cork
Tel 021-4886128

IMOGEELA (CASTLEMARTYR)
Sacred Heart, Mogeely
St Joseph's, Castlemartyr
St Peter's, Dungourney
St Lawrence's, Clonmult
Very Rev Francis O'Neill PP
Castlemartyr, Co Cork
Tel 021-4667133
Rev Finbarr O'Flynn CC
Dungourney, Co Cork
Tel 021-4668406

INNISCARRA
St Senan's, Cloghroe
St Mary's, Berrings
St Joseph's, Matehy
Very Rev Patrick Buckley PP
4 Upper Woodlands, Cloghroe, Co Cork
Tel 021-4385311
Rev Damien Lynch CC
Berrings, Co Cork
Tel 021-77332948

KANTURK
Immaculate Conception, Kanturk
St Joseph's, Lismire
Very Rev Canon Tobias Bluitt PP, VF
Tel 029-50192
Rev John Magner CC
Tel 029-50061
Kanturk, Co Cork

KILDORRERY
St Bartholomew's, Kildorrery
St Molaga's, Sraharla
Very Rev Eamonn Kelleher PP
Kildorrery, Co Cork
Tel 022-40703

KILLAVULLEN
St Nicholas', Kilavullen
St Crannacht's, Anakissa
Very Rev Gerard Condon PP
Ballygriffin, Killavullen, Co Cork
Tel 022-46578
Very Rev Richard Hegarty PE
Killavullen, Co Cork
Tel 022-26125

KILLEAGH
St John the Baptist, Killeagh
St Patrick's, Inch
Very Rev Tim Hazelwood PP
Killeagh, Co Cork
Tel 024-95133

KILWORTH
St Martin's, Kilworth
Immaculate Conception, Araglin
Very Rev Canon Donal Leahy PP
Kilworth, Co Cork
Tel 025-27186

LISGOOLD
St John the Baptist, Lisgoold
Sacred Heart, Leamlara
Very Rev Denis O'Hanlon PP
Lisgoold, Co Cork
Tel 021-4642363

MACROOM
St Colman's, Macroom
St John the Baptist, Caum
Very Rev Canon Donal Roberts PP, VF
Tel 026-21068
Rt Rev Mgr James O'Donnell AP
Tel 026-41042
Very Rev Joseph O'Mahony Adm
Tel 026-41092
Rev John Keane CC
Tel 089-7078770
Rev Patrick McCarthy CC *(protem)*
Tel 086-3831621
Macroom, Co Cork

MALLOW
St Mary's, Mallow
Resurrection, Mallow
Rt Rev Mgr Anthony O'Brien PP, VG
Tel 022-20391
Rev Thomas Lane CC
2 Bellevue Circle, Mallow, Co Cork
Tel 087-0660615
Rev James Greene CC
Tel 085-8471249
Rev Andrew Carvill CC
Tel 022-51606

DIOCESE OF CLOYNE

MIDLETON
Holy Rosary, Midleton
St Colman's, Ballintotas
Rt Rev Mgr Jim Killeen PP, VG
Tel 021-4631750
Very Rev John Ryan PE, CC
Tel 021-4631094
Rev Mark Hehir CC
Tel 021-4621670
Rt Rev Mgr Eamonn Goold PE
Tel 021-4633659
Midleton, Co Cork

MILFORD
Assumption of BVM, Milford
St Michael's, Freemount
St Berchert's, Tullylease
Very Rev Peter O'Farrell PP
Milford, Charleville, Co Cork
Tel 063-80038

MITCHELSTOWN
Our Lady Conceived Without Sin, Mitchelstown
Holy Family, Ballygiblin, Killacluig
Very Rev Canon Michael Leamy PP, VF
Tel 025-41765
Rev Patrick O'Donoghue CC
Tel 025-84077
Mitchelstown, Co Cork

MOURNE ABBEY
St Michael the Archangel, Analeentha
St John the Baptist, Burnfort
Rt Rev Mgr Anthony O'Brien Adm
Mallow, Co Cork
Tel 022-20391

NEWMARKET
Immaculate Conception, Newmarket
Holy Spirit, Taur
Very Rev Francis Manning PP
Newmarket, Co Cork
Tel 029-60999

NEWTOWNSHANDRUM
St Joseph's, Shandrum
St Peter & Paul's, Dromina
Very Rev Anthony Wickham PP
Newtownshandrum,
Charleville, Co Cork
Tel 063-70836

RATHCORMAC
Immaculate Conception, Rathcormac
St Bartholomew's, Bartlemy
Very Rev Joseph O'Keeffe PP
Main Street, Rathcormac, Co Cork
Tel 025-37371
Very Rev Cornelius O'Donnell PE
Rathcormac, Fermoy, Co Cork
Tel 025-36286

ROCKCHAPEL AND MEELIN
St Joseph's, Meelin
St Peter's, Rockchapel
Very Rev Denis Stritch PP
Meelin, Newmarket, Co Cork
Tel 029-68007

YOUGHAL
St Mary's, Our Lady of Lourdes, Holy Family, Youghal; St Ita's, Gortroe
Very Rev Canon William Bermingham PP
Tel 083-8687196
Rev Patrick Corkery CC
Tel 024-92336
Rev Brendan Mallon CC
Tel 024-92456
Rev Gerard Cremin CC
Tel 024-92270
Youghal, Co Cork
Very Rev Canon Tom Browne PE
South Abbey, Youghal, Co Cork
Tel 024-93199

PRIESTS OF THE DIOCESE ELSEWHERE

Rev Seán Corkery
Director of Formation,
St Patrick's College,
Maynooth, Co Kildare
Tel 086-2420240
Rev Daniel McCarthy CF
Office of the Chaplain,
James Stephens Barracks, Kilkenny City
Rev Eamonn McCarthy
Radio Maria Ireland,
Unit 8, St Anthony's Business Park,
Ballymount Road, Dublin 22
Tel 085-8585308
Very Rev Mgr Joseph Murphy
Head of Protocol, Secretariat of State,
00120 Vatican City
Tel 0039-0669883193
Rev P. J. O'Driscoll CF
First Battalion Royal Regiment of
Tusiliers, Mooltan Barracks, Tidworth,
Wiltshire SP9 7EN, England
Tel 0044-1980-651468

RETIRED PRIESTS

Rev Eamonn Barry
Gortacrue, Midleton, Co Cork
Tel 086-8157952
Very Rev Donal Broderick PE
Ballyhooly, Co Cork
Tel 025-39148
Very Rev Richard P. Browne PE
Nadrid, Coachford, Co Cork
Tel 021-7334059
Very Rev Canon Thomas Browne PE
Southabbey, Youghal, Co Cork
Tel 024-93199
Ven Archdeacon Gerard Casey PE
The Presbytery, Croke Park,
Doneraile, Co Cork
Tel 022-72789

Very Rev Donal Coakley
Buttevant, Co Cork
Very Rev John Cogan PE
Killeen, Vicarstown, Co Cork
Tel 021-4385535
Very Rev Canon Seán Cotter PE
Love Lane, Charleville, Co Cork
Tel 063-89778
Very Rev Mortimer Downing PE
Stuake, Donoughmore, Co Cork
Tel 021-7437815
Very Rev Canon Michael Fitzgerald PE
Garrycahera, Ballynoe,
Mallow, Co Cork
Rt Rev Mgr Eamonn Goold PE
Midleton, Co Cork
Tel 021-4633659
Very Rev Daniel Gould PE
Ballinadangan, Co Cork
Tel 025-85563
Dr Patrick Hannon
Emeritus Professor of Theology,
St Patrick's College, Maynooth,
Co Kildare
Tel 01-6285222
Very Rev Martin Heffernan PE, PhD
Skahardgannon, Doneraile, Co Cork
Tel 022-24570
Very Rev Richard Hegarty PE
Killavullen, Co Cork
Tel 022-26125
Very Rev Canon David Herlihy PE
Freemount, Charleville, Co Cork
Very Rev Canon Denis Kelleher PE
Inegrega, Midleton, Co Cork
Very Rev Liam Kelleher PE
4 Cathedral Terrace, Cobh, Co Cork
Tel 087-8516984
Very Rev Michael Madden PE
Ferry Road, Jamesbrook,
Midleton, Co Cork
Tel 087-6565072
Rev Kevin Mulcahy
Ballymacoda, Co Cork
Tel 024-98110
Rt Rev Mgr Denis O'Callaghan PE
Mallow, Co Cork
Tel 022-21112
Very Rev Peadar O'Callaghan PE
Suaimhneas, Charleville, Co Cork
Tel 086-8054040
Very Rev Cornelius O'Donnell PE
Rathcormac, Fermoy, Co Cork
Tel 025-36286
Very Rev Canon Colman O'Donovan PE
1 Youghal Road, Midleton, Co Cork
Tel 021-4621617
Very Rev Stephen O'Mahony PE
Liscarroll, Mallow, Co Cork
Tel 022-48128
Very Rev David O'Riordan PE
Midleton, Co Cork
Tel 086-3590047
Very Rev Mgr Denis Reidy PE
4 Carrig Downs, Carrigtwohill, Co Cork

DIOCESE OF CLOYNE

Very Rev Patrick Scanlan PE
Castlemagner, Co Cork
Very Rev Canon John Terry PE
Terriville, Ballylanders,
Cloyne, Co Cork
Tel 021-4646779
Very Rev Canon Patrick Twomey PE
Bellevue, Mallow, Co Cork
Tel 022-55632
Rev Denis Vaughan
45 The Oaks,
Maryborough Ridge,
Douglas, Cork

RELIGIOUS ORDERS AND CONGREGATIONS

SISTERS

ADORERS OF THE SACRED HEART OF JESUS OF MONTMARTRE, OSB
St Benedict's Priory,
The Mount, Cobh, Co Cork
Tel 021-4811354
Prioress: Mother M. Catherine
Community: 7
Contemplative Benedictines
Residential retreats
Contact person: Guest Mistress
Email cobhtyburnconvent@gmail.com

BON SECOURS SISTERS (PARIS)
38 Norwood Park,
Cobh, Co Cork
Tel 021-4815350
Co-ordinator: Sr Paschal Barry
Community: 4
Pastoral Ministry, Care of Elderly

St Martin's Carrignafoy,
Cobh, Co Cork
Community: 1

CONGREGATION OF THE SISTERS OF MERCY
'Trócaire', 6 Castleowen,
Blarney, Co Cork
Tel 021-4381745

Friaryville,
Buttevant, Co Cork
Tel 022-23014

Charleville, Co Cork
Tel 063-81276

Dan Corkery Place,
Macroom, Co Cork
Tel 026-42673

Holy Spirit Convent,
Bank Place, Mallow, Co Cork
Tel 022-21780

Convent of Mercy, Bathview,
Mallow, Co Cork
Tel 022-21395

3 Beechwood Grove,
Cluain Ard, Cobh, Co Cork
Tel 021-4815062

5 Ashgrove, Cluain Ard,
Cobh, Co Cork
Tel 021-4815305

41 Ivy Gardens, Mallow, Co Cork
Tel 022-58036

Island Road, Longacre,
Newmarket, Co Cork

17 Bromley Court,
Midleton, Co Cork

Mercy House, Church Street,
Kanturk, Co Cork

Convent Bungalow,
Bathview, Mallow, Co Cork

SISTERS OF ST FRANCIS OF PHILADELPHIA
2 Gouldshell,
Mallow, Co Cork
Contact: Sr Sheila Byrne

INFANT JESUS SISTERS
Bellevue, Mallow,
Co Cork P51 X658
Tel 022-43085
Retired sisters

12 Glenanaar Row,
Mallow, Co Cork P51 TK8N

Main Street, Ballyclough,
Mallow, Co Cork P51 AN8K

LITTLE COMPANY OF MARY
Little Company of Mary, 'Lima',
College Road, Fermoy,
Co Cork
Tel 025-40627
Community: 1

MISSIONARIES OF CHARITY
St Helen's Convent,
Blarney, Co Cork
Tel 021-4382041
Superior: Sr Vianita (MC)
Community: 6
Residential Treatment Centre

CONGREGATION OF THE SISTERS OF NAZARETH
Nazareth House, Mallow, Co Cork
Tel 022-21561 Fax 022-21147
Email
superior.mallow@nazarethcare.com
Superior: Sr Brigid Comerford
Email srbrigid.comerford@
sistersofnazareth.com
Community: 10
Home for elderly. Beds: 120

PRESENTATION SISTERS
Presentation Convent, Midleton, Co Cork
Tel 021-4631892
Email presmidleton@gmail.com
Team Leadership
Community: 6
Primary School Tel 021-4631593
St Mary's Secondary School
Tel 021-4631973

82 Brookdale,
Midleton, Co Cork P25 HV59
Community: 1

'Srahaun', 20 Barry's Court,
Duntahane, Fermoy, Co Cork P61 YD76
Tel 025-31248
Community: 3

Presentation Lodge, College Road,
Fermoy, Co Cork
Tel 025-49928
Community: 1

Presentation Convent,
Front Strand, Youghal, Co Cork
Tel 024-93039
Local Leader: Sr Placida Barry
Community: 3

Presentation Sisters, 'Darchno',
Castleredmond, Midleton, Co Cork
Tel 021-4631912
Community: 1

Presentation Primary School,
Mitchelstown, Co Cork
Tel 025-24264
Presentation Secondary School
Mitchelstown, Co Cork
Tel 025-24394

Nano Nagle Birthplace,
Presentation Sisters,
Ballygriffin, Mallow, Co Cork P51 CV91
Tel 022-26411 Fax 022-26953
Email secretary@nanonaglebirthplace.ie
Community: 4
Website www.nanonaglebirthplace.ie

20 Church View,
Charleville, Co Cork
Community: 1

31 Churchview,
Charleville, Co Cork
Community: 1

ST JOSEPH OF THE SACRED HEART SISTERS
Sisters of St Joseph of Sacred Heart,
Penola, 25B Harrison Place,
Charleville, Co Cork
Sr Maura Murphy

Cullinagh, Fermoy, Co Cork
Tel 089-2210409
Sr Christina Scannell
Email christine.scannell@sosj.org.au

EDUCATIONAL INSTITUTIONS

St Colman's College (Diocesan College)
Fermoy, Co Cork
Tel 025-31622 Fax 025-31634
Email stcolmansfermoy@eircom.net

Patrician Academy
Mallow, Co Cork
Tel 022-21884

Scoil Mhuire gan Smál
Blarney, Co Cork
Tel 021-4385331

De La Salle College
Macroom, Co Cork
Tel 026-41832

CHARITABLE AND OTHER SOCIETIES

St Mary's District Hospital
Youghal, Co Cork

County Hospital
Mallow, Co Cork

Society of St Vincent de Paul
Conferences at: Ballyvourney, Castlemartyr, Cobh, Fermoy, Doneraile, Kanturk, Macroom, Mallow, Midleton, Mitchelstown, Youghal, Carrigtwohill, Lisgoold, Aghada, Charleville

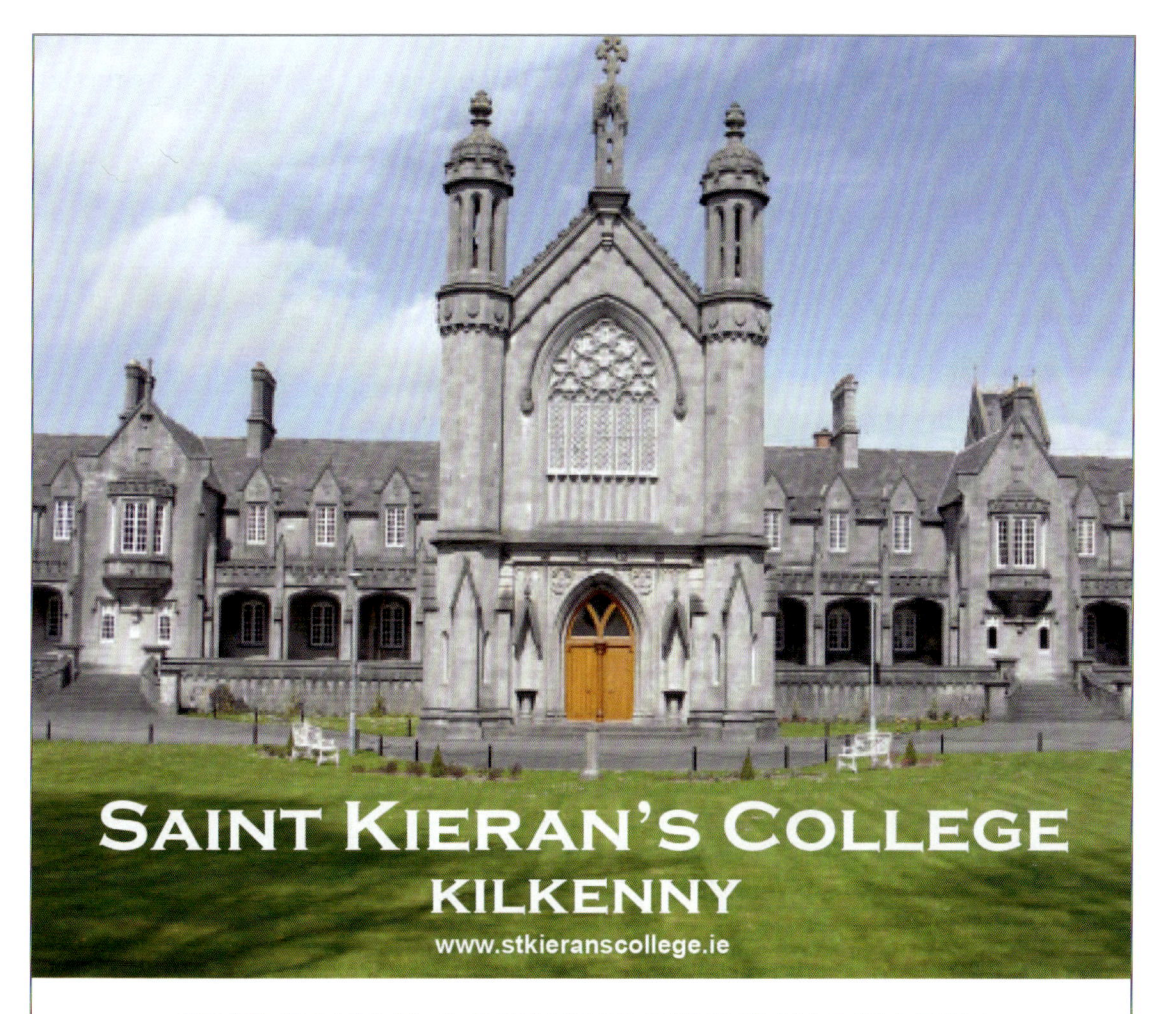

SAINT KIERAN'S COLLEGE
KILKENNY
www.stkieranscollege.ie

ST KIERAN'S IS A CATHOLIC DIOCESAN COLLEGE UNDER THE PATRONAGE OF THE BISHOP OF OSSORY.

Its objectives are the advancement of Catholic religion and education by providing a well-rounded academic education for second level students and supporting faith formation in the Diocese of Ossory as a pastoral centre and home for many diocesan initiatives.

- **SECONDARY SCHOOL** which promotes excellence in education and formation to 800 pupils, with a wide range of sporting, co-curricular and extra-curricular activities.
- **ASPAL** the home for the newly-designed digital learning platform for all involved in ministry and the faith life of our parishes and dioceses throughout Ireland.
- **CENTRE FOR RETREAT AND THEOLOGICAL REFLECTION** which offers parish evenings and weekend retreats and on-going formation courses for clergy and laity.
- **PASTORAL AND FAITH DEVELOPMENT** which supports parishes, various groups and people of our Diocese to deepen their understanding of faith, through reflection, lectures and various other initiatives.
- **THE KILKENNY RESEARCH & INNOVATION CENTRE** for teams from Telecommunication Software and Systems Group in Waterford IT and Carlow IT.

FOUNDED 1782

Further information:
The President, St Kieran's College, Kilkenny.
Tel: +353 (0)56 7721086 Email: president@stkieranscollege.ie

St Paul's College

Achieving excellence in a caring environment.

A school in the Vincentian Tradition.

St. Paul's College
Sybil Hill Road, Raheny, Dublin D05 C673

📞 (01) 831 4011

🐦 @stpaulscollege4

🌐 stpaulscollege.ie

MASON HAYES & CURRAN

Grounded in Wisdom

We are Ireland's leading provider of legal services to the Charity sector.

We have a deep appreciation of the mission, vision, charism and ethos of our clients and possess unparalleled knowledge and experience.

Our years of experience working with religious organisations give us excellent insight into your needs. We advise on:

- Charities Regulatory Compliance
- Data Protection
- Education Law
- Employment Law
- Fundraising
- Governance and Structures
- Property
- Safeguarding
- Wills & Probate

To find out how we can help you, please contact our team:

Niamh Callaghan
Head of Charities & Not-for-Profit
ncallaghan@mhc.ie

Alice Murphy
Charities Law & Governance
alicemurphy@mhc.ie

Edward Gleeson
Charities Law & Disputes
egleeson@mhc.ie

Catherine Allen
Charities & Data Privacy
callen@mhc.ie

Tom Davy
Charities Real Estate
tdavy@mhc.ie

Melanie Crowley
Employment Law
mcrowley@mhc.ie

Ian O'Herlihy
Education Law
ioherlihy@mhc.ie

Laura Rattigan
Dispute Resolution
lrattigan@mhc.ie

Dublin   London   New York   San Francisco

MHC.ie

New from Veritas Publications

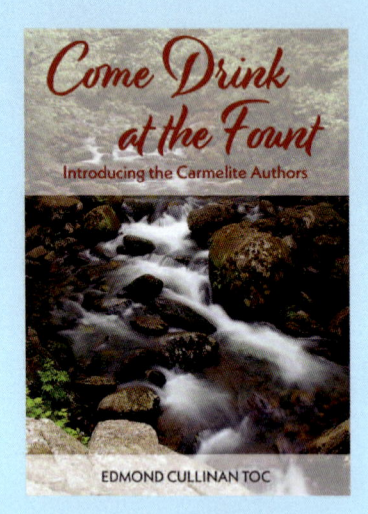

Come Drink at the Fount

Introducing the Carmelite Authors

EDMOND CULLINAN

978 1 80097 010 6
€12.99/£11.70

The title of this book, *Come Drink at the Fount*, suggests that people are thirsty. Christian spirituality seeks to respond to that thirst, which is, ultimately, a thirst for God. Carmelite spirituality is particularly accessible because it has been expressed in the writings of very gifted women and men. The authors introduced here are St Teresa of Ávila, St John of the Cross, Brother Lawrence of the Resurrection, St Thérèse of Lisieux and St Edith Stein (Teresa Benedicta of the Cross).

'Whoever opens the pages of this book will find a very attractive presentation of Carmelite saints and their spirituality. It may be dipped into at different times, or read chapter by chapter, or used by a study or reflection group. All will find it very helpful.'

Míceál O'Neill O. Carm., Prior General

Edmond Cullinan is a native of Dungarvan, County Waterford and a priest of the Diocese of Waterford and Lismore. He has worked in various ministries and is currently vice-rector of the Pontifical Irish College, Rome. He is a member of the Third Order of Carmel and is involved in the Focolare Movement. His previous publications include *The Story of the Liturgy in Ireland* (Columba Press, 2010) and *Pilgrims and Prophets: Biblical and Celtic Spirituality* (Veritas, 2016).

Abbey Street & Blanchardstown Centre, Dublin
Cork • Derry • Letterkenny • Newry

VERITAS
www.veritas.ie

DIOCESE OF CORK AND ROSS

PATRON OF THE DIOCESE OF CORK
ST FINBARR, 25 SEPTEMBER

PATRON OF THE DIOCESE OF ROSS
ST FACHTNA, 14 AUGUST

INCLUDES CORK CITY AND PART OF COUNTY CORK

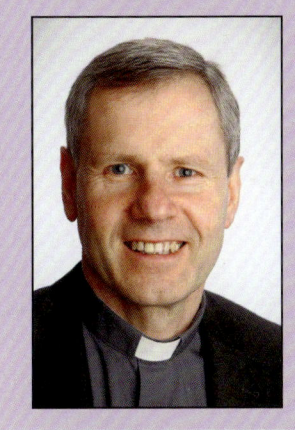

Most Rev Fintan Gavin DD
Bishop of Cork and Ross;
born 1966;
ordained priest 1991;
ordained Bishop of Cork & Ross
30 June 2019

Residence:
Cork and Ross Offices,
Redemption Road, Cork
Tel 021-4301717
Fax 021-4301557

CATHEDRAL OF ST MARY AND ST ANNE, CORK

The first cathedral on the site of the present Cathedral of St Mary and St Anne was the vision of Bishop Francis Moylan, who was Bishop of Cork from 1786 to 1815. The foundation stone was laid in 1799 and the cathedral was opened in 1808 as the parish church of the single parish then on the northside of the city – hence its local, popular name: the North Chapel. But in June 1820, the heat of the political climate struck the North Chapel when it was maliciously burned during the night.

Bishop John Murphy, one of the famous brewing family, wasted no time in calling a meeting to help restore the cathedral. The people of Cork generously rallied to the call.

The task of rebuilding was given to architect George Pain, who later designed Blackrock Castle, the court house and St Patrick's Church. The interior of the present-day cathedral, including the ornate ceiling, owes much to his creative gifts.

The next major alteration to the cathedral was undertaken in the 1870s when Canon Foley set about building the tower and the great Western Door – now the main door of the cathedral. The tower is higher than that of its more famous neighbour: St Anne's Church, Shandon, home of the much-played bells.

Almost a hundred years later, after the Second Vatican Council, Cornelius Lucey, then Bishop of Cork and Ross, added a further major extension at the other end of the cathedral. This included a completely new sanctuary and a smaller tower, and added capacity to the church, which served an area with a rapidly increasing population.

In 1994, major problems were discovered in the roof and other fabric of the building, which led to the closing of the cathedral for major refurbishment. The bishop, Michael Murphy, decided it was time to renovate the interior of the cathedral too. The task was entrusted to architect Richard Hurley, whose plan for the new interior saw a greater unity being achieved between the sanctuary and the rest of the floor area, and the new altar occupying the central place of prominence. The reordering and renovation was completed in 1996 at a cost of £2.5m and Bishop Murphy presided over its rededication – his last public function before he died a week later.

DIOCESE OF CORK AND ROSS

Most Rev John Buckley DD
Retired Bishop of Cork & Ross; born 1939; ordained priest 1965; ordained Titular Bishop of Leptis Magna 29 April 1984 and installed 6 February 1998
Residence: Cork and Ross Offices,
Redemption Road, Cork
Tel 021-4301717 Fax 021-4301557

CHAPTER

Dean: Very Rev Noel O'Sullivan
Archdeacon: Venerable Liam O'Driscoll
Precentor: Very Rev Canon James O'Donovan
Treasurer: Very Rev Canon Ted O'Sullivan
Chancellor:
Very Rev Canon John O'Donovan
Prebendaries
Kilbritain
Very Rev Canon Bartholomew O'Mahony
Desertmore
Very Rev Canon Martin Keohane
Kilnaglory: Very Rev Canon Dan Crowley
Holy Trinity
Very Rev Canon Martin O'Driscoll
Kilbrogan
Rt Rev Mgr Kevin O'Callaghan VF
Caherlag: Very Rev Canon John Kingston
Kilanully: Very Rev Canon George Murphy
Killaspugmullane
Very Rev Canon Michael Murphy
Liscleary: Very Rev Canon Robert Brophy
St Michael
Very Rev Canon Bernard Donovan
Inniskenny
Very Rev Canon John Paul Hegarty
Drimoleague: Vacant

Honorary Canons
Very Rev Canon Thomas Kelleher
Very Rev Canon John K. O'Mahony
Dean Michéal Ó Dálaigh
Archdeacon Kerry Murphy O'Connor
Very Rev Canon Tadhg Ó Mathuna
Very Rev Canon Liam O'Regan
Very Rev Canon Michael Riordan
Very Rev Canon Richard Hurley

ADMINISTRATION

Vicars General
Rt Rev Mgr Tom Hayes PP, VG
Parochial House, Ennniskeane, Co Cork
Tel 023-8847769
Rt Rev Mgr Aidan O'Driscoll PP, VG
Clonakilty, Co Cork
Tel 023-8833165

Vicars Forane
Rt Rev Mgr Kevin O'Callaghan AP, VF

Diocesan Secretary
Rev Michael Keohane
Cork & Ross Offices,
Redemption Road, Cork
Tel 021-4301717
Email secretary@corkandross.org

PASTORAL

Catechetics
Primary: Seamus Ó Dálaigh
Email diocesanadvisors@corkandross.org
Second-level: Ms Mary Scriven
Cork and Ross Offices,
Redemption Road, Cork
Tel 021-4301717
Email catechetics@corkandross.org

Child Protection
Diocesan Director: Ms Cleo Yates
Diocesan Offices, Redemption Road, Cork
Tel 021-4301717
Email safeguarding@corkandross.org

Marriage Counselling
ACCORD, 5 Main Street,
Bantry, Co Cork
Tel 027-50272

Diocesan Education Office
Cork and Ross Offices,
Redemption Road, Cork
Tel 021-4301717 Fax 021-4301557
Secretary for Education
Rev Michael Keohane *(Acting)*
Secretary: Seán Ó Caoimh
Email education@corkandross.org

Immigrants
Cois Tine, SMA Justice Office,
African Mission, Wilton, Cork
Tel 021-4933475
Email coistine@sma.ie
Diocesan Chaplain to Polish Community
c/o St Augustine's,
Washington Street, Cork
Tel 021-4275390

Marriage Tribunal
(See Marriage Tribunals section)

Office of Mission and Ministry
Cathedral Presbytery, Roman Street, Cork
Email missionandministry@corkandross.org
Episcopal Vicar
Rev Chris O'Donovan
Co-ordinator of Liturgy
Rev Christopher Fitzgerald
Email liturgy@corkandross.org

Pilgrimages
Director
Very Rev Canon James O'Donovan AP
The Presbytery, St Finbarr's West,
The Lough, Cork
Tel 087-2553021

Pontifical Mission Society
Rev Pat Fogarty PP
The Presbytery, Carrigaline, Co Cork
Tel 021-4371684

PARISHES

The mensal parishes are listed first. Other names follow alphabetically. Historical names are given in parentheses.

CATHEDRAL OF ST MARY & ST ANNE
Very Rev John O'Donovan Adm
Tel 021-4501022
Rev Seán Crowley CC
Rev Paul O'Donoghue CC
Cathedral Presbytery, Cork
Tel 021-4304325 Fax 021-4304204
Parish Office: Tel 021-4304325

ST PATRICK'S CATHEDRAL, SKIBBEREEN
Very Rev Michael Kelleher Adm
Rev Evin O'Brien CC
The Presbytery, Skibbereen, Co Cork
Tel 028-22878/22877
Parish Office: Tel 028-22828

ARDFIELD AND RATHBARRY
Rt Rev Mgr Aidan O'Driscoll Adm
Parochial House, Clonakilty, Co Cork
Tel 023-8833165

AUGHADOWN
Very Rev Donal Cahill Adm
Lisheen, Skibbereen, Co Cork
Tel 028-38111

BALLINCOLLIG
Very Rev Alan O'Leary PP
Parochial House, Ballincollig, Co Cork
Tel 021-4871206
Rev Cian O'Sullivan CC
The Bungalow, St Mary & St John,
Ballincollig, Co Cork
Tel 021-4877161
Rev Kamil Backara
64 Westcourt, Ballincollig, Co Cork
Parish Office: Tel 021-4871206

BALLINEASPAIG
Very Rev Canon Bartholomew O'Mahony PP
Tel/Fax 021-4346818
Very Rev Tom Clancy AP
Tel 021-4348588
Woodlawn, Model Farm Road,
Ballineaspaig, Cork
Parish Office: Tel 021-4344452

BALLINHASSIG
Very Rev Christopher Fitzgerald PP
Barrett's Hill, Ballinhassig, Co Cork
Tel 021-4885104
Parish Office: Tel 021-4805062

BALLINLOUGH
Rt Rev Mgr Gearóid Dullea PP
The Presbytery, Ballinlough, Cork
Tel 021-4292296
Parish Office: Tel 021-4294332

BALLINORA
Very Rev Declan Mansfield PP
Parochial House
Ballinora, Waterfall, near Cork
Tel 021-4872792

BALLYPHEHANE
Very Rev Canon Michael Murphy PP
The Presbytery, Ballyphehane, Cork
Tel 021-4965560
Very Rev Canon Jim O'Donovan AP
St Finbarr's Presbytery, The Lough, Cork
Parish Office: Tel 021-4311244

DIOCESE OF CORK AND ROSS

BANDON
Very Rev Canon John Kingston PP
Tel 023-8854666
Rev John C. O'Donovan CC
Tel 023-8865067
The Presbytery, Bandon, Co Cork
Parish Office: Tel 023-8841666

BANTRY
Very Rev Canon Martin O'Driscoll PP
The Presbytery, Bantry, Co Cork
Tel 027-50096
Rev John Heinhold (SPS) CC
The Presbytery, Bantry, Co Cork
Tel 027-50193
Parish Office: Tel 027-56398
Rev James MacSweeney
Chaplain to Coláiste Phobail Bheantraí
The Presbytery, Bantry, Co Cork

BARRYROE
Very Rev David O'Connell PP
Lislevane, Bandon, Co Cork
Tel 023-8846171

BLACKPOOL/THE GLEN
Very Rev John O'Donovan PP
Cathedral Presbytery, Roman Street, Cork
Tel 021-4501022
Rev Seán Crowley CC
Cathedral Presbytery, Roman Street, Cork
Tel 021-4304325
Parish Office: Tel 021-4300518

BLACKROCK
Very Rev Colin Doocey Adm
1 The Presbytery, Holy Cross Church,
Mahon, Co Cork
Tel 021-2414624
Rev Michael Keohane AP
1 The Presbytery, Blackrock, Cork
Very Rev Canon Tadhg Ó Mathúna AP
2 Parochial House, Blackrock, Cork
Tel 021-4358025

CAHERAGH
Very Rev Dr Daniel Pyburn PP
The Presbytery, Dromore,
Bantry, Co Cork
Tel 028-31126

CARRAIG NA BHFEAR
Very Rev Canon Martin Keohane PP
Parish House, Carraig na bhFear, Co Cork
Tel 021-4884119

CARRIGALINE
Very Rev Pat Fogarty PP
Tel 021-4371684
Rev Aidan Cremin CC
Tel 021-4372229
Rev Charles Nyhan CC
Cork Road, Carrigaline, Co Cork
Tel 021-4371860
Parish Office: Tel 021-4371109

CASTLEHAVEN
Very Rev Gerard Thornton (MSC) PP
Parish House, Union Hall,
Skibbereen, Co Cork, P81 C433
Tel 028-34940

CLOGHEEN (KERRY PIKE)
Very Rev Greg Howard Adm
St Mary's on the Hill,
Knocknaheeny, Cork
Parish Office: Tel 021-4392427

CLONAKILTY AND DARRARA
Rt Rev Mgr Aidan O'Driscoll PP, VG
Tel 023-8833165
Rev Fergus Tuohy (SMA) CC
Tel 023-8834441
The Presbytery, Clonakilty, Co Cork
Parish Office: Tel 023-8834441

CLONTEAD
Very Rev Michael Regan PP
Unit 1B, Riverside Grove,
Riverstick, Co Cork
Email clonteadbabhub@gmail.com

COURCEYS
Very Rev Michael O'Mahony PP
Ballinspittle, Co Cork
Tel 021-4778055

CROSSHAVEN
Very Rev Patrick Stevenson PP
Most Rev Patrick Coveney AP
The Presbytery, Crosshaven, Co Cork
Tel 021-4831218

CURRAHEEN ROAD
Very Rev Canon Robert Brophy PP
The Presbytery, Curraheen Road, Cork
Tel 021-4343535

DOUGLAS
Very Rev Canon Ted O'Sullivan PP
Parochial House, Douglas, Cork
Tel 021-4891265
Parish Office: Tel 021-4894128
St Patrick's, Rochestown:
Rev Pat O'Mahony (SMA) CC
St Patrick's Presbytery,
Rochestown Road, Cork
Tel 021-4892363
Parish Office: Tel 021-4896797

DRIMOLEAGUE
Very Rev Liam Crowley PP
Drimoleague, Co Cork
Tel 028-31133

DUNMANWAY
Very Rev Timothy Collins PP
Rev Rafal Zielonka CC
The Presbytery, Dunmanway, Co Cork
Tel 023-8845000
Parish Office: Tel 023-8856610

ENNISKEANE AND DESERTSERGES
Very Rev Tom Hayes PP, VG
Parochial House, Enniskeane, Co Cork
Tel 023-8847769
Parish Office:
parishoffice@enniskeaneparish.ie

FARRANREE
Very Rev John Walsh PP
The Presbytery, Farranree, Cork
Tel 021-4393815/4210111
Parish Office: Tel 021-4932230

FRANKFIELD-GRANGE
Very Rev Kevin O'Regan PP
The Presbytery, Frankfield, Cork
Tel 021-4361711
Parish Office: Tel 021-4897379

GLANMIRE
Very Rev John Newman PP
Glanmire, Co Cork
Tel 021-4866307
Rev Pat Nugent CC
Springhill, Glanmire, Co Cork
Tel 021-4866306/086-1689292
Parish Office: Tel 021-4820654

GLOUNTHAUNE
Very Rev Damian O'Mahony PP
Glounthaune, Co Cork
Tel 021-4232881
Rev Pat Nugent CC
Tel 086-1689292
Parish Office: Tel 021-4353366

GOLEEN
Very Rev Myles McSweeney Adm
Meenvane, Schull, Co Cork
Tel 028-28898
Rev Michael Anthony Buckley CC
The Presbytery, Goleen, Co Cork
Tel 028-35188

GURRANABRAHER
Very Rev Tomás Walsh (SMA) PP
Rev Aidan Vaughan (OFMCap) CC
Ascension Presbytery,
Gurranabraher, Cork
Tel 021-4303655
Parish Office: Tel 021-4303655

INNISHANNON
Very Rev Finbarr Crowley PP
Innishannon, Co Cork
Tel 021-4775348
Parish Office: Tel 021-4776794

KILBRITTAIN
Very Rev Jerry Cremin PP
Parochial House, Kilbrittain, Co Cork
Tel 023-8849637

KILMACABEA
Very Rev Terence O'Brien (MSC) PP
Parochial House, Leap, Co Cork
Tel 028-33177

KILMEEN AND CASTLEVENTRY
Very Rev John Collins PP
Rossmore, Clonakilty, Co Cork
Tel 023-8838630

DIOCESE OF CORK AND ROSS

KILMICHAEL
Very Rev Patrick O'Donovan PP
Parochial House, Tirelton,
Macroom, Co Cork
Tel 026-46012/086-2578065
Parish Office: Tel 085-8706204

KILMURRY
Very Rev Canon Bernard Donovan PP
Cloughdubh, Crookstown, Co Cork
Tel 021-7336054
Rt Rev Mgr Kevin O'Callaghan AP
The Presbytery, Lissarda, Co Cork
Tel 021-7336053

KINSALE
Very Rev Robert Young PP
Tel 021-4774019
Very Rev Canon Tom Kelleher PE
The Presbytery, Kinsale, Co Cork
Parish Office: Tel 021-4773821

KNOCKNAHEENY/HOLLYHILL
Very Rev Greg Howard PP
The Presbytery, Knocknaheeny, Cork
Parish Office: Tel 021-4392459

THE LOUGH
Very Rev Canon John Paul Hegarty PP
The Lough Presbytery,
St Finbarr's West, Cork
Tel 021-4322633
Very Rev Canon Jim O'Donovan AP
St Finbarr's Presbytery, The Lough, Cork

MAHON
Very Rev Colin Doocey PP
1 The Presbytery,
Holy Cross Church, Mahon, Cork
Tel 021-2414624
Rev John P. O'Riordan (CSsR) CC
2 The Presbytery, Mahon, Cork
Tel 021-4515460
Parish Office: 021-4357040

MONKSTOWN
Very Rev Sean O'Sullivan PP
Monkstown, Co Cork
Tel 021-4863267
Rev John Galvin PE
Passage West, Co Cork
Tel 021-4841267

MUINTIR BHÁIRE
Very Rev Canon Martin O'Driscoll Adm
The Presbytery, Bantry, Co Cork
Tel 027-56398
Email office@bantryparish.com

MURRAGH AND TEMPLEMARTIN
Very Rev Bernard Cotter PP
The Presbytery, Newcestown,
Bandon, Co Cork
Tel 021-7438000
Parish Office: maighratha@gmail.com

OVENS
Rev Liam Ó hÍcí PP
Ovens, Co Cork
Tel 021-4871180
Rt Rev Mgr Kevin O'Callaghan AP
The Presbytery, Lissarda, Co Cork
Tel 021-7336053

PASSAGE WEST
Very Rev Sean O'Sullivan PP
New Parochial House,
Monkstown, Co Cork
Tel 021-4863267
Rev John Galvin PE
Passage West, Co Cork
Tel 021-4841267

RATH AND THE ISLANDS
Very Rev Michael Kelleher Adm
2 The Presbytery, Skibbereen
Tel 028-22878
Rev Evin O'Brien CC
Tel 028-22877
The Presbytery, Skibbereen, Co Cork
Parish Office: Tel 028-22828

ROSSCARBERY AND LISSAVAIRD
Very Rev John McCarthy PP
Rosscarbery, Co Cork
Tel 023-8848168

SACRED HEART
Very Rev Tom Mulcahy PP
Rev John Fitzgerald CC
Sacred Heart Parish,
Western Road, Cork
Tel 021-4804120 Fax 021-4543823
Parish Office: Tel 021-4346711

ST FINBARR'S SOUTH
Very Rev Eoin Whooley PP
South Presbytery, Dunbar Street, Cork
Tel 085-1471147
Rev Jilson Kokkandathil CC
South Presbytery, Dunbar Street, Cork

ST JOSEPH'S (MAYFIELD)
Very Rev Chriostóir MacDonald PP
Murmont Lawn, Mayfield, Cork
Tel 021-4501861
Parish Office: Tel 021-4503531

ST JOSEPH'S (BLACKROCK ROAD)
Very Rev Alphonse Sekongo (SMA) PP
St Joseph's, Blackrock Road,
Cork T12 X281
Tel 021-4292871
Parish Office: Tel 021-4616327
Email parish.blackrock@sma.ie

ST PATRICK'S
Very Rev Eoin Whooley Adm
South Presbytery, Dunbar Street, Cork
Rev Jilson Kokkandathil CC
South Presbytery, Dunbar Street, Cork
Parish Office: Tel 021-4518191

ST VINCENT'S, SUNDAY'S WELL
Administered by Cathedral Parish
Tel 021-4304325
Email cathedral@corkandross.org

SS PETER'S AND PAUL'S
Very Rev Patrick A. McCarthy PP
35 Paul Street, Cork
Tel 021-4276573

SCHULL
Very Rev Myles McSweeney PP
Meenvane, Schull
Tel 028-28171
Rev Michael Anthony Buckley CC
The Presbytery, Goleen, Co Cork
Tel 028-35188

TIMOLEAGUE AND CLOGAGH
Very Rev Patrick Hickey PP
Parochial House, Timoleague, Co Cork
Tel 023-8839114
Rt Rev Mgr Finbarr O'Leary
The Presbytery, Clogagh, Co Cork
Tel 023-8869682

TOGHER
Rev Ben Hodnett Adm
The Presbytery, Togher, Cork
Tel 021-4316700
Parish Office: 021-4318899

TRACTON ABBEY
Very Rev Canon George Murphy PP
Tel 021-4887105
Minane Bridge, Co Cork

TURNER'S CROSS
Very Rev Billy O'Sullivan PP
Rev Chris O'Donovan AP
Tel 021-4313103
Ven Archdeacon Kerry Murphy O'Connor PE
Tel 021-4312466
The Presbytery, Turner's Cross, Cork

UIBH LAOIRE
Very Rev Anthony O'Mahony PP
Parochial House,
Inchigeela, Macroom, Co Cork
Tel 026-49838/087-2691432
Parish Office: Tel 087-1446958

UPPER MAYFIELD
Very Rev Dr Charles Kiely PP
The Presbytery, Our Lady Crowned,
Upper Mayfield, Cork
Tel 021-4503116
Parish Office: Tel 021-4551276

WATERGRASSHILL
Very Rev Donal Cotter PP
Parochial House,
Watergrasshill, Co Cork
Tel 021-4889103
Parish Office: Tel 021-4513671

WILTON, ST JOSEPH'S
Very Rev Michael O'Leary (SMA) PP
St Joseph's, Wilton, Cork T12 E436
Tel 021-4341362 Fax 021-4343940
Parish Office:
stjosephschurchwilton@yahoo.com

DIOCESE OF CORK AND ROSS

INSTITUTIONS AND THEIR CHAPLAINS

THIRD LEVEL COLLEGES

Cork Institute of Technology
Chaplaincy Office: 021-4326225
Chaplaincy Base: 3 Elton Lawn,
Rossa Avenue, Bishopstown, Cork
Tel 021-4326256
Chaplain: Rev Dr David McAuliffe
Tel 021-4346244
Co-ordinator of Pastoral Care
Ms Edel Dullea
Tel 021-4326778

University College, Cork
Chaplaincy Office: Iona, College Road, Cork
Tel 021-4902459
Chaplain: Rev Gerard Dunne (OP)
Tel 021-4902704

HOSPITALS

Bandon District Hospital
Bandon, Co Cork
Tel 023-8841403
Chaplain: Parish clergy, Bandon

Bantry Hospital
Bantry, Co Cork
Tel 027-50133
Chaplain: Parish clergy, Bantry

Bon Secours Hospital
College Road, Cork
Tel 021-4542807
Chaplain: Rev Jack Twomey (OFMCap)
Tel 021-4546682

Cork South Infirmary Victoria Hospital Ltd
Old Blackrock Road, Cork
Tel 021-4926100
Chaplains: Rev Adrian Curran (OFM Cap)
Rev Michael Forde
Tel 021-4926100

Cork University Hospital
Wilton, Cork
Tel 021-4546400
Chaplains: Rev Pierce Cormac
Tel 021-4546400
Rev Thomas Lyons
Tel 021-4546400/4922391
Rev Kieran O'Driscoll
Tel 021-4546400
Rev Joyel John Michael
Tel 021-4546400

Marymount Hospice
Curraheen, Co Cork
Tel 021-4501201
Chaplain: Rev John Manley

Mercy Urgent Care Centre
Baker's Road, Cork
Tel 021-4303264
Chaplains: Parish clergy, Gurranabraher
Tel 021-4303655

Mercy University Hospital
Grenville Place, Cork
Tel 021-4271971
Chaplain: Rev Marius O'Reilly

Mount Carmel Hospital
Clonakilty, Co Cork
Tel 023-8833205
Chaplain: Parish Clergy

Sacred Heart Hospital
Kinsale, Co Cork
Tel 021-4772202
Chaplain: Parish clergy, Kinsale

St Anthony's Hospital
Dunmanway, Co Cork
Tel 023-8845102
Chaplain: Parish clergy, Dunmanway

St Finbarr's Hospital
Douglas Road, Cork
Tel 021-4966555
Chaplains
Rev Adrian Curran (OFM Cap)
Rev Michael Forde
Tel 021-4926100

St Gabriel's Hospital
Schull, Co Cork
Tel 028-28120
Chaplain: Parish clergy, Schull

St Joseph's Hospital
Mount Desert, Lee Road, Cork
Tel 021-4541765

St Stephen's Hospital
Glanmire, Co Cork
Tel 021-4821411
Chaplain: Rev Des Farren (MSC)

Skibbereen Community Hospital
Skibbereen, Co Cork
Tel 028-21677
Chaplain: Parish Clergy

PORT

Port Chaplaincy
Rev Desmond Campion (SDB)
Tel 021-4378046

PRISONS

Cork Prison
Chaplain: Rev Ray Riordan
Tel 021-2388000

PRIESTS OF THE DIOCESE ELSEWHERE

Rev Dr Pádraig Corkery
St Patrick's College,
Maynooth, Co Kildare
Tel 01-7083639
Rev Joseph O'Leary
1-38-16 Ekoda, Nakanoku, Tokyo,
16J0022 Japan

Dean Noel O'Sullivan
St Patrick's College,
Maynooth, Co Kildare

RETIRED PRIESTS

Rev Michael O'Driscoll
Bushmount, Clonakilty, Co Cork
Tel 023-33991
Rev Pat Walsh
Priests House, Ahiohill,
Enniskeane, Co Cork
Rev Patrick Keating
Drumoleague, Co Cork
Very Rev Tom Riordan
Willow Lawn, Ballinlough, Cork
Very Rev Canon Thomas Kelleher
The Presbytery, Kinsale, Co Cork
Very Rev Timothy O'Sullivan
Villa Maria, Farnanes, Co Cork
Very Rev Canon Michael Riordan
Mount Desert, Lee Road, Cork
An tAth Seosaimh Ó Cochláin
c/o Cork & Ross Diocesan Office
Very Rev Denis Cashman
Ballincollig, Co Cork
Rev James Tobin
St Patrick's Presbytery,
Lower Road, Cork
Archdeacon Kerry Murphy O'Connor
The Bungalow, Turner's Cross, Cork
Rev Paul O'Donoghue
c/o Cork & Ross Diocesan Office
Very Rev Canon Tadhg O'Mathúna
The Presbytery, Blackrock, Cork
Very Rev Canon Richard Hurley
c/o Cork & Ross Diocesan Office
Very Rev Canon Dan Crowley PE
Woodlawn, Model Farm Road, Cork
Very Rev Patrick J. McCarthy PE
The Presbytery, O'Rahilly Street,
Clonakilty, Co Cork
Very Rev Canon Liam O'Regan PE
Cramer's Court Nursing Home,
Ballindeenisk, Kinsale, Co Cork
Rev John K. O'Mahony
Mount Desert, Lee Road, Cork

PERSONAL PRELATURE

OPUS DEI
Dunmahon Study Centre
Model Farm Road, Cork T12 KHC1
Tel 021-2029112
www.dunmahon.ie
Rev Brian McCarthy

RELIGIOUS ORDERS AND CONGREGATIONS

PRIESTS

AUGUSTINIANS
St Augustine's Priory,
Washington Street, Cork
Tel 021-4275398/4270410 Fax 021-4275381
Prior: Rev John Lyng (OSA)
Bursar: Rev Tom Sexton (OSA)

DIOCESE OF CORK AND ROSS

CAPUCHINS
Holy Trinity,
Fr Mathew Quay, Cork T12 PK24
Tel 021-4270827 Fax 021-4270829
Guardian: Rev Dermot Lynch (OFMCap)
Vicar: Br Declan O'Callaghan (OFMCap)

Capuchin Community,
Monastery Road, Rochestown,
Co Cork T12 NH02
Tel 021-4896244 Fax 021-4895915
Guardian
Rev Silvester O'Flynn (OFMCap)
Vicar: Rev John Manley (OFMCap)

St Francis Capuchin Franciscan College,
Rochestown, Co Cork
Principal: Mrs Marie Ring
Tel 021-4891417 Fax 021-4361254

CARMELITES (OCARM)
Carmelite Friary, Kinsale,
Co Cork P17 WR88
Tel 021-4772138
Email kinsale@irishcarmelites.com
Prior: Rev James Eivers (OCarm)

DOMINICANS
St Mary's, Pope Quay, Cork
Tel 021-4502267
Prior: Maurice Colgan (OP)

St Dominic's Retreat House,
Montenotte, Cork
Tel 021-4502520 Fax 021-4502712
Prior: Bernard Treacy (OP)

FRANCISCANS
Franciscan Friary, Liberty Street, Cork
Tel 021-4270302 Fax 021-4271841
Guardian: Rev Patrick Younge (OFM)

MISSIONARIES OF THE SACRED HEART
MSC Mission Support Centre,
PO Box 23, Western Road,
Cork T12 WT72
Tel 021-4545704/4543988
Fax 021-4343587
Director: Rev Michael O'Connell (MSC)
Email info@mscmissions.ie
www.mscmissions.ie

Western Road,
Cork, T12 TN80
Tel 021-4804120 Fax 021-4543823
Leader: Very Rev John Finn (MSC)
Parish Priest
Rev Thomas Mulcahy (MSC) PP

Carrignavor, Co Cork
Tel 021-4884404

(See also Castlehaven Parish and Kilmacabea Parish)

REDEMPTORISTS
Scala, Castle Mahon House,
Castle Road, Blackrock, Cork
Tel 021-4358800 Fax 021-4359696
Co-ordinator: Rev Brian Nolan (CSsR)

ROSMINIANS
Rosmini House, Dunkereen,
Innishannon, Cork, T12 N9DH
Tel 021-4776268/4776923
Fax 021-4776268
Rector: Rev Polachan Thettayil (IC)

ST COLUMBAN'S MISSIONARY SOCIETY
No. 2 Presbytery, Our Lady Crowned Church, Mayfield Upper, Cork
Tel 021-4508610
Rev Patrick O'Herlihy (SSC)

ST PATRICK'S MISSIONARY SOCIETY
Kiltegan House, 11 Douglas Road, Cork
Tel 021-4969371
House Leader: Rev James Kelleher (SPS)

SOCIETY OF AFRICAN MISSIONS
St Joseph's Provincial House, Feltrim,
Blackrock Road, Cork T12 N6C8
Tel 021-4292871 Fax 021-4292873
Email provincial@sma.ie
www.sma.ie
Provincial: Rev Malachy Flanagan (SMA)

SMA House, African Missions,
Blackrock Road, Cork T12 TD54
Superior: Rev Patrick O'Rourke (SMA)
Vice Superior: Rev Aidan J. McCrystal (SMA)

SMA House, Wilton, Cork T12 KR23
Tel 021-4541069/4541884
Fax 021-4541069
Superior: Rev Noel O'Leary (SMA)
Vice-Superior: Rev Colum O'Shea (SMA)

Justice Office,
SMA House, Wilton, Cork T12 KR23
Email justice@sma.ie
Mr Gerry Forde

(See also under parishes – St Joseph's (Blackrock Road))

BROTHERS

BROTHERS OF CHARITY
Our Lady of Good Counsel, Lota,
Glanmire, Co Cork
Tel 021-4821012 Fax 021-4821711
Chaplain: Fr Paul Thettayil (IC)

CHRISTIAN BROTHERS
Sunday's Well Life Centre,
6 Winter's Hill, Sunday's Well, Cork
Tel 021-4304391
Email corklifecentre@gmail.com
Director: Don O'Leary

PRESENTATION BROTHERS
4 Lynbrook, Glasheen Road, Cork
Tel 021-4679007
Community: 2

Mardyke House, Cork
Tel 021-4272239
Community: 2
Contact: Br John Hunt (FPM)

Maiville, Turner's Cross, Cork
Tel 021-4272649
Community: 16
Contact: Br Bede Minehane (FPM)

Mount St Joseph, Blarney Street, Cork
Tel 021-4392160
Community: 5
Contact: Br Kevin Mascerenhas (FPM)

SISTERS

BON SECOURS SISTERS (PARIS)
Bon Secours Convent,
College Road, Cork
Tel 021-4542416 Fax 021-4542533
Co-ordinator: Sr Martha Leamy
Email marthaleamy@gmail.com
Community: 7

Cnoc Mhuire, Fernhurst,
College Road, Cork
Tel 021-4345410 Fax 021-4345491
Co-ordinator: Sr Baptist Libby
Community: 31
Pastoral, community and hospital ministry

Casa Maria, Fernhurst,
College Road, Cork
Tel 021-4345411
Community: 2
Pastoral and vocation ministry

20 Old Quarry,
Coolroe, Ballincollig, Co Cork
Tel 021-4810622
Community: 1

St Enda's, College Road, Cork
Tel 021-4542750
Community: 2

CONGREGATION OF THE SISTERS OF MERCY
Provincial Offices, Bishop Street, Cork
Tel 021-4975380 Fax 021-4915220
Email provincialoffice@mercysouth.ie
Provincial: Sr Eileen O'Flynn

13 Kempton Park,
Ballyvolane, Cork
Tel 021-4551375

14 Kempton Park,
Ballyvolane, Cork

49 Hollymount,
Blarney Road, Cork
Tel 021-4302123

27 Ronayn's Court,
Rochestown Road, Cork

21 Mariner's Quay,
Passage West, Co Cork

19 Sheraton Court,
Glasheen Road, Cork

2 Woodbrook Grove,
Bishopstown, Cork
Tel 021-4342286

1 St Columba's,
Bishopstown Avenue West,
Model Farm Road, Cork

DIOCESE OF CORK AND ROSS

2 St Columba's,
Bishopstown Avenue West,
Model Farm Road, Cork

3 St Columba's,
Bishopstown Avenue West,
Model Farm Road, Cork

5 St Columba's,
Bishopstown Avenue West,
Model Farm Road, Cork

6 St Columba's,
Bishopstown Avenue West,
Model Farm Road, Cork

7 St Columba's,
Bishopstown Avenue West,
Model Farm Road, Cork

8 St Columba's,
Bishopstown Avenue West,
Model Farm Road, Cork

9 St Columba's,
Bishopstown Avenue West,
Model Farm Road, Cork

10 St Columba's,
Bishopstown Avenue West,
Model Farm Road, Cork

11 St Columba's,
Bishopstown Avenue West,
Model Farm Road, Cork

2 Parkview, Church Hill,
Passage West, Co Cork

1 Parkview, Church Hill,
Passage West, Co Cork

St Marie's Bungalow, Convent Place,
Crosses Green, Cork

St Marie's of the Isle,
Sharman Crawford Street, Cork
Tel 021-4316029

38 Sheares Street, Cork
Tel 021-4248755

9 Sharman Crawford Street, Cork

1 Kinloch Court, Bishopstown Avenue,
Model Farm Road, Cork

38 Ard na Rí, Closes Green,
Farranree, Cork

1 Sandymount Drive,
Glasheen Road, Cork
Tel 021-4541613

Cuan na Trócaire, 23 Benvoirlich Estate,
Bishopstown, Cork
Tel 021-4343371

Sunville, 36 Laburnum Drive,
Model Farm Road, Cork

Convent of Mercy, Winter's Hill, Kinsale,
Co Cork
Tel 021-4772165

Avila, Ard na Gaoithe Mór,
Bantry, Co Cork
Tel 027-50035

The Bungalow, Balindeasig,
Belgooly, Co Cork
Tel 021-4887954

Casa Maria Seskin,
Bantry, Co Cork
Tel 027-51198

Schull, Co Cork
Tel 028-28189

Arus Muire,
Scartagh, Clonakilty, Co Cork
Tel 023-8833391

Apt 1, Arus Muire,
Scartagh, Clonakilty, Co Cork

Apt 2, Arus Muire,
Scartagh, Clonakilty, Co Cork

Apt 3, Arus Muire,
Scartagh, Clonakilty, Co Cork

Apt 4, Arus Muire,
Scartagh, Clonakilty, Co Cork

Studio 26, Arus Muire,
Scartagh, Clonakilty, Co Cork

2 The Drive, Priory Court,
Watergrasshill, Co Cork
Tel 021-4513949

Studio 25 Arus Muire,
McCurtain Hill, Scartagh,
Clonakilty, Co Cork

Mercy House, Tullineasky West.
Clonakilty, Co Cork
Tel 023-8848116

DAUGHTERS OF CHARITY OF ST VINCENT DE PAUL
St Louise's, Hollyhill House,
Harbour View Road,
Knocknaheeny, Cork
Tel 021-4392762
Superior: Sr Marguerite Buckley
Community: 6
Parish and social work, pastoral care

FRANCISCAN MISSIONARIES OF ST JOSEPH
Convent of St Francis,
Blackrock Road, Cork
Tel 021-4317059
Community Leader: Sr Mary Coyne
Community: 12

CONGREGATION OF OUR LADY OF CHARITY OF THE GOOD SHEPHERD
Baile an Aoire,
Leycester's Lane, Montenotte,
Cork T23 WO85
Tel 021-4551200
Email rgscorklocalleader@gmail.com
Community: 7

17 Killiney Heights, Knockaheeny,
Cork T23 E3H1
Tel 021-4302660
Email jane.murphy100@gmail.com
Community: 2

INFANT JESUS SISTERS
19 Cherry Walk, Muskerry Estate,
Ballincollig, Co Cork P31 FN51
Tel 021-4873599
Pastoral ministry

St Joseph's, Model Farm Road,
Cork T12 EF24
Tel 021-4342348

LITTLE SISTERS OF THE ASSUMPTION
32 St Francis Gardens,
Thomas Davis Street,
Blackpool, Cork
Tel 021-4391407
Email isasfg33@gmail.com

2–3 College View,
Old Youghal Road, Cork
Tel 021-2357070
Email lsacollegev@gmail.com

SISTERS OF MARIE REPARATRICE
6 Knockrea Lawn,
Ballinlough Road, Cork T12 KV8P
Tel 087-9860536
7 Knockrea Lawn,
Ballinlough Road, Cork T12 H4FN
Tel 021-2357070
Email scoughlansmr@gmail.com
Contact: Sr Stephanie Coughlan
Community: 3

MISSIONARY SISTERS OF THE HOLY ROSARY
7 The Circle, Broadale, Douglas, Cork
Tel 021-4362424
Healthcare, work with refugees
Community: 2

OUR LADY OF THE CENACLE
19 St Francis' Gardens,
Blackpool, Cork
Tel 087-2891545
Email peggycronin.8@gmail.com
Contact: Sr Peggy Cronin
Ministry: Retreats and Spiritual Direction

POOR CLARES
Poor Clare Colettine Monastery,
College Road, Cork
Abbess: Sr Miriam Buckley
Community: 7
Contemplatives
Public chapel closed and all Masses,
Adoration, etc. suspended due to Covid-19 restrictions.

PRESENTATION SISTERS
Presentation Provincial Office,
Nano Nagle Place, Douglas Street,
Cork T12 X70A
Tel 021-4975190
Email presprovsw@gmail.com
Provincial Leader: Sr Grace McKernan

Presentation Community,
Nano Nagle Place, Douglas Street, Cork
Tel 021-4193586
Email sistersnanonagleplace@pbvm.org
Community: 3

South Presentation Convent,
Douglas Street, Cork T12 P7FE
Tel 021-4975042
Email southpres1@gmail.com
Local Leader: Sr Patricia O'Shea
Community: 9

115 Cathedral Road, Cork
Tel 021-4393086
Community: 2

Presentation Convent,
Ballyphehane, Cork
Tel 021-4321606
Email presballyork@gmail.com
Team Leadership
Community: 7
Primary School. Tel 021-4315724
Secondary School. Tel 021-4961765

18 The Orchards, Montenotte, Cork
Tel 021-4501456
Community: 2

North Presentation Convent,
Gerald Griffin Street, Cork
Tel 021-4302878
Email northpres.convent@gmail.com
Local Leader: Sr Angela Ryan
Community: 11
Primary School Tel 021-4307132
An Gleann Primary School
Tel 021-4504877

Regina Coeli Convent, Farranree, Cork
Tel 021-4302770
Email presfarranree@gmail.com
Non-resident Leader: Sr Helen Dobbyn
Community: 5
Aiséirí Chríost Primary School
Tel 021-4301383
Secondary School
Tel 021-4303330

126 Deerpark,
Friar's Walk, Cork T12 VY7X
Tel 021-4323321
Community: 2

Presentation Convent,
Bandon, Co Cork
Tel 023-8841476
Email bandonpresentation1@gmail.com
Non-resident Leader: Sr Jo McCarthy
Community: 9
Primary School. Tel 023-8841809
Secondary School. Tel 023-8841814

Apt 115, The Willows,
Boreenmanna Road, Cork
Tel 021-4292587
Community: 1

'Ruah', 33 Kingsbridge,
Turner's Cross, Cork
Tel 021-4809008
Community: 1

Ardán Mhuire, Togher Road, Cork
Tel 021-4961471
Community: 2

7 Churchfield Terrace West,
Gurranabraher, Cork
Tel 021-4306640
Community: 3

7 Old Waterpark,
Carrigaline, Co Cork
Tel 021-4372718
Community: 1

123 Comeragh Park,
The Glen, Cork
Tel 021-4504025
Community: 1

Dóchas, 21 Ashdene,
South Douglas Road, Cork
Tel 021-4897597
Email presdochas@gmail.com
Community: 2

44 Castlemeadows,
Mahon, Cork
Tel 021-4515944
Community: 2

44 Ashbrook Heights, Lehenaghmore,
Togher, Cork
Tel 021-4320006
Community: 1

78 Grange Way, Douglas, Cork
Tel 021-4899704
Community: 1

5 Abbey View, Nano Nagle Walk,
Douglas Street, Cork
Tel 021-4322097
Community: 1

18 Convent View, Nano Nagle Walk,
Douglas Street, Cork
Tel 021-4915380
Community: 1

Apt 15, Ard na Rí, Closes Green,
Farranree, Cork
Tel 021-4909704
Community: 1

Apt 31, Ard na Rí, Closes Green,
Farranree, Cork
Tel 021-4564733
Community: 1

Apt 37, Ard na Rí, Closes Green,
Farranree, Cork
Tel 021-4309262
Community: 1

Apt 39, Ard na Rí, Closes Green,
Farranree, Cork
Tel 021-4308784
Community: 1

35 Lios na Greine,
South Douglas Road, Cork
Community: 1

84 Earlwood Estate,
The Lough, Cork
Community: 2

RELIGIOUS SISTERS OF CHARITY
St Anthony's Convent,
Vincent's Avenue,
St Mary's Road, Cork T23 XVW8
Tel 021-4308162

SACRED HEARTS OF JESUS AND MARY
Sacred Heart Convent, Blackrock,
Cork T12 W200
Tel 021-4936200
Community Leader
Sr Annie Mary Nally
Email amnally@sacredheartsjm.org
Community: 25

SISTERS OF OUR LADY OF APOSTLES
Ardfoyle Convent,
Ballintemple, Cork T12 Y304
Tel 021-4291851 Fax 021-4291105
Email prov@ardfoyle.com
Provincial: Sr Kathleen McGarvey
Sister-in-Charge: Sr Katherine Donovan
Community: 35

URSULINES
Ursuline Convent, Blackrock, Cork
Tel 021-4358663 Fax 021-4356077
Email osucork@gmail.com
Community: 6
Primary School
Tel 021-4358476 Fax 021-4359073
Secondary School
Tel 021-4358012 Fax 021-4358012

58 Meadowgrove, Blackrock, Cork
Tel 021-4357249
Sr Máire O'Donohoe
Email mariefod55@gmail.com
Community: 1
Pastoral Ministry

68 Fort Hill, Moneygurney,
Douglas, Cork
Tel 021-4617091
Email
elizabethbradley010.eb@gmail.com
Community: 1
Pastoral Ministry

EDUCATIONAL INSTITUTIONS

Christ the King Secondary School
South Douglas Road, Cork
Tel 021-4961448 Fax 021-4314563

Christian Brothers College, Cork
Tel 021-4501653 Fax 021-4504113

Coláiste Chríost Rí, Cork
Tel 021-4274904 Fax 021-4964784

Coláiste an Spioraid Naoimh
Bishopstown, Cork
Tel 021-4543790 Fax 021-4543625

Coláiste Phobail Bheanntraí
Bantry, Co Cork
Tel 027-56434

Coláiste Éamann Rís
St Patrick's Road, Cork
Tel 021-4962025 Fax 021-4311792

Edmund Rice College
Carragline, Co Cork
Tel 021-4373785

Mercy Sisters Secondary School
Roscarbery, Co Cork
Tel 023-8848114 Fax 023-8848520

Mount Mercy College
Model Farm Road, Cork
Tel 021-4542366 Fax 021-4542709

North Monastery,
Our Lady's Mount, Cork
Tel 021-4301318 Fax 021-4309891

Presentation College, Cork
Tel 021-4272743 Fax 021-4273147

Presentation Convent
Bandon, Co Cork
Tel 023-8841814 Fax 023-8841385

Presentation Convent Secondary School
Crosshaven, Co Cork
Tel/Fax 021-4831604

Presentation Secondary School
Ballyphehane, Cork
Tel 021-4961765/4961767
Fax 021-4312864

Regina Coeli Convent Secondary School
Farranree, Cork
Tel 021-4303330 Fax 021-4303411

Sacred Heart College
Carrig na bhFear, Co Cork
Tel 021-4884104 Fax 021-4884442

Sacred Heart Secondary School
Clonakilty, Co Cork
Tel 023-8833737 Fax 023-8833908

St Aloysius School, Cork
Tel 021-4316017 Fax 021-4316007

St Angela's College, Cork
Tel 021-4500059 Fax 021-4504515

St Francis Capuchin College,
Rochestown, Co Cork
Tel 021-4891417 Fax 021-4361254

St Vincent's Secondary School, Cork
Tel 021-4307730 Fax 021-4307252

Skibbereen Community School
Gortnaclohy, Skibbereen, Co Cork
Tel 028-51272

Ursuline Convent Secondary School
Blackrock, Cork
Tel/Fax 021-435801

DIOCESE OF DERRY

PATRONS OF THE DIOCESE
ST EUGENE, 23 AUGUST; ST COLUMBA, 9 JUNE

INCLUDES ALMOST ALL OF COUNTY DERRY,
PARTS OF COUNTIES DONEGAL AND TYRONE
AND A VERY SMALL AREA ACROSS THE RIVER BANN IN COUNTY ANTRIM

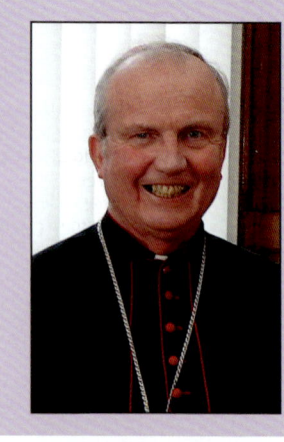

Most Rev Donal McKeown DD
Bishop of Derry
Born 12 April 1950; ordained priest 3 July 1977; appointed Auxiliary Bishop of Down and Connor 21 February 2001; ordained Bishop 29 April 2001; appointed Bishop of Derry 25 February 2014; installed 6 April 2014

Office Address:
Diocesan Offices,
St Eugene's Cathedral,
Francis Street, Derry BT48 9AP
Tel 028-71262302
Fax 028-71371960
Email office@derrydiocese.org

ST EUGENE'S CATHEDRAL, DERRY

In the 1830s, following the Catholic Emancipation Act of 1829, the Catholic community of Derry was able to contemplate building a cathedral. In the summer of 1838, a number of Catholics of the city met with the then Bishop of Derry, Peter McLaughlin, to consider such a project. Over the next thirteen years a weekly collection was made in the city and eventually, on 26 July 1851, the foundation stone was laid by Bishop Francis Kelly.

The construction of the cathedral was sporadic as the funds became available over twenty-five years, and owing to the difficulty in raising money, it was agreed to postpone the building of the tower, belfry and spire until a later date. Due to the lack of funds in the diocese, the windows were initially all of plain glass, and it was only in later years that the stained glass was installed.

J. J. McCarthy (1817–1882) was the architect commissioned to design St Eugene's Cathedral. He was one of the most outstanding church architects in Ireland in his time and he designed many churches and convents all over the country, including St Patrick's Cathedral, Armagh, St Macartan's Cathedral, Monaghan and the Cathedral of the Assumption, Thurles.

The actual construction work took twenty-two years to complete, at a cost of £40,000. It was not until 1873 that the building was brought to a stage where it could be dedicated and used for liturgical celebrations. The cathedral was dedicated by Bishop Francis Kelly on 4 May 1873.

In 1899 it was decided to add a spire to the tower, which was estimated to cost £15,000. The spire was completed on 19 June 1903, and on 27 June the eight-foot-high granite cross was put in position by Fathers John Doherty and Lawrence Hegarty. The full complement of stained-glass windows was achieved in the Spring and Autumn of 1896 at a cost of £2,270. The ten bells of the cathedral first rang out on Christmas Eve, 1902.

St Eugene's was solemnly consecrated on 21 April 1936, the seventh cathedral in Ireland to be consecrated, and the event is celebrated annually on 21 April.

DIOCESE OF DERRY

ADMINISTRATION

Vicars General
Rev Paul McCafferty VG
Rev Michael Canny PP, VG

Chancellor
Very Rev Francis Bradley PP

Vicars Forane
Derry City Deanery
Very Rev Colum Clerkin PP, VF
Co Derry Deanery
Very Rev Peter Madden PP, VF
Co Tyrone Deanery
Very Rev Kevin McElhennon PP, VF
Inishowen Deanery
Very Rev Brian Brady PP, VF

Derry Diocesan Trust
(St Columb's Diocesan Trust is Trustee of the Derry Diocesan Trust) *Directors:*
Most Rev Donal McKeown DD *(Chairperson)*
Rev Paul McCafferty
Rev Michael McCaughey PP
Very Rev Michael Canny PP
Mr Shaun McElhinney
Mr Sean O'Kane
Mr Ciaran Hampson
Ms Fiona Schlindwein
Ms Aine Gallagher
Ms Brenda Morris
Secretary: Teresa McMenamin

Diocesan Office
Bishop: Most Rev Donal McKeown DD
Rev Paul McCafferty VG
Administrative & Financial Secretary
Ms Teresa McMenamin
Executive Director, Derry Diocesan Trust
Mr Kevin McCauley
Diocesan Trust Support Officer
Mrs Oonagh Robinson
Diocesan Offices,
St Eugene's Cathedral,
Francis Street, Derry BT48 9AP
Tel 028-71262302 Fax 028-71371960
Email office@derrydiocese.org

Diocesan Notaries
Rev Kevin McElhennon PP, VF
Very Rev Colum Clerkin PP, VF
Rev Eamonn Graham PP
Ms Teresa McMenamin

CATECHETICS EDUCATION

Catholic Primary School Managers' Association
Contact: Rev Peter Devlin PP
Parochial House,
Malin, Co Donegal
Tel 074-9142022

Catechetical Centre
Derry Diocesan Catechetical Centre,
The Gate Lodge,
2 Francis Street,
Derry BT48 9DS
Tel 028-71264087 Fax 028-71269090
Email ddcc@derrydiocese.org
Director: Rev Paul Farren
Adviser: Miss Thérèse Ferry
Youth Co-ordinator: Ms Lizzie Rea
Secretary: Anne Marie Hickey

PASTORAL

ACCORD
Derry Centre
Diocesan Pastoral Centre,
164 Bishop Street,
Derry BT48 6UJ
Tel 028-71362475 Fax 028-71260970

Omagh Centre
Mount St Columba Pastoral Centre,
48 Brook Street, Omagh,
Co Tyrone BT78 5HD
Tel 028-82242439

Maghera Centre
Pastoral Centre,
159 Glen Road, Maghera
Tel 028-79642983

Inishowen Centre
Pastoral Centre
Church Road, Carndonagh,
Co Donegal
Tel 074-9374103

Chaplain to the Deaf
Rev Thomas Canning CC
143 Melmount Road, Sion Mills,
Strabane, Co Tyrone BT82 9EX
Tel 028-81658264

Charismatic Renewal
Director: Rev Seamus Kelly PP
19 Chapel Road, Dungiven,
Co Derry BT47 4RT

Columba Community
Director: Marguerite Hamilton
St Anthony's, Dundrean,
Burnfoot, Co Donegal
Tel 074-9368370
Email sarce@eircom.net
Columba House,
11 Queen Street, Derry BT48 7E6
Tel 028-71262407

Communications
Media Liaison Person:
Very Rev Michael Canny PP, VG
32 Chapel Road,
Derry BT47 2BB
Tel 028-71342303
Email michaelcanny1958@gmail.com

Ecumenism
Director: Rev Eamon McDevitt PP
78 Lisnaragh Road, Dunamanagh,
Strabane, Co Tyrone BT82 0QN
Tel 028-71398212

Library/Museum
Curators: Rev John R. Walsh CC
Rev Brian McGoldrick PEm

Marriage Tribunal
(See Marriage Tribunals section)

Migrants and Asylum Seekers
Rev Pat O'Hagan PP
Parochial House, Moville,
Co Donegal
Tel 074-9382057

NEST – New Existence for Survivors of Trauma
Ministry to adult victims of abuse of all kinds.
Centre: Pastoral Centre,
Maghera BT46 5JN
Tel 028-79642983
Email nest.int@btconnect.com

Pastoral Centres
Diocesan Pastoral Centre
164 Bishop Street,
Derry BT48 6UJ
Tel 028-71362475 Fax 028-71260970
Director: Rev Micheál McGavigan Adm

Inishowen Pastoral Centre
Carndonagh, Co Donegal
Tel 074-9374103
Director: Rev Con McLaughlin PP

Maghera Pastoral Centre
159 Glen Road,
Maghera, Co Derry
Tel 028-79642983
Director: Rev Patrick Doherty PP

Omagh Pastoral Centre
Mount St Columba Pastoral Centre,
48 Brooke Street, Omagh,
Co Tyrone BT78 5HD
Tel 028-82242439
Director: Rev Eugene Hasson PP

Pilgrimages
Lourdes Pilgrimages:
Mr Charles Glenn
Diocesan Pastoral Centre, 164 Bishop Street, Derry BT48 6HJ
Tel 028-71260293
Email derrypilgrim@outlook.com
Other Pilgrimages:
Rev Gerard Sweeney PP
Tel 028-71882274
Eail leckpatrick.rc@talktalk.net

DIOCESE OF DERRY

Pioneer Total Abstinence Association
Spiritual Director: Rev Karl Haan CC
Parochial House,
Culduff, Co Donegan
Tel 074-9379107

Travellers
Chaplain: Rev Brian Donnelly PP
20 Derbrough Road, Plumbridge,
Co Tyrone BT79 8EF

Trócaire
Diocesan Representative:
Rev Edward Gallagher PP
164 Greencastle, Omagh,
Co Tyrone BT79 7RU
Tel 028-81648474

Vocations
Director: Rev Pat O'Hagan PP
Tel 0770-3444280
Email pgoh2111@gmail.com

PARISHES

Mensal parishes are listed first, followed by other Derry city parishes. Other parishes follow alphabetically. Historical names are in parentheses. Church titulars are in italics.

DERRY CITY
Templemore (St Eugene's)
Rev Paul Farren Adm
Rev Patrick Lagan CC
Rev Ignacy Saniuta CC
Parochial House, St Eugene's Cathedral,
Derry BT48 9AP
Tel 028-71262894/71365712
Fax 028-71377494
Email steugenes@btconnect.com

Templemore (St Columba's)
Rev Patrick Baker Adm
St Columba's Presbytery,
6 Victoria Place, Derry BT48 6TJ
Tel 028-71262301
Fax 028-71372973
Email longtowerparish@aol.com

THE THREE PATRONS
Rev Michael M. Caughey PP
St Patrick's, Buncrana Road,
Pennyburn, Derry BT48 7QL
Tel 028-71262360
Rev Gerard Mongan CC
St Brigid's, Carnhill,
Derry BT48 8HJ
Tel 028-71351261

ST MARY'S, CREGGAN
Rev Joseph Gormley PP
Rev Daniel McFaul CC
Parochial House, St Mary's, Creggan,
Derry BT48 9QE
Tel 028-71263152
Fax 028-71264390
Email stmaryscreggan@derrydiocese.org

OUR LADY OF LOURDES, STEELSTOWN
Very Rev John McDevitt PP
The Presbytery, 11 Steelstown Road,
Derry BT48 8EU
Tel 028-71351718 F
ax 028-71357810
Email steelstownparish@derrydiocese.org

HOLY FAMILY, BALLYMAGROARTY
Rev Patrick O'Kane PP
1 Aileach Road, Ballymagroarty,
Derry BT48 0AZ
Tel 028-71267070 Fax 028-71308687
Email office@holyfamilyparish.com
Rev James Devine CC
c/o 1 Aileach Road, Ballymagroarty,
Derry BT48 0AZ

AGHYARAN (TERMONAMONGAN)
St Patrick's
Rev Paul Fraser PP
16 Castlefin Road,
Castlederg, Co Tyrone BT81 7BT
Tel 028-81670728
Email aghyaranparish@derrydiocese.org

ARDMORE
St Mary's
Rev James McGrory PP
Parochial House, 49 Ardmore Road,
Derry BT47 3QP
Tel 028-71349490
Email ardmoreparish@btinternet.com

BALLINASCREEN (DRAPERSTOWN)
St Columba's
Rev Peter Madden PP, VF
40 Derrynoid Road, Draperstown,
Magherafelt, Co Derry BT45 7DN
Tel 028-79628376
Email ballinascreenparish@gmail.com
Rev John Downey
36 Moneyneena Road, Draperstown,
Magherafelt, Co Derry BT45 7DZ
Tel 028-79628375
Rev Dermot McGirr CC
50 Tobermore Road, Desertmartin,
Magherafelt, Co Derry BT45 5LE
Tel 028-79632196

BANAGHER
St Joseph's, Fincairn
Rev Micheál McGavigan Adm
42 Glenedra Road, Feeny,
Co Derry BT47 4TW
Tel 028-77781223

BELLAGHY (BALLYSCULLION)
St Mary's
Rt Rev Mgr Andrew Dolan PP
25 Ballynease Road, Bellaghy,
Magherafelt, Co Derry BT45 8JS
Tel 028-79386259
Email info@bellaghyparish.com

BUNCRANA (DESERTEGNEY AND LOWER FAHAN)
St Mary's, Cockhill
Very Rev Francis Bradley PP
Cockhill, Buncrana, Co Donegal
Tel 074-9363455
Rev John Walsh CC
Parochial House, Buncrana,
Co Donegal
Tel 074-9361393 Fax 074-9361637
Parish Office: Tel 074-9361253
Fax 074-9361637
Email buncranaparish@eircom.net

CARNDONAGH (DONAGH)
Sacred Heart
Rev Con McLaughlin PP
Barrack Hill, Carndonagh,
Lifford, Co Donegal
Tel 074-9374104

CASTLEDERG (ARDSTRAW WEST AND CASTLEDERG)
St Patrick's
Rev Paul Fraser PP
16 Castlefin Road, Castlederg,
Co Tyrone BT81 7BT
Tel 028-81671393
Email castledergparish@derrydiocese.org

CLAUDY (CUMBER UPPER AND LEARMOUNT)
St Patrick's
Rev David O'Kane PP
9 Church Street, Claudy,
Co Derry BT47 4AA
Tel 028-71337727 Fax 028-71338236

CLONMANY
St Mary's
Very Rev Brian Brady PP, VF
Parochial House,
Ardnascanlon, Ballyliffin, Co Donegal
Tel 074-9376264
Rev Karl Haan CC
Parochial House, Culdaff, Co Donegal
Tel 074-9379107

COLERAINE (DUNBOE, MACOSQUIN AND AGHADOWEY)
St John's
Rev Neil Farren PP
Chapelfield, 59 Laurel Hill,
Coleraine, Co Derry BT51 3AY
Tel 028-70343130
Rev Gerald Hasson (CSSp) CC
Aghadowey, Coleraine

DIOCESE OF DERRY

CULDAFF
St Mary's, Bocan
Very Rev Brian Brady PP, VF
Parochial House, Ardnascanlon,
Ballyliffin, Co Donegal
Tel 074-9376264
Rev Karl Haan CC
Parochial House, Culdaff,
Co Donegal
Tel 074-9379107
Email culdaffnotes@gmail.com

CULMORE
Assumption
Very Rev Colum Clerkin PP, VF
23 Thornhill Park, Culmore,
Derry BT48 4PB
Tel 028-71358519 Fax 028-71353161
Email culmoreparish@derrydiocese.org
Website www.culmore.com

DESERTMARTIN (DESERTMARTIN AND KILCRONAGHAN)
St Mary's, Coolcalm
Rev Peter Madden PP, VF
40 Derrynoid Road, Draperstown,
Magherafelt, Co Derry BT45 7DN
Tel 028-79628376
Rev John Downey
36 Moneyneena Road, Draperstown,
Magherafelt, Co Derry BT45 7DZ
Tel 028-79628375
Rev Dermot Mcgirr CC
50 Tobermore Road, Desertmartin,
Magherafelt, Co Derry BT45 5LE
Tel 028-79632196

DONEYLOOP (URNEY AND CASTLEFINN)
St Columba's
Rev Ciaran Hegarty *(Down & Connor Diocese)* Adm
Doneyloop, Castlefin, Lifford, Co Donegal
Tel 074-9146183
Rev Oliver Crilly *(priest in residence)*
Parochial House, Castlefin,
Lifford, Co Donegal
Tel 074-9146251

DRUMQUIN (LANGFIELD)
St Patrick's
Rev Eugene Hasson Adm
52 Brook Street,
Omagh, Co Tyrone BT78 5HD
Tel 028-82243011
Rev Peter O'Kane CC
48 Brook Street,
Omagh, Co Tyrone BT78 5HD
Tel 028-82242092

DUNAMANAGH (DONAGHEADY)
St Patrick's
Rev Eamon McDevitt PP
78 Lisnaragh Road, Dunamanagh,
Strabane, Co Tyrone BT82 0QN
Tel 028-71398212

DUNGIVEN
St Patrick's
Rev Seamus Kelly PP
19 Chapel Road, Dungiven,
Co Derry BT47 4RT
Tel 028-77741219 Fax 028-77742633
Email dunpar@icloud.com
Rev Joseph Varghese CC
2 Station Road, Dungiven,
Co Derry BT47 4LN
Tel 028-77741256 Fax 028-77742953

FAHAN (BURT, INCH AND FAHAN)
St Mura's
Rev Francis Bradley PP
Cockhill, Buncrana, Co Donegal
Rev Kevin Mulhern (SMA) CC
Parochial House, Fahan,
Lifford, Co Donegal
Tel 074-9360151
Rev Fintan Diggin CC
Parochial House, Burt,
Lifford, Co Donegal
Tel 074-9368155

FAUGHANVALE (FAUGHANVALE AND LOWER CUMBER)
Star of the Sea
Rev Noel McDermott PP
91 Ervey Road, Eglinton,
Co Derry BT47 3AU
Tel 028-71810235

GARVAGH (ERRIGAL)
St Mary's, Ballerin
Very Rev Brendan Crowley PP
78 Ballerin Road, Garvagh,
Co Derry BT51 5EQ
Tel 028-29558251
Email errigalparish@gmail.com

GORTIN (BADONEY LOWER)
St Patrick's
Rev Edward Gallagher PP
164 Greencastle Road, Omagh,
Co Tyrone BT79 7RU
Tel 028-81648474
Email greencastlepp@yahoo.com
Email gortinparish@derrydiocese.org

GREENCASTLE
St Patrick's
Rev Edward Gallagher PP
164 Greencastle Road, Omagh,
Co Tyrone BT79 7RU
Tel 028-81648474 Fax 028-81647829
Email greencastlepp@yahoo.com

GREENLOUGH (TAMLAGHT O'CRILLY)
St Mary's
Rev Eamon Graham PP
65 Mayogall Road,
Knockloughrim,
Magherafelt, Co Derry BT45 8PG
Tel 028-79642458
Rev Dermott Harkin CC
230b Mayogall Road,
Clady, Portglenone,
Co Derry BT44 8NN
Tel 028-25821190

ISKAHEEN (ISKAHEEN AND UPPER MOVILLE)
St Mary's
Very Rev John Farren PP
Muff, Co Donegal
Tel 074-9384037 Fax 074-9384029
Email farrenjohn@eircom.net
Rev Anthony Mailey CC
Parochial House
Quigley's Point, Co Donegal
Tel 074-9383008

KILLYCLOGHER (CAPPAGH)
St Mary's
Very Rev Kevin McElhennon PP, VF
14 Killyclogher Road, Omagh,
Co Tyrone BT79 0AX
Tel 028-82243375
Email info@cappaghparish.com
Rev Declan McGeehan CC
5 Strathroy Road, Omagh,
Co Tyrone BT79 7DW
Tel 028-82251055
Email declan.mcgeehan@derrydiocese.org

KILLYGORDON (DONAGHMORE)
St Patrick's
Rev Patrick Arkinson PP
Sessiaghoneill, Ballybofey,
Co Donegal
Tel 074-9131149

KILREA (KILREA AND DESERTOGHILL)
St Mary's, Drumagarner
Very Rev John Cargan PP
4 Garvagh Road, Kilrea,
Co Derry BT51 5QP
Tel 028-29540343

DIOCESE OF DERRY

LAVEY (TERMONEENY AND PART OF MAGHERA)
St Mary's
Rev Eamon Graham PP
65 Mayogall Road, Knockloughrim,
Magherafelt, Co Derry BT45 8PG
Tel 028-79642458
Rev Dermott Harkin CC
230b Mayogall Road, Clady,
Portglenone, Co Derry BT44 8NN
Tel 028-25821190

LECKPATRICK (LECKPATRICK AND PART OF DONAGHEADY)
St Mary's, Cloughcor
Rev Gerard Sweeney PP
Parochial House, 447 Victoria Road,
Ballymagorry, Strabane,
Co Tyrone BT82 0AT
Tel 028-718802274 Fax 028-71884353
Email leckpatrick.rc@talktalk.net

LIFFORD (CLONLEIGH)
St Patrick's, Murlog
Rev Colm O'Doherty PP
6 Orchard Park, Murlog,
Lifford, Co Donegal
Tel 074-9142022
Parish Office: St Patrick's Church,
Murlog, Lifford, Co Donegal
Tel/Fax 074-9142001
Email clonleighparish@derrydiocese.org

LIMAVADY (DRUMACHOSE, TAMLAGHT, FINLAGAN AND PART OF AGHANLOO)
St Mary's, Irish Green Street
Rt Rev Mgr Bryan McCanny PP
119 Irish Green Street, Limavady,
Co Derry BT49 9AB
Tel 028-77765649
Fax 028-77765290
Email parishoflimavady@btinternet.com
Rev Christopher McDermott CC
20 Loughermore Road,
Ballykelly, Co Derry BT49 9PD
Tel 028-77762721
Email christopher.mcdermott@derrydiocese.org

MAGHERA
St Patrick's, Glen
Very Rev Patrick Doherty PP
Rev Kieran O'Doherty *(priest in residence)*
159 Glen Road, Maghera,
Co Derry BT46 5JN
Tel 028-79642496 Fax 028-79644593
Email accordmaghera@btconnect.com
Parish Office: 159A Glen Road,
Maghera, Co Derry BT46 5JN
Tel 028-79642983

MAGILLIGAN
St Aidan's
Rev Francis O'Hagan PP
71 Duncrun Road, Bellarena,
Limavady, Co Derry BT49 0JD
Tel 028-77750226
Email frohagan@aol.com

MALIN (CLONCA)
St Patrick's, Aghaclay
Rev Peter Devlin PP
Malin, Co Donegal
Tel 074-9370615
Email pnd4680@eircom.net
Rev Charles Logue CC
Malin Head, Co Donegal
Tel 074-9370134

MELMOUNT (MOURNE)
St Mary's, Melmount, Strabane
Rev Michael Doherty PP
39 Melmount Road, Strabane,
Co Tyrone BT82 9EF
Tel 028-71882648
Rev Thomas Canning CC
143 Melmount Road, Sion Mills,
Strabane, Co Tyrone BT82 9EX
Tel 028-81658264
Rev Malachy Gallagher CC
44 Barrack Street, Strabane,
Co Tyrone BT82 8HD
Email malachy.gallagher@derrydiocese.org
Parish Office: Melmount Parish Centre,
Melmount Road, Strabane,
Co Tyrone BT82 9EF
Tel 028-71383777 Fax 028-71886469
Email melparish@aol.com

MOVILLE (MOVILLE LOWER)
St Mary's, Ballybrack
Rev Patrick O'Hagan PP
Parochial House,
Moville, Co Donegal
Tel 074-9382057

NEWTOWNSTEWART (ARDSTRAW EAST)
St Eugene's, Glenock
Very Rev Brian Donnelly PP
Parochial House, Plumbridge,
Omagh, Co Tyrone BT79 8EF
Tel 028-81648283
Email bpdey@aol.co.uk
Rev Roland Colhoun CC
41 Moyle Road, Newtownstewart,
Co Tyrone BT78 4AP
Tel 028-81661445
Email ardstraweast@derrydiocese.org

OMAGH (DRUMRAGH)
St Mary's, Drumragh
Very Rev Eugene Hasson PP
52 Brook Street, Omagh,
Co Tyrone BT78 5HE
Tel 028-82243011 Fax 028-82252149
Email info@drumraghparish.com
Rev Peter O'Kane CC
48 Brook Street, Omagh,
Co Tyrone BT78 5HE
Tel 028-82242092
Parish Office: 48 Brook Street,
Omagh, Co Tyrone BT78 5HE
Tel 028-82442092

PLUMBRIDGE (BADONEY UPPER)
Sacred Heart
Very Rev Brian Donnelly PP
Parochial House, Plumbridge,
Omagh, Co Tyrone BT79 8EF
Tel 028-81648283
Email bpdey@aol.co.uk
Rev Roland Colhoun CC
41 Moyle Road, Newtownstewart,
Co Tyrone BT78 4AP
Tel 028-81661445
Email ardstraweast@derrydiocese.org

SION MILLS
St Theresa's
Very Rev Michael Doherty PP
39 Melmount Road, Strabane,
Co Tyrone BT82 9EF
Tel 028-71882648
Email frmdoc@aol.com
Rev Thomas Canning CC
143 Melmount Road, Sion Mills,
Strabane, Co Tyrone BT82 9EX
Tel 028-81658264
Rev Malachy Gallagher CC
44 Barrack Street, Strabane,
Co Tyrone BT82 8HD
Email malachy.gallagher@derrydiocese.org

STRABANE (CAMUS)
Immaculate Conception
Rev Declan Boland PP
44 Barrack Street, Strabane,
Co Tyrone BT82 8HD
Tel 028-71883293 Fax 028-71882615
Email declan@strabaneparish.com

STRATHFOYLE (STRATHFOYLE, ENAGH LOUGH)
St Oliver Plunkett
Served by the Parish of Glendermott
Parochial House, Parkmore Drive,
Strathfoyle, Co Derry BT47 1XA
Tel 028-71342303

SWATRAGH
St John the Baptist
Very Rev Charles Keaney PP
34 Moneysharvin Road,
Swatragh, Maghera,
Co Derry BT46 5PY
Tel 028-79401236
Email charleskeaney@derrydiocese.org

WATERSIDE (GLENDERMOTT)
St Columb's
Very Rev Michael Canny PP
Rev Sean O'Donnell CC
Rev Malachy Gallagher CC
Rev Roni Zacharis CC
Parochial House, 32 Chapel Road,
Waterside, Derry BT47 2BB
Tel 028-71342303 Fax 028-71345495
Email secretary@watersideparish.net
Website www.watersideparish.org

DIOCESE OF DERRY

INSTITUTIONS AND THEIR CHAPLAINS

Altnagelvin Hospital, Derry
Waterside General Hospital
Rev Daniel McFaul CC
Parochial House,
Creggan, Derry BT48 9QE
Tel 028-71263152
Rev Sean O'Donnell CC
Parochial House, 32 Chapel Road,
Waterside, Derry BT47 2BB
Tel 028-71342303

Community Hospital, Lifford
Rev Colm O'Doherty PP
6 Orchard Park, Lifford, Co Donegal
Tel 074-9142001

District Hospital, Carndonagh
Rev Con McLaughlin PP
Parochial House, Carndonagh
Tel 074-9174104

Gransha Hospital, Derry
Rev Daniel McFaul CC
Parochial House,
Creggan, Derry BT48 9QE
Tel 028-71263152
Rev Sean O'Donnell CC
Parochial House, 32 Chapel Road,
Waterside, Derry BT47 2BB
Tel 028-71342303

Magilligan Prison
Point Road, Magilligan,
Limavady BT49 OLR, Co Derry
Rev Francis O'Hagan PP
Tel 028-77763311

Nazareth House
Fahan, Co Donegal
Rev Francis Bradley PP
Tel 074-9360151

Tyrone County Hospital, Omagh
Very Rev Kevin McElhennon PP, VF

Tyrone and Fermanagh Hospital, Omagh
Very Rev Kevin McElhennon PP, VF

PRIESTS OF THE DIOCESE ELSEWHERE

Rev Manus Bradley
3690 Croissant Oscar,
Brossard, Quebec J4Y 2JB
Tel 00-1450-8127858

Rt Rev Mgr Brendan Devlin MA, DD
St Patrick's College,
Maynooth, Co Kildare
Tel 01-6285222

Rev Christopher Ferguson
On Sabbatical, c/o Diocesan Offices

RETIRED PRIESTS

Rev Joseph Donnelly PEm
Rev John Farrell PEm
Rev George McLaughlin PEm
Rev Peter McLaughlin PEm
Rev John Ryder PEm
Rev Michael Keaveny PEm
Rev Michael Collins PEm
Rev John Doherty PEm
Rev Patrick Crilly PEm
Rev Joseph O'Conor PEm
Rev Brian McGoldrick PEm
Rev James McGonagle PEm
Rev Liam Donnelly PEm
Rev Seamus O'Connell PEm
Rev Brendan Doherty PEm
Rev Patrick Mullan PEm
Rev Eugene Boland PEm
Rev John Gilmore PEm
Rev Edward Kilpatrick PEm
Rev Neil McGoldrick PEm
Rev Patrick McGoldrick PEm
Rev Art O'Reilly PEm
Rev Kevin Mullan PEm
Rev Michael Porter PEm

RELIGIOUS ORDERS AND CONGREGATIONS

PRIESTS

CARMELITES (OCD)
St Joseph's Retreat House,
Termonbacca, Derry BT48 9XE
Tel 028-71262512 Fax 028-71373589
Prior: Rev Stephen Quinn (OCD)
Community: 3

FRANCISCAN FRIARS OF THE RENEWAL (CFR)
St Columba Friary,
Fairview Road, Derry BT48 8NU
Tel 028-71419980 Fax 028-71417652
Email derryfranciscans@gmail.com
Local Servant (Superior)
Rev Francesco Gavazzi (CFR)

SALVATORIANS
'Naomh Mhuire', Upper Slavery,
Buncrana, Co Donegal
Tel 074-9322264
Contact: Rev Malachy McBride (SDS)

SISTERS

CONGREGATION OF THE SISTERS OF MERCY
St Catherine's,
123 Culmore Road, Derry BT48 8JF
Tel 028-71352209

22 Newtownkennedy Street,
Strabane, Co Tyrone BT82 8HT
Tel 028-71882269
Community: 8

8A Sheelin Park, Ballymagroarty,
Derry BT48 0PD
Tel 028-71260398
Community: 3

6 Ballycolman Road, Melmount,
Strabane, Co Tyrone BT82 9PH
Tel 028-71885913

60 Steelstown Village, Derry BT48 8JA
Tel 028-71352300

North Gate Lodge,
125 Culmore Road, Derry BT48 8JF
Tel 028-71350014

19 Towncastle Road,
Strabane, Co Tyrone BT82 0AH
Tel 028-71419891

3 Milestone Way, Fintona Road,
Tattyreagh, Omagh,
Co Tyrone BT78 2LY
Sr Mary Daly RSM
Sr Maura Twohig PBVM

32 Berkeley Heights, Killyclogher,
Omagh, Co Tyrone BT79 7PR

44 Ballynagard Crescent,
Culmore, Derry BT48 8JR
Tel 028-71355776

16 Papworth Avenue,
Derry BT48 8PT
Tel 028-71358827
Community: 4

27 Rockfield, Derry BT48 8AU
Tel 028-71350361

7 Culmore Park,
Culmore Road, Derry BT48 7AN

Flat 20, Abbey House,
Little Diamond, Derry BT48 9EJ

Flat 6, Abbey House,
Little Diamond, Derry BT48 9EJ

CONGREGATION OF OUR LADY OF CHARITY OF THE GOOD SHEPHERD
38 Dungiven Road, Waterside,
Derry BT47 6BW
Tel 028-71342429
Email rgsderry@hotmail.com
Leader: Sr Myriam McLaughlin
Community: 5

45 Virginia Court, Gobnascale,
Waterside, Derry BT47 2DX
Tel 028-71345127
Email vircourt@yahoo.com
Community: 2

LORETO (IBVM)
Convent Grammar, Omagh BT78 1DL
Tel 028-82243633
Primary School,
Brookmount Road, Omagh
Tel 028-82243551

Loreto Community, 1 Osborne Park,
Coleraine, Co Derry BT51 3LU
Tel 028-70344426
Leader: Sr Mary O'Kane
Community: 9
Loreto College, Coleraine BT51 3JZ
Tel 028-70343611

Loreto Sisters, 30 Buskin Way, Coleraine,
Co Derry BT51 3BD
Tel 028-70358065
Community: 2
Educational and pastoral work

CONGREGATION OF THE SISTERS OF NAZARETH
Nazareth House, Fahan,
Lifford, Co Donegal
Tel 074-9360113 Fax 074-9360561
Superior: Sr Margaret Gibbons
Email srmargaretgibbons@gmail.com
Community: 7
Home for aged. Beds: 48

Nazareth House Primary School
Principal: Mr Antoin Moran
Tel 028-71280212
Pupils: 253

EDUCATIONAL INSTITUTIONS
Christian Brothers Grammar School,
Kevlin Road, Omagh BT78 1LD
Tel 028-82243567 Fax 028-82240656
Principal: Mr Fonsie McConnell

CHARITABLE SOCIETIES
Society of St Vincent de Paul
4 Elagh Business Park, Buncrana Road,
Derry BT48 8QH
Tel 028-71265489

Allianz protecting dioceses, parishes and religious orders since 1902

At Allianz, we have the local presence, knowledge and expertise to provide you with the service and protection you need.

Allianz ROI: Allianz p.l.c. is regulated by the Central Bank of Ireland. Registered in Ireland.
Standard acceptance criteria apply.

Pioneer Total Abstinence Association of the Sacred Heart

Since 1898, Pioneers have been promoting sobriety and temperance through faith and prayer, by developing self-denial as a means to inner freedom, and by setting good example to others.

'The chains of habit are too weak to be noticed until they are too strong to be broken.'
(Samuel Johnson)

27-28 Marino Mart, Fairview, Dublin 3

www.pioneers.ie   Tel 01 804 5226

Prayer Requests welcome via www.pioneers.ie/connect

Registered Charity No. 20003579   CHY 2824

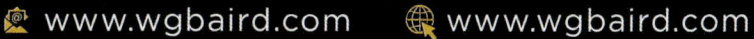

Allianz ⓘ

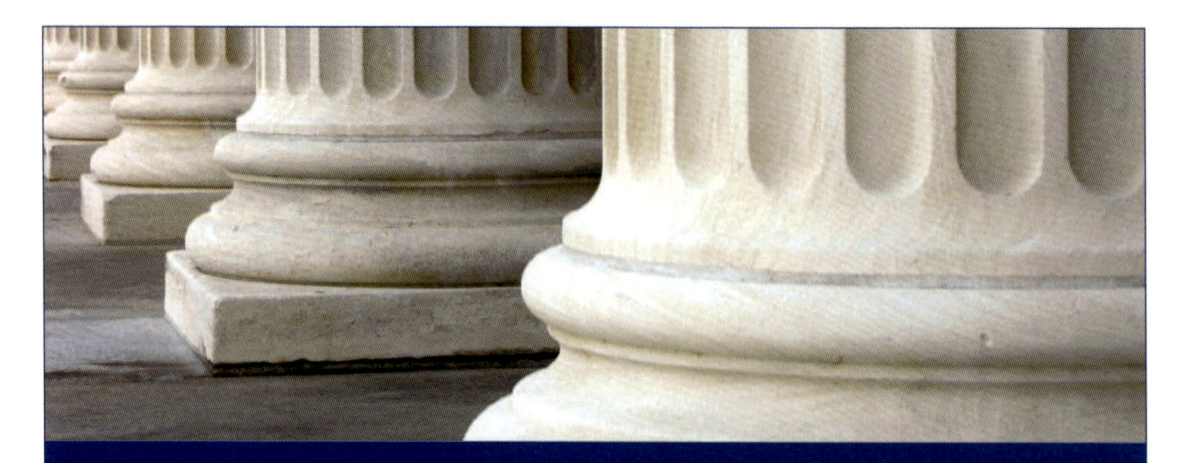

Providing Professional Ethical Advice

L&P specialises in providing ethical investment management and stewardship services to religious congregations, charities and non-profit organisations, trusts and endowments.

With over 30 years' experience, we work with many organisations worldwide. Our team of dedicated professionals specialises in the following areas:

CONSULTANCY
- Resource Assessment
- Strategic Planning
- Trust & Charity Law

STEWARDSHIP
- Accounting & Finance
- Business Management
- Corporate Governance
- Communication & Training

ETHICAL INVESTMENT MANAGEMENT

L&P forms part of the Cantor Fitzgerald Group, a leading global financial services firm with offices in 25 countries.

With a proud history of stockbroking and servicing our clients and financial advisors in Ireland since 1995, Cantor Fitzgerald Ireland provides a full suite of investment services and is committed to the highest level of service.

75 St Stephen's Green, Dublin 2, Ireland
Tel: + 353 1 633 3826
Email: L&P@cantor.com

www.cantorfitzgerald.ie/LPgroup

L&P

CANTOR Fitzgerald

Commercial Acumen with an Ethical Foundation

Cantor Fitzgerald Ireland is regulated by the Central Bank of Ireland and is a member firm of the Irish Stock Exchange and the London Stock Exchange.
L&P Trustee Services Ltd is authorised as a Trust & Company Service Provider.

DIOCESE OF DOWN AND CONNOR

PATRONS OF THE DIOCESE
ST MALACHY, 3 NOVEMBER; ST MACNISSI, 4 SEPTEMBER

INCLUDES COUNTY ANTRIM, THE GREATER PART OF COUNTY DOWN AND PART OF COUNTY DERRY

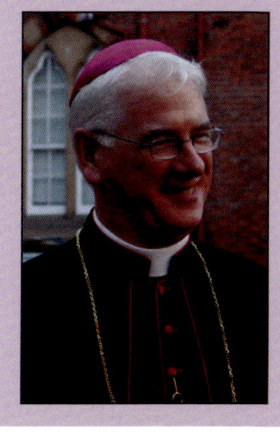

Most Rev Noel Treanor DD
Bishop of Down and Connor; ordained priest 13 June 1976; ordained Bishop of Down and Connor 29 June 2008

Residence: Lisbreen,
73 Somerton Road,
Belfast, Co Antrim BT15 4DE
Tel 028-90776185
Fax 028-90779377
Email
dcoffice@downandconnor.org

HISTORY OF THE DIOCESE

St Patrick does not provide many geographical details in his Confession about his sojourn in Ireland, yet a later tradition associated his work as a slave with Slemish in Co Antrim, his return as a missionary with Saul in Co Down and his burial place with Downpatrick.

In the course of his evangelisation of Ireland St Patrick ordained bishops to minister to local communities. Among those bishops was Mac Nissi, who, following his baptism by St Patrick, founded the church of Connor. However, by the sixth century, after Christianity had been well established, the monastic system was becoming the dominant form of ecclesiastical life. About 555 St Comgall founded a monastery at Bangor that was destined to become one of the most famous in Ireland. Monasteries were also founded in France, Switzerland and Italy, and these became influential centres for the conversion of many peoples. Other monasteries founded in the early centuries of Christianity in Down and Connor include those at Moville, Nendrum, Inch, Drumbo, Antrim and Comber. Some of these later adopted the Benedictine or Augustinian Rule.

The Norsemen cast greedy eyes on Irish monasteries, especially those near the coast, which could be easily attacked and plundered for silver and gold. Bangor fell victim to one such raid in 823, when many monks were killed and the shrine of St Comgall was destroyed. The loss of life and damage to buildings helped weaken the discipline and commitment of the monks. When St Malachy, the great reformer, became Abbot of Bangor in 1123, he found much of the abbey in ruins and the Rule being poorly observed.

In 1111, at the Synod of Rathbreasail, Ireland was at last given the diocesan territorial system that had been common in the western Church. Among the dioceses created were Connor for the Kingdom of Dalriada and Down for the Kingdom of Uladh. Though separate, these dioceses were united under St Malachy in 1124. He continued to reside at Bangor and pursue his reforms, but was driven from the monastery and forced to take refuge at Lismore. In 1129 he was appointed Archbishop of Armagh but because of local opposition, was not able to take control of the See until five years later. In 1137 he resigned and returned to the Diocese of Down, which was again separate from Connor. Invited by his fellow bishops to travel to Rome to obtain the pallia for the archbishops of Armagh and Cashel, Malachy set off in 1139 and visited St Bernard at Clairvaux. Though unsuccessful in his quest, he was appointed papal legate for Ireland. He left some monks at Clairvaux to be trained in the Cistercian way of life and they established the first Cistercian monastery at Mellifont in 1142. A second journey to Rome in 1148 to seek the pallia was cut short by his death on 2 November in the arms of St Bernard. The great Cistercian abbot later wrote Malachy's life story, which ensured that his fame spread widely on the Continent. Malachy was canonised in 1190.

In 1177 the Anglo-Norman adventurer, John de Courcy, carved out the Lordship of Ulster for himself and set up his base at Dunlethglaisse which he renamed Downpatrick. He took a keen interest in ecclesiastical affairs and brought Anglo-Norman Benedictine monks to the cathedral at Downpatrick. His wife founded the Cistercian Monastery at Greyabbey in the Ards Peninsula and he brought other Orders, such as the Premonstratensian and the Augustinian Canons to his territories.

In 1192 the Diocese of Dromore was cut off from Down to make provision for the native Irish, as the part that retained the name Down was by then regarded as Anglo-Norman. The Dioceses of Down and Connor continued to be administered separately until the fifteenth century. In 1439 Pope Eugene IV decided that, after the death of John Sely, the Bishop of Down, the two Sees should be united, and, although Sely was deprived of office three years later for misbehaviour, the Archbishop of Armagh resisted the union of the two dioceses for several years and it did not take place until 1453. In the 1220s the newly founded mendicant Orders, the Dominicans and Franciscans, established houses in the diocese. By the sixteenth century the Third Order of Franciscans had numerous friaries.

Robert Blyth, an English Benedictine, was Bishop of Down and Connor when Henry VIII demanded recognition as supreme Head of the Church. Blyth surrendered in 1539 and received a substantial pension. The Pope then deprived him of office and appointed in his place Eugene Magennis. Magennis also accepted the royal supremacy but later retracted his submission and was able to retain his See under Mary Tudor. The Franciscan pluralist, Miler McGrath, who succeeded in 1565 and accepted the royal supremacy in 1567, was deposed by Pope Gregory XIII in 1580 but had already been appointed Archbishop of Cashel by Queen Elizabeth. Two years later the Donegal Franciscan, Conor O'Devany, became bishop and after a lengthy episcopate of nearly thirty years was cruelly martyred in Dublin in 1612. (In 1992 he was one of the seventeen Irish martyrs beatified by Pope John Paul II)

During the upheavals of the seventeenth century and the harsh penal legislation of the early eighteenth century, the diocese was left vacant for long periods. After the death of Bishop Daniel Mackey in 1673 no appointment was made until Terence O'Donnelly became vicar apostolic in 1711. When O'Donnelly's successor, James O'Sheil, died in 1724 the See remained vacant until 1727. After the death of Bishop John Armstrong in 1739 all subsequent vacancies never lasted more than a year.

In 1825 William Crolly, who had been parish priest of Belfast for thirteen years, became bishop. Several of his predecessors had lived in or near Downpatrick but he chose to remain in the growing town which he rightly foresaw would become the largest in the diocese. Not only was Belfast geographically more central and convenient but its Catholic population soon dwarfed that of Downpatrick and of all other parishes in the diocese. By 1900 Catholics numbered 85,000 and represented just under a quarter of the city's population. The number of priests serving in it had greatly increased and religious orders of men and women had been brought in to care for the spiritual, educational and social needs of the people.

The continued increase in the number of Catholics in and around Belfast accounts for the position Down and Connor holds as the second largest diocese in Ireland, with a population of approximately 350,000.

DIOCESE OF DOWN AND CONNOR

Most Rev Anthony Farquhar DD
Titular Bishop of Ermiana; Former Auxiliary Bishop of Down and Connor; ordained priest 13 March 1965; ordained Bishop 15 May 1983
Residence: 24 Fruithill Park,
Belfast BT11 8GE Tel 028-90624252

Most Rev Patrick J. Walsh DD
Retired Bishop of Down and Connor; ordained priest 25 February 1956; ordained Titular Bishop of Ros Cré 15 May 1983; installed Bishop of Down and Connor 28 April 1991
Residence: Nazareth House Care Village, 516 Ravenhill Road, Belfast BT6 0BW
Tel 0044-77-32104366

CHAPTER

Dean: Vacant

Honorary Canons
Rt Rev Mgr Sean Connolly
Very Rev Canon Noel Conway
Very Rev Canon Robert Fullerton
Very Rev Canon Brendan Murray
Very Rev Canon Sean Rogan

ADMINISTRATION

Chancellor
Very Rev Eugene O'Hagan
Lisbreen, 75 Somerton Road,
Belfast BT15 4DE
Tel 028-90776185 Fax 028-90779377
Email chancellor@downandconnor.org

Vicars General
Very Rev Eugene O'Hagan VG
75 Somerton Road, Belfast BT15 4DE
Tel 028-90776185
The Rev Mgr Patrick Delargy VG
Parochial House, 4 Broughshane Road,
Ballymena, Co Antrim BT43 7DX
Tel 028-25641515

Diocesan Commission for Religious
Chairperson: Rev Willie McGettrick (CSsR)
Vice-Chair: Sr Nuala Kelly DC
Email mar_illac@yahoo.co.uk

Diocesan Safeguarding Office
120 Cliftonville Road, Belfast BT14 6LA
Acting Diocesan Director and Diocesan Liaison Person
Mr Philip O'Hara
Training and Parish Development Officer: Ms Susan Gordon
Safeguarding Champion for Safeguarding Adults: Mr Philip O'Hara
Office Tel 028-90492798
Emergency Tel 07534992124
Safeguarding Secretary
Ms Marion Adams
Vetting & Barring Co-ordinator for the Northern Dioceses: Mr Andrew Thomson
Vetting Supervisor (part-time)
Mrs Lorraine Moreland

Assistant Vetting Officer (Part-time)
Denise Rooney
Safeguarding Support Officers for Parish Safeguarding Committees can be contacted through the Safeguarding Office
Tel 028-90492798

Episcopal Vicar for Safeguarding
Very Rev Peter Owens

Safeguarding Tel 028-90492798
Safeguarding Email office@soddc.org
Vetting Tel 028-90492783
Vetting Email vetting@soddc.org or vetting@btinternet.com
Designated Liaison Person
Emergency Tel 07534-992124

Consultors
Very Rev Eugene O'Hagan VG
Very Rev Patrick Delargy VG
Very Rev Sean Emerson
Very Rev Canon Robert Fullerton
Very Rev Aidan Kerr
Very Rev Austin McGirr
Very Rev Thomas McGlynn
Very Rev Feargal McGrady
Very Rev Peter Owens

Episcopal Vicar for Clergy (Permanent Deacons)
Very Rev Michael Sheehan PP
Tel 028-90812238

Episcopal Vicar for Diocesan Forward Planning
Very Rev Timothy Bartlett
Tel 028-90320482

Council of Priests
Chairman: Very Rev Michael Spence
28 Willowbank Park, Belfast BT6 0LL
Tel 028-90793023
Secretary: Very Rev Conor McGrath
119A Glenravel Road, Carrowcowan
Co Antrim BT43 6QL
Tel 028-21758217

Judicial Vicar for Diocese of Down and Connor
Very Rev Joseph Rooney JCL
120 Cliftonville Road, Belfast BT14 6LA
Tel 028-90491990 Fax 028-90491440

Diocesan Trust Board
Chairman: Most Rev Noel Treanor
Secretary: Mr Gareth Hughes
Trustees: Very Rev Eugene O'Hagan VG
The Rev Mgr Patrick Delargy VG
The Rev Mgr Joseph M. Glover
Mr Joseph Higgins
Mr Gerard McGinn
Ms Orlaigh O'Neill
Ms Brenda Heenan
Mr Michael Scullion
Ms Rose Kelly
Mr Nicholas McKenna

Diocesan Director of Civil Administration
Mr Gareth Hughes
75 Somerton Road, Belfast BT15 4DE
Email g.hughes@downandconnor.org
Tel 028-90776185

DIOCESAN OFFICES
Finance Section
Ms Ann McColgan
Email ann@downandconnor.org
Mr Raymond Noade
Email raymond@downandconnor.org
Ms Sarah Mitchell
Email s.mitchell@downandconnor.org

Property Section
Property Liaison Officer
Mrs Martina Crilly
Email property@downandconnor.org

Secretarial Section
Mrs Frances Doran
Email dcoffice@downandconnor.org

HR Section
Ms Marie Toner
Email m.toner@downandconnor.org
Ms Mary Harrison
Email m.harrison@downandconnor.org

Media Liaison Officer
Very Rev Edward McGee
120 Cliftonville Road, Belfast BT14 6LA
Email dcpress@downandconnor.org

Diocesan Archivist
Very Rev Thomas McGlynn PP
St Agnes' Presbytery,
143 Andersonstown Road,
Belfast BT11 9BW
Tel 028-90615702
Email t.mcglynn@downandconnor.org

Diocesan Secretary
Very Rev Gerard Fox
Lisbreen, 75 Somerton Road,
Belfast BT15 4DE
Tel 028-90776185 Fax 028-90779377
Email g.fox@downandconnor.org

CATECHETICS AND EDUCATION

Episcopal Vicar for Education
Very Rev Gerard Fox
75 Somerton Road, Belfast BT15 4DE
Tel 028-90776185
Email education@downandconnor.org

Down & Connor Catholic Schools Support Service
Director: Very Rev Edward McGee
120 Cliftonville Road, Belfast BT14 6LA
Tel 028-90491886 Fax 028-90491440
Email dctrusteeservice@downandconnor.org

Council for Catholic Maintained Schools
Linen Hill House, 23 Linenhall Street,
Lisburn BT28 1FJ
Tel 028-92013014
Email info@ccmsschools.com

Diocesan Living Church Office
Director: Ms Paula McKeown
Assistant Director: Mr Jim Deeds
Faith Development Co-ordinator
Aisling Steen
SPRED Co-ordinator: Ms Louise McQuillan
120 Clifonville Road, Belfast BT14 6LA
Tel 028-90690920
Email livingchurch@downandconnor.org

DIOCESE OF DOWN AND CONNOR

LITURGY

Diocesan Commission on Liturgy
Chairman: Mr Malachy McKeever
Tel 075-98346011
Email liturgy@downandconnor.org

PASTORAL

ACCORD (NI) Catholic Marriage Care Service
Regional Office
Administration Officer: Ms Brenda Russell
68 Berry Street, Belfast BT1 1JF
Tel 028-90233002
Email info@accordni.com
www.accordni.com

Belfast
68 Berry Street, Belfast BT1 1JF
Tel 028-90339944

Ballymena
All Saints Parish Centre, 9 Cushendall Road,
Ballymena, Co Antrim
Tel 028-38334781

Downpatrick
Passionist Retreat Centre,
16A Downpatrick Road, Crossgar,
Co Down BT30 9EQ
Tel 028-90233002
Email downpatrick@accordni.com

Judicial Vicariate of Down & Connor
Very Rev Joseph G. Rooney, Judicial Vicar
120 Cliftonville Road,
Belfast BT14 6LA
Tel 028-90491990
Email judicialvicariate@downandconnor.org

Down & Connor Office of the Armagh Inter-Diocesan Marriage Tribunal
120 Cliftonville Road,
Belfast BT14 6LA
Tel 028-90491990
Email marriagetribunal@downandconnor.org
Judicial Vicar
Very Rev Joseph Rooney JCL
Associate Judge
Rev Vincent P. Cushnahan JCL
Tribunal/Chancery Administrators
Mrs Deirdre Rafferty
Mrs Maeve Laverty

Diocesan Ecumenical Commission
Secretary: Rev Colin Grant
Aquinas Grammar School,
518 Ravenhill Road, Belfast BT6 0BY
Tel 028-90643939

Pioneer Total Abstinence Association
Diocesan Director
Rev Raymond McCullagh
1 Seafield Park South,
Portstewart BT55 7LH
Tel 028-70832066

Pontifical Mission Societies
Diocesan Director: Rev Conor McGrath
119A Glenravel Road, Carrowcowan,
Ballymena, Co Antrim BT43 6QL
Tel 028-21758217

Diocesan Vocations Commission
Director: Very Rev Kevin McGuckien
23 Hannahstown Hill,
Belfast BT17 0LT
Tel 028-90614567
Email hannahstown@downandconnor.org

Diocesan Commission on Family Ministry
Secretary: Very Rev Michael McGinnity
St Malachy's Parish,
24 Alfred Street, Belfast BT2 8EN
Tel 028-90321713
Email m.mcginnity@btconnect.com

Diocesan Social Affairs Commission
Director: Rev Timothy Bartlett
75 Somerton Road, Belfast BT15 4DE
Tel 028-90776185

Youth Link Training Offices
Farset Enterprise Park,
683 Springfield Road,
Belfast BT12 7DY
Tel 028-90323217
Director: Rev Patrick White
Email info@youthlink.org.uk

PARISHES

Mensal parishes are listed first. Other parishes follow alphabetically, city parishes first. Historical names are in parentheses.

THE CATHEDRAL (ST PETER'S)
Very Rev Martin Graham Adm
Rev Brian Watters CC
Rev Aidan McCaughan *(priest in residence)*
Deacon Martin Whyte
St Peter's Cathedral Presbytery,
St Peter's Square, Belfast BT12 4BU
Tel 028-90327573

ST MARY'S
Very Rev Timothy Bartlett Adm, EV
Very Rev Paul Armstrong, PE
Rev Brian Watters, *Assistant Priest*
St Mary's, Marquis Street,
Belfast BT1 1JJ
Tel 028-90320482

ST PATRICK'S
Very Rev Eugene O'Neill Adm, VF
Rev Anthony Mc Aleese CC
St Patrick's Presbytery,
199 Donegall Street, Belfast BT1 2FL
Tel 028-90324597

HOLY FAMILY
Very Rev Paul Strain Adm
Rev Paul Morely CC and priest in charge (Chaplain) to the Syro-Malabar Community
Deacon Brendan Dowd
Holy Family Presbytery,
Newington Avenue, Belfast BT15 2HP
Tel 028-90743119
Very Rev Canon Brendan Murray *(priest in residence)*
Apt 13 Downview Manor, Belfast BT15 4JL

ST COLMCILLE'S
Very Rev Anthony Fitzsimons Adm
Rev Vincent Cushnahan JCL
191 Upper Newtownards Road,
Belfast BT4 3JB
Tel 028-90654157

CITY PARISHES

CHRIST THE REDEEMER, LAGMORE
Very Rev Colin Crossey PP
81 Lagmore Grove, Dunmurry,
Belfast BT17 0TD
Tel 028-90309011

CORPUS CHRISTI
Very Rev Patrick McCafferty PP
Corpus Christi Presbytery,
4-6 Springhill Grove, Belfast BT12 7SL
Tel 028-90246857

DERRIAGHY
Very Rev Brian McCann Adm
Deacon Kevin Webb
111 Queensway,
Lambeg, Lisburn BT27 4QS
Tel 028-92662896

GREENCASTLE
Very Rev David Delargy PP
824 Shore Road, Newtownabbey,
Co Antrim BT36 7DG
Tel 028-90370845

HOLY CROSS
Very Rev John Craven (CP) PP
Rev Frank Trias (CP) CC
Rev Gareth Thomas (CP) CC
Holy Cross Retreat, 432 Crumlin Road,
Ardoyne, Belfast BT14 7GE
Tel 028-90748231/2

HOLY ROSARY
Very Rev Brendan Hickland PP
503 Ormeau Road, Belfast BT7 3GR
Tel 028-90642446
Very Rev Canon Robert Fullerton CC
Holy Rosary Presbytery,
501 Ormeau Road, Belfast BT7 3GR
Tel 028-90641064

HOLY TRINITY
Very Rev Brendan Mulhall Adm
Holy Trinity Presbytery,
26 Norglen Gardens, Belfast BT11 8EL
Tel 028-90590985/6

DIOCESE OF DOWN AND CONNOR

THE NATIVITY
Very Rev Aidan Keenan PP
The Presbytery, Bell Steel Road,
Poleglass, Belfast BT17 0PB
Tel 028-90625739

OUR LADY QUEEN OF PEACE, KILWEE
Very Rev Rory Sheehan PP
Netherley Lodge,
130 Upper Dunmurry Lane,
Belfast BT17 0EW
Tel 028-90616300

SACRED HEART
Rev James Madden (OPraem) Adm
Deacon Joseph Baxter
Rev Manuelito Milo *(Chaplain, Belfast City Hospital)*
Sacred Heart Presbytery,
1 Glenview Street, Belfast BT14 7DP
Tel 028-90351851

ST AGNES'
Very Rev Thomas McGlynn PP
Deacon Gregory McGuigan
143 Andersonstown Road,
Belfast BT11 9BW
Tel 028-90615702/90603951

ST ANNE'S
Very Rev Peter O'Hare PP
Deacon Patrick McNeill
St Anne's Parochial House,
Kingsway, Finaghy, Belfast BT10 0NE
Tel 028-90610112

ST ANTHONY'S
Very Rev Henry McCann PP
St Anthony's Presbytery,
4 Willowfield Crescent, Belfast BT6 8HP
Tel 028-90458158

ST BERNADETTE'S
Very Rev Brendan Hickland Adm
Rev Michael Spence CC
28 Willowbank Park, Belfast BT6 0LL
Tel 028-90793023

ST BRIGID'S
Very Rev Edward O'Donnell PP
Deacon Brett Lockhart
42 Derryvolgie Avenue, Belfast BT9 6FP
Tel 028-90665409

ST GERARD'S
Redemptorist Fathers
Very Rev Kevin Browne (CSsR) PP and Rector
Rev Denis Luddy (CSsR) CC
722 Antrim Road, Newtownabbey,
Co Antrim BT36 7PG
Tel 028-90774833/4

ST JOHN'S
Very Rev Martin Magill PP
470 Falls Road, Belfast BT12 6EN
Tel 028-90321511
Very Rev Anthony McLaverty *(priest in residence)*
518 Donegall Road, Belfast BT12 6DY
Tel 028-90314112

ST LUKE'S
Very Rev Brian McCann PP, VF
St Luke's Presbytery, Twinbrook Road,
Dunmurry, Co Antrim BT17 0RP
Tel 028-90619459

ST MALACHY'S
Very Rev Michael McGinnity PP
St Malachy's Presbytery,
24 Alfred Street, Belfast BT2 8EN
Tel 028-90321713

ST MARY'S ON THE HILL
Very Rev Pat Sheehan PP, VF
Elmfield, 165 Antrim Road, Glengormley,
Newtownabbey, Co Antrim BT36 7QR
Tel 028-90832979
Very Rev Aidan Kerr PE
142 Carnmoney Road, Newtownabbey,
Co Antrim BT36 6JU
Tel 028-90832488
Very Rev Brendan Beagon CC
1 Christine Road, Newtownabbey,
Co Antrim BT36 6TG
Tel 028-90841507

ST MATTHEW'S
Very Rev Peter Carlin PP
St Matthew's Presbytery, Bryson Street,
Newtownards Road, Belfast BT5 4ES
Tel 028-90457626

ST MICHAEL'S
Very Rev Ciaran Feeney PP
200 Finaghy Road North, Belfast BT11 9EG
Tel 028-90617519

ST OLIVER PLUNKETT
Very Rev Aidan Brankin PP
27 Glenveagh Drive, Belfast BT11 9HX
Tel 028-90618180

ST PAUL'S
Very Rev Anthony Devlin PP, VF
Rev Joe Pazheparambil Davis CC
St Paul's Presbytery, 125 Falls Road,
Belfast BT12 6AB
Tel 028-90325034
Rev Eddie Craemer (CSsR) CC
Clonard Monastery, Clonard Gardens,
Belfast BT13 2RL

ST TERESA'S
Very Rev Gabriel Lyons PP
St Teresa's Presbytery, Glen Road,
Belfast BT11 8BL
Tel 028-90612855

ST VINCENT DE PAUL
Very Rev Patrick Devlin PP
St Vincent de Paul Presbytery,
169 Ligoniel Road, Belfast BT14 8DP
Tel 028-90713401

WHITEABBEY (ST JAMES'S)
Very Rev David Delargy PP
824 Shore Road,
Newtownabbey BT36 7DG

WHITEHOUSE
Very Rev David Delargy PP
824 Shore Road,
Newtownabbey BT36 7DG

COUNTRY PARISHES

AGHAGALLON AND BALLINDERRY
Very Rev Declan Mulligan PP
Parochial House, 5 Aghalee Road,
Aghagallon, Craigavon,
Co Armagh BT67 0AR
Tel 028-92651214

AHOGHILL
Very Rev Hugh J O'Hagan PP
Parochial House, 31 Ballynafie Road,
Ahoghill BT42 1LF
Tel 028-25871351

ANTRIM
Very Rev Sean Emerson PP, VF
Parochial House, 3 Oriel Road,
Antrim BT41 4HP
Tel 028-94428016
Rev James O'Reilly CC
St Joseph's Presbytery,
56 Greystone Road, Antrim BT41 1JZ
Tel 028-94429103
Rev Jain Matthew Mannathukaran CC
5 Oriel Road, Antrim BT41 4HP
Tel 028-94428086

ARMOY
Very Rev Robert Butler Adm *(pro tem)*
Parochial House, Armoy,
Ballymoney, Co Antrim BT53 8RL
Tel 028-20751205

BALLINTOY
Very Rev Brian Daly Adm
15 Moyle Road, Ballycastle,
Co Antrim BT54 6LB
Tel 028-20762223

BALLYCASTLE (RAMOAN)
Very Rev Brian Daly PP
Parochial House, 15 Moyle Road,
Ballycastle, Co Antrim BT54 6LB
Tel 028-20762223
Rev Barney McCahery (CSsR) CC
6 Market Street,
Ballycastle, Co Antrim BT54 6DP
Tel 028-20762202
Very Rev Raymond Fulton PE
4 Gortanclochair Park,
Ballycastle, Co Antrim BT54 6N1

BALLYCLARE AND BALLYGOWAN
Very Rev Joseph Rooney Adm, JCL
Parochial House, 69 Doagh Road,
Ballyclare, Co Antrim BT39 9BG
Tel 028-93342226

DIOCESE OF DOWN AND CONNOR

BALLYGALGET
Very Rev Feargal McGrady PP
Parochial House, 60 Windmill Hill,
Portaferry, Co Down BT22 1RH
Tel 028-42771212

BALLYMENA (KIRKINRIOLA)
The Rev Mgr Patrick Delargy PP, VF, VG
4 Broughshane Road, Ballymena,
Co Antrim BT43 7DX
Tel 028-25643828
Rev Aloysius Lumala
Parochial House, 4 Boughshane Road,
Ballymena BT43 7DX

BALLYMONEY AND DERRYKEIGHAN
Very Rev Damian McCaughan PP
81 Castle Street, Ballymoney,
Co Antrim BT53 6JT
Tel 028-27662003

BANGOR
Very Rev Joseph Gunn PP, VF
St Comgall's Presbytery,
27 Brunswick Road, Bangor,
Co Down BT20 3DS
Tel 028-91465522

CARNLOUGH
Very Rev Dermot McKay PP
51 Bay Road, Carnlough,
Ballymena, Co Antrim BT44 0HJ
Tel 028-28885220

CARRICKFERGUS
Very Rev Peter Owens PP
Parochial House,
8 Minorca Place, Carrickfergus,
Co Antrim BT38 8AU
Tel 028-93363269

CASTLEWELLAN (KILMEGAN)
Very Rev Denis McKinlay PP, VF
41 Lower Square,
Castlewellan BT31 9DN
Tel 028-43770377

COLERAINE
Very Rev Austin McGirr Adm
Rev Nideesh Varghese CC
72 Nursery Avenue, Coleraine,
Co Derry BT52 1LR
Tel 028-70343156

CROSSGAR (KILMORE)
Very Rev Brendan Smyth PP
Parochial House,
10 Downpatrick Street, Crossgar,
Downpatrick, Co Down BT30 9EA
Tel 028-44830229

CULFEIGHTRIN
Very Rev Con Boyle PP
87 Cushendall Road, Ballyvoy,
Ballycastle, Co Antrim BT54 6QY
Tel 028-20762248

CUSHENDALL
Very Rev Kieran Whiteford PP
Parochial House, 28 Chapel Road,
Cushendall, Ballymena BT44 0RS
Tel 028-21771240

CUSHENDUN
Very Rev Kieran Whiteford PP
Parochial House, 28 Chapel Road,
Cushendall, Ballymena,
Co Antrim BT44 0RS
Tel 028-21771240
Very Rev James O'Kane PE, CC
21 Knocknacarry Avenue,
Cushenden, Co Antrim BT44 0NX
Tel 028-21761269

DOWNPATRICK
Very Rev John Murray PP, VF
Very Rev Maurice Henry PE
Parochial House, 54 St Patrick's Avenue,
Downpatrick, Co Down BT30 6DN
Tel 028-44612443
Very Rev Liam Toland CC
29 Killough Road, Downpatrick,
Co Down BT30 6PX
Tel 028-44612443
Very Rev Canon Noel Conway *(priest in residence)*
23 Rathkeltair Road, Downpatrick,
Co Down BT30 6NL
Tel 028-44614777

DRUMAROAD AND CLANVARAGHAN
Very Rev Ciaran Dallat Adm
Parochial House, 15 Drumaroad Hill,
Castlewellan, Co Down BT31 9PD
Tel 028-44811474

DRUMBO AND CARRYDUFF
Very Rev Michael Sheehan PP
Parochial House, 546 Saintfield Road,
Carryduff, Belfast BT8 8EU
Tel 028-90812238
Very Rev Canon Sean Rogan PE
546 Saintfield Road, Carryduff,
Belfast BT8 8EU
Tel 028-90812238

DUNDRUM AND TYRELLA
Very Rev Robert Fleck PP
Parochial House, Dundrum,
Newcastle, Co Down BT33 0LU
Tel 028-43751212

DUNEANE
Very Rev Patrick McWilliams PP
103 Roguery Road, Moneyglass,
Toomebridge, Co Antrim BT41 3PT
Tel 028-79650225

DUNLOY AND CLOUGHMILLS
Very Rev Darren Brennan PP
Parochial House,
14 Presbytery Lane, Dunloy,
Co Antrim BT44 9DZ
Tel 028-27657223

DUNSFORD AND ARDGLASS
Very Rev Gerard McCloskey PP
Parochial House, Ardglass,
Co Down BT30 7TU
Tel 028-44841208

GLENARIFFE
Very Rev David White PP
Parochial House, 182 Garron Road,
Glenariffe, Co Antrim BT44 0RA
Tel 028-21771249

GLENARM (TICKMACREEVAN)
Very Rev Dermot McKay PP
51 Bay Road, Carnlough,
Co Antrim BT44 0HJ
Tel 028-28885220

GLENAVY AND KILLEAD
Very Rev Colm McBride PP, VF
Parochial House, 59 Chapel Road,
Glenavy, Crumlin,
Co Antrim BT29 4LY
Tel 028-94422262

GLENRAVEL AND THE BRAID (SKERRY)
Very Rev Conor McGrath PP
119A Glenravel Road, Martinstown,
Ballymena, Co Antrim BT43 6QL
Tel 028-21758217

HANNAHSTOWN
Very Rev Kevin McGuckien PP, VF
Parochial House, 23 Hannahstown Hill,
Belfast BT17 0LT
Tel 028-90614567

HOLYWOOD
Very Rev Stephen McBrearty PP
2A My Lady's Mile, Holywood,
Co Down BT18 9EW
Tel 028-90422167

KILCLIEF AND STRANGFORD
Very Rev John McManus PP
Parochial House, Strangford,
Co Down BT30 7NL
Tel 028-44881206

KILCOO
Very Rev Denis McKinlay PP, VF
41 Lower Square,
Castlewellan BT31 9DN
Tel 028-43770377

KILKEEL (UPPER MOURNE)
Very Rev Sean Dillon PP
Parochial House, Greencastle Road,
Kilkeel, Co Down BT34 4DE
Tel 028-41762242
Very Rev Sean Cahill CC
Curates' Residence, Massforth,
152 Newry Road, Kilkeel,
Co Down BT34 4ET
Tel 028-41762257

DIOCESE OF DOWN AND CONNOR

KILLOUGH (BRIGHT)
Very Rev Peter O'Kane PP
16 Rossglass Road, Killough,
Co Down BT30 7QQ
Tel 028-44841221

KILLYLEAGH
Very Rev Brendan Smyth PP
4 Irish Street, Killyleagh,
Co Down BT30 9QS
Tel 028-44828211

KIRCUBBIN (ARDKEEN)
Very Rev Anthony Alexander PP
46 Blackstaff Road, Ballycranbeg,
Kircubbin, Newtownards,
Co Down BT22 1AG
Tel 028-42738294

LARNE
Very Rev Francis O'Brien PP
Parochial House, 51 Victoria Road, Larne,
Co Antrim BT40 1LY
Tel 028-28273230/28273053

LISBURN (BLARIS)
Very Rev Dermot McCaughan PP
St Patrick's Presbytery,
29 Chapel Hill, Lisburn,
Co Antrim BT28 1EP
Tel 028-92662341
Rev Eamon Magorrian CC
Tel 028-92660206
Parochial House, 27 Chapel Hill, Lisburn,
Co Antrim BT28 1EP

LOUGHGUILE
Very Rev Patrick Mulholland PP
Parochial House, 44 Lough Road,
Loughguile, Ballymena,
Co Antrim BT44 9JN
Tel 028-27641206

LOUGHINISLAND
Very Rev Ciaran Dallat PP
Parochial House, Loughinisland,
Downpatrick, Co Down BT30 8QH
Tel 028-44811661

LOWER MOURNE
Very Rev Sean Gilmore PP
Parochial House,
284 Glassdrumman Road, Annalong,
Newry, Co Down BT34 4QN
Tel 028-43768208

NEWCASTLE (MAGHERA)
Very Rev James Crudden PP
24 Downs Road, Newcastle,
Co Down BT33 0AG
Tel 028-43722401

NEWTOWNARDS
Very Rev Martin O'Hagan PP, VF
Deacon James McAllister
71 North Street, Newtownards,
Co Down BT23 4JD
Tel 028-91812137

PORTAFERRY (BALLYPHILIP)
Very Rev Feargal McGrady PP
Parochial House, 60 Windmill Hill,
Portaferry, Co Down BT22 1RH
Tel 028-42728234

PORTGLENONE
Very Rev Anthony Curran PP
St Mary's Presbytery,
12 Ballymena Road,
Portglenone, Co Antrim BT44 8BL
Tel 028-25821218

PORTRUSH
Very Rev Austin McGirr Adm
Parochial House, 111 Causeway Street,
Portrush, Co Antrim BT56 8JE
Tel 028-70823388

PORTSTEWART
Very Rev Austin McGirr PP, VF
Deacon Terence Butcher
Parochial House, 4 The Crescent,
Portstewart, Co Derry BT55 7AB
Tel 028-70832534
Rev Raymond McCullagh *(priest in residence)*
1 Seafield Park South,
Portstewart BT55 7LH
Tel 028-70832066

RANDALSTOWN
Very Rev John Forsythe PP
Parochial House, 1 Craigstown Road,
Randalstown, Co Antrim BT41 2AF
Tel 028-94472640

RASHARKIN
Very Rev Luke McWilliams PP
Parochial House, 9 Gortahor Road,
Rasharkin, Ballymena,
Co Antrim BT44 8SB
Tel 028-29571212

SAINTFIELD AND CARRICKMANNON
Very Rev Anthony McHugh PP
Parochial House,
33 Crossgar Road, Saintfield,
Ballynahinch, Co Down BT24 7JE
Tel 028-97510237

SAUL AND BALLEE
Very Rev Paul Alexander PP
10 St Patrick's Road, Saul,
Downpatrick, Co Down BT30 7JG
Tel 028-44612525

INSTITUTIONS AND THEIR CHAPLAINS

HOSPITALS

Antrim Area Hospital
Tel 028-94424000
Rev James O'Reilly CC

Belfast City Hospital
Tel 028-90329241
Rev Manuelito Milo
St Paul's Presbytery,
125 Falls Road, Belfast BT12 6AB
Tel 028-90325034
Tel 028-90638621 *(chaplain's office)*

Causeway Hospital
Tel 028-70327032
Very Rev Damian McCaughan

Mater Hospital, Belfast
Tel 028-90741211
Rev Anthony McAleese
St Patrick's Presbytery,
199 Donegall Street,
Belfast BT1 2FL
Tel 028-90324597

Musgrave Park Hospital, Belfast
Tel 028-90902000
Rev Adrian Eastwood (CM)
99 Cliftonville Road,
Belfast BT14 6JQ
Tel 028-90751771

Royal Victoria Hospital, Belfast
Tel 028-95040503
Rev Robert Sloan
111 Queensway, Lambeg,
Lisburn, BT27 4QS
Tel 028-90606980

Ulster Hospital, Dundonald
Tel 028-90654157
Very Rev Anthony Fitzsimons Adm
Very Rev Martin O'Hagan PP
Very Rev Henry McCann PP
St Colmcille's Presbytery,
191 Upper Newtownards Road,
Belfast BT4 3JB

PENAL INSTITUTIONS

Maghaberry Prison
Old Road, Ballinderry Upper,
Lisburn,
Co Antrim BT28 2TP
Tel 028-92614825
Prison General Office: 028-92611888

Hydebank Wood College and Women's Prison
Hydebank Wood, Hospital Road,
Belfast BT8 8NA
Co-ordinating Lead Chaplain of Catholic Pastoral Team
Very Rev Stephen McBrearty
Tel 028-90253666
Rev Ciaran Dallat
Rev Frank Brady (SJ)
Sr Oonagh Hanrahan
Rev James Madden
Deacon Joseph Baxter
Deacon James McAllister

DIOCESE OF DOWN AND CONNOR

PRIESTS OF THE DIOCESE ELSEWHERE

Rev Andrew Black
Canadian Pontifical College,
Via Crescenzio 75, 00193 Roma, Italy
Very Rev Paul Byrne
3 Fortwilliam Demesne, Belfast BT15 4FD
Rev Ciarán Hegarty CC
Doneyloop, Castlefin,
Lifford, Co Donegal
Tel 074-9146183
Rev Martin Henry
Rev Oliver Treanor
Very Rev Hugh Kennedy
75 Somerton Road, Belfast BT15 4DE
Rev Gerard McFlynn
18 Maresfield Gardens, London NW3 5SX
Rev Darach MacGiolla Catháin
Pontificio Collegio Irlandese,
Via Dei SS Quattro 1, Roma 00184

RETIRED PRIESTS

Very Rev Paul Armstrong
5 Balmoral Mews, Belfast BT9 6NM
Rt Rev Mgr Sean Connolly VG
7 Tullyview, Loughguile,
Co Antrim BT44 9JY
Very Rev Peter Donnelly
c/o Diocesan Office
Email p.donnelly@downandconnor.org
Very Rev Raymond Fulton PE
4 Gortanclochair Park,
Ballycastle BT54 6NU
Very Rev Padraic Gallinagh
'Polperro', 8 Beverley Close,
Newtownards BT23 7FN
Very Rev Maurice Henry PE
28 Tyrella Road, Ballykinlar,
Co Down BT30 8DE
Tel 028-44851221
Very Rev John Hutton
Apt 2, Ceara Court, Windsor Avenue,
Belfast BT9 6EJ
Tel 028-90683002
Very Rev Martin Kelly
93 Ballylenaghan Park, Belfast BT8 6WR
Very Rev Sean McCartney
25 Alt-Min Avenue, Belfast BT8 6NJ
Rev Michael McConville
Nazareth House Care Village,
516 Ravenhill Road, Belfast BT6 0BW
Very Rev Laurence McElhill
43B Glen Road, Belfast BT11 8BL
Very Rev Patrick McKenna
19 Broughshane Road,
Ballymena BT43 7DX
Rev Gordon McKinstry
12 The Meadows, Randalstown,
Co Antrim BT41 2JB

Very Rev Anthony McLaverty
518 Donegall Road,
Belfast BT12 6DY
Very Rev Brendan McMullan
26 Willowbank Park,
Belfast BT6 0LL
Tel 028-90794440
Very Rev Kevin McMullan
418 Oldpark Road,
Belfast BT14 6QF
Very Rev Albert McNally
6 Hillside Avenue, Dunloy BT44 9DQ
Very Rev Vincent Maguire
26 Rodney Street, Portrush,
Co Antrim BT56 8LB
Very Rev John Moley
24 Mallard Road, Downpatrick,
Co Down BT30 6DY
Very Rev John Murray
c/o 75 Somerton Road,
Belfast BT15 4DE
Very Rev Michael Murray
c/o 75 Somerton Road,
Belfast BT15 4DE
Very Rev Patrick Neeson
Parochial House, Drumardan Road,
Ballygalget BT22 1NE
Rev John O'Connor
c/o Lisbreen, 75 Somerton Road,
Belfast BT15 4DE
Very Rev Gerard Patton
43 Head Road, Kilkeel,
Co Down BT34 4HX
Very Rev Jim Sheppard
189 Carrigenagh Road, Ballymartin,
Kilkeel, Co Down BT34 4GA
Very Rev Daniel Whyte
53 Marlo Park, Bangor,
Co Down BT19 6NL
Tel 078-12184624

PERSONAL PRELATURE

OPUS DEI
Dunraven,
104 Malone Road, Belfast BT9 5HP
Tel 028-90506947
Email dunraven104bt9@gmail.com
Rev Brendan O'Connor

RELIGIOUS ORDERS AND CONGREGATIONS

PRIESTS

CISTERCIANS
Our Lady of Bethlehem Abbey,
11 Ballymena Road, Portglenone,
Ballymena, Co Antrim BT44 8BL
Tel 028-25821211
Email cinfo@bethabbey.com
Website www.bethlehemabbey.com
Abbot/Superior
Rt Rev Dom Celsus Kelly (OCSO)

JESUITS
Peter Faber House,
28 Brookvale Avenue,
Belfast BT14 6BW
Tel 028-90757615 Fax 028-90747615
Email peter_faber@lineone.net
Superior: Rev Tom Layden (SJ)

PASSIONISTS
Holy Cross Retreat, Ardoyne,
Crumlin Road, Belfast BT14 7GE
Tel 028-90748231 Fax 028-90740340
Superior: Rev John Friel (CP)

Passionist Retreat Centre,
16A Downpatrick Road,
Crossgar, Downpatrick,
Co Down BT30 9EQ
Tel 028-44830242 Fax 028-44831382
Superior: Rev Thomas Scanlon (CP)

REDEMPTORISTS
Clonard Monastery,
1 Clonard Gardens,
Belfast BT13 2RL
Tel 028-90445950 Fax 028-90445988
Superior: Rev Peter Burns (CSsR)

St Gerard's Parish,
722 Antrim Road, Newtownabbey,
Co Antrim BT36 7PG
Tel 028-90774833 Fax 028-90770923
PP: Rev Kevin Browne (CSsR)

VINCENTIANS
99 Cliftonville Road, Belfast BT14 6JQ
Tel 028-90751771 Fax 028-90740547
Superior
Very Rev Adrian Eastwood (CM)

BROTHERS

CHRISTIAN BROTHERS
An Dúnán, 210 Glen Road,
Belfast BT11 8BW
Tel 028-90611343
Community Leader
Br Brian Monaghan
Community: 6

The Open Doors Learning Centre,
Barrack Street,
Belfast BT12 4AH
Tel 028-90325867 Fax 028-90241013
Coordinator: Cormac McArt
Email opendoorsbelfast@yahoo.co.uk

Education and Outreach Centre,
Westcourt Centre,
Barrack Street, Belfast BT12 4AH
Tel 028-90323009
Project Manager: Cormac McArt
Email westcourtcentre@btconnect.com

DE LA SALLE BROTHERS
De La Salle College,
Edenmore Drive,
Belfast BT11 8LT
Tel 028-90508800
Principal: Ms Claire Whyte

De La Salle Brothers,
Glanaulin, 141 Glen Road,
Belfast BT11 8BP
Tel 028-90614848
Superior: Br Ailbe Mangan
Community: 3

La Salle Pastoral Retreat Centre,
Glanaulin, 141 Glen Road,
Belfast BT11 8BP
Tel 028-90501932 Tax 028-90501932
Director: Ms Margaret McClory

La Salle House,
4 Stream Street, Downpatrick,
Co Down BT30 6DD
Tel 028-44612996
Superior: Br Mark Jordan
Community: 3

St Patrick's Grammar School,
Downpatrick,
Co Down BT30 6NJ
Tel 028-44619722
Principal: Mr Joseph McCann

Secondary School,
Struell Road, Downpatrick,
Co Down BT30 6JR
Tel 028-44612520
Principal: Mr Ciaran Maguire

SISTERS

CONGREGATION OF THE SISTERS OF MERCY
Convent of Mercy,
Beechmount, Ard Na Va Road,
Belfast BT12 6FF
Tel 028-90319496
Community: 6

21 Ardglass Road,
Downpatrick, Co Down BT30 6JQ
Tel 028-44615645

Mercy Convent,
Whiteabbey, 453 Shore Road,
Newtownabbey,
Co Antrim BT37 9SE
Tel 028-90863128

Convent of Mercy,
252 Limestone Road,
Belfast BT15 3AR
Tel 028-90749259

Sisters of Mercy
616 Crumlin Road,
Belfast BT14 7GL
Tel 028-90717112

23 Fortwilliam Fold,
Fortwilliam Park,
Belfast BT15 4AN
Tel 028-90371268

21 Camberwell Court,
Limestone Road,
Belfast BT15 3BH
Tel 028-90286584

618 Crumlin Road,
Belfast BT14 7GL
Tel 028-90715478

3 Ashgrove Lodge,
Glengormley, Newtownabbey,
Co Antrim BT36 6WY
Tel 028-90843890

25 Camberwell Court,
Limestone Road,
Belfast BT15 3BH
Tel 028-90290213

27 Camberwell Court,
Limestone Road,
Belfast BT15 3BH
Tel 028-90748830

45 Camberwell Court,
Limestone Road,
Belfast BT15 38H
Tel 028-90507842

CROSS AND PASSION CONGREGATION
St Teresa's Convent,
78 Glen Road,
Belfast BT11 8BH
Tel 028-90613955
Community: 4
Pastoral care, ecumenical work,
bereavement counselling

Villa Pacis, 78A Glen Road,
Belfast BT11 8BH
Tel 028-90621766
Community: 13
Care of sick and elderly

Drumalis Retreat Centre,
47 Glenarm Road, Larne,
Co Antrim BT40 1DT
Tel 028-28276455/28272196
Email drumalis@btconnect.com
Community: 2

5c Easton Avenue, Cliftonville road,
Belfast BT14 6LL
Tel 028-90749507
Community: 2
Retreat work, Vietnam project,
counselling and facilitation

DAUGHTERS OF CHARITY OF ST VINCENT DE PAUL
23 Glen Road,
Belfast BT11 8BA
Tel 028-90203052
and
Apt 6, 2 Glenhill Park,
Belfast BT11 8GB
Tel 028-90628483
Superior: Sr Claire Sweeney
Community: 5
Pastoral work and education

St Louise's Comprehensive College,
468 Falls Road,
Belfast BT 6EN
Tel 028-90325631

DOMINICAN SISTERS
St Catherine's, 133 Falls Road,
Belfast BT12 6AD
Tel 028-90327056
Email opfalls133@gmail.com
Prioress: Sr Alicia Mooney (OP)
Community: 12
Varied ministries
St Dominic's Grammar School
Tel 028-90320081

Dominican Convent,
Fortwilliam Park,
Belfast BT15 4AP
Tel 028-90370008
Email ionahouseop@gmail.com
Community: 7
Varied ministries
Grammar School
Tel 028-90370298

FAMILY OF ADORATION
63 Falls Road,
Belfast BT12 4PD
Tel 01232-325668
Email adorationsisters@utv.net
A contemplative community with
mission of adoration, making of altar
breads and Holy Shop

CONGREGATION OF OUR LADY OF CHARITY OF THE GOOD SHEPHERD
Lys Marie, 19 Rossmore Drive,
Belfast BT7 3LA
Tel 028-90641346
Email 25rossmoredrive@gmail.com
Community: 9

Congregation of Our Lady of Charity of
the Good Shepherd (Contemplative
Sisters)
Lys Marie, 19 Rossmore Drive,
Belfast BT7 3LA
Tel 028-90641346
Email lysmariesisters@yahoo.com
Community: 6

49 Knockbreda Park,
Belfast BT6 0HD
Tel 028-90582391
Community: 1

MISSIONARY SISTERS OF THE HOLY CROSS
86 Glen Road,
Belfast BT11 8BH
Tel 028-90614631
Email holycrossbelfast@gmail.com
Superior: Sr Patricia Kelly
Email patkelly8686@gmail.com
Community: 3

POOR SERVANTS OF THE MOTHER OF GOD
15 Martin's Lane, Carnagat,
Newry, Co Down BT35 8PJ
Tel 028-30268512
Contacts: Sr Rita Dempsey (SMG),
Sr Marie Slacke (SMG)
Comunity: 2
Pastoral

CONGREGATION OF THE SISTERS OF NAZARETH
Nazareth House Care Village,
516 Ravenhill Road,
Belfast BT6 0BX
Tel 028-90690600 Fax 028-90690601
Superior: Sr Cornelia Walsh
Email
superior.belfastuk@sistersofnazareth.com
srcornelia.walsh@sistersofnazareth.com
Community: 8
Home for the elderly. Beds: 88

Bethlehem Nursery School,
514 Ravenhill Road,
Belfast BT6 0BW
Tel 028-90640406
Pupils: 52
St Michael's Primary,
516 Ravenhill Road, Belfast BT6 0BW
Tel 028-90491529. Pupils: 410

RELIGIOUS OF SACRED HEART OF MARY
100 Hillsborough Road, Lisburn,
Co Antrim BT28 1JU
Tel 01846-678501
Community: 1
Ministry in local area

28 Upper Green, Dunmurry,
Belfast BT17 0EL
Tel 01232-600792
Community 3
Ministry in local area and education

Sacred Heart of Mary Grammar School
for Boys and Girls,
Rathmore, Finaghy,
Belfast BT10 0LF
Pupils: 1,350
Tel 01232-610115
Email
userid.rathmore@schools.class-ni.org.uk

ST CLARE SISTERS
St Clare's Convent, 43 Rosetta Park,
Belfast BT6 0DL
Tel 028-90694108
Community: 2

ST LOUIS SISTERS
14 Carndale Meadows,
Carniny Road,
Ballymena BT43 5NX
Tel 028-25651683
Community: 1

7 Riverdale Park Avenue,
Belfast BT11 9BP
Tel 028-90209074
Community: 1

22 Riverdale Park North,
Belfast BT11 9DL
Tel 028-90619375
Community: 1

Apartment 2 Hollycroft,
1-3 Inver Avenue,
Belfast BT15 5DG
Tel 028-90721037
Community: 1

49 Bracken Avenue,
Castlewellan Road,
Newcastle, Co Down BT33 0HG
Tel 028-43726282
Community: 1

THIRD LEVEL INSTITUTIONS AND THEIR CHAPLAINS

St Mary's University College
A College of Queen's University Belfast
191 Falls Road, Belfast 12 6FE
Tel 028-90327678
Principal
Professor Peter Finn BA MSSc KSG
Priest Lecturers
Rev Feidhlimidh Magennis MA, BD, LSS (Dromore)
Rev Edward McGee BSc, MA, DD
Rev Paul Fleming BA, BD, STL, PhD

Queen's University of Belfast
Chaplain: Rev Dominic McGrattan
Catholic Chaplaincy,
28 Elmwood Avenue,
Belfast BT9 6AY
Tel 028-90669739
Email qubcc@downandconnor.org
Facebook page The Catholic Chaplaincy at QUB

Ulster University
Coleraine Campus
Chaplain: Rev Raymond McCullagh
The Chaplaincy Office, L101,
University of Ulster, Coleraine
Tel 028-70124652
Home: 1 Seafield Park South,
Portstewart BT55 7LH
Tel 028-70831784
Email r.mccullagh@ulster.ac.uk

Jordanstown and Belfast Campuses
Chaplain: Rev Terry Howard (SJ)
Chaplains' Suit (SF01),
University of Ulster at Jordanstown,
Newtownabbey,
Co Antrim BT37 0QB
Tel 028-90366404
Email t.howard@ulster.ac.uk

EDUCATION TRUSTS

ST MACNISSI'S EDUCATIONAL TRUST
75 Somerton Road, Belfast BT15 4DE
Email education@downandconnor.org

EDMUND RICE SCHOOLS TRUST (NI)
Westcourt Centre
8-30 Barrack Street, Belfast BT12 4AH
Chief Executive: Mr Kevin Burke
Tel 028-90333205
Email erstni@live.com

CHARITABLE AND OTHER SOCIETIES

Apostolic Work Society
Xavier House, 156 Cliftonpark Avenue,
Belfast BT14 6DT
Tel 028-90351912
Email apostolic.work@btinternet.com
Office hours:
Monday-Wednesday 9.00 am-2.30 pm
Society for lay women
President: Ms Mary McGrath

Down and Connor Pioneer Association – DCPA
1st Floor, The McCoy Buildings,
68 Berry Street, Belfast BT1 7FJ
Tel 028-90894070
Email dandcpioneers@gmail.com
Spiritual Director
Rev Raymond McCullagh

Knights of Columbanus
Provincial Grand Knight Area 2
Charlie Clarke
67 Ballynahinch Road
Carryduff, Belfast, BT8 8DL
Tel 078-50203835
Email pgkarea2@outlook.com
Provincial Secretary Area 2
Con McLaughlin
2 Glenview Crescent
Newtownabbey BT37 0TW
Tel 077-75523937
Email provsecarea2@gmail.com

DIOCESE OF DOWN AND CONNOR

Legion of Mary
14 Cliftonville Road,
Belfast BT14 6JX
Tel 028-90746626

Morning Star House
2-12 Divis Street, Belfast
Tel 028-90333500

Regina Coeli Hostel
8-10 Lake Glen Avenue,
Belfast BT11 8FE
Tel 028-90612473
Night shelter for destitute and homeless women. Under the care of the Legion of Mary

Society of St Vincent de Paul
196-200 Antrim Road,
Belfast BT15 2AJ
Tel 028-90351561
Regional Administrator
Ms Pauline Brown

St Joseph's Centre for the Deaf
321 Grosvenor Road,
Belfast BT12 4LP
Tel 028-90713401
The Centre provides a wide range of facilities for the deaf.
Co-ordinator: Very Rev Patrick Devlin
Northern Diocesan Lay Chaplain:
Ms Denise Flack
Tel 078-77643961

Allianz

The Abbey Stained Glass Studios

FOUNDED IN 1944

BURNING THE WINTER MIDNIGHT OIL
JESUIT FATHERS, MANRESA HOUSE, CLONTARF, DUBLIN
FIVE EVIE HONE RHA STAINED GLASS WINDOWS

ABBEY STAINED GLASS STUDIOS WERE COMMISSIONED TO FIT PROTECTIVE LAMINATED STORMGLAZING PROPERLY VENTILATED AT THE TOP AND BOTTOM, OUTSIDE THIS FINE COLLECTION OF EVIE HONE RHA STAINED GLASS WINDOWS FOR MANRESA DIRECTOR, FR PIARAS JACKSON SJ

CONTACT: WILLIAM MALONE & KEN RYAN

TELEPHONE (01) 677 7285

18 OLD KILMAINHAM, KILMAINHAM, DUBLIN 8

MOBILE: 087 738 9749

Email enquiries@asgs.ie   Website www.abbeystainedglassstudios.ie

PAPAL ENCYCLICALS

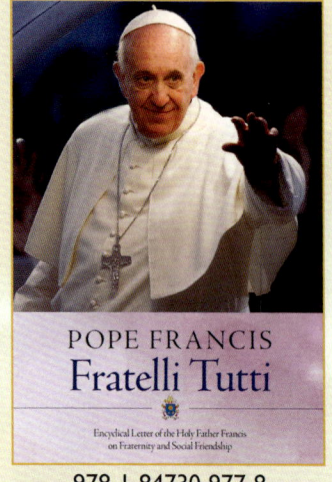

POPE FRANCIS
Fratelli Tutti
Encyclical Letter of the Holy Father Francis on Fraternity and Social Friendship
978 1 84730 977 8
€4.99/£4.50

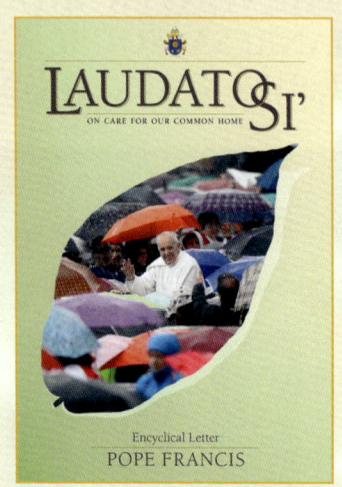

LAUDATO SI'
On Care for Our Common Home
Encyclical Letter
POPE FRANCIS
978 1 84730 597 8
€4.99/£4.50

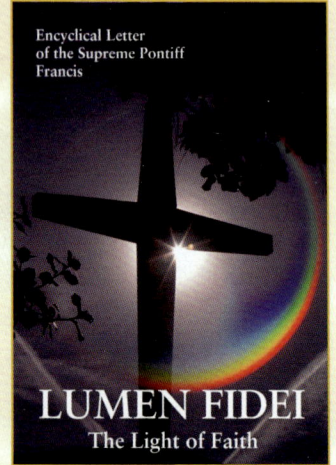

LUMEN FIDEI
The Light of Faith
Encyclical Letter of the Supreme Pontiff Francis
978 1 84730 524 4
€4.75/£4.30

ALSO AVAILABLE, THE FOLLOWING APOSTOLIC EXHORTATIONS

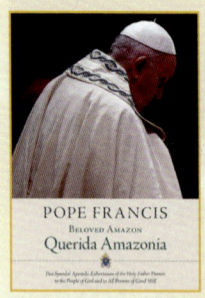

POPE FRANCIS
Beloved Amazon
Querida Amazonia
978 1 84730 964 8
€4.99/£4.50

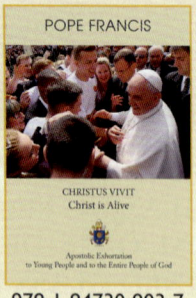

POPE FRANCIS
CHRISTUS VIVIT
Christ is Alive
Apostolic Exhortation to Young People and to the Entire People of God
978 1 84730 903 7
€4.99/£4.50

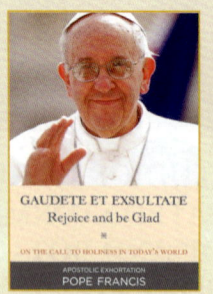

GAUDETE ET EXSULTATE
Rejoice and be Glad
On the Call to Holiness in Today's World
APOSTOLIC EXHORTATION
POPE FRANCIS
978 1 84730 856 6
€4.99/£4.50

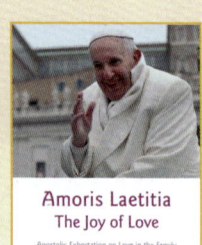

Amoris Laetitia
The Joy of Love
Apostolic Exhortation on Love in the Family
POPE FRANCIS
978 1 84730 735 4
€4.99/£4.50

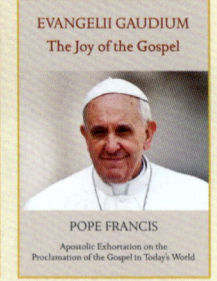

EVANGELII GAUDIUM
The Joy of the Gospel
POPE FRANCIS
Apostolic Exhortation on the Proclamation of the Gospel in Today's World
978 1 84730 542 8
€4.99/£4.50

Available from Veritas stores
Abbey Street & Blanchardstown Centre, Dublin
Cork • Derry • Letterkenny • Newry
www.veritas.ie

VERITAS
www.veritas.ie

Educating, reflecting and making a difference since 1795

St Patrick's Pontifical University, Maynooth offers a range of Undergraduate, Postgraduate and Continuing Education programmes in Theology and Philosophy, attracting students from home and abroad and a wide variety of careers. If you are interested in developing your critical thinking, analysis, reasoning and communication skills, why not take a look at what we offer.

maynoothcollege.ie/courses

St Patrick's
Pontifical University

INTERCOM
A CATHOLIC PASTORAL AND LITURGICAL RESOURCE

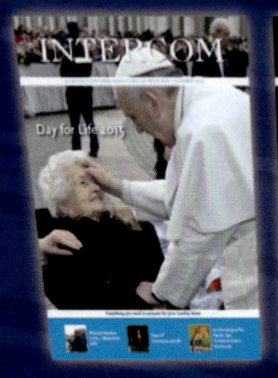

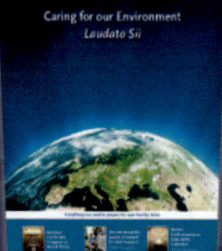

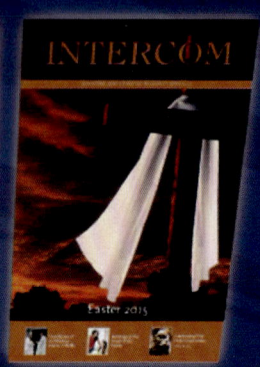

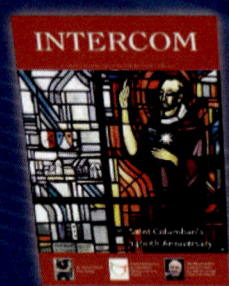

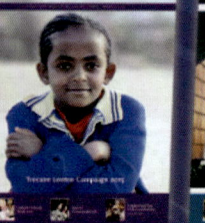

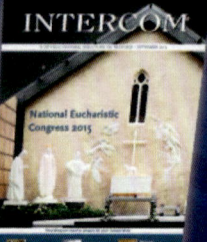

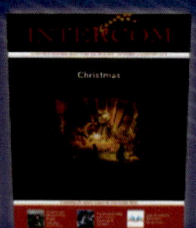

15% DISCOUNT ON NEW SUBSCRIPTIONS

To avail of a twelve-month subscription to *Intercom* for
IRL €59.50 · UK £58.65 · AIRMAIL €73.95, a saving of 15%,
contact Intercom Subscriptions: 01-8788177 · intercomsubscriptions@veritas.ie

Intercom is published on behalf of the Irish Catholic Bishops' Conference by
Veritas Publications, 7–8 Lower Abbey Street, Dublin 1, Ireland

DIOCESE OF DROMORE

PATRONS OF THE DIOCESE
ST PATRICK, 17 MARCH; ST COLMAN, 7 JUNE

INCLUDES PORTIONS OF COUNTIES ANTRIM, ARMAGH AND DOWN

SEDE VACANTE

Apostolic Administrator
Most Rev Eamon Martin DD

Residence:
Bishop's House,
44 Armagh Road,
Newry, Co Down BT35 6PN
Tel 028-30262444
Fax 028-30260496
Email
bishop@dromorediocese.org
Website dromorediocese.org

ST PATRICK AND ST COLMAN'S CATHEDRAL, NEWRY

Newry cathedral was founded in 1825, at the centre of a growing and prosperous town. It symbolised, in many ways, the increasing confidence of the local Catholic population of the day, especially the newly emerging Catholic middle class.

The cathedral was designed by Thomas J. Duff, a prominent architect in the northern part of Ireland at the turn of the century. The building was dedicated in May 1829 by the then Irish Primate, Dr Curtis. It was believed to be the first major dedication ceremony in Ireland following the granting of Catholic Emancipation.

Originally, the cathedral was sparsely furnished, and it received its first significant interior decoration in 1851. The building was developed considerably between 1888 and 1891. During these years, its two transepts were added and a handsome bell tower erected. From 1904 to 1909, Bishop Henry O'Neill oversaw a further major phase of building. The main body of the church was extended in length by some forty feet and a new sanctuary was added. Much of the internal fabric of the cathedral, as we know it today, belongs to this period. Rich interior mosaic decoration was undertaken, side chapels were constructed and the cathedral's tubular organ was installed. The cathedral was solemnly consecrated in July 1925 – a century after its foundation! It enjoys the joint patronage of Ss Patrick and Colman.

Interior renovation was necessary in the wake of the Second Vatican Council. This work of extending and refurbishing the sanctuary area was undertaken by Bishop Francis Gerard Brooks from 1989 to 1990. It included the construction of the present marble altar, the rebuilding of the reredos of the former high altar, now in three parts, and the relocation of the bishop's chair to the front of the sanctuary. This work of renovation has earned widespread praise in the field of contemporary ecclesiastical architecture.

DIOCESE OF DROMORE

Most Rev John McAreavey DD
Retired Bishop of Dromore; born 1949; ordained priest 10 June 1973; ordained Bishop of Dromore 19 September 1999; resigned 1 March 2018
Residence: Bishop's House,
44 Armagh Road, Newry,
Co Down BT35 6PN

CHAPTER

Prebendaries
Saint Colman and Lann: Vacant
Drumeragh: Vacant
Lanronan: Vacant
Aghaderg
Very Rev Canon Liam Stevenson PP, VF
Shankill
Clondallon: Vacant
Newry
Kilmycon: Vacant
Downaclone
Very Rev Canon Gerald Powell PP, VF
Tullylish
Retired Members, Honorary Canons:
Very Rev Francis Boyle
Rt Rev Mgr Arthur Byrne
Very Rev Michael Hackett
Rt Rev Mgr A. Hamill
Very Rev Canon John Kearney
Very Rev Canon Frank Kearney
Very Rev Gerard McCrory

ADMINISTRATION

Vicar General
Vacant

Chancellor/Diocesan Secretary
Very Rev Canon Gerald Powell PP, VF
Parochial House, 4 Holymount Road
Laurencetown, Craigavon BT63 6AT
Co Armagh
Tel 028-40624236
Email gpowellpp@aol.com

Council of Priests
Chairman
Vacant

Dromore Diocesan Trust
Diocese of Dromore Trustee is the Trustee for the Dromore Diocesan Trust
Most Rev Eamon Martin *(Chairperson)*
Very Rev Feidhlimidh Magennis,
Mr Michael Gillen,
Mr Brendan Jackson,
Mrs Nuala McKeagney
Mr Tony McCusker
Mrs Oonagh Murtagh

Finance Council
Administrator and Secretary
Very Rev Feidhlimidh Magennis
St Mary's University College, Belfast
Finance and Compliance Officer
Mrs Rosaleen Conway
c/o Diocesan Office, Bishop's House,
44 Armagh Road, Newry,
Co Down BT35 6PN
Tel 028-30262444
Email finance@dromorediocese.org

Members of Diocesan Finance Council
Chairman: Most Rev Eamon Martin DD
Minute Secretary: Agatha Larkin
Very Rev Canon Liam Stevenson
Mr Michael Gillen
Mr Cathal McHale
Mr Gerry Gray

Bishop's Secretary
Miss Agatha Larkin
Bishop's House, Newry, Co Down
Tel 028-30262444

CATECHETICS EDUCATION

Diocesan Advisers for Religious Education
Primary Schools: Mrs Joan Aldridge and
Mr Gerard McBrien
c/o Diocesan Office, Bishop's House,
44 Armagh Road, Newry,
Co Down BT35 6PN
Tel 028-30262444
Post-Primary Schools: Mrs Susan Morgan
c/o Diocesan Office, Bishop's House,
44 Armagh Road, Newry,
Co Down BT35 6PN
Tel 028-30262444

Diocesan Education Committee
Chairman: Vacant

PASTORAL

ACCORD
Director: Vacant
c/o Diocesan Office, 44 Armagh Road,
Newry, Co Down BT35 6PN
Tel 028-30262444

Adult Faith Development
Deacon Kevin Devine
c/o 70 North Street, Lurgan,
Co Armagh BT67 9AH
Tel 028-38323161
Eail afmcmahon@hotmail.co.uk

Chaplaincy to Deaf People
Contact: Fr Colum Wright
c/o Diocesan Office, Bishop's House,
44 Armagh Road, Newry,
Co Down BT35 6PN
Email colum.wright@btinternet.com

Communications
Press Officer
Rev Feidhlimidh Magennis
c/o Bishop's House, Newry, Co Down

Dromore Clerical Provident Society
c/o Bishop's House,
44 Armagh Road, Newry,
Co Down BT35 6PN
Tel 028-30262444

Ecumenism
Director: Deacon Frank Rice
c/o Parochial House, Maypole Hill,
Dromore, Co Down BT25 1BQ
Email ricefa@aol.com

Emigrant Services
Director: c/o Diocesan Office,
44 Armagh Road, Newry,
Co Down BT35 6PN
Tel 028-30262444

Immigrant Services
Rev Krzysztof Kosciolek (SC) CC
Burren
Tel 028-41772200

Knock Diocesan Pilgrimage
Director: c/o Diocesan Office,
44 Armagh Road, Newry,
Co Down BT35 6PN
Tel 028-30262444

Lourdes Diocesan Pilgrimage
Director: Rev Brian Fitzpatrick CC
c/o Diocesan Office, 44 Armagh Road,
Newry, Co Down BT35 6PN
Tel 028-30262444

Marriage Tribunal
Armagh Regional Marriage Tribunal,
Diocesan Office, 44 Armagh Road,
Newry, Co Down BT35 6PN
Tel 028-30269836

Permanent Diaconate
Director: Deacon Frank Rice,
c/o Parochial House, Maypole Hill,
Dromore, Co Down BT25 1BQ
Email ricefa@aol.com

Pioneer Total Abstinence Association
Diocesan Director
c/o Diocesan Office, 44 Armagh Road,
Newry, Co Down BT35 6PN
Tel 028-30262444

Pontifical Mission Societies and Dromore/Lodwar Mission Project
Diocesan Director: Vacant

Safeguarding Children
Diocesan Offices, 44 Armagh Road,
Newry, Co Down BT35 6PN
Designated person and Director
Ms Patricia Carville
Chair, Advisory Panel: Mrs Aileen Oates
Chair, Safeguarding Committee
Mr Paul Carlin

Special Needs Committee – Reachout
Mrs Anne Loughlin
22 Dallan Hill, Warrenpoint
Tel 077-34330336

Vocations
Director: Vacant

DIOCESE OF DROMORE

Youth
Chair Youth Commission: Vacant
Director: Mrs Frances Fox
Pastoral Centre, The Mall, Newry
Tel 028-30833898
Email dromoreyd@btconnect.com

Youth Ministry
Mrs Frances Fox
Pastoral Centre, The Mall, Newry
Tel 028-30833898
Email dromoreyd@btconnect.com

PARISHES

Mensal parishes are listed first. Other parishes follow alphabetically. Hostorical names are given in parentheses).

NEWRY
Very Rev Canon Francis Brown Adm
Rev Robert Markuszewski
Rev Alphonsus Chukwunenye (MSP)
Rev Callum Young
Cathedral Presbytery, 38 Hill Street,
Newry BT34 1AT
Tel 028-30262586 Fax 028-30267505
Email office@newrycathedralparish.org

CLONALLON, ST PETER'S (WARRENPOINT)
Very Rev Brendan Kearns PP
Parochial House, Great George's Street,
Warrenpoint, Co Down BT34 3NF
Tel 028-41754684 Fax 028-41754685
Rev Krzysztof Kosciolek (SC) CC
84 Milltown Street, Burren,
Warrenpoint, Co Down BT34 3PU
Tel 028-41772200
Rev John McClelland, Permanent Deacon
c/o Parish Office
Parish Office: Tel 028-41759981
Fax 028-41759980
Email
warrenpointparish@dromorediocese.org

AGHADERG
Very Rev Conor McConville PP
17 Monteith Road, Annaclone,
Banbridge, Co Down BT32 5AQ
Tel 028-40671201
Email
aghadergparish@dromorediocese.org

ANNACLONE
Very Rev Conor McConville PP
17 Monteith Road, Annaclone,
Banbridge, Co Down BT32 5AQ
Tel 028-40671201
Email
annacloneparish@dromorediocese.org

CLONALLON, ST MARY'S (BURREN)
Very Rev Brendan Kearns PP
Parochial House, Great George's Street,
Warrenpoint, Co Down BT34 3NF
Tel 028-41754684 Fax 028-41754685
Rev Krzysztof Kosciolek (SC) CC
84 Milltown Street, Burren,
Warrenpoint, Co Down BT34 3PU
Parish Office: Tel 028-41759981
Fax 028-41759980

CLONALLON, ST PATRICK'S (MAYOBRIDGE)
Very Rev Desmond Loughran PP
15 Chapel Hill, Mayobridge,
Newry, Co Down BT34 2EX
Tel 028-30850089
Parish Office: Tel 028-30850270

CLONDUFF (HILLTOWN)
Very Rev Charles Byrne PP
17 Castlewellan Road, Hilltown,
Newry, Co Down BT34 5UY
Tel/Fax 028-40630206

DONAGHMORE
Rev John Brown (SMA)
2 Moneymore Road, Glenn, Newry,
Co Down BT34 1RN
Parish Office: Tel 028-30821549
Email
donaghmoreparish@dromorediocese.org

DROMORE
Very Rev Feidhlimidh Magennis PP
Maypole Hill, Dromore,
Co Down BT35 1BQ
Rev Frank Rice, Permanent Deacon
c/o Maypole Hill, Dromore,
Co Down BT35 1BQ

DRUMGATH (RATHFRILAND)
Very Rev Charles Byrne
17 Castlewellan Road, Hilltown,
Newry, Co Down BT34 5UY
Tel/Fax 028-40630206

DRUMGOOLAND
Very Rev Peter C. McNeill PP
58 Ballydrumman Road,
Castlewellan, Co Down BT31 9UG
Tel 028-40650207 Fax 028-40650205
Email dromaradgooland@aol.co.uk

DROMARA
Very Rev Peter C. McNeill PP
58 Ballydrumman Road,
Castlewellan, Co Down BT31 9UG
Email dromaradgooland@aol.co.uk
Tel 028-40650207 Fax 028-40650205

KILBRONEY (ROSTREVOR)
Very Rev Demond Mooney PP
44 Church Street, Rostrevor,
Co Down BT34 3BB
Tel 028-41738277 Fax 028-41738315
Parish Office: Tel 028-41739495
Email
kilbroneyparish@dromorediocese.org

MAGHERADROLL (BALLYNAHINCH)
Very Rev Brian Brown PP
Church Street, Ballynahinch,
Co Down BT24 8LP
Tel/Fax 028-97562410
Email
magheradrollrc.parish@nireland.com
Parish Office: 028-97565429

MAGHERALIN
Very Rev Feidhlimidh Magennis PP
25 Bottier Road, Moira, Craigavon,
Co Armagh BT67 0PE
Tel 028-92611347
Parish Office: 028-92617435
Email
magheralinparish@dromorediocese.org

MOYRAVERTY (CRAIGAVON)
Rev Brian Fitzpatrick PP
The Presbytery, 11 Tullygally Road,
Legahory, Craigavon BT65 5BL
Tel 028-38341901
Very Rev Michael Maginn
The Presbytery, Tullygally Road,
Legahory, Craigavon BT65 5BY
Tel 028-38311872
Rev Gerry Heaney, Permanent Deacon
c/o The Presbytery, Tullygally Road,
Legahory, Craigavon BT65 5BL
Parish Office: Moyraverty,
10 Tullygally Road
Tel 028-38343013
Email
moyravertyparish@dromorediocese.org

SAVAL
Very Rev Canon Francis Brown PP
Cathedral Presbytery,
38 Hill Street, Newry BT34 1AT
Tel 028-30256372
Email savalparish@dromorediocese.org

SEAGOE (DERRYMACASH)
Very Rev Brian Fitzpatrick PP
The Presbytery, 11 Tullygally Road,
Legahory, Craigavon BT65 5BL
Tel 028-38341901
Very Rev Michael Maginn
The Presbytery, Tullygally Road,
Legahory, Craigavon BT65 5BY
Tel 028-38311872
Email seagoeparish@dromorediocese.org

SEAPATRICK (BANBRIDGE)
Very Rev Andrew McMahon PP
6 Scarva Road, Banbridge,
Co Down BT32 3AR
Tel 028-40662136
Rev Michael Rooney, Permanent Deacon
Parish Office
Tel 028-40624950 Fax 028-40626547
Email parishseapatrick@btconnect.com

SHANKILL, ST PAUL'S (LURGAN)
Very Rev Canon Liam Stevenson PP, VF
70 North Street, Lurgan,
Co Armagh BT67 9AH
Tel 028-38323161
Very Rev Colum Wright
Lisadell, 54 Francis Street,
Lurgan, Co Armagh BT66 6DL
Tel 028-38327173
Rev Josef Wozniak (SC) CC
68 North Street, Lurgan,
Co Armagh BT67 9AH
Tel 028-38323161 Fax 028-38347927
St Paul's Parish Office: Tel 028-38321289
Email office@stpaulsparishlurgan.org

SHANKILL, ST PETER'S (LURGAN)
Very Rev Canon Liam Stevenson PP, VF
70 North Street, Lurgan,
Co Armagh BT67 9AH
Tel 028-38323161
Very Rev Colum Wright
Lisadell, 54 Francis Street,
Lurgan, Co Armagh BT66 6DL
Tel 028-38327173
Rev Josef Wozniak (SC) CC
68 North Street, Lurgan,
Co Armagh BT67 9AH
Tel 028-38323161
Rev Kevin Devine, Permanent Deacon
c/o 70 North Street, Lurgan,
Co Armagh BT67 9AH
Email office@stpetersparishlurgan.org

TULLYLISH
Very Rev Canon Gerald Powell PP, VF
4 Holymount Road,
Gilford, Craigavon,
Co Armagh BT63 6AT
Tel 028-40624236 Fax 028-40625440
Email gpowellpp@aol.com
Parish Office: Tel 028-40624236
Email tullylish.dromore@btinternet.com
Website www.tullylish.com

HOSPITALS AND THEIR CHAPLAINS

Craigavon Area Hospital
Co Armagh
Chaplain: Very Rev Michael Maginn PP

District Hospital
Lurgan and Portadown, Co Armagh
Chaplain: Very Rev Michael Maginn PP

Hospice
Southern Area Hospice Services,
St John's House,
Courtenay Hill, Newry,
Co Down BT34 2EB
Tel 028-30267711 Fax 028-30268492
Chaplain: Sr Fiona Galligan

PRIESTS OF THE DIOCESE ELSEWHERE
Rt Rev Mgr Hugh Connolly BA, DD
Irish College Paris, 5 Rue des Irlandais,
75005 Paris
Very Rev Stephen Ferris
c/o Diocesan Office, Newry
Rev Matthew McConville
c/o Bishop's House
Rev Feidlimidh Magennis LSS
St Mary's University College, Belfast

RETIRED PRIESTS
Very Rev Canon Francis Boyle
Warrenpoint
Rt Rev Mgr Arthur Byrne
Castor's Bay Road, Lurgan
Very Rev John Joe Cunningham
Newcastle, Co Down
Rev Gerard Green
c/o Bishop's House, Newry, Co Down
Very Rev Canon Michael Hackett
Warrenpoint, Co Down
Rt Rev Mgr Aidan Hamill
c/o Bishop's House, Newry, Co Down
Very Rev Canon John Kearney
Warrenpoint, Co Down
Very Rev Canon Frank Kearney
Cabra, Hilltown, Co Down
Very Rev Canon Gerard McCrory
c/o Diocesan Office, Newry,
Co Down BT35 6PN
Very Rev Oliver Mooney
Newry, Co Down
Very Rev Patrick Joe Murray
c/o Diocesan Office, Newry,
Co Down BT35 6PN
Very Rev James Poland
Rostrevor, Co Down
Rev Niall Sheehan
Portadown, Co Armagh

RELIGIOUS ORDERS AND CONGREGATIONS

PRIESTS

BENEDICTINES
Holy Cross Abbey, 119 Kilbroney Road,
Rostrevor, Co Down BT34 3BN
Tel 028-41739979
Abbot: Rt Rev Dom Mark-Ephrem M. Nolan (OSB)
Email benedictinemonks@btinternet.com
Website www.benedictinemonks.co.uk

DOMINICANS
St Catherine's,
Newry, Co Down BT35 8BN
Tel 028-30262178
Superior: Very Rev David Tohill (OP)

SOCIETY OF AFRICAN MISSIONS
African Missions, Dromantine, Newry,
Co Down BT34 1RH
Tel 028-30821224
Email sma.dromantine@sma.ie
Superior: Rev Damian Bresnahan (SMA)

Dromantine Retreat and Conference
Centre, Newry, Co Down BT34 1RH
Tel 028-30821964 Fax 028-30281704
Email admin@dromantineconference.com
Website www.dromantineconference.com
Director: Rev Damian Bresnahan (SMA)

SISTERS

CONGREGATION OF THE SISTERS OF MERCY
Convent of Mercy, Catherine Street,
Newry, Co Down BT34 6JG
Tel 028-30262065/30264964
Community: 10

Convent of Mercy, 3 Glenashley,
Rostrevor, Co Down BT34 3FW
Tel 028-41738356
Community: 2

89 North Street, Lurgan,
Co Armagh BT67 9AH
Tel 028-38347858

Convent of Mercy, 9 Queen Street,
Warrenpoint, Co Down BT34 3HZ
Tel 028-41752221

12 Cloghogue Heights, Newry,
Co Down BT35 8BA
Tel 028-30261628

Sisters of Mercy, Edward Street,
Lurgan, Co Armagh BT66 6DB
Tel 028-38322635
Community: 8

No 4 Ummericam Road, Silverbridge,
Newry, Co Down BT35 9PB
Tel 028-30860441

8 The Woodlands,
Lower Dromore Road,
Warrenpoint, Co Down BT34 6WL
Tel 028-41752383

17 Oakleigh Grove, Lurgan,
Co Armagh BT67 9AY
Tel 028-38347984

204 Drumglass, Craigavon,
Co Armagh BT65 5BB
Tel 028-38343447

42 Antrim Road, Lurgan,
Co Armagh BT67 9BW
Tel 028-39328742

5A Catherine Street, Newry,
Co Down BT35 6JG
Tel 028-30264615

5B Catherine Street, Newry,
Co Down BT35 6JG
Tel 028-30265342

1 Kildarragh Close,
Old Warrenpoint Road, Newry,
Co Down BT34 2SU
Tel 028-30267141

Sisters of Mercy, 49 Ardfreelan,
Rathfriland Road, Newry,
Co Down BT34 1CD
Tel 028-30250951

7 Daly Park, Silverbridge,
Newry, Co Down BT35 9PJ

DIOCESE OF DROMORE

Sisters of Mercy, 2 Carrickree,
Bridle Loanan, Co Down BT34 3FA
Tel 028-41752347

27 Catherine Street, Newry,
Co Down, BT35 6JG
Tel 028-30833641

1 Dominican Court,
Newry, Co Down
Tel 028-30265184

Apt 4, Carlinn's Cove,
Warrenpoint Road, Rostrevor,
Co Down BT34 3GJ
Tel 028-41737751

6 Bracken Close,
Armagh Road, Newry,
Co Down BT35 6RW
Tel 028-30250630

2A Planting Road, Cashel,
Mullaghbawn, Newry,
Co Down BT35 9YU
Tel 028-30888990

MISSIONARY SISTERS OF THE ASSUMPTION
Assumption Convent,
34 Crossgar Road, Ballynahinch,
Co Down BT24 8EN
Tel 028-97561765 Fax 028-97565754
Superior: Sr Maureen Carville
Email maureen@msassumption.org
Community: 6
Assumption Grammar School
Tel 028-97562250
Pupils: 840

SISTERS OF OUR LADY OF APOSTLES
Rostrevor, Newry, Co Down
Tel 028-41737653 Fax 028-417377656
Community: 2
Email olagreendale@hotmail.com
1 Greendale Crescent, Greenpark Road,
Rostrevor, Newry, Co Down BT34 3HF

SISTERS OF ST CLARE
St Clare's Convent,
12 Ashgrove Avenue, Newry,
Co Down BT34 1PR
Tel 028-30252179
Contact: Sr Tarcisius Traynor
Community: 30

St Clare's Convent,
42 Glenvale Road, Newry,
Co Down BT34 2RD
Tel 028-30260116
Community: 3
Sacred Heart Grammar School,
10 Ashgrove Avenue,
Newry, Co Down BT34 1PR
Tel 028-30264632. Pupils: 875

EDUCATIONAL INSTITUTIONS

St Colman's College (Diocesan College)
Violet Hill,
Newry, Co Down
Tel 028-30262451
Principal: Mr Cormac McKinney
Vice Principal: Vacant

CHARITABLE AND OTHER SOCIETIES

ACCORD
Cana House,
Newry Parish Pastoral Centre, The Mall,
Newry, Co Down
Tel 028-30263577

Society of St Vincent de Paul
Conferences at:
Ballynahinch (St Patrick's)
Banbridge (St Patrick's)
Craigavon (St Anthony's)
Dromore (St Colman's)
Gilford (St John's)
Hilltown (St John's)
Laurencetown (St Patrick's)
Lurgan (St Peter's)
Newry (Cathedral)
Newry (St Brigid's)
Rathfriland (St Marys)
Rostrevor (St Bronach's)
Warrenpoint (St Patrick's)

DIOCESE OF ELPHIN

PATRONS OF THE DIOCESE
ST ASICUS, 27 APRIL; IMMACULATE CONCEPTION, 8 DECEMBER

INCLUDES PORTIONS OF COUNTIES ROSCOMMON, SLIGO AND GALWAY

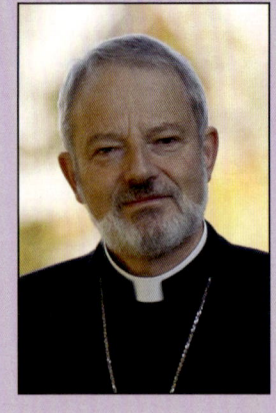

Most Rev Kevin Doran MA, PhD
Bishop of Elphin;
born 26 June 1953;
ordained priest 6 July 1977;
ordained Bishop of Elphin 13 July 2014

Residence: St Mary's,
Temple Street, Sligo
Tel 071-9150106
Email office@elphindiocese.ie

CATHEDRAL OF THE IMMACULATE CONCEPTION, SLIGO

The cathedral church dominates the skyline of Sligo town. It was erected during the episcopate of Bishop Laurence Gillooly (1858–1895), whose knowledge of ecclesiastical architecture is imprinted on every stone.

The foundation stone was laid on 6 October 1868. It was designed by a renowned English architect, George Goldie, and was modelled on Normano-Romano-Byzantine style. It was acclaimed by an eminent architect as a 'poem in stone'. It is 275 feet long, with transepts and nave, and can accommodate 4,000 people. A square tower incorporating the main entrance to the cathedral is surmounted by a four-sided pyramidal spire which reaches a height of 210 feet. The stained-glass windows and the original high altar are magnificent works of art.

Although the cathedral was open for public worship in 1874, it wasn't until 1882 that all construction work was completed. The cathedral was finally consecrated on 1 July 1897 and dedicated in honour of the Immaculate Conception of the Blessed Virgin Mary.

The cathedral has undergone extensive renovations on two occasions since it was erected, including the remodelling of the sanctuary to comply with liturgical norms in 1970.

DIOCESE OF ELPHIN

CHAPTER
Very Rev Canon Joseph Fitzgerald
Very Rev Canon Liam Devine
Very Rev Canon Eugene McLoughlin
Very Rev Canon Gerard Hanly VF
Very Rev Canon Niall Ahern VF
Very Rev Canon Ciaran Whitney
Very Rev Canon Thomas Hever VG

ADMINISTRATION

College of Consultors
Very Rev Canon Thomas Hever PP, VG
Very Rev John McManus PP, VG
Very Rev Canon Gerard Hanly PP, VF
Very Rev Raymond Milton PP, VF
Very Rev Michael Drumm PP
Very Rev Patrick Lombard PP
Very Rev Eamon O'Connor PP

Vicars General
Very Rev Canon Tom Hever PP, VG
Very Rev John McManus PP, VG

Diocesan Education Commission
Chairperson: Very Rev Michael Drumm PP
St Mary's, Sligo
Tel 071-9150106

Vicars Forane
Very Rev Canon Niall Ahern (Sligo)
Very Rev Michael Breslin (Roscommon)
Very Rev Canon Gerard Hanly (Boyle)
Very Rev Raymond Milton (Athlone)
Very Rev John McManus (Castlerea)
Very Rev Eamonn O'Connor (Strokestown)

Council of Priests
Very Rev Declan Boyce (SPS) Adm
Very Rev Canon Liam Devine PP
Very Rev Pravin Dhason PP
Very Rev Michael Drumm PP
Very Rev Stephan Ezenwegbu PP
Very Rev Canon Gerard Hanly PP, VF
Very Rev Canon Thomas Hever PP, VG
Very Rev Patrick Lombard PP
Very Rev Canon Eugene McLoughlin PE
Very Rev John McManus PP, VG
Very Rev Raymond Milton PP
Very Rev Dónal Morris PP
Very Rev Eamonn O'Connor PP, VF

Data Protection Officer
Email dpo@elphindiocese.ie

Diocesan Finance Council
Secretary
Very Rev Raymond Milton PP, VF
St Mary's, Temple Street, Sligo
Tel 071-9150106
Email finance@elphindiocese.ie

Diocesan Secretary and Diocesan Communications Officer
Ms Sheena Darcy
St Mary's, Temple Street, Sligo
Tel 071-9150106
Email office@elphindiocese.ie

Finance and Asset Manager
Mr Conor Ward
St Mary's, Temple Street, Sligo
Tel 071-9151080
Email finance@elphindiocese.ie

Chancellor
Very Rev Thomas Hever PP, VG
St Mary's, Temple Street, Sligo
Tel 071-9150106
Email chancellor@elphindiocese.ie

Safeguarding
Director: Ms Mary Nicholson
St Mary's, Temple Street, Sligo
Tel 071-9151086/086-3750277

Secretary to the Bishop
Ms Sheena Darcy
St Mary's, Temple Street, Sligo
Tel 071-9150106
Email bishopsecretary@elphindiocese.ie

CATECHETICS EDUCATION

Religious Education (Primary Schools)
Diocesan Advisors
Ms Teresa Melia
Ms Kathleen O'Dowd
c/o St Mary's, Temple Street, Sligo

Education (Post-Primary)
Religious Education Advisor
Dr Justin Harkin

Education (Primary)
Secretary
Sr Patricia Tomlinson (RSM)
St Mary's, Temple Street, Sligo
Tel 071-9150106

LITURGY

Liturgical Music
Adviser Church Organ Music:
Mr Charles O'Connor
Maugheraboy, Sligo
Tel 071-9145722

Diocesan Magazine
The Angelus, St Mary's, Sligo
Tel 071-9150106
Email angeluspaper@gmail.com

PASTORAL

ACCORD
Director: Rev James Murray CC
Carraroe, Sligo
Tel 071-9162136

Diocesan Catechists (Partners in the Gospel)
Co-ordinator: Very Rev Michael Drumm
St Columba's Rosses Point, Co Sligo
Tel 071-9177133

Diocesan Pastoral Council
Chair: Mr Tomás Kenny
Secretary: Ms Bernie Flynn

Ecumenism
Very Rev Pat Lombard PP
St Anne's, Sligo
Tel 071-9145028

Marriage Tribunal
(See Marriage Tribunals section)

Pastoral Development
Director: Dr Justin Harkin
Pastoral Development Office,
Church Grounds, St Coman's Club,
Abbey Street, Roscommon
Tel 087-6171526
Email justin@elphindiocese.ie

Permanent Diaconate
Director: Most Rev Kevin Doran
Director of Formation
Very Rev Michael Drumm

Pilgrimage Director (Lourdes)
Very Rev Raymond Milton PP
Knockcroghery, Co Roscommon
Tel 090-6661127

Pioneer Total Abstinence Association
Diocesan Director
Vacant

Pontifical Mission Societies
Diocesan Director
Deacon Wando deAraujo
33 Ardsallagh Woods,
Roscommon, Co Roscommon
Tel 087-2600338

Social Services
Director: Ms Christine McTaggart
Sligo Social Services, Charles Street, Sligo
Tel 071-9145682

Travellers
Chaplain: Rev John Carroll (SPS)
Cregg House, Rosses Point, Co Sligo
Tel 071-9177241

Vocations
Director: Deacon Frank McGuinness
St Mary's, Temple Street, Sligo
Tel 087-9880690
Assistant Director
Very Rev John Gannon PP
Tulsk, Co Roscommon
Tel 071-9639005
Email vocations@elphindiocese.ie

Youth Ministry
Diocesan Director
Deacon Frank McGuinness
St Mary's, Sligo, Co Sligo
Tel 087-9880690

DIOCESE OF ELPHIN

PARISHES

Mensal parishes are listed first. Other parishes follow alphabetically. Historical names are given in parentheses.

SLIGO, ST MARY'S
Very Rev Declan Boyce (SPS) Adm
Rev Willibrord Sakwe CC
Rev Victor Samugana (MSP) CC
St Mary's, Temple Street, Sligo
Tel 071-9162670/9162769

SLIGO, ST JOSEPH'S AND CALRY
Very Rev Noel Rooney PP
279 Sunset Drive, Cartron Point, Sligo
Tel 071-9142422
Rev Hugh McGonagle CC
7 Elm Park, Ballinode, Sligo
Tel 071-9143430

SLIGO, ST ANNE'S
Very Rev Patrick Lombard PP
Tel 071-9145028
Rev Stephen Walsh (CSSp) CC
Tel 071-9145028
St Anne's, Sligo
Rev James Murray CC
Carraroe, Co Sligo
Tel 071-9162136
Rev Stanislaw Kardas CC
Chaplain to Polish Community
Tel 071-9162670

AHAMLISH (GRANGE AND CLIFFONEY)
Very Rev Christopher McHugh PP
Grange, Co Sligo
Tel 071-9163100

AHASCRAGH (AHASCRAGH AND CALTRA)
Very Rev John Mahony PP
Ahascragh, Ballinasloe, Co Galway
Tel 090-9688617

ARDCARNE (COOTEHALL)
Very Rev Brendan McDonagh (SPS) PP
Cootehall, Boyle, Co Roscommon
Tel 071-9667004

ATHLEAGUE (ATHLEAGUE AND FUERTY)
Very Rev Christopher Edebianga (MSP) PP
Parochial House,
Athleague, Co Roscommon
Tel 090-6663338

ATHLONE, SS PETER AND PAUL'S
Very Rev John Deignan PP
10 Ashford, Monksland,
Athlone, Co Roscommon
Tel 090-6493262
Rev Glen Alipoyo, Pastoral Leader
Rev Bernard Ngalame CC
Forthill House, The Batteries, Athlone,
Co Westmeath
Tel 090-6492171
Rev Michael Hickey (CSSp) CC
Drum, Athlone, Co Roscommon
Tel 090-6437125

AUGHRIM (AUGHRIM AND KILMORE)
Very Rev Stephen Ezenwegbu PP
The Presbytery, Elphin, Co Roscommon
Tel 071-9630486

AGHANAGH (BALLINAFAD)
Rev Deacon Damien Kearns Adm
Ballinafad, Boyle, Co Roscommon
Tel 071-9666006

BALLINAMEEN (KILNAMANAGH AND ESTERSNOW)
Very Rev Lawrence Ebuk (MSP) PP
Ballinameen, Boyle, Co Roscommon
Tel 071-9668104

BALLINTUBBER (BALLINTOBER AND BALLYMOE)
Very Rev Julian Lupot PP
Tel 094-9655602
Rev Patrick O'Toole (CSSp) CC
Ballintubber, Castlerea,
Co Roscommon

BALLYFORAN (DYSART AND TISRARA)
Very Rev Francis Beirne PP
Tisrara, Four Roads, Co Roscommon
Tel 090-6623313

BALLYGAR (KILLIAN AND KILLERORAN)
Very Rev Michael Breslin PP, VF
Ballygar, Co Galway
Tel 090-6624637
Rev Louis Lohan
Parish Chaplain

BOYLE
Very Rev Canon Gerard Hanly PP, VF
Tel 071-9662218
Rev Jonas Rebamontan CC
Tel 071-9662012
Boyle, Co Roscommon

CASTLEREA (KILKEEVAN)
Very Rev John McManus PP, VG
Tel 094-9620040
Rev Kevin Reynolds (MHM) CC
Tel 094-9620039
Castlerea, Co Roscommon

CROGHAN (KILLUKIN AND KILLUMMOD)
Very Rev Alan Conway PP
Drumlion, Carrick-on-Shannon,
Co Roscommon
Tel 071-9620415

DRUMCLIFF/MAUGHEROW
Very Rev Canon Thomas Hever PP, VG
Drumcliff, Sligo
Tel 071-9142779

ELPHIN (ELPHIN AND CREEVE)
Very Rev Stephen Ezenwegbu PP
Elphin, Co Roscommon
Tel 071-9630486
Very Rev John J Gannon PE
Elphin, Co Roscommon
Tel 071-9635058

FAIRYMOUNT (TIBOHINE)
Very Rev Mícheál Donnelly PP
Parochial House, Ballingare,
Co Roscommon
Tel 094-9870039

FRENCHPARK (KILCORKEY AND FRENCHPARK)
Very Rev Mícheál Donnelly PP
Parochial House, Ballinagare,
Co Roscommon
Tel 094-9870039

GEEVAGH
Very Rev Laurence Cullen PP
Geevagh, Boyle, Co Roscommon
Tel 071-9647107

KILBEGNET AND GLINSK
Very Rev Donal Morris PP
Parochial House, Garraun South,
Creggs, Co Roscommon
Tel 090-6621127

KILBRIDE (FOURMILEHOUSE)
Deacon Seamus Talbot Adm
Email seamustalbot@gmail.com
Rev Eamon Conaty (SSC)
Parish Chaplain
Fourmilehouse, Roscommon
Tel 090-6629518

KILGEFIN (BALLAGH, CLOONTUSKERT, AND CURRAGHROE)
Very Rev Daniel Udofia (MSP) PP
Parochial House,
Ballyleague, Co Roscommon
Tel 043-3321171

KILGLASS (KILGLASS AND ROOSKEY)
Very Rev Evaristus Nkede PP
Rooskey, Carrick-on-Shannon,
Co Roscommon
Tel 071-9638014

KILTOOM (KILTOOM AND CAM)
Very Rev Michael McManus PP
Kiltoom, Athlone,
Co Roscommon
Tel 090-6489105

KNOCKCROGHERY/ST JOHN'S/RAHARA
Very Rev Raymond Milton PP, VF
Knockcroghery, Roscommon
Tel 090-6661115
Rev Joseph Ali CC
St John's Presbytery,
Lecarrow, Co Roscommon
Tel 090-6661115
Email knockcrogheyparish1@gmail.com

LOUGHGLYNN (LOUGHGLYNN AND LISACUL)
Very Rev Canon Liam Devine PP
Loughglynn, Castlerea, Co Roscommon
Tel 094-9880007

DIOCESE OF ELPHIN

ORAN (CLOVERHILL)
Very Rev Pravin Dhason PP
Cloverhill, Co Roscommon
Tel 090-6626275

RIVERSTOWN
Very Rev Yashin Jos PP
Parochial House,
Sooey, via Boyle, Co Sligo
Tel 071-9165144
Very Rev A.B. O'Shea PE
Rowantree Cottage, Church Grounds,
Riverstown, Co Sligo
Email aboshea@eircom.net

ROSCOMMON
Very Rev Kevin Fallon PP
Parochial House, Roscommon
Tel 090-6626298
Rev Douglas Zaggi CC
Curate's Residence, Abbey Street,
Roscommon
Tel 090-6626189
Rev Sean Beirne CC
Kilteevan, Roscommon
Tel 090-6626374
Very Rev Canon Joseph Fitzgerald
5 Hawthorn Park,
Ballygar, via Roscommon,
Co Galway

ROSSES POINT
Very Rev Michael Drumm PP
St Columba's, Rosses Point, Co Sligo
Tel 071-9177133

STRANDHILL/RANSBORO
Very Rev Canon Niall Ahern PP, VF
Strandhill, Co Sligo
Tel 071-9168147
Rev Christopher McCrann CC
Knocknahur, Sligo
Tel 071-9128470

STROKESTOWN (KILTRUSTAN, LISSONUFFY AND CLOONFINLOUGH)
Very Rev Eamonn O'Connor PP, VF
Rev Ciaran O'Flynn (SPS) CC
Strokestown, Co Roscommon
Tel 071-9633027

TARMONBARRY
Very Rev Jaroslaw (Jarek) Maszkiewicz PP
Carraun, Whitehall,
Tarmonbarry, Co Roscommon
Tel 043-3326020

TULSK (OGULLA AND BASLIC)
Very Rev John Gannon PP
Tulsk, Castlerea, Co Roscommon
Tel 071-9639005

CHAPLAINS

Chaplains to Overseas Communities
Re Deacon Wando de Araujo
Chaplain to Brazilian Community,
c/o Parish Office, Roscommon Town
Tel 090-6626298
Rev Stanislaw Kardas
Chaplain to Polish Community,
St Mary's, Temple Street, Sligo
Tel 071-9162670
Rev Julian Lupot
Chaplain to Filipino Community
Presbytery, Ballintubber,
Castlerea, Co Roscommon
Tel 094-9655602

Ballinode Vocational School
Sligo
Tel 071-9147111
Very Rev Noel Rooney PP

Castlerea Prison
Tel 094-9625278
Deacon Seamus Talbot
Prison General Office: 094-9625213

Christian Brothers School
Roscommon
Tel 090-6626189
Very Rev Joe Fitzgerald

Coláiste Chiaráin
Summerhill, Athlone, Co Roscommon
Chaplain: Deacon Tony Larkin
Tel 090-6492383

College of the Immaculate Conception
Summerhill, Sligo
Ms Denise McCann
Tel 071-9160311

Coola Vocational School
Riverstown, Boyle, Co Roscommon
Tel 071-9165144
Very Rev Yashin Jos PP

Cregg House, Sligo
Tel 071-9177241
Rev John Carroll (SPS)

Custume Barracks
Athlone, Co Westmeath
Tel 090-6421277
Rev Declan Shannon CF

Grange Vocational School, Sligo
Tel 071-9163100
Very Rev Christopher McHugh PP

Nazareth House, Sligo
Rt Rev Mgr Gerard Dolan
Church Hill, Sligo
Tel 071-9162278

Plunkett Home
Boyle, Co Roscommon
Tel 071-9662218
Very Rev Canon Gerard Hanly PP, VF

Post-Primary School, Elphin,
Co Roscommon
Tel 071-9635058
Clergy of the Parish

Post-Primary School, Strokestown
Co Roscommon
Tel 071-9633041
Very Rev Eamonn O'Connor PP, VF

Roscommon Hospital
Tel 090-6620039
Sr Gabriel Mee

St Angela's College
Lough Gill, Co Sligo
Tel 071-9143580
Rev Joseph Ali

St Cuan's College
Castleblakeney, Ballinasloe, Co Galway
Tel 090-9678127
Mr Kevin McGeeney

St Mary's Post-Primary School
Ballygar, Co Galway
Tel 090-664637
Very Rev Michael Breslin PP, VF

Sligo University Hospital
St Columba's, St John's
Tel 071-9171111
Chaplain: Rev Brian Conlon

PRIESTS OF THE DIOCESE ELSEWHERE

Rev Anthony Conry
Brazil
Rev John Coughlan
On Sabbatical
Rev John Cullen
Chaplain, Nazareth House,
Hammersmith, London

RETIRED PRIESTS

Rev Liam Sharkey
Ballyweelin, Rosses Point, Co Sligo
Rev Michael Glynn
c/o St Mary's, Temple Street, Sligo
Very Rev Dominick Gillooly
St Anne's, Sligo
Very Rev Ciarán Whitney
24 Kildallogue Heights,
Strokestown, Co Roscommon
Very Rev Francis Glennon
Presbytery, Castlecoote, Co Roscommon
Very Rev Michael Donnelly
c/o St Mary's, Temple Street, Sligo
Very Rev Canon Eugene McLoughlin
2 Essex Grove, Roscommon Town
Rt Rev Mgr Charles Travers
1 Convent Court, Roscommon
Tel 090-6628917

DIOCESE OF ELPHIN

PERMANENT DEACONS

Rev Wando de Araujo
Rev William Gacquin
Rev Damien Kearns
Rev Tony Larkin
Rev Frank McGuinness
Rev David Muldowney
Rev Martin Reidy
Rev Seamus Talbot

RELIGIOUS ORDERS AND CONGREGATIONS

PRIESTS

DIVINE WORD MISSIONARIES
Donamon Castle, Roscommon
Tel 090-6662222 Fax 090-6662511
Rector: Very Rev Pat Byrne (SVD)

DOMINICANS
Holy Cross, Sligo
Tel 071-9142700 Fax 071-9146533
Superior
Rev Augustine Champion (OP)
Email sligofriary@eircom.net

SISTERS

CONGREGATION OF THE SISTERS OF MERCY
Sisters of Mercy,
3 Newtown Terrace,
Athlone, Co Westmeath N37 D266
Tel 090-6473944
Community: 3

Sisters of Mercy,
Dún Mhuire, Lyster Street,
Athlone, Co Westmeath N37 E3V5
Tel 090-6494166 Fax 090-6440079
Community: 22

Sisters of Mercy,
Cois Abhann, Lyster Street,
Athlone, Co Westmeath
Community: 28

St Cecilias, Coosan Road West,
Athlone, Co Westmeath N37 K4X5
Tel 090-6472987
Community: 1

Sisters of Mercy, Bethany,
Chapel Hill, Sligo F91 KCH9
Tel 071-9138498
Community: 6

Our Lady of Mercy,
3 St Patrick's Avenue, Sligo F91 R85D
Tel 071-9142731 Fax 071-9147090
Community: 11

Sisters of Mercy,
No 1 St Patrick's Avenue,
Sligo F91 RK6C
Tel 071-9142393
Community: 2

Sisters of Mercy,
No 2 St Patrick's Avenue,
Sligo F91 E9TY
Tel 071-9145755
Community: 2

Sisters of Mercy,
1 Racecourt Manor,
Tonaphubble, Sligo F91 T91X
Tel 071-9154656
Community: 2

McAuley House,
Roscommon F42 XV70
Tel 090-6627904 Fax 090-6627581
Community: 7

Convent of Mercy,
St Catherine's,
Roscommon F42 CA26
Tel 090-6626767
Community: 5

Galilee Community,
Sisters of Mercy, Tintagh,
Boyle, Co Roscommon F52 TX93
Tel 071-9664101 Fax 071-9664684
Community: 3

Sisters of Mercy, Crubyhill,
Croscomon F42 VC55
Tel 090-6625725
Community: 3

Sisters of Mercy,
76 Oldwood, Ardsallagh,
Roscommon F42 YX88
Community: 1

DAUGHTERS OF WISDOM (LA SAGESSE)
2 The Greenlands,
Rosses Point,
Sligo F91 A6XE
Tel 071-9177607
Contact: Sr Margaret Morris
Email srmegmorris@gmail.com
Community: 2

DISCIPLES OF THE DIVINE MASTER
8 Castle Street, Athlone,
Co Westmeath N37 W9H6
Tel 090-6498755 *(Community)*
090-6492278 *(Liturgical Centre)*
Email kathrynwilliams@pddm.org
Sister-in-Charge: Sr Kathryn Williams
Community: 4
Contemplative-apostolic Congregation. Chapel of Adoration with daily Adoration, open to public. Prayer, support and intercession for priests. Liturgical Centre-distributor and producer of liturgical vestments/altar linens, high-quality liturgical art, religious gifts. Promotion of liturgical formation. Bethany House available for private retreats. Daily prayer and support groups.
Websites www.ppdm.ie
www.liturgicalcentre.ie

MISSIONARIES OF CHARITY
Temple Street, Sligo
Tel 071-9154843
Superior: Sr M. Bridget (MC)
Community: 6
Contemplative

CONGREGATION OF THE SISTERS OF NAZARETH
Nazareth House, Sligo
Tel 071-9162278 Public
Tel 071-9160664 Fax 071-9160344
Tel Convent 071-9154446
Superior: Sr Victoire Mulligan
Email srvictoire.mulligan@
sistersofnazareth.com
Community: 9
Home for the elderly. Beds 70
Nursing Home operated by Nazareth House Management
Director of Nursing: Mrs Linda Hallett
Tel 071-9180900

Ballymote Community Nursing Unit
Tel 071-9183195
Home for the Elderly: Beds 24
Owned by HSE
Operated by Nazareth House Management
Director of Service: Mrs Linda Hannon

PRESENTATION OF MARY SISTERS
4 Lower John Street,
Sligo
Tel 071-9160740
Superior: Sr Emma Dublan (PM)
Community: 4

DIOCESE OF ELPHIN

URSULINES
Ursuline Convent, Temple Street, Sligo
Tel 071-9161538
Community: 7
Primary School
Tel 071-9154573 Fax 071-9154573
Secondary School
Tel 071-9161653 Fax 071-9146141

Ursuline Sisters,
'Brescia', Ballytivnan, Sligo
Community: 5
Pastoral Ministry

EDUCATIONAL INSTITUTIONS OF CATHOLIC ETHOS (POST-PRIMARY)

College of the Immaculate Conception
Summerhill, Sligo
Tel 071-9160311
Principal
Mr Paul Keogh
Priest on Staff
Rev Gerard Cryan BA, HDE, STB, L Eccl Hist

Coláiste Chiaráin
Summerhill, Athlone, Co Roscommon
Tel 090-6492383
Principal: Mr Brendan Waldron

St Cuan's College
Castleblakeney,
Ballinasloe, Co Galway
Tel 090-9678127
Principal
Ms Colette Kennedy Walsh

CHARITABLE AND OTHER SOCIETIES

Legion of Mary
Assumpta House, John Street, Sligo

Social Services Centre
Charles Street, Sligo
Tel 071-9145682

Society of St Vincent de Paul
Conferences at Athlone, Boyle, Castlerea, Roscommon, Sligo

DIOCESE OF FERNS

PATRON OF THE DIOCESE
ST AIDAN, 30 JANUARY

INCLUDES ALMOST ALL OF COUNTY WEXFORD
AND PART OF COUNTY WICKLOW

Most Rev Ger Nash DD
Bishop of Ferns
Ordained Bishop
5 September 2021

Residence: Bishop's House,
Summerhill, Wexford
Tel 053-9122177
Fax 053-9123436
Email adm@ferns.ie

ST AIDAN'S CATHEDRAL, ENNISCORTHY

The foundation stone for St Aidan's Cathedral, Enniscorthy, was laid in 1843. The cathedral was designed by the architect Augustus Welby Northmore Pugin and is the largest church Pugin built in Ireland. The recent renovations of 1996 have restored to a great extent the original beautiful building as visualised by Pugin. The external stonework was executed by Irish stonemasons who were praised by Pugin. The restored stencilling of the interior gives some idea of what Pugin visualised for his churches.

Pugin, a Londoner, was as important an influence on the history of nineteenth-century English architecture as Frank Lloyd Wright was to be on American architecture. He was an extraordinarily gifted artist and designed ceramics, stained glass, wallpapers, textiles, memorial brasses, church plate, etc. His connection with the Diocese of Ferns came through the patronage of John, 16th Earl of Shrewsbury, Waterford and Wexford. Shrewsbury's wife was a native of Blackwater, Co Wexford. Her uncle, John Hyacinth Talbot, was the first Catholic MP for Co Wexford after Catholic Emancipation in 1829. A rich man through his marriage into the Redmond family, John Hyacinth Talbot introduced Pugin to Wexford, where through the patronage of the Talbot and Redmond family connections, he was to gain most of his Irish commissions.

Pugin was to die through overwork at the age of forty in 1852, but he has left a unique diocesan heritage to Ferns in his churches. His son and son-in-law, E.W. Pugin and George Ashlin, were to continue the building of Gothic Revival churches and monuments in Ireland.

DIOCESE OF FERNS

Most Rev Denis Brennan DD
Retired Bishop of Ferns
PO Box 40, Summerhill, Wexford

Most Rev Brendan Comiskey DD
Retired Bishop of Ferns
PO Box 40, Summerhill, Wexford

CHAPTER
Very Rev James B. Canon Curtis
Very Rev Seamus De Val
Very Rev Felix Byrne
Very Rev Lorenzo Cleary
Very Rev Patrick C. O'Brien
Very Rev Seamus Larkin
Very Rev Thomas Doyle
Very Rev Richard Hayes
Rt Rev Mgr James Hammel
Very Rev Diarmuid Desmond
Rt Rev Mgr Denis Lennon
Very Rev Thomas McGrath

ADMINISTRATION

College of Consultors
Very Rev Brian Broaders
Rt Rev Joseph McGrath
Very Rev Matthew Boggan
Very Rev William Swan
Very Rev Jim Doyle
Very Rev Barry Larkin

Vicar General
Rt Rev Mgr Joseph McGrath VG, VF
New Ross, Co Wexford
Tel 051-447080

Vicar for Clergy
Very Rev Brian Broaders PP, VF
Rathnure, Enniscorthy,
Co Wexford

Vicars Forane
Very Rev Brian Broaders PP, VF
Rt Rev Mgr Joseph McGrath VG, VF
Very Rev Aodhan Marken PP, VF
Very Rev Denis Browne PP, VF

Diocesan Finance Council
Rt Rev Mgr Joseph McGrath VG, VF
Very Rev Patrick Cushen PP
Very Rev James Fegan PP
Mr Liam Gaynor
Mr John Murphy
Mr Patrick F. Dore
Ms Eleanor Furlong
Ms Pauline O'Neill
Ms Annette McCarthy
Ms Martha Cooney
Very Rev Tom Dalton
Finance Officer and Chairman:
Mr Eugene Doyle

Diocesan Archivist
Rt Rev Mgr James Hammel
Ballygarron, Kilmuckridge
Gorey, Co Wexford
Tel 086-1688295

Diocesan Chancellery
Rev James Murphy
PO Box 40, Bishop's House,
Summerhill, Wexford
Tel 053-9124368

Diocesan Secretary
Ms Patricia Murphy
PO Box 40, Bishop's House,
Summerhill, Wexford
Tel 053-9124368

Diocesan Pastoral Council
Co-ordinator: Sr Stephanie O'Brien
Ferns Diocesan Centre,
St Peter's College, Wexford
Tel 053-9145511
Email
diocesanpastoralcentrestpeters@gmail.com

CATECHETICS EDUCATION

Catholic Primary School Management Association (CPSMA)
Mr Colm O'Tiarnaigh
Tel 053-9122177
Email fernsed@gmail.com

Diocesan Adviser for Primary School Catechetics
Ms Mairin Jackson
Fushia Cottage, Aughclare,
New Ross, Co Wexford
Tel 087-2222522

Director of Religious Education
Ms Colette O'Doherty
Ferns Diocesan Centre,
St Peter's College, Wexford
Tel 053-9145511
Email fernsda@ferns.ie

PASTORAL

Apostolic Work Society
Diocesan Director
Very Rev Joseph Power PP
Kilrush, Bunclody, Enniscorthy,
Co Wexford
Tel 053-9377262

Chaplain to Special Needs Groups
Very Rev Tom Dalton PP
Riverchapel, Gorey, Co Wexford
Tel 053-9425241

CORI (Ferns Branch)
Secretary: To be confirmed

Ecumenism
Director: Rev James Murphy PP
St Brigid's, Rosslare,
Co Wexford
Tel 053-9132118

Fatima Pilgrimage
Director: Very Rev Denis Browne
Kilanerin, Gorey, Co Wexford

House of Mission
Rev Thaddeus Doyle
Shillelagh, Arklow, Co Wicklow
Tel 053-9429926

Knock Pilgrimage
Director
Very Rev Gerald O'Leary PP
Horeswood, Campile,
Co Wexford

Legion of Mary
Very Rev Seamus Canon De Val
1 Irish Street, Bunclody,
Co Wexford
Tel 053-9376140

Lourdes Pilgrimage
Director
Very Rev Matthew Boggan PP
Parochial house, Clongeen,
Foulksmill, Co Wexford

Marriage Tribunal
(See also Marriage Tribunals section)
Ferns Diocesan Auditor for Dublin Regional Marriage Tribunal
Very Rev Kevin Cahill (DCL)
c/o Bishop's House,
Summerhill, Wexford

Our Lady's Island Pilgrimage
Director
Very Rev James Cogley PP
Our Lady's Island, Broadway,
Co Wexford
Tel 053-9131167

Pioneer Total Abstinence Association
Diocesan Director
Very Rev Robert McGuire Adm
Parochial House, Taghmon, Co Wexford
Tel 053-9134123

Pontifical Mission Societies
Diocesan Director
Very Rev Patrick Cushen PP
Parochial House, Ferns,
Enniscorthy, Co Wexford

St Aidan Retirement Fund
Chairman
Very Rev James Murphy PP
Parochial House, Rosslare, Co Wexford
Tel 053-9132118

St Joseph's Young Priests' Society
Diocesan Chaplain
Right Rev Mgr Joseph McGrath PP, VF, VG
New Ross, Co Wexford
Tel 051-447080

DIOCESE OF FERNS

Travellers
Diocesan Co-ordinator
Rev Thomas Orr CC
Traveller Resource Centre,
Mary Street, New Ross,
Co Wexford
Tel 051-422272

Vocations
Director
Very Rev William Swan Adm
The Presbytery,
School Street, Wexford
Tel 053-9122055

PARISHES

Mensal parishes are listed first. Other parishes follow alphabetically.

ENNISCORTHY, CATHEDRAL OF ST AIDAN
Very Rev Odhrán Furlong Adm
Rev James Doyle CC
St Aidan's, Enniscorthy,
Co Wexford
Tel 053-9235777
Fax 053-9237700

WEXFORD
Very Rev William Swan Adm
Rev Michael O'Shea CC
Rev James Cullen CC
The Presbytery,
12 School Street, Wexford
Tel 053-9122055 Fax 053-9121724

ADAMSTOWN
Very Rev Robert Nolan PP
Adamstown, Enniscorthy,
Co Wexford
Tel 053-9240512

ANNACURRA
Very Rev John-Paul Sheridan PP
Annacurra, Aughrim, Co Wicklow
Tel 0402-36119

BALLINDAGGIN
Very Rev James Fegan PP
Ballindaggin, Enniscorthy,
Co Wexford
Tel 053-9388559

BALLYCULLANE
Very Rev William Byrne PP
Ballycullane, New Ross, Co Wexford
Tel 051-562123
Very Rev Sean Laffan CC
Gusserane, Co Wexford
Tel 051-562111

BALLYGARRETT
Very Rev James Butler PP
Ballygarrett, Gorey, Co Wexford
Tel 053-9427330

BALLYMORE AND MAYGLASS
PP Appointment pending

BANNOW
Very Rev James Kehoe PP
Carrig-on-Bannow,
Wellington Bridge, Co Wexford
Tel 051-561192
Rev Martin Pender CC
Ballymitty, Co Wexford
Tel 051-561128

BLACKWATER
Very Rev Brendan Nolan PP
Blackwater, Enniscorthy,
Co Wexford
Tel 053-9127118

BREE
Very Rev Michael Byrne PP
Bree, Enniscorthy, Co Wexford
Tel 053-9247843
Rev Billy Caulfield CC
Galbally, Ballyhogue, Enniscorthy,
Co Wexford
Tel 053-9247814

BUNCLODY
(*Parish Office:* Tel/Fax 053-9376190)
Very Rev Laurence O'Connor PP
Bunclody, Enniscorthy, Co Wexford
Tel 053-9377319
Rev Patrick Duffy CC
Kilmyshall, Enniscorthy, Co Wexford
Tel 053-9377188

CAMOLIN
Very Rev Joseph Kavanagh PP
Camolin, Co Wexford
Tel 053-9383136
Rev Tomás Kehoe CC
Ballycanew, Gorey, Co Wexford
Tel 053-9427184

CARNEW
Very Rev Martin Casey PP
Woolgreen, Carnew, Co Wicklow
Tel 053-9426888

CASTLEBRIDGE AND CURRACLOE
Very Rev Denis Kelly PP
Ballymore, Screen,
Enniscorthy, Co Wexford
Tel 053-9137140

CLONARD
(*Parish Office:* Tel 053-9123672
Fax 053-9146699)
Very Rev Barry Larkin Adm
1 Clonard Park, Clonard,
Co Wexford
Tel 053-9147686
Rt Rev Mgr Denis Lennon PE
39 Beechlawn, Wexford
Tel 053-9124417

CLONGEEN
Very Rev Matthew Boggan PP
Clongeen, Foulksmills, Co Wexford
Tel 051-565610

CLOUGHBAWN AND POULPEASTY
Very Rev Bernard Cushen PP
Clonroche, Enniscorthy,
Co Wexford
Tel 053-9244115

CRAANFORD
Rev Brian Whelan Adm
Craanford, Gorey, Co Wexford
Tel 053-9428163
Very Rev Felix Canon Byrne CC
Monaseed, Gorey, Co Wexford
Tel 053-9428207

CROSSABEG AND BALLYMURN
Very Rev James Finn PP
Crossabeg, Co Wexford
Tel 053-9159015

CUSHINSTOWN AND RATHGAROGUE
Very Rev Sean Devereux PP
Cushinstown, Newbawn,
Co Wexford
Tel 051-428347

DAVIDSTOWN AND COURTNACUDDY
Very Rev James Nolan PP
Davidstown, Enniscorthy,
Co Wexford
Tel 053-9238240

DUNCANNON
Very Rev John P. Nolan PP
Duncannon, New Ross,
Co Wexford
Tel 051-389118

FERNS
Very Rev Patrick Cushen PP
Ferns, Enniscorthy, Co Wexford
Tel 053-9366152

GLYNN
Very Rev John Carroll PP
Barntown, Co Wexford
Tel 053-9120853

GOREY
Very Rev William Flynn PP
St Michael's, Gorey, Co Wexford
Tel 053-9421112
Rev Roger O'Neill CC
St Michael's, Gorey, Co Wexford
Tel 053-9421117

HORESWOOD AND BALLYKELLY
Very Rev Gerald O'Leary PP
Horeswood, Campile, Co Wexford
Tel 051-388129

DIOCESE OF FERNS

KILANERIN AND BALLYFAD
Very Rev Denis Browne PP
Kilanerin, Gorey,
Co Wexford
Tel/Fax 0402-37120

KILLAVENEY AND CROSSBRIDGE
Very Rev Raymond Gahan PP
Killaveney, Tinahely,
Co Wicklow
Tel 0402-38188

KILMORE AND KILMORE QUAY
Very Rev Pat Mernagh PP
Kilmore, Co Wexford
Tel 053-9135181

KILMUCKRIDGE (LITTER) AND MONAMOLIN
Very Rev Francis Murphy PP
Kilmuckridge, Gorey, Co Wexford
Tel 053-9130116
Very Rev Seamus Canon Larkin *(priest in residence)*
Monamolin, Gorey, Co Wexford

KILRANE AND ST PATRICK'S
Very Rev Diarmuid Desmond PP
Kilrane, Co Wexford
Tel 053-9133128

KILRUSH AND ASKAMORE
Very Rev Joseph Power PP
Kilrush, Bunclody, Enniscorthy,
Co Wexford
Tel 053-9377262

MARSHALLSTOWN AND CASTLEDOCKRELL
Very Rev Daniel McDonald PP
Marshallstown, Enniscorthy,
Co Wexford
Tel 053-9388521

MONAGEER
Very Rev William Cosgrave PP
Monageer, Ferns, Enniscorthy,
Co Wexford
Tel 053-9233530
Rev Morgan White CC
Boolavogue, Ferns, Wexford
Tel 053-9366282

NEWBAWN AND RAHEEN
Very Rev James Moynihan PP
Newbawn, Co Wexford
Tel 051-428227

NEW ROSS
Rt Rev Mgr Joseph McGrath PP, VF, VG
New Ross, Co Wexford
Tel 051-447080
Rev Tom Orr CC
New Ross, Co Wexford

OULART AND BALLAGHKEENE
Very Rev Patrick Browne PP
Oulart, Gorey, Co Wexford
Tel 053-9136139

OUR LADY'S ISLAND AND TACUMSHANE
Very Rev James Cogley PP
Our Lady's Island, Broadway,
Co Wexford
Tel 053-9131167

OYLEGATE AND GLENBRIEN
Very Rev John Byrne PP
Oylegate, Co Wexford
Tel 053-9138163

PIERCESTOWN AND MURRINTOWN
Very Rev Aodhan Marken PP
Piercestown, Co Wexford
Tel 053-9158000

RAMSGRANGE
Very Rev Richard Redmond PP
Ramsgrange, New Ross,
Co Wexford
Tel 051-389148

RATHANGAN AND CLEARIESTOWN
PP Appointment pending
Rathangan, Duncormick,
Co Wexford
Tel 051-563104
Very Rev James Ryan *(priest in residence)*
Cleariestown, Co Wexford
Tel 053-9139110

RATHNURE AND TEMPLEUDIGAN
Very Rev Brian Broaders PP
Rathnure, Co Wexford
Tel 053-9255122

RIVERCHAPEL, COURTOWN HARBOUR
Very Rev Thomas Dalton PP
Riverchapel, Courtown Harbour,
Gorey, Co Wexford
Tel 053-9425241

ST SENAN'S, ENNISCORTHY
Parish Office: Tel 053-9237611
Very Rev Patrick Banville Adm
The Presbytery, Templeshannon,
Enniscorthy, Co Wexford
Tel 053-9237611

TAGHMON
Very Rev Robert McGuire Adm
Taghmon, Co Wexford
Tel 053-9134123

TAGOAT
Rev James Murphy PP
St Brigid's, Rosslare,
Co Wexford
Tel 053-9132118

TEMPLETOWN AND POULFUR
Very Rev Michael Doyle PP
Poulfur, Fethard-on-Sea,
New Ross, Co Wexford
Tel 051-397113

INSTITUTIONS AND THEIR CHAPLAINS

Community School
Gorey, Co Wexford
Tel 053-9421000

Vocational College Wexford
Rev James Cullen CC
The Presbytery, Wexford
Tel 053-9122753

Wexford General Hospital
Tel 053-9142233
Chaplain: Rev Ken Quinn
General Hospital, Wexford
Tel 053-9142233

Community School
Ramsgrange
Tel 051-389211
Ms Maria McCabe

St John of God Convent
Newtown Road, Wexford
Chaplain: Vacant

St John's Hospital
Enniscorthy, Co Wexford
Chaplain: Rev Odhran Furlong
Tel 053-9233228

PRIESTS OF THE DIOCESE ELSEWHERE IN IRELAND

Rev David Murphy CF
Chaplain to Defence Forces
Rev Chris Hayden
c/o Bishop's House
Rev Richard Lawless
c/o Bishop's House

PRIESTS OF THE DIOCESE ABROAD

Rev Thomas Brennan, USA
Rev Dermot Gahan, USA

DIOCESE OF FERNS

RETIRED PRIESTS

Most Rev Denis Brennan DD
PO Box 40, Wexford
Very Rev James Byrne
Ballylannon, Wellingtonbridge,
Co Wexford
Rev Michael Byrne
Serene Valley, Borris Road, Kiltealy,
Enniscorthy, Co Wexford
Very Rev Matthew L. Cleary
The Stables, Bridgetown, Co Wexford
Most Rev Brendan Comiskey (SSCC) DD
PO Box 40, Wexford
Very Rev James Curtis
3 Oldtown Court,
Clongreen, Foulksmills,
New Ross, Co Wexford
Very Rev James B. Canon Curtis
Rathjarney, Drinagh, Co Wexford
Very Rev Seamus Canon De Val
1 Irish Streeet, Bunclody, Co Wexford
Very Rev Denis Doyle
Starvehall, Coolballon, Co Wexford
Very Rev Thomas Canon Doyle
3 Priory Court, Gorey, Co Wexford
Very Rev Thomas Eustace
The Cools, Barntown, Wexford
Very Rev John French
Horeswood, New Ross, Co Wexford
Tel 051-593196
Very Rev James Furlong
Tomgarrow, Adamstown, Co Wexford
Very Rev Sean Gorman
Ballask, Kilmore,
Co Wexford
Very Rev James Hammel
Ballygarron, Kilmuckridge,
Gorey, Co Wexford
Very Rev William Howell
c/o Bishop's House
Very Rev Richard Hayes
Collinstown, Duncormick,
Co Wexford
Very Rev John Jordan
Kyle, Oulart, Gorey, Co Wexford
Rt Rev Mgr Don Kenny
Cois Cuan Arthurstown,
New Ross, Co Wexford
Very Rev Seamus Canon Larkin
Monamolin, Gorey, Co Wexford
Tel 053-9389223
Very Rev Thomas McGrath
Cois Tra, Chapel Road,
Duncannon, Co Wexford
Very Rev Colm Murphy
'Villa Maria', Kilrane,
Rosslare Harbour, Co Wexford
Very Rev Patrick Canon O'Brien
No 9 Bungalow, Chambersland,
New Ross, Co Wexford
Very Rev Anthony O'Connell
5 Parkside, Stoneybatter, Wexford
Very Rev John O'Reilly
Rosslare, Co Wexford
Very Rev James Ryan
Cleariestown, Co Wexford
Rev Patrick Sinnott
Parkannesley, Ballyarrett,
Gorey, Co Wexford
Very Rev Patrick Stafford
Tomsollagh, Ferns,
Enniscorthy, Co Wexford
Very Rev Oliver Sweeney
24 The Willows, Wellingtonbridge,
Co Wexford

RELIGIOUS ORDERS AND CONGREGATIONS

PRIESTS

AUGUSTINIANS
Good Counsel College,
New Ross, Co Wexford
Tel 051-421363/421909
Fax 051-421909
Prior: Rev Michael Collender (OSA)
Bursar: Rev David Crean (OSA)

CONVENTUAL FRANCISCANS
The Friary,
St Francis Street, Wexford
Tel 053-9122758
Guardian
Rev Aquino Maliakkal (OFMConv)

BROTHERS

CHRISTIAN BROTHERS
Christian Brothers' House,
Joseph Street, Wexford
Tel 053-45659
Community Leader
Br Éamonn Mac Loughlainn
Community: 5

SISTERS

CARMELITES
Mount Carmel Monastery,
New Ross, Co Wexford
Tel 051-421076
Email nrcarmelites@gmail.com
Prioress: Sr Anne McGlynn
Community: 13
Contemplatives
Altar breads

CONGREGATION OF THE SISTERS OF MERCY
Convent of Mercy,
Clonard Road, Wexford
Tel 053-9123024

Sisters of Mercy,
Lower South Knock,
New Ross, Co Wexford
Tel 051-425340

The Lodge, 38 Irishtown, New Ross,
Co Wexford

40 Willow Park, Mountgarret,
New Ross, Co Wexford

77 Pineridge, Summerhill,
Wexford

21 Castle Gardens, St Helen's Village,
Kilrane, Co Wexford

FAMILY OF ADORATION
St Aidan's Monastery of Adoration,
Ferns, Co Wexford
Tel 053-9366634
Email staidansferns@eircom.net
Contemplative life with adoration of the Eucharist. 8 hermitages for private retreats. Icon reproduction workshop.

LORETO (IBVM)
Loreto Community, Railway Road,
Gorey, Co Wexford
Tel 055-21257
Shared Leaders
Sr Mary O'Dwyer, Sr Carmel Swords
Community: 6
Primary School

Conabury,
11 Newtown Court, Wexford
Tel 053-43470
Shared Leaders
Sr Jane Bailey, Sr Ethel Keegan,
Sr Phil Murphy
Community: 3
Secondary School

PERPETUAL ADORATION SISTERS
Perpetual Adoration Convent,
Newtown Road, Wexford Town,
Co Wexford
Tel 053-9124134
Email sisterpeterleech@gmail.com
Superior: Sr M. Peter Leech
Community: 6
Perpetual adoration of the Blessed Sacrament

PRESENTATION SISTERS
Presentation Sisters,
Francis Street, Wexford
Tel 053-9122504
Community: 6

SISTERS OF ST JOHN OF GOD
St John of God Congregational Centre,
Newtown Road, Wexford
Tel 053-9142396
Email stjohnogoffice@ssjgcc.ie
Congregational Leader
Sr Geraldine Fitzpatrick

DIOCESE OF FERNS

St John of God Convent,
Sallyville House,
Newtown Road, Wexford
Tel 053-9142276
Local Leader: Sr Mary Cahill
Community: 23

St John of God Heritage Centre,
Sallyville, Newtown Road,
Wexford
Tel 053-9142293

Sisters of St John of God,
1 Summerhill Heights, Wexford
Tel 053-9171625

Sisters of St John of God,
'Granada', Ballyvaloo, Blackwater,
Enniscorthy, Co Wexford Y21 HX73
Tel 053-9137160
Retreat ministry

Sisters of St John of God,
Moorefield House, Loreto Village,
Enniscorthy, Co Wexford
Tel 053-9239734
Sheltered homes for the elderly

Sisters of St John of God,
6 Parkside, Stoneybatter,
Wexford
Tel 053-9146058

Sisters of St John of God,
Ard Coilm, 15 Millpark,
Castlebridge, Co Wexford
Tel 053-9159862
Community: 2

Sisters of St John of God,
1 Beechville, Clonard, Wexford
Tel 053-9142601
Community: 3

Sisters of St John of God,
26 Mansfield Drive,
Coolcots, Wexford
Tel 053-9144427

Sisters of St John of God, Caritas,
Glenbrook, Newtown Road,
Wexford
Tel 053-9143752
Community: 2

Sisters of St John of God,
3 Cluain Aoibhinn,
Clonard, Wexford
Community: 3

Sisters of St John of God,
Rectory Mews,
Spawell Road, Wexford
Community: 9

EDUCATIONAL INSTITUTIONS

St Peter's Diocesan College
Tel 053-9142071
Principal: Mr John Banville
Chaplain/Counsellor
Very Rev William Swan

CHARITABLE AND OTHER SOCIETIES

Aiseiri
Roxborough House,
Wexford
Tel 053-9141818

Christian Media Trust
Tel 053-9145176

FDYS Youth Work Ireland
Wexford
Tel 053-9123262/9123358

Society of St Vincent de Paul
17 Conferences in the Diocese of Ferns
South Ferns President
Ms Annette Beckett
Barntown, Co Wexford
North Ferns President: Brian Keenan
SVDP, Market Square,
Enniscorthy, Co Wexford

Traveller Resource Centre
Tel 051-422272

Special Schools
Our Lady of Fatima, Wexford
Tel 053-9123376
St John of God, Enniscorthy
Tel 053-9233419
St Patrick's, Enniscorthy
Tel 053-9233657
Dawn House, Wexford
Tel 053-9145351
Community Workshop
Enniscorthy Ltd
Tel 053-9233069
Community Workshop
New Ross Ltd
Tel 051-421956

DIOCESE OF GALWAY, KILMACDUAGH AND KILFENORA

Patrons of the Diocese
Galway – Our Lady Assumed into Heaven, 15 August
Kilmacduagh – St Colman, 29 October
Kilfenora – St Fachanan, 20 December

Includes portions of counties Galway, Mayo and Clare
Kilfenora is in the province of Cashel but the Bishop of Galway and Kilmacduagh is its Apostolic Administrator

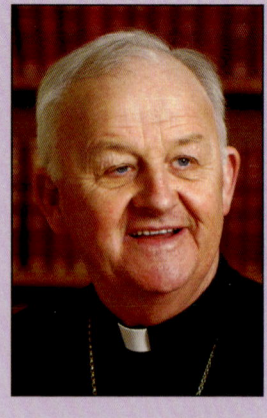

Most Rev Brendan Kelly DD
Bishop of Galway
born 20 May 1946;
ordained priest 20 June 1971;
ordained Bishop of Achonry
27 January 2008;
installed Bishop of Galway
11 February 2018

Residence: Mount Saint Mary's,
Taylor's Hill, Galway
Tel 091-563566
Email info@galwaydiocese.ie
Website www.galwaydiocese.ie

CATHEDRAL OF OUR LADY ASSUMED INTO HEAVEN AND ST NICHOLAS, GALWAY

In 1484, the Church of St Nicholas in Galway became a collegiate church, with a warden and vicars. However, with the Reformation, after 1570, the Catholic people of Galway lost the right to practise their religion publicly. Mass was celebrated in private houses until the rigour of persecution moderated and a parish chapel was built in Middle Street about 1750. The Diocese of Galway was established in 1831, and the parish chapel became its pro-cathedral. A fund for the building of a more fitting cathedral was inaugurated in 1876 and was built up by successive bishops. In 1883 the Diocese of Kilmacduagh was joined with Galway, and the Bishop of Galway was made Apostolic Administrator of Kilfenora.

In 1941, Galway County Council handed over Galway Jail to Bishop Michael Browne as a site for the proposed new cathedral. The jail was demolished, and in 1949 John J. Robinson of Dublin was appointed architect for the new cathedral. Planning continued until 1957, when Pope Pius XII approved the plans submitted to him by Dr Browne. Cardinal D'Alton, the Archbishop of Armagh, blessed the site and the foundation stone on 27 October 1957. The construction, which began in February 1958, was undertaken by Messrs John Sisk Ltd of Dublin. The people of the diocese contributed to a weekly collection, and donations were received from home and abroad. The total cost, including furnishing, was almost one million pounds.

Pope Paul VI appointed Cardinal Richard Cushing, Archbishop of Boston, Pontifical Legate to dedicate the cathedral. The cathedral was dedicated on the Feast of the Assumption, 15 August 1965.

DIOCESE OF GALWAY, KILMACDUAGH AND KILFENORA

Most Rev Martin Drennan DD
Born 2 January 1944;
ordained priest 16 June 1968; ordained Auxiliary Bishop of Dublin 21 September 1997; installed Bishop of Galway 3 July 2005; Retired 29 July 2016
Residence: 17 Doughiska Road, Galway

CHAPTER

Very Rev Dean Michael McLoughlin VF, Moycullen, Galway
Very Rev Mgr Peter Rabbitte PP, VG The Cathedral
Very Rev Canon Martin Downey, St Joseph's, Galway
Very Rev Canon Derek Feeney, Craughwell, Co Galway
Very Rev Michael Canon Reilly PP, Castlegar, Galway
Very Rev Canon Thomas Marrinan VF, Gort, Co Galway
Very Rev Canon Martin Glynn Mervue, Galway
Very Rev Canon Ian O'Neill Claregalway, Co Galway
Very Rev Canon Tadhg Quinn Knocknacarra, Galway

ADMINISTRATION

Vicar General
Very Rev Mgr Peter Rabbitte
The Cathedral, Galway
Tel 091-563577

Vicars Forane
Very Rev Mgr Peter Rabbitte, Galway West
Very Rev Dean Michael McLoughlin, Galway Rural
Very Rev Canon Thomas Marrinan, Kilmacduagh
Very Rev Canon Martin Glynn, Galway East
Very Rev Richard Flanagan, Kilfenora

Chancellor
Very Rev Canon Ian O'Neill PP
Claregalway, Co Galway
Tel 091-798104

Diocesan Council of Priests
Chairman: Rev Ian O'Neill
Secretary: Rev Hugh Clifford
Rev Martin Glynn
Rev John O'Halloran
Rev Joseph Roche
Rev Edward Crosby
Rev Declan Lohan
Rt Rev Mgr Malachy Hallinan
Rev Des Foley (OSA)
Rev Daniel Gallagher
Rev Diarmuid Hogan
Rev Michael McLoughlin
Rev Martin Downey
Ex officio
Rt Rev Mgr Peter Rabbitte VG
Bishop Brendan Kelly

Finance Committee
Mr Enda McGowan
Rev Martin Whelan
Mr Thomas Hansberry, Secretary
Mr Peter Casserly
Very Rev Michael Dean McLoughlin
Very Rev Mgr Peter Rabbitte

Financial Administrator
Mr Thomas Hansberry
Diocesan Office,
The Cathedral, Galway
Tel 091-563566

Diocesan Development (Meitheal)
Secretary
Mr Thomas Hansberry
Diocesan Office,
The Cathedral, Galway
Tel 091-563566

Diocesan Secretary
Rev Martin Whelan
Diocesan Office,
The Cathedral, Galway
Tel 091-563566
Email secretary@galwaydiocese.ie

Diocesan Archivist
Mr Thomas Hansberry
Tel 091-563566
Email info@archive.galwaydiocese.ie

CATECHETICS EDUCATION

Primary Education
Diocesan Adviser: Sr Breda Coyne (RJM)
Diocesan Pastoral Centre,
Árus De Brún,
Newtownsmith, Galway
Tel 091-575050

Post-primary Education
Diocesan Adviser: Rev Martin Whelan
Diocesan Office,
The Cathedral, Galway
Tel 091-563566

LITURGY

Liturgical Committee
Chairperson: Very Rev Joseph Roche
Parochial House, Labane,
Adrahan, Co Galway
Tel 091-635164
Email kaparishes@gmail.com
Members
Vacant

Sacred Music
Diocesan Director
Mr Raymond O'Donnell MA, HDE, LTCL
Tel 091-563577/087-2241365
Fax 091-534881
Email music@galwaycathedral.ie

PASTORAL

ACCORD
Árus de Brún,
Newtownsmith, Galway
Tel 091-562331
Diocesan Director
Very Rev Michael Dean McLoughlin PP
Parochial House,
Moycullen, Co Galway
Tel 091-555106
Email accordgalway@eircom.net

Apostolic Work Society
President: Mrs Marie Dempsey
Cregboy, Claregalway, Co Galway
Tel 091-798125
Secretary: Mrs Eileen Flannery
102 Hazel Park, Newcastle, Galway
Tel 091-523845

Brazilian Community
Chaplain: Rev Kevin Keenan (SVD)
Church of the Sacred Heart,
Seamus Quirke Road, Galway
Tel 091-524751

Safeguarding Office
Director: Mr Kevin Duffy
Administrator: Ms Ita O'Mahony
Diocesan Pastoral Centre,
Arús de Brún,
Newtownsmith, Galway
Tel 091-575051
Email info@safeguarding.galwaydiocese.ie

Communications Committee
Diocesan Communications Officer (DCO)
Very Rev Diarmuid Hogan PP
Parochial House,
Oranmore, Co Galway
Tel 087-1037452
Email info@comms.galwaydiocese.ie

Diocesan Education Office
Pastoral Centre, Árus de Brún,
Newtownsmith, Galway
Tel 091-565066
Co-ordinator: Mr Patrick Kelly
Email education@galwaydiocese.ie

Diocesan Pastoral Centre
Árus de Brún, Newtownsmith, Galway
Tel 091-565066
Director: Rev Gerard McCarthy (SVD)
Email pastoral@galwaydiocese.ie

Diocesan Pilgrimage Committee
Pilgrimage Director
Very Rev Dean Martin Moran PP
Rosscahill, Co Galway
Tel 091-550106

Ecumenism
Rev Barry Horan
Clarinbridge, Go Galway
Tel 091-776741
Email thebridgeparish@gmail.com

DIOCESE OF GALWAY, KILMACDUAGH AND KILFENORA

Emigrants Committee
Director
Very Rev Gearóid Ó Griofa PP
Lettermore, Co Galway
Tel 091-551169
Email gogriofa@gmail.com
Secretary
Very Rev Canon Michael Reilly PP
Castlegar, Galway
Tel 091-751548
Email
castlegar@parishes.galwaydiocese.ie

Legion of Mary
Annunciata House,
15 Fr Griffin Road, Galway
Tel 091-521871
Contact: Mr Bernard Finan

Marriage Tribunal
Officials: Rev Barry Horan
(see also Marriage Tribunals section)

Missions Committee
Chairman
Very Rev Canon Martin Downey PP
24 Presentation Road, Galway
Tel 091-562276
Email
stjosephs@parishes.galwaydiocese.ie

Pioneer Total Abstinence Association
Diocesan Director
Very Rev Patrick Dean Callanan
Kilbeacanty, Gort, Co Galway
Tel 091-631691

Polish Community
Chaplain: Rev Marek Cul (OP)
St Mary's Priory, Claddagh, Galway
Tel 091-582884
Email mcul@dominikanie.pl

Pontifical Mission Societies
Diocesan Director: Rev Declan Lohan
Renmore, Co Galway
Tel 091-751707
Email
renmore@parishes.galwaydiocese.ie

St Joseph's Young Priests' Society
Diocesan Chaplain: Rev Martin Whelan
Diocesan Office, The Cathedral, Galway
Tel 091-563566

Trócaire
Diocesan Director: Rev Declan Lohan
St Oliver Plunkett Church,
Renmore, Galway
Tel 091-751707
Email
renmore@parishes.galwaydiocese.ie

Vocations
Director: Very Rev Ian Canon O'Neill PP
Parochial House, Claregalway, Co Galway
Tel 091-798741
Email galwaypriesthood@gmail.com

PARISHES

Church titulars, if different from parish name, are in italics.

CATHEDRAL
Our Lady Assumed into Heaven and St Nicholas
Very Rev Mgr Peter Rabbitte PP, VG
Tel 091-563577
Rev John Gerard Acton CC
18 University Road, Galway
Tel 091-524875/563577
Email info@galwaycathedral.ie

City Parishes

BALLYBANE
St Brigid
Very Rev Canon Martin Glynn Adm
St Brigid's, Ballybane, Galway
Tel 091-755381
Email info@stbrigidsparishballybane.com

GOOD SHEPHERD
Very Rev Canon Martin Glynn PP
Parochial House, Mervue, Galway
Tel 091-751721/087-2527124
Rev Jose Thomas CC
Curate's House
129 Túr Uisce, Doughiska, Galway
Tel 091-756823
Email goodshepherdgalway@gmail.com
Website www.goodshepherdgalway.com

MERVUE
Holy Family
Very Rev Canon Martin Glynn PP
Mervue, Galway
Tel 091-751721/087-2527124
Email mervuechurch@gmail.com

RENMORE
St Oliver Plunkett
Rev Declan Lohan CC
Parochial House, Renmore, Galway
Tel 091-751707
Email
renmore@parishes.galwaydiocese.ie

SACRED HEART CHURCH
Very Rev Kevin Keenan PP
Church of the Sacred Heart
Seamus Quirke Road, Galway
Tel 091-524751
Email
sacredheart@parishes.galwaydiocese.ie

ST AUGUSTINE'S
Rev Des Foley (OSA)
St Augustine's Priory,
St Augustine's Street, Galway
Tel 091-562524

ST JOHN THE APOSTLE
Very Rev Tadhg Canon Quinn PP
Rev James Clesham (SMA) CC
St John the Apostle,
Knocknacarra, Galway
Tel 091-590059
Email tadhgknocknacarra@gmail.com

ST JOSEPH'S
Very Rev Canon Martin Downey PP
24 Presentation Road, Galway
Tel 091-562276
Email
stjosephs@parishes.galwaydiocese.ie

ST MARY'S
Very Rev Donal Sweeney (OP) PP
Email dsyop@eircom.net
Rev Denis Murphy (OP) CC
Email murphydenis345@gmail.com
St Mary's Priory,
The Claddagh, Galway
Tel 091-582884

ST PATRICK'S
Very Rev Patrick Whelan PP
St Patrick's Presbytery,
Forster Street, Galway
Tel 091-567994
Email pgcwhelan@gmail.com

SALTHILL
Christ the King
Very Rev Gerard Jennings PP
Tel 091-523413
Email salthill@parishes.galwaydiocese.ie
Monksfield, Salthill, Galway
Rev Charles Sweeney (MSC)
Cruí Nua, Rosary Lane,
Taylor's Hill, Galway
Email charles.sweeney4@gmail.com

TIRELLAN
Resurrection
Very Rev Tony Horgan (MSC) PP
Church of the Resurrection,
Headford Road, Galway, H91 W298
Tel 091-762883
Email ballinfoyleparish@eircom.net

Country Parishes

ARDRAHAN
St Teresa's
Very Rev Joseph Roche PP
Ardrahan, Co Galway
Tel 091-635164
Email kaparishes@gmail.com

BALLINDERREEN
St Colman's
Very Rev Hugh Clifford PP
Parochial House, Kinvara, Co Galway
Tel 091-637154
Email
bkoffice@parishes.galwaydiocese.ie

BALLYVAUGHAN
St John the Baptist
Rev Richard Flanagan PP, VF
Ballyvaughan, Co Clare
Tel 065-7077045
Email bvfanore@icloud.com

BEARNA
Mary Immaculate Queen
Very Rev Michael Brennan PP
Bearna, Galway
Tel 091-590956
Email bearna@parishes.galwaydiocese.ie

DIOCESE OF GALWAY, KILMACDUAGH AND KILFENORA

CARRON AND NEW QUAY
St Columba's, Carron,
St Patrick's, New Quay
Rev Colm Clinton (SPS) *(Administrator)*
New Quay, Co Clare
Tel 065-7078026
Email colmcc@gmail.com

CASTLEGAR
St Columba's
Rev Kevin Blade (MSC) Adm
Castlegar, Co Galway
Tel 091-751548
Email castlegar@parishes.galwaydiocese.ie

CLAREGALWAY
Assumption and St James
Very Rev Ian Canon O'Neill PP
Claregalway, Co Galway
Tel 091-798104
Email claregalway@parishes.galwaydiocese.ie

CLARINBRIDGE
Annunciation of the BVM
Very Rev Barry Horan PP
Main Street, Clarinbridge, Co Galway
Tel 091-776741
Email thebridgeparish@gmail.com

CRAUGHWELL
St Colman's
Very Rev Canon Derek Feeney PP
Craughwell, Co Galway
Tel 091-846057
Email craughwell@parishes.galwaydiocese.ie

ENNISTYMON
Our Lady and St Michael
Very Rev William Cummins PP
Ennistymon, Co Clare
Tel 065-7071063
Rev Des Forde CC
Curate's House, Sea Park,
Lahinch, Co Clare
Tel 065-7081307
Email ennistymon@parishes.galwaydiocese.ie

GORT/BEAGH
St Colman's and St Ann
Very Rev Thomas Canon Marrinan PP, VF
Gort, Co Galway
Tel 091-631220
Email gort.beagh@parishes.galwaydiocese.ie

KILBEACANTY/PETERSWELL
St Columba and St Thomas Apostle
RVery Rev Joseph Roche PP
Ardrahan, Co Galway
Tel 091-635164
Email kandpnewsletter@gmail.com

KILCHREEST
Nativity and Church of St Teresa
Very Rev Joseph Roche (*priest in charge*)
Parochial House, Ardrahan, Co Galway
Tel 091-635164
Email kaparishes@gmail.com

KILFENORA
St Fachanan's
Very Rev Edward Crosby Adm
Kilfenora, Co Clare
Tel 065-7088006
Email crosby32000@yahoo.com

KINVARA
St Colman's
Very Rev Hugh Clifford PP
Parochial House, Kinvara, Co Galway
Tel 091-637154
Email bkoffice@parishes.galwaydiocese.ie

LETTERMORE
Naomh Colmcille
Very Rev Gearóid Ó Griofa PP
Lettermore, Co Galway
Tel 091-551169
Email gogriofa@gmail.com

LISCANNOR
St Brigid's
Very Rev Denis Crosby PP
Liscannor, Co Clare
Tel 065-7081248
Email denis.crosby@icloud.com

LISDOONVARNA AND KILSHANNY
Corpus Christi
Very Rev Robert McNamara PP
The Rectory, Lisdoonvarna, Co Clare
Tel 065-7074142
Email lisdoonpp@parish.galwaydiocese.ie

MOYCULLEN
Immaculate Conception
Very Rev Michael Dean McLoughlin PP
Parochial House, Moycullen, Co Galway
Email moycullen@parishes.galwaydiocese.ie
Website www.moycullenparish.com

ORANMORE
Immaculate Conception
Very Rev Diarmuid Hogan PP
Oranmore, Co Galway
Tel 091-794634
Email oranmorepp@gmail.com
Rev Martin Whelan CC
Maree, Oranmore, Co Galway
Tel 091-794113
Email oranmorecc@gmail.com

OUGHTERARD
Immaculate Conception
Very Rev Michael Connolly PP
Oughterard, Co Galway
Tel 091-552290
Email oughterparish@gmail.com

ROSMUC
Séipéal an Ioncolnaithe
Very Rev Gearóid Ó Griofa (*priest in charge*)
Rosmuc, Co Galway
Tel 091-551169
Email gogriofa@gmail.com

ROSSCAHILL (KILLANNIN)
Immaculate Heart of Mary
Very Rev Martin Dean Moran PP
Rosscahill, Co Galway
Tel 091-550106
Email killannin@parishes.galwaydiocese.ie

SHRULE
St Joseph's
Very Rev Vivian Loughrey PP
Shrule, Galway
Tel 093-31262
Email parishofshrule3@gmail.com

AN SPIDÉAL
Cill Éinne
Rev Daniel Gallagher Adm
Teach an Sagairt, An Spidéal,
Co na Gaillimhe
Tel 091-553155
Email ce@parishes.galwaydiocese.ie

INSTITUTIONS AND THEIR CHAPLAINS

Bon Secours Hospital
Renmore, Galway
Tel 091-751534/757711
Co-ordinator: Very Rev Martin Glynn

Coláiste Muire Máthair
Chaplain's Office
Rev Martin Whelan
Tel 091-563566

Dún Uí Mhaoilíosa
Renmore Barracks, Renmore, Galway
Rev Paul Murphy
Tel 091-751156

Extraordinary Form (Latin Mass)
Canon Wulfran Lebocq
Institute of Christ the King Sovereign Priest, 12-14 The Crescent, Limerick

Galway/Mayo Insititute of Technology
Dublin Road, Galway
Tel 091-753161/757298
Chaplain: Br Ronan Sharpley
Email chaplain@gmit.ie

Galway Clinic
Doughiska, Galway
Chaplain's Office
Very Rev John D. Keane
Tel 091-785000

Gort Community School
Chaplain's Office
Tel 091-632163
Ms Orla Duggan

DIOCESE OF GALWAY, KILMACDUAGH AND KILFENORA

Merlin Park University Hospital
Chaplains Office
Tel 091-757631
Very Rev John D. Keane

NUI, Galway
University Road, Galway
Chaplain's Office
Tel 091-495055
Rev Ben Hughes
Email ben.hughes@nuigalway.ie

St Enda's College
Threadneedle Road, Salthill, Galway
Sr Pauline Uhlemann (RJM)
Tel 091-522458

St Joseph's Secondary College
Nun's Island, Galway
Priests of Augustinian Parish
Tel 091-562524

St Thomas Syro-Malabar Chaplaincy
Holy Family Church, Mervue, Galway
Rev Jose Thomas
Tel 091-756823
Email goodshepherdgalway@gmail.com

University Hospital
Chaplain's Office
Tel 091-524222
Rev Seán McHugh
Rev John O'Halloran
Email jmtohalloran@gmail.com

PRIESTS OF THE DIOCESE ELSEWHERE

Very Rev Thomas Brady
26 Cloonarkin Drive,
Oranmore, Co Galway
Rev Michael Conway
St Patrick's College,
Maynooth, Co Kildare
Tel 01-6285222
Rev Conor Cunningham
5 Pine Grove, Moycullen, Co Galway
Rev Peter Joyce
c/o Diocesan Office, The Cathedral,
Galway
Rev Michael King
c/o Diocesan Office, The Cathedral,
Galway
Rev Thomas Lyons
Cork University Hospital,
Wilton, Cork
Tel 021-4546109
Rev Patrick O'Donohue
FSSP Chaplain, Waterford & Lismore,
2 John's Hill, Waterford City X91 FWY1
An tAth Dáithí Ó Murchú
Chaplain, Holy Cross Hospital,
Hindhead Road, Haslemere,
Surrey GU27 1NQ, UK
Very Rev Canon Michael Reilly
Parochial House, Gastlegar, Galway
Tel 0981-751548

RETIRED PRIESTS

Rev Patrick Canon Callanan PE
Kilbeacanty, Gort, Co Galway
Tel 091-631691
Rev Michael Carney PE
c/o Diocesan Office, The Cathedral,
Galway
Tel 091-563566
Rev Patrick Connaughton
St Columban's, Dalgan Park,
Navan, Co Meath
Tel 046-21525
Very Rev Dean Patrick Considine PE
No. 2 St Mary's Apartments,
Shantalla Road, Galway
Tel 091-563566
Very Rev Michael Crosby
Main Street, Ballinrobe, Co Mayo
Very Rev Canon Joseph Delaney
Castlelawn Heights, Headford Road,
Galway
Very Rev Canon Eamonn Dermody PE
Clarinbridge, Co Galway
Tel 091-796208
Very Rev Enda Glynn
13 Lios Na Mara, Station Road,
Lahinch, Co Clare
Rt Rev Mgr Malachy Hallinan
Church of the Sacred Heart,
Seamus Quirke Road, Galway
Tel 091-522713
Rev Barry Hogg
15 Parklands, Tubbercurry, Co Sligo
Very Rev Canon Francis Larkin
7 Presentation Road, Galway
Very Rev Canon Michael Mulkerrins PE
Curate's Residence, Renmore, Galway
Tel 091-757859
Very Rev Dean Christopher O'Connor PE
Kilkerrin, Ballinasloe, Co Galway
Very Rev Canon John O'Dwyer PE
20 Cloonarkin Drive,
Oranmore, Co Galway
Tel 091-484501
Rt Rev Mgr Seán O'Flaherty PE
St Mary's Nursing Home,
Shantalla Road, Galway
Tel 091-540500
Rev Gregory Raftery
Zum Holzfeld 25, 30880 Loatzen,
Germany

PERSONAL PRELATURE

Opus Dei
Gort Ard University Residence,
Rockbarton North, Salthill,
Galway H91 KH94
Tel 091-523846
Rev Charles Connolly

RELIGIOUS ORDERS AND CONGREGATIONS

PRIESTS

AUGUSTINIANS
St Augustine's Priory, Galway
Tel 091-562524
www.augustinians.ie/galway
Prior & PP: Rev Desmond Foley (OSA)
Bursar: Rev Sean MacGearailt (OSA)

DOMINICANS
St Mary's, The Claddagh, Co Galway
Tel 091-582884
Prior: Very Rev Donal Sweeney (OP) PP

FRANCISCANS
The Abbey, 8 Francis Street, Galway
Tel 091-562518 Fax 091-565663
Guardian: Rev David Collins (OFM)

JESUITS
St Ignatius Community & Church
27 Raleigh Row, Salthill, Galway
Tel 091-523707
Email galway@jesuit.ie
Rector: Rev Martin Curry (SJ)

Coláiste Iognáid,
24 Sea Road, Galway
Tel 091-501500 Fax 091-501551
Email colaisteiognaid@eircom.net
Secondary School Principal
Mr David O'Sullivan
Scoil Iognaid (National School) Principal
Ms Laoise Breathnach

MISSIONARIES OF THE SACRED HEART
Croí Nua, Rosary Lane,
Taylor's Hill, Galway, H91 WY2A
Tel 091-520960 Fax 091-521168
Leader: Rev Charles Sweeney (MSC)

SALVATORIANS
Parochial House,
Pairc Na Mara, Lahinch, Co Clare
Tel 065-7081307
Email henrynevinsds@hotmail.com
Superior: Rev Henry Nevin (SDS)

Ard Mhuire, Kilmoon,
Lisdoonvarna, Co Clare
Tel 086-1030261
Email seamusoduill@eircom.net
Rev Seamus O'Duill (SDS)

SOCIETY OF AFRICAN MISSIONS
Cloonbigeen, Claregalway,
Co Galway H91 YK64
Tel 091-798880 Fax 091-798879
Email sma.claregalway@sma.ie
Superior
Rev Seamus Nohilly (SMA)
Bursar
Rev James Clesham (SMA)

DIOCESE OF GALWAY, KILMACDUAGH AND KILFENORA

BROTHERS

BROTHERS OF CHARITY
Regional Office,
Kilcornan Centre,
Clarinbridge, Co Galway
Tel 091-796389/796413
Regional Leader: Br John O'Shea
Community: 4

CHRISTIAN BROTHERS
Christian Brothers' House,
Mount St Joseph,
Ennistymon, Co Clare
Tel 065-7071130
Community: 2

PATRICIAN BROTHERS
Manor Drive, Kingston, Galway
Tel 091-523267
Superior: Br Niall Coll (FSP)
Community: 4

St Patrick's Primary School,
Lombard Street, Galway
Tel 091-568707. Pupils: 616
Principal: Ms Marian Barrett
Email saintpatricksgalway@gmail.com

St Joseph's Patrician College,
Nun's Island, Galway
Tel 091-565980
Pupils: 747
Principal: Mr John Madden

SISTERS

BRIGIDINE SISTERS
27 Cimín Mór,
Cappagh Road,
Bearna, Co Galway
Tel 091-592234
Contact: Sr Margaret Coyle
Community: 1
Retired

CONGREGATION OF THE SISTERS OF MERCY
Convent of Mercy,
St Vincent's, Newtownsmith,
Galway H91 N7PW
Tel 091-565519 Fax 091-564739
Community: 20

Aisling Court,
Ballyloughaun Road,
Renmore, Galway
Community: 4

Sisters of Mercy,
3 Greenview Heights,
Inishannagh Park,
Newcastle, Galway H91 T8FT
Tel 091-526126
Community: 1

146 Seacrest Road,
Knocknacarra, Galway H91 EEP0
Tel 091-591685
Community: 2

Sisters of Mercy, McAuley House,
7A Francis Street, Galway H91 W6X4
Community: 3

17 Newtownsmith,
Galway H91 W7X3
Apt 1 Tel 091-563297
Apt 2 Tel 091-563698
Community: 1

Sisters of Mercy, Teaghlach Mhuire,
Ballyloughane Road,
Renmore, Galway
Community: 39

St Anne's Lodge, Taylor's Hill Road,
Taylor's Hill, Galway H91 DCW9
Tel 091-527710
Community: 1

147 Seacrest Road,
Knocknacarra, Galway H91 DE0C
Tel 091-591598
Community: 1

Sisters of Mercy, Stella Maria,
Taylor's Hill, Galway H91 XY93
Community: 41

Sisters of Mercy,
Cnoc Mhuire, Ballyloughaun Road,
Renmore, Galway H91 TDY9
Community: 5

Sister of Mercy, 61 The Green,
College Road, Galway H91 R5FY
Community: 1

DAUGHTERS OF CHARITY OF ST VINCENT DE PAUL
65 Shantalla Road, Galway
Tel 091-584410
Superior: Sr Bríd Fahy
Community: 3
SVP, pastoral work, chaplaincy Limerick

DAUGHTERS OF MARY MOTHER OF MERCY
Sr Magdalena Ohaja
Apt 10 Bridgewater Court, Fairhill Lower,
Claddagh, Galway

DOMINICAN SISTERS
Dominican Convent,
Taylor's Hill, Galway H91 P8HW
Tel 091-522124
Email dominicancg@eircom.net
Community: 7
Varied ministries
Primary School. Tel 091-521517
Secondary School. Tel 091-523171

JESUS AND MARY, CONGREGATION OF
Convent of Jesus and Mary,
23 Lenaboy Gardens,
Salthill, Galway
Tel 091-524277
Superior: Sr Maria O'Toole
Community: 7
Sisters in principalship and chaplaincy of post-primary schools
Scoil Íde Primary School
Tel 091-522716. Pupils: 279
Salerno Post-Primary School
Tel 091-529500. Pupils: 720

LA RETRAITE SISTERS
2 Distillery Road, Galway
Tel 091-524548
Contact: Sr Moira McDowall
Email moiramcdlr@gmail.com

LA SAINTE UNION DES SACRES COEURS
Sarsfield Road,
Ballinasloe, Co Galway
Community: 2
Pastoral

2 Boherbradagh House,
Coy's Boreen, Old Galway Road,
Loughrea, Co Galway
Community: 1
Healthcare

St Mary's Residential Care Centre,
Shantalla Road,
Galway

10 Dún na Carraige,
Blackrock, Salthill, Galway
Community: 1
Pastoral

Milltown, Dysart,
Ballinasloe, Co Galway
Community: 1
Pastoral

LITTLE SISTERS OF THE ASSUMPTION
50 St Finbarr's Terrace,
Bohermore, Galway
Tel 091-568870

POOR CLARES
St Clare's Monastery,
Nuns' Island, Galway
www.poorclares.ie
www.clairinibochta.ie
Abbess: Sr M. Colette
Community: 10
Contemplatives. Adoration of the Blessed Sacrament. Altar breads

PRESENTATION SISTERS

Presentation Convent,
Presentation Road, Galway
Tel 091-561067 Fax 091-562384
Community: 17

Shantalla Road, Galway
Tel 091-522598
Community: 6
School and pastoral ministry

160 Corrib Park,
Newcastle, Galway
Tel 091-581715
Community: 2
Pastoral

Apt 103, Duirling, Roscam,
Galway
Community 1

Apt 100 Duirling, Roscam,
Galway
Community 1

ASSOCIATION OF THE FAITHFUL

FRATERNITY OF MARY IMMACULATE QUEEN
'Síiol Dóchas',
Ballard, Barna, Galway
Tel/Fax 091-592196
Email miq@eircom.net

EDUCATIONAL INSTITUTIONS

Coláiste Einde, Gaillimh
Tel 091-521407
Principal: Ms Deirbhle Quinn
Chaplain's Office: Tel 091-522458/524904
Sr Pauline Uhlemann (RJM)

Coláiste Muire Máthais, Galway
Tel 091-522369
Principal: Mrs Betty Hernon
Chaplain: Fr Martin Whelan
Email info@cmmg.ie

Gort Community School
Principal: Mr Brian Crossan
Chaplain's Office
Tel 091-632163
Ms Orla Duggan

St Joseph's Secondary College
Nun's Island, Galway
Priests of Augustinian Parish
Tel 091-562524

Seamount College
Tel 091-637362
Principal: Mairéad Mhic Dhomhnaill
Email seamount.ias@eircom.net
Chaplain: Rev Hugh Clifford

CHARITABLE AND OTHER SOCIETIES

COPE Galway
(Crisis Housing, Caring Support) Ltd
3–5 Calbro House,
Tuam Road, Galway
Tel 091-778750
CEO: Michael Smyth
Cope provides emergency accommodation for homeless persons and families and women and children experiencing domestic violence. It also provides a community catering service in Galway City and runs a day centre for older people in Mervue.

Society of St Vincent de Paul
Ozanam House,
St Augustine Street, Galway
Tel 091-563233/562254
Administrator: Ms Deirdre Swords

DIOCESE OF KERRY

PATRON OF THE DIOCESE
ST BRENDAN, 16 MAY

INCLUDES COUNTY KERRY, EXCEPT KILMURRILY, AND PART OF COUNTY CORK

Most Rev Raymond Browne DD
Bishop of Kerry;
born 23 January 1957;
ordained priest 4 July 1982
ordained Bishop of Kerry
21 July 2013

Residence:
Bishop's House, Killarney,
Co Kerry
Tel 064-6631168
Fax 064-6631364
Email admin@dioceseofkerry.ie

ST MARY'S CATHEDRAL, KERRY

The Cathedral of Our Lady of the Assumption, better known as St Mary's, was designed by Augustus Welby Pugin. The main part of the cathedral was built between 1842 and 1855. Work was suspended between 1848 and 1853 because of the Famine and the building was used as a shelter for victims of the Famine.

Between 1908 and 1912 the nave and side aisles were extended and the spire, sacristy and mortuary chapel were added.

In 1972/3 the cathedral was extensively renovated. The interior was reordered to meet the demands of the liturgical renewal that followed the Second Vatican Council.

DIOCESE OF KERRY

Most Rev William Murphy DD
Retired Bishop of Kerry; born 6 June 1936; ordained priest 18 June 1961; ordained Bishop of Kerry 10 September 1995; retired 2 May 2013
Residence: No. 2 Cathedral Place, Killarney, Co Kerry
Tel 064-663833
Email bfmurphy13@gmail.com

CHAPTER

Very Rev Tadhg Fitzgerald VG
Tralee, Dean of Kerry
Rt Rev Mgr Sean Hanafin,
Ballybunion
Very Rev Maurice Canon Brick
Castleisland
Very Rev Declan Canon O'Connor
Listowel
Archdeacon: Venerable George Hayes
Kenmare
Very Rev Larry Canon Kelly, Cahirciveen
Very Rev Noel Canon Spring,
Castletownbere
Very Rev Kevin Canon Sullivan,
Killorglin
Very Rev Jack Canon Fitzgerald,
Millstreet
Very Rev Michael Canon Moynihan,
Dingle

Honorary Canons
Very Rev Pat Canon O'Donnell, Rathmore
Very Rev Gearóid Canon Walsh,
Ballymacelligott
Very Rev Joseph Canon Begley,
Glengarriff

Retired Members
Very Rev Michael O'Doherty
Very Rev Patrick Sheehan
Very Rev Seamus Linnane
Very Rev Eoin Mangan
Rt Rev Mgr Daniel O'Riordan
Very Rev Thomas Looney
Venerable Thomas Crean

ADMINISTRATION

College of Consultors
Rt Rev Mgr Tadhg Fitzgerald
Rev Gearóid Godley
Very Rev Nicholas Flynn
Very Rev Pat O'Donnell
Rev Niall Howard
Very Rev Padraig Walsh
Very Rev John Buckley

Vicar General
Rt Rev Mgr Tadhg Fitzgerald
c/o Diocesan Office, Cathedral Walk,
Killarney, Co Kerry

Vicars Forane
Very Rev Pat Canon O'Donnell
Venerable George Hayes
Very Rev Larry Canon Kelly
Very Rev Kevin Canon Sullivan
Very Rev Declan Canon O'Connor
Very Rev Denis O'Mahony
Very Rev Kieran O'Brien
Very Rev Tadhg Fitzgerald
Very Rev John Buckley
Very Rev Michael Canon Moynihan
Very Rev Noel Canon Spring
Rt Rev Mgr Sean Hanafin

Finance Council
Very Rev Nicholas Flynn,
Very Rev Gearóid Walsh,
Mr Liam Chute, Mr Brian Durran,
Rev Gearóid Godley,
Mr Patrick McElligott,
Ms Bridget McGuire, Mr John Collins,
Mr John O'Connor,
Mr Pádraig O'Sullivan

Foreign Missions Committee
Chairman: Rev Gearóid Godley
John Paul II Pastoral Centre,
Rock Road, Killarney, Co Kerry
Tel 064-6630535 Fax 064-6631170

Diocesan Archivist
Diocesan Centre, Cathedral Walk,
Killarney, Co Kerry
Tel 064-6631168 Fax 064-6631364

Diocesan Secretary
Very Rev Nicholas Flynn
Bishop's House, Killarney, Co Kerry
Tel 064-6631168
Email nicholasflynn@dioceseofkerry.org

Diocesan Communications Officer
Ms Mary Fagan
Tel 087-1301555/066-7123787
Email maryfagan@dioceseofkerry.ie

Property Committee
Chairman: Mr Bill Looney
Secretary: Mr Shane O'Donoghue
Diocesan Centre, Cathedral Walk,
Killarney, Co Kerry
Tel 064-6631168
Email shaneodonoghue@dioceseofkerry.org

CATECHETICS EDUCATION

Post-Primary Religious Education
Director: Mr Tomás Kenny
John Paul II Pastoral Centre,
Rock Road, Killarney, Co Kerry
Tel 064-6632644 Fax 064-6631170

Primary Religious Education
Director: Sr Noreen Quilter
Assistant Director: Mr Kieran Coffey
c/o John Paul II Pastoral Centre,
Rock Road, Killarney, Co Kerry
Tel 064-6632644

Primary School Management
St Senan's Education Office
Tel 061-347777

LITURGY

Liturgical Committee
Chair: Ms Eileen Burke
Secretary: Tomás Kenny
Tel 064-6632644

PASTORAL

ACCORD
Killarney Centre: John Paul II Pastoral Centre, Killarney, Co Kerry
Tel 064-6632644
Email jp2centre@eircom.net
Director: Very Rev John Buckley
Tralee Centre: St John's Parish Centre, Castle Street, Tralee, Co Kerry
Tel 066-7122280
Director: Rev Francis Nolan

Council of Priests
Chairman
Very Rev Pádraig Walsh PP
Secretary
Very Rev Joseph Begley PP

Diocesan Pastoral Centre
Director: Rev Gearóid Godley
John Paul II Pastoral Centre,
Rock Road, Killarney, Co Kerry
Tel 064-6632644

Diocesan Pastoral Council
Chairperson: Mr Shane O'Donoghue
Secretary: Mr Tomás Kenny
John Paul II Pastoral Centre,
Rock Road, Killarney, Co Kerry
Tel 064-6632644

Diocesan Safeguarding Children Committee
Chairperson: Ms Rosarii O'Connor
c/o Diocesan Office, Cathedral Walk,
Killarney, Co Kerry
Director of Safeguarding:
Ms Jacklyn McCarthy,
c/o Diocesan Office, Cathedral Walk,
Killarney, Co Kerry
Tel 087-6362780

Ecumenism
Secretary: Very Rev Pat Crean-Lynch
The Presbytery, Ardfert, Co Kerry
Tel 066-7134131

Marriage Tribunal
(See Marriage Tribunals Section)

Pastoral Renewal Team
Rev Gearóid Godley
Ms Frances Rowland
Mr Des Bailey
John Paul II Pastoral Centre,
Killarney, Co Kerry
Tel 064-6632644

DIOCESE OF KERRY

Pilgrimage Director
Diocesan Secretary
Very Rev Nicholas Flynn
Bishop's House, Killarney, Co Kerry
Tel 064-6631168

Pioneer Total Abstinence Association
Diocesan Director
Very Rev Noel Spring PP
The Presbytery, Castletownbere,
Co Cork
Tel 027-70849

Pontifical Mission Societies
Diocesan Director
Rev Gearóid Godley
John Paul II Pastoral Centre,
Killarney, Co Kerry
Tel 064-6632644 Fax 064-6631170

Vocations
Director
Very Rev Joseph Begley
Tel 027-63045

Youth Director
c/o John Paul II Pastoral Centre,
Rock Road, Killarney, Co Kerry
Tel 064-6632644

PARISHES

The mensal parish is listed first. Other parishes follow alphabetically Historical names are given in parentheses. Church titulars are in italics.

KILLARNEY
St Mary's Cathedral, Killarney
Holy Spirit, Muckross
Resurrection, Park Road
Very Rev Kieran O'Brien Adm, VF
Very Rev Jim Lenihan CC
Rev Niall Howard CC
Killarney, Co Kerry
Tel 064-6631014
Email killarney@dioceseofkerry.ie

ABBEYDORNEY
St Bernard's, Abbeydorney
St Mary's, Kilflynn
Very Rev Denis O'Mahony PP, VF
Abbeydorney, Co Kerry
Tel 066-7135146
Email abbeydorney@dioceseofkerry.ie

ADRIGOLE
St Fachtna's
Very Rev Martin Sheehan
Adrigole, Bantry, Co Cork
Tel 027-60006
Email adrigole@dioceseofkerry.ie

ALLIHIES
St Michael's, Allihies,
St Michael's, Cahermore
Rev Jerry Keane, Moderator
Allihies, Bantry, Co Cork
Tel 027-73012
Email allihies@dioceseofkerry.ie

ANNASCAUL
Sacred Heart, Annascaul
St Mary's, Camp
St Joseph's, Inch
Rev Michael Moynihan, Moderator
Annascaul, Co Kerry
Tel 066-9157103
Email annascaul@dioceseofkerry.ie

ARDFERT
St Brendan's, Ardfert
Sacred Heart, Kilmoyley
Very Rev Pat Crean-Lynch PP
Ardfert, Co Kerry
Tel 066-7134131
Email ardfert@dioceseofkerry.ie

BALLINSKELLIGS (PRIOR)
St Michael the Archangel, Ballinskelligs,
St Patrick's, Portmagee,
Sacred Heart and St Finan, The Glen
Rev Patsy Lynch (SMA)
St Michael's, Ballinskelligs, Co Kerry
Tel 066-9479108
Email ballinskelligs@dioceseofkerry.ie

BALLYBUNION
St John's
Rt Rev Mgr Sean Hanafin PP
Ballybunion, Co Kerry
Tel 068-27102
Email ballybunion@dioceseofkerry.ie

BALLYDESMOND
St Patrick's
Very Rev Joseph Tarrant PP
Ballydesmond, Mallow, Co Cork
Tel 064-7751104
Email ballydesmond@dioceseofkerry.ie

BALLYDONOGHUE
St Teresa's
Rev Sean Hanafin, Moderator
Ballydonoghue, Lisselton, Co Kerry
Tel 068-47103
Email ballydonoghue@dioceseofkerry.ie

BALLYFERRITER
Uinseann Naofa, Baile an Fheitearaigh
Naomh Gobnait, Dún Chaoin
Séipéal na Carraige
Very Rev Eugene Kiely PP
Tel 066-9156131
Email baileanfheirtearaigh@dioceseofkerry.ie

BALLYHEIGUE
St Mary's
Rev Brendan Walsh, Moderator
Ballyheigue, Tralee, Co Kerry
Tel 066-7133110
Email ballyheigue@dioceseofkerry.ie

BALLYLONGFORD
St Michael the Archangel, Ballylongford
Very Rev Michael Hussey PP
Ballylongford, Co Kerry
Tel 068-43110
Email ballylongford@dioceseofkerry.ie
St Mary's, Asdee

BALLYMACELLIGOTT
Immaculate Conception, Ballymacelligott
St Brendan's, Clogher
Very Rev Gearóid Canon Walsh PP
Ballymacelligott, Co Kerry
Tel 066-7137118
Email ballymacelligott@dioceseofkerry.ie

BEAUFORT (TUOGH)
St Mary's, Beaufort
Our Lady of the Valley, The Valley
Very Rev Fergal Ryan PP
The Presbytery, Beaufort, Co Kerry
Tel 064-6644128
Email beaufort@dioceseofkerry.ie

BOHERBUE/KISKEAM
Immaculate Conception, Boherbue
Sacred Heart, Kiskeam
Very Rev Séamus Kennelly PP
Boherbue, Mallow, Co Cork
Tel 029-76151
Email boherbue@dioceseofkerry.ie

BROSNA
St Carthage, Brosna
Our Lady of the Assumption, Knockaclarig
Very Rev Martin Spillane PP
Brosna, Co Kerry
Tel 068-44112
Email brosna@dioceseofkerry.ie

CAHIRCIVEEN
Holy Cross, O'Connell Memorial,
Immaculate Conception, Filemore;
St Joseph's, Aghatubrid
Very Rev Larry Canon Kelly PP, VF
Cahirciveen, Co Kerry
Tel 066-9472210
Email cahersiveen@dioceseofkerry.ie

CAHERDANIEL
St Crohan's, Mary Immaculate, Lohar
Most Precious Blood, Castlecove
Rev Gerard Finucane, Moderator
Caherdaniel, Co Kerry
Tel 066-9475111
Email caherdaniel@dioceseofkerry.ie

CASTLEGREGORY
St Mary's, Castlegregory
St Brendan's, Cloghane
Very Rev Eamon Mulvihill PP
Castlegregory, Co Kerry
Tel 066-7139145
Email castlegregory@dioceseofkerry.ie

CASTLEISLAND
SS Stephen and John, Castleisland
Our Lady of Lourdes, Scartaglin
Immaculate Conception, Cordal
Very Rev Maurice Canon Brick PP
Castleisland, Co Kerry
Tel 066-7141241
Email castleisland@dioceseofkerry.ie

DIOCESE OF KERRY

CASTLEMAINE
St Gobnait, Keel
St Carthage, Kiltallagh
Rev Danny Broderick, Moderator
Castlemaine, Co Kerry
Tel 066-9767322
Email castlemaine@dioceseofkerry.ie

CASTLETOWNBERE AND BERE ISLAND
Sacred Heart, Castletownbere
St Bartholomew, Rossmacowen
St Michael's, Bere Island
Very Rev Noel Canon Spring PP, VF
Castletownbere, Co Cork
Tel 027-70849
Email castletownbere@dioceseofkerry.ie

CAUSEWAY
St John the Baptist, Causeway
SS Peter and Paul, Ballyduff
Very Rev Brendan Walsh PP
Causeway, Co Kerry
Tel 066-7131148
Email causeway@dioceseofkerry.ie

DINGLE
St Mary's, Dingle
St John the Baptist, Lispole
Naomh Caitlín, Ceann Trá
Very Rev Michael Canon Moynihan PP
Dingle, Co Kerry
Tel 066-9151208
Email dingle@dioceseofkerry.ie

DROMTARIFFE
St John's, Dromagh
Presentation of the BVM, Derrinagree
Very Rev Tom Leane PP
Dromagh, Mallow, Co Cork
Tel 029-78096
Email dromtariffe@dioceseofkerry.ie

DUAGH
St Brigid's, Duagh
Sacred Heart, Lyreacrompane
Rev Declan Canon O'Connor, Moderator
Duagh, Listowel, Co Kerry
Tel 068-45102
Email duagh@dioceseofkerry.ie

EYERIES
St Kentigern, Eyeries
Resurrection, Ardgroom
Very Rev Jerry Keane PP
Eyeries, Co Cork
Tel 027-74008
Email eyeries@dioceseofkerry.ie

FIRIES
St Gertrude, Firies
Sacred Heart, Ballyhar
Very Rev Padraig Kennelly PP
Firies, Killarney, Co Kerry
Tel 066-9764122
Email firies@dioceseofkerry.ie

FOSSA
Christ, Prince of Peace
Very Rev Niall Geaney PP
Fossa, Killarney, Co Kerry
Tel 064-6631996
Email fossa@dioceseofkerry.ie

GLENBEIGH
St James's, Glenbeigh
St Stephen's, Glencar
Very Rev Kieran O'Sullivan PP
Glenbeigh, Co Kerry
Tel 066-9768209
Email glenbeigh@dioceseofkerry.ie

GLENFLESK
St Agatha, Glenflesk
Sacred Heart, Barraduff
Our Lady of the Wayside, Clonkeen
Very Rev Kevin McNamara PP
St Agatha's Parish Centre, Headford,
Killarney, Co Kerry
Tel 064-7754008
Email glenflesk@dioceseofkerry.ie

GLENGARRIFF (BONANE)
Sacred Heart, Glengarriff
St Fachtna's, Bonane
Very Rev Joseph Canon Begley PP
Glengarriff, Co Cork
Tel 027-63045
Email glengarriff@dioceseofkerry.ie

KENMARE
Holy Cross, Kenmare
Our Lady of Perpetual Help,
Derreenderagh
Our Lady of the Assumption,
Templemore
Venerable George Hayes PP, VF
Kenmare, Co Kerry
Tel 064-6641352
Email kenmare@dioceseofkerry.ie

KILCUMMIN
Our Lady of Lourdes
Rev Kieran O'Brien, Moderator
Kilcummin, Killarney, Co Kerry
Tel 064-6643176
Email kilcummin@dioceseofkerry.ie

KILGARVAN
St Patrick's
Rev Joesph Begley, Moderator
Kilgarvan, Co Kerry
Tel 064-6685313
Email kilgarvan@dioceseofkerry.ie

KILLEENTIERNA
Immaculate Conception, Currow
SS Thérèse & Colmcille, Currans
Very Rev John Buckley PP
Killeentierna, Killarney, Co Kerry
Tel 066-9764141
Email killeentierna@dioceseofkerry.ie

KILLORGLIN
St James, Killorglin
Our Lady, Star of the Sea, Cromane
Very Rev Kevin Canon Sullivan PP, VF
Killorglin, Co Kerry
Tel 066-9761172
Email killorglin@dioceseofkerry.ie

KNOCKNAGOSHEL
St Mary's
Rev John Buckley, Moderator
Knocknagoshel, Co Kerry
Tel 068-46107
Email knocknagoshel@dioceseofkerry.ie

LISTOWEL
St Mary's
Very Rev Declan Canon O'Connor PP, VF
Listowel, Co Kerry
Tel 068-21188
Email listowel@dioceseofkerry.ie

LIXNAW
St Michael's, Lixnaw
Our Lady of the Assumption, Rathea
Our Lady of Fatima and St Senan,
Irremore
Very Rev Anthony O'Sullivan PP
The Presbytery, Lixnaw, Co Kerry
Tel 066-7132111 Fax 066-7132171
Email lixnaw@dioceseofkerry.ie

MILLSTREET
St Patrick's, Millstreet
Our Lady of Lourdes, Ballydaly
Blessed Virgin Mary, Cullen
Very Rev Jack Canon Fitzgerald PP
Millstreet, Co Cork
Tel 029-70043
Email millstreet@dioceseofkerry.ie

MILLTOWN
Sacred Heart, Milltown
Immaculate Conception, Listry
Very Rev Daniel Broderick PP
Milltown, Killarney, Co Kerry
Tel 066-9767312
Email milltown@dioceseofkerry.ie

MOYVANE
Assumption of the BVM, Moyvane
Corpus Christi, Knockanure
Very Rev Brendan Carmody (SJ) PP
Moyvane, Listowel, Co Kerry
Tel 068-49308
Email moyvane@dioceseofkerry.ie

RATHMORE
Christ the King, Knocknagree
St Joseph's, Rathmore
Our Lady of Perpetual Succour, Shrone
Holy Rosary, Gneeveguilla
Very Rev Pat Canon O'Donnell PP, VF
Rathmore, Co Kerry
Tel 064-7758026
Email rathmore@dioceseofkerry.ie

SNEEM
St Michael, Sneem; St Brendan,
Glenlough; St Patrick, Tahilla
Very Rev Liam O'Brien PP
Sneem, Co Kerry
Tel 064-6645141
Email sneem@dioceseofkerry.ie

SPA
Church of the Purification, Churchill
St Joseph's, Fenit
Very Rev Francis Nolan PP
Fenit, Tralee, Co Kerry
Tel 066-7136145
Emailspa@dioceseofkerry.ie

DIOCESE OF KERRY

TARBERT
St Mary's
Rt Rev Mgr Sean Hanafin, Moderator
The Presbytery, Tarbert, Co Kerry
Tel 068-36111
Email tarbert@dioceseofkerry.ie

TRALEE, ST BRENDAN'S
Our Lady and St Brendan, Rock Street
Very Rev Pádraig Walsh PP
Rev Amos Surungai Ruto
St Brendan's, Tralee, Co Kerry
Tel 066-7125932
Email stbrendans@dioceseofkerry.ie

TRALEE, ST JOHN'S
St John the Baptist, Castle Street, Tralee
Immaculate Conception, Rathass
St Brendan's, Curaheen
Rt Rev Mgr Tadhg Fitzgerald PP, VG
Rev Sean Jones
Rev Bernard Healy
Rev Vitalis Barasa
St John's Presbytery, Tralee, Co Kerry
Tel 066-7122522
Email stjohns@dioceseofkerry.ie
Email stjohnscastlestreet@eircom.net

TUOSIST
St Killian's, Lauragh
Dawros, Dawros
Very Rev John Kerin PP
St Joseph's, Lauragh, Killarney, Co Kerry
Tel 064-6683107
Email tuosist@dioceseofkerry.ie

VALENTIA
Immaculate Conception, Knightstown
SS Derarca and Teresa, Chapeltown
Rev Larry Canon Kelly, Moderator
Valentia Island, Co Kerry
Tel 066-9476104
Email valentia@dioceseofkerry.ie

WATERVILLE (DROMOD)
St Finian's, Dromod
Our Lady of the Valley, Cillin Liath
Very Rev Gerard Finucane PP
The Presbytery, Waterville, Co Kerry
Tel 066-9474703
Email waterville@dioceseofkerry.ie

INSTITUTIONS AND THEIR CHAPLAINS

Boherbue Comprehensive School
Mallow, Co Cork
Ms Fiona O'Donoghue
Tel 029-76032

Castletownbere Community School,
Co Cork
Ms Marie Murphy
Tel 027-70177

Causeway Comprehensive School
Mr Paul Montgomery
Tel 066-7131197

Coláiste na Sceilge
Cahirciveen
Tel 066-9473335
Liam Egan

Kenmare Pobalscoil Inbhear Scéine
Ms Mairéad Hickey
Tel 064-6640846

Kerry General Hospital
Rev Teddy Linehan
Rev Gerard O'Leary
Tel 066-7126222

Killarney Community College
Rev Niall Howard
Tel 064-6632764

Killarney St Columbanus Home
Killarney Parish Clergy
Tel 064-6631014

Killorglin Post-Primary Schools
Parish Clergy
Tel 066-9761172

Millstreet Community School
Co Cork
Mr John Magee
Tel 029-70087/79028

Listowel Presentation Convent
Sr Eilis Daly
Tel 068-21452

Our Lady of Fatima Home
Oakpark, Tralee, Co Kerry
Tel 066-7125900
St John's Parish Clergy

Pobalscoil Chorca Dhuibhne
Dingle
Mr Antóin Ó Braoin
Tel 066-9150055

Rathmore Community School
Ms Aggie Riordan
Parish Clergy
Tel 064-7758135

St Brendan's College
Killarney, Co Kerry
Parish Clergy
Tel 064-6631021

St Michael's College
Listowel, Co Kerry
Parish Clergy
Tel 068-21049/21188

Tarbert, Comprehensive School
Listowel, Co Kerry
Ms Yvonne O'Connor
Tel 068-36105

Munster Technology University
Tralee, Co Kerry
Rev Donal O'Connor
Tel 066-7145639/7135236

Tralee Mercy Secondary Mounthawk
Tel 066-7102550
Our Lady and St Brendan's Parish Clergy
Tel 066-7125932

PRIESTS OF THE DIOCESE ELSEWHERE

Rev Liam Lovell
c/o Diocesan Office, Killarney, Co Kerry
Rev Seamus McKenna BA, HDE
Cork Regional Marriage Tribunal,
The Lough, Cork
Tel 021-4963653
Rev Tomás O'Caoimh
c/o Diocesan Office, Killarney, Co Kerry
Rev Seamus O'Connell
St Patrick's College,
Maynooth, Co Kildare
Tel 01-6285222
Rev Richard O'Connor
Villa Maria Assenta, Via Aurellia 284,
00-165 Roma, Italy
Rev Anthony O'Reilly
Newry, Co Armagh

RETIRED PRIESTS

Rev Pat Ahern
Rev Con Buckley
Rev Tom Crean
Rev Brendan Harrington
Rev Martin Hegarty
Rev Roger Kelleher
Rev John Lawlor
Rev Seamus Linnane
Rev Tom Looney
Rev Eoin Mangan
Rev Pat McCarthy
Rev Patrick Murphy
Rev Joseph Nolan
Rev Philip O'Connell
Rev Michael O'Dochartaigh
Rev Tadhg Ó Dochartaigh
Rev Michael O'Doherty
Rev Dan O'Riordan
Rev John Quinlan
Rev Bill Radley
Rev Luke Roche
Rev John Shanahan
Rev P. Sheehan
Rev Patrick Sugrue

RELIGIOUS ORDERS AND CONGREGATIONS

PRIESTS

DOMINICANS
Holy Cross,
Tralee, Co Kerry
Tel 066-7121135/7129185
Superior: Gregory Carroll (OP)
Email domstralee@gmail.com

DIOCESE OF KERRY

FRANCISCANS
Franciscan Friary,
Killarney, Co Kerry
Tel 064-6631334/6631066
Fax 064-6637510
Email friary@eircom.net
Guardian: Rev Pat Lynch (OFM)
Vicar: Rev Rev Antony Jukes (OFM)

OBLATES OF MARY IMMACULATE
Department of Chaplaincy,
Tralee General Hospital, Co Kerry
Rev Edward Barrett
Tel 066-7126222

BROTHERS

CHRISTIAN BROTHERS
Christian Brothers,
14 The Orchard, Ballyrickard,
Tralee, Co Kerry
Tel 066-713910
Community Leader: Br Daithi O'Connell
Community: 2

PRESENTATION BROTHERS
Port Road,
Killarney, Co Kerry
Tel 064-6631267
Contact: Br Richard English (FPM)
Community: 6

SAINT JOHN OF GOD BROTHERS
Killorglin,
Co Kerry V93 EY96
Community Superior
Br Martin Taylor (OH)
Community: 2

SAINT JOHN OF GOD KERRY SERVICES
Cloonanorig, Monavalley,
Tralee, Co Kerry J92 HK73
Tel 066-7124333 Fax 066-7126197
Email kerry@sjog.ie
Regional Director: Ms Claire O'Dwyer
Training and supported employment service with back-up residential and community services

St Mary of the Angels,
Beaufort, Co Kerry V92 K738
Tel 064-44133 Fax 064-44302
Training, residential and community services for people with an intellectual disability

St Francis Special School,
Beaufort, Co Kerry
Tel 064-44452 Fax 064-24884
School Principal: Liam Twomey

SISTERS

BON SECOURS SISTERS (PARIS)
Bon Secours Convent,
Strand Street, Tralee, Co Kerry
Tel 066-7149800 Fax 066-7129068
Co-ordinator: Sr Teresita Hoare
Community: 4
Pastoral ministry

6 Strand Street,
Tralee, Co Kerry
Tel 066-7194647
Community: 1

CONGREGATION OF THE SISTERS OF MERCY
Sisters of Mercy, Convent of Mercy,
Rock Road, Killarney, Co Kerry
Tel 064-6671498

Apartment 1, Convent of Mercy,
Rock Road, Killarney, Co Kerry

21 The Grove, Mounthawk,
Tralee, Co Kerry
Tel 066-7189029

St Brigid's Convent,
Greenville, Listowel, Co Kerry
Tel 068-21557

14 Brandon Place, Basin Road,
Tralee, Co Kerry
Tel 066-7144997

9 Carraig Lí, Killerisk,
Tralee, Co Kerry

10 Carraig Lí, Killerisk,
Tralee, Co Kerry
Tel 066-7192364

Goodwin House, The Mall,
Dingle, Co Kerry
Tel 066-9151943

Mercy Sisters, Aoibhneas,
103 Gort na Sidhe, Mounthawk,
Tralee, Co Kerry
Tel 066-7128056

7 Woodview, Moyderwell, Tralee,
Co Kerry
Tel 066-7118027

2 Carrigeendaniel Court, Caherslee,
Tralee, Co Kerry
Tel 066-7127517

1 St Brendan's Park,
Tralee, Co Kerry

3 Siena Court, Oakpark,
Tralee, Co Kerry

7 Siena Court, Oakpark,
Tralee, Co Kerry

10 Siena Court, Oakpark,
Tralee, Co Kerry

Apartment 7, Riverville House,
Oakview Village, Tralee, Co Kerry

15 Castlemorris Orchard,
Ballymullen,
Tralee, Co Kerry

Apartment 6, Closheen Lane,
Roscarbery, Co Cork
Tel 023-8851753

Apartment 16,
Riverville House, Oakview Village,
Tralee, Co Kerry

DOMINICAN SISTERS (KING WILLIAM'S TOWN)
Oakpark, Tralee, Co Kerry
Tel 066-7125641
Community: 4
Our Lady of Fatima Retirement Home
Tel 066-7125900 Fax 066-7180834
Email dominicansistersstralee@gmail.com
Beds: 66
Siena Court for Active Retired:
Bungalows: 10 en suite
Contact Person: Sr Teresa McEvoy OP
Email teresamcevoy@fatimahome.com

FRANCISCAN MISSIONARIES OF THE DIVINE MOTHERHOOD
Sancta Chiara,
5 St Margaret's Road,
Killarney, Co Kerry W93 Y47P
Tel 064-6626866 Fax 064-6626414
Community: 4

INFANT JESUS SISTERS
12 West End,
Millstreet, Co Cork P51 YF76

No. 1 Cois Locha,
Coolea, Co Cork P12 VH67

7 Blackrock, St Brendan's Road,
Tralee, Co Kerry V92 KC0E
Tel 066-7124455
Teaching and pastoral ministry

DIOCESE OF KERRY

LITTLE COMPANY OF MARY
Park Road,
Killarney, Co Kerry
Tel 064-6671220
Community: 4

PRESENTATION SISTERS
Teach na Toirbhirte,
Miltown, Co Kerry
Tel 066-9767387
Non-resident Leader: Sr Marie Wall
Community: 3
Primary School. Tel 066-9767626
Post-Primary School. Tel 066-9767168

Presentation Convent,
Killarney, Co Kerry
Tel 064-6631172
Team Leadership
Community: 5
Secondary School. Tel 064-6632209

Presentation Convent,
Castle Street,
Tralee, Co Kerry
Tel 066-7122128
Email presentationconvtralee@gmail.com
Local Leader: Sr Mary Hoare
Community: 10
Primary School. Tel 066-7123314
Secondary School. Tel 066-7122737

20 Baile and Toirín,
Killorglin, Co Kerry
Community: 1

Apt. 1, Presentation Convent,
Castle Street, Tralee, Co Kerry
Tel 066-7181627

Apt. 2, Presentation Convent,
Castle Street, Tralee, Co Kerry
Tel 066-7118539
Community: 1

Apt. 3, Presentation Convent,
Castle Street, Tralee, Co Kerry
Tel 066-7122828
Community: 1

Apt. 4, Presentation Convent,
Castle Street, Tralee, Co Kerry
Tel 066-7102862
Community: 1

Apt. 5, Presentation Convent,
Castle Street, Tralee, Co Kerry
Tel 066-7121827
Community: 1

Presentation Convent,
Castleisland, Co Kerry
Tel 066-7141256
Email prescastle1@gmail.com
Non-resident Leader: Sr Miriam Pollard
Community: 4
Primary School. Tel 066-7141147
Secondary School. Tel 066-7141178

Presentation Convent,
Lixnaw, Co Kerry
Tel 066-7132138
Email lixnawpbvm@gmail.com
Non-resident Leader
Sr Bríd Clifford
Community: 6
Primary School. Tel 066-7132600

Presentation Convent,
Rathmore, Co Kerry
Tel 064-7758027
Email rathmoreconvent@gmail.com
Non-resident Leader: Sr Lelia Finn
Community: 3
Primary School. Tel 064-7758499

48 Hawley Park,
Tralee, Co Kerry
Tel 066-7122111
Community: 2

'Tigh na Féile', Ballygologue Road,
Listowel, Co Kerry
Tel 068-21156
Community: 1
Primary School. Tel 068-22294
Secondary School. Tel 068-21452
Nano Nagle School. Tel 068-21942

9 Beech Grove, Cahirdown,
Listowel, Co Kerry
Tel 068-53951
Community: 1

Mail Road, Cahirdown,
Listowel, Co Kerry
Tel 068-22500
Community: 2

7 Tamhnach Lí,
Monavalley, Tralee, Co Kerry
Tel 066-7180800
Community: 1

8 Tamhnach Lí,
Monavalley, Tralee, Co Kerry
Tel 066-7194174
Community: 1

9 Tamhnach Lí,
Monavalley, Tralee, Co Kerry
Tel 066-7195312
Community: 2

9 Woodbrooke Manor,
Monavalley, Tralee, Co Kerry
Tel 066-7185454
Community: 2

15 St Joseph's Gardens,
Millstreet, Co Cork
Tel 029-71655
Community: 1

31 St Joseph's Gardens,
Millstreet, Co Cork
Tel 029-71627
Community: 1

SISTERS OF ST CLARE
St Clare's Convent,
Kenmare, Co Kerry
Tel 064-6641385
Email stclareskenmare@eircom.net
Community: 3
St Clare's Primary. Pupils: 151
Kenmare Community School
Tel 064-6640846/7

ST JOSEPH OF ANNECY SISTERS
St Joseph's Convent,
Killorglin, Co Kerry
Tel 066-9761809 Fax 066-9761127
Superior: Sr Helena Lyne
Email margaret.lyne@talk21.com
Community: 4

St Joseph's Home for the Aged,
Killorglin, Co Kerry
Tel 066-9761124 (H)
Tel 066-9761808 (Patients)
Beds: 40

ST JOSEPH OF THE SACRED HEART SISTERS
Sisters of St Joseph of Sacred Heart,
St Joseph's, Brosna Road,
Castleisland, Co Kerry
Tel 066-7141472
Sr Theresa Herlihy

Sisters of St Joseph of Sacred Heart,
St Joseph's, 5 Allman's Terrace,
Killarney, Co Kerry
Tel 064-6623528
Sr Ellen Lane
Email eireregion@gmail.com

Sisters of St Joseph of Sacred Heart,
Apt 2, Park Avenue, Oakdale,
Killarney, Co Kerry V93 W3KN
Tel 064-6671662
Sr Eily Deasy

DIOCESAN SECONDARY SCHOOLS

St Brendan's College (Diocesan College)
Killarney, Co Kerry
Tel 064-6631021
Principal: Mr Sean Coffey

St Michael's College
Listowel, Co Kerry
Tel 068-21049
Principal: Mr John Mulvihill

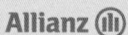

CHARITABLE AND OTHER SOCIETIES

Legion of Mary
Dingle, Firies, Fossa, Glenflesk, Kilcummin, Killarney, Killeentierna, Knocknagree, Millstreet, Milltown, Scartaglin, Tralee

St Vincent de Paul
Conferences at: Abbeydorney, Annascaul, Ardfert, Ballybunion, Ballyduff, Ballyferiter, Ballyheigue, Ballylongford, Boherbue, Cahirciveen, Castlemaine, Castlegregory, Castleisland, Castletownbere, Dingle, Firies, Kenmare, Killarney (four conferences), Killorglin, Knocknagoshel, Listowel, Lixnaw, Millstreet, Milltown, Moyvane, Rathmore, Tralee (five conferences)

COMPREHENSIVE SELECTION OF CHURCH FURNISHINGS & SUPPLIES

Church Candles | Altar Wine | Incense & Charcoal
Mass Kits | Priest's Sick Call Sets | Indoor & Outdoor Statuary
Vestments | Stations of the Cross | Lecterns | Priedieux
Tabernacles | Papal Blessings | Chalices | Ciboria

CBC DISTRIBUTORS

Greenbank, Newry, Co. Down BT34 2JP
Tel: (028) 3026 5216 **Fax:** (028) 3026 3927
If dialling from the Irish Republic: **Tel:** (042) 93 32321/2 **Fax:** (042) 93 37248
www.cbcdistributors.co.uk E.Mail: sales@cbcdistributors.co.uk

Children in Crossfire — 25 YEARS

STOP MALNUTRITION
SAVE CHILDREN'S LIVES

Children in Crossfire have supported St Luke's Hospital in Wolisso, Ethiopia since 2009. Through our partnership, the lives of more than 5,500 very sick children have been saved.

Here you see community health checks, where early signs of severe acute malnutrition are identified and vulnerable children are referred to St Luke's.

Please support this vital work.

TO DONATE...

Go to:
www.childrenincrossfire.org/donate

Call us on:
028 / 048 7126 9898

Send a cheque to:
2 St Joseph's Avenue, Derry, BT48 6TH

Allianz

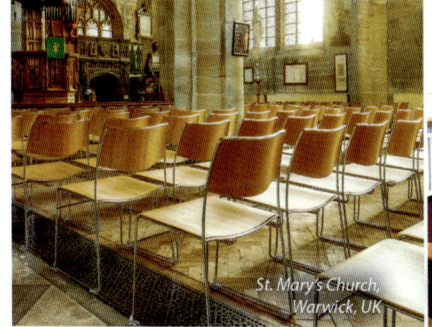

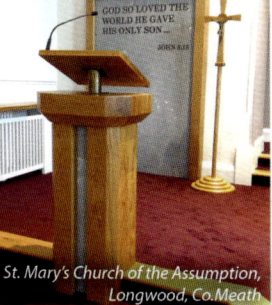

ICS
CHURCH FURNISHERS

St. Patrick's Church, Donaghmore, Co. Tyrone

St. Mary's Church, Warwick, UK

St. Mary's Church of the Assumption, Longwood, Co. Meath

St. Patrick's Church, Drumshanbo, Co. Leitrim

St. Patrick's Church, Drumshanbo, Co. Leitrim

Knock Basilica, Co. Mayo

Beautifully handcrafted Church Furniture.
Design, Manufacture, Restoration and Installation
of Church Furniture Worldwide.

ICS Furniture – Head Office: Dromod, Carrick-on-Shannon, Co Leitrim, Ireland. **IRL Tel:** +353 71 963 8230 **Fax:** +353 71 963 8290
UK Tel: 020 8906 6878 **Email:** info@icsfurniture.com **Web:** www.icsfurniture.com **twitter:** twitter.com/ICS_Furniture

VERITAS

FOR ALL YOUR PARISH NEEDS

We have the widest range of religious titles, missals, chalices, ciboria, thuribles, statues, holy water fonts, prayer cards, celebration cards and everything you need for Baptisms, Communions, Confirmations and more …

Mass Kit

Gold- & Silver-Plated Chalice

Gold- & Silver-Plated Ciborium

Large HIS Pxy

Gold-Plated Chalice

Gold-Plated Thurible

Gold-Plated Incense Boat

20% Parish Discount Available!

Drop into one of our stores throughout Ireland ·
Dublin City Centre · Blanchardstown · Cork
Derry · Letterkenny · Newry
Or order online at www.veritas.ie

DIOCESE OF KILDARE AND LEIGHLIN

PATRONS OF THE DIOCESE
ST BRIGID, 1 FEBRUARY; ST CONLETH (KILDARE), 4 MAY;
ST LAZERIAN (LEIGHLIN) 18 APRIL

INCLUDES COUNTY CARLOW AND PARTS OF COUNTIES KILDARE, LAOIS,
OFFALY, KILKENNY, WICKLOW AND WEXFORD

Most Rev Denis Nulty DD
Bishop of Kildare and Leighlin
Born 1963;
ordained priest 1988;
ordained Bishop of Kildare &
Leighlin 4 August 2013

Residence:
Bishop's House, Carlow
Tel 059-9176725/059-9142796
Email bishop@kandle.ie

CATHEDRAL OF THE ASSUMPTION, CARLOW

The ancient cathedrals of the Diocese of Kildare and Leighlin passed into Protestant usage in the period of the Reformation. Thus the cathedrals of Kildare and Old Leighlin stand on the sites of the ancient monasteries of St Brigid and St Laserian. Even before the Catholic Emancipation Act passed through the Westminster Parliament (1829), Bishop James Doyle OSA was working on the building of the Cathedral of the Assumption, Carlow. It is built on the site of and incorporates parts of the previous parish church of Carlow, which had been built in the 1780s by Dean Henry Staunton.

Carlow cathedral is not particularly large, having more the dimensions of a big parish church. The architectural work was begun by Joseph Lynch, but the final building is stamped with the design of Thomas Cobden, who replaced Lynch in 1829. Cobden gave the cathedral quite an elaborate exterior, with the obvious influence of the Bruges Town Hall tower. The cost of the building work was about £9,000. At its opening in November 1833, the interior decoration was incomplete. In fact, many elements were integrated over the following hundred years, sometimes adding to the mixture of styles.

The cathedral was consecrated on the occasion of its centenary, on 29 November 1933. A thorough reordering of the interior was completed in 1997, giving a very bright, welcoming, prayerful location for both diocesan and parish liturgical celebrations. The most notable elements are: the baptistry, the aumbry, the bishop's and president's chairs, the Hogan statue of James Doyle, former Bishop of Kildare and Leighlin popularly known as JKL, and the newly installed reliquary of St Willibrord, patron saint of Luxembourg who was educated in the Carlow area in the 7th century.

DIOCESE OF KILDARE AND LEIGHLIN

Most Rev James Moriarty DD
Retired Bishop of Kildare and Leighlin, born 1936; ordained priest 1961; ordained Bishop 22 September 1991; installed as Bishop of Kildare & Leighlin on 31 August 2002; retired April 2010

ADMINISTRATION

Diocesan Website
www.kandle.ie

Vicar General
Rt Rev Mgr John Byrne PP, VG
Dublin Road, Portlaoise, Co Laois
Tel 057-8621142

Vicars Forane
Very Rev Thomas Little PP, VF
(K&L South Deanery)
St Mary's Presbytery,
Brownshill Avenue, Carlow
Tel 059-9131559
Very Rev Mícheál Murphy PP, VF
(K&L West Deanery)
Mountmellick, Co Laois
Tel 057-8679302
Very Rev Liam Morgan PP, VF
(K&L North Deanery)
Sallins Road, Naas, Co Kildare
Tel 045-949576

Episcopal Vicar for the Pastoral Care of Priests
Very Rev Andy Leahy PP
The Presbytery, Kildare Town, Co Kildare
Tel 045-520347

Episcopal Vicar for Parish Renewal and Development
Very Rev Liam Morgan PP
Sallins Road, Naas, Co Kildare
Tel 045-949576

Consultors
Rt Rev Mgr Brendan Byrne, Chancellor
Rt Rev Mgr John Byrne PP, VG
Very Rev Andy Leahy PP
Very Rev Thomas Little PP, VF
Very Rev Mícheál Murphy PP, VF
Very Rev Liam Morgan PP, VF

Chancellor/Diocesan Secretary
Rt Rev Mgr Brendan Byrne
Email chancellor@kandle.ie
c/o Bishop's House, Carlow
Tel 059-9176725
Assistant Chancellor:
Very Rev Thomas O'Byrne Adm
c/o Bishop's House, Carlow
Tel 059-9176725
Email frthomas@kandle.ie

Diocesan Communications Liaison
Very Rev Mícheál Murphy PP, VF
Tel 057-8679302
Email mfmurphy59@gmail.com

Diocesan Communications
Very Rev Bill Kemmy PP
Tel 087-2308053
www.icatholic.ie
Rev David Vard CC
Te 057-8600121

Finance Committee
Chairperson: Mrs Anna-May McHugh
Fallaghmore, Ballylinan, Athy, Co Kildare
Recording Secretary: Rosie Boyd
Bishop's House, Carlow
Tel 059-9176725
Email rosie@kandle.ie

Diocesan Commission for Church, Art and Architecture
Chairman
Very Rev Francis MacNamara PE
Mountmellick, Co Laois
Tel 057-8624198
Secretary: Very Rev Denis Harrington PE
Clane, Co Kildare
Tel 045-868224

Director of Vocations
Very Rev Ruairí Ó Domhnaill PP
Chapel Lane, Newbridge, Co Kildare
Tel 045-431741
Email vocations@kandle.ie

Director of Diaconal Formation
Rt Rev Mgr John McEvoy PP
Rathvilly, Co Carlow
Tel 059-9161114
Email permanentdiaconate@kandle.ie

Diocesan Commission for Liturgical Formation
Chairperson: Ms Eileen Good
c/o Bishop's House, Carlow
Tel 059-9176725

Patron's Secretary for Primary Schools
Mr Bryan O'Reilly
c/o Bishop's House, Carlow
Tel 059-9176725/086-3400141
Email bryan@kandle.ie

Safeguarding Office
Director of Safeguarding & Diocesan Designated Liaison Person
Ms Kathleen Sherry
c/o Bishop's House, Carlow
Tel 085-8021633
Email safeguarding@kandle.ie
Deputy Designated Liaison Persons
Ms Michele Hughes
c/o Bishop's House, Carlow
Tel 086-1710643
Fr Mícheal Murphy PP
Mountmellick
Tel 057-8679302
Mr Mick Daly
c/o Bishop's House, Old Dublin Road
Carlow
Tel 059-9176725
Diocesan Garda Vetting Administrator
Rosie Boyd
c/o Bishop's House, Carlow
Tel 059-9176725
Email rosie@kandle.ie

Archivist
Diocesan Archivist: Bernie Deasy
Bishop's House, Carlow
Tel 059-9153200
Email bdeasy@carlowcollege.ie

FAITH DEVELOPMENT SERVICES

Faith Development Services
Cathedral Parish Centre, College Street,
Carlow Town
Tel 059-9164084 Fax 059-9164020
Email fds@kandle.ie
Primary Diocesan Advisor
Ms Maeve Mahon
Email maeve.mahon@kandle.ie
Post-Primary Diocesan Advisor
Ms Hilda Campbell
Email hilda.campbell@kandle.ie
Youth Ministry/Meitheal Co-ordinator
Mr Robert Norton
Email robert.norton@kandle.ie
Ms Cathriona Kelly
Email cathriona.kelly@kandle.ie
Pastoral Resource Person
Ms Julie Kavanagh
Email julie.kavanagh@kandle.ie

Church Music
Rev Liam Lawton Adm
Edenderry, Co Offaly Tel 046-9732352
Email liamlawtonireland@gmail.com

Catholic Primary School Managers Association
Chairman
Very Rev Thomas O'Byrne Adm
the Presbytery, Old Dublin Road, Carlow
Tel 059-9131227
Secretary: Br Camillus Regan
c/o Bishop's House, Carlow
Tel 087-2244175
Email patbros@iol.ie

PASTORAL

ACCORD
Centre Directors
Carlow: Very Rev Patrick Hennessy PP
The Presbytery,
Leighlinbridge, Co Carlow
Tel 059-9721463
Ms Mary Merrigan
Tel 059-9138738
Portlaoise: Fr Paddy Byrne PP
Tel 087-9948505
Accord, Parish Office, Portlaoise, Co Laois
Newbridge: Very Rev Joseph McDermott
Accord Office, Parish Centre,
Station Road, Newbridge, Co Kildare
Tel 045-431695

ALPHA
Very Rev James O'Connell Adm
The Parochial House, Ballon, Co Carlow
Tel 059-9159329

Conciliators
Rt Rev Mgr John McDonald PE, CC
Curragh Camp, Co Kildare
Tel 045-441369
Very Rev William O'Byrne PP
Kill, Co Kildare
Tel 045-878008
Mr Brian O'Sullivan
Drumcooley, Edenderry, Co Offaly
Tel 046-9731522 (W) 046-31435 (H)

Diocesan Committee for Adoration
Chairperson: Br Matthew Hayes
Tel 057-8755964
Secretary: Elizabeth Murphy
Email murphylizls@gmail.com

DIOCESE OF KILDARE AND LEIGHLIN

Ecumenism
Director: Very Rev Tom Lalor PE
Tinryland, Co Carlow
Tel 087-2360355

Pioneer Total Abstinence Association
Diocesan Director
Very Rev Mark Townsend PP
Graignamanagh, Co Kilkenny
Tel 059-9724238

Pontifical Mission Societies
Diocesan Director
Very Rev George Augustine PP
Kilcock, Co Kildare
Tel 01-6103512

Polish Chaplaincy
Rev Piotr Jakubiak
The Presbytery, Ballymany,
Newbridge, Co Kildare
Tel 045-434069

Prisons
Contact Priest: Rev Eugene Drumm (SPS)
Portlaoise Prison, Portlaoise, Co Laois
Tel 057-8622549

Travellers
Chaplains
Very Rev Thomas Dooley PP
Portarlington, Co Laois
Tel 057-8643004
Very Rev John Brickley PP
Cooleragh, Coill Dubh, Naas, Co Kildare
Tel 045-860281

Youth Ministry Team
Meitheal Co-ordinator: Mr Robert Norton
Email robert.norton@kandle.ie
Ms Cathriona Kelly
Faith Development Services,
Cathedral Parish Centre,
College Street, Carlow
Tel 059-9164084 Fax 059-9164020

PARISHES

Mensal parishes are listed first. Other parishes follow alphabetically. Historical names are given in parentheses. Church titulars are in italics.

CATHEDRAL, CARLOW
Cathedral of the Assumption
Email info@carlowcathedral.ie
Website www.carlowcathedral.ie
Very Rev Thomas O'Byrne Adm
The Presbytery, Carlow
Tel 059-9131227 Fax 059-9130805
Rev Gaspar Habara (SVD) CC
The Presbytery, Carlow
Tel 059-9131227
Rev Yanbo Chen (SVD) *(Priest in Residence)*
Rev Martin Smith (SPS) CC
1 Green Road, Carlow
Tel 059-9142632
Permanent Deacon: Rev David O'Flaherty
Tel 059-9164086
Cathedral/Parish Shop & Office
Tel 059-9164087

ASKEA
Holy Family
Email office@askeaparish.ie
Very Rev Thomas Little PP, VF
Browneshill Avenue, Carlow
Tel 059-9131559
Email tomedwardlittle@gmail.com
Rev Tommy Dillon PE, CC
Parochial House, Askea, Carlow
Tel 059-9164882
Email dillontommy@gmail.com

ABBEYLEIX
Holy Rosary, Abbeyleix
St Patrick, Ballyroan
Very Rev Paddy Byrne PP
Abbeyleix, Co Laois
Tel 057-8731135
Rev Petru Medves CC
Abbeyleix Parish Office,
Abbeyleix, Co Laois
Tel 085-1853069

ALLEN
Holy Trinity, Allen
St Brigid's, Milltown
Immaculate Conception, Allenwood
Very Rev William Byrne PP
Allen, Kilmeague, Naas, Co Kildare
Tel 045-860135
Rev Brian Kavanagh CC
St Patrick's College, Maynooth, Co Kildare
Tel 045-890559

ARLES
Sacred Heart, Arles, St Anne's, Ballylinan
St Abban's, Maganey
Email arlesparish@gmail.com
Very Rev Padraig Shelley PP
The Presbytery, Arles, Co Carlow
Tel 059-9147637

BALLINAKILL
St Brigid's, Ballinakill
St Lazarian's, Knock
Very Rev Paddy Byrne PP
Abbeyleix, Co Laois
Tel 087-9948505
Rev Petru Medves CC
Tel 085-1853069
Very Rev Seán Conlon PE, CC
Ballinakill, Co Laois
Tel 057-8733336

BALLON
SS Peter and Paul, Ballon
St Patrick's, Rathoe
Very Rev James O'Connell Adm
Parochial House, Ballon, Co Carlow
Tel 059-9159329

BALLYADAMS
St Joseph's, Ballyadams
St Mary's, Wolfhill
Holy Rosary, Luggacurren
Very Rev Daniel Dunne PP
Tullamoy, Stradbally, Co Laois
Tel 059-8627123

BALLYFIN
St Fintan's
Very Rev Joseph Brophy PP
Ballyfin, Portlaoise, Co Laois
Tel 057-8755227
Rev P.J. Fitzgerald (SPS) CC
Mountrath, Co Laois
Tel 057-8732234

BALTINGLASS
St Joseph's, Baltinglass
St Oliver's, Grange Con
St Mary's, Stratford
Email admin@baltinglassparish.ie
Very Rev Gerard Ahern PP
Parkmore, Baltinglass, Co Wicklow
Tel 059-6298881
Email aherngerard22@gmail.com

BALYNA
St Mary's, Broadford,
St Patrick's Johnstownbridge,
St Brigid's, Clogherinchoe
Email balynaparish2020@gmail.com
Website www.balynaparish.ie
Very Rev Séan Maher PP
Broadford, Co Kildare
Tel 046-9551203

BENNEKERRY
St Mary's
Email office@askeaparish.ie
Very Rev Thomas Little PP, VF
St Mary's, Browneshill Avenue, Carlow
Tel 059-9131559
Email tomedwardlittle@gmail.com
Rev Tommy Dillon PE, CC
Parochial House, Askea, Carlow
Tel 059-9164882
Email dillontommy@gmail.com

BORRIS
Sacred Heart, Borris
St Patrick's, Ballymurphy
St Forchan's, Rathanna
Email borrisparish@gmail.com
Very Rev Rory Nolan PP
Borris, Co Carlow via Kilkenny
Tel 059-9773128

CARAGH
Our Lady and St Joseph, Caragh,
Email parishoffice@caragh.net
Very Rev Rúairí O'Domhnaill Adm
Chapel Lane, Newbridge, Co Kildare
Tel 045-431741
Very Rev Joseph McDermott PE, CC
Parochial House, Caragh,
Naas, Co Kildare
Tel 045-903889

CARBURY
Holy Trinity, Carbury
Holy Family, Derrinturn
Email carburyparish@gmail.com
Very Rev John Fitzpatrick PP
Carbury, Co Kildare
Tel 046-9553355

CLANE
SS Patrick and Brigid, Clane
Sacred Heart, Rathcoffey
Email claneparish@eircom.net
Website www.claneparish.com
Very Rev Paul O'Boyle PP
Clane, Naas, Co Kildare
Tel 045-868249
Email oboylepaul@eircom.net
Permanent Deacon: Rev John Dunleavy
Tel 045-861393

CLONASLEE
St Manman's
Email clonaslee@eircom.net
Very Rev Thomas O'Reilly Adm
Clonaslee, Co Laois
Tel 057-8648030

CLONBULLOGUE
Sacred Heart, Clonbullogue
St Brochan's, Bracknagh,
Immaculate Conception, Walsh Island
Very Rev Gregory Corcoran PP
Rhode, Co Offaly
Tel 087-9402669
Rev Sean Hyland CC
29 Pine Villa, Portarlington, Co Laois
Tel 057-8645582/087-9486769
Permanent Deacon: Rev Gary Moore
Tel 046-9737579

CLONEGAL
St Brigid's, Clonegal
St Lasarian's, Kildavin
Very Rev Pat Hughes PP
Myshall, Co Carlow
Tel 059-9157635
Very Rev Joseph Fleming PE, CC
Clonegal, Enniscorthy, Co Wexford
Tel 053-9377298

CLONMORE
St Mary's, Ballyconnell
St Finian's, Kilquiggan
Our Lady of the Wayside, Clonmore
St Finian's Oratory, Killinure
Email clonmoreoffice.parish@gmail.com
Very Rev John O'Brien PP
Parochial House, Killinure,
Tullow, Co Carlow
Tel 059-9156344
Email frjohn51@gmail.com

COOLERAGH AND STAPLESTOWN
Christ the King, Cooleragh,
St Benignus, Staplestown
Email standco100@gmail.com
Very Rev John Brickley PP
Cooleragh, Coill Dubh, Naas, Co Kildare
Tel 045-860281

CURRAGH CAMP
St Brigid's
Very Rev P. J. Somers PP
Chaplain's House, Curragh Camp,
Co Kildare
Tel 045-441277
Email spj44@hotmail.com
Rt Rev Mgr John McDonald PE, CC
Chaplain's House, Curragh Camp,
Co Kildare
Tel 045-441369

DAINGEAN
Mary Mother of God, Daingean
SS Peter and Paul, Kilclonfert
St Francis of Assisi and St Brigid,
Ballycommon; Oratory of the
Immaculate Conception, Cappincur
Email daingeanparish@eircom.net
Very Rev Declan Thompson (SPS) PP
St Mary's Road, Daingean, Co Offaly
Tel 057-9362653
Very Rev Patrick O'Byrne PE, CC
St Mary's Road, Daingean, Co Offaly
Tel 057-9353064

DOONANE
St Abban's, Doonane
Blessed Virgin Mary, Mayo
Very Rev Denis Murphy Adm
Tolerton, Ballickmoyler, Carlow
Tel 056-4442126

DROICHEAD NUA/NEWBRIDGE
St Conleth's, Newbridge
Cill Mhuire, Ballymany
St Eustace's, Dominican Church
Parish Office: 045-431394
Email parishoffice@newbridgeparish.ie
Very Rev Rúairí O'Domhnaill PP
Chapel Lane, Newbridge, Co Kildare
Tel 045-431741
Rev Michal Cudzilo
Curate's House, Chapel Lane,
Newbridge, Co Kildare
Very Rev Joseph McDermott PE, CC
Caragh, Naas, Co Kildare
Tel 045-903889
Email jmcder44@gmail.com
Rev Eugen Dragos Tamas CC
Curate's House, Chapel Lane,
Newbridge, Co Kildare
Tel 045-433979
Rev Piotr Jakubiak
The Presbytery, Ballymany,
Newbridge, Co Kildare
Tel 045-434069
Website www.newbridgeparish.ie
Permanent Deacon: Rev Jim Stowe
c/o Parish Office, Station Road,
Droichead Nua, Co Kildare
Tel 045-431394

EDENDERRY
St Mary's
Email edenderryparishcentre@gmail.com
Very Rev Liam Lawton Adm
Very Rev P.J. McEvoy PP
St Mary's, Edenderry, Co Offaly
Tel 046-9732352
Rev Larry Malone *(in residence)*
Edenderry, Co Offaly
Tel 046-9732352
Permanent Deacon: Rev Paul Wyer
Tel 046-9733311

EMO
St Paul's, Emo; Sacred Heart, Rath
Email portarlingtonparishoffice@eircom.net
Very Rev Thomas Dooley Adm
Patrick Street, Portarlington, Co Laois
Tel 057-8643004
Email frtomdooley@eircom.net
Rev Joe O'Neill CC
Priest's House, Emo, Portlaoise, Co Laois
Tel 089-4535533

GRAIGNAMANAGH
Duiske Abbey, Graignamanagh
Our Lady of Lourdes,
Skeoughvosteen, Co Kilkenny
Email graigparish@kandle.ie
Very Rev Mark Townsend PP
Parochial House,
Graignamanagh, Co Kilkenny
Tel 059-9724238
Abbey Centre: 059-9724238

GRAIGUECULLEN
St Clare's, Graiguecullen
Holy Cross, Killeshin
Email gkparish@gmail.com
www.graiguecullenkilleshin.com
Very Rev John Dunphy PP
Graiguecullen, Carlow
Tel 059-9141833
Email dunphiej@gmail.com
Permanent Deacon: Rev Joe O'Rourke
c/o Parish Office, Graiguecullen, Carlow
Tel 059-9141833

HACKETSTOWN
St Brigid's, Hacketstown
Our Lady, Killamoate
Church of the Immaculate Conception, Knockananna
Church of Our Lady, Askinagap
Email hacketstownparish@gmail.com
Very Rev Terence McGovern PP
Main Street, Hacketstown, Co Carlow
Tel 087-6754811

KILCOCK
St Coca, Kilcock
Nativity of the BVM, Newtown
Email info@kilcockandnewtownparish.ie
Website www.kilcockandnewtownparish.ie
Very Rev George Augustine PP
Mill Lane, Kilcock, Co Kildare
Tel 01-6103512

KILDARE
St Brigid's, Kildare
Our Lady of Victories, Kildangan
Sacred Heart, Nurney
Parish Office: 045-521352
Email kildareparish@gmail.com
Website www.kildareparish.ie
Very Rev Andy Leahy PP
The Presbytery, Kildare Town
Tel 045-520847
Very Rev Adrian Carbery PE, CC
26 Beech Grove, Kildare
Tel 045-521900

KILL
St Brigid's, Kill
St Anne's, Ardclough
Email admin@killparish.ie
Website www.killparish.ie
Very Rev William O'Byrne PP
Kill, Naas, Co Kildare
Tel 045-878008
Very Rev Matthew Kelly PE, CC
60 Hartwell Green, Kill, Naas, Co Kildare
Tel 045-877880

KILLEIGH
St Patrick's, Killeigh
St Joseph's, Ballinagar
St Mary's, Raheen
Email office@killeigh.com
Website www.killeigh.com
Very Rev John Stapleton PP
Killeigh, Co Offaly
Tel 057-9344161
Email john@killeigh.com
Rt Rev Mgr Thomas Coonan PE, CC
Geashill, Co Offaly
Tel 057-9343517

DIOCESE OF KILDARE AND LEIGHLIN

LEIGHLIN
St Laserian's, Leighlin
St Fintan's, Ballinabranna
Very Rev Patrick Hennessy PP
Leighlinbridge, Co Carlow
Tel 059-9721463
Permanent Deacon: Rev Pat Roche
Leighlinbridge, Co Carlow
Tel 059-9722607

MONASTEREVIN
SS Peter and Paul, Monasterevin
Email monasterevin.parish@gmail.com
Very Rev Liam Merrigan PP
Tougher Road, Monasterevin, Co Kildare
Tel 045-525346

MOUNTMELLICK
St Joseph's, Mountmellick
St Mary's, Clonaghadoo
Email stjosephs1878@gmail.com
Very Rev Mícheál Murphy PP, VF
11 Ashgrove, Mountmellick, Co Laois
Tel 057-8679302
Very Rev Noel Dunphy PE, CC
Mountmellick, Co Laois
Tel 057-8624141

MOUNTRATH
St Fintan's, Mountrath
Sacred Heart, Hollow
Very Rev Joseph Brophy PP
Ballyfin, Portlaoise, Co Laois
Tel 057-8755227
Rev P.J. Fitzgerald (SPS) CC
Mountrath, Co Laois
Tel 057-8732234

MUINEBHEAG/BAGENALSTOWN
St Andrew's, Bagenalstown
St Patrick's Newtown
St Laserian's, Ballinkillen
Email bagenalstownparish@gmail.com
Website www.bagenalstownparish.ie
Very Rev Declan Foley PP
The Presbytery, Muinebheag, Co Carlow
Tel 059-9721154
Email pdlfoley@gmail.com
Rev Shem Furlong CC
Muinebheag Parish Office,
Bagenalstown, Co Carlow
Tel 087-2400582

MYSHALL
Exaltation of the Cross, Myshall
St Laserian's, Drumphea
Very Rev Pat Hughes PP
Myshall, Co Carlow
Tel 059-9157635

NAAS
Our Lady and St David, Naas
Irish Martyrs, Ballycane
Very Rev Liam Morgan PP, VF
Sallins Road, Naas, Co Kildare
Tel 045-949576
Rev Robert Petrisor CC
Sallins Road, Naas, Co Kildare
Tel 045-897703
Rev Alex Kochatt CC
77 The Lakelands, Naas, Co Kildare
Tel 045-949576
Rev Michael Flattery (SMA) CC
364 Sundays Well, Naas, Co Kildare
Tel 045-876197
Permanent Deacon: Rev Fergal O'Neill
Tel 086-3816133

PAULSTOWN
The Assumption, Paulstown
Holy Trinity, Goresbridge
Email gbptparish@gmail.com
Very Rev James Kelly PP
Goresbridge, Co Kilkenny
Tel 059-9775180

PORTARLINGTON
St Michael's, Portarlington
St John the Evangelist, Killenard
Email portarlingtonparishoffice@eircom.net
Very Rev Thomas Dooley PP
Patrick Street, Portarlington, Co Laois
Tel 057-8643004
Email frtomdooley@eircom.net
Rev Joe O'Neill CC
Emo, Portlaoise, Co Laois
Tel 057-8646517

PORTLAOISE
SS Peter and Paul, Portlaoise
The Assumption, The Heath
The Holy Cross, Ratheniska
Email info@portlaoiseparish.ie
Website www.portlaoiseparish.ie
Rt Rev Mgr John Byrne PP, VG
Parochial House,
Portlaoise, Co Laois
Tel 057-8692153
Email john@portlaoiseparish.ie
Rev David Vard CC
Annebrook, Stradbally Road,
Portlaoise, Co Laois
Tel 057-8688440
Rev Ciprian Matei CC
Tower Hill, Portlaoise, Co Laois
Tel 057-8621142

PROSPEROUS
Our Lady and St Joseph, Prosperous
Email prosperousparishoffice@eircom.net
Rev Bernard Reyhart CC
Curate's House,
Prosperous, Co Kildare
Tel 045-868187

RAHEEN
St Fintan's, Raheen
St Brigid's, Shanahoe
Very Rev Paddy Byrne PP
The Presbytery, Ballinakill Road,
Abbeyleix, Co Laois
Tel 057-8731135
Rev Petru Medves CC
Abbeyleix Parish Office,
Abbeyleix, Co Laois
Tel 087-1853069

RATHANGAN
Assumption and St Patrick
Very Rev Bill Kemmy PP
Rathangan, Co Kildare
Tel 087-2308053
Very Rev Gerard O'Byrne PE, CC
Rathangan, Co Kildare
Tel 045-524316
Email gerobyrne@eircom.net

RATHVILLY
St Patrick's, Rathvilly
St Brigid's, Talbotstown
Blessed Virgin Mary, Tynock
Email office@rathvillykilteganparish.ie
Rt Rev Mgr John McEvoy PP
Rathvilly, Co Carlow
Tel 059-9161114
Rev Pat O'Brien (SPS) CC
Kiltegan, Co Wicklow
Tel 059-6473211

RHODE
St Peter's, Rhode
St Anne's, Croghan
Website www.rhodeparish.ie
Very Rev Gregory Corcoran PP
Rhode, Co Offaly
Tel 046-9737010
Rev Sean Hyland CC
29 Pine Villa, Portarlington, Co Laois
Tel 057-8645582/087-9486769
Permanent Deacon: Rev Gary Moore
Tel 046-9737579

ROSENALLIS
St Brigid's
Email rosenallisparish@eircom.net
Website www.rosenallis.com
Very Rev Thomas Walshe PP
Rosenallis, Portlaoise, Co Laois
Tel 057-8628513

ST MULLINS
St Moling's, Glynn
St Brendan's, Drummond
Very Rev Edward Aughney Adm
Glynn, St Mullins via Kilkenny
Tel 051-424563

SALLINS
Our Lady of the Rosary & Guardian Angels
Email office@naasparish.net
Very Rev Liam Morgan PP,VF
Sallins Road, Naas, Co Kildare
Tel 045-949576

STRADBALLY
Sacred Heart, Stradbally
Assumption, Vicarstown
St Michael, Timahoe
Email stradballychurch@gmail.com
Very Rev Gerard Breen PP
Parochial House, Stradbally, Co Laois
Tel 057-8625132
Very Rev Seán Kelly PE, CC
Stradbally, Co Laois
Tel 057-8625831

SUNCROFT
St Brigid's
Email suncroftparish@eircom.net
Very Rev Barry Larkin PP
Suncroft, Curragh, Co Kildare
Tel 045-441586

TINRYLAND
St Joseph's
Website www.tinryland.ie
Very Rev Thomas Little Adm, VF
Brownshill Avenue, Carlow
Tel 059-9131559
Email tomedwardlittle@gmail.com

TULLOW
Most Holy Rosary, Tullow
Immaculate Conception, Ardattin
St John the Baptist, Grange
Email tullowparish@outlook.com
Website www.tullowparish.com
Very Rev Brian Maguire (SPS) PP
The Shroughaun, Tullow, Co Carlow
Tel 059-9180377

TWO-MILE-HOUSE
Very Rev Liam Morgan PP, VF
Sallins Road, Naas, Co Kildare
Tel 045-949576

INSTITUTIONS AND THEIR CHAPLAINS

Abbeyleix District Hospital
Very Rev Paddy Byrne PP
Tel 057-8731135

Baltinglass District Hospital
Very Rev Gerard Ahern PP
Tel 087-6298881

County Hospital, Portlaoise
Rt Rev Mgr John Byrne PP, VG
Portlaoise, Co Laois
Tel 057-8621142

Curragh Camp
Very Rev P.J. Somers PP
Tel 045-441369

Edenderry Hospital
Very Rev P. J. McEvoy PP
Tel 046-9731296

Institute of Technology, Carlow
Rev Martin Smith (SPS)
Tel 059-9142632

Naas General Hospital, Co Kildare
Sr Mary Lalor
Tel 045-897221

Portlaoise Prison
Rev Eugene Drumm (SPS)
Tel 057-8622549

Sacred Heart Hospital, Carlow
Very Rev Thomas O'Byrne Adm
Tel 059-9131227

St Brigid's Hospital
Shaen, Portlaoise, Co Laois
Rt Rev Mgr John Byrne PP, VG
Tel 057-8621142

St Dympna's Hospital, Carlow
Very Rev Thomas O'Byrne Adm
Tel 059-9131227

St Fintan's Hospital, Portlaoise
Rt Rev Mgr John Byrne PP, VG
Dublin Road, Portlaoise, Co Laois
Tel 057-8621142

St Vincent's Hospital, Mountmellick
Very Rev Micheál Murphy PP, VF
Mountmellick, Co Laois
Tel 057-8679302

PRIESTS OF THE DIOCESE ELSEWHERE

Rev Kilian Byrne
Dublin Regional Marriage Tribunal
Very Rev Peter Cribbin
c/o Bishop's House, Dublin Road, Carlow
Very Rev Patrick Dunny
Wood Road, Graignamanagh,
Co Kilkenny
Tel 059-9724518
Rev Paul McNamee
c/o Bishop's House, Dublin Road, Carlow

RETIRED PRIESTS

Rt Rev Mgr Brendan Byrne PE
c/o Bishop's House, Carlow
Tel 059-9176725
Very Rev Charles Byrne
c/o Bishop's House, Carlow
Very Rev Gerald Byrne PE
15 New Road, Leighlinbridge,
Co Carlow
Very Rev Patrick Daly PE
Braganza, Athy Road, Carlow
Very Rev James Gahan PE
c/o Bishop's House, Carlow
Very Rev Denis Harrington PE
Clane, Co Kildare
Tel 045-868224
Very Rev Brendan Howard PE
Hillview Nursing Home,
Tullow Road, Carlow
Very Rev Edward Kavanagh PE
Rath, Emo, Co Laois
Very Rev Tom Lalor PE
The Presbytery, Tinryland, Co Carlow
Tel 087-2360355
Rev James McCormack
c/o Bishop's House
Very Rev Francis McNamara PE
Parochial House, Davitt Road,
Mountmellick, Co Laois
Tel 057-8624198
Rev Michael Moloney PE
43 The Waterways, Sallins,
Naas, Co Kildare
Very Rev Edward Moore PE
Marian House, Sallins Road,
Naas, Co Kildare
Very Rev Alphonsus Murphy PE
Carbury, Co Kildare
Tel 046-9553020
Very Rev Michael Noonan PE
Portarlington, Co Laois
Tel 057-8623431
Very Rev John O'Connell PE
The Presbytery, Two-Mile-House,
Naas, Co Kildare
Tel 045-876160
Rt Rev Mgr Caomhín O'Neill
Emmaus, Abbeyleix, Co Laois
Very Rev Philip O'Shea PE
Clonagoose, Borris, Co Carlow
Very Rev Thomas O'Shea PE
Gowran Abbey Nursing Home,
Gowran, Co Kilkenny
Very Rev Denis O'Sullivan PE
c/o Bishop's House, Carlow
Very Rev Colum Swan PE
c/o Bishop's House, Carlow

RELIGIOUS ORDERS AND CONGREGATIONS

PRIESTS

CAPUCHINS
Capuchin Friary,
43 Dublin Street, Carlow R93 PH27
Tel 059-9142543 Fax 059-9142030
Guardian
Rev Desmond McNaboe (OFMCap)
Vicar: Br Philip Tobin (OFMCap)

CARMELITES (OCARM)
Carmelite Priory, White Abbey,
Co Kildare R51 X827
Tel 045-521391 Fax 045-522318
Email carmeliteskildare@gmail.com
Prior: Rev Chacko Antony
Thandiparahibil (OCarm)

DOMINICANS
Newbridge College,
Droichead Nua, Co Kildare
Tel 045-487200
Prior: Vacant
Secondary School

JESUITS
Clongowes Wood College,
Clane, Co Kildare
Tel 045-868663/868202 Fax 045-861042
Email *(College)* reception@clongowes.ie
(Community) reception@clongowes.ie
Rector: Rev Michael Sheil (SJ)
Headmaster: Mr Chris Lumb
Vice-Rector: Rev Bernard McGuckian (SJ)
Minister: Br Tom Phelan (SJ)
Boarding School for Secondary Pupils

ST PATRICK'S MISSIONARY SOCIETY
St Patrick's,
Kiltegan, Co Wicklow
Tel 059-6473600 Fax 059-6473622
Email spsoff@iol.ie (office)
Society Leader: Rev Victor Dunne (SPS)
Assistant Society Leader
Rev John Marren (SPS)
Fax *(Society Leader & Council)*
059-6473644

BROTHERS

PATRICIAN BROTHERS
10 Hawthorn Drive,
Tullow, Co Carlow
Tel 059-9181727 Fax 059-9181728
Province Leader:
Br Camillus Regan (FSP)
Community: 1

Newbridge, Co Kildare
Tel 045-431475 Fax 045-431505
Superior: Br James O'Rourke (FSP)
Community: 2
Monastery National School
Tel 045-432174
Principal: Mr John O'Donovan
Patrician Secondary School
Tel 045-432410
Principal: Mr Pat Maloney

DIOCESE OF KILDARE AND LEIGHLIN

Patrician Brothers,
Cavansheath, Mountrath, Co Laois
Tel 057-8755964
Superior: Br Gerard Reburn (FSP)
Community: 3

The Irish Province has seven houses in Kenya
Regional Superior
Br Placido Kaburu (FSP)
Patrician Formation House,
PO Box 5064, via Eldoret, Kenya
Tel/Fax 0321-61134
Email pbroskam@africaonline.co.ke
Community: 9

SISTERS

BRIGIDINE SISTERS
16 Mount Clare,
Graguecullen, Co Carlow
Tel 059-9135869
Contact: Sr Maureen O'Leary
Community: 1
Retired

Brigidine Convent, Tullow, Co Carlow
Tel 059-9151308
Community Co-ordinator
Sr Thomasina Murphy
Community: 7
Education, Parish Work, Pastoral Care and Retired

Brigidine Sisters,
Delany Court, New Chapel Lane,
Tullow, Co Carlow
Contact: Sr Elizabeth Mary McDonald
Community: 5
Parish Work, Education, Retired

Teach Bhríde, Tullow, Co Carlow
Tel/Fax 059-9152465
Email teachbhride@eircom.net
Contact: Sr Carmel McEvoy
Community: 1
Holistic education centre

11 The Rise,
Ballymurphy Road, Tullow, Co Carlow
Tel 059-9152498
Contact: Sr Betty McDonald
Community: 1

1 Salem House,
Chantiere Gate, Portlaoise, Co Laois
Tel 057-8665516
Contact: Sr Angela Phelan
Community: 1

Sue Ryder Centre
Kilminchy, Portlaoise, Co Laois
Community: 1

Carlow Road, Abbeyleix, Co Laois
Tel 057-8731467
Community: 2
Contact: Sr Mary Hiney
Parish, Adult education

Brigidine Sisters,
Castletown Road, Mountrath, Co Laois
Tel 057-8732799
Contact: Sr Mary Sheedy
Community: 4
Parish and Pastoral Work

Solas Bhríde, 14 Dara Park, Kildare
Tel 045-522890 Fax 045-522212
Contact: Sr Rita Minehan
Community: 1
Education, spirituality centre

Solas Bhride Centre & Hermitages
Tully Road, Kildare Town, Co Kildare
Tel 045-522890
Contact: Sr Mary Minehan
Community: 2
Spirituality Centre

Brigidine Sisters, 22 Marble Court,
Paulstown, Co Kilkenny
Tel 059-9726156
Contact: Sr Margaret Walsh
Community: 2
Parish Ministry

CHARITY OF JESUS AND MARY, SISTERS OF
Ros Glas, Moore Abbey,
Monasterevan, Co Kildare
Tel 045-525478
Matron: Majella Keefe
Email maryannal@eircom.net
Community: 5
Assisted Living Community

Grove House Community, Moore Abbey,
Monasterevin, Co Kildare
Contact: Sr Philomena Enright
Tel 087-2480738
Email philomena194@hotmail.com
Community: 1

Suaimhneas, Cappakeel, Emo, Co Laois
Tel 057-8626541
Community: 3

CONGREGATION OF THE SISTERS OF MERCY
The Sisters of Mercy minister throughout the diocese in pastoral and social work, community development, counselling, spirituality, education and health care, answering current needs.

St Leo's Convent of Mercy,
Carlow R93 CX81
Tel 059-9131158 Fax 059-9142226
Community: 7

4 Pinewood Avenue,
Rathnapish, Carlow R93 X242
Tel 059-9140408
Community: 2

Convent of Mercy,
Monasterevin, Co Kildare W34 HH79
Tel/Fax 045-525372
Community: 2

St Helen's Convent of Mercy,
Naas, Co Kildare W91 H9TC
Tel 045-897673
Community: 4

Convent of Mercy,
Leighlinbridge, Co Carlow R93 CP80
Tel 059-9721350 Fax 059-9721350
Community: 3

4 Lacken View, Naas,
Co Kildare W91 R8AF
Tel 045-874168
Community: 1

37 Lakelands, Naas,
Co Kildare W91 XR9Y
Tel 045-875496
Community: 2

9 Spring Gardens, Naas,
Co Kildare W91 A5DF
Tel 045-876013
Community: 2

DAUGHTERS OF MARY AND JOSEPH
3/4 Sycamore Road, Connell Drive,
Newbridge, Co Kildare
Tel 045-431842
Community: 3
Pastoral

SISTERS OF THE HOLY FAMILY OF BORDEAUX
Holy Family Convent,
Droichead Nua, Co Kildare
Tel 045-431268
Contact: Sr Colette Keegan
Community: 23
Retired sisters, parish work, teaching English to non-nationals, counselling

'Sonas Chríost',
Moorfield Park, Droichead Nua,
Co Kildare
Tel 045-431939
Contact: Sr Eileen Murphy
Community: 3
Sisters involved in community, parish work, chaplaincy to secondary school

LA SAINTE UNION DES SACRES COEURS
Mountpleasant Lodge
Nursing Care Home,
Kilcock, Co Kildare
Community: 4

POOR CLARES
Poor Clare Colettine Monastery,
Graiguecullen, Carlow
Email poorclarescarlow@gmail.com
Abbess: Mother Rosario Byrne
Community: 10
Perpetual adoration, contemplatives

DIOCESE OF KILDARE AND LEIGHLIN

PRESENTATION SISTERS
Generalate, Monasterevin,
Co Kildare W34 PV32
Tel 045-525335/525503 Fax 045-525209
Email admin@pbvm.org
www.pbvm.org
Congregational Leader
Sr Julie Watson
Community: 6

Mount St Anne's
Retreat and Conference Centre,
Killenard, Portarlington, Co Laois
Tel 057-8626153 Fax 057-8626700
Director: Dr Oonagh O'Brien
Email ceo.mountstannes@gmail.com
Facilities available for seminars, retreats, conferences and meetings on request
Community: 2 (Intercongregational)
Tel 057 9647057

Presentation Convent, Ashbrook Gardens,
Mountrath Road, Portlaoise, Co Laois
Tel 057-8670877
School, counselling and pastoral
Community: 10
School and pastoral work

Apr 6, 53 Beechfield,
Portlaoise, Co Laois
Community: 1

56 Oakley Park,
Tullow Road, Carlow
Tel 059-9143103
Community: 2
School ministry and pastoral

Presentation Convent,
Bridge Street, Mountmellick,
Co Laois
Tel 057-8624129
Community: 12
Parish and pastoral ministry

Shalom, Kilcock, Co Kildare
Tel 01-6287018 Fax 01-6287316
Community: 19
Care of sick and elderly sisters

Cul na Cille, Kilcock, Co Kildare
and
No. 2 Dean's Court, Kilcock, Co Kildare
Tel 01-6284502
Community: 8

Presentation Sisters,
27 Abbeyfield, Kilcock,
and No. 1 Dean's Court, Kilcock,
Co Kildare
Tel 01-6284579
Community: 4
Spirituality, pastoral ministry

SISTERS OF ST JOHN OF GOD
49 Blundell Wood,
Edenderry, Co Offaly
Tel 046-9731582

EDUCATIONAL INSTITUTIONS

Carlow College (founded 1782)
College Street, Carlow
Tel 059-9153200 Fax 059-9140258
Email infocc@carlowcollege.ie
Website www.carlowcollege.ie
President
Rev Conn Ó Maoldhomhnaigh MA
Vice-President and Bursar
Rt Rev Mgr John McEvoy
Chaplain: Rev Liam Dunne, Deacon
Priests on Staff
Rev Dr Fergus Ó Fearghaill DSS
Rev Dr Dermot Ryan DD

Holy Family Secondary School
Newbridge, Co Kildare
Principal: Ms Sarah Allen
Chaplain: Sr Kate Cuskelly

St Mary's, Knockbeg College
Knockbeg, Carlow
Tel 059-9142127 Fax 059-9134437
Email info@knockbegcollege.ie
Headmaster: Mr Michael Carew
Chaplain: Fr John Dunphy
www.knockbegcollege.ie

St Mary's Secondary School
Edenderry
Principal: Emmett McDonnell
Chaplain: Fr P. J. McEvoy

St Paul's Secondary School
Monasterevin
Principal: Brian Bergin
Chaplain: Fr Liam Merrigan

CHARITABLE AND OTHER SOCIETIES

Community Services
St Catherine's
Community Services Centre,
St Joseph's Road, Carlow
Tel 059-9138700

DIOCESE OF KILLALA

PATRON OF THE DIOCESE
ST MUREDACH, 12 AUGUST

INCLUDES PORTIONS OF COUNTIES MAYO AND SLIGO

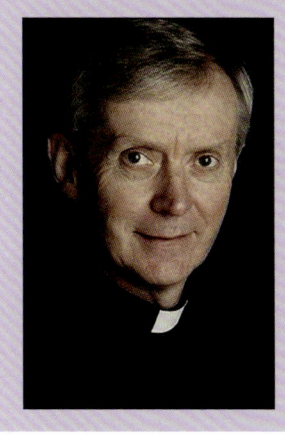

Most Rev John Fleming DD, DCL
Bishop of Killala;
born 16 February 1948;
ordained priest 18 June 1972;
ordained Bishop of Killala
7 April 2002

Residence: Bishop's House,
Ballina, Co Mayo
Tel 096-21518
Fax 096-70344
Email bishop@killaladiocese.org

ST MUREDACH'S CATHEDRAL, BALLINA

Built between 1827 and 1831, St Muredach's Cathedral is the fourth oldest Roman Catholic Cathedral in Ireland. It follows a building tradition begun by Waterford and Lismore in 1796 and followed by Dublin in 1825 and Dromore in 1829. While Bishop Peter Waldron (1814-1835) put forward the idea of building a cathedral, Bishop John McHale was the force which saw the Cathedral open its doors for the celebration of the Eucharist in 1831.

Ten years later the ornate ceiling, which is a distinguishing mark of the cathedral, was put in place. Work on the cathedral was suspended during the Famine and only resumed in 1853, when the construction of the Spire began. The entire work was completed in 1892.

Marcus Murray, the architect of the cathedral, gave the work of creating the very ornate ceiling to Arthur Canning. This work was interrupted by the Famine and only completed in 1855. In 2014 marks on the ceiling indicated some deterioration. Following examination, all the timbers supporting the entire ceiling were replaced and the ceiling itself repaired by George O'Malley. During 2015 and 2016 a major program of restoration has taken place and the work continues.

Photo: David Farrell, *The Western People*, Ballina

DIOCESE OF KILLALA

CHAPTER

Dean: Vacant
Chancellor
Rt Rev Mgr Seán Killeen PP, VG
Archdeacon: Vacant
Members
Very Rev John George Canon MacHale PP, VF

ADMINISTRATION

Vicar General
Rt Rev Mgr Seán Killeen VG
Cloghans, Ballina, Co Mayo

Vicars Forane
Very Rev Michael Reilly PP, VF
Very Rev Brian Conlon PP, VF
Very Rev Dr Aidan O'Boyle VF
Very Rev Gerard O'Hora PP, VF

College of Consultors
Most Rev John Fleming DD, DCL
Very Rev Michael Flynn PP
Very Rev Brian Conlon PP
Very Rev Michael O'Horo PP
Very Rev Edward Rogan AP
Very Rev Dr Michael Gilroy PP
Rev Liam Reilly CC

Finance Secretary
Very Rev Dr Michael Gilroy DD, PP
Skreen, Co Sligo
Tel 071-9166629

Diocesan Secretary
Mrs Anne Forbes
Bishop's House, Ballina, Co Mayo
Tel 096-21518 Fax 096-70344
Email secretary@killaladiocese.org

CATECHETICS EDUCATION

Diocesan Advisers for Religious Education
Primary: Sr Patricia Lynott
Post-Primary: Vacant
Newman Institute, Cathedral Close,
Ballina, Co Mayo
Tel 096-72066

Diocesan Education Council
Chairman: Mr John Cummins

LITURGY

Church Music
Director: Ms Regina Deacy
c/o The Pastoral Centre, Ballina, Co Mayo
Tel 096-70555

Diocesan Liturgy and Music Commission
Chairman: Very Rev Michael Flynn PP
Parochial House, Knockmore,
Ballina, Co Mayo
Tel 094-58108

PASTORAL

ACCORD
Director: Very Rev Gerard O'Hora
The Pastoral Centre, Ballina, Co Mayo
Tel 096-70555

Building Committee
Chairperson
Rt Rev Mgr Seán Killeen VG

Child Safeguarding Committee
Chairperson: Dr Mairín Glynn

Communications
Director: Very Rev Gerard O'Hora

Council of the Laity
Chairperson: Peter McLoughlin

Council of Priests
Chairperson: Very Rev Francis Judge PP
Parochial House, Mullenmore Road,
Crossmolina, Co Mayo
Tel 096-31677
Secretary: Very Rev Michael Reilly PP
Parochial House, Belmullet, Co Mayo
Tel 097-81426

Diocesan Finance Committee
Chairman
Most Rev John Fleming DD, DCL
Secretary: Ms Anne Forbes

Ecumenism
Director: Very Rev Anthony Gillespie PP
Dromore West, Co Sligo
Tel 096-47012

Emigrants
Advisor: Very Rev Michael Harrison PP
Killala, Co Mayo
Tel 096-32176

Immigrants
Diocesan Representative
Vacant

Legion of Mary
Director
Very Rev John Loftus, Co-Pastor
Tel 097-82350

Marriage Tribunal
(See Marriage Tribunals section)

Pilgrimages
Director: Rev Tom Doherty CC
Cathedral Presbytery, Ballina, Co Mayo
Tel 096-71365

Pioneer Total Abstinence Association
Diocesan Director
Very Rev Patrick Munnelly PP
Ardagh, Ballina, Co Mayo
Tel 096-31144

Pontifical Mission Societies
Diocesan Director: Vacant

Travellers
Chaplain: Very Rev Michael Reilly PP, VF
Belmullet, Co Mayo
Tel 097-81426

Trócaire
Secretary: Rev Michael Nallen
Aughoose, Ballina, Co Mayo
Tel 097-87990

Vocations
Director: Rev Tom Doherty CC
Cathedral Presbytery, Ballina, Co Mayo
Tel 096-71365

Youth Ministry
Co-ordinator: Rev Francis Judge

PARISHES

BALLINA (KILMOREMOY)
St Muredach's Cathedral, St Patrick's
Very Rev Dr Aidan O'Boyle PP
Cathedral Presbytery, Ballina, Co Mayo
Tel 096-71365
Rev Tom Doherty CC
Cathedral Presbytery, Ballina, Co Mayo
Tel 096-71355
Rev Billy Sheridan CC
St Patrick's Presbytery, Ballina, Co Mayo
Tel 096-71360

BACKS
Christ the King
Very Rev Michael Flynn PP
Knockmore, Ballina, Co Mayo
Tel 094-9258108
St Teresa's
Rev Des Smith (SMA)
Rathduff, Ballina, Co Mayo
Tel 096-21596

ARDAGH
Very Rev Patrick Munnelly PP
Ardagh, Ballina, Co Mayo
Tel 096-31144

BALLYCASTLE (KILBRIDE AND DOONFEENY)
St Bridget's, St Teresa's
Very Rev Brian Conlon PP, VF
Ballycastle, Co Mayo
Tel 096-43010

BALLYCROY
Holy Family
Very Rev Christopher Ginnelly PP
Parochial House, Ballycroy,
Westport, Co Mayo
Tel 098-49134

BALLYSOKEARY
Very Rev James Corcoran PP
Cooneal, Ballina, Co Mayo
Tel 096-32242

DIOCESE OF KILLALA

BELMULLET
Sacred Heart, Our Lady of Lourdes
Very Rev Michael Reilly PP, VF
Belmullet, Co Mayo
Tel 097-81426

CASTLECONNOR
St Joseph's
Very Rev Desmond Kelly PP
Corballa, Ballina, Co Mayo
Tel 096-36266

CROSSMOLINA
St Tiernan's, Holy Souls,
Our Lady of Mercy, St Mary's
Very Rev Francis Judge PP
Crossmolina, Co Mayo
Tel 096-31677
Rev Gabriel Rosbotham CC
Chapel Road, Crossmolina, Co Mayo
Tel 096-31344

DROMORE-WEST (KILMACSHALGAN)
Very Rev Anthony Gillespie PP
Dromore West, Co Sligo
Tel 096-47012

EASKEY
St James's
Very Rev Kieran Holmes PP
Easkey, Co Sligo
Tel 096-49011

KILCOMMON-ERRIS
Very Rev Michael Nallen PP
Aughoose, Ballina, Co Mayo
Tel 097-87990
Rev Joseph Hogan CC
Cornboy, Rossport, Ballina, Co Mayo
Tel 097-88939

KILFIAN
Sacred Heart
Very Rev Gerard O'Donnell PP
Kilfian, Killala, Co Mayo
Tel 096-32420

KILGLASS
Holy Family, Christ the King
Very Rev Gerard O'Hora PP
Enniscrone, Ballina, Co Mayo
Tel 096-36164
Very Rev Canon John George MacHale
(Priest in residence)
Kilglass, Enniscrone,
Ballina, Co Mayo
Tel 096-36191

KILLALA
St Patrick's
Very Rev Michael Harrison PP
Killala, Co Mayo
Tel 096-32176

KILMORE-ERRIS
St Joseph's, Holy Family, Seven Dolours
Rev John Loftus, Co-Pastor
Binghamstown,
Belmullet, Co Mayo
Tel 097-82350
Rev Kevin Hegarty, Co-Pastor
Carne, Belmullet, Co Mayo
Tel 097-81011

KILTANE
Sacred Heart
St Pius X
Very Rev James Cribbin, PP
Geesala, Bangor, Ballina, Co Mayo
Tel 097-86740

LACKEN
St Patrick's
Very Rev Michael Harrison PP
Carrowmore, Ballina, Co Mayo
Tel 096-34014

LAHARDANE (ADDERGOOLE)
St Patrick's
Very Rev John Reilly PP
Lahardane, Ballina, Co Mayo
Tel 096-51007

MOYGOWNAGH
St Cormac's
Very Rev Martin McGrath PP *(protem)*
Moygownagh,
Ballina, Co Mayo
Tel 096-31288

SKREEN AND DROMARD
St Adamnan's
Very Rev Dr Michael Gilroy DD, PP
Skreen, Co Sligo
Tel 071-9166629

TEMPLEBOY
Very Rev Dr Michael Gilroy DD, PP
Skreen, Co Sligo
Tel 071-9166629

INSTITUTIONS AND THEIR CHAPLAINS

An Coláiste
Rossport, Ballina, Co Mayo
Tel 097-88940

Convent of Mercy
Belmullet, Co Mayo
Tel 097-81044
Rev Kevin Hegarty

Convent of Jesus and Mary
Enniscrone, Ballina, Co Mayo
Tel 096-36151
Rev Gerard O'Hora

Convent of Jesus and Mary
Crossmolina, Co Mayo
Tel 096-30876/30877
Very Rev Francis Judge PP

Distrist Hospital
Ballina, Co Mayo
Tel 096-21166
Very Rev Dr Aidan O'Boyle

District Hospital
Belmullet, Co Mayo
Tel 097-81301
Very Rev John Loftus

St Mary's Secondary School
Ballina, Co Mayo
Tel 096-70333

Vocational School
Easkey, Co Sligo
Tel 096-49021
Very Rev Kieran Holmes

Vocational School
Ballina, Co Mayo
Tel 096-21472
Rev Tom Doherty

Vocational School
Crossmolina, Co Mayo
Tel 096-31236
Rev Gabriel Rosbotham CC

Vocational School
Belmullet, Co Mayo
Tel 097-81437
Rev Michael Nallen

Vocational School
Lacken Cross, Co Mayo
Tel 096-32177
Very Rev Michael Harrison

PRIESTS OF THE DIOCESE ELSEWHERE

Very Rev Martin Keveny
Paroquia Sao Sebastiao,
Caixa Postal 94, CEP 77760-000
Colinas Do Tocantins, Brazil
Tel 63-8311427
Rev Liam Reilly
On loan to Diocese of Reno, Nevada
Rev Edward Rogan
St On loan to Diocese of Chulucanas

RETIRED PRIESTS

Very Rev Michael Conway
Barr Trá, Enniscrone, Co Sligo
Very Rev Gerard Gillespie
Rathball, Ballina, Co Mayo
Very Rev Brendan Hoban
Sliabh Rua, Breaffy, Ballina, Co Mayo
Very Rev Patrick Hoban
St Jude's Avenue,
Crossmolina, Co Mayo
Rev John Judge
Killaser, Swinford, Co Mayo
Rt Rev Mgr Sean Killeen
Cloghans, Ballina, Co Mayo
Rt Rev Mgr Kevin Loftus
Enniscrone, Co Sligo
Very Rev Peter O'Brien
Ballina, Co Mayo
Very Rev Michael O'Horo
Templeboy, Co Sligo

Retired Priests (Other Dioceses)
Very Rev Joseph Cahill (SSC)
Bohernasup, Ballina, Co Mayo
Very Rev Leonard Taylor
Rathlee, Easkey, Co Sligo

RELIGIOUS ORDERS AND CONGREGATIONS

PRIESTS

SPIRITUAL LIFE INSTITUTE
Holy Hill Hermitage, Skreen, Co Sligo
Tel 071-66021
Superior: Sr Patricia McGowan
Community: 2

SISTERS

CONGREGATION OF THE SISTERS OF MERCY
Sisters of Mercy, 'Bethany',
8/9 Rockwell Estate, Killala Road,
Ballina, Co Mayo F26 H7D5
Tel 096-23066
Community: 6

Sisters of Mercy,
28 Moy Heights, Ballina,
Co Mayo F26 D8P6
Community: 1

35 Amana Estate,
Ballina, Co Mayo F26 H9N6
Community: 2

96 Knocknalyre, Sligo Road,
Ballina, Co Mayo F26 T6X9
Community: 1

JESUS AND MARY, CONGREGATION OF
Convent of Jesus and Mary,
Mullinmore Road,
Crossmolina, Co Mayo
Tel 096-30877
Contact person: Sr Anne Dyar
Headmistress: Tel 096-31194/096-31597
Community: 4
Post-Primary Coeducational Day School
Tel 096-31131
Principal: Mr John Mangan
Pupils: 520

'St Claudines',
Convent of Jesus and Mary,
Church Road, Enniscrone, Co Sligo
Tel 096-36151
Animator: Sr Mary Kelly
Community: 4
Post-Primary, Coeducational School
Tel 096-36496
Principal: Sr Mary Kelly
Pupils: 370

EDUCATIONAL INSTITUTIONS

St Muredach's College
Ballina, Co Mayo
Tel 096-21298
Principal: Mr Leo Golden
Chaplain: Rt Rev Mgr Sean Killeen

Newman Institute Ireland
Centre for Pastoral Care,
Cathedral Place, Ballina, Co Mayo
Tel 096-72066
Chancellor
Most Rev John Fleming, DD, DCL
Director: Very Rev Dr Michael Gilroy DD

CHARITABLE AND OTHER SOCIETIES

Society of St Vincent de Paul
Ozanam House, Teeling Street,
Ballina, Co Mayo
Tel 096-72905

St Joseph's Young Priests Society
c/o Pastoral Centre, Ballina, Co Mayo
Tel 096-70555

Legion of Mary
c/o Pastoral Centre, Ballina, Co Mayo
Tel 096-70555

ACCORD
CMAC Centre
c/o Pastoral Centre, Ballina, Co Mayo
Tel 096-70555

DIOCESE OF KILLALOE

Patron of the Diocese
St Flannan, 18 December

Includes portions of counties Clare, Laois, Limerick, Offaly and Tipperary

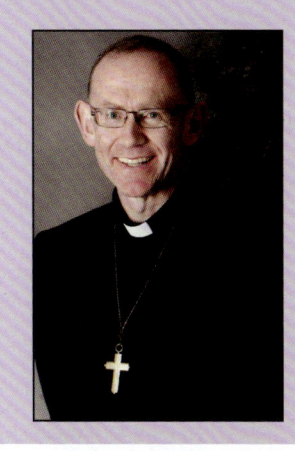

Most Rev Fintan Monahan DD
Bishop of Killaloe;
born 23 January 1967,
ordained priest 16 June 1991,
ordained Bishop of Killaloe
25 September 2016

Residence:
Westbourne, Ennis, Co Clare
Tel 065-6828638
Fax 065-6842538
Email office@killaloediocese.ie
Website www.killaloediocese.ie

CATHEDRAL OF SS PETER AND PAUL, ENNIS

The church that now serves as the cathedral of the Diocese of Killaloe was originally built to serve as the parish church of Ennis. The diocese had not had a permanent cathedral since the Reformation. In 1828, Francis Gore, a Protestant landowner, donated the site for the new Catholic church. Dominick Madden, who also designed the cathedrals in Ballina and Tuam, was chosen as the architect.

The construction of the new church was a protracted affair. Shortly after the work began, the project ran into financial difficulties and was suspended for three years. Aided by generous donations from local Protestants, including Sir Edward O'Brien of Dromoland and Vesey Fitzgerald, the work began again in 1831. Progress was slow throughout the 1830s and there were many problems. In September 1837 there was a serious accident on the site when the scaffolding collapsed, killing two and seriously injuring two more. Finally, in 1842, the roof was on and the parish priest, Dean O'Shaughnessy, was able to say the first Mass inside the still-unfinished building.

On 26 February 1843, the new church was blessed and placed under the patronage of Saints Peter and Paul, by Bishop Patrick Kennedy. Fr Matthew, 'The Apostle of Temperance', preached the sermon.

Much still remained to be done on the project, but the Great Famine brought the work to a halt. After the Famine, the work recommenced. J. J. McCarthy, one of the leading church architects in nineteenth-century Ireland, was commissioned to oversee the interior decoration of the building. Much of this is still visible, including the internal pillars and arches and the organ gallery.

A local committee decided in 1871 to complete the tower and spire, but owing to financial difficulties, it was not until 23 October 1874 that the final stone was put in place.

In 1889 Dr Thomas McRedmond was appointed coadjutor bishop and he was consecrated in 1890. He had full charge of the diocese, owing to the illness of Bishop Flannery. Though he was already Parish Priest of Killaloe, the new bishop chose to make Ennis his home, remaining there after he succeeded to the office of diocesan bishop, on the death of Dr Flannery. The Parish Church of Ss Peter and Paul was thus designated the pro-cathedral of the diocese.

Major renovations were carried out in 1894. The present main entrance under the tower was constructed, a task that necessitated breaking through a six-foot-thick wall. The building was also redecorated. The improvements were under the direction of Joshua Clarke, father of the stained-glass artist Harry Clarke. The large painting of the Ascension, which dominates the sanctuary, the work of the firm Nagle and Potts, was also installed at this time. The building remained largely unchanged for the next eighty years. A new sacristy and chapter room were added in the 1930s, as were the pipe organ and chapter stalls for the canons.

Another major renovation was carried out in 1973 to bring the building into line with the requirements of the Second Vatican Council. The architect for the work was Andrew Devane and the main contractors were Ryan Brothers, Ennis. The artistic adviser was Enda King. The building was reopened after six months in December 1973. The Clare Champion reported: 'The main features of the renovation included new altar, ambo, new tabernacle on granite pillar, baptismal font located near sanctuary, new flooring. New heating system, new amplification system and complete reconstruction of the sanctuary.'

In 1990, 163 years after work on the building began, Bishop Harty named it The Cathedral of the Diocese. The solemn dedication of the cathedral and the altar took place on 18 November 1990. A fire at a shrine in the cathedral in October 1995 caused serious internal damage. The sanctuary had to be rebuilt and the building redecorated. The restoration was celebrated with Solemn Evening Prayer in November 1996.

In 2006 major repair and refurbishment was completed on the Cathedral spire.

DIOCESE OF KILLALOE

Most Rev William Walsh DD
Retired Bishop of Killaloe;
born 1935; ordained priest 21 February 1959; ordained Bishop of Killaloe 2 October 1994
Residence: 'Camblin', College View, Clare Road, Ennis, Co Clare
Tel 065-6842540

CHAPTER

Dean: Vacant
Archdeacon: Vacant
Chancellor: Very Rev Brendan Canon O'Donoghue AP, Shannon
Precentor: Vacant
Treasurer: Vacant
Members
Very Rev Seamus Canon Mullin AP, Miltown Malbay

COLLEGE OF CONSULTORS

Rev Des Hillery VG
Rev Pat Malone
Rev Albert McDonnell, Chancellor
Rev Tom Ryan
Rev Ger Jones
Rev John Molloy

ADMINISTRATION

Killaloe Diocesan Office
Diocesan Chancellor
Rev Albert McDonnell
Email a.mcdonnell@killaloediocese.ie
Diocesan Secretary: Rev Ger Jones
Email g.jones@killaloediocese.ie
Diocesan Finance Manager
Ms Cathy Sheehan
Email c.sheehan@killaloediocese.ie
Diocesan Office Administrator
Ms Claire Thynne
Secretarial: Ms Mary Brohan
Westbourne, Ennis, Co Clare
Tel 065-6828638 Fax 065-6842538
Email office@killaloediocese.ie
Education Secretary: Rev Gerry Kenny
Westbourne, Ennis, Co Clare
Tel 085-7858344

Vicar General
Rev Des Hillery Co-PP, VG
Church Road, Nenagh, Co Tipperary

Safeguarding
Ms Cleo Yates
Westbourne, Ennis, Co Clare
Tel 086-8096027
Email c.yates@killaloediocese.ie

Finance Committee
Chairman: Mr Aidan Spooner
Recording Secretary: Ms Cathy Sheehan
Mr David Williams
Rev Gerard Kenny Co-PP, VF
Mr Owen Smyth
Mr Des Leahy
Rev Albert McDonnell Co-PP, VF
Bishop Fintan Monahan
Rev Des Hillery VG
Rev Ger Jones Co-PP

Killaloe Priests' Benevolent Fund
Secretary: Ms Cathy Sheehan
c/o Westbourne, Ennis, Co Clare
Tel 065-6828638 Fax 065-6842538

Killaloe Priests' Subsidy Fund
Secretary: Ms Cathy Sheehan
c/o Westbourne, Ennis, Co Clare
Tel 065-6828638 Fax 065-6842538

Killaloe Priests' Hospital Fund
Secretary: Ms Cathy Sheehan
c/o Westbourne, Ennis, Co Clare
Tel 065-6828638 Fax 065-6842538

Diocesan Archivist
c/o Diocesan Chancellor
Westbourne, Ennis, Co Clare
Tel 065-6828638 Fax 065-6842538

Diocesan Secretary
Rev Ger Jones
c/o Westbourne, Ennis, Co Clare
Tel 065-6828638

Episcopal Vicars for Retired Priests
Rev Tony Casey Co-PP, VF
Cooraclare, Co Clare
Tel 065-9059008
Rev Pat Larkin Co-PP, VF
Kilmaley, Co Clare
Tel 065-6839735
Rev Michael Cooney Co-PP
Terryglass, Co Tipperary
Tel 067-22017

CATECHETICS EDUCATION

Boards of Management
Primary Schools
St Senan's Education Office,
Diocesan Pastoral Centre,
St Munchin's College, Limerick
Tel 061-347777
Director: Fiona Shanley
Email sseo@ldo.ie
Acting Director: Alan Hynes

Religious Education in Primary Schools
Directors: Sr Essie Hayes
Ashe Road, Nenagh, Co Tipperary
Tel 067-33835
Mr Joe Searson
Mullagh, Co Clare
Tel 065-7087875/087-6762023

Religious Education in Post-Primary Schools
c/o Diocesan Office
Westbourne, Ennis, Co Clare
Tel 065-6828638

PASTORAL

Diocesan Pastoral Development
Pastoral Worker: Ms Maureen Kelly
Secretary: Ms Jean Gaynor
45 Garden View, Greggaun na Hilla,
Clarecastle, Co Clare
Tel 065-6847096

Biblical Ministry
Sr Marie McNamara
c/o Killaloe Diocesan Office,
Westbourne, Ennis, Co Clare
Tel 065-6842235

Diocesan Pastoral Council
Chair: Don O'Sullivan
Secretary: Jean Gaynor
45 Garden View, Creggaun na Hilla,
Clarecastle, Co Clare
Tel 065-6847096

ACCORD
Director: Rev Damien Nolan Co-PP, VF
Ennis ACCORD Centre,
7 Carmody Street Business Park,
Ennis, Co Clare
Tel 1850-585000
Director: Very Rev Willie Teehan
Nenagh Centre, Loretto House,
Kenyon Street, Nenagh, Co Tipperary
Tel 067-31272

Communications
Director
Rev Brendan Quinlivan Co-PP, VF
c/o Bishop's House, Westbourne,
Ennis, Co Clare
Tel 065-6828638

Child Protection Committee
Chairperson: Tracey Murray
Delegates:
Ms Cleo Yates, Director of Safeguarding
Tel 086-8096027
Mr Joe Searson
Tel 085-2535326

Ecumenism
Director: Dr Susan O'Brien
Westbourne, Ennis, Co Clare
Tel 065-6724721
Email se.obrien@me.com

Lourdes Pilgrimage
Director: Very Rev Tom Ryan Co-PP, VF
Cathedral House, Ennis, Co Clare
Te 065-6824043

Marriage Tribunal
(See Marriage Tribunals section)

Pastoral Care of Immigrants
c/o Bishop's House,
Westbourne, Ennis, Co Clare
Tel 065-6828638

Pioneer Total Abstinence Association
Diocesan Director: Vacant

DIOCESE OF KILLALOE

Polish Chaplain
Rev Dariusz Plasek Co-PP
Bodyke, Co Clare
Tel 087-7036053
Email dariuszplasek@ennisparish.com

Pontifical Mission Societies
Diocesan Director
Rev Tom O'Halloran Co-PP, VF
Borrisokane, Co Tipperary
Tel 067-27105

Social Services
North Tipperary Community Services
Kenyon Street,
Nenagh, Co Tipperary
Tel 067-31800
Clarecare
Harmony Row, Ennis, Co Clare
Tel 065-6828178

Travellers
Chaplain
c/o Bishops House, Westbourne,
Ennis, Co Clare
Tel 065-6828638

Vocations
Director: Rev Ignatius McCormack
St Flannan's College,
Ennis, Co Clare
Tel 065-6828019/086-2777139

PARISHES

The Diocese of Killaloe was divided into 15 Pastoral Areas in July 2018. Historical names are given in parentheses. Church titulars are in italics.

PASTORAL AREA 1 – COIS FHARRAIGE

PARISHES: CARRIGAHOLT, CROSS, DOONBEG & KILKEE
Our Lady of Lourdes, Cross; St John the Baptist, Kilbaha; Blessed Virgin Mary, Carrigaholt; The Holy Spirit, Doonaha; Lady Assumed into Heaven, Doonbeg; St Senan, Belaha; The Immaculate Conception and St Senan, Kilkee; St Flannan, Lisdeen

Co-PPs
Rev Gerard Kenny Co-PP, VF
1 Circular Road, Kilkee, Co Clare
Tel 065-9056580
Rev Michael Casey Co-PP
Parochial House, Cross,
Kilrush, Co Clare
Tel 065-9058008

Pastoral Offices
KILKEE: Parish Office, Circular Road,
Kilkee, Co Clare
Tel 065-9056580
Parish email office@kilkeeparish.com
Parish Website www.doonbeginfo.com
CROSS: Parish Office, Cross,
Kilrush, Co Clare
Tel 065-9058008
Parish email kilballyowen@eircom.net
Parish Website www.loopheadclare.com

PASTORAL AREA 2 – INIS CATHAIGH

PARISHES: COORACLARE, KILMIHIL, KILLIMER & KILRUSH
St Senan, Cooraclare; St Mary, Cree; St Michael, Kilmihil; St Senan, Knockerra; St Imy, Killimer; St Senan, Kilrush; Little Senan Church, Monmore

Co-PPs
Rev Anthony Casey Co-PP, VF
Kilmacduane, Cooraclare, Co Clare
Tel 065-9059008
Rev Pat Larkin Co-PP
47 Woodfield Crescent, Kilrush, Co Clare
Tel 065-9262729

Priest in Residence
Rev Peter O'Loughlin AP
Kilmihil, Co Clare
Tel 065-9050016

Pastoral Offices
KILRUSH: Toler Street, Kilrush, Co Clare
Tel 065-9051093
Parish email kilrushparishoffice@gmail.com
COORACLARE: Kilmacduane,
Cooraclare, Co Clare
Tel 065-9059008
Parish email cooraclareandcreeparish@gmail.com
KILMIHIL: Parish Office, Kilmihil, Co Clare
Tel 065-9050824
Parish email kilmihilparishoffice@gmail.com

PASTORAL AREA 3 – RADHARC NA NOILEÁN

PARISHES: BALLYNACALLY/LISSYCASEY, COOLMEEN, KILDYSART & KILMURRY MCMAHON
Our Lady of the Wayside, Lissycasey; Christ the King, Ballynacally; St Benedict, Coolmeen; St Mary, Cranny; St Michael, Kildysart; St Mary, Kilmurry McMahon; St Kieran, Labasheeda

Co-PPs
Rev Albert McDonnell Co-PP, VF
The Presbytery, Kings Road,
Kildysart, Co Clare
Tel 085-7811823
Rev Brendan Kyne Co-PP
The Presbytery, Ballycorick, Co Clare

Priests in Residence
Rev Joseph Hourigan
Parochial House, Lissycasey, Co Clare
Tel 065-6834145
Rev Tom McGrath (MHM)
Mountshannon, Labasheeda, Co Clare
Rev Paddy McMahon
The Presbytery, Labasheeda, Co Clare
Tel 065-6830932

Pastoral Office
RADHARC NA NOILEAN: Community
Centre, Kildysart, Co Clare V95 XKP3
Tel 065-6832838
Email radharcpastoralarea@gmail.com

PASTORAL AREA 4 – CRÍOCHA CALLAN

PARISHES: INAGH/KILNAMONA, KILMALEY, MILTOWN MALBAY & MULLAGH
St Mary, Mullagh; Our Lady, Star of the Sea, Quilty; The Most Holy Redeemer, Coore; St Joseph, Milltown Malbay; St Mary, Moy; Immaculate Conception, Inagh; The Blessed Virgin Mary, Cloonanaha; St Joseph, Kilnamona; St John the Baptist, Kilmaley; Our Lady of the Wayside, Inch; St Michael the Archangel, Connolly

Co-PPs
Rev John McGovern Co-PP
Parochial House, Kilmaley,
Ennis, Co Clare V95 ENK6
Tel 065-6839735
Rev Donagh O'Meara Co-PP, VF
Parochial House, Carhuligane,
Mullagh, Co Clare
Tel 065-7087012
Rev Martin Shanahan Co-PP
Parochial House, Inagh, Co Clare
Tel 087-7486935

Priests in Residence
Rev Seán Murphy AP
The Presbytery,
Miltown Malbay, Co Clare
Tel 065-7084129
Canon Seamus Mullin AP
The Presbytery,
Miltown Malbay, Co Clare
Tel 065-7084003
Rev Sean Sexton AP
Kilnamona, Ennis, Co Clare
Tel 065-6829507
Canon Michael McLaughlin
Airfield, Inch, Co Clare
Tel 065-6839332

Pastoral Offices
INAGH-KILNAMONA: Parish office,
Inagh, Ennis, Co Clare
Tel 085-2315709
Parish email parishofficeik@gmail.com
KILMALEY: Parish Office, Parochial
House, Kilmaley, Ennis, Co Clare
Tel 065-6839735
Parish email kilmaleyparish@gmail.com
MILLTOWN MALBAY: Parish Office, The
Presbytery, Miltown Malbay, Co Clare
Tel 065-7079829
Parish email malbayparish@eircom.net
MULLAGH: Parish Office, Carhuligane,
Mullagh, Co Clare
Tel 065-7087161
Parish email:office@kibparish.ie

DIOCESE OF KILLALOE

PASTORAL AREA 5 – ABBEY

PARISHES: ENNIS, CLARECASTLE, DOORA-BAREFIELD & QUIN
Cathedral of St Peter and Paul, Ennis; St Joseph's Lifford; Christ the King, Cloughleigh; St Breckan, Doora; The Immaculate Conception, Barefield; Church of Our Lady, Roslevan; St Mary's, Quin; St Stephen's, Maghera; St John XXIII, Clooney

Co-PPs
Rev Tom Ryan Co-PP, VF
Cathedral Presbytery, O'Connell Street, Ennis, Co Clare
Tel 065-6824043
Rev Ger Jones Co-PP
The Presbytery, 1 Shallee Drive, Cloughleigh, Ennis, Co Clare
Tel 065-6840715
Rev David Carroll Co-PP
St Joseph's Presbytery, 52 Kincora Park, Lifford, Ennis, Co Clare
Tel 065-6822166
Rev Tom O'Gorman Co-PP
The Presbytery, Quin, Co Clare
Tel 065-6824043
Rev Patrick Malone Co-PP
Parochial House, Church Drive, Clarecastle, Co Clare
Tel 065-6823011
Rev Tom Fitzpatrick Co-PP
3 The Woods, Cappahard, Tulla Road, Ennis, Co Clare
Tel 065-6822225

Curate
Rev Joy Njarakattuvely CC
Catherdral Presbytery,
O'Connell Street, Ennis, Co Clare
Tel 065-6824043

Priests in Residence
Rev Harry Brady AP
10 Beechwood, Lissane, Clarecastle, Co Clare
Tel 065-6797256
Rev Ignatius McCormack
St Flannan's College, Ennis

Pastoral Sisters
Sr Betty Curtin, Ennis
Tel 065-6868542

Pastoral Offices
CLARECASTLE: Parish Office, Church Drive, Clarecastle, Co Clare
Tel 065-6823011
Parish email
clarecastleballyea@eircom.net
Parish website
www.clarecastleballyeaparish.ie
DOORA-BAREFIELD: 3 The Woods, Cappahard, Tulla Road, Ennis, Co Clare
Tel 065-6822225
Parish email
doorabarefieldparish@eircom.net
ENNIS: Cathedral House, O'Connell Street, Ennis, Co Clare
Tel 065-6824043 Fax 065-6842541
Parish email info@ennisparish.com
Parish website www.ennisparish.com
QUIN: Parish Office, Parochial House, Quin, Co Clare
Tel 065-6825612
Parish email gcm@gmail.com
Parish website guimclooneymaghaca.ie

PASTORAL AREA 6 – TRADAREE

PARISHES: NEWMARKET-ON-FERGUS, SHANNON, SIXMILEBRIDGE
BVM of the Rosary, Newmarket on Fergus; Our Lady of the Wells, Clonmoney; St Conaire, Carrigerry; The Immaculate Mother of God, Shannon; SS John & Paul, Shannon; St Finaghta, Sixmilebridge; St Mary's Kilmurry

Co-PPs
Rev Arnold Rosney Co-PP, VF
SS John & Paul Presbytery, 4 Dún na Rí, Shannon, Co Clare
Tel 061-364133
Rev Michael Collins Co-PP
Parochial House, 19 Goodwood Estate, Newmarket-on-Fergus, Co Clare
Tel 061-700883

Curate
Rev Francis Xavier Kochuveettil CC
The Presbytery, 5 Drumgeely Avenue, Shannon, Co Clare
Tel 061-471513
Rev James Michael CC
The Presbytery, 5 Drumgeely Avenue, Shannon, Co Clare
Tel 061-471513

Priests in Residence
Rev Harry Bohan AP
172 Drumgeely Hill, Shannon, Co Clare
Canon Brendan O'Donoghue AP
12 Tullyglass Square, Shannon, Co Clare
Tel 061-361257

Pastoral Offices
NEWMARKET ON FERGUS: 19 Goodwood, Newmarket-on-Fergus, Co Clare
Tel 061-368127
Parish email
office@newmarketonfergusparish.ie
Parish website
www.newmarketonfergusparish.ie
SHANNON: Parish Office, 4 Dún na Rí, Shannon, Co Clare
Tel 061-363243 Fax 061-364516
Parish email office@shannonparish.ie
Parish website www.shannonparish.ie
SIXMILEBRIDGE: Parish Office, The Green, Sixmilebridge, Co Clare
Tel 061-713682
Parish email
office@sixmilebridgeparish.ie
Parish website
www.sixmilebridgeparish.ie

PASTORAL AREA 7 – CEANNTAR NA LOCHANNA

PARISHES: BROADFORD, O'CALLAGHAN'S MILLS, TULLA
St Peter, Broadford; St Mary, Kilbane; St Joseph, Kilmore; St Patrick, O'Callaghan's Mills; St Senan, Kilkishen; St Vincent de Paul, Oatfield; SS Peter & Paul, Tulla; The Immaculate Conception, Tulla; St James, Knockjames

Co-PPs
Rev Brendan Quinlivan Co-PP, VF
Parochial House, Newline, Tulla, Co Clare
Tel 065-6835117
Rev Donal Dwyer Co-PP
Parochial House,
O'Callaghan's Mills, Co Clare
Tel 065-6835148

Priest in Residence
Rev Brendan Lawlor AP
2 Powerscourt, Tulla, Co Clare
Tel 065-6835284

Pastoral Offices
BROADFORD: Parochial House, Gortnaglough, Broadford, Co Clare
Tel 061-473123
Parish email broadfordclare@gmail.com
O'CALLAGHAN'S MILLS: Parochial House, O'Callaghan's Mills, Co Clare
Tel 065-6835148
Parish email
ocallaghansmillskot@gmail.com
TULLA: Parish Office, Newline, Tulla, Co Clare
Tel 065-6835117

PASTORAL AREA 8 – IMEALL BOIRNE

PARISHES: COROFIN, CRUSHEEN, RUAN, TUBBER
St Brigid, Corofin; St Joseph, Kilnaboy; St Mary, Rath; St Cronan, Crusheen; The Immaculate Conception, Ballinruan; St Mary, Ruan; St Tola, Dysart; St Michael, Tubber; All Saints, Boston

Co-PPs
Rev Damien Nolan Co-PP, VF
1A Laghtagoona, Corofin, Co Clare
Tel 065-6837178

Priests in Residence
Rev Patrick O'Neill Co-PP
Ruan, Co Clare
Tel 065-6827799

Pastoral Offices
IMEALL BOIRNE PASTORAL OFFICE:
Parish Centre, Crusheen, Co Clare
Tel 065-6890865
Email imeallboirne@outlook.com

DIOCESE OF KILLALOE

CRUSHEEN (INCHICRONAN): Parish Centre, Crusheen, Co Clare
Parish email
inchicronanparish@gmail.com
COROFIN: Parish Office, 1A Laghtagoona, Corofin, Co Clare
Tel 065-6837178
Parish email corofinparish@yahoo.co.uk
RUAN/DYSART: Parish Office, Ruan, Co Clare
Tel 065-6827799
Parish email ruandysartparish@gmail.com

PASTORAL AREA 9 – INIS CEALTRA

PARISHES: BODYKE, FEAKLE, KILLANENA, MOUNTSHANNON, OGONNELLOE, SCARIFF
Our Lady, Assumed into Heaven, Bodyke; St Joseph, Tuamgraney; St Mary, Feakle; St Joseph, Kilclarin; St Mary, Killanena; St Mary, Flagmount; St Caimin, Mountshannon; St Flannan, Whitegate; St Molua, Ogonnelloe; St Mary, Ballybrohan; The Sacred Heart, Scariff; St Mary, Clonusker

Co-PPs
Rev Darius Plasek Co PP
Parochial House, Bodyke, Co Clare
Tel 061-921060
Rev Joe McMahon Co-PP, VF
Parochial House, Scariff, Co Clare
Tel 061-921051

Priests in Residence
Rev John Jones AP
St Caimin's, Mountshannon, Co Clare
Tel 061-927213
Rev James O'Brien AP
Parochial House, Feakle, Co Clare
Tel 061-924035
Rev Jackie Sharpe
Ogonnelloe, Co Clare
Tel 086-8940556

Pastoral Offices
BODYKE-TUAMGRANEY: Parochial House, Bodyke, Co Clare
Tel 061-921060
Parish email
bodykeparishnewsletter@gmail.com
Parish website
www.bodyketuamgraneyparish.ie
FEAKLE: Parochial House, Fossabeg, Scariff, Co Clare
Tel 061-921051
Parish email feakleparish@gmail.com
KILLANENA-FLAGMOUNT: Parochial Office, Fossabeg, Scariff, Co Clare
Tel 061-921051
Parish email killanenaparish@gmail.com
MOUNTSHANNON: St Caimin's, Mountshannon, Co Clare
Tel 061-927213
OGONNELLOE: Ballybrohan, Killaloe, Co Clare
Parish email newsletter@ogonnelloe.ie
Parish website www.ogonnelloeparish.ie
SCARIFF: Parochial House, Fossabeg, Scariff, Co Clare
Tel 061-921051
Parish email scariffparish@gmail.com

PASTORAL AREA 10 – SCÁTH NA SIONNAINE

PARISHES: CASTLECONNELL, CLONLARA, KILLALOE
St Joseph, Castleconnell; St Patrick, Ahane; St Senan, Clonlara; Mary, Mother of God, Truagh; St Flannan's Killaloe; St Thomas, Bridgetown; The Sacred Heart & St Lua, Garraunboy

Co-PPs
Rev William Teehan Co-PP, VF
The Spa, Castleconnell, Co Limerick
Tel 061-377170
Rev James Grace Co-PP
Parochial House, Killaloe, Co Clare
Tel 061-376137
Rev Pat Mulcahy Co-PP
Parochial House, 18 Churchfield, Clonlara, Co Clare
Tel 061-354334
Rev Tom Whelan Co-PP
The Spa, Castleconnell, Co Limerick
Tel 061-219482

Priests in Residence
Rev Jerry O'Brien AP
Bridgetown, Co Clare
Tel 061-376137

Pastoral Offices
CASTLECONNELL: Parochial House, Castleconnell, Co Limerick
Tel 061-377170
Parish email
castleconnellrcchurch@gmail.com
CLONLARA: Parish Office, Clonlara Community Sports Centre, Clonlara, Co Clare
Tel 061-354977
Parish email senanclon@gmail.com
KILLALOE: Parochial House, Killaloe, Co Clare
Tel 061-376137
Parish email killaloeparish@gmail.com

PASTORAL AREA 11 – ODHRAN

PARISHES: NENAGH, PORTROE, PUCKANE, SILVERMINES, TEMPLEDERRY, YOUGHALARRA
St Mary of the Rosary, Nenagh; St John the Baptist, Tyone; Blessed Virgin Mary, Portroe; Our Lady & St Patrick, Puckane; St Mary's, Carrig; Our Lady of Lourdes, Silvermines; Our Lady of the Wayside, Ballinclough; The Immaculate Conception, Templederry; Our Lady of the Wayside, Killeen; Our Lady of the Wayside, Curreeney; The Holy Spirit, Youghalarra; The Immaculate Conception, Ballywilliam

Co-PPs
Rev Des Hillery Co-PP, VG, VF
The Presbytery, Church Road, Nenagh, Co Tipperary
Tel 067-37130
Rev Michael Geraghty Co-PP
The Presbytery, Church Road, Nenagh, Co Tipperary
Tel 067-37134
Rev William McCormack Co-PP
Puckane, Nenagh, Co Tipperary
Tel 067-24105
Rev Rexon Chullickal Co-PP
The Presbytery, Church Road, Nenagh, Co Tipperary
Tel 067-37130

Priests in Residence
Rev Timothy O'Brien AP
Carrigatogher, Nenagh, Co Tipperary
Tel 067-31231
Rev Brendan Moloney AP
Silvermines, Nenagh, Co. Tipperary
Tel 067-25864

Pastoral Offices
NENAGH: Parish Office, Church Road, Nenagh, Co Tipperary
Tel 067-31272/37136
Parish email
parishoffice@nenaghparish.com
Parish website www.nenaghparish.ie
Nenagh Pastoral Centre
Church Road, Nenagh, Co Tipperary
Tel 067-37590
Email nenaghpastoralcentre@gmail.com
SILVERMINES: Silvermines, Nenagh, Co Tipperary
Tel 067-25864
Parish email
silverminesparish@gmail.com
TEMPLEDERRY: Parochial House, Templederry, Co Tipperary
Tel 0504-52988
Parish email
templederryparish@gmail.com
PORTROE: Teach a t'Sagairt, Portroe, Nenagh, Co Tipperary
Tel 067-23105
Parish email portroeparish@gmail.com
PUCKANE: Parochial House, Puckane, Nenagh, Co Tipperary
Tel 067-24105
YOUGHLARRA: Carrigatogher, Nenagh, Co Tipperary
Tel 067-31231
Parish email burgess.youghal@gmail.com

PASTORAL AREA 12 – OLLATRIM

PARISHES: CLOUGHJORDAN, DUNKERRIN, TOOMEVARA
St Michael & St John, Cloughjordan; St Flannan, Ardcroney; St Ruadhán, Kilruane; St Mary, Dunkerrin; St Joseph, Moneygall; Sacred Heart, Barna; St Joseph, Toomevara; St Joseph, Ballinree; St Joseph, Gortagarry; St Joseph, Grennanstown

Co-PPs
Rev Patrick Greed Co-PP, VF
Parochial House, Templemore Road, Cloughjordan, Co Tippeary
Tel 0505-42266
Rev John Molloy Co-PP
Parochial House, Toomevara, Co Tipperary
Tel 067-26023

Priests in Residence
Rev Joseph Kennedy AP
Parochial House, Moneygall, Birr, Co Offaly
Tel 0505-45110

DIOCESE OF KILLALOE

Pastoral Offices
CLOUGHJORDAN: Parish Office,
Templemore Road,
Cloughjordan, Co Tipperary
Tel 0505-42266
Parish email
cloughjordanrcparish@gmail.com
DUNKERRIN: Moneygall, Birr, Co Offaly
Tel 0505-45110
Parish email:dunkerrinparish@eircom.net
TOOMEVARA: Toomevara, Co Tipperary
Tel 067-26023
Parish email toomevaraparish@gmail.com

PASTORAL AREA 13 – COIS DEIRGE

PARISHES: BORRISOKANE, LORRHA, TERRYGLASS
SS Peter & Paul, Borrisokane; St Michael the Archangel, Aglish; St Ruadhan, Lorrha; Our Lady Queen of Ireland, Rathcabban; Holy Redeemer, Redwood; The Immaculate Conception, Terryglass; St Barron, Kilbarron

Co-PPs
Rev Tom O'Halloran Co-PP, VF
Parochial House,
Borrisokane, Co Tipperary
Tel 067-27105
Rev Michael Cooney Co-PP
Parochial House, Terryglass, Co Tipperary
Tel 067-22017

Priests in Residence
Rev Pat Deely AP
Lorrha, Co Tipperary
Tel 086-8330225

Pastoral Offices
BORRISOKANE: Parochial House,
Borrisokane, Co Tipperary
Tel 067-27105
Parish email
borrisokaneparish@gmail.com
LORRHA: Parochial House, Lorrha,
Nenagh, Co Tipperary
Parish email
lorrhaparishoffice@gmail.com
TERRYGLASS: Parochial House,
Terryglass, Co Tipperary
Tel 067-22017
Parish email terryglasskilbarron@gmail.com

PASTORAL AREA 14 – BRENDAN

PARISHES: BIRR, KILCOLMAN, KINNITTY, SHINRONE
St Brendan, Birr; Our Lady of the Annunciation, Carrig; St Colman, Kilcolman; St Ita, Coolderry; St John, Ballybritt; St Flannan, Kinnitty; St Luna, Cadamstown; St Finan Cam, Longford; St Molua, Roscomroe; St Mary, Shinrone; St Patrick, The Pike

Co-PPs
Rev Tom Hogan Co-PP, VF
The Presbytery, John's Mall,
Birr, Co Offaly
Tel 057-9121757

Rev Kieran Blake Co-PP
Kilcolman, Sharavogue, Birr, Co Offaly
Tel 057 9120812
Rev Michael O'Meara Co-PP
Kinnitty, Birr, Co Offaly
Tel 057-9137021

Priests in Residence
Rev Antony Puthiyaveettil CC
The Presbytery, John's Mall,
Birr, Co Offaly
Tel 057-9120098

Pastoral Offices
BIRR: Parish Office, St Brendan's Church,
Birr, Co Offaly
Tel 057-9122028
Parish email info@stbrendansbirr.ie
KILCOLMAN: Parish Office Kilcolman,
Sharavogue, Birr, Co Offaly
Tel 057-9120812 Fax 057-9120812
Parish email
kilcolmanparishoffaly@gmail.com
KINNITTY: Parochial House, Kinnitty,
Birr, Co Offaly
Tel 057-9137021

PASTORAL AREA 15 – CRONAN

PARISHES: BOURNEA, KYLE & KNOCK, ROSCREA
St Patrick, Bournea; St Brigid, Clonakenny; St Molua, Ballaghmore; St Patrick, Knock; St Cronan, Roscrea; St John the Baptist, Camblin

Co-PPs
Rev Michael Harding Co-PP, VF
Templemore Road,
Roscrea, Co Tipperary
Tel 0505-21218
Rev Patrick Treacy Co-PP
The Presbytery, Convent Hill,
Roscrea, Co Tipperary
Tel 0505-21370

Priests in Residence
Dr Thomas Corbett AP
Convent Hill, Roscrea, Co Tipperary
Tel 0505-21108
Rev Noel Kennedy AP
Bournea, Roscrea, Co Tipperary
Tel 0505-43211
Rev Lorcan Kenny (Chaplain)
Curates' Residence, Convent Hill,
Roscrea, Co Tipperary
Tel 0505-23637

Pastoral Offices
ROSCREA: Parish Office, Abbey Street,
Roscrea, Co Tipperary
Tel 0505-31835
Parish email rosrc@eircom.net
Parish website stcronanscluster.ie
BOURNEA: Parish email
bourneaparish@eircom.net
KYLE & KNOCK: Parish Office
Tel 0505-31835
Parish email rosrc@eircom.net

INSTITUTIONS AND THEIR CHAPLAINS

Carrigoran House
Newmarket-on-Fergus, Co Clare
Tel 061-368100
Priests of Tradaree Pastoral Area
Tel 061-700883

Community Hospital
Kilrush, Co Clare
Tel 065-9051966
Priests of Inis Cathaigh Pastoral Area
Tel 065-9051093

General Hospital, Ennis
Tel 065-6824464
Acute Psychiatric Unit
Tel 065-6863218
Priests of Abbey Pastoral Area
Tel 065-6824043

Cahercalla Community Hospital and Hospice
Cahercalla, Ennis, Co Clare
Tel 065-6824388
Priests of Abbey Pastoral Area
Tel 065-6824043

Community Nursing Unit, Birr
Co Offaly
Tel 057-9123200
Priests of Brendan Pastoral Area

County Hospital, Nenagh
Co Tipperary
Tel 067-31491
Priests of Odhran Pastoral Area
Tel 067-37130

District Hospital, Raheen
Tuamgraney, Co Clare
Tel 061-923007
Priests of Inis Cealtra Pastoral Area
Tel 061-921060

St Joseph's Hospital
Ennis, Co Clare
Tel 065-6840666
Priests of Abbey Pastoral Area
Tel 065-6824043

Welfare Home, Nenagh
Co Tipperary
Tel 067-31893
Priests of Odhran Pastoral Area

Welfare Home, Roscrea
Co Tipperary
Tel 0505-21389
Priests of Cronan Pastoral Area
Tel 0505-21108

Regina House
Kilrush, Co Clare
Tel 065-9051209
Priests of Inis Cathaigh Pastoral Area
Tel 065-9051209

Community School, Roscrea
Co Tipperary
Tel 0505-21454
Rev Lorcan Kenny
Tel 0505-23637

St Anne's Community College
Killaloe, Co Clare
Tel 061-376257
Veronica Molloy

DIOCESE OF KILLALOE

St Brendan's Community School
Birr, Co Offaly
Tel 0509-20510
Ms Kate Liffey
Tel 057-9120098

St Caimin's Community School
Shannon, Co Clare
Tel 061-364211
Cora Guinnane

Kilrush Community School
Tel 065-9051359
Mr Karol Torpey

St Joseph's Community College
Kilkee, Co Clare
Tel 065-9056138
Mrs Ann Healy

St Patrick's Comprehensive School
Shannon, Co Clare
Tel 061-361428
Nuala Murray

Kiladysart Community College
Co Clare
Tel 065-6832300
Joanne O'Brien

PRIESTS OF THE DIOCESE ELSEWHERE

Rev Martin Blake
c/o Diocesan Office
Rev Patrick Gilbert
c/o Diocesan Office
Rev Pascal Hanrahan HCF
(from 1 March) Head Chaplain,
Defence Forces Headquarters,
McKee Barracks, Blackhorse Avenue,
Dublin 7
Tel 01-8042637
Mgr Seamus Horgan
Apostolic Nunciature,
3339 Massachusetts Avenue,
Washington DC 20008-3610, USA
Archbishop Eugene M. Nugent
Apostolic Nunciature, Yarmouk Block 1,
Street 2, Villa NI, Kuwait City, Kuwait
Tel +965-25337767
Rev Martin O'Brien
1 Cuan an Chlair, Cahercalla,
Ennis, Co Clare
Tel 087-2504075

RETIRED PRIESTS

Rev John Bane
3 Cottage Gardens, Station Road,
Ennis, Co Clare
Tel 086-8246555

Rev Enda Burke
Cloughjordan, Co Tipperary
Tel 0505-42120
Rev Paschal Flannery
Ballinderry, Nenagh, Co Tipperary
Tel 067-22916/086-2225099
Rev Seamus Gardiner
Portroe, Co Tipperary
Tel 067-23101/086-8392741
Rev Brian Geoghegan
Carrigoran Nursing Home,
Newmarket on Fergus, Co Clare
Tel 087-2387067
Rev Tom Hannon
The Bungalow, Moynure,
Brosna, Birr, Co Offaly
Tel 086-8768116
Rev Leo Long
Cahercalla, Ennis, Co Clare
Tel 086-8353388
Rev Pat Sexton
5 Cottage Gardens, Station Road,
Ennis, Co Clare
Tel 065-6840828/087-2477814

RELIGIOUS ORDERS AND CONGREGATIONS

PRIESTS

CISTERCIANS
Mount Saint Joseph Abbey
Roscrea, Co Tipperary E53 D6S1
Tel 0505-25600 Fax 0505-25610
Email info@msjroscrea.ie
Website www.msjroscrea.ie
Superior ad nutum
Rev Dom Malachy Thompson (OCSO)
Prior: Rev Aodhán McDunphy (OCSO)

FRANCISCANS
Franciscan Friary, Ennis, Co Clare
Tel 065-6828751 Fax 065-6822008
Email friars.ennis@eircom.net
Guardian: Rev Brendan McGrath (OFM)

BROTHERS

CHRISTIAN BROTHERS
Christian Brothers' House,
New Road, Ennis, Co Clare
Tel 065-6821471/6828469 (office)
Community Leader: Br Dan V. Healy
Community: 5

Christian Brothers' House,
Nenagh, Co Tipperary
Tel 067-31557
Community Leader: Br Seamus C. Whelan
Community: 4

PRESENTATION BROTHERS
Presentation Brothers, Birr, Co Offaly
Tel 0509-20247
Contact: Br Walter Hurley (FPM)
Community: 4

SISTERS

BRIGIDINE SISTERS
Sue Ryder House, The Streame,
Limerick Road, Nenagh, Co Tipperary
Contact: Sr Mary Slattery
Community: 1

SISTERS OF CHARITY OF THE INCARNATE WORD
St Michael Convent, Carrigoran,
Newmarket-on-Fergus, Co Clare
Tel 061-368381
Contact person: Sr Marisa Revert Font
Email marisarevert@yahoo.com
Community: 3

CONGREGATION OF THE SISTERS OF MERCY
The Sisters of Mercy minister throughout the diocese in pastoral and social work, community development, counselling, spirituality, education and health care, answering current needs.

Mercy Sisters,
Garinis Clonroadmore,
Ennis, Co Clare V95 RF3A
Tel 065-6820768
Community: 2

St Xavier's, Ennis, Co Clare V95 P9KT
Tel 065-6828024 Fax 065-6828776
Community: 22

1 Corovorrin Crescent,
Ennis, Co Clare V95 N15P
Tel 065-6841375
Community: 4

7 Shallee Drive,
Cloughleigh, Ennis, Co Clare V95 F3CN
Tel 065-6828894 Fax 065-6828892
Community: 3

8 Greendale, Clonroad,
Ennis, Co Clare V95 R3KH
Tel 065-6840385
Community: 6

5 & 6 Rosanore, Gort Road,
Ennis, Co Clare V95 Y7DY
Tel 065-6821554
Community: 4

Milltown Road, Kilkee,
Co Clare V15 HD92
Tel 065-9056116
Community: 4

Convent of Mercy,
Kilkee Road, Kilrush, Co Clare V15 NC58
Tel 065-9051068
Community: 6

20 Sycamore Drive,
Kilrush, Co Clare V15 T218
Tel 065-9051957
Community: 2

Ashe Road, Nenagh,
Co Tipperary E45 X773
Tel 067-33835
Community: 7

DIOCESE OF KILLALOE

5 Dromin Court, Nenagh,
Co Tipperary E45 WV38
Tel/Fax 067-31591
Community: 2

Church Road, Tulla,
Co Clare V95 P1H3
Tel 065-6835118
Community: 3

2 Fergus Drive, Shannon,
Co Clare V14 F825
Tel 061-471637
Community: 4

St Mary's, Nenagh,
Co Tipperary E45 D283
Tel 067-31357 Fax 067-31151
Community: 14

33 Yewston Estate,
Nenagh, Co Tipperary E45 Y290
Tel 067-32830
Community: 4

St John's, Riverside, Birr,
Co Offaly R42 XP40
Tel 057-9120891
Community: 9

10/11 Ardlea Close,
Clare Road, Ennis, Co Clare V95 K2K0
Tel 065-6842399
Community: 4

DAUGHTERS OF CHARITY OF ST VINCENT DE PAUL
St Vincent's, Lisnagry, Co Limerick
Tel 061-501400
St Vincent's Special School, day and residential centre for people with intellectual disability, chaplaincy service

St Anne's Centre, Roscrea, Co Tipperary
Services for persons with intellectual disability, chaplaincy service
Tel 0505-22046

LA SAINTE UNION DES SACRES COEURS
LSU Sisters, 40 Cregaun,
Tobartaoscáin, Ennis, Co Clare
Community: 2
Education, pastoral, therapy

POOR CLARES
Poor Clare Monastery,
Francis Street, Ennis, Co Clare V95 VNP5
Email bernardinemeskell@live.ie
Abbess: Sr Bernardine Meskell
Community: 9
Contemplative

SISTERS OF ST JOHN OF GOD
Sisters of St John of God,
9 Cuan an Chlair, Ennis Co Clare
Tel 065-6843579

ST JOSEPH OF THE SACRED HEART SISTERS
57 Woodlands, Kilrush Road,
Ennis, Co Clare
Tel 065-6891178
Sr Betty Curtin

ST MARY MADELEINE POSTEL SISTERS
Mount Carmel Nursing Home,
Abbey Street, Roscrea, Co Tipperary
Tel 0505-21146
Apply Provider: Sr Marie Keegan
Community: 8

Ard Mhuire Convent, Parkmore,
New Line, Roscrea, Co Tipperary
Regional Superior: Sr M. Luke Minogue
Community: 6

EDUCATIONAL INSTITUTIONS

St Flannan's College (Diocesan College)
Ennis, Co Clare
Tel 065-6828019 Fax 065-6840644
Principal: Rev Ignatius McCormack
Tel 086-2777139

CHARITABLE AND OTHER SOCIETIES

Apostolic Work Society
Diocesan Headquarters at Maria
Assumpta Hall, Station Road, Ennis,
Co Clare

Birr Social Service Council
c/o 47 New Road, Birr, Co Offaly

Clarecare
Clarecare, Harmony Row,
Ennis, Co Clare
Tel 065-6828178

Clare Youth Service
Carmody Street, Ennis, Co Clare
Tel 065-6845350

Geriatric Centre
Carrigoran House,
Newmarket-on-Fergus, Co Clare
Tel 061-368100

Legion of Mary
Headquarters at Maria Assumpta Hall,
Station Road, Ennis, Co Clare

Mount Carmel Nursing home
Parkmore, Abbey Street, Roscrea,
Co Tipperary
Tel 0505-21146

North Tipperary Community Services
Loreto House, Kenyon Street,
Nenagh, Co Tipperary
Tel 067-31800

Roscrea Community Service Centre
Rosemary Street, Roscrea, Co Tipperary
Tel 0505-21498

Schools for children with Special Needs
St Vincent's, Woodstown House,
Lisnagry, Co Limerick
(Daughters of Charity)
Tel 061-501400

St Anne's, residential and day school,
Sean Ross Abbey, Roscrea, Co Tipperary
Tel 0505-21187

St Clare's, day school,
Gort Road, Ennis, Co Clare
Tel 065-6821899

St Anne's, day school,
Ennis, Co Clare
Tel 065-6829072

Society of St Vincent de Paul
Conferences at: Birr, Castleconnell,
Clarecastle, Cloughjordan, Ennis, Kilrush,
Kilkee, Nenagh, Newmarket-on-Fergus,
Roscrea, Scariff/Tuamgraney and
Shannon

DIOCESE OF KILMORE

PATRONS OF THE DIOCESE
ST PATRICK, 17 MARCH; ST FELIM, 9 AUGUST

INCLUDES ALMOST ALL OF COUNTY CAVAN,
AND A PORTION OF COUNTIES LEITRIM, FERMANAGH, MEATH AND SLIGO

Most Rev Martin Hayes DD
Bishop of Kilmore;
born 24 October 1959;
ordained priest 10 June 1989;
ordained Bishop of Kilmore
20 September 2020

Residence:
Bishop's House,
Cullies, Co Cavan
Tel 049-4331496
Email admin@kilmorediocese.ie
Website www.kilmorediocese.ie

CATHEDRAL OF ST PATRICK AND ST FELIM, CAVAN

The original cathedral of the diocese was situated about four miles south of Cavan in the present parish of Kilmore. Some time in the sixth century, St Felim had established a church there. Bishop Andrew MacBrady (1445–1455) rebuilt the ancient church of St Felim and received permission from Pope Nicholas V to raise it to the status of a cathedral. After the confiscation of the Cathedral of St Felim at Kilmore, the diocese had no cathedral for three hundred years. Bishop James Browne extended Cavan parish church and erected it into a cathedral in 1862. It was replaced by the new Cathedral of St Patrick and St Felim, built by Bishop Patrick Lyons in the years 1938–1942. The architects were W. H. Byrne & Son and the contractors John Sisk & Son. The cathedral cost £209,000 and was opened and dedicated in 1942. It was consecrated in 1947.

The cathedral is neo-classical in style with a single spire rising to 230 feet. The portico consists of a tympanum supported by four massive columns of Portland stone with Corinthian caps. The tympanum figures of Christ, St Patrick and St Felim were executed by a Dublin sculptor, George Smith. The twenty-eight columns in the cathedral, the pulpit on the south side and all the statues are of Pavinazetto marble and came from the firm of Dinelli Figli of Pietrasanta in Italy.

The fine work of George Collie can be seen in the Stations of the Cross and in the mural of the Risen Christ on the wall of the apse. Directly above the mural are twelve small windows, showing the heads of the twelve apostles. The High Altar is of green Connemara marble and pink Middleton marble, while the altar rails are of white Carrara marble. The apse has two side-chapels on the north and two on the south. The Blessed Sacrament is now reserved in the south chapel closest to the altar. The six splendid stained-glass windows in the nave and one in the south transept came from the studios of Harry Clarke.

DIOCESE OF KILMORE

Most Rev Leo O'Reilly DD
Retired Bishop of Kilmore
born 1944; ordained priest 15 June 1969;
ordained bishop 2 February 1997;
installed as Bishop of Kilmore 15
November 1998; retired 31 December
2018
Residence: 4 Carraig Beag,
Cootehill Road, Cavan

ADMINISTRATION

College of Consultors
Rt Rev Mgr Liam Kelly PP
Very Rev John Gilhooly PP
Very Rev Sean Mawn PP, VF
Very Rev John McTiernan PP, VF
Very Rev Kevin Fay Adm, VF
Very Rev Donal Kilduff PP
Very Rev Brian Flynn
Very Rev Andrew Tully
Very Rev Ultan McGoohan

Vicar General
Rt Rev Mgr Liam Kelly

Council of Priests
Chairman: Very Rev John Gilhooly
Secretary: Very Rev Donal Kilduff

Deanery Vicars
Very Rev John Gilhooly VF
Very Rev Sean Mawn PP, VF
Very Rev Ultan McGoohan PP, VF
Very Rev John McTiernan PP, VF

Diocesan Finance Officer
Ms Jennifer O'Reilly
Bishop's House, Cullies, Cavan
Tel 049-4331496
Email accounts@kilmorediocese.ie

Finance Committee
Bishop Martin Hayes
Rt Rev Mgr Liam Kelly PP
Very Rev Gerard Alwill PP
Mrs Joan Quinn
Ms Carmel Denning
Mr Paul Kelly
Ms Lauren Tierney
Secretary: Very Rev Donal Kilduff

Chancellor/Diocesan Secretary
Very Rev Donal Kilduff
Bishop's House, Cullies, Co Cavan
Tel 049-4331496 Fax 049-4361796
Email diocesansecretary@kilmorediocese.ie

Bishop's Secretary
Ms Ann-Marie Kilduff
Bishop's House, Cullies, Co Cavan
Tel 049-4331496
Email admin@kilmorediocese.ie

Diocesan Archivist
Rev Thomas McKiernan
Bishop's House, Cullies, Co Cavan
Tel 049-4331496
Email admin@kilmorediocese.ie

CATECHETICS EDUCATION

Catholic Primary School Managers' Association
Secretary: Kathy McGoldrick
Kilmore Diocesan Pastoral Centre,
Cullies, Cavan
Tel 049-4375004 (ext 4) Fax 049-4327497
Email edsec@kilmorediocese.ie

Diocesan Catechetical Advisers
Primary: Sr Anna Smith
Sisters of Mercy, 2 Dún na Bó,
Willowfield Road, Ballinamore,
Co Leitrim
Tel 071-9645973
Mr Terence Leddy
Drumsilla, Butlersbridge, Co Cavan
Second level: Mrs Patricia Sheridan
Kells Road, Bailieborough,
Co Cavan

LITURGY

Pastoral Team: Kilmore Diocesan Pastoral
Centre, Cullies, Cavan
Tel 049-4375004
Advisor: Vacant

Church Music
Director: Rev Thomas Hanley
The Presbytery, Farnham Street, Cavan
Tel 049-4375004

Art, Architecture and Buildings
Chairman: Vacant

PASTORAL

Kilmore Diocesan Pastoral Centre
Cullies, Cavan
Director: Mr Sean Coll
Tel 049-4375004 Ext 102 Fax 049-4327497
Email directorkdpc@kilmorediocese.ie

ACCORD
Kilmore Diocesan Pastoral Centre
Tel 049-4375004
Diocesan Director: Angela Flynn
Email cavanaccord@eircom.net

Apostolic Society
Diocesan President
Ms Suzanna Tinnenny
Quivvy, Belturbet, Co Cavan
Tel 049-9522928
Spiritual Director
Rev John McMahon
Carrigallen
Tel 049-4339610

Communications
Diocesan Director: Very Rev Donal Kilduff
Bishop's House, Cullies, Co Cavan
Tel 049-4331496
Email diocesansecretary@kilmorediocese.ie

Diocesan Pastoral Council
Chairperson: Mr Christy Dooley
c/o Pastoral Centre, Cavan

Ecumenism
Director: Rev Gerry Comiskey PP
Staghall, Belturbet, Co Cavan
Tel 049-9522140

Eucharistic Adoration
Chairperson: Rev John Cooney
Parochial House, Cootehill, Co Cavan
Tel 049-5552120

Knock Pilgrimage
Director: Very Rev Sean Maguire
Parochial House, Bawnboy
Tel 049-9523103

Legion of Mary
Spiritual Director: Rev Tom McKiernan

Lourdes Pilgrimage
Director: Very Rev Tom Mannion PP
Ballinglera, Carrick-on-Shannon,
Co Leitrim
Tel 071-9643014

Marriage Tribunal
Kilmore Office of Armagh Regional
Marriage Tribunal: Sr Kathleen Gormley
Kilmore Diocesan Pastoral Centre,
Cullies, Cavan
Tel 049-4375004
Email tribunal@kilmorediocese.ie

Safeguarding Children & Vulnerable Adults Diocesan Committee
Chairperson: Ms Rita Martin
Director: Sr Suzie Duffy
Kilmore Diocesan Pastoral Centre
Tel 049-4375004 Ext 105
Designated Persons
Sr Suzie Duffy, Mr Paul Cullen
Kilmore Diocesan Pastoral Centre
Tel 049-437500 4 Ext 105
Email safeguarding@kilmorediocese.ie

Pastoral Services
Director: Ms Martina Gilmartin
Kilmore Diocesan Pastoral Centre,
Cullies, Cavan
Tel 049-4375004 Ext 108
Email pastoralservices@kilmorediocese.ie

Permanent Diaconate
Director: Mgr Michael Cooke PE
15 Meadow Park, Dublin Road, Cavan
Tel 049-4365417

Pioneer Total Abstinence Association
Diocesan Director: Rev John Cusack CC
Ballinamore, Co Leitrim
Tel 071-9644050

Pontifical Mission Societies
Diocesan Director
Very Rev John McMahon PP
Parochial House, Carrigallen, Co Leitrim
Tel 049-4339610

DIOCESE OF KILMORE

St Joseph's Young Priests' Society
Diocesan President: Mr Pat Denning
Drumcave, Cavan
Tel 049-4331362

Travellers
Chaplain: Very Rev Sean McDermott PP, VF
Lacken, Ballinagh, Co Cavan
Tel 049-4337106

Immigrants
Diocesan Representive: Vacant

Vocations
Director: Very Rev Ultan McGoohan
St Anne's, Baileborough, Co Cavan

Youth Ministry
Director: Mr Francis Keaney
Kilmore Diocesan Pastoral Centre,
Cullies, Cavan
Tel 049-4375004 Ext 103
Email youthministry@kilmorediocese.ie

PARISHES

Mensal parishes are listed first. Other parishes follow alphabetically. Historical names are given in parentheses. Church titulars appear in italics

CAVAN (URNEY AND ANNAGELLIFF)
Cathedral of SS Patrick and Felim, Cavan
St Clare's, Cavan
St Brigid's, Killygarry
St Aidan's, Butlersbridge
Rev Kevin Fay Adm, VF
Rev Peter Okpetu CC
Rev Martin Gilcreest
Rev Thomas Small
The Presbytery, Cavan
Tel 049-4331404/4332269 Fax 049-4332000
Information line 049-4371787
Email cavan@kilmorediocese.ie
Rev Brian McElhinney CC
Butlersbridge, Co Cavan
Tel 049-4365266
Deacon Andrew Brady

BAILIEBORO (KILLANN)
St Anne's, Bailieboro; *St Anne's, Killann*
St Patrick's, Shercock
Very Rev Ultan McGoohan PP, VF
St Anne's, Bailieboro, Co Cavan
Tel 042-9665117
Email bailieboro@kilmorediocese.ie
Curate Vacant
Parochial House, Shercock, Co Cavan
Tel 042-9669127
Email shercock@kilmorediocese.ie

BALLAGHAMEEHAN
St Aidan's, Ballaghameehan
St Mary's, Rossinver
St Aidan's, Glenaniff
St Patrick's, Kiltyclogher
Very Rev John Sexton Adm
Parochial House, Rossinver, Co Leitrim
Tel 071-9854022
Email rossinver@kilmorediocese.ie

BALLINAGLERA
St Hugh's, Ballinaglera
St Columcill, Newbridge
Immaculate Conception, Doobally
Very Rev Tom Mannion PP
Ballinaglera, Carrick-on-Shannon,
Co Leitrim
Tel 071-9643014
Email ballinaglera@kilmorediocese.ie

BALLINAMORE/DRUMREILLY LOWER
St Patrick's Ballinamore,
St Mary's Aughnasheelin
St Bridgid's, Coraleehan
St Patrick's Aughawillan
Very Rev Sean Mawn PP, VF
Ballinamore, Co Leitrim
Tel 071-9644039
Email ballinamore@kilmorediocese.ie
Rev John Cusack CC
Ballinamore, Co Leitrim
Tel 071-9644050

BALLINTEMPLE
St Michael's, Potahee
St Mary's, Bruskey
St Patrick's, Aghaloora
Very Rev Sean McDermott PP, VF
Lacken, Ballinagh, Co Cavan
Tel 049-4337106
Email potahee@kilmorediocese.ie

BELTURBET (ANNAGH)
Immaculate Conception, Belturbet
St Patrick's, Drumalee
St Brigid's, Redhills
Very Rev John McTiernan PP, VF
Bridge Street, Belturbet, Co Cavan
Tel 049-9522109
Email belturbet2@kilmorediocese.ie
Rev Joseph Long CC
Curate's House, Fairgreen,
Belturbet, Co Cavan
Tel 049-9522151
Rev Jason Murphy *(priest in residence)*
Killoughter, Redhills, Co Cavan
Tel 047-55021

CARRIGALLEN
St Mary's, Carrigallen
St Mary's, Drumeela
St Mary's, Drumreilly
Very Rev John McMahon PP
Carrigallen, Co Leitrim, via Cavan
Tel 049-4339610
Email carrigallen@kilmorediocese.ie

CASTLERAHAN AND MUNTERCONNAUGHT
St Bartholomew's, Munterconnaught
St Mary's, Castlerahan
St Joseph's, Ballyjamesduff
Very Rev Kevin Donohoe PP, VF
Ballyjamesduff, Co Cavan
Tel 049-8544410
Email ballyjamesduff@kilmorediocese.ie
Rev Anthony Kildarathil CC
Knocktemple, Virginia, Co Cavan
Tel 049-8547435

CASTLETARA
St Mary's Ballyhaise,
St Patrick's, Castletara
Very Rev Gerard Cassidy PP
Ballyhaise, Co Cavan
Tel 049-4338121
Email ballyhaise@kilmorediocese.ie

CLOONCLARE AND KILLASNETT
St Clare's, Manorhamilton
Annunciation, Mullies
St Osnat's, Glencar
Very Rev John Gilhooly PP, VF
Manorhamilton, Co Leitrim
Tel 071-9855042
Email manorhamilton@kilmorediocese.ie
Curate vacant
Glencar, Manorhamilton, Co Leitrim
Tel 071-9855433
Email glencar@kilmorediocese.ie
Deacon Padraig Kelly

COOTEHILL (DRUMGOON)
St Michael's, Cootehill
St Mary's, Middle Chapel
St Patrick's, Maudabawn
Very Rev John Cooney PP, VF
Cootehill, Co Cavan
Tel 049-5552120
Email cootehill@kilmorediocese.ie
Rev Michael Gilsenan (SSCC) CC
Gallonreagh, Maudabawn,
Cootehill, Co Cavan

CORLOUGH/TEMPLEPORT
St Patrick's, Corlough,
St Patrick's, Kilnavart,
St Mogue's, Bawnboy
Very Rev Sean Maguire PP
Bawnboy, Co Cavan
Tel 049-9523103
Email bawnboy@kilmorediocese.ie

CROSSERLOUGH
St Patrick's, Kilnaleck
St Mary's, Crosserlough
St Joseph's, Drumkilly
Very Rev Peter McKiernan PP
Crosserlough, Co Cavan
Tel 049-4336122
Email crosserlough@kilmorediocese.ie
Rev Darragh Connolly *(priest in residence)*
Drumkilly, Co Cavan
Tel 049-4336120

DENN
St Matthew's, Crosskeys
St Matthew's, Drumavaddy
Very Rev Donal Kilduff PP
Crosskeys, Co Cavan
Tel 049-4336102
Email crosskeys@kilmorediocese.ie

DIOCESE OF KILMORE

DERRYLIN (KNOCKNINNY)
St Ninnidh's, Derrylin
St Mary's, Teemore
Very Rev Gerard Alwill PP
56 Main Street, Derrylin,
Co Fermanagh BT92 9PD
Tel 028-67748315
Email derrylin@kilmorediocese.ie

DRUMAHAIRE AND KILLARGUE
St Patrick's, Drumahaire
St Mary's, Newtownmanor
St Brigid's, Killargue
Very Rev Paul Casey PP
Drumahaire, Co Leitrim
Tel 071-9164143
Email drumahaire@kilmorediocese.ie

DRUMKEERIN (INISHMAGRATH)
St Brigid's, Drumkeerin
St Patrick's, Tarmon
St Brigid's, Creevalea
Very Rev Tom McManus PP, VF
Drumkeerin, Co Leitrim
Tel 071-9648025
Email drumkeerin@kilmorediocese.ie

DRUMLANE
St Mary's, Staghall
St Patrick's, Milltown
Very Rev Gerard Comiskey PP
Staghall, Belturbet,
Co Cavan
Tel 049-9522140
Email staghall@kilmorediocese.ie

GLENFARNE
St Michael's, Glenfarne
St Mary's, Brockagh
Very Rev Oliver Kelly Adm
West Barrs, Glenfarne,
Co Leitrim
Tel 071-9855134
Email glenfarne@kilmorediocese.ie

KILDALLAN AND TOMREGAN
Our Lady of Lourdes, Ballyconnell
St Dallan's, Kildallan
Very Rev Oliver O'Reilly PP, VF
Ballyconnell, Co Cavan
Tel 049-9526291
Email ballyconnell@kilmorediocese.ie

KILLESHANDRA
St Brigid's, Killeshandra
Sacred Heart, Arva
Immaculate Conception, Coronea
Very Rev Charles O'Gorman PP
Killeshandra, Co Cavan
Tel 049-4334179
Email killeshandra@kilmorediocese.ie
Rev Donald Hannon CC
Arva, Co Cavan
Tel 049-4335246
Email arva@kilmorediocese.ie

KILLINAGH AND GLANGEVLIN
St Patrick's, Killinagh
St Patrick's, Glangevlin
St Felim's, Gowlan
Very Rev Loughlain Carolan, Parish Administrator
Blacklion, Co Cavan
Tel 071-9853012
Email blacklion@kilmorediocese.ie

KILLINKERE
St Ultan's, Killinkere
St Mary's, Clanaphilip
Very Rev Eamonn Lynch PP
Killinkere, Virginia, Co Cavan
Tel 049-8547307
Email killinkere@kilmorediocese.ie

KILMAINHAMWOOD AND MOYBOLOGUE
Sacred Heart
St Patrick's
Very Rev Addison Okpeh PP
Kilmainhamwood, Kells, Co Meath
Tel 046-9052129
Email kilmainhamwood@kilmorediocese.ie

KILMORE
St Felim's, Ballinagh
St Patrick's, Drumcor
Very Rev Peter Casey PP
Ballinagh, Co Cavan
Tel 049-4337232
Email ballinagh@kilmorediocese.ie

KINAWLEY/KILLESHER
St Mary's, Swanlinbar
St Naile's, Kinawley
St Patick's, Killesher
St Lasir's, Wheathill
Very Rev Maurice McMorrow PP, VF
Kinawley, Enniskillen,
Co Fermanagh BT92 4FH
Tel 028-66348250
Email kinawley@kilmorediocese.ie

KILSHERDANY AND DRUNG
Immaculate Conception, Drung
St Patrick's, Corick
St Patrick's, Bunnoe
St Brigid's, Kill
Rt Rev Mgr Liam Kelly PP
Parochial House, Bunnoe,
Cootehill, Co Cavan
Tel 049-5553035
Email drung@kilmorediocese.ie
Rev Yusuf Bamai CC
Kill, Cootehill, Co Cavan
Tel 049-5553218
Email kill@kilmorediocese.ie

KINLOUGH AND GLENADE
St Aidan's, Kinlough
St Patrick's, Tullaghan
St Michael's, Glenade
St Brigid's, Ballintrillick
Very Rev John Phair PP
Kinlough, Co Leitrim
Tel 071-9841428
Email kinlough@kilmorediocese.ie

KNOCKBRIDE
St Brigid's, Tunnyduff
St Brigid's, East Knockbride
Very Rev Anthony Fagan PP
Knockbride, Bailieboro, Co Cavan
Tel 042-9660112
Email tunnyduff@kilmorediocese.ie

LARAGH
St Brigid's, Laragh
St Brigid's, Carrickallen
St Michael's, Clifferna
Very Rev Brian Flynn PP
Laragh, Stradone, Co Cavan
Tel 049-4330142
Email laragh@kilmorediocese.ie

LAVEY
St Dympna's, Upper Lavey
St Dympna's, Lower Lavey
Very Rev Andrew Tully PP
Lavey, Stradone, Co Cavan
Tel 049-4330125
Email lavey@kilmorediocese.ie

MULLAGH
St Kilian's, Mullagh
St Mary's, Cross
Very Rev Paul Prior PP
Mullagh, via Kells, Co Meath
Tel 046-42208
Email mullagh@kilmorediocese.ie

VIRGINIA (LURGAN)
Mary Immaculate, Virginia
St Patrick's, Lurgan
St Matthew's, Maghera
Very Rev Dermot Prior PP, VF
Virginia, Co Cavan
Tel 049-8547063
Email virginia@kilmorediocese.ie
Parish Office: 049-8548727

INSTITUTIONS AND THEIR CHAPLAINS

Bailieboro Community School
Chaplain: Ms Alison Holton
Tel 042-9665295

Ballinamore Community School
Ballinamore, Co Leitrim
Chaplain: Mr Micheál Kane
Email office@ballinamorecs.ie
Website www.ballinamorecs.ie

DIOCESE OF KILMORE

Breifne College
Cootehill Road, Cavan
Catechist: Rev Jason Murphy
Tel 049-4331735

Carrigallen Vocational School
Visiting Chaplain: Rev John McMahon PP
Tel 049-4339640

Cavan General Hospital
Tel 049-4361399
Rev Gerard Kearns
Rev Gabriel Kelly
Cavan General Hospital,
Lisdaran, Cavan

Cavan Institute
Cathedral Road, Cavan
Chaplaincy and Pastoral Care
Rev Gerard Kearns
Tel 049-4332334

Loreto College, Cavan
Tel 049-4331354
Visiting Chaplain: Rev Gabriel Kelly

Lough Allen College
Drumkeerin, Co Leitrim
Visiting Chaplain: Rev Tom McManus
Tel 071-9648025

Loughan House
Blacklion, Co Cavan
Visiting Chaplain: Rev Loughlain Carolan
General Office: 071-9853059

St Aidan's Comprehensive School
Cootehill, Co Cavan
Tel 049-5552161
Chaplain: Mr Gabriel McQuillan

St Aidan's High School
Derrylin, Co Fermanagh
Visiting Chaplain: Rev Gerard Alwill
Tel 028-67748337

St Bricin's Vocational School
Belturbet, Co Cavan
Tel 049-9522170

St Clare's College
Ballyjamesduff, Co Cavan
Visiting Chaplain: Rev Anthony Kidarathil
Tel 049-8547435

St Clare's Comprehensive School, Manorhamilton
Chaplain: Rev John Sexton
Tel 071-9855060

St Mogue's College
Bawnboy, Co Cavan
Visiting Chaplain: Rev Sean Maguire PP
Tel 049-9523112

St Patrick's College, Cavan
Chaplain: Rev Andrew Tully
Tel 049-4330125

Virginia College
Virginia, Co Cavan
Visiting Chaplain: Rev Dermot Prior
Tel 049-8547063

PRIESTS OF THE DIOCESE ELSEWHERE

Rev Enda Murphy
Rome

RETIRED PRIESTS

Rev Patrick Bannon
15 Lisdarn Heights, Cavan

Rev Philip Brady
Creighan, Cavan

Rev Owen Collins
22 River Crescent,
Virginia, Co Cavan

Rt Rev Mgr Michael Cooke
15 Meadow Park,
Dublin Road, Cavan

Rev Bernard Doyle
51 Drumnavanagh, Cavan

Very Rev Patrick Farrelly
Knocknagilla, New Inn,
Ballyjamesduff, Co Cavan

Rev Frank Kelleher
15 The Drumlins,
Virginia, Co Cavan

Very Rev Thomas Keogan
7 Quary Park, Mullaghmore, Co Sligo

Rev Patrick McHugh
Derrylester,
Enniskillen, Co Fermanagh
Tel 048-66349984

Rev Thomas McKiernan
Rosskeeragh, Belturbet, Co Cavan

Rev John Murphy
Bailieborough Road,
Virginia, Co Cavan

Very Rev Denis Murray
Parochial House,
Derrylin, Co Fermanagh

Rev Thomas Woods
Edenville, Kinlough, Co Leitrim

Rev Patrick V. Brady
Rev Eamonn Bredin
Rev Colm Hurley

RELIGIOUS ORDERS AND CONGREGATIONS

PRIESTS

NORBERTINE CANONS
Holy Trinity House
Lismacanican, Mountnugent, Co Cavan
Email kilnacrottabbeytrust@gmail.com
Prior: Rt Rev James J. Madden (OPraem)

SISTERS

CONGREGATION OF THE SISTERS OF MERCY
Church Street,
Belturbet, Co Cavan H14 Y300
Tel 049-9522110

No. 4 Oriel Lodge, Church Street,
Belturbet, Co Cavan H14 V188
Tel 049-9524657

16 Castlemanor,
Billis, Cavan, Co Cavan H12 RX25
Tel 049-4379267

No 2 Dún na Bó,
Willowfield Road, Ballinamore,
Co Leitrim N41 EH94
Tel 071-9645973
Community: 2

3 Drumalee, Co Cavan

55 Cavan Road, Cootehill, Co Cavan
Tel 049-5552904

No. 16 Dún na Bó, Willowfield Road,
Ballinamore, Co Leitrim N41 TY38
Tel 071-9644006
Community: 2

LORETO (IBVM)
Loreto Post-Primary School
Tel 049-4331354

MISSIONARY SISTERS OF THE HOLY ROSARY
Cavan Town
House 1
Tel 049-4332735
Superior: Sr Benen Mullen
Community: 7

House 2
Tel 049-4332733
Superior: Sr Kathleen O'Brien
Community 8

27 Cherrymount,
Keadue, Cavan Town
Tel 049-4372936
Pastoral, healthcare
Community: 2

SISTERS OF ST CLARE
St Clare's, Keadue Lane, Cavan
Tel 049-4331134
Primary School. Pupils: 550
Tel 049-4332671

EDUCATIONAL INSTITUTIONS

St Clare's College
Ballyjamesduff, Co Cavan
Tel 049-8544551
Fax 049-8544081
Principal: Ms Teresa Donnellan
Visiting Chaplain: Rev Anthony Kidarathil
Tel 049-8547435

Bailieborough Community School
Virginia Road, Bailieborough, Co Cavan
Tel 042-966295
Principal: Ms Martha Lievens
Chaplain: Ms Alison Holton
Email info@bailieborocs.ie
Website www.bailieborocs.ie

Ballinamore Community School
Ballinamore, Co Leitrim
Tel 071-9644049
Principal: Mr Diarmuid McCaffrey
Chaplain: Mr Micheál Kane
Email office@ballinamorecs.ie
Website www.ballinamorecs.ie

St Aidan's Comprehensive School
Cootehill, Co Cavan
Tel 049-5552161
Principal: Ms Mary Ann Smith
Chaplain: Mr Gabriel McQuillan
Email office@staidans.ie

St Aidan's High School
Derrylin,
Tel 048-67748337
Principal: Mr Pat McTeggart
Visiting Chaplain: Rev Gerard Alwill

St Clare's Comprehensive School
Manorhamilton, Co Leitrim
Tel 071-9855087
Principal: Mr John Irwin
Chaplain: Rev John Sexton
Email stclares@iol.ie
Website www.stclarescomprehensive.ie

St Patrick's College
Cullies, Co Cavan
Tel 049-4361888
Email stpats@kilmorediocese.ie
Website www.stpatscavan.com
Principal: Mr Christopher Rowley
Chaplain: Rev Andrew Tully

Partner With An Expert IT Company

IT should be responsive, adaptive and smart.
Now more than ever, you need a business that runs effeciently
and can adapt to today's challenges.
We can help with custom IT solutions designed to meet your needs.

Outsourcing and Managed IT Services
Expert support, consulting and implementation

Managed IT Security Services
Protect your data and your brand

Cloud
Increase business agility and improve productivity

ORACLE NETSUITE

ERP, CRM, eCommerce
Unify your business on one platform

📞 Shannon: (061) 708 820
📞 Dublin: (01) 531 3777

https://newtecservices.ie

NEWTEC
Thinking Ahead

EDITING, DESIGN, PRINTING

– we do it all!

- Booklets
- Brochures
- Fliers
- Leaflets
- Annual Reports
- Catalogues
- Prayer Cards
- Bookmarks
- Business Stationery

Find out how we can help you with your next project.

CONTACT
Colette Dower
colette.dower@veritas.ie
(01) 878 8177

✳ VERITAS

www.veritas.ie

NEED TO GET YOUR MESSAGE ACROSS?

We can Print it

PARISH NEWSLETTERS
OFFERING ENVELOPES
CHRISTMAS CARDS
CALENDARS
AND MORE...

CALL (01) 660 6618
FOR YOUR NEXT PRINTING PROJECT TO BE DELIVERED AT PACE.
FAST TURNAROUND, RELIABLE SERVICE COMPETITIVE PRICES,
ON TIME, EVERY TIME...

Paceprint Trading Limited

Shaws Lane, Bath Avenue, Sandymount, Dublin 4
p: (01) 660 6618   w: www.paceprint.ie   e: sales@paceprint.ie

VERITAS STORES

Dublin City Centre
7–8 Lower Abbey Street, Dublin 1
T: 01-878 8177 • E: sales@veritas.ie

Blanchardstown
Unit 309, Blanchardstown Centre, Dublin 15
T: 01-886 4030 • E: blanchardstownshop@veritas.ie

Cork
Carey's Lane, Cork
T: 021-425 1255 • E: corkshop@veritas.ie

Derry
20 Shipquay Street, Derry BT48 6DW
T: 028-7126 6888 • E: derryshop@veritas.ie

Letterkenny
13 Lower Main Street, Letterkenny, Co Donegal
T: 074-912 4814 • E: letterkennyshop@veritas.ie

Newry
The Mall, Newry, Co Down BT34 1AN
T: 028-3025 0321 • E: newryshop@veritas.ie

www.veritas.ie

VERITAS
For Books and Gifts with a Difference · www.veritas.ie

DIOCESE OF LIMERICK

PATRONS OF THE DIOCESE
ST MUNCHIN, 3 JANUARY; ST ITA, 15 JANUARY

INCLUDES THE GREATER PART OF COUNTY LIMERICK, PART OF COUNTY CLARE AND ONE TOWNLAND IN COUNTY KERRY

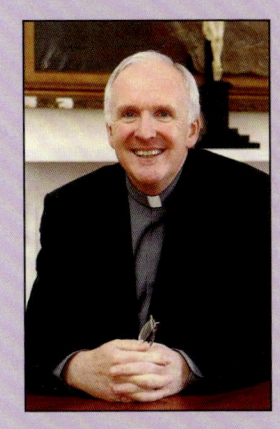

Most Rev Brendan Leahy DD
Bishop of Limerick;
born 28 March 1960;
ordained priest 5 June 1986;
ordained Bishop of Limerick
14 April 2013

Diocesan Office:
Limerick Diocesan Centre,
St Munchin's, Corbally, Limerick
Tel 061-350000
Email
bishop@limerickdiocese.org
Website
www.limerickdiocese.org

ST JOHN'S CATHEDRAL, LIMERICK

Since the twelfth century, a church dedicated to St John has stood in the area of Limerick city known as Garryowen. The earliest reference to the first church comes from the year 1205 when the Cathedral Chapter of the Diocese of Limerick was founded by Bishop Donatus O'Brien, Bishop of Limerick from 1195 to 1207. In the document of foundation, the revenues from the Church of St John were given to the Archdeacon of Limerick. This medieval church was replaced by a penal church, which in turn was supplanted by the parish church of St John in the middle of the eighteenth century. With an increase in population in the area around Garryowen, it was decided to build a new church to accommodate the estimated 15,000 parishioners of St John's. An appeal for funds was so well received that the decision was made to abandon the plans for a parish church and build a cathedral for the diocese instead.

Designed by Philip Charles Hardwick, a contemporary and associate of Pugin, St John's Cathedral is revival Gothic in the early English style. It was opened for worship in 1861 and consecrated in 1894 by Cardinal Logue. The spire, standing at 265 feet, 9 inches, was built between 1878 and 1883.

DIOCESE OF LIMERICK

Most Rev Donal Murray DD
Bishop Emeritus
born 29 May 1940; ordained priest 22 May 1966; ordained bishop 18 April 1982; installed as Bishop of Limerick 24 March 1996; retired December 2009

CHAPTER

Dean: Canon Anthony Mullins VG
Archdeacon
Rt Rev Mgr Michael Lane
Theologian: Canon Donough O'Malley
Penitentiary
Canon Gerard Garrett
Chancellor: Canon Frank Duhig
Precentor: Canon James Ambrose
Prebendaries and Canons
Ardcanny: Canon John Daly
Croagh: Canon Joseph Shire
Dysart: Canon John O'Shea
Tullybrackey: Canon Anthony O'Keeffe
Donoghmore
Rt Rev Mgr Daniel Neenan
Ballycahane
Canon William Fitzmaurice
Killeedy: Canon Donal McNamara

Honorary Canons (Pastores Emeriti)
Canon James Ambrose *(Precentor)*
Canon Gary Bluett
Canon Micheál Liston
Canon James Costello
Canon Patrick Kelly

COLLEGE OF CONSULTORS

Most Rev Brendan Leahy
Very Rev Anthony Canon Mullins VG
Very Rev Éamonn Fitzgibbon EV
Very Rev Timothy Curtin
Very Rev John Daly
Very Rev Gerard Garrett
Very Rev Joseph Hayes (SJ)
Rev Seán Harmon
Very Rev Michael Noonan
Rev Frank O'Connor
Rev Chris O'Donnell

ADMINISTRATION

Vicars General
Very Rev Anthony Canon Mullins VG
Very Rev Eamon Fitzgibbon VG

Episcopal Vicars
Episcopal Vicar for Pastoral Care of Priests
Very Rev Frank Canon Duhig VG

Episcopal Vicar for Pastoral Planning
Very Rev Éamonn Fitzgibbon VG

Vicar for Religious
Sr Phyllis Moynihan (RSM)

Episcopal Vicar for Evangelisation
Rev Chris O'Donnell EV

Vicar for Vocations
Sr Mara Rose McDonnell (OP)

Diocesan Chancellor
Very Rev Donough Canon O'Malley
Tel 086-2586908
Email donough@ldo.ie

Council of Priests
Most Rev Brendan Leahy
Very Rev Canon Anthony Mullins VG, ex officio
Very Rev Éamonn Fitzgibbon VG, ex officio
Rev Chris O'Donnell EV, ex officio
Rev Joe Hayes (SJ), religious congregation
Rev Krzysztof Tyburowski, bishop's nominee
Very Rev Canon O'Malley, retired priests representative
Rev Eugene Boyce, Curraghchase Area
Rev Frank O' Connor, Cathedral Area
Rev David Casey, Pobal Mocheallog Area
Canon John Daly, Maigue Area
Very Rev Michael Noonan, Our Lady's Area
Rev Gerard O'Leary, Thomond Area
Rev Tim Curtin, Tuath Phadraig Naofa
Rev Denis Mullane, Íde Naofa Area
Rev Seán Harmon, Pobal Neasain
Very Rev Canon Gerard Garrett, bishop's nominee

General Manager/Diocesan Secretary
Catherine Kelly
Limerick Diocesan Centre,
St Munchin's, Corbally, Limerick
Tel 061-350000
Email catherine.kelly@limerickdiocese.org
Website www.limerickdiocese.org
Finance Manager: Patricia Quirke
Secretarial Staff: Stephanie Cleary
Diocesan Spokesperson and Communications: Catherine Kelly
Finance Administrator: Karen Kiely

Diocesan Archivist
David Bracken
Limerick Diocesan Centre, St Munchin's, Corbally, Limerick
Tel 061-350000
Email david.bracken@limerickdiocese.org

DIOCESAN PASTORAL COUNCIL

Bishop Brendan Leahy
Very Rev Éamonn Fitzgibbon VG
Ms Rose O'Connor
Very Rev Mike Cussen
Ms Veronica Garvey
Very Rev Tony Mullins
Ms Siobhán Barrett
Very Rev Michael O'Shea
Mr Pat Condon
Sr Caitríona Kavanagh OP
Ms Ann Breen

CATECHETICS EDUCATION

Primary Level Religious Education
Veronica Behan
Email veronica.behan@limerickdiocese.org
Sr Rose Miriam Collins (OP)
Email srrosemiriam@limerickdiocese.org
Limerick Diocesan Centre,
St Munchin's, Corbally, Limerick
Tel 061-350000

Second Level Religious Education
Dermot Cowhey
Limerick Diocesan Centre,
St Munchin's, Corbally, Limerick
Tel 061-350000
Email dermot.cowhey@limerickdiocese.org

Primary Education Secretary
Acting Director: Alan Hynes
Email alan.hynes@limerickdiocese.org
Assistant Director: Ms Aoife Foley
Email aoife.foley@limerickdiocese.org
St Senan's Education Office,
Limerick Diocesan Centre,
St Munchin's, Corbally, Limerick
Tel 061-347777
Administration Staff
Linda Fleming Email linda@ldo.ie
Gwen O'Sullivan Email gwen@ldo.ie

LITURGY

Liturgy Advisory Committee
Chair: Rev Frank O'Connor
Very Rev Gerard Garrett, Paudie Hurley, Bernadette Kiely, Sarah Murphy, Josie Sweeney
Cathedral House,
Cathedral Place, Limerick
Tel 061-414624
Email oconfrank@eircom.net

PASTORAL

ACCORD
Limerick City Centre:
Social Service Centre,
Henry Street, Limerick
Contact: Ms Jacinta Tierney
Email accordlimerick@eircom.net
www.accord.ie
Spiritual Director: Rev Joseph Hayes (SJ)
Enquiries: Tel 061-343000 Fax 061-350000
Newcastle West Centre:
Parish Centre, Newcastle West,
Co Limerick
Contact: Helen Ahern
Tel 069-61000
Spiritual Director
Rev Frank Canon Duhig VF
St Ita's Presbytery,
Newcastle West, Co Limerick
Tel 069-62141/087-6380299

Apostleship of the Sea, Foynes
Director and Port Chaplain
Rev Anthony Canon O'Keeffe VF
Shanagolden, Co Limerick
Tel 069-60112

Charismatic Renewal Groups
Liaison Priest: Rev Damian Ryan
Manister, Co Limerick
Tel 061-397335/087-2274412

Neocatechumenal Way
Contacts: Rev Nikola Mladineo
Tel 083-4578388
Emanuele and Bernadetta Cuinaglia
Tel 086-2198186

DIOCESE OF LIMERICK

Ecumenism
Director: Rev Noel Hession (OSA)
St Augustine's, O'Connell Street, Limerick
Tel: 061-415374

Emigrant Apostolate
Director: Rev John McCarthy
Tel 085-8066468

Marriage Tribunal
Contact: Rev Richard Keane
Judicial Vicar of the Cork Regional
Marriage Tribunal
Tel 021-4963653

Military Chaplain
Rev Piotr Delimat
Sarsfield Barracks, Limerick
Tel 061-314233

Pioneer Total Abstinence Association
Spiritual Director: Rev Eamon Purcell

Pilgrimage
(Lourdes) Director
Rev Frank O'Dea
Tel 087-2443106
Email frankodea@eircom.net

Pontifical Mission Societies
Diocesan Director
Rev Derek Leonard
Tel 087-6261287

Safeguarding Children
*Director of Safeguarding and
Designated Person:* Ger Crowley
Email ger.crowley@limerickdiocese.org

Social Service Council
General Manager: Brian Ryan
Henry Street, Limerick
Tel 061-314111/314213

Travelling Community
Diocesan Chaplain: Rev Pat Hogan
Tel 087-6522746

Trócaire
Director: Rev Derek Leonard
St Mary's, Athlunkard Street, Limerick
Tel 087-6261287
Email derekleonard@eircom.net

Vocations
Sr Mara Rose McDonnell (OP)
Limerick Diocesan Centre, St Munchin's,
Corbally, Limerick
Tel 061-350000

Youth Apostolate
Contact: Ms Aoife Walsh
Limerick Diocesan Centre,
St Munchin's, Corbally, Limerick
Tel 061-350000/085-2527465

PARISHES

The Diocese of Limerick has been divided into 16 Pastoral Units. Church titulars are in italics.

PASTORAL UNIT 1

PARISHES: ST JOHN'S, MONALEEN, ST PATRICK'S, ST MICHAEL'S, OUR LADY HELP OF CHRISTIANS (associated parish)
*St John's Cathedral, St Mary Magdalene, St Patrick's, St Brigid's, St Michael's.
Associated Parish: Our Lady Help of Christians*

Co Parish Priests
Rev Noel Kirwan *(Moderator)*
Cathedral House,
Cathedral Place, Limerick
Tel 061-414624/087-2616843
Email nkirwan62@gmail.com
Rev Frank O'Connor
Cathedral House,
Cathedral Place, Limerick
Tel 061-414624/087-2642393
Email oconfrank@eircom.net
Rev Leo McDonnell
Cathedral House,
Cathedral Place, Limerick
Tel 061-414624/087-2200366
Email revleomcdonnell@yahoo.co.uk
Rev Gerard Garrett
1 Trinity Court, Monaleen Road,
Monaleen, Limerick
Tel 061-330974/086-3233268
Email gergarrett54@gmail.com
Rev David Gibson
St Patrick's Presbytery,
Dublin Road, Limerick
Tel 061-415397/087-2528738
Email brookhaven@eircom.net

Assistant Priest
Rev Krzysztof Tyburowski
134 Cosgrove Park, Moyross, Limerick
Tel 087-4110997
Email vincensleo@hotmail.com

Associated Parish: Our Lady Help of Christians
Rev Koenraad Van Gucht (SDB)
Salesian House, Milford,
Castletroy, Limerick
Tel 061-330268/086-3814353
Email koenraad@sdb.ie
Rev Robbie Swinburne (SDB)
Salesian House, Milford,
Castletroy, Limerick
Tel 061-330268
Email robei2iq@eircom.net

PASTORAL UNIT 2

PARISHES: ST JOSEPH'S, ST SAVIOUR'S, OUR LADY OF LOURDES
St Joseph's, St Saviour's, Our Lady of Lourdes

Co Parish Priests
Rev John Walsh *(Moderator)*
Mount David, North Circular Road, Limerick
Tel 087-4493228
Email frjohnwalsh1963@gmail.com

Rev Liam Enright
5 Lifford Avenue, Ballinacurra, Limerick
Tel 087-7415603
Sr Catríona Kavanagh (OP)
Administrator St Saviour's and team member of pastoral unit

Assistant Priests
Rev Deogratias Kisweka
Augustinian Priory, O'Connell Street, Limerick
Tel. 086-7248236
Rev Donough Canon O'Malley
19 School House Lane,
rear of Barrington Street, Limerick
Tel 086-2586908

PASTORAL UNIT 3

PARISHES: DONOUGHMORE/KNOCKEA/ROXBORO, OUR LADY QUEEN OF PEACE, HOLY FAMILY
St Patrick, Our Lady Queen of Peace, Holy Family

Co Parish Priests
Rev Tom Mangan *(Moderator)*
Donoghmore, Co Limerick
Tel 087-2348226
Email tjmangan86@gmail.com
Rev Daniel Tomasik
Elm View, Roxboro Road, Limerick
Tel 061-410846/087-6092086
Email dantomasik@gmail.com
Rev Joseph Hayes (SJ)
Della Strada, Dooradoyle, Co Limerick
Tel 061-480929/087-4647634
Email jhayessj@gmail.com

PASTORAL UNIT 4

SUB UNIT A – PARISHES: ST MUNCHIN'S/ST LELIA'S, CORPUS CHRISTI, PARTEEN/MEELICK
St Munchin's/St Lelia's, Corpus Christi, St Patrick's, St John the Baptist

Co Parish Priests
Rev Canon Donal McNamara *(Moderator)*
St Munchin's, Clancy Strand, Limerick
Tel 061-455635/087-2402518
Email donal.mcnamara@limerickdiocese.org
Rev Pat Hogan
Sruth Lan, South Circular Road, Limerick
Tel 087-6522746
Email pkfhogan@gmail.com
Rev Pat Seaver
4 Glenview Terrace, Farranshone, Limerick
Tel 061-328838/086-0870297
Email patseaver@gmail.com
Rev Eamonn Purcell
Parteen, Co Clare
Tel 087-7635617
Email eamon.purcell@hse.ie

Assistant Priest
Rev Oliver Plunkett
13 Castle Court, Clancy Strand, Limerick]
Tel 087-6593176
Email bohereenop@gmail.com

SUB UNIT B – PARISHES: ST NICHOLAS, ST MARY'S
St Nicholas, St Mary's

Co Parish Priests
Rev Derek Leonard *(Moderator)*
St Mary's, Athlunkard Street, Limerick
Tel 087-6261287
Email derekleonard0007@gmail.com
Rev John O'Byrne
St Mary's, Athlunkard Street, Limerick
Tel 085-7491268
Email johnbyrne.beda@yahoo.co.uk
Rev Gerard O'Leary
The Curate's House,
Athlunkard Street, Limerick
Tel 087-9378685
Email gerardoleary58@gmail.com

Assistant Priest
Rev Liam Enright
St Nicholas Presbytery, Westbury, Limerick
Tel 087-2546335

PASTORAL UNIT 5

PARISHES: CHRIST THE KING, CRATLOE/SIXMILEBRIDGE, OUR LADY OF THE ROSARY
Christ the King, St John's, Little Church, Our Lady of the Rosary

Co Parish Priests
Rev Richard Keane *(Moderator)*
Parochial House, Cratloe, Co Clare
Tel 087-9552729
Email richardkeane2002@yahoo.co.uk
Rev Patrick O'Sullivan
17 Alderwood Avenue,
Caherdavin, Limerick
Tel 087-2376032
Rev Des McAuliffe
'Sheen Lodge', Ennis Road, Limerick
Tel 061-324825/087-2336476
Email desmondmcauliffe@gmail.com

Assistant Priest
Rev Tom Ryan
Gleneden, North Circular Road,
Limerick
Tel 087-2997733

PASTORAL UNIT 6

PARISHES: PATRICKSWELL/BALLYBROWN, MUNGRET/RAHEEN/CRECORA, ST PAUL'S
Blessed Virgin Mary, St Joseph's, St Nessan's, St Oliver Plunkett, Ss Peter & Paul's, St Paul's

Co Parish Priests
Rev Michael Cussen *(Moderator)*
The Presbytery, Ballybrown, Co Limerick
Tel 061-353711/087-1279015
Email mikecussen@outlook.com
Rev Canon John O'Shea
St Nessan's Presbytery,
Raheen, Co Limerick
Tel 061-210869/087-9708282
Email frjohnoshea@gmail.com
Rev Richie Davern
Ballyduane, Clarina, Co Limerick
Tel 087-2977500
Email frrichie@hotmail.com
Rev Noel Murphy (CSSp)
14 Springfield, Dooradoyle, Limerick
Tel 061-304508/087-2228971

Assistant Priests
Rev Éamonn Fitzgibbon
The Presbytery, Patrickswell, Co Limerick
Tel 087-6921191
Email eamonn.fitzgibbon@limerickdiocese.org
Mgr Michael Lane
2 Meadowvale, Raheen, Limerick
Tel 087-2544450
Email michaellane@outlook.ie
Rev Robin Thomas
42 Nessan Court, Lower Church Road,
Raheen, Limerick
Tel 089-4333124
Email robinkooru@gmail.com
Rev Shoji Varghese
42 Nessan Court, Lower Church Road,
Raheen, Limerick
Tel 089-4431922
Email shojiputhenpurackal@gmail.com
Rev Seán Harmon
37 Gouldavoher, Dooradoyle, Limerick
Tel 087-9870284

PASTORAL UNIT 7

SUB UNIT A – PARISHES: MANISTER, FEDAMORE, BRUFF/MEANUS/GRANGE
St Michael's, St John the Baptist, Ss Peter & Paul's, St Mary's, Ss Patrick & Brigid

Co Parish Priests
Rev John Canon Daly *(Moderator)*
The Presbytery, Bruff, Co Limerick
Tel 061-32990/087-8180815
Email jgdaly2013@gmail.com
Rev Damian Ryan
Manister, Croom, Co Limerick
Tel 061-523954/087-2274412
Email 4dlord@eircom.net

Assistant Priests
Rev Michael Hanley
Parochial House, Fedamore, Co Limerick
Tel 086-8595733
Email hanleymichaelangelo@gmail.com
Rev James Canon Costello
Bruff, Co Limerick
Tel 061-382555

SUB UNIT B – PARISHES: CROOM, BANOGUE, DROMIN/ATHLACCA
St Mary's, Ss Peter & Paul's, Holy Trinity, St John the Baptist

Co Parish Priests
Rev William Canon Fitzmaurice *(Moderator)*
Croom, Co Limerick
Tel 061-397231/0862423728
Email croomchurch@eircom.net
Rev John McCarthy
Parochial House, Dromin,
Kilmallock, Co Limerick
Tel 085-8066468
Email johnipcboston@hotmail.com

PASTORAL UNIT 8

PARISHES: ROCKHILLL/BRUREE, BALLYAGRAN/COLMANSWELL
St Munchin's, Immaculate Conception, St Michael's, St Colman's

Co Parish Priests
Rev Joseph Canon Shire *(Moderator)*
Ballyagran, Kilmallock, Co Limerick
Tel 087-6924563
Email bentarsna@gmail.com
Rev Tim O'Connor CC
St Munchin's Church,
Rockhill, Co Limerick
Tel 087-7859028
Email timoconnor@rcdow.org.uk

PASTORAL UNIT 9

SUB UNIT A – PARISHES: BULGADEN/MARTINSTOWN, EFFIN/GARRIENDERK, KILMALLOCK
Our Lady of the Assumption (Bulgaden), Our Lady of the Assumption (Martinstown), Our Lady Queen of Peace, St Patrick's (Garrienderk), Ss Peter & Paul's, St Mary's

Co Parish Priests
Rev David Casey *(Moderator)*
Parochial House, Kilmallock, Co Limerick
Tel 087-2272791
Email daibhidhc@hotmail.com

Assistant Priests
Rev Chris O'Donnell
Jerpoint, Sheares Street,
Kilmallock, Co Limerick.
Tel. 087-6323309
Email chris.odonnell@limerickdiocese.org
Rev Tom Coughlan
Effin, Kilmallock, Co Limerick
Tel 063-71314/087-2229223
Email frtomcoughlan@hotmail.com
Rev Joseph Kennedy
'Suaimhneas' Glenfield Road, Kilmallock,
Co Limerick
Tel 087-9217622
Rev Anthony Bluett
Parochial House, Ardpatrick, Co Limerick
Tel 087-1848833
Email frtonybluett@gmail.com

SUB UNIT B – PARISHES: ARDPATRICK, GLENROE/BALLYORGAN, KILFINANE
St Patrick's (Ardpatrick), Our Lady of Ransom, St Joseph's, St Andrew

Co Parish Priests
Rev Michael O'Shea *(Moderator)*
Parochial House, Kilfinane, Co Limerick
Tel 087-9791432
Email mjtoshea@gmail.com

PASTORAL UNIT 10

PARISHES: RATHKEALE, BALLINGARRY/GRANAGH, KNOCKADERRY/CLONCAGH
St Mary's, Our Lady of the Immaculate Conception, St Joseph's, St Munchin's, St Mary's

DIOCESE OF LIMERICK

Co Parish Priests
Rev Thomas Carroll *(Moderator)*
Turrett Street, Ballingarry,
Co Limerick
Tel 087-2036229
Email carrollgtom@gmail.com
Rev Robert Coffey
35 Orchard Avenue, Rathkeale,
Co Limerick
Tel 087-6540908
Email coffeyrobert@gmail.com
Rev Ed Irwin
Cloncagh, Ballyhahill, Co Limerick
Tel 069-83972/087-2547707
Email edwinirwin48@gmail.com
Rev William Russell
Riddlestown, Rathkeale, Co Limerick
Tel 087-2272825
Email wfruss@gmail.com

PASTORAL UNIT 11

PARISHES: CROAGH/KILFINNY, ADARE, CAPPAGH
St John the Baptist, St Kieran, Holy Trinity, St James

Co Parish Priests
Rev Eugene Boyce *(Moderator)*
Croagh, Rathkeale, Co Limerick
Tel 069-64185/086-2542517
Email croaghkilfinny@eircom.net
Rev Mgr Daniel Neenan
Holy Trinity Abbey Church,
Adare, Co Limerick
Tel 061-396172/ 087-2208547
Email danneenan@outlook.com

Assistant Priests
Rev Joe Noonan
Adare, Co Limerick
Tel 087-2400700

PASTORAL UNIT 12

PARISHES: KILDIMO/PALLASKENRY, KILCORNAN, ASKEATON/BALLYSTEEN
St Joseph, St Mary, St John the Baptist, St Mary, St Patrick

Co Parish Priests
Rev John Donworth *(Moderator)*
Parochial House, Kildimo, Co Limerick
Tel 061-394134/087-2237501
Email johndonworth@hotmail.com
Rev Seán O'Longaigh
Askeaton, Co Limerick
Tel 061-392249
Email seanolongaigh@eircom.net

Assistant Priest
Rev Muiris O'Connor
Askeaton, Co Limerick
Tel 086-6075628
Email muiris.oconnor@limerickdiocese.org

PASTORAL UNIT 13

PARISHES: SHANAGOLDEN/FOYNES/ ROBERTSTOWN, LOUGHILL/ BALLYHAHILL, GLIN, COOLCAPPA/ KILCOLMAN
St Senan (Shanagolden), St Senan (Foynes), St Senan (Robertstown), Church of the Assumption, Ballyhahill, Immaculate Conception, St Kyran, St Colman

Co Parish Priests
Rev Tim Curtin *(Moderator)*
The Presbytery, Carrons,
Kilcolman, Co Limerick
Tel 069-60126 /086-3697735
Email frtcurtin@gmail.com
Rev Anthony Canon O'Keeffe
Shanagolden, Co Limerick
Tel 069-60112/087-4163401
Email ctokeeffe@eircom.net
Rev Austin McNamara
Parochial House, Ballyhahill,
Co Limerick
Tel 069-82103/087-2615471
Email austinmcnamara1896@yahoo.com

PASTORAL UNIT 14

PARISHES: ABBEYFEALE, ATHEA, TEMPLEGLANTINE, TOURNAFULLA/ MOUNTCOLLINS
Our Lady of the Assumption, St Bartholomew's, Most Holy Trinity, St Patrick's, Our Lady of the Assumption

Co Parish Priests
Rev Denis Mullane *(Moderator)*
The Presbytery, Templeglantine,
Co Limerick
Tel 069-84021/087-2621911
Email 3parishesttm@gmail.com
Very Rev Canon Anthony Mullins
The Presbytery, Abbeyfeale,
Co Limerick
Tel 068-31157
Email mullinstrev@gmail.com
Rev Brendan Duggan (CSSp)
Parochial House, Athea, Co Limerick
Tel 087-0562674
Email ebduggan@kimmagemanor.ie

Assistant Priest
Rev Daniel Lane
1 Cedarville, Abbeyfeale, Co Limerick
Tel 087-2533030
Email danfl44@outlook.com

PASTORAL UNIT 15

PARISHES: NEWCASTLEWEST, MAHOONAGH, MONAGEA, ARDAGH/ CARRICKERRY
Immaculate Conception of the Blessed Virgin Mary, St John the Baptist & St Nicholas, St Mary's, Church of Visitation of BVM, St Molua, St Mary's

Co Parish Priests
Rev Frank Canon Duhig *(Moderator)*
St Ita's Presbytery,
Newcastlewest, Co Limerick
Tel 069-62141/087-6380299
Email ncwparish@yahoo.co.uk
Rev John Mockler
Gortboy, Newcastlewest, Co Limerick
Tel 086-2342242
Email jmmockler@gmail.com
Rev Joseph Cussen, Lisieux, Gortboy,
Newcastlewest, Co Limerick
Tel 069-77090
Email cussenjos@gmail.com
Rev Michael Noonan
Parochial House, Ardagh, Co Limerick
Tel 069-76121/087-6796217
Email manoonan2@eircom.net

Assistant Priest
Rev Tom Crawford
Gortboy, Newcastlewest,
Co Limerick
Tel 087-2218078
Email frtdec@gmail.com

PASTORAL UNIT 16

PARISHES: DROMCOLLOGHER/ BROADFORD, KILEEDY/ASHFORD, FEENAGH/KILMEEDY
St Bartholomew, Our Lady of the Snows, St Ita (Kileedy), St Ita (Ashford), St Ita (Feenagh), St Ita (Kilmeedy)

Co Parish Priests
Rev Frank O'Dea *(Moderator)*
Parochial House, The Square,
Dromcollogher, Co Limerick
Tel 063-83718/087-2443106
Email frank.odea@limerickdiocese.org
Rev John Keating
Parochial House, Raheenagh,
Ballagh, Co Limerick
Tel 069-85014/087-6322212

SYRO MALABAR CHAPLAIN

Chaplain: Rev Robin Thomas
Email robinkooru@gmail.com
Tel 089-4333124

INSTITUTIONS, COLLEGES AND THEIR CHAPLAINS

Askeaton Community College
Coláiste Mhuire, Askeaton, Co Limerick
Diane Brown
Tel 061-392368

Castletroy Community College
Castletroy, Limerick
Tel 061-330785
Ms Brenda Cribben

Coláiste Iósaef
Kilmallock, Co Limerick
Theresa Mulcaire
Tel 063-98275

DIOCESE OF LIMERICK

Coláiste Na Trócaire
Rathkeale, Co Limerick
Olivia Giltenane
Tel 069-64094

Coláiste Ide & Iosef
Abbeyfeale, Co Limerick
Ms Noirín McCarthy
Tel 068-30631

Thomond Community College
Dooneen Road, Woodview Park, Limerick
Tel 061-452422
Suzanne O'Connor

Brothers of Charity Services
Bawnmore, Clonlong Road, Limerick
Rev Joseph Young
The House of Bernadette, Dooneen,
Crecora, Co Limerick
Tel 061-405835

Prison, Limerick
Mulgrave Street, Limerick
Prison General Office: Tel 061-415111
Christine Hoctor
Rev Michael Kelleher (CSsR)

Croom County Hospital
Croom, Co Limerick
Rev Garrett Canon Bluett
Tel 061-397335

St Camillus's Hospital
Shelbourne Road, Limerick
Clergy, St Munchin's Parish

St Ita's Hospital
Newcastle West, Co Limerick
Tel 069-62311
Rev Frank Canon Duhig
Tel 069-62141

St John's Hospital, Limerick
Pastoral Care Department
Tel 061-462111
Clergy, St John's Parish
Tel 061-414624

Sarsfield Barracks, Limerick
Rev Piotr Delimat
Tel 061-314233

University Maternity Hospital
Ennis Road, Limerick
Parish clergy, Our Lady of the Rosary
087-2997733

University Hospital
Dooradoyle, Limerick
Tel 061-301111
Chaplains: Rev Shoji Varghese
42 Nessan Court, Lower Church Road,
Raheen, Limerick
Tel 089-4431922
Rev Seán Harmon
37 Gouldavoher Estate,
Dooradoyle, Limerick
Tel 087-9870284

University of Limerick
Chaplains: Rev John Campion (SDB)
Salesian House, Milford,
Castletroy, Limerick
Tel 061-330268/202180
Email johncampion@ul.ie
Sr Sarah O'Rourke (FMA)

PRIESTS OF THE DIOCESE ELSEWHERE

Rev David Costello
c/o The Missionary Society of St James
the Apostle, 24 Clark Street,
Boston, MA 02109, USA
Email perudavid@gmail.com
Rev Paul Finnerty, Rector
Pontificio Collegio Irlandese,
Via dei Santi Quattro 1,
00184 Roma, Italy
Tel +39-06-772631
Email paulfinnerty@irishcollege.org
Rev. Seamus Madigan, HCF
Office of the Head Chaplain, McKee
Barracks, Blackhorse Avenue, Dublin 7.
Tel (H) 01-8042637 (O) 01-8042638
Email seamusmadigan@hotmail.com

RETIRED PRIESTS

Very Rev James Canon Ambrose
Very Rev Garrett Canon Bluett
Very Rev Patrick Bluett
Very Rev Patrick Bowen
Rev Jeremiah Brouder
Rev James Costello
Rev Maurice Costello
Rev Patrick Costelloe
Very Rev Thomas Coughlan
Rev Sean Condon
Very Rev Tom Crawford
Very Rev John Duggan
Very Rev Liam Enright
Very Rev Patrick Howard
Very Rev Thomas Hurley
Very Rev Patrick Canon Kelly
Very Rev David Kennedy
Very Rev Joseph Kennedy
Very Rev Daniel Lane
Venerable Archdeacon Michael Lane
Very Rev John Leonard
Very Rev Micheál Canon Liston
Very Rev Laurence Madden
Very Rev Martin Madigan
Very Rev Anthony Mulvihill
Very Rev Frank Moriarty
Most Rev Donal Murray, Bishop Emeritus
Very Rev Joseph Noonan
Rev Terence O'Connell
Very Rev Timothy O'Leary
Very Donough Canon O'Malley
Rev Charles O'Neill
Very Rev Oliver Plunkett
Very Rev Seamus Power
Very Rev Tom A. Ryan
Rev Willie Walsh

PERSONAL PRELATURE

OPUS DEI
Rev Brian McCarthy
Castleville Study Centre, Golf Links Road,
Castletroy, Limerick V94 YC95
Tel 061-331223 Fax 061-331204
Email castleville@eircom.net

RELIGIOUS ORDERS AND CONGREGATIONS

PRIESTS

AUGUSTINIANS
St Augustine's Priory,
O'Connell Street, Limerick
Tel 061-415374
Prior: Rev Noel Hession (OSA)
Bursar: Rev Flor O'Callaghan (OSA)

FRANCISCAN FRIARS OF THE RENEWAL (CFR)
St Patrick Friary, 64 Delmege Park,
Moyross, Limerick V94 859Y
Tel 061-458071 Fax 061-457626
Email limerickfranciscans@gmail.com
Local Servant (Superior)
Rev Joseph Mary Deane

INSTITUTE OF CHRIST THE KING SOVEREIGN PRIEST
Sacred Heart Church, The Crescent,
Limerick V94 HK29
Tel 061-315812
Email limerick@icrsp.org
Prior: Canon Lebocq
1st Vicar: Canon Arrasate
2nd Vicar: Canon O'Connor

JESUITS
Crescent College Comprehensive SJ,
Dooradoyle, Limerick
Tel 061-229655 Fax 061-229013
Email dooradoyle@jesuit.ie
Superior: Rev Joseph Hayes (SJ)
Principal: Ms Karin Fleming

REDEMPTORISTS
Mount St Alphonsus Mission House,
South Circular Road, Limerick
Tel 061-315099 Fax 061-315303
Superior: Rev Seamus Enright (CSsR)

St Clement's College, Laurel Hill Avenue,
South Circular Road, Limerick
Tel 061-315878 Fax 061-316640
Email cssrlimerick@eircom.net
Secondary school for boys
Principal: Mr Pat Talty

SALESIANS
Salesian College, Don Bosco Road,
Pallaskenry,
Co Limerick, V94 WP86
Tel 061-393105 Fax 061-393298
Rector: Rev John Horan (SDB)
Email salesian@indigo.ie
Secondary and agricultural schools

Salesian House, Milford,
Castletroy, Limerick, V94 DK44
Tel 061-330268/330194
Rector: Very Rev John Campion (SDB)
Vice-Rector: Vacant
Parish Priest
Very Rev Koenraad Van Guch (SDB) PP
Student hostel and parish

DIOCESE OF LIMERICK

BROTHERS

BROTHERS OF CHARITY
Bawnmore, Clonlong Road, Limerick
Tel 061-412288 Fax 061-412389
Residential & Day Care for persons with learning disabilities
Chaplain: Rev Joe Young

CHRISTIAN BROTHERS
Christian Brothers, St Teresa's,
North Circular Road, Limerick
Tel 061-451811
Community Leader: Br Senan Ryan
Community: 5

SISTERS

SISTERS OF BON SECOURS DE TROYES
St Paul's Nursing Home, Dooradoyle, Limerick
Tel 061-304690
Email bonsecours792@gmail.com
Contact: Sr Margaret Costello
Community: 2

CHARITY OF ST PAUL THE APOSTLE SISTERS
St Paul's Convent,
Kilfinane, Co Limerick
Tel 063-91025 Fax 063-91639
Email stpaulsfin@gmail.com
Contact: Sr Eileen Kelly
Community: 2
Education and parish work

St Paul's, Glenfield Road,
Kilmallock, Co Limerick
Tel 063-98086
Email sisterskilm@eircom.net
Contact: Sr Mary Hannigan
Community: 2
Parish work

CONGREGATION OF THE SISTERS OF MERCY
The Sisters of Mercy minister throughout the diocese in pastoral and social work, community development, counselling, spirituality, education and health care, answering current needs.

Convent of Mercy, Westbourne,
Ashbourne Avenue, Limerick V94 A5NA
Tel 061-229388/229605
Community: 6

Mount St Vincent,
O'Connell Avenue, Limerick V94 K6EH
Tel 061-314965 Fax 061-404175
Community: 13

Sisters of Mercy, St Mary's Convent,
Bishop Street, Limerick V94 CT9X
Tel 061-317356 Fax 061-317361
Community: 8

16 Portland Estate,
St Clare's, Newcastlewest,
Co Limerick V42 V302
Tel 069-62373
Community: 2

33 Danesfort, Corbally,
Limerick V94 YE2X
Tel 061-341214
Community: 1

34 Danesfort, Corbally,
Limerick V94 H66E
Tel 061-349131
Community: 2

7 Fitzhaven Square,
Ashbourne Avenue,
Limerick V94 H2HW
Tel 061-304614
Community: 2

1 Greenfields, Rosbrien,
Limerick V94 X7WE
Tel 061-229773
Community: 3

Catherine McAuley House Nursing Home,
Old Dominic Street, Limerick V94 DX58
Tel 061-315313/315384 Fax 061-315455
Community: numbers vary

136 Fortview Drive,
Ballinacurra Gardens, Limerick V94 HHN4
Tel 061-304798
Community: 2

1 Mount Vincent Place,
O'Connell Avenue, Limerick V94 KN29
Tel 061-468448
Community: 2

22 Galtee Drive,
O'Malley Park, Southill,
Limerick V94 N5TF
Tel 061-416706
Community: 2

Sisters of Mercy,
St Ita's Voluntary Housing,
Convent Street,
Abbeyfeale, Co Limerick V94 R283
Tel 068-310203
Community: 2

DOMINICAN SISTERS OF ST CECILIA
St Saviours, Glentworth Street, Limerick
Tel 085-2255796
Parish mail
stsavioursdominican@gmail.com
Convent email limerick@op-tn.org
Superior: Sr Caitríona Kavanagh (OP)
Community: 3

FRANCISCAN MISSIONARIES OF MARY
Castle View Gardens,
Clancy Strand, Limerick
Tel 061-455320
Email jomcglynnfmm@yahoo.co.uk
Superior: Sr Josephine McGlynn
Community: 6
Pastoral work

SISTERS OF ST FRANCIS OF PHILADELPHIA
Delamarie, Hassett's Cross, Limerick
Email bajosf@gmail.com
Contact: Sr Barbara Jackson

Cuan Mhuire, Bruree, Co Limerick
Email moman@osfphila.com
Contact: Sr Marie Oman

CONGREGATION OF OUR LADY OF CHARITY OF THE GOOD SHEPHERD
Good Shepherd Avenue,
12 Pennywell Road,
Limerick V94 AFP3
Tel 061-415178
Leader: Sr Noreen O'Shea
Community: 13

Omega B, Roxboro Road,
Janesboro, Limerick V94 K2N7
Tel 061-416676
Email rgsroxboro@hotmail.com
Community: 4

LA SAINTE UNION DES SACRES COEURS
Apartment 14, Sylvan House,
Park Village, Castletroy, Limerick
Tel 061-332598
Community: 1
Pastoral

LITTLE COMPANY OF MARY
Milford Convent
Plassey Park Road,
Castletroy, Limerick
Tel 061-485800 Fax 061-330351
Email lcm.milfordc@gmail.com
Community: 11
Milford Care Centre Nursing Home: 4

St Joseph's Convent,
Plassey Park Road,
Castletroy, Limerick
Tel 061-331144
Email stjoslcm@gmail.com
Community: 3

1 Mary Potter Court,
Plassey Park Road,
Castletroy, Limerick
Tel/Fax 061-332798
Community: 1

2 Mary Potter Court,
Plassey Park Road,
Castletroy, Limerick
Tel 061-332777
Community: 1

3 Mary Potter Court,
Plassey Park Road,
Castletroy, Limerick
Tel 061-332755
Community: 1

DIOCESE OF LIMERICK

SISTERS OF MARIE REPARATRICE
Laurel Hill Avenue,
South Circular Road, Limerick V94 XN29
Tel 061-315045
Contact: Sr Eileen Carroll
Email eileencarrollsmr@gmail.com
Community: 10
Spiritual direction/retreats
Regional Animator: Sr Eileen Carroll

POOR SERVANTS OF THE MOTHER OF GOD
43 Liosan, Sheehan Road,
Newcastle West, Co Limerick
Tel 069-20936
Community: 2
Daycare Centre

Dún Íosa, Main Street,
Drumcollogher, Co Limerick
Tel 063-83844
Community: 3
Pastoral

PRESENTATION SISTERS
8-9 Oakvale Drive,
Dooradoyle, Limerick
Tel 061-302011
Community: 2

Roxboro Road, Limerick
Tel 061-417204
Email presconvent@gmail.com
Team Leadership
Community: 13

34 McDonagh Avenue,
Janesboro, Limerick
Tel 061-594777
Community: 2

Apartment A,
6 Sexton Street, Limerick
Tel 061-467866
Community: 1

Apartment B,
6 Sexton Street, Limerick
Tel 061-467983
Community: 1

Apt 1 Presentation House,
Parnell Place, Parnell Street, Limerick
Tel 061-481674
Community: 1

Apt 3 Presentation House,
Parnell Place, Parnell Street, Limerick
Tel 061-419370
Community: 1

Apt 4 Presentation House,
Parnell Place, Parnell Street, Limerick
Tel 061-467867
Community: 1

Apt 8 Presentation House,
Parnell Place, Parnell Street, Limerick
Tel 061-310036
Community: 1

SALESIAN SISTERS OF ST JOHN BOSCO
'Bethel',
Caherdavin Heights, Limerick
Contact person: Sr Anne Collins

33/34 Bracken Crescent,
North Circular Road, Limerick
Tel 061-455132
Email brken@gofree.indigo.ie
Superior: Sr Mary McInerney
Community: 4
Teaching, related activities

Salesian Convent, Dun Ide,
Lower Shelbourne Road, Limerick
Tel 061-454511
Superior: Sr Frances Beggan
Community: 6
Parish work, spiritual accompaniment, pioneers, clubs

Salesian Convent, Ard Mhuire,
Caherdavin Heights, Limerick
Tel 061-451322
Email caherdavinhouse@eircom.net
Superior: Sr Catherine Sweeney
Community: 9
Ministry to the elderly, Parish ministry

Salesian Sisters, Cill Leala, New Road,
Thomondgate, Limerick
Tel 061-453099
Email cillela@gofree.indigo.ie
Contact person: Sr Noelle Costello
Community: 4
Involvement in parish and Blue Box

Salesian Sisters, 'Sonas', 3 Oakton Road,
Westbury, Corbally, Limerick
Email 3oaktonroad@eircom.net
Superior: Sr Patricia Murtagh
Community: 3
Parish and youth work

ST JOSEPH OF THE SACRED HEART SISTERS
Coolcranogue, Upper Dunganville,
Ardagh, Co Limerick
Tel 069-76668
Regional Leader: Sr Margaret O'Sullivan
Email margaretosullivan1@outlook.ie

7 Plassey Grove, Castletroy, Limerick
Tel 061-335794
Sr Cecilia Keating

Mackillop House, Dromcollogher,
Co Limerick
Tel 063-83911
Sr Maureen Cahill

No. 2 St Ita's Centre, Convent Street,
Abbeyfeale, Co Limerick
Tel 068-51984
Sr Elizabeth Kirby

4 Clover Field, Glin, Co Limerick
Tel 068-26015
Sr Mary Doody

St Catherine's, Bungalow 1, Bothar Buí,
Newcastle West, Co Limerick
Tel 069-62584
Sr Anne Keaty

St Catherine's, Bungalow 2, Bothar Buí,
Newcastle West, Co Limerick
Tel 069-62584
Sr Mary Keating

St Catherine's, Bungalow 3, Bothar Buí,
Newcastle West, Co Limerick
Tel 069-62579
Sr Margaret Hanrahan

St Catherine's, Bungalow 5, Bothar Buí,
Newcastle West, Co Limerick
Tel 069-62607
Sr Kathleen Murphy

Apt 15, Liosan Court, Gort Boy,
Newcastle West, Co Limerick
Tel 069-69603
Sr Catherine Duggan

'St Joseph's' Banogue Cross,
Croom, Co Limerick
Tel 061-600932
Sr Eileen Lenihan
Email eileen.lenihan@sosj.org.au

Apt. 39, Halcyon Place,
The Park Village,
Castletroy, Co Limerick 94N CC7
Tel:061-332725
Sr Sarah Hogan

Apt. 20, Sylvan House,
The Park Village,
Castletroy, Co Limerick
Tel 061-276545
Sr Bridget Moloney

Rose Cottage, Ballyloughane,
Newcastle West, Co Limerick
Tel 069-76655
Sr Bridie O'Sullivan
Email bridie06os@eircom.net

Beechwood House,
Newcastle West, Co Limerick
Sr Dymphna O'Brien
Email dymphna.obrien@sosj.org.au

DIOCESE OF LIMERICK

EDUCATIONAL INSTITUTIONS

Mary Immaculate College of Education
Tel 061-204300
Chaplain: Rev Michael Wall
Tel 061-204331
Email michael.wall@mic.ul.ie
Head of Department of Theology & Religious Studies: Rev Eamonn Conway
Tel 061-204353
Email eamonn.conway@mic.ul.ie
Director of Institute for Pastoral Studies
Rev Eamonn Fitzgibbon
St Patrick's Campus, Thurles, Co Tipperary
Email eamonn.fitzgibbon@mic.ul.ie

St Munchin's College (Diocesan College)
Corbally, Limerick
Tel 061-348922 Fax 061-340465
Email stmunchins@eircom.net
Principal: David Quilter
Email davequilter@hotmail.com
Chaplain: Tom Conneely

Gaelscoileanna
Chaplain: Rev Micheál Canon Liston
21 Sullane Crescent, Raheen Heights, Limerick
Tel 087-2314804

CHARITABLE AND OTHER SOCIETIES

Apostolic Work Society
Contact: Brid Shine
Glenbrohane, Garryspillane,
Kilmallock, Co Limerick
Tel 062-46612
Email dirb@iol.ie

Catholic Institute Athletic Club
Rosbrien, Limerick
President: Tel 061-455635
Secretary: Tel 061-452023

Doras Luimní
(Development organisation for Refugees and Asylum Seekers)
Central Buildings,
51A O'Connell Street, Limerick
Tel 061-609960
Email dorasluimni@eircom.net

Knights of St Columbanus
Contact: Mr William Ryan
Tel 061-414173 (work)/061-227530 (home)

Legion of Mary
Assumpta House, Windmill Street, Limerick
Tel 061-314071

Limerick Youth Service
5 Lower Glentworth Street, Limerick
Tel 061-412444/412545 Fax 061-412795
CEO: Fiona O'Grady
Email lys@limerickyouthservice.net

Order of Malta
7A Davis Street, Limerick
Tel/Fax 061-314250

St Joseph's Young Priests' Society
Contact: Una Nunan
10 Garravogue Road, Raheen, Limerick
Tel 061-227852

St Vincent de Paul Society
Ozanam House, Hartstonge Street, Limerick
Tel 061-317327 Fax 061-310320
Email info@svpmw.com
Administrator: Mary Leahy
Drop-In Centre
The Lane, Hartstonge Street, Limerick
Manager: Tom Flynn
Tel 061-313557

DIOCESE OF MEATH

PATRON OF THE DIOCESE
ST FINIAN, 12 DECEMBER

INCLUDES THE GREATER PART OF COUNTIES MEATH, WESTMEATH AND OFFALY, AND A PORTION OF COUNTIES LONGFORD, LOUTH, DUBLIN AND CAVAN

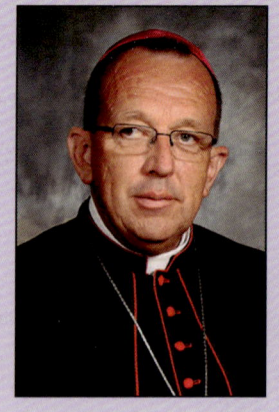

Most Rev Tom Deenihan DD, Ed.D
Bishop of Meath;
born 1967;
ordained priest 1 June 1991;
ordained Bishop of Meath
2 September 2018

Residence: Bishop's House,
Dublin Road, Mullingar,
Co Westmeath N91 DW32
Tel 044-9348841 Fax 044-9343020
Email secretary@dioceseofmeath.ie
Website www.dioceseofmeath.ie

CATHEDRAL OF CHRIST THE KING, MULLINGAR

As the Penal Laws began to be relaxed, Bishop Patrick Plunkett was appointed Bishop of Meath in 1778. He was to spend the next forty-nine years of his life restoring and rebuilding the diocese. He had no cathedral, but providing one was not his immediate priority. Towards the end of his time as bishop, work began on the magnificent new Church of St Mary in Navan. This was opened in 1830 and was considered the Cathedral Church of the Diocese. In 1870 Bishop Thomas Nulty decided to locate the bishop's residence in Mullingar, and the parish church there was designated Cathedral Church of the Diocese. It had been built in 1828 but was quite small.

On his appointment as bishop in 1900, Matthew Gaffney called a public meeting to discuss the building of a cathedral for the Diocese of Meath. This meeting adopted the following resolution: 'The Diocese of Meath not having a cathedral nor the parish of Mullingar a suitable church, be it resolved that a church be built in Mullingar which will fulfil this double purpose.' A building fund was established, and £15,000 was subscribed at this first meeting – a very sizeable sum at that time. It was not until the day of his consecration as bishop in 1929 that Thomas Mulvany was able to announce the decision to proceed with the project. Ralph A. Byrne, chief architect with William H. Byrne & Son, Dublin, prepared plans, which were accepted. Work began in 1932, and the Cathedral of Christ the King was opened for worship in September 1936. It was consecrated on 30 August 1939, the debt having been cleared. In recent years, a major renovation, including the replacement of the roof, has been completed.

DIOCESE OF MEATH

Most Rev Michael Smith DCL, DD
Bishop Emeritus of Meath
born 1940; ordained priest 1963;
consecrated Bishop 29 January 1984;
Co-adjutor Bishop of Meath 10 October 1988; succeeded 16 May 1990;
retired 18 June 2018.
Residence: St Oliver's, Beechfield,
Dublin Road, Mullingar, Co Westmeath
Tel 044-9340636
Email msmith@dioceseofmeath.ie

ADMINISTRATION

Diocesan website
www.dioceseofmeath.ie

Vicars General
Very Rev Declan Hurley Adm, VG
St Mary's, Navan, Co Meath
Tel 046-9027518
Very Rev Joseph Gallagher PP, VG
Parochial House, Tullamore, Co Offaly
Tel 057-9321587

Chancellor
Very Rev Paul Connell Phd
Meath Diocesan Office, Dublin Road,
Mullingar, Co Westmeath
Tel 044-9348841
Email chancellor@dioceseofmeath.ie

Vicars Forane
Very Rev John Byrne PP, VF
Parochial House, Kells, Co Meath
Tel 046-9240213
Very Rev Gerry Stuart PP, VF
Parochial House, Ratoath, Co Meath
Tel 01-8256207
Very Rev Tom Gilroy PP, VF
Parochial House,
Kinnegad, Co Westmeath
Tel 044-9375117
Very Rev Joseph Gallagher PP, VF
Parochial House, Tullamore, Co Offaly
Tel 057-9321587
Very Rev Patrick Moore PP, VF
Parochial House,
Castlepollard, Co Westmeath
Tel 044-9661126 Fax 044-9661881
Very Rev Andrew Doyle PP, VF
Parochial House, Durhamstown,
Bohermeen, Navan, Co Meath
Tel 046-9073805
Very Rev Denis McNelis PP, VF
Parochial House, Laytown, Co Meath
Tel 041-9827258
Very Rev Padraig McMahon PP, VF
Parochial House, Athboy, Co Meath
Tel 046-9432184 Fax 046-9430021

College of Consultors
Most Rev Tom Deenihan DD, Ed.D
Very Rev Declan Hurley Adm, VG
Very Rev John Byrne PP, VF
Very Rev Phil Gaffney PP
Very Rev Joseph Gallagher PP, VG
Very Rev Derek Darby Adm
Very Rev Sean Henry PP
Very Rev Denis McNelis PP, VF
Very Rev Patrick Moore PP, VF
Very Rev Paul Connell Phd

Episcopal Vicar for Pastoral Development
Very Rev Derek Darby
Meath Diocesan Office, Dublin Road,
Mullingar, Co Weatmeath
Tel 044-9348841
Email pastoral@dioceseofmeath.ie

Secretary
Ms Irene Carton
Bishop's House, Dublin Road, Mullingar,
Co Westmeath
Tel 044-9348841 Fax 044-9343020
Email secretary@dioceseofmeath.ie

EDUCATION

Diocesan Office for Education
Very Rev Paul Connell Phd
Meath Diocesan Office, Dublin Road,
Mullingar, Co Westmeath
Tel 044-9348841
Email education@dioceseofmeath.ie

Post-Primary Religious Education
Diocesan Director: Mr Seán Wright
The Whinnies, Tierworker,
Kells, Co Meath
Tel 042-9665547 Fax 042-9666969
Email ppdd@eircom.net

Primary Religious Education
Diocesan Advisers
Antoinette Shaw
Eileen Burns
Kathleen Duffy
Mairin Fanning
Bishop's House, Dublin Road, Mullingar,
Co Westmeath
Tel 044-9348841

LITURGY

Liturgical Commission
Chairman: Vacant
Secretary: Mr James Walsh
18 Beechgrove, Laytown, Co Meath

PASTORAL

ACCORD
Secretary, Mullingar Centre
Ms Angie Daly
Tel 044-9348707
Secretary, Navan Centre
Ms Mary McCabe
Tel 046-9023146
Secretary, Tullamore Centre
Ms Michelle Cleary
Tel 057-9341831
www.dioceseofmeath.ie/marriage

Apostolic Work Society
Mullingar Branch
Chaplain
Vacant

Navan Branch
Chaplain: Vacant
St Mary's, Navan, Co Meath
Tel 046-9027518

Chaplain to Polish Community
Rev Janusz Lugowski
Parochial House, Moynalvey, Co Meath
Tel 087-9908922

Council of Priests
Chairman: Very Rev Denis McNelis PP, VF
Parochial House, Laytown, Co Meath
Tel 041-9827258
Secretary: Rev Brendan Ludlow CC
c/o Diocesan Office, Dublin Road,
Mullingar, Co Westmeath

Diocesan Eucharistic Adoration Committee
St Anne's Centre,
Fairgreen, Navan, Co Meath
John Howard 087-2478519
Bartle Ó Curraoin 086-3020848
Email info@eucharisticadoration.ie

Ecumenism
Secretary: Very Rev William Coleman PP
Parochial House, Rochfortbridge,
Co Westmeath
Tel 044-9222107

Fr Matthew Union
Secretary: Very Rev Séamus Houlihan PP
Parochial House, Ballycumber Road,
Moate, Co Westmeath
Tel 090-6481951

Knock Pilgrimage
Director: Very Rev Martin Halpin PP
Parochial House, Ballinabrackey,
Kinnegad, Co Westmeath
Tel 046-9739015

Laity Commission
Diocesan Representative
Mrs Molly Buckley
Moylena, Clara Road,
Tullamore, Co Offaly
Tel 0506-41357

Lourdes Pilgrimage
Director
Very Rev Joseph Gallagher PP, VG
Parochial House, Tullamore, Co Offaly
Tel 057-9321587

Marriage Tribunal
(See Marriage Tribunals section)

Pioneer Total Abstinence Association
Very Rev Seamus Houlihan PP
Parochial House,
Kilcormac, Co Offaly
Tel 057-9135989

Pontifical Mission Societies
Diocesan Director
Vacant

Travellers
Chaplain: Very Rev Patrick O'Connor PP
Parochial House Dunboyne, Co Meath
Tel 01-8255342

DIOCESE OF MEATH

Vocations and Youth
Directors: Rev Tony Gonoude
Parochial House, Ballynacargy,
Co Westmeath
Tel 044-9373923
Email vocations@dioceseofmeath.ie

PARISHES

Mensal parishes are listed first. Other parishes follow alphabetically.

MULLINGAR
Cathedral of Christ the King
St Paul's, Mullingar
Assumption, Walshestown
Immaculate Conception, Gainstown
Little Flower and Our Lady of Good Counsel, Brotenstown
Very Rev Phil Gaffney Adm
Rev Vincent Daka CC
Rev Andrei Stolnicu CC
Rev Norman Allred CC
Cathedral House, Mullingar,
Co Westmeath
Tel 044-9348338/9340126
Fax 044-9340780
Email office@mullingarparish.ie
Website www.mullingarparish.ie

NAVAN
St Mary's; St Oliver's
Very Rev Declan Hurley Adm, VG
Rev Robert McCabe CC
Rev Noel Weir CC
Rev Eusebius Tulbure CC
St Mary's, The Fairgreen,
Navan, Co Meath C15 X0A3
Tel 046-9027518
Email office@navanparish.ie
Website www.navanparish.ie

ARDCATH
St Mary's, Ardcath
St John the Baptist, Clonalvy
Very Rev Gerry Stuart Adm (see Ratoath Parish)
Rev Kevin Heery CC
Parochial House, Curraha, Co Meath
Tel 01-8350136
Email accparish@gmail.com
www.ardcath.com

ASHBOURNE-DONAGHMORE
Immaculate Conception, Ashbourne
St Patrick, Donaghmore
Parish Office: Tel/Fax 01-8353149
Email ashbournedonaghmoreparish@gmail.com
Website www.ashbourneparish.ie
Very Rev Michael Kilmartin PP
54 Brookville, Ashbourne, Co Meath
Rev Ciaran Clarke CC
Parochial House, Ashbourne, Co Meath

ATHBOY
St James', Athboy
St Lawrence, Rathmore
Naomh Pádraig, Rathcairn
Very Rev Padraig McMahon PP, VF
Parochial House, Athboy, Co Meath
Tel 046-9432184 Fax 046-9430021
Email athboyensis@gmail.com
Website www.athboyparish.ie

BALLINABRACKEY
Assumption, Ballinabrackey
Trinity, Castlejordan
Very Rev Martin Halpin PP
Parochial House, Ballinabrackey,
Kinnegad, Co Westmeath
Tel/Fax 046-9739015
Email martinhalpin@gmail.com
Parish ballinabrackeyparish@gmail.com
Website www.ballinabrackeyandcastlejordan.com

BALLYNACARGY
The Nativity, Ballynacargy
St Michael, Sonna
Very Rev Tony Gonoude PP
Parochial House, Ballynacargy,
Co Westmeath
Tel 044-9373923

BALLIVOR
St Columbanus
Very Rev Mark Mohan PP
Parochial House, Ballivor, Co Meath
Tel/Fax 046-9546488
Parish email bkparishoffice@gmail.com
Website www.ballivorkildalkey.ie

BALLYMORE
The Holy Redeemer, Ballymore
St Brigid's, Boher
Very Rev Oliver Devine PP
Parochial House, Drumraney,
Athlone, Co Westmeath
Tel 044-9356207
Email oliver_devine@eircom.net
Website www.ballymoreanddrumraneyparishes.ie

BEAUPARC
The Assumption, Beauparc
The Assumption, Kentstown
Very Rev David Brennan PP
Parochial House,
Kentstown, Navan, Co Meath
Tel 041-9825276 Fax 041-9825252
Email bkyfparish@gmail.com
Website www.beauparcparish.ie
Very Rev Peter Farrelly AP
Parochial House, Beauparc,
Navan, Co Meath
Tel 046-9024114
Email peterfarrelly9@gmail.com

BOHERMEEN
St Ultan's, Bohermeen
St Cuthbert's, Boyerstown
Christ the King, Cortown
Very Rev Andrew Doyle PP, VF
Durhamstown, Bohermeen,
Navan, Co Meath
Tel 046-9073805
Email bohermeenparish1@gmail.com

CARNAROSS
St Ciaran, Carnaross
Sacred Heart, Mullaghea
Very Rev Michael Walsh PP
Parochial House, Carnaross,
Kells, Co Meath
Tel 046-9245904

CASTLEPOLLARD
St Michael's, Castlepollard
St Michael's, Castletown
St Mary's, Finea
Very Rev Patrick A. Moore PP, VF
Parochial House, Castlepollard,
Co Westmeath
Tel 044-9661126/087-2510855
Fax 044-9661881
Email fr.patrick.moore@gmail.com

CASTLETOWN-GEOGHEGAN
St Michael, Castletown-Geoghegan
St Stephen, Tyrrellspass
St Peter, Raheenmore
Very Rev Barry Condron PP
Tyrrellspass, Co Westmeath
Tel 044-9223115
Email tyrrellspass1@eircom.net

CASTLETOWN-KILPATRICK
St Patrick's, Castletown-Kilpatrick
St Colmcille's, Fletcherstown
Very Rev Maurice Henry Adm
Parochial House,
Castletown-Kilpatrick,
Navan, Co Meath
Office: Tel 046-9054142
Email castletownkpparish@gmail.com

CLARA
St Brigid's, Clara
Sts Peter & Paul, Horseleap
Very Rev Joseph Deegan PP
St Brigid's Parish Office, Church Street,
Clara, Co Offaly R35 PW97
Tel 057-9331170
Email claraparish7@gmail.com

CLONMELLON
Sts Peter & Paul, Clonmellon
St Bartholomew, Killallon
Very Rev Sean Garland PP
Parochial House, Clonmellon
Navan, Co Meath
Tel 046-9433124
Email clonmellonparish@gmail.com

DIOCESE OF MEATH

COLLINSTOWN
St Mary's, Collinstown
St Feichin's, Fore
Very Rev Patrick Donnelly PP
Parochial House, Collinstown,
Co Westmeath
Tel 044-9666326
Email collinstownforeparish@gmail.com

COOLE (MAYNE)
Immaculate Conception, Coole
St John the Baptist, Whitehall
Very Rev Oliver Skelly PP
Parochial House, Coole, Co Westmeath
Tel 044-9661191
Email cooleparish@gmail.com
Website coolemayneparish.ie

CURRAHA
St Andrew's
Very Rev Gerry Stuart Adm (see Ratoath Parish)
Rev Kevin Heery CC
Parochial House, Curraha, Co Meath
Tel 01-8350136
Email accparish@gmail.com
Website www.currahaparish.ie

DELVIN
Assumption, Delvin
St Livinus, Killulagh
Very Rev Seamus Heaney PP
Parochial House, Delvin, Co Westmeath
Tel 044-9664127
Email info@delvinparish.ie
Website www.delvinparish.ie

DONORE
The Nativity of Our Lady, Donore
The Nativity of Our Lady, Rosnaree
Very Rev Mark English Adm
Parochial House, Duleek, Co Meath
Tel 041-9823137
Email donorerossnareeparish@gmail.com

DROGHEDA, HOLY FAMILY
Rev Stepen Kennedy
Rev Brendan O'Rourke
The Presbytery, Ballsgrove,
Drogheda, Co Louth
Tel 041-9831991
Email holyfamilyballsgrove@outlook.com
Website www.holyfamilydrogheda.ie

DROGHEDA, ST MARY'S
Very Rev John Conlon PP
Rev Cyprian Solomon CC
St Mary's, Drogheda, Co Louth
Tel 041-9834958 Fax 041-9845144
Parish Office: Tel 041-9834587
Email stmarysdrogheda@gmail.com
Website www.stmarysdrogheda.ie

DRUMCONRATH
Sts Peter & Paul, Drumconrath
Sts Brigid & Patrick, Meath Hill
Very Rev Finian Connaughton PP
Parochial House, Drumconrath,
Navan, Co Meath
Tel 041-6854146
Email drumconrathparish@topmail.ie
Website www.drumconrathparish.ie

DRUMRANEY
Immaculate Conception, Drumraney
Immaculate Conception, Tang
Immaculate Conception, Forgney
Very Rev Oliver Devine PP
Drumraney, Athlone,
Co Westmeath
Tel 044-9356207
Email drumraneyparish@gmail.com
Website www.ballymoreanddrumraneyparishes.ie
Rev Godwin Atede CC
St Mary's, Tang,
Ballymahon, Co Longford
Tel 0906-432214
Email atedegodwin@hotmail.com

DULEEK
St Cianan, Duleek
St Thérèse, Bellewstown
Very Rev Mark English PP
Rev Anthony Ayola
Parochial House, Duleek, Co Meath
Tel 041-9823205
Email duleekparish@gmail.com
Rev David Jones
The Hemitage, Duleek, Co Meath
Website www.duleekbellewstownparish.com

DUNBOYNE
SS Peter & Paul, Dunboyne
St Brigid & Sacred Heart, Kilbride
Very Rev Patrick O'Connor PP
Parochial House,
Dunboyne, Co Meath
Tel 01-8255342 Fax 01-8252321
Email dunboynekilbride.parish@gmail.com
Website www.dunboynekilbrideparish.org
Rev Declan Kelly CC
2 Orchard Court, Dunboyne, Co Meath
Rev John Hogan (OCDS)
1 Orchard Court, Dunboyne, Co Meath

DUNDERRY
Assumption, Dunderry
Assumption, Robinstown
Assumption, Kilbride
Very Rev Noel Horneck PP
Parochial House, Dunderry,
Navan, Co Meath
Tel 046-9431433
Email dunderryparish@gmail.com

DUNSHAUGHLIN
Sts Patrick & Seachnall, Dunshaughlin
St Martin of Tours, Culmullen
Very Rev Sean Henry PP
Parochial House, Dunshaughlin,
Co Meath
Tel 01-8259114
Rev Joseph Clavin AP
St Martin's, Culmullen, Drumree,
Co Meath
Tel 01-8241976
Email office@dcparish.ie
Website www.dunshaughlin-culmullenparish.ie

DYSART
St Patrick's, Dysart
Assumption, Loughanavalley
Very Rev David O'Hanlon PP
Parochial House, Dysart, Mullingar,
Co Westmeath
Tel 044-9226122
Email ppdysartwestmeath@gmail.com

EGLISH
St James, Eglish
St John the Baptist, Rath
Very Rev John Moorhead PP
Parochial House, Eglish,
Birr, Co Offaly
Tel 057-9133010
Website www.eglishdrumcullen.com

ENFIELD
St Michael, Rathmolyon
Assumption, Jordanstown
Very Rev Michael Whittaker PP
The Presbytery, Enfield, Co Meath
Tel 046-9541282
Email michaeljwhittaker@gmail.com
Rev John Kennedy
Parochial House,
Rathmolyon, Co Meath
Tel 046-9555212
Website www.enfieldparish.ie

GLASSON–TUBBERCLAIRE
Immaculate Conception, Tubberclaire
Very Rev Seamus Mulvany PP
Parochial House, Tubberclaire-Glasson,
Athlone, Co Westmeath
Tel 090-6485103
Email tubberclairchurch@gmail.com
Website www.tubberclairchurch.com

JOHNSTOWN
Nativity of Our Lady, Johnstown
Assumption, Walterstown
Very Rev Michael Cahill PP
Parochial House, Johnstown,
Navan, Co Meath
Tel 046-9021731
Email johnsnavan@eircom.net

DIOCESE OF MEATH

KELLS
St Columcille, Kells
Immaculate Conception, Girley
Very Rev David Bradley PP
Email jplowebyrne@gmail.com
Rev John Byrne AP
Parochial House, Kells, Co Meath
Tel 046-9240213
Email info@kellsparish.ie
Website www.kellsparish.ie

KILBEG
Nativity of Our Lady, Kilbeg
St Michael, Staholmog
Very Rev Liam Malone Adm
Parochial House, Kilbeg, Kells, Co Meath
Tel 046-9246604
Email kilbegparish@gmail.com

KILBEGGAN
St James, Kilbeggan
St Hugh, Rahugh
Very Rev Brendan Corrigan PP
Parochial House, Harbour Road,
Kilbeggan, Co Westmeath
Tel 057-9332155
Email info@kilbegganparish.ie
Website www.kilbegganparish.ie

KILCLOON
St Oliver Plunkett, Kilcloon
The Assumption, Batterstown
Little Chapel of the Assumption, Kilcock
Very Rev Declan Kelly PP
Parochial House, Batterstown,
Dunboyne, Co Meath
Tel 01-8259267
Email kilcloonparish@gmail.com
Website www.kilcloonparish.com

KILCORMAC
Nativity of the Blessed Virgin Mary, Kilcormac
St Brigid, Mountbolus
Very Rev Michael Meade PP
Parochial House, Kilcormac, Co Offaly
Tel 057-9135989
Email kilcormacparish@outlook.ie
Website www.kilcormackillougheyparish.com

KILDALKEY
St Dympna's
Very Rev Mark Mohan PP
Parochial House, Ballivor, Co Meath
Tel 046-9546488
Parish email bkparishoffice@gmailcom
Website www.ballivorkildalkey.ie

KILLUCAN
St Joseph's, Rathwire
St Brigid's, Raharney
Very Rev Stan Deegan PP
St Joseph's Parochial House,
Killucan, Co Westmeath N91 F292
Tel 044-9374127
Email parishofkillucan@gmail.com

KILMESSAN
Nativity of Our Lady, Kilmessan
Assumption, Dunsany
Very Rev Terence Toner PP
Parochial House, Kilmessan, Co Meath
Tel 046-9025172
Email kilmessanparish@gmail.com

KILSKYRE
St Alphonsus Liguori, Kilskyre
Assumption, Ballinlough
Very Rev Patrick Kearney PP
Parochial House, Kilskyre,
Kells, Co Meath
Tel 046-9243623
Email kilskyreparish@gmail.com
Website www.kilskyreballinlough.ie

KINGSCOURT
Immaculate Conception, Kingscourt
St Joseph's, Corlea
Our Lady of Mount Carmel, Muff
Very Rev Gerard MacCormack PP
Parochial House, Kingscourt, Co Cavan
Tel 042-9667314
Email info@kingscourtparish.ie
Website www.kingscourtparish.ie

KINNEGAD
Assumption, Kinnegad
St Agnes, Coralstown
St Finian, Clonard
Very Rev Thomas Gilroy PP
Parochial House, Kinnegad, Co Meath
Tel 044-9375117
Email info@kinnegadparish.ie
Website www.kinnegadparish.ie
Parish Office: 044-9391030
Fridays 10.00 am-4.00 pm

LAYTOWN-MORNINGTON
Sacred Heart, Laytown
Star of the Sea, Mornington
Very Rev Denis McNelis PP, VF
Parochial House, Laytown, Co Meath
Tel 041-9827258
Email parishoffice@sacredheartlaytown.com
Website www.sacredheartlaytown.com
Rev Joseph Apust CC
Parochial House,
Mornington, Co Meath
Tel 041-9827384
Email mgtparish@gmail.com
Website www.morningtonchurch.com

LOBINSTOWN
Holy Cross
Very Rev Gerry Boyle Adm
Rev Timothy Mejida
Parochial House, Lobinstown,
Navan, Co Meath
Tel 046-9053155

LONGWOOD
Church of the Holy Family, Longwood
Our Lady & St Dominic, Killyon
Very Rev Tom Gilroy Adm (see Kinnegad Parish)
Rev Louis Illah CC
52 Edgeworth Court,
Longwood, Co Meath
Parish mobile 087-1723903
Email longwoodparish@gmail.com

MILLTOWN
St Matthew, Milltown
St Matthew, Empor
St Patrick, Moyvore
Very Rev William Fitzsimons PP
Parochial House, Milltown,
Rathconrath, Co Westmeath
Tel 044-9355106

MOUNTNUGENT
St Brigid, Mountnugent
Sts Brigid & Fiach, Ballinacree
Very Rev Philip O'Connor PP
Parochial House,
Mountnugent, Co Cavan
Tel 049-8540123
Email stbrigids.parish@outlook.com

MOYNALTY
Assumption, Moynalty
Assumption, Newcastle
Very Rev Joseph McEvoy PP
Parochial House, Moynalty,
Kells, Co Meath
Tel 046-9244305
Email moynaltyparish@gmail.com

MOYNALVEY
Nativity, Moynalvey
Assumption, Kiltale
Very Rev Declan Kelly Adm (see Kilcloon Parish)
Rev Janusz Lugowski CC
Parochial House, Moynalvey,
Summerhill, Co Meath
Tel 046-9557031
Email mknotices@gmail.com
Website www.moynalveykiltaleparish.com

MULTYFARNHAM
St Nicholas, Multyfarnham
St Patrick's, Leney
Very Rev Paul Connell Adm
Rev Conor McGee CC
Parochial House, Rathganny,
Multyfarnham, Co Westmeath N91 E186
Tel 044-9371124
Email stnicholasmultyfarnham@gmail.com

NOBBER
St John the Baptist
Very Rev Liam Malone PP
Parochial House, Nobber, Co Meath
Tel 046-9052197
Email nobberparish@gmail.com
Tel (office) 046-9089688

DIOCESE OF MEATH

OLDCASTLE
St Brigid, Oldcastle
St Mary, Moylough
Very Rev Ray Kelly PP
Parochial House, Oldcastle, Co Meath
Tel 049-8541142
Email oldcastleparish@gmail.com
Website
www.oldcastleandmoylaghparish.com

ORISTOWN
St Catherine, Oristown
St John the Baptist, Kilberry
Very Rev John O'Brien PP
Parochial House, Oristown,
Kells, Co Meath
Tel 046-9054124
Email oristownparish@gmail.com
Website www.oristownparish.com

RAHAN
St Carthage, Killina
St Patrick, The Island
St Colman, Mucklagh
Very Rev Martin Carley PP
Parochial House, Killina, Rahan,
Tullamore, Co Offaly
Tel 057-9355917
Rev Frank Guinan
The Presbytery, Mucklagh,
Tullamore, Co Offaly
Tel 057-9321892
Email rahanparish@gmail.com
Website www.rahanparish.ie

RATHKENNY
Sts Louis & Mary, Rathkenny
St Patrick, Rushwee
St Brigid, Grangegeeth
Very Rev Gerry Boyle PP
Parochial House, Rathkenny, Co Meath
Tel 046-9054138
Website www.rathkennyparish.ie

RATOATH
Holy Trinity
Very Rev Gerard Stuart PP
Rev Yohanna Jacob CC
Parochial House, Ratoath, Co Meath
Tel 01-8256207 Fax 01-8256662
Email ratoathparish@gmail.com
Website www.ratoathparish.ie

ROCHFORTBRIDGE
Immaculate Conception, Rochfortbridge
Sacred Heart, Meedin
St Joseph, Milltownpass
Very Rev William Coleman PP
Parochial House, Rochfortbridge,
Co Westmeath
Tel 044-9222107
Email rochfortbridgeparish@gmail.com

SKRYNE
St Colmcille, Skryne
Immaculate Conception, Rathfeigh
Very Rev Thomas O'Mahony PP
Parochial House, Skryne, Tara, Co Meath
Tel 046-9025152
Email office@skryneandrathfeighparish.ie
Website
www.skryneandrathfeighparish.ie

SLANE
St Patrick, Slane
Assumption, Monknewtown
Very Rev Richard Matthews PP
Parochial House, Slane, Co Meath
Tel 041-9824249 Office 041-9884429
Email slaneparish@gmail.com
Website www.slaneparish.com

STAMULLEN
St Patrick, Stamullen
St Mary's, Julianstown
Very Rev Brendan Ferris PP
Preston Hill, Stamullen, Co Meath
Tel/Fax 01-8412647
Parish Email secretary@sjparish.ie

SUMMERHILL
Our Lady of Lourdes, Dangan
Assumption, Coole
Very Rev Paul Crosbie Adm (see Trim Parish)
Rev Vincent McKay (CSSp)
Parochial House, Summerhill, Co Meath
Tel 046-9557021
Email coolsummerhillparish@gmail.com
Website www.summerhillparish.ie

TAGHMON
Assumption, Taghmon
St Joseph, Turin
Very Rev Declan Smith PP
Parochial House, Taghmon,
Mullingar, Co Westmeath
Tel 044-9372140

TRIM
St Patrick, Trim
St Brigid, Boardsmill
Very Rev Paul Crosbie PP
Rev Warren Collier CC
Parochial House, Trim, Co Meath
Tel 046-9431251
Parish email spcctrim@gmail.com

TUBBER
Holy Family, Tubber
St Thomas the Apostle, Rosemount
Rev Seamus Houlihan PP
Parochial House, Ballycumber Road,
Moate, Co Westmeath
Tel 090-6481951
Email tubberrosemountparish@gmail.com

TULLAMORE
Assumption, Tullamore
St Colmcille, Durrow
Very Rev Joseph Gallagher PP, VG
Rt Rev Mgr Seán Heaney AP
Email heaneysean@eircom.net
Rev Fergal Cummins CC
Email fergalcummins100@yahoo.ie
Rev Luke Ohiemi CC
Rev Joe Campbell CC
Parochial House, Tullamore, Co Offaly
Tel 057-9321587
Email tullamoreparishsecretary@gmail.com
Website www.tullamoreparish.ie

INSTITUTIONS AND THEIR CHAPLAINS

St Loman's Hospital
Mullingar, Co Westmeath
Tel 044-9340191
Priests of the parish

Longford & Westmeath General Hospital
Mullingar, Co Westmeath
Tel 044-9340221
Priests of the parish

Our Lady's Hospital
Navan, Co Meath
Tel 046-9021210
Priests of the parish

Tullamore General Hospital
Tullamore, Co Offaly
Tel 057-9321501
Priests of the parish

PRIESTS OF THE DIOCESE ELSEWHERE

Rev Shane Crombie
c/o Meath Diocesan Office, Mullingar
Rev Gabriel Flynn
DCU, Dublin
Rev Tony Gavin
c/o Meath Diocesan Office, Mullingar
Rev David Hanratty
Tierhogar, Portarlington, Co Laois
Tel 057-8645719
Rev Michael Hinds
Chaplain to the Defence Forces
Rev Stephen Kelly
Apostolic Nunciature, Burundi
Rev Brendan Ludlow
Chaplain UCD
Rev Martin McErlean
c/o Meath Diocesan Office, Mullingar
Rev John Nally
Waterford
Rev Thomas O'Connor DD
St Patrick's College,
Maynooth, Co Kildare

RETIRED PRIESTS

Very Rev Ray Brady
c/o Bishop's House, Mullingar
Rev Anthony Draper DD
Millbury Nursing Home,
Navan, Co Meath
Rev Jim Lynch
Dunboyne, Co Meath
Rt Rev Mgr Eamonn Marron PE
The Presbytery,
Raharney, Co Westmeath
Tel 044-9374271
Very Rev Frank McNamara PE
Cluan Lir, Mullingar, Co Westmeath
Very Rev Matthew Mollin PE
Elm Hall, Loughlinstown Road,
Celbridge, Co Kildare
Very Rev Colm Murtagh PE
1 Greenville, Kildalkey, Co Meath
Tel 046-9435133
Very Rev Eamonn O'Brien PE
Newbrook Nursing Home,
Mullingar, Co Westmeath
Very Rev Michael Sheerin PE
Woodlands Nursing Home,
Navan, Co Meath
Rev Philip Smith PE
Tir-ee, Harbourstown,
Stamullen, Co Meath
Tel 01-8020708
Rt Rev Mgr Thomas Woods DD
Newbrook Nursing Home,
Mullingar, Co Westmeath

PERSONAL PRELATURE

OPUS DEI
Lismullin Conference Centre
Navan, Co Meath C15 XW40
Tel 046-9026936
Rev Philip Griffin, Chaplain

RELIGIOUS ORDERS AND CONGREGATIONS

PRIESTS

BENEDICTINE MONKS OF PERPETUAL ADORATION
Silverstream Priory
Stamullen, Co Meath K32 T189
Tel 01-8417142
Email info@cenacleosb.org
Prior
Very Rev Dom Elijah Carroll (OSB)
Monastery Website http://cenacleosb.org/
Vocations Website
http://cenacleosb.org/vocations/
Vultus Christi Weblog
http://vultus.stblogs.org/

CAMILLIANS
St Camillus Community,
Killucan, Co Westmeath
Tel 044-74115
Superior: Rev Frank Monks (OSCam)
Nursing Centre
Tel 044-74196

CARMELITES (OCARM)
Carmelite Priory,
Moate, Co Westmeath
Tel 090-6481160/6481398
Fax 090-6481879
Email carmelitemoate@eircom.net
Prior: Rev Jaison Kuthanapillil (OCarm)

FRANCISCANS
Franciscan Abbey,
Multyfarnham, Co Westmeath
Tel 044-9371114/9371137
Fax 044-9371387
Email theabbeymulty@gmail.com
Provincial Delegate
Rev Kieran Cronin (OFM)

HOLY SPIRIT CONGREGATION
Spiritan Missionaries,
Ardbraccan, Navan, Co Meath
Tel 046-9021441
Community Leader
Rev Peter Conaty (CSSp)

ST COLUMBAN'S MISSIONARY SOCIETY
St Columban's, Dalgan Park,
Navan, Co Meath
Tel 046-9021525
Regional Director
Rev Raymond Husband (SSC)
Regional Vice-Director
Rev Gerard Neylon (SSC)

St Columban's Retirement Home,
Dalgan Park, Navan, Co Meath
Tel 046-9021525
Person in Charge: Ms Anne McNally
Provider Nominee
Rev Gerry Neylon (SSC)
Email ngneylon@gmail.com

BROTHERS

FRANCISCAN BROTHERS
The Monastery, Clara, Co Offaly
Tel 057-9331130
Local Minister: Br Charles Conway
Community: 3

SISTERS

BLESSED SACRAMENT SISTERS
Denene, New Road,
Tullamore, Co Offaly R35 N528
Tel 057-9351371
Email imelda.doorley@gmail.com
Community: 2

CHARITY OF JESUS AND MARY SISTERS
Residential centre transferred to
Muiriosa Foundation

Aisling, Mitchelstown,
Delvin, Co Westmeath
Tel 044-64379
Contact: Sr Kathleen O'Connor
Community: 2

CONGREGATION OF THE SISTERS OF MERCY
St Mary's Convent of Mercy,
Athlumney, Navan,
Co Meath C15 PK72
Tel 046-9021271
Facilitator: Sr Consilio Rock
Community: 6

Sisters of Mercy,
3 St Brigid's Court, Connaught Street,
Athboy, Co Meath C15 E433
Tel 046-9400032

Sisters of Mercy, Charlestown,
Clara, Co Offaly
Tel 057-9331184

202 Ballsgrove,
Drogheda, Co Louth A92 NY5E
Tel 041-9830160

Convent of Mercy, Kells,
Co Meath A82 C7P3
Tel 046-9240159
Community: 13

Cill na Gréine, Convent of Mercy,
Kells, Co Meath
Tel 046-9252536

Sisters of Mercy,
13 Grand Priory, Kells,
Co Meath A82 H1F2
Tel 046-9249027

Convent of Mercy, Tullamore Road,
Kilbeggan, Co Westmeath
Tel 057-9332161
Community: 6

Sisters of Mercy, Loughcrew,
Laytown, Co Meath
Tel 041-9827432
Community: 2

29 Green Road,
Mullingar, Co Westmeath N91 E6D6
Tel 044-9341680

10 College Court, College Street,
Mullingar, Co Westmeath N91 E276
Tel 044-9330768

DIOCESE OF MEATH

St Joseph's,
Leighsbrook, Navan,
Co Meath C15 HW32
Tel 046-9071760
Community: 5

Sisters of Mercy,
Mount Carmel, 15 Aylesbury Lodge,
Navan, Co Meath C15 P9P9
Tel 046-9071757
Community: 3

Sisters of Mercy, 4 Ferndale,
Navan, Co Meath C15 T2W7
Tel 046-9023844

Sisters of Mercy, Sacre Coeur,
The Commons, Navan, Co Meath
Tel 046-9021970

Sisters of Mercy,
1 Mornington Way, Trim,
Co Meath C15 V064
Tel 046-9437025 Fax 046-9437025
Community: 3

Convent of Mercy,
St Joseph's, Tullamore,
Co Offaly R35 PC80
Tel 057-9321221
Community: 27
Leaders: Srs Cecilia Cadogan &
Maeve Hyland & Ann O'Neill

Sisters of Mercy,
130 Arden Vale, Tullamore,
Co Offaly R35 ED66
Tel 057-9352733

Sisters of Mercy,
47 Tara Crescent, Clonminch,
Tullamore, Co Offaly R35 Y526
Tel 057-9322150

69 Carne Hill, Johnstown,
Navan, Co Meath C15 RRN2
Tel 046-9091772

42 Blackcastle Estate,
Navan, Co Meath C15 Y9P9

Sisters of Mercy,
Blackfriary, Trim, Co Meath C15 R276
Tel 046-9437759

Sisters of Mercy, 5 Headfort Road,
Kells, Co Meath A82 T6T8
Tel 046-9249775
Community: 3

6 Friars Park, Trim,
Co Meath C15 Y861
Tel 046-9437037
Community: 3

Shunem, Laytown,
Co Meath A92 T6R0

Sisters of Mercy, 133 College Hill,
Irishtown, Mullingar,
Co Westmeath N91 X6H0
Tel 044-9335303

135 Droim Liath, Collins Lane,
Tullamore, Co Offaly R35 C3W7
Tel 057-9361133

Apartment 6, Knightsbridge Village,
Longwood Road, Trim,
Co Meath C15 AX22
Tel 046-9486028

1 Summerhill Road,
Trim, Co Meath

1 Oakfield, Church Road,
Tullamore, Co Offaly R35 YC83

Harbour Road,
Kilbeggan, Co Westmeath
Tel 057-9332147

3 Roselawn, High Street,
Tullamore, Co Offaly R35 CV04
Tel 057-9352077

Apt B6, Friar's Court,
McCurtain Street,
Mullingar, Co Westmeath

'Solanus',
St Joseph's Convent of Mercy,
Tullamore, Co Offaly

Santa Maria Apartment,
Convent Road, Athlumney,
Navan, Co Meath C15 PK72
Tel 046-9071298

9 Derravagh Mews,
Castlepollard,
Co Westmeath N91 N4A4

DAUGHTERS OF MARY AND JOSEPH
22 Northlands, Eastham Road,
Bettystown, Co Meath
Community: 1

FRANCISCAN MISSIONARIES OF OUR LADY
La Verna Centre,
Franciscan House of Spirituality &
Hospitality, Franciscan Convent,
Ballinderry, Mullingar,
Co Westmeath N91 K680
Tel 044-9352000/087-3935613
Email lavernacentre@gmail.com
Website www.fmoireland.ie
lavernacentre on Facebook
Superior: Sr Clare Brady
Email info@fmoireland.ie
Commmunity: 3
House of solitude for those wishing to
spend time in solitude and quiet space

FRANCISCAN SISTERS OF THE RENEWAL
St Anthony Convent, Dublin Road,
Drogheda, Co Louth A92 X044
Tel 041-9830441 Fax 041-9842321
Website www.franciscansisterscfr.com
Superior: Sr Agnes Holtz
Community: 4

HOLY FAMILY OF ST EMILIE DE RODAT
Arden Road,
Tullamore, Co Offaly
Tel 057-9321577
Superior: Sr Margaret O'Riordan
Email oriordan.margaret@yahoo.ie
Community: 7

LORETO (IBVM)
Loreto Community,
St Michael's, Navan, Co Meath
Tel 046-9021740
Email loretonavan@eircom.net
Co-Leaders: Sr Maire Carr, Sr Siobhan Quill
Community: 13
Loreto Secondary School
Tel 046-9023830
Day Care Centre

Loreto Sisters, Athlumney Road,
Navan, Co Meath
Tel 046-9073423
Community: 2
Education

Anam Aras, Laytown,
Drogheda, Co Louth
Tel 041-9828952
Retreat centre

MEDICAL MISSIONARIES OF MARY
Bruach na Mara, Golf Links Road,
Bettystown, Co Meath A92 X2N1
Tel 041-9888541
Email btown.mmm@gmail.com
Community: 3

MISSIONARY SISTERS OF THE HOLY ROSARY
Holy Rosary Convent,
Dublin Road, Bettystown, Co Louth
Tel 041-9827362
Community: 8
Pastoral

EDUCATIONAL INSTITUTIONS

St Finian's College
Mullingar, Co Westmeath
Tel 044-9348313 Fax 044-9345275
President: Very Rev Paul Connell PhD
Tel 044-9348672
Principal: Mr John McHale
Chaplain: Very Rev Phil Gaffney

DIOCESE OF MEATH

St Mary's Diocesan School
Beamore Road,
Drogheda, Co Louth
Tel Office: 041-9837581
Staff: 041-9838001 Fax 041-9841151
Principal: Mr Ciaran O'Hare
Chaplain: Priests of Parish

St Patrick's Classical School
Mount Rivers, Moatlands,
Navan, Co Meath
Tel 046-9021847
Principal: Mr Colm O'Rourke
Chaplain: Mr Mark Donnelly

Coláiste Choilm
Tullamore, Co Offaly
Tel 057-9351756
Headmaster: Mr Tadhg O'Sullivan
Chaplain: Fr Fergal Cummins

Boyne Community School
Trim, Co Meath
Tel 046-9431358
Principal: Ms Elizabeth Cahill
Chaplain: Ms Aoife Daly

Ashbourne Community School
Ashbourne, Co Meath
Tel 01-8353066
Principal: Ms Susan Duffy
Chaplain: Ms Frances Gildea

St Peter's College
Dunboyne, Co Meath
Tel 01-8252552
Principal: Ms Deirdre Maye
Chaplain: Mr John Tighe

St Ciaran's Community School
Kells, Co Meath
Tel 046-9241551
Principal: Ms Cora McLoughlin
Chaplain: Mr Sean Wright

Athboy Community School
Athboy, Co Meath
Tel 046-9487894
Principal: Mr Anthony Leavy
Chaplain: Mr Joe Tynan

Ratoath College
Jamestown, Ratoath, Co Meath
Tel 01-8254102
Principal: Mr Seamus Meehan
Chaplain: Vacant

CHARITABLE AND OTHER SOCIETIES

Bethany Pastoral Care
Cathedral Social Services Centre,
Mullingar, Co Westmeath
Tel 087-6309808

Parish Community Centre
Bishopsgate Street,
Mullingar, Co Westmeath
Tel 044-9343432

Society of St Vincent de Paul
Ozanam Holiday Home, Mornington,
Co Meath
Tel 041-9827924

DIOCESE OF OSSORY

Patron of the Diocese
St Kieran, 5 March

Includes most of County Kilkenny and portions of Counties Laois and Offaly

SEDE VACANTE

Apostolic Administrator
Most Rev Denis Nulty DD

Ossory Diocesan Office,
James' Street,
Kilkenny R95 NH60
Tel 056-7762448
Email bishop@ossory.ie
Website www.ossory.ie

ST MARY'S CATHEDRAL, KILKENNY – RESTORATION – RENOVATION – RECONNECTION

St Mary's Cathedral, Kilkenny, dates from 1857 and is one of the finest cathedrals of pure Gothic design in Ireland. Along with being the Mother Church of the Diocese of Ossory and a prayerful sacred space for the faithful, it is of special interest in a number of architectural, historical, archaeological, artistic, cultural and social categories. It forms the centrepiece of St Mary's Architectural Conservation Area within Kilkenny City. It is in this context also that the essential restoration works to the building fabric commenced on site in January 2015, with the replacement of the roof over the Sanctuary and the appropriate cleaning and repainting of the highly ornate ceiling below. The repair works were undertaken by a specialist team of restoration painters over a period of many months and ranged through plaster repair, paint matching, gold leaf work, and paint stencilling, all done by hand by local specialist craftsmen and women. Painted features adorning the window surround, and supporting columns were also revealed and reinstated with particular attention paid to investigating and recording the underlining history as evidenced throughout the works.

Beneath the ceiling the hand-cut mosaics which decorate all the Sanctuary walls were also in need of cleaning and restoration. This was undertaken through the application of non-abrasive pumice to the entire area and removal after drying, which lifted the build-up of carbonation, dirt and smoke gathered over the decades, all carried out without damage to the mosaics themselves. In tandem, the magnificent and original stained glass windows running to over five metres tall were fully removed, repaired, re-leaded, and replaced by a local stained glass expert, securing their integrity for future generations.

Work was completed in time for the first ordination to priesthood in our diocese in fourteen years, celebrated in our beautiful cathedral by Bishop Seamus on 28 June 2015.

At floor level a number of statues were cleaned and reinstated to their positions, bespoke furniture was designed and installed within the alcoves, the altar was repaired, and the floor mosaics cleaned. Appropriate modern lighting systems were added in concealed locations to highlight the complete works, and the dramatic impact of the restoration works is now evident for the citizens of Kilkenny, the faithful of the forty-two parishes in the Diocese of Ossory and the many visitors who come to view, to be uplifted and to appreciate its beauty and craftsmanship.

'They devoted themselves to the apostles' teaching and to fellowship, to the breaking of bread and to prayer.' (Acts 2:42)

We welcome you to come to our diocese, to come see and pray, and experience our newly restored Sanctuary, the most sacred space of St Mary's Cathedral, the Mother Church of the Diocese of Ossory.

DIOCESE OF OSSORY

Most Rev Séamus Freeman (SAC) DD
Bishop Emeritus of Ossory
born 23 February 1944;
ordained priest 12 June 1971;
Consecrated Bishop of Ossory
2 December 2007;
Retired 29 July 2016
Diocesan Office,
James's Street, Kilkenny R95 NH60
Tel 086-3103934
Email seamusfreeman@ossory.ie

CHAPTER

Dean: Very Rev Seamus McEvoy
Archdeacon
Very Rev Sean Canon O'Doherty
Members
Very Rev James Canon Crotty
Very Rev Patrick Canon Dalton
Very Rev Patrick Canon Duggan
Very Rev Laurence Canon Dunphy
Very Rev Brian Canon Flynn
Very Rev Frank Canon Maher
Very Rev Noel Canon Maher
Very Rev Thomas Canon Murphy

ADMINISTRATION

Chancellor
Very Rev William Dalton
c/o Diocesan Office, James's Street,
Kilkenny
Tel/Fax 056-7725287

College of Consultors
Rev Patrick Carey
Very Rev Daniel Carroll
Rt Rev Mgr Daniel Cavanagh
Very Rev Patrick Dalton
Very Rev Martin Delaney
Very Rev Frank Purcell
Rev Dermot Ryan

Financial Administrator
Mr Tom Keating
Diocesan Office, James's Street, Kilkenny
Tel 056-7762448

Diocesan Secretary
Mrs Frances Lennon
Diocesan Office, James's Street, Kilkenny
Tel 056-7762448 Fax 056-7763753
Email admin@ossory.ie

Finance Secretary
Mrs Sheila Walshe
Diocesan Office, James's Street, Kilkenny
Tel 056-7762448 Fax 056-7763753
Email sheilawalshe@ossory.ie

Priest Secretary to Apostolic Administrator
Rt Rev Dr Dermot Ryan
Diocesen Office, James's Street, Kilkenny
Tel 056-7762448
Email dermotryan@ossory.ie

Diocesan Accountant
Mr Michael Dundon
Diocesen Office, James's Street, Kilkenny
Tel 056-7762448
Email accounts@ossory.ie

Data Protection Officer
Diocesan Office, James's Street, Kilkenny
Tel 056-7762448
Email admin@ossory.ie

Finance Committee
Chairperson: Mr Geoff Meagher
Diocesan Office, James's Street, Kilkenny
Tel 056-7762448

Episcopal Vicars
Primary Education
Rev Dr Dermot Ryan
St Kieran's College, Kilkenny
Family and Social Affairs
Rt Rev Mgr Kieron Kennedy PP
Freshford, Co Kilkenny
Retired Priests
Very Rev Thomas O'Toole PP
Glenmore, Co Kilkenny
Care of Clergy
Very Rev Roderick Whearty TL
St Patrick's Parish Centre,
Loughbay, Kilkenny

Director of Youth Ministry
Very Rev Brian Griffin
Parochial House, Camross, Co Laois
Tel 087-0644158
Email griffinmilepost@yahoo.ie

Diocesan Forum Co-ordinator
Sr Helen Maher
St Kieran's College, Kilkenny
Tel 056-7789714
Email diocesanforum@ossory.ie

Diocesan Pastoral Plan Co-ordinator
Ms Gemma Mulligan
St Kieran's College, Kilkenny
Tel 087-7571250
Email gemmamulligan@ossory.ie

CATECHETICS EDUCATION

Diocesan Advisers for Religious Education
Primary Education: Sr Maria Comerford
Convent of Mercy, Callan, Co Kilkenny
Tel 087-2350719
Email mgcomerford@hotmail.com
Post Primary: Ms Olivia Maher
Email office@cbskilkenny.ie

Catholic Primary School Managers Association
Secretary
Rev Dr Dermot Ryan
St Kieran's College, Kilkenny
Tel 086-6097483
Email education@ossory.ie

LITURGY

Liturgy Chairperson
Very Rev Richard Scriven Adm
St Mary's Cathedral, Kilkenny
Tel 056-7721253/087-2420033
Email rscriven2009@gmail.com

PASTORAL

Adult Faith Formation
Director: Rev Dr Dermot Ryan
St Kieran's College, Kilkenny
Tel 056-7721086/086-6097483
Email afd@ossory.ie

Vocations
Director: Very Rev Kieran O'Shea PP
Ferrybank, Waterford
Tel 086-8272828
Email kieranoshea@ossory.ie

Safeguarding Children
Director of Safeguarding and Diocesan Liaison Person: Ms Kathleen Sherry
Safeguarding Office, Waterford Road,
Kilkenny
Tel 056-7721685/085-8021633
Email safeguarding@ossory.ie
Safeguardinfg Vetting Authorised Signatories
Sr Ena Kennedy
Tel 087-1953850
Email vetting@ossory.ie
Ms Frances Lennon
Tel 056-7762448
Email admin@ossory.ie

Chaplain to the Travelling Community
Very Rev Sean O'Connor PP
Ballyhale, Co Kilkenny
Tel 086-3895911
Email seanoconnor@ossory.ie

Communications Officer
Rev Dr Dermot Ryan
St Kieran's College, Kilkenny
Tel 056-7721086
Email communications@ossory.ie

ACCORD
Seville Lodge, Callan Road, Kilkenny
Tel 056-7722674
Chaplain: Very Rev Daniel Bollard

Ecumenism
Very Rev Dan Carroll
St John's Presbytery, Kilkenny
Tel 056-7721072/087-9077769
Email dancarroll@ossory.ie

Emigrant Commission
Very Rev Laurence Wallace PP
Muckalee, Ballyfoyle, Co Kilkenny
Tel 056-4441271/087-2326807
Fax 056-4440007
Email muckalee@ossory.ie

Trócaire
Very Rev Raymond Dempsey
St John's Presbytery, Kilkenny
Tel 087-2859682
Email 1dempseyr@gmail.com

Lourdes Pilgrimage
Director: Very Rev Anthony O'Connor PP
Kilmacow, via Waterford, Co Kilkenny
Tel/Fax 051-885269/087-2517766

Marriage Tribunal
(See Marriage Tribunals section)

DIOCESE OF OSSORY

Ossory Adoption and Referral Services
Information and Guidance in all matters in relation to adoption
Tel 056-7721685
Ms Mary Curtin, Social Service Centre, Waterford Road, Kilkenny
Tel 056-7721685

Ossory Priests Fraternal Fund
Administrator: Mr Donal Cadogan
Dicoesan Office, James's Street, Kilkenny
Tel 056-7762448
Email kilfera2008@live.com

Ossory Priests Society
Administrator: Mrs Maura Joyce
Dicoesan Office, James's Street, Kilkenny
Tel 056-7762448

Ossory Youth
Desart Hall, New Street, Kilkenny
Tel 056-7761200 Fax 056-7752385
Chairperson: Padraig Fleming
CEO: Ms Mary Mescal

Pioneer Total Abstinence Association
Diocesan Director
Very Rev Thomas Canon Murphy
Ballyragget, Co Kilkenny
Tel 086-8130694

Pontifical Mission Societies
Diocesan Director
Very Rev Sean O'Connor PP
Ballyhale, Co Kilkenny
Tel 086-3895911
Email rsoc1973@gmail.com

PARISHES

Kilkenny city parishes are listed first. Other parishes follow alphabetically. Church titulars are in italics.

ST MARY'S
St Mary's Cathedral
Very Rev Richard Scriven Adm
St Mary's Cathedral, Kilkenny R95 CP46
Tel 056-7721253/087-2420033
Email rscriven2009@gmail.com
Parish sister: Sr Maria Comerford
Tel 056-7721253
Email mgcomerfordrsm@gmail.com
Email stmaryscathedral@ossory.ie
Website www.stmaryscathedral.ie

ST JOHN'S
St John the Evangelist, Holy Trinity, St John the Baptist
St John's Presbytery, Kilkenny R95 ND2W
Email stjohns@ossory.ie
Website www.stjohnskilkenny.com
Very Rev Daniel Carroll
Tel 056-7721072/087-9077769
Email dancarroll@ossory.ie
Very Rev Raymond Dempsey
Tel 087-2859682
Email ldempseyr@gmail.com
Very Rev Lorcan Moran
Tel 086-8550521
Email lorcanmoran5@gmail.com

ST CANICE'S
St Canice's
Very Rev James Murphy PP
St Canice's Presbytery, Dean Street, Kilkenny R95 K6PH
Tel 056-7752991/087-2609545
Fax 056-7721533
Email jimmurphy@ossory.ie
Rev Thomas Norris CC
St Canice's Presbytery, Kilkenny R95 VY0T
Tel 056-7752994/083-3241438

ST PATRICK'S
St Patrick's, St Fiacre's, St Joseph's
St Fiacre's Gardens, Bohernatownish Road, Loughboy, Kilkenny R95 RF97
Tel 056-7764400 Fax 056-7770173
Email stpatricksparish@ossory.ie
Website www.patricksparish.com
Very Rev Roderick Whearty
Tel 056-7764400/086-8133661
Email roderick1@eircom.net
Very Rev Peter Muldowney
Tel 086-8265955
Email peter.muldowney@hotmail.com

AGHABOE
Immaculate Conception, St Canice
Very Rev Noel Canon Maher PP
Clough, Ballacolla, Portlaoise, Co Laois
Tel 057-8738513/087-2326200 Fax 057-8738909
Email nmaher@outlook.ie

AGHAVILLER
St Brendan's, Stoneyford, St Brendan's, Newmarket Holy Trinity
Very Rev Liam Cassin PP
Hugginstown, Co Kilkenny
Tel/Fax 056-7768693/087-2312354
Email liamcassin@ossory.ie

BALLYCALLAN
Queen of Peace, St Molua, St Brigid
Parish email ballycallan@ossory.ie
Very Rev Liam Taylor PP
Ballycallan, Co Kilkenny R95 E8N0
Tel 056-7769564/086-8180954
Email frliamtaylor@gmail.com

BALLYHALE
St Martin of Tours, Our Lady of the Assumption, All Saints
Very Rev Sean O'Connor PP
Ballyhale, Co Kilkenny R95 Y9F4
Tel 086-3895911
Email rsoc1973@gmail.com

BALLYRAGGET
St Patrick's, Assumption of BVM
Very Rev Eamonn O'Gorman PP
Ballyragget, Co Kilkenny
Tel 087-2236145
Email eamonnogorman123@gmail.com

BORRIS-IN-OSSORY
St Canice, Assumption, St Kieran
Very Rev John Robinson PP
Borris-in-Ossory, Portlaoise, Co Laois
Tel 0505-41148/087-2431412
Fax 0505-41148
Email binoparish@gmail.com

CALLAN
Assumption, All Saints, Nativity of BVM
Very Rev William Dalton PP
Callan, Co Kilkenny
Tel 056-7725287/086-8506215
Fax 056-7725287
Email williamdalton@ossory.ie
Website www.callanparish@irishchurch.net

CAMROSS
St Fergal
Very Rev Brian Griffin Adm
Camross, Co Laois
Tel 087-0644158
Email griffinmilepost@yahoo.ie

CASTLECOMER
Immaculate Conception
Rt Rev Mgr Michael Ryan PP
Castlecomer, Co Kilkenny
Tel 056-4441262/086-3693863
Fax 056-4441969
Parish email castlecomer@ossory.ie

CASTLETOWN
St Edmund
Very Rev Brian Griffin Adm
Camross, Co Laois
Tel 087-0644158
Email griffinmilepost@yahoo.ie

CLARA
St Coleman
Very Rev William Purcell PP
Clifden Villa, Clifden, Co Kilkenny
Tel 056-7726560/087-6286858
Fax 056-7726558
Email wpurcell@eircom.net
Parish email clara@ossory.ie

CLOGH
St Patrick's, Sacred Heart
Very Rev Thomas Corcoran PP
Clogh, Castlecomer, Co Kilkenny
Tel 056-4442135/085-2543904
Email tomjcorcoran1@gmail.com

CONAHY
St Coleman, Our Lady of Perpetual Help
Very Rev William Hennessy Adm
Conahy, Jenkinstown, Co Kilkenny
Tel 087-8736155
Email williehennessy@ossory.ie

DANESFORT
St Michael the Archangel, Holy Cross, Kells Holy Cross, Cuffesgrange
Very Rev Mark Condon PP
Danesfort, Co Kilkenny
Tel 056-7727137/086-6005402
Email markcondon@ossory.ie

DIOCESE OF OSSORY

DUNAMAGGAN
St Leonard, St Eoghan
Very Rev Fergus Farrell PP
Windgap, Co Kilkenny
Tel 086-0782066/051-648111

DURROW
Holy Trinity, St Tighearnach
Very Rev Martin Delaney Adm
Rathdowney, Co Laois
Tel 0505-46282/086-2444594
Email delaneymartindl@gmail.com
Rev Thomas McGree CC
Durrow, Cullohill, Co Laois
Tel 087-7619235 Fax 057-8736226
Email frtommcgree@gmail.com

FERRYBANK
Sacred Heart
Very Rev Kieran O'Shea PP
Ferrybank, Waterford
Tel 086-8272828
Email kieranoshea@ossory.ie
Website www.ferrybankparish.com

FRESHFORD
St Lachtain, St Nicholas
Rt Rev Mgr Kieron Kennedy PP
Freshford, Co Kilkenny R95 X2E0
Tel 056-8832426/087-2523521
Email kieronkennedy@ossory.ie
Email freshford@ossory.ie
Website parishoffreshford.com

GALMOY
Immaculate Conception
Very Rev Oliver Maher PP
Urlingford, Co Kilkenny
Tel 086-8323010
Email olivermaher@ossory.ie

GLENMORE
St James
Very Rev Thomas O'Toole PP
Glenmore, via New Ross, Co Kilkenny
Tel 051-880080/087-2240787
Email tm5-tle@hotmail.com

GOWRAN
Assumption
Very Rev Patrick Canon Dalton PP
Gowran, Co Kilkenny R95 E2Y4
Tel 056-7726128/086-8283478
Fax 056-7726134
Email daltonpadraig@gmail.com

INISTIOGE
St Columcille, Assumption, St Brendan
Very Rev Frank Purcell PP
Inistioge, Co Kilkenny
Tel 051-423619/086-6010001
Email sevillelawns@gmail.com

JOHNSTOWN
St Kieran, St Michael
Very Rev Oliver Maher PP
Urlingford, Co Kilkenny
Tel 056-883112/086-8323010
Email olivermaher@ossory.ie

Very Rev Frank Canon Maher CC
Johnstown via Thurles, Co Kilkenny
Tel 056-8831219/087-2402487
Fax 056-8831219
Email frankmaher@ossory.ie

KILMACOW
St Senan
Very Rev Anthony O'Connor PP
Kilmacow, via Waterford, Co Kilkenny
Tel 087-2517766
Email maoc50@me.com
Email kilmacowparish@ossory.ie

LISDOWNEY
St Brigid, St Munchin, St Fiacre
Very Rev Eamonn O'Gorman PP
Ballyragget, Co Kilkenny
Tel 087-2236145
Email eamonnogorman@gmail.com
Very Rev Patrick O'Farrell CC
Lisdowney, Co Kilkenny
Tel 056-8833138/087-2353520
Fax 056-8833701
Email patofarrell@ossory.ie
Parish email lisdowney@ossory.ie

MOONCOIN
Assumption, St Kevin, St Kilgoue
Very Rev Martin Tobin Adm
Mooncoin, Co Kilkenny
Tel 086-2401278
Email frmartintobin@ossory.ie
Parish Office
Tel 051-895123
Email mooncoin@ossory.ie

MUCKALEE
St Brendan, St Brigid, St Joseph
Very Rev Laurence Wallace PP
Muckalee, Ballyfoyle, Co Kilkenny
Tel 056-4441271/087-2326807
Fax 056-4440007
Email lwallace@gmail.com
Parish email muckalee@ossory.ie

MULLINAVAT
St Beacon, St Paul
Very Rev Liam Barron PP
Tel 051-898108/087-2722824
Fax 051-898108
Mullinavat, via Waterford, Co Kilkenny
Email mullinavat@ossory.ie

RATHDOWNEY
Holy Trinity, Our Lady, Queen of the Universe
Very Rev Martin Delaney PP
Rathdowney, Portlaoise, Co Laois
Tel 0505-46282/086-2444594
Email delaneymartindl@gmail.com
Email rathdowney@ossory.ie

ROSBERCON
Assumption, St David, St Aidan
Rt Rev Mgr Daniel Cavanagh PP
Rosbercon, New Ross, Co Wexford
Tel 051-421515/087-2335432
Fax 051-425093
Email danieljcavanagh49@gmail.com

SEIR KIERAN
St Kieran
Very Rev Michael Reddan (SVD) Adm
Seir Kieran, Clareen, Birr, Co Offaly
Tel 057-9131080/087-4345898
Email mjreddan2016@gmail.com
Parish email seirkierparish35@gmail.com

SLIEVERUE
Assumption
Very Rev Kieran O'Shea PP
Ferrybank, Waterford
Tel 086-8272828
Parish email slieverue@ossory.ie
Website www.slieverue.com

TEMPLEORUM
Assumption
Very Rev Paschal Moore PP
Piltown, Co Kilkenny
Tel 051-643112/087-2408078
Fax 051-644911
Email templeorum@ossory.ie
Website www.templeorum.ie

THOMASTOWN
Assumption
Very Rev Daniel Bollard PP
Tel/Fax 056-7724279/087-6644858
Email bollard.dan@gmail.com
Parish email thomastown@ossory.ie

TULLAHERIN
St Bennet, St Kieran
Very Rev Patrick Canon Dalton PP
Tel 056-7726128/086-8283478
Email daltonpadraig@gmail.com
Very Rev Patrick Canon Duggan PE
Tel 056-7727140/086-2557471
Fax 056-7727755
Bennetsbridge, Co Kilkenny
Email patduggan@ossory.ie

TULLAROAN
Assumption
Very Rev Liam Taylor Adm
Ballycallan, Co Kilkenny
Tel 056-7769564/086-8180954
Email frliamtaylor@gmail.com
Very Rev Patrick Guilfoyle CC
Tullaroan, Co Kilkenny
Tel 056-7769141/087-9932117
Fax 056-7769141
Email guilfoylepat@eircom.net

URLINGFORD
Assumption, St Patrick
Very Rev Oliver Maher PP
Urlingford, Co Kilkenny
Tel 056-8831121/086-8323010
Email olivermaher@ossory.ie

DIOCESE OF OSSORY

WINDGAP
St Nicholas, Windgap
St Nicholas, Tullahought
Very Rev Fergus Farrell PP
Windgap, Co Kilkenny
Tel 051-648111/086-0782066
Email fearghus.ofearghail@dcu.ie

INSTITUTIONS AND THEIR CHAPLAINS

Aut Even Hospital
Aut Even, Kilkenny
Priests of St Canice's Parish
Tel 056-7721523/087-9335663

City Vocational School, Kilkenny
Very Rev William Purcell
Tel 087-6286858
Email wpurcell@eircom.net

Community School
Castlecomer, Co Kilkenny
Ms Edel O'Connor
Tel 056-4441447

Abbey Community College
Ferrybank, Waterford
Ms Claire Bolger
Tel 051-832930

District Hospital
Castlecomer, Co Kilkenny
Rt Rev Mgr Michael Ryan
Tel 056-4441262/086-3034155

Orthopaedic Hospital
Kilcreene, Kilkenny
Very Rev Richard Scriven Adm
St Mary's Parish
Tel 056-7721253/087-2420033

St Canice's Hospital, Kilkenny
Priests of St John's Parish
Tel 056-7721072

St Columba's Hospital
Thomastown, Co Kilkenny
Very Rev Daniel Bollard
Tel 056-7724279/087-6644858

St Luke's Hospital, Kilkenny
Rev Patrick Carey
Tel 056-7785000/7771815/087-2599087
Email patrick.carey@hse.ie

Stephen Barracks, Kilkenny
Rev Daniel McCarthy
Tel 056-7761852

PRIESTS OF THE DIOCESE ELSEWHERE

Rt Rev Mgr Liam Bergin
St Brigid's Parish, 841 East Broadway,
Boston, MA 02127, USA
Tel 001-617-4477770
Email lbergin@ossory.ie

Very Rev Laurence O'Keeffe
The Presbytery, Slieverue, Co Kilkenny
Tel 051-832773

RETIRED PRIESTS

Very Rev Pat Comerford
Drakelands Nursing Home,
Ballycallan Road, Kilkenny
Tel 086-1038430
Email patcomerford@ossory.ie

Rev John Condon
Owing House, Piltown, Co Kilkenny
Tel 086-8394615

Very Rev Thomas Coyle
Friary Street, Kilkenny
Tel 087-7668969

Very Rev James Canon Crotty
Ferrybank, Waterford
Tel 086-8317711
Email jimcrotty@ossory.ie

Rev John Delaney
Beechwood Nursing Home,
Leighlinbridge, Co Carlow
Tel 086-2326807

Very Rev Liam Dunne
The Forge, Martin's Lane,
Upper Main Street,
Arklow, Co Wicklow
Tel 0402-32779

Very Rev Laurence Canon Dunphy
Urlingford, Co Kilkenny
Tel 087-2300849

Vey Rev Brian Canon Flynn
Kilmacow,
Via Waterford, Co Kilkenny
Tel 051-885122/087-2828391
Email brianflynn@ossory.ie

Very Rev Eamon Foley
6 Woodlawn, Archers Avenue,
Kilkenny
Tel 087-7828784

Very Rev Peter Hoyne
Newmarket,
Hugginstown, Co Kilkenny
Tel 056-7768678

Very Rev Dean Seamus McEvoy
Drakelands Nursing Home,
Ballycallan Road, Kilkenny
Tel 086-2634093

Very Rev Thomas Canon Murphy
Brookhaven Nursing Home,
Ballyragget, Co Kilkenny
Tel 086-8130694

Very Rev Archdeacon Sean O'Doherty
Durrow, Co Laois
Tel 057-8736156

RELIGIOUS ORDERS AND CONGREGATIONS

PRIESTS

CAPUCHINS
Capuchin Friary, Friary Street,
Kilkenny R95 NX60
Tel 056-7721439 Fax 056-7722025
Guardian: Rev Eddie Dowley (OFMCap)
Vicar: Rev Christy Twomey (OFMCap)

DOMINICANS
Black Abbey, Kilkenny, Co Kilkenny
Tel 056-7721279 Fax 056-7721297
Superior: Rev Thomas Monahan (OP)
Email blackabbey@dominicans.ie

BROTHERS

BROTHERS OF CHARITY
St Vincent's Brothers' Community,
9 Arbourmount, Rockshire Road,
Ferrybank, Waterford
Tel 051-832180 Fax 051-833490
Community Leader: Br Joseph Killoran
Email
jkilloran@waterford.brothersofcharity.ie
Community: 3

CHRISTIAN BROTHERS
Christian Brothers, Edmund Rice House,
Westcourt, Callan, Co Kilkenny
Tel 056-7725141
Community Leader
Br Chrisy O'Carroll
Community: 6

Edmund Rice Centre,
Callan, Co Kilkenny
Tel 056-7725993

DE LA SALLE BROTHERS
De La Salle Monastery,
Castletown, Portlaoise, Co Laois
Tel 057-8732359 (residence)
Fax 057-8732925
Superior: Br Stephen Deignan
Community: 3

Miguel House, Castletown,
Portlaoise, Co Laois
Tel 057-8732136 Fax 057-8756648
Superior: Br Martin Curran
Community: 16
House for retired brothers

La Salle Pastoral Centre,
Castletown, Portlaoise, Co Laois
Tel 057-8732442 Fax 057-872925
Director: Mr Derek Doherty
Retreat centre

SISTERS

CONGREGATION OF THE SISTERS OF MERCY
Convent of Mercy, Ballyragget,
Co Kilkenny
Tel 056-8833114

Convent of Mercy,
Callan, Co Kilkenny
Tel 056-7725223

1 Mountain View, Borris-in-Ossory,
Portlaoise, Co Laois
Tel/Fax 0505-41964

Villa Maria, Talbot's Inch, Kilkenny
Tel 056-7765774

20 Archer's Court, Loughboy,
Kilkenny
Tel 056-7780437

DAUGHTERS OF MARY AND JOSEPH
10 Parcnagowan, Waterford Road,
Kilkenny
Community: 2

10 Hazelwood,
Parcnagowan, Kilkenny

LITTLE COMPANY OF MARY
Troy's Court, Kilkenny
Tel 056-7763117
Community: 3

LITTLE SISTERS OF THE POOR
St Joseph's, Abbey Road,
Ferrybank, Waterford
Tel 051-833006
Superior: Sr Roseline
Email ms.waterford@lspireland.com
Community: 14
Care for the elderly

LORETO (IBVM)
Loreto Community,
Freshford Road, Kilkenny
Tel 056-7721187
Shared Leaders
Sr Louvenagh Heffernan,
Sr Nan O'Mahony
Community: 14
Loreto Secondary School
Tel 056-7765131
Education and pastoral work

PRESENTATION SISTERS
Presentation Sisters, Kilkenny
Tel 056-7721351
Community: 16

Presentation Sisters,
8 Rosemount,
Newpark Drive, Kilkenny
Tel 056-7721693

Presentation Sisters,
33 Newpark Close,
Newpark Drive, Kilkenny
Tel 056-7708544
Community: 1

RELIGIOUS OF SACRED HEART OF MARY
Ferrybank, Waterford
Tel 051-832592
Community: 14
Primary School. Pupils: 200+
Secondary School. Pupils: 630

22 Castle Oaks, Rockshire Road,
Ferrybank, Waterford
Tel 051-851606
Community: 1
Education, pastoral work

An Grianán, Ferrybank, Waterford
Community: 8

Naomh Bríd, Ferrybank, Waterford
Community: 8

SISTERS OF ST JOHN OF GOD
Regional Centre,
College Road, Kilkenny
Tel 056-7722870 Fax 056-7751411
Email sjgregionaloffice@eircom.net
Regional Leader
Sr Geraldine Fitzpatrick

Sisters of St John of God,
Galtrim, Waterford Road, Kilkenny
Tel 056-7775510

Sisters of St John of God,
7 Maudlin Court,
Thomastown, Co Kilkenny
Tel 056-7724046

Sisters of St John of God,
11 Dean's Court,
Waterford Road, Kilkenny
Tel 056-7764576

St John of God House,
College Road, Kilkenny
Tel 056-7756790

Sisters of St John of God,
'Fermoyle', Greenshill, Kilkenny
Tel 056-7751259

Sisters of St John of God,
Aut Even Convent, Kilkenny
Tel 056-7761451

EDUCATIONAL INSTITUTIONS

St Kieran's College
Kilkenny
Tel 056-7721086 Fax 056-7770001
Email school@stkieranscollege.ie
President: Rev Dr Dermot Ryan
Principal: Mr Adrian Finan
Tel 056-7721086 Ext 223/7761707
Chaplain: Mr Ken Maher
Tel 056-7761707

Our Lady of Lourdes Secondary School
Rosbercon, via New Ross, Co Kilkenny
Principal: Ms Toni Ormond
Tel 051-422177

Adult Educational Institute
Seville Lodge, Callan Road, Kilkenny
Tel/Fax 056-7721453
Business Manager: Mr Richard Curtin

CHARITABLE AND OTHER SOCIETIES

Cathedral Bookshop
St Mary's Cathedral,
James's Street, Kilkenny
Contact: Very Rev Richard Scriven
Tel 056-7721253
Email rscriven2009@gmail.com

Cathedral Cafe
St Mary's Cathedral,
James's Street, Kilkenny
Contact: Very Rev Richard Scriven
Tel 056-7721253
Email rscriven2009@gmail.com

Good Shepherd Centre
Administrator: Mr Seamus Roche
Hostel for transient homeless men
Tel 056-7722566

Homes for Elderly People
Kilkenny: Troy's Court
Tel 056-7763117
St Patrick's Parish: Tel 056-7764400
St Johns' Parish: Tel 056-7721072
Ballyragget: O'Gorman House
Tel 056-8833377
St Mary's: Tel 056-7721253
Callan: Mount Carmel
Tel 056-7725301
Freshford: Prague House
Tel 056-8832281
Kilmacow: Rosedale
Tel 051-885125
Kilmoganny: St Joseph's
Tel 051-648091
Owning, Piltown: Lady Sue Ryder Home
Tel 051-643136
Rathdowney: Cuan Bhríde
Tel 0505-46521

L'Arche, Workshops and Accommodation for People with Learning Difficulties
Moorefield House, Kilmoganny,
Co Kilkenny
Tel 051-64809
An Siol: 42 West Street, Callan,
Co Kilkenny
Tel 056-7725230
Cluain Aoibhin: Fairgreen, Callan,
Co Kilkenny
Tel 056-7725628

Ossory Social Services
Social Service Centre,
Waterford Road, Kilkenny
Tel 056-7721685 Fax 056-7763636
Email kilkennysocialservices@gmail.com
Director: Rt Rev Mgr Kieron Kennedy

Local Social Services Centres:
Callan: Sr Cecilia Dowley
Tel 056-7725223
Castlecomer: Ms Bridget McLean
Tel 056-4441679
Ferrybank: Sr Constance O'Sullivan
Tel 051-832592
Freshford: Sr Brigid Lonergan
Tel 056-8832281
Rathdowney Cuan Bhride
Sr Catherine O'Brien
Tel 0505-46521

SOS (Kilkenny) Ltd,
Sheltered Workshop and
Accommodation for People with
Learning Difficulties
SOS (Kilkenny) Ltd,
Callan Road, Kilkenny
Tel 056-7764000 Fax 056-7761212

Apostolic Work Society
Secretary: Mrs Nora Ryan
Ross, Rathdowney, Co Laois
Tel 0505-46524

St Joseph's Young Priests' Society
Chairperson: Mr Paul Clarke
Clonkil, Callan, Co Kilkenny
Tel 056-7725108/086-2523534
Email paulfclarke@eircom.net
Chaplain: Rev William Purcell
St Kieran's College, Kilkenny
Tel 056-7721086/087-6286858
Email wpurcell@eircom.net

DIOCESE OF RAPHOE

PATRON OF THE DIOCESE
ST EUNAN, 23 SEPTEMBER

INCLUDES THE GREATER PART OF COUNTY DONEGAL

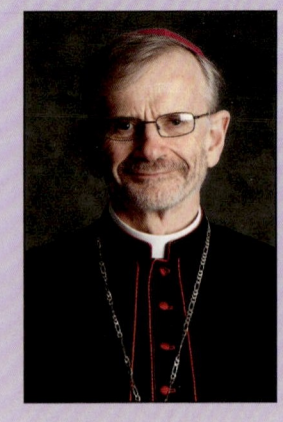

Most Rev Alan McGuckian (SJ) DD
Bishop of Raphoe;
born 26 Ferbruary 1953;
ordained priest 22 June 1984;
ordained Bishop of Raphoe
6 August 2017

Residence: Ard Adhamhnáin,
Cathedral Road, Letterkenny,
Co Donegal F92 W2W9
Tel 074-9121208
Fax 074-9124872
Email
diocesanoffice@raphoediocese.ie
Website www.raphoediocese.ie

ST EUNAN'S CATHEDRAL, LETTERKENNY

The old cathedral of Raphoe passed into Protestant hands at the Reformation. In the eighteenth century the Catholic bishops came to live in Letterkenny. A church was built circa 1820 and, having been extended by Bishop Patrick McGettigan, was used as a pro-cathedral. Bishop McDevitt (1871–1879) thought of building a new cathedral, and Lord Southwell promised a site, but it was not until 1891, when Bishop O'Donnell was in office, that actual building began. The cathedral was completed in 1901. Besides overseeing the cathedral project, Bishop O'Donnell had the task of providing a house for the bishop and priests of the cathedral parish.

The main benefactors were Fr J.D. McGarvey PP, Killygarvan, and Mr Neil Gillen of Airdrie. Various priests of the diocese spent considerable time fund-raising in Britain, the US and Canada. The style is Gothic, with some Hiberno-Romanesque features, and the building is of white Mountcharles sandstone. The cathedral dominates the Letterkenny skyline. Among the artistic features to be noted are the 'Drumceat' window, by Michael Healy (North Transept); the pulpit, by Messrs Pearse (Patrick Pearse's family); the Great Arch, with its St Columba and St Eunan columns; and, outside, the fine statue of Bishop O'Donnell, by Doyle of Chelsea.

Remodelling of the cathedral took place in 1985, with the addition of an altar table and chairs; great care was taken to preserve the style and materials of the original altar. Bishop Hegarty promoted this tasteful restoration work, which left intact the architectural character of the building.

Local Social Services Centres:
Callan: Sr Cecilia Dowley
Tel 056-7725223
Castlecomer: Ms Bridget McLean
Tel 056-4441679
Ferrybank: Sr Constance O'Sullivan
Tel 051-832592
Freshford: Sr Brigid Lonergan
Tel 056-8832281
Rathdowney Cuan Bhride
Sr Catherine O'Brien
Tel 0505-46521

SOS (Kilkenny) Ltd,
Sheltered Workshop and
Accommodation for People with
Learning Difficulties
SOS (Kilkenny) Ltd,
Callan Road, Kilkenny
Tel 056-7764000 Fax 056-7761212

Apostolic Work Society
Secretary: Mrs Nora Ryan
Ross, Rathdowney, Co Laois
Tel 0505-46524

St Joseph's Young Priests' Society
Chairperson: Mr Paul Clarke
Clonkil, Callan, Co Kilkenny
Tel 056-7725108/086-2523534
Email paulfclarke@eircom.net
Chaplain: Rev William Purcell
St Kieran's College, Kilkenny
Tel 056-7721086/087-6286858
Email wpurcell@eircom.net

DIOCESE OF RAPHOE

PATRON OF THE DIOCESE
ST EUNAN, 23 SEPTEMBER

INCLUDES THE GREATER PART OF COUNTY DONEGAL

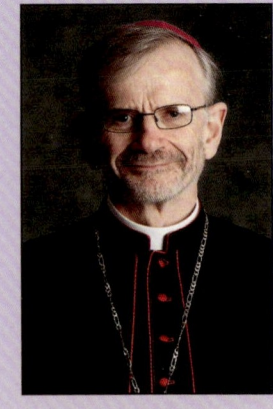

Most Rev Alan McGuckian (SJ) DD
Bishop of Raphoe;
born 26 Ferbruary 1953;
ordained priest 22 June 1984;
ordained Bishop of Raphoe
6 August 2017

Residence: Ard Adhamhnáin,
Cathedral Road, Letterkenny,
Co Donegal F92 W2W9
Tel 074-9121208
Fax 074-9124872
Email
diocesanoffice@raphoediocese.ie
Website www.raphoediocese.ie

ST EUNAN'S CATHEDRAL, LETTERKENNY

The old cathedral of Raphoe passed into Protestant hands at the Reformation. In the eighteenth century the Catholic bishops came to live in Letterkenny. A church was built circa 1820 and, having been extended by Bishop Patrick McGettigan, was used as a pro-cathedral. Bishop McDevitt (1871–1879) thought of building a new cathedral, and Lord Southwell promised a site, but it was not until 1891, when Bishop O'Donnell was in office, that actual building began. The cathedral was completed in 1901. Besides overseeing the cathedral project, Bishop O'Donnell had the task of providing a house for the bishop and priests of the cathedral parish.

The main benefactors were Fr J.D. McGarvey PP, Killygarvan, and Mr Neil Gillen of Airdrie. Various priests of the diocese spent considerable time fund-raising in Britain, the US and Canada. The style is Gothic, with some Hiberno-Romanesque features, and the building is of white Mountcharles sandstone. The cathedral dominates the Letterkenny skyline. Among the artistic features to be noted are the 'Drumceat' window, by Michael Healy (North Transept); the pulpit, by Messrs Pearse (Patrick Pearse's family); the Great Arch, with its St Columba and St Eunan columns; and, outside, the fine statue of Bishop O'Donnell, by Doyle of Chelsea.

Remodelling of the cathedral took place in 1985, with the addition of an altar table and chairs; great care was taken to preserve the style and materials of the original altar. Bishop Hegarty promoted this tasteful restoration work, which left intact the architectural character of the building.

DIOCESE OF RAPHOE

Most Rev Philip Boyce (OCD)
Bishop Emeritas of Raphoe;
born 25 January 1940;
ordained priest 17 April 1966;
ordained Bishop of Raphoe 1 October 1995; Retired 6 August 2017
Residence: 'Columba House', Windyhall, Letterkenny, Co Donegal F92 EK4W
Tel 074-9122729

CHAPTER

Dean
Very Rev Canon Austin Laverty PP, Ardara
Archdeacon
Ven Archdeacon William McMenamin PE Raphoe
Members
Very Rev Canon Denis McGettigan PE Raphoe
Very Rev Canon John Gallagher PE Ardara
Very Rev Canon Francis McAteer AP Glencolmcille
Very Rev Canon James Friel PE Rathmullan
Very Rev Canon Michael Herrity AP Cnoc Fola

ADMINISTRATION

Vicars General
Very Rev Francis McLoone PP, VG
Parochial House, Killymard,
Donegal Town, Co Donegal F94 C6T7
Rev Michael McKeever CC, VG
Parochial House, Church Hill,
Letterkenny, Co Donegal F92 H2V6

Diocesan Secretary
Rev Michael McKeever
Diocesan Office, Ard Adhamhnáin,
Letterkenny, Co Donegal F92 W2W9
Tel 074-9121208 Fax 074-9124872
Email diocesanoffice@raphoediocese.ie

Administration Secretary
Ms Marie McGill
Diocesan Office, Ard Adhamhnáin,
Letterkenny, Co Donegal R92 W2W9
Tel 074-9121208 Fax 074-9124872
Email diocesanoffice@raphoediocese.ie

Diocesan Chancellor
Rt Rev Mgr Kevin Gillespie Adm, VF
Ard Choluim, Cathedral Road,
Letterkenny, Co Donegal F92 CF88

College of Consultors
Very Rev Francis McLoone PP, VG Killymard
Rev Michael McKeever CC, VG Church Hill
Rt Rev Mgr Kevin Gillespie Adm, VF Letterkenny
Very Rev Michael Carney PP, Ramelton
Very Rev Paddy Dunne PP, Kilmacrennan
Very Rev Ciaran Harkin PP Newtowncunningham
Rev Danny McBrearty
Rev Brian O'Fearraigh CC, Gaoth Dobhair

Vicars Forane
Rt Rev Mgr Kevin Gillespie Adm, VF Letterkenny
Very Rev Cathal O'Fearrai PP, VF Ballyshannon
Very Rev Gerard Cunningham PP, VF Glenties
Very Rev Pat Ward PP, VF Burtonport
Very Rev Kieran McAteer PP, VF Stranorlar

Financial Administrator
Mrs Carmel Doherty
Ard Adhamhnáin,
Letterkenny, Co Donegal

Finance Committee
Bishop Alan McGuckian (SJ),
Rev Michael McKeever
Rev Stephan Gorman *(Secretary)*

Building Committee
Very Rev Canon Austin Laverty PP
Very Rev Canon John Gallagher PE

Diocesan Archives
Faíche Ó Dónaill Building
Ard Adhamhnáin, Letterkenny,
Co Donegal
Tel 074-9161109
Email archives@raphoediocese.ie

CATECHETICS EDUCATION

Religious Education in Primary Schools
Co-ordinator
Very Rev Aodhan Cannon PP
Dungloe, Co Donegal
Tel 074-9521008

Religious Education in Secondary Schools
Vacant

LITURGY

Perpetual Eucharistic Adoration
Diocesan Director: Vacant

PASTORAL

ACCORD
Pastoral Centre,
Monastery Ave, Letterkenny
Tel 074-9122218
LoCall 1850-201878

Child Safeguarding Office
Pastoral Centre, Monastery Avenue,
Letterkenny, Co Donegal
Tel 074-9125669
Email raphoesafeguarding@gmail.com

Ecumenism
Diocesan Director
Very Rev Canon Francis McAteer AP
Glencolmcille, Co Donegal
Tel 074-9730888

Family Ministry Centre
The Pastoral Centre,
Letterkenny, Co Donegal
Tel 074-9121853 Fax 074-9128433

Fatima Pilgrimage
Director: Very Rev James Sweeney PP
Frosses, Co Donegal
Tel 074-9736006

Knock Pilgrimage
Director: Rev Michael McKeever CC, VG
Church Hill, Co Donegal
Tel 074-9137057

Lourdes Pilgrimage
Director: Rev Stephen Gorman CC
Parochial House, Milford,
Co Donegal
Tel 074-9153236/074-9125090 *(Lourdes office)*

Marriage Tribunal
(See also Marriage Tribunals section)
Secretary: Rhona Healy
Judicial Vicar/Instructor
Mgr Kevin Gillespie
Assistant: Rev John Joe Duffy
The Pastoral Centre, Letterkenny,
Co Donegal
Tel 074-9121853

Pioneer Total Abstinence Association
Diocesan Director
Very Rev Canon James Friel PE
Rathmullan, Co Donegal
Very Rev James Sweeney PP
Frosses, Co Donegal
Tel 074-9736006

Religious Broadcasting
Diocesan Director
Very Rev Patrick Dunne PP
Parochial House, Kilmacrennan,
Letterkenny
Tel 074-9139018

Vocations
Director
Very Rev Rory Brady PP
Parochial House,
Bruckless, Co Donegal
Tel 074-9737015

Missio Ireland
Diocesan Director
Rev Damien Nejad CC
Parochial House,
Letterkenny, Co Donegal F92 CF88
Tel 074-9121021

DIOCESE OF RAPHOE

PARISHES

The mensal parish is listed first. Other parishes follow alphabetically. Historical names are given in parentheses.

LETTERKENNY (CONWAL AND LECK)
Cathedral of St Eunan and St Columba
Mgr Kevin Gillespie Adm, VF
Rev Philip Kemmy CC
Rev Damien Nejad CC
Parochial House, Letterkenny,
Co Donegal F92 CF88
Tel 074-9121021
Email office@steunanscathedral.ie
Website www.steunanscathedral.ie
Letterkenny General Hospital
Rev Martin Chambers
2 Chaplain's House, Knocknamona,
Letterkenny, Co Donegal
Tel 074-9125090
Rev Shane Gallagher
1 Chaplain's House, Knocknamona,
Letterkenny, Co Donegal
Tel (Hospital) 074-9125888

ANNAGRY
Very Rev Nigel Ó Gallachóir PP
Annagry, Co Donegal
Tel 074-9548902

ARDARA
Very Rev Canon Austin Laverty PP
Tel 074-9541135
Rev Johnny Moore CC
Tel 074-9537033
Ardara, Co Donegal
Rev Philip Daly CC
Kilclooney, Co Donegal
Tel 074-9545114

AUGHANINSHIN
Website www.irishmartyrs.com
Very Rev Brian Quinn PP
Ballyraine, Letterkenny, Co Donegal
Tel 074-9127600
Rev Brendan Ward CC
Carnamuggagh Lower,
Letterkenny, Co Donegal
Tel 074-9122608

BALLINTRA (DRUMHOLM)
Very Rev Adrian Gavigan PP
Parochial House, Lisminton,
Ballintra, Co Donegal
Tel 074-9734642

BALLYSHANNON (KILBARRON)
Website www.kilbarron.org
Very Rev Cathal Ó Fearraí PP, VF
Kilbarron House, College Street,
Ballyshannon, Co Donegal
Tel 071-9851295

BRUCKLESS (KILLAGHTEE)
Very Rev Rory Brady PP
Bruckless, Co Donegal
Tel 074-9737015

BURTONPORT (KINCASSLAGH)
Very Rev Pat Ward PP, VF
Burtonport, Co Donegal
Tel 074-9542006
Rev John Boyce CC
Arranmore Island, Co Donegal
Tel 074-9520504
www.kincasslagh.ie

CARRICK (GLENCOLMCILLE)
Very Rev Denis Quinn PP
Carrick, Co Donegal
Tel 074-9739008
Very Rev Canon Francis McAteer AP
Glencolmcille, Co Donegal
Tel 074-9730888

CARRIGART (MEEVAGH)
Very Rev Charles Byrne PP
Carrigart, Co Donegal
Tel 074-9155154

CLOGHAN (KILTEEVOGUE)
Very Rev Lorcan Sharkey PP
Cloghan, Lifford, Co Donegal
Tel 074-9133007

DONEGAL TOWN (TAWNAWILLY)/CLAR
Very Rev Niall Coll PP
Donegal Town, Co Donegal
Tel 074-9721026

DRUMOGHILL (RAYMOCHY)
Very Rev Martin Cunningham PP
Drumoghill, Co Donegal
Tel 074-9157169

DUNFANAGHY (CLONDAHORKEY)
Very Rev Martin Doohan PP
Dunfanaghy, Co Donegal
Tel 074-9136163
Rev John Joe Duffy CC
Creeslough, Co Donegal
Tel 074-9138011

DUNGLOE (TEMPLECRONE AND LETTERMACAWARD)
Very Rev Aodhan Cannon PP
Dungloe, Co Donegal
Tel 074-9521008
Very Rev Eddie Gallagher AP
Leitirmacaward, Co Donegal
Tel 074-9544102

FALCARRAGH
Very Rev James Gillespie PP
Falcarragh, Co Donegal
Tel 074-9135196

GLENSWILLY (GLENSWILLY AND TEMPLEDOUGLAS)
Rev Liam Boyle CC
Glenswilly, New Mills, Letterkenny,
Co Donegal
Tel 074-9137456

GLENTIES (INISKEEL)
Very Rev Gerard Cunningham PP, VF
Glenties, Co Donegal
Tel 074-9551117
Rev Donnchadh Ó Baoill CC
Fintown, Donegal Town, Co Donegal
Tel 074-9546107

GORTAHORK/TORY ISLAND
Very Rev Seán Ó Gallchóir PP
Gortahork, Co Donegal
Tel 074-9135214

GWEEDORE
Very Rev Pádraig Ó Baoighill PP
Tel 074-9531310
Rev Brian O'Fearraigh CC
Tel 074-9531947
Derrybeg, Letterkenny
Very Rev Canon Michael Herrity AP
Bun-a-leaca, Letterkenny,
Co Donegal
Tel 074-9531155

INVER
Very Rev James Sweeney PP
Frosses, Co Donegal
Tel 074-9736006
Rev Francis Ferry CC
Mountcharles, Co Donegal
Tel 074-9735009
Rev Morty O'Shea (SOLT) CC
Ardaghey, Co Donegal
Tel 074-9736007

KILCAR
Very Rev William Peoples PP
Kilcar, Co Donegal
Tel 074-9738007

KILLYBEGS
www.killybegsparish.com
Very Rev Colm O'Gallchoir PP
Killybegs, Co Donegal
Tel 074-9731030

KILLYMARD
Very Rev Francis McLoone PP, VG
Killymard, Co Donegal
Tel 074-9721929

KILMACRENNAN
Very Rev Patrick Dunne PP
Kilmacrennan, Co Donegal
Tel 074-9139018

NEWTOWNCUNNINGHAM & KILLEA
Very Rev Ciaran Harkin PP
Parochial House,
Newtowncunningham,
Lifford, Co Donegal
Tel 074-9156138

RAMELTON (AUGHNISH)
Very Rev Michael Carney PP
Ramelton, Co Donegal
Tel 074-9151304

DIOCESE OF RAPHOE

RAPHOE
www.parishofraphoe.com
Very Rev Eamonn Kelly PP
Convoy, Lifford, Co Donegal
Tel 087-9077985

RATHMULLAN (KILLYGARVAN AND TULLYFERN)
www.mrparishes.ie
Very Rev Martin Collum PP
Rathmullan, Co Donegal
Tel 074-9158156
Rev Stephen Gorman CC
Milford, Co Donegal
Tel 074-9153236
Rev Paul McGeehan
Glenvar, Rathmullan, Co Donegal
Tel 074-9150014

ST JOHNSTON (TAUGHBOYNE)
Rt Rev Mgr Daniel Carr PP
St Johnston, Lifford, Co Donegal
Tel 074-9148203

STRANORLAR
www.stranorlarparish.com
Very Rev Kieran McAteer PP, VF
Parochial House, Ballybofey,
Co Donegal
Tel 074-9131135
Rev Anthony Briody CC
Parochial House, Stranorlar,
Co Donegal
Tel 074-9131157

TAMNEY (CLONDAVADDOG)
Very Rev Patrick McGarvey PP
Fanavolty, Kindrum,
Letterkenny, Co Donegal
Tel 074-9159007

TERMON (GARTAN AND TERMON)
Very Rev Patrick McHugh PP
Termon, Letterkenny,
Co Donegal
Tel 074-9139016
Rev Michael McKeever CC, VG
Church Hill, Letterkenny,
Co Donegal
Tel 074-9137057
www.gartantermonparish.ie

INSTITUTIONS AND THEIR CHAPLAINS

General Hospital
Letterkenny, Co Donegal
Tel 074-9125888
Rev Martin Chambers
c/o General Hospital, Letterkenny
or 2 Chaplain's House,
Knocknamona, Letterkenny
Rev Shane Gallagher
1 Chaplain's House,
Knocknamona, Letterkenny

St Joseph's Hospital
Stranorlar, Co Donegal
Tel 074-9131038
Parochial clergy Stranorlar

PRIESTS OF THE DIOCESE ELSEWHERE

Rev Patrick Bonner
c/o Diocesan Office,
Letterkenny, Co Donegal
Rev Joseph Briody
St John's Seminary, 127 Lake Street,
Brighton, MA 02135, USA
Rev Jonathan Flood
c/o Diocesan Office,
Letterkenny, Co Donegal
Rev Brendan McBride
St Philip's Church,
725 Diamond Street, San Francisco,
California, 94114
Rev Eamonn McLaughlin
Congregation for the Clergy, Rome

RETIRED PRIESTS

Very Rev Connell Cunningham PE
c/o Diocesan Office,
Letterkenny, Co Donegal
Rev Anthony Griffith
Rushbrook, Laghey, Co Donegal
Tel 074-9734021
Very Rev Daniel O'Doherty PE
St Eunan's Nursing Home,
Letterkenny, Co Donegal
Very Rev Desmond Sweeney PE
17 Meadowvale, Ramelton
Tel 074-9151085
Very Rev Michael Connaghan PE
c/o Hillcrest Nursing Home, Letterkenny,
Co Donegal
Very Rev Canon James Friel PE
Massreagh, Rathmullen, Co Donegal
Tel 074-9158306
Archdeacon William McMenamin PE
'St Columba's',
Meeting House Street,
Raphoe, Co Donegal
Tel 074-9144834
Very Rev Dermot McShane PE
c/o Community Hospital, Killybegs,
Co Donegal
Very Rev Seamus Meehan PE
Main Street, Dungloe, Co Donegal
Tel 074-9521895
Very Rev Canon John Gallagher PE
Ardara, Co Donegal
Tel 087-6636434
Very Rev Seamus Dagens PE
Drimarone, Co Donegal
Tel 085-8590936

Very Rev Michael Sweeney PE
Ballynabrockey, Fanad, Co Donegal
Very Rev Canon Dinny McGettigan PE
Meetinghouse Street,
Raphoe, Co Donegal
Rev Daniel McBrearty
Gortnavern, Coolboy,
Letterkenny, Co Donegal

RELIGIOUS ORDERS AND CONGREGATIONS

PRIESTS

CAPUCHINS (OFMCAP)
Capuchin Friary, Ard Mhuire,
Creeslough, Letterkenny,
Co Donegal F92 Y23R
Tel 074-9138005 Fax 074-9138371
Guardian: Rev Philip Baxter (OFMCap)
Vicar: Rev Kieran Shorten (OFMCap)

FRANCISCANS (OFM)
Franciscan Friary, Rossnowlagh,
Co Donegal
Tel 072-9851342 Fax 072-9852206
Email info.rossnowlagh@franciscans.ie
Guardian: Rev Eugene Barrett (OFM)
Vicar: Rev Vincent Finnegan (OFM)

SISTERS

CONGREGATION OF THE SISTERS OF MERCY
Convent of Mercy, Donegal Town,
Co Donegal F94 D8Y8
Tel 074-9721175
Shared leadership
Community: 5

17 Blackrock Drive, Ballybofey,
Co Donegal F93 VW1X
Tel 074-9132721

St Catherine's,
Ballyshannon, Co Donegal F94 D309
Tel 071-9851268
Community: 14

Dia Linn, Gortnamucklagh,
Glenties, Co Donegal
Tel 074-9551125

Sisters of Mercy,
Ceoil na Coille, Stranorlar,
Lifford, Co Donegal F93 ET28
Tel 074-9131711

35 Brookfield Manor,
Donegal Town, Co Donegal F94 K2N5
Tel 074-9725996

No 7 Slí Na mBroc,
Arkeskin, Donegal Town F94 H2K4
Tel 074-9742652

St Anne's, Ballyshannon,
Co Donegal F94 FD85

DIOCESE OF RAPHOE

EDUCATIONAL INSTITUTIONS

Coláiste Ailigh
Carnamuggagh, Letterkenny,
Co Donegal
Tel 074-9125943
Príomh-Óide:
Mr Michael Gibbons
Séiplineadh:
Ms Annmarie Canning

Coláiste Cholmcille
Ballyshannon, Co Donegal
Tel 071-9858288/9851369/9852459
Principal: Ms Cora Fagan
Chaplain: Vacant

Coláiste Phobail Cholmcille
Oileán Thoraigh, Co Dhún na nGall
Tel 074-9165448
Príomh-Óide
Mr Patrick Queenan

Rosses Community School
Dungloe, Co Donegal
Tel 074-9521122
Principal: Mr John Gorman

Comprehensive School
Glenties, Lifford, Co Donegal
Tel 074-9551172
Fax 074-9551664
Principal: Mrs Frances Bonner
Chaplain: Mr Hugh Doyle

Institute of Technology, Letterkenny
Director: Mr Paul Hannigan
Tel 074-9124888
Chaplain: Rev Liam Boyle

Loreto Convent Secondary School
Letterkenny, Co Donegal
Tel 074-9121850
Principal: Ms Geraldine Mullin
Chaplain: Parish Clergy

Loreto Community School
Milford, Co Donegal
Tel 074-9153253 Fax 074-9153518
Principal: Ms Margaret O'Connor
Tel 074-9153399
Chaplain: Mr John Lynch

Pobalscoil Chloich Cheannfhaola
Falcarragh,
Letterkenny, Co Donegal
Tel 074-9135424/9135231
Fax 074-9135019
Príomh-Oide: Ms Maeve Sweeney
Séiplineach: Mr Oliver Gallagher

Pobalscoil Ghaoth Dobhair
Derrybeg,
Letterkenny, Co Donegal
Tel 074-9531040
Príomh-Oide: Seamus Ó Briain
Séiplineach: Rev Brian O'Fearraigh CC

St Columba's College
Stranorlar, Co Donegal
Tel 074-9131246
Principal: Mr Tom Rowan
Chaplain: Parish Clergy

St Eunan's College
Letterkenny, Co Donegal
Tel 074-9121143
Principal: Mr Damien McCroary
Chaplaincy: Rev Brendan Ward and
Rev Damien Nejad

Donegal ETB Schools
Arranmore Island, Co Donegal
Tel 074-9520747
Principal: Mrs Mary Doherty
Chaplain: Vacant

Ballinamore, Co Donegal
Tel 074-9546133 Fax 074-9546256
Principal: Mr Ciarán Mac Ruaidhrí
Chaplain: Vacant

Carrick, Co Donegal
Tel 074-9739071 Fax 074-9739265
Principal: Mr Sean MacSuibhne
Chaplain: Vacant

*Abbey Vocational School,
Donegal Town, Co Donegal*
Tel 074-9721105 Fax 074-9722851
Principal: Mrs Geraldine Diver
Chaplain: Vacant

*Gairm Scoil Catríona,
Killybegs, Co Donegal*
Tel/Fax 074-9731491
Principal: Ms Anne Marie Luby

*Errigal College,
Letterkenny, Co Donegal*
Tel 074-9121047/9121861
Fax 074-9121861
Principal: Mr Danny McFadden

*Mulroy College,
Milford, Co Donegal*
Tel 074-9153346
Principal: Ms Fiona Temple

*Deele College,
Raphoe, Co Donegal*
Tel 074-9145493
Principal: Mr Joe Boyle

*Finn Valley College,
Stranorlar, Co Donegal*
Tel 074-9131684 Fax 074-9131355
Principal: Mr Alan Thompson

CHARITABLE AND OTHER SOCIETIES

Ards Friary Retreat Centre
Manager: Mr Joe Conroy
Tel 074-9138909
Email info@ardsfriary.ie
Website www.ardsfriary.ie

Trócaire
Very Rev Aodhan Cannon PP
Parochial House, Dungloe, Co Donegal
Tel 074-9521008

DIOCESE OF WATERFORD AND LISMORE

PATRONS OF THE DIOCESE
ST OTTERAN, 27 OCTOBER; ST CARTHAGE, 15 MAY;
ST DECLAN, 24 JULY

INCLUDES COUNTY WATERFORD
AND PART OF COUNTIES TIPPERARY AND CORK

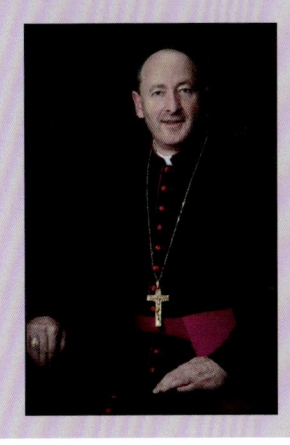

Most Rev Alphonsus Cullinan DD
Bishop of Waterford and Lismore
born 7 May 1959;
ordained priest 12 June 1994;
ordained Bishop of Waterford and Lismore 12 April 2015

Residence: Bishop's House, John's Hill, Waterford
Tel 051-874463
Email info@waterfordlismore.ie

CATHEDRAL OF THE MOST HOLY TRINITY, WATERFORD

The Cathedral of the Most Holy Trinity, Barronstrand Street, Waterford is the oldest Roman Catholic cathedral in Ireland. The work began in 1793 with the Protestant Waterford man, John Roberts, as architect. Roberts also designed the Church of Ireland cathedral.

Over the years, additions and alterations have been made. Most of the present sanctuary was added in the 1830s; the apse and a main altar in 1854. The beautiful baldachin, which is supported by five Corinthian columns, was erected in 1881.

The carved oak Baroque pulpit, the chapter stalls and bishop's chair, designed by Goldie and Sons of London and carved by Buisine and Sons of Lille, were installed in 1883.

The stained-glass windows, mainly by Meyer of Munich, were installed between 1883 and 1888.

The Stations of the Cross, which are attached to the columns in the cathedral, are nineteenth-century paintings by Alcan of Paris. The cut-stone front was built in 1892–1893 for the centenary of the cathedral.

In 1977, a new wooden altar was placed in the redesigned sanctuary. The Belgian walnut panels of the base of the altar were originally part of the altar rails at St Carthage's Church, Lismore.

There are many plaques in the cathedral. One of them commemorates fourteen famous Waterford men: Luke Wadding OFM; Peter Lombard; Patrick Comerford OSA; James White; Michael Wadding SJ: Peter Wadding SJ; Thomas White; Paul Sherlock SJ; Ambrose Wadding SJ; Geoffrey Keating; Luke Wadding SJ; Stephen White SJ; Thomas White SJ and Bonaventure Barron OFM.

Ten Waterford Crystal chandeliers were presented by Waterford Crystal in 1979.

In 1993 the Bicentenary of the Cathedral was celebrated.

DIOCESE OF WATERFORD AND LISMORE

Most Rev William Lee DD
Retired Bishop of Waterford and Lismore
born 1941;
ordained priest 19 June 1966;
ordained Bishop of Waterford and Lismore 25 July 1993;
retired 1 October 2013
Residence: 5 The Brambles,
Ballinakill Downs, Waterford
Tel 051-821485

CHAPTER

Right Rev Mgr Nicholas O'Mahony PP, VG
Tramore
Very Rev Canon William Ryan PP, VG
Dungarvan
Very Rev Canon Daniel O'Connor PE
Dungarvan
Very Rev Canon Brendan Crowley PP, VF
SS Peter & Paul's, Clonmel
Very Rev Canon Edmond Cullinan Adm, VF
Holy Trinity Cathedral
Very Rev William Meehan PP
St Mary's, Clonmel

College of Consultors
Right Rev Mgr Nicholas O'Mahony PP
Very Rev Patrick Fitzgerald PP
Very Rev Canon William Ryan
Very Rev Robert Power PP
Rev Shane O'Neill CC
Very Rev Michael Toomey Adm
Very Rev Paul Waldron PP

ADMINISTRATION

Diocesan Development Committee
Right Rev Mgr Nicholas O'Mahony PP
Very Rev Michael Cullinan PP
Very Rev Milo Guiry PP
Very Rev Richard O'Halloran PP

Diocesan Finance Committee
Most Rev Alphonsus Cullinan
Right Rev Mgr Nicholas O'Mahony
Mr Jim Kennedy
Mr Lee Walsh
Mr David O'Brien
Mr Patrick Slevin
Mr Paul L'Estrange
Very Rev John Harris

Diocesan Secretary and Director of Finance
Mr Lee Walsh
Bishop's House, John's Hill, Waterford
Tel 051-874463

Episcopal Vicar for Retired Priests
Very Rev John Kiely PP
Cappoquin, Co Waterford
Tel 058-54216

Vicars for Clergy
Very Rev Brian Power PP
Parochial House, Killea,
Dunmore East, Co Waterford
Tel 051-383127
Very Rev Patrick Butler
Parochial House, Youghal Road,
Tallow, Co Waterford

CATECHETICS EDUCATION

Catechetics
Primary Schools Religious Education:
Sr Antoinette Dilworth
St John's Pastoral Centre, John's Hill, Waterford
Tel 051-874199
Sr De Lourdes Breen
Presentation Sisters, 158 Larchville, Waterford
Tel 051-355496
Rev Richard O'Halloran PP
Portlaw, Co Waterford
Tel 051-387227
Director Post-Primary Schools Religious Education: Mr Declan Browne
St John's Pastoral Centre, John's Hill, Waterford
Tel 051-874199

Catholic Primary School Managers' Association
Secretary: Very Rev Paul Waldron PP
Parochial House, Chapel Street,
Carrick-on-Suir, Co Tipperary
Tel 051-640168

LITURGY

Assistant to Parishes
Ms Mary Dee
St John's Pastoral Centre,
John's Hill, Waterford
Tel 051-874199

Diocesan Liturgy and Sacred Music Committee
Assistant to Parishes: Mary Dee
St John's Pastoral Centre
Very Rev Canon William Ryan PP
Very Rev Paul Waldron PP
Very Rev William Meehan PP
Mr Noel Casey
Ms Deirdre Moore
Ms Mary Dunphy
Ms Anna Fennessey
Ms Fidelma Nugent
Mr Donal Kenefick
Mr Nicholas de Paor

PASTORAL

ACCORD
Director: Very Rev Liam Power PP
St John's Pastoral Centre, John's Hill
Waterford
Tel 051-874199

Bereavement Counselling
Director: Ms Ann O'Farrell
Family Ministry Office,
St John's Pastoral Centre,
John's Hill, Waterford
Tel 051-874199/858772

Communications Office
Email media@waterfordlismore.ie

Charismatic Groups
Very Rev Patrick Gear PP
Parochial House, Cappoquin,
Co Waterford
Tel 058-54216

Diocesan Archivist
Bishop's House, John's Hill, Waterford
Tel 051-874463

Emigrant Bureau
Director: Very Rev Michael Enright PE
Dunabrattin, Annestown, Co Waterford
Tel 087-2371546

Historic Churches Advisory Committee
Mr Eamonn McEneaney
Very Rev Canon William Ryan PP, VF
Very Rev Michael Walsh PE
Tel 051-874463

Marriage Tribunal
Diocesan Official: Cork Marriage Tribunal
(See also Marriage Tribunals section)

Ministry to Polish Community
Rev Marek Kowalkowski
The Presbytery, Kill, Co Waterford

Ministry to the Latin Mass Chaplaincy
Rev Patrick O'Donohue (FSSP)
St John's Parish, Waterford
Email office@fssp.ie

Pilgrimage
Director: Very Rev Martin Keogh
Parochial House, Newtown,
Kilmacthomas, Co Waterford
Te 051-294261

DIOCESE OF WATERFORD AND LISMORE

Pontifical Mission Societies
Diocesan Director
Mr Gerard Deegan
Cúil Mhuire, 12 Grange Road, Waterford
Tel 051-876847

Travellers
Chaplain
Very Rev Robert Grant PP

Trócaire
Diocesan Director
Very Rev Conor Kelly Adm
The Orchard, Dungarvan, Co Waterford
Tel 058-64284

Youth Ministry Officer
Ms Nodlaig Lilis
St John's Pastoral Centre,
John's Hill, Waterford
Tel 051-874199

PARISHES

City parishes are listed first. Other parishes follow alphabetically. Italics denote church titulars where they differ from parish names.

TRINITY WITHIN AND ST PATRICK'S
Holy Trinity Cathedral
Very Rev John Harris Adm
Holy Family Presbytery,
Luke Wadding Street, Waterford
Tel 051-350023
Sacristy: Tel 051-875166

ST JOHN'S
Very Rev Thomas Rogers PP
2 Carmel, Priest's Road,
Tramore, Co Waterford
Tel 051-511275
Sacristy: Tel 051-875849

SS JOSEPH AND BENILDUS
SS Joseph & Benildus, Newtown
St Mary, Ballygunner
Very Rev Liam Power PP
Parish Office, SS Joseph and Benildus,
Newtown, Waterford
Tel 051-873073
Very Rev Raymond Liddane AP
Newtown, Waterford
Tel 051-874284
Rev PJ Breen CC
14 Heathervue Road, Riverview,
Knockboy, Waterford
Tel 051-820452
Sacristy: Tel 051-878977

BALLYBRICKEN
Holy Trinity Without
Very Rev Thomas Rogers Adm
Very Rev Michael Mullins PE
St Anne's Presbytery, Convent Hill,
Waterford
Tel 051-855819
Sacristy: Tel 051-874519

HOLY FAMILY
Very Rev Gerard Langford PP
Holy Family Presbytery,
Luke Wadding Street, Waterford
Tel 051-375274

ST PAUL'S
Very Rev Patrick Fitzgerald PP
Parochial House,
Lisduggan, Waterford
Tel 051-372257
Sacristy: Tel 051-378073

SACRED HEART
Very Rev Gerard Chestnutt PP
The Presbytery, The Folly, Waterford
Tel 051-878429
Sacristy: Tel 051-873792
Rev Francis Xavier Vijaykumar CC
Sacred Heart Presbytery,
21 The Folly, Waterford
Tel 051-873759

ST SAVIOUR'S
Very Rev Robert Grant PP
Parochial House, Fenor, Co Waterford
Tel 051-376032

ABBEYSIDE
St Augustine, Abbeyside
St Laurence, Ballinroad
St Vincent de Paul, Garranbane
Very Rev Edmond Hassett PP
Strandside South, Abbeyside,
Dungarvan, Co Waterford
Tel 058-42036

AGLISH
Our Lady of the Assumption, Aglish
St James, Ballinameela
St Patrick, Mount Stuart
Very Rev Conor Kelly Adm
The Orchard, Dungarvan,
Co Waterford
Tel 058-64284
Very Rev Philip Amooti Balikuddembe CC
Parochial House, Aglish,
Co Waterford
Tel 024-96287

ARDFINNAN
Holy Family, Ardfinnan
St Nicholas, Grange, Ballybacon Church
Very Rev Michael Toomey Adm
Ardfinnan, Clonmel, Co Tipperary
Tel 052-7466216

ARDMORE
St Declan, Ardmore
Our Lady of the Assumption, Grange
Very Rev Michael Guiry PP
Ardmore, Youghal, Co Waterford
Tel 024-94275

BALLYDUFF
St Michael
Very Rev Gerard McNamara PP
Ballyduff, Co Waterford
Tel 058-60227

BALLYLOOBY
Our Lady & St Kieran, Ballylooby
St John the Baptist, Duhill
Rev Jude Ronayne Forde (OSA)
Ballylooby, Cahir, Co Tipperary
Tel 052-7441489

BALLYNEALE AND GRANGEMOCKLER
St Mary, Ballyneale
St Mary, Grangemockler
Very Rev Paul Waldron PP *(priest in charge)*
Rev James Browne (IC) CC
Ballyneale, Carrick-on-Suir, Co Tipperary
Tel 051-640148

BALLYPOREEN
Our Lady of the Assumption
Very Rev Bobby Power Adm
Very Rev Joseph Flynn AP
Ballyporeen, Cahir, Co Tipperary
Tel 052-7467105

BUTLERSTOWN
St Mary
Very Rev Patrick Fitzgerald PP *(priest in charge)*
Parochial House, Lisduggan,
Waterford
Tel 051-372257

CAHIR
St Mary
Rev Peter Cullen Adm
20 Bengurragh, Cahir, Co Tipperary
Tel 052-7441585

CAPPOQUIN
St Mary's
Very Rev Patrick Gear PP
Tel 058-54216
Very Rev James Denmead AP
Tel 058-54221
Cappoquin, Co Waterford

CARRICKBEG
St Molleran, Carrickbeg
St Bartholomew, Windgap
Very Rev Thomas Flynn PP
Carrickbeg, Carrick-on-Suir, Co Tipperary
Tel 051-640340

CARRICK-ON-SUIR
St Nicholas, Carrick-on-Suir
St Patrick, Faugheen
Very Rev Paul Waldron PP
Parochial House, Carrick-on-Suir,
Co Tipperary
Tel 051-640168

DIOCESE OF WATERFORD AND LISMORE

CLASHMORE
St Cronan, Clashmore
St Bartholomew, Piltown
Very Rev Michael Guiry *(Moderator)*
Ardmore, Co Waterford
Tel 024-94275

CLOGHEEN
St Mary, Clogheen
Our Lady of the Assumption, Burncourt
Very Rev Robert Power PP
Parochial House, Clogheen, Cahir,
Co Tipperary
Tel 052-7465268

CLONMEL, ST MARY'S
St Mary
Very Rev. William Meehan PP
St Mary's, Clonmel, Co Tipperary
Tel 052-6122954

CLONMEL, ST OLIVER PLUNKETT
St Oliver Plunkett
Very Rev Michael Hegarty (IC) PP
Rev Deacon Lazarus Gidolf
Cooleens, Glenconnor, Clonmel,
Co Tipperary, E91 N578
Tel 052-6125679

CLONMEL, SS PETER AND PAUL'S
SS Peter and Paul's,
Church of the Resurrection
Very Rev John Treacy PP
Very Rev Canon Brendan Crowley PE
SS Peter and Paul's, Clonmel,
Co Tipperary
Tel 052-6126292

DUNGARVAN
St Mary
Very Rev Canon William Ryan PP, VF
Parochial House, Dungarvan,
Co Waterford
Tel 058-42374
Rev John McEneaney
The Presbytery, Mitchell Street,
Dungarvan, Co Waterford
Rev Matthew Cooney (OSA)
The Presbytery, Dungarvan,
Co Waterford

DUNHILL
Sacred Heart, Dunhill
Immaculate Conception, Fenor
Rt Rev Mgr Nicholas O'Mahony PP (priest in charge)
Priest's Road, Tramore,
Co Waterford
Tel 051-381525

KILGOBINET
St Gobnait, Kilgobinet
St Anne, Colligan
St Patrick, Kilbrian
Very Rev Canon William Ryan PP
Kilgobinet

KILLEA (DUNMORE EAST)
Holy Cross, Killea
St John the Baptist, Crooke
St Nicholas, Faithlegg
Very Rev Brian Power PP
Dunmore East, Co Waterford
Tel 051-383127

KILROSSANTY
St Brigid, Kilrossanty
St Anne, Fews
Very Rev John Delaney PP
Parochial House, Kilrossanty,
Kilmacthomas, Co Waterford
Tel 051-291985

KILSHEELAN
St Mary, Gambonsfield
St John the Baptist, Kilcash
Very Rev William Carey PP
Kilsheelan, Clonmel, Co Tipperary
Tel 052-6133118

KNOCKANORE
Very Rev Patrick T. Condon PP
Knockanore, Tallow, Co Waterford
Tel 024-97140

LISMORE
St Carthage
Very Rev Michael Cullinan PP, VF
Parochial House,
Lismore, Co Waterford
Tel 058-54246

MODELIGO
Our Lady of the Assumption, Modeligo
St John the Baptist, Affane
Priest in charge:
Very Rev Patrick Gear
Cappoquin, Co Waterford
Tel 058-54216

NEWCASTLE AND FOURMILEWATER
Our Lady of the Assumption, Newcastle
Our Lady & St Laurence, Fourmilewater
Very Rev Michael Toomey Adm
Newcastle, Clonmel, Co Tipperary
Tel 052-6136387

NEWTOWN
All Saints, Newtown
St Mary, Saleen, Kill Church
Very Rev Martin Keogh PP
Parochial House, Newtown,
Kilmacthomas, Co Waterford
Tel 051-294261

PORTLAW
St Patrick, Portlaw
St Nicholas, Ballyduff
Very Rev Richard O'Halloran PP
Portlaw, Co Waterford
Tel 051-387227
Very Rev Michael O'Byrne AP
Kilmeaden, Co Waterford
Tel 051-384117

POWERSTOWN
St John the Baptist, Powerstown
St John the Baptist, Lisronagh
Very Rev Peter Ahearne PP
Rathronan, Clonmel, Co Tipperary
Tel 052-6121891

RATHGORMACK
SS Quan & Broghan, Clonea
Sacred Heart, Rathgormack
Rev P. J. Fegan (IC) (priest in charge)
Rathgormack, Carrick-on-Suir,
Co Waterford
Tel 051-646006

RING AND OLD PARISH
Nativity of the BVM
St Nicholas
Very Rev William Canon Ryan Adm
The Orchard, Dungarvan,
Co Waterford
Tel 058-64284

STRADBALLY
Exaltation of the Holy Cross, Stradbally
St Anne, Ballylaneen, Faha Church
Very Rev Jeremiah Condon PP
Stradbally, Kilmacthomas,
Co Waterford
Tel 051-293133

TALLOW
Immaculate Conception
Priest in Charge
Very Rev Gerard McNamara PP
Ballyduff Upper, Co Waterford
Tel 058-60227

TOURANEENA
St Mary, Touraneena, Nire Church
Very Rev Garrett Desmond PP
Tournaneena, Ballinamult,
Clonmel, Co Tipperary
Tel 058-47138

TRAMORE
Holy Cross, Tramore
Our Lady, Carbally
Right Rev Mgr Nicholas O'Mahony PP
Parochial House, Tramore,
Co Waterford
Tel 051-381525
Rev Shane O'Neill CC
Tel 051-391868
Rev Paul Yang
Rev Tadeusz Durajczyk
Tel 051-338291
Priest's Road, Tramore, Co Waterford

INSTITUTIONS AND CHAPLAINS

Bon Sauveur Services
Carriglea, Dungarvan, Co Waterford
Tel 058-41322 Fax 058-41432
Email bonsav@eircom.net

University Hospital, Waterford
Tel 051-873321
Chaplains
Rev John Philip Kakkarakunel
Rev Bobit Augusthy (OSCam)
Rev Russell Jacom (OSCam)
Waterford University Hospital,
Dunmore Road, Waterford
Tel 051-848000

South Tipperary General Hospital
Chaplain: Rev Deogratias Mayanja
Tel 052-6177000

Waterford Institute of Technology
Chaplain: Rev David Keating
10 Claremont, Cork Road, Waterford
Tel 051-378878

Military Chaplaincy
Very Rev Paul F. Murphy (CF)
Chaplain's House, Dún Uí Mhaoilíosa,
Renmore, Galway
Tel 091-751156

PRIESTS OF THE DIOCESE ELSEWHERE

Very Rev Edmond Cullinan
Vice-Rector, Irish College, Rome
Very Rev Michael O'Connor
c/o St John's Pastoral Centre,
John's Hill, Waterford
Email mnoc@iol.ie

RETIRED PRIESTS

Rev Thomas Burns
St John's Presbytery, New Street,
Waterford
Very Rev William Callanan AP
Mowlam Healthcare, Ballinakill Downs,
Dunmore Road, Waterford
Very Rev Eanna Condon PE
St Mary's, Clonmel, Co Tipperary
Tel 052-6127870
Very Rev Joseph Condon PP
Apartment 2, St John's College,
The Folly, Waterford
Tel 051-876843
Very Rev Canon Brendan Crowley PE
SS Peter and Paul's, Clonmel,
Co Tipperary
Rev James Curran
61 Tournane Court, Dungarvan,
Co Waterford
Tel 058-45177
Very Rev Michael Enright PE
Dunabrattin,
Annestown, Co Waterford
Tel 087-2371546
Rev Pat Hayes
Dunabbey House,
Dungarvan, Co Waterford

Very Rev Michael Kennedy PE
Parochial House, Colligan, Dungarvan,
Co Waterford
Tel 058-41629
Very Rev John Kiely PE
'The Cottage', Ballinaparka,
Aglish, Co Waterford
Very Rev Francis Lloyd PE
The Presbytery, Dungarvan,
Co Waterford
Very Rev Finbarr Lucey PE
Ardmore, Youghal, Co Cork
Tel 024-94177
Very Rev Michael Mullins PE
St Anne's Presbytery, Convent Hill,
Waterford
Very Rev Paul Murphy PE
St John's Presbytery, New Street,
Waterford
Rev Michael O'Brien
St Anne's Presbytery, Convent Hill,
Waterford
Very Rev Canon Daniel O'Connor PE
The Presbytery, Dungarvan,
Co Waterford
Tel 058-42381
Very Rev Gerard O'Connor PE
Clashmore, Co Waterford
Tel 024-96110
Very Rev Sean O'Dwyer PE
Clonmel Road, Cahir, Co Tipperary
Tel 087-4184213
Rev Charles Scanlan
Ballinwillin, Lismore, Co Waterford
Very Rev Michael F. Walsh PE
Ballinarrid, Bonmahon, Co Waterford
Tel 051-292992

RELIGIOUS ORDERS AND CONGREGATIONS

PRIESTS

AUGUSTINIANS
St Augustine's Priory, Dungarvan,
Co Waterford
Tel 058-41136   Fax 058-44534
Prior & Bursar: Rev Tony Egan (OSA)

St Augustine's College,
Dungarvan, Co Waterford
Tel 058-41140/41152 Fax 058-41152

Duckspool House (Retirement Community)
Abbeyside, Dungarvan, Co Waterford
Tel 058-23784
Prior: Rev Ben O'Brien (OSA)

CISTERCIANS
Mount Melleray Abbey,
Cappoquin, Co Waterford P51 R8XW
Tel 058-54404 Fax 058-52140
Email info@mtmelleray.ie
Abbot
Rt Rev Dom Richard Purcell (OCSO)
Prior: Rev Patrick Ryan (OCSO)

DOMINICANS
Bridge Street, Waterford
Tel 051-875061 Fax 051-858093
Superior
Very Rev Krzsztof Kupczakiewiczy (OP)

FRANCISCANS
Franciscan Friary,
Clonmel, Co Tipperary
Tel 052-6121378 Fax 052-6125806
Email franciscans.clonmel@outlook.com
Guardian: Rev Jim Hasson (OFM)
Vicar: Rev Liam McCarthy (OFM)

Franciscan Friary,
Lady Lane, Waterford
No longer resident community. Church served from Clonmel

ROSMINIANS
St Joseph's Doire na hAbhann
Tickincor, Clonmel,
Co Tipperary, E91 XY71
Tel 052-26914 Fax 052-26915
Residential centre for children in care.

(See also under parishes – St Oliver Plunkett)

BROTHERS

CHRISTIAN BROTHERS
Mount Sion,
Barrack Street, Waterford
Tel 051-879580 Fax 051-841578
Community Leader
Br Peadar Gleeson
Community: 4

International Heritage Centre & Chapel
Mount Sion,
Barrack Street, Waterford
Tel 051-874390 Fax 051-841578

DE LA SALLE BROTHERS
De La Salle College, Newtown,
Waterford
Tel 051-875294 Fax 051-841321
Email delasall@iol.ie
Superior: Br Benedict Hanlon
Community: 5
Secondary School
Principal: Mr Michael Walsh

De La Salle Brothers
25 Patrick Street, Waterford
Tel 051-874623
Community: 3
Superior: Br Francis McCallig
St Stephen's Primary School
Principal: Ms Sinead Lowe
Tel 051-871716

PRESENTATION BROTHERS
Glór na hAbhann,
Ballinamona Lower, Old Parish,
Dungarvan, Co Waterford
Tel 058-46904
Contact: Br John Hunt (FPM)
Community: 2

SISTERS

CARMELITES
St Joseph's Carmelite Monastery, Tallow,
Co Waterford
Tel 058-56205
Email carmeltallow@eircom.net
Superior: Sr Patrice Buckley
Community: 12
Contemplatives

CISTERCIANS
St Mary's Abbey,
Glencairn, Lismore,
Co Waterford P51 X725
Tel 058-56168
Email info@glencairnabbey.org
Abbess: Sr Marie Fahy
Tel 058-56197
Email mariebfahy@gmail.com
Community: 26
Monastic

CONGREGATION OF THE SISTERS OF MERCY
Teach Bride, Convent Road,
Townspark, Cahir, Co Tipperary
Tel 052-7443809

St Mary's, Mount Anglesby,
Clogheen, Cahir, Co Tipperary
Tel 052-7465255

Greenhill, Carrick-on-Suir,
Co Tipperary
Tel 051-640059

Springwell, Pill Road,
Carrick-on-Suir, Co Tipperary
Tel 051-642870

12 Comeragh View,
Carrick-on-Suir, Co Tipperary
Tel 051-645012

10 Ash Park, Carrick-on-Suir,
Co Tipperary
Tel 051-640814

31 Willow Park,
Clonmel, Co Tipperary
Tel 052-6128903

Convent of Mercy, Church Street,
Dungarvan, Co Waterford
Tel 058-41293/41337

1 Park Lane Drive, Abbeyside,
Dungarvan, Co Waterford
Tel 058-48795

22 Blackrock Court,
Youghal Road, Dungarvan,
Co Waterford
Tel 058-48286

16 Blackrock Court,
Youghal Road, Dungarvan,
Co Waterford
Tel 058-45713

17 Blackrock Court,
Youghal Road, Dungarvan,
Co Waterford
Tel 058-44865

11 Blackrock Court,
Youghal Road, Dungarvan,
Co Waterford
Tel 058-24656

Convent of Mercy,
Military Road, Waterford
Tel 051-374161/377909

104 Glenville,
Dunmore Road, Waterford

2 Chestnut Grove,
Waterford
Tel 051-373542

93 Clonard Park,
Ballybeg, Waterford
Tel 051-379110

7 Aisling Court,
Hennessy's Road, Waterford

Apartment 57, College House,
St John's College,
John's Hill, Waterford

CONGREGATION OF OUR LADY OF CHARITY OF THE GOOD SHEPHERD
Virginia Crescent, Hennessy's Road,
Waterford X91 N267
Tel 051-874294
Email rgswat33@hotmail.co.uk
Leader: Sr Bernie McNally
Community: 10

Good Shepherd Sisters,
37 Clonard Park, Ballybeg,
Waterford X91 CH02
Email rgsanna18@gmail.com
Community: 1

LITTLE COMPANY OF MARY
36 Willowbrook,
Tallow, Co Waterford
Tel 058-55962
Community: 1

LORETO (IBVM)
Loreto Secondary School,
Clonmel, Co Tipperary
Tel 052-21402
Community: 2

MISSIONARY SISTERS OF THE GOSPEL
Carriglea,
Dungarvan, Co Waterford
Tel 058-45884 (office line)
Email mary.fitzgeraldmsg20@gmail.com
Superior: Sr Mary Fitzgerald (MSG)
Community: 5
Pastoral Ministry to Carriglea Cairde Service – Residential and day care services for persons with an intellectual disability

PRESENTATION SISTERS
Presentation Sisters,
Clonmel, Co Tipperary
Tel 052-6121538
Community: 18
Community and pastoral

Presentation Sisters,
Youghal Road, Dungarvan,
Co Waterford
Tel 058-41359
Community: 7

Presentation Play School Ltd.
Tel 087-6204077
Email presplayschool@eircom.net

Presentation Sisters,
81 Treacy Park, Carrick-on-Suir,
Co Tipperary
Tel 051-641733
Community: 1

11 Convent Lodge,
Mitchell Street, Dungarvan,
Co Waterford
Community: 1

SISTERS OF ST JOHN OF GOD
9 The Cloisters, John's Hill, Waterford
Tel 051-874370

Sisters of St John of God,
41 Grange Cove, Waterford
Tel 051-855585

URSULINES
Ursuline Convent, Waterford
Tel 051-874068
Email stangurs@yahoo.com
Community: 7
Primary School
Tel 051-873788/852855
Fax 051-852855
Secondary School
Tel 051-8766510 Fax 051-879022

DIOCESE OF WATERFORD AND LISMORE

18 Shannon Drive,
Avondale, Waterford
Tel 051-854680
Email bolandmaureen88@gmail.com
Community: 2

1 St Anne's,
Ursuline Court, Waterford
Tel 051-857015
Email brettelizabeth9@gmail.com
Community: 2

ST JOHN'S PASTORAL CENTRE

St John's Pastoral Centre
John's Hill, Waterford
Tel 051-874199 Fax 051-843107
Email
pastoralcentre@waterfordlismore.ie
Administrator: Ms Mary Dee

CHARITABLE AND OTHER SOCIETIES

Holy Family Mission
Glencomeragh House,
Kilsheelan, Co Waterford
Tel 052-6133636
House of Formation for Young People
Retreat House

Hostels
Men's Hostel, Ozanam House,
Lady Lane, Waterford
(St Vincent de Paul)

PERSONAL PRELATURES

Prelature of the Holy Cross and Opus Dei

Founded by Saint Josemaría Escrivá in 1928, it was erected as a Personal Prelature (cf CIC 294-297) in 1982, and is constituted by the Prelate (Mgr Fernando Ocáriz), incardinated clergy, and lay people, married and celibate. The faithful of the Prelature try to promote a deep consciousness of the universal call to holiness and apostolate in all sectors of society and, more specifically, an awareness of the sanctifying value of ordinary work.

Information Office:
10 Hume Street, Dublin D02 VY39
Tel 087-7690049

Website www.opusdei.ie
Email info.ie@opusdei.org

Vicar for Ireland
Rev Donncha Ó hAodha
Harvieston,
22 Cunningham Road, Dalkey,
Co Dublin A96 CX59
Tel 01-2859877
Fax 01-2073144

Archdiocese of Dublin
Harvieston, 22 Cunningham Road,
Dalkey, Co Dublin A96 CX59
Tel 01-2859877
Rev Patrick Gorevan
Rev Donncha Ó hAodha
Rev Francis Planell

30 Knapton Road,
Dun Laoghaire, Co Dublin A96 XA46
Tel 01-2804353
Rev Daniel Cummings
Rev James Gavigan
Rev Martin Hannon
Rev Thomas McGovern
Rev Oliver Powell

Cleraun Study Centre,
90 Fosters Avenue, Mount Merrion,
Co Dublin A94 VX73
Tel 01-2881734
Rev Brendan O'Connor
Rev Philip Griffin
Rev Walter Macken

Ely University Centre
10 Hume Street, Dublin D02 VY39
Tel 01-6767420
Rev Gavan Jennings
Rev Thomas Dowd

Diocese of Cork & Ross
Dunmahon Study Centre
Model Farm Road, Cork T12 KHC1
Tel 021-2029112
www.dunmahon.ie
Rev Brian McCarthy

Diocese of Down & Connor
Dunraven
104 Malone Road, Belfast BT9 5HP
Tel 028-90506947
Email dunraven104bt9@gmail.com
Rev Brendan O'Connor

Diocese of Galway
Gort Ard University Residence,
Rockbarton North, Galway H91 KH94
Tel 091-523846
Rev Charles Connolly

Diocese of Limerick
Castleville Study Centre,
Golf Links Road, Castletroy,
Limerick V94 YC95
Tel 061-331223
Rev Brian McCarthy

Diocese of Meath
Lismullin Conference Centre
Navan, Co Meath C15 XW40
Tel 046-9026936
Rev Philip Griffin, Chaplain

RELIGIOUS ORDERS AND CONGREGATIONS

MALE RELIGIOUS

AUGUSTINIANS (OSA)

Irish Province
www.augustinians.ie

Archdiocese of Dublin

Dublin South Community
St Augustine's
Taylor's Lane,
Ballyboden, Dublin 16
Tel 01-4241000
Fax 01-4939915

Provincial: Rev John Hennebry
Tel 01-4241030
Fax 01-4932457
Email osaprov@eircom.net
Secretary: Tel 01-4241040
Email hibprovsec@irishbroadband.net
Prior: Rev Francis Aherne CC
Sub-prior & Provincial Secretary: Rev Dick Lyng (CC Ballyboden)

Rev John Byrne
Rev Gabriel Daly
Rev Senan Doran
Rev Patrick Farrell
Rev Michael Fitzgerald
Rev John Hughes (PP Ballyboden)
Rev Richard Hughes
Br Giles O'Halloran
Rev Aidan O'Leary
Rev Liam Ryan
Rev David Slater
Rev John Williams

St John's Priory
Thomas Street, Dublin 8
Tel 01-6770393/0415/0601
Fax 01-6713102 (Mission Office)
Fax 01-6770423 (House)

Prior: Rev Padraig A. Daly
Sub-Prior: Rev Niall Coghlan (PP Meath St)
Bursar: Rev Bernard Twomey

Rev Pat Gayer
Rev Richard Goode
Rev Nicholas Kearney
Rev Michael Mernagh
Rev John Joe O'Connor
Bishop Louis O'Donnell
Rev Kieran O'Mahony
Rev Brian O'Sullivan

Meath Street Parish
St Catherine's Presbytery,
Dublin 8
Tel 01-4543356
Fax 01-4738303

No Resident Community

Rivermount Parish
Parochial House,
5 St Helena's Drive, Dublin 11
Tel 01-8343444/8343722
Fax 01-8642192

Prior: Rev Paddy O'Reilly

Very Rev Seamus Ahearne PP
Rev Paul O'Connor

Archdiocese of Armagh

St Augustine's Priory
Shop Street,
Drogheda, Co Louth
Tel 041-9838409
Fax 041-9831847

Prior and Master of Pre-Novices: Rev Colm O'Mahony
Bursar: Rev Declan Brennan

Rev Lazarus Barkindo
(Hospital Chaplain)
Rev Malachy Loughran

Archdiocese of Cashel and Diocese of Emly

The Abbey
Fethard, Co Tipperary
Tel 052-31273

Prior
Rev Ignatius O'Donovan
Bursar: Rev Gerard Horan

Rev David Fitzgerald
Rev Henry MacNamara
Rev Paul O'Brien

Diocese of Cork & Ross

St Augustine's Priory
Washington Street, Cork
Tel 021-4275398/4270410
Fax 021-4275381

Prior: Rev John Lyng
Bursar: Rev Tom Sexton

Rev Michael Boyle
Rev Martin Crean
Rev Michael Leahy
Rev James Maguire
Rev Tommy McManus
Rev Pat Twohig

Diocese of Ferns

Good Counsel College
New Ross, Co Wexford
Tel 051-421182
Fax 051-421909

Prior
Rev Michael Collender
Bursar
Rev David Crean

Diocese of Galway

St Augustine's Priory
St Augustine's Street,
Galway
Tel 091-562524
www.augustinians.ie/galway

Prior & PP
Rev Desmond Foley
Bursar
Rev Sean MacGearailt

Rev Declan Deasy
Rev Anthony Finn
Rev John Whelan

Diocese of Limerick

St Augustine's Priory
O'Connell Street,
Limerick
Tel 061-415374

Prior
Rev Noel Hession
Bursar & Rector Ecclesiae
Rev Flor O'Callaghan

Rev Michael Danaher
Rev Paul Flynn
Rev David Kelly (Provincial Archivist)

Diocese of Waterford & Lismore

St Augustine's College
Dungarvan, Co Waterford
Tel 058-41140/41152
Fax 058-41152

No Resident Community

St Augustine's Priory
Dungarvan,
Co Waterford
Tel 058-41136
Fax 058-44534

Prior & Bursar
Rev Tony Egan
Sub-prior
Rev Seamus Humphreys

Rev Michael Brennock
Rev Matthew Cooney
Rev Finbarr Spring

Duckspool House
(Retirement Community)
Abbeyside, Dungarvan,
Co Waterford
Tel 058-23784

Prior
Rev Ben O'Brien
Bursar
Rev Patrick Lennon

Rev Ailbe Brennan
Rev Vincent McCarthy
Rev John O'Connor

The Irish Province of the Augustinians also has missions in Ecuador and Nigeria.

Irish Augustinian Personnel on Other Assignments

USA
Rev John Grace

BENEDICTINES (OSB)

Archdiocese of Cashel and Diocese of Emly

Attached to the Benedictine Congregation of the Annunciation, Belgium.

Glenstal Abbey
Murroe,
Co Limerick V94 A725
Tel 061-621000 Fax 061-386328
Email monks@glenstal.org

Abbot
Rt Rev Dom Brendan Coffey
Prior
Very Rev Senan Furlong
Sub-Prior
Rev Christopher Dillon

RELIGIOUS ORDERS AND CONGREGATIONS

Headmaster
Rev Martin Browne
Novice Master
Br Pádraig McIntyre

Rev Anselm Barry
Rev Cuthbert Brennan
Rev Alan Crawford
Rev William Fennelly
Br Ciarán Forbes
Rev Mark Patrick Hederman
Rev Denis Hooper
Br Anselm Hurt
Rev Anthony Keane
Br Jaroslaw Kurek
Br Cyprian Love
Rev Fintan Lyons
Rev Columba McCann
Br Timothy McGrath
Br Oscar McDermott
Rev Luke Macnamara
Rev Lino Moreira
Rev Brian Murphy
Rev Placid Murray
Rev John O'Callaghan
Br Colmán Ó Clabaigh
Br Emmaus O'Herlihy
Br Cillian Ó Sé
Rev Henry O'Shea
Rev Simon Sleeman
Br Justin Robinson
Rev Philip Tierney

Diocese of Dromore

Attached to the Benedictine Congregation of St Mary of Monte Oliveto.

Benedictine Monks
Holy Cross Abbey,
119 Kilbroney Road,
Rostrevor,
Co Down BT34 3BN
Tel 028-41739979
Email benedictinemonks@btinternet.com
Website
www.benedictinemonks.co.uk

Abbot: Rt Rev Dom Mark-Ephrem M. Nolan

Rev D. Eric M. Loisel
Rev D. Thierry M. Marteaux
D. Gregory M. Foret
D. Benoît M. Charlet
D. Joshua M. Domenzain Canul
D. David Joseph M. Mayer
D. Laurent M. Salud Abila

Dependent House
Monastery of Christ our Saviour
Turvey,
Bedfordshire, England

BENEDICTINE MONKS OF PERPETUAL ADORATION OF THE MOST HOLY SACRAMENT (OSB)

Diocese of Meath

Silverstream Priory
Stamullen, Co Meath K32 T189
Tel 01-8417142
Email info@cenacleosb.org

Prior
Very Rev Dom Elijah Carroll

Very Rev Dom Mark Daniel Kirby
Rev Dom Benedict Andersen
Dom Finnian King
Dom Cassian Aylward
Rev Dom Hildebrand Houser
Dom John Baptist DeCant
Dom Chrysostom Gryniewicz
Dom Thomas Aquinas Borders
Dom Placid McKee
Dom Isaias Kwasniewski
Dom Isaac Conard
Dom Theodore Lee
Dom Aelred Tillotson
Dom David Watters

BLESSED SACRAMENT CONGREGATION (SSS)

Provincial
Rev James Campbell
Blessed Sacrament Chapel,
20 Bachelors Walk,
Dublin D01 NW14

Archdiocese of Dublin

Blessed Sacrament Chapel
20 Bachelors Walk,
Dublin D01 NW14
Tel 01-8724597 Fax 01-8724724
Email sssdublin@eircom.net
Web
www.blessedsacramentuki.org

Superior
Rev Dr Darren Maslen
Email
dunstanmaslen@gmail.com

Rev James Campbell
Rev Renato Esoy
Br Andrew McTeigue
Rev Don Anthony Priyantha Angodage

CAMILLIANS (OSCam)
Order of St Camillus

Anglo-Irish Province

Archdiocese of Dublin

St Camillus
South Hill Avenue,
Blackrock, Co Dublin
Tel 01-2882873/2833380

Superior: Rev Denis Sandham

Rev Suresh Babu
Rev Jayan Joseph *(Chaplain to St James' Hospital)*
Rev Tom O'Connor

St Camillus
11 St Vincent Street North,
Dublin 7
Tel 01-8300365 (residence)
Tel 01-8301122 (Mater Hospital)

Superior & Provincial
Rev Stephen Forster
Tel 01-8304635

Rev Bobit Augusthy
Rev Russel Jacob
Rev Prince Mathew *(Chaplain to Mater Hospital)*
Rev Tomy Paradiyil
Rev John Philip *(Chaplain to Waterford Hospital)*
Rev Vincent Xavier *(Chaplain to Mater Hospital)*
4 St Vincent Street North,
Dublin 7

Diocese of Meath

St Camillus
Killucan, Co Westmeath
Tel 044-74196 (nursing centre)
Tel 044-74115 (community)
Fax 044-74309

Superior: Rev Frank Monks

Rev Martin Geraghty
Rev Suneesh Mathew
(Chaplain to Mater Hospital)
Br John O'Brien

CAPUCHINS (OFM Cap)

Province of Ireland

Includes nine friaries in Ireland, Provincial Custodies in South Africa, Zambia, and South Korea and delegation of Great Britain.

Archdiocese of Dublin

Provincial Office
12 Halston Street,
Dublin D07 Y2T5
Tel 01-8733205 Fax 01-8730294
Email capcurirl@eircom.net

Provincial Minister
Very Rev Seán Kelly
Guardian: Br John Wright
Vicar, Secretary of the Province: Rev Paul Murphy

Rev Martin Bennett (PP Halston Street Parish)

Capuchin Friary
137-142 Church Street,
Dublin D07 HA22
Tel 01-8730599 Fax 01-8730250

Guardian
Rev Richard Hendrick
Email brorick50@gmail.com
Vicar: Rev Kevin Kiernan
Email frklkiernan@gmail.com

Rev Peter Rodgers
Rev Kevin Crowley
Rev Patrick Flynn
Rev Paul Tapley
Rev Owen O'Sullivan *(Assigned)*
Br Alphonsus Ryan
Rev Severino Pinheiro da Salva Neto

Capuchin Friary
Station Road,
Raheny, Dublin D05 T9E4
Tel 01-8313886 Fax 01-8511498

Guardian: Rev Seán Donohoe
Email
seandonohoe25@gmail.com
Vicar: Br Joseph Gallagher

Rev Jude McKenna
Rev Alexius Healy *(Assigned)*
Rev Eustace McSweeney
Rev Anthony Boran *(Assigned)*
Rev Pádraig Ó Cuill
Rev Matthew Clerkin
Email
matthewclerkin@gmail.com
Rev Dan Joe O'Mahony
Rev Michael Duffy
Br Bernard McAllister
Br Bibin Antony Kurian

Capuchin Friary
Clonshaugh Drive,
Priorswood, Dublin D17 RP20
Tel 01-8474469
Fax 01-8487296

Guardian
Rev Terence Harrington
Email tharr@eircom.net
Vicar: Rev William Ryan

Rev Bryan Shortall PP

Diocese of Cork & Ross

Capuchin Friary
Holy Trinity, Fr Mathew Quay,
Cork T12 PK24
Tel 021-4270827
Fax 021-4270829

Guardian
Rev Dermot Lynch
Vicar
Br Declan O'Callaghan

Rev Kenneth Reynolds
Br John Hickey
Rev Aidan Vaughan *(Assigned)*

RELIGIOUS ORDERS AND CONGREGATIONS

Rev Anthony O'Keeffe
Br Ignatius Galvin
Email iggy.galvin@yahoo.com
Rev Joseph Nagle
Rev Jack Twomey *(Assigned)*
Rev Michael Burgess

St Francis Capuchin Friary
Rochestown,
Co Cork T12 NH02
Tel 021-4896244
Fax 021-4895915

Guardian
Rev Silvester O'Flynn
Vicar: Rev John Manley

Rev Edwin Flynn
Rev Leo McAuliffe
Br Albert Cooney
Rev Adrian Curran

St Francis Capuchin Franciscan College
Rochestown, Co Cork
Tel 021-4891417
Fax 021-4361254

Principal
Mrs Marie Ring

Diocese of Kildare & Leighlin

Capuchin Friary
43 Dublin Street,
Carlow R93 PH27
Tel 059-9142543
Fax 059-9142030

Guardian
Rev Desmond McNaboe
Vicar: Br Philip Tobin

Rev Patrick Lynch
Rev Damien Loughrey

Diocese of Ossory

Capuchin Friary
Friary Street,
Kilkenny R95 NX60
Tel 056-7721439
Fax 056-7722025

Guardian: Rev Eddie Dowley
Vicar: Rev Christy Twomey

Rev Benignus Buckley
Rev Pius Higgins
Rev Michael Murphy
Rev Jerzy Stopa

Diocese of Raphoe

Capuchin Friary
Ard Mhuire, Creeslough,
Letterkenny,
Co Donegal F92 Y23R
Tel 074-9138005
Fax 074-9138371

Guardian: Rev Philip Baxter
Vicar: Rev Kieran Shorten

Br Vianney Holmes
Rev Flannan Lynch
Br Bosco Connolly
Br Charles Stewart
Rev Thomas Forde
Rev Jeremy Heneghan

Custody of Zambia

Capuchin Franciscans
Post Net Box 147,
P/Bag E891,
Lusaka, Zambia
Tel 00260-211-250969
Fax 00260-211-252828
Email capzam@iconnect.zm

Custody of South Africa

Capuchin Franciscans
PO Box 118,
Howard Place 7450,
South Africa
Tel 00272-16370026
Fax 00272-16370014
Email capadmin@iafrica.com

Custody of South Korea

Capuchin Franciscans
Hyochang Won Ro 70 Gil 13,
Yong San-Gu, Seoul,
South Korea 140-896
Tel 0082-2-7015727
Fax 0082-2-7176128
Email capuchin@capuchin.or.kr

Delegate
Franciscan Friary,
Carlton Drive, Erith,
Kent KA8 1DN, UK

For further details concerning the Missions contact:

Capuchin Mission Office
Church Street, Dublin 7
Tel 01-8731022
Fax 01-8740478

CARMELITES (OCarm)

Irish Province

Archdiocese of Dublin

Provincial Office and Carmelite Community
Gort Muire, Ballinteer,
Dublin D16 EI67
Tel 01-2984014 Fax 01-2987221

Provincial
Very Rev Michael Troy
Email provincial@gortmuire.com

Assistant Provincial
Rev David Twohig
Prior & Bursar
Rev Fintan Burke
Sub-Prior
Rev David Twohig

Rev Fintan Burke
Rev Ambrose Costello
Rev Genildo De Queiroz
Rev Laurence Frost
Rev Gerard Galvin
Rev John Keating
Rev Robert Kelly
Rev Fred Lally
Rev Anthony McKinney
Rev Michael Morrissey
Rev Bernard Murphy
Rev Francis O'Gara
Rev Bernard O'Reilly
Rev Patrick Mullins
Rev Martin Ryan
Rev Michael Troy
Rev David Weakliam

Whitefriar Street Church
56 Aungier Street,
Dublin D02 R598
Tel 01-4758821
Fax 01-4758825
Email whitefriars@eircom.net

Prior
Rev Simon Nolan
Parish Priest
Rev Seán MacGiollarnáth
Bursar
Rev Martin Baxter

Rev Donal Byrne
Rev Christopher Conroy
Rev Patrick Graham
Rev Thomas Higgins
Rev Desmond Kelly
Rev Frank McAleese
Rev Anthony McDonald
Rev Joseph Mothersill
Rev Patrick Smyth

Terenure College
Terenure,
Dublin D6W DK72
Tel 01-4904621
Fax 01-4902403
Email admin@terenurecollege.ie

Prior/Bursar
Rev Éanna Ó hÓbain
Principal Senior School
Rev Éanna Ó hÓbáin

Rev Peter Kehoe
Rev Martin Kilmurray
Rev Martin Parokkaran

Diocese of Cork & Ross

Carmelite Friary
Kinsale,
Co Cork P17 WR88
Tel 021-4772138
Email kinsale@irishcarmelites.com

Prior: Rev James Eivers
Bursar
Rev Benedict O'Callaghan

Rev Stan Hession
Rev Laurence Lynch
Rev Eoin Moore

Diocese of Kildare & Leighlin

Carmelite Priory
White Abbey,
Co Kildare R51 X827
Tel 045-521391
Fax 045-522318
Email carmeliteskildare@gmail.com

Prior
Rev Chacko Anthony Thandiparahbil
Bursar
Rev Rojan Peter Pazhampilly

Rev Yesuoas Asariparambil Abraham

Diocese of Meath

Carmelite Priory
Moate,
Co Westmeath N37 AW34
Tel 090-6481160/6481398
Fax 090-6481879
Email carmelitemoate@eircom.net

Prior/Bursar
Rev Jaison Kuthanapillil

Rev Daniel Callaghan
Rev Brian Mckay
Rev James Murray

CARMELITES (OCD)

Anglo-Irish Province

The Province has five communities in Ireland and thirteen overseas including five in Nigeria.

Provincial
Rev John Grennan
Avila Carmelite Centre,
Bloomfield Avenue,
Morehampton Road, Dublin 4
Tel 01-6430200
Fax 01-6430281
Email jtgrennan@hotmail.com
Website www.ocd.ie

RELIGIOUS ORDERS AND CONGREGATIONS

Archdiocese of Dublin

St Teresa's
Clarendon Street,
Dublin 2
Tel 01-6718466/6718127
Fax 01-6718462

Prior
Very Rev Jim Noonan
Email stteresa@ocd.ie

Rev Michael Brown
Rev Sean Conlon
Rev David Donnellan
Rev Patrick Keenan
Rev Nicholas Madden
Rev Vincent O'Hara
Rev Edmond Smyth

Avila
Bloomfield Avenue,
Morehampton Road,
Dublin 4
Tel 01-6430200
Fax 01-6430281
Email avila@ocd.ie

Prior
Rev Liam Finnerty

Rev Joseph Birmingham
Rev Willie Moran
Br Noel O'Connor
Rev Felix Okolo
Rev Tom Stone

Diocese of Clonfert

The Abbey
Loughrea, Co Galway
Tel 091-841209
Fax 091-842343

Prior
Rev Mícheál MacLaifeartaigh

Rev Patrick Beecher
Rev Christopher Clarke
Rev Cronan Glynn
Rev Ambrose McNamee
Rev Tom Shanahan

Diocese of Derry

St Joseph's Carmelite
Retreat Centre
Termonbacca,
Derry BT48 9XE
Tel 028-71262512
Fax 028-71373589

Prior: Rev Stephen Quinn

Rev Michael McGoldrick
Rev Michael Spain

CISTERCIAN ORDER (OCSO)

The mother house of the Cistercian Order is the Arch-abbey of Citeaux, Cóte d'Or, France.

Archdiocese of Armagh

Mellifont Abbey
Collon, Co Louth
Tel 041-9826103
Fax 041-9826713
Email info@mellifontabbey.ie

Superior
Rt Rev Brendan Freeman
Email
frbrendan@newmelleray.org

Br Brian Berkeley
Rev Michael Burleigh
Br Denis Bernard Cazes
Br Andrew Considine
Rev William Cullinan
Br William Foster
Br Brendan Garry
Br Thomas Maher
Rev Rufus Pound

Archdiocese of Dublin

Bolton Abbey
Moone, Co Kildare
Tel 059-8624102
Mobile 087-9366723
Email
boltonabbeymoone@gmail.com
Website www.boltonabbey.ie

Abbot
Rt Rev Dom Michael Ryan
Prior
Br Anthony Jones
Guestmaster
Br Francis McLean
Novice Director

Rev Eoin de Bhaldraithe

Diocese of Down & Connor

Our Lady of Bethlehem Abbey
11 Ballymena Road,
Portglenone, Ballymena,
Co Antrim BT44 8BL
Tel 028-25821211
Email info@bethabbey.com
www.bethlehemabbey.com

Abbot/Superior
Rt Rev Dom Celsus Kelly

Prior
Rev Martin Dowley
Sub-Prior
Rt Rev Dom Charles Kaweesi

Br Simon Cassidy
Br Robert Folian
Br Michael McCourt
Br Finbar McLoughlin
Rev Aelred Magee
Rev Francis Morgan
Br Vianney O'Donnell
Rev Finnian Owens
Rev Philip Scott

Diocese of Killaloe

Mount Saint Joseph Abbey
Roscrea,
Co Tipperary E53 D6S1
Tel 0505-25600
Fax 0505-25610
Email info@msjroscrea.ie
www.msjroscrea.ie

Superior ad nutum
Dom Malachy Thompson
Email malachy@msjroscrea.ie
Prior
Rev Aodhán McDunphy
Sub-prior
Rev Laurence Walsh

Rev Laurence Walsh
Rev Kevin Daly
Br Laurence Molloy
Rev Anthony O'Brien (at Tautra, Norway)
Rev Liam O'Connor
Rev Bavo Samosir
Br Vladimir Tkachenko

Diocese of Waterford & Lismore

Mount Melleray Abbey
Cappoquin,
Co Waterford P51 R8XW
Tel 058-54404 Fax 058-52140
Email info@mtmelleray.ie

Abbot
Rt Rev Dom Richard Purcell
Prior
Rev Patrick Ryan

Br Seamus Corrigan
Br Edmund Costin
Rev Donal Davis
Rev John Dineen
Rt Rev Dom Eamon Fitzgerald
(Abbot General)
Rev Ignatius Hahessy
Rt Rev Augustine McGregor
Rev Denis Luke O'Hanlon

COMBONI MISSIONARIES (MCCJ)

Verona Fathers

Provincial
Rev Alberto Pelucchi
Comboni Missionaries,
London Road, Sunningdale,
Berks SL5 OJY, UK

Archdiocese of Dublin

8 Clontarf Road
Clontarf, Dublin 3
Tel/Fax 01-8330051
Email
combonimission@eircom.net

Superior
Rev Ruben Padilla Rocha

Rev Sean Dempsey
Rev Jose Manuel Casillas
Hernandez

Congregation of the Sacred Hearts of Jesus and Mary (SSCC)

Sacred Hearts Community

Archdiocese of Dublin

Provincialate
Coudrin House,
27 Northbrook Road,
Dublin 6 D06 W294
Tel 01-6604898 (Provincialate)
Email
ssccdublin@sacredhearts.ie
Website
www.sacred-hearts.net

Provincial
Very Rev Michael Ruddy
Tel 01-6473750
Provincial Secretary
Sheila O'Dowd

Rev Eamon Aylward
Tel 01-6473756
Email eamonmoz@yahoo.com
Most Rev Brendan Comiskey DD
Rev Michael F. Foley
Tel 01-6473759
Email
michaelffoley@gmail.com

Sacred Heart Presbytery
St John's Drive,
Clondalkin,
Dublin D22 W1W6
Tel 01-4570032

Rev Vincent Fallon
Email renovin@aol.com
Rev Ultan Naughton
Email
ultan.naughton@hotmail.com

RELIGIOUS ORDERS AND CONGREGATIONS

Diocese of Clogher

Cootehill
Co Cavan H16 CA22
Tel 049-5552188

Rev Jerry White
Email jerryssсc@gmail.com
Rev Kieran Murtha

Rockcorry
Co Monaghan

Rev Jerry White CC
Email jerryssсc@gmail.com

Diocese of Kilmore

Gallonreagh
Maudabawn, Cootehill,
Co Cavan H16 K576

Rev Michael Gilsenan CC
Email gilsenbawn@gmail.com

DIVINE WORD MISSIONARIES (SVD)

Irish & British Province

Each Province of the Society is independent. When members are assigned to work in the missions, they automatically become members of the territory to which they are assigned and are no longer members of the Irish British Province.

Archdiocese of Dublin

1 & 3 Pembroke Road,
Dublin 4
Tel 01-6680904
Rector: Rev Liam Dunne
Email pembroke@svdireland.com

Provincial
Rev Timothy Lehane
Email provincial@svdireland.com
provsec@svdireland.com

Rev Binoy Mathew
Rev John McAteer

133 North Circular Road,
Dublin 7
Tel 01-8386743

Praeses
Rev Anthony O'Riordan

Rev Michael Egan
Rev John Feighery
Rev Paul St John

Church of St Philip the Apostle,
Mountview, Dublin 15
Tel 01-8249695

Parish Priest: Rev George Adzato

Rev John Owens

Maynooth
Co Kildare
Tel 01-6286391/2
Fax 01-6289184
Email secretary@svdireland.com

Rector
Rev Finbarr Tracey
Provincial Treasurer
Rev Gerhard Osthues

Rev Gaspar Habara
Rev Gerard McCarthy
Rev George Millar
Rev Pat Moroney
Rev Sean Moynihan
Rev Jim Perry
Rev Justinus Purba
Rev Garrett Roche
Rev Jega Susai
Rev Teodor Tomasik

Diocese of Elphin

Donamon Castle
Roscommon
Tel 090-6662222
Fax 090-6662511
accounts@dwmcards.ie

Rector: Rev Pat Byrne

Rev George Agger
Rev Tony Coote
Rev Norman Davitt
Rev Tadeusz Durajczyk
Rev Charles Guthrie
Rev Michael Joyce
Rev Tom Kearney
Rev Jerry Lanigan
Rev Peter Maloney
Rev Peter McHugh
Rev Bert Parys
Rev Michael Reddan
Rev Krzysztof Sikora
Rev Vincent Twomey

British District

London
8 Teignmouth Road,
London, NW2 4HN
Tel 020-84528430

Praeses: Rev Albert Escoto

Rev John Bettison
Rev Eamonn Donnelly
Rev Krzyskow Krsysztof
Rev Vinsensius Mbu'i
Rev John McCarthy
Rev Martin McPake
Rev Kevin O'Toole
Rev Sanjeeb Xaxa

Bristol
St Mary-on-the-Quay
Presbytery, 20 Colston Street,
Bristol BS1 5AE
Tel 0117-9264702

Parish Priest: Rev Pat Hogan

Isleworth, London
Our Lady of Sorrows &
St Bridget of Sweden,
112 Twickenham Road,
Isleworth TW7 6DL

Parish Priest
Rev Nico Lobo Ratu

Rev Kieran Fitzharris

DOMINICAN ORDER (OP)
Order of Preachers

Irish Province

Archdiocese of Dublin

Provincial Office
St Mary's,
Tallaght, Dublin D24 X585
Tel 01-4048118
Email provincial@dominicans.ie

Provincial
Very Rev John Harris

Secretary of the Province
Rev Joseph Bulman
Email provincialsecretary@dominicans.ie
Provincial Bursar
Rev David Walker
Email provincialbursar@dominicans.ie
Children Protection Officer
Ms Mary Tallon
Email safeguardingoffice@dominicans.ie

Dominican Community
St Mary's Priory
Tallaght, Dublin 24
Tel 01-4048100
Parish 01-4048188
Email parish@stmarys-tallaght.ie
Retreat House
Tel 01-4048123/8191
Email dominicanretreats@gmail.com

Prior
Very Rev Donal Roche Adm

Rev Wilfrid Harrington
Rev Patrick Brennan
Rev Vincent Travers
Rev Philip Gleeson
Rev Donagh O'Shea
Rev Thomas O'Flynn
Rev Brian McKevitt
Rev Philip McShane
Br Martin Cogan

Br Eamonn Moran
Rev Gerard Norton
Rev Séamus Touhy
Rev Michael Dunleavy
Rev Robert Regula CC
Rev Atanasio Flores
Rev Albert Leonard
Rev Leo Donavan
Rev Colm Mannion

St Saviour's
Upper Dorset Street,
Dublin 1
Tel 01-8897610
Fax 01-8734003
Email stsaviours@eircom.net

Prior
Very Rev Joseph Dineen PP

Rev Edward Foley
Rev Liam Walsh
Rev Diarmuid Clifford
Rev Martin Boyle
Rev Bernard McCay-Morrissey
Rev Terence Crotty
Rev Joseph O'Brien
Rev Alan O'Sullivan
Rev John Cunningham
Rev John H. Walsh
Rev Patryk Zaczrewski
Rev Conor McDonough
Br Anthony Kavanagh
Br Kellan Scott
Br Ruaidhi Crieve
Br Ciaran Egan
Br Darran McGlinchey
Br Christopher Gault
Br Blazej Bialek
Br Bruno Kelleher
Br Mark Murphy
Br Nathan Peer
Br Sean Blackwell
Br Desmond Conway
Br Ivan Maher

St Aengus's
Tymon North,
Balrothery, Tallaght,
Dublin 24
Tel 01-4513757
Fax 01-4624038

Superior
Very Rev Benedict Moran PP
Email ben.moran25@gmail.com

Rev Pat Lucey CC

St Dominic's
St Dominic's Road,
Tallaght, Dublin 24
Tel 01-4510620
Fax 01-4623223

Superior
Very Rev Laurence Collins Adm
Email collinsl11@eircom.net

Rev Timothy Mulcahy CC
Rev Stephen Hutchinson

RELIGIOUS ORDERS AND CONGREGATIONS

Archdiocese of Armagh

St Malachy's
Dundalk, Co Louth
Tel 042-9334179/9333714
Fax 042-9329751

Superior: Rev David Barrins

Rev Bede McGregor
Rev Ronan Cusack
Rev Anthony McMullan
Rev Columba Mary Toman

Diocese of Cork & Ross

St Mary's
Pope Quay, Cork
Tel 021-4502267

Prior: Rev Maurice Colgan

Rev Finian Lynch
Rev Brendan Clifford
Rev Damian Polly
Rev Luuk Jansen
Rev Philip Mulryne

St Dominic's Retreat House
Montenotte, Co Cork
Tel 021-4502520
Fax 021-4502712

Prior: Rev Bernard Treacy

Br Thomas Casey
Rev Stephen Cummins
Rev Frank Downes
Rev Archie Byrne
Rev Benedict Hegarty
Rev Joseph Kavanagh
Rev Gerard Dunne

Diocese of Dromore

St Catherine's
Newry,
Co Down BT35 8BN
Tel 028-30262178

Superior
Very Rev David Tohill

Rev Noel Molloy
Br Mark McGreevy
Rev Stephen Tumilty
Rev Noel McKeown
Rev Adrian Farrelly
Rev Cesare Decio
Rev Joseph Ralph

Diocese of Elphin

Holy Cross
Sligo, Co Sligo
Tel 071-9142700
Fax 071-9146533

Superior
Rev Augustine Champion
Email sligofriary@eircom.net

Rev Anthony Morris
Rev Richard Walsh

Diocese of Galway

St Mary's
The Claddagh, Co Galway
Tel 091-582884

Prior
Very Rev Donal Sweeney PP
Email dsyop@eircom.net

Rev Denis Murphy
Rev Marek Cul
Rev Ambrose O'Farrell
Rev Jordan O'Brien
Rev Thomas McCarthy
Br James Ryan

Diocese of Kerry

Holy Cross
Tralee, Co Kerry
Tel 066-7121135/7129185

Superior: Rev Gregory Carroll
Email
domstralee@gmail.com

Rev James Duggan
Rev John O'Rourke
Rev David McGovern
Rev Matthew Farrell

Diocese of Kildare & Leighlin

Newbridge College
Droichead Nua, Co Kildare
Tel 045-487200
Fax 045-487234
Email
newbridgepriory@ireland.com
Secondary School

Prior: Vacant

Rev Edmund Murphy
Rev Benedict MacKenna
Rev Michael Commane
Rev Laurence Kelly
Rev Eoin Casey
Rev Jesse Maingot

Diocese of Ossory

Black Abbey
Kilkenny, Co Kilkenny
Tel 056-7721279
Fax 056-7721297

Superior:
Rev Thomas Monahan
Email
blackabbey@dominicans.ie

Rev Thomas Jordan
Rev Joseph Bulman

Diocese of Waterford & Lismore

St Saviour's
Bridge Street, Waterford
Tel 051-875061
Fax 051-858093

Superior: Very Rev Krzysztof Kupczakiewicz

Rev Canice Murphy
Rev Declan Corish
Rev Donal Mehigan

Rome

Convent of SS Xystus and Clement
Collegio San Clemente,
Via Labicana 95,
00184 Roma,
Italy
Tel 0039-06-7740021

Prior: Rev Paul Lawlor

Rev Paul Murray
Rev Michael Carragher
Rev Vivian Boland
Rev Fergus Ryan
Rev Patrick Desmond
Rev Kevin O'Reilly
Rev Brian Doyle
Rev Ronan Connolly
Rev Matthew Martinez

Lisbon

Convento dos Padres Dominicanos Irlandeses
Praceta Infante D. Henrique,
No 34, I-Dto, Rua do Murtal
San Pedro do Estoril, 2765-531
Estoril, Portugal
Tel 351-21-4673771

Superior and Parish Priest
Rev David Walker PP
Email stmarys@netcabo.pt

Tehran

St Abraham's Church
PO Box 14185-868
Jamalzadeh Shomali 252,
Tehran, Iran
Tel 98-21-66926535

PP Vacant

Trinidad

St Finbar's
Morne Coco Road,
Four Roads, Diego Martin,
Republic of Trinidad and
Tobago, West Indies
Tel 001-868-6328119

Superior: Rev Thomas Lawson

Rev Carlyle Fortune
Rev Alan Mohammed

Holy Cross
Arina, Republic of Trinidad
and Tobago, West Indies
Tel 001-868-6673208

Superior
Rev Ferdinand Warner

Rev Matthew Ahye
Rev Dwight Black
Rev Urban Hudlin

FRANCISCAN ORDER (OFM)

Province of Ireland

Provincial Office,
Franciscan Friary,
4 Merchant's Quay,
Dublin D08 XY19
Tel 01-6742500
Fax 01-6742549
Email info@franciscans.ie

Provincial
Rev Aidan McGrath
Email
provincial@franciscans.ie

Vicar Provincial and Secretary of the Province
Rev Joseph Condren
4 Merchants' Quay,
Dublin D08 XY19
Email sec.prov@franciscans.ie

Archdiocese of Dublin

Adam & Eve's
4 Merchants' Quay,
Dublin D08 XY19
Tel 01-6771128
Fax 01-6771000

Guardian
Br Niall O'Connell
Vicar
Rev Joseph Condren

Rev Brian Allen
Br Laurence Brady
Rev Damien Casey
Rev Richard Kelly
Rev Angelus Lee
Rev Aidan McGrath
Rev Fintan O'Shea
(96 Fr Scully House, Middle
Gardiner Street, Dublin 1)

RELIGIOUS ORDERS AND CONGREGATIONS

Franciscan House of Studies
Dún Mhuire,
Seafield Road,
Killiney, Co Dublin
Tel 01-2826760
Fax 01-2826993
Email franciscans.killiney@franciscans.ie

Guardian
Br Stephen O'Kane
Vicar
Rev Micheál Mac Craith

Rev Michael Bailey
Br Ronald Bennett
Rev Patrick Conlan
Rev Francis Cotter
Rev John Dalton
Rev Ignatius Fennessy
Rev John Harty
Rev Hugh O'Donnell
Rev Maelisa Ó Huallacháin
Rev Declan Timmons
Br Bonaventure Ward

Diocese of Ardagh & Clonmacnois

Franciscan Friary
Friary Lane, Athlone,
Co Westmeath
Tel 090-6472095
Fax 090-6424713

Guardian
Rev Gabriel Kinahan
Vicar
Rev Seamus Donohoe

Br Salvador Kenny
Rev Ralph Lawless
Rev Feargus McEveney
Rev Ulic Troy

Diocese of Cork & Ross

Franciscan Friary
Liberty Street, Cork
Tel 021-4275481
Fax 021-4271841

Guardian: Rev Patrick Younge
Vicar: Br Isidore Cronin

Br Denis Aherne
Rev Louis Brennan
Rev Colin Garvey
Rev Tony Hardiman
Rev Michael Holland
Rev Peter O'Grady
Rev Oscar O'Leary
Rev Ultan McCaffrey
Rev Brendan Scully
Br Nicholas Shanahan
Rev Hilary Steblecki

Diocese of Galway

The Abbey
8 Francis Street,
Galway
Tel 091-562518
Fax 091-565663
Email galwayabbey@franciscans.ie

Guardian
Rev David Collins
Vicar
Rev Frank McGrath

Rev Liam Kelly
Rev Adrian Peelo
Rev Jacopo Pozzerle
Br Ronan Sharpley

Diocese of Kerry

Franciscan Friary
Killarney, Co Kerry
Tel 064-6631334/6631066
Fax 064-6637510
Email friary@eircom.net

Guardian
Br Pat Lynch
Vicar:
Rev Antony Jukes

Rev PJ Brady
Rev Lars Frendel
Rev Walter Gallahue
Rev Eamonn O'Driscoll
Rev Caoimhín Ó Laoide
Rev Augustinus Wehrmeier

Diocese of Killaloe

Franciscan Friary
Ennis, Co Clare
Tel 065-6828751
Fax 065-6822008
Email ennis.friary@franciscans.ie

Guardian
Rev Brendan McGrath
Vicar
Rev Joseph MacMahon

Br Philip Lane
Rev Paschal McDonnell
Rev Cletus Noone
Br Elzear O'Brien
Rev Ailbe Ó Murchú

Diocese of Meath

Franciscan Abbey
Multyfarnham,
Co Westmeath
Tel 044-9371114/9371137
Fax 044-9371387
Email theabbeymulty@gmail.com

Provincial Delegate
Rev Kieran Cronin

Rev Sean Cassin
Rev John Kealy
Rev Lomán Mac Aodha
Rev John O'Brien
Rev Diarmaid Ó Riain
Rev Malcolm Timothy
Rev Joseph Walsh

Diocese of Raphoe

Franciscan Friary
Rossnowlagh, Co Donegal
Tel 071-9851342
Fax 071-9852206
Email info.rossnowlagh@franciscans.ie

Guardian
Rev Eugent Barrett
Vicar: Rev Vincent Finnegan

Rev Florian Farrelly
Rev Vincent Gallogley
Rev Pius McLaughlin

Diocese of Waterford & Lismore

Franciscan Friary
Clonmel, Co Tipperary
Tel 052-6121378
Fax 052-6125806
Email franciscans.clonmel@outlook.com

Guardian
Rev Jim Hasson
Vicar
Rev Liam McCarthy

Rev Billy Hoyne
Rev Larry Mulligan
Br Sean Murphy
Rev Jude Ronayne-Ford
Rev Thomas Russell

Franciscan Friary
Lady Lane, Waterford
*No longer resident community.
Church served from Clonmel.*

Filia House of Clonmel
Rev Patrick Cogan
*(15 Orchard Drive, Ursuline Court, Waterford/
Tel 087-2360239/Respond!
Office Tel 051-876865)*

Other Individual Addresses

Rev Jim Hynes
17 Rue du Faubourg La Grappe,
28000 Chartre, France

Franciscan Communities Abroad

St Anthony's Parish
(English-Speaking Chaplaincy)
23/25 Oudstrijderslaan,
1950 Kraainem, Belgium
Tel 0032-2-7201970
Fax 0032-2-7255810
Email stanthonyparish@telnet.be

Rev Michael Nicholas
(Provincial Delegate/Parish Priest)
Rev Patrick Power *(Associate Pastor)*

Collegio S. Isidoro
Via degli Artisti 41,
00187 Roma, Italy
Tel 0039-06-4885359
Fax 0039-06-4884459
Email collegio_s_isidoro@libero.it

Guardian
Rev Hugh McKenna

Rev Padraig Breheny
Br Ian Cunningham
Br Philip McMahon

Franciscan Custody in Zimbabwe
Custos: Rev Naison Manjovha

CONVENTUAL FRANCISCANS (OFMConv)

Provincial Custodial Office
St Patrick's Friary
26 Cornwall Road, Waterloo,
London SE1 8TW, England
Tel +44-2079288897

Provincial Custos
Very Rev Ciprian Budau

Archdiocese of Dublin

Friary of the Visitation of the BVM
Fairview Strand, Dublin 3
Tel 01-8376000 (office)
Tel 01-4825821 (priest)

Rev Maximilian McKeown PP
Rev Joseph Connick CC
Rev Aidan Walsh CC *(Guardian)*
Rev Marius Tomulesei
Br Joseph Fenton

Diocese of Ferns

The Friary
St Francis Street, Wexford
Tel 053-9122758

Rev Aquino Maliakkal
(Guardian)
Rev Robert Cojoc
Rev Kazimierz Trzcinski
Br Solanus Mary

FRANCISCAN FRIARS OF THE RENEWAL (CFR)

Community of the Franciscan Friars of Renewal
Community Servant
Rev John-Paul Ouellette
Our Lady of the Angels,
427 East 155th Street,
Bronx, NY 10455
Tel 001-718-4028255

Vocation Contact
Br Angelo Lefever
St Pio Friary,
Sedgefield Terrace,
Westgate,
Bradford BD1 2RU, UK
Tel 01274-721989
Fax 01274-740038
Email cfrfriar@cfrfranciscan.co.uk

Diocese of Derry

St Columba Friary
Fairview Road,
Derry BT48 8NU
Tel 028-71419980
Fax 028-71417652
Email derryfranciscans@gmail.com

Local Servant (Superior)
Rev Francesco Gavazzi

Rev Isaac Spinharney
Rev Thomas Cacciola
Br Benedict Joseph Deiarmi
Rev Charles-Benoit Reche

Diocese of Limerick

St Patrick Friary
64 Delmege Park,
Moyross, Limerick V94 859Y
Tel 061-458071
Fax 061-457626
Email limerickfranciscans@gmail.com

Local Servant (Superior)
Rev Joseph Mary Deane

Rev Oisin Martin
Rev Gabriel Joseph Kyte
Br Seraphim Roycourt
Rev Bernardino Maria Soukup

HOLY SPIRIT CONGREGATION (CSSp)

Province of Ireland

Archdiocese of Dublin

Holy Spirit Provincialate
Temple Park, Richmond Avenue South,
Dublin D06 AW02
Tel 01-4975127/4977230
Fax 01-4975399
Website www.spiritan.ie

Provincial Leadership Team
Rev Martin Kelly (Provincial)
Rev Peter Conaty
Rev Patrick Moran
Rev Colm Reidy
Rev David Conway (Provincial Bursar)
Rev Michael Kilkenny (Provincial Secretary)

Rev Brendan Carr (in residence)

Communications Manager
Mr Peter O'Mahony
Email communications@spiritanplt.ie

Safeguarding Office
Mr Liam Lally (Safeguarding Coordinator/Designated liaison person)
Tel 087-6709461
Email liam.lally@spiritanplt.ie

Spiritan Education Trust
Kimmage Manor,
Dublin 12
Tel 01-4997610
www.spiritaneducation.ie
Mr Patrick Kitterick (Chair)

Heritage and Archives Centre
Kimmage Manor,
Dublin 12
Manager: Vacant
Email archives@spiritan.ie

Holy Spirit Missionary College
Kimmage Manor,
Whitehall Road,
Dublin D12 P5YP
Tel 01-4064300
Fax 01-4920062
Email kimmagereception@spiritan.ie

Community Leader
Rev Colm Reidy

Rev Desmond Arigho
Rev Joseph Beere
Rev John Brown
Br Albert Buckley
Rev Tony Byrne
Rev James Byrnes
Rev Michael Casey
Rev Brendan Cogavin
Rev David Conway
Rev Kevin Corrigan
Rev Brian Cronin
Rev Patrick Cully
Rev Roderick Curran
Rev Hugh de Blacam
Rev Seán de Léis
Rev Patrick Doody
Rev Dermot Doran
Rev Patrick Doran
Rev James Duncan
Most Rev Robert Ellison
Rev Hugh Fagan
Rev John Flavin
Rev Michael Fillie
Rev John Flavin
Rev Michael Foody
Rev Denis Gavin
Rev Reginald Gillooly
Rev Brian Gogan
Rev Austin Healy
Rev James Heneghan
Rev Gregory Iwuozor
Rev Michael Kane
Rev Martin Keane
Rev Patrick James Kelly
Rev Daithí Kenneally
Rev John Laizer
Rev Owen Lambert
Rev Patrick Leonard
Rev Anthony Little
Rev Jude Lynch
Rev Naos Mac Cumhaill
Rev John Mahon
Rev Liam Martin
Rev Vincent McDevitt
Rev Martin McDonagh
Rev Peter J. McEntire
Rev Patrick McGlynn
Rev Brian McLaughlin
Rev Michael McMahon
Rev Walter McNamara
Rev Michael Moore
Rev Noel Moynihan
Rev Brian Murtagh
Rev John O'Brien
Rev James O'Connell
Rev Eddie O'Farrell
Rev Vincent O'Grady
Rev Michael O'Looney
Rev Noel O'Meara
Rev Sean O'Shaughnessy
Rev Joseph Poole
Rev Noel Redmond
Rev Desmond Reid
Rev Michael B. Reynolds
Rev Patrick J. Ryan
Rev Patrick M. Ryen
Rev Larry Shine
Rev Maurice Shortall
Rev Terence Smith
Rev Jim Stapleton
Br Conleth Tyrrell
Rev Paul Walsh
Rev Tom Whelan

Church of the Holy Spirit
Kimmage, Dublin 12
Tel 01-4064377
www.kimmagemanorparish.com

Church of the Holy Spirit
Greenhills, Dublin 12
Tel 01-4504040
www.holyspiritparishgreenhills.ie

Team Leader
Rev Raphael Annan

Rev Isaac Antwi-Boasiako CC
Rev John Mahon

Blackrock College
Blackrock, Co Dublin
Tel 01-2888681 Fax 01-2834267
www.blackrockcollege.com
Email info@blackrockcollege.com

Community Leader
Rev Cormac Ó Brolcháin
Principal: Alan MacGinty

Rev Vincent Browne
Rev Patrick Dundon
Rev Myles Healy
Rev Liam Kehoe
Rev Denis Kennedy
Rev John Kevin
Rev Thomas McDonald
Rev Tom Nash

Willow Park
Tel 01-2881651
Fax 01-2783353
Email admin@willowparkschool.ie

Principal Senior School
Mr Alan Rogan
Principal Junior School
Mr James Docherty

St Mary's College
Rathmines, Dublin 6
Community Tel 01-4995760
Fax 01-4972621
www.stmarys.ie
Junior School Tel 01-4995721
Email junsec@stmarys.ie
Senior School Tel 01-4995700
Fax 01-4972574
Email sensec@stmarys.ie

Community Leader
Rev Patrick Moran
Principal Secondary School
Mr Denis Murphy
Principal Junior School
Ms Judith Keane

Rev Martin Andama (Studies)
Br Ignatius Curry
Rev Richard Olin
Wilfred Otubo (Student)

RELIGIOUS ORDERS AND CONGREGATIONS

St Michael's College
Ailesbury Road,
Dublin 4
Tel 01-2189400
www.stmc.com
Email admin@stmc.ie

Principal: Mr Tim Kelleher
Principal Junior School
Ms Lorna Heslin

Duquesne University
Duquesne in Dublin,
St Michael's College,
1 Ailesbury Road,
Ballsbridge, Dublin 4
Tel/Fax 01-2080940
www.duq.edu/ireland
Resident Director:
Ms Nora McBurney
Email
nora.mcburney@gmail.com

Spiritan House
Spiritan Asylum Services Initiative (SPIRASI)
213 North Circular Road,
Dublin 7
Tel 01-8389664
Fax 01-8823547
www.spirasi.ie
Mr Rory Halpin *(Executive Director, SPIRASI)*
Commmunity Leader
Rev Michael Kilkenny

Rev Edward Flynn
Br Michael Liston
Rev Samson Mann
Br Liam Sheridan

Templeogue College
Templeville Road,
Dublin 6W
Tel 01-4903909
Fax 01-4920903
www.templeoguecollege.ie
Email
info@templeoguecollege.ie

Principal: Ms Niamh Quinn

Rev William Bradley
Rev Ronan Grimshaw
Rev Thomas Raftery

Church of the Transfiguration
Presbytery, Bawnogue,
Clondalkin, Dublin 22
Tel 01-4519810
www.facebook.com/
bawnogueparishclondalkin

Parish of St Ronan's
Deansrath, Clondalkin,
Dublin 22
Tel 01-4570380
Email stronansdeansrath@hotmail.com

Team Leader
Rev Brian Starken

Rev Patrick Coughlan
Rev Edvaldo Rodrigues da Silva

Archdiocese of Cashel and Diocese of Emly

Rockwell College
Cashel, Co Tipperary
Tel 062-61444 Fax 062-61661
www.rockwell-college.ie
Email info@rockwellcollege.ie

Secondary Residential and Day School

Principal
Ms Audrey O'Byrne

Br Gerard Cummins
Rev Patrick Downes
Rev Brendan Duggan
Rev Bernard M. Frawley
Rev Gerard Griffin
Rev Thomas Hogan
Rev William Kingston
Rev Jeremiah Kirwin *(Bursar)*
Rev Matthew Knight
Rev Patrick McGeever
Rev John Meade
Rev Noel Murphy

Diocese of Meath

Spiritan Missionaries
Ardbraccan,
Navan,
Co Meath C15 T884
Tel 046-9021441

Community Leader
Rev Peter Conaty

Rev Niall Greene
Lewis Kapchanga *(Student)*
Edmund Chipulu *(Student)*

Rome

Clivo di Cinna 195, 00136
Roma, Italy
Tel +39-06-35404609
Fax +39-06-35450676

Superior General
Most Rev John Fogarty

JESUITS (SJ)
SOCIETY OF JESUS

Irish Province

Archdiocese of Dublin

Irish Jesuit Provincialate
Milltown Park,
Sandford Road, Dublin 6
Tel 01-4987333
Fax 01-4987334
Email curia@jesuit.ie

Provincial
Rev Leonard Moloney
Assistant Provincial
Rev Declan Murray

Jesuit Centre for Faith and Justice
54/57 Upper Gardiner Street,
Dublin 1
Tel 01-8556814
Email info@jcfj.ie
www.jcfj.ie
Director: Mr Kevin Hargaden

Jesuit Communication Centre
Irish Jesuit Provincialate,
Milltown Park,
Sandford Road, Dublin 6
Tel 01-4987347/4987348
Director: Ms Pat Coyle
Email coylep@jesuit.ie
Irish Jesuit News
amdg@jesuit.ie
jcc@jesuit.ie
Sacred Space
Website www.sacredspace.ie

Jesuit Curia Community
Loyola House,
Milltown Park,
Sandford Road, Dublin 6
Tel 01-2180276
Email loyola@jesuit.ie

Rector: Rev Declan Murray

Rev Shane Daly
Rev Leonard Moloney
Rev Leon Ó Giolláin
Rev Peter Sexton

Applications for *retreats* to
Rev Piaras Jackson
Manresa House, Dollymount,
Dublin 3
Tel 01-8331352
or online at www.manresa.ie

Enquiries in respect of *foreign missions* to Rev Director, Jesuit Foreign Missions,
20 Upper Gardiner Street,
Dublin 1
Tel 01-8366509
Fax 01-8366510

St Francis Xavier's
Upper Gardiner Street,
Dublin 1
Tel 01-8363411 Fax 01-8555624
Email sfxcommunity@jesuit.ie
Parish church and residence

Superior
Rev Richard O'Dwyer
Vice-Superior
Rev Dermot Mansfield
Parish Priest
Very Rev Richard O'Dwyer PP

Rev Patrick Carberry
Patrick Corkery (Scholastic)
Rev Eddie Cosgrove
Br Eamonn Davis
Rev Paul Farquharson
Rev Niall S. Leahy
Rev Micheál MacGréil
Rev Krzysztof Madel
Rev Fergus O'Keefe
Rev Brendan Staunton

Residing Elsewhere
Rev Brian Lennon
Rev Peter McVerry
Rev Kevin O'Higgins
Rev James Smyth

Belvedere College SJ
Great Denmark Street, Dublin 1
Jesuits reside in SFX Gardiner Street

Secondary day school
Tel 01-8586600 (College)
Fax 01-8744374
Rector: Rev Patrick Greene
Headmaster: Mr Gerard Foley

St Ignatius House of Writers
35 Lower Leeson Street
Dublin 2
Tel 01-6761248 Fax 01-7758598
Residence

Superior: Rev Jim Culliton
Vice-Superior
Rev Michael Kirwan (Bri)

Rev Arunmozhi
Rev Galaz Carvajal (Chilean Province)
Rev Nemo Castelli
Rev David Coughlan
Rev Patrick Davis
Rev Juan Diego
Rev Michael O. Gallagher
Rev Edmond Grace
Rev Brian Grogan
Rev John Looby
Rev Donal Neary
Rev Myles O'Reilly
Rev Michael O'Sullivan

Residing Elsewhere
Rev Ronan Geary
Br Gerard Marks

Sacred Heart Messenger – a Jesuit Publication
37 Lower Leeson Street,
Dublin 2
Tel 01-6767491
Editor: Rev Donal Neary
Commissioning Editor
Rev Paddy Carberry
Manager: Ms Cecilia West
Email manager@messenger.ie

Manresa House
426 Clontarf Road,
Dollymount, Dublin 3
Tel 01-8331352
Fax 01-8331002
Email manresa@jesuit.ie
Retreat House

Rector: Rev William Reynolds
Director of Retreat House
Rev Piaras Jackson

Rev Brendan Comerford
Rev Michael Drennan
Rev Patrick Greene
Rev Peter Hannan
Rev Dermot O'Connor

Milltown Park
Sandford Road,
Dublin D06 V9K7
Tel 01-2698411/2698113
Fax 01-2600371
Email milltown@jesuit.ie

Rector
Rev Tom Casey
Vice-Rector
Rev Declan Murray

Br John Adams
Rev Noel Barber
Rev Bruce Bradley
Rev Fergal Brennan
Rev William Callanan
Rev Tom Casey
Rev Brendan Duddy
Br George Fallon
Rev John K. Guiney
Rev Finbarr Lynch
Rev William Mathews
Br James McCabe
Rev Thomas Morrissey
Rev Laurence Murphy
Rev Brian O'Leary
Rev Frank Sammon
Rev Patrick Sheary

Residing Elsewhere
Rev John Dooley
Rev Henry Grant
Rev Conor Harper
Rev Alan Mowbray

Gonzaga College SJ
Sandford Road, Dublin 6
Tel 01-4972943 (community)
Fax 01-4960849 (community)
Tel 01-4972931 (college)
Fax 01-4967769
Email
(Community) gonzaga@jesuit.ie
(College) office@gonzaga.ie

Rector: Rev John O'Keeffe
Headmaster
Mr Damon McCaul

Rev John Callanan
Rev Edward O'Donnell
Rev Fergus O'Donoghue
Rev Desmond O'Grady
Rev Colin Warrack

25 Croftwood Park
Cherry Orchard, Dublin 10
Tel 01-6267413

Rev Gerard O'Hanlon
Rev William Toner

Archdiocese of Armagh

Iona
211 Churchill Park
Portadown, BT62 1EU
Tel 028-38330366
Fax 028-38338334
Email iona@jesuit.ie

Superior
Rev Brendan MacPartlin
Rev Michael Bingham *(British Province)*
Rev Prionsias Mac Brádaigh

Diocese of Down & Connor

Peter Faber House
28 Brookvale Avenue
Belfast BT14 6BW
Tel 028-90757615
Fax 028-90747615
Email
peter_faber@lineone.net

Superior: Rev Tom Layden

Rev Gerry Clarke
Rev Terence Howard
Rev Brendan McManus

Diocese of Galway

St Ignatius Community & Church
27 Raleigh Row, Salthill,
Galway
Tel 091-523707
Email galway@jesuit.ie

Rector: Rev Martin Curry

Rev Liam O'Connell
Rev Enda O'Callaghan
Rev Ciaran Quirke
Rev Patrick Tyrrell

Residing Elsewhere
Rev Paul Brassil *(Zambia)*

Coláiste Iognáid SJ
24 Sea Road, Galway
College Tel 091-501550
Fax 091-501551
Email
colaisteiognaid@eircom.net

Secondary School Principal
Mr David O'Sullivan
Scoil Iognaid (National School) Principal
Ms Laoise Breathnach
Tel 091-584491

Diocese of Kildare & Leighlin

Clongowes Wood College SJ
Clane, Co Kildare
W91 DN40
Tel 045-868663/868202
Fax 045-861042
Email *(College)*
reception@clongowes.net
(Community)
reception@clongowes.net
Secondary Boarding School

Rector
Rev Michael Sheil
Headmaster: Mr Chris Lumb
Email hm@clongowes.net
Vice-Rector
Rev Bernard McGuckian
Minister: Br Tom Phelan
Sub-Minister
Br Charles Connor

Residing Elsewhere
Rev Dermot Murray

Diocese of Limerick

Crescent College Comprehensive SJ
Dooradoyle, Limerick
(Community)
Tel 061-229655 Fax 061-229013
Email dooradoyle@jesuit.ie
(College)
Email ccadmin.ias@eircom.net
Comprehensive Day School for Boys and Girls

Superior: Rev Joseph Hayes
Minister: Rev James Maher
Principal: Mr Diarmuid Mullins

Jesuits temporarily outside Ireland

Correspondence to
Irish Jesuit Provincialate
Milltown Park,
Sandford Road, Dublin 6
Tel 01-4987333
Email curia@jesuit.ie

Rev Kevin Casey
Rev James Corkery
Rev John Dardis
Rev Cathal Doherty
Rev Edmond Grace
Rev Timothy Healy
Rev Niall F.X. Leahy
Rev Brian Mac Cuarta
Rev Michael McGuckian
Rev James Murphy
Rev Caoimhín Ó Ruairc
Rev Anthony O'Riordan
Rev Patrick Riordan
Rev Gerard Whelan

Diocese of Raphoe

Most Rev Alan McGuckian
Bishop of Raphoe

LEGIONARIES OF CHRIST (LC)

Archdiocese of Dublin

Community
Leopardstown Road,
Foxrock, Dublin 18
Tel 01-2955902
Email ireland@legionaries.org

Superior: Rev Joseph Fazio
Vocations Director
Rev Timothy Moran
Email tmoran@legionaries.org
Regnum Christi
Rev Aaron Vinduska
Email
avinduska@legionaries.org
Community Secretary
Rev Timothy Moran
Email tmoran@legionaries.org

Creidim Centre
Leopardstown Road,
Dublin D18 FF64
Tel 01-2955902
Email
faithandfamilycentre@arcol.org
School Retreats
Email team@clonlost.ie
School retreats, Communion and Confirmation retreats, Children and Adult Catechesis Programmes, Marriage Enrichment days, Spiritual retreats, Courses on the Faith, Spiritual Direction

Director: Rev Aaron Vinduska
Email
avinduska@legionaries.org

RELIGIOUS ORDERS AND CONGREGATIONS

Dublin Oak Academy
Kilcroney, Bray,
Co Wicklow
Tel 01-2863290
Fax 01-2865315
Email secretary@
dublinoakacademy.com

Director: Rev Oscar Sanchez
Chaplain: Rev Joseph Fazio

Woodlands Academy
Wingfield House, Bray
Co Wicklow
Tel 01-2866323
Fax 01-2864918

Chaplain
Rev Vincent McMahon

MARIANISTS (SM)
Society of Mary

Provincial Headquarters
4425 West Pine Boulevard,
St Louis, MO 63108-2301,
USA
Tel 314-533-1207

Provincial
Rev Oscar Vasquez

Archdiocese of Dublin

Marianist Community
13 Coundon Court, Killiney,
Co Dublin A96 K0T9
Tel 01-2858301
Residence for Religious

Director: Br Gerard McAuley
Email
gerardmcauley001@gmail.com

Rev Michael Reaume
Br Fred Rech
Br James Contadino

St Laurence College
Loughlinstown, Dublin 18
Tel 01-2826930
Coeducational Secondary Day School

Principal: Mr Shane Fitzgerald

MARIST FATHERS (SM)
Society of Mary

Archdiocese of Dublin

Marist Fathers Chanel
Finance & Administrative Office, Coolock Village,
Dublin D05 KU62
Tel 01-8505022/086-2597905

Administrator
Rev Declan Marmion
Email
dmarmion50@gmail.com

St Brendan's Parish
Coolock Village, Dublin 5
Tel 01-8484799

Parish Priest
Rev Edwin McCallion PP

Rev John Harrington CC
Rev Paddy Stanley CC

Chanel Community
Coolock, Dublin 5
Tel 01-8477133

Superior
Rev Edwin McCallion PP

Rev Frank Corry
Rev Edmund Duffy
Rev Cormac McNamara
Archbishop Adrian Smith,
Nazareth House,
Malahide Road, Dublin 9
Rev Ray Staunton

Chanel College
Coolock, Dublin 5
Tel 01-8480655/8480896

Headmaster: Mr Dara Gill

St Teresa's
Donore Avenue, Dublin 8
Tel 01-4542425/4531613

Parish Priest
Rev David Corrigan PP
Superior
Rev John O'Gara

Catholic University School
89 Lower Leeson Street,
Dublin 2
Tel 01-6762586

Headmaster
Mr Clive Martin

Archdiocese of Armagh

Cerdon
Marist Fathers,
St Mary's Road,
Dundalk, Co Louth
Tel 042-9334019

Superior
Rev James O'Connell

Rev Kevin Cooney
Rev Bernard (Barney) King
Rev Michael Maher

St Mary's College
Dundalk, Co Louth
Tel 042-9339984

Principal: Mr Alan Craven

Marist Fathers elsewhere in Ireland

Armagh
Rev Sean McArdle
Parochial House,
Louth Village,
Dundalk, Co Louth

Dublin
Rev Kieran Butler
Little Sisters of the Poor,
Sybill Hill Road, Raheny
Rev P. G. Byrne
Little Sisters of the Poor,
Sybill Hill Road, Raheny

Marist Fathers outside Ireland

Rev Aidan Carvill, Australia
Rev Larry Duffy, Italy
Rev Patrick Muckian,
Philippines
Rev Paddy O'Hare, France
Rev Martin McAnaney, Paris
Rev James McElroy, France
Rev Seamus McMahon,
Australia
Rev Rory Mulligan, Norway
Rev Jim Ross, Fiji
Rev Paul Walsh
Communaté Mariste
22 Rue Victor Clappier,
83000 Toulon, France

MILL HILL MISSIONARIES (MHM)

Archdiocese of Dublin

St Joseph's House
50 Orwell Park,
Rathgar,
Dublin D06 C535
Tel 01-4127700
Email josephmhm@eircom.net

Regional Superior
Rev Philip O'Halloran
Tel 01-4127773/4127735/
089-4385320
Email
millhillregional.irl@gmail.com

Rector
Rev Philip O'Halloran
Vice Rector: Position vacant
Bursar
Rev Patrick Murray
Email millhill@iol.ie

Rev John Ambrose
Rev Matt Carpenter
Rev Tom Connors
Rev Christopher Fox
Rev Donal Harney
Rev Maurice McGill
(Organising Secretary)
Email
organisingmhm@gmail.com
Rev Sean O'Brien
Rev Jim O'Connell
(Editor, St Joseph's Advocate)
Email jimocmhm@eircom.net
Rev John Nevin
Rev Philip Shube Bawe
Rev Patrick O'Connell
Rev Matthew Grier
Rev Tom Keane
Rev Anthony Murphy
Rev Michael O'Brien
Rev Patrick Molloy
Rev Desmond McGillicuddy

Archdiocese of Tuam

St James Apartments
Knock Shrine,
Knock, Co Mayo

Rev Denis Hartnett
Rev Gerald Doyle

Elsewhere in Ireland

Rev Tom McGrath, Diocese of Killaloe
Rev Kevin Reynolds, Diocese of Elphin
Care of St Joseph's House:
Rev Christopher O'Connor
Rev Kevin O'Rourke
Rev Thomas Sinnott
Rev James A. Boyle
Rev Patrick Ryan
Rev Daniel O'Connor,
St Laurence O'Toole,
Kilmacud Parish

Generalate

Mill Hill Missionaries
1 Colby Gardens,
Cookham Road,
Maidenhead SL6 7GZ,
England
Tel 0044-1628-789752

Superior General
Very Rev Michael Corcoran

MISSIONARIES OF AFRICA (White Fathers)

Province of Europe
Irish Community

Archdiocese of Dublin

Community House
Cypress Grove Road,
Templeogue,
Dublin D6W, YV12
Tel 01-4055263 (House)
Tel 01-4063966
Email pep.irl.del@mafr.org

Community Superior
Rev Michael P. O'Sullivan
Bursar
Br Karl Kaelin

Cypress Grove
Templeogue,
Dublin D6W YV12
Tel 01-4055263
Tel 01-4055526 (Promotion)
Email m.africaprom@yahoo.com
House of promotion/retired priests and brothers/studies

Superior
Rev Michael P. O'Sullivan
Promotion Director
Rev Neil Loughrey
Mite Boxes
Rev Neil Loughrey

Rev Ian Buckmaster
Rev Eugene Lewis
Rev Neil Loughrey
Rev Jim McTiernan
Rev Sean O'Leary
Rev Michael P. O'Sullivan
Rev Diarmuid Sheehan
Rev Charles Timoney

Members of the Irish sector outside Ireland
Rev P. J. Cassidy (South Africa)
Rev James Greene (South Sudan)
Br Raymond Leggett (Scotland)
Rev Ciaran McGuinness (England)
Rev Joseph McMenamin (Zambia)
Rev Raymond McQuarrie (South Africa)
Rev Gerard Murphy (Ethiopia)
Rev John O'Donoghue (Malawi)
Rev Brendan O'Shea (Malawi)
Rev Peter Reilly (Uganda)
Rev David Sullivan (Jerusalem)

MISSIONARIES OF THE SACRED HEART (MSC)

The Missionaries of the Sacred Heart is a congregation of 16 provinces. Members of the Irish Province work in Ireland, England, USA, South Africa and Venezuela.

Archdiocese of Dublin

Provincialate
65 Terenure Road West,
Dublin 6W, D6W P295
Tel 01-4906622
Fax 01-4920148

Provincial Leader
Rev Carl Tranter

Woodview House
Mount Merrion Avenue,
Blackrock, Co Dublin
A94 DW95
Tel 01-2881644 (community)

Leader: Rev Manus Ferry

Rev John Bennett
Rev Eugene Clarkson
Rev Joseph Falloon
Rev Patrick McGlanaghy
Rev Martin McNamara
Rev John O'Sullivan
Rev Michael Screene
Rev David Smith
Mr Tadhg Ó Dálaigh
(community member)

Sacred Heart Parish
Killinarden,
Tallaght, Dublin D24 R521
Tel 01-4522251

Rev Fintan O'Dricsoll PP
Rev Con O'Connell

Formation House
Rev Joseph McGee
Rev Con O'Connell
Rev Diarmuid Ó Murchú
56 Mulvey Park, Dundrum,
Dublin D14 K223
Tel 01-2951856

Diocese of Cork & Ross

MSC Mission Support Centre
PO Box 23, Western Road,
Cork, T12 WT72
Tel 021-4545704/4543988
Fax 021-4343587
info@mscmissions.ie
www.mscmissions.ie

Rev Michael O'Connell

Western Road
Cork T12 TN80
Tel 021-4804120
Fax 021-4543823

Leader: Rev John Finn

Parish Priest
Rev Thomas Mulcahy

Rev Charles Conroy
Rev Jeremiah Daly
Rev Desmond Farren
Rev John Fitzgerald
Br Donal Hallissey
Rev Seamus Kelly
Rev Donncha Mac Cárthaigh
Rev Alan Neville
Rev Michael O'Connell
Rev Daniel O'Neill

Carrignavar
Co Cork
Tel 021-4884044

Rev Christopher Coleman
Rev Seán Horgan
Rev Jimmy Stubbs

Castlehaven Parish
Parish House,
Union Hall, Skibbereen,
Co Cork, P81 C433
Tel 028-34940

Parish Priest
Rev Gerard Thornton PP

Leap-Glandore Parish
Parish House, Leap,
Skibbereen, Co Cork,
P81 NN52
Tel 028-33177

Parish Priest
Rev Terence O'Brien PP

Rev Michael Curran

Diocese of Galway

'Croí Nua'
Rosary Lane,
Taylor's Hill,
Galway H91 WY2A
Tel 091-520960
Fax 091-521168

Leader
Rev Charles Sweeney

Rev Kevin Blade
Rev Con Doherty
Rev Eamon Donohoe
Rev Hugh Hanlon
Rev Patrick Kelly
Rev Martin Morrissey
Rev Michael Smyth
Rev Augustine O'Brien
Rev Thomas Plower

Parish of the Resurrection
Ballinfoyle, Headford Road,
Galway, H91 W298
Tel 091-762883

Parish Priest
Rev Anthony Horgan PP

NORBERTINE CANONS (OPraem)

Diocese of Kilmore

Holy Trinity House
Lismacanican,
Mountnugent, Co Cavan
Email kilnacrottabbeytrust@gmail.com

Prior
Rt Rev James J. Madden
Email kilnacrottabbeytrust@gmail.com

Rev Kilian Mitchell
Br Kevin O'Brien
Rev Joseph O'Donohoe
Rev Terry Smyth

Priests working elsewhere in Ireland
Rt Rev James J. Madden
Rev Pat Reilly

Priests working outside Ireland
Rt Rev William M. Fitzgerald

OBLATES OF MARY IMMACULATE (OMI)

Archdiocese of Dublin

Provincial Residence
Oblates of Mary Immaculate
House of Retreat,
Tyrconnell Road, Inchicore,
Dublin 8
Tel 01-4541160/4541161
Fax 01-4541138
Email provincialoffice@oblates.ie

Provincial
Very Rev Oliver Barry
Provincial Treasurer
Rev Liam Griffin
Provincial Secretary
Angela Malone

Oblate House of Retreat
Inchicore, Dublin 8
Tel 01-4534408/4541805
Fax 01-4543466

Superior
Rev William Fitzpatrick
Rev Anthony Clancy

Rev Edward Carolan
Rev Peter Clucas
Rev Peter Daly
Rev Jeremiah Donovan
Br Francis Flanagan
Br Patrick Flanagan
Rev Liam Griffin
Rev Michael Hughes
Rev Gerard Kenny
Rev Patrick McGrath

RELIGIOUS ORDERS AND CONGREGATIONS

Rev Vincent Mulligan
Rev Conor Murphy
Rev Kevin O'Connor
Rev Desmond O'Donnell
Rev Martin O'Keeffe
Rev Joseph O'Melia
Rev Thomas O'Shea
Rev John Poole

170 Merrion Road
Ballsbridge, Dublin 4
Tel 01-2693658
Fax 01-2600597

Rev Brian de Burca
Rev Noel Ormonde

Oblate Scholasticate
St Anne's,
Goldenbridge Walk,
Inchicore, Dublin 8
Tel 01-4540841/4542955
Fax 01-4731903

Rev Oliver Barry
Rev Thomas McCabe

Inchicore
St Michael's Parish
52a Bulfin Road,
Inchicore, Dublin 8
Tel 01-4531660
Fax 01-4548191

Rev Michael Brady
Rev L. McDermott
Rev D. Mills

Bluebell Parish
Our Lady of the Wayside
118 Naas Road,
Bluebell, Dublin 12
Tel 01-4501040
Email
olowbluebell@oceanfree.net

*Moderator of Bluebell/
Inchicore Pastoral Area*
Rev Leo Philomin
Rev Dominik Zwierzychowski

Darndale Parish
The Presbytery,
Darndale, Dublin 17
Tel 01-8474547
Fax 01-8479295
Email omiddale@eircom.net

Superior
Very Rev Michael O'Connor CC

Rev Eduardo Nunez Yepez Co-PP
Rev Edward Quinn

Diocese of Kerry

Department of Chaplaincy
Tralee General Hospital,
Tralee, Co Kerry
Tel 066-7126222

Rev Edward Barrett

PALLOTTINES (SAC)
Society of the Catholic Apostolate

The Pallottine houses in Ireland and Britain are united in the Irish Province, as are the houses in Kenya, Tanzania, Rome, Argentina and the USA.

Archdiocese of Dublin

Provincial House
'Homestead',
Sandyford Road,
Dundrum, Dublin 16
Tel 01-2956180/2954170
Email
motherofdivinelove@gmail.com

Provincial
Very Rev Liam McClarey
Rector
Rev Michael Irwin
Email
mirwinyawl99@gmail.com
Provincial Bursar/Secretary for Missions
Rev John Kelly
Email pallbursar@gmail.com
Director of Formation
Rev John Egan

Br Tony Doherty
Rev Jeremiah Murphy

Attached to Provincial House
Rev Gerard Fleming CC
(Springfield/Jobstown/
Brookfield parishes)
Rev Liam Sweeney
Sacred Heart Residence,
Sybil Hill Road, Raheny,
Dublin 5

St Anne's
Shankill, Co Dublin
Rev Emmet O'Hara *(protem)*
St Benin's, Dublin Road,
Shankill, Co Dublin
Tel 01-2824425

Rev Michael O'Dwyer CC
Rev Jaimie Twohig CC
St Benin's, Dublin Road,
Shankill, Co Dublin
Tel 01-2824381

St Patrick's
Corduff, Blanchardstown,
Dublin 15
Tel 01-8213596/8215930

Rev John O'Connor PP
Rev John Regan CC

Archdiocese of Cashel and Diocese of Emly

Pallottine College
Thurles, Co Tipperary
Tel 0504-21202

Rector
Very Rev George Ranahan
Vice-Rector
Br Stephen Buckley

Rev John Casey
Rev John Coen
Rev Michael Coen
Rev Patrick Dwyer
Rev John Bergin
Rev Philip Barry
Rev Martin Mareja *(Director, Mission Promotion Office)*
Bishop Seamus Freeman
Rev Brendan Walsh
Rev Kevin Ward
Rev Michael Barry
Rev Donal McCarthy

Attached to Pallottine College
Rev Vincent Kelly
18 Silvercourt,
Silversprings, Cork

PASSIONISTS (CP)
Congregation of the Passion

Province of St Patrick: houses in Ireland, Scotland and Paris.

Archdiocese of Dublin

St Paul's Retreat
Mount Argus, Dublin 6W
Tel 01-4992000
Fax 01-4992001
Email
passionistsmtargus@eircom.net
Provincial Office
Tel 01-4992050
Fax 01-4992055
passionistprov@eircom.net

Provincial: Rev James Sweeney
Superior: Rev Bernard Lowe

Rev Kenneth Brady
Rev Kieran Creagh
Rev Ralph Egan
Rev James Feehan
Rev Dermot Gallagher
Rev Augustine Hourigan
Rev Joseph Kennedy
Rev Eugene McCarthy
Rev Brian Mulcahy
Rev Patrick Rogers
Rev James Sheridan
Rev Patrick Sheridan
Rev Paul Francis Spencer PP
Rev Ignatius Waters

Applications for missions and retreats to Rev Superior of any of our local Communities

Diocese of Clogher

St Gabriel's Retreat
The Graan, Enniskillen,
Co Fermanagh BT7 45PB
Tel 028-66322272
Fax 028-66325201

Superior
Rev Charles Cross
Email
charlescrosscp@gmail.com

Rev Victor Donnelly
Br Brendan Gallagher
Rev Arthur McCann
Rev Anthony O'Leary

Diocese of Down & Connor

Passionist Retreat Centre
16 A Downpatrick Road,
Crossgar,
Downpatrick,
Co Down BT30 9EQ
Tel 028-44830242
Fax 028-44831382

Superior
Rev Thomas Scanlon

Rev Ephrem Blake
Rev Mel Byrne
Rev Brian D'Arcy
Rev Aidan O'Kane

Holy Cross Retreat
Ardoyne,
Crumlin Road,
Belfast BT14 7GE
Tel 028-90748231
Fax 028-90740340

Parish Priest
Rev John Craven
Superior
Rev John Friel

Rev Gary Donegan
Rev Patrick Duffy
Rev Myles Kavanagh
Rev Terence McGuckin
Rev Gareth Thomas
Rev Francis Trias

Scotland

Passionist Community
26 Plantation Parkway,
Bishopbriggs,
Glasgow G64 2FD, Scotland
Tel 141-7729697

France

St Joseph's Church
50 Avenue Hoche,
75008 Paris
Tel 33-1-42272856
Fax 33-1-42278649

RELIGIOUS ORDERS AND CONGREGATIONS

REDEMPTORISTS (CSSR)
Congregation of the Most Holy Redeemer

The Irish Province of the Redemptorists is a complete province, with one dependent. Vice-Province in Brazil, ten other members assigned to the Province of CEBU/Philippines, one member assigned to the Province of Bangalore, India, and two members in Mozambique.

Office of the Provincial
St Joseph's Monastery,
St Alphonsus Road,
Dundalk,
Co Louth A91 F3FC
Email provincial@cssr.ie
Provincial Secretary
Email secretary@cssr.ie

Provincial
Rev Dan Baragry
Provincial Vicar
Rev Ciarán O'Callaghan
2nd Provincial Consultor
Rev Gerry O'Connor

Archdiocese of Dublin

Dún Mhuire
461/463 Griffith Avenue,
Dublin D09 X651
Tel 01-5180196
Fax 01-8369655

Rev Thomas Hogan (*Hospital Chaplain, Our Lady of Lourdes*)
Rev Patrick Kelly
Rev Denis O'Connor (*parish*)
Rev Brendan O'Rourke

Most Holy Sacrament Parish
Cherry Orchard, Dublin 10
Tel 01-6267930

Rev Michael Murtagh PP

Ballyfermot Assumption Parish
197 Kylemore Road,
Ballyfermot, Dublin 10
Parish Tel 01-6264691
Community Tel 01-5356977

Rev Adrian Egan PP & Coordinator
Rev Séamus Devitt
Rev Cornelius J. Casey

Archdiocese of Armagh

St Joseph's
St Alphonsus Road,
Dundalk, Co Louth A91 F3FC
Tel 042-9334042/9334762
Fax 042-9330893
Provincial administration, parish and Redemptorist Communications

Superior
Rev Noel Kehoe PP
Vicar-Superior
Rev Richard Delahunty

Rev Dan Baragry (*Provincial*)
Rev John Bermingham
Rev Cathal Cumiskey
Br Patrick Doherty
Rev Eamonn Hoey
Rev Patrick Horgan
Rev Eamon Kavanagh
Rev Stan Mellett
Rev Tony Rice
Rev Derek Ryan

Diocese of Clonfert

St Patrick's
Esker, Athenry, Co Galway
Tel 091-844007
Fax 091-845698
Outside office hours
086-8440619
Mission house, retreat house and Youth Village

Superior
Rev Brendan Callanan
Vicar Superior
Rev Patrick O'Keeffe

Rev James Buckley
Br James Casey
Rev Seán Cannon
Rev John F. Corbett
Rev Anthony Flannery
Rev Philip Hearty
Rev Clement MacMánuis
Rev Richard McMahon
Rev Anthony Mulvey
Rev Michael O'Flynn
Rev Richard Tobin

Diocese of Cork & Ross

Scala
Castlemahon House,
Castle Road, Blackrock, Cork
Tel 021-4358800
Fax 021-4359696

Co-ordinator: Rev Brian Nolan

Rev Michael Forde
Rev Gerard O'Connor
Rev John P. O'Riordan CC
Mahon Parish,
2 The Presbytery, Mahon, Cork
Rev Pat Sugrue

Diocese of Down & Connor

Clonard Monastery
1 Clonard Gardens,
Belfast, BT13 2RL
Tel 028-90445950
Fax 028-90445988

Superior
Rev Peter Burns
Vicar
Rev Ciaran O'Callaghan

Rev Anthony Branagan
Rev Edmond Creamer
Rev Michael Dempsey
Rev Johnny Doherty
Rev Alphonsus Doran
Rev John Hanna
Rev Brendan Keane
Rev Sean Keeney
Rev Barney McCahery
Rev Brendan McConvery
Rev Anthony McCrave
Rev William McGettrick
Rev Sean Moore
Rev Pat O'Connor
Rev Paul Turley

St Gerard's Parish
722 Antrim Road,
Newtownabbey,
Co Antrim BT36 7PG
Tel 028-90774833
Fax 028-90770923
PP: Rev Kevin Browne

Rev Denis Luddy

Diocese of Limerick

Mount Saint Alphonsus
South Circular Road, Limerick
Tel 061-315099 Fax 061-315303
Mission House

Superior
Rev Seamus Enright
Vicar-Superior
Rev Gerard Moloney

Rev Eamonn Breslin
Rev Laurence Gallagher
Rev Raphael Gallagher
Rev John Goode
Br Nicholas Healy
Rev Michael Kelleher
Rev Cornelius Kenneally
Rev John Lucey
Br Dermot McDonagh
Rev Aidan McMahon
Rev David McNamara
Rev Derek Meskell
Rev Gerard Moloney
Rev Michael G. O'Connor
Rev John J. Ó Ríordáin

St Clement's College
Laurel Hill Avenue,
South Circular Road,
Limerick
Tel 061-315878/318749 (staff)
Tel 061-310294 (students)
Fax 061-316640
Secondary school for boys

Principal: Mr Pat Talty

Province of Cebu (Philippines)

PO Box 280
6000 Cebu City,
Philippine Islands
Tel +63-32-2536341/2536315

Provincial: Vacant

Province of Bangalore (India)

Redemptorist Community
R.C. Church,
Morrispet PO, Tenali, Guntur
DT 522 202,
Andhra Pradesh,
India
Tel +91-8644-223382

Rev Martin Cushnan

Vice-Province of Fortaleza (Brazil)

Missionarios Redentoristas
Caixa Postal 85
60,001-970 Fortaleza
Est. do Ceara, Brazil
Tel +55-8532232016

Mission in Rome

Via Merulana 31
CP 2458,
00185 Roma-PT158, Italy
Tel 0039-06-494901

Rev Brendan Kelly (*Administration*)
Rev Martin McKeever (*Alphonsian Academy*)

Mission in Mozambique

Santa Maria dei Monti Mission
Furancungo,
Mozambique, Africa

Rev Eridian Goncalves de Lima
Rev Brian Holmes
Contact: c/o Provincial, Dublin

RELIGIOUS ORDERS AND CONGREGATIONS

ROSMINIANS (IC)
Institute of Charity

Irish Province

Archdiocese of Dublin

Clonturk House
Ormond Road, Drumcondra,
Dublin 9, D09 F821
Tel 01-6877014

*Provincial & Vocations
Director:* Rev Joseph O'Reilly
Mission Secretaries
Rev Frank Quinn
Rev Christopher McElwee
Rev Emilian Kibiriti

Rector: Rev Matt Gaffney

Rev James Flynn
Rev Gerald Cunningham
Rev Sean Walsh
Rev John Mullen
Rev William Stuart
Rev Michael O'Neill
Rev Michael O'Shea
Rev Christanand Varghese
Kuttikkatt
Br Eamon Fitzpatrick

**Rosminian Mission
Development Office**
Clonturk House,
Ormond Road,
Drumcondra,
Dublin D09 F821
Tel 01-6877023

Rev Emilian Kibiriti

Archdiocese of Armagh

Faughart Parish
St Brigid's, Kilcurry,
Dundalk,
Co Louth A91 E8N8
Tel 042-9334410

Parish Priest
Rev Vinod Thennattil Kurian
Rev Oliver Stansfield

Parochial House,
Knocknagoran,
Omeath,
Co Louth A91 HK76

Rev Christopher McElwee

Diocese of Cork & Ross

Rosmini House
Dunkereen, Innishannon,
Co Cork, T12 N9DH
Tel 021-4776268/4776923
Fax 021-4776268

Rector
Rev Polachan Thettayil

Rev Joyce John Michael

Diocese of Waterford & Lismore

St Joseph's
Doire na hAbhann,
Tickincar, Clonmel,
Co Tipperary, E91 XY71
Tel 052-6126914
Fax 052-6126915

Rev James Browne
Rev Tom Coffey
Rev P. J. Fegan
Rev Michael Melican
Rev Patrick Pierce

St Oliver Plunkett's Parish
Cooleens, Glenconnor,
Clonmel, Co Tipperary
E91 N578
Tel 052-6125679

Rev Michael Hegarty PP

*Enquiries concerning the
missions to:* Rev Frank Quinn
or Rev Emilian Kibiriti
Clonturk House,
Ormond Road,
Drumcondra, Dublin 9

SACRED HEART FATHERS (SCJ) Congregation of the Priests of the Sacred Heart of Jesus

British-Irish Province

Archdiocese of Dublin

Sacred Heart Fathers
Fairfield,
66 Inchicore Road,
Dublin 8
Tel 01-4538655
Email scjdublin@eircom.net

Provincial
Rev John Kelly

Rev Thomas Stanley
Br Daniel Yentsa

Ardlea Parish
St John Vianney
Ardlea Road,
Dublin 5
Tel 01-8474123/8474173
Email jvianney@indigo.ie

Rev Hugh Hanley *(Moderator)*
Rev Marian Szalwa
Rev Michel Simo Temgo

ST COLUMBAN'S MISSIONARY SOCIETY (SSC)

Maynooth Mission to China – Ireland

Superior General
Rev Tim Mulroy
No 3 and 4, Ma Yau Tong
Village,
Po Lam Road, Tseung Kwan O,
Hong Kong, SAR
Email
columban@columban.org.hk
Vicar General: Rev Brian Vale
Email
societyvicar@columban.org.hk
Councillors
Kang Seung-Won Joseph
Email
jkswing@columban.org.hk
Rev Alvaro Martinez Ibánez
Email
amartinezgc@columban.org.hk

Procurator General
Rev Robert McCulloch
Collegio San Colombano,
Corso Trieste 57, 00198 Roma
Email procol.roma@gmail.com
Bursar General
Rev Jovito Dales
Hong Kong
Email
jovitodales@columban.org.hk
Columban Intercom Editor
Rev Peter Woodruff
PO Box 752, Vic 3042,
Australia
Email
intercom@columban.org.au

*Research on Mission and
Culture:* Rev Sean Dwan
Columban Fathers,
c/o St Columban's,
Dalgan Park,
Navan, Co Meath
Tel 046-9021525
Email seandwan@gmail.com
Research on JPIC Priorities
Rev Sean McDonagh
St Columban's, Dalgan Park,
Navan, Co Meath
Tel 046-9021525
Email
seanmcdonagh10@gmail.com
*Society Archivist and
Columban History
Coordinator*
Rev Patrick O'Donoghue
St Columban's, Dalgan Park,
Navan, Co Meath
Tel 046-9021525
Email neilcollins93@gmail.com
Assistant Archivist
Barbara Scally
Email
barbara.scally@columban.ie

Archdiocese of Dublin

St Columban's
67-68 Castle Dawson,
Rathcoffey Road, Maynooth,
Co Kildare
Tel 01-6286036
Rev Hugh MacMahon
(Priest in charge)
Email hugh.macmahonssc@
columban.ie

Columban Centre
13 Store Street,
Dublin 1
Tel 01-8942078
Contact person
Michael O'Sullivan
Email michael.osullivan@
columban.ie

Diocese of Meath

St Columban's
Dalgan Park, Navan,
Co Meath
Tel 046-9021525

Regional Director
Rev Raymond Husband
Tel 046-9021525
Email
ray.husbandssc@columban.ie
Regional Vice-Director
Rev Gerry Neylon
Email mgneylon@gmail.com
Regional Secretary
Evelyn Honan
Email
evelynhonan@columban.ie

Regional Council
Rev Padraig O'Donovan
Email padraigssc@gmail.com
Rev Patrick Dooher
Email pgdooher@gmail.com
Rev Oliver McCrossan
omccrossanss@gmail.com

Regional Offices
Fax 046-9071297
Email
missionoffice@columban.com
Regional Bursar
Evelyn Maguire *(Head of
Finance/Regional Board)*
Email
regionalbursar@columban.ie

Mission Outreach Co-ordinator
Vacant
Email missionoutreach@
columban.com

Communications Co-ordinator
Rev Cyril Lovett
Email cyrillovet39@gmail.com

Ongoing Education
Rev Cyril Lovett
Email cyril.lovett@columban.ie

JPIC Outreach
Michael O'Sullivan
Email michael.osullivan@columban.ie
Rev Frank Nally
Email frank.nallyssc@columban.ie

Lay Missionary Contact Person
Kyumg-Ja Lee
Email clm.ireland@columban.ie

Vocations Contact Person
Rev Padraig O'Donovan
Email padraigssc@gmail.com

Inter-faith Dialogue
Michael O'Sullivan
Email michael.osullivan@columban.ie
Sean Dwan
Email sean.dwanssc@columban.ie

Regional Newsletter
Rev Hugh MacMahon

Office Manager
Ada Coughlan
Email irishfareast@gmail.com

Focus on China
Rev Hugh MacMahon
Rev Gerard Neylon

Far East Editor
Sarah MacDonald
Email sarah.mcdonald@columban.ie
www.columbans.ie

Board of Reconciliation
Rev Gerald French
Rev Joseph Hargaden
Rev Conal O'Connell

Alcoholic Advisory Board
Rev Brendan Hoban
Email brendan.hobanssc@columban.ie
John Norris *(Lay Advisor)*

Safeguarding Officer and Designated Liaison Person
Sandra Neville
Tel 087-9844779
Email sandra.neville@columban.ie

Deputy Safeguarding Officer
Rev Donal Hogan
Email doniehogan@gmail.com

HR Manager
Denis Kelly
Email hrmanager@columban.ie

St Columban's
Dalgan Park,
Navan, Co Meath
Tel 046-9021525
Fax 046-9022799

House Superior
Rev Padraig O'Donovan
Email padraig.odonovanssc@columban.ie

Bursar & Vice-Superior
Rev Joseph McDonnell
Email joe.mcdonnell@columban.ie

House Council
Rev Patrick Dooher
Email paddy.doohersc@columban.ie
Rev John Hogan
Email hoganheaven@yahoo.com

Residents
Rev Sean Brazil
Rev John Colgan (Ret)
Rev Neil Collins
Rev Sean Coyle
Email scoylumban@gmail.com
Rev Noel Daly
Email noel.dalyssc@columban.ie
Rev Michael Dodd
Rev Patrick Dooher
Rev Noel Doyle
Rev Owen Doyle (Ret)
Rev Sean Dwan
Rev Patrick Egan (Ret)
Rev Gerald French
Rev John Gilmore
Rev Malachy Hanratty (Ret)
Rev Jeremiah Healy
Rev Brendan Hoban
Rev Donal Hogan
Rev John Hogan
Rev Maurice Hogan
Rev Raymond Husband
Rev Norman Jennings
Rev David Kenneally
Rev Cyril Lovett
Rev Barry Maguire
Rev Bernard Martin (Ret)
Rev Brendan MacHale
Rev Oliver McCrossan
Rev Sean McDonagh
Rev Joseph McDonnell
Rev Austin McGuinness
Rev Kevin McHugh
Rev John McLaughlin (Ret)
Rev Patrick McManus
Rev Charles Meagher
Rev John Molloy (Ret)
Rev Michael Molloy (Ret)
Rev Bernard Mulkerins
Rev Cornelius Murphy (Ret)
Rev Brendan Murray (Ret)
Rev Frank Nally
Rev Gerry Neylon
Rev Kevin O'Boyle
Rev Anthony O'Brien (Ret)
Rev Conal O'Connell
Rev Padraig O'Donovan
Rev Donal O'Hanlon
Rev Peter O'Neill
Rev Thomas O'Reilly
Rev Brian Oxley (Ret)
Rev Patrick Raleigh
Email praleighssc@gmail.com
Rev Patrick Smyth
Rev Bernard Steed

St Columban's Retirement Home
Dalgan Park,
Navan, Co Meath
Tel 046-9021525

Provider Nominee
Rev Gerry Neylon
Email ngneylon@gmail.com

Person in Charge
Ms Anne McNally

Pastoral Care Team
Rev Sean Brazil
Rev Sean Coyle
Rev Brendan Hoban
Rev John Hogan
Rev Bernard Mulkerins
Rev Brendan Murray

Residents
Rev William Byrne
Rev John Chute
Rev Patrick Clarke
Rev Sean Corr
Rev Padraig Digan
Rev Michael Doohan
Rev Seamus Egan
Rev Gerard McNicholas
Rev Cyril Murphy
Rev Michael O'Farrell
Rev Daniel O'Gorman
Rev Francis O'Kelly
Rev Richard O'Sullivan

Columbans living outside Dalgan (Retired)
Rev Dan Ahern, Tralee
Rev Donal N. Bennett, Omagh, Co Tyrone
Rev Jody Cahill, Ballina, Co Mayo
Rev William Carrigan, Kilkenny
Rev Timothy Collins, Cork
Rev Patrick Conway, Ennis
Rev Joseph Hargaden, Wexford
Rev Derek Harris, Dublin
Rev Michael Irwin, Limerick
Rev Sean McNulty, Galway
Rev Eamonn O'Brien, Kerry
Rev Michael O'Loughlin, Ennis
Rev Myles Roban, Enniscorthy
Rev James Sheehy, Dungarvan, Co Waterford

Promotion Work/Mission Awareness
Rev Barry Maguire
Rev Oliver McCrossan
Rev Donal O'Hanlon
Rev Bernard Steed
Angie Escarsa LM

Priests on Special Work
Rev P. Aloysius Connaughton (Thailand)
Rev John Hickey (Columban Sisters, Magheramore, Co Wicklow)

Rev John Gilmore (Immigration Apostolate)
Rev Donal Hogan (Deputy Safeguarding Office)
Rev Sean McDonagh (Research JPIC)

Priests on diocesan work in Ireland
Rev Eamon Conaty (Elphin)
Rev Sean Connaughton (Meath)
Rev Kevin Fleming (Meath)
Rev Jeremiah Murphy (Meath)
Rev Seamus O'Neill (Derry)

Columban Lay Missionaries from the Philippians working in Ireland
Angie Escarsa (Co-ordinator)

ST PATRICK'S MISSIONARY SOCIETY (SPS)

Diocese of Kildare & Leighlin

St Patrick's
Kiltegan,
Co Wicklow W91 YO22
Tel 059-6473600
Fax 059-6473622

Society Leader
Rev Victor Dunne

Assistant Society Leader
Rev John Marren

Councillors
Rev Bosco Kamau
Rev Cathal Moriarty
Email ccullen@spms.ie

Bursar General
Rev Seamus O'Neill

RELIGIOUS ORDERS AND CONGREGATIONS

District Leader for Ireland
Rev Thomas O'Connor
Email
districtleaderireland@spms.ie
Assistant District Leader
Rev Pat Murphy
Tel 059-6473600
Email pmurphysps@gmail.com
District Secretary
Ms Carly Cullen
Tel 059-6473615
Kiltegan House Leader
Rev Enda Kelly
Assistant House Leader
Rev John Roche
Director of Promotion
Rev David Walsh
Office Manager
Ms Joanne Fortune
Kiltegan House Manager
Ms Fiona Hawkins
Editor, Africa
Rev Sean Deegan
Email africa@spms.ie
Director of Slí an Chroí
Rev Pat Murphy
Tel 059-6473488

Rev Anthony Barrett
Rev Jim Bermingham
Rev Bernard Bohan
Rev Jim Brady
Rev Richie Brennan
Rev Tom Browne
Rev Joe Cantwell
Rev John P. Carroll
Rev Noel Connolly
Rev Colm Cooke
Rev Michael Conroy
Rev Patrick Corcoran
Rev Jim Crowe
Rev Sean Cullen
Rev Paddy Feeney
Rev Peter Finegan
Rev Padraig Flanagan
Rev Leo Flynn
Rev Dermot Foley
Rev William Fulton
Rev John Garry
Rev Ned Grace
Rev Thomas Greenan
Rev Thomas Grenham
Rev Patrick Hagan
Rev Eamonn Hayden
Rev Bobby Kavanagh
Rev Andy Keating
Rev Michael Kelly
Rev Liam Kelly
Rev Maurice Kelly

Rev Michael Kelly
Rev Edward Lalor
Rev John Lalor
Rev Oliver Leavy
Rev Michael Long
Rev James McAuliffe
Rev Patrick McCallion
Rev Donald McDonagh
Rev Fintan McDonald
Rev James McDonnell
Rev Thomas McDonnell
Rev Patrick McGivern
Rev Martin McGrath
Rev Sean McGrath
Rev Noel McHenry
Rev Oliver McHugh
Rev Gregory McManus
Rev Frank Minogue
Rev Frank Morgan
Rev Nicholas Motherway
Rev Ray Murtagh
Rev Rory O'Brien
Rev Thomas O'Connor
Rev Bartie O'Doherty
Rev Seamus O'Reilly
Rev Denis O'Rourke
Rev Brendan Payne
Rev Joseph Rabbitt
Rev Norbert Reid
Rev James Regan
Rev Seamus Reihill
Rev Edmond Ryan
Rev Tom Ryan
Rev Sean Rynn
Rev Liam V. Scanlan
Rev Thomas Scott
Rev Tony Sheerin
Rev Joe Taylor
Rev Donal Twomey
Rev David Walsh
Rev Edward Walsh
Rev William Walshe
Rev Seamus Whelan
Rev Seamus Whitney

Archdiocese of Dublin

St Patrick's
21 Leeson Park,
Dublin D06 DE76
Tel 01-4977897
Fax 01-4962812

House Leader
Rev David Larkin

Rev Michael Browne
Rev Brendan Cooney
Rev Peter Coyle
Rev Dermot Connolly
Rev Donal Dorr
Rev Danny Gibbons
Rev David Larkin
Rev George O'Brien
Rev Brendan McCarron
Rev Con Ryan

Archdiocese of Tuam

St Patrick's
Main Street,
Knock, Co Mayo
Tel 094-9388661

House Leader
Rev Gary Howley

Rev Steve Donohue
Rev Gerard O'Carroll

Diocese of Cork & Ross

Kiltegan House
11 Douglas Road,
Cork
Tel 021-4969371

House Leader
Rev James Kelleher

Rev Martin Barry
Rev William Greene
Rev John O'Brien

Priests on special ministries
Rev Michael Rodgers,
Tearmann Spirituality Centre,
Brockagh, Glendalough,
Co Wicklow
Tel 0404-45208
Rev Martin Smith

Priests on temporary diocesan work

Rev Liam Blayney
Rev Declan Boyce
Rev John Carroll
Rev Colm Clinton
Rev Frank Conlisk (Tuam – Milltown, Co Galway)
Rev Bernard Conway
Rev Eugene Drumm
Rev PJ Fitzgerald (Kildare & Leighlin)
Rev Niall Geaney (Kerry)
Rev John Heinhold
Rev John Kearns
Rev Joseph Long (Kilmore)
Rev Brian Maguire (Kildare & Leighlin)
Rev Brendan McDonagh
Rev Michael Morris (Ardagh & Clonmacnois)
Rev Patrick O'Brien
Rev Sean O'Dowd
Rev Ciaran O'Flynn
Rev Martin Spillane
Rev Declan Thompson

SALESIANS (SDB)

Archdiocese of Dublin

Provincialate
Salesian House,
45 St Teresa's Road,
Crumlin,
Dublin D12 XK52
Tel 01-4555787
Email (secretary)
office@salesians.ie
www.salesiansireland.ie

Provincial
Very Rev Eunan McDonnell
Email
provincial@salesiansireland.ie
Provincial Secretary
Rev Lukasz Nawrat

Salesian House
45 St Teresa's Road,
Crumlin, Dublin D12 XK52
Tel 01-4555605
House of residence

Rector
Rev Martin McCormack
Vice-Rector
Rev Raymond McIntyre
Bursar
Rev Selvaraj Mallavarappu

Rev Hugh Boyle
Rev Patrick Brewster
Rev Michael Browne
Rev Thomas Clowe CC
Rev Charles Cunningham
Rev John Finnegan
Br Colm Kennedy
Br Colum Maguire
Rev Alan Mowles
Rev James Somers

Rinaldi House
72 Sean McDermott Street,
Dublin D01 K2O1
Tel 01-8363358
Fax 01-8552320

Rector
Rev Michael Casey Adm

Vice-Rector
Rev Hugh O'Donnell
Bursar: Rev John Quinn

Rev Val Collier
Br David O'Hara

Don Bosco Houses
12 Clontarf Road,
Dublin D03 V3P4
Tel 01-8336009/8337045

Priest-in-Charge
Rev Val Collier

Our Lady of Lourdes Parish
Seán McDermott Street,
Dublin D01 AD73
Tel 01-8363554

Rev Michael Casey Adm

Salesian College
Maynooth Road, Celbridge,
Co Kildare, W23 W0XK
Tel 01-6275058/60
Fax 01-6272208
Secondary School
Tel 01-6272166/6272200

Rector: Rev Patrick Hennessy
Vice-Rector
Rev Apap Jesmond
Bursar
Rev Tran Xuan Binh Paul

Rev Lukasz Nawrat
Rev A. McEvoy
Rev George McCaughey
Br James O'Hare

Diocese of Limerick

Salesian College
Don Bosco Road, Pallaskenry,
Co Limerick V94 WP86
Tel 061-393105 Fax 061-393298
Secondary and agricultural
schools

Rector: Rev John Horan
Vice-Rector: Rev Daniel Devitt
Bursar
Rev Nguyen Viet Binh Dominic

Rev John Butler
Rev Daniel Carroll
Rev Timothy Wrenn

Salesian House
Milford, Castletroy,
Limerick, V94 DK44
Tel 061-330268/330914
Student hostel and parish

Rector and Chaplain,
University of Limerick
Rev John Campion
Vice-Rector: Vacant
Economer
Rev Koenraad Van Gucht PP

Rev John Fagan
Rev Martin Loftus
Rev Michael Smyth
Rev Bob Swinburne

Elsewhere in Ireland
Rev Desmond Campion
(Chaplain Naval Service,
Haulbowline, Cobh, Cork)
Rev G. Dowd
(Chaplain, Custume Barracks,
Athlone)
Rev James O'Halloran
(St Catherine's Centre, North
Campus, Maynooth, Co
Kildare)

Rev P.J. Healy
(Chaplain, Mount Carmel
Nursing Home,
Roscrea, Co Tipperary)

SALVATORIANS (SDS)

Diocese of Derry

Rev Malachy McBride
'Naomh Mhuire',
Upper Slavery, Buncrana,
Co Donegal
Tel 074-9322264

Diocese of Galway

Rev Seamus O'Duill
Ard Mhuire, Kilmoran,
Lisdoonvarna, Co Clare
Tel 086-1030261
Email seamusoduill@eircom.net

SERVITES (OSM)
Order of Friar Servants of Mary

Prior Provincial
Rev Colm M. McGlynn
Servite Priory
36 Grangewood Estate,
Rathfarnham,
Dublin D16 V263
Tel 01-4936755/086-4060124
Email
colmmcglynn154@hotmail.com

Province of the Isles

Archdiocese of Dublin

Servite Priory
St Peregrine,
36 Grangewood Estate,
Rathfarnham, Dublin 16
Tel 01-4936755

Prior: Rev Jimmy M. Kelly
(Chaplain, Cloverhill Prison,
Clondalkin, Dublin 24

Rev Timothy M. Flynn
(Director, St Peregrine
Ministry)

Church of the Divine Word
Marley Grange,
25–27 Hermitage Downs,
Rathfarnham, Dublin 16
Tel 01-4944295/4941064
Fax 01-4941069

Prior: Rev Liam Tracey CC

Rev Jim Mulherin PP
Rev Camillus McGrane
Our Lady's Manor, Dalkey,
Dublin

Monthly St Peregrine Mass on
first Saturday of every month at
10.00 a.m. – also on webcam.

Archdiocese of Armagh

Servite Priory
Benburb, Dungannon,
Co Tyrone, BT71 7JZ
Northern Ireland
Tel 028-37548241
Tel 01861-548241/548533
Retreat, Conference Centre
and youth centre

Prior: Rev Bernard Thorne

Rev Gabriel Bannon
Br Patrick Gethins
Rev Sean Lennon
Rev Dermot MacNeice
Rev Eamonn McCreave
Very Rev Raymond O'Connell

SOCIETY OF AFRICAN MISSIONS (SMA)
Societas Missionum Ad Afros

Diocese of Cork & Ross

African Missions
Provincial House, Feltrim,
Blackrock Road,
Cork T12 N6C8
Tel 021-4292871
Fax 021-4292873
www.sma.ie
Email provincial@sma.ie

Provincial
Rev Malachy Flanagan
Vice Provincial
Rev Eamonn Finnegan
Provincial Councillor
Rev Anthony Kelly
Provincial Secretary
Rev Martin Kavanagh
Safeguarding and Data
Protection
Ms Elizabeth Murphy
Compiance Officer
Ms Thora McMahon

African Missions
Blackrock Road,
Cork T12 TD54
Tel 021-4292871
Email sma.blackrock@sma.ie

Superior
Rev Patrick O'Rourke
Provincial Bursar
Rev Jarlath Walsh
Assistant Bursar
Mr Paul Murphy
Provincial Archivist
Rev Edmund M. Hogan

Rev John Bowe
Rev Lee Cahill
Most Rev Timothy Carroll
(Retired Bishop)
Rev Denis Collins
Rev Francis Coltsmann
Rev Patrick Connolly
Rev Bernard Cotter
Rev Timothy Cullinane
Br Patrick Dowd
Rev Christopher Emokhare
Rev thomas Fenlon
Rev Alphonsus Flatley
Rev John Flynn
Rev Joseph Foley
Rev Francis Geoghegan
Rev William Ghent
Rev Hugh Harkin
Rev Valentine Hynes
Rev Michael Igoe
Rev Martin Kavanagh
Rev Michael Kidney
Rev Angelo Lafferty
Rev Sean Lynch
Rev Michael McCabe
Rev Aidan McCrystal
Rev Michael McGrath
Rev Gerard Murray
Rev Michael Nohilly
Rev Matthew O'Connell
Rev Edward O'Connor
Rev Fionnbarra O'Cuilleanáin
Rev Martin O'Hare
Rev John O'Hea
Rev Michael O'Shea
Rev Andrew O'Sullivan
Rev Denis J. Ryan
Rev Thomas Treacy
Rev Thomas Wade
Rev Jarlath Walsh
Rev Michael Waters
Rev Oscar Welsh

SMA House
Wilton, Cork T12 KR23
Tel 021-4541069/4541884
Email sma.wilton@sma.ie

Superior
Rev Noel O'Leary
Vice-Superior
Rev Colum O'Shea
Local Bursar
Mr Pat Coughlan

Rev Cormac Breathnach
Rev Daniel Cashman
Rev John Dunne
Rev Thomas Harlow
Most Rev Patrick Harrington
(Retired Bishop)
Rev John Horgan
Rev Thomas Kearney
Rev Maurice Kelleher
Rev Cornelius Murphy
Rev Augustine O'Driscoll
Rev Kevin O'Gorman

RELIGIOUS ORDERS AND CONGREGATIONS

Rev John O'Keeffe
Most Rev Noel O'Regan
(Retired Bishop)
Rev Denis O'Sullivan
Rev Richard Wall

St Joseph's SMA Parish
Blackrock Road, Cork T12 X281
Tel 021-4293325
Email parish.blackrock@sma.ie

Rev Alphonse Sekongo PP

St Joseph's SMA Parish
Wilton, Cork T12 E436
Tel 021-4341362
Fax 021-4343940
Email stjosephschurchwilton@yahoo.com

Rev Michael O'Leary PP

Justice Office
SMA House, Wilton,
Cork T12 KR23
Email justice@sma.ie
Mr Gerry Forde

Archdiocese of Dublin

SMA House
81 Ranelagh Road,
Dublin D06 WT10
Tel 01-4968162 Fax 01-4968164
Email sma.dublin@sma.ie

Superior
Rev Joseph Egan
Vice-Superior
Rev John O'Brien
Bursar
Rev Thomas Curran

Rev Patrick Kelly
Rev Owen McKenna
Rev Paul Monahan

Also in Dublin
Rev Sean Healy
Social Justice Ireland,
Arena House, Arena Road,
Sandyford, Dublin 18
Tel 01-2130724
www.socialjustice.ie
Rev Kevin O'Gorman
St Patrick's College,
Maynooth, Co Kildare

Diocese of Galway

SMA House
Cloonbigeen Claregalway,
Co Galway H91 YK64
Tel 091-798880
Fax 091-798879
Email sma.claregalway@sma.ie

Superior
Rev Seamus Nohilly
Bursar
Rev James Clesham

Rev Martin Costello
Rev John Dunleavy
Rev Alphonsus Kelly
Rev Paraic Kelly
Rev Francis McGrath
Rev Eugene McLoughlin
Rev Kieran Morahan
Rev Colman Nilan
Rev Gerard Sweeney

Diocese of Dromore

African Missions
Dromantine,
Newry,
Co Down BT34 1RH
Tel 028-30821224
Fax 028-30821704
Email sma.dromantine@sma.ie

Superior
Rev Damian Bresnahan
Vice-Superior & Bursar
Rev John Brown

Rev Desmond Corrigan
Rev Edward Deeney
Rev Thomas Faherty
Rev John Gallagher
Rev Hugh Lagan
Rev Daniel McCauley
Rev Cathal McKenna
Rev Hugh O'Kane
Rev James O'Kane
Rev Peter Thompson

Dromantine Retreat and Conference Centre
Newry,
Co Down BT34 1RH
Tel 028-30821964
Fax 028-30821704
Email admin@dromantineconference.com
www.dromantineconference.com

Accommodation:
42 single en suite rooms,
30 double en suite rooms,
8 conference rooms

Director
Rev Damian Bresnahan

Temporary diocesan work in Ireland
Rev Chris Brennan
Rev Michael Flattery
Rev Anthony Gill
Rev Patrick Lynch
Rev Thomas McNamara
Rev Kevin Mulhern
Rev Patrick O'Mahony
Rev Billy Sheridan
Rev Desmond Smith
Rev Donal Toal
Rev Fergus Tuohy
Rev Thomas Walsh

Church of Our Lady of the Rosary and St Patrick
61 Blackhorse Road,
Walthamstow,
London E17 7AS, England
Tel +44-208-5203647

Rev Kevin Conway
Rev Freddy Warner

Rome

Generalate
Missioni Africane,
Via della Nocetta 111,
00164 Roma, Italy
Tel +39-06-6616841
Fax +39-06-66168490
Email secgen@smainternational.org

Superior General
Rev Antonio Porcellato
Email supgen@smainternational.org

SOCIETY OF ST PAUL (SSP)

The Society of St Paul in Ireland operates exclusively through the mass media.

Archdiocese of Dublin

Society of St Paul
Moyglare Road,
Maynooth, Co Kildare
Tel 01-6285933
Fax 01-6289330
Email sspireland@gmail.com

Rev Alexander Anandam
Rev Jose Nunes
Rev Thomas Devasia Perumparambil
Rev Paul Kottackal Varkey

St Paul Book Centre
Moyglare Road,
Maynooth,
Co Kildare W23 NX34
Email sspireland@gmail.com
www.stpauls.ie

St Paul's Books and Mass Leaflets
Moyglare Road,
Maynooth,
Co Kildare W23 NX34
Email sales@stpauls.ie

SONS OF DIVINE PROVIDENCE (FDP)

The Irish Foundation is part of the Missionary English-speaking Delegation of 'Mary Mother of the Church'.

Regional Superior
Rev Marcelo Boschi
c/o Via Etruria 6,
00183 Rome, Italy
Local Co-ordinator
Rev Philip Kehoe
25 Lower Teddington Road,
Kingston-on-Thames,
Surrey
Tel 208-9775130

Archdiocese of Dublin

Sarsfield House
Sarsfield Road,
Ballyfermot,
Dublin 10
Tel 01-6266193/6266233
Fax 01-6260303
Email don-orion@clubi.ie

Rev John Perrotta
Email jperrotta16@yahoo.ie

VINCENTIANS (CM)

Vincentian communities of the Irish Province are established in Ireland and England.

Archdiocese of Dublin

Provincial Office
Sybil Hill, Raheny,
Dublin D05 AE38
Tel 01-8510842 Fax 01-8510846
Email cmdublin@vincentians.ie
www.vincentians.ie

Provincial
Very Rev Paschal Scallon
Secretary to the Provincial
Ms Avril Gibson
Email cmdublin@vincentians.ie

St Paul's
Raheny, Dublin D05 AE38
Tel 01-8314011/2 (college)
Tel 01-8318113 (community)
Fax 01-8316387
Secondary School

Superior
Very Rev Michael McCullagh

Rev Roderic Crowley
Rev Michael Dunne
Rev John Gallagher
Rev Joseph McCann
Rev James McCormack
Rev Bernard Meade
Rev Harry Slowey
Rev Philip Walshe

RELIGIOUS ORDERS AND CONGREGATIONS

Phibsborough
St Peter's, Dublin 7
Tel 01-8389708/8389841
Email info@stpetersphibsboro.ie

Superior
Very Rev Eamon Devlin Co-PP
Email pp@stpetersphibsboro.ie

Rev John Concannon
Rev Sean Farrell
Rev Eamon Flanagan
Rev Joseph Loftus
Rev Kieran MaGovern
Rev Mark Noonan
Rev Padraig Regan

St Joseph's
44 Stillorgan Park, Blackrock,
Co Dublin A94 PC62
Tel 01-2886961

Superior
Very Rev Patrick Collins

Rev Aidan Galvin
Rev Jack Harris
Rev Colm McAdam

St Vincent's College
Castleknock,
Dublin D15 PD95
Tel 01-8213051
Secondary Day School for Boys

Superior
Very Rev Paschal Scallon

Rev Stephen Monaghan
Rev Cornelius Nwaogwugwu

Diocese of Down & Connor

99 Cliftonville Road
Belfast BT14 6JQ
Tel 028-90751771
Fax 028-90740547

Superior
Very Rev Adrian Eastwood

Rev Peter Gildea
Rev James Rafferty

COMMUNITIES OF RELIGIOUS BROTHERS

In this section, details of each community's main house are given, followed by a list of the dioceses in which the community is present. For more information on houses in particular dioceses, please see the entry for the appropriate diocese.

ALEXIAN BROTHERS (CFA)

Anglo-Irish Province

Regional Residence
Churchfield, Knock,
Co Mayo
Tel 094-9376996
Email cellerbruders@gmail.com

Regional Leader
Br Barry Butler

Tuam

BROTHERS OF CHARITY

St Joseph's Region

Regional Office
Regional Administration
Kilcornan Centre,
Clarinbridge, Co Galway
Tel 091-796389/796413
Fax 091-796352
Email john.oshea@bocsi.ie

Regional Leader
Br John O'Shea

Cork & Ross, Galway,
Limerick, Ossory

CHRISTIAN BROTHERS (CFC)

European Province

Province Centre
Marino, Griffith Avenue,
Dublin 9

Leadership Team
Province Leader
Br Edmund Garvey
Deputy Leader
Br David Gibson
Councillor: Br John Burke
Councillor: Br Chris Glavey
Councillor: Br Tom Costello

Dublin, Cork, Down & Connor,
Ferns, Kerry, Killaloe, Limerick,
Ossory, Waterford & Lismore

DE LA SALLE BROTHERS (FSC)

Provincialate
121 Howth Road,
Dublin D03 XN15
Tel 01-8331815 Fax 01-8339130
Email province@iol.ie

Assistant Provincial
Br Ben Hanlon

Armagh, Dublin, Tuam,
Down & Connor, Ossory,
Waterford & Lismore

FRANCISCAN BROTHERS (OSF)

Franciscan Brothers of the
Third Order Regular

A branch of the Regular Third
Order of Penance of St Francis
of Asissi, with communities in
East Africa and the USA as
well as Ireland.

Generalate
Mountbellew, Co Galway
Tel 090-9679295
Fax 090-9679687
Email franciscanbrs@eircom.net

Minister General
Br Tony Dolan
Assistant General
Br Sean Conway
Councillors
Br Hilarion O'Connor
Br Charles Lagu
Br Boniface Kyalo
Procurator General
Br Boniface Kyalo
Bursar General
Br Hilarion O'Connor
Secretary General
Br Bernard Kariuki

Dublin, Tuam, Meath

MARIST BROTHERS (FMS)

The Marist Brothers in Ireland
are part of the province of
West Central Europe principally
involved in education.

Provincialate
Frères Maristes,
Rue de Linthout 91,
1030 Bruxelles, Belgium
Tel +32-27342641
Fax +31-27341599
Email provincial@maristen.org

Provincial Superior
Frère Robert Thunus

Dublin, Ardagh &
Clonmacnois

PATRICIAN BROTHERS (FSP)

Brothers of St Patrick

Patrician Brothers
Fairfield, PO Box 980,
NSW 1860, Australia

Congregation Leader
Br Peter D. Ryan *(Australia)*
Email bropryan@gmail.com
*Deputy Congregation Leader
& First Councillor:* Br George
Xavier Thlaikat (India)
Second Councillor: Br George
Mangara (India Prov)
Third Councillor: Br Stephen
Sweetman (Australia–PNG)
Fourth Councillor: Br Nicholas
Harsan (Australia–PNG)

Irish Province Leader
Br Camillus Regan
Tullow, Co Carlow

Dublin, Kildare & Leighlin,
Galway

PRESENTATION BROTHERS (FPM)

Generalate
Mount St Joseph,
Blarney Street, Cork
Tel 021-4392160
Fax 021-4398200
Email generalate@presentationbrothers.org

Congregation Leader
Br Francis Agoah

Provincial Office
Mardyke House,
Mardyke, Cork
Tel 021-4251819
Email aiprovince@presentationbrothers.org

Province Leader
Br Raymond Dwyer

Dublin, Cork & Ross, Kerry,
Killaloe, Waterford & Lismore

SAINT JOHN OF GOD BROTHERS (OH)

Hospitaller Order of
Saint John of God

West European Province of
Saint John of God (Great
Britain, Ireland, Malawi)

Saint John of God Brothers
Provincial Curia,
Granada, Stillorgan,
Co Dublin A94 D9N1
Tel 01-5333313
Email provincial@sjog.ie

Provincial
Br Donatus Forkan (OH)

RELIGIOUS ORDERS AND CONGREGATIONS

Saint John of God Hospitaller Ministries
Hospitaller House,
Stillorgan,
Co Dublin A94 X5K8
Tel 01-5333300
Fax 01-2831257
Group Chief Executive
Mr Conor McCarthy
Email groupchiefexecutive@sjog.ie

Saint John of God Hospitaller Services
Suite 1-3 Yarn,
Lingfield House,
Lingfield Point,
Darlington DL1 1RW,
Co Durham, England
Tel +44-1325-373700
Fax +44-1325-373707
Interim Chief Executive
Mr Paul Bott

Saint John of God Communty Services CLG
Crinken House, Crinken Lane,
Shankill, Co Dublin C18 K2Y8
Website www.sjog.ie
Chief Executive
Ms Clare Dempsey
Tel 01-5333395
Email clare.dempsey@sjog.ie

Armagh, Dublin, Kerry

COMMUNITIES OF RELIGIOUS SISTERS

In this section, details of each community's main house are given, followed by a list of the dioceses in which the community is present. For more information on houses in particular dioceses, please see the entry for the appropriate diocese.

ADORERS OF THE SACRED HEART OF JESUS OF MONTMARTRE (OSB)

St Benedict's Priory
The Mount, Cobh, Co Cork
Tel 021-4811354

Prioress
Mother M. Catherine

Cloyne

BENEDICTINE NUNS (OSB)

Kylemore Abbey
Kylemore, Connemara,
Co Galway H91 VR90
Tel 095-52011
Email info@kylemoreabbey.ie

Abbess: Sr Máire Hickey

Tuam

BLESSED SACRAMENT SISTERS

Blessed Sacrament Convent
Denene, New Road,
Tullamore,
Co Offaly R35 N528
Email imelda.doorley@gmail.com

Dublin, Meath

BON SECOURS SISTERS (Paris)

Leadership Office
College Road, Cork
Tel 021-4543310
Fax 021-4542533

Country Leader
Sr Eileen O'Connor
Email leadership@congregation.bonsecours.ie

Dublin, Cloyne, Cork & Ross, Kerry

SISTERS OF BON SECOURS DE TROYES

St Paul's Nursing Home,
Dooradoyle, Limerick
Tel 061-304690
Email bonsecours792@gmail.com

Contact: Sr Margaret Costello

Limerick

BRIGIDINE SISTERS
Sisters of St Brigid

106 The Edges 1,
Beacon South Quarter,
Sandyford, Dublin D18 WY00

Congregational Leader
Sr Catherine O'Connor
Email coconnorcsb07@gmail.com

Dublin, Galway, Kildare & Leighlin, Killaloe

CARMELITE MONASTERIES

Archdiocese of Dublin

Carmelite Monastery of the Immaculate Conception
Roebuck, Dublin D14 T1H9
Tel 01-2884732
Altar Breads
Email altarbreads@roebuckcarmel.com
Email carmel@roebuckcarmel.com

Prioress: Sr Teresa Whelan

Star of the Sea Carmelite Monastery
Seapark, Malahide,
Dublin K36 P586
Tel 01-8454259
Tel 087-9643953
Email rmebodc@gmail.com
www.malahidecarmelites.ie
Contemplative Community

Prioress: Sr Rosalie Burke

Carmelite Monastery of St Joseph
Upper Kilmacud Road,
Stillorgan, Blackrock,
Co Dublin A94 YY33
Tel 01-2886089
Email contact@kilmacudcarmel.ie
www.kilmacudcarmel.ie

Prioress
Sr Mary Brigeen Wilson

Archdiocese of Tuam

Carmelite Monastery
Tranquilla, Knock,
Claremorris,
Co Mayo F12 AH64
Email tranquilla.knock@gmail.com

Prioress: Sr Claire

Diocese of Ferns

Mount Carmel Monastery
New Ross,
Co Wexford

Prioress: Sr Anne McGlynn

Diocese of Waterford & Lismore

St Joseph's Carmelite Monastery
Tallow, Co Waterford
Tel 058-56205
Email carmeltallow@eircom.net

Prioress: Sr Patrice Buckley

CARMELITE SISTERS FOR THE AGED AND INFIRM

Our Lady's Manor
Bulloch Castle,
Dalkey, Co Dublin
Tel 01-2806993 Fax 01-2844802
Email ourladysmanor1@eircom.net

Superior
Sr Mary Therese Healy
Email smtjhealy57@gmail.com
Administrator
Sr Bernadette Murphy

Dublin

SISTERS OF CHARITY OF THE INCARNATE WORD

Carrigoran House
Newmarket-on-Fergus,
Co Clare
Tel 061-368100
Fax 061-368170
Email info@carrigoranhouse.ie

Contact person
Sr Marisa Revert Font

Administrator
Ms Mary O'Dowd

Killaloe

RELIGIOUS ORDERS AND CONGREGATIONS

CHARITY OF JESUS AND MARY SISTERS

Anglo-Irish Province
Moore Abbey
Monasterevin, Co Kildare
Tel 045-525478

Contact
Sr Mary-Anna Lonergan
Email maryannal@eircom.net
Provincial Superior
Sr Elizabeth Roche
108 Spring Road, Letchworth,
Hertfordshire SG6 3B
Tel 0462-675694

Our residential centres have been transferred to Muiriosa Foundation since 1 January 2012

Kildare & Leighlin, Meath

CHARITY OF NEVERS SISTERS

76 Cherrywood
Loughlinstown Drive,
Dun Laoghaire, Co Dublin

Contact person
Sr Rosaleen Cullen
Tel 01-4585654/086-8411466
Email
rosaleencullen@upcmail.ie

Dublin

CHARITY OF ST PAUL THE APOSTLE SISTERS

St Paul's Convent
Selly Park,
Birmingham B29 7LL
Tel 0044-121-4156100

Superior: Sr Kathleen Neenan
Email
kathleen.neenan@sellypark.org

Dublin, Limerick

CHRISTIAN RETREAT SISTERS

'The Demesne'
Mountbellew, Ballinasloe,
Co Galway H53 RH61
Tel 090-9679311

Contact: Sr Assumpta Collins
Email assumptahrc@gmail.com

Superior General
Sr Rose Marie Prongue
17 Rue Du Couvent,
25210 Les Fontenelles,
France

Tuam

CISTERCIANS

St Mary's Abbey
Glencairn, Lismore,
Co Waterford P51 X725
Tel 058-56168
Email
info@glencairnabbey.org

Abbess: Sr Marie Fahy

Waterford & Lismore

CLARISSAN MISSIONARY SISTERS OF THE BLESSED SACRAMENT

Our Lady of Guadalupe Residence for Students
28 Waltersland Road,
Stillorgan, Co Dublin
Tel/Fax 01-2886600
Email misclaridub@hotmail.com
www.guadaluperesidence.com

Superior: Sr Elisa Padilla
Tel 087-0510783

Dublin

CONGREGATION OF THE SISTERS OF MERCY

The Congregation of the Sisters of Mercy is an International Congregation. It has 1,572 members currently serving in Ireland, Britain, Brazil, Kenya, South Africa, Peru, Zambia and the US.

Congregational Leadership Team
Sr Marie Louise White
(Congregational Leader)
Sr Anna Burke
Sr Cait O'Dwyer
Sr Bernie Ryan
Sr Helena O'Donoghue

Congregational Offices
'Rachamim', 13/14 Moyle Park,
Convent Road, Clondalkin,
Dublin 22
Tel 01-4673737
Email mercy@csm.ie
Website www.sistersofmercy.ie

The Northern Province
comprising the dioceses of
Raphoe, Derry, Down &
Connor, Armagh, Dromore,
Clogher, Kilmore and Meath.

Provincial
Sr Rose Marie Conlan

Sr Áine Campbell
Sr Mary De Largy
Sr Mabel Marron
Sr Perpetua McNulty

Provincial Office
74 Main Street, Clogher,
Co Tyrone BT76 0AA
Tel 028-85548127
Fax 028-85549459
Email mercy@mercynth.org

The Western Province
Comprising the dioceses of
Killala, Achonry, Elphin,
Galway, Tuam, Clonfert,
Ardagh & Clonmacnois.

Provincial: Sr Breege O'Neill

Sr Áine Barrins
Sr Maura Bane
Sr Margaret Casey
Sr Una Purcell

Provincial Office
Caoineas, Society Street,
Ballinasloe, Co Galway
Tel 090-9645202
Fax 090-9645203
Email caoineas@smwestprov.ie

The South Central Province
Comprising the dioceses of
Dublin, Cashel & Emly,
Kildare & Leighlin, Killaloe,
Limerick.

Provincial: Sr Brenda Dolphin

Sr Patricia O'Meara
Sr Nóirín Long
Sr Margaret Prendergast

Provincial Office,
Oldtown, Sallins Road,
Naas, Co Kildare W91 A5RK
Tel 045-876784
Fax 045-871509
Email
provoffice@mercyscp.ie

The Southern Province
Comprising the dioceses of
Cork & Ross, Cloyne, Kerry,
Ferns, Ossory, Waterford &
Lismore.

Provincial: Sr Eileen O'Flynn

Sr Nora Anne Lombard
Sr Julianne Sullivan
Sr Anna Mai Middleton
Sr Bríd Biggane

Provincial Office
Bishop Street, Cork
Tel 021-4975380
Fax 021-4915220
Email
provincialoffice@mercysouth.ie

CROSS AND PASSION CONGREGATION

Province Office,
299 Boarshaw Road,
Middleton,
Manchester M24 2PF
Tel 0044-161-6553184
Fax 0044-161-6533666

Province Leader
Sr Therese O'Regan

Dublin, Down & Connor

DAUGHTERS OF CHARITY OF ST VINCENT DE PAUL

St Catherine's Provincial House
Dunardagh, Blackrock,
Co Dublin
Tel 01-2882669/2882896/
2882660 Fax 01-2834485

Local Superior
Sr Marie Fox
Provincial Superior
Sr Goretti Butler

Dublin, Tuam, Cork & Ross,
Down & Connor, Galway and
Killaloe

DAUGHTERS OF THE CROSS OF LIÈGE

Daughters of the Cross
Beech Park Convent,
Beechwood Court, Stillorgan,
Co Dublin
Tel 01-2887401/2887315
Fax 01-2881499
Email
beechpark1833@gmail.com

Superior
Sr Kathleen McKenna

Dublin

DAUGHTERS OF THE HEART OF MARY

St Joseph's
1 Crosthwaite Grove,
Crosthwaite Park South,
Dun Laoghaire, Co Dublin
Tel 01-2801204

Dublin

DAUGHTERS OF THE HOLY SPIRIT

9 Walnut Park
Drumcondra,
Dublin 9
Tel 01-8371825

Contact person: Sr Ita Durnin
Email itadhs@yahoo.co.uk

RELIGIOUS ORDERS AND CONGREGATIONS

Provincial Superior
Sr Anne Morris
22 Holyrood Road,
Northhampton, NN5 7AH,
England

Dublin

DAUGHTERS OF MARY AND JOSEPH

Leadership Team
Email dmjireland@gmail.com

Dublin, Kildare & Leighlin, Meath, Ossory

DAUGHTERS OF OUR LADY OF THE SACRED HEART

Provincial House
14 Rossmore Avenue,
Templeogue, Dublin 6W
Tel 01-4903200
Tel/Fax 01-4903113
Email olshprov@eircom.net

Provincial: Sr Mairéad Kelleher

Dublin, Clogher

DAUGHTERS OF WISDOM (LA SAGESSE)

2 The Greenlands
Rosses Point, Sligo F91 A6XE
Tel 071-9177607

Contact: Sr Margaret Morris
Email srmegmorris@gmail.com

Dublin, Elphin

DISCIPLES OF THE DIVINE MASTER

Newtownpark Avenue,
White's Cross, Blackrock,
Co Dublin A94 V2N8
Tel 01-2114949/2886414

Delegation Superior
Sr M. Kathryn Williams
Email kathrynwilliams@pddm.org
www.pddm.ie

Dublin, Elphin

DOMINICAN CONTEMPLATIVE NUNS

Monastery of St Catherine of Siena
The Twenties, Drogheda,
Co Louth A92 KR84
Tel 041-9838524
Email sienamonastery@gmail.com

Prioress: Sr Mairéad Mullen OP

Armagh

DOMINICAN SISTERS (King William's Town)

Our Lady of Fatima Convent
Oakpark, Tralee, Co Kerry
Tel 066-7125641/066-7125900
Fax 066-7180834
Email teresamcevoy@fatimahome.com

Contact: Sr Teresa McEvoy OP

Kerry

DOMINICAN SISTERS

Congregation of Dominican Sisters
Mary Bellew House,
Dominican Campus, Cabra,
Dublin D07 Y2E7
Tel 01-8299700 Fax 01-8299799
Email domgen@dominicansisters.com

Congregation Prioress
Sr Martina Phelan OP

Dublin, Down & Connor, Galway

DOMINICAN SISTERS OF ST CECILIA

St Saviour's
Glentworth Street, Limerick
Tel 085-2255796

Superior
Sr Caitríona Kavanagh OP
Email limerick@op-tn.org

Limerick

FAMILY OF ADORATION SISTERS

St Aidan's Monastery
Ferns, Co Wexford
Tel 053-9366634
Email staidansferns@eircom.net

Ferns, Down & Connor

FRANCISCAN MISSIONARIES OF THE DIVINE MOTHERHOOD

Franciscan Convent
Gorbally Drive, Ballinasloe,
Co Galway H53 RF84

Trustee: Sr Kathleen Murphy
Tel 090-9643642

Armagh, Dublin, Clonfert, and Kerry

FRANCISCAN MISSIONARIES OF MARY

Provincial House
5 Vaughan Avenue,
London W6 0XS
Tel 020-87484077

Provincial Superior
Sr Lillian Hunt
Email provincial@fmmuk.org

Provincial Secretary
Email provsec@fmmuk.org

Dublin, Limerick

FRANCISCAN MISSIONARIES OF OUR LADY

La Verna Centre
Franciscan House of Spirituality & Hospitality,
Ballinderry, Mullingar,
Co Westmeath N91 K680
Tel 044-9352000/087-3935613
Email lavernacentre@gmail.com
www.fmoireland.ie
lavernacentre on Facebook

Regional Superior
Sr Clare Brady
Email info@fmoireland.ie

Meath

FRANCISCAN MISSIONARIES OF ST JOSEPH

St Joseph's
16 Innismore,
Crumlin Village, Dublin 12
Tel 01-4563445

Regional Leader
Sr Mary Butler

Dublin, Cork & Ross

FRANCISCAN MISSIONARY SISTERS FOR AFRICA

Central Team
34a Gilford Road,
Sandymount, Dublin 4
Tel 01-2838376
Fax 01-2602049
Email generalate@fmsa.net

Leader: Sr Jeanette Watters

Armagh, Dublin

FRANCISCAN SISTERS OF THE IMMACULATE CONCEPTION

Franciscan Sisters,
97/99 Riverside Park,
Clonshaugh, Dublin 17
Tel 087-6703715

Contact person
Sr Immaculata Owhotemu
99 Riverside Park, Clonshaugh,
Dublin 17
Tel 01-8771778
Email immachwo@hotmail.com

Dublin

FRANCISCAN SISTERS OF THE RENEWAL

St Anthony Convent
Dublin Road, Drogheda,
Co Louth A92 D044
Tel 041-9830441
Fax 041-9842321
Website
www.franciscansisterscfr.com

Superior: Sr Agnes Holtz

Meath

FRANCISCAN SISTERS OF LITTLEHAMPTON

Eden
Knock, Claremorris,
Co Mayo FT12 YC83
Tel 094-9388302
Registered charity 232931

Leader
Sr Anastasia McGonagle

Tuam

SISTERS OF ST FRANCIS OF PHILADELPHIA

Our Lady of Angels Convent
609 S. Convent Road,
Aston, PA 19014
Tel 6105587733
Fax 6104500195

Congregational Minister
Sr Mary Kathryn Dougherty

Dublin, Cloyne, Limerick

RELIGIOUS ORDERS AND CONGREGATIONS

CONGREGATION OF OUR LADY OF CHARITY OF THE GOOD SHEPHERD

Province Administration
63 Lower Sean McDermott Street, Dublin D01 NX93
Tel 01-8711109
Email province.office@rgs.ie
www.goodshepherdsisters.com

Province Leader
Sr Cait O'Leary

Dublin, Cork & Ross, Derry, Down & Connor, Limerick, Waterford & Lismore

HANDMAIDS OF THE SACRED HEART OF JESUS

St Raphaela's
Upper Kilmacud Road,
Stillorgan,
Co Dublin A94 TP38
Tel 01-2889963
Fax 01-2889536

Superior: Sr Irene Guia
Email iguiaci@gmail.com

Dublin

HOLY CHILD JESUS, SOCIETY OF THE

European Province
Sr Angela O'Connor
14 Norham Gardens,
Oxford OX2 6QB, England

Provincial Representative
Sr Eileen Crowley
21 Grange Park Avenue,
Raheny, Dublin D05 AY65
Email crowley.eileen@gmail.com

Dublin

HOLY FAITH SISTERS

Generalate
Aylward House,
Glasnevin, Dublin D11 YEF1
Tel 01-8520306
Email congregationalleader@hfaith.ie

Congregational Leader
Sr Rosaleen Cunniffe

Dublin

SISTERS OF THE HOLY FAMILY OF BORDEAUX

65 Griffith Downs
Drumcondra, Dublin 9
Tel 01-5477709

Councillor for Ireland
Sr Claire McGrath
Email clairemcgrath.hfb@gmail.com

Dublin, Kildare & Leighlin

HOLY FAMILY OF SAINT EMILIE DE RODAT

Contact
Sr Leyla Abon Rjeily
Superior General
6 Rus des Cordeliers,
12200 Villefrancle-de-Rgue
Email leylasf@msn.com

Meath, Tuam

INFANT JESUS SISTERS

Provincial House
56 St Lawrence Road,
Clontarf, Dublin D03 Y5F2
Tel 01-8338930

Provincial: Sr Kitty Ellard
Email kittyijs@gmail.com

Dublin, Cloyne, Cork & Ross, Kerry

JESUS AND MARY, CONGREGATION OF

The sisters from the Irish Province work in Haiti, Cameroon, Ekpoma, Lagos and Pakistan. The sisters are involved in education, working with the handicapped and in formation, including a house of formation in Nigeria.

Provincialate, 'Errew House'
110 Goatstown Road,
Dublin 14
Tel 01-2966059

Provincial Superior
Sr Marie O'Halloran
Tel 01-2969150/087-7203649
Email marieohalloran68@gmail.com

Dublin, Galway, Killala

SISTERS OF LA RETRAITE

77 Grove Park
Rathmines, Dublin 6
Tel 01-491171

Congregational Leader
Sr Avril O'Regan
Email avriloreganrlr@gmail.com

Dublin, Galway

LA SAINTE UNION DES SACRES COEURS

Provincial Office
53 Croftdown Road,
London NW5 1EL
Tel 020-74827225
Email lsuahtprovince@gmail.com

Province leadership Team
Sr Annemarie Egan
Sr Michele Totman

Dublin, Ardagh & Clonmacnois, Galway, Kildare & Leighlin, Killaloe, Limerick, Tuam

LITTLE COMPANY OF MARY

Provincialate
Cnoc Mhuire, 29 Woodpark, Ballinteer Avenue, Dublin 16
Tel 01-2987040
Email lcom@lcm.ie

Province Leader
Sr Mary Flanagan

Dublin, Cloyne, Kerry, Limerick, Ossory, Waterford & Lismore

LITTLE SISTERS OF THE ASSUMPTION

Administration Office
42 Rathfarnham Road,
Terenure, Dublin 6W
Tel 01-4909850 Fax 01-4925740
Email pernet42r@gmail.com

Sr Mary O'Sullivan, Sr Maria Flynn, Sr Mary Malone

Dublin, Cork & Ross, Galway

LITTLE SISTERS OF THE POOR

Mother Provincial
St Peter's Residence,
2A Meadow Road,
South Lambeth,
London SW8 1QH
Tel 0044-020-73350788
Email mp.lond@lsplondon.co.uk

Provincial: Sr Anthony Francis

Dublin, Ossory

LORETO (IBVM)

Provincialate
Loreto House, Beaufort,
Rathfarnham, Dublin 14
Tel 01-4933827
Email provadmin@loreto.ie

Provincial: Sr Ita Moynihan

Dublin, Derry, Ferns, Kilmore, Meath, Ossory, Waterford & Lismore

MARIE AUXILIATRICE SISTERS

7 Florence Street,
Portobello, Dublin 8
Tel/Fax 01-4537622

Dublin

SISTERS OF MARIE REPARATRICE

Laurel Hill Avenue,
South Circular Road,
Limerick V94 XN29
Tel 061-315045

Contact
Sr Eileen Carroll
Email eileencarrollsmr@gmail.com

Cork & Ross, Limerick

MARIST SISTERS

Provincialate
51 Kenilworth Square,
Dublin 6
Tel 01-4972196
Email secirlmarists@gmail.com

Leader – Ireland
Sr Miriam McManus

Dublin, Achonry, Ardagh & Clonmacnois

MEDICAL MISSIONARIES OF MARY

Rosemount,
Rosemount Terrace,
Booterstown, Blackrock,
Co Dublin A94 AH63
Tel 01-2882722
Fax 01-2834626
Email rcsmmm@mmm37.org

Armagh, Dublin, Meath

RELIGIOUS ORDERS AND CONGREGATIONS

MISSIONARIES OF CHARITY

Gift of Love
223 South Circular Road,
Dublin 8

Regional Superior
Sr M. Chantal
177 Bravington Road
London W9 3AR
Tel 0208-9602644

Armagh, Dublin, Cloyne, Elphin

MISSIONARY FRANCISCAN SISTERS OF THE IMMACULATE CONCEPTION

Franciscan Convent
Assisi House, Navan Road,
Dublin 7
Tel 01-8682216

Dublin

MISSIONARY SISTERS OF THE ASSUMPTION

Assumption Convent
34 Crossgar Road,
Ballynahinch,
Co Down BT24 8EN
Tel 028-97561765
Fax 028-97565754

Superior
Sr Maureen Carville

Dromore

MISSIONARY SISTERS OF THE GOSPEL

Carriglea
Dungarvan, Co Waterford
Tel 058-45884
Email
mary.fitzgeraldmsg20@gmail.com

Superior: Sr Mary Fitzgerald

Waterford & Lismore

MISSIONARY SISTERS OF THE HOLY CROSS

86 Glen Road,
Belfast BT11 8BH
Tel 028-90614631
Email
holycrossbelfast@gmail.com

Superior
Sr Patricia Kelly

Down & Connor

MISSIONARY SISTERS OF THE HOLY ROSARY

Regional Administration
41 Westpark,
Artane, Dublin 5
Tel 01-8510010
Email mshrreg@eircom.net

Regional Superior for Ireland and England: Sr Paula Molloy

Dublin, Cork & Ross, Kilmore, Meath

MISSIONARY SISTERS OF ST COLUMBAN

St Columban's Convent
Magheramore,
Wicklow A67 HY02
Tel 0404-67348

Community Leaders
Sr Anne Ryan (Main House)
Sr Margaret Murphy (Nursing Home)

Dublin

MISSIONARY SISTERS OF ST PETER CLAVER

81 Bushy Park Road,
Terenure, Dublin D06 V6Y9
Tel 01-4909360

Contact Person
Sr Juli Thottungal
Email
missiondublin@stpeterclaver.ie

Dublin

MISSIONARY SISTERS SERVANTS OF THE HOLY SPIRIT

143 Philipsburgh Avenue,
Fairview, Dublin D03 HF80
Tel 01-8369383
Email
sspsfairview1@gmail.com

Community Leader
Sr Joan Quirke

Dublin

CONGREGATION OF OUR LADY OF THE MISSIONS

Notre Dame Convent
Upper Churchtown Road,
Leading to Sweetmount
Avenue, Dublin D14 N8E8
Tel 01-2983306

Dublin, Ardagh & Clonmacnois

OUR LADY OF THE CENACLE

19 St Francis' Gardens,
Blackpool, Cork
Tel 087-2891545

Contact: Sr Peggy Cronin
Email
peggycronin.8@gmail.com

Dublin, Cork & Ross

PERPETUAL ADORATION SISTERS

Perpetual Adoration Convent
Wexford
Tel 053-9124134
Email adoration44@eircom.net

Superior: Sr M. Peter Leech

Ferns

POOR CLARES

Archdiocese of Dublin

St Damian's
3A Simmonscourt Road,
Ballsbridge,
Dublin D04 P8A0
Fax 01-6685464
Email pccdamians@mac.com

Abbess/Contact
Sr Mary Brigid Haran

Diocese of Ardagh & Clonmacnois

Poor Clare Monastery of Perpetual Adoration
Drumshanbo,
Co Leitrim

Abbess
Mother Jemma Hayag

Diocese of Cork & Ross

Poor Clare Colettine Monastery
College Road, Cork

Abbess: Sr Miriam Buckley

Diocese of Galway

St Clare's Monastery
Nuns' Island, Galway

Abbess
Sr M. Colette

Diocese Kildare & Leighlin

Poor Clare Colettine Monastery
Graiguecullen, Carlow

Abbess
Mother Rosario Byrne

Diocese of Killaloe

Poor Clare Monastery
Francis Street, Ennis,
Co Clare V95 VNP5
Email
bernardinemeskell@live.ie

Abbess
Sr Bernardine Meskell

POOR SERVANTS OF THE MOTHER OF GOD

Generalate
Maryfield Convent,
Mount Angelus Road,
Roehampton SW15 4JA,
England
Tel 0208-7884351

General: Sr Rosarii O'Connor

Local Leader (Dublin region North): Sr Mary Beecher
Email
mary.beecher@psmgs.org
Local Leader (Dublin region West): Sr Ann Coughlan
Email
acoughlan1942@gmail.com
Local Leader (outside Dublin)
Sr Nora Daly
Email nora.daly@psmgs.org

Dublin, Tuam, Down & Connor, Limerick

CONGREGATION OF THE SISTERS OF NAZARETH

Nazareth House
Malahide Road, Dublin 3
Tel 01-8338205
Email
regional.ie@nazarethcare.com

Regional Superior
Sr Patricia Enright

Dublin, Cloyne, Derry, Down & Connor, Elphin

PRESENTATION SISTERS

Generalate
Monasterevin,
Co Kildare W34 PV32
Tel 045-525335/525503
Fax 045-525209
Email admin@pbvm.org
Website www.pbvm.org

RELIGIOUS ORDERS AND CONGREGATIONS

Congregational Leader
Sr Julie Watson

Armagh, Dublin, Cashel & Emly, Tuam, Clogher, Cloyne, Cork & Ross, Ferns, Galway, Kerry, Kildare & Leighlin, Limerick, Ossory, Waterford & Lismore

PRESENTATION OF MARY SISTERS

4 Lower John Street,
Sligo
Tel 071-9160740

Superior: Sr Emma Dublan

Elphin

REDEMPTORISTINES

Monastery of St Alphonsus
St Alphonsus Road Upper,
Dublin D09 HN53

Superior: Sr Lucy & Sr Gabrielle
Email
lucy.conway@redemptorists.ie

Dublin

RELIGIOUS OF CHRISTIAN EDUCATION

Provincial Office
3 Bushy Park House,
Templeogue Road, Dublin 6W
Tel 01-4901668 Fax 01-4901101
Email rodyolooney@yahoo.co.uk

Provincial Superior
Sr Rosemary O'Looney

Dublin

RELIGIOUS OF SACRED HEART OF MARY

13/14 Huntstown Wood,
Dublin D15 XT9X
Tel 01-8223566/086-0876154

Contact person
Sr Catherine Gough
Email catherinegoughshm@yahoo.co.uk

Dublin, Down & Connor, Ossory

RELIGIOUS SISTERS OF CHARITY

Generalate
Caritas, 15 Gilford Road,
Sandymount, Dublin 4
Tel 01-2697833/2697935

Provincialate, Provincial House, Our Lady's Mount, Harold's Cross, Dublin D6W W934
Tel 01-4973177

Dublin, Cork & Ross

SACRED HEART SOCIETY

Provincial Administration Office
76 Home Farm Road,
Drumcondra, Dublin D09 R903
Tel 01-8375412

Provincial Secretary
Email provsec@rscjirs.org
Canonical Leader
Sr Dairne McHenry
Executive Officer
Email executive@rscjirs.org

Armagh, Dublin

SACRED HEARTS OF JESUS AND MARY (PICPUS)

Delegation House
11 Northbrook Road
Ranelagh,
Dublin D06 Y962
Tel 01-4974831 (Community)

Contact
Sr Aileen Kennedy (SSCC)

Dublin

SACRED HEARTS OF JESUS AND MARY

Sacred Heart Convent
Blackrock, Cork T12 W200
Tel 021-4936200

Community Leader
Sr Annie Mary Nally

Tuam, Cork & Ross

SALESIAN SISTERS OF ST JOHN BOSCO

Provincialate
203 Lower Kilmacud Road,
Stillorgan, Co Dublin
Tel 01-2985188
Email
provincial@salesiansisters.net

Provincial Superior
Sr Bridget O'Connell

Dublin, Limerick

SERVANT SISTERS OF THE HOME OF THE MOTHER

Knockaire, Galway Road,
Roscommon Town

Superior: Sr Ruth O'Callaghan

Elphin

SISTERS OF OUR LADY OF APOSTLES

Provincialate
Ardfoyle Convent,
Ballintemple, Cork T12 Y304
Tel 021-4294076
Fax 021-4291019
Email prov@ardfoyle.com

Provincial
Sr Kathleen McGarvey

Dublin, Tuam, Cork & Ross, Dromore

SISTERS OF ST CLARE

St Clare's Generalate
63 Harold's Cross Road,
Dublin 6W
Tel 01-4966880/4995135
Fax 01-4966388
Email annedkelly@yahoo.com

Abbess General
Sr Anne Kelly

Dublin, Down & Connor,
Dromore, Kerry, Kilmore

Regional Superior
Sr Zita Daly
St Clare's Convent,
12 Ashgrove Avenue, Newry,
Co Down BT34 1PR
Tel 028-30253877
Email zitadaly@gmail.com

SISTERS OF ST JOHN OF GOD

St John of God Congregational Centre
Newtown Road,
Wexford
Tel 053-9142396
Email stjohnogoffice@ssjgcc.ie

Congregational Leader
Sr Geraldine Fitzpatrick

Dublin, Ferns, Kildare & Leighlin, Killaloe, Ossory, Waterford & Lismore

ST JOSEPH OF ANNECY SISTERS

St Joseph's Convent
Killorglin, Co Kerry
Tel 066-9761809
Fax 066-9761127
Email
margaret.lyne@talk21.com

Superior: Sr Helena Lyne

Kerry

ST JOSEPH OF THE APPARITION SISTERS

St Joseph's Convent
Dun Bríd, Ballymote, Co Sligo
Tel 071-9183973
Email stjsligo@eircom.net

Achonry

SISTERS OF ST JOSEPH OF CHAMBERY

St Joseph's Convent
Springdale Road, Raheny,
Dublin 5
Tel 01-8478351 (Convent)
Email silkegalway@gmail.com

Superior: Sr Eileen Silke
Email silkegalway@gmail.com
Regional Superior
Sr Sarah Goss
Email sarahgoss@ymail.com

Dublin

ST JOSEPH OF CLUNY SISTERS

Mt Sackville Convent
Chapelizod, Dublin 20
Tel 01-8213134
Fax 01-8224002
Email provirlgb@sjc.ie
Website www.sjc.ie

Provincial Superior
Sr Maeve Guinan

Dublin, Ardagh & Clonmacnois

ST JOSEPH OF THE SACRED HEART SISTERS

Coolcranogue
Dunganville Upper, Ardagh,
Co Limerick
Tel 069-76794

Regional Leader
Sr Margaret O'Sullivan
margaretosullivan1@outlook.ie

Dublin, Tuam, Achonry, Cloyne, Kerry, Killaloe, Limerick

ST LOUIS SISTERS

131 Beaufort Downs
Rathfarnham, Dublin 14
Tel 01-4934194
Email regionalate@stlouisirl.ie

Regional Leader
Sr Uainín Clarke

Armagh, Dublin, Tuam, Clogher, Down & Connor

ST MARY MADELEINE POSTEL SISTERS

Ard Mhuire Convent
Parkmore, New Line,
Roscrea, Co Tipperary

Regional Superior
Sr M. Luke Minogue

Killaloe

ST PAUL DE CHARTRES SISTERS

6-8 Garville Avenue,
Rathgar, Dublin 6
Tel 01-4975381/4972366
Email fabiolapak@gmail.com

Regional Superior
Sr Fabiola Pak

Dublin

URSULINES

Ursuline Provincialate
17 Trimleston Drive,
Booterstown, Co Dublin
Tel 01-2693503
Email angemeriwk@gmail.com
Website www.ursulines.ie

Provincial
Sr Anne Harte Barry

Dublin, Cashel & Emly, Cork & Ross, Elphin, Waterford & Lismore

URSULINES OF JESUS

26 The Drive
Seatown Park,
Swords, Co Dublin
Tel 01-8404323

Delegated Councillor
Sr Hilary Brown
Ursulines of Jesus,
Flat 14 Kimpton Court,
2 Murrain Road,
London N4 2BN
Email hiliaryuj@gmail.com

Dublin

INSTITUTES

LAY SECULAR INSTITUTES

Lay secular institutes come under the jurisdiction of the Sacred Congregation for Religious Secular Institutes as laid down by the Apostolic Constitution, *Provida Mater Ecclesia*.

Caritas Christi
Secular institute of pontifical right founded in 1937 for laywomen.

Priest Assistant
Rev Jordan O'Brien (OP)
St Mary's, The Claddagh,
Galway H91 CD36
Tel 091-582884
Email pjobpjob@gmail.com

Priest Assistant for Dublin
Rev Gregory Carroll (OP)
St Mary's Priory,
Tallaght, Dublin 24
Tel 01-4048118
Fax 01-4515584
Email gregcop@eircom.net

Contacts: www.ccinfo.org
Veronica Doolan
Tel 086-8660384
Kathleen Tel 087-9005767

Columba Community
Private association of the faithful involved in prayer, Christian teaching, counsel, reconciliation and healing and rehabilitation from drugs and alcohol.

Columba House,
11 Queen Street,
Derry BT48 7EG
Tel 028-71262407
Email columbacommunity@hotmail.com
Website www.columbacommunity.com

Spiritual Director
Rev Neal Carlin
Treasurer: Ms Kathleen Devlin
Contact: Tommy McCay

Servitium Christi
A Secular Institute of Pontifical right for women in the Eucharistic Family of St Peter Julian Eymard (also includes the Congregation of the Blessed Sacrament).

Enquiries: Mary Keane
58 Moyne Road,
Ranelagh, Dublin 6

CATHOLIC EDUCATION

COMMISSION FOR CATHOLIC EDUCATION AND FORMATION

Executive Secretary to the Episcopal Commission/Department
Rev Paul Connell PhD
Tel 01-5053014
Email education@iecon.ie

COUNCIL FOR CATECHETICS OF THE IRISH EPISCOPAL CONFERENCE

Members of the Council
Most Rev Brendan Leahy DD *(Chair)*
Most Rev William Crean DD, Ms Maura Hyland, Rt Rev Mgr Dermot A. Lane, Dr Gerry O'Connell, Dr Cora O'Farrell, Ms Hilda Campbell, Fr Edward McGee, Sr Antoinette Dilworth (RSJ), Dr Aiveen Mullaly, Ms Olivia Dolan, Ms Kate Liffey, Dr Daniel O'Connell
National Director & Executive Secretary of the Council for Catechetics
Dr Alexander O'Hara
Columba Centre, Maynooth, Co Kildare
Tel 01-5053000 Fax 01-6016401
Email catechetics@iecon.ie

COUNCIL FOR EDUCATION OF THE IRISH EPISCOPAL CONFERENCE [WITH NORTHERN IRELAND COUNCIL FOR CATHOLIC EDUCATION (NICCE)]

The Council for Education articulates policy and vision for Catholic Education in Ireland, north and south, on behalf of the Episcopal Conference. It has responsibility for the forward planning necessary to ensure the best provision for Catholic Education in the country. It liaises with other Catholic Education Offices, the Department of Education and Skills and the Department of Education, Northern Ireland. The Council advises the Conference on all government legislation as applied to education. It responds to and acts as spokesperson for the Episcopal Conference on issues related to the work of education. It seeks also to develop long-term strategies in education for the Episcopal Conference

Members of the Council for Education
Most Rev Brendan Kelly DD *(Chair)*
Most Rev Donal McKeown DD
Most Rev Thomas Deenihan DD
Most Rev Francis Duffy DD
Rt Rev Mgr Dan O'Connor,
Sr Evelyn Byrne
Mr Seamus Mulconry
Mr John Curtis
Dr Marie Griffin

Executive Secretary
Rev Paul Connell PhD
Council for Education of the IEC,
Columba Centre, Maynooth, Co Kildare
Tel +353-1-5053014
Email education@iecon.ie
Administrative Assistant
Ms Cora Hennelly
Tel +353-1-5053027
Email chennelly@iecon.ie

Northern Ireland Commission for Catholic Education (NICCE)
Until 2005, there was no central body seeking to offer leadership across the Catholic education sector in NI. The 'Maintained' schools (nursery, primary and non-selective post-primary) were managed by CCMS (a statutory body) while the Voluntary Grammar schools had a considerable degree of independence. The Northern Ireland Commission for Catholic Education (NICCE) was set up in 2005 by the Trustees in order to provide co-ordination of the Catholic sector in a time of rapid change. Today, there are 460 Maintained Schools and 29 Voluntary Grammar Schools.

Current Directors of the Northern Ireland Commission for Catholic Education (NICCE)
Most Rev Donal McKeown DD (Chair),
Most Rev Eamon Martin DD, Most Rev Noël Treanor DD, Sr Eithne Woulfe (SSL), Mr Dermot McGovern (ERST NI), Monsignor Peter O'Reilly, Dean Kevin Donaghy, Sr Maureen O'Dee (Sister of St Clare), Rev Feidhlimidh Magennis, Rev Timothy Bartlett, Rev Gerard Fox and Sr Brighde Vallely

In attendance
Mr Sean Dogherty
Mr Jim Clarke
Rev Paul Connell
Northern Ireland Commission for Catholic Education (NICCE)
St Eugene's Cathedral, Francis Street,
Derry, BT48 9AP
Tel 028-71262302
Email bishop@derrydiocese.org
Website info@catholiceducation-ni.com

The Catholic Education Services Committee (CESC)

The CESC is an education committee established by the Irish Episcopal Conference (IEC) and the Association of Leaders of Missionaries and Religious of Ireland (AMRI). Formally consisting of six Bishops and six Religious nominated by AMRI, it was reconstituted in 2019. The membership now consists of six Bishops, four Religious nominated by AMRI, two representatives of the six educational Trusts that have Public Juridic Person status (PJPs), and a representative of third level Catholic Education. As such, it is now representative of the entire Catholic Education sector.

CESC aims to support a vibrant Catholic education sector in response to changing social, economic and political conditions in Ireland. It promotes the Catholic education sector nationally and assists providers and practitioners in encouraging people to choose Catholic education at all stages of lifelong learning. The development of a co-ordinated and strategic approach to education across the entire Catholic sector in Ireland is a priority for CESC.

Members of the Catholic Education Services Committee (CESC)
Most Rev Thomas Deenihan DD (Chair), Most Rev Francis Duffy DD, Most Rev Brendan Kelly DD, Most Rev Donal McKeown DD, Most Rev Dermot Farrell DD, Most Rev Fintan Monahan DD, Fr Leonard Moloney (SJ), Fr John Hennebry (OSA), Sr Ella McGuinness (RSM), Sr Aideen Kinlen (RSCJ), Dr Sandra Cullen, Mr Paul Meany and Mr Richard Leonard. In attendance Dr Marie Criffin (Chair CEP).

Executive Secretaries: Sr Eithne Woulfe; Rev Paul Connell
Catholic Education Service
Columba Centre, Maynooth, Co Kildare
Tel +353-1-5053014
Email education@iecon.ie

Catholic Education Service Trust (CEST)

The Catholic Education Service is a charity created by Deed of Trust. The Trustees of CEST are four Catholic Bishops who are Ordinaries of Catholic dioceses in Ireland and each representing one of the four ecclesiastical provinces of Ireland (Most Rev Thomas Deenihan DD, Most Rev Fintan Monahan DD, Most Rev Dermot Farrell DD, Most Rev Brendan Kelly DD) and two Religious appointed by AMRI, Rev Leonard Moloney (SJ) and Rev John Hennebry (OSA). The Trustees of the CEST are *ex officio* members of Catholic Education Service Committee (CESC).

Catholic Education Partnership (CEP)

In November 2020, a new structure for the management and trusteeship of Catholic Post-Primary Education came into being. As part of this new structure, two new companies have been established: the Association of Patrons and Trustees of Catholic Schools (APTCS) (see below), and the Catholic Education Partnership (CEP). The CEP replaces the Catholic Schools Partnership (CSP) and will continue its work of providing support for all the partners in Catholic education at first, second and third level in the Republic of Ireland. The CEP going forward will be closely aligned with the Secretariat of Secondary Schools (SSS) which provides support for Boards of Management and Principals in Catholic Post Primary Schools. In addition, it will also be closely aligned with the APTCS which provides support and advice for Patrons and Trustees of Catholic Schools. The activities of the CEP will be supported and funded by CEST.

The Directors of the new CEP Company are:
Most Rev Leo O'Reilly DD, Dr Marie Griffin, Fr Gareth Byrne, Ms Mary Bergin, Mr Declan Lawlor, Dr John McCafferty, Dr Andrew McGrady, Ms Deirdre Matthews, Dr Amalie Meehan, Dom Richard Purcell (OCSO), Mr Jonathan Tiernan and Sr Eithne Woulfe (SSL).

Chair: Dr Marie Griffin
CEO: Ms Gillian McGrath
Company Secretary: Fr Paul Connell
Columba Centre,
Maynooth, Co Kildare
Tel 01-5053100
Email office@catholicschools.ie
Website www.catholicschools.ie

Association of Patrons and Trustees of Catholic Schools (APTCS)

The Association of Patrons and Trustees of Catholic Schools (APTCS) came into being in November 2020. The APTCS is the representative body for the 'Catholic Trustee Voice' in Irish education at primary and post-primary level. Its membership includes members of the Irish Episcopal Conference, representatives of various religious congregations, representatives of the PJP trusts, as well as the trustees of a number of other Catholic schools.

Members of the APTCS Board
Mr Brian Flannery, Mr Paul Meany, Mr Michael Sexton, Ms Sheila McManamly, Ms Clare Ryan, Fr Paul Connell, Mr Gerry Bennett, Mr Edmund Corrigan.

Contact details:
Association of Patrons and Trustees of Catholic Schools (APTCS)
Chairperson: Mr Paul Meany
CEO: Dr Eilis Humphreys
New House, St Patrick's College,
Maynooth, Co Kildare
Tel 01-5053164
Email info@aptcs.ie

Secretariat of Secondary Schools (SSS)

Chair: Ms Deirdre Matthews
General Secretary: Mr John Curtis
Secretariat of Secondary Schools,
Emmet House, Dundrum Road,
Milltown, Dublin 14
Tel +353-1-2838255 Fax +353-1-2695461
Email info@jmb.ie
Website www.jmb.ie

The Secretariat of Secondary Schools is the company which governs the Association of Management of Catholic Secondary Schools (AMCSS). The AMCSS promotes, advises and supports Catholic Voluntary Secondary Schools in Ireland. Founded in the 1960s, it adopted its present structure in 1987. Its membership includes a principal and chairperson of a Board of Management from each of its ten constituent regions. It also includes a representative of the Irish Episcopal Conference and a representative of AMRI (Association of Leaders of Missionaries and Religious of Ireland). The Council cooperates and maintains links with other national and international groups interested in Catholic education. Its Secretariat provides a wide range of educational services and advice to its members. When the Council joins with representatives of the Protestant Voluntary Secondary Schools the Irish School Heads (ISA) it forms the Council of the Joint Managerial Body ((JMB). The JMB is recognised by the Department of Education & Skills as the negotiating body for Voluntary Secondary Schools.

Catholic Primary School Management Association (CPSMA)

Chair: Ms Anne Fay
General Secretary: Mr Seamus Mulconry
New House, St Patrick's College,
Maynooth, Co Kildare
Tel +353-1-6292462/1850-407200
Fax +353-1-6292654
Email info@cpsma.ie
Website www.cpsma.ie

CPSMA represents the boards of management of all Catholic primary schools. Its standing committee has close links with the Episcopal Commission for Education.

* * *

CEIST

Chairperson, Board of Directors
Mr Bernard Keeley
CEO: Ms Clare Ryan
CEIST Ltd, Summit House,
Embassy Office Park, Kill, Co Kildare
Tel 01-6510350 Fax 01-6510180
Email info@ceist.ie
www.ceist.ie

CEIST: Catholic Education – An Irish Schools Trust is a collaborative trustee body for the voluntary secondary schools of the following congregations:
- Presentation Sisters
- Sisters of the Christian Retreat
- Congregation of the Sisters of Mercy
- Missionaries of the Sacred Heart
- Daughters of Charity

CEIST CLG was incorporated in May 2007

Vision: A compassionate and just society inspired by the life and teachings of Jesus Christ.

Mission Statement: To provide a holistic education in the Catholic tradition

Values: Promoting spiritual and human development, achieving quality in teaching and learning, showing respect for every person, creating community and being just and responsible.

ERST – Edmund Rice School Trust

Chairperson: Mr Brendan McAuley
Chief Executive: Mr Gerry Bennett
Co-ordinator of Ethos: Mr Eddie Bourke
Co-ordinator of Governance Services
Ms Helen O'Brien
Finance/Property Officer
Ms Louise Callaghan
Meadow Vale, Clonkeen Road
Blackrock, Co Dublin A94 YN96
Tel 01-2897511 Fax 01-2897540
Email reception@erst.ie
www.erst.ie

The Edmund Rice Schools Trust, an independent lay company based in Dublin, ensures that the schools in the former Christian Brothers Network (currently 96) will continue to provide a Catholic education into the future, in the spirit and tradition of Blessed Edmund Rice, for the people of Ireland.

ERST was incorporated in May 2008.

Vision: Promoting full personal and social development in caring Christian communities of learning and teaching.

Mission Statement: To provide Catholic Education in the Edmund Rice tradition.

The five keys elements of an Edmund Rice Schools Trust School are:
- nurturing faith, Christian spirituality and Gospel-based values;
- promoting partnership in the school community;
- excelling in teaching and learning;
- creating a caring school community;
- inspiring transformational leadership.

ERST – Edmund Rice School Trust (NI)

Chairperson, Board of Directors
Mr Dermot McGovern
Chief Executive: Mr Kevin Burke
Office Administrator
Mrs Gráinne McCann
Edmund Rice Schools Trust,
Westcourt Centre, 8-30 Barrack Street,
Belfast. BT12 4AH
Tel 028-90333205
Email erstni1@live.com

Edmund Rice Schools Trust (NI) is a body of lay people and an autonomous Public Juridical Person in canon law. It is also a limited company in civil law. The Trust has eight schools which were formerly under the Trusteeship of the Christian Brothers.

The Trust was incorporated in February 2009.

Vision: Promoting full personal and social development in caring Christian communities of learning and teaching.

Mission Statement: To provide Catholic Education in the Edmund Rice tradition.

The five keys elements of an Edmund Rice Schools Trust School are:
- Nurturing faith, Christian spirituality and Gospel-based values
- Promoting partnership in the school community
- Excelling in teaching and learning
- Creating a caring school community
- Inspiring transformational leadership.

National Association of Primary Diocesan Advisors (NAPDA)

Chairperson: Mr John McDonagh

The National Association of Primary Diocesan Advisors in Religious Education is a national organisation whose members support, educate and resource the partners in religious education at a primary school level in Ireland.

Membership of the Association is open to all full-time or part-time primary Diocesan Advisers. Associate membership is open to others who work in the area of Religious Education in primary schools.

The association aims to:
- support individual members in their work.
- provide a forum for discussion and debate.
- offer further formation and education for the members.
- review nationally the work of religious education in the Primary School and to actively encourage continual evaluation of progress.
- liaise with other agencies involved in the field of Religious Education.
- articulate nationally the needs of Religious Education at primary level.
- foster co-operation between the three partners involved in Religious Education – home, school and parish.

The association holds an Annual Conference and a minimum of two other meetings during the year. It is represented and organised by an executive, which is elected by the membership and holds office for three years. Members of the Executive represent the Association at the Catholic Primary School Management Association, the Episcopal Commission on Catechetics, and the Consultation Group for the National Primary School Programme.

National Association of Post-Primary Diocesan Advisors (NAPPDA)

Chairperson
Mr Tomás Kenny, Diocese of Kerry
Secretary
Mrs Patricia Sheridan, Diocese of Kilmore
Council Members
Mrs Lily Barry, Dublin Archdiocese
Mrs Eileen Gallagher, Clogher Diocese (North)
Mrs Mary Scriven, Cork and Ross Diocese.

The National Association of Post-Primary Diocesan Advisers provides support, resources, in-service and pastoral care for Religious Education teachers and chaplains working in Post-Primary schools. Membership of the association is open to all full-time and part-time Post-Primary DAs.

The association:
- provides continuous support for all members of the association – full-time and part-time.
- provides faith and professional development opportunities for all members.
- participates in ongoing review of the current situation of Post-Primary RE.
- collaborates with the Council for Catechetics of the Irish Bishops' Conference.
- liaises with the National Director for Catechetics.
- collaborates with the National Association of Post-Primary Chaplains.
- collaborates with all parties involved in Post-Primary RE.

The association holds four meetings a year, including the AGM. These meetings are organised by the executive committee. The NAPPDA currently has representatives on the National Council for Catechetics and on Consultation Group for Post-Primary education.

PBST – Presentation Brothers Schools Trust

Chairperson, Board of Directors:
Ms Carmel Murphy
CEO: Mr Michael Sexton
Presentation Brothers Schools Trust,
10 Deerpark Court,
Friars Walk, Cork T12 D8H3
Tel 021-2417144
Email michaelsexton@pbst.ie
www.pbst.ie

PBST is the trustee body for five voluntary secondary schools and three primary schools formerly in the trusteeship of the Presentation Brothers.

Presentation Brothers Schools Trust CLG was incorporated in January 2009.

Vision: to ensure that the 'characteristic spirit' of each school is in keeping with Christ's teaching as exemplified by Blessed Edmund Rice and, as legal owner, to take overall responsibility for the properties and finances of the schools and to ensure compliance with statutory requirements.

Mission Statement: 'to make Christ's Gospel of love known and relevant to each succeeding generation' ... ' seeing education as the key to growth and transformation in the context of the search for meaning, happiness and the common good'.

Values: The four core elements of a PBST education (as outlined in our Charter) are:
- a genuine and tangible spirit of respect and caring for each member of the school community
- a comprehensive and holistic education
- a vibrant experience of community and partnership
- a deep commitment to Gospel values as lived in the Edmund Rice tradition

Le Chéile Schools Trust

Chairperson: Mr Ciaran Flynn
Executive Director
Ms Marie-Therese Kilmartin
Le Chéile Schools Trust, Moibhi Block B,
Alexandra College,
96 Rathmines Road Upper, Rathmines,
Dublin D06 W9N4
Tel 01-5380104
Email admin@lecheiletrust.ie

The Le Chéile Schools Trust is a collaborative Trust set up by twelve religious congregations (now fifteen) to affirm their commitment to the future of Catholic Education in Ireland and to work in partnership with the government in the education system.

Le Chéile schools provide an education that acknowledges and affirms the dignity and uniqueness of every human being as a child of God. Our main motivation is the holistic flourishing of every student – 'the glory of God is humanity fully alive' (St Irenaeus) and embraces the physical, mental, emotional, social, moral and spiritual growth of each student. It seeks to build a learning community that welcomes and witnesses through the Gospel values. We use the three words Welcome, Wisdom and Witness to draw together the core elements of what we call a Le Chéile spirituality. This vision reflects the rich heritage of the founding congregations in providing for the needs of the students and communities in its schools.

The Trust was incorporated in October 2008 and is now patron of 63 post primary schools and will welcome primary schools into the Trust in 2019-2020. Together with its sister company, Síol Schools Trust, Le Cheile Education Trust is a recognised Catholic body, with juridic person status granted by the Irish Episcopal Commission in 2012.

Educena

Chairperson, Board of Directors
Mr James Corbett
CEO: Mr John D'Arcy
The Educena Foundation, Summit House, Embassy Office Park, Kill, Co Kildare
Tel 01-6510434
Email info@educena.ie

The Educena Foundation is responsible for the ownership and management of CEIST school properties, licensing these to providing finance to CEIST in fulfilling its responsibility as trustees.

The Company was incorporated in May 2007

Vision: A thriving community of faith-based schools

Mission Statement: Our mission is to secure faith-based education in the Catholic tradition for second- level students.

Values: Collaboration, Faith-based education, Integrity, Commitment and Compassion.

SEMINARIES AND HOUSES OF STUDY

SEMINARIES

PONTIFICAL IRISH COLLEGE, ROME
Founded in 1628 the Irish National College in Rome provides formation to seminarians and priests for the diocesan priesthood in Ireland and beyond.
Via dei SS Quattro 1, 00184 Roma, Italy
Tel 003906-772631 Fax 003906-77263323
Email ufficio@irishcollege.org
www.irishcollege.org
Rector
Rev Paul Finnerty BA, BD, STL
Email paul.finnerty@irishcollege.org
Vice-Rector
Rev John Coughlan BA, BD, STL
Email john.coughlan@irishcollege.org
Spiritual Director
Rev Aidan Ryan STL
Email aidanryan1946@gmail.com

ST PATRICK'S COLLEGE, MAYNOOTH
Founded in 1795, the National Seminary for Ireland and Pontifical University, Maynooth, Co Kildare W23 TW77

President
Rev Professor Michael Mullaney BA, BD, JCD
Tel 01-7083958
Email president@spcm.ie

Seminary
Seminary Rector
Rev Tomás Surlis B.Rel.Sc, BD, STL, SThD
Tel 01-7083727
Email rector@spcm.ie
Director of Formation (Coordinator of Human and Pastoral Formation)
Rev Sean Corkery
Email sean.corkery@spcm.ie
Coordinator of Intellectual Formation
Rev Michael Shortall
Email michael.shortall@spcm.ie
Spiritual Director
Rev Chris Hayden
Email chris.hayden@spcm.ie
Vocational Growth Counsellor
Rev Leon Ó Giolláin SJ
Email leon.ogiollain@spcm.ie
Human Formation Advisor
Rev Hugh Lagan (SMA)
Email hugh.lagan@spcm.ie
Director of Sacred Music
John O'Keeffe KSG, PhD, HDE, LTCL
Email john.okeeffe@spcm.ie

College Officers
Financial Officer
Ms Fidelma Madden ACA, AITI
Registrar and Supervisor of Examinations
Maurice Garde BATh, MSocSci
Email registrar@spcm.ie
Librarian: Cathal McCauley
Archivist: archives@spcm.ie

Pontifical University Officers
Dean, Faculty of Theology
Dr Jessie Rogers
Dean, Faculty of Philosophy
Rev Professor Thomas Casey (SJ)
Dean, Postgraduate Studies
Rev Dr Michael Shortall
Academic Registrar
Maurice Garde
Marketing Director
Paul Hurley

Pontifical University Courses – Professors/Department Heads
Systematic Theology
Rev Professor Declan Marmion (SM) Mth, STD, HDE, Dip Pastoral Theology
Sacred Scripture
Rev Professor Seamus O'Connell BSc, LSS
Moral Theology
Rev Dr Pádraig Corkery BSc, STD
Faith and Culture
Rev Professor Michael A. Conway MSC, D.Theol
Canon Law
Rev Professor Michael Mullaney BA, BD, JCD
Liturgy
Rev Professor Liam Tracey (OSM) STB, SLD, DipMar, DipPastoral Theology
Ecclesiastical History
Professor Salvador Ryan BA, PhD
Director of Pastoral Theology
Dr Aoife McGrath PhD, MACSPW

SEMINARIES AND HOUSES OF STUDY

HOUSES OF STUDY

For details see Religious Orders and Congregations Section

Camillians (OSCam)
St Camillus, South Hill Avenue,
Blackrock, Co Dublin
Tel 01-2882873/2833380

Carmelites (OCarm)
Prior: Rev Fintan Burke
Gort Muire, Ballinteer, Dublin D16 E167
Tel 01-2984014 Fax 01-2987221
Email gortmuire@gortmuire.com

Dominicans (OP)
St Saviour's Priory, Upper Dorset Street,
Dublin 1
Tel 01-8897610 Fax 01-8734003
Email dominican.studium@dominicans.ie
Regent: Rev Terence Crotty (OP)

St Mary's Priory, Tallaght, Dublin 24
Tel 01-4048100
The Priory Institute
Tel 01-4048124 Fax 01-4626084
Email enquiries@prioryinstitute.com

Franciscans (OFM)
Dún Mhuire, Seafield Road,
Killiney, Co Dublin A96 R590
Tel 01-2826760 Fax 01-2826993
Email franciscans.killiney@franciscans.ie
Guardian: Br Stephen O'Kane
Vicar: Rev Micheál Mac Craith

Missionaries of Africa (White Fathers)
Cypress Grove, Templeogue,
Dublin 6W YV12
Tel 01-4055263
Contact Person: Rev Sean O'Leary
Email dep.irl.del@mafr.org

Oblates (OMI)
St Anne's, Goldenbridge Walk, Inchicore,
Dublin 8
Tel 01-4540841

Mona,
12 Tyrconnell Road, Inchicore, Dublin 8
Rev Patrick Carolan (OMI)
Rev Paul Horrocks

Salesians (SDB)
St Catherine's Centre, North Campus,
Maynooth, Co Kildare W23 TN90
Tel 01-6286111 Fax 01-6286268
Email sdbmaynooth@iol.ie
Rector: Rev Cyril Odia
Vice-Rector: Rev Michael Connell
Bursar: Rev Miroslaw Niechwiej
Dean of Studies
Rev Arkadiusz Orzechowski
Br Bénoit Kufika Beya
Br António Paulo Cristovao
Br Mulugeta Woldemeskel
Rev Mark Anthony Okpalire
Rev Michael Scott
Br Vincent Tran Hien Vinh

SPECIAL INSTITUTES OF EDUCATION

Irish School of Ecumenics
Trinity College Dublin
School of Religion
ISE-LI Building,
Trinity College, Dublin 2
Contact: Prof. Andrew Pierce, Head of Discipline, Religious Studies
Tel 01-8964778 Fax 01-6725024
Email isedir@tcd.ie
www.tcd.ie/ise

Irish School of Ecumenics
Trinity College Dublin
School of Religion
9 Lennoxvale, Belfast BT9 5BY
Tel 028-90775010 Fax 028-90373986
Email isedir@tcd.ie
www.tcd.ie/ise

Redemptoris Mater Archdiocesan Missionary Seminary
(Archdiocese of Armagh)
Founded in 2012 to form priests for the New Evangelisation who are both diocesan and missionary.

De La Salle Terrace,
Dundalk, Co Louth A91 C5D6
Tel 042-9336584
Email seminary@redmatarmagh.org
Web www.redmatarmagh.org
Rector: Rev Giuseppe Pollio
Director of Studies
Rev Maciej Zacharek
Spiritual Director
His Eminence Cardinal Seán Brady
Spiritual Director
Rev Bede McGregor (OP)

Mater Dei Centre for Catholic Education
DCU Institute of Education,
DCU St. Patrick's Campus,
Upper Drumcondra Road,
Dublin D09 DY00
Tel 01-8842003
Email materdei.cce@dcu.ie
www.dcu.ie/materdei.cce
Director: Dr Cora O'Farrell
Tel 01-7009154
Email cora.ofarrell@dcu.ie

RETREAT AND PASTORAL CENTRES

RETREAT HOUSES

ANTRIM
Drumalis Retreat & Conference Centre,
Glenarm Road, Larne,
Co Antrim BT40 1DT
Tel 028-28272196/28276455
Email drumalis@btconnect.com
www.drumalis.co.uk
Offering an organised programme of events as well as catering for groups, conferences, retreats and chapters, on a residential or non-residential basis.
Facilities include:
• Chapel, Oratory and Prayer Spaces.
• 2 large conference tooms (1 of which can also be used as a chapel),variety of smaller meeting rooms and breakout rooms, craft room, library, spacious dining room and 2 lounges with teas/coffee-making facilities.
• Accommodation in custom built retreat building (39 double/twin en-suite rooms – 4 of which are disabled friendly) and 15 additional bedrooms in Heritage House. Lift access and free wifi available throughout centre.
Set in spacious grounds overlooking Larne Lough and the sea, Drumalis offers space for contamplation and prayer – 'an oasis on the journey of life'.
In light of COVID-19 restrictions, Drumalis is closed to in-house guests until Spring 2021.

CORK
St Benedict's Priory Retreat House,
The Mount, Cobh, Co Cork
Tel 021-4811354
Acc: 6 single rooms, 2 double rooms available for private individual or group retreats, private day retreats, opportunity to share in the liturgical life of the Sisters – Holy Mass, Liturgy of the Hours and Eucharistic Adoration. Quiet peaceful setting, Bible Garden, all meals supplied.
Contact for private retreats
Guest Mistress
Email cobhtyburnconvent@gmail.com

Ennismore Retreat & Conference Centre,
Ennismore, Montenotte, Cork
Tel 021-4502520 Fax 021-4502712
Email info@ennismore.ie
www.ennismore.ie
Contact person: The Secretary
Acc: singles 31, doubles 2
Dominicans

DERRY
Carmelite Retreat Centre,
Termonbacca, Derry BT48 9XE
Tel 028-71262512
Email ocdderry@hotmail.co.uk
www.ocd.ie
Contact person: The Secretary
Acc: singles 15, twin 20, ensuite rooms 12
Carmelites (OCD)

DONEGAL
St Anthony's Retreat Centre,
Dundrean, Burnfoot, Co Donegal
Tel 074-9368370
Email stanthonysretreat7@gmail.com
Acc: 5 hermitages, 1 double (all en suite)
Director: Vacant
Spiritual direction available
Full board: €60 per day

DOWN
Dromantine Retreat and Conference,
Centre, Newry, Co Down BT34 1RH
Tel 028-30821964 (048 from ROI)
Email admin@dromantineconference.com
www.dromantineconference.com
Contact: Rev Damian Bresnahan (SMA)
Accommodation: 47 single en suite rooms, 25 double en suite rooms, 8 conference rooms

An Cuan, Youth with a Mission,
44 Shore Road, Rostrevor, Newry,
Co Down BT34 3ET
Tel 028-41738492
Email info@ywamrostrevor.com
Acc: singles 3, double/family 1, twin 5
Contact: Scott Sotomayor (Director)
www.ywamrostrevor.com

Passionist Retreat Centre,
16 A Downpatrick Road, Crossgar,
Downpatrick, Co Down BT30 9EQ
Tel 028-44830242
Email managertobarmhuire@gmail.com
Accommodation: 18 bedrooms
Superior: Rev Thomas Scanlon

DUBLIN
Avila Carmelite Centre
Bloomfield Avenue
Morehampton Road, Dublin 4
Tel 01-6430200 Fax 01-6430281
Email info@avilacentre.ie
Prior: Fr Vincent O'Hara (OCD)
Carmelites (OCD)

Dominican Retreat Centre
Tallaght Village, Dublin D24 KA40
Tel 01-4048123/4048189
Email dominicanretreats@gmail.com
www.goodnews.ie or
www.retreats.dominicans.ie
Secretary/Contact: Anita Kenny
Acc: singles 26, doubles 2, 1 large, 5 medium conference rooms, oratory.
Free wifi and parking. Extensive gardens.
Dominicans

The Emmaus Centre, Ennis Lane,
Lissenhall, Swords, Co Dublin K67 Y2X
Tel 01-8700050
Email emmauscentre@emmauscentre.ie
www.emmauscentre.ie
Acc: 63 ensuite bedrooms, 3 prayer rooms, 13 meeting rooms
Director: Julie Cosden
Assistant Director: Nora Meenaghan
Christian Brothers

Tallaght Rehabilitation Project
Kiltalown House, Jobstown,
Tallaght, Dublin 24
Tel 01-4597705 Fax 01-4148123
Email info@tallaghtrehabproject.ie
Co-ordinator: Marie Hayden

Manresa Jesuit Centre of Spirituality
426 Clontarf Road,
Dollymount, Dublin D03 FP52
Tel 01-8331352
Email reception@manresa.ie
www.manresa.ie
Located on Dublin Bay, Manresa offers the Spiritual Exercises of Saint Ignatius in a variety of forms. The retreat house has forty ensuite rooms and a number of prayer and meeting spaces to facilitate quiet retreats, reflection and prayer.
Director: Rev Piaras Jackson (SJ)

RETREAT AND PASTORAL CENTRES

GALWAY
Emmanuel House of Providence,
Clonfert, Ballinasloe,
Co Galway H53 E5N6
Tel 057-9151552
Email contact@emmanuelhouse.ie
www.emmanuelhouse.ie
No Accommodation
Eddie and Lucy Stones
Catholic centre for prayer and evangelisation. It is a new community of Christ's faithful, a spiritual hospital where people can experience the healing power of God in spirit, mind and body.

Esker Retreat House and Youth Village,
Athenry, Co Galway
Tel 091-844549 Fax 091-845698
Email eskerret@indigo.ie
www.eskercommunity.net
Acc: singles 17, doubles 26 in retreat house, 70 in 2 dorms in youth village
Retreat House Co-ordinator
Fr Fonsie Doran CSsR
Email rev_dorancssr@yahoo.com
Youth Village Co-ordinator
Fr Michael Cusack CSsR
Contact: The Secretary

KERRY
Ardfert Retreat Centre,
Abbeylands, Ardfert, Tralee,
Co Kerry V92 D438
Tel 066-7134276
Email ardfertretreat@eircom.net
Acc: 29 rooms
Contact Person: Sr Elizabeth Gilmartin
Kerry Diocese
Website www.ardfertretreatcentre.org

LAOIS
La Salle Pastoral Centre, Castletown,
Portlaoise, Co Laois R32 N6D8
Tel 057-8732442
Email castletownretreats@gmail.com
Contact: Derek Doherty
Administrator: Br Kevin McEvoy (FSC)
Email kevinmcevoy@lasalleigbm.org
Tel 087-1763729
Acc: 40. De La Salle Brothers

Mount St Anne's Retreat and Conference
Centre, Killenard,
Portarlington, Co Laois
Tel 057-8626153
Email secretary@mountstannes.com
http://www.mountstannes.com
Acc: 35 rooms (incl. 3 individual apartments)
CEO: Dr Oonagh O'Brien
Email ceo@mountstannes.com
Contact Person: Catherine Gorey (Secretary)
Operations Manager: Marian Keightley

LOUTH
Dominican Nuns
Monastery of St Catherine of Siena,
The Twenties, Drogheda,
Co Louth A92 KR84
Tel 041-9838524
Email sienasilence@gmail.com
www.dominicannuns.ie
In a quiet country setting – self-catering Retreat House
Acc: 4 en suite rooms. Oratory with reserved Blessed Sacrament; fully equipped kitchen; private garden. Conference room suitable for day groups. Eucharistic Adoration; opportunity to attend the monastic liturgy
Contact: Sister in Charge (Retreat Rooms)

TYRONE
Servite Priory, Benburb, Dungannon,
Co Tyrone BT71 7JZ
Tel 028-37548241
Email servitecommunity@gmail.com
Contact: Retreats 028-37548241
Residential groups and conferences
Tel 028-87659201
Email hello@benburbpriory.com

WEXFORD
Sisters of St John of God,
Ballyvaloo Retreat & Conference Centre,
Ballyvaloo, Blackwater, Enniscorthy,
Co Wexford Y21 X392
Tel 053-9137160
Email office@ballyvaloo.ie
www.ballyvaloo.ie
Director: Sr Mary Rowsome
Acc: 32 ensuite rooms

PASTORAL CENTRES

CORK
Dominican Pastoral Centre,
Popes Quay, Cork
Tel 021-4502067/021-4502267
Email dompastoralcentre@gmail.com
Director: Rev Damian Polly (OP)
Acc: 2 conference rooms, 1 hall
Non-residential

Nano Nagle Birthplace,
Ballygriffin, Mallow, Co Cork
Tel 022-26411
Email secretary@nanonaglebirthplace.ie
www.nanonaglebirthplace.ie
Presentation Sisters
Heritage, Spirituality and Ecology Centre.
Retreats, workshops and courses.
Conference Centre for Hire.
Self-catering accommodation:
2 bungalows and 3 apartments.

DONEGAL
Whiteoaks Rehabilitation Centre
Derryvane, Muff, Co Donegal
Tel 07493-84400 Fax 07493-84883
Email info@whiteoakscentre.com
www.whiteoaksrehabcentre.com
Director: Fr Neal Carlin
Manager: Sharon McMullan
The purpose of White Oaks is to aid the recovery of people suffering from addictions. We offer a 30-day residential treatment programme, for people addicted to drugs, alcohol and gambling, based on the 12-step model. There is a two year aftercare programme.
The Centre has full international accreditation with CHKS Ltd for the quality of its services. It is approved by the main Healthcare Insurances.

KERRY
St John Paul II Pastoral Centre
Rock Road, Killarney, Co Kerry
Tel 064-6632644
Email pastoralcentre@dioceseofkerry.ie
Non-residential
Director: Rev Gearóid Godley
Kerry Diocese

RETREAT AND PASTORAL CENTRES

MEATH
Dowdstown Counselling Services,
Cyws Hall, Fairgreen, Navan, Co Meath
Tel 046-9031196
Email
dowdstowncounsellingservices1@gmail.com
www.dowdstowncounsellingservices.com
Administrator: Mary Mahon
Dowdstown Counselling Services offers affordable counselling to all in the Meath and surrounding areas.
Meath Diocese

WATERFORD
St John's Pastoral Centre
John's Hill, Waterford
Tel 051-874199
Administrator: Ms Mary Dee
Email
pastoralcentre@waterfordlismore.ie

PRIVATE RETREATS

ANTRIM
Adoration Sisters
63 Falls Road, Belfast BT12 4PD
Tel 02890-325668
www.adorationsisters.info
Altar Bread Suppliers
'Saint Joseph's House of Bread'
Tel 02890 247175
Email stjosephsltd@gmail.com
Superior General
Mother Mary Josephine Caldwell
Email info@adorationsisters.info

Our Lady of Bethlehem Abbey
11 Ballymena Road, Portglenone,
Co Antrim BT44 8BL
Tel 028-25821211
Email info@bethabbey.com
www.bethlehemabbey.com
Contact: Rev Guestmaster
9.30am-5.00 pm, Monday-Saturday
Acc: 10 rooms: 8 singles/doubles, 2 singles
Cistercians

DERRY
Columba Community,
Columba House of Prayer and Reconciliation
11 Queen Street, Derry BT48 7EG
Tel 028-71262407
Email columbacommunity@hotmail.com
www.columbacommunity.com
Director: Rev Neal Carlin
Contact: Tommy McCay
Email columbacommunity@hotmail.com
A basic Christian community with 20 members offering opportunities for private reflection and group worship. Prayer and pastoral counselling available on a one-to-one and group basis.
Blessed Sacrament Chapel open daily 9.30am-5.00pm
Monday to Friday: all welcome
Thursday 7.30pm Mass and Prayer for Healing

DOWN
Holy Cross Abbey
119 Kilbroney Road, Rostrevor,
Co Down BT34 3BN
Tel 028-41739979
Email benedictinemonks@btinternet.com
www.benedictinemonks.co.uk
Contact: The Guestmaster
Accommodation: 8 singles
Benedictines

GALWAY
Spiritual Direction – La Retraite
3 St Mary's Mews, Shantalla Road,
Galway H91 WF6N
Tel 091-524548
Contact: Sr Moira McDowall
Tel 086-3505779
Email moira.mcdowall@outlook.com
La Retraite Sisters

LEITRIM
La Verna, Convent Avenue,
Drumshanbo, Co Leitrim
Tel 071-9641308
Contact: Sr Helen Keegan
Self-catering: 3 bedroom retreat house
Poor Clare Monastery of Perpetual Adoration

LIMERICK
Glenstal Abbey, Monastic Guest House,
Murroe, Co Limerick
Tel 061-621000
Contact: The Guestmaster
Email guestmaster@glenstal.org
Acc: 12
Benedictines

MEATH
Silverstream Priory,
Stamullen, Co Meath K32 T189
Tel 01-8417142
Contact: Dom Cassian Aylward (OSB)
Email guestmaster@cenacleosb.org
Acc: 2 rooms, clergy and seminarians only (en suite)
Benedictines Monks of Perpetual Adoration

WEXFORD
St Aidan's Monastery of Adoration
Ferns, Enniscorthy, Co Wexford
Tel 053-9366634
Email staidansferns@eircom.net
Web www.adorationsisters.info
Acc: 8 hermitages, 1 wheelchair-friendly.

PERMANENT DEACONS

The Church teaches that there are three degrees within the Sacrament of Holy Orders: bishops, priests and deacons.

In recent centuries the Order of Deacon within the Roman Rite, tended to be seen as a step towards becoming a priest. This was revisited during the Second Vatican Ecumenical Council in the 1960s. At this Council a decision was taken to restore the diaconate as a distinct ministry of service within the Church to help renew and enrich the Church's missionary endeavours.

In recent years, many of the Irish dioceses have ordained permanent deacons and they are listed as follows:

ARMAGH
Rev Martin Barlow
Rev Martin Brennan
Rev Philip Carder
Rev Paul Casey
Rev Dermot Clarke
Rev Martin Cunningham
Rev Kevin Duffy
Rev David Durrigan
Rev Andrew Hegarty
Rev Tony Hughes
Rev Paul Mallon
Rev Malachy McElmeel
Rev Eamon Quinn
Rev John Taaffe

DUBLIN
Rev Jim Adams
Rev Declan Barry
Rev Frank Browne
Rev Declan Colgan
Rev Eric Cooney
Rev Gabriel Corcoran
Rev Don Devaney
Rev James Fennell
Rev Paul Ferris
Rev Victor Garvin
Rev Michael Giblin
Rev John Graham
Rev Thomas Groves
Rev Paul Kelly
Rev Gerard Larkin
Rev Tom Larkin
Rev Derek Leonard
Rev Steve Maher
Rev Gerard Malone
Rev Dermot McCarthy
Rev Damian Murphy
Rev Matthew Murphy
Rev Tim Murphy
Rev Eamonn Murray
Rev Michael O'Connor
Rev John O'Neill
Rev Padraic O'Sullivan
Rev Greg Pepper
Rev Gerard Reilly
Rev Noel Ryan
Rev Jeremy Seligman
Rev Joseph Walsh

ACHONRY
Rev Kevin Flynn
Rev Martin Lynch

CLOGHER
Rev Martin Donnelly

CLOYNE
Rev Paul Alapini
Rev Leonard Cleary
Rev Garrett Cody
Rev Damian McCabe
Rev John McCarthy
Rev Edward Mulhare
Rev John Nestor
Rev Gerard Rooney
Rev James Sheahan
Rev Brian Williams

CORK & ROSS
Rev David Lane
Rev John Guirey
Rev Frank McKevitt

DOWN & CONNOR
Rev Joseph Baxter
Rev Terence Butcher
Rev Brendan Dowd
Rev Brett Lockhart
Rev James McAllister
Rev Gregory McGuigan
Rev Patrick McNeill
Rev Kevin Webb
Rev Martin Whyte

DROMORE
Rev Kevin Devine
Rev Gerry Heaney
Rev John McClelland
Rev Frank Rice
Rev Michael Rooney

ELPHIN
Rev Wando de Araujo
Rev William Gacquin
Rev Damien Kearns
Rev Tony Larkin
Rev Frank McGuinness
Rev David Muldowney
Rev Martin Reidy
Rev Seamus Talbot

KERRY
Rev Conor Bradley
Rev Jean Yves Letanneur
Rev Denis Kelleher
Rev Thady O'Connor
Rev Pat Coffey
Rev Francis White

KILDARE & LEIGHLIN
Rev Vincent Crowley
Rev John Dunleavy
Rev Liam Dunne
Rev Eugene Keyes
Rev Gary Moore
Rev David O'Flaherty
Rev Fergal O'Neill
Rev Joe O'Rourke
Rev Patrick Roche
Rev Jim Stowe
Rev Paul Wyer

KILMORE
Rev Andrew Brady
Rev Padraig Kelly

WATERFORD & LISMORE
Rev Lazarus Gidolf
Rev Brendan Gallagher
Rev Hugh Nugent

MARRIAGE TRIBUNALS

By Decree dated 24 March 1975, the Irish Episcopal Conference decided to establish four Regional Marriage Tribunals of first instance to be located at Armagh, Dublin, Cork and Galway. This decree was formally approved by the Supreme Tribunal of the Apostolic Signatur on 6 May 1975. In accordance with the terms of the Roman rescript, the Episcopal Conference, in a decision of 30 September 1975, determined the Regional Tribunals would come into effect on 1 January 1976. From that date they replaced all previous diocesan marriage tribunals.

By the same process which established in Ireland Regional Marriage Tribunals of first instance, the Episcopal Conference set up a sole Appeal Tribunal, located in Dublin, to hear cases on appeal from each of the four Regional Tribunals. It also came into effect on 1 January 1976. Its personnel and administration are wholly distinct from the Dublin Regional Marriage Tribunal.

NATIONAL MARRIAGE APPEAL TRIBUNAL

Columba Centre, Maynooth, Co Kildare
Tel 01 5053119 Fax 01-5053122
Judicial Vicar
Rev Michael Smyth (MSC), STL, JUD
Administrator: Mrs Stephanie Walpole
Vice Officialis
Rt Rev Mgr Joseph Donnelly PP, VF
Associate Judges
Very Rev Canon Eugene Mangan PP, Very Rev Gerard McNamara PP, Very Rev Patrick Gill AP, Very Rev John Canon O'Boyle BA, Very Rev Patrick Williams AP, Very Rev S.J. Clyne PP, VF, Rev Patrick Connolly DCL, Rev Brendan Kilcoyne LCL, Rev Michael Mullaney DCL, Rev Brian Flynn PP,Rev John Whelan (OSA), Mr Michael V. O'Mahony, Rev Seán O'Neill, Very Rev Francis Maher PP, Rev Lorcan Moran PP, Rt Rev Mgr Gerard Dolan PP, LCL, Very Rev Patrick Canon Twomey PE, Most Rev William Walsh DD, Sr Máirín McDonagh (RJH), Very Rev Patrick McCarthy BL, PP

Defenders of the Bond
Rev Brian Kavanagh LCL,
Rev Michael Bannon
Rev Gabriel Kelly, Rev Kevin O'Gorman
Correspondence to: Administrator

REGIONAL MARRIAGE TRIBUNALS

ARMAGH INTER-DIOCESAN MARRIAGE TRIBUNAL

Regional Office: 15 College Street, Armagh BT61 9BT
Tel 028-37524537 Fax 028-37528763
Email armagh@marriagetribunal.org
Judicial Vicar
Very Rev Joseph Rooney JCL
Administrator
Very Rev John McKeever LLB, STL
Presiding Judges
Very Rev Joseph Rooney JCL;
Rev Vincent Cushnahan JCL
Contact Person for Constituent Dioceses
Armagh
Very Rev John McKeever LLB, STL;
Rev Colm Hagan LLB, STB
Tel 028-37524537
Clogher: Mr Kevin Slowey
Tel 028-66327222
Derry: Rev Micheál McGavigan JCL;
Rev Brendan Ward
Tel 028-71362475
Down & Connor
Very Rev Joseph Rooney SCL;
Rev Vincent Cushnahan JCL
Tel 028-90491990
Dromore: Rev Mr Michael Rooney
Tel 028-37524537
Kilmore: Sr Kathleen Gormley (RSM)
Tel 049-4375004
Raphoe: Rt Rev Mgr Kevin Gillespie;
Tel 074-9121853

DUBLIN INTER-DIOCESAN MARRIAGE TRIBUNAL

Diocesan Offices,
Archbishop's House, Dublin D09 C42Y
Tel 01-8087564
Email dublinrmt3@gmail.com
Judicial Vicar: Rev Paul Churchill
Tribunal Staff Members
Rev Kilian Byrne LCL (Kildare and Leighlin)
Sr Mary Grennan LCL (PBVM)
Rev William Richardson PhD, JCD (Dublin)
Mgr Alex Stenson DCL (Dublin)
Very Rev Laurence Collins (OP)
Maeve Cotter, Rev Tom Dowd,
Anne Giblin (RSC), Jane O'Donoghue,
Mrs Pamela van de Poll
Correspondence to: The Rev Judicial Vicar
Constituent Dioceses: Dublin, Ferns, Kildare and Leighlin, Meath, Ossory

CORK REGIONAL MARRIAGE TRIBUNAL

Tribunal Offices, The Lough,
Cork T12 C654
Tel 021-4963653 Fax 021-4314149
Judicial Vicar
Very Rev Richard Keane BA, BD, MTh, JCL
Email frrichard.tribunal@gmail.com
Associate Judicial Vicar: Vacant
Judge: Very Rev Seamus McKenna BA, HDE, LCL
Constituent Dioceses
Cashel, Cloyne, Cork and Ross, Kerry, Limerick, Waterford and Lismore
Correspondence to: Aileen Coleman (Tribunal Secretary)
Email aileen.tribunal@gmail.com

GALWAY REGIONAL MARRIAGE TRIBUNAL

7 Waterside, Woodquay,
Galway H91 PF61
Tel 091-565179
Email 7waterside@eircom.net
Website
www.galwayregionalmarriagetribunal.org
Moderator
Most Rev Brendan Kelly, Bishop of Galway, Kilmacduagh & Kilfenora
Judicial Vicar
Very Rev Barry Horan JCL
Associate Judicial Vicar: Vacant
Judge Instructor
Mairéad Uí Mhurchadha
Correspondence to the Administrator:
Nicola Burke
Constituent Dioceses: Tuam, Achonry, Ardagh and Clonmacnois, Clonfert, Elphin, Galway, Killala, Killaloe

CHAPLAINS

THE DEFENCE FORCES CHAPLAINCY SERVICE

Head Chaplain
Rev Seamus Madigan HCF
Rev Pascal Hanrahan HCF (from 1 March)
Defence Forces Headquarters,
McKee Barracks, Blackhorse Avenue,
Dublin 7
Tel 01-8042637
Email seamusmadigan@hotmail.com
Administration Secretary
Sgt Liam Bellew
Defence Forces Headquarters,
McKee Barracks, Blackhorse Avenue,
Dublin 7
Tel 01-8042638
Email liam.bellew@defenceforces.ie

Aiken Barracks
Dundalk, Co Louth
Rev Michael Hinds CF
Tel 087-3940186
Email: Michaelhinds1@hotmail.com

Casement Aerodrome
Baldonnel, Co Dublin
Tel 01-4037536
Rev Bernard McCay-Morrissey CF
Email bernardmccaymorrissey@gmail.com

Cathal Brugha Barracks
Rathmines, Dublin 6
Tel 01-8046484
Vacant

Collins Barracks (Cork)
Tel 021-4502734
Rev Edward Sheehan CF
Email tedsheehan64@gmail.com

Curragh Camp
Co Kildare
Rt Rev Mgr John McDonald CF
Tel 045-441369
Email frjohnmcdonald@gmail.com
Rev P.J. Somers CF
Tel 045-445071
Email somerspj@gmail.com

Custume Barracks
Athlone, Co Westmeath
Tel 090-6421277
Rev Declan Shannon
Email declanjjshannon@gmail.com

Finner Camp
Ballyshannon, Co Donegal
Tel 071-9842294
Rev Jeremiah Carroll CF
Email jerryzulu@gmail.com

Gormanston Camp
Co Meath
Rev Michael Hinds CF
Tel 087-3940186
Email: Michaelhinds1@hotmail.com

McKee Barracks
Dublin 7
Tel 086-2256794
Rev Damian Farnon
Email damian.farnon@defenceforces.ie

The Naval Base
Haulbowline, Co Cork
Tel 021-4378046
Rev Desmond Campion (SDB) CF
Email campiond@eircom.net

Renmore Barracks
Galway
Tel 091-751156
Rev Paul Murphy CF
Email papamurfi@gmail.com
Tel 086-2326851

Saint Bricin's Hospital
Infirmary Road, Dublin 7
Tel 01-8042637
Rev Seamus Madigan HCF

Sarsfield Barracks
Limerick
Tel 087-6381489
Rev Piotr Delimat CF
Email pieetro@wp.pl

James Stephens Barracks
Kilkenny
Tel 056-7772015
Rev Dan McCarthy CF
Tel 086-8575155
Email danielmaccarthy@icloud.com

International Military Pilgrimage to Lourdes (Pèlerinage Militaire International)
Director: Rev Seamus Madigan HCF
Defence Forces Headquarters,
McKee Barracks, Blackhorse Avenue,
Dublin 7
Tel 01-8042637

Substitute Chaplain
Tel 087-2511488
Rev David Murphy CF
Email revcorporal@gmail.com

CHAPLAINS

BRITAIN

Irish Chaplaincy
52 Camden Square
London NW1 9XB
Tel 0044-2074825528
Fax 0044-2074824815
Email info@irishchaplaincy.org.uk
Trustees: Mr John Walsh (Chair),
Mgr Canon Tom Egan (Hon. Treasurer)

EUROPE

Brussels
Rev Michael Nicholas (OFM)
23/25 Oudstrijderslaan,
1950 Kraainem, Belgium
Tel 0032-2-7201970
Fax 0032-2-7255810

Copenhagen
Skt Annae Kirke, Hans Bogbinders Alle 2,
2300 Copenhagen S, Denmark
Tel 0045-31-582102

Lisbon
Rev Gus Champion
St Mary's, Rua do Murtal 368
San Pedro do Estoril
2765 Estoril, Portugal
Tel 00-351-1-4673771 *(Residence)*
Tel 00-351-1-4681676 *(Parish)*

Luxembourg
Rev Michael Cusack (CSsR)
European Parish, 34 Rue des Capucins,
Luxembourg BP 175
Tel 00352-470039 Fax 00352-220859

Munich
Rev Chetus Cohace
Landsberger Strasse 39,
80399 Munich, Germany
Email englischsprachige-
mission.muenchen@erzbistum-
muenchen.de
Tel 0049-89-5003580
Fax 0049-89-50035826
Website
www.englishspeking-mission-munic.de

Paris
Rev Tom Scanlon (CP)
Rev Anthony Behan (CP)
St Joseph's Church,
50 Avenue Hoche, 75008 Paris, France
Tel 0033-1-42272856
Fax 0033-1-42278649
Rev Sean Maher
Irish College, Paris, 5 Rue des Irlandais,
75005 Paris, France
Tel 0033-1-58521030 *(College)*
Email dechurley@eircom.net

Rome
Redentoristi, Via Merulana 31,
CP2458, Rome, Italy Tel 0039-6-494932
Email rgallagher@alfonsiana.edu

AUSTRALIA

Sydney
Rev Tom Devereux OMI
Parish of St Patrick's,
2 Wellington St, Bondi, NSW 2026
Tel 0061-02-93651195
Fax 0061-02-93654002
Mobile 0061-04-07347301
Email stpatbon@bigpond.net.au

CHAPLAINS

UNITED STATES OF AMERICA

Director: Rev Brendan McBride
Irish Immigration Pastoral Centre
5340 Geary Boulevard #206,
San Francisco, CA 94121
Tel 001-4157526006
Fax 001-4157526910
Email nationaloffice@usairish.org
Cellphone 001-4157609818
Administrator: Ms Geri M. Garvey
Irish Apostolate USA
1005 Downs Drive,
Silver Spring, MD 20904
Tel/Fax 001-3013843375
Email administrator@usairish.org

Boston
Irish Pastoral Centre
Executive Director: Sr Marguerite Kelly
953 Hancock Street,
Quincy, MA 02170
Tel 001-617-4797404
Fax 001-617-4790541
Email ipcboston@yahoo.com
Chaplain: Rev John McCarthy
15 Rita Road, Dorchester, MA 02124
Tel 001-617-4797404
Fax 001-617-4790541
Cellphone 001-617-4121331
Email jmccarthyipc@yahoo.com

Chicago
Chicago Irish Immigrant Support
Chaplain: Rev Michael Leonard
3525 S. Lake Park Avenue,
Chicago, IL 60653
Tel 312-5348445
Fax 312-5348446
Email irishoverhere@sbcglobal.net
Website www.ci-is.com

Ocean City, Maryland
(Open June–September)
Irish Student Outreach
Co-ordinator: William Ferguson
13701 Sailing Rd, Ocean City, MD 21842
Tel 001-410-2500362
001-443-7837893
Email wfergus4@aol.com

Milwaukee
Irish Immigrant Service of Milwaukee
John Gleeson, 2133 Wisconsin Ave,
Milwaukee, WI 53233-1910
Tel 001-414-3458800
Email gleeson@uwm.edu
Website www.ichc.net

New York
Project Irish Outreach
Co-ordinator: Patricia O'Callaghan
1011 First Avenue, New York NY 10022
Tel 001-212-3171011
Fax 001-212-7551526
Email patricia.ocallaghan@archny.org

Aisling Irish Community Centre
990 McLean Avenue, Yonkers, NY 10704
Chaplain: Sr Christine Hennessey
Tel 001-914-2375121
Fax 001-914-2375172
Email Sr.Christine.Hennessy@archny.org,
aislingirishcc@mindspring.com
Website www.aislingirishcenter.org

Philadelphia
Philadelphia Immigration Resource Centre
Executive Director: Siobhan Lyons
7 South Cedar Lane
Upper Darby, PA 19082 2816
Tel 001-610-7896355 Fax 001-7896352
Email irishimmigration@aol.com
Website www.irishimmigrants.org

San Diego
Irish Outreach San Diego Inc.
Bernadette Cashmann
2725 Congress Street 2G,
San Diego, CA 92110
Tel 001-619-2911630
Email irishsd@sbcglobal.net
Website www.irishoutreachsd.org

San Francisco
Irish Immigration Pastoral Centre
Celine Kennelly
5340 Geary Boulevard #206,
San Francisco, CA 94121
Tel 001-415-7526006
Fax 001-415-7526910
Email iipc@pacbell.net
Website www.sfiipc.org
Cellphone 001-415-7605762

Seattle
Seattle Immigration Support Group
Chairman: James Cummins
5819 St Andrews Drive, Mukileto,
WA 98275
Tel 001-425-2445147
Email siisg@irishclub.org

GENERAL INFORMATION

OBITUARY LIST

Beata mortui qui in Domino moriuntur
Rv 14:13

PRIESTS AND BROTHERS

Arthure, Robert (Waterford & Lismore) 27 April 2021
Bennett, Terry (SSC) 12 November 2020
Bohan, James P. (SPS) 20 December 2020
Boyle, Liam (Limerick) 2 December 2021
Boylan, Noel (Kilmore) 15 June 2021
Boyle, Michael (SMA) 17 February 2021
Brady, Edward (White Fathers) 11 July 2021
Breen, Albert (OCarm) 25 August 2021
Browne, Raymond (Elphin) 25 November 2020
Burke, Christopher (CSSp) 23 January 2021
Burke, Daniel (Don) (SMA) 31 March 2021
Burke, Edward (OFM) 12 August 2021
Byrne, James A. (SPS) 7 September 2021
Byrne, Martin (Ferns) 13 October 2021
Caffery, Frank (CSSp) 14 April 2020
Callaghan, Kevin (CFC) 12 May 2021
Campion, Seamus (CSsR) 15 June 2021
Caputo, Sal (SSC) 16 November 2020
Carlin, Neal (Derry) 6 August 2021
Carr, Frank (SSC) 28 July 2021
Carroll, Gerard (Ardagh & Clonmacnois) 5 July 2021
Carroll, William (OSCam) 3 June 2021
Casey, John (CSsR) 14 January 2021
Casey, Patrick (Meath) 3 June 2021
Cassidy, Eoin (Dublin) 10 March 2021
Cassin, James (Ossory) 5 June 2020
Clarke, Eugene (Kilmore) 1 January 2021
Cleary, Michael J. (CSSp) 3 September 2020
Collins, Peter Seamus (OP) 21 October 2020
Commins, Cormac (FSP) 22 December 2020
Condon, Kevin (OP) 14 June 2021
Connolly, Diarmuid (Dublin) 20 November 2020
Cooney, Tom (OSA) 27 June 2021
Corkery, Jackie (Cloyne) 20 August 2021
Corr, Anthony (Dromore) 6 June 2021
Corry, James (CSSp) 10 April 2020
Cox, Noel (CSSp) 15 March 2020
Coyle, Harry (Armagh) 18 April 2021
Cronin, Con (SPS, Cork & Ross) 3 August 2021
Cronin, Peter (SSC) 10 July 2021
Crotty, Fintan Gerard (SSCC) 6 January 2021
Crotty, Oliver (Dublin) 4 September 2021
Crowley, Michael (Cork & Ross) 27 January 2021
Culloty, Tom (Galway) 29 July 2021
Cunningham, Colum (CSSp) 1 April 2020
Cunningham, Sean (OP) 13 June 2021
Cunningham, Tom (CSSp) 29 January 2021
Daly, Michael V. (Meath) 11 March 2021
Darragh, Anthony (CSSp) 28 January 2021
Davies, Anthony (Dromore) 19 January 2021
Delaney, James (CSSp) 28 January 2021
Denny, Martin (CP) 11 July 2021
Dillon, Michael (SPS) 7 February 2021
Dollard, James (Ossory) 24 February 2020
Donnelly, John (Killaloe) 9 May 2021
Donovan, Patrick (CSSp) 30 January 2021
Doyle, Eamonn (CFC) 24 November 2020
Doyle, James (Kildare & Leighlin) 23 October 2020
Doyle, John A. (Seán) (CSSp) 3 April 2021
Duggan, John (Ossory) 4 November 2021
Dulaine, Connla (SJ) 10 January 2021
Fallon, John (Tuam) 9 April 2021
Farrington, Ambrose (OCSO) 16 January 2021
Fegan, James (SMA) 9 November 2020
Ferrie, Frank (SSC) 9 November 2020
Fitzpatrick, Bernard (Kilmore) 30 April 2021
Flannery, Peter (CSsR) 13 November 2020
Flynn, Joe (SPS) 19 January 2021
Fogarty, Declan (OSA) 8 January 2021
Foley, Gerard (CSSp) 26 August 2021
Foley, Joseph (Limerick) 20 August 2021
Gallagher, Colm (Dublin) 17 April 2021
Galvin, Gerard (Cork & Ross) 13 October 2021
Galvin, Séamus (CSSp) 9 April 2020
Gaynor, Patrick (Kildare & Leighlin) 26 April 2021
Gildea, Seán (OFM) 11 June 2021
Grimes, Edward (CSSp) 15 April 2020
Hand, John (SM) 16 March 2021
Harrington, Michael (Cloyne) 29 June 2021
Hartley, Noel (Ferns) 1 January 2021
Heagney, Michael (CSsR) 8 January 2021
Heeran, Brendan (CSSp) 26 January 2021
Heffernan, John (OP) 8 January 2021
Herlihy, Cornelius (OFM Cap) 2 January 2021
Houlihan, Henry (OFM) 22 January 2021
Hughes, Bernard (IC) 10 October 2020
Jones, Bernard (OFM) 26 May 2021
Joyce, Michael (Achonry) 15 March 2021
Kane, Andrew (OP) 2 June 2021
Kane, Michael (SPS) 19 August 2021
Kavanagh, Dermot (CSSp) 8 January 2021
Kearney, Stephen (Derry) 13 November 2020
Keating Crispin (OFM) 1 February 2021
Keating, Denis (OP) 12 July 2021
Kelly, Edward (Galway) 29 May 2021
Kelly, Patrick (SPS) 30 October 2020
Kelly, Robert (OCSO) 26 January 2021
Kenny, Michael (Tuam) 16 January 2021
Kenny, Paul (SSC) 29 June 2021
Kilcoyne, Colm (Tuam) 15 October 2020
Kirwan, Pius Joseph (OSA) 14 November 2020
Lagan, Francis (Derry) 9 June 2020
Lalor, John (Ossory) 19 February 2020
Lambe, Jeremiah (CSSp) 17 June 2021
Lumsden, David (Dublin) 31 August 2020
MacMahon, James Ardle (Dublin) 6 May 2021
Mauric, William P. (SPS) 6 April 2021
McAteer, Thomas (Dromore) 12 September 2021
McCaffrey, Eugene (OCD) 8 September 2021
McCarrick, Roger (SM) 16 October 2020

OBITUARY LIST

McCarthy, Florence (SDB) 20 January 2021
McCaughey, Vincent (CP) 30 July 2021
McDonagh, Enda (Tuam) 24 February 2021
McDonnell, James (CSSp) 12 April 2020
McDonnell, Thomas (CFC) 11 May 2021
McElhatton, Frank (SPS) 24 November 2020
McGarry, Leo (CSSp) 14 January 2021
McGauran, Francis (Elphin) 10 September 2021
McGee, Brendan (Down & Connor) 9 February 2021
McGeough, Thomas (Armagh) 25 January 2021
McGhee, Patrick (CSSp) 12 March 2021
McGillicuddy, Cornelius (Dublin) 10 July 2021
McGoldrick, Patrick (Derry) 16 December 2020
McGovern, Patrick (CFC) 10 August 2021
McHugh, James (OSCam) 31 May 2021
McKeever, Joseph (Armagh) 23 January 2021
McKiernan, Fintan (Kilmore) 21 April 2021
McLaughlin, Pat (CSsR) 14 July 2021
McLoughlin, Joseph (CSsR) 29 November 2020
McLoughlin, Timothy (SSS) 21 September 2020
McNamara, Leslie (Limerick) 5 February 2021
McQuillan, Ignatius (Derry) 20 August 2021
Moran, John (SSC) 11 June 2021
Mortell, Tony (SSC) 20 November 2020
Mullan, Aidan (Derry) 9 September 2021
Mullan, Michael (Derry) 25 December 2020
Mullan, Patsy (Derry) 2 September 2021
Murphy, Brendan (Limerick) 10 October 2020
Murphy, James (CSsR) 31 March 2021
Murphy, John (OSA) 21 November 2020
Murphy, Martin (SSC) 12 December 2020
Norton, Michael (Ossory) 11 November 2021
Nyland, Patrick Joseph (SDB) 11 August 2021
Ó Dálaigh, Micheál (Cork & Ross) 5 October 2021
Ó Dúláine, Connla (SJ) 10 January 2021
Ó hIceadha, Tomás (Kerry) 12 April 2021
O'Brien, Brendan (CSSp) 17 June 2021
O'Brien, Christopher (Armagh) 14 August 2021
O'Brien, Donal (Cloyne) 7 July 2021
O'Brien, Pat (Tuam) 21 November 2021
O'Brien, Valentine (CSSp) 15 February 2021
O'Carroll, Caimin (Killaloe) 3 November 2021
O'Connell, Patrick (CSsR) 13 January 2021
O'Connor, Dermot (CSsR) 15 August 2021
O'Connor, Erill (Dublin) 29 April 2021
O'Donnell, Brian (Derry) 25 May 2021
O'Donnell, Terence (IC) 14 July 2021
O'Donoghue, James (Waterford & Lismore) 17 February 2020
O'Driscoll, Liam (Cork & Ross) 7 October 2021
O'Farrell, Anthony (CSSp) 9 May 2020
O'Grady, Nicholas (CP) 11 May 2021
O'Laoghaire, Seán (Jack) (Kildare & Leighlin) 14 August 2021
O'Leary, John (Armagh) 27 October 2020
O'Mahony, Brendan (OFM Cap) 14 September 2020
O'Mahony, George (Cork & Ross) 10 June 2021
O'Reilly, Patrick M. (SPS) 4 April 2021
O'Rourke, Charles (SSC) 6 November 2020
O'Rourke, John Joe (Cashel & Emly) 23 July 2021
O'Rourke, Kevin (SSC) 23 October 2020
O'Sullivan, Paul (OCD) 12 February 2021
O'Toole, Brian (CSSp) 1 November 2020
Olden, Michael (Waterford & Lismore) 30 August 2021
Peters, James (CSSp) 27 January 2021
Rafferty, Thomas (MHM) 9 May 2021
Reedy, Patrick (CSSp) 31 January 2021
Regan, Christy (OFM) 14 May 2021
Ruddy, Joseph (MSC) 18 July 2021
Ryan, Liam (Cashel & Emly) 23 April 2021
Seery, Michael (Armagh) 14 January 2021
Sheedy, Michael (Killaloe) 2 November 2021
Sheehan, Joseph (CSSp) 21 August 2020
Silke, Leo (SMA) 16 April 2021
Slattery, Gabriel (Dublin) 18 June 2021
Smith, Kevin (OPraem) 28 January 2021
Smyth, Brendan (CSSp) 12 April 2020
Stack, Thomas (Dublin) 27 December 2020
Tallon, Edward (CFC) 5 October 2020
Talty, Robert (OP) 27 September 2020
Tarpey, Richard (Galway) 28 February 2021
Timmins, Thomas (CSSp) 18 July 2020
Tuohy, Thomas (SM) 10 July 2021
Turner, Alberic (OCSO) 15 February 2021
Wadding, George (CSsR) 24 August 2021
Walsh, Thomas (SSC) 17 March 2021
Ward, Conor (Dublin) 18 July 2021
Webster, George (SSC) 29 December 2020
Wilmsen, Jerry (SSC) 6 April 2021

SISTERS

Adigo, Fidelia (MMM) 13 June 2021
Amadi, Patricia (MMM) 6 December 2020
Beggar, Brigid Nuala (Salesian Sisters of St John Bosco) 15 October 2020
Bird, Breda (Missionary Sisters of the Holy Rosary) 18 April 2021
Blewitt, Brigid (Sisters of Mercy) 30 January 2021
Brady, Elizabeth (Sisters of Mercy) 3 March 2021
Breslin, Finbarr (Sisters of Mercy) 7 November 2020
Buckley, Catherine Mary (Presentation Sisters) 1 February 2021
Byrne, Annette (Our Lady of the Cenacle) 16 February 2021
Byrne, Patricia (St Joseph of Cluny Sisters) 14 March 2021
Carroll, Mary (LSA) 4 January 2020
Carroll, Elizabeth (LCM) 21 June 2021
Cassidy, Veronica (Sisters of Mercy) 7 August 2021
Caulfield, Nora (Sisters of Mercy) 18 April 2021
Chambers, Nora (Missionary Sisters of the Holy Rosary) 9 October 2020
Clancy, Brídín (Senan) (Brigidine) 17 January 2021
Clancy, Phyl (Sisters of Mercy) 22 February 2021
Clark, Rose Imelda (Dominican Sisters) 20 August 2021
Coffey, Anne (Presentation Sisters) 25 October 2020
Collins, Angelique (Bon Secours Sisters) 8 October 2020
Connolly, Teresa (MMM) 26 October 2020
Conway, Nuala (Sisters of Mercy) 27 July 2021
Corkery, Rupert (Presentation Sisters) 20 May 2021
Coughlan, Teresa (OLCGS) 16 May 2021
Culhane, Rita (LCM) 21 January 2021
Cullen, Rosarii (LCM) 18 April 2021

OBITUARY LIST

Cunningham, Lucy (Daughters of Charity) 14 January 2021
Curtin, Anne (MMM) 5 December 2020
Daly, Mary Hilary (Society of the Holy Child Jesus) 21 December 2020
Davis, Sally (MMM) 14 November 2020
Daye, Anne (Presentation Sisters) 9 July 2021
Delaney, M. Catherine (Carmelite) 27 February 2021
Dempsey, Angela (Sisters of Mercy) 30 December 2020
Dempsey, Una (Dominican Sisters) 26 April 2021
Devitt, Raphael (Perpetual Adoration Sisters) 13 March 2021
Donnellan, Cecilia (Sisters of Mercy) 22 January 2021
Donnelly, Maura (Sacred Heart Society) 2 March 2021
Doran, Mary (Daughters of Charity) 4 May 2021
Doyle, Helena Josephine (Lena) (Franciscan Missionary Sisters for Africa) 11 July 2021
Dromey, Elizabeth Rose (Discalced Carmelite) 16 April 2021
Duffy, Jerome (Sisters of Mercy) 13 September 2021
Duggan, Laurence Mary (Bon Secours Sisters) 18 September 2021
Dunne, Anne (Presentation Sisters) 5 April 2021
Egan, Brigid (Presentation Sisters) 21 November 2020
Egan, Eileen (Sisters of Mercy) 1 June 2021
Eivers, Mai (Sisters of Mercy) 25 March 2021
Farquharson, Barbara (Sacred Heart Society) 27 November 2020
Farragher, May (Sisters of Mercy) 13 May 2021
Fennell, Rita (Sisters of Mercy) 30 June 2021
Fennelly, Noreen May (Presentation Sisters) 23 August 2021
Ferriter, Cora (Sisters of Mercy) 8 April 2021
Fitzgerald, Alexis (Presentation Sisters) 27 May 2021
Fitzgibbon, Teresa Philomena (Bon Secours Sisters) 4 May 2021
Flynn, Bernadette (Sisters of Our Lady of Apostles) 4 January 2021
Flynn, Mary (Presentation Sisters) 9 January 2021
Fortune, Mary Brigid (Presentation Sisters) 2 February 2021
Gillen, Brigid (Dominican Sisters) 13 January 2021
Gleeson, Catherine Bernadette (Presentation Sisters) 1 November 2020
Griffin, John Bosco (Sisters of Mercy) 7 July 2021
Halpin, Theophane (St Joseph of Cluny Sisters) 21 August 2021
Harrington, Patricia (Sisters of Mercy) 13 November 2020
Hayden, Mairéad (Daughters of Charity) 28 December 2020
Healy, Mary Martin (Sisters of Our Lady of Apostles) 13 November 2020
Hegarty, Eibhlín (Dominican Sisters) 27 November 2020
Hendron, Kathleen Brigid (Presentation Sisters) 18 January 2021
Hennessy, Gregory (Bon Secours Sisters) 6 February 2021
Hickey, Maureen (Franciscan Missionary Sisters for Africa) 16 March 2021
Hilliard, Fidelis (Missionary Sisters of the Holy Rosary) 28 June 2021
Holohan, Teresa (Presentation Sisters) 2 September 2021
Horgan, de Sales (Presentation Sisters) 4 April 2021
Howard, Stella (IBVM) 19 October 2020
Hughes, Marian Corona (Sisters of Mercy) 18 April 2021
Hurley, Eileen (Missionary Sisters of the Assumption) 2 May 2021
Hutton, Joseph Dolores (Discalced Carmelite) 20 February 2021
Johns, M. Winefride (Sisters of St Clare) 15 April 2021
Keane, Catherine (Sisters of Nazareth) 5 September 2021
Kearney, Sheila (Sisters of Mercy) 13 January 2021
Keary, Mary Jane (Presentation Sisters) 9 July 2021
Kelly, Bridget (Dominican Sisters) 23 July 2021
Kelly, Philomena (Sisters of Mercy) 20 August 2021
Kenny, Inez (Marist Sisters) 3 August 2021
Kenny, Regina (Sisters of Mercy) 3 March 2021
Kett, Maria (FMDM) 11 June 2021
Kilroy, Perpetua (Sisters of Mercy) 7 March 2021
Kinane, Kathleen (Presentation Sisters) 3 September 2021
Lacey, Kathleen (Sisters of Mercy) 15 October 2020
Lamont, Ethel (Sacred Heart Society) 1 November 2020
Lawlor, Anne (Presentation Sisters) 12 November 2020
Lee, M. Cecilia (Carmelite) 22 August 2021
Loftus, Pauline (Sisters of Mercy) 10 November 2020
Looby, Edmund (Dominican Sisters) 14 July 2021
Loughran, Monica (Sisters of Mercy) 6 December 2020
Lynch, Bernard (Sisters of Mercy) 5 October 2020
Lynch, Goretti (Missionary Sisters of the Holy Rosary) 15 February 2021
Lynch, M. Eugene (Sisters of St Clare) 11 December 2020
Lyne, Genevieve (Presentation Sisters) 3 April 2021
MacCurtain, Margaret (Dominican Sisters) 5 October 2020
Madden, Mary Bernadette (Presentation Sisters) 13 February 2021
Malone, M. Anne (Carmelite) 6 June 2021
Marmion, Maria Goretti (Sisters of St Clare) 7 January 2021
Mascarenhas, Bernadette (Daughters of the Cross of Liège) 17 January 2021
McAuliffe, Sheila (Sacred Heart Society) 28 August 2021
McCarthy, Kathleen (Presentation Sisters) 21 August 2021
McCarthy, Nora Agatha (Presentation Sisters) 21 January 2021
McCaver, Elizabeth (Sisters of Mercy) 14 August 2021
McClory, Annunciata (Sisters of Mercy) 14 July 2021
McCormick, Luarena (Sisters of Mercy) 29 July 2021
McElroy, Monique Kathleen (Little Sister of the Poor) 30 April 2021
McEvoy, Teresa (Dominican Sisters) 20 August 2021
McFadden, Joan (OLCGS) 21 December 2020
McGrath, Jacinta (Bon Secours Sisters) 20 January 2021
McGrath, Patricia (Dominican Sisters) 28 June 2021
McGuinness, Brigid Jane (Marist Sisters) 25 February 2021
McGuire, Anne Marie (Blessed Sacrament Sisters) 24 August 2021
McInerney, Clare (LCM) 4 February 2021
McKenna, Anita (Sisters of Mercy) 13 March 2021
McKenna, Dympna (Missionary Sisters of the Holy Rosary) 14 March 2021
McLoughlin, Peggy (St Joseph of Cluny Sisters) 23 July 2021

McNamara, Anne (Salesian Sisters of St John Bosco) 9 May 2021
Meagher, Mary Teresa (Presentation Sisters) 23 February 2021
Minogue, Maria (OLCGS) 28 October 2020
Morgan, Mary (Sisters of Nazareth) 9 April 2021
Morton, Elizabeth (Sisters of Mercy) 7 May 2021
Morton, Ellen (Sisters of Mercy) 8 February 2021
Mullen, Vianney (Sisters of Mercy) 29 October 2020
Mulligan, M. Bridget (Sisters of St Clare) 24 January 2021
Murphy, Agnus (Dominican Sisters) 20 August 2021
Murphy, Marie (Presentation Sisters) 1 May 2021
Murray, Clare (LSA) 15 October 2020
Murray, Clement (Sisters of Mercy) 20 April 2021
Murray, Mairéad (Sisters of Mercy) 24 March 2021
Murray, Mary (LSA) 2 November 2020
Normoyle, Ethel (LCM) 16 August 2021
O'Brien, Breda (Sisters of Nazareth) 5 March 2021
O'Brien, Brigid (Daughters of Charity) 10 May 2021
O'Brien, Claire (Dominican Sisters) 23 October 2020
O'Brien, Deirdre (Sacred Heart Society) 5 March 2021
O'Brien, Margaret Mary (Presentation Sisters) 9 June 2021
O'Byrne, Ellen Mary (Presentation Sisters) 29 July 2021
O'Connell, Angela (Sisters of Mercy) 31 August 2021
O'Connell, Teresa (Sisters of Mercy) 9 May 2021
O'Connor, Áine (Sisters of Mercy) 8 February 2021
O'Connor, Mary (Sisters of Mercy) 3 March 2021
O'Donnell, Enda (Sisters of Mercy) 9 February 2021
O'Farrell, M. Malachy (Sisters of St Clare) 29 November 2020
O'Keeffe, Majella (Sisters of Mercy) 14 October 2020
O'Leary, Anne (Presentation Sisters) 26 January 2021
O'Neill, Anna Maria (Poor Clares) 23 December 2020
O'Neill, Bridie (Daughters of Charity) 31 March 2021
O'Regan, Ursula (LSA) 24 September 2020
O'Reilly, Carmel (Sisters of Mercy) 27 June 2021
O'Sullivan, Ann (Sisters of Mercy) 17 October 2020
O'Sullivan, Mary Catherine (Sisters of Our Lady of Apostles) 15 January 2021
Parlon, Celsus (Bon Secours Sisters) 30 August 2021
Pender, Ellen (Presentation Sisters) 20 November 2020
Phelan, Louise (Sisters of Mercy) 27 February 2021
Power, Angela (Sisters of Mercy) 22 July 2021
Power, Henrietta (Sisters of Our Lady of Apostles) 30 November 2020
Raftery, Ellen Elizabeth (Bon Secours Sisters) 6 September 2021
Ramsbottom, Elizabeth Anne (Presentation Sisters) 4 February 2021
Reilly, Assumpta (Sisters of Mercy) 15 October 2020
Reilly, Imelda (St Joseph of Cluny Sisters) 4 February 2021
Roche, Brigid (Sisters of Mercy) 12 May 2021
Roche, Frances (OLCGS) 18 December 2020
Roe, Patricia (Presentation Sisters) 11 October 2020
Ryan, Breda (Brigidine) 15 February 2021
Ryan, Goretti Gabriel (Bon Secours Sisters) 25 May 2021
Ryan, Mary (Sisters of Mercy) 5 November 2020
Ryan, Rita (Sisters of Mercy) 14 February 2021
Ryder, Margaret (Daughters of Charity) 6 October 2020
Sands, Maoil Iosa (Sisters of Mercy) 25 July 2021
Scanlon, Scholastica (Presentation Sisters) 13 December 2020
Sheahan, Michael Nora (Redemptoristines) 19 June 2021
Sheridan, Augustine (MMM) 17 November 2020
Sherlock, Bridget (Sisters of Mercy) 13 April 2021
Shine, Maura (Missionary Sisters of the Holy Rosary) 26 December 2020
Somers, Hanoria Elizabeth (Presentation Sisters) 15 November 2020
Stakelum, Imelda (Sisters of Mercy) 21 October 2020
Sullivan, Margaret Irene (Presentation Sisters) 23 February 2021
Tarpey, Jo (Sisters of Mercy) 18 October 2020
Thomas, Ann (LSA) 10 October 2020
Treacy, Marie (Sisters of Our Lady of Apostles) 19 February 2021
Troy, Michaela (FMDM) 26 April 2021
Twomey, Concepta (Sisters of Mercy) 21 May 2021
Walker, Betty (Sacred Heart Society) 7 March 2021
Walsh, Annie Josephine (Presentation Sisters) 6 February 2021
Whelan, Nora Bridget (Presentation Sisters) 9 April 2021
Williams, Mary B. (Sisters of Mercy) 1 June 2021

ORDINATIONS

Acton, John Gerard (Galway) 1 August 2021
Casey, Damian (OFM) 24 April 2021
Dineen, John (OCSO) 26 September 2021
González-Borrallo, Juan Jesus (Armagh) 29 June 2021
Holovlasky, Ryan (CSSR) 5 September 2021
Mahony, John (Elphin) 8 December 2020
McEneaney, John (Waterford & Lismore) 24 October 2021
Pasalic, Antun (Killaloe) 8 September 2021 (Deacon)
Shields, Stephen (OSA) 25 July 2021 (Deacon)
Young, Callum (Armagh) 29 June 2021

IRISH COUNCIL OF CHURCHES

Irish Council of Churches
President: Very Rev Dr Ivan Patterson
Vice-President: Rt Rev Andrew Forster

Inter-Church Centre
48 Elmwood Avenue, Belfast BT9 6AZ
Tel 028-90663145
Email info@irishchurches.org
Website www.irishchurches.org
General Secretary: Dr N. Brady

Member Churches of Council
Antiochian Orthodox Church in Ireland; Church of Ireland; Greek Orthodox Church in Ireland; Lutheran Church in Ireland; Methodist Church in Ireland; Moravian Church, Irish District; Non-Subscribing Presbyterian Church in Ireland; Presbyterian Church in Ireland; Religious Society of Friends; Cherubim and Seraphim Church; Romanian Orthodox Church in Ireland; Salvation Army (Ireland Division); Redeemed Christian Church of God; Indian Orthodox Church; Syrian Orthodox Church

Leaders of Member Churches
Antiochian Orthodox Church in Ireland
Mr William Hunter (Sec to St Ignatius the God-bearer of Antioch Parish, Belfast)
Antiochian Orthodox Church,
8 Wheatfield Gardens, Belfast BT14 7HU
Tel 028-90712523

Church of Ireland
Most Rev John McDowell
Archbishop of Armagh, Primate of All Ireland, Church House, 46 Abbey Street, Armagh BT61 7DZ
Tel 028-37527144
Email archbishop@armagh.anglican.org

Greek Orthodox Church
Church of the Annunciation
46 Arbour Hill, Dublin 7
Rev Fr Tom Carroll PP
Moneygall, Roscrea, Co Tipperary
Tel 0505-45849/086-2394539
Email fr.tomcarroll@gmail.com
Contact Person
Rev Fr Tom Carroll PP

Lutheran Church in Ireland
Lutherhaus,
24 Adelaide Road, Dublin 2
Tel 01-6766548
Pastor: Stephan Arras
Email info@lutheran-ireland.org
Website www.lutheran-ireland.org

Methodist Church in Ireland
President: Rev T. H. Samuel McGuffin
'Wesley House', 34 Dalewood,
Newtownabbey, Co Antrim BT36 5WR
Secretary: Rev Dr Heather M. E. Morris
Edge Hill House, 9 Lennoxvale,
Belfast BT9 5BY
Tel 028-90767969

Moravian Church, Irish District
Rev Sarah Groves, Chairman
Moravian Church, Irish District,
25 Church Road, Gracehill,
Ballymena BT42 2NL
Email sarah.groves@moravian.org.uk

Non-Subscribing Presbyterian Church
Moderator: Right Rev Christopher Hudson
20 Myrtlefield Manor, Belfast BT9 6NE
Tel 028-90663830/079-69059993
Email minister@allsoulsbelfast.org
Clerk: Very Rev Robert A. McKee
10 Dalwass Bawn Road, Carrickfergus,
Co Antrim BT38 9BY
Tel 028-93372257/078-77631737
Email clerkofnspci@gmail.com
Rev Dr Heather Catherine Walker *(Editor, Non-Subscribing Presbyterian Magazine)*
6 Love Lane, Carrickfergus BT38 8SL
Tel 079-03803391/028-93365482
Email hwalker.research@gmail.com
Clerk of the Presbytery of Antrim
Rev Dr J. W. Nelson
102 Carrickfergus Road,
Larne, Co Antrim BT40 3JX
Tel 028-28272600
Clerk of the Presbytery of Bangor
Rev Brian Moodie
33 Beechgrove, Dromore,
Co Down BT25 1BS
Tel 074-27662828
Email deomorensp@gmail.com
Clerk of the Synod of Munster
Rev Simon Henning
61 Beechfield Crescent, Bangor BT19 7ZJ
Tel 077-40362093
Email simon.henning@hotmail.co.uk

Presbyterian Church in Ireland
Right Rev Dr David Bruce
Moderator, c/o Assembly Buildings,
Fisherwick Place, Belfast BT1 6DW
Tel 028-90322284 Fax 028-90417301
Email moderator@presbyterianireland.org
Rev Trevor D. Gribben, Clerk
Assembly Buildings, Belfast BT1 6DW
Tel 028-90417208 Fax 028-90417301
Email clerk@presbyterianireland.org

Religious Society of Friends
Denise C. Gabuzda
Clerk of Yearly Meeting
For information contact
Mary F. McNeilly
National Administrative Office,
Quaker House Dublin,
Stocking Lane, Dublin D16 V3F8
Tel 01-4998003
Email office@quakers.ie

Rock of Ages Cherubim & Seraphim Church in Ireland
Mother Cherub Prophetess Agnes Oluyinka Olushoo-Aderanti
Rock of Ages Cherubim & Seraphim Church, 46 Priory Gate, Athboy, Co Meath
Tel 086-8134747/087-9727699
Email rockofagescs@hotmail.com
Website rockofagescs@hotmail.com

Romanian Orthodox Church in Ireland
Romanian Orthodox Parish of the Exaltation of the Holy Cross,
Christ Church, Leeson Park, Dublin 6
Dean: Fr Calin Florea
St John the Baptist Missionary & Cultural Centre, Drimnagh Castle, Dublin 12
Tel 087-6148140
Email revcalin.florea@gmail. com

Salvation Army
Colonel Neil Webb
Divisional Commander,
Divisional Headquarters, 12 Station Mews, Sydenham, Belfast BT4 1TL
Tel 028-90675000
Email neil.webb@salvationarmy.org.uk
Major Eleanor Haddick
Dublin Chaplain
Tel 01-8476415
Email eleanor.haddick@salvationarmy.ie

IRISH COUNCIL OF CHURCHES

ANTIOCHIAN ORTHODOX CHURCH IN IRELAND

Dublin
Rev Fr John Hickey PP
Tel 086-7913689
Email hickeyjohnp@gmail.com
Parish of the Three Patrons
(Ss Patrick, Columba and Bridget)
Worshipping @ 7 Grange Terrace,
Deansgrange, Blackrock, Co Dublin

Tralee
Parish of the 'Pantanassa'
Worshipping @ Collis Sandes House,
Tralee, Co Kerry

Belfast
Fr John Hickey and Fr Gregory Hoban
Parish of St Ignatius the God-bearer of Antioch
Worshipping at Belfast Central Mission,
3rd Floor, Grosvenor House,
Belfast BT12 5AD
Mr William Hunter (Secretary to Parish of St Ignatius, Belfast)
8 Wheatfield Gardens, Belfast BT14 7HU
Tel 028-90712523

CHURCH OF IRELAND ARCHBISHOPS AND BISHOPS

Armagh
Most Rev John McDowell
Archbishop of Armagh, Primate of All Ireland and Metropolitan,
Church House, 46 Abbey Street,
Armagh BT61 7DZ
Tel 028-37527144
Email archbishop@armagh.anglican.org
Diocesan Secretary: Mrs J. Leighton
Church House, 46 Abbey Street,
Armagh BT61 7DZ
Tel 028-37522858
Email secretary@armagh.anglican.org

Dublin and Glendalough
Most Rev Dr M.G. St A. Jackson MA, PhD, DPhil
Archbishop of Dublin, Bishop of Glendalough, Primate of Ireland and Metropolitan, Church of Ireland House,
Church Avenue, Rathmines, Dublin 6
Tel 01-4125663
Email archbishop@dublin.anglican.org
Diocesan Secretary: Mrs S. Heggie
Diocesan Office, Church of Ireland House,
Church Avenue, Rathmines, Dublin 6
Tel 01-4966981
Email secretary@dublin.anglican.org

Meath and Kildare
Most Rev P.L. Storey MA(Hons), BTh
Bishop of Meath and Kildare,
Bishop's House, Moyglare,
Maynooth, Co Kildare
Tel 01-6289825
Email bishop@meath.anglican.org
Diocesan Secretary: Mrs K. Seaman
Meath & Kildare Diocesan Centre
Moyglare, Maynooth, Co Kildare
Tel 01-6292163
office@meath.anglican.org

Cashel, Ferns and Ossory
Rt Rev M.A.J. Burrows MA, MLitt, Prof.Dip.Th
Bishop of Cashel, Ferns and Ossory,
Bishop's House, Troysgate, Kilkenny
Tel 056-7786633
Email cfobishop@gmail.com
Diocesan Secretary: Ms Elizabeth Keyes
The Diocesan Office,
The Palace Coach House, Church Lane,
Kilkenny R95 A032
Tel 056-7761910
Mon-Fri 10.00 am-2.30 pm
Email palacecoachhouse@gmail.com
Assistant Diocesan Secretary
Ms Rita Cammaer
Email cfo.asec@gmail.com

Down and Dromore
Rt Rev David McClay BTh, MA
Bishop of Down and Dromore,
Church of Ireland House,
61-67 Donegall Street, Belfast BT1 2QH
Tel: 028-90828850
Email bishop@downdromorediocese.org
Diocesan Secretary: Mr R. Lawther
Diocesan Office, Church of Ireland House,
61-67 Donegall Street, Belfast BT1 2QH
Tel 028-90828830
Email rlawther@downdromorediocese.org

Derry and Raphoe
Rt Rev A. J. Forster BA (Hons), BTh
Bishop of Derry and Raphoe,
The See House, 112 Culmore Road,
Londonderry BT48 8JF
Tel 028-71377013
Email bishopsoffice@derryandraphoe.org
Diocesan Secretary
Mr G. Harkin
Diocesan Office, 24 London Street,
Londonderry BT48 6RQ
Tel 028-71262440
Email gavin@derryandraphoe.org

Limerick and Killaloe
Bishop of Limerick and Killaloe Vacant

Bishop's Secretary
Ms Anne Donegan
Email bishopsecretary@limerick.anglican.org
Office Hours: Tuesday, Wednesday and Thursday 9.30 am-1.00 pm
Diocesan Secretary
Mrs Lorna Sharpe
Kellysgrove, Ballinasloe, Galway
Tel 087-6130063
Email diocesansecretary@limerick.anglican.org

Tuam
Bishop of Tuam, Killala and Achonry Vacant

Diocesan Administrator
Mrs Heather Pope
11 Ros Ard, Cappagh Road,
Barna, Co Galway H91 XW9A
Tel 086-8336666
Email secretary@tuam.anglican.org

Clogher
Rt Rev Dr Ian W. Ellis BTh, BSc, PGCE, EdD
Bishop of Clogher, The See House,
152A Ballagh Road,
Co Tyrone BT75 0QP
Tel 028-89522461
Email bishop@clogher.anglican.org
Diocesan Secretary: Mr G. M. T. Moore
Clogher Diocesan Office,
St Macartin's Cathedral Hall, Hall's Lane,
Enniskillen, Co Fermanagh BT74 7DR
Tel 028-66347879
Email secretary@clogher.anglican.org

Cork
Rt Rev W.P. Colton BCL (Hons), DipTh, MPhil (Ecum), LL.M, PhD
Bishop of Cork, Cloyne and Ross,
St Nicholas' House, 14 Cove Street,
Cork T12 RP40
Tel 021-5005080
Email bishop@corkchurchofireland.com
Diocesan Secretary: Mr Billy Skuse
St Nicholas House, 14 Cove Street,
Cork T12 RP40
Tel 021-5005080 Fax 021-4320960
Email secretary@corkchurchofireland.com

Kilmore, Elphin and Ardagh
Rt Rev S.F. Glenfield MA, MTh, PhD
Bishop of Kilmore, Elphin and Ardagh,
The See House, Kilmore Upper,
Co Cavan
Tel 049-5559954
Diocesan Administrator: Mrs Sarah Taylor
Email dkeatreasurer@gmail.com
Diocesan Office, 20A Market Street,
Cootehill, Co Cavan
Tel 049-5559954
(From NI) 00353-49-5559954
Email office@kilmore.anglican.org

Connor
Rt Rev G. T. Davison BTh, BD
Bishop of Connor, Bishop's House,
27 Grange Road, Doagh,
Ballyclare BT39 0RQ
Tel 028-90828870 (office)
Email bishop@connor.anglican.org
Finance and Administration Manager
Mr R. Cotter
The Diocesan Office,
Church of Ireland House,
61-67 Donegall Street, Belfast BT1 2QH
Tel 028-90828830
Email richardcotter@connordiocese.org

GREEK ORTHODOX CHURCH IN IRELAND

Greek Orthodox Church of the Annunciation,
46 Arbour Hill, Dublin 7
Rev Tom Carroll PP
Monegall, Roscrea, Co Tipperary
Tel 0505-45849/086-2394539
Email fr.tomcarroll@gmail.com
Contact Person: Rev Tom Carroll PP

METHODIST CHURCH IN IRELAND

District Superintendents
Southern District
Rev Andrew J. Dougherty
Mayo House,
16 Meadowfield, Sandyford,
Dublin D18 HF80
North Eastern District
Rev W. Philip Agnew
1 Royal Lodge Road,
Belfast BT8 7UL
Tel 028-90402202
North Western District
Rev Dr Stephen F. Skuce
19 Derry Road, Strabane
Co Tyrone BT82 8DU

PRESBYTERIES OF THE PRESBYTERIAN CHURCH

Ards
Rev J.H. Flaherty
The Manse, 17 Ballywalter Road,
Millisle BT22 2HS
Email jflaherty@presbyterianireland.org

Armagh
Rev E.P. Gamble
'Greenfield Manse',
72 Newry Road, Armagh BT60 1ER
Tel 028-37525522
Email pgamble@presbyterianireland.org

Ballymena
Rev J.J. Andrews
1 Forthill Park, Ballymena BT42 2HL
Tel 028-25645544
Email jandrews@presbyterianireland.org

East Belfast
Rev Stephen Moore
234 Lower Braniel Road, Belfast BT5 7NJ
Tel 028-90795136
Email smoore@presbyterianireland.org

North Belfast
Mr T. Long OBE
12 Shinningdale Park North,
Belfast BT14 6RZ
Tel 028-90710012
Email taslong@hotmail.com

South Belfast
Rev M.S. Gault
15 Park Road, Belfast BT7 2FW
Tel 028-90642981
Email mgault@presbyterianireland.org

Carrickfergus
Rev Dr C.D. McClure
5 Whitla's Brae, Larne BT40 3BY
Tel 028-28272441
Email cmcclure@presbyterianireland.org

Coleraine and Limavady
Rev Dr T.J. McCormick
6 Garvagh Road, Kilrea,
Coleraine BT51 5QP
Tel 028-29540256
Email tmccormick@presbyterianireland.org

Derry and Donegal
Rev Paul Linkens
19 Clearwater, Caw,
Londonderry BT47 6BE
Tel 028-71311425
Email plinkens@presbyterianireland.org

Down
Rev D.M. Spratt
17 Downpatrick Road, Crossgar,
Downpatrick BT30 1EQ
Tel 028-44830041
Email iabraham@presbyterianireland.org

Dromore
Rt Rev Dr William J. Henry
47 Kesh Road, Maze,
Lisburn BT27 5RR
Tel 028-92621269
Email whenry@presbyterianireland.org

Dublin and Munster
Mr Stuart Ferguson
'Brianna', Ballyclough, Camolin,
Enniscorthy, Co Wexford
Tel 053-9383854
Email stuartfer@gmail.com

Iveagh
Rev G.E Best
28 Manse Road, Portadown,
Craigavon BT63 5NW
Tel 028-38831265
Email gbest@presbyterianireland.org

Monaghan
Rev D.T.R. Edwards
The Manse, Old Bridge Road,
Cootehill, Co Cavan
Tel 049-5555456
Email dedwards@presbyterianireland.org

Newry
Rev S.A. Finlay
156 Glassdrumman Road, Annalong,
Newry BT34 4QL
Tel 028-43768232
Email sfinlay@presbyterianireland.org

Omagh
Rev Robert Herron
10 Mullaghmenagh Avenue,
Omagh BT78 5QH
Tel 028-82243776
Email rherron@presbyterianireland.org

Route
Rev Noel McClean
Kilraughts Manse, 24 Topp Road,
Ballymoney BT53 8LT
Tel 074-69719000
Email nmcclean@presbyterianireland.org

Templepatrick
Rev D.J. Paul
50 Killead Road, Aldergrove,
Crumlin BT29 4EN
Tel 028-94422436
Email jmurdock@presbyterianireland.org

Tyrone
Rev T.J. Conway
29 Belvedere Park, Castlerock,
BT51 4XW
Tel 077-84105843
Email tconway@presbyterianireland.org

ROMANIAN ORTHODOX CHURCH IN IRELAND

www.mitropolia.eu

Parish of the Exaltation of the Holy Cross
Christ Church, Leeson Park, Dublin 6
www.romanianorthodox.ie

St Colman of Oughaval's Church
Stradbally Hall, Abbeyleix Road,
Stradbally, Co Laois
Fr Calin Florea
St John the Baptist Missionary & Cultural Centre, Drimnagh Castle, Longmile Road, Dublin 12
Tel 087-6148140
Email revcalin.florea@gmail.com
Fr Constantin Uncu
2 Charnwood Gardens,
Clonsilla, Dublin 15
Tel 087-2512101
Email uncu_expres@yahoo.com

Parish of St Columba
Hartstown Community Centre,
Hartstown Road, Dublin 15
www.bisericaortodoxadublin.com
Fr Raul Simion
Hartstown Community Centre,
Hartstown, Dublin 15
Tel 01-8131969/087-6394530
Email pr_simion@yahoo.com
Deacon Dragos Blanaru
24 Littlepace Close, Clonee, Dublin 11
Tel 086-6087652
Email dragosblanaru85@yahoo.com

Parish of the Annunciation & All Saints of Romania
52B Western Way, Broadstone, Dublin 7
www.bisericasfintiiromani.com
Rev Dr Irineu Craciun
38 Ardmore Crescent, Artane, Dublin 5
Tel 01-8474956
Email i.craciun@iolfree.ie
· Fr Petru Vlaic
Tel 086-3940784
Email petruioanvlaic@yahoo.com

IRISH COUNCIL OF CHURCHES

Romanian Orthodox Community (2nd & 4th Sunday)
Sacred Heart Church, Arles, Co Laois
Fr Petru Vlaic
32 Paddocks Square, Adamstown,
Lucan, Co Dublin
Tel 086-3940784
Email petruioanvlaic@yahoo.com

St John the Baptist Missionary & Cultural Centre, Drimnagh Castle, Longmile Road, Dublin 12
Fr Calin Florea
Tel 087-6148140

Parish of St Nicholas & St Brigid of Kildare, Collegiate Church of St Nicholas (COI), Lombard Street, Galway

Romanian Orthodox Community (3rd Sunday of Month)
Sisters of Mercy Chapel,
Westbourne Convent,
Courtbrack Avenue, Limerick
Fr Tudor Ghita
102 Friar Hill, Rahoon, Galway
Tel 086-2282690
Email tuxghita@yahoo.com

Parish of St Calinic of Cernica & St Patrick
Fr Collins Community Centre,
Cork Road, Passage West, Cork
Fr Viorel Hurjui
6 Marriner's Quay, Passage West, Co Cork
Tel 089-4423580
Email viohur@yahoo.com

Parish of St John the Evangelist Parish Centre, All Saints RC Church, 4 Broughshane Road,
Ballymena BT43 7DX, Co Antrim
www.romanianparish.com
Fr Cornel Clepea
4 Broughshane Road,
Ballymena BT43 7DX,
Co Antrim, Northern Ireland
Email clepiai@yahoo.com

St Paul's RC Church
Falls Road, Belfast BT12 6AB
Fr Toma Romeo Puiu
Tel +44-7598845950
Email puiu_romeotoma@oo.com

Romanian Orthodox Parish
Edmund Rice Heritage Centre,
Mount Sion, Barrack Street, Waterford
Fr Calin Florea
Tel 087-6148140
email revcalin.florea@gmail.com

Romanian Missionary Parish, Mullingar
Contact: Fr Calin Florea
Tel 087-6148140

Romanian Missionary Parish, Sligo
Contact: Fr Tudor Ghitá
Tel 086-2282690
Email tuxghita@yahoo.com

IRELAND'S CARDINALS

Since 1866, when Ireland received its first residential cardinal, to the present, eleven Irish bishops have been elected to the Sacred College. By 'Irish bishops' is meant those who, while exercising actual pastoral government, were cardinals; not included are those Irish prelates who were made cardinals but whose ministry was spent overseas (e.g. Cardinal Glennon), or in the service of the Roman Curia (e.g. Cardinal Browne), or those who, having been territorial bishops in Ireland, were elevated to the Sacred College while exercising pastoral government in a diocese overseas (e.g. Cardinal Moran).

Paul Cullen (1803-78)
Ordained Archbishop of Armagh (1850); translated to Dublin (1852); created Cardinal (22 June 1866) by Pius IX.

Edward McCabe (1816-85)
Ordained Bishop of Gadara and appointed auxiliary to the Archbishop of Dublin, Cardinal Cullen (1877); appointed Archbishop of Dublin, following Cardinal Cullen's death (1879); created Cardinal (27 March 1882) by Leo XIII.

Michael Logue (1840-1924)
Ordained Bishop of Raphoe (1879); translated to be Co-adjutor to Archbishop Daniel McGettigan of Armagh (March 1887), whom he succeeded (December 1887); created Cardinal (16 January 1893) by Leo XIII.

Patrick O'Donnell (1856-1927)
Ordained Bishop of Raphoe (1888); translated to be Co-adjutor to Cardinal Logue (1922), whom he succeeded as Archbishop of Armagh (1924); created Cardinal (14 December 1925) by Pius XI.

Joseph MacRory (1861-1945)
Ordained Bishop of Down and Connor (1915); translated to Armagh as Archbishop in succession to Cardinal O'Donnell (1928); created Cardinal (12 December 1929) by Pius XI.

John D'Alton (1882-1963)
Ordained Bishop of Binda and appointed Co-adjutor to the Bishop of Meath (1942), whom he succeeded (1943); translated to Armagh in succession to Cardinal MacRory (1946); created Cardinal (12 January 1953) by Pius XII.

William Conway (1913-77)
Ordained Bishop of Neve and appointed auxiliary to the Archbishop of Armagh, Cardinal D'Alton (1958), whom he succeeded (1963); created Cardinal (22 February 1965) by Paul VI.

Tomás Ó Fiaich (1923-90)
Ordained Archbishop of Armagh (1977) and created Cardinal (30 June 1979) by John Paul II.

Cahal Brendan Daly (1917-2009)
ordained priest 22 June 1941; ordained Bishop of Ardagh and Clonmacnois 16 July 1967; installed Bishop of Down and Connor 17 October 1982; installed Archbishop of Armagh 16 December 1990; created Cardinal 28 June 1991 by John Paul II; retired 1 October 1996.

Cardinal Desmond Connell (1926-2017)
Ordained priest 19 May 1951; ordained Archbishop of Dublin 6 March 1988; created Cardinal 21 February 2001; retired 26 April 2004.

The eleventh Irish Cardinal is the Emeritus Archbishop of Armagh, H. E. **Cardinal Seán Brady** *(see Diocese of Armagh)*

STATISTICS

TABLE 1: CATHOLIC CHURCH PERSONNEL 2012

	Number
Diocesan	2,800
Clerical Religious Orders	1,888
Sisters' Orders	6,912
Brothers' Orders	628
TOTAL	12,228

Source: Statistical Yearbook of the Church

TABLE 2: VOCATIONS 2006

		Entrants
Diocesan		28
Clerical Religious Orders		15
Sisters' Orders		9
Brothers' Orders		1
TOTAL		53

Source: Council for Research and Development 2007

TABLE 3: NULLITY OF MARRIAGE

Year	Applications Nationwde	Decrees of Nullity
2011	292	253
2012	224	259
2013	231	188
2014	215	191
2015	188	215
2016	395	216
2017	321	231
2018	23	18
2019	33	30
2020	14	16

EXPLANATORY NOTES:

1. The above figures relate to the 32 counties.
2. Only a minority of applications persist beyond the preliminary stages. About 40% are found to have no *prima facie* case for nullity and do not reach the stage of formal investigation; a further third are withdrawn by the applicants.
3. In about 75–80% of cases ending with a nullity decree, a veto – technically called a *vetitum* – on marriage in the Church is imposed on one or both parties. This is because the defect which caused the nullity is judged to be still present, putting at risk the validity of a future marriage. The *vetitum* may be lifted by the local bishop only if he is satisfied, after investigation, of the person's fitness for marriage in all essential respects. The purpose of the *vetitum* is to prevent the sacrament of marriage being brought into disrepute and to protect the genuine interests of any future spouse.
4. Before a decree is granted it must be judged by a Religion Tribunal. It must be established with moral certainty – probability alone is not enough – that nullity exists in a particular case; that is, that, because of fundamental defect of capacity for, or consent to, that marriage, established to have been present at the time of marriage, there was in fact, no valid marriage. The tribunal starts with the presumption that the marriage is valid; the onus is on the applicants to provide convincing evidence that it is not. The decision of the First Instance Tribunal, whether it is in favour of the nullity of marriage or not, can be appealed to the National Marriage Appeal Tribunal, located in St Patrick's College, Maynooth, Co Kildare. Futher evidence may be presented in the Appeal Process before the Judgement is made and a Decree is issued.
5. COST OF THE PROCEDURE: The costs involved for the applicant are kept as low as possible and are, in fact, very modest. Applicants are expected to pay if they can afford it. However, each applicant is formally told that the progress of the case or its outcome does not in any way depend on the ability or willingness to pay any or all of these expenses. If they genuinely cannot pay, the Church will come to their aid. In practice, only a minority pay the full case fee. Over half pay nothing.

TABLE 4: CATHOLICS & TABLE 5: CATHOLIC SCHOOLS

	Parishes	Catholic Population	Churches	Schools (no) Primary	Schools (no) Secondary[1]	School Population Primary	School Population Secondary[1]
Armagh	61	263,505	146	151	27	30,221	20,660
Dublin	197	1,093,095	246	450	182	141,038	103,866
Cashel	46	78,935	84	115	20	12,143	11,143
Tuam	56	148,000	31	193	18	19,200	8,200
Achonry[2]	23	34,826	47	49	9	3,780	3,969
Ardagh[2]	41	74,000	80	76	6	11,256	7,857
Clogher[2]	37	83,882	85	89	16	12,026	6,947
Clonfert[2]	24	36,000	47	49	7	6,800	3,200
Cloyne	46	157,752	107	122	29	22,879	15,194
Cork & Ross[2]	68	220,000	124	173	35	n/a	n/a
Derry	51	259,689	104	111	21	19,017	17,062
Down & Connor	86	368,263	147	124	33	32,174	24,986
Dromore[2]	22	63,400	48	51	14	10,270	11,524
Elphin	37	90,559	90	110	13	10,385	4,116
Ferns[2]	49	116,001	101	96	20	16,598	16,276
Galway	39	116,752	71	84	14	14,030	7,607
Kerry	53	139,650	111	150	30	17,077	12,973
Kildare & Leighlin	56	256,186	117	163	41	36,048	24,634
Killala	22	36,012	48	63	10	3,387	4,217
Killaloe	58	124,211	133	145	21	19,512	11,327
Kilmore	34	69,794	95	81	14	10,674	6,046
Limerick[2]	60	154,836	94	102	25	16,512	14,186
Meath	69	265,151	149	186	36	37,820	25,338
Ossory	42	86,115	88	85	16	11,795	8,914
Raphoe[2]	33	82,505	71	100	20	10,662	13,151
Waterford & Lismore[2]	45	155,643	85	97	23	16,439	12,527
Totals[3]	1,355	4,574,732	2,549	3,215	700	541,743	395,920

Notes:
1. Includes voluntary secondary schools and state schools.
Source: Diocesan returns

2. Data unchanged from 2020.
3. Total estimates only.

TABLE 6: NUMBER OF PRIESTS, RELIGIOUS AND PERMANENT DEACONS

	Active in Ministry				Members of Religious Congregations		
	Incardinated Priests[1]	Other priests[2]	Permanent Deacons	Others[3]	Clerical[4]	Brothers	Sisters
Armagh	77	16	14	31	40	12	211
Dublin	331	171	33	82	558	205	1,739
Cashel	72	4	0	-	56	12	92
Tuam	46	12	0	6	0	8	16
Achonry[5]	24	0	2	9	1	0	30
Ardagh	46	5	0	16	11	6	94
Clogher	61	-	1	5	3	0	104
Clonfert[5]	25	6	0	6	22	0	92
Cloyne	64	3	10	36	0	0	140
Cork & Ross[5]	92	-	3	22	40	29	195
Derry	64	5	0	30	6	2	64
Down & Connor	96	34	9	34	12	15	120
Dromore[5]	25	-	5	18	7	1	134
Elphin	33	28	8	14	8	0	145
Ferns[5]	75	2	1	28	9	6	131
Galway	38	8	0	23	43	11	180
Kerry	47	4	6	26	9	12	85
Kildare & Leighlin	66	18	11	21	0	17	131
Killala[5]	31	3	0	13	0	0	35
Killaloe	58	6	0	22	10	13	129
Kilmore	43	6	2	17	0	0	44
Limerick[5]	58	18	-	45	42	9	233
Meath	78	16	-	20	80	3	80
Ossory	43	2	0	17	9	26	111
Raphoe[5]	54	2	0	17	9	2	23
Waterford & Lismore[5]	61	-	3	19	46	34	266
Totals[6]	1,708	369	108	577	1,021	423	4,624

Notes:
1. Priests incardinated in the Diocese are in active ministry in the Dioceses.
2. Priests who are in active ministry in the Diocese but who are incardinated elsewhere.
3. Priests incardinated in the Diocese who are either retired or working outside the Diocese
4. Priests of religious orders who are not in active ministry in the Diocese.
5. Data unchanged from 2020.
6. Totals estimates only.

Source: Diocesan returns

CATHOLIC ARCHBISHOPS AND BISHOPS OF BRITAIN

APOSTOLIC NUNCIO

Mgr Claudio Gugerotti
54 Parkside, London SW19 5NF
Tel 020-89447189
Fax 020-89472494

ENGLAND AND WALES

PROVINCE OF WESTMINSTER

H.E. Cardinal Vincent Nichols
Archbishop of Westminster

Auxiliaries
Rt Rev John Sherrington
Rt Rev Nicholas Hudson
Rt Rev Paul McAleenan

Suffragans
Right Rev Alan Williams
Bishop of Brentwood
Right Rev Patrick McKinney
Bishop of Nottingham
Right Rev Alan Hopes
Bishop of East Anglia
Right Rev David Oakley
Bishop of Northhampton

PROVINCE OF BIRMINGHAM

Most Rev Bernard Longley
Archbishop of Birmingham

Auxilary
Rt Rev David Evans
Rt Rev Stepen Wright

Suffragans
Right Rev Mark Davies
Bishop of Shrewsbury
Right Rev Declan Lang
Bishop of Clifton

PROVINCE OF LIVERPOOL

Most Rev Malcolm McMahon
Archbishop of Liverpool

Auxilary
Right Rev Thomas Williams
Right Rev Thomas Neylon

Suffragans
Right Rev John Arnold
Bishop of Salford
Right Rev Marcus Stock
Bishop of Leeds
Right Rev Ralph Heskett
Bishop of Hallam
Right Rev Terence Drainey
Bishop of Middlesbrough
Right Rev Robert Byrne
Bishop of Hexham and Newcastle
Right Rev Paul Swarbrick
Bishop of Lancaster

PROVINCE OF CARDIFF

Most Rev George Stack
Archbishop of Cardiff and Apostolic Administrator, Menevia

Suffragans
Vacant See Menevia
Most Rev George Stack, Apostolic Administrator
Right Rev Peter Brignall
Bishop of Wrexham

PROVINCE OF SOUTHWARK

Most Rev John Wilson
Archbishop of Southwark

Auxiliaries
Rt Rev Paul Hendricks

Suffragans
Right Rev Mark O'Toole
Bishop of Plymouth
Right Rev Richard Moth
Bishop of Arundel and Brighton
Right Rev Philip Egan
Bishop of Portsmouth

Bishop of the Forces
Right Rev Paul Mason

BISHOPS' CONFERENCE OF ENGLAND AND WALES

Bishops' Conference
39 Eccleston Square, London SW1V 1BX
Tel 020-76308220 Fax 020-79014821
Email secretariat@cbcew.org.uk

H.E. Cardinal Vincent Nichols
Archbishop's House, Ambrosden Avenue,
London SW1P 1QJ
Tel 020-77989033 Fax 020-77989077

Right Rev Declan Lang
Bishop of Clifton, St Ambrose,
North Road, Leigh Woods,
Bristol BS8 3PW
Tel 0117-9733027 Fax 0117-9735913

Most Rev John Wilson
Archbishop of Southwark,
Archbishop's House, St George's Road,
Southwark, London SE1 6HX
Tel 020-79282495 Fax 020-79287833

Right Rev Paul Swarbrick
Bishop of Lancaster,
Bishop's Office, Balmoral Road,
Lancaster LA1 3BT
Tel 01524-596050

Right Rev Mark O'Toole
Bishop of Plymouth,
45 Cecil Street, Plymouth,
Devon PL1 5HW
Tel 01752-224414 Fax 01752-223750

Right Rev Alan Hopes
The White House, 21 Upgate,
Poringland, Norwich, Norfolk NR14 7SH
Tel 01586-2202/3956 Fax 01586-5358

Most Rev Bernard Longley
Archbishop of Birmingham,
8 Shadwell Street, Birmingham B4 6EY
Tel 0121-2369090 Fax 0121-2120171

Right Rev Mark Davies
Bishop of Shrewsbury,
Curial Offices, 2 Park Road South,
Prenton, Wirral CH43 4UX
Tel 0151-6529855

Right Rev Peter Brignall
Bishop of Wrexham, Bishop's House,
Sontley Road, Wrexham,
Clwyd LL13 7EW
Tel 01978-262726 Fax 01978-354257

Right Rev Terence Drainey
Bishop of Middlesbrough,
Bishop's House, 16 Cambridge Road,
Middlesbrough, Cleveland TS5 5NN
Tel 01642-818253 Fax 01642-850548

Right Rev Philip Egan
Bishop of Portsmouth, Bishop's House,
Bishop Crispian Way, Portsmouth PO1 3HG
Tel 01705-820894 Fax 01705-863086

Right Rev John Arnold
Bishop of Salford, Wardley Hall, Worsley,
Manchester M28 5ND
Tel 0161-7942825 Fax 0161-7278592

Right Rev Marcus Stock
Bishop's House,
13 North Grange Road, Headingley,
Leeds LS6 2BR
Tel 01532-304533 Fax 01532-789890

Right Rev Robert Byrne
Bishop of Hexham and Newcastle,
Bishop's House,
East Denton Hall, 800 West Road,
Newcastle Upon Tyne NE5 2BJ
Tel 0191-2280003 Fax 0191-2740432

Right Rev David Oakley
Bishop of Northampton,
Bishop's House, Marriott Street,
Northhampton NN2 6AW
Tel 01604-715635 Fax 01604-792186

CATHOLIC ARCHBISHOPS AND BISHOPS OF BRITAIN

Right Rev Patrick McKinney
Bishop of Nottingham, Bishop's House,
27 Cavendish Road East, The Park,
Nottingham NG7 1BB
Tel 0115-9474786 Fax 0115-9475235

Right Rev Alan Williams
Bishop of Brentwood,
Cathedral House, Ingrave Road,
Brentwood, Essex CM15 8AT
Tel 01277-232266 Fax 01277-214060

Right Rev John Sherrington
Auxiliary Bishop of Westminster
Archbishop's House,
Ambrosden Avenue, London SWIP IQJ
Tel 020-7798 9033 Fax 020-7798 9077

Right Rev Ralph Heskett
Bishop of Hallam, Bishop's House
75 Norfolk Road, Sheffield 52 2SZ
Tel 0114 278 7988 Fax 0114 278 7988

Right Rev Richard Moth
Bishop of Arundel and Brighton
Highoaks, Old Brighton Road North,
Pease Pottage, West Sussex RH11 9AJ
Tel 01293-526428 Fax 01293-385276

Right Rev Paul Mason
Bishop of the Forces, Bishop's Oak,
26 The Crescent, Farnborough Park,
Farnborough, Hants GU14 7AS
Tel 01252-543649 Fax 01252-373748

Most Rev George Stack
Archbishop of Cardiff,
Archbishop's House,
42-43 Cathedral Road, Cardiff CF1 9HD
Tel 01222-20411 Fax 01222-345950

Most Rev Malcolm McMahon
Archbishop of Liverpool,
Archbishop's House, 19 Salisbury Road,
Cressington Park, Liverpool L10 0PH
Tel 0151-4940686

Right Rev Thomas Williams
14 Hope Place, Liverpool L1 9BG
Tel 0151-7030109 Fax 0151-7030267

Right Rev Paul Hendricks
Auxiliary Bishop of Southwark,
95 Carshalton Road, Sutton,
Surrey SMI 4LL
Tel 020-86438007

Right Rev Nicholas Hudson
Auxiliary Bishop of Westminster
Archbishop's House, Ambrosden Avenue,
London SW1P 1QJ
Tel 020-77989033 Fax 020-77989077

Right Rev Paul McAleenan
Auxiliary Bishop of Westminster
Archbishop's House, Ambrosden Avenue,
London SW1P 1QJ
Tel 020-77989033 Fax 020-77989077

Right Rev Tom Neylon
Auxiliary Bishop of Liverpool
The Priory, 5 Lancaster Lane,
Parbold, Wigan WN8 7HS

UKRAINIAN APOSTOLIC EPARCHY

Right Rev Kenneth Nowlakowski
Eparch of the Ukrainians
90 Binney Street, London W1Y 1YN
Tel 0171-6291534

SYRO-MALABAR EPARCHY

Right Rev Joseph Srampickal
Eparch of the Syro-Malabar Church of
Great Britain, Bishop's Office,
St Alphonsa of Immaculate Conception,
St Ignatius Square, Preston PR1 1TT
Tel 01772-396065

RETIRED BISHOPS IN ENGLAND AND WALES

Right Rev Howard Tripp
Former Auxiliary in Southwark
Little Sisters of the Poor,
2A Meadow Road,
London SW8 1QH

Right Rev Philip Pargeter
Auxiliary in Birmingham,
Grove House, 90 College Road,
Sutton Coldfield,
West Midlands B73 5AH

Right Rev Mark Jabalé
Emeritus Bishop of Menevia,
Belmont Abbey,
Ruckhall Lane,
Hereford HR2 9RZ

Most Rev Kevin McDonald
Emeritus Archbishop of Southwark,
c/o Archbishop's House,
St George's Road, Southwark,
London SE1 6HX

Most Rev Patrick Kelly
Emeritus Archbishop of Liverpool,
c/o Archbishop's House, Lowood,
Carnatic Road, Liverpool L18 8BY

Right Rev Edwin Regan
Emeritus Bishop of Wrexham,
c/o Bishop's House, Sontley Road,
Wrexham, Clwyd LL13 7EW

Right Rev Crispian Hollis
Emeritus Bishop of Portsmouth,
c/o Bishop's House,
Bishop Crispian Way,
Portsmouth PO1 3HG

Right Rev Christopher Budd
Emeritus Bishop of Plymouth
The Presbytery, Silver Street,
Lyme Regis DT7 3HS

Right Rev John Hine
Former Auxiliary in Southwark
St Andrews, 47 Ashford Road,
Tenterden, Kent TN30 6LL

Right Rev John Rawsthorne
Emeritus Bishop of Hallam
Bishop's House, 75 Norfolk Road,
Sheffield S2 2SZ

Right Rev Thomas McMahon
Bishop's House, Stock,
Ingatestone, Essex CM4 9BU

Right Rev Terence Brain
c/o Diocese of Salford Cathedral Centre,
3 Ford Street, Salford M3 6DP

Right Rev Michael Campbell
St Augustine's Priory,
55 Fulham Palace Road, Hammersmith,
London W6 8AU

Right Rev Thomas Burns
St Anne's Presbytery, Oliphant Circle,
Malpas, Newport NP20 6PF

Right Rev Seamus Cunningham
9 Clifton Road, Sunderland SR6 9DW

Right Rev David McGough
Former Auxiliary Bishop of Birmingham,
160 Draycott Road, Tean,
Stoke on Trent ST10 4JT

Right Rev Patrick Lynch
Former Auxiliary in Southwark,
Park House, 6a Cresswell Park,
Blackheath, London SE3 9RD

Right Rev William Kenney
Former Auxiliary in Birmingham,
St Hugh's House, 27 Hensington Road,
Woodstock, Oxfordshire OX20 1JH

CATHOLIC ARCHBISHOPS AND BISHOPS OF BRITAIN

THE HIERARCHY OF SCOTLAND

PROVINCE OF ST ANDREWS AND EDINBURGH

Most Rev Archbishop Leo Cushley
Archbishop of St Andrews and
Edinburgh, 42 Greenhill Gardens,
Edinburgh EH10 4BJ
Tel 0131-4473337 Fax 0131-4470816
Email Abp.Cushley@staned.org.uk

Suffragans
Right Rev Hugh Gilbert
Bishop of Aberdeen,
Bishop's House, St Mary's House,
14 Chanonry, Old Aberdeen AB24 1RP
Tel 01224-319154 Fax 01224-325570
Email bishop.hugh@gmx.com

Right Rev Stephen Robson
Bishop of Dunkeld, Diocese of Dunkeld,
24028 Lawside Road, Dundee DD3 6XY
Tel 01382-225453 Fax 01382-204585
Email bishop@dunkelddiocese.org.uk

Right Rev Brian McGee
Bishop of Argyll and The Isles
Bishop's House, Esplanade, Oban,
Argyll PA34 5AB
Tel 01631-571395 Fax 01631-564930
Email Brian-Mcgee@btconnect.com

Right Rev William Nolan
Bishop of Galloway, Candida Casa,
8 Corsehill Road, Ayr KA7 2ST
Tel 01292-266750 Fax 01292-289888
Email bishop@gallowaydiocese.org.uk

PROVINCE OF GLASGOW

Suffragans
Right Rev Joseph A. Toal
Bishop of Motherwell,
Diocesan Centre, Coursington Road,
Motherwell ML1 1PP
Tel 01698-269114
Email bishop@rcdom.org.uk

Right Rev John Keenan
Bishop of Paisley, Diocesan Centre,
Cathedral Precincts, Incle Street,
Paisley PA1 1HR
Tel 0141-8476130
Email bishopjohn@rcdop.org.uk

BISHOPS' CONFERENCE OF SCOTLAND

General Secretary
Rev Dr Gerard Maguiness
General Secretariat,
64 Aitken Street, Airdrie,
Lanarkshire ML6 6LT
Tel 01236-764061 Fax 01236-762489
Email gensec@bcos.org.uk
www.bcos.org.uk

Assistant General Secretary
Mr Michael McGrath
64 Aitken Street,
Airdrie ML6 6LT

RETIRED BISHOPS IN SCOTLAND

Right Rev Maurice Taylor
Bishop Emeritus (Galloway Diocese)
41 Overmills Road, Ayr KA7 3LH
Email mauricetaylor1926@sky.com

Right Rev Peter A. Moran
Bishop Emeritus of Aberdeen,
10 Cathedral Square, Fortrose IV10 8TB
email pmoran@bcos.org.uk

Most Rev Mario Joseph Conti
Archbishop Emeritus of Glasgow,
40 Newlands Road, Glasgow G43 2JD
Email Mario.Conti@rcag.org.uk

Right Rev John Cunningham
Bishop Emeritus (Galloway)
29 Johnstone Terrace,
Greenock PA16 8BD

FORMS OF ECCLESIASTICAL ADDRESS

These notes should be understood as a guide to present-day practice in Ireland, rather than as 'prescriptive' rules. Forms of address – for example, whether someone is 'Very Rev', 'Right Rev', or 'Most Rev' – vary from country to country and language to language. The aim here has been to reflect Irish usage. These conventions are not static but are subject to gradual change. Some of the more involved forms of address have disappeared, and a dual standard of formality has emerged. For instance, 'Canon John Nonnullus' has in recent years tended to replace 'John Canon Nonnullus'. Where the older form is still found, the norm of normal address is given with the older form in parentheses ( ) as the more formal form of address. Since the form used is often a matter of preference of the person addressed, or the customary usage of a particular diocese or religious order, where this is known it should be followed. This directory uses what is considered to be the normal Irish form.

THE HIERARCHY

The Apostolic Nuncio
Written address: His Excellency Most Rev Dr John Nonnullus
Spoken address: same
In conversation: Your Excellency.
Reference to: 'The Nuncio said...'
('His Excellency said...')

Cardinals
Written address: His Eminence Cardinal John Nonnullus (H.E. John Cardinal Nonnullus)
Spoken address: Cardinal John Nunnullus (the more formal address is either of the written forms)
In conversation: Cardinal (Your Eminence)
Reference to: 'The Cardinal said...'
('His Eminence said...')

Note: The majority of cardinals are bishops, and they are divided into three groups, a small number known as the 'cardinal bishops', another small group who are the 'cardinal deacons', and the majority, who are called 'cardinal priests'. From this has arisen the form 'Cardinal-Archbishop of ...' or 'the cardinal-archbishop said', sometimes used in the media for emphasis. There is no category of 'cardinal-archbishops'; rather there are bishops and archbishops who are also cardinals. If one wishes to refer to a cardinal and also to draw attention to the see of which he is bishop, the following form should be used: 'Cardinal John Nunnullus, the Archbishop of Nusquam'.

Archbishops
Written address: The Most Rev John Nonnullus
Spoken address: Archbishop Nonnullus (His Grace the Archbishop of Nusquam)
In conversation: Your Grace
Reference to: 'The Archbishop said...' ('His Grace said...')

Bishops
Written address: The Most Rev John Nonnullus
Spoken address: Dr John Nonnullus, Bishop of Nusquam (His Lordship Dr...)
In conversation: Doctor (My Lord)
Reference to: 'The Bishop said...'

Note: The practice of using the word 'Bishop' in spoken address (e.g. Bishop John Nonnullus of Nusquam) and in conversation (e.g. 'Bishop, I am pleased to meet you') is becoming increasingly common.

CLERGY

Secular:
Monsignor
Written: Right Rev Mgr
Spoken: Monsignor

Capitular Dignitaries:
Archdeacon
Written: The Venerable John Nonnullus, Archdeacon of Nusquam
Spoken: Archdeacon

Dean
Written: The Very Rev Dean Nonnullus
Spoken: Dean

Canon
Written: The Very Rev Canon John Nonnullus (John Canon Nonnullus)
Spoken: Canon

Others
Those holding other capitular offices (e.g. precentor) are addressed as canons.

Parish Priest
Written: The Very Rev John Nonnullus PP
Spoken: Father

Curates
Written: The Very Rev John Nonnullus CC
Spoken: Father

Other Priests
Secular priests not included above:
Written: Rev John Nonnullus
Spoken: Father
Priests using academic titles are referred to by these titles, and in writing these are prefixed by 'Rev', e.g. Rev Prof John Nonnullus

Deacons
Written: Rev John Nonnullus
Spoken: Mister (Rev Mister)

Regular
The conventional protocol varies with religious orders, many of whom preserve forms of address peculiar to themselves. A general rule is that priests are addressed as found under Other priests above, and superiors (of houses or provinces) are addressed in writing as 'The Very Rev'.

Abbots
Written: 'The Right Rev' is placed before the conventional form of address of a member of that community.

NON-CLERICAL RELIGIOUS

Men
Non-clerical religious orders of men and non-clerical members of clerical religious orders are referred to as 'Br John Nonnullus' in writing, and `Brother' in speech.

Note 1. The use of Christian name or surname (e.g. 'Br John' or 'Br Nonnullus') depends on the usage of the order.

Note 2. Some orders have traditional ways of referring to their non-clerical members other than 'Brother'.

Women
Members of religious orders of women are referred to as 'Sr' in writing and 'Sister' in speech, irrespective of the position they hold in their institute.
Note 1. The form 'Reverend Mother' is obsolete and its use does not arise.
Note 2. The use of Christian name, name in religion, or surname, or the prefixing of the forename with 'M' (Mary) depends on the usage of the order.
Note 3. Some orders, in particular monastic and enclosed orders, use titles derived from their own traditions (e.g. abbess and prioress). There is no consistent usage with regard to these titles (e.g. it may be `Mother Abbess' or 'Sr Mary, the Abbess') and the usage depends on the order or the house.

THE ROMAN PONTIFFS

Information includes the name of the Pope, in many cases his name before becoming Pope, his birth-place or country of origin, the date of accession to the Papacy, and the date of the end of reign which, in all but a few cases, was the date of death. Double dates record the day of election and coronation.
Source: *Annuario Pontificio*

St Peter (Simon Bar-Jona) of Bethsaida, in Galilee, Prince of the Apostles, who received from Jesus Christ supreme pontifical power to be transmitted to his successors, resided first at Antioch, then at Rome, where he was martyred in the year 64 or 67, having governed the Church from that city for twenty-five years.
St Linus, Tuscany, 67-76
St Anacletus (Cletus), Rome 76-88
St Clement, Rome 88-97
St Evaristus, Greece, 97-105
St Alexander I, Rome, 105-25
St Sixtus I, Rome, 115-25
St Telesphorus, Greece, 125-36
St Hyginus, Greece, 136-40
St Pius I, Aquilea, 140-55
St Anictus, Syria, 155-66
St Soter, Campania, 166-75
St Eleutheius, Nicopolis in Epirus, 175-89

Up to the time of St Eleutherius, the years indicated for the beginning and end of pontificates are not certain. Also, up to the middle of the eleventh century, there are some doubts about the exact days and months given in chronological tables.

St Victor I, Africa, 189-99
St Zephyrinus, Rome, 199-217
St Callistus I, Rome, 217-22
St Urban I, Rome, 222-30
St Pontian, Rome, 21 July 230 to 28 Sept 235
St Anterus, Greece, 21 Nov 235 to 3 Jan 236
St Fabian, Rome, 10 Jan 236 to 20 Jan 250
St Cornelius, Rome, Mar 251 to June 253
St Lucius I, Rome, 12 May 254 to 2 Aug 254
St Stephen I, Rome, 12 May 254 to 2 Aug 257
St Sixtus II, Greece, 30 Aug 257 to 6 Aug 258
St Dionysius, birthplace unknown, 22 July 259 to 26 Dec 268
St Felix I, Rome, 5 Jan 269 to 30 Dec 274
St Eutychian, Luni, 4 Jan 275 to 7 Dec 283
St Caius, Dalmatia, 17 Dec 283 to 22 Apr 296
St Marcellinus, Rome, 30 June 296 to 25 Oct 304
St Marcellus I, Rome, 27 May 308 or 26 June 308 to 16 Jan 309

St Eusebius, Greece, 18 Apr 309 or 310 to 17 Aug 309 or 310
St Melchiades (Miltiades), Africa, 2 July 311 to 11 Jan 314
St Sylvester I, Rome, 31 Jan 314 to 31 Dec 335

Most of the popes before St Sylvester I were martyrs.

St Marcus, Rome, 18 Jan 336 to 7 Oct 336
St Julius I, Rome, 6 Feb 337 to 12 Apr 352
Liberius, Rome, 17 May 352 to 24 Sept 366
St Damasus I, Spain, 1 Oct 366 to 11 Dec 384
St Siricius, Rome, 15 or 22 or 29 Dec 384 to 26 Nov 399
St Anastasius I, Rome, 27 Nov 399 to 19 Dec 401
St Innocent I, Albano, 22 Dec 401 to 12 Mar 417
St Zozimus, Greece, 18 Mar 417 to 26 Dec 418
St Bonifice I, Rome, 28 or 29 Dec 418 to 4 Sept 422
St Celestine I, Campania, 10 Sept 422 to 27 July 432
St Sixtus III, Rome, 31 July 432 to 19 Aug 440
St Leo I (the Grant), Tuscany, 29 Sept 440 to 10 Nov 461
St Hilary, Sardinia, 19 Nov 461 to 29 Feb 468
St Simplicius, Tivoli, 3 Mar 468 to 10 Mar 483
St Felix III (II), Rome, 13 Mar 483 to 1 Mar 492

He should be called Felix II, and his successors of the same name should be numbered accordingly. The discrepancy in the numerical designation of popes named Felix was caused by the erroneous insertion in some lists of the name of St Felix of Rome, a martyr.

St Gelasius I, Africa, 1 Mar 492 to 21 Nov 496
Anastasius II, Rome, 24 Nov 496 to 19 Nov 498
St Symmachus, Sardinia, 22 Nov 498 to 19 July 514
St Hormisdas, Frosinone, 20 July 514 to 6 Aug 523
St John I, Martyr, Tuscany, 13 Aug 523 to 18 May 526
St Felix IV (III), Samnium, 12 July 526 to 22 Sept 530

Boniface II, Rome, 22 Sept 530 to 17 Oct 532
John II, Rome, 2 Jan 533 to 8 May 535

John II was the first pope to change his name. His given name was Mercury.

St Agapitus I, Rome, 13 May 535 to 22 Apr 536
St Silverius, Martyr, Campania, 1 or 8 June 536 to 11 Nov 537 (d. 2 Dec 537)

St Silverius was violently deposed in March 537 and abdicated on 11 Nov 537. His successor, Vigilius, was not recognised as pope by all the Roman clergy until his abdication.

Vigilius, Rome, 29 Mar 537 to 7 June 555
Pelagius I, Rome, 16 Apr 556 to 4 Mar 561
John III, Rome, 17 July 561 to 13 July 574
Benedict I, Rome, 2 June 575 to 30 July 579
Pelagius II, Rome, 26 Nov 579 to 7 Feb 590
St Gregory I (the Great), Rome, 3 Sept 590 to 12 Mar 604
Sabinian, Blera in Tuscany, 13 Sept 604 to 22 Feb 606
Bonifcace III, Rome, 19 Feb 607 to 12 Nov 607
St Boniface IV, Abruzzi, 25 Aug 608 to 8 May 615
St Deusdedit (Adeodatus I), Rome, 19 Oct 615 to 8 Nov 618
Boniface V, Naples, 23 Dec 619 to 25 Oct 625
Honorius I, Campania, 27 Oct 625 to 12 Oct 638
Severinus, Rome, 28 May 640 to 2 Aug 640
John IV, Dalmatia, 24 Dec 640 to 12 Oct 642
Theodore I, Greece, 24 Nov 642 to 14 May 649
St Martin I, Martyr, Todi, July 649 to 16 Sept 655 (in exile from 17 June 653)
St Eugene I, Rome, 10 Aug 654 to 2 June 657

St Eugene I was elected during the exile of St Martin I, who is believed to have endorsed him as pope.

St Vitalian, Segni, 30 July 657 to 27 Jan 672

THE ROMAN PONTIFFS

Adeodatus II, Rome, 11 Apr 672 to 17 June 676
Donus, Rome, 2 Nov 676 to 11 Apr 678
St Agatho, Sicily, 27 June 678 to 10 Jan 681
St Leo II, Sicily, 17 Aug 682 to 3 July 683
St Benedict II, Rome, 26 June 684 to 8 May 685
John V, Syria, 23 July 685 to 2 Aug 686
Conon, birthplace unkown, 21 Oct 686 to 21 Sept 687
St Sergius I, Syria, 15 Dec 687 to 8 Sept 701
John VI, Greece, 30 Oct 701 to 11 Jan 705
John VII, Greece, 1 Mar 705 to 18 Oct 707
Sisinnius, Syria, 15 Jan 708 to 4 Feb 708
Constantine, Syria, 25 Mar 708 to 9 Apr 715
St Gregory II, Rome, 19 May 715 to 11 Feb 731
St Gregory II, Syria, 18 May 731 to Nov 741
St Zachary, Greece, 10 Dec 741 to 22 Mar 752
Stephen II (III), Rome, 26 Mar 752 to 26 Apr 757

After the death of St Zachary, a Roman priest named Stephen was elected but died (four days later) before his consecration as Bishop of Rome, which would have marked the beginning of his pontificate. Another Stephen was elected to succeed Zachary as Stephen II. (The first pope with this name was St Stephen 254-7). The ordinal III appears in parentheses after the name of Stephen II because the name of the earlier elected but deceased priest was included in some lists. Other Stephens have double numbers.

St Paul I, Rome, Apr (29 May) 757 to 28 June 767
Stephen III (IV), Sicily, 1 (7) Aug 768 to 24 Jan 772
Adrian I, Rome, 1 (9) Feb 772 to 25 Dec 795
St Leo III, Rome, 26 (27) Dec 795 to 12 June 816
Stephen IV (V), Rome, 22 June 816 to 24 Jan 817
St Paschal I, Rome, 25 Jan 817 to 11 Feb 824
Eugene II, Rome, Feb (May) 824 to Aug 827
Valentine, Rome, Aug 827 to Sept 827
Gregory IV, Rome, 827 to Jan 844
Sergius II, Rome, Jan 844 to 27 Jan 847
St Leo IV, Rome, Jan (10 Apr) 847 to 17 Jan 855
Benedict III, Rome, July (29 Sept) 855 to 17 Apr 858

St Nicholas I (the Great), Rome, 24 Apr 858 to 13 Nov 867
Adrian II, Rome, 14 Dec 867 to 14 Dec 872
John VIII, Rome, 14 Dec 872 to 16 Dec 882
Marinus I, Gallese, 16 Dec 882 to 15 May 884
St Adrian III, Rome, 17 May 884 to Sept 885
Stephen V (VI), Rome, Sept 885 to 14 Sept 891
Formosus, Portus, 6 Oct 891 to 4 Apr 896
Boniface VI, Rome, Apr 896 to Apr 896
Stephen VI (VII), Rome, May 896 to Aug 897
Romanus, Gallese, Aug 897 to Nov 897
Theodore II, Rome, Dec 897 to Dec 897
John IX, Tivoli, Jan 898 to Jan 900
Benedict IV, Rome, Jan (Feb) 900 to July 903
Leo V, Ardea, July 903 to Sept 903
Sergius III, Rome, 29 Jan 904 to 14 Apr 911
Anastasius III, Rome, Apr 911 to June 913
Landus, Sabina, July 913 to Feb 914
John X, Tossignano (Imola), Mar 914 to May 928
Leo VI, Rome, May 928 to Dec 928
Stephen VII (VIII), Rome, Dec 928 to Feb 931
John XI, Rome, Feb (Mar) 931 to Dec 935
Leo VII, Rome, 3 Jan 936 to 13 July 939
Stephen VIII (IX), Rome, 14 July 939 to Oct 942
Marinus II, Rome, 30 Oct 942 to May 946
Agapitus II, Rome, 10 May 946 to Dec 955
John XII (Octavius), Tusculum, 16 Dec 955 to 14 May 964 (date of his death)
Leo VIII, Rome, 4 (6) Dec 963 to 1 Mar 965
Benedict V, Rome, 22 May 964 to 4 July 966

Confusion exists concerning the legitamcy of claims to the pontificate by Leo VII and Benedict V. John XII was deposed on 4 Dec 963 by a Roman council. If this deposition was invalid, Leo was an antipope. If the deposition of John was valid, Leo was the legitimate pope and Benedict was an antipope.

John XIII, Rome, 1 Oct 965 to 6 Sept 972
Benedict VI, Rome, 19 Jan 973 to June 974
Benedict VII, Rome, Oct 974 to 10 July 983
John XIV (Peter Campenora), Pavia, Dec 983 to 20 Aug 984
John XV, Rome, Aug 985 to Mar 996
Gregory V (Bruno of Carinthia), Saxony, 3 May 996 to 18 Feb 999
Sylvester II (Gerbert), Auvergne, 2 Apr 999 to 12 May 1003

John XVII (Siccone), Rome, June 1003 to Dec 1003
John XVIII (Phasianus), Rome, Jan 1004 to July 1009
Sergius IV (Peter), Rome, 31 July 1009 to 12 May 1012

The custom of changing one's name on election to the papacy is generally considered to date from the time of Sergius IV. Before his time, several popes had changed their names. After his time, this became a regular practice, with few exceptions, e.g. Adrian VI and Marcellus II.

Benedict VIII (Theophylactus), Tusculum, 18 May 1012 to 9 Apr 1024
John XIX (Rosmanus), Tusculum, Apr (May) 1024 to 1032
Benedict IX (Theophylactus), Tusculum, 1032-44
Sylvester III (John), Rome, 20 Jan 1045 to 10 Feb 1045

Sylvester III was an antipope if the forcible removal of Benedict IX in 1044 was not legitimate.

Benedict IX (second time), 10 Apr 1045 to 1 May 1045
Gregory VI (John Gratian), Rome, 5 May 1045 to 20 Dec 1046
Clement II (Suitger, Lord of Morsleben and Homburg), Saxony, 24 (25) Dec 1046 to 9 Oct 1047

If the resignation of Benedict IX in 1045 and his removal at the December 1046 synod were not legitimate, Gregory VI and Clement II were antipopes.

Benedict IX (third time), 8 Nov 1047 to 17 July 1028 (d. c.1055)
Damasus II (Poppo), Bavaria, 17 July 1028 to 9 Aug 1028
St Leo IX (Bruno), Alsace 12 Feb 1049 to 19 Apr 1054
Victor II (Gebhard), Swabia, 16 Apr 1055 to 28 July 1057
Stephen IX (X) (Frederick), Lorraine, 3 Aug 1057 to 29 Mar 1058
Nicholas II (Gerard), Burgundy, 24 Jan 1059 to 27 July 1061
Alexander II (Anselmo da Baggio), Milan, 1 Oct 1061 to 21 Apr 1073
St Gregory VII (Hildebrand), Tuscany, 22 Apr (30 June) 1073 to 25 May 1085
Bl Victor III (Dauferius; Desiderius), Benevento, 24 May 1086 to 15 Sept 1087
Bl Urban II (Otto di Lagery), France, 12 Mar 1088 to 29 July 1099
Paschall II (Raniero), Ravenna, 13 (14) Aug 1099 to 21 Jan 1118
Gelasius II (Giovanni Caetani), Gaeta, 24 Jan (10 Mar) 1118 to 28 Jan 1119
Callistus II (Guido of Burgundy), Burgundy, 2 (9) Feb 1119 to 13 Dec 1124

THE ROMAN PONTIFFS

Honorius II (Lamberto), Fiagnano (Imola), 15 (21) Dec 1124 to 13 Feb 1130
Innocent II (Gregorio Paperschi), Rome, 14 (23) Feb 1130 to 24 Sept 1143
Celestine II (Guido), Città di Castello, 26 Sept (3 Oct) 1143 to 8 Mar 1144
Lucius II (Gerardo Caccianemici), Bologna, 12 Mar 1144 to 15 Feb 1145
Bl Eugene III (Bernardo Paganelli di Montemagno), Pisa, 15 (18) Feb 1145 to 8 July 1153
Anastasius IV (Corrado), Rome, 12 July 1153 to 3 Dec 1154
Adrian IV (Nicholas Breakspear), England, 4 (5) Dec 1154 to 1 Sept 1159
Alexander III (Rolando Bandinelli), Siena, 7 (20) Sept 1159 to 30 Aug 1181
Lucius III (Ubaldo Allucingoli), Lucca, 1 (6) Sept 1181 to 25 Sept 1185
Urban III (Uberto Crivelli), Millan, 25 Nov (1 Dec) 1185 to 20 Oct 1187
Gregory VIII (Alberto de Morra), Benevento, 21 (25) Oct 1187 to 17 Dec 1187
Clement III (Paolo Scolari), Rome, 19 (20) Dec 1187 to Mar 1191
Celestine III (Giacinto Bobone), Rome, 30 Mar (14 Apr) 1191 to 8 Jan 1198
Innocent III (Lotario dei Conti di Segni), Anagni, 8 Jan (22 Feb) 1198 to 16 July 1216
Honorius III (Cencio Savelli), Rome, 18 (24) July 1216 to 18 Mar 1227
Gregory IX (Ugolino, Count of Segni), Anagni, 19 (21) Mar 1227 to 22 Aug 1241
Celestine IV (Goffredo Castiglioni), Milan, 25 (28) Oct 1241 to 10 Nov 1241
Innocent IV (Sinibaldo Fieschi), Genoa, 25 (28) June 1243 to 7 Dec 1254
Alexander IV (Rinaldo, Count of Segni), Anagni, 12 (20) Dec 1254 to 25 May 1261
Urban IV (Jacques Pantaléon), Troyes, 29 Aug (4 Sept) 1261 to 2 Oct 1264
Clement IV (Guy Foulques or Guido le Gros), France, 5 (15) Feb 1265 to 29 Nov 1268
Bl Gregory X (Teobaldo Visconti), Piacenza, 1 Sept 1271 (27 Mar 1272) to 10 Jan 1276
Bl Innocent V (Peter of Tarentaise), Savoy, 21 Jan (22 Feb) 1276 to 22 June 1276
Adrian V (Ottobono Fieschi), Genoa, 11 July 1276 to 18 Aug 1276
John XXI (Petrus Juliani or Petrus Hispanus), Portugal, 8 (20) Sept 1276 to 20 May 1277

Elimination was made of the name of John XX in an effort to rectify the numerical designation of popes named John. The error dates back to the time of John XV.

Nicholas III (Giovanni Gaetano Orsini), Rome, 25 Nov (26 Dec) 1277 to 22 Aug 1280

Martin IV (Simon de Brie), France, 22 Feb (23 Mar) 1281 to 28 Mar 1285

The names of Marinus I (882-4) and Marinus II (942-6) were construed as Martin. In view of these two pontificates and the earlier reign of St Martin I (649-55), this pope was called Martin IV.

Honorius IV (Giacomo Savelli), Rome, 2 Apr (20 May) 1285 to 3 Apr 1287
Nicholas IV (Girolamo Masci), Ascoli, 22 Feb 1288 to 4 Apr 1292
St Celestine V (Pietro del Murrone), Isernia, 5 July (29 Aug) 1294 to 13 Dec 1294; d. 1296. Canonised 5 May 1313
Boniface VIII (Benedetto Caetani), Anagni, 24 Dec 1294 (23 Jan 1295) to 11 Oct 1303
Bl Benedict XI (Niccolo Boccasini), Treviso, 22 (27) Oct 1303 to 7 July 1304
Clement V (Bertrand de Got), France, 5 June (14 Nov) 1305 to 20 Apr 1314 (first of Avignon popes)

From 1309 to 1377 Avignon was the residence of a series of French popes during a period of power struggles between the rulers of France, Bavaria and England and the Church. Despite some positive achievments it was the prologue to the Western Schism which began in 1378.

John XXII (Jacques d'Euse), Cahors, 7 Aug (5 Sept) 1316 to 4 Dec 1334
Benedict XII (Jacques Fournier), France, 20 Dec 1334 (8 Jan 1335) to 25 Apr 1342
Clement VI (Pierre Roger), France, 7 (19) May 1342 to 6 Dec 1352
Innocent VI (Etienne Aubert), France, 18 (30) Dec 1352 to 12 Sept 1362
Bl Urban V (Guillaume de Grimoard), France, 28 Sept (6 Nov) 1362 to 19 Dec 1370
Gregory XI (Pierre Roger de Beaufort), France, 30 Dec 1370 (5 Jan 1371) to 26 Mar 1378 (last of Avignon popes)
Urban VI (Bartolomeo Prignano), Naples, 8 (18) Apr 1378 to 15 Oct 1389
Boniface IX (Pietro Tomacelli), Naples, 2 (9) Nov 1389 to 1 Oct 1404
Innocent VII (Cosma Migliorati), Sulmona, 17 Oct (11 Nov) 1404 to 6 Nov 1406
Gregory XII (Angelo Correr), Venice, 30 Nov (19 Dec)1406 to 4 July 1415 when he voluntarily resigned from the papacy to permit the election of his successor.

This brought to an end in the Council of Constance the Western Schism which had divided Christendom into two and then three papal obediences from 1370 to 1417. Gregory XII died on 18 Oct 1417.

Martin V (Oddone Colonna), Rome, 11 (21) Nov 1417 to 20 Feb 1431

Eugene IV (Gabriel Condulmer), Venice, 3 (11) Mar 1431 to 23 Feb 1447
Nicholas V (Tommaso Parentucelli), Sarzana, 6 (19) Mar 1447 to 24 Mar 1455
Callistus III (Alfonso Borgia), Jativa (Valencia), 8 (20) Apr 1455 to 6 Aug 1458
Pius II (Enea Silvio Piccolomini), Siena, 19 Aug (3 Sept) 1458 to 14 Aug 1464
Paul II (Pietro Barbo), Venice, 30 Aug (16 Sept) 1464 to 26 July 1471
Sixtus IV (Francesco della Rovere), Savona, 9 (25) Aug 1471 to 12 Aug 1484
Innocent VIII (Giovanni Battista Cibo), Genoa, 29 Aug (12 Sept) 1484 to 25 July 1492
Alexander VI (Rodrigo Borgia), Jativa (Valencia), 11 (26) Aug 1492 to 18 Aug 1503
Pius III (Francesco Todeschini-Piccolomini), Siena, 22 Sept (1, 8 Oct) 1503 to 18 Oct 1503
Julius II (Guiliano della Rovere), Savona, 31 Oct (26 Nov) 1503 to 21 Feb 1513
Leo X (Giovanni de' Medici), Florence, 9 (19) Mar 1513 to 1 Dec 1521
Adrian VI (Adrian Florensz), Utrecht, 9 Jan (31 Aug) 1522 to 14 Sept 1523
Clement VII (Giulio de' Medici), Florence, 19 (26) Nov 1523 to 25 Sept 1534
Paul III (Alessandro Farnese), Rome, 13 Oct (3 Nov) 1534 to 10 Nov 1549
Julius III (Giovanni Maria Ciocchi del Monte), Rome, 7 (22) Feb 1550 to 23 Mar 1555
Marcellus II (Marcello Cervini), Montepulciano, 9 (10) Apr 1555 to 1 May 1555
Paul IV (Gian Pietro Carafa), Naples, 23 (26) May 1555 to 18 Aug 1559
Pius IV (Giovan Angelo de' Medici), Milan, 25 Dec 1559 (6 Jan 1560) to 9 Dec 1565
St Pius V (Antonio-Michele Ghislieri), Bosco (Alexandria), 7 (17) Jan 1566 to 1 May 1572. Canonised 22 May 1712
Gregory XIII (Ugo Buoncompagni), Bologna, 13 (25) May 1572 to 10 Apr 1585
Sixtus V (Felice Peretti), Grottammare (Ripatransone), 24 Apr (1 May) 1585 to 27 Aug 1590
Urban VII (Giovanni Battista Castagna) Rome, 15 Sept 1590 to 27 Sept 1590
Gregoryy XIV (Niccolo Sfondrati), Cremona, 5 (8) Dec 1590 to 16 Oct 1591
Innocent IX (Giovanni Antonio Facchinetti), Bologna, 19 Oct (3 Nov) 1591 to 30 Dec 1591
Clement VIII (Ippolito Aldobrandini), Florence, 30 Jan (9 Feb) 1592 to 3 Mar 1605
Leo XI (Alessandro de' Medici), Florence, 1 (10) Apr 1605 to 27 Apr 1605
Paul V (Camillo Borghese), Rome, 16 (29) May 1605 to 28 Jan 1621
Gregory XV (Alessandro Ludovisi), Bologna, 9 (14) Feb 1621 to 8 July 1623

THE ROMAN PONTIFFS

Urban VIII (Maffeo Barberini), Florence, 6 Aug (29 Sept) 1623 to 29 July 1644
Innocent X (Giovanni Battista Pamfili), Rome, 15 Sept (4 Oct) 1644 to 7 Jan 1655
Alexander VII (Fabio Chigi), Siena, 7 (18) Apr 1655 to 22 May 1667
Clement IX (Giulio Rospigliosi), Pistoia, 20 (26) June 1667 to 9 Dec 1669
Clement X (Emilio Altieri), Rome, 29 Apr (11 May) 1670 to 22 July 1676
Bl Innocent XI (Benedetto Odescalchi), Como, 21 Sept (4 Oct) 1676 to 12 Aug 1689. Beatified 7 Oct 1956
Alexander VIII (Pietro Ottoboni), Venice, 6 (16) Oct 1689 to 1 Feb 1691
Innocent XII (Antonio Pignatelli), Spinazzola, 12 (15) July 1691 to 27 Sept 1700
Clement XI (Giovanni Francesco Albani), Urbino, 23, 30 Nov (8 Dec) 1700 to 19 Mar 1721
Innocent XIII (Michelangelo dei Conti), Rome, 8 (18) May 1721 to 7 Mar 1724
Benedict XIII (Pietro Francesco [in religion Vincenzo Maria] Orsini), Gravina (Bari), 29 May (4 June) 1724 to 21 Feb 1730
Clement XII (Lorenzo Corsini), Florence, 12 (16) July 1730 to 6 Feb 1740
Benedict XIV (Prospero Lambertini), Bologna, 17 (22) Aug 1740 to 3 May 1758
Clement XIII (Carlo Rezzonico), Venice, 6 (16) July 1758 to 2 Feb 1769
Clement XIV (Giovanni Vincenzo Antonio [in religion Lorenzo] Gaganelli), Rimini, 19, 28 May (4 June) 1769 to 22 Sept 1774
Pius VI (Giovanni Angelo Braschi), Cesena, 15 (22 Feb) 1775 to 29 Aug 1799
Pius VII (Barnabà [in religion Gregirio] Chiaramonti, Cesena, 14 (21) Mar 1800 to 20 Aug 1823
Leo XII (Annibale della Genga), Genga (Fabriano), 28 Sept (5 Oct) 1823 to 10 Feb 1829
Pius VIII (Francesco Saverio Castiglioni), Cingoli, 31 Mar (5 Apr) 1829 to 30 Nov 1830
Gregory XVI (Bartolomeo Alberto [in relgion Mauro] Cappellari), Belluno, 2 (6) Feb 1831 to 1 June 1846
Pius IX (Giovanni M. Mastai-Ferretti), Senigallia, 16 (21) June 1846 to Feb 1878
Leo XIII (Gioacchino Pecci), Carpineto (Anagni), 20 Feb (3 Mar) 1878 to 20 July 1903
St Pius X (Giuseppe Sarto), Riese (Treviso), 4 (9) Aug 1903 to 20 Aug 1914. Canonised 29 May 1954
Benedict XV (Giacomo della Chiesa), Genoa, 3 (6) Sept 1914 to 22 Jan 1922
Pius XI (Achille Ratti), Desio (Milan), 6 (12) Feb 1922 to 10 Feb 1939
Pius XII (Eugenio Pacelli), Rome, 2 (12) Mar 1939 to 9 Oct 1958
John XXIII (Angelo Giuseppe Roncalli), Sotto il Monte (Bergamo), 28 Oct (4 Nov) 1958 to 3 June 1963
Paul VI (Giovanni Battista Montini), Concessio (Brescia, 21 (30) June 1963 to 6 Aug 1978
John Paul I (Albino Luciani), Forno di Canale (Belluno), 26 Aug (3 Sept) 1978 to 28 Sept 1978
John Paul II (Karol Wojtyla), Wadowice, Poland, 16 (22) Oct 1978 to 2 April 2005
Benedict XVI (Joseph Ratzinger), Germany, 19 April 2005 to 28 Feb 2013A
Francis (Jorge Mario Bergoglio) 13 March 2013A

CHURCH OF ST COLUMBANUS, BALLIVOR, CO MEATH, CELEBRATES ITS BI-CENTENARY

Top: Newly refurbished sanctuary of Church of St Columbanus.

Above: Missal from 1821 used by Fr Laurence Shaw OP; Brievary of Fr Patrick Farrell, PP of Ballivor in 1921; Chalice and Paten of the current PP of Ballivor, Fr Mark Mohan.

In medieval times Ballivor was a very different place to what it is today and the parish was known as Killaconnigan. It is not clear if there was a regular site of worship in the parish at that time. About 1793, Fr Laurence Shaw OP, who was attached to the Friary at Donore, built a small thatched chapel about 300 metres from Ballivor village. He used this chapel until he built the current church, in the village in 1821 on land donated by the Earl of Darnley. Fr Shaw was the last Dominican to live in the area and died in 1833. He is buried beneath the chapel.

Father Patrick Farrell (grand uncle of the current Archbishop of Dublin), who was parish priest from 1908 to 1950, substantially renovated the church in 1920–21 and dedicated it to St Columbanus.

Fr William Kiernan who succeeded Fr Farrell as Parish Priest (1950–72) carried out further renovations to the church. Wooden steps to the altar were replaced by marble steps and a central marble tabernacle was erected on the high altar.

New stained glass windows replaced those installed in 1920. The large window behind the altar depicting the crucifixion, which we see today, was donated by Dr Sean Coughlan in memory of his wife Lily.

Nine other stained glass windows on the ground floor also replaced those installed in 1920. These depict St Philomena, St Joseph, St Maria Goretti, St Patrick, St Therese, St Pius X, St Brigid, St Columbanus and the Immaculate Conception. These were donated by parishioners. There are also two stained glass windows on the gallery depicting St Jude and the Holy Infant of Prague.

In order to comply with changes to the liturgy, the altar was separated from the wall in 1971.

BICENTENARY OF CHURCH OF ST COLUMBANUS, BALLIVOR, CO MEATH

St Columbanus Stained Glass Window

St Patrick Stained Glass Window

St Joseph Stained Glass Window

Fr Sean Kenny (Parish Priest, 1972–77) had a Rieger organ installed.

Further modernisation, including housing the Church Bell was carried out in 1992–93 by Fr Matthew Mollin (Parish Priest, 1988–2004).

Modification to the outbuildings around St Columbanus', including creation of a car park in 2009 was carried out by Fr Oliver Devine (Parish Priest, 2004–2016) assisted by the parish finance committee.

Now, two hundred years after the church was built, current Parish Priest, Fr Mark Mohan, has overseen the beautiful renovation. The bicentenary was celebrated with Mass on the evening of Tuesday, 23 November 2021. The main celebrate was Most Rev Tom Deenihan, Bishop of Meath and was concelebrated by Most Rev Dermot Farrell, Archbishop of Dublin; Most Rev Michael Smith, Bishop Emeritus of Meath; Fr Matthew Mollin, former PP of Ballivor, Fr John Conlon PP, St Mary's, Drogheda and Fr Robert McCabe CC, St Mary's, Navan.

The sermon was preached by Fr John Harris OP, Provincial of Dominican Order in Ireland:

'Fr Shaw built this church looking to the future, we must not use it to look back, but like Shaw continue to build our faith on the contemplation of God and to bring to others the fruits of that contemplation. This is a soul of the Dominican Order. It gave life to men like Shaw, it must still be our foundation stone. We come to this sacred temple to

Our Lady's Altar

be filled with the life of God through the celebration of the sacraments, the listening of the Word of God and the prayerful contemplation within our own souls. How many hours have you spent in this sacred place praying to God, asking for mercy and forgiveness, seeking his help and guidance? And going out from this place to be a Christian neighbour.

We are entering into a new age in the Irish church, the devotional revolution has run its course. But our

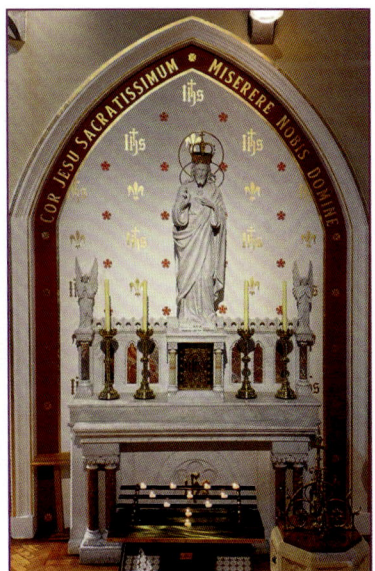

Sacred Heart Altar

future must be union with Christ and love of our neighbours. This house of God is dedicated to St Columbanus, a monk who became a missionary, a contemplative who became a preacher. The pearl of great price that we discover in this sacred place must be shared with the Ireland of today and tomorrow.'

That's us dear brothers and sisters. This is our time.'

Index of Advertisers

Accountants/Financial Advisers
L&P Financial Trustees   148 & Bookmark

Charities/Fundraising
Children in Crossfire   196
Trócaire   37

Church Services/Parish Resources
Cathedral Candle Company   87
CBC Distributors   195
Disciples of Divine Master   77
RPD Limited   79
Veritas   90, 198

Design/Proofing Services
Veritas   226 & Bookmark

Educational Institutes
St Kieran's College, Kilkenny 125
St Patrick's Pontifical University, Maynooth 161
St Paul's College, Raheny   126

Furniture
ICS Furniture   197

Glass
Abbey Stained Glass Studios   159

Health & Safety Training
Darren Whelan   89

Insurance
Allianz   145

Legal Services
Mason Hayes & Curran   127

IT Solutions
Newtec   225

Pioneers
Pioneer Total Abstinence Association 146

Publishers/Publications
Intercom   162
Veritas, *Grow in Love: In the Parish* 78
Veritas Publications   38, 80, 88, 128, 160

Printers
W & G Baird   147
Paceprint   227

Radio
Radio Maria   36

Religious Bookshops
Veritas   228

Website
www.veritas.ie   35

ALPHABETICAL LIST OF CLERGY IN IRELAND

DIOCESAN, RELIGIOUS AND MISSIONARY

Irish Diocesan clergy working or studying abroad are also listed.
Telephone numbers are included in this list.
For all other forms of telephonic or electrical communications, including mobiles, faxes, email addresses and websites, please refer to the main entries in this directory.

**All STD numbers in this Directory are listed with both the number and the local area code.
Callers from the Irish Republic to Northern Ireland simply need to dial 048 followed by the 8-digit local number.**

A

Abraham, Yesuoas Asariparambil (OCarm)
Carmelite Priory,
White Abbey,
Co Kildare R51 X827
Tel 045-521391

Acton, John Gerard, CC
18 University Road,
Galway
Tel 091-524875/563577
(*Cathedral*, Galway)

Adzato, George (SVD), Co-PP
c/o St Philip the Apostle Church, No. 2 Presbtery,
Mountview,
Blanchardstown, Dublin 14
Tel 01-8249695
(*Blakestown/Huntstown/Mountview*, Dublin)

Agger, George (SVD)
Donamon Castle,
Roscommon
Tel 090-6662222

Aguilar, Arturo (SSC), VG
No 3 and 4,
Ma Yau Tong Village,
Po Lam Road,
Tseung Kwan O, Hong Kong, SAR

Aguilar-Díez, Juan José (SJ)
John Sullivan House,
56/56A Mulvey Park,
Dundrum, Dublin 14
Tel 01-2983978

Ahearne, Peter, Very Rev, PE
(Waterford & L., retired)

Ahearne, Seamus (OSA), Very Rev, PP
The Presbytery,
60 Glenties Park,
Finglas South, Dublin 11
Tel 01-8343722/
087-6782746
(*Rivermount*, Dublin)

Ahern, Dan (SSC)
c/o St John's Parish Centre,
Castle Street, Tralee,
Co Kerry

Ahern, Gerard, Very Rev, PP
Parkmore,
Baltinglass, Co Wicklow
Tel 087-6298881
(Kildare & L.)

Ahern, Niall, Very Rev Canon, PP, VF
Strandhill, Co Sligo
Tel 071-9168147
(*Strandhill/Ransboro*, Elphin)

Ahern, Pat
(Kerry, retired)

Aherne, Francis (OSA), CC
Prior, St Augustine's,
Taylor's Lane,
Ballyboden, Dublin 16
Tel 01-4241000

Akubuenyi, Samuel, PC
c/o Parish Office,
Balgaddy Road, Lucan,
County Dublin K78 NH05
Tel 01-4572900
(*Lucan South*, Dublin)

Alexander, Anthony, Very Rev, PP
46 Blackstaff Road,
Ballycranbeg, Kircubbin,
Newtownards,
Co Down BT22 1AG
Tel 028-42738294
(*Kircubbin (Ardkeen)*, Down & C.)

Alexander, Paul, Very Rev, PP
10 St Patrick's Road, Saul,
Downpatrick,
Co Down BT30 7JE
Tel 028-44612525
(*Saul and Ballee*, Down & C.)

Ali, Joseph, CC
St John's Presbytery,
Lecarrow, Co Roscommon
Tel 090-6661115
(*Knockcroghery*, Elphin)

Alipoyo, Glen, CC
(Pastoral Leader)
Forthill House,
The Batteries,
Athlone, Co Westmeath
Tel 0906-492171
(*Ss Peter and Paul's*, Athlone, Elphin)

Allen, Brian (OFM)
Adam & Eve's
4 Merchants' Quay
Dublin, D08 XY19
Tel 01-6771128

Allman, Colm, Very Rev, BA, HDE
President,
St Joseph's College,
Garbally Park, Ballinasloe,
Co Galway
Tel 090-9642504/9642254
(*Ballinasloe, Creagh And Kilclooney*, Clonfert)

Allred, Norman, CC,
Cathedral House,
Mullingar,
Co Westmeath
Tel 044-9348338/9340126
(*Mullingar*, Meath)

Alwill, Gerard, Very Rev, PP
56 Main Street, Derrylin
Co Fermanagh BT92 9PD
Tel 028-67748315
(*Derrylin (Knockninny)*, Kilmore)

Ambrose, James, Very Rev Canon
Dromcollogher,
Charleville, Co Limerick
Tel 087-7740753
(Limerick, retired)

Ambrose, John Rev (MHM)
St Joseph's House,
50 Orwell Park,
Rathgar, Dublin D06 C535
Tel 01-4127700

Ameh, Christian, PC
c/o The Sacristy, St Vincent de Paul Church,
Griffith Avenue, Dublin 9
Tel 01-8339756
(*Marino*, Dublin)

Anandam, Alexander (SSP)
Society of Saint Paul,
Moyglare Road,
Maynooth Co Kildare
Tel 01-6285933

Andama, Martin (CSSp)
St Mary's College,
Rathmines, Dublin 6
Tel 01-4995760

Andersen, Dom Benedict Maria (OSB)
Silverstream Priory,
Stamullen,
Co Meath K32 T189

Angodage, Anthony Priyantha (SSS)
Blessed Sacrament Chapel,
20 Bachelors Walk,
Dublin 1 D01 NW14
Tel 01-8724597

Annan, Raphael Kobina (CSSp)
Team Leader
Church of the Holy Spirit
Greenhills, Dublin 12
Tell 01-4504040

Antwi-Boasiako, Isaac (CSSp)
55 Fernhill Road,
Greenhills, Dublin 12
Tell 01-4504040
(*Greenhills, Kimmage Manor*, Dublin)

Apap, Jesmond (SDB)
Vice-Rector,
Salesian College,
Maynooth Road,
Celbridge,
Co Kildare W23 W0XK

Apust, Joseph, CC
Parochial House,
Mornington, Co Meath
Tel 01-9827384
(*Laytown-Mornington*, Meath)

Arigho, Desmond (CSSp)
Holy Spirit Missionary College
Kimmage Manor,
Whitehall Road,
Dublin D12 P5YP
Tel 01-4064300

Arkinson, Patrick, PP
Sessiaghoneill, Ballybofey,
Co Donegal
Tel 074-9131149
(*Killygordon (Donaghmore)*, Derry)

Armstrong, Paul, Very Rev, PE
5 Balmoral Mews,
Belfast BT9 6NM
(Down & C., retired)

LIST OF CLERGY IN IRELAND

Arnasius, Egidijus
48 Westland Row,
Dublin 2
Tel 01-6761030/
087-7477554
(*Westland Row*, Dublin)
Arunmozhi (SJ)
35 Lower Leeson Street,
Dublin 2
Tel 01-6761248
Atede, Godwin, CC
St Mary's, Tang,
Ballymahon, Co Longford
Tel 090-6432214
(*Drumraney*, Meath)
Attoh, John, PC
7 Cardiff Castle Road,
Finglas West, Dublin 11
Tel 01-8343928
(*Finglas West*, Dublin)
Audley, Pádraig, Very Rev,
PE
Leitir Mealláin,
Co na Gaillimhe
(Tuam, retired)
Aughney, Edward, Very Rev,
Adm
Glynn, St Mullins via
Kilkenny
Tel 051-424563
(*St Mullins*, Kildare & L.)
Augusthy, Bobit (OSCam)
Chaplain, Waterford
University Hospital,
Dunmore Road, Waterford
Tel 051-848000
(Waterford & L.)
Augustine, George, Very
Rev, PP
Mill Lane, Kilcock,
Co Kildare
Tel 01-6103512
(*Kilcock*, Kildare & L.)
Aylward, Cassian (OSB)
Silverstream Priory,
Stamullen,
Co Meath K32 T189
Tel 01-8417142
Aylward, Eamon (SSCC)
27 Northbrook Road,
Ranelagh, Dublin 6
Tel 01-4570032
Ayola, Anthony, CC
Parochial House, Duleek,
Co Meath
Tel 041-9823205
(*Duleek*, Meath)
Ayuba, James
Parish Chaplain,
Holy Redeemer Parish,
Main Street, Bray,
Co Wicklow
Tel 089-9646741
(*Bray (Holy Redeemer)*,
Dublin)

B

Babu, Suresh (OSCam)
St Camillus,
South Hill Avenue,
Blackrock, Co Dublin
Tel 01-2882873/2833380
Bachara, Kamil, CC
64 Westcourt,
Ballincollig, Co Cork
(*Ballincollig*, Cork & R.)
Bailey, Michael (OFM)
Dún Mhuire,
Seafield Road,
Killiney, Co Dublin
Tel 01-2826760
Baker, Eugene, Very Rev, PP
The Presbytery,
Richmond Street,
Buttevant, Co Cork
Adm, Churchtown
Tel 086-8031876
(*Buttevant, Churchtown
(Liscarroll)*, Cloyne)
Baker, Patrick, Adm
St Columba's Presbytery,
6 Victoria Place,
Derry BT48 6TJ
Tel 028-71262301
(*Derry City*, Derry)
Balikuddembe, Philip
Amooti, CC
Parochial House,
Aglish, Co Waterford
Tel 024-96287
(*Aglish*, Waterford and L.)
Bamai, Yusuf, CC
Kill, Cootehill, Co Cavan
Tel 049-5553218
(*Kilsherdany and Drung*,
Kilmore)
Bane, John
3 Cottage Gardens,
Station Road,
Ennis, Co Clare
Tel 086-8246555
(Killaloe, retired)
Bannon, Gabriel (OSM),
Very Rev
Servite Priory, Benburb,
Dungannon,
Co Tyrone BT71 7JZ
Northern Ireland
Tel 028-37548241
Bannon, Michael, PP
Gowna, Co Cavan
Tel 043-6683120
(*Lough Gowna and
Mullinalaghta*, Ardagh &
Cl.)
Bannon, Patrick
15 Lisdarn Heights, Cavan
(Kilmore, retired)

Banville, Patrick, Very Rev,
Adm
The Presbytery,
Templeshannon,
Enniscorthy, Co Wexford
Tel 053-9237611
(*St Senans*, Enniscorthy,
Ferns)
Baragry, Dan (CSsR)
Provincial, St Joseph's,
St Alphonsus Road,
Dundalk,
Co Louth A71 F3FC
Tel 042-9334042/9334762
Barasa, Vitalis
St John's Presbytery,
Tralee, Co Kerry
Tel 066-7122522
(*Tralee, St John's*, Kerry)
Barber, Noel (SJ)
Milltown Park,
Sandford Road,
Dublin D04 NX39
Tel 01-269898411
Barden, Thomas, PP
Kenagh, Co Longford
Tel 043-3322127
(*Kilcommoc*, Ardagh & Cl.)
Barkindo, Lazarus (OSA)
St Augustine's Priory,
Shop Street, Drogheda,
Co Louth
Barrett, Anthony (SPS)
St Patrick's, Kiltegan,
Co Wicklow W91 Y022
Tel 059-6473600
Barrett, Edward (OMI)
Department of Chaplaincy,
Tralee General Hospital,
Tralee, Co Kerry
Tel 066-7126222
Barrett, Eugene (OFM)
Guardian,
Franciscan Friary,
Rossnowlagh,
Co Donegal F94 PH21
Tel 071-9851342
Barrins, David (OP),
Superior,
Dundalk, Co Louth
Tel 042-9334179/9333714
(*Droichead
Nua/Newbridge*, Kildare &
L.)
Barron, Liam, Very Rev, PP
Mullinavat, via Waterford,
Co Kilkenny
Tel 051-898108/
087-2722824
(*Mullinavat*, Ossory)
Barry, Anselm (OSB)
Glenstal Abbey, Murroe,
Co Limerick
Tel 061-621000
Barry, Eamonn
Gortacrue
Midleton, Co Cork
Tel 086-8157952
(Cloyne, retired)

Barry, Martin (SPS)
Kiltegan House,
11 Douglas Road, Cork
Tel 021-4969371
Barry, Maurice (OCarm)
Carmelite Friary, Kinsale,
Co Cork
Tel 021-772138
Barry, Michael (SAC)
Pallottine College,
Thurles, Co Tipperary
Tel 0504-21202
Barry, Oliver (OMI), Very
Rev
Provincial,
Oblates of Mary
Immaculate House of
Retreat,
Tyreconell Road,
Inchicore, Dublin 8
Tel 01-4541160/4541160
Barry, Philip (SAC)
Pallottine College,
Thurles, Co Tipperary
Tel 0504-21202
Bartlett, Timothy, Very Rev,
Adm
St Mary's, Marquis Street,
Belfast BT1 1JJ
Tel 028-90320482
(*St Mary's*, Down & C.)
Bartley, Kevin, Very Rev,
Adm
The Presbytery,
Chapel Green, Rush,
Co Dublin
Tel 01-8437208
(*Rush*, Dublin)
Baxter, Martin (OCarm)
Bursar, Carmelite Priory,
Whitefriar Street Church,
56 Aungier Street,
Dublin 2 D02 R598
Tel 01-4758821
Baxter, Philip (OFMCap)
Guardian, Capuchin Friary,
Ard Mhuire,
Creeslough, Letterkenny,
Co Donegal
Tel 074-9138005
Baxter, Turlough, Adm
Parochial House, Killashee
Co Longford
Tel 043-3345546
(*Killashee*, Ardagh & Cl.)
Bayaca, Darwin (SSC)
No 3 and 4,
Ma Yau Tong Village,
Po Lam Road,
Tseung Kwan O,
Kow Loon, Hong Kong,
SAR
Beagon, Brendan, Very Rev,
CC
1 Christine Road,
Newtownabbey,
Co Antrim BT36 6TG
Tel 028-90841507
(*St Mary's on the Hill*,
Down & C.)

LIST OF CLERGY IN IRELAND

Beatty, John, Very Rev, AP
St Michael's Street,
Tipperary Town,
Co Tipperary
Tel 062-80475
(*Tipperary*, Cashel & E.)

Beecher, Patrick (OCD)
The Abbey, Loughrea,
Co Galway
Tel 091-841209

Beere, Joseph (CSSp)
Holy Spirit Missionary
College,
Kimmage Manor,
Whitehall Road, Dublin 12
Tel 01-4064300

Beggan, Nguekam Tiernach,
Very Rev, PP
6 Boa Island, Belleek,
Enniskillen,
Co Fermanagh BT93 3AE
Tel 028-68658229
(*Belleek-Garrison*, Clogher)

Beglan, Peter, PE
The Presbytery,
Edgeworthstown,
Co Longford
(Ardagh & Cl., retired)

Begley, George P., Adm
Parochial House,
Chapel Road,
Lusk, Co Dublin
Tel 01-8949229
(*Lusk*, Dublin)

Begley, Joseph, Very Rev
Canon, PP
Glengarriff, Co Cork
Tel 027-63045
Moderator, Kilgarvin
Kilgarvan, Co Kerry
Tel 064-6685313
(*Glengarriff (Bonane)*,
Kilgarvan, Kerry)

Behan, Laurence, Very Rev
On Leave
(Dublin)

Behan, Richard, Very Rev,
PP
The Presbytery,
Main Street,
Blessington, Co Wicklow
Tel 045-865442
(*Blessington, Valleymount*,
Dublin)

Beirne, Francis, Very Rev, PP
Tisrara, Four Roads,
Co Roscommon
Tel 090-6623313
(*Ballyforan (Dysart and
Tisrara)*, Elphin)

Beirne, Seán, CC
Kilteevan, Roscommon
Tel 090-6626374
(*Roscommon*, Elphin)

Belton, Liam, Very Rev
Canon,
Moderator
Presbytery No 1,
Ballinteer Avenue,
Dublin D16 PY54
Tel 01-4944448
(*Ballinteer, Dundrum,
Meadowbrook*, Dublin)

Bennett, Donal N. (SSC)
Omagh, Co Tyrone

Bennett, John (MSC)
Woodview House,
Mount Merrion Avenue,
Blackrock, Co Dublin
Tel 01-2881644

Bennett, Mark, CC
St Mary's,
Carrick-on-Shannon,
Co Leitrim
Tel 071-9620347
(*Carrick-on-Shannon
(Kiltoghert)*, Ardagh & Cl.)

Bennett, Martin (OFMCap),
PP
Capuchin Friary,
Church Street, Dublin 7
Tel 01-8730599
(*Halston Street and
Arran Quay*, Dublin)

Bennett, Paul, CC
2 Cathedral Terrace,
Cobh, Co Cork
Tel 021-4908317
(*Cobh*, Cloyne)

Bennett, Roch (OFMCap)
Capuchin Friary,
Ard Mhuire, Creeslough,
Letterkenny,
Co Donegal F92 Y23R
Tel 074-9138005

Bennett, Terence (SSC)
St Columban's Retirement
Home,
Dalgan Park,
Navan, Co Meath
Tel 046-9021525

Bergin, John (SAC)
Pallottine College,
Thurles, Co Tipperary
Tel 0504-21202

Bergin, Liam, Rt Rev Mgr
St Brigid's Parish,
841 East Broadway,
Boston, MA 02127, USA
Tel 001-617-4477770
(Ossory)

Bermingham, Jim (SPS)
St Patrick's, Kiltegan,
Co Wicklow
Tel 059-6473600

Bermingham, John (CSsR)
St Joseph's,
St Alphonsus Road,
Dundalk,
Co Louth A71 F3FC
Tel 042-9334042

Bermingham, William, Very
Rev Canon, PP
Youghal, Co Cork
Tel 083-8687196
(*Youghal*, Cloyne)

Berney, Donal, PP
Kilanerin, Gorey,
Co Wexford
Tel 0402-37120
(*Kilanerin and Ballyfad*,
Ferns)

Bettison, John (SVD)
8 Teignmouth Road,
London, NW2 4HN
Tel 020-84528430

Binh, Dominic Nguyen Viet
(SDB)
Salesian College, Don
Bosco Road
Pallaskenry,
Co Limerick V94 WP86
Tel 061-393105

Binh, Paul Tran Xuan Rev
(SDB)
Salesian College,
Maynooth Road,
Celbridge,
Co Kildare W23 W0XK

Bingham, Michael (SJ)
(British Province)
Iona, 211 Churchill Park,
Portadown BT62 1EU
Tel 028-38330366

Birmingham, Joseph (OCD)
Avila Carmelite Centre,
Bloomfield Avenue,
Morehampton Road,
Dublin 4
Tel 01-6430200

Black, Andrew
Canadian Pontifical
College,
Via Crecenzio, 75,
00193 Rome
(Down & C.)

Blade, Kevin (MSC), Adm
Castlegar, Galway
Tel 091-751548
(*Castlegar*, Galway)

Blake, Ciarán, Very Rev, PP
Cummer, Tuam,
Co Galway
(*Cummer (Kilmoylan and
Cummer)*, Tuam)

Blake, Declan, Very Rev
Presbytery 2,
Shangan Road, Dublin 9
Tel 01-8421486
(*St Pappin's, Ballymun*,
Dublin)

Blake, Ephrem (CP)
Passionist Retreat Centre,
Downpatrick Road,
Crossgar,
Co Down BT30 9EQ
Tel 028-44830242

Blake, Kieran, Very Rev,
Co-PP
Kilcolman, Sharavogue,
Birr, Co Offaly
Tel 057-9120812/
087-9302214
(*Brendan Pastoral Area*,
Killaloe)

Blake, Martin,
c/o Diocesan Office,
Westbourne, Ennis,
Co Clare
(Killaloe)

Blayney, Liam (SPS), Very
Rev
12 Bellaghy Road,
Dunloy, Ballymena
Co Antrim BT44 9AE

Bluett, Anthony
Parochial House,
Ardpatrick, Co Limerick
Tel 087-1934525
(*Pastoral Unit 9*, Limerick)

Bluett, Garrett, Very Rev
Canon
Croom, Co Limerick
Tel 061-397335
(Limerick, retired)

Bluett, Patrick,
Glenfield,
Kilmallock,
Co Limerick.
(Limerick, retired)

Bluitt, Tobias, Very Rev
Canon, PP, VF
Kanturk, Co Cork
Tel 029-50192
(*Kanturk/Castlemanger*,
Cloyne)

Boggan, Matthew, PP
Clongeen, Foulksmills,
Co Wexford
Tel 051-565610
(*Clongeen*, Ferns)

Bohan, Bernard (SPS)
St Patrick's, Kiltegan,
Co Wicklow
Tel 059-6473600

Bohan, Harry, Very Rev, AP
172 Drumgeely Hill,
Shannon, Co Clare
Tel 061-713682/086-
8223362
(*Tradaree Pastoral Area*,
Killaloe)

Bohan, Seamus, Very Rev,
PP
Tynagh, Loughrea,
Co Galway H62 DH32
Tel 090-9745113
Moderator, Duniry and
Abbey
(*Duniry and Kilnelehan*)
(*Duniry and Abbey*
Duniry and Kilnelehan),
Tynagh and Killeen,
Clonfert)

Boland, Declan, PP
44 Barrack Street,
Strabane,
Co Tyrone BT82 8HD
Tel 028-71883293
(*Strabane*, Derry)

Boland, Eugene
c/o Diocesan Offices,
St Eugene's Cathedral,
Francis Street,
Derry BT48 9AP
(Derry, retired)

Boland, Vivian (OP)
Convent of SS Xystus and Clement
Collegio San Clemente,
Via Labicana 95,
00184 Roma
Tel 0039-06-7740021

Bollard, Daniel, Very Rev, PP
Thomastown, Co Kilkenny
Tel 056-7724279/
087-6644858
(*Thomastown*, Ossory)

Bonner, Patrick
c/o Diocesan Office,
Letterkenny, Co Donegal
(Raphoe)

Boran, Anthony (OFMCap)
Capuchin Friary,
Station Road, Raheny,
Dublin D05 T9E4
Tel 01-8313886

Borders, Thomas Aquinas (OSB)
Silverstream Priory,
Stamullen,
Co Meath K32 T189
Tel 01-8417142

Boschi, Marcelo (FDP)
Regional Superior,
c/o Via Etruria 6, 00183
Rome, Italy

Bourke, Eamonn, Very Rev
Head Chaplain, UCD,
Belfield, Dublin 4
Tel 01-7161971
(Dublin)

Bourke, George, Very Rev, AP
Moycarkey, Thurles,
Co Tipperary
Tel 0504-44227
(*Moycarkey*, Cashel & E.)

Bowe, John (SMA)
African Missions,
Blackrock Road,
Cork T12 TD54
Tel 021-4292871

Bowen, Patrick, Very Rev, PP
Glenmore Avenue
Tel 0876532482
(Limerick, retired)

Boyce, Eugene,
Croagh, Rathkeale,
Co Limerick
Tel 069-64185/087-2542517
(*Pastoral Unit 11*, Limerick)

Boyce, Declan (SPS), Adm,
St Mary's, Temple Street,
Co Sligo
Tel 071-9162670
(*St Mary's, Sligo*, Elphin)

Boyce, John, CC
Arranmore Island,
Co Donegal
Tel 074-9520504
(*Burtonport (Kincasslagh)*, Raphoe)

Boyce, Philip (OCD), Most Rev, DD
Bishop Emeritus of Raphoe,
'Columba House',
Windyhall, Letterkenny,
Co Donegal F92 EK4W
Tel 074-9122729
(Raphoe)

Boyers, John
16 'Wilfield',
Sandymount Avenue,
Ballsbridge, Dublin 4
Tel 087-1557887
(*Donnybrook*, Dublin)

Boyle, Brian, Very Rev, Adm
The Presbytery,
Ravenswood,
Fermoy, Co Cork
Tel 025-34467
(*Fermoy*, Cloyne)

Boyle, Con, Very Rev, PP
87 Cushendall Road,
Ballyvoy, Ballycastle,
Co Antrim BT54 6QY
Tel 028-20762248
(*Culfeightrin*, Down & C.)

Boyle, Francis, PE
(Dromore, retired)

Boyle, Gerry, Very Rev, PP
Parochial House,
Rathkenny, Co Meath
Tel 046-9054138
Administrator,
Parochial House,
Lobinstown, Navan,
Co Meath
Tel 046-9053155
(Meath)

Boyle, Hugh (SDB)
Salesian House,
45 St Teresa's Road,
Crumlin, Dublin D12 XK52
Tel 01-4555605

Boyle, James A. (MHM)
c/o St Joseph's House,
50 Orwell Park,
Rathgar, Dublin D06 C535
Tel 01-4127700

Boyle, Laurence, Very Rev, PP
Parochial House,
1 Convert Road,
Cookstown,
Co Tyrone BT80 8QA
Tel 028-86763370
(*Cough, Cookstown (Desertcreight & Derryloran)*, Armagh)

Boyle, Liam
Parochial House,
Newmills, Glenswilly,
Co Donegal
Tel 074-9137456
Chaplain,
Letterkenny Institute of Technology,
(*Glenswilly*, Raphoe)

Boyle, Liam, Rt Rev
Knockaderry, Co Limerick
(Limerick, retired)

Boyle, Martin (OP)
St Saviour's,
Upper Dorset Street,
Dublin 1
Tel 01-8897610

Boyle, Michael (OSA)
St Augustine's Priory,
Washington Street, Cork
Tel 021-2753982

Boyle, Patrick, Very Rev, Adm
67 Edenvale Road,
Dublin 6
Tel 01-4972165
(*Edenmore*, Dublin)

Boyle, Ronnie, Very Rev, PP
Parochial House,
Chapel Field,
Abbeyknockmoy, Tuam,
Co Galway H54 DR02
Tel 093-43510
(*Abbeyknockmoy*, Tuam)

Bracken, John, Co-PP
Emmaus, Main Street,
Dundrum, Dublin 14
Tel 01-2983494
(*Dundrum*, Dublin)

Bracken, P. J., Very Rev, PP
Portumna Retirement Village,
Portumna, Co Galway
(Clonfert, retired)

Bradley, Bruce (SJ)
Milltown Park,
Sandford Road, Dublin 6
Tel 01-2698411/2698113

Bradley, David, Very Rev, PP
Parochial House,
Kells, Co Meath
Tel 046-9240213
(*Kells*, Meath)

Bradley, Francis, Very Rev, PP, Chancellor
Cockhill, Buncrana,
Co Donegal
Tel 074-9363455
(*Buncrana, Fahan (Burt, Inch and Fahan)*, Derry)

Bradley, John, Very Rev, PE
8 Killymeal Road,
Dungannon,
Co Tyrone BT71 6BE
Tel 028-87722183
(Armagh, retired)

Bradley, Manus
3690 Croissant Oscar,
Brossard,
Quebec J4Y 2JB
Tel 001-1450-8127858
(Derry)

Bradley, Philip, Very Rev, Adm, VF
Parochial House,
83 Terenure Road East,
Dublin 6
Tel 01-4905520
(*Terenure*, Dublin)

Bradley, William (CSSp)
Templeogue College,
Templeville Road,
Dublin 6W
Tel 01-4903909

Brady, Brian, Very Rev, PP, VF
Parochial House,
Ardnascanlon, Co Donegal
Tel 074-9376264
(Derry)

Brady, Enda, Very Rev, PP
Bohereenglas, Cashel,
Co Tipperary
Tel 062-61127
(*Cashel*, Cashel & E.)

Brady, Frank, (SJ), PC
The Presbytery,
Shangan Road, Ballymun,
Dublin 9
Tel 01-8421551
(*Ballymun*, Dublin)

Brady, Frank Rev
Hydebank Wood,
Hospital Road,
Belfast BT8 8NA
(Down & C.)

Brady, Gerard, PP
Carrick, Finea,
Mullingar,
Co Westmeath
Tel 043-6681129
(*Carrick-Finea*, Ardagh & Cl.)

Brady, Harry, Very Rev, AP
10 Beechwood, Lissane,
Clarecastle, Co Clare
Tel 086-2349798
(*Abbey Pastoral Area*, Killaloe)

Brady, Jim (SPS)
St Patrick's, Kiltegan,
Co Wicklow W91 Y022
Tel 059-6473600

Brady, Kenneth (CP)
St Paul's Retreat,
Mount Argus, Dublin 6W
Tel 01-4992000

Brady, Michael (OMI)
52a Bulfin Road,
Dublin 8
Tel 01-4531660

Brady, P. J. (OFM)
Franciscan Friary,
Killarney, Co Kerry
Tel 064-6631334/6631066

LIST OF CLERGY IN IRELAND

Brady, Patrick V.
  (Kilmore, retired)
Brady, Peter, PE
  Lenamore, Co Longford
  Tel 044-9357404
  (Ardagh & Cl., retired)
Brady, Philip, Very Rev
  Creighan, Co Cavan
  (Kilmore, retired)
Brady, Ray, Very Rev
  c/o Bishop's House,
  Mullingar, Co Westmeath
  (Meath, retired)
Brady, Rory, Very Rev, PP
  Bruckless, Co Donegal
  Tel 074-9737015
  (Bruckless (Killaghtee),
  Raphoe)
Brady, Seán, His Eminence
  Cardinal, DCL, DD
  Archbishop Emeritus of
  Armagh,
  Parochial House,
  86 Maydown Road
  Tullysaran, Benburb,
  Co Tyrone BT71 7LN
  (Armagh)
Brady, Thomas, Very Rev
  26 Cloonarkin Drive,
  Oranmore, Co Galway
  Tel 091-751707
  (Galway)
Branagan, Anthony (CSsR)
  Clonard Monastery,
  1 Clonard Gardens,
  Belfast BT13 2RL
  Tel 028-90445950
Branigan, Desmond, CC
  Our Lady of Lourdes
  Presbytery,
  Hardman's Gardens,
  Drogheda,
  Co Louth A92 PXF3
  Tel 041-9831899
  (Drogheda, Armagh)
Brankin, Aidan, Very Rev, PP
  27 Glenveagh Drive,
  Belfast BT11 9HX
  Tel 028-90618180
  (St Oliver Plunkett, Down
  & C.)
Brannigan, David, Very Rev,
  Co-PP
  89 Sperrin Road,
  Drimnagh, Dublin 12
  Tel 01-4652418
  (Mourne Road, Dublin)
Brassil, Paul (SJ) (Zambia)
  c/o St Ignatius Community
  & Church,
  27 Raleigh Row,
  Salthill, Galway
  Tel 091-523707
Brazil, Sean (SSC)
  St Columban's,
  Dalgan Park,
  Navan, Co Meath
  Tel 046-9021525

Breathnach, Cormac (SMA)
  SMA House, Wilton,
  Cork, T12 KR23
  Tel 021-4541069/4541884
Bredin, Eamonn
  (Kilmore, retired)
Breen, Gerard, Very Rev, PP
  Parochial House,
  Stradbally, Co Laois
  Tel 057-8625132
  (Stradbally, Kildare & L.)
Breen, P. J., CC
  14 Heathervue Road,
  Riverview,
  Knockboy, Co Waterford
  Tel 051-820452
  (Ss Joseph and Benildus,
  Waterford and L.)
Breen, Thomas O., Very Rev,
  PP
  Ballylanders, Kilmallock,
  Co Limerick
  Tel 062-46705
  (Ballylanders, Cashel & E.)
Breheny, Pádraig (OFM)
  Collegio S. Isidoro
  Via degli Artisti 41
  00187 Roma, Italy
  Tel 0039-06-4885359
Brennan, Ailbe (OSA)
  Duckspool House
  (Retirement Community),
  Abbeyside, Dungarvan,
  Co Waterford
  Tel 058-23784
Brennan, Brian, PE
  Hollybrook, Drumanure,
  Abbeyshrule, Co Longford
  (Ardagh & Cl., retired)
Brennan, Christopher Very
  Rev (SMA), Adm,
  Islandeady, Castlebar,
  Co Mayo
  Tel 094-9024125
  (Islandeady, Tuam)
Brennan, Darren, PP
  Parochial House,
  14 Presbytery Lane,
  Dunloy,
  Co Antrim BT44 9DZ
  Tel 028-27657223
  (Dunloy and Cloughmills,
  Down & C.)
Brennan, David, Very Rev,
  PP
  Parochial House,
  Kentstown,
  Navan, Co Meath
  Tel 041-9825276
  (Beauparc, Meath)
Brennan, Declan (OSA)
  Hospital Chaplain
  St Augustine's Priory,
  Shop Street,
  Drogheda, Co Louth
  Tel 041-9838409

Brennan, Denis, Most Rev,
  DD
  Retired Bishop of Ferns,
  PO Box 40, Summerhill,
  Wexford
  (Ferns)
Brennan, Fergal (SJ)
  Milltown Park,
  Sandford Road, Dublin 6
  Tel 01-2698411/2698113
Brennan, Kilian
  Apartment 3, Seascape,
  366 Clontarf Road,
  Dublin 3
  (Dublin, retired)
Brennan, Loughlin, Very
  Rev, PP
  Liscreagh, Murroe,
  Co Limerick
  Tel 061-386227
  (Murroe and Boher, Cashel
  & E.)
Brennan, Louis (OFM)
  Franciscan Friary,
  Liberty Street,
  Cork T12 D376
  Tel 021-4270302/4275481
Brennan, Michael, Very Rev,
  PP
  Bearna, Co Galway
  Tel 091-590956
  (Bearna, Galway)
Brennan, Oliver, Very Rev,
  PP
  Parochial House,
  114 Battlehill Road,
  Richhill,
  Co Armagh BT61 8QJ
  Tel 028-38871661
  (Kilmore, Armagh)
Brennan, Patrick (OP)
  Dominican Community,
  St Mary's Priory, Tallaght,
  Dublin 24
  Tel 01-4048100
Brennan, Peter, Very Rev, PP
  The Parochial House,
  Clerihan, Clonmel,
  Co Tipperary
  Tel 087-2362603
  (Clerihan, Cashel & E.)
Brennan, Richard (SPS)
  St Patrick's, Kiltegan,
  Co Wicklow W91 YO22
  Tel 0596473600
Brennan, Thomas
  USA
  (Ferns)
Brennock, Michael (OSA)
  St Augustine's Priory,
  Dungarvan, Co Waterford
  Tel 058-41136
Breslan, Fergus, PE
  Parochial House,
  17 Carnmore Drive,
  Newry, Co Down
  Tel 028-30269047
  (Armagh, retired)

Breslan, Patrick, Very Rev,
  PE, AP
  Parochial House,
  55 Dermanaught Road,
  Galbally, Dungannon,
  Co Tyrone BT70 2NR
  Tel 028-87758277
  (Donaghmore, Armagh)
Breslin, Eamonn (CSsR)
  Mount Saint Alphonsus,
  South Circular Road,
  Limerick
  Tel 061-315099
Breslin, Michael, Very Rev,
  PP, VF
  Ballygar, Co Galway
  Tel 090-6624637
  (Ballygar (Killian and
  Killeroran), Elphin)
Bresnahan, Damian (SMA)
  Superior,
  African Missions,
  Dromantine, Newry,
  Co Down BT34 1RH
  Tel 028-30821224
Brewster, Patrick (SDB)
  Salesian House,
  45 St Teresa's Road,
  Crumlin, Dublin 12
  Tel 01-4555605
Brick, Maurice, Very Rev,
  Canon, PP
  The Presbytery,
  Castleisland, Co Kerry
  Tel 066-7141241
  (Castleisland, Kerry)
Brickley, John, Very Rev, PP
  Cooleragh, Coill Dubh,
  Naas, Co Kildare
  Tel 045-860281
  (Kilcock, Kildare & L.)
Briody, Anthony, CC
  Parochial House,
  Stranorlar,
  Co Donegal
  Tel 074-9131157
  (Stranorlar, Raphoe)
Briody, Joseph
  St John's Seminary,
  127 Lake Street,
  Brighton, MA 01235, USA
  (Raphoe)
Briscoe, Peter, Rt Rev Mgr,
  Adm
  67 Ramleh Park, Milltown,
  Dublin 6
  Tel 01-2196600
  (Milltown, Dublin)
Broaders, Brian, Very Rev,
  PP, VF
  Rathnure, Enniscorthy,
  Co Wexford
  Tel 053-9255122
  (Rathnure and
  Templeudigan, Ferns)

LIST OF CLERGY IN IRELAND

Broderick, Daniel, Very Rev, PP
Milltown,
Killarney, Co Kerry
Tel 066-9767312
Moderator, Castlemaine Parish
(*Milltown, Castlemaine, Kerry*)

Broderick, Donal, Very Rev, PE
Ballyhooly, Co Cork
Tel 025-39148
(Cloyne, retired)

Brodie, Thomas (OP)
St Saviour's,
Glentworth Street,
Limerick
Tel 061-412333

Brophy, Joseph, Very Rev, CC
Ballyfin, Portlaoise,
Co Laois
Tel 057-8755227
(*Mountrath*, Kildare & L.)

Brophy, Robert, Very Rev Canon, PP
The Presbytery,
Curraheen Road, Cork
Tel 021-4343535
(*Curraheen Road*, Cork & R.)

Brouder, Jeremiah
49 Halcyon Place,
Park Village,
Castletroy, Limerick
(Limerick, retired)

Brough, David, Very Rev, Co-PP
2, St Mary's Terrace,
Arklow, Co Wicklow
Tel 0402-3296
(*Arklow*, Dublin)

Brown, Brian, Very Rev, PP
Church Street,
Ballynahinch,
Co Down BT24 8LP
Tel 028-97562410
(*Magheradroll* (*Ballynahinch*), Dromore)

Brown, Francis, Very Rev Canon, Adm
Cathedral Presbytery,
38 Hill Street,
Newry BT34 1AT
Tel 028-30262586/ 028-30256372
(*Newry, Saval*, Dromore)

Brown, John (SMA)
Vice-Superior & Bursar
African Missions,
Dromantine, Newry,
Co Down BT34 1RH
Tel 028-30821224

Brown, John (CSSp)
Holy Spirit Missionary College
Kimmage Manor,
Whitehall Road,
Dublin D12 P5YP
Tel 01-4064300

Brown, Michael (OCD)
St Teresa's,
Clarendon Street, Dublin 2
Tel 01-6718466/6718127

Browne, Colm
c/o Bishop's House,
Dublin Road,
Mullingar, Co Westmeath
(Meath)

Browne, Denis, Very Rev, PP
Kilanerin, Gorey
Co Wexford
Tel 0402-37120
(*Kilanerin & Ballyfad*, Ferns)

Browne, James (IC)
Doire na hAbhann,
Tickincor, Clonmel,
Co Tipperary
Tel 052-6126914

Browne, Kevin (CSsR), Very Rev, PP, Rector
722 Antrim Road,
Newtownabbey,
Co Antrim BT36 7PG
Tel 028-90774833/4
(*St Gerard's*, Down & C.)

Browne, Martin (OSB)
Glenstal Abbey, Murroe,
Co Limerick
Tel 061-621000

Browne, Michael (SPS)
St Patrick's,
21 Leeson Park,
Dublin D06 DE76
Tel 01-4977897

Browne, Michael (SBD)
Vice-Rector,
Salesian House,
45 St Teresa's Road,
Crumlin, Dublin 12
Tel 01-4555605

Browne, Patrick, Very Rev, PP
Oulart, Gorey, Co Wexford
Tel 053-9136139
(*Oulart and Ballaghkeene*, Ferns)

Browne, Raymond, Most Rev, DD
Bishop of Kerry,
Bishop's House, Killarney,
Co Kerry
Tel 064-6631168
(Kerry)

Browne, Richard, Very Rev, PP
Cappamore, Co Limerick
Tel 061-381288
(*Cappamore*, Cashel & E.)

Browne, Richard, Very Rev, PE
Nadrid, Coachford,
Co Cork
(Cloyne, retired)

Browne, Thomas, Very Rev, PE
Southabbey,
Youghal, Co Cork
Tel 024-93199
(Cloyne, retired)

Browne, Tom (SPS)
St Patrick's, Kiltegan,
Co Wicklow W91 Y022
Tel 059-6473600

Browne, Vincent (CSSp)
Blackrock College,
Blackrock, Co Dublin
Tel 01-2888681

Bucciarelli, Robert, Rt Rev, DD
Vicar for Ireland,
Harvieston,
Cunningham Road,
Dalkey, Co Dublin
Tel 01-2859877
(Opus Dei)

Buckley, Benignus (OFMCap)
Capuchin Friary,
Friary Street,
Kilkenny R95 NX60
Tel 056-7721439

Buckley, Con
(Kerry, retired)

Buckley, James (CSsR)
St Patrick's, Esker,
Athenry, Co Galway
Tel 091-844007

Buckley, John, Most Rev, DD
Bishop Emeritus of Cork and Ross,
Cork and Ross Offices,
Redemption Road, Cork
Tel 021-4301717
(Cork & R., retired)

Buckley, John, Very Rev, PP
Killeentierna, Killarney,
Co Kerry
Tel 066-974141
Moderator,
Knocknagoshel
Tel 068-46107
(*Killeentierna, Knocknagoshel*, Kerry)

Buckley, Michael Anthony, CC
The Presbytery, Goleen,
Co Cork
Tel 028-35188
(*Goleen, Schull*, Cork & R.)

Buckley, Patrick, Very Rev, PP
4 Upper Woodlands,
Cloghroe, Co Cork
Tel 021-4385311
(*Inniscarra*, Cloyne)

Buckmaster, Ian (White Fathers)
Cypress Grove Road,
Templeogue, Dublin 6W
Tel 01-4055263

Budau, Ciprian (OFMConv), Very Rev
Custodial Office,
St Patrick's Friary,
26 Cornwall Road,
Waterloo,
London SE1 8TW, England
Tel 020-79288897/ 0044-2079288897

Buggy, James
Castlebar, Co Mayo
(Tuam retired)

Bulman, Joseph (OP)
Secretary of the Province,
Provincial Office,
St Mary's, Tallaght,
Dublin D24 X585
Tel 01-4048118
Black Abbey
Kilkenny, Co Kilkenny
Tel 056-7721279

Burger, John (SSC)
Knock, Mayo
(retired)

Burgess, Michael (OFMCap)
Capuchin Friary,
Holy Trinity,
Fr Mathew Quay,
Cork T12 PK24
Tel 021-4270827

Burke, Colm, PE
Queen of Peace Nursing Home, Knock, Co Mayo
(Tuam, retired)

Burke, Enda, Very Rev
Cloughjordan,
Co Tipperary
Tel 0505-42120
(Killaloe, retired)

Burke, Fintan (OCarm)
Carmelite Community,
Gort Muire, Ballinteer,
Dublin 16 D16 EI67
Tel 01-2984014

Burke, Gabriel,
5 Lavallin Drive,
Whitechurch, Co Cork
Tel 021-4200184
(*Blarney*, Cloyne)

Burke, Kieran, Very Rev, CC
Parochial House,
Letterbrickaun, Leenane,
Co Galway, H91 EC5R
Tel 095-42251
(*Ballyhaunis (Annagh)*, Tuam)

Burke, Peter, PP
Ferbane, Co Offaly
Tel 090-6454380
(*Ferbane High Street and Boora*, Ardagh & Cl.)

LIST OF CLERGY IN IRELAND

Burke, Sean, CC
  Mohill, Co Leitrim
  Tel 071-9631097
  (Mohill (Mohill-Manachain), Ardagh & Cl.)
Burleigh, Michael (OCSO)
  Mellifont Abbey,
  Collon, Co Louth
  Tel 041-9826103
Burns, Gerard, Very Rev, PP
  The Parochial House,
  Clonbur, via Claremorris,
  Co Galway
  Tel 094-9546030
  (Clonbur (Ross), Tuam)
Burns, John
  On sick leave
  (Down & C.)
Burns, Karl, Very Rev, PP
  Mount Bellew, Ballinasloe,
  Co Galway
  Tel 090-9679235
  (Moylough and Mountbellew/Menlough (Killascobe), Tuam)
Burns, Pat, PP
  Bohermore, Cashel,
  Co Tipperary
  Tel 087-2036763
  (Cashel, Cashel & E.)
Burns, Peter (CSsR)
  Superior,
  Clonard Monastery,
  1 Clonard Gardens,
  Belfast BT13 2RL
  Tel 028-90445950
Burns, Thomas
  St John's Presbytery,
  New Street, Waterford
  Tel 051-874271
  (St John's, Waterford & L.)
Butler, James, PP
  Ballygarrett, Gorey,
  Co Wexford
  Tel 053-9427330
  (Ballygarrett, Ferns)
Butler, John (SDB)
  Salesian College, Don Bosco Road
  Pallaskenry, Co Limerick
  V94 WP86
  Tel 061-393105
Butler, Kieran (SM),
  Little Sisters of the Poor,
  Sybil Hill Road,
  Raheny, Dublin 5
  (Retired)
Butler, Patrick, Very Rev
  Vicar for Clergy,
  Chaplaincy for Religious Houses
  Parochial House,
  Youghal Road,
  Tallow, Co Waterford
  Tel 086-1737499
  (Waterford & L.)

Butler, Robert, Very Rev,
  Adm (Pro-tem)
  Parochial House,
  Armoy, Ballymoney,
  Co Antrim BT53 8RL
  (Armoy, Down & C.)
Byrne, Archie (OP)
  St Dominic's Retreat House,
  Montenotte, Co Cork
  Tel 021-4502520
Byrne, Arthur, Rt Rev Mgr
  Castor's Bay Road, Lurgan
  (Dromore, retired)
Byrne, Brendan, Rt Rev Mgr,
  Chancellor
  c/o Bishop's House, Carlow
  Tel 059-9176725
  (Kildare & L., retired)
Byrne, Charles, Very Rev
  c/o Bishop's House, Carlow
  (Kildare & L., retired)
Byrne, Charles, Very Rev, PP
  17 Castlewellan Road,
  Hilltown, Newry,
  Co Down BT34 5UY
  Tel 028-40630206
  (Clonduff (Hilltown), Drumgath (Rathfriland), Dromore)
Byrne, Charles, Very Rev, PP
  Carrigart, Co Donegal
  Tel 074-9155154
  (Carrigart, Raphoe)
Byrne, Desmond (CSSp), TA
  45 Woodford Drive,
  Monastery Road,
  Clondalkin, Dublin 22
  Tel 01-4592323
  (Clondalkin/Rowlagh/Neilstown/Deansrath/Bawnogue, Dublin)
Byrne, Diarmuid, Very Rev, Co-PP
  Parochial House,
  Arklow, Co Wicklow
  Tel 0402-32294
  (Aughrim, Dublin)
Byrne, Donal (OCarm),
  Whitefriar Street Church,
  56 Aungier Street,
  Dublin 2 D02 R598
  Tel 01-4758821
Byrne, Felix, Very Rev
  Canon, CC
  Monaseed, Gorey,
  Co Wexford
  Tel 053-9428207
  (Craanford, Ferns)
Byrne, Gareth, Very Rev, VG
  Moderator of the Curia,
  Office of the Moderator,
  Archbishop's House,
  Dublin 9
  Tel 01-8379347
  Team Assistant, Ballygall,
  Ballymun Road,
  Drumcondra, Glasnevin,
  Iona Road parishes
  (Dublin)

Byrne, Gerald, Very Rev, PP
  15 New Road,
  Leighlinbridge, Co Carlow
  (Kildare & L., retired)
Byrne, James, Very Rev
  Ballylannon,
  Wellingtonbridge,
  Co Wexford
  (Ferns, retired)
Byrne, John (OSA)
  St Augustine's,
  Taylor's Lane,
  Balyboden, Dublin 16
  Tel 01-4241000
Byrne, John, Very Rev, PP
  Oylegate, Co Wexford
  Tel 053-9138163
  (Oylegate and Glenbrien, Ferns)
Byrne, John, Rt Rev Mgr, PP, VG
  Parochial House,
  Dublin Road, Portlaoise,
  Co Laois
  Tel 057-8621142/057-8692153
  (Portlaoise, Kildare & L.)
Byrne, John, Very Rev, AP, VF
  Parochial House, Kells,
  Co Meath
  Tel 046-9240213
  (Kells, Meath)
Byrne, Kilian
  Archbishop's House,
  Dromcondra, Dublin 9
Byrne, Martin, Very Rev, PP
  Ballymore, Killinick,
  Co Wexford
  Tel 053-9158966
  (Ballymore and Mayglass, Ferns)
Byrne, Mel (CP)
  Passionist Retreat Centre,
  Downpatrick Road,
  Crossgar,
  Co Down BT30 9EQ
  Tel 028-44830242
Byrne, Michael
  Serene Valley, Borris Road,
  Kiltealy, Enniscorthy,
  Co Wexford
  (Ferns, retired)
Byrne, Michael, Very Rev, PP
  Bree, Enniscorthy,
  Co Wexford
  Tel 053-9247843
  (Bree, Ferns)
Byrne, Paddy, PP
  The Presbytery,
  Ballinakill Road,
  Abbeyleix, Co Laois
  Tel 0578731135/087-9948505
  (Abbeyleix, Ballinakill, Raheen, Kildare & L.)
Byrne, Patrick (SVD)
  Rector, Donamon Castle,
  Roscommon
  Tel 090-6662222

Byrne, Paul, Very Rev
  3 Fortwilliam Demesne,
  Belfast BT15 4FD
  (Down & C.)
Byrne, Paul, Very Rev, PP
  Parochial House,
  Termonfeckin,
  Drogheda,
  Co Louth A92 W403
  Tel 041-9822121
  (Techmonfechin, Armagh)
Byrne, Peter F.,
  On Sabbatical
  (Dublin)
Byrne, Tony (CSSp)
  Holy Spirit Missionary College
  Kimmage Manor,
  Whitehall Road,
  Dublin D12 P5YP
  Tel 01-4064300
Byrne, William Rev (SSC)
  St Columban's Retirement Home, Dalgan Park,
  Navan, Co Meath
  Tel 046-9021525
Byrne, William, PP
  Ballycullane, New Ross,
  Co Wexford
  Tel 051-562123
  (Ballycullane, Ferns)
Byrne, William, Very Rev, PP
  Allen, Kilmeague, Naas,
  Co Kildare
  Tel 045-860135
  (Allen, Kildare & L.)
Byrnes, James (CSSp)
  Holy Spirit Missionary College
  Kimmage Manor,
  Whitehall Road,
  Dublin D12 P5YP
  Tel 01-4064300
Byrnes, Michael, Very Rev, PP JV
  Dunkellin Terrace,
  Portumna,
  Co Galway H53 F584
  Tel 090-9741092
  Moderator, Fahy and Quansborough
  (Fahy and Quansborough (Fahy and Kilquain), Portumna, Clonfert)

LIST OF CLERGY IN IRELAND

C

Cacciola, Thomas (CFR)
St Columba Friary,
Fairview Road,
Derry BT48 8NU
Tel 028-71419980

Cadam, Simon, PP, VF
St Mary's, Granard,
Co Longford
Tel 043-6686550
(*Granard*, Ardagh & Cl.)

Caffrey, Jim, CC
The Presbytery,
Hawthorns Road,
Dublin 18
Tel 01-2952869
(*Balally*, Sandyford,
Dublin)

Cahill, Donal, Very Rev,
Adm
Lisheen, Skibbereen,
Co Cork
Tel 028-38111
(*Aughadown*, Cork & R.)

Cahill, Éamonn, PP
4 The Lawn,
Finglas West, Dublin 7
Tel 01-8341000
(*Finglas West*, Dublin)

Cahill, Joseph (SSC)
Bohernasup, Ballina,
Co Mayo
Tel 096-22984
(retired)

Cahill, Kevin, Very Rev, DCL,
c/o Bishop's House,
Summerhill, Wexford
(Ferns)

Cahill, Lee (SMA)
African Missions,
Blackrock Road,
Cork T12 TD54
Tel 021-4292871

Cahill, Michael, Very Rev, PP
Parochial House,
Johnstown, Navan,
Co Meath
Tel 046-9021731
(*Johnstown*, Meath)

Cahill, Sean, Very Rev, CC
Curates' Residence,
Massforth,
152 Newry Road,
Kilkeel, Co Down BT34 4ET
Tel 028-41762257
(*Kilkeel (Upper Mourne)*,
Down & C.)

Callaghan, Daniel (OCarm)
Carmelite Priory, Moate,
Co Westmeath N37 AW34
Tel 090-6481160/6481398

Callan, Paul, Very Rev Mgr
On Sabbatical
(Dublin)

Callanan, Brendan (CSsR),
Superior,
St Patrick's, Esker,
Athenry, Co Galway
Tel 091-844007

Callanan, John (SJ)
Gonzaga College,
Sandford Road, Dublin 6
Tel 01-4972943

Callanan, Patrick, Very Rev
Canon, PE
Kilbeacanty, Gort,
Co Galway
Tel 091-631691
(Galway, retired)

Callanan, William (SJ)
Milltown Park,
Sandford Road,
Dublin 6 D06 V9K7
Tel 01-2698411/2698113

Campbell, Garrett, PP
Parochial House,
17 Eagralougher Road,
Loughgall,
Co Armagh BT61 8LA
Tel 028-38891231
(*Loughgall*, Armagh)

Campbell, Gerard, Very Rev,
PP, EV,
Parochial House,
Knockbridge, Dundalk,
Co Louth A91 NA03
Tel 042-9374125
(*Knockbridge*, Armagh)

Campbell, James (SSS)
Provincial,
Blessed Sacrament Chapel,
20 Bachelors Walk,
Dublin D01 NW14
Tel 01-8724597

Campbell, Joseph, CC
Parochial House,
Tullamore, Co Offaly
Tel 057-9321587
(*Tullamore*, Meath)

Campbell, Noel
Ballysmutton, Manor
Kilbride, Blessington,
Co Wicklow
(Dublin, retired)

Campion, Desmond (SDB)
Chaplain Naval Service,
Haulbowline, Cobh, Cork

Campion, John (SDB), Very
Rev
Rector, Salesian House,
Milford, Castletroy,
Limerick
Tel 061-330268

Canning, Thomas, CC
143 Melmount Road,
Sion Mills, Strabane,
Co Tyrone BT82 9EX
Tel 028 81658264
(Derry)

Cannon, Aodhan, Very Rev,
PP
Parochial House, Dungloe,
Co Donegal
Tel 074-9521008
(*Dungloe (Templecrone
and Lettermacaward)*,
Raphoe)

Cannon, Seán (CSsR)
St Patrick's, Esker,
Athenry, Co Galway
Tel 091-844007

Canny, Michael, Very Rev,
PP, VG
Parochial House,
32 Chapel Road,
Derry BT47 2BB
Tel 028-71342303
(*Waterside (Glendermott)*,
Derry)

Cantwell, Joe (SPS)
St Patrick's, Kiltegan,
Co Wicklow
Tel 059-6473600

Caraher, Laurence, Very
Rev, PE, AP
The Ravel, School Lane,
Tullyallen, Drogheda,
Co Louth
Tel 041-9834293
(Armagh, retired)

Carberry, Patrick (SJ)
St Francis Xavier's,
Upper Gardiner Street,
Dublin 1
Tel 01-8363411

Carbery, Adrian, Very Rev,
PE, CC
26 Beech Grove, Kildare
Tel 045-521900
(*Kildare*, Kildare & L.)

Carey, John
Sacred Heart Residence,
Sybil Hill Road, Raheny,
Dublin 5
(Dublin, retired)

Carey, Michael, Very Rev, PP
Parochial House,
Blanchardstown, Dublin 15
Tel 01-8213660
(*Blanchardstown*, Dublin)

Carey, Patrick
Chaplain,
St Luke's Hospital,
Kilkenny
Tel 056-7785000
(Ossory)

Carey, William, Very Rev, PP
Kilsheelan, Clonmel,
Co Tipperary
Tel 052-6133118
(*Kilsheelan*, Waterford &
L.)

Cargan, John, Very Rev, PP
4 Garvagh Road, Kilrea,
Co Derry BT51 5QP,
Tel 028-29540343
Adm, Garvagh (Errigal)
Parish
Tel 028-29558251
(*Kilrea*, Derry)

Carley, Martin, CC
St Mary's, Drogheda,
Co Louth
Tel 041-9834958
(*Drogheda, St Mary's*,
Meath)

Carlin, Peter
St Matthew's Presbytery,
Bryson Street,
Newtowntownards Road,
Belfast BT5 4E5
Tel 028-90457626
(*St Matthew's*, Down & C.)

Carmody, Brendan (SJ), Very
Rev, PP
Moyvane, Listowel,
Co Kerry
Tel 068-49308
(*Moyvane*, Kerry)

Carney, Denis, Very Rev, PP
Balla, Co Mayo F23 ED65
Tel 094-9365025
Administration Mayo
Abbey (Mayo and Rosslea)
(*Balla and Manulla*,
*Mayo Abbey (Mayo and
Rosslea)*, Tuam)

Carney, Michael, PE
c/o Diocesan Office,
The Cathedral, Galway
Tel 091-563566
(Galway, retired)

Carney, Michael, Very Rev,
PP
Ramelton, Co Donegal
Tel 074-9151304
(*Ramelton*, Raphoe)

Carolan, Edward (OMI)
Oblate House of Retreat,
Inchicore, Dublin 8
Tel 01-4534408/4541805

Carolan, Loughlain,
Parish Administration,
Blacklion, Co Cavan
Tel 071-9853012
(*Killinagh and Glangevlin*,
Kilmore)

Carolan, Patrick (OMI)
12 Tyrconnell Road,
Inchicore, Dublin 8
Tel 01-4541117

Carpenter, Matt (MHM)
St Joseph's House,
50 Orwell Park,
Rathgar, Dublin D06 C535
Tel 01-4127700

Carr, Brendan (CSSp)
Holy Spirit Provincialate,
Temple Park, Richmond
Avenue South,
Dublin 6 D06 AW02
Tel 01-4977230

Carr, Daniel, Rt Rev Mgr, PP
St Johnston, Lifford,
Co Donegal
Tel 074-9148203
(*St Johnston
(Taughboyne)*, Raphoe)

Carragher, Michael (OP)
Convent of SS Xystus and
Clement,
Collegio San Clemente,
Via Labicana 95,
00184 Roma
Tel 039-06-7740021

Carrigan, William (SSC)
58 Aylesbury,
Freshford Road, Kilkenny
(retired)
Carrigy, Colman
Clonee, Killoe,
Co Longford
(Ardagh & Cl.)
Carroll, Aidan
9 Hillcrest Manor,
Templeogue, Dublin 6W
(Dublin, retired)
Carroll, Daniel (SDB), Very Rev
Salesian College, Don Bosco Road
Pallaskenry, Co Limerick
V94 WP86
Tel 061-393105
Carroll, Daniel, Very Rev
St John's Presbytery,
Kilkenny
Tel 056-7721072/
087-9077769
(*St John's*, Ossory)
Carroll, David, Very Rev, Co-PP
St Joseph's Presbytery,
52 Kincora Park, Lifford,
Ennis, Co Clare
Tel 065-6822166/086-3467909
(*Abbey Pastoral Area*,
Killaloe)
Carroll, Declan, Very Rev, PP
Cong, Co Mayo
Tel 094-9546030
(*Cong and Neale*, Tuam)
Carroll, Denis
Marymount Care Centre,
Westmanstown,
Lucan, Co Dublin
(Dublin, retired)
Carroll, Dom Elijah (OSB),
Prior
Silverstream Priory,
Stamullen,
Co Meath K32 T189
Tel 01-8417142
Carroll, Gregory (OP), Very Rev
Superior, Holy Cross,
Tralee, Co Kerry
Tel 066-7121135/7129185
Carroll, John (SPS)
Cregg House,
Rosses Point, Sligo
(Elphin, retired)
Carroll, James, Rt Rev Mgr, PP, EV
Parochial House,
Big Strand Road,
Clogherhead,
Drogheda, Co Louth
(*Togher*, Armagh)

Carroll, Jeremiah (Jerry), CF
Finner Camp,
Ballyshannon,
Co Donegal F94 C985
Tel 071-9842294
(Clogher)
Carroll, John, PP
Diocesan Secretary and Chancellery,
PO Box 40, Bishop's House,
Summerhill, Wexford
Tel 053-9124368
Diocesan Secretary,
Barntown, Co Wexford
Tel 053-9120853
(*Glynn*, Ferns)
Carroll, John P. (SPS)
St Patrick's, Kiltegan,
Co Wicklow
Tel 059-6473600
Carroll, Patrick, Very Rev
Canon, VF
124 New Cabra Road,
Dublin 7
Tel 01-8385244
(Dublin, retired)
Carroll, Thomas, Moderator
Turrett Street
Ballingarry, Co Clare
Tel 087-2036229
(*Pastoral Unit 10*, Limerick)
Carroll, Timothy (SMA) Most Rev
(Retired Bishop)
African Missions,
Blackrock Road,
Cork T12 TD54
Tel 021-4292871
Carvill, Aidan (SM)
Australia
Carvill, Andrew, CC
Mallow, Co Cork
Tel 022-51606
(*Mallow*, Cloyne)
Carvill, Gregory, Very Rev, PP
Parochial House,
194 Newton Hamilton Road, Ballymacnab,
Armagh, BT60 2QS
Tel 028-37531641
(*Killcluney*, Armagh)
Casey, Anthony, Co-PP, VF
Cooraclare, Co Clare
Tel 065-9059008/
087-9936950
(*Inis Cathaigh Pastoral Area*, Killaloe)
Casey, Aquin, Very Rev, CC
Cobh, Co Cork
Tel 021-4908657
(*Cobh, St Colman's Cathedral*, Cloyne)
Casey, Cornelius J. (CSsR)
97 Kylemore Road,
Ballyfermot, Dublin 10
Tel 01-6264691/5356977

Casey, Damian (OFM)
Adam & Eve's
4 Merchants' Quay
Dublin D08 XY19
Tel 01-6771128
Casey, David
Parochial House,
Kilmallock, Co Limerick
Tel 087-2272791
(*Pastoral Unit 9*, Limerick)
Casey, Eoin (OP)
Newbridge College,
Droichead Nua, Co Kildare
Tel 045-487200
Casey, Gerard, Ven
Archdeacon, PE,
Doneraile, Co Cork
Tel 022-72789
(*Cloyne*, retired)
Casey, John (SAC)
Pallottine College,
Thurles, Co Tipperary
Tel 0504-21202
Casey, Kevin (SJ)
Irish Jesuit Provincialate,
Milltown Park,
Sandford Road, Dublin 6
Tel 01-4987333
Casey, Martin, Very Rev, PP
Woolgreen, Carnew,
Co Wicklow
Tel 053-9426888
(*Carnew*, Ferns)
Casey, Michael (CSSp)
Holy Spirit Missionary College
Kimmage Manor,
Whitehall Road,
Dublin D12 P5YP
Tel 01-4064300
Casey, Michael, Co-PP
Cross, Kilrush, Co Clare
Tel 065-9058008/
086-0842216
(*Cois Fharraige Pastoral Area*, Killaloe)
Casey, Michael (SDB), Very Rev, Adm
Rector, Rinaldi House,
72 Sean McDermott Street, Dublin D01 K2O1
Casey, Paul, PP
Drumahaire, Co Leitrim
Co Cavan
Tel 071-9164143
(*Drumahaire and Killargue*, Kilmore)
Casey, Peter, Very Rev, PP
Ballinagh, Co Cavan
Tel 049-4337232
(*Kilmore*, Kilmore)
Casey, Seamus
11 Auburn Heights,
Athlone, Co Westmeath
Tel 090-6478318
(Ardagh & Cl.)
Casey, Sean, PP
Ennybegs, Longford
Tel 043-3323119
(*Killoe*, Ardagh & Cl.)

Casey, Thomas (SJ)
Rector, Milltown Park,
Sandford Road, Dublin 6
Tel 01-2698411/2698113
Cashman, Daniel (SMA)
SMA House, Wilton,
Cork, T12 KR23
Tel 021-4541069/4541884
Cashman, Denis, Very Rev
Ballincollig, Co Cork
(Cork & R., retired)
Cassidy, Gerard, Very Rev, PP
Ballyhaise, Co Cavan
Tel 049-4338121
(*Castletara*, Kilmore)
Cassidy, Gerard, Very Rev (CSsR)
1 Clonard Gardens,
Belfast BT13 2RL
Tel 028-90445950
Cassidy, Seamus, Very Rev
Tavis, Kilmainham Wood,
Kells, Co Meath
(Dublin, retired)
Cassin, Liam, Very Rev, PP
Hugginstown, Co Kilkenny
Tel 087-2312354/
056-7768693
(*Aghaviller*, Ossory)
Cassin, Seán (OFM)
Franciscan Abbey,
Multyfarnham,
Co Westmeath N91 X279
Tel 044-9371114/9371137
Castelli, Nemo S. (SJ)
35 Lower Leeson Street,
Dublin 2
Tel 01-6761248
Caulfield, Billy, CC
Galbally, Ballyhogue,
Enniscorthy, Co Wexford
Tel 053-9247814
(*Bree*, Ferns)
Cavanagh, Daniel, Rt Rev Mgr, PP
Rosbercon, New Ross,
Co Wexford
Tel 051-421515/
087-2335432
(*Rosbercon*, Ossory)
Cawley, Farrell, Very Rev, PE
Ballinacarrow,
Co Sligo
Tel 086-0864347
(*Achonry*, retired)
Cawley, Michael, Very Rev
River View Nursing Home,
Ballina, Co Mayo
(Killala, retired)
Chamakalayil, Jayan Joseph (MI)
Chaplain,
St James's Hospital
St Camillus,
South Hill Avenue,
Blackrock, Co Dublin

Chambers, Martin, PP
 2 Chaplain's House,
 Knocknamona,
 Letterkenny, Co Donegal
 Tel 074-9125090
 (*Letterkenny*, Raphoe)
Champion, Augustine (OP)
 Holy Cross, Sligo
 Co Sligo
 Tel 071-9142700
Charles, Nigel, Adm
 Parochial House, Mohill,
 Co Leitrim
 Tel 071-9631024
 (*Mohill (Mohill-Manachain)*, Ardagh & Cl.)
Charlet, Benoît M. (OSB)
 Benedictine Monks,
 Holy Cross Abbey,
 119 Kilbroney Road,
 Rostrevor,
 Co Down BT34 3BN
 Tel 028-41739979
Chen, Yanbo (SVD)
 (Priest in Residence)
 The Presbytery,
 Old Dublin Road, Carlow,
 Tel 059-9131227
 (*Cathedral, Carlow*,
 Kildare & L.)
Chester, John, PP
 4a Monaghan Road,
 Roslea. Co Fermanagh,
 Tel 028-67751227
 (*Roslea*, Clogher)
Chestnutt, Gerard, Very Rev, PP
 Sacred Heart Presbytery,
 The Folly, Waterford
 Tel 051-878429
 (*Sacred Heart*, Waterford & L.)
Chukwunenye, Alphonsus (MSP)
 Cathedral Presbytery,
 38 Hill Street,
 Newry BT34 1AT
 Tel 028-30262586
 (*Newry Pastoral Area*,
 Dromore)
Chullickal, Rexon, Co-PP
 The Presbytery,
 Church Road,
 Nenagh, Co Tipperary
 Tel 067-37130
 (*Odhran Pastoral Area*,
 Killaloe)
Churchill, Paul, Very Rev, PP
 St Joseph's, Berkeley Road,
 Dublin 7
 Tel 01-8306336
 (*Berkeley Road*, Dublin)
Chute, John (SSC), Very Rev
 St Columban's Retirement Home, Dalgan Park,
 Navan, Co Meath
 Tel 046-9021525

Cirhakarhula, Jean Paul
 (White Fathers)
 Promotion Director,
 Cypress Grove,
 Templeogue, Dublin 6W
 Tel 01-4055263
Claffey, Pat (SVD), CC
 The Presbytery,
 Haddington Road,
 Dublin 4
 Tel 085-7123675
 (*Haddington Road*,
 Dublin)
Clancy, Anthony (OMI), Very Rev, Co-PP
 Oblate Fathers House of Retreat,
 Inchicore, Dublin 8
 Tel 01-4534408/4541805
 (*Bluebell*, Dublin)
Clancy, Peter, CC
 75 Newtown Park, Leixlip,
 Co Kildare
 Tel 01-6243533
 (*Confey*, Dublin)
Clancy, Tom, Very Rev, AP
 Woodlawn,
 Model Farm Road,
 Ballineaspaig, Cork
 Tel 021-4348588
 (*Ballineaspaig*, Cork & R.)
Clarke, Christopher (OCD)
 The Abbey, Loughrea,
 Co Galway
 Tel 091-841209
Clarke, Ciaran, CC
 Parochial House,
 Ashbourne, Co Meath
 Tel 01-8353149
 (*Ashbourne-Donaghmore*,
 Meath)
Clarke, Eamonn, CC
 The Presbytery,
 Beechwood Park,
 Kilcoole, Co Wicklow
 Tel 01-2876207
 (*Kilquade*, Dublin)
Clarke, Gerard (SJ)
 28 Brookvale Avenue,
 Belfast BT14 6BW
 Tel 028-90757615
Clarke, Joseph, Very Rev,
 Foxhall, Gurlymadden,
 Loughrea, Co Galway
 (Clonfert, retired)
Clarke, Patrick (SSC)
 St Columban's Retirement Home, Dalgan Park,
 Navan, Co Meath
 Tel 046-9021525
Clarke, Peter, Very Rev
 Parochial House,
 11 Moy Road, Portadown,
 Co Armagh BT62 1QL
 Tel 028-38332218
 (*Portadown (Drumcree)*,
 Armagh)

Clarkson, Eugene (MSC)
 Woodview House,
 Mount Merrion Avenue,
 Blackrock, Co Dublin
 Tel 01-2881644
Clavin, Joseph, Very Rev, AP
 St. Martin's,
 Culmullen, Drumree,
 Co Meath
 Tel 01-8241976
 (*Dunshaughlin*, Meath)
Clayton-Lea, Paul, Very Rev, PE
 Woodside, Strand Road,
 Termonfeckin,
 Drogheda,
 Co Louth A92 W7W6
 Tel 041-9822631
 (Armagh, retired)
Cleary, Edward, Very Rev, PP
 Knockainey, Hospital,
 Co Limerick,
 Tel 061-584873
 (*Knockainey*, Cashel & E.)
Cleary, Lorenzo, Very Rev
 The Stables, Hayestown,
 Wexford
 Tel 053-9144346
 (Ferns)
Cleary, Matthew L., Very Rev
 The Stables, Bridgetown,
 Co Wexford
 (Ferns, retired)
Clerkin, Colum, Very Rev, PP, VF
 23 Thornhill Park,
 Culmore, Derry BT48 4PB
 Tel 028-71358519
 (*Culmore*, Derry)
Clerkin, Matthew (OFMCap)
 Capuchin Friary,
 Station Road, Raheny,
 Dublin 5 D05 T9E4
 Tel 01-8313886
Clesham, James (SMA), CC
 St John the Apostle,
 Knocknacarra, Galway
 Tel 091-590059
 (*St John the Apostle*,
 Galway)
Clifford, Brendan (OP)
 St Mary's, Pope's Quay,
 Cork
 Tel 021-4502267
Clifford, Dermot, Most Rev, PhD, DD
 Archbishop Emeritus of
 Cashel and Emly,
 The Green, Holycross,
 Thurles, Co Tipperary
 (Cashel & E.)
Clifford, Diarmuid (OP)
 St Saviour's,
 Upper Dorset Street,
 Dublin 1
 Tel 01-8897610

Clifford, Hugh, Very Rev PP
 Parochial House,
 Kinvara, Co Galway
 Tel 091 637154
 (*Ballinderreen*, Galway)
Clinton, Colm (SPS), Adm
 New Quay, Co Clare
 Tel 065-7078026
 (*Carron and New Quay*,
 Galway)
Clowe, Thomas (SDB), TA
 45 St Teresa's Road,
 Crumlin, Dublin 12
 Tel 01-4555383
 (*Crumlin*, Dublin)
Clucas, Peter (OMI)
 Oblate House of Retreat,
 Inchicore, Dublin 8
 Tel 01-4534408/4541805
Clyne, S. James, Very Rev
 Canon, PE, AP
 Parochial House,
 24 Chapel Road, Killeavy,
 Newry, Co Down BT35 8JY
 Tel 028-30848222
 (*Cloghogue (Killeavy Upper)*, Armagh)
Coady, Michael, Very Rev, PP
 St Mary's Presbytery,
 Willbrook Road,
 Rathfarnham, Dublin 14
 Tel 01-4932390/
 087-2401441
 (*Rathfarnham*, Dublin)
Coakley, Donal, Very Rev, PE
 Buttevant, Co Cork
 (Cloyne, retired)
Coen, John (SAC)
 Pallottine College,
 Thurles, Co Tipperary
 086-3103934
Coen, Michael (SAC)
 Pallottine College, Thurles,
 Co Tipperary
 Tel 0504-21202
Coffey, Brendan (OSB)
 Glenstal Abbey, Murroe,
 Co Limerick
 Tel 061-621000
Coffey, Patrick, Rev, PP
 Golden, Co Tipperary
 Tel 062-72146
 (*Golden*, Cashel & E.)
Coffey, Robert
 35 Orchard Avenue,
 Rathkeale, Co Limerick
 Tel 087-6540908
 (*Pastoral Unit 10,* Limerick)
Coffey, Thomas, Very Rev
 Parochial House,
 Corcaghan,
 Monaghan H18 H673
 Tel 042-9744806
 (*Corcaghan*, Clogher)

LIST OF CLERGY IN IRELAND

Coffey, Tom (IC)
Doire na hAbhann,
Tickincor, Clonmel,
Co Tipperary
Tel 052-6126914

Cogan, John, Very Rev, PE
Killeen, Vicarstown,
Tel 021-4385535
(Cloyne, retired)

Cogan, Patrick (OFM)
15 Orchard Drive,
Ursuline Court, Waterford
Tel 087-2360239
Respond! Office
Tel 051-876865

Cogavin, Brendan (CSSP)
Holy Spirit Missionary College
Kimmage Manor,
Whitehall Road,
Dublin D12 P5YP
Tel 01-4064300

Coghlan, David (SJ)
Vice-Superior,
Dominic Collins' House Residence,
129 Morehampton Road,
Dublin 4 D04 NX39
Tel 01-2693075

Coghlan, Kieran, Very Rev, Moderator
Presbytery, Bawnogue,
Clondalkin, Dublin 22
Tel 01-4519810
(Bawnogue, Clondalkin, Deansrath, Neilstown, Rowlagh and Quarryvale, Dublin)

Coghlan, Niall (OSA), Very Rev, Co-PP
St Catherine's Church,
Meath Street, Dublin 8
Tel 01-4543356
(Meath Street and Merchants' Quay, Dublin)

Cogley, James, Very Rev, PP
Our Lady's Island,
Broadway,
Co Wexford
Tel 053-9131167
(Our Lady's Island and Tacumshane, Ferns)

Cojoc, Robert (OFMConv)
The Friary,
St Francis' Street,
Wexford
Tel 053-9122758

Colclough, Robert, Very Rev, Adm, VF
Parochial House,
49 Seville Place, Dublin 1
Tel 01-2865457
(North Wall-Seville Place, Dublin)

Coleman, Christopher (MSC)
Carrignavar,
Co Cork
Tel 021-4884044

Coleman, Gerard, Very Rev, PP
Castlelyons, Co Cork
Tel 025-36372
(Castlelyons, Cloyne)

Coleman, Gerard, Very Rev, PP
Dromahane, Mallow,
Co Cork
Tel 087-9580420
(Glantane, Cloyne)

Coleman, William, Very Rev, PP
Parochial House,
Rochfortbridge,
Co Westmeath
Tel 044-9222107
(Rochfortbridge, Meath)

Colgan, John (SSC),
St Columban's, Dalgan Park, Navan, Co Meath
Tel 046-9021525

Colgan, Maurice (OP)
St Mary's, Pope's Quay,
Cork
Tel 021-4502267

Colgan, Pat (SSC)
No 3 and 4,
Ma Yau Tong Village,
Po Lam Road,
Tseung Kwan O,
Kow Loon, Hong Kong, SAR

Colhoun, Roland, CC
41 Moyle Road,
Newtownstewart,
Co Tyrone BT78 4AP
Tel 028-81661445
(Newtownstewart and Plumbridge, Derry)

Coll, Francis, CC
Parochial House,
Hanover Square,
Coagh, Cookstown,
Co Tyrone BT80 0EF
Tel 028-86737212
(Coagh, Armagh)

Coll, Niall
Donegal Town,
Co Donegal
Tel 074-9721026
(Donegal Town (Tawnawilly)/Clar, Raphoe)

Collender, Michael (OSA)
Good Counsel College,
New Ross, Co Wexford
Tel 051-421182

Collery, Seamus
St Attracta's Community School,
Tubbercurry, Co Sligo
Tel 071-9120184
(Achonry)

Collier, Warren
Parochial House,
Trim, Co Meath
Tel 046-9431251
(Trim, Meath)

Collier, Val (SDB)
Rinaldi House,
72 Sean McDermott Street, Dublin D01 K2O1
Tel 01-8363358

Collins, Brendan, CC
c/o Bishop's House,
St Eugene's Cathedral,
Francis Street,
Derry BT48 6AP
(Derry)

Collins, David (OFM)
The Abbey,
8 Francis Street, Galway
H91 C53K
Tel 091-562518

Collins, Denis (SMA)
African Missions,
Blackrock Road,
Cork T12 TD54
Tel 021-4292871

Collins, Gregory (OSB)
Dormition Abbey,
Mount Sion, PO Box 22,
IL-91000, Jerusalem, Israel

Collins, John, Very Rev, Co-PP
18 Aspen Road,
Kinseely Court,
Swords, Co Dublin
Tel 01-4531143
(Swords, Dublin)

Collins, John, Very Rev, PP
Rossmore, Clonakilty,
Co Cork
Tel 023-8838630
(Kilmeen and Castleventry, Cork & R.)

Collins, Laurence (OP), Very Rev, Adm
The Presbytery,
St Dominic's,
St Dominic's Road,
Tallaght, Dublin 24
Tel 01-4510620
(Tallaght, Dodder, Dublin)

Collins, Michael
2 Traverslea Woods,
Glenageary Road Lower,
Dun Laoghaire, Co Dublin,
(Dublin, retired)

Collins, Michael, PEm
119 Irish Green Street,
Limavady,
Co Derry BT49 9AB
Tel 028-77765649
(Derry, retired)

Collins, Michael, Co-PP
Parochial House, 19
Goodwood Estate,
Newmarket-on-Fergus
Tel 061-700883
(Tradaree Pastoral Area, Killaloe)

Collins, Neil (SSC)
St Columban's,
Dalgan Park,
Navan, Co Meath
Tel 046-9021525

Collins, Owen,
22 River Crescent,
Virginia, Co Cavan
(Kilmore, retired)

Collins, P. Gerard, Very Rev
The Presbytery,
Passage West,
Co Cork
(Cork & R., retired)

Collins, Patrick (CM)
St Joseph's,
44 Stillorgan Park,
Blackrock,
Co Dublin A94 PC62
Tel 01-2886961

Collins, Timothy (SSC)
Cork

Collins, Timothy, Very Rev, PP
The Presbytery,
Dunmanway,
Co Cork
Tel 023-8845000
(Dunmanway, Cork & R.)

Collum, Martin, Very Rev, PP
Rathmullan, Co Donegal
Tel 074-9158156
(Rathmullan, Raphoe)

Coltsmann, Francis (SMA)
African Missions,
Blackrock Road,
Cork T12 TD54
Tel 021-4292871

Comer, Micheál, Very Rev, Adm
The Presbytery,
Eadestown, Naas,
Co Kildare
Tel 045-862187
(Eadestown, Dublin)

Comerford, Brendan (SJ)
Manresa House,
426 Clontarf Road,
Dollymount, Dublin 3
Tel 01-8331352

Comerford, Patrick, Very Rev, PP
Drakelands Nursing Home,
Ballycallan Road,
Kilkenny
Tel 086-1038430
(Ossory, retired)

Comiskey, Brendan, Most Rev, DD
Retired Bishop of Ferns,
PO Box 40, Summerhill,
Wexford
(Ferns, retired)

Comiskey, Gerard, Very Rev, PP
Staghall, Belturbet,
Co Cavan
Tel 049-9522140
(Drumlane, Kilmore)

Commane, Michael (OP)
Chaplain,
St Luke's Hospital,
Highfield Road,
Rathgar, Dublin 6
Tel 01-4065000

Commins, Thomas, PP
Kilkerrin, Ballinasloe,
Co Galway H53 Y326
Tel 094-9659212
(*Kilkerrin and Clonberne*,
Tuam)

Conaghan, Michael, Very
Rev, PE
6 Fields Court,
Kilmacrennan, Co Donegal
Tel 074-91198711
(*Raphoe*, retired)

Conard, Isaac (OSB)
Silverstream Priory,
Stamullen,
Co Meath K32 T189
Tel 01-8417142

Conaty, Eamonn (SSC), Very
Rev, PP
4 Cuan Mhuire,
Fourmilehouse,
Roscommon
Tel 090-6629518
(*Kilbride* (*Fourmilehouse*),
Elphin)

Conaty, Peter (CSSp)
Community Leader,
Spiritan Missionaries,
Ardbraccan, Navan,
Co Meath C15 T884
Tel 046-9021441

Concannon, Eamonn, Very
Rev Canon, PE
Ballyhowley, Knock,
Co Mayo F12 C920
(Tuam, retired)

Concannon, John (CM)
St Peter's, Phibsboro,
Dublin 7
Tel 01-8389708/8389841

Condon, Eanna, Very Rev,
PE
St Mary's, Clonmel,
Co Tipperary
Tel 052-6127870
(Waterford & L., retired)

Condon, Gerard, Very Rev,
PP
Diocesan Advisor for
Religious Education,
Ballygriffin, Killavullen,
Co Cork
Tel 022-46578
(*Killavullen*, Cloyne)

Condon, Jeremiah, Very
Rev, PP
Stradbally, Kilmacthomas,
Co Waterford
Tel 051-293133
(*Stradbally*, Waterford &
L.)

Condon, John
Owing House,
Piltown, Co Kilkenny
Tel 086-8394615
(Ossory, retired)

Condon, Joseph, Very Rev,
PP
Apartment 2,
St John's College,
The Folly, Waterford
Tel 051-876843
(Waterford & L., retired)

Condon, Mark, CC
Danesfort, Co Kilkenny
Tel 086-6005402
(*Danesfort*, Ossory)

Condon, Patrick T., Very
Rev, PP
Knockanore, Tallow,
Co Waterford
Tel 024-97140
(*Knockanore*, Waterford &
L.)

Condon, Sean
Cathedral House,
Cathedral Place, Limerick
Tel 061-414624
(Limerick, retired)

Condren, Joseph (OFM)
Vicar Provincial,
Secretary of the Province,
4 Merchants' Quay
Dublin, D08 XY19
Tel 01-6771128

Condron, Barry, Very Rev,
PP
Tyrrellspass,
Co Westmeath
Tel 044-9223115
(*Castletown-Geoghegan*,
Meath)

Conlan, Anthony
Chaplain,
St Vincent's University
Hospital, Elm Park,
Dublin 4
Tel 01-2694533
(Dublin)

Conlan, Patrick (OFM)
Dún Mhuire,
Seafield Road,
Killiney, Co Dublin
Tel 01-2826760

Conlisk, Frank (SPS), Adm
Parochial House
Milltown, Co Galway
Tel 089-2064773
(*Kilconly and Kilbannon*,
Milltown (*Addergole and
Liskeevey*), Tuam)

Conlon, Alex, Very Rev, PP
213B Harold's Cross,
Dublin 6W
Tel 01-4972816
(*Harold's Cross*, Dublin)

Conlon, Brian
Chaplain,
Sligo University Hospital
The Mall, Co Sligo
Tel 071-9171111
(Elphin)

Conlon, Brian, Very Rev, PP,
VF
Ballycastle, Co Mayo
Tel 096-43010
(*Ballycastle* (*Kilbride and
Doonfeeny*), Killala)

Conlon, John, Very Rev, PP
St Mary's, Drogheda,
Co Louth
Tel 041-9834958
(*Drogheda, St Mary's*,
Meath)

Conlon, Malachy, Very Rev,
PP, VF, EV, Adm
Top Rath, Carlingford,
Co Louth A91 XW24
Tel 042-9376105
(*Cooley*, Armagh)

Conlon, Noel,
(priest in residence)
Inniskeen, Dundalk,
Co Louth
Tel 042-9378678
(*Inniskeen*, Clogher)

Conlon, Sean (OCD)
St Teresa's
Claredon Street, Dublin 2
Tel 01-6718466/6718127

Conlon, Seán, Very Rev, PE,
CC
Ballinakill, Co Laois
Tel 057-8733336
(*Ballinakill*, Kildare & L.)

Connaughton, Finian, Very
Rev, PP
Parochial House,
Drumconrath, Navan,
Co Meath
Tel 041-6854146
(*Drumconrath*, Meath)

Connaughton, P. Aloysius
(SSC)
Thailand

Connaughton, Patrick
St Columban's,
Dalgan Park,
Navan, Co Meath
Tel 046-9021525
(Galway, retired)

Connaughton, Sean (SSC)
St Columban's,
Dalgan Park, Navan,
Co Meath
Tel 046-9021525

Connaughton, Vincent, PP
Ardagh, Co Longford
Tel 043-6675006
(*Ardagh and Moydow*,
Ardagh & Cl.)

Connell, Michael (SDB)
Vice-Rector,
St Catherine's Centre,
North Campus, Maynooth

Connell, Paul, Very Rev,
PhD, Adm
Parochial House,
Rathganny,
Multyfarnham,
Co Westmeath N91 E186
Tel 044-9371124
Chancellor, Meath
Diocesan Office,
Dublin Road, Mullingar,
Co Westmeath
Tel 044-9348841
(*Multyfarnharm*, Meath)

Connell, Seamus, Very Rev,
Adm
56 Foxfield St John,
Kilbarrack, Dublin 5
(Dublin, retired)

Connell, Seamus (SSC)
Padres de San Columbano,
Apartado 073/074,
Lima 39, Peru

Connelly, Christopher (OFM)
Franciscan Friary,
Killarney, Co Kerry
Tel 064-6631334/6631066

Connick, Joseph (OFMConv)
Friary of the Visitation,
Fairview Strand, Dublin 3
Tel 01-8376000

Connolly, Charles, (Opus
Dei)
Gort Ard University
Residence
Rockbarton North, Galway
Tel 091-523846

Connolly, Darragh
(priest in residence)
Drumkilly, Co Cavan
(*Crosserlough*, Kilmore)

Connolly, David (OFM)
4 Merchants' Quay
Dublin, D08 XY19
Tel 01-6711228

Connolly, Dermot (SPS)
St Patrick's,
21 Leeson Park,
Dublin 6 D06 DE76
Tel 01-4977897

Connolly, Hugh, Rt Rev Mgr,
BA, DD, President,
Irish College, Paris
5 Rue des Irlandais,
75005 Paris, France
(Dromore)

Connolly, John, Very Rev
c/o Ara Coeli,
Armagh BT61 7QY
(Armagh)

Connolly, Joseph, Very Rev,
PP
Parochial House,
Ballymore Eustace, Naas
Co Kildare
Tel 045-864114
(*Ballymore Eustace*,
Dublin)

LIST OF CLERGY IN IRELAND

Connolly, Kevin, CC
St Joseph's,
Carrickmacross,
Co Monaghan A81 WP68
Tel 042-9661231
(*Carrickmacross (Machaire Rois)*, Clogher)

Connolly, Michael, Very Rev, PP
Oughterard, Co Galway
Tel 091-456527
(*Oughterard*, Galway)

Connolly, Noel (SPS)
St Patrick's, Kiltegan,
Co Wicklow W91 Y022
Tel 059-6473600

Connolly, Patrick, Dr
Theology Department,
Mary Immaculate College,
South Circular Road,
Limerick
V94 VN26
Tel 061-204575
(Clogher)

Connolly, Patrick (SMA)
African Missions,
Blackrock Road,
Cork T12 TD54
Tel 021-4292871

Connolly, Philip, Very Rev
Canon, PE
Doohamlet, Castleblayney,
Co Monaghan A75 PX09
Tel 042-9741239
(*Clontibret*, Clogher)

Connolly, Ronan (OP)
Convent of Ss Xystus and Clement,
Collegio San Clemente
Via Labicana 95,
00184 Roma, Italy
Tel 0039-067740021

Connolly, Sean, Rt Rev Mgr, VG
7 Tullyview, Loughguile,
Co Antrim BT44 9JY
(Down & C., retired)

Connolly, Terence, Very Rev, PE
178 Newtownsaville Road,
Omagh,
Co Tyrone BT78 2RJ
Tel 028-82841306
(*Eskra*, Clogher)

Connolly, Vincent, Rt Rev Mgr, PE
Magherarney,
Smithborough,
Co Monaghan H18 H297
Tel 047-57011
(*Roslea*, Clogher)

Connors, Tom Rev (MHM)
St Joseph's House,
50 Orwell Park,
Rathgar, Dublin D06 C535
Tel 01-4127700

Conroy, Charles (MSC)
Western Road,
Cork T12 TN80
Tel 021-4804120

Conroy, Christopher (OCarm)
Whitefriar Street Church,
56 Aungier Street,
Dublin 2 D02 R598
Tel 01-4758821

Conroy, Michael (SPS)
St Patrick's, Kiltegan,
Co Wicklow
Tel 059-6473600

Conroy, Patrick, Very Rev, PP
Ballinakill, Loughrea,
Co Galway H62 AW68
Tel 090-9745021
(*Ballinakill and Derrybrien*, Clonfert)

Conry, Anthony
Brazil
(Elphin)

Considine, Patrick, Very Rev
Dean, PE
2 St Mary's Apartments,
Shantalla Road, Galway
(Galway, retired)

Convey, Martin, Very Rev,
BSc, MLitt, PhD, PP
Straide, Foxford, Co Mayo
Tel 094 9031029
(*Straide*, Achonry)

Conway, Alan, Very Rev, PP
Parochial House, Drumlion
Carrick-on-Shannon,
Co Roscommon
Tel 071-9620415
(*Croghan*, Elphin)

Conway, Brian (SPS)
18 Cartron Court,
Catron, Sligo
(Elphin, retired)

Conway, Bernard (SPS)
On temporary diocesan work

Conway, David (CSSp)
Provincial Bursar,
Holy Spirit Missionary College
Kimmage Manor,
Whitehall Road,
Dublin D12 P5YP
Tel 01-4064300

Conway, Eamon
Head of Department of Theology & Religious Studies,
Mary Immaculate College,
University of Limerick,
South Circular Road,
Limerick
Tel 061-204353
(Limerick)

Conway, Edward, Very Rev, PC
1 Maretimo Gardens West,
Blackrock, Co Dublin
Tel 01-2882248
(*Blackrock*, Dublin)

Conway, Kevin (SMA)
Church of Our Lady of the Rosary and St Patrick,
61 Blackhorse Road,
Walthamstow,
London E17 7AS, UK

Conway, Michael
St Patrick's College,
Maynooth, Co Kildare
Tel 01-6285222
(Galway)

Conway, Michael, Very Rev
Barr Trá, Enniscrone,
Co Sligo
(Killala, retired)

Conway, Noel, Very Rev
Canon
(priest in residence)
23 Rathkeltair Road,
Downpatrick,
Co Down BT30 6NL
Tel 024-4461477
(*Downpatrick*, Down & C.)

Conway, Paddy,
(Killaloe, retired)

Conway, Patrick (SSC)
c/o Bishop's Residence,
Westbourne,
Ennis, Co Clare
Tel 065-6828638

Cooke, Colm (SPS)
St Patrick's, Kiltegan,
Co Wicklow W91 Y022
Tel 059-6473600

Cooke, Michael, Rt Rev Mgr
15 Meadow Park,
Dublin Road, Cavan,
Co Cavan
(Kilmore, retired)

Coonan, Thomas, Rt Rev Mgr, PE, CC
Geashill, Co Offaly
Tel 057-9343517
(*Killeigh*, Kildare & L.)

Cooney, Brendan (SPS)
St Patrick's,
21 Leeson Park,
Dublin 6 D06 DE76
Tel 01-4977897

Cooney, John, Very Rev, PP
Parochial House,
Station Road,
Cootehill, Co Cavan
Tel 049-5552120
(*Cootehill (Drumgoon)*, Kilmore)

Cooney, Kevin (SM)
Superior,
Cerdon, Marist Fathers,
St Mary's Road,
Dundalk, Co Louth
Tel 042-9334019

Cooney, Matthew (OSA)
The Presbytery,
Dungarvan, Co Waterford
(*Dungarvan*, Waterford & L.)

Cooney, Michael, CC
Presbytery 1,
Thormanby Road, Howth,
Co Dublin
Tel 01-8323193
(*Howth*, Dublin)

Cooney, Michael, Very Rev, Co-PP
Parochial House,
Terryglass,
Nenagh, Co Tipperary
Tel 067-22017/087-6548331
(*Cois Deirge Pastoral Area*, Killaloe)

Coote, Tony (SVD)
Donamon Castle,
Roscommon
Tel 090-6662222

Corbett, John F. (CSsR)
St Patrick's, Esker,
Athenry, Co Galway
Tel 091-844007

Corbett, Padraig
Castleiney, Co Tipperary
(Cashel & E., retired)

Corbett, Thomas, Very Rev Dr, AP
Convent Hill, Roscrea,
Co Tipperary
Tel 0505-21108/086-8418570
(*Cronan Pastoral Area*, Killaloe)

Corcoran, Gerard, Very Rev, (Moderator),
12 Grangemore Grove
Donaghmede,
Dublin D13 A264
Tel 01-8474652
(*Ayrfield, Donaghmede-Clongriffin-Balgriffin*, Dublin)

Corcoran, Gregory, Very Rev, PP
Rhode, Co Offaly
Tel 087-9402669/046-9737010
(*Clonbullogue, Rhode*, Kildare & L.)

Corcoran, James, Very Rev, PP
Cooneal, Ballina, Co Mayo
Tel 096-32242
(*Ballysokeary*, Killala)

Corcoran, Michael (MHM)
Superior General,
1 Colby Gardens,
Cookham Road,
Maidenhead SL6 7GZ,
England
Tel 0044-1628-789752

Corcorcan, Patrick (SM)
Chanel Community,
Coolock, Dublin 5
Tel 01-8477133

Corcoran, Patrick (SPS)
St Patrick's, Kiltegan,
Co Wicklow
Tel 059-6473600

LIST OF CLERGY IN IRELAND

Corcoran, Philip, Very Rev, PE
542 River Forest Estate,
Leixlip, Co Kildare
(Dublin, retired)

Corcoran, Thomas, Very Rev, PP
Clogh, Castlecomer,
Co Kilkenny
Tel 056-4442135/
085-2543904
(*Clogh*, Ossory)

Corish, Declan (OP), PP
St Saviour's, Bridge Street,
Waterford
Tel 051-875061

Corkery, Eamonn, PE
Aughnacliffe,
Co Longford N39 T2P1
(Ardagh & Cl., retired)

Corkery, James (SJ)
c/o Irish Jesuit
Provincialate,
Milltown Park,
Sandford Road, Dublin 6
Tel 01-4987333

Corkery, Michael, Very Rev, PP
Glanworth, Co Cork
Tel 025-38123
(*Glanworth*, Cloyne)

Corkery, Pádraig, Dr
St Patrick's College,
Maynooth, Co Kildare
Tel 01-7083639
(Cork & R.)

Corkery, Patrick, CC
Youghal, Co Cork
Tel 024-92336
(*Youghal*, Cloyne)

Corkery, Seán
Director of Formation
St Patrick's College,
Maynooth, Co Kildare
Tel 086-2420240
(*Mallow*, Cloyne)

Cormac, Pierce
Chaplain,
Mercy University Hospital,
Grenville Place,
Cork
Tel 021-4271971
(Cork & R.)

Corr, Sean (SSC)
St Columban's Retirement
Home,
Dalgan Park,
Navan, Co Meath
Tel 046-9021525

Corrigan, Brendan, Very Rev, PP
Parochial House,
Harbour Road,
Kilbeggan,
Co Westmeath
Tel 057-9332155
(*Kilbeggan*, Meath)

Corrigan, David (SM), PP
St Teresa's,
Donore Avenue, Dublin 8
Tel 01-4542425/4531613

Corrigan, Desmond
17 Chapel Street,
Poyntzpass, Newry
Co Down BT35 6SY
Tel 028-38318217
(Armagh, retired)

Corrigan, Desmond (SMA)
African Missions,
Dromantine, Newry,
Co Down BT34 1RH
Tel 028-30821224

Corrigan, Kevin (CSSp)
Holy Spirit Missionary
College
Kimmage Manor,
Whitehall Road,
Dublin D12 P5YP
Tel 01-4064300

Corrigan, Peter, Very Rev, PE
Shanco, Newbliss,
Co Monaghan H18 K303
Tel 047-54011
(*Killeevan*, Clogher)

Corry, Edward
Presbytery 2,
Treepark Road,
Kilnamanagh, Dublin 24
(Dublin, retired)

Corry, Francis (SM),
The Presbytery,
Coolock Village, Dublin 5
Tel 01-8477133
(*Coolock*, Dublin)

Cosgrave, William, Very Rev, PP
Monageer, Ferns,
Enniscorthy, Co Wexford
Tel 053-9233530
(*Monageer*, Ferns)

Cosgrove, Edward (SJ)
St Francis Xavier's,
Upper Gardiner Street,
Dublin 1
Tel 01-8363411

Cosgrove, John, Very Rev Canon, PE
Claremorris, Co Mayo
(Tuam, retired)

Cosgrove, Martin, Very Rev Canon (Moderator), PP, VF
St Mary's Presbytery,
Willbrook,
Rathfarnham, Dublin 14
Tel 01-4954554
(*Rathfarnham*, Dublin)

Costello, Aidan, CC
The Presbytery, Loughrea,
Co Galway H62 YE09
Tel 091-841212
(*Loughrea, St Brendan's Cathedral*, Clonfert)

Costello, Ambrose (OCarm)
Carmelite Community,
Gort Muire, Ballinteer,
Dublin D16 EI67
Tel 01-2984014

Costello, Bernard
13 Garbally Oaks,
Ballinasloe,
Co Galway H53 KW27
Tel 087-2396208
(*Lawrencetown and Kiltormer*, Clonfert)

Costello, David
c/o The Missionary Society
of St James the Apostle,
24 Clark Street, Boston,
MA 02109, USA
(Limerick)

Costello, James, Very Rev Canon
Bruff, Kilmallock,
Co Limerick
Tel 061-382555
(Limerick, retired)

Costello, Martin (SMA)
SMA House, Cloonbigeen,
Claregalway,
Co Galway H91 YK64
Tel 091-798880

Costello, Maurice
Main Street, Rathkeale,
Co Limerick
Tel 069-63452
(Limerick, retired)

Costello, Padraig, Very Rev, PP, VF
Chaplain, St Joseph's
Secondary School,
Foxford, Co Mayo
Tel 094-9860010
Parish: Foxford, Co Mayo
Tel 094-9256131
(*Foxford,* Achonry)

Costello, Shane, CC
Castlebar, Co Mayo
Tel 094-9021844
(*Castlebar*, Tuam)

Costelloe, Morgan
Our Lady's Manor,
Bullock Harbour,
Dalkey, Co Dublin
Tel 01-2718007
(Dublin, retired)

Costelloe, Patrick,
Mount Sarto, Lower Park,
Corbally, Limerick
Tel 061-342276/
086-2444528
(Limerick, retired)

Cotter, Bernard (SMA)
African Missions,
Blackrock Road,
Cork T12 TD54
Tel 021-4292871

Cotter, Bernard, Very Rev, PP
The Presbytery,
Newcestown,
Bandon, Co Cork
Tel 021-7438000
(*Murragh and Templemartin*, Cork & R.)

Cotter, Donal, Very Rev, PP
Parochial House,
Watergrasshill, Co Cork
Tel 021-4889103
(*Watergrasshill*, Cork & R.)

Cotter, Francis (OFM)
Franciscan House of
Studies, Dún Mhuire,
Seafield Road,
Killiney, Co Dublin
Tel 01-2826760

Cotter, Seán, Very Rev Canon, PE
Love Lane,
Charleville, Co Cork
(Cloyne, retired)

Coughlan, David Rev (SJ)
35 Lower Leeson Street,
Dublin 2
Tel 01-6761248

Coughlan, John, CC
On Sabbatical
(Elphin)

Coughlan, Patrick (CSSp)
The Presbytery,
Bawnogue, Clondalkin,
Dublin 22
Tel 01-4519810

Coughlan, Thomas, PC
The Presbytery, Avoca,
Co Wicklow
Tel 0402-35204
(Dublin, retired)

Coughlan, Thomas, Very Rev
Effin, Limerick
Tel 0872229223
(Limerick, retired)

Coveney, Patrick, Most Rev, AP
Crosshaven, Co Cork
Tel 021-4831218
(*Crosshaven*, Cork & R.)

Cox, Tom, Adm
Shannonbridge,
Athlone, Co Offaly
Tel 090-9674125
(*Shannonbridge*)
(*Clonmacnois*), Ardagh & Cl.)

Coyle, Mark (OFMCap)
Ard Mhuire, Creeslough,
Letterkenny,
Co Donegal F92 Y23R
Tel 074-9138005

Coyle, Patrick
c/o Ara Coeli,
Armagh BT61 7QY
(Armagh)

LIST OF CLERGY IN IRELAND

Coyle, Paul, Co-PP
159 Botanic Road,
Glasnevin, Dublin 9
Tel 01-83773455
Acting Chancellor,
The Chancellery,
Archbishop's House,
Dublin 9
Tel 01-8379253
(*Glasnevin*, Dublin)

Coyle, Peter (SPS)
St Patrick's, 21 Leeson Park,
Dublin 6 D06 DE76
Tel 01-4977897

Coyle, Rory
c/o Ara Coeli,
Armagh, BT61 7QY
Tel 028-37522045
(*Armagh*, Armagh)

Coyle, Séan (SSC)
St Columban's,
Dalgan Park, Navan Road,
Co Meath
Tel 046-9021525

Coyle, Thomas, Very Rev, PP
Galmoy, Crosspatrick,
via Thurles, Co Kilkenny
Tel 056-8831227/
087-7668969
(*Galmoy*, Ossory)

Coyne, Joseph, Very Rev, Moderator
36 Ashfield Lawn,
Huntstown, Dublin 15
Tel 01-8216447
(*Blakestown, Hartstown, Huntstown, Mountview*, Dublin)

Coyne, Vincent (OSM)
Acting Provincial,
The Servite Priory,
500 Bury New Road,
Salford,
Manchester M7 4ND
Tel 01-617922152

Craemer, Eddie (CSsR)
Clonard Monastery,
Clonard Gardens
Belfast BT13 2RL

Craven, John, PP
Holy Cross Retreat,
Crumlin Road, Ardoyne,
Belfast BT14 7GE
Tel 028-90748231
(*Holy Cross*, Down & C.)

Crawford, Alan (OSB)
Glenstal Abbey, Murroe,
Co Limerick
Tel 061-386103

Crawford, Thomas, AP
9 Chestnut Gardens,
Newcastlewest,
Co Limerick
Tel 087-2218078
(*Pastoral Unit 15*, Limerick)

Crawley, Michael, Very Rev Canon, PE,
Parochial House,
89 Derrynoose Road,
Keady,
Co Armagh BT60 3EZ
Tel 028-3751222
(*Armagh*, retired)

Creagh, Kieran (CP)
Chaplain, Our Lady's Hospice and Care Services,
Harold's Cross, Dublin 6W
Tel 01-4068700
(Dublin)

Creamer, Edmond (CSsR)
Clonard Monastery,
1 Clonard Gardens,
Belfast BT13 2RL
Tel 028-90445950

Crean, David (OSA)
Good Counsel College
New Ross, Co Wexford

Crean, Jack (OSA)
Duckspool House
(Retirement Community),
Abbeyside, Dungarvan,
Co Waterford
Tel 058-23784

Crean, Martin (OSA)
St Augustine's Priory,
Washington Street,
Cork

Crean, Thomas, Venerable
(Kerry, retired)

Crean, William, Most Rev, DD
Bishop of Cloyne,
Cloyne Diocesan Centre,
Cobh, Co Cork
Tel 021-4811430
(Cloyne)

Crean-Lynch, Pat, Very Rev, PP
Ardfert, Co Kerry
Tel 066-7134131
(*Ardfert*, Kerry)

Creelman, Leo, CC
St Joseph's Presbytery,
Park Street
Co Monaghan H18 C588
Tel 047-81220
(*Monaghan*, Clogher)

Cremin, Aidan, CC
Cork Road, Carrigaline,
Co Cork
Tel 021-4372229
(*Carrigaline*, Cork & R.)

Cremin, Gerard, CC
Upper strand, Youghal,
Co Cork
Tel 024-90296
(*Youghal*, Cloyne)

Cremin, Jerry, Very Rev, PP,
Parochial House,
Kilbrittain, Co Cork
Tel 023-8849637
(*Kilbrittain*, Cork & R.)

Cribbin, James, Very Rev, PP
Geesala, Bangor,
Ballina, Co Mayo
Tel 097-86740
(*Kiltane*, Killala)

Cribbin, Peter, Very Rev
c/o Bishop's House,
Dublin Road, Carlow
(Kildare & L.)

Crilly, Oliver
(priest in residence)
Parochial House, Castlefin,
Lifford, Co Donegal
Tel 074-9146251
(*Doneyloop (Urney and Castlefinn)*, Derry)

Crilly, Patrick, PEm
35 Rocktown Lane,
Knockloughrim,
Magerafelt,
Co Derry BT45 8QF
(Derry, retired)

Cristóbal, Jimenez A. (SJ)
Jesuit Community,
27 Leinster Road,
Rathmines, Dublin 6
Tel 01-4970250

Crombie, Shane, CC
c/o Bishop's House,
Dublin Road, Mullingar,
Co Westmeath N91 DW32
(Meath)

Cronin, Brian (Cssp)
Holy Spirit Missionary College
Kimmage Manor,
Whitehall Road,
Dublin D12 P5YP
Tel 01-4064300

Cronin, Kieran (OFM)
Provincial Delegate,
Franciscan Abbey,
Multyfarnham,
Co Westmeath N91 X279
Tel 044-9371114/9371137

Crosbie, Paul, PP
Parochial House, Trim,
Co Meath
Tel 046-9431251
Adm, Summerhill
(*Summerhill, Trim*, Meath)

Crosby, Denis, Very Rev, PP
Liscannor, Co Clare
Tel 065-7081248
(*Liscannor*, Galway)

Crosby, Edward, Adm
Parochial House,
Kilfenora, Co Clare
Tel 065-7088006
(*Kilfenora*, Galway)

Crosby, Michael, Very Rev
Main Street, Ballinrobe,
Co Mayo
(Galway, retired)

Cross, Charles (CP), CC
St Gabriel's Retreat, The Graan, Enniskillen
Co Fermanagh
Tel 028-66322272
(Down & C.)

Crossan, Stephen, CC,
c/o Bishop's House, Newry
Co Down BT32 4DW
(Dromore, retired)

Crossey, Colin, CC
81 Lagmore Grove,
Dunmurry,
Belfast, BT17 0TD
Tel 028-90309011
(*Christ the Redeemer, Lagmore*, Down & C.)

Crosson, Eamonn, Very Rev, Adm
Parochial House, Ashford,
Co Wicklow
Tel 0404-40540
(*Ashford*, Dublin)

Crotty, James, Very Rev Canon, PP
Ferrybank, Waterford
Tel 051-832787/
086-8317711
(Ossory, retired)

Crotty, Terence (OP)
St Saviour's,
Upper Dorset Street,
Dublin 1
Tel 01-8897610

Crowe, Jim (SPS)
St Patrick's, Kiltegan,
Co Wicklow
Tel 059-6473600

Crowe, Philip (CSSp), CC
Drumgossatt,
Carrickmacross,
Co Monaghan
Tel 042-9661388
(*Magheracloone*, Clogher)

Crowley, Adrian, CC
4 Summerfield Lawn,
Clonsilla Road,
Blanchardstown, Dublin 15
(*Mulhuddart*, Dublin)

Crowley, Aidan, Very Rev, PP
Doneraile, Co Cork
Tel 086-0434911
(*Doneraile*, Cloyne)

Crowley, Brendan, PP
78 Ballerin Road, Garvagh,
Co Derry BT51 5EQ
Tel 028-29558251
(*Garvagh (Errigal)*, Derry)

Crowley, Brendan, Very Rev Canon, PE, VF
SS Peter and Paul's,
Clonmel, Co Tipperary
Tel 052-6126292
(*Clonmel, SS Peter and Paul's*, Waterford & L.)

Crowley, Dan, Very Rev Canon, PE
Woodlawn,
Model Farm Road,
Co Cork.
(Cork & R, retired)

Crowley, Finbarr, PP
Innishannon, Co Cork
Tel 021-4775348
(*Innishannon*, Cork & R.)

LIST OF CLERGY IN IRELAND

Crowley, Kevin (OFMCap)
Capuchin Friary,
137-142 Church Street,
Dublin D07 HA22
Tel 01-8730599

Crowley, Liam, PP
Drimoleague, Co Cork
Tel 028-31133
(*Drimoleague*, Cork & R.)

Crowley, Roderic (CM)
St Paul's, Sybil Hill,
Raheny, Dublin D05 AE38
Tel 01-8318113

Crowley, Sean, CC
Cathedral Presbytery,
Roman Street, Co Cork
Tel 021-4304325
(*Cathedral of St Mary & St Anne,
Blackpool/The Glen*, Cork & R.)

Crudden, James, Very Rev, PP
24 Downs Road,
Newcastle,
Co Down BT33 0AG
Tel 028-43722401
(*Newcastle (Maghera)*,
Down & C.)

Cryan, Gerard, BA, HDE, STB, L Eccl Hist
(priest in residence)
St Mary's, Sligo
Tel 071-9162670/9162769
College of the Immaculate Conception, Summerhill,
Sligo
Tel 071-9160311
(*Elphin*)

Cudzilo, Michal
Curate's House, Chapel Lane,
Newbridge, Co Kildare
Tel 045-434069
(*Droichead Nua/Newbridge*, Kildare & L.)

Cuffe, Liam
Chaplain,
St Vincent's University Hospital,
Elm Park, Dublin 4
Tel 01-2094325
(*Ardagh & Cl.*)

Cul, Marek (OP)
St Mary's, The Claddagh,
Co Galway
Tel 091-582884

Cullen, James, CC
The Presbytery,
12 School Street, Wexford
Tel 053-9122055
(*Wexford*, Ferns)

Cullen, John, Very Rev
Chaplain, Nazareth House,
Hammersmith, London
(*Elphin*)

Cullen, Kevin, Very Rev, PP
Parochial House,
9A Newry Road
Crossmaglen, Newry,
Co Down BT35 9HH
(*Cullyhanna (Creggan Lower)*, Armagh)

Cullen, Laurence, Very Rev, PP
Geevagh, Boyle,
Co Roscommon
Tel 071-9647107
(*Geevagh*, Elphin)

Cullen, Michael, Very Rev, Adm
5 St Assam's Road West,
Raheny, Dublin 5
Tel 01-8313806
(*Raheny*, Dublin)

Cullen, Peter, Adm
20 Bengurragh, Cahir
Co Tipperary
Tel 052 7441585
(*Cahir*, Waterford & L.)

Cullen, Sean
St Patrick's, Kiltegan,
Co Wicklow
Tel 059-6473600

Cullinan, Alphonsus, Most Rev, DD
Bishop of Waterford and Lismore
Bishop's House, John's Hill,
Waterford
Tel 051-874463
(*Waterford & L.*)

Cullinan, Edmond, Very Rev Canon, VF
Vice-Rector,
Pontifical Irish College,
Via Dei SS Quattro 1,
00184 Roma, Italy
(*Waterford & L.*)

Cullinan, William (OCSO)
Mellifont Abbey,
Collon, Co Louth
Tel 041-9826103

Cullinane, Michael, Very Rev, PP, VF
Parochial House, Lismore,
Co Waterford
Tel 058-54246
(*Lismore*, Waterford & L.)

Cullinane, Timothy (SMA)
African Missions,
Blackrock Road,
Cork T12 TD54
Tel 021-4292871

Culliton, Jim (SJ)
Superior, St Ignatius House of Writers,
35 Lower Leeson Street,
Dublin 2
Tel 01-6761248

Cully, Patrick (CSSp)
Cherry Orchard Hospital,
Ballyfermot, Dublin 10
Tel 01-6264702
Holy Spirit Missionary College
Kimmage Manor,
Whitehall Road,
Dublin D12 P5YP
Tel 01-4064300

Cumiskey, Cathal (CSsR)
St Joseph's,
St Alphonsus Road,
Dundalk,
Co Louth A71 F3FC
Tel 042-9334042/9334762

Cummings, Daniel
30 Knapton Road,
Dun Laoghaire, Co Dublin
Tel 01-2804353
(*Opus Dei*)

Cummins, Fergal
Parochial House,
Tullamore, Co Offaly
Tel 057-9321587
(*Tullamore*, Meath)

Cummins, Stephen (OP)
St Dominic's Retreat House,
Montenotte, Co Cork
Tel 021-4502520

Cummins, William, Very Rev, PP
Parochial House,
Ennistymon, Co Clare
Tel 065-7071063
(*Ennistymon*, Galway)

Cunnane, Fergal, Very Rev, PP, VF
The Parochial House,
Dunmore,
Co Galway H54 E893
Tel 093-38124
(*Dunmore*, Tuam)

Cunnane, Seamus, Very Rev Canon,
Grove House,
Vicar street, Tuam,
Co Galway H54 KW02
(*Tuam*, retired)

Cunningham, Charles (SDB)
Salesian House,
45 St Teresa's Road,
Crumlin, Dublin D12 XK52
Tel 01-4555605

Cunningham, Connell, Very Rev, PE
c/o Diocesan Office,
Letterkenny,
Co Donegal
(*Raphoe*, retired)

Cunningham, Conor, Very Rev,
5 Pine Grove, Moycullen,
Co Galway
(*Galway*)

Cunningham, Donal, AP
Upperchurch, Thurles,
Co Tipperary
Tel 0504-54181
(*Upperchurch*, Cashel & E.)

Cunningham, Enda, Very Rev
47 Westland Row,
Dublin 2
Tel 01-6765517
(*Westland Row/University Church*, Dublin)

Cunningham, Gerald (IC)
Clonturk House,
Ormond Road,
Drumcondra, Dublin 9
Tel 01-6877014

Cunningham, Gerard, Very Rev, PP, VF
Glenties, Co Donegal
Tel 074-9551117
(*Glenties*, Raphoe)

Cunningham, John Joe, Very Rev
Newcastle, Co Down
(*Dromore*, retired)

Cunningham, John M. (OP)
St Saviour's,
Upper Dorset Street,
Dublin 1
Tel 01-8897610

Cunningham, Martin, Very Rev, PP
Drumoghill, Co Donegal
Tel 074-9157169
(*Drumoghill (Raymochy)*, Raphoe)

Cunningham, Seán, Very Rev, CC
Parochial House,
Corrandulla, Co Galway
Tel 091-791125
(*Corrandulla (Annaghdown)*, Tuam)

Curran, Adrian (OFMCap),
Very Rev
St Francis Capuchin Friary,
Rochestown,
Co Cork T12 NH02
Tel 021-4896244

Curran, Anthony, Very Rev, PP,
St Mary's Presbytery,
12 Ballymena Road,
Portglenone,
Co Antrim BT44 8BL
Tel 028-25821218
(*Portglenone*, Down & C.)

Curran, Colum, Very Rev
Parochial House,
22 Ballymartin Village,
Kilkeel,
Co Down BT34 4PA
Tel 028-43768208
(*Lower Mourne*, Down & C.)

LIST OF CLERGY IN IRELAND

Curran, James
61 Tournane Court,
Dungarvan, Co Waterford
Tel 058-45177
(Waterford & L., retired)

Curran, Michael (MSC)
Parish House, Union Hall,
Skibbereen, Co Cork
Tel 028-34940
(Castlehaven, Cork & R.)

Curran, Michael, Very Rev, PE
c/o Bishop's House,
John's Hill, Waterford
(Waterford & L., retired)

Curran, Philip, Very Rev, Moderator,
231 Beech Park, Lucan,
Co Dublin
Tel 01-2533804
(Esker-Doddboro-Adamstown, Lucan, Lucan South, Dublin)

Curran, Roderick (CSSp)
Holy Spirit Missionary College
Kimmage Manor,
Whitehall Road,
Dublin D12 P5YP
Tel 01-4064300

Curran, Thomas (SMA)
Bursar, SMA House,
81 Ranelagh Road,
Ranelagh, Dublin 6
Tel 01-4968162/3

Currivan, Patrick, Very Rev, AP
Caherconlish, Co Limerick
Tel 061-351248
(Caherconlish, Cashel & E.)

Curry, Colum, Rt Rev Mgr, PP, VG
Parochial House,
Beragh, Omagh,
Co Tyrone BT790SY
(Beragh, Armagh)

Curry, Martin (SJ)
Rector
St Ignatius Community & Church,
27 Raleigh Row, Salthill,
Galway
Tel 091-523707

Curtin, Timothy,
The Presbytery,
Carrons, Kilcolman,
Co Limerick
Tel 069-60126/086-3697735
(Patoral Unit 13, Limerick)

Curtis, James, Very Rev
3 Oldtown Court,
Clongreen, Foulksmills,
New Ross, Co Wexford
(Ferns, retired)

Curtis, James B., Very Rev Canon
Rathjarney, Drinagh,
Co Wexford
(Ferns, retired)

Cusack, John, CC
Ballinamore, Co Leitrim
Tel 071-9644050
(Ballinamore (Oughteragh), Kilmore)

Cusack, Ronan (OP), Very Rev
St Malachy's, Dundalk,
Co Louth
Tel 042-9334179

Cushen, Bernard, Very Rev, PP
Clonroche, Enniscorthy,
Co Wexford
Tel 053-9244115
(Cloughbawn and Poulpeasty, Ferns)

Cushen, Patrick, Very Rev, PP
Ferns, Enniscorthy,
Co Wexford
Tel 053-9366152
(Ferns, Ferns)

Cushnahan, Vincent, CC, JCL
Armagh Regional Marriage Tribunal Down & Connor Office,
The Good Shepherd Centre,
511 Ormeau Road,
Belfast BT7 3GS
191 Upper Newtownards Road, Belfast BT4 3JB
Tel 028-90654157
(Down & C.)

Cushnan, Martin (CSsR)
Redemptorist Community,
R.C. Church,
Morrispet P.O., Tenali,
Guntur DT 522 202,
Andhra Pradesh, India
Tel 0091-8644-223-382

Cussen, Joseph,
Lisieux, Gortboy,
Newcastlewest,
Co Limerick
Tel 069-77090
(Pastoral Unit 15, Limerick)

Cussen, Michael,
The Presbytery,
Ballybrown, Clarina,
Co Limerick
Tel 061-353711/
087-1279015
(Pastoral Unit 6, Limerick)

D

D'Arcy, Brian (CP)
Passionist Retreat Centre
Downpatrick Road,
Crossgar, Downpatrick,
Co Down BT30 9EQ
Tel 028-44830242

D'Souza, Darryl (SDB)
c/o Salesian House,
45 St Teresa's Road,
Crumlin, Dublin 12
Tel 01-4555605
(India)

Dagens, Seamus, PE
Drimarone, Co Donegal
(Raphoe, retired)

Daka, Vincent, CC
Cathedral House,
Mullingar, Co Westmeath
Tel 044-9348338/9340126
(Mullingar, Meath)

Dales, Jovito Rev (SSC)
Bursar General,
No 3 and 4,
Ma Yau Tong Village,
Po Lam Road,
Tseung Kwan O, Kow Loon, Hong Kong, SA

Dallat, Ciaran, Very Rev, PP
Parochial House,
Loughinisland,
Downpatrick,
Co Down BT30 8QH
Tel 028-44811661
(Loughinisland, Down & C.)

Dalton, John (OFM)
4 McSweeney House,
Berkeley Road, Dublin 7
Tel 01-2826760

Dalton, Patrick, Very Rev Canon, PP, VF
Gowran,
Co Kilkenny R95 E2Y4
Tel 056-7726128/
086-8283478
(Gowran, Tullaherin, Ossory)

Dalton, Thomas, Very Rev, PP
Riverchapel,
Courtown Harbour,
Gorey, Co Wexford
Tel 053-9425241
(Riverchapel, Courtown Harbour, Ferns)

Dalton, William, Very Rev, PP
Callan, Co Kilkenny
Tel 056-7725287/
086-8506215
(Callan, Ossory)

Daly, Brian, Very Rev, PP
Parochial House,
15 Moyle Road,
Ballycastle,
Co Antrim BT54 6LB
Tel 028-20762223
Administration Ballintoy
(Ballintoy, Ballycastle (Ramoan), Down & C.)

Daly, Gabriel (OSA)
St Augustine's,
Taylor's Lane,
Ballyboden, Dublin 16
Tel 01-4241000

Daly, James, Very Rev, PP
Parochial House, St Anne's Church,
Bohernabreena, Tallaght,
Dublin 24
Tel 01-4626893
(Bohernabreena, Tallaght, Oldbawn, Dublin)

Daly, Jeremiah (MSC)
Western Road,
Cork T12 TN80
Tel 021-4804120

Daly, John, Very Rev, PP
Parochial House,
La Touche Road,
Greystones, Co Wicklow
Tel 01-2874278
(Greystones, Kilquade, Dublin)

Daly, John
The Presbytery, Bruff,
Kilmallock, Co Limerick
Tel 061-32990/087 8180815
(Pastoral Unit 7, Limerick)

Daly, Kevin (OCSO)
Mount Saint Joseph Abbey, Roscrea,
Co Tipperary E53 D651
Tel 0505-25600

Daly, Martin (SM)
2 Beresford House,
Custom House Square,
Mayor Street Lower,
IFSC, Dublin 1
(retired)

Daly, Martin, CC
'Renvyle', Corrig Avenue,
Dun Laoghaire, Co Dublin
Tel 01-2802100
(Dun Laoghaire, Dublin)

Daly, Michael, Very Rev Canon, PP
Broomfield, Castleblayney,
Co Monaghan
A75 A344
Tel 042-9743617
(Donaghmoyne, Clogher)

Daly, Noel (SSC)
St Columban's,
Dalgan Park, Navan,
Co Meath
Tel 046-9021525

Daly, Pádraig A. (OSA)
Prior, St John's Priory,
Thomas Street, Dublin 8
Tel 01-6770393/0415/0601

Daly, Patrick, Very Rev, PE
Braganza, Athy Road,
Carlow
(Kildare & L., retired)

Daly, Peter (OMI)
Oblate House of Retreat,
Inchicore, Dublin 8
Tel 01-4534408/4541805

Daly, Philip, CC
Kilclooney, Co Donegal
Tel 074-9545114
(Ardara, Raphoe)

LIST OF CLERGY IN IRELAND

Daly, Shane (SJ)
Loyola House,
Milltown Park,
Sandford Road, Dublin 6
Tel 01-2180276

Daly, Thomas, Very Rev, PE, AP
Parochial House,
Boicetown, Togher,
Drogheda,
Co Louth A92 C597
Tel 041-6852110
(*Togher*, Armagh)

Dalzell, Tom, Moderator,
Parochial House,
Church Avenue
Killiney, Co Dublin
Tel 01-2826404
(*Ballybrack-Killiney,
Loughlinstown*, Dublin)

Danaher, Michael (OSA)
St Augustine's Priory,
O'Connell Street, Limerick
Tel 061-415374

Daniels, Iomar, Very Rev, PP
Parochial House,
Leitrim, Loughrea,
Co Galway H62 RP40
(*Leitrim and Ballyduggan
(Kilcooley and Leitrim)*,
Clonfert)
Killoran, Ballinasloe,
Co Galway
Tel 091-841758 for both parishes
(*Kilmeen*, Tuam)

Darby, Derek
Meath Diocesan Office,
Dublin Road, Mullingar
Tel 044-9348841
(Meath)

Darby, Gary, Very Rev, Co-PP
St Luke's, Kilbarron Road,
Kilmore West, Dublin 5
Tel 01-8486806
(*Kilmore Road West*,
Dublin)

Dardis, John (SJ)
c/o Irish Jesuit
Provincialate,
Milltown Park,
Sandford Road, Dublin 6
Tel 01-4987333

Darko, Michael, CC
St Patrick's Presbytery,
Roden Place, Dundalk
Co Louth A91 K2P4
Tel 042-9334648
(*Dundalk, St Patrick's*,
Armagh)

Davern, Richard,
Ballyduane, Clarina,
Co Limerick
Tel 087-2977500
(*Pastoral Unit 6*, Limerick)

Davey, Gerard, Very Rev, Adm
Carracastle,
Ballghaderreen,
Co Mayo F45 W822
Tel 094-9254301
(*Ballghaderreen*, Achonry)

David, Jerald, Adm, CC
Parochial House,
Aghamore, Ballyhaunis,
Co Mayo F35 WF51
Tel 094-9367024
(*Aghamore*, Tuam)

Davis, Donal (OCSO)
Mount Melleray Abbey,
Cappoquin,
Co Waterford P51 R8XW
Tel 058-54404

Davis, Patrick (SJ)
St Ignatius House of Writers,
35 Lower Leeson Street,
Dublin 2
Tel 01-6761248

Davis, Joe Pazheparambil, CC
St Paul's Presbytery,
125 Falls Road,
Belfast BT12 6AB
Tel 028-90325034
(*St Paul's*, Down & C.)

Davitt, Norman (SVD)
Donamon Castle,
Roscommon
Tel 090-6662222

Dawson, Laurence, Very Rev Canon, PE
25 Teiges Hill,
Brookeborough,
Co Fermanagh BT94 4EZ
Tel 028-89531770
(*Brookeboro (Aghavea-Aghintaine)*, Clogher)

De Bhaldraithe, Eoin (OCSO)
Bolton Abbey, Moone,
Co Kildare
Tel 059-8624102

De Blacam, Hugh (CSSp)
Holy Spirit Missionary College
Kimmage Manor,
Whitehall Road,
Dublin D12 P5YP
Tel 01-4064300

De Burca, Brian (OMI), Very Rev
170 Merrion Road,
Ballsbridge, Dublin 4
Tel 01-2693658

De Léis, Seán (CSSp)
Holy Spirit Missionary College
Kimmage Manor,
Whitehall Road,
Dublin D12 P5YP
Tel 01-4064300

De Querioz, Genildo (OCarm)
Gort Muire, Ballinteer,
Dublin D16 EI67
Tel 01-2984014

De Val, Seamus, Very Rev Canon
1 Irish Street, Bunclody,
Co Wexford
Tel 053-9376140
(Ferns, retired)

Deane, Joseph Mary (CFR)
Local Servant (Superior),
St Patrick Friary,
64 Delmege Park,
Moyross,
Limerick V94 859Y
Tel 061-458071

Deasy, Declan (OSA)
St Augustine's Priory,
St Augustine's Street,
Galway
Tel 091-562524

Deasy, John F., Very Rev Mgr,
(Team Assistant)
55 St Agnes' Road,
Crumlin, Dublin 12
Tel 01-4550955
(*Crumlin*, Dublin)

DeCant, John Baptist (OSB)
Silverstream Priory,
Stamullen,
Co Meath K32 T189
Tel 01-8417142

Decio, Cesare (OP)
St Catherine's, Newry,
Co Down BT35 8BN
Tel 028-30262178

Deegan, Gerard, Co-PP
28 Glentworth Park,
Ayrefield, Dublin 13
Tel 01-8674007
(*Ayrefield*, Dublin)

Deegan, Joseph, Very Rev, PP
St Brigid's Parish Office,
Church Street, Clara,
Co Offaly R35 PW97
Tel 057-9331170
(*Clara*, Meath)

Deegan, Sean (SPS)
Editor, *Africa*,
St Patricks,
Kiltegan, Co Wicklow
Tel 059-6473600

Deegan, Stan, Very Rev, PP
St Joseph's Parochial House, Killucan,
Co Westmeath N91 F292
Tel 044-9374127
(*Killucan*, Meath)

Deely, Patrick, AP
Lorrha, Co Tipperary
Tel 086-8330225
(*Cronan Pastoral Area*,
Killaloe)

Deeney, Edward (SMA)
African Missions,
Dromantine, Newry,
Co Down BT34 1RH
Tel 028-30821224

Deenihan, Thomas, Most Rev, DD, EdD
Bishop of Meath,
Bishop's House
Dublin Road, Mullingar
Co Meath
Tel 044-9348841
(Meath)

Deery, Cathal, Very Rev, CC
15 Knockmore Road,
Drumary, Derrygonnelly,
Co Fermanagh BT93 6GA
Tel 028-68641207
(*Derrygonnelly (Botha)*,
Clogher)

Deighan, Gerard, Very Rev, Adm
Parochial House,
Harrington Street,
Dublin 8
Tel 01-4751506
(*Harrington Street*, Dublin)

Deignan, John, PP
10 Ashford, Monksland,
Athlone, Co Roscommon
Tel 090-6493262
(*Athlone, SS Peter and Paul's*, Elphin)

Delahunty, Richard (CSsR), CC
Holy Family Parish,
Hoey's Lane,
Muirhevnamor,
Dundalk, Co Louth
A91 K761
Tel 042-9336301
(*Dundalk, Holy Family*,
Armagh)

Delaney, Joseph, Very Rev Canon
Castlelawn Heights,
Headford Road, Galway
(Galway, retired)

Delaney, John, Very Rev Canon,
Moderator,
Parochial House, St Mary's,
Sandyford, Dublin 18
Tel 01-2956317
(*Balally*, Dublin)

Delaney, John, CC
Beechwood Nursing Home,
Leighlinbridge, Co Carlow
Tel 086-2326807
(Ossory)

Delaney, John, Very Rev, PP
Parochial House,
Kilrossanty, Kilmacthomas,
Co Waterford
Tel 051-291985
(*Kilrossanty*, Waterford & L.)

LIST OF CLERGY IN IRELAND

Delaney, Joseph, Very Rev, AP
Clonbealy, Newport,
Co Tipperary
Tel 061-378126
(*Newport*, Cashel & E.)

Delaney, Martin, Very Rev, PP
Rathdowney, Co Laois
Tel 0505-46282/
086-2444594
Adm, Durrow
(*Durrow, Rathdowney*, Ossory)

Delany, John, Very Rev Canon, Moderator, VF
Parochial House, St Mary's
Sandyford Village,
Dublin 18
Tel 01-2956317
(*Balally*, Dublin)

Delargy, David, Very Rev, PP
824 Shore Road,
Newtownabbey,
Co Antrim BT36 7 DG
Tel 028-90370845
(*Greencastle, Whiteabbey (St James), Whitehouse*, Down & C.)

Delargy, Patrick, Rev Mgr, PP, VG
4 Broughshane Road,
Ballymena BT43 7DX
Tel 028-25643828
(*Ballymena (Kirkinriola)*, Down & C.)

Delimat, Piotr
Sarsfield Barracks,
Limerick
Tel 061-314233
(*Limerick*)

Dempsey, Michael (CSsR)
Clonard Monastery,
1 Clonard Gardens,
Belfast BT13 2RL
Tel 028-90445950

Dempsey, Michael Vincent
The Presbytery,
Kilmeade, Narraghmore,
Co Wicklow
(*Dublin*, retired)

Dempsey, Paul, Most Rev, DD
Bishop of Achonry
Bishop's House,
Convent Road,
Ballaghaderreen,
Co Roscommon F45 H004
Tel 094-9860034
(*Achonry*)

Dempsey, Raymond
St John's Presbytery,
Kilkenny
Tel 087-2859682
(*St John's*, Ossory)

Dempsey, Sean (MCCJ)
8 Clontarf Road, Clontarf,
Dublin 3
Tel 01-8330051

Denmead, James, AP
Cappoquin, Co Waterford
Tel 058-54221
(*Cappoquin*, Waterford & L.)

Dennehy, Philip, Very Rev, PE
4 Stanhope Place, Athy,
Co Kildare
Tel 059-8631696
(*Dublin*, retired)

Dermody, Eamonn, Very Rev Canon, PE
Clarinbridge, Co Galway
Tel 091-796208
(*Galway*, retired)

Desmond, Diarmuid, Very Rev, PP
Kilrane, Co Wexford
Tel 053-9133128
(*Kilrane and St Patrick's*, Ferns)

Desmond, Garrett, Very Rev, PP
Tournaneena, Ballinamult,
Clonmel, Co Tipperary
Tel 058-47138
(*Tournaneena*, Waterford & L.)

Desmond, Patrick
The Lodge, Mount
Sackville, Chapelizod,
Dublin 20
Tel 01-8214004
(*Dublin*)

Desmond, Patrick (OP)
Newbridge College,
Droichead Nua, Co Kildare
Tel 045-487200

Devaney, Owen, PE
Treanlawn, Killoe,
Co Longford, N39 79F3
(*Ardagh & Cl.*, retired)

Deveney, Cathal, PP, VF
Parochial House,
19 Caledon Road,
Aughnacloy,
Co Tyrone BT69 6HX
Tel 028-85557212
(*Aughnacloy (Aghaloo)*, Armagh)

Devereux, Sean, Very Rev, PP
Cushinstown, Newbawn,
Co Wexford
Tel 051-428347
(*Cushingtown and Rathgarogue*, Ferns)

Devine, James, CC
1 Aileach Road,
Ballymagroarty,
Derry BT48 0AZ
Tel 028-71267070
(*Holy Family, Ballymagroarty*, Derry)

Devine, Liam, Very Rev Canon, PP
Parochial House,
Loughglynn, Castlerea,
Co Roscommon
Tel 090-9880007
(*Loughglynn*, Elphin)

Devine, Oliver Very Rev, PP
Parochial House,
Drumraney, Athlone,
Co Westmeath
Tel 044-9356207

Devitt, Patrick, Adm
17 Prospect Lawn,
The Park, Cabinteely,
Dublin 18
(*Dublin*, retired)

Devitt, Séamus (CSsR), CC
The Presbytery,
197 Kylemore Road,
Ballyfermot, Dublin 10
Tel 01-6264789
(*Ballyfermot*, Dublin)

Devlin, Anthony, Very Rev, PP
St Paul's Presbytery,
125 Falls Road,
Belfast BT12 6AB
Tel 028-90325034
(*St Paul's*, Down & C.)

Devlin, Brendan, Rt Rev Mgr, MA, DD
St Patrick's College,
Maynooth, Co Kildare
Tel 01-6285222
(*Derry*)

Devlin, Eamon (CM), Very Rev, Co-PP
Superior,
St Peter's, Phibsboro,
Dublin 7
Tel 01-8389708/8389841
(*Phibsborough*, Dublin)

Devlin, Patrick, PP
St Vincent de Paul
Presbytery,
169 Ligoniel Road,
Belfast BT14 8DP
Tel 028-90713401
(*St Vincent de Paul*, Down & C.)

Devlin, Peter, PP
Parochial House,
Malin, Co Donegal
Tel 074-9370615
(*Malin (Clonca)*, Derry)

Digan, Padraig (SSC)
St Columban's Retirement
Home, Dalgan Park,
Navan, Co Meath
Tel 046-9021525

Diggin, Fintan, CC
Parochial House, Burt,
Lifford, Co Donegal
Tel 074-9368155
(*Fahan (Burt, Inch and Fahan)*, Derry)

Dillon, Christopher (OSB), Rev
Glenstal Abbey, Murroe,
Co Limerick
Tel 061-621000

Dillon, Sean, Very Rev, PP
Parochial House,
Greencastle Road, Kilkeel,
Co Down BT34 4DE
Tel 028-41762242
(*Kilkeel (Upper Mourne)*, Down and C.)

Dillon, Thomas, Very Rev, PE, CC
Parochial House,
Askea, Carlow
Tel 059-9164882
(*Bennekerry*, Kildare & L.)

Dineen, John (OCSO)
Mount Melleray Abbey,
Cappoquin,
Co Waterford P51 R8XW
Tel 058-54404

Dineen, Joseph (OP), PP
Prior, St Saviour's,
Upper Dorset Street,
Dublin 1
Tel 01-8897610
(*Dominick Street*, Dublin)

Dhason, Pravin, Very Rev, PP
Parochial House,
Cloverhill, Co Roscommon
Tel 090-6626275
(*Oran*, Elphin)

Dobbin, Séamus, CC
c/o Ara Coeli,
Armagh BT61 7QY
(*Armagh*)

Dodd, Michael (SSC)
St Columban's,
Dalgan Park,
Navan, Co Meath
Tel 046-9021525

Doherty, Brendan, PEm,
4 Garvagh Road, Kilrea,
Co Derry BT51 5QP
Tel 028-29540343
(*Derry*, retired)

Doherty, Cathal (SJ)
Irish Jesuit Provincialate,
Milltown Park,
Sandford Road, Dublin 6
Tel 01-4987333

Doherty, Con Rev (MSC)
'Croí Nua', Rosary Lane,
Taylor's Hill Road,
Galway H91 WY2A
Tel 091-520960

Doherty, John (CSsR)
Clonard Monastery,
1 Clonard Gardens,
Belfast BT13 2RL
Tel 028-90445950

Doherty, John, PEm
Parochial House,
447 Victoria Road,
Ballymagorry, Strabane,
Co Tyrone BT82 0AT
Tel 028-718802274
(*Derry*, retired)

Doherty, John, Rt Rev Mgr, PE
(priest in residence),
Charlestown, Co Mayo
Tel 094-9255793
(Achonry, retired)

Doherty, Kevin, CC
No 1 the Glebe,
Peamount Road,
Newcastle Lyons,
Co Dublin
Tel 01-4589230
(Newcastle, Dublin)

Doherty, Michael, PP
39 Melmount Road,
Strabane,
Co Tyrone BT82 9EF
Tel 028-71882648
(Melmount, Sion Mills, Derry)

Doherty, Patrick, Very Rev, PP
159 Glen Road, Maghera,
Co Derry BT46 5JN
Tel 028-79642496
(Maghera, Derry)

Doherty, Tom, CC
Cathedral Presbytery,
Ballina, Co Mayo
Tel 096-71365
(Ballina (Kilmoremoy), Killala)

Dolan, Andrew, Rt Rev Mgr, PP
25 Ballynease Road,
Bellaghy, Magherafelt,
Co Derry BT45 8JS
Tel 028-79386259
(Bellaghy (Ballyscullion), Derry)

Dolan, Denis, Very Rev, PE
Shanmullagh, Dromore
Co Tyrone BT78 3DZ
Tel 028-82898641
(Dromore, Clogher)

Dolan, Gerard, Rt Rev Mgr,
St Mary's, Temple Street,
Co Sligo
Tel 071-9162670
Nazareth House,
Churchill, Sligo
Tel 071-9162278
(Elphin, retired)

Dolan, John, Rt Rev Mgr, LCL
The Chancellery,
Archbishop's House,
Dublin 9
Tel 01-8379253
(Dublin)

Dolan, Martin, Adm
The Presbytery,
Francis Street, Dublin 8
Tel 01-4544861/
086-4035318
(Francis Street, Dublin)

Domenzain Canul, Joshua M. (OSB)
Benedictine Monks,
Holy Cross Abbey,
119 Kilbroney Road,
Rostrevor,
Co Down BT34 3BN
Tel 028-41739979

Donaghy, Kevin, Very Rev, PP, Adm, VG, VF
4 Circular Road,
Dungannon,
Co Tyrone BT71 6BE
Tel 028-87722775
(Dungannon (Drumglas, Killyman
and Tullyniskin), Armagh)

Donegan, Gary, Very Rev (CP)
Holy Cross Retreat,
Crumlin Road, Ardoyne,
Belfast BT14 7GE
Tel 028-90748231

Donlon, Chris, Very Rev. PP
Ladysbridge, Co Cork
Tel 021-4667173
(Ballymacoda & Ladysbridge, Cloyne)

Donnellan, David (OCD)
St Teresa's,
Clarendon Street, Dublin 2
Tel 01-6718466/6718127

Donnellan, Patrick, Very Rev, PE
25 Drisín, Knocknacarra,
Galway
(Tuam, retired)

Donnelly, Brian, PP
Parochial House,
Plumbridge, Omagh,
Co Tyrone, BT79 8EF
Tel 028-81648283
(Newtownstewart and Plumbridge, Derry)

Donnelly, Eamonn (SVD)
8 Teignmouth Road,
London, NW2 4HN
Tel 020-84528430

Donnelly, James, Very Rev, PP,
Doon, Co Limerick
Tel 061-380165
(Doon, Cashel & E.)

Donnelly, Joseph, PEm
52 Brook Street, Omagh,
Co Tyrone BT78 5HE
Tel 028-82243011
(Derry, retired)

Donnelly, Liam, PEm
20 Loughermore Road,
Ogill, Ballykelly,
Co Derry BT49 9PD
Tel 028-77762721
(Derry, retired)

Donnelly, Michael, Very Rev,
c/o St Mary's, Temple
Street, Sligo
(Elphin, retired)

Donnelly, Micheál, Very Rev, PP,
Parochial House,
Ballinagare,
Co Roscommon
Administration
Fairymount Parish
Tel 094-9870039
(Fairymount, Frenchpark, Elphin)

Donnelly, Patrick, PP
Parochial House,
Collinstown,
Co Westmeath
Tel 044-9666326
(Collinstown, Meath)

Donnelly, Peter, Very Rev, VF
c/o Diocesan Office,
Lisbreen,
73 Somerton Road,
Belfast,
Co Antrim BT15 4DE
(Down & C.)

Donnelly, Peter, Very Rev, PP, VF
Parochial House,
130 Ballinderry Bridge
Road, Coagh, Cookstown,
Co Tyrone BT80 0AY
Tel 028-79418244
(Ballinderry, Armagh)

Donnelly, Raymond CC
4 Darling Street,
Enniskillen,
Co Fermanagh BT74 7DP
Tel 028-66322075
(Enniskillen, Clogher)

Donnelly, Victor (CP)
St Gabriel's Retreat,
The Graan, Enniskillen,
Co Fermanagh
Tel 028-66322272

Donohoe, Eamon (MSC)
'Croí Nua', Rosary Lane,
Taylor's Hill, Galway
Tel 091-520960

Donohoe, Kevin, PP, VF
Ballyjamesduff, Co Cavan
Tel 049-8544410
(Castlerahan & Munterconnaught, Kilmore)

Donohoe, Séamus (OFM)
Vicar,
Franciscan Friary,
Friary Lane, Athlone,
Co Westmeath
Tel 090-6472095

Donohoe, Sean (OFMCap)
Guardian, Capuchin Friary,
Station Road, Raheny,
Dublin 5 D05 T9E4
Tel 01-8313886

Donohue, Steve (SPS)
St Patrick's, Main Street,
Knock, Co Mayo
Tel 094-9388661

Donovan, Bernard, Very Rev Canon, PP
Cloughdubh, Crookstown,
Co Cork
Tel 021-7336054
(Kilmurry, Cork & R.)

Donovan, Jeremiah (OMI)
Oblate House of Retreat,
Inchicore, Dublin 8
Tel 01-4534408/4541805

Donovan, Leo (OP)
Dominican Community,
St Mary's Priory,
Tallaght, Dublin 24
Tel 01-4048100

Donovan, Roy, PP
Caherconlish,
Co Limerick
Tel 061-450730
(Caherconlish, Cashel & E.)

Donworth, John,
Parochial House,
Kildimo, Co Limerick
Tel 061-394134/
087-2237501
(Pastoral Unit 12, Limerick)

Doocey, Colin, Very Rev, PP, Adm
1 The Presbytery,
Holy Cross Church,
Mahon, Cork
Tel 021-2414624
(Blackrock, Mahon, Cork & R.)

Doody, Patrick (CSSp)
Holy Spirit Missionary College
Kimmage Manor,
Whitehall Road,
Dublin D12 P5YP
Tel 01-4064300

Doohan, Martin, Very Rev, PP
Dunfanaghy,
Co Donegal
Tel 074-9136163
(Dunfanaghy, Raphoe)

Doohan, Michael (SSC)
St Columban's Retirement Home, Dalgan Park,
Navan, Co Meath
Tel 046-9021525

Dooher, Patrick G. (SSC)
St Columban's,
Dalgan Park,
Navan, Co Meath
Tel 046-9021525

Dooley, Francis Desmond, Very Rev
45 Westfield, Sion Hill
Blackrock, Co Dublin
(Dublin, retired)

Dooley, John (SJ)
c/o Milltown Park,
Sandford Road, Dublin 6
Tel 01-2698411/2698113

LIST OF CLERGY IN IRELAND

Dooley, Maurice, Rt Rev Mgr, AP
Loughmore, Templemore, Co Tipperary
Tel 0504-31375
(*Loughmore*, Cashel & E.)

Dooley, Seán, Very Rev, PP
Parochial House,
Tullyallen, Drogheda,
Co Louth
Tel 041-9838520
(*Mellifont*, Armagh)

Dooley, Thomas, Very Rev, PP, Adm
Patrick Street,
Portarlington,
Co Laois A92 H243
Tel 057-8643004
Administration Emo
(*Emo, Portarlington*, Kildare & L.)

Dooley, Tom (SM),
Chanel Community,
Coolock Village, Dublin 5
Tel 01-8484799

Doran, Dermot (CSSp)
Holy Spirit Missionary College
Kimmage Manor,
Whitehall Road,
Dublin D12 P5YP
Tel 01-4064300

Doran, Alphonsus (CSsR)
Clonard Monastery,
Clonard Gardens
Belfast BT13 2RL
Tel 028-90445950

Doran, Joseph, Very Rev, Adm
Parochial House,
Kilbride, Co Wicklow
Tel 087-2288579
(*Kilbride and Barndarrig*, Dublin)

Doran, Kevin, Most Rev, MA, PhD
Bishop of Elphin
St Mary's, Temple Street,
Sligo
Tel 071-9150106
(Elphin)

Doran, Patrick (CSsp)
Holy Spirit Missionary College,
Kimmage Manor,
Whitehall Road, Dublin 12
Tel 01-4064300

Doran, Senan (OSA)
St Augustine's,
Taylor's Lane,
Ballyboden, Dublin 16
Tel 01-4241000

Dorgan, Michael, Very Rev, PE
Curate's House,
Ballycotton, Co Cork
Tel 083-8230854
(*Cloyne*, Cloyne)

Dorr, Donal (SPS)
St Patrick's, 21 Leeson Park,
Dublin 6 D06 DE76
Tel 01-4977897

Dowd, Gerard (SDB)
c/o Salesian House,
45 St Teresa's Road,
Crumlin, Dublin D12 XK52

Dowd, Thomas
Ely University Centre,
10 Hume Street, Dublin 2
Tel 01-6767420
(Opus Dei)

Dowley, Eddie (OFMCap)
Guardian
Capuchin Friary,
Friary Street,
Kilkenny R95 NX60
Tel 056-7721439

Dowley, Martin (OCSO)
Prior,
Our Lady of Bethlehem Abbey,
11 Ballymena Road,
Portglenone, Ballymena,
Co Antrim BT44 8BL
Tel 028-25821211

Dowling, Cornelius
Our Lady's Manor,
Bullock Harbour, Dalkey,
Co Dublin
(Dublin, retired)

Downes, Edward, CC
Sacred Heart Residence,
Sybil Hill Road, Raheny,
Dublin 5
(Dublin, retired)

Downes, Frank (OP)
St Dominic's Retreat House, Montenotte,
Co Cork
Tel 021-4502520

Downes, Patrick (CSSp)
Rockwell College,
Cashel, Co Tipperary
Tel 062-61444

Downey, John
36 Moneyneena Road,
Draperstown,
Magherafelt,
Co Derry BT45 7DZ
Tel 028-79628375
(*Ballinascreen* (*Draperstown*), Derry)

Downey, Martin, Very Rev Canon, PP
24 Presentation Road,
Galway
Tel 091-562276
(*St Joseph's*, Galway)

Downing, Mortimer, Very Rev, PE
Stuake, Donoughmore,
Co Cork
Tel 021-7437815
(*Cloyne*, retired)

Doyle, Andrew, Very Rev, PP
Durhamstown,
Bohermeen, Navan,
Co Meath
Tel 046-9073805
(*Bohermeen*, Meath)

Doyle, Bernard
51 Drumnavanagh, Cavan
(Kilmore, retired)

Doyle, Brian (OP)
Convent of Ss Xystus and Clement,
Collegio San Clemente
Via Labicana 95,
00184 Roma, Italy
Tel 0039-067740021

Doyle, Derek, Very Rev, Moderator
Parochial House,
Rathdrum, Co Wicklow,
Tel 0404-46229
(*Glendalough, Rathdrum, Roundwood*, Dublin)

Doyle, Denis, Very Rev,
Starvehall,
Coolballon, Co Wexford
(Ferns, retired)

Doyle, Desmond G., Very Rev, Moderator
Chaplain's Residence,
Dublin Airport, Co Dublin
Tel 01-8405948/8447283
(*Brackenstown, River Valley, Swords*, Dublin)

Doyle, Gerald (MHM),
St James Apartments,
Our Lady of Knock Shrine,
Knock, Co Mayo
F12 R982

Doyle, James, CC
St Aidan's Cathedral,
Enniscorthy,
Co Wexford
Tel 053-9235777
(*Enniscorthy, Cathedral of St Aidan*, Ferns)

Doyle, Michael A.,
Poulfur, Fethard-on-Sea,
New Ross, Co Wexford
Tel 051-397048
(*Templetown and Poulfur*, Ferns)

Doyle, Noel (SSC)
St Columban's,
Dalgan Park, Navan,
Co Meath
Tel 046-9021525

Doyle, Owen (SSC)
St Columban's,
Dalgan Park,
Navan, Co Meath
Tel 046-9021525

Doyle, Rory (OFMConv)
Fairview Strand, Dublin3
Tel 01-8376000

Doyle, Thaddeus
Shillelagh, Arklow,
Co Wicklow
Tel 053-9429926
(Ferns)

Doyle, Thomas, Very Rev Canon
3 Priory Court, Gorey
Co Wexford
(Ferns, retired)

Draper, Anthony, Rev DD
Millbury Nursing Home,
Navan, Co Meath
(Meath, retired)

Drennan, Martin, Most Rev, DD
Retired Bishop of Galway,
17 Doughiska Road,
Galway
(Galway)

Drennan, Michael (SJ)
Manresa House,
Dollymount, Dublin 3
Tel 01-8331352

Drescher, Frank,
Presbytery,
44 Woodview Grove,
Blanchardstown, Dublin 15
Tel 01-5485038
(*Blanchardstown*, Dublin)

Drumm, Eugene (SPS)
On temporary diocesan work

Drumm, Michael PP
St Columba's,
Rosses Point, Co Sligo
Tel 071-9177133
(*Rosses Point*, Elphin)

Duddy, Brendan (SJ)
Milltown Park,
Sandford Road, Dublin 6
Tel 01-2698411/2698113

Duffy, Aquinas T., Very Rev, Acting Moderator,
19 Woodlands Road,
Johnstown
Glenageary, Co Dublin
Tel 01-5672374
(*Cabinteely, Foxrock*, Dublin)

Duffy, Eddie (SM)
Chanel Community,
Coolock, Dublin 5
Tel 01-8477133

Duffy, Eugene, DD
Convent Road,
Balaghaderreen,
Co Roscommon
Tel 087-9621410
(Achonry)

Duffy, Francis, Most Rev, DD
Archbishop of Tuam,
Archbishop's House,
Tuam,
Co Galway H54 HP57
Tel 093-24166
(Tuam)

Duffy, John Joe, CC
Creeslough,
Co Donegal
Tel 074-9138011
(*Dunfanaghy* (*Clondahorkey*), Raphoe)

LIST OF CLERGY IN IRELAND

Duffy, Joseph, Most Rev, DD
Bishop Emeritus,
Doire na gCraobh,
Monaghan
Tel 047-62725
(Clogher)

Duffy, Kevin, Very Rev, PP
42 Church Street,
Burfits Hill, Irvinestown,
Co Fermanagh BT94 1EN
Tel 028-68621856
(Irvinestown, Clogher)

Duffy, Larry (SM)
Italy

Duffy, Lawrence, Most Rev DD
Bishop of Clogher,
Bishop's House,
Monaghan H18 PN35
Tel 047-81019
(Clogher)

Duffy, Michael (OFMCap)
Capuchin Friary,
Station Road, Raheny,
Dublin 5 D05 T9E4
Tel 01-8313886

Duffy, Patrick (CP)
Holy Cross Retreat,
Crumlin Road, Ardoyne,
Belfast BT14 7GE
Tel 028-90748231

Duffy, Patrick, CC
Kilmyshall, Enniscorthy,
Co Wexford
Tel 053-9377188
(Bunclody, Ferns)

Duffy, Stephen, CC
Parochial House,
Beech Corner,
Castleblaney,
Co Monaghan A75 PF98
Tel 042-9740637
(Castleblaney, Clogher)

Duffy, Stephen, Very Rev,
Adm
Parochial House,
Ravensdale, Dundalk,
Co Louth A91 V523
Tel 042-9371327
(Lordship (and
Ballymascanlon), Armagh)

Duggan, Brendan (CSSp),
Parochial House,
Athea, Co Limerick
Tel 087-0562674
(Pastoral Unit 14, Limerick)

Duggan, Frank
(Dublin, retired)

Duggan, James (OP)
Holy Cross, Tralee,
Co Kerry
Tel 066-7121135/29185

Duggan, John, Very Rev, PE
44 An Cuirt,
Monard, Co Tipperary
(Limerick, retired)

Duggan, Patrick, Very Rev
Canon, PE
Bennetsbridge,
Co Kilkenny
Tel 056-7727140/
086-2557471
(Tullaherin, Ossory)

Duhig, Frank,
St Ita's Presbytery,
Newcastle West,
Co Limerick
Tel 069-62141/
087-6380299
(Pastoral Unit 15, Limerick)

Duignan, Michael, Most
Rev, SThD, DD
Bishop of Clonfert,
Coorheen, Loughrea
Co Galway H62 TD82
Tl 091-841560
(Clonfert)

Dullea, Gearóid, Rt Rev
Mgr, PP
The Presbytery,
Ballinlough, Cork
(Ballinlough, Cork & R.)

Duncan, James (CSSp)
Holy Spirit Missionary
College
Kimmage Manor,
Whitehall Road,
Dublin D12 P5YP
Tel 01-4064300

Dundon, Patrick (CSSp)
Blackrock College,
Blackrock, Co Dublin
Tel 01-2888681

Dunleavy, John (SMA)
SMA House, Cloonbigeen,
Claregalway,
Co Galway H91 YK64
Tel 091-798880

Dunleavy, Michael, Very Rev (OP)
Dominican Community,
St Mary's Priory, Tallaght,
Dublin 24
Tel 01-4048100

Dunne, Aidan, Very Rev, PP
Parochial House,
11 Chapel Road,
Bessbrook, Newry,
Co Down BT35 7AU
Tel 028-30830206
(Bessbrook (Killeavy
Lower), Armagh)

Dunne, Daniel, Very Rev, PP
Tullamoy, Stradbally,
Co Laois
Tel 059-8627123
(Ballyadams, Kildare & L.)

Dunne, Gerard (OP)
Univerisity College, Cork
Chaplaincy Office: Iona
College Road
Tel 021-4902704
St Dominic's Retreat
House
Montenotte, Co Cork
Tel 021-4502520

Dunne, John (SMA)
SMA House, Wilton,
Cork, T12 KR23
Tel 021-4541069/4541884

Dunne, Kieran, Very Rev,
Co-PP
Parochial House, Foxrock,
Dublin 18
Tel 01-2893229
(Foxrock, Dublin)

Dunne, Liam (SVD), Rector,
1 & 3 Pembroke Road,
Dublin 4
Tel 01-6680904

Dunne, Liam, Very Rev
The Forge, Martin's Lane,
Upper Main Street,
Arklow, Co Wicklow
Tel 0402-32779
(Ossory, retired)

Dunne, Michael (CM)
St Paul's College, Raheny,
Dublin 5
Tel 01-8318113

Dunne, Patrick, Very Rev, PP
Parochial House,
Kilmacrennan,
Letterkenny
Co Donegal
Tel 074-9139018
(Kilmacrennan, Raphoe)

Dunne, Paul, CC
24 Watermill Road,
Raheny, Dublin 5
Tel 01-8313232
(Raheny, Dublin)

Dunne, Ronald
(priest in residence)
60 Grange Park Grove,
Raheny, Dublin 5
Tel 086-4513904
(Edenmore, Grange Park,
Dublin)

Dunne, Thomas (SDB)
Salesian House,
45 St Teresa's Road,
Crumlin, Dublin 12
Tel 01-4555605

Dunne, Thomas, CC
Ballinree, Boherlahan,
Cashel, Co Tipperary
Tel 083-4854776
(Boherlahan and Dulla,
Cashel & E.)

Dunne, Victor (SPS)
Society Leader, St Patrick's
Kiltegan, Co Wicklow
Tel 059-6473600

Dunny, Patrick, Very Rev
Wood Road,
Graignamanagh,
Co Kilkenny
Tel 059-9724518
(Kildare & L.)

Dunphy, John, Very Rev
Chaplain, Children's
Health Ireland at Crumlin
(Our Lady's Children's
Hospital),
Crumlin, Dublin 12
Tel 01-4096100
(Dublin)

Dunphy, John, Very Rev,
Adm
Graiguecullen, Co Carlow
Tel 059-9141833
(Graiguecullen, Kildare &
L.)

Dunphy, Laurence, Very Rev
Canon
Urlingford, Co Kilkenny
Tel 087-2300849
(Ossory, retired)

Dunphy, Noel, Very Rev, PE,
CC
Mountmellick, Co Laois
Tel 057-8624141
(Mountmellick, Kildare &
L.)

Dunphy, Paul
Two-Mile-House,
Naas, Co Kildare
Tel 045-876160
(Naas, Kildare & L.)

Durajczyk, Tadeusz (SVD)
Priest's Road,
Tramore, Co Tipperary
(Tramore, Waterford & L.)

Durkan, John, Very Rev, PP
Killasser, Swinford,
Co Mayo
Tel 094-9024761
(Killasser, Achonry)

Durnin, Brian, CC
12 Brookwood Grove,
Artane, Dublin 5
Tel 01-8187996
(Artane, Dublin)

Dwan, Sean (SSC)
St Columban's,
Dalgan Park,
Navan, Co Meath
Tel 046-9021525

Dwyer, Donal, Very Rev, Co-PP
Parochial House,
O'Callaghan's Mills,
Co Clare
Tel 065-6835148/
086-1050090
(Ceanntar na Lochanna
Pastoral Area, Killaloe)

Dwyer, Patrick (SAC)
Pallottine College, Thurles,
Co Tipperary
Tel 0504-21202

Dziduch, Włodzimierz
(SCHR)
Chaplain to Polish
Community,
201 Donegall Street,
Belfast BT1 2FL
Tel 075-87101979
(Down & C.)

LIST OF CLERGY IN IRELAND

E

Earley, Patrick, Mgr, PE
Parochial House,
Rathowen, Co Westmeath
Tel 043-6676044
(*Ardagh & Cl.*, retired)

Early, Brian, Very Rev, PE
St Dympna's, Tydavnet,
Co Monaghan H18 Y190
Tel 047-79434
(*Tydavnet*, Clogher)

Eastwood, Adrian (CM)
Superior,
99 Cliftonville Road,
Belfast BT14 6JQ
Tel 028-90751771

Ebuk, Lawrence (MSP), PP
Ballinameen, Boyle,
Co Roscommon
Tel 071-9668104
(*Ballinameen*
(*Kilnamanagh and
Estersnow*), Elphin)

Ebuka, Martins, TA
75 Ludford Road,
Ballinteer, Dublin 16
(*Meadowbrook*, Dublin)

Echavarria, John (SSP)
c/o Society of St Paul,
Moyglare Road,
Maynooth, Co Kildare
Tel 01-6285933

Edebianga, Christopher
(MSP), Very Rev, PP
Parochial House,
Roscommon
Tel 090-6663338
(*Athleague*, Elphin)

Edwards, Brian, Very Rev,
Co-PP
23 Oakdown Road,
Dublin 14
Tel 01-2981744
(*Churchtown*, Dublin)

Egan, Adrian (CSsR), PP
The Presbytery,
197 Kylemore Road,
Ballyfermot, Dublin 10
Tel 01-6264789
(*Ballyfermot*, Dublin)

Egan, James, Very Rev, PP
Knockavilla, Dundrum,
Co Tipperary
Tel 062-71157
(*Knockavilla*, Cashel & E.)

Egan, John, Very Rev, AP
Lattin, Co Tipperary
Tel 062-55240
(*Lattin and Cullen*, Cashel
& E.)

Egan, John (SAC)
Provincial House,
'Homestead',
Sandyford Road,
Dundrum, Dublin 16
Tel 01-2956180/2954170

Egan, Joseph (SMA)
Superior,
SMA House,
81 Ranelagh Road,
Ranelagh, Dublin 6
Tel 01-4968162/3

Egan, Joseph, Very Rev, PP
Boherlahan, Cashel,
Co Tipperary
Tel 0504-41114
(*Boherlahan and Dualla*,
Cashel & E.)

Egan, Michael (SVD)
133 North Circular Road,
Dublin 7
Tel 01-8386743

Egan, Patrick (SDB)
c/o Salesian House,
45 St Teresa's Road,
Crumlin, Dublin D12 XK52

Egan, Patrick (SSC)
St Columban's,
Dalgan Park, Navan
Co Meath
Tel 046-9021525

Egan, Ralph (CP), CC
St Paul's Retreat,
Mount Argus, Dublin 6W
Tel 01-4992000

Egan, Seamus (SSC)
St Columban's Retirement
Home, Dalgan Park,
Navan, Co Meath
Tel 046-9021525

Egan, Sean
Kilrickle, Loughrea,
Co Galway H62 PO27
(*Clonfert*, retired)

Egan, Thomas F., Very Rev
Clonoulty, Cashel,
Co Tipperary
Tel 086-8199678
(*Clonoulty & Rossmore*,
Cashel & E.)

Egan, Tony (OSA)
Prior,
St Augustine's Priory,
Dungarvan, Co Waterford
Tel 058-41136

Eivers, James (OCarm)
Prior, Carmelite Priory,
Kinsale,
Co Cork P17 WR88
Tel 021-4772138

Ellison, Robert (CSSp), Most
Rev
Holy Spirit Missionary
College
Kimmage Manor,
Whitehall Road,
Dublin D12 P5YP
Tel 01-4064300

Emechebe, Anselm (MSP),
CC
Parochial House,
Kilsaran,
Castlebellingham,
Dundalk,
Co Louth A91 A256
Tel 042-9372255
(*Kilsaran*, Armagh)

Emerson, Sean, Very Rev,
Adm, VF
Parochial House,
3 Oriel Road,
Antrim BT41 4HP
Tel 028-94428016
(*Antrim, St Comgall's and
St Joseph's*, Down & C.)

Emokhare, Christopher
(SMA)
African Missions,
Blackrock Road,
Cork T12 TD54
Tel 021-4292871

English, Mark, Very Rev, PP
Parochial House, Duleek,
Co Meath
Tel 041-9823205
Adm, Donore Parish
Tel 041-9823137
(*Donore, Duleek*, Meath)

Ennis, John Very Rev, Adm
1 Maypark,
Malahide Road, Dublin 5
Tel 01-8313033
(*Donnycarney*, Dublin)

Enright, Ciarán, Very Rev,
Co-PP
30 Willow Park Crescent,
Dublin 11
Tel 01-8423865
(*St Pappin's Ballymun*,
Dublin)

Enright, Liam
5 Lifford Avenue,
Ballinacurra, Co Limerick
Tel 087-7415603
(*Pastoral Unit 2*, Limerick)

Enright, Liam, Very Rev, PP
St Nicholas Presbytery,
Westbury, Limerick
(*Limerick*, retired)

Enright, Michael, Very Rev,
PE
Dunabratlin, Annestown,
Co Waterford
(*Waterford & L.*, retired)

Enright, Séamus (CSsR)
Superior, Mount Saint
Alphonsus, Limerick
Tel 061-315099

Escoto, Albert (SVD)
Praeses,
8 Teignmouth Road,
London, NW2 4HN
Tel 020-84528430

Esoy, Renato (SSS)
Blessed Sacrament Chapel,
20 Bachelors Walk,
Dublin 1
Tel 01-8724597

Etomike, Hilary, PC
The Presbytery,
St Martin de Porres Parish,
Firhouse Road West
Dublin 24 D24 K198
Tel 01-4510160
(*Bohernabreena*, Dublin)

Eustace, Conal, Very Rev
Canon, PP, VF
The Parochial House
Castlebar,
Co Mayo F31 YA29
Tel 094-9541784/9021844
(*Castlebar*, Tuam)

Eustace, Thomas, Very Rev
The Cools, Barntown,
Wexford
(*Ferns*, retired)

Evans, Ian
Assistant Chaplain General
to the Forces, England
(Dublin)

Everard, Eugene, Venerable
Archdeacon, PP, VG
St Michael's Street,
Tipperary Town,
Co Tipperary
Tel 062-51536
(*Templemore*, Cashel & E.)

Everard, Liam, Very Rev, PP
The Parochial House,
Fethard, Clonmel,
Co Tipperary
Tel 052 6131178
(*Fethard*, Cashel & E.)

Eze, John (MSP), CC
St Mary's Athlone,
Co Westmeath
Tel 090-6472088
(*Athlone*, Ardagh & Cl.)

Ezenwata, Anastasius, PC
Parochail House,
Parish of the Assumption,
Booterstown, Co Dublin
(*Booterstown*, Dublin)

Ezenwegbu, Stephen, Very
Rev, PP
The Presbytery,
Elphin, Co Roscommon
Tel 071-9630486
(*Aughrim, Elphin*, Elphin)

F

Faber, Dixy, CC
The Presbytery,
Chapel Street, Castlebar,
Co Mayo F23 DF82
Tel 094-9021844
(*Castlebar (Aglish,
Ballyheane and
Breaghwy)*, Tuam)

Fagan, Anthony, Very Rev,
PP
Knockbride, Bailieboro,
Co Cavan
Tel 042-9660112
(*Knockbride*, Kilmore)

LIST OF CLERGY IN IRELAND

Fagan, Hugh (CSSp)
Holy Spirit Missionary College
Kimmage Manor,
Whitehall Road,
Dublin D12 P5YP
Tel 01-4064300

Fagan, John (SDB)
Salesian House, Milford,
Castletroy, Limerick
Tel 061-330268/330914

Fagan, Patrick, Very Rev Canon, PE
Our Lady's Manor,
Bullock Harbour,
Dalkey, Co Dublin
(Dublin, retired)

Faherty, Thomas (SMA)
African Missions,
Dromantine, Newry,
Co Down BT34 1RH
Tel 028-30821224

Fahey, Francis, CC
Ballintubber,
Claremorris, Co Mayo
(Tuam, retired)

Fallon, Kevin, Very Rev, PP
Parochial House,
Roscommon
Tel 090-662698
(Roscommon, Elphin)

Fallon, Vincent, (SSCC), Very Rev, PP
Sacred Heart,
St John's Drive,
Clondalkin,
Dublin D22 W1W6
Tel 01-4570032
(Sruleen, Dublin)

Falloon, Joseph (MSC)
Woodview House,
Mount Merrion Avenue,
Blackrock, Co Dublin

Farnon, Damian CF
McKee Barracks, Dublin 7
Tel 086-2256794
(Dublin)

Farquhar, Anthony, Most Rev, DD
Titular Bishop of Ermiana and Former Auxiliary Bishop of Down & Connor,
24 Fruithill Park,
Belfast BT11 8GE
Tel 028-90624252
(Down & C.)

Farquharson, Paul (SJ)
Vice-Superior,
St Francis Xavier's,
Upper Gardiner Street,
Dublin 1
Tel 01-8363411

Farragher, Michael, Very Rev, PP
The Parochial House,
Carnacon, Claremorris,
Co Mayo
Tel 094-9360205
(Burriscarra and Ballintubber, Tuam)

Farragher, Patrick, Very Rev, Adm
The Presbytery, Tuam,
Co Galway H54 HR58
Tel 093-24250
(Tuam (Cathedral of the Assumption), Tuam)

Farragher, Stephen, Very Rev Canon, PP
Parochial House,
Ballyhaunis,
Co Mayo F35 YY65
Tel 094-9630006
(Ballinlough (Kiltullagh), Ballyhaunis (Annagh), Tuam)

Farrell, Derek Very Rev Canon, Moderator,
Parochial House,
Main Street, Garristown,
Co Dublin A42 PF64
Tel 01-8412932
(Garristown, Naul, Rolestown-Oldtown, Dublin)

Farrell, Dermot, Most Rev, DD
Archbishop of Dublin,
Archbishop's House,
Drumcondra,
Dublin D09 H4C2
(Dublin)

Farrell, Fergus, Very Rev, PP
Windgap, Co Kilkenny
Tel 051-648111/
086-0782066
(Dunamaggan, Windgap, Ossory)

Farrell, Fergus, PC
St Laurence O'Toole's Presbytery,
49 Seville Place, Dublin 1
Tel 01-8740796
(North Wall-Seville Place, Dublin)

Farrell, John, PEm
5 Ballyreagh Road,
Portrush, Co Antrim
(Derry, retired)

Farrell, Liam, CC
Moate, Co Westmeath
Tel 090-6481189
(Moate and Mount Temple, Ardagh & Cl.)

Farell, Matthew (OP)
Holy Cross, Tralee,
Co Kerry
Tel 066-7121135

Farrell, Patrick (OSA)
St Augustine's,
Taylor's Lane,
Ballyboden, Dublin 16
Tel 01-4241000

Farrell, Sean (CM)
Phibsboro, St Peter's,
Dublin 7
Tel 01-8389708/8389841

Farrell, William, Very Rev, CC
Parochial House,
St Joseph's, Glasthule,
Co Dublin
Tel 01-2801226
(Glasthule, Dublin)

Farrelly, Adrian (OP) Very Rev
St Catherine's,
Newry, Co Down BT35 8BN
Tel 028-30262178

Farrelly, Florian (OFM)
Guardian,
Franciscan Abbey,
Mulyfarnham,
Co Westmeath
Tel 044-9371114

Farrelly, Pat, Very Rev, PP
Knocknagilla, New Inn,
Ballyjamesduff, Co Cavan
(Kilmore, retired)

Farrelly, Peter, Very Rev, AP
Parochial House,
Beauparc, Navan,
Co Meath
Tel 046-9024114
(Beauparc, Meath)

Farren, Desmond (MSC)
Western Road,
Cork T12 TN80
Tel 021-4804120

Farren, John, Very Rev, PP
Muff, Co Donegal
Tel 074-9384037
(Iskaheen Iskaheen & Upper Moville), Derry)

Farren, Neil, PP
Chapelfield,
59 Laurel Hill,
Coleraine,
Co Derry BT51 3AY
Tel 028-70343130
(Coleraine (Dunboa, Macosquin and Aghadowney), Derry)

Farren, Paul, Adm
Parochial House,
St Eugene's Cathedral,
Derry BT48 9AP
Tel 028-71262894/
028-71365712
(Derry City, Derry)

Faruna, Pius, PC
c/o Parish Office,
Balgaddy Road, Lucan,
County Dublin, K78 NH05
Tel 01-4572900
(Lucan South, Dublin)

Fasakin, Emmanuel (MSP), CC
Parochial House,
42 Abbey Street,
Armagh BT61 7D2
Tel 028-37522802
(Armagh, Armagh)

Faughnan, Cathal, PP
Keadue, Boyle,
Co Roscommon
Tel 071-9647212
(Keadue, Arigna & Ballyfarnon (Kilronan), Ardagh & Cl.)

Fay, Kevin, Adm, VF
(priest in residence)
The Presbytery,
Cavan Town, Co Cavan
Tel 049-4331404
(Cavan (Urney & Annagelliff), Kilmore)

Fazio, Joseph (LC)
Chaplain, Dublin Oak Academy,
Kilcroney, Bray,
Co Wicklow
Tel 01-2863290

Fee, Benedict, Very Rev Canon, PP, EV, VF
Teac na h'Ard Croise,
3 Cloghog Road,
Clonoe, Coalisland,
Co Tyrone, BT71 5EH
Tel 028-87749184
(Clonoe, Armagh)

Fee, Ian, Rev, CC
The Rock, Ballyshannon,
Co Donegal
Tel 071-9851221
(Magh Ene, Clogher)

Feehan, James (CP)
St Paul's Retreat,
Mount Argus, Dublin 6W
Tel 01-4992000

Feeney, Ciaran, Very Rev, Adm
200 Finaghy Road North,
Belfast BT11 9EG
Tel 028-90617519
(St Michael's, Down & C.)

Feeney, Derek, Very Rev Canon, PP
Parochial House,
Craughwell, Co Galway
Tel 091-846057
(Craughwell, Galway)

Feeney, Joseph, Very Rev Canon, AP
The Prochial House,
Ballinlough,
Co Roscommon F45 R208
Tel 094-9640155
(Ballinlough (Kiltullagh), Tuam)

Feeney, Paddy (SPS)
St Patrick's, Kiltegan,
Co Wicklow
Tel 059-6473600

Fegan, James, Very Rev, PP
Ballindaggin, Enniscorthy,
Co Wexford
Tel 053-9388559
(Ballindaggin, Ferns)

LIST OF CLERGY IN IRELAND

Fegan, P. J. (IC) (Priest in Charge)
Rathgormack,
Carrick-on-suir,
Co Waterford
Tel 051-646006
(*Rathgormack*, Waterford & L.)

Fehily, G. Thomas, Rt Rev Mgr, PE
Hampstead Hospital,
Glasnevin, Dublin 11
(Dublin, retired)

Feighery, John (SVD)
133 North Circular Road,
Dublin 7
Tel 01-8386743

Fenlon, Thomas (SMA)
African Missions,
Blackrock Road,
Cork T12 TD54
Tel 021-4292871

Fennelly, Sean,
Chaplain,
St John the Baptist Community School,
Barrysfarm, Hospital,
Co Limerick
Tel 061-383565
(*Hospital*, Cashel & E.)

Fennelly, William (OSB)
Glenstal Abbey, Murroe,
Co Limerick
Tel 061-386103

Fennessy, Ignatius (OFM)
Franciscan House of Studies, Dún Mhuire,
Seafield Road,
Killiney, Co Dublin
Tel 01-2826760

Fergus, Austin, Very Rev Canon, AP
The Parochial House,
Mayo Abbey, Claremorris,
Co Mayo F12 D6P9
Tel 094-9365086
(*Mayo Abbey (Mayo and Rosslea)*, Tuam)

Ferguson, Christopher,
c/o Diocesan Offices,
St Eugene's Cathedral,
Francis Street,
Derry BT48 9AP
(Derry)

Ferris, Brendan, Very Rev, PP
Preston Hill,
Stamullen, Co Meath
Tel 01-8412647
(Meath)

Ferris, John, Co-PP
14 The Coral, The Grange,
Stillgorgan, Co Dublin
(Dublin, retired)

Ferris, Stephen, Very Rev, PP
c/o Diocesan Office, Newry
(Dromore)

Ferry, Francis, CC
Mountcharles, Co Donegal
Tel 074-9735009
(*Inver*, Raphoe)

Ferry, Manus (MSC)
Leader, Woodview House,
Mount Merrion Avenue,
Blackrock, Co Dublin
Tel 01-2881644

Field, Raymond, Most Rev, DD
Auxiliary Bishop Emeritus of Dublin,
3 Castleknock Road,
Blanchardstown,
Dublin 15
Tel 01-8209191
(Dublin)

Fillie, Michael (CSSp)
Holy Spirit Missionary College
Kimmage Manor,
Whitehall Road,
Dublin D12 P5YP
Tel 01-4064300

Finan, James, Very Rev Canon, CC
Colloney, Co Sligo
Tel 071-9167109
(*Collooney (Kilvarnet)*, Achonry)

Finegan, Peter (SPS)
St Patrick's, Kiltegan,
Co Wicklow W91 Y022
Tel 059-6473600

Fingleton, James, Very Rev Canon
279 Howth Road, Raheny,
Dublin 5
(Dublin, retired)

Finn, John (MSC)
Leader,
Western Road,
Cork T12 TN80
Tel 021-4804120

Finn, Tony (OSA)
St Augustine's Priory
St Augustine's Street
Co Galway
Rector Ecclesiae,
St Patrick's College and Church,
Via Piemonte 60,
00187 Rome, Italy
Tel 00396-4203121

Finn, William (OCD)
St Teresa's,
Clarendon Street, Dublin 2
Tel 01-6718466/6718127

Finnegan, Eamonn (SMA)
Vice Provincial, African Missions,
Provincial House, Feltrim,
Blackrock Road,
Cork T12 N6C8
Tel 021-4292871

Finnegan, John (SDB)
Salesian House,
45 St Teresa's Road,
Crumlin, Dublin 12
Tel 01-4555605

Finnegan, John, Very Rev Canon, PE
51 Arney Road,
Mullymesker, Enniskillen,
Co Fermanagh BT92 2AB
Tel 028-66348217
(*Arney (Cleenish)*, Clogher)

Finnegan, Vincent F. (OFM)
Vicar, Franciscan Friary,
Rossnowlagh, Co Donegal
F94 PH21
Tel 071-9851342

Finneran, Michael, Very Rev, PP
Clontuskert, Ballinasloe,
Co Galway H53 CV99
Tel 090-9642256
(*Clontuskert*, Clonfert)

Finnerty, Liam (OCD)
Prior,
Avila Carmelite Centre,
Bloomfield Avenue,
Morehampton Road,
Dublin 4
Tel 01-6430200

Finnerty, Paul
Rector,
Pontifico Collegio Irlandese,
Via dei Santi Quattro 1,
00184 Roma, Italy
Tel 0039-06-772631
(Limerick)

Finnerty, Peter, Very Rev, Adm
Parochial House, Bayside Square North,
Sutton, Dublin 13
Tel 01-8323150
Administrator,
St John the Evangelist,
Killbarrack-Killiney,
Living in Bayside
(*Bayside*, Dublin)

Finucane, Gerard, Very Rev, PP
Our Lady of the Valley,
Cillin Liath
Tel 066-9474703
Moderator, Caherdaniel
Caherdaniel, Co Kerry
Tel 066-9475111
(*Caherdaniel, Waterville (Dromod)*, Kerry)

Fitzgerald, Brendan
St Barnabas Church,
409 East 241 Street,
Bronx, New York 10470
USA

Fitzgerald, Christopher, PP
Barrett's Hill,
Ballinhassig, Co Cork
Tel 021-4885104
Parish Office:
Tel 021-4294332
(*Ballinhassig*, Cork & R.)

Fitzgerald, David (OSA)
The Abbey, Fethard,
Co Tipperary
Tel 052-31273

Fitzgerald, Eamon (OCSO), Rt Rev Dom,
Abbot General,
Mount Melleray Abbey,
Cappoquin,
Co Waterford P51 R8XW
Tel 058-54404

Fitzgerald, Jack, Very Rev Canon, PP
Millstreet, Co Cork
Tel 029-70043
(*Millstreet*, Kerry)

Fitzgerald, John, Rev, CC (MSC)
Sacred Heart Parish,
Western Road,
Cork T12 TN80
Tel 021-4804120
(*Sacred Heart*, Cork & R.)

Fitzgerald, John, Very Rev, PP
Abbeydorney, Co Kerry
Tel 066-7135146
(*Abbeydorney*, Kerry)

Fitzgerald, John, Very Rev, PP
Parish Administrator
Rockhill, Bruree,
Co Limerick
087-6522746
(Limerick)

Fitzgerald, Joseph,
5 Hawthorn Park, Ballygar,
via Roscommon,
Co Galway
(*Roscommon*, Elphin)

Fitzgerald, Michael, Very Rev, PP
Blarney, Co Cork
Tel 021-4385105
(*Blarney*, Cloyne)

Fitzgerald, Michael, Very Rev Canon, PE
Garrycahera, Ballynoe,
Mallow, Co Cork
(Cloyne, retired)

Fitzgerald, Michael (OSA)
St Augustine's,
Taylor's Lane,
Ballyboden, Dublin 16
Tel 01-4241000

Fitzgerald, P. J. (SPS), CC
Mountrath, Co Laois
Tel 057-8732234
(*Ballyfin/Mountrath*, Kildare & L.)

Fitzgerald, Patrick (CP), CC
St Paul's Retreat,
Mount Argus, Dublin 6W
Tel 01-4992000
(*Mount Argus*, Dublin)

Fitzgerald, Patrick, Very Rev, PP
Parochial House,
Lisduggan, Waterford
Tel 051-372257
Also: Priest in Charge of Butlerstown Parish
(*St Paul's*, Waterford & L.)

Fitzgerald, Tadhg, Rt Rev Mgr, VG
St John's Presbytery
Ballybunion, Co Kerry
Tel 066-7122522
Ardfert, Co Kerry
Tel 066-7134131
Ardfert Retreat Centre
Tel 066-7134276
(Kerry)

Fitzgibbon, John, Very Rev Canon, PE
Parochial House,
Chapel Road, Lusk,
Co Dublin
Tel 01-8438023
(Dublin, retired)

Fitzharris, Kieran (SVD)
Our Lady of Sorrows & St Bridget of Sweden
112 Twickenham Road
Ilseworth, TW7 6DL

Fitzmaurice, William, Canon,
Croom, Co Limerick
Tel 061-397231/
086-2423728
(*Pastoral Unit 7*, Limerick)

Fitzpatrick, Brian, CC
The Presbytery,
11 Tullygally Road,
Legahory,
Craigavon BT65 5BL
Tel 028-38341901
(*Moyraverty (Craigavon),
Seagoe (Derrymacash),
Shankill, St Paul's & St Peter's (Lurgan)*, Dromore)

Fitzpatrick, Jeremiah (OCD)
Prior, St Joseph's
Carmelite Retreat Centre,
Termonbacca, Derry BT48 9XE
Tel 028-71262512

Fitzpatrick, John, Very Rev, PP
Carbury, Co Kildare
Tel 046-9553355
(*Carbury*, Kildare & L.)

Fitzpatrick, P. J., CC
6 St Ciaran Park,
Tullamore Road,
Shannonbridge,
Co Offaly
(*Ardagh & Cl.*, retired)

Fitzpatrick, Tom, Co-PP
3 The Woods, Cappahard,
Tulla Road, Ennis, Co Clare
Tel 065-6822225/
087-2720187
(*Abbey Pastoral Area*, Killaloe)

Fitzpatrick, William (OMI), Co-PP
Superior, Oblate Fathers,
House of Retreat,
Inchicore, Dublin 8
Tel 01-4541117
(*Inchicore, Mary Immaculate*, Dublin)

Fitzsimons, Anthony, Very Rev, PP
191 Upper Newtownards Road, Belfast BT4 3JB
Tel 028-90654157
(*St Colmcille's*, Down & C.)

Fitzsimons, Patrick, Very Rev Canon
Holy Family Residence,
Roebuck, Dundrum,
Dublin 14
(Dublin, retired)

Fitzsimons, William, Very Rev, PP
Parochial House,
Milltown, Rathconrath,
Co Westmeath
Tel 044-9355106
(*Milltown*, Meath)

Flaherty, John, Very Rev Canon, VF, Co-PP
St Anne's, Strand Road,
Portmarnock, Co Dublin
Tel 01-8461081
(*Portmarnock*, Dublin)

Flaherty, Raymond, Very Rev, PP
The Parochial House,
Headford,
Co Galway H91 PXH5
Tel 093-35448
(*Headford (Killursa and Killower)*, Tuam)

Flanagan, Benny, PE
14 Kilgarve Gardens,
Creagh, Ballinasloe,
Co Galway
(Clonfert, retired)

Flanagan, Eamon (CM)
Phibsboro, St Peter's,
Dublin 7
Tel 01-8389708/8389841

Flanagan, John, Very Rev, PP
Ballyoisin, Emyvale,
Co Monaghan H18 F207
Tel 047-87152
(*Errigal Truagh*, Clogher)

Flanagan, Malachy (SMA)
Provincial, African Missions,
Provincial House, Feltrim,
Blackrock Road,
Cork T12 N6C8
Tel 021-4292871

Flanagan, Padraig Rev (SPS)
St Patrick's, Kiltegan,
Co Wicklow W91 Y022

Flanagan, Richard, PP, VF
Ballyvaughan, Co Clare
Tel 065-7077045
(*Ballyvaughan*, Galway)

Flannery, Anthony (CSsR)
St Patrick's, Esker,
Athenry, Co Galway
Tel 091-844007

Flannery, John D., Very Rev Canon, PE
Cartron, Milltown,
Co Galway H54 YD54
(Tuam, retired)

Flannery, Paschal, Very Rev
Ballinderry, Nenagh,
Co Tipperary
Tel 067-22916/086-2225099
(Killaloe, retired)

Flatley, Alphonsus (SMA)
African Missions,
Blackrock Road,
Cork T12 TD54
Tel 021-4292871

Flattery, Michael (SMA), CC
364 Sundays Well, Naas,
Co Kildare
Tel 045-876197
(*Naas*, Kilare & L.)

Flavin, John P. (CSSp)
Holy Spirit Missionary College
Kimmage Manor,
Whitehall Road,
Dublin D12 P5YP
Tel 01-4064300

Fleck, Robert, Very Rev, PP
Parochial House,
Dundrum, Newcastle,
Co Down BT33 0LU
Tel 028-43751212
(*Dundrum and Tyrella*, Down & C.)

Fleming, David, CC
87 Beechwood Lawns,
Rathcoole, Co Dublin
Tel 01-4587187
(*Newcastle, Saggart/Rathcoole/Brittas*, Dublin)

Fleming, Gerard (SAC)
Parochial House,
Sperrin Road,
Drimnagh, Dublin 12
Tel 01-4556103
(*Mourne Road*, Dublin)

Fleming, John Kevin (MSC)
(Resident elsewhere)

Fleming, John, Most Rev, DD, DCL
Bishop of Killala,
Bishop's House, Ballina,
Co Mayo
Tel 096-21518
(Killala)

Fleming, Joseph, Very Rev, CC
Clonegal, Enniscorthy,
Co Wexford
Tel 053-9377298
(*Clonegal*, Kildare & L.)

Fleming, Kevin (SSC)
St Columban's, Dalgan Park, Navan, Co Meath
Tel 046-9021525
(Meath)

Fleming, Paul, BA, BD, STL, PhD
St Mary's University College, 191 Falls Road,
Belfast 12 6FE
Tel 028-90327678
(Down & C.)

Fletcher, Robert, CC,
New Inn, Cashel,
Co Tipperary
Tel 086-1927455
(*New Inn*, Cashel & E.)

Flood, Jonathan, CC
c/o Diocesan Office,
Letterkenny, Co Donegal
(Raphoe)

Flores, Atanasio (OP)
Dominican Community,
St Mary's Priory, Tallaght,
Dublin 24
Tel 01-4048100

Flynn, Brian, Very Rev Canon, PP
Laragh, Stradone,
Co Cavan
Tel 049-4330142
(*Laragh*, Kilmore)

Flynn, Brian, Very Rev, PE
Kilmacow, via Waterford,
Co Kilkenny
Tel 051-885122/
087-2828391
(Ossory, retired)

Flynn, Edward (CSSp)
Spiritan House,
213 North Circular Road,
Dublin 7
01-8389664

Flynn, Edwin (OFMCap)
St Francis Capuchin Friary,
Rochestown,
Co Cork T12 NH02
Tel 021-4896244

Flynn, Gabriel, TA
1 The Presbytery,
Greenfield Road,
Sutton, Dublin 13
(*Sutton*, Dublin)
(Meath)

Flynn, James (IC)
Clonturk House,
Ormond Road,
Drumcondra,
Dublin D09 F821
Tel 01-6877014

LIST OF CLERGY IN IRELAND

Flynn, John (SMA)
African Missions,
Blackrock Road,
Cork T12 TD54
Tel 021-4292871

Flynn, Joseph, Very Rev, PP
Ballyporeen, Cahir, AP
Co Tipperary
Tel 052-7467105
(*Ballyporeen*, Waterford & L.)

Flynn, Laurence, Rt Rev Mgr, Adm
Priest's House,
Main Street, Pettigo,
Co Donegal F94 FYN7
Tel 071-9861666
(*Pettigo*, Clogher)

Flynn, Leo (SPS)
St Patrick's, Kiltegan,
Co Wicklow W91 Y022
Tel 059-6473600

Flynn, Michael, Very Rev, PP
Christ the King Church,
Knockmore, Ballina,
Co Mayo
Tel 094-9258108
(*Backs*, Killala)

Flynn, Nicholas, Very Rev
Diocesan Secretary,
Bishop's House,
Killarney, Co Kerry
Tel 064-6631168
(Kerry)

Flynn, Patrick (OFMCap)
Capuchin Friary,
137-142 Church Street,
Dublin D07 HA22
Tel 01-8730599

Flynn, Paul (OSA)
St Augustine's Priory
O'Connell Street,
Co Limerick

Flynn, Seán, CC
The Presbytery,
Dublin Road, Tuam,
Co Galway H54 HR58
Tel 093-24250
(*Tuam (Cathedral of the Assumption)*, Tuam)

Flynn, Thomas, Very Rev, PP
Carrickbeg,
Carrick-on-Suir, Co Tipperary
Tel 051-640340
(*Carrickbeg*, Waterford & L.)

Flynn, Timothy (OSM)
Director, St Peregrine Ministry
Servite Priory,
St Peregrine,
36 Grangewood Estate,
Rathfarnham, Dublin 16
Tel 01-4936755

Flynn, Tomás, PP
Drumcong,
Carrick-on-Shannon,
Co Leitrim
Tel 071-9642021
(*Kiltubrid*, Ardagh & Cl.)

Flynn, William, PP
St Patrick's, Gorey,
Co Wexford
Tel 053-9421117
(*Gorey*, Ferns)

Fogarty, John (CSSp), Most Rev
Superior General,
Clivo di Cinna 195,
00136, Roma, Italy
Tel 0039-06-35404609

Fogarty, Pat, Very Rev, PP
Cork Road, Carrigaline,
Co Cork
Tel 021-4371684
(*Carrigaline*, Cork & R.)

Fogarty, Thomas, Very Rev, PP
Ballydavid, Littleton,
Thurles, Co Tipperary
Tel 0504-44317
(*Moycarkey*, Cashel & E.)

Fokchet, Augustine, PC
St Mary's, Donabate,
Co Dublin
Tel 01-8434604
(*Donabate*, Dublin)

Foley, Declan, Very Rev, PP
Bagenalstown, Co Carlow
Tel 059-9721154
(*Muinebheag/Bagenalstown*, Kildare & L.)

Foley, Denis, Very Rev, PE
c/o Archbishop's House,
Dromcondra, Dublin 9
(Dublin, retired)

Foley, Dermot (SPS)
St Patrick's, Kiltegan,
Co Wicklow W91 Y022
Tel 059-6473600

Foley, Desmond (OSA)
Prior & Bursar,
St Augustine's Priory,
St Augustine's Street,
Galway
Tel 091-562524

Foley, Eamon, Very Rev, PE
6 Woodlawn, Archers Avenue, Kilkenny
Tel 087-7828784
(Ossory, retired)

Foley, Edward (OP)
St Saviour's,
Upper Dorset Street,
Dublin 1
Tel 01-8897610

Foley, Joseph (SMA)
African Missions,
Blackrock Road,
Cork T12 TD54
Tel 021-4292871

Foley, Michael F. (SSCC)
Coudrin House,
27 Northbrook Road,
Dublin 6
Tel 01-6686590

Foley, Niall, BSc, BD, HDE
Vice-President,
St Joseph's College,
Garbally Park, Ballinasloe,
Co Galway H62 AR27
Tel 090-9642504/9642254
(Clonfert)

Foody, Michael (CSSp)
Holy Spirit Missionary College
Kimmage Manor,
Whitehall Road,
Dublin D12 P5YP
Tel 01-4064300

Forbes, John PE
(Derry, retired)

Ford, Seán (OCarm), Very Rev, PP, VF
Our Lady of Mount Carmel Parish,
Whitefriar Street Church,
56 Aungier Street,
Dublin 2
(*Whitefriar Street*, Dublin)

Forde, Denis, Very Rev
Tigh an tSagairt,
Clogheen, Cork
(Cork & R.)

Forde, Des, CC
Curate's House, Sea Park,
Lahinch, Co Clare
Tel 065-7081307
(*Ennistymon*, Galway)

Forde, Jude Ronayne, (OFM)
Ballylooby, Cahir,
Co Tipperary
Tel 052-7441489
(*Ballylooby*, Waterford & L.)

Forde, Michael (CSsR)
Scala, Castlemahon House,
Castle Road,
Blackrock, Cork
Tel 021-4358800

Forde, Tom (OFMCap)
Capuchin Friary,
Ard Mhuire,
Creeslough, Letterkenny,
Co Donegal
Tel 074-9138005

Foret, Gregory M. (OSB)
119 Kilbroney Road,
Rostrevor,
Co Down BT34 3BN
Tel 028-41739979

Forster, Stephen (MI)
Superior and Provincial,
St Camillus,
4 St Vincent Street North,
Dublin 7
Tel 01-8300365

Forsythe, John, Very Rev, PP
Parochial House,
1 Craigstown Road,
Randalstown,
Co Antrim BT41 2AF
Tel 028-94472640
(*Randalstown*, Down & C.)

Fortune, William, PC
32 Newtownpark Avenue,
Blackrock, Co Dublin
Tel 01-2100337
(*Newtownpark*, Dublin)

Fox, Christopher (MHM)
St Joseph's House,
50 Orwell Park, Rathgar,
Dublin 6
Tel 01-4127700

Fox, Gerard, Very Rev
Lisbreen,
75 Somerton Road,
Belfast BT15 4DE
Tel 028-90776185
(Down & C.)

Fox, John, Very Rev, PP
Parochial House,
153 Aughrim Road,
Toombridge,
Antrim BT41 3SH
Tel 028-79468277
(*Newbridge*, Armagh)

Francis, Britus Kadavunkal, Very Rev, Adm
Aughagower, Westport,
Co Mayo F28 PH61
Tel 098-25057
(*Aughagower*, Tuam)

Fraser, Paul, PP
16 Castlefin Road,
Castlederg
Co Tyrone BT81 7BT
Tel 028-81670728
(*Castlederg (Ardstraw West and Castlederg)*, *Aghyaran (Termonamongan)*, Derry)

Frawley, Bernard M. (CSSp)
Rockwell College,
Cashel, Co Tipperary
Tel 062-61444

Freeman, Brendan (OCSO),
Rt Rev, Dom, Superior
Mellifont Abbey,
Collon, Co Louth
Tel 041-9826103

Freeman, Séamus (SAC),
Most Rev, DD
Bishop Emeritus of Ossory,
Diocesan Office,
James Street, Kilkenny
R95 NH60
086-3103934
(Ossory, retired)

Freeney, Paul, Very Rev, PE
Oghill Nursing Home,
Oghill, Monasterevin,
Co Kildare
(Dublin, retired)

LIST OF CLERGY IN IRELAND

French, Gerry (SSC)
St Columban's,
Dalgan Park,
Navan, Co Meath
Tel 046-9021525
(Dublin)

French, John, Very Rev
Horeswood, New Ross,
Co Wexford
Tel 051-593196
(Ferns, retired)

Frendel, Lars (OFM)
Franciscan Friary
Killarney, Co Kerry
Tel 064-6631334/6631066

Friel, James, Very Rev
Canon, PE
Massreagh, Rathmullan,
Co Donegal
Tel 074-9158306
(Raphoe, retired)

Friel, John (CP)
Superior,
Holy Cross Retreat,
432 Crumlin Road,
Ardoyne, Belfast BT14 7GE
Tel 028-90748231
(Holy Cross, Down & C.)

Frost, Laurence (OCarm)
Gort Muire, Ballinteer,
Dublin D16 EI67
Tel 01-2984014

Fuentes, Alejandro (LC)
Chaplain,
Woodlands Academy,
Wingfield House, Bray,
Co Wicklow
Tel 01-2866323

Fullerton, Robert, Very Rev
Canon
501 Ormeau Road,
Belfast BT7 3GR
Tel 028-90641064
(Holy Rosary, Down & C.)

Fulton, Raymond, Very Rev, PP
4 Gortanclochair Park,
Ballycastle BT54 6NV
(Down & C., retired)

Fulton, William (SSC)
St Patrick's, Kiltegan,
Co Wicklow
Tel 059-6473600

Furlong, James, Very Rev
Tomgarrowm,
Adamstown,
Co Wexford
(Ferns, retired)

Furlong, Odhrán, Very Rev,
Adm
St Aidan's, Enniscorthy,
Co Wexford
Tel 053-9235777
Chaplain to St John's
Hospital
(Enniscorthy, Cathedral of
St Aidan, Ferns)

Furlong, Senan (OSB), Very
Rev
Prior, Glenstal Abbey,
Murroe, Co Limerick
Tel 061-621000

Furlong, Shem
Muinebheag Parish Office,
Bagenalstown, Co Carlow
Tel 087-2400582
(Muinebheag/
Bagenalstown, Kildare &
L.)

Furlong, Tadhg, Very Rev,
PP
Cappawhite, Co Tipperary
Tel 062-75427
(Cappawhite, Cashel & E.)

G

Gaffney, Matthew (IC)
Rector, Clonturk House,
Ormond Road,
Drumcondra, Dublin 9
Tel 01-6877014

Gaffney, Philip, Very Rev,
Adm
Cathedral House,
Mullingar, Co Westmeath
Tel 044-9348338/9340126
(Mullingar, Meath)

Gahan, Dermot
c/o PO Box 40, Bishop's
House, Wexford
(Ferns)

Gahan, James, Very Rev, PE
c/o Bishop's House, Carlow
(Kildare & L., retired)

Gahan, Raymond, Very Rev,
PP
Killaveney, Tinahely,
Co Wicklow
Tel 0402-38188
(Killaveney and
Crossbridge, Ferns)

Galaz Carvajal, Juan Diego
(SJ)
35 Lower Leeson Street,
Dublin 2
Tel 01-6761248

Gallagher, Brendan, PP
146 Ballagh Road,
Fivemiletown,
Co Tyrone BT75 OQP
Tel 028-89521291
(Brookeboro (Aghavea-
Aghintaine), Clogher)

Gallagher, Daniel, Adm
Teach an Sagairt,
An Spidéal, Co na Gaillimhe
Tel 091-553155
(An Spidéal, Galway)

Gallagher, Declan, CC
No. 3 Prebytery,
Castle Street, Dalkey,
Co Dublin
Tel 01-2859212
(Dalkey, Dublin)

Gallagher, Denis
c/o Archbishop's House,
Tuam
(Tuam)

Gallagher, Dermot (CP)
St Paul's Retreat,
Mount Argus, Dublin 6W
Tel 01-4992000

Gallagher, Edward, PP
164 Greencastle Road,
Omagh,
Co Tyrone BT79 7RU
Tel 028-81648474
(Gortin (Badoney Lower),
Greencastle, Derry)

Gallagher, Edward, Very
Rev, AP
Leitrimacaward,
Co Donegal
Tel 074-9544102
(Dungloe (Templecrone
and Lettermacaward)
Raphoe)

Gallagher, John (CM)
St Paul's, Raheny,
Dublin 5
Tel 01-8318113

Gallagher, John, (SMA), CC
African Missions,
Dromantine, Newry,
Co Down BT34 1RH
Tel 028-30821224

Gallagher, John, Very Rev
Canon, PE,
Ardara, Co Donegal
Tel 087-6636434
(Raphoe, retired)

Gallagher, Joseph, Very Rev,
PP, VG
Parochial House,
Tullamore, Co Offaly
Tel 057-9321587
(Tullamore, Meath)

Gallagher, Laurence (CSsR)
Mount Saint Alphonsus,
South Circular Road,
Limerick
Tel 061-315099

Gallagher, Malachy, CC
44 Barrack Street,
Strabane
Co Tyrone BT82 8HD
(Melmount (Mourne), Sion
Hills, Derry)

Gallagher, Michael O. (SJ)
35 Lower Leeson Street,
Dublin 2
Tel 01-6761248

Gallagher, Peter, Very Rev,
PP
Lavagh, Ballymote,
Co Sligo
Tel 071-9184002
(Achonry, Achonry)

Gallagher, Raphael (CSsR)
Mount Saint Alphonsus,
South Circular Road,
Limerick
Tel 061-315099

Gallagher, Shane, CC
1 Chaplain's House,
Knocknamona,
Letterkenny, Co Donegal
Tel 074-9125888 (Hospital)
(Letterkenny (Conwal and
Leck), Raphoe)

Gallagher, Thomas
Cloughmore,
Achill, Co Mayo
(Tuam)

Gallahue, Walter (OFM)
Franciscan Friary,
Killarney, Co Kerry
Tel 064-6631334/6631066

Gallinagh, Padraic, Very Rev
'Polperro',
8 Beverley Close,
Newtownards BT23 7FN
(Down & C., retired)

Gallogley, Vincent (OFM)
Franciscan Friary,
Rossnowlagh, Co Donegal
Tel 071-9851342

Galvin, Aidan (CM)
St Joseph's,
44 Stillorgan Park,
Blackrock,
Co Dublin A94 PC62
Tel 01-2886961

Galvin, Gerald (OCarm)
Carmelite Community,
Gort Muire, Ballinteer,
Dublin D16 EI67
Tel 01-2984014

Galvin, Ignatius (OFMCap)
Capuchin Friary,
Holy Trinity,
Fr Mathew Quay,
Cork T12 PK24
Tel 021-4270827

Galvin, John, PE
Passage West, Co Cork
Tel 021-4841267
(Monkstown, Passage
West, Cork & R.)

Galvin, John
60 Lower Mount Pleasant
Avenue,
Rathmines, Dublin 6
(Dublin, retired)

Gannan, John
St James' Apts,
Knock, Co Mayo F12 HE19
(Knock, Tuam)

Gannon, John, Very Rev, PP
Parochial House, Tulsk,
Co Roscommon
Tel 071-9639005
(Tulsk, Elphin)

Gannon, John J., Very Rev,
PE
Parochial House
Elphin, Co Roscommon
Tel 071-9635058
(Elphin, Elphin)

LIST OF CLERGY IN IRELAND

Gannon, Peter, Very Rev, PP
Dalton Street, The
Presbytery, Claremorris,
Co Mayo F12 X8C2
Tel 094-9362477
(*Claremorris (Kilcolman)*,
Tuam)

Gardiner, Seamus, Very Rev
Portroe, Nenagh,
Co Tipperary
Tel 067-23101/
086-8392741
(*Killaloe, retired*)

Garland, Sean, Very Rev, PP
Parochial House,
Clonmellon, Navan,
Co Meath
Tel 046-9433124
(*Clonmellon*, Meath)

Garrett, Gerard,
1 Trinity Court,
Monaleen Road,
Monaleen, Limerick,
Tel 061-330974/
086-3233268
(*Pastoral Unit 1*, Limerick)

Garry, John (SPS)
St Patrick's, Kiltegan,
Co Wicklow
Tel 059-6473600

Garvey, Colin (OFM)
Franciscan Friary,
Liberty Street,
Cork T12 D376
Tel 021-4270302/4275481

Garvey, Francis, PP, VF
Carrick-on-Shannon,
Co Leitrim
Tel 071-9620118
(*Carrick-on-Shannon*,
Ardagh & Cl.)

Garvey, John, Very Rev, PP
St Michael's, Creagh,
Ballinasloe,
Co Galway H53 EC98
Tel 090-9643916
(*Ballinasloe, Creagh and
Kilclooney*, Clonfert)

Garvey, John, Very Rev, PE
Clonbur Road,
Ballinrobe,
Co Mayo F31 WF70
(*Tuam, retired*)

Gates, John, Very Rev, PP, VF
Parochial House,
30 King Street,
Magherafelt,
Co Derry BT45 6AS
Tel 028-79632439
(*Magherafelt and Ardtrea North*, Armagh)

Gaughan, J. Anthony, Very Rev Canon, PE
56 Newtownpark Avenue,
Blackrock, Co Dublin
(*Dublin, retired*)

Gavazzi, Francesco (CFR)
Local Servant (Superior),
St Columba Friary,
Fairview Road,
Derry, BT48 8NU
Tel 028-71419980

Gavigan, Adrian, PP
Parochial House,
Lisminton, Ballintra,
Co Donegal
Tel 074-9734642
(*Ballintra*, Raphoe)

Gavigan, James
30 Knapton Road,
Dun Laoghaire, Co Dublin
Tel 01-2804353
(*Opus Dei*)

Gavigan, Joseph, Very Rev, PP
Parochial House,
Kilmovee,
Ballaghadereen, Co Mayo
Tel 094-9649137
(*Kilmovee*, Achonry)

Gavin, Aiden (CM)
St Paul's, Sybil Hill,
Raheny, Dublin D05 AE38
Tel 01-8318113

Gavin, Denis J. (CSSp)
Holy Spirit Missionary College,
Kimmage Manor,
Whitehall Road, Dublin 12
Tel 01-4064300

Gavin, Fintan, Most Rev, DD
Bishop of Cork and Ross,
Cork and Ross Offices,
Redemption Road, Cork
Tel 021-4301717
(Cork & R.)

Gavin, Tony, Very Rev, PP
c/o Bishop's House,
Dublin Road, Mullingar,
Co Westmeath N91 DW32
(Meath)

Gayer, Pat (OSA)
St John's Priory,
Thomas Street, Dublin 8
Tel 01-6770393

Gaynor, Harry, Very Rev, Co-PP
112 Ballygall Road East,
Glasnevin, Dublin 11
Tel 01-8342248
(*Ballygall*, Dublin)

Geaney, Niall, PP
Fossa, Killinary, Co Kerry
Tel 064-6631996
(*Fossa*, Kerry)

Gear, Patrick, Very Rev, PP
Cappoquin, Co Waterford
Tel 058-54216
(*Cappoquin, Modeligo,
Waterford & L.*)

Geary, Ronan (SJ)
c/o 35 Lower Leeson Street, Dublin 2
Tel 01-6761248

Geelan, John, Very Rev, PP
Parochial House,
Bonniconlon,
Ballina, Co Mayo
Tel 096-45016
(*Bonniconlon*, Achonry)

Geoghegan, Brian, Very Rev
Carrigoran Nursing Home
Newmarket On Fergus,
Co Clare
Tel 087-2387067
(*Killaloe, retired*)

Geoghegan, Francis (SMA)
African Missions,
Blackrock Road,
Cork T12 TD54
Tel 021-4292871

George, Roy, PC
500 South Circular Road,
Rialto, Dublin 8
(*Rialto/Dolphin's Barn*, Dublin)

Geraghty, Cathal, Rt Rev Mgr, PP, VG
Chancellor,
The Presbytery,
Barrack Street,
Loughrea,
Co Galway H62 YE09
Tel 091-841212
Moderator, Kilnadeema and Aille
(*Loughrea, St Brendan's Cathedral,
Kilnadeema and Aille
(Kilnadeema and Kilteskill)*, Clonfert)

Geraghty, Gerard, Very Rev, PP
Aughrim, Ballinasloe,
Co Galway H53 PY13
Tel 090-9673724
(*Aughrim and Kilconnell*, Clonfert)

Geraghty, Martin (MI)
St Camillus, Killucan,
Co Westmeath
Tel 044-74196/044-74115

Geraghty, Michael, Co-PP
The Presbytery,
Church Road,
Nenagh, Co Tipperary
Tel 067-37134/0879926519
(*Odhran Pastoral Area*, Killaloe)

Gesla, Marceli (OFM)
Chaplain to Polish Community,
Franciscan Friary,
Killarney, Co Kerry
Tel 064-6631334/6631066

Ghent, William (SMA)
African Missions,
Blackrock Road,
Cork T12 TD54
Tel 021-4292871

Gibbons, Danny (SPS)
St Patrick's,
21 Leeson Park,
Dublin D06 DE76
Tel 01-4977897

Gibbons, Richard, Very Rev, PP
The Presbytery,
Knock Shrine,
Knock, Co Mayo
Tel 094-9388100
(*Knock*, Tuam)

Gibson, David
St Patrick's Presbytery,
Dublin Road, Limerick
Tel 061-415397/087-2528738
(*Pastoral Unit 1*, Limerick)

Gibson, Steve (CSC)
Fr Patrick Peyton Centre,
Attymass, Co Mayo
Tel 096-45374

Gilbert, Patrick
c/o Diocesan Office,
Westbourne, Ennis,
Co Clare
(Killaloe)

Gilcreest, Martin
The Presbytery,
Cavan Town
Tel 049-4331404
(*Cavan (Urney and Annagilliff)*, Kilmore)

Gildea, Peter (CM), Very Rev
99 Cliftonville Road,
Belfast BT14 6JQ
Tel 028-90751771

Gildea, Seán (OFM)
Drumderrig House Nursing Home,
Abbeytown, Boyle,
Co Rosscommon F52 RC95

Gilhooly, Anthony, CC
The Presbytery, Longford
Tel 043-3346465
(*Longford (Templemichael, Ballymacormack)*, Ardagh & Cl.)

Gilhooly, John, Very Rev, PP
Manorhamilton,
Co Leitrim
Tel 071-9855042
(*Cloonclare and Killasnet*, Kilmore)

Gill, Patrick, Very Rev
Louisburgh, Co Mayo
(*Tuam, retired*)

Gill, Anthony (SMA)
Apt 1, Parochial House,
Balbriggan, Co Dublin
Tel 087-3695332
(*Balbriggan*, Dublin)

Gillan, Hugh (OH)
St John of God Hospital,
Stillorgan, Co Dublin
Tel 01-2771400
(Dublin)

LIST OF CLERGY IN IRELAND

Gillespie, Anthony, Very Rev, PP
Dromore West, Co Sligo
Tel 096-47012
(*Dromore-West (Kilmacshalgan)*, Killala)

Gillespie, Gerard, Very Rev, PE
Rathball, Ballina, Co Mayo
(Killala, retired)

Gillespie, James, Very Rev, PP
Falcarragh, Co Donegal
Tel 074-9135196
(*Falcarragh*, Raphoe)

Gillespie, Kevin, Mgr, Adm, VF
Parochial House,
Letterkenny, Co Donegal
Tel 074-9121021
(*Letterkenny*, Raphoe)

Gilligan, John, Very Rev, Moderator
St Mary's Parochial House,
Saggart, Co Dublin
Tel 087-4103239
(*Newcastle*, Dublin)

Gillooly, Dominick, Very Rev, PE
St Anne's, Sligo
(Elphin, retired)

Gillooly, Reginald (CSSp)
Holy Spirit Missionary College
Kimmage Manor,
Whitehall Road,
Dublin D12 P5YP
Tel 01-4064300

Gilmore, John (SSC)
St Columban's, Dalgan Park, Navan, Co Meath
Tel 046-9021525

Gilmore, John, PE
(Derry, retired)

Gilmore, Sean, Very Rev, PP
Parochial House,
284 Glassdrumman Road,
Annalong, Newry,
Co Down BT34 4QN
Tel 028-43768208
(*Lower Mourne*, Down & C.)

Gilroy, Michael, Very Rev Dr, DD, PP
Skreen, Co Sligo
Tel 071-9166629
(*Skreen and Dromard, Templeboy*, Killala)

Gilroy, Thomas, Very Rev, PP, VF
Parochial House,
Kinnegad, Co Westmeath
Tel 044-9375117
Adm, Longwood
Tel 087-1723903
(*Kinnegad, Longwood*, Meath)

Gilsenan, Michael (SSCC), CC
Gallonreagh,
Maudabawn, Cootehill,
Co Cavan H16 K576
(*Cootehill (Drumgoon)*, Kilmore)

Gilton, Michael, CC
48 Aughrim Street,
Dublin 7
Tel 01-8386176
(*Aughrim Street*, Dublin)

Ginnelly, Christopher, Very Rev, PP
Parochial House, Ballycroy,
Westport, Co Mayo
Tel 098-49134
(*Ballycroy*, Killala)

Gleeson, Martin, Very Rev Canon, PE
Tuam, Co Galway
(Tuam, retired)

Gleeson, Padraig, Adm
St Kevin's Presbytery,
Pearse Street, Sallynoggin,
Co Dublin
Tel 01-2854667
(*Sallynoggin*, Dublin)

Gleeson, Patrick
14 Deerpark Road,
Mount Merrion,
Dublin A94 Y0C1
(Dublin, retired)

Gleeson, Philip (OP)
St Mary's Priory, Tallaght,
Dublin 24
Tel 01-4048100

Glennon, Francis, Very Rev
Presbytery, Castlecoote,
Co Roscommon
(Elphin, retired)

Glennon, Paul, PP
162 Walkinstown Road,
Dublin 12 D12 YOF1
Tel 01-4501372
(*Walkinstown*, Dublin)

Glover, Joseph M., Rt Rev Mgr
c/o Lisbreen,
73 Somerton Road,
Belfast BT15 4DE
(Down & C.)

Glynn, Cronan (OCD)
The Abbey, Loughrea,
Co Galway
Tel 091-841209

Glynn, Enda, Very Rev
c/o 13 Lios Na Mara,
Station Road, Lahinch,
Co Clare
(Galway, retired)

Glynn, John, Very Rev, PP
Parochial House,
Tourlestrane, Ballymote,
Co Sligo
Tel 071-9181105
(*Tourlestrane (Kilmactigue)*, Achonry)

Glynn, Martin, Very Rev Canon, PP
Parochial House, Mervue,
Galway
Tel 091-751721/087-2527124
Administrator, Ballybane
(*Ballybane, Good Shepherd, Mervue*, Galway)

Glynn, Michael
c/o St Mary's, Temple Street, Sligo
(Elphin, retired)

Goaley, Michael, Very Rev Canon, PE,
8 Lake View,
Creggs Road, Glenamaddy,
Co Galway F45 XF29
(Tuam, retired)

Godley, Gearóid
John Paul II Pastoral Centre, Rock Road,
Killarney, Co Kerry
Tel 064-6632644
(Kerry)

Gogan, Brian M. (CSSp)
Holy Spirit Missionary College
Kimmage Manor,
Whitehall Road,
Dublin D12 P5YP
Tel 01-4064300

Goncalves de Lima, Eridian (CSsR)
Santa Maria dei Monti Mission,
Furancungo,
Mozambique, Africa
c/o Marianella,
75 Orwell Road,
Rathgar, Dublin 6
Tel 01-4067100

Gonoude, Anthony, Very Rev, PP
Parochial House,
Ballynacargy,
Co Westmeath
Tel 044-9373923
(*Ballynacargy*, Meath)

Gonzalez-Borrallo, Juan Jesus, CC
Parochial House,
12 Aughrim Road,
Magherafelt,
Co Derry BT45 6AY
Tel 077-36955013
(*Magherafelt and Ardtrea North*, Armagh)

Goode, John (CSsR)
Mount Saint Alphonsus,
Limerick
Tel 061-315099

Goode, Richard (OSA)
St John's Priory,
Thomas Street, Dublin 8
Tel 01-6770393

Goold, Eamonn, Rt Rev Mgr, PE,
Midleton, Co Cork
Tel 021-4633659
(Cloyne, retired)

Gorevan, Patrick
Harvieston,
Cunningham Road,
Dalkey, Co Dublin
Tel 01-2859877
(Opus Dei)

Gormally, Michael, Very Rev, PP
Parochial House,
Ballinrobe, Co Mayo
Tel 094-9541085/541784
Administration for Kilmaine
(*Ballinrobe, Kilmaine*, Tuam)

Gorman, Owen, (OCDS), CC
(Priest in Residence)
Priest's House,
Shantonagh,
Castleblayney,
Co Monaghan A75 NN12
Tel 042-9745015
(*Aughnamullen East*, Clogher)

Gorman, Seán, Very Rev,
Ballask, Kilmore,
Co Wexford
(Ferns, retired)

Gorman, Stephen, CC
Parochial House,
Milford, Co Donegal
Tel 074-9153236
(*Rathmullan (Killygarvan and Tullyfern)*, Raphoe)

Gormey, Frank (OMI)
Oblate House of Retreat,
Inchicore, Dublin 8
Tel 01-4534408/4541805

Gormley, Joseph, PP
Parochial House,
St Mary's, Creggan,
Derry BT48 9QE
Tel 028-71263152
(*St Mary's, Creggan*, Derry)

Gough, Brian
Chaplain,
St James's Hospital,
James's Street, Dublin 8
Tel 01-4103659/4162023
(Dublin)

Gould, Daniel, Very Rev, PE
Ballindangan,
Mitchelstown, Co Cork
(Cloyne, retired)

Grace, Edmond (SJ)
c/o Irish Jesuit Provincialate,
Milltown Park,
Sandford Road, Dublin 6
Tel 01-4987333

LIST OF CLERGY IN IRELAND

Grace, James, Very Rev, Co-PP
Parochial House, Killaloe,
Co Clare
Tel 061-376137/
087-6843315
(*Scáth na Sionnaine Pastoral Area*, Killaloe)

Grace, John (OSA)
On assignment in USA

Grace, Ned (SPS)
St Patrick's, Kiltegan,
Co Wicklow
Tel 059-6473600

Graham, Eamon, PP
65 Mayogall Road,
Knockloughrim,
Magherafelt,
Co Derry BT45 8PG
Tel 028-7964248
(Derry)

Graham, Martin, Very Rev, PP, Adm
81 Lagmore Grove,
Dunmurry,
Belfast BT17 0TD
Tel 028-90309011
Cathedral Presbytery,
St Peter's Square,
Belfast BT12 4BU
Tel 028-90327573
(Down & C.)

Graham, Patrick (OCarm)
Whitefriar Street Church,
56 Aungier Street,
Dublin 2 D02 R598
Tel 01-4758821

Grant, Colin, MA, STL, PGCE
Diocesan Ecumenical Commission,
Aquinas Grammar School,
518 Ravenhill Road,
Belfast BT6 0BY
Tel 028-90643939
(Down & C.)

Grant, Henry (SJ)
c/o Milltown Park,
Sandford Road, Dublin 6
Tel 01-2698411/2698113

Grant, Robert, Very Rev, PP
Parochial House,
Fenor, Co Waterford
Tel 051-376032
(*St Saviour's*, Waterford & L.)

Gray, Francis, PE
'Shalom', Tamlaght Beg,
Mohill, Co Leitrim
(Ardagh & Cl., retired)

Greed, Patrick, Very Rev, Co-PP, VF
Parochial House,
Templemore Road,
Cloughjordan, Co Clare
Tel 0505-42266/
086-6067003
(*Ollatrim Pastoral Area*, Killaloe)

Green, Gerard
c/o Bishop's House, Newry,
Co Down
(Dromore, retired)

Greenan, Thomas (SPS)
St Patrick's
Kiltegan, Co Wicklow
Tel 059-6473600

Greene, James (White Fathers)
c/o Cypress Grove Road,
Templeogue, Dublin 6W
Tel 01-4055263

Greene, James, CC
Mallow, Co Cork
Tel 085-8471249
(*Mallow*, Cloyne)

Greene, John, CC
Parochial House,
St Kevin's Parish,
Laragh, Glendalough,
Co Wicklow
Tel 044-45140
(*Glendalough, Rathdrum, Roundwood*, Dublin)

Greene, Niall (CSSp)
Holy Spirit Missionaries,
Ardbraccan, Navan,
Co Meath C15 T884
Tel 046-9021441

Greene, Patrick (SJ)
Manresa House,
426 Clontarf Road,
Dollymount, Dublin 3
Tel 01-8331352

Greene, William (SPS)
House Leader,
Kiltegan House,
11 Douglas Road, Cork
Tel 021-4969371

Grenham, Thomas (SPS)
St Patrick's, Kiltegan,
Co Wicklow W91 Y022
Tel 059-6473600

Grennan, John (OCD)
Provincial
Avila Carmelite Centre
Bloomfield Avenue
Morehampton Road,
Dublin 4
Tel 01-643 0200

Grier, Matthew (MHM)
St Joseph's House,
50 Orwell Park,
Rathgar, Dublin D06 C535
Tel 01-4127700

Griffin, Brian, Very Rev, Adm
Camross, Co Laois,
Tel 087-0644158
(*Camross, Castletown*, Ossory)

Griffin, Edward, Very Rev
10 Connawood, Bray,
Co Wicklow
(Dublin, retired)

Griffin, Gerard (CSSp)
Rockwell College,
Cashel, Co Tipperary
Tel 062-61444

Griffin, Liam (OMI)
Oblates of Mary Immaculate House of Retreat, Tyrconnell Road,
Inchicore, Dublin 8
Tel 01-4541160/4541161
Oblate House of Retreat,
Inchicore, Dublin 8
Tel 01-4534408/4541805

Griffin, Pat
Ashborough Lodge, Lyre,
Milltown, Co Kerry
(Kerry, retired)

Griffin, Philip
Nullamore, Richmond Avenue South, Dublin 6
Tel 01-4971239
(Opus Dei)

Griffin, Thomas (IC),
Parochial House,
Kilcurry,
Dundalk, Co Louth
Tel 042-9334410

Griffith, Anthony
Rushbrook, Laghey,
Co Donegal
Tel 074-9734021
(Raphoe, retired)

Grimshaw, Ronan (CSSp)
Templeogue College,
Templeville Road,
Dublin 6W
Tel 01-4903909

Grogan, Brian (SJ)
35 Lower Leeson Street,
Dublin 2
Tel 01-6761248

Grogan, Desmond, Very Rev Canon, PE
Partry, Claremorris,
Co Mayo
Tel 094-9543013
(Tuam, retired)

Gryniewicz, Chrysostom (OSB)
Silverstream Priory,
Stamullen,
Co Meath K32 T189
Tel 01-8417142

Guilfoyle, Patrick, Very Rev, CC
Tullaroan, Co Kilkenny
Tel 056-7769141/
087-9932117
(*Tullaroan*, Ossory)

Guinan, Frank
The Presbytery, Mucklagh,
Tullamore, Co Offaly
Tel 057-9321892
(*Rahan*, Meath)

Guiney, John K. (SJ)
Milltown Park,
Sandford Road,
Dublin 6 D06 V9K7
Tel 01-2698411/2698113

Guiry, Michael, Very Rev, PP
Ardmore, Youghal,
Co Waterford
Tel 024-94275
Moderator, Clashmore
(*Ardmore, Clashmore*, Waterford & L.)

Gunn, Joseph, Very Rev, PP, VF
St Comgall's Presbytery,
27 Brunswick Road,
Bangor,
Co Down BT20 3DS
Tel 028-91465522
(*Bangor*, Down & C.)

Guthrie, Charles (SVD)
Donamon Castle,
Roscommon
Tel 090-6662222

Gutu, Lovemore (OCarm)
Provincial Office and Carmelite Community,
Gort Muire, Ballinteer,
Dublin 16
Tel 01-2984014

H

Haan, Karl, CC
Parochial House, Culdaff,
Co Donegal
Tel 074-9379107
(*Culdaff*, Derry)

Habara, Gaspar (SVD), CC
The Presbytery,
Old Dublin Road, Carlow,
Tel 059-9131227
(*Catheral*, Kildare & L.)

Hackett, Michael, Very Rev Canon, PE
Warrenpoint, Co Down
(Dromore, retired)

Hagan, Patrick (SPS)
St Patrick's, Kiltegan,
Co Wicklow
Tel 059-6473600

Hahessy, Ignatius (OCSO)
Mount Melleray Abbey,
Cappoquin,
Co Waterford P51 R8XW
Tel 058-54404

Hallinan, Malachy, Rt Rev Mgr, PP, VG, VF
Church of the Sacred Heart,
Seamus Quirke Road,
Galway
Tel 091-522713
(*Sacred Heart Church*, Galway)

Halpin, Martin, Very Rev, PP
Parochial House,
Ballinabrackey,
Kinnegad, Co Westmeath
Tel 046-9739015
(*Ballinabrackey*, Meath)

Halton, John, Very Rev, PE
26 Cullion Road,
Tempo, Enniskillen,
Co Fermanagh BT94 3LY
Tel 028-89541344
(*Tempo*, Clogher)

Hamill, Aidan, Rt Rev Mgr
c/o Bishop's House, Newry
(Dromore, retired)

Hammel, James, Rt Rev
MgrDiocesan Archivist,
Ballygarron, Kilmuckridge
Gorey, Co Wexford
Tel 086 1688295
(Ferns, retired)

Hampson, Paul
St Patricks Campus,
Drumcondra Road Upper,
Dublin 9
Tel 01-8842000
(Dublin)

Hanafin, Sean, Rt Rev Mgr,
PP
Ballybunion, Co Kerry
Tel 068-27102
Moderator,
Ballydonoghue, Tarbert
(*Ballybunion*,
Ballydonoghue, *Tarbert*,
Kerry)

Hanley, Hugh, Very Rev
(SCJ)
(Moderator)
Parochial House,
St John Vianney,
Ardlea Road, Dublin 5
Tel 01-8474173
(*Ardlea*, Dublin)

Hanlon, Hugh, (MSC)
'Croí Nua', Rosary Lane,
Taylor's Hill Road,
Galway H91 WY2A
Tel 091-520960

Hanlon, Joseph, Very Rev
(Assistant Priest)
St Mary's Presbytery,
Willbrook Road,
Rathfarnham, Dublin 14
Tel 01-4932390
(*Rathfarnham*, Dublin)

Hanly, Gerard, Very Rev
Canon, PP, VF
Boyle, Co Roscommon
Tel 071-9662218
(*Boyle*, Elphin)

Hanna, John (CSsR)
Clonard Monastery,
1 Clonard Gardens,
Belfast BT13 2RL
Tel 028-90445950

Hannan, John (SM) PC
The Presbyerty,
78A Donore Avenue,
Dublin 8
Tel 01-4542425
(*Donore Avenue*, Dublin)

Hannan, Peter (SJ)
Manresa House,
426 Clontarf Road,
Dollymount, Dublin 3
Tel 01-8331352

Hannigan, Patrick, Very Rev,
PP,
Parochial House,
65 Tullyallen Road,
Dungannon,
Co Tyrone BT70 3AF
Tel 028-87769111/
028-87769211
(*Killeeshil*, Armagh)

Hannon, Donald, CC
Arva, Co Cavan
Tel 049-4335246
(*Killeshandra*, Kilmore)

Hannon, Martin
30 Knapton Road,
Dun Laoghaire, Co Dublin
Tel 01-2804353
(Opus Dei)

Hannon, Patrick, Dr
Emeritus Professor of
Theology,
St Patrick's College,
Maynooth, Co Kildare
Tel 01-6285222
(Cloyne, retired)

Hannon, Timothy, CC
3 Stanhope Place, Athy
Tel 059-8631698
(*Athy*, Dublin)

Hannon, Tom, Very Rev
The Bungalow, Moynure,
Bosna, Bir, Co Offaly
(Killaloe, retired)

Hanrahan, Paschal, HCF
Head Chaplain,
Defence Forces
Headquarters,
McKee Barracks,
Blackhorse Avenue
Dublin 7
Tel 01-8042637
(Killaloe)

Hanratty, David
Tierhogar, Portarlington,
Co Laois
Tel 057-8645719
(Meath)

Hanratty, Malachy (SSC)
St Columban's, Dalgan
Park, Navan, Co Meath
Tel 046-9021525

Hanratty, Oliver
The Bungalow,
Crescent Road,
Rogerstown, Rush,
Co Dublin
(Dublin, retired)

Hardiman, Tony (OFM)
Franciscan Friary,
Liberty Street, Cork
Tel 021-4270302/4275481

Harding, Michael, Co-PP
Templemore Road,
Roscrea, Co Tipperary
Tel 0505-21218
(*Cronan Pastoral Area*,
Killaloe)

Hargaden, Joseph (SCC)
Wexford, retired

Harkin, Ciarán, Very Rev, PP
Parochial House,
Newtowncunningham,
Lifford, Co Donegal
Tel 074-9156138
(*Newtowncunningham &
Killea*, Raphoe)

Harkin, Dermott, CC
230b Mayogall Road,
Clady, Portglenone,
Co Derry BT44 8NN
Tel 028-25821190
(*Greenlough and Lavey*,
Derry)

Harkin, Hugh (SMA)
African Missions,
Blackrock Road,
Cork T12 TD54
Tel 021-4292871

Harlow, Thomas (SMA)
SMA House, Wilton, Cork
Tel 021-4541069/4541884

Harmon, Sean,
37 Gouldavoher,
Dooradoyle, Limerick
Tel 087-9870284
(*Pastoral Unit 4,* Limerick)

Harnan, Nick (MSC)
c/o Formation House,
56 Mulvey Park, Dundrum,
Dublin 16
Tel 01-2951856

Harney, Donal (MHM)
St Joseph's House,
50 Orwell Park,
Rathgar, Dublin D06 C535
Tel 01-4127700

Harper, Conor (SJ), PC
Jesuit House,
Milltown Park,
Sandford Road, Dublin 6
Tel 01-2698411
(*Donnybrook*, Dublin)

Harrington, Brendan
(Kerry, retired)

Harrington, Denis, Very Rev,
PE
Clane, Naas, Co Kildare
Tel 045-868224
(Kildare & L., retired)

Harrington, John (SM), TA
The Presbytery,
Coolock Village, Dublin 5
Tel 01-8477133

Harrington, Patrick (SMA)
Retired Bishop,
SMA House, Wilton,
Cork T12 KR23
Tel 021-4541069/4541884

Harrington, Terence
(OFMCap)
Guardian, Capuchin Friary,
Clonshaugh Drive,
Priorswood,
Dublin D17 RP20
Tel 01-8474469

Harrington, Wilfred (OP)
St Mary's Priory, Tallaght,
Dublin 24
Tel 01-4048100

Harris, Derek (SSC)
44 Harbour View, Howth,
Co Dublin
Tel 01-8395161

Harris, Jack (CM)
St Joseph's,
44 Stillorgan Park,
Blackrock,
Co Dublin A94 PC62
Tel 01-2886961

Harris, John (OP), Very Rev
Provincial, St Mary's,
Tallaght,
Dublin 24 D24 X585
Tel 01-4048118

Harris, John, CC
Holy Family Presbytery,
Luke Wadding Street,
Waterford
Tel 051-323947
(*Cathedral*, Waterford &
L.)

Harris, Walter, Very Rev
Canon, PE
151 Clonsilla Road,
Blanchardstown, Dublin 15
Tel 01-8213716
(Dublin, retired)

Harrison, Michael, Very Rev,
PP
Killala, Co Mayo
Tel 096-32176
Carrowmore, Ballina,
Co Mayo
Tel 096-34014
(*Killala/Lacken*, Killala)

Harte, Martin, CC
Presbytery,
Kilcullen, Co Kildare
Tel 045-481222
(*Kilcullen*, Dublin)

Hartnett, Denis (MHM)
St James Apartments,
Our Lady of Knock Shrine,
Knock, Co Mayo F12 R982

Harty, John (OFM)
Dún Mhuire,
Seafield Road,
Killiney, Co Dublin
Tel 01-2826760

Hassett, Edmond, Very Rev,
PP
Strandside South,
Abbeyside, Dungarvan,
Co Waterford
Tel 058-42036
(*Abbeyside*, Waterford &
L.)

LIST OF CLERGY IN IRELAND

Hassett, John, Co-PP
127 Castlegate Way,
Adamstown, Co Dublin
Tel 01-62812088
(*Esker-Doddsboro-Adamstown*, Dublin)

Hasson, Eugene, PP
52 Brook Street, Omagh,
Co Tyrone BT78 5HE
Tel 028-82243011
Adm, Drumquin
(Langfield)
(*Drumquin (Langfield)*,
Omagh (Drumragh),
Derry)

Hasson, Gerald (CSSp), CC
33 Cullycapple Road,
Aghadowney,
Co Derry BT51 4AR
Tel 048-70869019
(*Coleraine*, Derry)

Hasson, James (OFM)
Guardian, Franciscan
Friary,
Clonmel, Co Tipperary
Tel 052-6121378

Hastings, Mícheál, Very Rev
Benevin Lodge Nursing
Home,
Glasnevin, Dublin 11
(Dublin, retired)

Hayden, Chris
c/o Bishop's House,
Summerhill, Wexford
(Ferns)

Hayden, Desmond
Ampleforth Abbey,
York YO62 4EN, UK
(Dublin)

Hayden, Eamonn Rev (SPS)
St Patrick's Kiltegan,
Co Wicklow W91 Y022

Hayes, Conor, Very Rev, PP
Templemore, Co Limerick
Tel 0504-31684
(*Templemoore*, Cashel &
E.)

Hayes, George, Venerable
Archdeacon, PP, VF
Kenmare, Co Kerry
Tel 064-6641352
(*Kenmare*, Kerry)

Hayes, Joseph (SJ)
Superior, Della Strada,
Dooradoyle, Limerick
Tel 061-480929/
087-4647634
(*Pastoral Unit 3*, Limerick)

Hayes, Patrick,
Dunabbey House,
Dungarvan,
Co Waterford
(*Waterdord & L.*, retired)

Hayes, Richard, Very Rev
Collinstown, Duncormack,
Co Wexford
(Ferns, retired)

Hayes, Tom, Very Rev, PP,
VG
Parochial House,
Enniskeane, Co Cork
Tel 023-8847769
(*Enniskeane and
Desertserges*, Cork & R.)

Hazelwood, Timothy, Very
Rev, PP
Killeagh, Co Cork
Tel 024-95133
(*Killeagh*, Cloyne)

Heagney, John, Very Rev,
PP, VF
124 Eglish Road,
Dungannon,
Co Tyrone BT70 1LB
Tel 028-37549661
(*Eglish*, Armagh)

Healy, Alexius (OFMCap)
Capuchin Friary,
Station Road, Raheny,
Dublin D05 T9E4
Tel 01-8313886

Healy, Austin (CSSp)
Holy Spirit Missionary
College
Kimmage Manor,
Whitehall Road,
Dublin D12 P5YP
Tel 01-4064300

Healy, Bernard,
St John's Presbytery,
Tralee, Co Kerry
Tel 066-7122522
(*Tralee, St John's*, Kerry)

Healy, Charles, PP
Carrickedmond, Colehill
Co Longford
Tel 044-9357442
(*Carrickedmond And
Abbeyshrule,
Legan and Ballycloghan*,
Ardagh & Cl.)

Healy, Jeremiah (SSC)
St Columban's,
Dalgan Park,
Navan, Co Meath
Tel 046-9021525

Healy, Myles (CSSp)
Blackrock College,
Blackrock, Co Dublin
Tel 01-2888681

Healy, Patrick J. (SDB)
Chaplain,
Mount Carmel Nursing
Home, Roscrea,
Co Tipperary

Healy, Peter, Rev, Co-PP
Parochial House,
Roundwood, Co Wicklow
Tel 01-2818149/087-
2463876
(*Roundwood*, Dublin)

Healy, Sean (SMA)
Social Justice Ireland,
Arena House
Arena Road, Sandyford,
Dublin 18
Tel 01-2130724

Healy, Thomas, PP
Diocesan Office,
St Michael's,
Edgeworthstown,
Co Longford
Tel 043-3346432/6671046
(*Longford
(Templemichael,
Ballymacormack)*, Ardagh
& Cl.)

Healy, Timothy (SJ)
Irish Jesuit Provincialate,
Milltown Park,
Sandford Road, Dublin 6
Tel 01-4987333

Heaney, Seamus, Very Rev,
PP
Parochial House, Delvin,
Co Westmeath
Tel 044-9664127
(*Delvin*, Meath)

Heaney, Seán, Rt Rev Mgr,
AP
Parochial House,
Tullamore, Co Offaly
Tel 057-9321587/
057-9351510
(*Tullamore*, Meath)

Hearne, Thomas, PP
Bohermore, Cashel,
Co Tipperary
Tel 052-7462810
(*Clonoulty*, Cashel & E.)

Hearty, Philip (CSsR)
St Patrick's, Esker,
Athenry, Co Galway
Tel 091-844007

Hederman, Mark Patrick
(OSB)
Abbot, Glenstal Abbey,
Murroe, Co Limerick
Tel 061-621000

Heery, Kevin, CC
Parochial House, Curraha,
Co Meath
Tel 01-8350136
(*Ardcath, Curraha*, Meath)

Heffernan, Martin, Very
Rev, PE, PhD
Skahardgannon,
Doneraile, Co Cork
Tel 022-24570
(Cloyne, retired)

Hegarty, Benedict (OP), Very
Rev,
St Dominic's Retreat
House,
Montenotte, Co Cork
Tel 021-4502520

Hegarty, Ciarán, Adm
(Down & Connor Diocese)
Doneyloop, Castlefin,
Lifford, Co Donegal
Tel 074-9146183
(*Doneyloop (Urney and
Castlefinn)*, Derry)

Hegarty, John Paul, Very
Rev Canon, PP
The Lough Presbytery,
St Finbarr's West, Cork
Tel 021-4322633
(*The Lough*, Cork & R.)

Hegarty, Kevin, Very Rev
Carne, Belmullet, Co Mayo
Tel 097-81011
(*Kilmore-Erris*, Killala)

Hegarty, Martin
(Kerry, retired)

Hegarty, Michael (IC), Very
Rev, PP
St Oliver Plunkett's Parish,
Cooleens, Clonmel,
Co Tipperary
Tel 052-6125679
(*Clonmel, St Oliver
Plunkett*, Waterford & L.)

Hegarty, Richard, Very Rev,
PE,
Killavullen, Co Cork
Tel 022-26125
(Cloyne, retired)

Hehir, Mark, CC
Midleton, Co Cork
Tel 021-4621670
(*Midleton*, Cloyne)

Heinhold, John (SPS), CC
The Presbytery, Bantry,
Co Cork
Tel 027-50193
(*Bantry*, Cork & R.)

Hendrick, Richard (OFMCap)
Guardian, Capuchin Friary,
Church Street,
Raheny, Dublin D07 HA22
Tel 01-8730599

Heneghan, James (CSSp)
Holy Spirit Missionary
College
Kimmage Manor,
Whitehall Road,
Dublin D12 P5YP
Tel 01-4064300

Heneghan, Jeremy
(OFMCap)
Ard Mhuire, Creeslough,
Letterkenny,
Co Donegal F92 Y23R
Tel 074-9138005

Hennebry, John (OSA)
Provincial, St Augustine's
Taylor's Lane, Ballyboden,
Dublin 16
Tel 01-4241000

Hennessy, Gerard, PP
The Parochial House,
Borrisoleigh, Thurles,
Co Tipperary
Tel 0504-51935
(*Borrisoleigh*, Cashel & E.)

Hennessy, Patrick (SDB)
Salesian College,
Maynooth Road,
Celbridge,
Co Kildare W23 W0XK
Tel 01-62755058/60

LIST OF CLERGY IN IRELAND

Hennessy, Patrick, Very Rev, PP
Leighlinbridge, Co Carlow
Tel 059-9722607
(*Leighlin*, Kildare & L.)

Hennessy, William, Very Rev, Adm
Conahy, Jenkinstown,
Co Kilkenny
Tel 087-8736155
(*Conahy*, Ossory)

Hennigan, Frank (SM)
181 South Circular Road,
Dublin 8

Henry, Denis, Co-PP
1A Ballydowd Grove,
Lucan, Co Dublin
Tel 01-2955541
(*Lucan*, Dublin)

Henry, Leo, Very Rev, BA, HDE, PP
Curry, Ballymote,
Co Sligo
Tel 087-6306938
(*Curry*, Achonry)

Henry, Martin
St Patrick's College,
Maynooth, Co Kildare
Tel 01-6285222
(Down & C.)

Henry, Martin
St Nathy's College,
Ballaghaderreen,
Co Roscommon
Tel 094-9861728
(Achonry)

Henry, Maurice, Very Rev, PE
54 St Patrick's Avenue,
Downpatrick,
Co Down BT30 6DN
Tel 028-44851221
(*Downpatrick*, Down & C.)

Henry, Maurice, Very Rev, Adm
Parochial House,
Castletown-Kilpatrick,
Navan, Co Meath
(*Castletown-Kilpatrick*, Meath)

Henry, Seán, Very Rev, PP
Parochial House,
Dunshaughlin, Co Meath
Tel 01-8259114
(*Dunshaughlin*, Meath)

Heraty, Jarlath, PP
Killererin, Barnderg,
Tuam, Co Galway
Tel 093-49222
(*Killererin*, Tuam)

Herlihy, David, Very Rev Canon, PE
Freemount, Charleville,
Co Cork
(*Cloyne*, retired)

Hernandez, Jose Manuel Casillas (MCCJ)
8 Clontarf Road,
Clontarf, Dublin 3
Tel 01-8330051

Herrity, Michael, Very Rev Canon, AP
Bun-a-leaca,
Letterkenny,
Co Donegal
Tel 074-9531155
(*Gweedore*, Raphoe)

Herron, Frank, Very Rev, PP
Parochial House, Foxrock,
Dublin 18
Tel 01-2893229
(Dublin)

Hession, Noel (OSA)
Prior and Bursar,
St Augustine's Priory,
O'Connell Street,
Limerick
Tel 061-415374

Hession, Stan (OCarm)
Carmelite Friary,
Kinsale,
Co Cork P17 WR88
Tel 021-4772138

Hever, Thomas, Very Rev, PP, VG
Parochial House
Rathcormac, Co Sligo
Tel 071-9635058
(*Drumcliff-Maugherow*, Elphin)

Hickey, John (SSC)
Columban Sisters,
Magheramore,
Co Wicklow

Hickey, Michael (CSSp)
Drum, Athlone,
Co Roscommon
Tel 090-6437125
(*Athlone, SS Peter and Paul*, Elphin)

Hickey, Michael, Very Rev, PP
Bansha, Co Tipperary
Tel 062-54132
(*Bansha and Kilmoyler*, Cashel & E.)

Hickey, Patrick, Very Rev, PP
Parochial House,
Timoleague, Co Cork
Tel 023-8869682
(*Timoleague and Clogagh*, Cork & R.)

Hickland, Brendan, Very Rev, PP
503 Ormeau Road,
Belfast BT7 3GR
Tel 028-90642446
Administrator,
St Bernadette's Parish
(*Holy Rosary*, St Bernadette's, Down & C.)

Higgans, Pius (OFMCap)
Capuchin Friary,
Friary Street,
Kilkenny R95 NX60
Tel 056-7721439

Higgins, Thomas (OCarm)
Whitefriar Street Church,
56 Aungier Street,
Dublin 2 D02 R598
Tel 01-4758821

Hillery, Desmond, Very Rev, Co-PP, VG, VF
The Presbytery,
Church Street,
Nenagh, Co Tipperary
Tel 067-37130
(*Odhran Pastoral Area*, Killaloe)

Hilliard, Alan
Technological University Dublin,
Coordinator, Pastoral Care and Chaplaincy Service,
Room 254, TU Dublin,
Bolton Street D01 K822
(Dublin)

Hinds, Michael, CF
Aiken Barracks,
Dundalk, Co Louth
Tel 042-9331759
Gormanston Army Camp,
Stamullen, Co Meath
Tel 087-3940186
(Meath)

Hoban, Brendan (SSC)
Alcoholic Advisory Board,
St Columban's,
Dalgan Park,
Navan, Co Meath
Tel 046-9021525

Hoban, Brendan, Very Rev, PP
Sliabh Rua, Breaffy,
Ballina, Co Mayo
Tel 096-31288
(Killala, retired)

Hoban, Patrick, Very Rev
St Jude's Avenue,
Crossmolina, Co Mayo
(Killala, retired)

Hodnett, Ben, Adm
The Presbytery,
Togher, Cork
Tel 021-4316700
(*Togher*, Cork & R.)

Hoey, Eamonn, (CSsR)
St Joseph's,
St Alphonsus Road,
Dundalk,
Co Louth A71 F3FC
Tel 042-9334042

Hogan, Bernard, PP, VF
Drumlish, Co Longford
Tel 043-3324132
(*Drumlish*, Ardagh & Cl.)

Hogan, Diarmuid, Very Rev, PP
Parochial House,
Oranmore, Co Galway
Tel 091-794634/
087-1037452
(*Oranmore*, Galway)

Hogan, Donal (SSC)
Deputy Safeguarding Office, St Columban's,
Dalgan Park,
Navan, Co Meath
Tel 046-9021525

Hogan, Edmund M. (SMA)
African Missions,
Blackrock Road,
Cork T12 TD54
Tel 021-4292871

Hogan, John Rev (SSC)
St Columban's,
Dalgan Park,
Navan, Co Meath

Hogan, John, CC
St Mary's, Drogheda,
Co Louth
Tel 041-9834958
(*Drogheda, St Mary's*, Meath)

Hogan, John Very Rev (OCD) PP
1 Orchard Court,
Dunboyne, Co Meath
(*Dunboyne*, Meath)

Hogan, Joseph, CC
Cornboy, Rossport, Ballina,
Co Mayo
Tel 097-88939
(*Kilcommon-Erris*, Killala)

Hogan, Martin, Very Rev Canon, VF
(Moderator)
186 Clontarf Road,
Clontarf,
Dublin D03 HK59
Tel 01-8338575
(*Clontarf, St John's,
Clontarf, St Anthony's,
Dollymount*, Dublin)

Hogan, Maurice (SSC)
St Columban's,
Dalgan Park, Navan,
Co Meath
Tel 046-9021525

Hogan, Patrick (SVD)
St Mary-on-the-Quay Presbytery,
20 Colston Street,
Bristol BS1 5AE

Hogan, Patrick,
Sruth Lan,
South Circular Road,
Limerick
Tel 087-6522746
(*Pastoral Unit 4*, Limerick)

Hogan, Thomas (CSSp)
Rockwell College,
Cashel, Co Tipperary
Tel 062-61444

Hogan, Thomas (CSsR)
Dún Mhuire,
461/463 Griffith Avenue,
Dublin D09 X651
Tel 01-5180196
Chaplain,
Our Lady of Lourdes,
Drogheda, Co Louth

LIST OF CLERGY IN IRELAND

Hogan, Tom, Very Rev, Co-PP, VF
The Presbytery,
John's Mall,
Birr, Co Offaly
Tel 055-9121757/
087-6446410
(*Brendan Pastoral Area*, Killaloe)

Hogg, Barry, Very Rev
15 Parkelands
Tubbercurry
Co Sligo
Tel 091-522458/524904
(*Galway*)

Holland, Michael (OFM)
Franciscan Abbey,
Liberty Street, Cork
Tel 021-4270302/4275481

Holleran, Patrick, Very Rev, PP
Coolaney, Co Sligo
Tel 071-9167745
(*Coolaney (Killoran)*, Achonry)

Holmes, Brian (CSSR)
c/o Provincial Office,
St Joseph's,
St Alphonsus Road,
Dundalk,
Co Louth A71 F3FC

Holmes, Kieran, PP
Easkey, Co Sligo
Tel 096-49011/49021
(*Easkey*, Killala)

Holovlasky, Ryan (CSSR), CC
St Joseph's,
St Alphonsus Road,
Dundalk,
Co Louth A71 F3FC
Tel 042-9334042
(*Dundalk, St Joseph's*, Armagh)

Horan, Barry PP
Main Street,
Clarinbridge, Co Galway
Tel 091-776741
(*Clarinbridge*, Galway)

Horan, Gerard (OSA)
Bursar, The Abbey,
Fethard, Co Tipperary
Tel 052-31273

Horan, John (SDB), Very Rev
Rector, Salesian College,
Don Bosco Road,
Pallaskenry,
Co Limerick V94 WP86
Tel 061-393105

Horgan, John (SMA),
SMA House, Wilton,
Cork T12 KR23
Tel 021-4541069/4541884

Horgan, Patrick (CSsR)
St Joseph's,
St Alphonsus Road,
Dundalk,
Co Louth A71 F3FC
Tel 042-9334042/9334762

Horgan, Seamus, Mgr
Apostolic Nunciature,
3339 Massachusetts Ave.
Washington DC,
20008-3610
USA
(Killaloe)

Horgan, Seán (MSC), CC
(pro tem)
Carrignavar, Co Cork
Tel 021-4884044

Horgan, Tony (MSC) PP
Church of the
Resurrection,
Headford Road,
Galway H91 W298
Tel 091-762883
(*Tirellan*, Galway)

Horneck, Noel, Very Rev, PP
Parochial House,
Dunderry, Navan,
Co Meath
Tel 046-9431433
(*Dunderry*, Meath)

Horrocks, Paul (OMI)
Oblates Fathers, House of Retreat,
Inchicore, Dublin 8
Tel 01-4541117

Hou, Anthony
Chaplain to Chinese Community,
Westland Row, Dublin 2
Tel 01-6761270
(*Westland Row*, Dublin)

Houlihan, Séamus, Very Rev, PP,
Parochial House,
Ballycumber Road
Moate, Co Westmeath,
Tel 090-6481951
(*Tubber*, Meath)

Hourigan, Augustine (CP)
St Paul's Retreat,
Mount Argus, Dublin 6W
Tel 01-4992000

Hourigan, Joseph, Very Rev, AP
Parochial House,
Lissycasey, Ennis,
Co Clare
Tel 065-6834145
(*Radharc na nOileán Pastoral Area*, Killaloe)

Houser, Dom Hildebrand (OSB)
Silverstream Priory,
Stamullen,
Co Meath K32 T189
Tel 01-8417142

Howard, Brendan, Very Rev, PE
Hillview Nursing Home,
Tullow Road, Carlow
(Kildare & L. retired)

Howard, Greg, PP, Adm
The Prebytery,
Knocknaheeny, Cork
Tel 021-4392459
Adm, Clogheen (Kerry Pike)
St Mary's on the Hill,
Knocknaheeny,
Tel 021-4392427
(*Clogheen (Kerry Pike)*, *Knocknaheeny*, Cork & R.)

Howard, Niall, CC
Killarney, Co Kerry
Tel 064-6631014
(*Killarney*, Kerry)

Howard, Patrick, Very Rev
Athlacca, Kilmallock,
Co Limerick
Tel 063-90540
(Limerick, retired)

Howard, Terence (SJ)
Peter Faber House,
28 Brookvale Avenue,
Belfast BT14 6BW
Tel 028-90757615

Howell, William, Very Rev
C/o Bishop's House,
Summerhill, Wexford
(Ferns, retired)

Howley, Enda, Very Rev
Canon, PE
College Road, Galway
(Tuam, retired)

Howley, Gary (SPS)
St Patrick's Missionary Society, Main Street,
Knock, Co Mayo F12 KX34
Tel 094-9388661

Hoyne, Peter, Very Rev, PE
Newmarket,
Hugginstown,
Co Kilkenny
Tel 056-7768678
(Ossory, retired)

Hoyne, William (OFM)
Franciscan Friary,
Clonmel, Co Tipperary
Tel 052-6121378

Hughes, Augustine (OFM)
Franciscan Friary,
Clonmel, Co Tipperary
Tel 052-6121378

Hughes, Benedict
(On study leave)
Chaplaincy Centre,
NUI Galway,
University Road, Galway
H91 TK 33
Tel 086-3864907
(Clogher)

Hughes, Eoin
Chaplain,
Beaumont Hospital,
Beaumont Road, Dublin 9
Tel 01-8477573
(Dublin)

Hughes, John (OSA), PP
St Augustine's,
Taylor's Lane,
Ballyboden, Dublin 16
(*Ballyboden*, Dublin)

Hughes, John, Very Rev, PE, CC
30 Jockey Lane, Moy,
Dungannon,
Co Tyrone BT71 7SR
Tel 028-87784240
(Armagh, retired)

Hughes, Martin,
Team Assistant,
447 The Oaks,
Belgard Heights
Tallaght, Dublin 24
Tel 01-4519399
(*Brookfield*, Dublin)

Hughes, Michael (OMI)
Oblate House of Retreat,
Inchicore, Dublin 8
Tel 01-4534408/4541805

Hughes, Michael (SCJ)
Sacred Heart Fathers,
Fairfield,
66 Inchicore Road,
Dublin 8
Tel 01-4538655

Hughes, Pat, CC
Parochial House, Myshall,
Co Carlow
Tel 059-9157635
(*Clonegal, Myshall*, Kildare & L.)

Hughes, Patrick, Very Rev, PP, Adm
Parochial House,
10 Cloughfin Road,
Kildress, Cookstown,
Co Tyrone BT80 9JB
Administration Kildress
Tel 028-86751206
(*Kildress, Lissan*, Armagh)

Hughes, P. J., PP
Mullahoran,
Kilcogy via Longford,
Co Cavan
Tel 043-6683141
(*Mullahoran and Loughduff*, Ardagh & Cl.)

Hughes, Richard (OSA),
St Augustine's,
Taylor's Lane,
Ballyboden, Dublin 16

Humphries, Seamus (OSA)
St Augustine's Priory,
Dungarvan, Co Waterford
Tel 058-41136

Hunt, Anselm (OSB)
Abbot, Glenstal Abbey,
Murroe, Co Limerick
Tel 061-386103

Hurley, Colm
(Kilmore, retired)

LIST OF CLERGY IN IRELAND

Hurley, Declan, Very Rev, Adm, VG
St Mary's Presbytery,
The Fairgreen, Navan,
Co Meath C15 X0A3
Tel 046-9027518
(*Navan*, Meath)

Hurley, James, CC
31 Herbert Avenue,
Merrion Road, Dublin 4
Tel 01-2692001
(*Merrion Road*, Dublin)

Hurley, Michael C., Very Rev Canon, PP, VF
Killeshandra, Co Cavan
Tel 049-4334155
(*Killeshandra*, Kilmore)

Hurley, Michael, Very Rev Canon PC
85 Tymon Crescent,
Oldbawn, D24 FK0W,
Tel 01-4627080
(*Bohernabreena, Tallaght, Oldbawn*, Dublin)

Hurley, Richard, Very Rev Canon
c/o Cork & Ross Offices
Redemption Road,
Co Cork
Tel 085-1471147
(*Cork & R.*, retired)

Hurley, Thomas, Very Rev
Templeglantine,
Co Limerick
Tel 068-84021
(*Limerick*, retired)

Husband, Raymond (SSC)
Regional Director,
St Columban's,
Dalgan Park,
Navan, Co Meath
Tel 046-9021525

Hussey, Michael, Very Rev, PP
Ballylongford, Co Kerry
Tel 06843110
(*Ballylongford*, Kerry)

Hutchinson, Stephen (OP), Very Rev
St Dominic's,
St Dominic's Road,
Tallaght, Dublin 24
Tel 01-4510620

Hutton, John, Very Rev
Apt 2, Ceara Court,
Windsor Avenue,
Belfast BT9 6EJ
Tel 028-90683002
(*Down & C.*, retired)

Hyland, Richard, Very Rev, PP
5 The Lawn, Finglas
Dublin 1,
Tel 01-8341894
(*Finglas*, Dublin)

Hyland, Sean, CC
29 Pine Villa,
Portarlington, Co Laois
Tel 057-8645582/
087-9486769
(*Clonbollogue and Rhode*, Kildare & L.)

Hynes, James (OFM)
17 Rue de Faubourg La Grappe,
28000 Chartre, France

Hynes, Valentine (SMA)
African Missions,
Blackrock Road,
Cork T12 TD54
Tel 021-4292871

I

Ifunanya, Onwe (OCSO)
Our Lady of Bethlehem Abbey,
11 Ballymena Road,
Portglenone, Ballymena,
Co Antrim, BT44 8BL
Tel 028-25822795

Igoe, Michael (SMA)
African Missions,
Blackrock Road,
Cork T12 TD54
Tel 021-4292871

Illah, Louis, CC
52 Edgeworth Court,
Longwood, Co Meath
Tel 087-1723903
(*Longwood*, Meath)

Irwin, Charles,
Kevin Villa,
O'Connell Avenue,
Limerick
Tel 061-348922
(*Limerick*)

Irwin, Edwin,
Cloncagh, Ballyhahill,
Co Limerick
Tel 069-83972/087-2547707
(*Pastoral Unit 10*, Limerick)

Irwin, John
c/o Diocesan Offices,
St Eugene's Cathedral,
Francis Street,
Derry BT48 9AP
(Derry)

Irwin, Michael (SAC)
Rector, 'Homestead',
Sandyford Road,
Dundrum, Dublin 16
Tel 01-2956180/2954170

Irwin, Michael (SSC)
36 Clonmore, Kilteragh,
Dooradoyle,
Co Limerick
Tel 069-83972

Irwin, Nicholas J., Very Rev, PP
Diocesan Secretary/Chancellor,
Archbishop's House,
Thurles, Co Tipperary
Tel 0504-21512
PP, Gortnahoe
The Parochial House,
Gortnahoe, Thurles,
Co Tipperary
Tel 056-8834855
(*Gortnahoe*, Cashel & E.)

Issac, Sunil (SCJ)
Sacred Heart Fathers,
Fairfield,
66 Inchicore Road,
Dublin 8
Tel 01-4538655

Iwuozor, Gregory (CSSp)
Holy Spirit Missionary College
Kimmage Manor,
Whitehall Road,
Dublin D12 P5YP
Tel 01-4064300

J

Jachym, Mario (SC), CC
15 Chapel Hill,
Mayobridge,
Co Down BT34 2EX
Tel 028-30851225

Jackson, Piaras (SJ)
Director of Retreat House,
Manresa House,
426 Clontarf Road,
Dollymount, Dublin 3
Tel 01-8331352
Director, Sacred Space

Jacob, Bibin (CST), CC
Parochial House,
Brackenstown Road,
Swords, Co Dublin
Tel 01-8408926
(*Brackenstown*, Dublin)

Jacob, John, CC
12 Walkinstown Road,
Dublin 12
Tel 01-4502541
(*Walkinstown*, Dublin)

Jacob, Russel (OSCam)
Chaplain, Waterford University Hospital,
Dunmore Road, Waterford
Tel 051-848000
(Waterford & L.)

Jacob, Yohanna, CC
Parochial House,
Ratoath, Co Meath
Tel 01-8256207
(*Ratoath*, Meath)

Jakubiak, Piotr
Polish Chaplaincy
The Presbytery, Ballymany,
Newbridge, Co Kildare
Tel 045-434069
(*Droichead Nua/Newbridge*, Kildare & L.)

Jansen, Luuk (OP)
St Mary's,
Pope's Quay, Cork
Tel 021-4502267

Jennings, Gavan
Harvieston,
Cunningham Road,
Dalkey, Co Dublin
Tel 01-2859877
(Opus Dei)

Jennings, Gerard, Very Rev, PP
Monksfield, Salthill,
Galway
Tel 091-523413
(*Salthill*, Galway)

Jennings, Martin, Very Rev, PE
4 St Mary's House
Shantalla, Galway
Tel 087-9476115
(*Achonry*, retired)

Jennings, Norman (SSC)
St Columban's,
Dalgan Park,
Navan, Co Meath
Tel 046-9021525

Jjooga, Matthias, CC
1 Grangemore Avenue,
Donaghmede, Dublin 13
01-5556232
(*Donaghmede-Clongriffin-Balgriffin*, Dublin)

Johnston, Anthony
8 Corrig Park,
Dun Laoghaire, Co Dublin
Tel 01-2805594
(Dublin, retired)

Johnston, Cecil
Sacred Heart Residence,
Sybil Hill Road,
Raheny, Dublin 5
(Dublin, retired)

Johnston, Thomas, Rt Rev Mgr, PP
Charlestown, Co Mayo
Tel 094-9254315
(*Charlestown (Kilbeagh)*, Achonry)

Jones, Bernard (OFM)
Franciscan Friary,
Rossnowlagh, Co Donegal F94 PH21
Tel 071-9851342

Jones, David
The Hermitage
Duleek, Co Meath
Tel 041-9823205
(*Duleek*, Meath)

LIST OF CLERGY IN IRELAND

Jones, Gerard, Co-PP
 The Presbytery,
 1 Shallee Drive,
 Cloughleigh,
 Ennis, Co Clare
 Tel 065-6840715
 Diocesan Office,
 Westbourne,
 Ennis, Co Clare
 Tel 065-6828638
 (*Abbey Pastoral Area*,
 Killaloe)
Jones, John (SPS)
 Dysart, Mullingar,
 Co Westmeath
Jones, John, Very Rev, PC
 151 Swords Road,
 Whitehall, Dublin 9
 Tel 01-8374887
 (*Larkhill-Whitehall-Santry*,
 Dublin)
Jones, John, Very Rev, AP
 St Caimin's,
 Mountshannon, Co Clare
 Tel 061-927213/
 086-1933479
 (*Inis Cealtra Pastoral Area*,
 Killaloe)
Jones, Joseph
 (Moderator)
 122 Greencastle Road,
 Dublin 17
 Tel 01-8487657
 (*Bonnybrook*, Dublin)
Jones, Patrick, Very Rev,
 Team Assistant
 87 Iona Road,
 Dublin 9
 Tel 01-8308257
 (*Iona Road*, Dublin)
Jones, Sean
 St John's Parish Centre,
 Castle Street,
 Tralee, Co Kerry
 Tel 066-7122522
 (*Tralee, St John's*, Kerry)
Jordan, John, Very Rev, PP
 Kyle, Oulart,
 Gorey, Co Wexford
 (*Ferns*, retired)
Jordan, Michael, CC
 (Priest in Residence)
 Parochial House, Killanny
 Carrickmacross,
 Co Monaghan
 A81 PX31
 Tel 042-9661452
 (*Killanny*, Clogher)
Jordan, Thomas (OP), Very
 Rev
 Black Abbey, Kilkenny,
 Co Kilkenny
 Tel 056-7721279
Jos, Yashin, Very Rev, PP
 Parochial House
 Sooey, Coola,
 Via Boyle, Co Sligo
 Tel 071-9165144
 (*Riverstown*, Elphin)

Joseph, Nelson, CC
 Achill Sound, Achill,
 Co Mayo
 Tel 098-45109
 (*Achill*, Tuam)
Joseph, Rajesh, CC
 Presbytery No. 2
 Shangan Road,
 Ballymun, Dublin 9
 (*Ballymun, St Pappin's*,
 Dublin)
Joyce, Michael (SVD)
 Donamon Castle,
 Roscommon
 Tel 090-6662222
Joyce, Peter
 c/o Diocesan Office.
 The Cathedral, Galway
 (Galway, retired)
Joyce, Stephen, Very Rev, PP
 Parochial House,
 Stracrunnion,
 Scotstown,
 Co Monaghan H18 X620
 Tel 047-89204
 (*Tydavnet*, Clogher)
Joyel John Michael,
 Rosmini House,
 Dunkereen,
 Innishannon,
 Co Cork T12 N9DH
 Tel 021-4776268/4776923
 Chaplain, Cork University
 Hospital,
 Tel 021-4546400
 (Cork & R.)
Judge, Francis, Very Rev, PP
 Parochial House,
 Mullenmore Road
 Crossmolina, Ballina
 Co Mayo
 Tel 096-31677
 (*Crossmolina*, Killala)
Judge, John
 Killaser,
 Swinford, Co Mayo
 (Killala, retired)
Jukes, Antony (OFM)
 Franciscan Friary
 Killarney, Co Kerry
 Tel 064-6631334/6631066

K

Kakkadampallil, Vincent
 Xavier (OSCam)
 Chaplain, Mater Hospital,
 Eccles Street, Dublin 7
 Tel 01-8301122
 (Dublin)
Kakkarakunel, John Philip
 Chaplain, Waterford
 University Hospital,
 Dunmore Road,
 Co Waterford
 Tel 051-848000
 (Waterford & L.)

Kalema, Godfrey
 Team Assistant, Holy
 Redeemer Parish,
 Herbert Road, Bray,
 Co Dublin
 Tel 01-2868413
 (*Bray, Holy Redeemer*,
 Dublin)
Kamau, Bosco (SPS)
 Councillor, St Patrick's
 Kiltegan, Co Wicklow
 Tel 059-6473600
Kane, Gerry, Very Rev, PP
 52 Booterstown Avenue,
 Blackrock, Co Dublin
 Tel 01-2882162
 (*Booterstown*, Dublin)
Kane, Michael (CSSp)
 Holy Spirit Missionary
 College
 Kimmage Manor,
 Whitehall Road,
 Dublin D12 P5YP
 Tel 01-4064300
Kardas, Stanislaw, Rev, CC
 Chaplain to the Polish
 Community
 St Mary's,
 Temple Street, Sligo,
 Tel 071-9162670
 (*Sligo, St Anne's*, Elphin)
Kavanagh, Bobby (SPS)
 St Patrick's, Kiltegan,
 Co Wicklow W91 Y022
 Tel 059-6473600
Kavanagh, Brian, Very Rev,
 CC
 St Patricks College,
 Maynooth, Co Kildare
 Tel 045-890559
 (*Allen*, Kildare & L.)
Kavanagh, Eamon (CSsR), CC
 St Joseph's,
 St Alphonsus Road,
 Dundalk, Co Louth
 Tel 042-9334042
 (*Dundalk*, Armagh)
Kavanagh, Edward, Very
 Rev, PE
 Rath, Emo, Co Laois
 (Kildare & L., retired)
Kavanagh, Hugh, Very Rev,
 Co-PP
 The Prebytery, Neilstown
 Clondalkin, Dublin 22,
 Tel 01-6263920
 (*Neilstown, Rowlagh and
 Quarryvale*, Dublin)
Kavanagh, Joseph (OP)
 St Dominic's Retreat
 House,
 Montenotte, Co Cork
 Tel 021-4502520
Kavanagh, Joseph, Very Rev,
 PP
 Camolin, Co Wexford
 Tel 053-9383136
 (*Camolin*, Ferns)

Kavanagh, Martin (SMA)
 Provincial Secretary,
 African Missions,
 Blackrock Road,
 Cork T12 TD54
 Tel 021-4292871
Kavanagh, Myles (CP), CC
 Holy Cross Retreat,
 432 Crumlin Road,
 Ardoyne, Belfast BT14 7GE
 Tel 028-90748231/2
 (*Holy Cross*, Down & C.)
Kaweesi, Charles (OCSO), Rt
 Rev Dom
 Sub-Prior, Our Lady of
 Bethlehem Abbey,
 11 Ballymena Road,
 Portglenone, Ballymena,
 Co Antrim BT44 8BL
 Tel 028-25821211
Kealy, Brendan, Very Rev,
 Adm
 Parochial House,
 46 North William Street,
 Dublin1
 Tel 01-8556474
 (*North William Street*,
 Dublin)
Kealy, John (OFM)
 Franciscan Abbey,
 Multyfarnham,
 Co Westmeath
 Tel 044-9371114/9371137
Keane, Anthony (OSB)
 Glenstal Abbey, Murroe,
 Co Limerick
 Tel 061-621000
Keane, Brendan (CSsR)
 Clonard Monastery,
 1 Clonard Gardens,
 Belfast, BT13 2RL
 Tel 028-90445950
Keane, Jerry, Very Rev, PP
 Eyeries, Co Cork
 Tel 027-74008
 Moderator, Allihies Parish,
 Tel 027-73012
 (*Eyeries*, Kerry)
Keane, John, CC
 53 Ros Álainn,
 Gurteenroe,
 Macroom, Co Cork
 Tel 089-7078770
 (*Macroom*, Cloyne)
Keane, John D., Very Rev
 Chaplain's Office,
 Galway Clinic,
 Doughiska, Galway
 Tel 091-785000
 Chaplain's Office,
 Merlin Park University
 Hospital, Galway
 (Galway)
Keane, Martin
 No. 3 St Mary's College
 House,
 Shantalla Road, Galway
 (Galway, retired)

Keane, Martin (CSSp)
  Holy Spirit Missionary College
  Kimmage Manor,
  Whitehall Road,
  Dublin D12 P5YP
  Tel 01-4064300
Keane, Richard,
  Cratloe, Co Clare
  Tel 087-9552729
  (Pastoral Unit 5, Limerick)
Keane, Tom (MHM)
  St Joseph's House,
  50 Orwell Park,
  Rathgar, Dublin D06 C535
  Tel 01-4127700
Keaney, Charles, PP
  34 Moneysharvin Road,
  Swatragh, Maghera,
  Co Derry BT46 5PY
  Tel 028-79401236
  (Swatragh, Derry)
Kearney, Francis, Very Rev Canon
  Cabra, Hilltown, Co Down
  (Dromore, retired)
Kearney, John, Very Rev Canon
  Warrenpoint, Co Down
  (Dromore, retired)
Kearney, Patrick, Very Rev, PP
  Parochial House, Kilskyre,
  Kells, Co Meath
  Tel 046-9243623
  (Kilskyre, Meath)
Kearney, Thomas (SMA),
  SMA House, Wilton,
  Cork T12 KR23
  Tel 021-4541069/4541884
Kearney, Thomas (SVD)
  Donamon Castle,
  Roscommon
  Tel 090-6662222
Kearney, Thomas, PC
  137 Shantalla Road,
  Whitehall, Dublin 9
  Tel 01-8420260
  (Larkhill-Whitehall-Santry, Dublin)
Kearney, Tom (SVD)
  St Mary-on-the-Quay Presbytrey,
  20 Colston Street,
  Bristol BS1 5AE
  Tel 0117-9264702
Kearns, Brendan, PP
  Parochial House,
  Great George's Street,
  Warrenpoint,
  Co Down, BT34 3NF
  Tel 028-41754684
  (St Peter's (Warrenpoint),
  St Mary's (Burren),
  Dromore)
Kearns, Gerard
  Cavan General Hospital
  Tel 049-4361399
  (Kilmore)
Kearns, John (SPS)
  On temporary diocesan work
Kearns, John, CC
  Loughside Road, Garrison,
  Enniskillen
  Co Fermanagh BT93 4AE
  Tel 028-68658238
  (Belleek-Garrison (Inis Muighe Samh), Clogher)
Kearney, Nicholas (OSA)
  St John's Priory,
  Thomas Street, Dublin 8
  Tel 01-6770393/0415/0601
Keating, Andy (SPS)
  St Patrick's, Kiltegan,
  Co Wicklow
  Tel 059-6473600
Keating, David
  Chaplain, Waterford Institute of Technology,
  10 Claremont, Cork Road,
  Waterford
  Tel 051-378878
  (Waterford & L.)
Keating, John,
  Raheenagh, Ballagh,
  Co Limerick
  Tel 069-85014/087-6322212
  (Pastoral Unit 16, Limerick)
Keating, John (OCarm)
  Terenure College,
  Terenure,
  Dublin D6W DK72
  Tel 01-4904621
Keating, Patrick, Very Rev, PP
  Drimoleague
  (Cork & R., retired)
Keaveny, Michael, PEm
  53 Brisland Road,
  Eglinton,
  Co Derry BT47 3EA
  Tel 028-71810234
  (Derry, retired)
Keegan, John F., Very Rev, Co-PP
  Rolestown, Swords,
  Co Dublin
  Tel 01-8401514
  (Rolestown-Oldtown, Dublin)
Keenan, Aidan, Very Rev, PP
  The Presbytery,
  Bell Steel Road,
  Poleglass
  Belfast BT17 0PB
  Tel 028-90625739
  (Portglenone, Down & C.)
Keenan, Brian (SM)
  CUS Community,
  89 Lower Leeson Street,
  Dublin 2
  Tel 01-6762586
Keenan, Kevin, Very Rev, PP
  Church of the Sacred Heart,
  Seamus Quirke Road,
  Galway
  Tel 091-524751
  (Sacred Heart Church, Galway)
Keenan, Pádraig, Very Rev, PP
  Parochial House,
  Chapel Road,
  Haggardstown,
  Dundalk,
  Co Louth A91 XOPR
  Tel 042-9321621
  (Haggardstown and Blackrock, Armagh)
Keenan, Patrick (OCD)
  St Teresa's,
  Clarendon Street, Dublin 2
  Tel 01-6718466/6718127
Keeney, Sean (CSsR)
  Clonard Monastery,
  1 Clonard Gardens,
  Belfast, BT13 2RL
  Tel 028-90445950
Kehoe, James, Very Rev, PP
  Carrig-on-Bannow,
  Wellington Bridge,
  Co Wexford
  Tel 051-561192
  (Bannow, Ferns)
Kehoe, Liam (CSsp)
  Blackrock College,
  Blackrock, Co Dublin
  Tel 01-2888681
Kehoe, Noel (CSsR) PP
  Superior, St Joseph's,
  Alphonsus Road, Dundalk,
  Co Louth A71 F3FC
  Tel 042-9334042
  (Dundalk, St Joseph's, Armagh)
Kehoe, Peter, (OCarm)
  Terenure College,
  Terenure,
  Dublin D6W DK72
  Tel 01-4904621
Kehoe, Philip (FDP)
  25 Lower Teddington Road,
  Kingston-on-Thames,
  Surrey
  Tel 208-9775130
Kehoe, Tomás, CC
  Ballycanew, Gorey,
  Co Wexford
  Tel 053-9427184
  (Camolin, Ferns)
Kelleher, Anthony, CC
  Priest's House,
  Kilcornan, Co Limerick
  Tel 0862666822
  (Limerick)
Kelleher, Denis, Very Rev Canon, PE
  Inegrega,
  Middleton, Co Cork
  (Cloyne, retired)
Kelleher, Eamonn, Very Rev PP
  Kildorrery, Co Cork
  Tel 022-40703
  (Kildorrery, Cloyne)
Kelleher, Francis, Very Rev, PP
  The Drumlins, Virginia,
  Co Cavan
  (Kilmore, retired)
Kelleher, James (SPS)
  Kiltegan House,
  11 Douglas Road, Cork
  Tel 021-4969371
Kelleher, Liam, Very Rev, PE
  Cobh, Co Cork
  Tel 087-8516984
  (Cloyne, retired)
Kelleher, Maurice (SMA)
  SMA House, Wilton,
  Cork, T12 KR23
  Tel 021-4541069/4541884
Kelleher, Michael, Very Rev, Adm
  2 The Presbytery,
  Skibbereen, Co Cork
  Tel 028-22878/22877
  (St Patrick's Cathedral, Skibbereen, Rath and the Islands, Cork & R.)
Kelleher, Michael G. (CSsR)
  Mount Saint Alphonsus,
  South Circular Road,
  Limerick
  Tel 061-315099
Kelleher, Roger
  (Kerry, retired)
Kelleher, Thomas, Very Rev Canon, PE
  The Presbytery, Kinsale,
  Co Cork
  (Cork & R., retired)
Kelliher, Padraig, CC
  St Mary's, Athlone,
  Co Westmeath
  Tel 090-6472088
  (Athlone, Ardagh & Cl.)
Kelly, Anthony (SMA)
  Provincial Councillor,
  African Missions,
  Provincial House, Feltrim,
  Blackrock Road,
  Cork T12 N6C8
  Tel 021-4292871
Kelly, Alphonsus Rev (SMA)
  SMA House Cloonbigeen,
  Claregalway,
  Co Galway H91 YK64
  Tel 091-798880
Kelly, Brendan (CSsR), Adm
  Via Merulana 31, CP 2458,
  00185 Roma-PT158, Italy
  Tel 0039-06-494901
Kelly, Brendan, Most Rev, DD
  Bishop of Galway,
  Mount Saint Mary's,
  Taylor's Hill, Galway
  Tel 091-563566
  (Galway)

LIST OF CLERGY IN IRELAND

Kelly, Celsus (OCSO), Rt Rev Dom
Abbot and Superior, Our Lady of Bethlehem Abbey,
11 Ballymena Road,
Portglenone, Ballymena,
Co Antrim BT44 8BL
Tel 028-25821211

Kelly, Conor, Very Rev, Adm
1 The Orchard,
Dungarvan,
Co Waterford
Tel 058-64284
(*Aglish*, Waterford & L.)

Kelly, David (OSA)
St Augustine's Priory,
O'Connell Street,
Limerick

Kelly, Declan, CC
2 Orchard Court,
Dunboyne, Co Meath
(*Dunboyne*, Meath)

Kelly, Declan, Very Rev, PP
Parochial House,
Batterstown,
Dunboyne, Co Westmeath
Tel 01-8259267
Adm, Moynalvey
(*Kilcloon, Stamullen*, Meath)

Kelly, Denis, Very Rev, PP
Ballymore, Screen,
Enniscorthy, Co Wexford
Tel 053-9137140
(*Castlebridge and Curracloe*, Ferns)

Kelly, Dermot (OCarm)
Director of Vocations,
Gort Muire Centre,
Ballinteer, Dublin 16
Tel 01-2984014

Kelly, Desmond (OCarm)
Whitefriar Street Church,
56 Aungier Street,
Dublin 2 D02 R598
Tel 01-4758821

Kelly, Desmond, Very Rev, PP
Corballa, Ballina,
Co Mayo
Tel 096-36266
(*Castleconnor*, Killala)

Kelly, Eamonn, PP, VF
Raphoe, Convoy,
Co Donegal
Tel 087-9077985
(*Raphoe*, Raphoe)

Kelly, Enda, (SPS)
Kiltegan House Leader,
St Patrick's, Kiltegan,
Co Wicklow
Tel 059-6473600

Kelly, Fergus, Very Rev (CM)
Sacred Heart Presbytery
2 Flower Lane, Mill Hill,
London NW7 2JB
Tel 0044-2089591021

Kelly, Gabriel, Very Rev
Chaplain,
Cavan General Hospital,
Lisdaran, Co Cavan
Tel 049-4361399
(Kilmore)

Kelly, James, PP
Goresbridge, Co Kilkenny
Tel 059-9775180
(*Paulstown*, Kildare & L.)

Kelly, Jimmy (OSM)
Chaplain, Cloverhill Prison,
Clondalking, Dublin 24
c/o Prior, Servite Priory,
St Peregrine,
36 Grangewood Estate,
Rathfarnham, Dublin 16
Tel 01-4517115

Kelly, Jimmy, Very Rev, PP
Raheen, Abbeyleix,
Co Laois
Tel 057-8731182
(*Raheen*, Kildare & L.)

Kelly, Joe, CC
5 Bayside Square East,
Sutton, Dublin 13
Tel 01-8322305
(*Bayside*, Dublin)

Kelly, John
Director of Pastoral Care,
Tallaght Hospital,
22 Nugent Road,
Churchtown, Dublin 14
Tel 01-4142482
(Dublin)

Kelly, John (SAC)
Bursar/Secretary for Missions,
Provincial House,
'Homestead',
Sandyford Road,
Dundrum, Dublin 16
Tel 01-2956180/2954170

Kelly, John (SCJ)
Provincial,
Sacred Heart Fathers,
Fairfield, 66 Inchicore Road, Dublin 8
Tel 01-4538655

Kelly, Larry, Rev Canon,
Modereator,
Cahirciveen, Co Kerry
Tel 066-9472210
Valentia Island, Co Kerry
Tel 066-9476104
(*Cahirciveen, Valentia Island*, Kerry)

Kelly, Laurence (OP)
Newbridge College,
Droichead Nua, Co Kildare
Tel 045-487200

Kelly, Liam (OFM)
The Abbey,
8 Francis Street,
Galway H91 C53K
Tel 091-562518

Kelly, Liam, Rt Rev Mgr, PP
Diocesan Administrator,
Parochial House,
Bunnoe, Cootehill,
Co Cavan
Tel 049-5553035
(*Kilsherdany and Drung*, Kilmore)

Kelly, Liam (SPS)
St Patrick's, Kiltegan,
Co Wicklow W91 Y022

Kelly, Martin Rev (CSSp)
Provincial, Holy Spirit Provincialate,
Temple Park,
Richmond Avenue South,
Dublin 6
Tel 01-4977230

Kelly, Martin, Very Rev
93 Ballyenaghan Park,
Belfast BT8 6WR
(Down & C., retired)

Kelly, Matthew, Very Rev, PE, CC
60 Hartwell Green, Kill,
Naas, Co Kildare
Tel 045-877880
(*Kill*, Kildare & L.)

Kelly, Maurice (SPS)
St Patrick's, Kiltegan,
Co Wicklow
Tel 059-6473600

Kelly, Michael
Crumlin, Dublin 12
Tel 01-4542308
(Dublin)

Kelly, Michael (SPS)
St Patrick's, Kiltegan,
Co Wicklow
Tel 059-6473600

Kelly, Michael (SPS)
St Patrick's, Kiltegan,
Co Wicklow
Tel 059-6473600

Kelly, Oliver, Very Rev, PP, VF
West Barrs, Glenfarne,
Co Leitrim
Tel 071-9855134
(*Glenfarne*, Kilmore)

Kelly, Paddy (CSSR)
Dún Mhuire,
461/463 Griffith Avenue,
Dublin D09 X651
Tel 01-5180196

Kelly, Paraic (SMA)
SMA House, Cloonbigeen,
Claregalway,
Co Galway H91 YK64
Tel 091-798880

Kelly Jnr, Patrick (CSsR)
Dún Mhuire
461/463 Griffith Avenue,
Dublin D09 X651
Tel 01-5180196

Kelly Snr, Patrick (CSsR)
St Joseph's, Dundalk,
Co Louth

Kelly, Patrick (MSC)
'Croí Nua', Rosary Lane,
Taylor's Hill,
Co Galway
Tel 091-520960

Kelly, Patrick
(Limerick, retired)

Kelly, Patrick James (CSSp)
Holy Spirit Missionary College
Kimmage Manor,
Whitehall Road,
Dublin D12 P5YP
Tel 01-4064300

Kelly, Paul, Very Rev, CC
The Presbytery,
18 Straffan Way,
Maynooth, Co Kildare
Tel 087-2463876
(*Maynooth*, Dublin)

Kelly, Ray, Very Rev, PP
Parochial House,
Oldcastle, Co Meath
Tel 049-8541142
(*Oldcastle*, Meath)

Kelly, Richard (OFM)
Adam & Eve's,
4 Merchants' Quay
Dublin, D08 XY19
Tel 01-6771128

Kelly, Richard, Very Rev, PP
Kilbehenny, Mitchelstown,
Co Cork
Tel 025-24040
(*Kilbehenny*, Cashel & E.)

Kelly, Robert (OCarm)
Gort Muire, Ballinteer,
Dublin D16 EI67
Tel 01-2984014

Kelly, Seamus, PP
19 Chapel Road,
Dungiven,
Co Derry BT47 4RT
Tel 028-77741219
(*Dungiven*, Derry)

Kelly, Seamus (MSC)
Western Road,
Cork T12 TN80
Tel 021-4804120

Kelly, Seán (OFMCap)
Provincial Minister,
Provincial Office,
12 Halston Street,
Dublin D07 Y2T5
Tel 01-8733205

Kelly, Seán, Very Rev, PE, CC
Stradbally, Co Laois
Tel 057-8625831
(*Stradbally*, Kildare & L.)

Kelly, Stephen
Apostolic Nunciature
Burundi
(Meath)

Kelly, Vincent (SAC)
(attached to Pallottine College, Thurles)
18 Silvercourt,
Silversprings, Cork

Kemmy, Bill, PP
Diocesan Communications,
c/o Bishops House, Carlow
Tel 087-2308053
Rathangan, Co Kildare
Tel 045-524316
(*Rathangan*, Kildare & L.)

Kemmy, Philip, CC
Parochial House,
Letterkenny,
Co Donegal
Tel 074-9121021
(*Letterkenny (Conwal and Leck)*, Raphoe)

Kenneally, Cornelius (CSsR)
Mount St Alphonsus,
South Circular Road,
Limerick
Tel 061-315099

Kenneally, Daithí (CSSp)
Kimmage Manor,
Whitehall Road, Dublin 12
Tel 01-4064300

Kennedy, Bernard, MA, MSc, Adm
Parochial House,
Enniskerry, Co Wicklow
Tel 01-2863506
(*Enniskerry/Kilmacnogue (Bray Grouping)*, Dublin)

Kennedy, Colm Rev (SDB)
Salesian House,
45 St Teresa's Road,
Crumlin,
Dublin D12 XK52

Kennedy, David, Very Rev
Clonlusk Doon,
Co Limerick
(*Limerick, retired*)

Kennedy, Denis, (CSSp)
c/o St Joseph's Pastoral Centre,
Glasthule, Co Dublin
Blackrock College,
Blackrock, Co Dublin
Tel 01-2888681
(*Glasthule*, Dublin)

Kennedy, Hugh, Very Rev
More House,
53 Cromwell Road,
London SW7 2EH
(Down & C.)

Kennedy, James, Very Rev, PP
Anacarty,
Co Tipperary
Tel 062-71104
(*Anacarty*, Cashel & E.)

Kennedy, Joseph, Very Rev, AP
Parochial House,
Moneygall, Birr, Co Offaly
Tel 0505-45110/
086-4072488
(*Ollatrim Pastoral Area*, Killaloe)

Kennedy, John
Parochial House,
Rathmolyon, Co Meath
Tel 046-9555212
(*Enfield*, Meath)

Kennedy, John, Rt Rev Mgr
(Congregation for the Doctrine of the Faith)
Via del Mascherino 12,
00193 Roma, Italy
(Dublin)

Kennedy, Joseph (CP), PC
St Paul's Retreat,
Mount Argus, Dublin 6W
Tel 01-4992000
(*Mount Argus*, Dublin)

Kennedy, Joseph, Very Rev
Glenfield Road,
Kilmallock, Co Limerick
(*Limerick, retired*)

Kennedy, Kieron, Rt Rev Mgr, PP
Freshford,
Co Kilkenny R95 X2EO
Tel 056-8832426/
087-2523521
(*Freshford*, Ossory)

Kennedy, Michael (CSSp)
Chaplain, NRH,
Rochestown Avenue,
Dun Laoghaire, Co Dublin
Tel 01-2355272

Kennedy, Michael, Very Rev
Ballylaneen,
Kilmacthomas,
Co Waterford
(Waterford & L.)

Kennedy, Michael, Very Rev, PP
Lusmagh, Banagher,
Co Offaly R42 WP40
Tel 0509-51358
(*Lusmagh*, Clonfert)

Kennedy, Michael, Very Rev, PP
Lattin, Co Tipperary
Tel 087-4147229
(*Lattin and Cullen*, Cashel & E.)

Kennedy, Michael, Very Rev, PE
Parochial House, Colligan,
Dungarvan, Co Waterford
Tel 058-41629
(*Kilgobinet*, Waterford & L.)

Kennedy, Noel, Very Rev, PP
Bournea, Roscrea,
Co Tipperary
Tel 0505-43211/
086-3576775
(*Cronan Pastoral Area*, Killaloe)

Kennedy, Stephen
The Presbytery, Ballsgrove,
Drogheda, Co Louth
Tel 041-9831991
(*Drogheda, Holy Family*, Meath)

Kennedy, Thomas, Very Rev, Co-PP
14 Roselawn, Lucan,
Co Dublin
Tel 01-6280205
(*Lucan*, Dublin)

Kennelly, Daithí (CSSp)
Holy Spirit Missionary College
Kimmage Manor,
Whitehall Road,
Dublin D12 P5YP
Tel 01-4064300

Kennelly, Pádraig, PP
Firies, Killarney, Co Kerry
Tel 066-9764122
(*Firies*, Kerry)

Kennelly, Séamus, Very Rev, PP
Boherbue, Mallow,
Co Cork
Tel 029-76151
(*Boherbue/Kiskeam*, Kerry)

Kenny, Donald, Rt Rev Mgr
Cois Cuan, Arthurstown,
New Ross, Co Wexford
(Ferns, retired)

Kenny, Gerard, Co-PP, VF
Circular Road, Kilkee,
Co Clare
Tel 065-9056580
(*Cois Fharraige Pastoral Area*, Killaloe)

Kenny, Gerard (OMI)
Oblate House of Retreat,
Inchicore, Dublin 8
Tel 01-4534408/4541805

Kenny, John, Very Rev, PP, VF
Partry, Claremorris,
Co Mayo
Tel 094-9543013
(*Partry (Ballyovey)*, Tuam)

Kenny, Lorcan
Curates House,
Convent Hill,
Roscrea, Co Tipperary
Tel 0505-21454
Chaplain, The Valley,
Roscrea, Co Tipperary
Tel 0505-23637/
087-6553402
(*Cronan Pastoral Area (Roscrea)*, Killaloe)

Kenny, Merlyn, PP
Newtowncashel,
Co Longford
Tel 043-3325112
(*Newtowncashel (Cashel)*, Ardagh & Cl.)

Kenny, Pat, Very Rev, PP
St Killian Church, Newinn,
Ballinasloe,
Co Galway H53 P6C0
Tel 090-9675819
(*New Inn and Bullaun*, Clonfert)

Kenny, Paul, PP
(Moderator)
149 Swords Road,
Whitehall, Dublin 9
Tel 01-8375274
(*Larkhill-Whitehall-Santry*, Dublin)

Kenny, Paul (SSC)
St Columban's Retirement Home,
Dalgan Park, Navan,
Co Meath
Tel 046-9021525

Keogan, Thomas M., Adm
7 Quary Park,
Mullaghmore, Co Sligo
(Kilmore, retired)

Keogh, Martin, Very Rev, PP
Parochial House,
Newtown,
Kilmacthomas,
Co Waterford
Tel 051-294261
(*Newtown*, Waterford & L.)

Keohane, Martin, Very Rev Canon, PP
Parish House,
Carraig na bhFear,
Co Cork
Tel 021-4884119
(*Carraig na bhFear*, Cork & R.)

Keohane, Michael, Very Rev, AP
Diocesan Secretary,
1 The Presbytery,
Blackrock,
Tel 021-4301717
(*Blackrock*, Cork & R.)

Kerin, John, Very Rev, PP
St Joseph's, Lauragh,
Killarney, Co Kerry
Tel 064-6683107
(*Tuosist*, Kerry)

Kerr, Aidan, Very Rev, PE
142 Carnmoney Road,
Newtownabbey,
Co Antrim BT36 6JU
Tel 028-90832488
(*St Mary's on the Hill*, Down & C.)

Kerr, Peter, Very Rev, PE, AP
42 Innishatieve Road,
Carrickmore, Omagh,
Co Tyrone BT79 9HS
Tel 028-80761837
(Armagh, retired)

Kett, Patrick J., Very Rev
27 Huntsgrove,
Ashbourne, Co Meath
(Dublin, retired)

Keveny, Martin, Very Rev
Paroquia Sao Sebastiao,
Caixa Postal 94,
CEP 77760-000,
Colinas Do Tocantins,
Brazil
Tel 63-8311427
(Killala)

LIST OF CLERGY IN IRELAND

Kevin, John (CSSp)
Blackrock College,
Blackrock, Co Dublin
Tel 01-2888681

Kibiriti, Emilian (IC)
Mission Secretary,
Clonturk House,
Ormond Road,
Drumcondra,
Dublin D09 F821
Tel 01-6877014

Kidney, Michael (SMA)
African Missions,
Blackrock Road,
Cork T12 TD54
Tel 021-4292871

Kiely, Charles, Dr, PP
The Presbytery,
Our Lady Crowned,
Upper Mayfield, Cork
Tel 021-4503116
(Upper Mayfield, Cork & R.)

Kiely, Eugene, Very Rev, PP
Ballyferriter West,
Tralee, Co Kerry
Tel 066-9156131
(Ballyferriter, Kerry)

Kiely, John, Very Rev, PE
'The Cottage',
Ballinaparka,
Aglish, Co Waterford
(Waterford & L., retired)

Kieran, Aidan, Adm, VF
Parochial House
Castledermot, Co Kildare
Tel 059-9144164
(Castledermot, Dublin)

Kiernan, Brian (OCarm)
Gort Muire, Ballinteer,
Dublin 16
Tel 01-2984014

Kiernan, Kevin (OFMCap)
Vicar, Capuchin Friary,
Church Street,
Dublin D07 HA22
Tel 01-8730599

Kiernan, Patrick, PP
Banagher, Co Offaly
Tel 057-9151338
(Cloghan and Banagher (Gallen and Reynagh), Ardagh & Cl.)

Kilcoyne, Brendan, Very Rev Canon, PP, VF
The Parochial House,
St Mary's Presbytery,
Athenry,
Co Galway H65 VX67
Tel 091-844076
(Athenry, Tuam)

Kildarathil, Anthony, CC
Knocktemple, Virginia,
Co Cavan
Tel 049-8547435
(Castlerahan & Munterconnaught, Kilmore)

Kilduff, Donal, Very Rev, PP
Crosskeys, Co Cavan
Tel 049-4336102
(Denn, Kilmore)

Kilkelly, Christopher
c/o Archbishop's House,
Tuam, Co Galway
(Tuam, retired)

Kilkenny, Michael (CSSP), Very Rev, Moderator
66 Rockfield Avenue,
Dublin 12
Tel 01-4558316
Community Leader,
Spiritan House,
213 North Circular Road
Dublin 7
(Greenhills, Kimmage Manor, Dublin)

Killeen, Jim, Rt Rev Mgr, PP, VG
Midleton, Co Cork
Tel 021-4631750
(Midleton, Cloyne)

Killeen, John, Very Rev, Canon, CC
20 Abbey Court,
Abbey Road, Monkstown
Co Dublin
Tel 01-2802533
(Kill-O'-The-Grange, Dublin)

Killeen, Seán, Rt Rev Mgr, VG
Cloghans, Ballina,
Co Mayo
(Killala, retired)

Killenga, Malasi S. (AOR)
John Sullivan House of Formation,
27 Leinster Road,
Rathmines, Dublin 6
Tel 01-5242134

Kilmartin, Michael, Very Rev, PP
54 Brookville, Ashbourne,
Co Meath
Tel 01-8353149
(Ashbourne-Donaghmore, Meath)

Kilmurray, Martin (OCarm)
Terenure College,
Terenure,
Dublin D6W DK72
Tel 01-4904621

Kilpatrick, Edward, PE
(Derry, retired)

Kilroy, Peter
64 Cherbury Court,
Booterstown, Co Dublin
(Dublin, retired)

Kinahan, Gabriel (OFM)
Guardian,
Franciscan Friary,
Friary Lane, Athlone,
Co Westmeath
Tel 090-6472095

King, Anthony, Very Rev Canon, PE
Parklands, New Road,
Westport,
Co Mayo F28 K236
(Tuam, retired)

King, Bernard (SM), CC
Marist Fathers,
St Mary's Road,
Dundalk, Co Louth
Tel 0429334019

King, Finnian (OSB)
Silverstream Priory,
Stamullen,
Co Meath K32 T189
Tel 01-8417142

King, Michael
c/o Diocesan Office,
The Cathedral, Galway
(Galway)

King, Michael, Very Rev, PE
21 Wattlebridge Road,
Drumquilla,
Newtownbutler,
Co Fermanagh BT92 8JP
Tel 028-67738229
(Newtownbutler (Galloon), Clogher)

King, William, Very Rev
156b Rathgar Road,
Dublin 6
(Dublin, retired)

Kingston, John, Very Rev Canon, PP
The Presbytery, Bandon,
Co Cork
Tel 023-8854666
(Bandon, Cork & R.)

Kingston, William (CSSp)
Rockwell College,
Cashel, Co Tipperary
Tel 062-61444

Kirby, John, Most Rev, DD, PP
Retired Bishop of Clonfert,
Cappatagle, Balinasloe,
Co Galway, H53 X206
Tel 091-843017
(Cappataggle and Killrickle (Killalaghtan and Kilickle), Clonfert)

Kirby, Dom Mark Daniel (OSB), Very Rev
Silverstream Priory,
Stamullen,
Co Meath K32 T189
Tel 01-8417142

Kirwan, Michael Rev (SJ)
Vice Superior,
35 Lower Leeson Street,
Dublin 2
Tel 01-6761248

Kirwan, Noel, Very Rev, (Moderator)
Cathedral House,
Cathedral Place, Limerick
Tel 061-414624/
087-2616843
(Pastoral Unit 1, Limerick)

Kirwin, Jeremiah M (CSSp)
Bursar, Rockwell College,
Cashel, Co Tipperary
Tel 062-61444

Kitching, Ciaran, Very Rev, PP
St Joseph's,
Killimor, Ballinasloe,
Co Galway H53 R8C4
Tel 090-9676151
(Killimor & Tiranascragh, Clonfert)

Kivlehan, Paul, Very Rev, Adm
The Presbytery,
Ballaghdereen,
Co Roscommon
Tel 094-9860011
(Ballaghaderreen (Castlemore and Kilcolman), Achonry)

Knight, Matthew J. (CSSp)
Rockwell College,
Cashel, Co Tipperary
Tel 062-61444

Kochatt, Alex CC
77 The Lakelands,
Naas, Co Kildare
Tel 045-949576
(Naas, Kildare & L.)

Kochuveettil, Francis Xavier, CC
The Presbytery, Shannon,
Co Clare
Tel 089-4494090
(Tradaree Pastoral Area, Killaloe)

Kokkandathil, Jilson, CC
South Presbytery,
Dunbar Street, Cork
Tel 085-1471147
(St Finbarr's South, St Patrick's, Cork & R.)

Kornitsky, Vasil
Chaplain to Ukranian Community,
3 Maypark,
Malahide Road, Dublin 5
Tel 01-5164752
(Donnycarney, Dublin)

Kosciolek, Krzysztof (SC), CC
84 Milltown Street,
Burren, Warrenpoint,
Co Down BT34 3PU
Tel 028-41772200
(St Peter's (Warrenpoint), St Mary's (Burren), Dromore)

Kottackal Varkey, Paul (SSP)
Society of Saint Paul,
Moyglare Road,
Maynooth Co Kildare
Tel 01-6285933

Kowalkowski, Marek
Ministry to Polish Community,
The Presbytery
Kill, Co Waterford
(Waterford & L.)

Kowalski, Wojciech (SJ)
  Jesuit Community,
  27 Leinster Road,
  Rathmines, Dublin 6
  Tel 01-4970250
Krawiec, Jaroslaw (OP)
  St Saviour's,
  Upper Dorset Street,
  Dublin 1
  Tel 01-8897610
Krzystof, Krzysków (SVD)
  8 Teignmouth Road,
  London, NW2 4HN
  Tel 020-84528430
Kupczakiewicz, Krzysztof (OP)
  St Saviour's, Bridge Street,
  Waterford
  Tel 051-875061
Kuthanapillil, Jaison (OCarm)
  Prior, Bursar,
  Carmelite Priory, Moate,
  Co Westmeath N37 AW34
  Tel 090-6481160/6481398
Kuttikkatt, Christanand Varghese (IC)
  Clonturk House,
  Ormond Road,
  Drumcondra,
  Dublin D09 F821
  Tel 01-6877014
Kwasniewski, Isaias (OSB)
  Silverstream Priory,
  Stamullen,
  Co Meath K32 T189
  Tel 01-8417142
Kwikirza, Dominic, CC
  Presbytery 1,
  Montrose Park,
  Beaumont, Dublin 5
  Tel 01-8477740
  (*Beaumont*, Dublin)
Kyne, Brendan, Very Rev, Co-PP
  The Prebytery,
  Ballycoricick, Co Clare
  (*Radharc na nOileán Pastoral Area*, Killaloe)
Kyte, Gabriel Joseph (CFR)
  St Patrick Friary,
  64 Delmege Park,
  Moyross,
  Limerick V94 859Y
  Tel 061-458071

L

Lacey, Liam, Very Rev, PP
  No. 1 Prebytery,
  Castle Street, Dalkey,
  Co Dublin
  Tel 01-2857773
  (*Dalkey*, Dublin)
Laffan, Sean, Very Rev, CC
  Gusserane, Co Wexford
  Tel 051-562111
  (*Ballycullane*, Ferns)

Lafferty, Angelo (SMA)
  African Missions,
  Blackrock Road,
  Cork T12 TD54
  Tel 021-4292871
Lagan, Hugh (SMA)
  African Missions,
  Dromantine, Newry,
  Co Down BT34 1RH
  Tel 028-30821224
Lagan, Patrick, CC
  Parochial House,
  St Eugene's Cathedral,
  Derry BT48 9AP
  Tel 028-71262894/71365712
  (*Cathedral, St Eugene's*, Derry)
Laizer, John (CSSp)
  Holy Spirit Missionary College
  Kimmage Manor,
  Whitehall Road,
  Dublin D12 P5YP
  Tel 01-4064300
Lally, Fredrick (OCarm)
  Gort Muire, Ballinteer,
  Dublin 16 D16 EI67
  Tel 01-2984014
Lalor, Eddie (SPS)
  St Patrick's, Kiltegan,
  Co Wicklow W91 YO22
  Tel 0596473600
Lalor, John (SPS)
  St Patrick's, Kiltegan,
  Co Wicklow
  Tel 059-6473600
Lalor, Thomas, Very Rev, PE
  The Presbytery,
  Tinryland, Co Carlow
  Tel 087-2360355
  (*Kildare & L.*, retired)
Lambe, Anthony, Very Rev, PP
  Drangan, Thurles,
  Co Tipperary
  Tel 052-9152103
  (*Drangan*, Cashel & E.)
Lambert, Owen (CSSp)
  Holy Spirit Missionary College
  Kimmage Manor,
  Whitehall Road,
  Dublin D12 P5YP
  Tel 01-4064300
Lane, Daniel, AP
  1 Cedarville,
  Abbeyfeale, Co Limerick
  Tel 087-2533030
  (*Pastoral Unit 14*, Limerick)
Lane, Dermot A., Rt Rev Mgr, PC
  162 Sandyford Road,
  Dublin 16
  Tel 01-2956165
  (*Balally*, Dublin)

Lane, Michael, Venerable Archdeacon, PE,
  2 Meadowvale, Raheen,
  Limerick
  Tel 061-228761/087-2544450
  (Limerick, retired)
Lane, Thomas, CC
  2 Bellevue Circle,
  Mallow, Co Cork
  Tel 087-0660615
  (*Mallow*, Cloyne)
Langford, Gerard, Very Rev, PP
  Holy Family Presbytery,
  Luke Wadding Street,
  Waterford
  Tel 051-323213
  (*Holy Family*, Waterford & L.)
Lanigan-Ryan, Thomas, PP
  Ballina, Killaloe,
  Co Clare
  Tel 061-376178
  (*Ballina*, Cashel & E.)
Lanigan, Jerry (SVD)
  Donamon Castle,
  Roscommon
  Tel 090-6662222
Larkin, Barry, Very Rev, Adm
  1 Clonard Park,
  Clonard, Co Wexford
  Tel 053-9147686
  (*Clonard*, Ferns)
Larkin, Barry, Very Rev, PP
  Suncroft, Curragh,
  Co Kildare
  Tel 045-441586
  (*Suncroft*, Kildare & L.)
Larkin, David (SPS)
  House Leader,
  St Patrick's,
  21 Leeson Park,
  Dublin 6 D06 DE76
  Tel 01-4977897
Larkin, Francis, Very Rev Canon, AP
  7 Presentation Road,
  Co Galway
  Tel 091-449727
  (Galway, retired)
Larkin, James,
  Chaplain to Loreto Sisters, Rathfarnham/
  Chaplain to Coiste Treadach, 72 Bird Avenue, Clonskeagh, Dublin 14
  Tel 01-2196869
  (Dublin)
Larkin, Pat, Very Rev, Co-PP, VF
  47 Woodfield Crescent,
  kilrush, Co Clare
  Tel 065-9262729
  (*Inis Cathaigh Pastoral Area*, Killaloe)

Larkin, Patrick, Very Rev, PE
  Carlingford Nursing Home
  Old Dundalk Road,
  Carlingford, Co Louth
  (Armagh, retired)
Larkin, Seamus, Very Rev Canon
  (priest in residence)
  Monamolin,
  Gorey, Co Wexford
  (Ferns, retired)
Larkin, Seán, PE, AP
  Parochial House,
  9 Chapel Road,
  Bessbrook, Newry,
  Co Down BT35 7AU
  Tel 028-30830272
  (*Bessbrook (Killeavy Lower)*, Armagh)
Lavelle, Paul, Very Rev
  123 Foxfield Grove,
  Kilbarrack, Dublin 5
  (Dublin, retired)
Laverty, Austin, Very Rev Canon, PP
  Ardara, Co Donegal
  Tel 074-9541135
  (*Ardara*, Raphoe)
Laverty, Denis
  47 Silken Vale,
  Maynooth, Co Kildare
  (Dublin, retired)
Lawless, Brendan, Very Rev, PP
  Carrabane, Athenry,
  Co Galway H65 EP04
  Tel 091-841103
  (*Clostoken and Kilconieran*, Clonfert)
Lawless, Brian, Very Rev, Adm
  54 Clogher Road
  Dublin 12
  Tel 01-4536988
  (*Clogher Road*, Dublin)
Lawless, Ralph (OFM)
  Franciscan Friary,
  Friary Lane, Athlone,
  Co Westmeath
  Tel 090-6472095
Lawless, Richard, Very Rev
  c/o Bishop's House,
  Summerhill, Wexford
  (Ferns)
Lawlor, Brendan, AP
  2 Powerscourt, Tulla,
  Co Clare
  Tel 065-6835284/087-9845417
  (*Ceanntar na Lochanna Pastoral Area*, Killaloe)
Lawlor, John, Very Rev
  (Kerry, retired)
Paul Lawlor (OP), Prior
  Convent of SS Xystus and Clement
  Collegio San Clemente,
  Via Labicana 95,
  00184 Roma
  Tel 0039-06-7740021

LIST OF CLERGY IN IRELAND

Lawton, Liam, Adm
St Mary's,
Edenderry, Co Offaly
Tel 046-9732352
(*Edenderry*, Kildare & L.)

Layden, Thomas (SJ)
Superior,
Peter Faber House,
28 Brookvale Avenue,
Belfast BT14 6BW
Tel 028-90757615

Leader, Mícheál, Very Rev, PP
Ballyclough, Mallow,
Co Cork
Tel 022-27650
(*Ballyclough*, Cloyne)

Lehane, Timothy (SVD)
Provincial,
1 & 3 Pembroke Road,
Dublin 4
Tel 01-6680904

Leahy, Andy, Very Rev, PP
Episcopal Vicar for the
Pastoral Care of Priests,
The Presbytery,
Kildare Town, Kildare
Tel 045-520347
(*Kildare*, Kildare & L)

Leahy, Brendan, Most Rev, DD
Bishop of Limerick,
Limerick Diocesan Centre,
St Munchin's,
Corbally, Limerick
Tel 061-350000
(Limerick)

Leahy, Donal, Very Rev Canon, PP
Kilworth, Co Cork
Tel 025-27186
(*Kilworth*, Cloyne)

Leahy, Michael (OSA)
St Augustine's Priory,
Washington Street, Cork
Tel 021-2753982

Leahy, Niall F.X. (SJ)
Irish Jesuit Provincialate,
Milltown Park,
Sandford Road, Dublin 6
Tel 01-4987333

Leahy, Niall S. (SJ)
The Presbytery,
Upper Gardiner Street,
Dublin 1
Tel 01-8363411
(*Gardiner Street*, Dublin)

Leamy, Michael, Very Rev Canon, PP, VF
Mitchelstown, Co Cork
Tel 025-41765
(*Mitchelstown*, Cloyne)

Leane, Thomas, Very Rev, PP
Dromagh, Mallow,
Co Cork
Tel 029-78096
(*Dromtariffe*, Kerry)

Leavy, Oliver (SPS)
St Patrick's, Kiltegan,
Co Wicklow W91 Y022
Tel 059-6473600

Lebocq, Wulfran, Canon
Institute of Christ the King Sovereign Priest
12–14 The Crescent,
Limerick
(Galway)

Lee, Angelus (OFM)
Adam & Eve's,
4 Merchants' Quay
Dublin, D08 XY19
Tel 01-6771128

Lee, Theodore (OSB)
Silverstream Priory,
Stamullen,
Co Meath K32 T189
Tel 01-8417142

Lee, William, Most Rev, DD
Retired Bishop of
Waterford and Lismore,
5 The Brambles,
Ballinakill Downs,
Waterford
Tel 051-821485
(Waterford & L.)

Lenihan, Jim, Very Rev, CC
Killarney, Co Kerry
Tel 064-6631014
Chaplain,
St Brendan's College,
Killarney, Co Kerry
Tel 064-6631021
(*Killarney*, Kerry)

Lennon, Brian (SJ)
St Francis Xavier's,
Upper Gardiner Street,
Dublin 1
Tel 01-8363411
(Zam-Mal)

Lennon, Denis, Rt Rev Mgr, CC
39 Beechlawn, Clonard,
Wexford
Tel 053-9124417
(*Clonard*, Ferns)

Lennon, James, CC
(Hexham & Newcastle)
Castledockrell,
Ballycarney, Enniscorthy,
Co Wexford
Tel 053-9388569
(*Marshallstown*, Ferns)

Lennon, Patrick, PP
Dromard, Moyne,
Co Longford
Tel 049-4335248
(*Dromard*, Ardagh & Cl.)

Lennon, Patrick (OSA)
Duckspool House
(Retirement Community),
Abbeyside, Dungarvan,
Co Waterford
Tel 058-23784

Lennon, Sean (OSM)
Servite Priory,
Benburb, Dungannon,
Co Tyrone, BT71 7JZ
Tel 028-37548241

Leonard, Albert (OP), Very Rev
St Mary's Priory,
Tallaght, Dublin 24
Tel 01-4048100

Leonard, Derek, Very Rev,
St Mary's,
Athlunkard Street,
Limerick
Tel /087-6261287
(*Pastoral Unit 4*, Limerick)

Leonard, John
(Limerick, retired)

Leonard, Patrick (CSSp)
Holy Spirit Missionary College
Kimmage Manor,
Whitehall Road,
Dublin D12 P5YP
Tel 01-4064300

Levakovic, Josip, CC
(Chaplain to the Croatian Community)
The Presbytery,
Haddington Road,
Dublin 4
Tel 01-660075

Lewis, Eugene (White Fathers)
Cypress Grove,
Templeogue, Dublin 6W
Tel 01-4055263/4055264

Leycock, Dermot, Very Rev, PP
64 Newtownpark Avenue,
Blackrock, Co Dublin
Tel 01-2784860
(*Newtownpark*, Dublin)

Liddane, Raymond, Very Rev, AP
Newtown, Waterford
Tel 051-874284
(*SS Joseph and Benildus*, Waterford & L.)

Linehan, Patrick, Very Rev, PP
Cloyne, Midleton, Co Cork
Tel 021-4652597
(*Cloyne*, Cloyne)

Linehan, Terry,
Kerry General Hospital,
Tralee, Co Kerry
Tel 066-7126222
(Kerry)

Linnane, Seámus, Very Rev,
(Kerry, retired)

Liston, Mícheál, Very Rev Canon
Chaplain to
Gaelscoileanna,
21 Sullane Crescent,
Raheen Heights, Limerick
Tel 087-2314804
(Limerick, retired)

Little, Anthony G. (CSSp)
Holy Spirit Missionary College
Kimmage Manor,
Whitehall Road,
Dublin D12 P5YP
Tel 01-4064300

Little, Thomas, Very Rev, Adm, PP, VF,
Brownshill Avenue, Carlow
Tel 059-9131559
(*Askea, Tinryland*, Kildare & L.)

Littleton, John
The Priory Institute,
Tallaght Village,
Dublin 24
Tel 01-4048100
(Cashel & E.)

Littleton, Patrick
2 May Park, Donnycarney,
Dublin 5
(Dublin, retired)

Lloyd, Enda, Rt Rev Mgr, EV, Co-PP
10 The Oaks,
Loughlinstown Drive,
Dun Laoghaire
Tel 01-2826895
(*Loughlinstown, Ballybrack-Killiney*, Dublin)

Lloyd, Francis, Very Rev, PE
The Presbytery,
Dungarvan, Co Waterford
(Waterford & L., retired)

Loftus, Hughie, Very Rev, PP
Carraroe, Co Galway
Tel 091-595452
(*Carraroe (Kileen)*,
Spiddal/Knock, Tuam)

Loftus, John,
Co-Pastor
Binghamstown, Belmullet
Co Mayo
Tel 097-82350
(*Kilmore-Erris*, Killala)

Loftus, Joseph (CM)
Room RD-117,
Rathdown House,
TU Dublin, Grangegorman
Dublin D07 H6K8
(Dublin)

Loftus, Kevin, Rt Rev Mgr, VG
St James's,
Enniscrone, Co Sligo
Tel 096-49011
(Killala, retired)

Loftus, Martin (SDB)
Salesian House, Milford,
Castletroy, Limerick
Tel 061-330268

Logue, Charles, CC
Malin Head, Co Donegal
Tel 074-9370134
(*Malin (Clonca)*, Derry)

LIST OF CLERGY IN IRELAND

Lohan, Declan, CC
Parochial House,
Renmore, Galway
Tel 091 751707
(*Renmore*, Galway)

Lohan, Louis
Parish Chaplain,
Ballygar, Co Galway
(*Ballygar (Kilian and Killeroran)*, Elphin)

Loisel, D. Eric M. (OSB)
Benedictine Monks,
Holy Cross Abbey,
119 Kilbroney Road,
Rostrevor,
Co Down BT34 3BN
Tel 028-41739979

Lombard, Patrick, Very Rev, PP
St Anne's, Sligo
Tel 071-9145028
(*Sligo, St Anne's*, Elphin)

Long, Joseph (SPS), CC
Curate's House, Fairgreen,
Belturbet, Co Cavan
Tel 049-9522151
(*Belturbet (Annagh)*, Kilmore)

Long, Leo
Cahercalla,
Ennic, Co Clare
Tel 086-8353388
(*Killaloe*, retired)

Long, Martin, Very Rev, PP
The Parochial House,
Westport Road,
Louisburgh,
Co Mayo F28 PH00
Tel 098-66198
(*Louisburgh (Kilgeever)*, Tuam)

Long, Michael (SPS)
St Patrick's, Kiltegan,
Co Wicklow W91 Y022
Tel 059-6473600

Looby, John (SJ)
35 Lower Leeson Street,
Dublin 2
Tel 01-6761248

Looney, Thomas, Very Rev,
(Kerry, retired)

Loughran, Alfred (OFM)
Franciscan Friary,
Killarney, Co Kerry
Tel 064-6631334/6631066

Loughran, Desmond, Very Rev,
15 Chapel Hill,
Mayobridge, Newry,
Co Down BT34 2EX
Tel 028-30850089
(*St Patrick's (Mayobridge)*, Dromore)

Loughran, Malachy (OSA)
St Augustine's Priory,
Shop Street,
Drogheda, Co Louth
Tel 041-9838409

Loughrey, Damien (OFMCap)
St Anthony's Capuchin Friary,
43 Dublin Street,
Carlow R93 PH27
Tel 059-9142543

Loughrey, Neil (White Fathers)
Promotion Director/Mite Boxes
Cypress Grove,
Templeogue, Dublin 6W
Tel 01-4055263/4055264

Loughrey, Vivian, Very Rev, PP
Shrule, Galway
Tel 093-31262
(*Shrule*, Galway)

Lovell, Liam
c/o Diocesan Office,
Killarney, Co Kerry
(Kerry)

Lovett, Cyril (SSC)
(Editor, Far East Magazine),
St Columban's,
Dalgan Park, Navan,
Co Meath
Tel 046-9021525

Lowe, Bernard (CP)
Superior, St Paul's Retreat,
Mount Argus, Dublin 6W
Tel 01-4992000

Lucey, Finbarr, Very Rev, PP
Ardmore, Youghal,
Co Cork
Tel 024-94177
(Waterford & L., retired)

Lucey, John (CSsR)
Mount Saint Alphonsus,
Limerick
Tel 061-315099

Lucey, Pat (OP), CC
St Mary's, Tallaght,
Dublin D24 X585
Tel 01-4048100

Ludden, Paul, Very Rev, Co-PP
c/o St Mary's, Sandyford,
Dublin 18
(*Sandyford*, Dublin)

Luddy, Denis (CSsR), CC
722 Antrim Road,
Newtownabbey,
Co Antrim BT36 7PG
Tel 028-90774833
(*St Gerard's*, Down & C.)

Ludlow, Brendan,
Chaplain, UCD
Chaplains' Room, UCD
Belfield, Dublin 4
Tel 01-7168317
(Meath)

Lugowski, Janusz
Chaplain to Polish Community,
Parochial House,
Moynalvey, Summerhill,
Co Meath
Tel 046-9557031/
087-9908922
(*Moynalvey*, Meath)

Lumala, Aloysius, AP
43b Glen Road,
Belfast BT11 8BB
Tel 028-90613949
(*St Teresa's*, Down & C.)

Lumsden, David, Very Rev, PP
Director, Knock Diocesan Pilgrimage,
83 Tonlegee Drive,
Raheny, Dublin 5
Tel 01-8480917/
087-2569873
(*Edenmore, Grange Park*, Dublin)

Lupot, Julian, PP
The Presbytery,
Ballintubber
Castlerea, Co Roscommon
Tel 094-9655602
(*Ballintubber (Ballintubber and Ballymoe)*, Elphin)

Lynch, Damien CC
Berrings, Co Cork
Tel 021-7332948
(*Inniscarra*, Cloyne)

Lynch, Dermot (OFMCap)
Guardian, Holy Trinity,
Fr Mathew Quay,
Cork T12 PK24
Tel 021-4270827

Lynch, Dermot (SJ)
St Ignatius Community & Church, 27 Raleigh Row,
Salthill, Galway
Tel 091-523707

Lynch, Eamonn, Very Rev, PP
Killinkere, Virginia,
Co Cavan
Tel 049-8547307
(*Killinkere*, Kilmore)

Lynch, Finbarr (SJ)
Milltown Park,
Sandford Road, Dublin 6
Tel 01-2698411/2698113

Lynch, Finian (OP)
St Mary's,
Pope's Quay, Cork
Tel 021-4502267

Lynch, Flannan (OFMCap), CC
Capuchin Friary,
Ard Mhuire,
Creeslough, Letterkenny,
Co Donegal
Tel 074-9138005

Lynch, Jim,
Dunboyne, Co Meath
(Meath, retired)

Lynch, Jude (CSSp)
Holy Spirit Missionary College
Kimmage Manor,
Whitehall Road,
Dublin D12 P5YP
Tel 01-4064300

Lynch, Laurence (OCarm)
Carmelite Friary,
Kinsale,
Co Cork P17 WR88
Tel 021-4772138

Lynch, Lorcan, Very Rev
St Anne's Nursing Home,
Clones Road, Ballybay,
Co Monaghan A75 K193
(Clogher, retired)

Lynch, Owen
c/o Archbishop's House
Drumcondra,
Dublin D09 H4C2
(Dublin, retired)

Lynch, Patrick (OFM)
Guardian,
Franciscan Friary,
Killarney, Co Kerry
Tel 064-6631334/6631066

Lynch, Patrick (OFMCap)
St Anthony's Capuchin Friary,
43 Dublin Street,
Carlow R93 PH27
Tel 059-9142543

Lynch, Patrick, Very Rev, PE
(priest in residence)
Kiltimagh, Co Mayo
(Achonry, retired)

Lynch, Patsy (SMA), PP
St Michael's, Ballinskelligs,
Co Kerry
Tel 066-9479108
(*Ballinskelligs (Prior)*, Kerry)

Lynch, Sean (SMA)
African Missions,
Blackrock Road,
Cork T12 TD54
Tel 021-4292871

Lyng, Dick (OSA), CC
Provincial Secretary,
St Augustine's,
Taylor's Lane,
Ballyboden, Dublin 16
Tel 01-4241000
(*Ballyboden*, Dublin)

Lyng, John (OSA)
Prior,
St Augustine's Priory,
Washington Street, Cork
Tel 021-4275398/4270410

Lyon, Kevin, Archdeacon, CC
Archdeacon of Glendalough,
Parochial House,
Crosschapel, Blessington,
Co Wicklow
Tel 045-865215
(*Blessington*, Dublin)

LIST OF CLERGY IN IRELAND

Lyons, Fintan (OSB)
Glenstal Abbey, Murroe,
Co Limerick
Tel 061-386103

Lyons, Gabriel, Very Rev, PP
St Teresa's Presbytery,
Glen Road,
Belfast BT11 8BL
(*St Teresa's*, Down & C.)

Lyon, Kevin, Rev
Archdeacon, CC,
Parochial House,
Crosschapel,
Blessington, Co Wicklow
Tel 01-865215
(*Blessington*, Dublin)

Lyons, Thomas
Chaplain,
Cork University Hospital,
Wilton, Cork
Tel 021-4546400/4922391/4546109
(Galway)

M

MacAodh, Lomán (OFM)
Franciscan Abbey,
Multyfarnham,
Co Westmeath
Tel 044-9371114/9371137

MacBradaigh, Proinsias (SJ)
Superior,
Arrupe Community,
127 Shangan Road,
Ballymun, Dublin 9
Tel 01-8625345

MacCárthaigh, Donncha (MSC)
Western Road,
Cork T12 TN80
Tel 021-4804120

MacCarthaigh, Pádraig
Irremore, Listowel,
Co Kerry
(Kerry, retired)

MacCormack, Gerard, Very Rev, PP
c/o Bishop's House,
Dublin Road,
Mullingar, Co Westmeath
(Meath)

MacCraith, Micheál (OFM)
Dún Mhuire,
Seafield Road,
Killiney, Co Dublin
Tel 01-2826760

Mac Cuarta, Briain (SJ)
c/o Irish Jesuit
Provincialate,
Milltown Park,
Sandford Road, Dublin 6
Tel 01-4987333

Mac Cumhaill, Naos (CSSp)
Holy Spirit Missionary
College
Kimmage Manor,
Whitehall Road,
Dublin D12 P5YP
Tel 01-4064300

MacDaid, Liam S., Most Rev, DD
Retired Bishop of Clogher,
Drumhirk, Dublin Road,
Co Monaghan H18 YE30
Tel 047-82208
(Clogher)

MacDonagh, Fergal, Very Rev
(Moderator)
18 St Anthony's Road,
Rialto, Dublin 8
Tel 01-4534469
(*Dolphin's Barn/Rialto*, Dublin)

MacDonald, Criostóir, Very Rev, PP
Murmont Lawn,
Mayfield, Cork
Tel 021-4501861
(*St Joseph's (Mayfield)*, Cork & R.)

MacEntee, Patrick, Very Rev Canon, PP
35A Esker Road, Dromore,
Co Tyrone BT78 3LE
Tel 028-82898641
(*Dromore, Fintona (Donacavey)*, Clogher)

MacGearailt, Sean (OSA)
St Augustine's Priory,
St Augustine's Street,
Galway

MacGiolla Catháin, Darach
Pontifical Irish College,
Via Dei SS Quattro 1,
00184 Roma, Italy
(Down & C)

MacGiollarnáth, Seán, (OCarm)
Carmelite Priory,
56 Aungier Street,
Dublin 2 D02 R598
Tel 01-4758821

MacGréil, Mícheál (SJ)
St Francis Xavier's,
Upper Gardiner Street,
Dublin 1
Tel 01-8363411

MacHale, Brendan (SSC)
St Columban's,
Dalgan Park, Navan,
Co Meath
Tel 046-9021525

MacHale, John George, Very Rev Canon
(Priest in Residence)
Kilglass, Enniscrone,
Ballina, Co Mayo
Tel 096-36191
(*Kilglass*, Killala)

Macken, Walter
Ely University Centre,
10 Hume Street, Dublin 2
Tel 01-6767420
(Opus Dei)

MacKenna, Benedict (OP)
Newbridge College,
Droichead Nua,
Co Kildare
Tel 045-487200

Mackey, Niall, Very Rev, Adm
Parochial House,
Kilcullen, Co Kildare
Tel 045-481230
(*Kilcullen*, Dublin)

MacKiernan, James, Adm
The Presbytery, Longford,
Co Offaly
Tel 043-3346465
(*Longford (Templemichael, Ballymacormack)*, Ardagh & Cl.)

MacLaifeartaigh, Micheál (OCD)
Prior, The Abbey,
Loughrea, Co Galway
Tel 091-841209

MacLochlainn, Piaras, CC
No. 2 Presbytery,
148A Blackditch Road
Dublin 10
Tel 01-6265119
(*Ballyfermot Upper*, Dublin)

MacMahon, Hugh (SSC)
Priest in Charge,
St Columban's,
67-68 Castle Dawson,
Rathcoffey Road,
Maynooth, Co Kildare
Tel 01-8286036

MacMahon, Joseph (OFM)
Vicar, Franciscan Friary,
Ennis, Co Clare
Tel 065-6828751

MacMánuis, Clement (CSsR)
St Patrick's, Esker,
Athenry, Co Galway
Tel 091-844007

MacNamara, Francis, Very Rev, PE, CC
Mountmellick,
Co Laois
Tel 057-8624198
(Kildare & L., retired)

MacNamara, Henry (OSA)
The Abbey, Fethard,
Co Tipperary
Tel 052-31273

MacNamara, Luke (OSB)
Glenstal Abbey, Murroe,
Co Limerick
Tel 061-386103

MacNeice, Dermot (OSM)
Servite Priory,
Benburb, Dungannon,
Co Tyrone, BT71 7JZ
Tel 028-37548241

MacPartlin, Brendan (SJ)
Superior,
Iona, 211 Churchill Park,
Portadown BT62 1EU
Tel 028-38330366

MacRaois, Brian, Very Rev, PP, AP
The Holly Tree, Grange
Knockbridge, Dundalk,
Co Louth A91 VK18
Tel 042-6827409
(*Kilkerley*, Armagh)

MacSuibhne, Domhnall (OP), Very Rev, PP
Prior, St Mary's,
The Claddagh, Co Galway
Tel 091-582884
(*The Claddagh*, Galway)

MacSweeney, James
Chaplain to Coláiste
Phobail Bheantraí,
The Presbytery, Bantry
(*Bantry*, Cork & R.)

Madden, Brendan, Very Rev, PP
2 Rossmore Road
Dublin 6W
Tel 01-4508432
(*Willington*, Dublin)

Madden, James J. (OPraem)
Sacred Heart Presbytery,
1 Glenview Street,
Belfast BT14 7DP
Tel 028-90351851
(*Sacred Heart*, Down & C)

Madden, Laurence, Very Rev
Doonmore, Doonbeg,
Co Clare
(Limerick, retired)

Madden, Michael, Very Rev, PE
Ferry Road, Jamesbrook,
Midleton
Tel 087-6565072
(Cloyne, retired)

Madden, Nicholas (OCD)
St Teresa's,
Clarendon Street, Dublin 2
Tel 01-6718466/6718127

Madden, Patrick, Very Rev, Adm
Parochial House,
34 Aughrim Street,
Dublin 7
Tel 01-8386571
(*Aughrim Street*, Dublin)

Madden, Peter, PP, VF
40 Derrynoid Road,
Draperstown,
Magherafelt,
Co Derry BT45 7DN
Tel 028-79628376
(*Ballinascreen (Draperstown) and Desertmartin*, Derry)

Madel, Krzysztof (SJ)
St Francis Xavier's,
Upper Gardiner Street,
Dublin 1
Tel 01-8363411

LIST OF CLERGY IN IRELAND

Madigan, Martin, Very Rev
Suaimhneas Church,
Foynes, Co Limerick,
(Limerick, retired)

Madigan, Seamus, HCF
Defence Forces
Headquarters, McKee
Barracks,
Blackhorse Avenue,
Dublin 7
Tel 01-8042637/018042638
(Limerick)

Magee, Aelred (OCSO)
Our Lady of Bethlehem
Abbey,
11 Ballymena Road,
Portglenone, Ballymena,
Co Antrim BT44 8BL
Tel 028-25821211

Magee, Gerard
The Chaplaincy,
28 Elmwood Avenue,
Belfast BT9 6AY
Tel 028-90669737
(Down & C.)

Magee, John, Most Rev, DD
Retired Bishop of Cloyne,
'Carnmeen', Convent Hill,
Mitchelstown, Co Cork
Tel 025-41887
(Cloyne)

Magennis, Feidlimidh, Very
Rev, PP, Adm
Maypole Hill, Dromore
Co Down BT35 1BQ
(Dromore, Magheralin,
Dromore)

Magill, Martin, Very Rev,
Adm
470 Falls Road,
Belfast BT12 6EN
Tel 028-90321511
(St John, Down & C.)

Maginn, Michael, Very Rev
The Presbytery,
Tullygally Road, Legahory,
Craigavon BT65 5BY
Tel 028-38311872
(Moyraverty (Craigavon),
Seagoe (Derrymacash),
Dromore)

Magner, John, CC
Church Street, Kanturk,
Co Cork
Tel 029-50061
(Kanturk, Cloyne)

Magorrian, Eamon, CC
Parochial House,
27 Chapel Hill, Lisburn,
Co Antrim BT28 1EP
Tel 028-92660206
(Lisburn (Blaris), Down &
C.)

Maguire, Barry (SSC)
St Columban's,
Dalgan Park,
Navan, Co Meath
Tel 046-9021525

Maguire, Brian (SPS) CC
The Shroughaun, Tullow
Co Carlow
Tel 059-9180377
(Tullow, Kildare & L.)

Maguire, James (OSA)
St Augustine's Priory,
Washington Street, Cork
Tel 021-2753982

Maguire, Sean, Very Rev, PP
Parochial House,
Bawnboy, Co Cavan
Tel 049-9523103
(Courlough/Templeport,
Kilmore)

Maguire, Vincent, Very Rev
26 Rodney Street,
Portrush,
Co Antrim BT56 8LB
(Down and C., retired)

Maher, Frank, Very Rev
Canon, CC
Johnstown via Thurles,
Co Kilkenny
Tel 056-8831219/
087-2402487
(Johnstown, Ossory)

Maher, James (SJ) Minister,
Crescent College
Comprehensive,
Dooradoyle, Limerick
Tel 061-480920

Maher, Jerry, Very Rev, PP,
Presbytery, Idrone Avenue
Knocklyon, Dublin 16
(Knocklyon, Dublin)

Maher, Michael (SM)
Cerdon, Marist Fathers,
St Mary's Road, Dundalk,
Co Louth
Tel 042-9334019

Maher, Noel, Very Rev
Canon, PP
Clough, Ballacolla,
Portlaoise, Co Laois
Tel 057-8738513/
087-2326200
(Aghaboe, Ossory)

Maher, Oliver, Very Rev, PP
Urlingford, Co Kilkenny
Tel 056-883112/
086-8323010
(Urlingford, Ossory)

Maher, Sean, PP
The Presbytery,
Broadford, Co Kildare
Tel 046-9551203
(Balyna, Kildare & L.)

Mahon, John (CSSp)
Holy Spirit Missionary
College
Kimmage Manor,
Whitehall Road,
Dublin D12 P5YP
Tel 01-4064300

Mahony, John, Very Rev, PP
Ahascragh, Ballinasloe,
Co Galway
Tel 090-9688617
(Ahascragh (Ahascragh
and Caltra), Elphin)

Mailey, Anthony, CC
Parochial House,
Quigley's Point,
Co Donegal
Tel 074-9383008
(Iskaheen (Iskaheen &
Upper Moville), Derry)

Maingot, Jesse (OP)
Newbridge College,
Droichead Nua, Co Kildare
Tel 045-487200

Malcolmson, Kevin, CC
3 Landbrook Road,
Drumquilla,
Newtownbutler,
Co Fermanagh BT92 8JJ
Tel 028-67738244
(Newtownbutler
(Galloon), Clogher)

Maliakkal, Aquino
(OFMConv)
Guardian, The Friary,
St Francis' Street, Wexford
Tel 053-9122758

Mallavarappu, Selvaraj
(SDB)
Bursar, Salesian House,
45 St Teresa's Road,
Crumlin, Dublin D12 XK52
Tel 01-4555605

Mallon, Brendan, CC
Youghal, Co Cork
Tel 024-92456
(Youghal, Cloyne)

Mallon, Dominic
13 Richview Heights,
Keady,
Co Armagh BT60 3SW
(Armagh)

Mallon, Thomas, Very Rev,
PE, AP
Parochial House,
170 Loughmacrory Road,
Loughmacrory, Omagh,
Co Tyrone BT79 9LG
Tel 028-80761230
(Termonmaguirc
(Carrickmore,
Loughmacrory & Creggan),
Armagh)

Malone, Douglas, Adm
The Presbytery, Dunlavin,
Co Wicklow
Tel 045-401227
(Dunlavin, Dublin)

Malone, Larry
(priest in residence)
Edenderry, Co Offaly
Tel 046-9732352
(Edenderry, Kildare & L.)

Malone, Liam, Very Rev, PP,
Adm
Administrator
Parochial House, Kilbeg,
Kells, Co Meath
Tel 046-9246604
Parish Priest
Parochial House,
Nobber, Co Meath
Tel 046-9089688
(Kilbeg/Nobber, Meath)

Maloney, Dermot, Very Rev,
PP
Parochial House,
9 Newry Road,
Crossmaglen, Newry,
Co Down BT35 9HH
(Crossmaglen (Cregan
Upper) Armagh)

Maloney, John, Very Rev,
Adm
Attymass, Ballina,
Co Mayo
Tel 096-29990
(Ballina, Achonry)

Malone, Patrick, Co-PP,
Parochial House,
Church Drive,
Clarecastle, Co Clare
Tel 065-6823011
(Abbey Pastoral Area,
Killaloe)

Maloney, Peter (SVD)
Donamon Castle,
Roscommon
Tel 090-6662222

Mandi, Josephat
Parish Chaplain,
287 South Circular Road,
Dublin 8
Tel 01-4533490
(Dolphin's Barn, Dublin)

Mangan, Cyril, Very Rev,
Moderator
8 Greenfield Road, Sutton,
Dublin 13
Tel 01-8322396
(Baldoyle, Howth, Sutton,
Dublin)

Mangan, Eoin, Very Rev
Canon, PP
(Kerry, retired)

Mangan, Patrick J., Very
Rev,
Dún Mhuire,
44 Beechwood Avenue
Upper, Dublin 6
Tel 01-4975180/
087-9857264
(Dublin, retired)

Mangan, Thomas,
Donaghmore,
Co Limerick
Tel 087-2348226-313898
(Pastoral Unit 3, Limerick)

Manik, Robert (OCarm)
Gort Muire, Ballinteer,
Dublin 16
Tel 01-2984014

LIST OF CLERGY IN IRELAND

Manley, John (OFMCap)
Vicar,
St Francis Capuchin Friary,
Rochestown, Co Cork T12 NH02
Tel 021-4896244

Mann, Robert (SCJ), Very Rev
On sabbatical
(Dublin)

Mann, Samson (CSSp)
Spiritan House,
213 North Circular Road,
Dublin 7
01-8389664
Chaplain,
St Mary's Hospital,
Pheonix Park, Dublin 20
Tel 01-6250300
Chaplain,
Stewart's Hospital,
Palmerstown
Tel 01-6264444
(Dublin)

Mannathukara, Jain Matthew, CC
5 Oriel Road, Antrim
BT41 4HP
Tel 028-94428086
(Antrim, Down & C.)

Manning, Francis, Very Rev, PP
Newmarket, Co Cork
Tel 029-60999
(Newmarket, Cloyne)

Mannion, Colm (OP)
Dominican Community,
St Mary's Priory, Tallaght,
Dublin 24
Tel 01-4048100

Mannion, Tom, Very Rev PP
Ballinaglera,
Carrick-on-Shannon,
Co Leitrim
Tel 071-9643014
(Ballinaglera, Kilmore)

Mansfield, Declan, Very Rev, Adm
Parochial House, Ballinora,
Waterfall, near Cork
Tel 021-4872792
(Ballinora, Cork & R.)

Mansfield, Dermot (SJ)
Vice-Superior,
St Francis Xavier's,
Upper Gardiner Street,
Dublin 1
Tel 01-8363411

Mareja, Martin (SAC)
Pallottine College,
Thurles, Co Tipperary
Tel 0504-21202

Marken, Aodhan, Very Rev, PP, VF
Piercestown, Co Wexford
Tel 053-9158000
(Piercestown and Murrintown, Ferns)

Markuszewski, Robert,
Cathedral Presbytery,
38 Hill Street,
Newry, BT34 1AT
Tel 028-30262586
(Newry, Dromore)

Marmion, Declan (SM)
Administrator, Marist Fathers Chanel,
Finance & Administrative Office,
Coolock Village,
Dublin D05 KU62
Tel 01-8505022/086-2597905

Marren, John (SPS)
Assistant Society Leader,
St Patrick's
Kiltegan, Co Wicklow
Tel 059-6473600

Marrinan, Thomas, Very Rev Canon, PP, VF
Gort, Co Galway
Tel 091-631220
(Gort/Beagh, Galway)

Marrion, Declan (SM)
181 South Circular Road,
Dublin 8

Marron, Eamonn, Rt Rev Mgr, PE
The Presbytery, Raharney,
Co Westmeath
Tel 044-9374271
(Meath, retired)

Marron, Patrick, Very Rev Canon, PE
St Anne's Nursing Home,
Clones Road, Ballybay,
Co Monaghan A75 K193
(Clogher, retired)

Marteaux, D. Thierry (OSB)
Benedictine Monks,
Holy Cross Abbey,
119 Kilbroney Road,
Rostrevor,
Co Down BT34 3BN
Tel 028-41739979

Martin, Bernard (SSC)
St Columban's,
Dalgan Park, Navan,
Co Meath
Tel 046-9021525

Martin, Diarmuid, Most Rev, DD
Archbishop Emeritus of Dublin
c/o Archbishop's House,
Drumcondra,
Dublin D09 H4C2
Tel 01-8373732
(Dublin)

Martin, Eamon, Most Rev, DD
Archbishop of Armagh,
Primate of All Ireland,
Ara Coeli, Cathedral Road,
Armagh BT61 7QY
Tel 028-37522045
Apostlic Administrator of Dromore
Bishop's House,
44 Armagh Road, Newry,
Co Down
Tel 028-300262444
(Armagh)

Martin, Hubert, Very Rev, PP
Parochial House, Glennan, Glaslough, Monaghan
H18 FV10
Tel 047-88120
(Donagh, Clogher)

Martin, Liam (CSSp)
Holy Spirit Missionary College
Kimmage Manor,
Whitehall Road,
Dublin D12 P5YP
Tel 01-4064300

Martin, Oisin (CFR)
St Patrick Friary,
64 Delmege Park,
Moyross,
Limerick V94 859Y
Tel 061-458071

Martin, Valentine, Very Rev, PP
Logatryna, Dunlavin,
Co Wicklow
(Dublin, retired)

Martinez, Matthew (OP)
Convent of SS Xystus and Clement
Collegio San Clemente,
Via Labicana 95,
00184 Roma
Tel 0039-06-7740021

Maslen, Darren, Rev Dr, (SSS)
Superior,
Blessed Sacrament Chapel,
20 Bachelors Walk,
Dublin D01 NW14
Tel 01-8724597

Maszkiewicz, Jaroslaw (Jarek), PP
Carraun, Whitehall,
Tarmonbarry,
Co Roscommon
Tel 043-3326020/0852727279
(Tarmonbarry, Elphin)

Matei, Ciprian, CC
Tower Hill,
Portlaoise, Co Laois
Tel 057-8621142
(Portlaoise, Kildare & L.)

Mathew, Prince (OSCam)
St Camillus,
11 St Vincent Street North,
Dublin 7
Tel 01-8300365

Mathew, Suneesh (OSCam)
Chaplain, Mater Hospital,
Eccles Street, Dublin 7
Tel 01-8301122
(Dublin)

Mathews, William (SJ)
Milltown Park,
Sandford Road, Dublin 6
Tel 01-2698411/2698113

Matthew, Binoy (SVD),
1 & 3 Pembroke Road,
Dublin 4
Tel 01-6680904

Matthews, Barry, CC
Parochial House,
42 Abbey Street,
Armagh BT61 7DZ
Tel 028-37522802
(Armagh, Armagh)

Matthews, Richard, Very Rev, PP
Parochial House,
Slane, Co Meath
Tel 041-9824249/041-9884429
(Slane, Meath)

Mawn, Sean, Very Rev, PP, VF
Ballinamore, Co Leitrim
Tel 071-9644039
(Ballinamore/Drumreilly Lower, Kilmore)

Mayanja, Deogratias,
Chaplain,
South Tipperary General Hospital
Tel 052-6177000
(Waterford & L.)

Mayer, David Joseph (OSB)
Benedictine Monks,
Holy Cross Abbey,
119 Kilbroney Road,
Rostrevor,
Co Down BT34 3BN
Tel 028-41739979

McAdam, Colm (CM), Very Rev
St Joseph's,
44 Stillorgan Park,
Blackrock,
Co Dublin A94 PC62
Tel 01-2886961

McAleer, Brendan, Very Rev, PP
Parochial House,
Garristown, Co Dublin
Tel 01-8354138
(Garristown, Dublin)

LIST OF CLERGY IN IRELAND

McAleer, Gerard, Very Rev, PP, VF
Parochial House,
63 Castlecaulfield Road,
Donaghmore,
Dungannon,
Co Tyrone BT70 3HF
Tel 028-87761327
(*Donaghmore*, Armagh)

McAleer, Ryan
Amerikaans College,
Naamsestraat 100/01.02,
3000 Leuven Belgium
(Armagh)

McAleese, Anthony CC
St Patrick's Presbytery,
199 Donegall Street,
Belfast BT1 2FL
Tel 028-90324597
(*St Patrick's*, Down & C.)

McAleese, Frank (OCarm)
Whitefriar Street Church,
56 Aungier Street,
Dublin 2 D02 R598
Tel 01-4758821

McAlinden, John, PP
Parochial House,
Slane Road, Mell,
Drogheda,
Co Louth A92 WAC4
Tel 041-983 8278
(*Mell*, Armagh)

McAnaney, Martin (SM)
Paris

McAnenly, Peter, Very Rev, Adm
Parochial House,
42 Abbey Street,
Armagh BT61 7D2
Tel 028-37522802
(*Armagh*, Armagh)

McAnerney, Arthur, Very Rev, PE, AP
Parochial House,
10 Aughrim Road,
Magherafelt,
Co Derry BT45 6AY
Tel 028-79632351
(*Magherafelt and Ardtrea North*, Armagh)

McArdle, Martin, Very Rev, PP, VF
Parochial House,
10 Springhill Road,
Moneymore, Magherafelt,
Co Derry BT45 7NG
Tel 028-86748242
(*Moneymore (Ardtrea)*, Armagh)

McArdle, Sean (SM)
Parochial House,
Louth Village, Dundalk,
Co Louth AP1 XE42
Tel 042-9374285
(*Louth*, Armagh)

McAreavey, John, Most Rev, DD
Bishop Emeritus of Dromore,
Bishop's House,
44 Armagh Road, Newry,
Co Down BT35 6PN
Tel 028-30262444
(*Dromore*)

McAteer, Francis, Very Rev Canon, AP
Glencolmcille, Co Donegal
Tel 074-9730888
(*Carrick (Glencolmcille)*, Raphoe)

McAteer, John (SVD)
1 & 3 Pembroke Road,
Dublin 4
Tel 01-6680904

McAteer, Kieran, Very Rev, PP, VF
Parochial House,
Ballybofey, Co Donegal
Tel 074-9131135
(*Stranorlar*, Raphoe)

McAuliffe, David, Dr
Chaplaincy Base, Cork Institute of Technology,
3 Elton Lawn,
Rossa Avenue,
Bishopstown, Cork
Tel 021-4346244
(*Cork & R.*)

McAuliffe, Desmond,
Sheen Lodge, Ennis Road,
Co Limerick
Tel 063-324825/
087-2336476
(*Pastoral Unit 5*, Limerick)

McAuliffe, James (SPS)
St Patrick's, Kiltegan,
Co Wicklow
Tel 059-6473600

McAuliffe, Leo (OFMCap)
St Francis Capuchin Friary,
Rochestown,
Co Cork T12 NH02
Tel 021-4896244

McBrearty, Danny,
Gortnavern, Coolboy,
Letterkenny, Co Donegal
(Raphoe, retired)

McBrearty, Stephen, Very Rev, PP
2A My Lady's Mile,
Holywood,
Co Down BT18 9EW
Tel 028-90422167
(*Holywood*, Down & C.)

McBride, Brendan
St Philip's Church,
725 Diamond Street,
San Francisco,
California 94114
(Raphoe)

McBride, Colm, Very Rev, PP
Parochial House,
59 Chapel Road,
Glenavy, Crumlin,
Co Antrim, BT29 4LY
Tel 028-94422262
(*Glenavy and Killead*, Down & C.)

McBride, Malachy (SDS)
'Naomh Mhuire',
Upper Slavery,
Buncrana, Co Donegal
Tel 074-9322264

McCabe, Michael (SMA)
African Missions,
Feltrim, Blackrock Road,
Cork T12 N6C8
Tel 021-4292871

McCabe, Robert, CC
St Mary's Presbytery,
The Fairgreen, Navan,
Co Meath C15 X0A3
Tel 046-9027518
(*Navan*, Meath)

McCabe, Thomas (OMI)
Oblate Scholasticate,
St Anne's,
Goldenbridge Walk,
Inchicore, Dublin 8
Tel 01-4540841/4542955

McCafferty, Patrick, PP
Corpus Christi Presbytery,
4-6 Springhill Grove,
Belfast BT12 7SL
Tel 028-90246857
(*St Luke's*, Down & C.)

McCafferty, Paul
Derry Diocesan Office,
St Eugene's Cathedral,
Francis Street,
Derry BT48 9AP
Tel 028-71262302
(Derry)

McCaffrey, Ultan (OFM)
Franciscan Friary,
Liberty Street, Cork
Tel 021-4275481

McCague, Brendan, CC
Castleross Retirement Home,
Castleross Village,
Carrickmacross,
Co Monaghan
A81 X242
(Clogher, retired)

McCahery, Barney (CSsR), CC
6 Market Street,
Ballycastle,
Antrim BT54 6DP
Tel 028-20762202
(*Ballycastle (Ramoan)*, Down & C.)

McCallion, Edwin (SM), Very Rev, PP
Superior, The Presbytery,
Coolock Village,
Dublin 5
Tel 01-8477133
(*Coolock*, Dublin)

McCallion, John, CC
Parochial House,
140 Mountjoy Road,
Brocagh, Dungannon,
Co Tyrone BT71 5DY
Tel 028-87738381
(*Clonoe*, Armagh)

McCallion, Patrick (SPS)
St Patrick's, Kiltegan,
Co Wicklow W91 Y022
Tel 059-6473600

McCamley, Eamonn, Very Rev, PP, VF
Parochial House,
6 Circular Road,
Dungannon,
Co Tyrone BT71 6BE
Tel 028-87722631
(*Dungannon (Drumglass, Killyman and Tullyniskin)*, Armagh)

McCann, Aidan, CC
Parochial House,
34 Madden Row, Keady,
Co Armagh BT60 3RW
Tel 028-3751242
(*Keady (Derrynoose)*, Armagh)

McCann, Arthur (CP)
St Gabriel's Retreat,
The Graan,
Enniskillen, Co Fermanagh
Tel 028-66322272
(Clogher)

McCann, Brian, Very Rev, PP, VF
St Luke's Presbytery,
Twinbrook Road,
Dunmurry,
Co Antrim BT17 0RP
Tel 028-90619459
Administrator, Derriaghy Parish
(*St Luke's, Derriaghy*, Down & C.)

McCann, Columba (OSB)
Glenstal Abbey, Murroe,
Co Limerick
Tel 061-621000

McCann, Henry, Very Rev, PP
St Anthony's Presbytery,
4 Willowfield Crescent,
Belfast BT6 8HP
Tel 028-90458158
(*St Anthony's*, Down & C.)

McCann, Joseph (CM)
St Paul's, Sybil Hill,
Raheny, Dublin 5
D05 AE38
Tel 01-8318113

McCanny, Bryan, Rt Rev Mgr, PP
119 Irish Green Street,
Limavady,
Co Derry BT49 9AB
Tel 028-77729759
(*Limavady*, Derry)

LIST OF CLERGY IN IRELAND

McCarney, Eugene, Very Rev, PE
Parochial House,
Castletown, Gorey,
Co Wexford
Tel 0402-37112
(*Castletown*, Dublin)

McCarron, Brendan (SPS)
St Patrick's,
21 Leeson Park,
Dublin D06 DE76
Tel 01-4977897

McCarron, Peter,
(Dublin, retired)

McCartan, Seán, Very Rev
(priest in residence)
Parochial House,
Ardee Street,
Collon, Co Louth A92 F2P7
(*Ardee and Collon*, Armagh)

McCarthy, Brian
Castleville Study Centre,
Golf Links Road,
Castletroy, Limerick
Tel 061-331223
(Opus Dei)

McCarthy, Daniel, CF
(Cloyne)
Chaplain,
James Stephens Barracks,
Kilkenny
Tel 056-7761852
(Ossory)

McCarthy, Dermod
26 Brackenbush Road,
Killiney, Co Dublin
(Dublin, retired)

McCarthy, Donal (SAC)
Pallottine College,
Thurles, Co Tipperary
Tel 0504-21202

McCarthy, Eamonn, CC
Radio Maria Ireland,
Unit 8,
St Anthony's Business Park, Ballymount Road,
Dublin 22
Tel 085-8585308
(Cloyne)

McCarthy, Eamonn, CC
The Presbytery, Donard,
Co Wicklow
Tel 045-404614
(*Dunlavin*, Dublin)

McCarthy, Eugene (CP)
St Paul's Retreat,
Mount Argus, Dublin 6W
Tel 01-4992000

McCarthy, Fachtna, Very Rev, Adm,
Parochial House,
St Mary's,
Haddington Road,
Dublin 4
Tel 01-6600075/
087-3936327
(*Haddington Road*, Dublin)

McCarthy, Francis
Parochial House,
Crookstown, Co Kildare
Tel 087-6978143
(*Athy*, Dublin)

McCarthy, John, Very Rev, PP
Ballyvourney, Co Cork
Tel 086-8212101
(*Ballyvourney*, Cloyne)

McCarthy, John, Very Rev
Carrowmore Meadows,
Knock, Co Mayo F12 T8X8
(*Tuam*, retired)

McCarthy, John, Very Rev, PP
Parochial House,
Rosscarbery, Co Cork
Tel 023-8848168
(*Rosscarbery and Lissavaird*, Cork & R.)

McCarthy, John,
Dromin, Kilmallock,
Co Limerick
Tel 085-8676317
(*Pastoral Unit 7*, Limerick)

McCarthy, John (SVD)
8 Teignmouth Road,
London, NW2 4HN
Tel 020-84528430

McCarthy, Liam (OFM)
Vicar, Franciscan Friary,
Clonmel,
Co Tipperary E91 X9T8
Tel 052-6121378

McCarthy, Pat
(Kerry, retired)

McCarthy, Patrick A., Very Rev, PP
35 Paul Street, Cork
Tel 021-4276573
(*SS Peter and Paul*, Cork & R.)

McCarthy, Patrick J., Very Rev, PE
The Presbytery,
O'Rahilly Street,
Clonakilty, Co Cork
(Cork & R., retired)

McCarthy, Patrick, CC (pro tem)
Macroom, Co Cork
Tel 086-3831621
(*Macroom*, Cloyne)

McCarthy, Thomas
Ferndene Nursing Home,
Newtown Park,
Blackrock,
Co Dublin
(Dublin, retired)

McCarthy, Thomas (OP), Very Rev
St Mary's, The Claddagh,
Co Galway
Tel 091-582884

McCarthy, Vincent (OSA)
Duckspool House
(Retirement Community),
Abbeyside, Dungarvan,
Co Waterford
Tel 058-23784

McCartney, Sean, Very Rev, PP
25 Alt-Min Avenue,
Belfast BT8 6NJ
(Down & C., retired)

McCaughan, Aidan
(priest in residence)
St Peter's Cathedral Presbytery,
St Peter's Square,
Belfast BT12 4BU
(*Cathedral (St Peter's)*, Down & C.)

McCaughan, Damian, CC
81 Castle Street,
Ballymoney,
Co Antrim BT53 6JT
Tel 028-27662003
(*Ballymoney and Derrykeighan*, Down & C.)

McCaughan, Dermot, Very Rev, PP
St Patrick's Presbytery,
29 Chapel Hill, Lisburn,
Co Antrim BT28 1EP
Tel 028-92662341
(*Lisburn (Blaris)*, Down & C.)

McCaughey, George (SDB)
Salesian College,
Maynooth Road,
Celbridge, Co Kildare
Tel 01-6275058/60

McCaughey, Michael M., PP
St Patrick's,
Buncrana Road,
Pennyburn,
Derry BT48 7QL
Tel 028-71262360
(*The Three Patrons*, Derry)

McCaughey, Shane, Rt Rev Mgr Canon, PP, VG,
St Joseph's,
Carrickmacross,
Co Monaghan A81 F688
Tel 047-81019
(*Carrickmacross (Machaire Rois)/Magheracloone*, Clogher)

McCaul, Dermot (SMA)
(Priest in residence)
Parochial House,
56 Minterburn Road,
Lairakean, Caledon
Co Tyrone BT68 4XH
Tel 028-37568288
(*Aughnacloy (Aghaloo)*, Armagh)

McCauley, Daniel (SMA)
African Missions,
Dromantine, Newry,
Co Down BT34 1RH
Tel 028-30821224

McCay-Morrissey, Bernard (OP)
Casement Aerodome,
Baldonnel, Co Dublin
Tel 01-4037536

McClarey, Liam Very Rev, (SAC)
Provincial, 'Homestead',
Sandyford Road,
Dundrum, Dublin 16
Tel 01-2956180/2954170

McCloskey, Gerard, Very Rev, PP
Parochial House, Ardglass,
Co Down BT30 7TU
(*Dunsford and Ardglass*, Down & C.)

McCluskey, Brian, Very Rev Canon, PE
Apt 2,
2 Danesfort Park North,
Stranmillis Road,
Belfast BT9 5RB
Tel 028-90683544
(Clogher, retired)

McConvery, Brendan (CSsR)
Clonard Monastery,
1 Clonard Gardens,
Belfast BT13 2RL
Tel 028-90445950

McConville, Conor, Very Rev, PP
17 Monteith Road,
Annaclone, Banbridge,
Co Down BT32 5AQ
Tel 028-40671201
(*Aghaderg*, *Annaclone*, Dromore)

McConville, Matthew
c/o Bishop's House,
44 Armagh Road,
Newry, Co Down
(Dromore)

McConville, Michael,
Nazareth House Care Village
516 Ravenhill Road,
Belfast BT15 0BW
(Down & C., retired)

McCormack, Christy
Fohenagh, Ahascragh,
Ballinasloe,
Co Galway H53 K037
Tel 090-9688623
(*Fohenagh and Killure*, Clonfert)

McCormack, Gerard, Very Rev, PP
Parochial House,
Kingscourt, Co Cavan
Tel 042-966734
(*Kingscourt*, Meath)

McCormack, Ignatius,
St Flannan's College,
Ennis, Co Clare
Tel 065-68280/086-2777139
(*Abbey Pastoral Area*, Killaloe)

LIST OF CLERGY IN IRELAND

McCormack, James (CM)
St Paul's College, Raheny,
Dublin 5
Tel 01-8314011/2

McCormack, James, PE,
c/o Bishop's House, Carlow
(Kildare & L., retired)

McCormack, Martin (SDB),
Rector, Salesian House,
45 St Teresa's Road,
Crumlin,
Dublin D12 XK52
Tel 01-4555605

McCormack, William, Very
Rev, Co-PP
Puckane, Nenagh,
Co Tipperary
Tel 067-24105/087-4168855
(*Odhran Pastoral Area*,
Killaloe)

McCrann, Christopher, CC
Knocknahur, Sligo
Tel 071-9128470
(*Strandhill/Ransboro*,
Elphin)

McCreave, Eamon (OSM)
St Michael's Presbytery,
200 Finaghy Road North,
Belfast BT11 9EG
Tel 028-95904304

McCrory, Gerard, Very Rev
Canon
c/o Diocesan Office,
Armagh Road,
Newry, Co Down BT35 6PN
(*Dromore*, retired)

McCrory, Patrick, J., Very
Rev, PE
Parochial House,
Sixemilecross, Omagh,
Co Tyrone BT79 9NF
Tel 028-80758344
(*Armagh*, retired)

McCrossan, Oliver (SSC)
St Columban's,
Dalgan Park, Navan,
Co Meath
Tel 046-9021525

McCrystal, Aidan (SMA)
African Missions,
Blackrock Road,
Cork T12 TD54
Tel 021-4292871

McCullagh, Michael (CM)
Superior,
St Paul's, Sybil Hill,
Raheny, Dublin D05 AE38
Tel 01-8318113

McCullagh, Raymond
(priest in residence)
1 Seafield Park South,
Portstewart,
Co Derry BT55 7LH
Tel 028-70832066
(*Portstewart*, Down & C.)

McCulloch, Robert (SSC)
Collegio San Colombano,
Corso Trieste 57,
00198 Roma

McDermott, Christopher, CC
20 Loughermore Road,
Ballykelly,
Co Derry BT49 9PD
(*Limavady*, Derry)

McDermott, Joseph, Very
Rev, PE, CC
Parochial House, Caragh,
Naas, Co Kildare
Tel 045-903889
(*Caragh, Droichead Nua/
Newbridge*, Kildare & L.)

McDermott, Kieran, Very
Rev, Adm
Pro-Cathedral House,
83 Marlborough Street,
Dublin 1
Tel 01-8745441
(*Pro-Cathedral*, Dublin)

McDermott, Louis (OMI)
Our Lady of the Wayside,
118 Naas Road,
Bluebell, Dublin 12
Tel 01-4501040
(*Inchicore, St Michael's*,
Dublin)

McDermott, Niall, Very Rev
The Presbytery,
91 Grange Road,
Baldoyle, Dublin 13
(*Dublin*, retired)

McDermott, Noel, PP
91 Ervey Road, Eglinton,
Co Derry BT47 3AU
Tel 028-71810235
(*Faughanvale*, Derry)

McDermott, Padraic, (CSSp),
CC
The Presbytery,
Manor Kilbride,
Blessington, Co Wicklow
Tel 01-4582154
(*Blessington*, Dublin)

McDermott, Patsy, PP
Killenummery, Dromahair,
via Sligo,
Co Leitrim
Tel 071-9164125
(*Killenummery and
Ballintogher*
(*Killenummery and
Killery*), Ardagh & Cl.)

McDermott, Sean, Very Rev,
PP, VF
Lacken, Ballinagh,
Co Cavan
Tel 049-43331404
(*Ballintemple*, Kilmore)

McDermott, Thomas, Very
Rev, Adm
1 Cathedral Terrace, Cobh,
Co Cork
Tel 021-4815934
(*Cobh*, Cloyne)

McDevitt, Eamon, PP
78 Lisnaragh Road,
Dunamanagh, Strabane,
Co Tyrone BT82 0QN
Tel 028-71398212
(*Dunamanagh
(Donaghedy)*, Derry)

McDevitt, John, PP
The Presbytery,
11 Steelstown Road,
Derry BT48 8EU
Tel 028-71351718
(*Our Lady of Lourdes,
Steelstown*, Derry)

McDevitt, Vincent (CSSp)
Holy Spirit Missionary
College
Kimmage Manor,
Whitehall Road,
Dublin D12 P5YP
Tel 01-4064300

McDonagh, Brendan (SPS),
Very Rev, PP
Cootehall, Boyle,
Co Roscommon
Tel 071-9667004
(*Ardcarne (Cootehall)*,
Elphin)

McDonagh, Donald (SPS)
St Patrick's, Kiltegan,
Co Wicklow
Tel 059-6473600

McDonagh, James, Very
Rev, PP, VF
Ballymote, Co Sligo
Tel 071-9191770
(*Ballymote (Emlefad and
Kilmorgan)*, Achonry)

McDonagh, John, Very Rev,
PP
'Stella Maris',
15 Oswald Road,
Sandymount, Dublin 4
Tel 01-6684265
(*Sandymount*, Dublin)

McDonagh, Martin, (CSSp)
Holy Spirit Missionary
College
Kimmage Manor,
Whitehall Road,
Dublin D12 P5YP
Tel 01-4064300

McDonagh, Sean (SSC)
(Research JPIC)
St Columban's,
Dalgan Park,
Navan, Co Meath
Tel 046-9021525

McDonald, Anthony
(OCarm)
Carmelite Priory,
Whitefriar Street Church,
56 Aungier Street,
Dublin 2 D02 R598
Tel 01-4758821

McDonald, Daniel, Very Rev,
PP
Marshallstown,
Enniscorthy, Co Wexford
Tel 053-9388521
(*Marshallstown*, Ferns)

McDonald, Fintan (SPS)
St Patrick's, Kiltegan,
Co Wicklow W91 YO22

McDonald, John, CC
3 Stanhope Place, Athy,
Co Kildare
Tel 059-8631698
(*Athy*, Dublin)

McDonald, John, Rt Rev
Mgr, PE, CC
Chaplains House,
Curragh Camp,
Co Kildare
Tel 045-441369
(*Curragh Camp*, Kildare &
L.)

McDonald, Joseph, PP
Presbytery, Main Street,
Celbridge, Co Kildare
Tel 01-6275874
(*Celbridge*, Dublin)

McDonald, Thomas (CSSp)
Blackrock College,
Blackrock, Co Dublin
Tel 01-2888681

McDonnell, Albert, Rev, Co-PP, VF
The Presbytery,
King's Road,
Kildysart, Co Clare
Tel 085-7811823
(*Radharc na nOileán
Pastoral Area*, Killaloe)

McDonnell, Charles, Very
Rev, Adm, VF
The Presbytery,
Westport,
Co Mayo F28 TN28
Administration Kilmeena
(*Westport*, Tuam)

McDonnell, Eunan (SDB)
Pronvicial, Salesian House,
45 St Teresa's Road,
Crumlin,
Dublin D12 XK52

McDonnell, Joseph (SSC)
Bursar, St Columban's,
Dalgan Park,
Navan, Co Meath
Tel 046-9021525

McDonnell, Leo, Very Rev,
Cathedral House,
Cathedral Place, Limerick
Tel 061-414624/087-2200366
(*Pastoral Unit 1*, Limerick)

McDonnell, Paschal (OFM)
Franciscan Friary,
Ennis, Co Clare
Tel 065-6828751

LIST OF CLERGY IN IRELAND

McDonnell, Patrick, Very Rev Canon, PE
Our Lady of Lourdes Presbytery,
Hardman's Gardens,
Drogheda, Co Louth
Tel 041-9831899
(Armagh, retired)

McDonnell, Paudge, Very Rev, PE
Parochial House,
Annyalla, Castleblayney,
Co Monaghan
A75 PX20
Tel 042-9740121
(Clontibret, Clogher)

McDonnell, Thomas (SPS)
St Patrick's, Kiltegan,
Co Wicklow
Tel 059-6473600

McDonough, Conor (OP)
St Saviour's,
Upper Dorset Street,
Dublin 1
Tel 01-8897610

McDunphy, Aodhán (OCSO)
Prior,
Mount Saint Joseph Abbey,
Roscrea,
Co Tipperary E53 D651
Tel 0505-25600

McElhennon, Kevin Very Rev, PP, VF
14 Killyclogher Road,
Omagh,
Co Tyrone BT79 0AX
Tel 028-82243375
(Killyclogher (Cappagh), Derry)

McElhill, Laurence, Very Rev, PE
(priest in residence),
43B Glen Road,
Belfast BT11 8BB
Tel 028-90613949
(St Teresa's, Down & C.)

McElhinney, Brian, Very Rev, PP
Butlersbridge, Co Cavan
Tel 049-4365266
(Cavan (Urney & Annagelliff) Kilmore)

McElroy, James (SM)
France

McElwee, Christopher (IC), CC,
Knocknagoran, Omeath,
Co Louth A91 HK76
Tel 042-9375198
(Carlingford and Clogherny, Armagh)

McEneaney, John
The Presbytery,
Mitchell Street,
Dungarvan,
Co Waterford
(Dungarvan, Waterford & L.)

McEneaney, Owen J., Very Rev Canon, PP
Parochial House, St Patrick's,
Ballybay, Co Monaghan
A75 K299
Tel 042-9741032
(Ballybay (Tullycorbet), Latton (Aughnamullen West), Rockcorry (Ematris), Clogher)

McEnroe, Patrick, Very Rev, PP
Darver, Readypenny,
Dundalk,
Co Louth A91 YC60
Tel 042-9379147
(Darver and Dromiskin, Armagh)

McEntee, Patrick, Very Rev, PP
8 Abbey Court, Dromore,
Co Tyrone BT78 3JB
(Dromore, Clogher)

McEntee, Seamus
Chaplain Dublin City University, St Mary's,
New Road, Clondalkin,
Dublin 22
(Clondalkin, Dublin)

McEntire, Peter J. (CSSp)
Holy Spirit Missionary College
Kimmage Manor,
Whitehall Road,
Dublin D12 P5YP
Tel 01-4064300

McErlean, Martin
c/o Bishop's House,
Mullingar
Co Westmeath
(Meath)

McEveney, Feargus (OFM)
Franciscan Friary,
Friary Lane,
Athlone, Co Westmeath
Tel 090-6472095

McEvoy, A. (SDB)
Salesian College,
Maynooth Road,
Celbridge, Co Kildare
Tel 01-6275058/60

McEvoy, Francis, Very Rev Canon, Adm
Parochial House,
Moyglare Road,
Maynooth
Tel 01-6286220
(Maynooth, Dublin)

McEvoy, John, Rt Rev Mgr, PP
Rathvily, Co Carlow
Tel 059-961114
(Paulstown, Kildare & L.)

McEvoy, Joseph, Very Rev, PP
Parochial House,
Moynalty, Kells, Co Meath
Tel 046-9244305
(Moynalty, Meath)

McEvoy, P. J., Very Rev, PP
Francis Street, Edenderry,
Co Offaly
Tel 046-9732352
(Edenderry, Kildare & L.)

McEvoy, Seamus, Very Rev Dean
Drakelands Nursing Home,
Ballycallan Road, Kilkenny
Tel 086-2634093
(Ossory, retired)

McEvoy, Seán, Very Rev, PP
St Moninna's Hermitage,
207 Dublin Road,
Newry, Co Down BT35 8RL
Tel 028-30849424
(Armagh)

McFaul, Daniel, CC
Parochial House,
St Mary's, Creggan
Derry BT48 9QE
Tel 028-71263152
(St Mary's, Creggan, Derry)

McFlynn, Gerard
18 Maresfield Gardens,
London NW3 5SX
(Down & C.)

McGahan, Noel, Very Rev Canon, PP
25 Augher Road, Clogher,
Co Tyrone BT76 0AD
Tel 028-85549604
Priest in charge Eskra
(Clogher, Eskra, Clogher)

McGarvey, Patrick, Very Rev, PP
Fanavolty, Kindrum,
Letterkenny, Co Donegal
Tel 074-9159007
(Tamney (Clondavaddog), Raphoe)

McGavigan, Micheál, Adm
42 Glenedra Road,
Feeny, Co Derry BT47 4TW
Tel 028-77781223
(Banagher, Derry)

McGee, Conor, CC,
Parochial House,
Rathganny,
Multyfarnham,
Co Westmeath N91 E186
Tel 044-9371124
(Multyfarnharm, Meath)

McGee, Edward, Very Rev, BSc, MA, DD
120 Cliftonville Road,
Belfast BT14 4DE
Tel 078-11144268
(Down & C.)

McGee, Joseph (MSC)
Formation House,
56 Mulvey Park, Dundrum,
Dublin 16
Tel 01-2951856

McGeehan, Declan, CC
5 Strathroy Road, Omagh,
Co Tyrone, BT79 7DW
Tel 028-82251055
(Killyclogher (Cappagh), Derry)

McGeehan, Paul, CC
Glenvar, Rathmullan,
Co Donegal
Tel 074-9150014
(Rathmullan (Killygarvan and Tullyfern), Raphoe)

McGeever, Patrick (CSSp)
Rockwell College,
Cashel, Co Tipperary
Tel 062-61444

McGettigan, Denis, Very Rev Canon, PE
Meetinghouse Street,
Raphoe
Co Donegal
(Raphoe, retired)

McGettrick, William (CSsR)
Clonard Monastery,
1 Clonard Gardens,
Belfast BT13 2RL
Tel 028-90445950

McGill, Maurice (MHM)
Organising Secretary,
St Joseph's House,
50 Orwell Park,
Rathgar, Dublin D06 C535
Tel 01-4127700

McGillicuddy, Desmond (MHM)
St Joseph's House,
50 Orwell Park,
Rathgar, Dublin D06 C535
Tel 01-4127700

McGinley, Séamus, Very Rev, PP
Parochial House,
2 Tullynure Road,
Cookstown,
Co Tyrone BT809XH
Tel 028-86769921
(Lissan, Armagh)

McGinn, Emlyn, PP, VF
Parochial House,
9a Forkhill Road,
Mullaghbawn, Newry,
Co Down BT35 9RA
Tel 028-30888286
(Mullaghbawn (Forkhill), Armagh)

McGinn, Patrick, Very Rev Canon, PP
St Joseph's Presbytery,
Park Street,
Co Monaghan H18 C588
Tel 047-81220
Adm, Monaghan,
Tyholland
(Corcaghan, Monaghan, Tyholland, Clogher)

McGinnity, Gerard, Very Rev, PE
Rowan Road,
Co Armagh BT60 3DR
(Armagh, retired)

McGinnity, Michael, PP
St Malachy's Presbytery,
24 Alfred Street,
Belfast BT2 8EN
Tel 028-90321713
(St Malachy's, Down & C.)

McGirr, Austin, Very Rev, PP, VF
Parochial House,
4 The Crescent,
Portstewart,
Co Derry BT55 7AB
Tel 028-70832534
Adm, Coleraine and Portrush
(*Coleraine, Portstewart, Portrush,* Down & C.)

McGirr, Dermot, CC
50 Tobermore Road,
Desertmartin,
Magherafelt,
Co Derry BT45 5LE
Tel 028-79632196
48 Brook Street, Omagh
Co Tyrone, BT78 5HE
Tel 028-82242092
(*Omagh (Drumragh),* Derry)

McGivern, Patrick (SPS)
Assistant House Leader,
St Patrick's, Kiltegan,
Co Wicklow
Tel 059-6473600

McGlanaghy, Patrick (MSC)
Woodview House,
Mount Merrion Avenue,
Blackrock, Co Dublin
Tel 01-2881644

McGlynn, Colm (OSM)
Prior Provincial
Servite Priory,
St Peregrine,
36 Grangewood Estate,
Rathfarnham,
Dublin D16 V263
Tel 01-4517115/
086-4060124

McGlynn, Fergus
43 Chestnut Grove,
Ballymount Road,
Dublin 24
Tel 01-4515570
(Dublin, retired)

McGlynn, Patrick (CSSp)
Holy Spirit Missionary College
Kimmage Manor,
Whitehall Road,
Dublin D12 P5YP
Tel 01-4064300

McGlynn, Thomas, Very Rev, PP
143 Andersonstown Road,
Belfast BT11 9BW
Tel 028-90615702/
028-90603951
(*St Agnes',* Down & C.)

McGoldrick, Brian, PEm
St Orans Road,
Buncrana, Co Donegal
(Derry, retired)

McGoldrick, John, Very Rev
9999 Military Trail,
Palm Beach Gardens,
Florida 33410, USA
Tel 001-215-9291326/
001-772-2875044
(Armagh)

McGoldrick, Michael (OCD)
St Joseph's Carmelite Retreat Centre
Termonbacca
Derry BT48 9XE
Tel 028-71262512

McGoldrick, Neil, PE
(Derry, retired)

McGonagle, Hugh, CC
7 Elm Park, Ballinode,
Sligo
Tel 071-9143430
(*Sligo, St Joseph's-Calry,* Elphin)

McGonagle, James, Very Rev, PEm
Radharc an Lochan,
New Road, Stroove,
Greencastle, Co Donegal
Tel 074-9325736
(Derry, retired)

McGoohan, Ultan, Very Rev, PP, VF
St Anne's, Bailieborough
Co Cavan
Tel 042-9665117
(*Bailieboro (Killann),* Kilmore)

McGourty, Michael, Very Rev Canon, PE
Lisnarick Road,
Irvinestown,
Co Fermanagh
Tel 071-9871221
(*Bundoran (Magh Ene),* Clogher)

McGovern, Ciarán, PP
Newtownforbes,
Co Longford
Tel 043-3346805
(*Newtownforbes,* Ardagh & Cl.)

McGovern, David (OP)
Holy Cross, Tralee,
Co Kerry
Tel 066-7121135

McGovern, John, Very Rev, Co-PP
Parochial House, Kilmaley,
Co Clare V95 ENK6
Tel 065-6839735/086-3221210
(*Críocha Callan Pastoral Area,* Killaloe)

McGovern, Kieran (CM)
St Peter's, Phibsboro,
Dublin 7
Tel 01-8389708/8389841

McGovern, Terence, Very Rev, PP
Main Street, Hacketstown,
Co Carlow
Tel 087-6754811
(*Hacktstown,* Kildare & L.)

McGovern, Thomas
30 Knapton Road,
Dun Laoghaire, Co Dublin
Tel 01-2804353
(Opus Dei)

McGowan, Michael, PC
7 St Patrick's Crescent,
Rathcoole, Co Dublin
Tel 01-4589210
(*Saggart,* Dublin)

McGowan, Thomas
Beechtree Nursing Home,
Murragh,
Oldtown, Co Dublin
(Dublin, retired)

McGrady, Feargal, Very Rev, PP
Parochial House,
60 Windmill Hill,
Portaferry,
Co Down BT22 1RH
Tel 028-42728234
(*Ballygalget, Portaferry,* Down & C.)

McGrane, Camillus (OSM)
Church of the Divine Word,
Marley Grange,
25-27 Hermitage Downs,
Rathfarnham Dublin 16
Tel 01-4944295/4941064

McGrath, Aidan (OFM)
Provincial Office,
Franciscan Friary
4 Merchants' Quay
Dublin, D08 XY19
Tel 01-67425000

McGrath, Brendan (OFM)
Gaurdian, Franciscan Friary,
Ennis, Co Clare V95 A4N2
Tel 065-6828751

McGrath, Conor, PP
119A Glenravel Road,
Martinstown, Ballymena,
Co Antrim BT43 6QL
Tel 028-21758217
(*Glenravel and The Braid, Skerry,* Down & C.)

McGrath, Frank (OFM)
Vicar, The Abbey,
8 Francis Street,
Galway H91 C53K
Tel 091-562518

McGrath, Francis (SMA)
SMA House,
Cloonbigeen, Claregalway,
Co Galway H91 YK64
Tel 091-798880

McGrath, Joseph, CC
Mount Temple, Moate
Co Westmeath
Tel 090-6481239
(*Moate and Mount Temple,* Ardagh & Cl.)

McGrath, Joseph, Rt Rev, PP, VG, VF
New Ross, Co Wexford
Tel 051-447080
(*New Ross,* Ferns)

McGrath, Martin, PP (pro tem)
Moygownagh,
Ballina, Co Mayo
Tel 096-31288
(*Moygownagh,* Killala)

McGrath, Martin (SPS)
St Patrick's, Kiltegan,
Co Wicklow
Tel 059-6473600

McGrath, Matthew, Very Rev, AE, AP
Cashel, Co Tipperary
Tel 0504-42494
(*Clonoulty,* Cashel & E.)

McGrath, Michael
The Presbytery, Longford
Tel 043-3346465
(*Longford (Templemichael, Ballymacormack),* Ardagh & Cl.)

McGrath, Michael (SMA)
African Missions,
Blackrock Road,
Cork T12 TD54
Tel 021-4292871

McGrath, Patrick (OMI)
Oblate House of Retreat,
Inchicore, Dublin 8
Tel 01-4534408/4541805

McGrath, Sean (SPS)
St Patrick's, Kiltegan,
Co Wicklow W91 Y022
Tel 059-6473600

McGrath, Thomas, Very Rev
Cois Tra, Chapel Road,
Duncannon,
Co Wexford
(Ferns, retired)

McGrath, Tom (MHM)
Mountshannon,
Labasheeda, Co Clare
Tel 065-6830932
(*Radharc na nOileán Pastoral Area,* Killaloe)

McGrattan, Dominic
Cliftonville Road,
Belfast BT14 6LA
028-90690920
(Down and C.)

McGree, Thomas
Durrow, Cullohill,
Co Laois
Tel 087-7619235
(*Durrow,* Ossory)

LIST OF CLERGY IN IRELAND

McGregor, Augustine (OCSO), Rt Rev
Retired Abbot,
Mount Melleray Abbey,
Cappoquin,
Co Waterford P51 R8XW
Tel 058-54404

McGregor, Bede (OP)
St Malachy's, Dundalk,
Co Louth
Tel 042-9334179/9333714

McGrory, James, CC
Parochial House,
49 Ardmore Road,
Derry BT47 3QP
Tel 028-71349490
(*Ardmore*, Derry)

McGuckian, Alan, Most Rev (SJ)
Bishop of Raphoe,
Ard Adhamháin,
Cathedral Road,
Letterkenny,
Co Donegal F92 W2W9
(Raphoe)

McGuckian, Bernard (SJ)
Vice-Rector and Minister,
Clongowes Wood College,
Clane,
Co Kildare W91 DN40
Tel 045-868663/868202

McGuckian, Michael (SJ)
c/o Milltown Park,
Sandford Road,
Dublin D06 V9K7
Tel 01-4987333

McGuckien, Kevin, Very Rev, PP
Director of Vocations,
Parochial House,
23 Hannahstown Hill,
Belfast BT17 0LT
Tel 028-90614567
(*Hannahstown*, Down & C.)

McGuckin, Terence (CP)
Holy Cross Retreat,
Ardoyne, Crumlin Road,
Belfast BT14 7GE
Tel 028-90748231

McGuckin, Patrick, Very Rev, PE
79 Reclain Road, Galbally,
Dungannon,
Co Tyrone BT70 2PG
Tel 028-87759692
(Armagh, retired)

McGuigan, Seán, PP
Parochial House,
19 Ardoe Road,
Moortown, Cookstown
Co Tyrone BT80 0HT
Tel 028-86737236
(*Ardboe*, Armagh)

McGuinness, Austin (SSC)
St Columban's,
Dalgan Park,
Navan, Co Meath
Tel 046-9021525

McGuinness, Brendan, Very Rev, PP
The Parochial House,
Bekan, Claremorris,
Co Mayo F12 HC79
Tel 094-9380203
(*Bekan*, Tuam)

McGuinness, David
St Joseph's Catholic Church,
134 Prince Avenue,
Athens, Georgia 30601,
USA
(Waterford & L.)

McGuinness, Joseph, Rt Rev Mgr,
Executive Secretary to the Irish Episcopal Conference,
Columba Centre,
Maynooth,
Co Kildare W23 P6D3
Tel 01-5053000
(Clogher)

McGuire, Robert, Adm
Parochial House,
Taghmon,
Mullingar, Co Westmeath
Tel 053-9134123
(*Taghmon*, Ferns)

McHale, Benny, CC
The Parochial House,
New Line, Athenry,
Co Galway H65 DW20
Tel 091-844227
(*Athenry*, Tuam)

McHenry, Noel (SPS)
St Patrick's, Kiltegan,
Co Wicklow
Tel 059-6473600

McHugh, Anthony, Very Rev, PP
Parochial House,
33 Crossgar Road,
Saintfield, Ballynahinch,
Co Down BT24 7JE
Tel 028-97510237
(*Saintfield and Carrickmannon*, Down & C.)

McHugh, Christopher, Very Rev, PP,
Grange, Co Sligo
Tel 071-9163100
(*Ahamlish (Grange and Cliffoney)*, Elphin)

McHugh, Kevin (SSC)
St Columban's,
Dalgan Park,
Navan, Co Meath
Tel 046-9021525

McHugh, Oliver (SPS)
St Patrick's, Kiltegan,
Co Wicklow
Tel 059-6473600

McHugh, Patrick
Derrylester, Enniskillen,
Co Fermanagh
Tel 048-66349984
(Kilmore, retired)

McHugh, Patrick, Very Rev Canon, PP
5 Killynoogan, Kesh,
Co Fermanagh BT93 8DF
Tel 042-9740027
(Clogher)

McHugh, Patrick, Very Rev, PP
Parochial House, Termon,
Co Donegal
Tel 074-9139016
(*Termon*, Raphoe)

McHugh, Peter (SVD)
Donamon Castle,
Roscommon
Tel 090-6662222

McHugh, Seán
Chaplain,
University Hospital,
Galway
Tel 091-524222
(Galway)

McHugh, Thomas, Very Rev, Adm
75 Clonfeacle Road,
Blackwatertown,
Dungannon,
Co Tyrone BT71 7HP
Tel 028-87511215
(*Eglish, Moy (Clonfeacle)*, Armagh)

McIlraith, Cormac, Adm
10 Cranfield Place,
Sandymount, Dublin 4
Tel 01-6686845
(*Sandymount*, Dublin)

McInerney, Declan, Very Rev, PP
Eyrecourt, Ballinasloe
Co Galway H53 KX85
Tel 090-9675113
(*Eyrecourt, Clonfert and Meelick*), Clonfert)

McIntyre, Raymond (SDB)
Vice-Rector,
Salesian House,
45 St Teresa's Road,
Crumlin, Dublin 12
Tel 01-4555605

McKay, Brian (OCarm)
Carmelite Priory, Moate,
Co Westmeath N37 AW34
Tel 090-6481160/6481398

McKay, Dermot, Very Rev, PP
51 Bay Road, Carnlough,
Ballymena,
Co Antrim BT44 0HJ
Tel 028-28885220
(*Carnlough/Glenarm (Tickmacreevan)*, Down & C.)

McKay, Vincent (CSSp)
Parochial House,
Summerhill, Co Meath
Tel 046-9557021
(*Summerhill*, Meath)

McKee, Placid (OSB)
Silverstream Priory,
Stamullen,
Co Meath K32 T189
Tel 01-8417142

McKeever, John, Very Rev, PP, VF
Assistant Chancellor of the Diocese
Parochial House,
35 St Patrick Street, Keady,
Co Armagh BT60 3TQ
Tel 028-37531246
(*Keady (Derrynoose)*, Armagh)

McKeever, Martin (CSsR)
Alphonsian Academy,
Via Merulana 31, CP 2458,
00185 Roma-PT158, Italy
Tel 0039-06494901

McKeever, Michael, CC, VG
Church Hill, Letterkenny,
Co Donegal
Tel 074-9137057
(*Termon*, Raphoe)

McKenna, Cathal (SMA)
African Missions,
Dromantine, Newry,
Co Down BT34 1RH
Tel 028-30821224

McKenna, Hugh (OFM)
Collegio S. Isidoro,
Via degli Artisti 41,
00187 Roma, Italy
Tel 0039-06-4885359

McKenna, John F., CC
Scotshouse, Clones,
Co Monaghan H23 YTI0
Tel 047-56016
(*Killeevan (Currin, Killeevan and Aghabog)*, Clogher)

McKenna, John, Very Rev Canon, PP
Trillick, Omagh,
Co Tyrone BT78 3RD
Tel 028-89561350
(*Trillick*, Clogher)

McKenna, Joseph
(Birmingham Diocese)
Shannagh Nursing Home,
Belleek, Co Fermanagh
(Clogher, retired)

McKenna, Jude (OFMCap)
Capuchin Friary,
Station Road,
Raheny, Dublin D05 T9E4
Tel 01-8313886

McKenna, Owen (SMA)
SMA House,
81 Ranelagh Road,
Ranelagh, Dublin 6
Tel 01-4968162/3

383

LIST OF CLERGY IN IRELAND

McKenna, Pádraig, Very Rev, PP
Parochial House, Millbank,
Trillick, Co Tyrone
Tel 028-89561982k
(*Trillick (Kilskeery)*,
Clogher)

McKenna, Patrick, Very Rev, PE
19 Broughshane Road,
Ballymena BT43 7DX
Tel 028-25643828
(*Ballymena (Kirkinriola)*,
Down & C.)

McKenna, Robert, Very Rev, PE, AP
Parochial House,
26 Newtown Road,
Camlough, Newry,
Co Down BT35 7JJ
Tel 028-30830237
(*Armagh*, retired)

McKenna, Seamus, BA, HDE
Cork, Regional Marriage Tribunal,
The Lough, Cork
Tel 021-4963653
(*Kerry*)

McKeon, Seamus, PP
Aughnacliffe, Co Longford
Tel 043-6684118
(*Colmcille*, Ardagh & Cl.)

McKeown, Donal, Most Rev, DD
Bishop of Derry,
Diocesan Offices,
St Eugene's Cathedral,
Francis Street,
Derry BT48 9AP
Tel 028-71262302
(*Derry*)

McKeown, Noel (OP)
St Catherine's, Newry,
Co Down BT35 8BN
Tel 028-30262178

McKeown, Maximilian (OFMConv), Very Rev
Friary of the Visitation of the BVM,
Fairview Strand, Dublin 3
Tel 01-8376000
(*Fairview*, Dublin)

McKevitt, Brian (OP)
St Mary's Priory, Tallaght,
Dublin 24
Tel 01-4048100

McKiernan, Peter, Very Rev, PP
Crosserlough, Co Cavan
Tel 049-4336122
(*Crosserlough*, Kilmore)

McKiernan, Thomas
Rosskeeragh, Belturbet,
Co Cavan
(*Kilmore*, retired)

McKinlay, Denis, Very Rev, PP
Parochial House,
41 Lower Square,
Castlewellan,
Co Down BT31 9DN
Tel 028-43770377
Administrator, Kilcoo
(*Castlewellan (Kilmegan)*,
Kilcoo, Down & C.)

McKinley, Patrick, Very Rev
Moderator Brookfield,
Jobstown and Springfield
68 Maplewood Road,
Springfield, Tallaght,
Dublin 24
(*Brookfield*, *Jobstown*,
Springfield, Dublin)

McKinney, Anthony (OCarm)
Gort Muire, Ballinteer,
Dublin 16 D16 EI67
Tel 01-2984014

McKinney, Liam, Very Rev, Adm
'Glenshee',
9 Dublin Road, Newry,
Co Down BT35 8DA
Tel 028-30262376
(*Middle Killeavy (Newry)*,
Armagh)

McKinstry, Gordon
12 The Meadows,
Randalstown,
Co Antrim BT41 2JB
(Down & C., retired)

McKittrick, Brian, CC
Parochial House, Avoca,
Co Wicklow
(*Avoca*, Dublin)

McLaughlin, Brian (CSSp)
Holy Spirit Missionary College
Kimmage Manor,
Whitehall Road,
Dublin D12 P5YP
Tel 01-4064300

McLaughlin, Con, PP
Barrack Hill, Carndonagh,
Lifford, Co Donegal
Tel 074-9374104
Director,
Inishowen Pastoral Centre,
Carndonagh, Co Donegal
Tel 074-9374103
(*Carndonagh (Donagh)*,
Derry)

McLaughlin, Eamonn, CC
Congregation for the Clergy, Rome
(Raphoe)

McLaughlin, George, PEm
Chez Nous, Drumawier,
Greencastle, Co Donegal
(*Derry*, retired)

McLaughlin, John (SSC)
St Columban's,
Dalgan Park,
Navan, Co Meath
Tel 046-9021525

McLaughlin, Kevin (OMI)
An Tobar, Ardbraccan,
Navan, Co Meath

McLaughlin, Michael, Very Rev, Canon,
Airfield, Inch, Ennis,
Co Clare
Tel 065-6839332
(*Críocha Callan Pastoral Area*, Killaloe)

McLaughlin, Peter, PEm
c/o Bishop's Office,
St Eugene's Cathedral,
Francis Street,
Derry BT48 9AP
Tel 028-71262302
(*Derry*, retired)

McLaughlin, Pius (OFM)
Franciscan Friary,
Rossnowlagh,
Co Donegal
Tel 071-9851342

McLaverty, Anthony, Very Rev, CC
518 Donegall Road,
Belfast BT12 6DY
Tel 028-90314112
(*St John's*, Down & C.)

McLoone, Francis, Very Rev, PP
Parochial House,
Killymard, Donegal Town,
Co Donegal F94 C6T7
Tel 074-9721929
(*Killymard*, Raphoe)

McLoughlin, Eamonn, CC
Parochial House,
Letterkenny, Co Donegal
Tel 074-9121021
(*Letterkenny (Conwal and Leck)*, Raphoe)

McLoughlin, Eugene Rev (SMA)
SMA House Cloonbigeen,
Claregalway,
Co Galway H91 YK64
Tel 091-798880

McLoughlin, Eugene, Very Rev Canon, PE
2 Essex Grove,
Roscommon Town
(*Elphin*, retired)

McLoughlin, Michael, Very Rev Dean, PP, VF
Parochial House,
Moycullen, Co Galway
Tel 091-555106
(*Moycullen*, Galway)

McMahon, Aidan (CSsR)
Mount Saint Alphonsus,
South Circular Road,
Limerick
Tel 061-315099

McMahon, Andrew, Very Rev PP
6 Scarva Road, Banbridge,
Co Down BT32 3AR
Tel 028-40662136
(*Annaclone*, Dromore)

McMahon, John, Very Rev, PP
Carrigallen, Co Leitrim,
via Cavan
Tel 049-4339610
(*Carrigallen*, Kilmore)

McMahon, Joseph (OFM)
Vicar, Franciscan Friary,
Ennis, Co Clare
Tel 065-6828751

McMahon, Joseph, Very Rev, Co-PP, VF
Parochial House,
Scariff, Co Clare
Tel 061-921051/087-2665793
(*Inis Cealtra Pastoral Area*,
Killaloe)

McMahon, Michael (CSSp)
Holy Spirit Missionary College
Kimmage Manor,
Whitehall Road,
Dublin D12 P5YP
Tel 01-4064300

McMahon, Padraig, Very Rev, PP, VF
Parochial House, Athboy,
Co Meath
Tel 046-9432184
(*Athboy*, Meath)

McMahon, Patrick,
The Presbytery,
Labasheeda, Co Clare
Tel 065-6830126
(*Radharc na nOilean Pastoral Area*, Killaloe)

McMahon, Paul (SSC)
Belfast (on compassionate leave)

McMahon, Richard (CSsR)
St Patrick's, Esker,
Athenry, Co Galway
Tel 091-844007

McMahon, Richard (CSsR)
St Patrick's, Esker,
Athenry, Co Galway
Tel 091-844007

McMahon, Seamus (SM)
Australia

McMahon, Vincent (LC)
Woodlands Academy,
Wingfield House, Bray,
Co Wicklow
Tel 01-2866323

MacManus, Clement (CSsR)
St Joseph's, Dundalk,
Co Louth
Tel 042-9334042/9334762

McManus, Brendan (SJ)
Peter Faber House,
28 Brookvale Avenue,
Belfast BT14 6BW
Tel 028-90757615

McManus, Clement, AP
Knock, Inverin, Co Galway
Tel 091-593122
(*Spiddal/Knock*, Tuam)

LIST OF CLERGY IN IRELAND

McManus, Frank, Very Rev, PP,
19 Ardvarney Road,
Ederney, Enniskillen,
Co Fermanagh BT93 0EG
Tel 028-68631315
(*Ederney (Cúl Máine)*,
Clogher)

McManus, Gregory (SPS)
St Patrick's,
21 Leeson Street,
Kiltegan,
Co Wicklow W91 YO22

McManus, John, Very Rev, PP, VG
Parochial House, Castlerea,
Co Roscommon
Tel 094-9620040
(*Castlerea (Kilkeevan)*,
Elphin)

McManus, John
Parochial House,
Strangford,
Co Down BT30 7NL
Tel 028-44881206
(*Kilclief and Strangford*,
Down & C.)

McManus, Kevin (OSA), PP
St John's Priory,
Thomas Street, Dublin 8
Tel 01-6770393

McManus, Michael, PP
Kiltoom, Athlone
(*Kiltoom*, Elphin)

McManus, Patrick (SSC)
St Columban's,
Dalgan Park, Navan,
Co Meath
Tel 046-9021525

McManus, Patrick, Very Rev, CC
34 Dollymount Grove,
Clontarf, Dublin 3
Tel 01-8057692/
087-2371089
(*Dollymount*, Dublin)

McManus, Thomas, VF
Drumkeerin, Co Leitrim
Tel 071-9648025
(*Drumkeerin
(Inisgmagrath)*, Kilmore)

McManus, Tommy (OSA)
St Augustine's Priory,
Washington Street, Cork
Tel 021-4275398/4270410

McMenamin, Joseph (White Fathers)
Promotion Director,
Cypress Grove,
Templeogue, Dublin 6W
Tel 01-4055526

McMenamin, William, Very Rev Archdeacon, PE
'St Columba's'
Meeting House Street,
Raphoe, Co Donegal
Tel 074-9144834
(*Raphoe*, retired)

McMorrow, Maurice, Very Rev, PP, VF
Kinawley, Enniskillen
Co Fermangh BT92 4FH
Tel 028-6638250
(*Kinawley/Killesher*,
Kilmore)

McMullan, Anthony (OP)
St Malachy's, Dundalk,
Co Louth
Tel 042-9334179/9333714

McMullan, Brendan, Very Rev
26 Willowbank Park,
Belfast BT6 0LL
Tel 028-90794440
(*Down & C.*, retired)

McMullan, Kevin, Very Rev
418 Oldpark Road
Belfast BT14 6QF
(*Down & C.*, retired)

McNaboe, Desmond (OFMCap),
Guardian, St Anthony's
Capuchin Friary,
43 Dublin Street,
Carlow R93 PH27
Tel 059-9142543

McNally, Albert, Very Rev, PP, VF
6 Hillside Avenue,
Dunloy BT44 9DQ
(*Down and C.*, retired)

McNamara, Austin, Very Rev, PP
Parochial House,
Ballyhahill, Co Limerick
Tel 069-82103/
087-2615471
(*Pastoral Unit 13*, Limerick)

McNamara, Cormac (SM),
Chanel Community,
Coolock, Dublin 5
Tel 01-8477133

McNamara, David (CSsR)
Mount Saint Alphonsus,
South Circular Road,
Limerick
Tel 061-315099

McNamara, Donal, Very Rev Canon,
St Munchin's,
Clancy Strand, Limerick
Tel 061-455635/
087-2402518
(*Pastoral Unit 4*, Limerick)

McNamara, Henry (OSA)
The Abbey, Fethard,
Co Tipperary
Tel 052-31273

McNamara, Francis, Very Rev, PE
Parochial House,
Davitt Road,
Mountmellick, Co Laois
057-8624198
(*Kildare & L.*, retired)

McNamara, Frank, Very Rev, PE
Cluan Lir,
Mullingar, Co Westmeath
(*Meath*, retired)

McNamara, Gerard, Very Rev, PP
Ballyduff Upper,
Co Waterford
Tel 058-60227
(*Ballyduff*, Waterford & L.)

McNamara, John, Very Rev Canon, PP, VF
Apt 2, The Presbytery,
Dublin Road, Balbriggan,
Co Dublin
Tel 01-8020185
(*Balbriggan*, Dublin)

McNamara, Kevin, PP
St Agatha's Parish Centre,
Headford, Killarney,
Co Kerry
Tel 064-7754008
(*Glenflesk*, Kerry)

McNamara, Liam, Very Rev Canon, AP
Tipperary Town
Co Tipperary
Tel 062-82664
(*Tipperary*, Cashel & E.)

McNamara, Martin (MSC)
Woodview House,
Mount Merrion Avenue,
Blackrock, Co Dublin
Tel 01-2881644

McNamara, Martin, Very Rev, PP
Kiltulla, Athenry,
Co Galway H65 DYM0
Tel 091-848021
(*Kiltullagh, Killimordaly & Clooncagh*, Clonfert)

McNamara, Oliver, CC
Annaghdown, Co Galway
Tel 091-791142
(*Corrandulla
(Annaghdown)*, Tuam)

McNamara, Robert, CC
The Rectory,
Lisdoonvarna, Co Clare
Tel 065-7074142
(*Lisdoonvarna and Kilshanny*, Galway)

McNamara, Thomas (SMA)
SMA House,
81 Ranelagh Road,
Ranelagh, Dublin 6
Tel 01-4968162/3

McNamara, Walter (CSSp)
Holy Spirit Missionary College
Kimmage Manor,
Whitehall Road,
Dublin D12 P5YP
Tel 01-4064300

McNamee, Ambrose (OCD)
The Abbey, Loughrea,
Co Galway
Tel 091-841209

McNamee, Paul
c/o Bishop's House,
Dublin Road, Carlow
(Kildare & L.)

McNeice, Damian, PP
6 Beechpark Lawn,
Castleknock, Dublin 15
Tel 01-6408595
(*Castleknock, Laurel Lodge-Carpenterstown*,
Dublin)

McNeice, Dermot (OSM)
Servite Priory, Benburb,
Dungannon,
Co Tyrone, BT71 7JZ

McNeill, Peter, Very Rev, PP
58 Ballydrumman Road,
Ballyward, Castlewellan,
Co Down BT31 9UG
Tel 028-40650207
(*Drumgooland, Dromara*,
Dromore)

McNelis, Denis, Very Rev, PP, VF
Parochial House, Laytown,
Co Meath
Tel 041-9827258
(*Laytown-Mornington*,
Meath)

McNerney, John
Chaplains' Residence,
St Stephen's, UCD,
Belfield, Dublin 4
Tel 01-7164789
(Dublin)

McNicholas, Gerard (SSC)
St Columban's Retirement Home, Dalgan Park,
Navan, Co Meath
Tel 046-9021525

McNulty, Sean (SSC)
Gortnalea, Dunmore,
Tuam,
Co Galway H54 ET02

McNulty, Thomas
Goretti Cottage,
Acre Road, Carlingford,
Co Louth, A91 PW95
Tel 042-9376577
(*Armagh*, retired)

McPartland, Jimmy, Very Rev, Co-PP
St Fergal's, Killarney Road,
Bray, Co Wicklow
(*Bray (Ballywaltrim)*,
Dublin)

McPhillips, James, Very Rev, PP, VG
10 Knocks Road,
Lisnaskea,
Co Fermanagh BT92 0GA
Tel 028-67721324
(*Linaskea (Aghalurcher)*,
Clogher)

LIST OF CLERGY IN IRELAND

McQuaid, Macartan, Very Rev Canon
Priest in Residence,
Parochial House,
Threemilehouse,
Co Monaghan H18 E290
Tel 047-81501/087-2454705
(Corcaghan (Kilmore and Drumsnat, Clogher)

McShane, Dermot, Very Rev, PE
c/o Community Hospital,
Killybegs, Co Donegal
(Raphoe, retired)

McShane, Philip (OP)
St Mary's Priory,
Tallaght, Dublin 24
Tel 01-4048100

McSorley, Gerard, Rt Rev Mgr
St Anne's Nursing Home,
Clones Road, Ballybay,
Co Monaghan A75 K193
(Clogher, retired)

McSweeney, Eustace (OFMCap)
Capuchin Friary,
Station Road, Raheny,
Dublin D05 T9E4
Tel 01-8313886

McSweeney, Myles, Very Rev, PP
Meenvane, Schull,
Co Cork
Tel 028-28171
Adm, Goleen
Tel 028-28898
(Goleen, Schull, Cork & R.)

McTiernan, Jim (White Fathers)
Cypress Grove,
Templeogue, Dublin 6W
Tel 01-4055263/4055264

McTiernan, John, Very Rev, PP, VF
Bridge Street, Belturbet,
Co Cavan
Tel 049-9522109
(Belturbet (Annagh), Kilmore)

McVeigh, Joseph
(priest in residence)
4 Darling Street,
Enniskillen,
Co Fermanagh BT74 7EW
Tel 028-66322075
(Enniskillen, Clogher)

McVeigh, Martin, Very Rev, PP
Parochial House,
Clogherhead,
Drogheda,
Co Louth A92 K970
Tel 041-9822224
(Clogherhead, Armagh)

McVerry, Peter (SJ)
Arrupe Community,
217 Silloge Road,
Ballymun, Dublin 11
Tel 01-8420886
(Zam-Mal)

McWilliams, Luke, Very Rev, PP
Parochial House,
9 Gortahor Road,
Rasharkin, Ballymena,
Co Antrim BT44 8SB
Tel 028-29571212
(Rasharkin, Down & C.)

McWilliams, Patrick, Very Rev, PP
103 Roguery Road,
Moneyglass, Toomebridge,
Co Antrim BT41 3PT
Tel 028-79650225
(Duneane, Down & C.)

Meade, Bernard (CM)
St Paul's, Sybil Hill,
Raheny, Dublin D05 AE38
Tel 01-8318113

Meade, John (CSSp)
Rockwell College,
Cashel, Co Tipperary
Tel 062-61444

Meade, Michael, Very Rev PP
Parochial House,
Kilcormac, Co Offaly
Tel 057-9135989
(Kilcormac, Meath)

Meagher, Charles (SSC)
St Columban's, Dalgan Park, Navan, Co Meath
Tel 046-9021525

Medina, Nelson (OP)
St Saviour's,
Upper Dorset Street,
Dublin 1
Tel 01-8897610

Medves, Petru, CC
Abbeyleix Parish Office
Abbeyleix, Co Laois
Tel 085-1853069
(Abbeyleix, Ballinakill, Raheen, Kildare & L.)

Meehan, Conleth, Co-PP
21 Wheatfield Grove,
Portmarnoc, Co Dublin
Tel 01-8461561
(Kinsealy, Dublin)

Meehan, Dermot, Very Rev, PP, VG
Swinford, Co Mayo
Tel 094-9251790
(Swinford (Kilconduff and Meelick), Achonry)

Meehan, Dominic, Very Rev, PP
Church Avenue,
Templemore,
Co Tipperary
Tel 0504-31492
(Loughmore, Cashel & E.)

Meehan, Séamus, Very Rev, PE
Main Street, Dungloe,
Co Donegal
Tel 074-9521895
(Raphoe, retired)

Meehan, William, Very Rev, PP
St Mary's, Clonmel,
Co Tipperary
Tel 052-6122954
(Clonmel, St Mary's, Waterford & L.)

Mehigan, Donal (OP)
St Saviour's, Bridge Street,
Waterford
Tel 051-875061

Mejida, Timothy
Parochial House,
Lobinstown, Navan,
Co Meath
Tel 046-9053155
(Lobinstown, Meath)

Melican, Michael (IC)
Doire na hAbhann,
Tickincor, Clonmel,
Co Tipperary
Tel 052-6126914

Mellett, Stan (CSsR),
St Joseph's,
St Alphonsus Road,
Dundalk,
Co Louth A71 F3FC
Tel 042-9334042/9334762

Mernagh, Michael (OSA)
St John's Priory,
Thomas Street, Dublin 8
Tel 01-6770393/0415/0601

Mernagh, Patrick, Very Rev, PP
Kilmore, Co Wexford
Tel 053-9135181
(Kilmore and Kimore Quay, Ferns)

Merrigan, Liam, Very Rev, PP
Drogheda Road,
Monasterevin, Co Kildare
Tel 045-525346
(Monasterevin, Kildare & L.)

Meskell, Derek (CSsR)
Mount Saint Alphonsus,
Limerick
Tel 061-315099

Mhamwa, Thaddeus, PC
128 Roselawn Road,
Blanchardstown, Dublin 15
Tel 01-8219014
(Blanchardstown, Dublin)

Michael, James, CC
The Presbytery,
5 Drumgeely Avenue,
Shannon, Co Clare
Tel 061-471513
(Tradaree Pastoral Area, Killaloe)

Michael, Shajan Panachickal, CC
Ard Easmuinn,
Dundalk, Co Louth
Tel 042-9334259
(Dundalk, Holy Redeemer, Armagh)

Millar, George (SVD)
Maynooth, Co Kildare
Tel 01-6286391/2

Mills, Dermot (OMI), Co-PP
52a Bulfin Road, Dublin 8
Tel 01-4531660
(Inchicore, St Michaels, Dublin)

Milo, Manuelito,
(Chaplain, Belfast City Hospital)
Sacred Heart Presbytery,
1 Glenview Street
Belfast BT14 7DP
Tel 028-90351851
(St Paul's, Down & C.)

Milton, Raymond, Very Rev, PP, VF
Knockcroghery,
Co Roscommon
Tel 090-666115
(Knockcroghery/ St John's/Rahara, Elphin)

Minogue, Frank (SPS)
St Patrick's, Kiltegan,
Co Wicklow W91 Y022

Mitchell, Francis, Rev,
Archbishop's House,
Tuam,
Co Galway H54 HP57
Tel 093-24166
(Tuam)

Mitchell, Kilian (OPraem)
Holy Trinity House,
Lismacanican,
Mountnugent, Co Cavan

Mockler, John,
Gortboy, Newcastlewest,
Co Limerick
Tel 086-2342242
(Pastoral Unit 15, Limerick)

Mohan, Mark, Very Rev, PP
Parochial House,
Ballivor, Co Meath
Tel 046-9546488
(Ballivor/kildalkey, Meath)

Mohan, Richard, Rt Rev Mgr, PE
34 Lacky Road,
Drumswords, Roslea,
Co Fermanagh BT92 YNQ
Tel 048 67751374
(Clones, Clogher)

Moley, John, Very Rev
24 Mallard Road,
Downpatrick,
Co Down BT30 6DY
(Down & C., retired)

LIST OF CLERGY IN IRELAND

Mollin, Matthew, Very Rev, PE
Elm Hall,
Loughlinstown Road,
Celbridge, Co Kildare
(Meath, retired)

Molloy, John, Co-PP
Parochial House,
Toomevara, Co Tipperary
Tel 067-26023/0868152828
(*Ollatrim Pastoral Area*, Killaloe)

Molloy, John (SSC)
St Columban's,
Dalgan Park, Navan,
Co Meath
Tel 046-9021525

Molloy, Michael (SSC)
St Columban's,
Dalgan Park,
Navan, Co Meath
Tel 046-9021525

Molloy, Michael, Very Rev, PP, VF
The Presbytery, Moore
Ballydangan, Athlone,
Co Roscommon
Tel 090-9673539
(*Moore*, Tuam)

Molloy, Noel (OP)
St Catherine's, Newry,
Co Down BT35 8BN
Tel 028-30262178

Molloy, Patrick (MHM)
St Joseph's House,
50 Orwell Park,
Rathgar, Dublin D06 C535
Tel 01-4127700

Moloney, Bernie, Very Rev, PP
Emly, Co Tipperary
Tel 062-57111
(*Emly*, Cashel & E.)

Moloney, Brendan, Very Rev, AP, VF
Silvermines, Nenagh,
Co Tipperary
Tel 067-25864
(*Odhran Pastoral Area*, Killaloe)

Moloney, Dermot, Rt Rev Mgr, PE
5 Gold Cave Crescent,
Tuam, Co Galway
Tel 093-52946
(Tuam, retired)

Moloney, Gerard (CSsR)
Vicar-Superior,
Mount Saint Alphonsus,
South Circular Road,
Limerick
Tel 061-315099

Moloney, Joseph, Very Rev, PE
Grove House, Vicar Street,
Tuam, Co Galway
(Tuam, retired)

Moloney, Leonard (SJ)
Provincial, Milltown Park
Sanford Road, Dublin 6
Tel 01-4987333

Moloney, Michael, PE
43 The Waterways, Sallins,
Naas, Co Kildare
(Kildare & L., retired)

Molovlasky, Ryan (CSsR)
Clonard Monastery,
1 Clonard Gardens,
Belfast BT13 2RL
Tel 028-90445950

Monaghan, Stephen (CM), Very Rev
St Paul's, Raheny,
Dublin 5
Tel 01-8318113

Monahan, Fintan, Most Rev, DD
Bishop of Killaloe,
Westbourne, Ennis,
Co Clare V95 W63H
Tel 065-6828638
(Killaloe)

Monahan, Patrick
Earlsfort,
291A Old Greenfield,
Maynooth,
Co Kildare
(Dublin, retired)

Monahan, Paul (SMA)
SMA House,
81 Ranelagh Road,
Ranelagh, Dublin 6
Tel 01-4968162/3

Monahan, Thomas (OP)
Black Abbey, Kilkenny,
Co Kilkenny
Tel 056-7721279

Mongan, Gerard, CC
St Patrick's,
Buncrana Road,
Pennyburn,
Co Derry BT48 7QL
Tel 028-71262360
(*The Three Patrons*, Derry)

Monks, Frank (MI)
Superior,
St Camillus, Killucan,
Co Westmeath
Tel 044-74115

Montades, Rudy (SVD), CC
The Presbytery, City Quay,
Dublin 2
Tel 01-6773706
(*City Quay*, Dublin)

Montague, Paul, Very Rev, PP
Parochial House,
Reaghstown, Ardee,
Co Louth A92 KW68
Tel 041-6855117
(*Tallanstown*, Armagh)

Mooney, Desmond, Very Rev, PP
44 Church Street,
Rostrevor,
Co Down BT34 3BB
Tel 028-41738277
(*Kilbroney (Rostrevor)*, Dromore)

Mooney, Oliver, Very Rev
Newry, Co Down
(Dromore, retired)

Mooney, Patrick, Very Rev Canon
Glenamaddy, Co Galway
(Tuam, retired)

Moore, David, Very Rev, Adm
c/o Parochial House,
9 Cavanakeeran Road,
Pomeroy, Dungannon,
Co Tyrone, BT70 2RD
Tel 028-87757867
(*Pomeroy*, Armagh)

Moore, Edward, Very Rev, PE
Marian House, Sallins,
Naas, Co Kildare
(Kildare & L., retired)

Moore, Eóin (OCarm)
Carmelite Friary,
Kinsale, Co Cork P17 WR88
Tel 021-4772138

Moore, Gerard, PP
23 Wainsfort Park
Terenure, Dublin 6W
Tel 01-4900218
(*Templeogue*, Dublin)

Moore, James,
Co-ordinator of Mission and Ministry,
Cloyne Diocesan Centre,
Cobh, Co Cork
Tel 086-8694744
Rushbrooke, Cobh,
Co Cork
Tel 086-8694744
(*Cobh, St Colman's Cathedral*, Cloyne)

Moore, James, Very Rev, PP
Clonkeencole, Clones,
Co Monaghan H23 V895
Tel 047-51048
(*Clones, Killeevan*, Clogher)

Moore, Johnny, CC
Ardara, Co Donegal
Tel 074-9537033
(*Ardara*, Raphoe)

Moore, Kevin, Very Rev, Moderator,
Apartment No. 1,
St Sylvester's Church,
Malahide, Co Dublin
Tel 01-8451244
(*Kinsealy, Malahide, Portmarnock, Yelow Walls, Malahide*, Dublin)

Moore, Michael (CSSp)
Holy Spirit Missionary College
Kimmage Manor,
Whitehall Road,
Dublin D12 P5YP
Tel 01-4064300

Moore, Paschal, Very Rev, PP
Piltown, Co Kilkenny
Tel 051-643112/
087-2408078
(*Templeorum*, Ossory)

Moore, Patrick, Very Rev, PP, VF
Parochial House,
Castlepollard,
Co Westmeath
Tel 044-9661126/
087-2510855
(*Castlepollard*, Meath)

Moore, Sean (CSsR)
Clonard Monastery,
1 Clonard Gardens,
Belfast, BT13 2RL
Tel 028-90445950

Moore, Seán, Very Rev, PP
Parochial House,
290 Monaghan Road,
Middletown,
Co Armagh BT60 4HS
Tel 028-37568406
(*Middletown (Tynan)*, Armagh)

Moorhead, John, Very Rev, PP
Parochial House, Eglish,
Birr, Co Offaly
Tel 057-9133010
(*Eglish*, Meath)

Morahan, Kieran (SMA)
SMA House, Cloonbigeen,
Claregalway,
Co Galway H91 YK64
Tel 091-798880

Moran, Benedict (OP), Very Rev, PP
Dominican Community,
St Aengus's, Balrothery,
Tallaght, Dublin 24
Tel 01-4624038
(*Tallaght, Tymon North*, Dublin)

Moran, John F., CC
192 Navan Road, Dublin 7
Tel 01-8387902
(Dublin, retired)

Moran, Lorcan, Very Rev
St John's Presbytery,
Kilkenny
R95 ND2W
Tel 086-8550521
(*St John's*, Ossory)

Moran, Martin, Very Rev Dean, PP
Rosscahill, Co Galway
Tel 091-550106
(*Rosscahill (Killannin)*, Galway)

LIST OF CLERGY IN IRELAND

Moran, Patrick (CSSp)
Community Leader,
St Mary's College,
Rathmines, Dublin 6
Tel 01-4995760

Moran, Patrick
1 Seapark,
Mount Prospect Avenue
Dublin 3
(Dublin, retired)

Moran, Timothy (LC)
Vocations Director,
Leopardstown Road,
Foxrock, Dublin 18
Tel 01-2955902

Moran, Willie (OCD)
Avila Carmelite Centre,
Bloomfield Avenue,
Morehampton Road,
Dublin 4
Tel 01-6430200

Moreira, Lino (OSB)
Glenstal Abbey,
Murroe, Co Limerick
Tel 061-621000

Morely, Paul, CC
Chaplain to the Syro-
Malabar Community
Holy Family Presbytery
Newington Avenue,
Belfast BT15 2HP
Tel 028-90743119
(*Holy Family*, Down and C.)

Morgan, Francis (OCSO)
Our Lady of Bethlehem
Abbey,
11 Ballymena Road,
Portglenone, Ballymena,
Co Antrim BT44 8BL
Tel 028-25821211

Morgan, Frank (SPS)
St Patrick's, Kiltegan,
Co Wicklow
Tel 059-6473600

Morgan, Liam, Very Rev, PP, VF
Sallins Road, Naas,
Co Kildare
Tel 045-949576
(*Two-Mile-House*, Kildare & L.)

Moriarty, Cathal (SPS)
Councillor, St Patrick's
Kiltegan, Co Wicklow
Tel 059-6473600

Moriarty, Declan
Sacred Heart Residence,
Sybil Hill Road, Raheny,
Dublin 5
(Dublin, retired)

Moriarty, Frank, Very Rev
Adare, Co Limerick
Tel 061-396177
(Limerick, retired)

Moriarty, James, Most Rev, DD
Retired Bishop of Kildare
and Leighlin,
c/o Bishop's House, Carlow
(Kildare & L.)

Moroney, Pat (SVD)
Maynooth, Co Kildare
Tel 01-6286391/2

Morris, Anthony (OP)
Holy Cross, Sligo,
Co Sligo
Tel 071-9142700

Morris, Dónal, Very Rev, PP
Parochial House,
Garraun South,
Creggs, Co Roscommon
Tel 090-6621127
(*Kilbegnet and Glinsk*, Elphin)

Morris, John, Very Rev, PP
Solohead, Co Limerick
Tel 062-47614
(*Solohead*, Cashel & E.)

Morris, Michael, (SPS), CC
Curate, The Presbytery,
Ferbane, Co Offaly.
Tel 090-6454309
(*Ferbane High Street and Boora*, Ardagh & Cl.)

Morrissey, Martin (MSC)
'Croí Nua', Rosary Lane,
Taylor's Hill Road,
Galway H91 WY2A
Tel 091-520960

Morrissey, Michael (OCarm)
Carmelite Community,
Gort Muire, Ballinteer,
Dublin 16 D16 EI67
Tel 01-2984014

Morrissey, Robin, Very Rev, PP
Castletownroche, Co Cork
Tel 087-6727925
(*Castletownroche*, Cloyne)

Morrissey, Thomas (SJ)
Milltown Park,
Sandford Road,
Dublin D06 V9K7
Tel 01-2698411/2698113

Mortell, Anthony (SSC)
St Columban's Retirement
Home, Dalgan Park,
Navan, Co Meath
Tel 046-9021525

Mothersill, Joseph (OCarm), CC
Carmelite Priory,
Whitefriar Street Church,
56 Aungier Street,
Dublin 2 D02 R598
Tel 01-4758821

Motherway, Nicholas (SPS)
St Patrick's, Kiltegan,
Co Wicklow
Tel 059-6473600

Mowbray, Alan (SJ),
c/o Milltown Park,
Sandford Road,
Dublin 6 D06 V9K7
Tel 01-2698411/2698113

Mowles, Alan (SDB)
Salesian House,
45 St Teresa's Road,
Crumlin, Dublin 12
Tel 01-4555605

Moynihan, James, Very Rev, PP
Newbawn, Co Wexford
Tel 051-428227
(*Newbawn and Raheen*, Ferns)

Moynihan, Michael, Very Rev, Canon, PP, VF
Dingle, Co Kerry
Tel 066-9151208
Moderator, Annascaul
Tel 066-9157103
(*Annascaul, Dingle*, Kerry)

Moynihan, Noel (CSSp)
Holy Spirit Missionary
College
Kimmage Manor,
Whitehall Road,
Dublin D12 P5YP
Tel 01-4064300

Moynihan, Seán (SVD)
Maynooth, Co Kildare
Tel 01-6286391/2

Muckian, Patrick (SM)
Philippines

Muhindo, Ubaldo
Curate in charge,
c/o Parish Office,
Balgaddy Road, Lucan,
Co Dublin, K78 NH05
Tel 01-4572900
(*Lucan South*, Dublin)

Mulcahy, Brian (CP)
St Paul's Retreat,
Mount Argus, Dublin 6W
Tel 01-4992000

Mulcahy, Kevin
Ballymacoda, Co Cork
Tel 024-98110
(Cloyne, retired)

Mulcahy, Pat, Very Rev, Co-PP
Parochial House,
18 Churchfield
Clonlara, Co Clare
Tel 061-354334/
087-6329913
(*Scáth na Sionnaine Pastoral Area*, Killaloe)

Mulcahy, Richard, Rt Rev
30 Knapton Road,
Dun Laoghaire, Co Dublin
Tel 01-2804353
(Opus Dei)

Mulcahy, Thomas (MSC), PP
Western Road,
Cork T12 TN80
Tel 021-4804120
(*Sacred Heart*, Cork & R.)

Mulcahy, Timothy (OP), CC
St Dominic's,
St Dominic's Road,
Tallaght, Dublin 24
Tel 01-4510620
(*Tallaght, Dodder*, Dublin)

Muldowney, Peter, Very Rev
St Fiacre's Gardens,
Bohernatownish Road,
Loughboy,
Kilkenny R95 RF97
Tel 056-77701730/
086-8265955
(*St Patrick's*, Ossory)

Mulhall, Brendan (CSsR)
Clonard Monastery,
1 Clonard Gardens,
Belfast BT13 2RL
Tel 028-90445950

Mulhall, Brendan, Very Rev, Adm
Holy Trinity Presbytery,
26 Norglen Gardens,
Belfast BT11 8EL
Tel 028-90590985/6
(*Coleraine*, Down & C.)

Mulherin, Jim (OSM), CC
Church of the Divine
Word,
Marley Grange,
25–27 Hermitage Downs,
Rathfarnham, Dublin 16
Tel 01-4944295/4941064
(*Marley Grange*, Dublin)

Mulhern, Kevin (SMA), CC
Parochial House, Fahan,
Lifford, Co Donegal
Tel 074-9360151
(*Fahan (Burt, Inch and Fahan)*, Derry)

Mulholland, Patrick, Very Rev, PP
Parochial House,
44 Lough Road,
Loughguile, Ballymena,
Co Antrim BT44 9JN
Tel 028-27641206
(*Loughguile*, Down & C.)

Mulkerins, Bernard (SSC)
St Columban's,
Dalgan Park,
Navan, Co Meath
Tel 046-9021525

Mulkerrins, Michael, Very Rev Canon, PE
Curate's Residence,
Renmore, Galway
Tel 091-757859
(Galway, retired)

Mullaly, Kevin
8 Finglaswood Road,
Finglas West, Dublin 11
Tel 01-8238354
(*Blanchardstown*, Dublin)

Mullan, Joseph, Very Rev, Adm
79 The Rise,
Mount Merrion,
Co Dublin
Tel 01-2889879
Moderator, Kilmacud-
Stillorgan and Mount
Merrion.
(*Clonskeagh, Kilmacud-Stillorgan,
Mount Merrion*, Dublin)

LIST OF CLERGY IN IRELAND

Mullan, Kevin, PE
(Derry, retired)

Mullane, Denis,
The Presbytery,
Templeglantine,
Co Limerick
Tel 069-84021/
087-2621911
(*Pastoral Unit 14*, Limerick)

Mullaney, Michael Very Rev
DD
St Patrick's College,
Maynooth, Co Kildare
Tel 01-7084700
(Dublin)

Mullan, Joseph, PP
49 Rathgar Road,
Dublin 6
Tel 01-4970039/
087-2326254
(*Rathgar*, Dublin)

Mullen, John (IC)
Clonturk House,
Ormond Road,
Drumcondra, Dublin 9
Tel 01-6877014

Mulligan, Ben, Very Rev, PE
(priest in residence)
42 Corke Abbey, Little
Bray, Co Wicklow
Tel 01-2720224
(Dublin, retired)

Mulligan, Declan, Very Rev,
PP
Parochial House,
5 Aghalee Road,
Aghagallon, Craigavon,
Co Armagh BT67 0AR
Tel 028-92651214
(*Aghagallon and
Ballinderry*, Down & C.)

Mulligan, Larry (OFM)
Franciscan Friary,
Clonmel, Co Tipperary
Tel 052-6121378

Mulligan, Rory (SM)
Norway

Mulligan, Seán, CC
Parochial House,
25 Lisdergan Road,
Fintona,
Co Tyrone BT78 2NR
Tel 028-82841907
(*Fintona (Donacavey)*,
Clogher)

Mulligan, Thomas, Very Rev,
PE
Árd Aoibhinn,
Madogue, Swinford,
Co Mayo
Tel 083 8997039
(Achonry, retired)

Mulligan, Vincent (OMI)
Oblate House of Retreat,
Inchicore, Dublin 8
Tel 01-4534408/4541805

Mullin, Joseph, Very Rev
Canon, PE
c/o 10 Knock's Road,
Lisnaskea,
Co Fermanagh BT92 0JA
(Clogher, retired)

Mullin, Seamus, Very Rev
Canon, AP
Miltown Malbay, Co Clare
Tel 065-7084003
(*Críocha Callan Pastoral
Area*, Killaloe)

Mullins, Anthony, Canon,
VG
The Presbytery,
Abbeyfeale, Co Limerick
Tel 068-31157
(*Pastoral Unit 14*, Limerick)

Mullins, Melvyn, Very Rev,
PP
42 Strand Street,
Skerries, Co Dublin
Tel 01-8491250
(*Skerries*, Dublin)

Mullins, Michael, Very Rev,
PE
St Anne's Presbytery,
Convent Hill, Waterford
(*Ballybricken*, Waterford &
L.)

Mullins, Patrick (OCarm)
Carmelite Community,
Gort Muire, Ballinteer,
Dublin D16 EI67
Tel 01-2984014

Mullins, Patrick, Very Rev
Canon, PE
Tuam, Co Galway
(Tuam, retired)

Mulroy, Tim (SSC)
No 3 and 4,
Ma Yau Tong Village,
Po Lam Road,
Tseung Kwan O,
Kowloon, Hong Kong, SAR

Mulryne, Philip Rev (OP)
St Mary's, Pope's Quay,
Cork
Tel 021-4502267

Mulvany, Seamus, Very Rev,
PP
Parochial House,
Tubberclaire-Glasson,
Athlone, Co Westmeath
Tel 090-6485103
(*Glasson*, Meath)

Mulvey, Anthony (CSsR)
St Patrick's, Esker,
Athenry, Co Galway
Tel 091-844007

Mulvihill, Anthony, Very Rev
Ballymarkham, Quin,
Co Clare
(Limerick)

Mulvihill, Eamonn, Very
Rev, PP
Castlegregory, Co Kerry
Tel 066-7139145
(*Castlegregory*, Kerry)

Mundisye, Simon, PC
Presbytery, Blackditch
Road
Ballyfermot, Dublin 10
Tel 01-6265695
(*Ballyfermot Upper*,
Dublin)

Mundow, Sean, Rev
The Presbytery,
Chapelizod, Dublin 20
Tel 01-6264645/
087-8195073
(*Chapelizod*, Dublin)

Munnelly, Patrick, Very Rev,
PP
Ardagh, Ballina, Co Mayo
Tel 096-31144
(*Ardagh*, Killala)

Munster, Ramon, Very Rev
Canon, PP
Parochial House,
Church Road,
Bundoran, Co Donegal
F94 AK80
Tel 071-9841290
(*Bundoran*, Clogher)

Muresan, Coriolan, CC
Presbytery No 2,
St Joseph's Road, Dublin 7
Tel 01-8386571
(*Aughrim Street*, Dublin)

Murney, Peadar, Very Rev
Archdeacon,
25 Thomastown Road,
Dun Laoghaire, Co Dublin
Tel 01-2856660
(Dublin, retired)

Murphy O'Connor, Kerry,
Venerable Archdeacon, PE
The Bungalow,
Turner's Cross, Cork
Tel 021-4312466
(*Turner's Cross*, Cork & R.)

Murphy, Aidan, Very Rev,
PP
St Peter's Presbytery,
10 Fair Street,
Drogheda,
Co Louth A92 NX3T
Tel 041-9838239
(*Drogheda*, Armagh)

Murphy, Alphonsus, Very
Rev, PE
Carbury, Co Kildare
Tel 046-9553020
(Kildare & L., retired)

Murphy, Anthony (MHM)
St Joseph's House,
50 Orwell Park,
Rathgar, Dublin D06 C535
Tel 01-4127700

Murphy, Bernard (OCarm)
Gort Muire, Ballinteer,
Dublin 16 D16 EI67
Tel 01-2984014

Murphy, Brian (OSB)
Glenstal Abbey, Murroe,
Co Limerick
Tel 061-386103

Murphy, Canice (OP)
St Saviour's, Bridge Street,
Waterford
Tel 051-875061

Murphy, Colm, Very Rev,
Clongeen,
Foulksmills,
Co Wexford
Tel 051-565610
(Ferns, retired)

Murphy, Colum
Cathedral Presbytery,
38 Hill Street,
Newry, BT34 1AT
Tel 028-30262586
(*Newry Pastoral Area*,
Dromore)

Murphy, Conor (OMI)
Oblates House of Retreat
Inchicore, Dublin 8
Tel 01-4534408/4541805

Murphy, Cornelius (SMA)
SMA House,
Wilton,
Cork, T12 KR23
Tel 021-4541069/4541884

Murphy, Cornelius (SSC)
St Columban's,
Dalgan Park, Navan,
Co Meath
Tel 046-9021525

Murphy, Cyril (SSC)
St Columban's Retirement
Home, Dalgan Park,
Navan, Co Meath
Tel 046-9021525

Murphy, Daniel, Very Rev,
PP
Church Road, Aghada,
Co Cork
Tel 086-0224682
(*Aghada*, Cloyne)

Murphy, David, CC, CF
Chaplain to Defence
Forces
c/o Bishop's House,
Summerhill,
Wexford
(Ferns)

Murphy, Denis (OP)
(leave of absence)
St Catherine's, Newry,
Co Down BT35 8BN
Tel 028-30262178

Murphy, Denis, Very Rev,
Adm
Tolerton, Ballickmoyler,
Carlow
Tel 056-4442126
(*Doonane*, Kildare & L.)

Murphy, Derry (SAC), Very
Rev, PP
St Benin's Parish,
Dublin Road,
Shankill, Co Dublin
Tel 01-2824425
(*Shankill*, Dublin)

Murphy, Edmund (OP)
Newbridge College,
Droichead Nua, Co Kildare
Tel 045-487200

Murphy, Enda
Rome
(Kilmore)

Murphy, Eoin,
25 The Haven, Glasnevin,
Dublin 9
(Dublin, retired)

Murphy, Francis, Very Rev, PP
Kilmuckridge, Gorey,
Co Wexford
Tel 053-9130116
(*Kilmuckridge (Litter) and Monamolin*, Ferns)

Murphy, Gabriel, Very Rev, PP
Keash, Ballymote,
Co Sligo
Tel 086-3249686
(*Keash (Drumrat)*, Achonry)

Murphy, George, Very Rev Canon, PP
Minane Bridge, Co Cork
Tel 021-4887105
(*Tracton Abbey*, Cork & R.)

Murphy, James (SJ)
Irish Jesuit Provincialate,
Milltown Park,
Sandford Road, Dublin 6
Tel 01-4987333

Murphy, James, Very Rev, PP
St Brigid's, Rosslare,
Co Wexford
Tel 053-9132118
(*Tagoat*, Ferns)

Murphy, James, Very Rev, PP
St Canice's Presbytery,
Dean Street,
Kilkenny R95 K6PH
Tel 056-7752991/
087-2609545
(*St Canice's*, Ossory)

Murphy, Jason
(priest in residence)
Killougher, Redhills,
Co Cavan
Tel 047-55021
(*Belturbet (Annagh)*, Kilmore)

Murphy, Jeremiah (SAC),
Very Rev
Provincial House,
'Homestead',
Sandyford Road,
Dundrum, Dublin 16
Tel 01-2956180/2954170

Murphy, Jerry (SSC)
St Columban's,
Dalgan Park, Navan,
Co Meath
Tel 046-9021525

Murphy, John
Bailieborough Road
Virginia, Co Cavan
(Kilmore, retired)

Murphy, Joseph, Very Rev Mgr
Head of Protocol, Office of Secretariat of State,
(Section for Relations with States),
00120 Vatican City
Tel 0039-0669883193
(Cloyne)

Murphy, Laurence (SJ)
Milltown Park,
Sandford Road,
Dublin D06 V9K7
Tel 01-2698411/2698113

Murphy, Malachy, PP
Parochial House,
25 Priestbush Road,
Whitecross,
Co Armagh BT60 2TP
Tel 028-37507214
(*Whitecross (Loughilly)*, Armagh)

Murphy, Martin, Very Rev, PP
Drom, Thurles,
Co Tipperary
Tel 0504-51196
(*Drom and Inch*, Cashel & E.)

Murphy, Michael, Very Rev, Adm
Presbytery No 1,
Treepark Road,
Kilnamanagh, Dublin 24
Tel 01-4523805/
086-2408188
(*Kilnamanagh-Castleview*, Dublin)

Murphy, Michael (OFMCap)
Capuchin Frary,
Friary Street,
Kilkenny R95 NX60
Tel 056-7721439

Murphy, Michael, CC
The Parochial House,
Roundfort,
Hollymount,
Co Mayo F12 A3Y8
Tel 094-9540026
(*Robeen*, Tuam)

Murphy, Michael, Very Rev Canon, PP
The Presbytery,
Ballyphehane, Co Cork
Tel 021-4965560
(*Ballyphehane*, Cork & R.)

Murphy, Mícheál, Very Rev, PP, VF
11 Ashgrove,
Mountmellick, Co Laois
Tel 057-8679302
(*Mountmellick*, Kildare & L.)

Murphy, Noel (CSSp)
Rockwell College,
Cashel, Co Tipperary
Tel 062-61444

Murphy, Noel, (CSSp)
14 Springfield Drive,
Dooradoyle, Limerick
Tel 061-304508/
087-2228971
(*Pastroal Unit 6*, Limerick)

Murphy, Pádraig, Very Rev, PE
Parochial House,
Jenkinstown, Dundalk,
Co Louth A91 CC79
Tel 042-9371328
(Armagh, retired)

Murphy, Patrick (SPS)
Assistant District Leader,
Director of Slí an Chroí,
St Patrick's, Kiltegan,
Co Wicklow W91 Y022

Murphy, Patrick, Adm
St Mary's, Athlone,
Co Westmeath
Tel 090-6472088
(*Athlone*, Ardagh & Cl.)

Murphy, Patrick
(Kerry, retired)

Murphy, Patrick, Very Rev, PP
Templetuohy, Thurles,
Co Tipperary
Tel 0504-53114
(*Templetuohy*, Cashel & E.)

Murphy, Paul, CC
Our Lady of Lourdes Presbytery,
Hardman's Gardens,
Drogheda, Co Louth
Tel 041-9831899
(*Drogheda*, Armagh)

Murphy, Paul (OFMCap)
Vicar, Secretary of the Province,
Provincial Office,
12 Halston Street,
Dublin D07 Y2T5
Tel 01-8733205

Murphy, Paul F., Very Rev, CF
Chaplain's House,
Dún Uí Mhaoilíosa
Renmore, Galway
Tel 091-751156
(Waterford & L.)

Murphy, Paul, Very Rev, Co-PP
St John's Presbytery,
New Street, Waterford
(Waterford & L., retired)

Murphy, Peadar, Very Rev, PP
Aghabullogue, Co Cork
Tel 021-7334035
(*Aghabullogue*, Cloyne)

Murphy, Peter
Chaplain,
Mater Private Hospital,
Dublin 7
Tel 01-8858888
(Dublin)

Murphy, Peter, Very Rev Canon, PP, VF
Parochial House,
Hale Street, Ardee,
Co Louth A92 PXF3
Tel 041-6850920
(*Ardee & Collon*, Armagh)

Murphy, Seán, Very Rev, PP
Miltown Malbay, Co Clare
Tel 065-7084129
(*Críocha Callan Pastoral Area*, Killaloe)

Murphy, Thomas, Very Rev Canon,
Brookhaven Nursing Home,
Ballyragget, Co Kilkenny
086-8130694
(Ossory, retired)

Murphy Timothy, PC
St Mary's, Barndarrig
Co Wicklow
(*Kilbride and Barndarrig*, Dublin)

Murphy, William, Most Rev, DD
Retired Bishop of Kerry
No. 2 Cathedral Place,
Killarney, Co Kerry
Tel 064-6633833
(Kerry)

Murray, Brendan (SSC)
St Columban's,
Dalgan Park,
Navan, Co Meath
Tel 046-9021525

Murray, Brendan, Very Rev Canon
(priest in residence)
Apt 13 Downview Manor,
Belfast BT15 4JL
(*Holy Family*, Down & C.)

Murray, Declan (SJ)
Assistant Provincial,
Milltown Park
Sandford Road, Dublin 6
Tel 01-4987333

Murray, Denis, Very Rev
Parochial House,
Derrylin, Co Fermanagh
(Kilmore, retired)

Murray, Dermot (SJ)
Cherryfield Lodge,
Milltown Park, Ranelagh,
Dublin D06 V9K7
Tel 01-4985800

LIST OF CLERGY IN IRELAND

Murray, Donal, Most Rev, DD
Bishop Emeritus, Former Bishop of Limerick,
Limerick Diocesan Centre,
St Munchin's,
Corbally, Limerick
Tel 061-350000
(Limerick, retired)

Murray, Francis, PP
Drumshanbo, Co Leitrim
Tel 071-9641010
(*Drumshanbo (Murhaun)*, Ardagh & Cl.)

Murray, Gerard, (SMA)
African Missions,
Blackrock Road,
Cork T12 TD54
Tel 021-4292871

Murray, James (OCarm)
Carmelite Priory, Moate,
Co Westmeath N37 AW34
Tel 090-6481160/6481398

Murray, James, CC
Director of ACCORD,
Carraroe, Sligo, Co Sligo
Tel 071-9162136
(*Sligo, St Anne's*, Elphin)

Murray, John, Very Rev, PP
Achill Sound, Achill,
Co Mayo
Tel 098-45288
(*Achill*, Tuam)

Murray, John, Very Rev
c/o 75 Somerton Road
Belfast BT15 4DE
(Down & C., retired)

Murray, Liam, PP
Ballymahon, Co Longford
Tel 090-6432253
(*Ballymahon (Shrule)*, Ardagh & Cl.)

Murray, Michael, CC
Belcarra, Castlebar,
Co Mayo
Tel 094-9032006
(*Balla and Manulla*, Tuam)

Murray, Michael, Very Rev
c/o 73 Somerton Road,
Belfast, BT15 4DE
(Down & C., retired)

Murray, Patrick J., Very Rev, PP
c/o Diocesan Office, Newry
(Dromore, retired)

Murray, Patrick (MHM)
St Joseph's House,
50 Orwell Park,
Rathgar, Dublin D06 C535
Tel 01-4127700

Murray, Paul (OP)
Convent of SS Xystus and Clement
Collegio San Clemente,
Via Labicana 95,
00184 Roma
Tel 0039-06-7740021

Murray, Placid (OSB)
Glenstal Abbey, Murroe,
Co Limerick
Tel 061-386103

Murray, Raymond, Rt Rev Mgr, PE
60 Glen Mhacaha,
Cathedral Road,
Armagh BT61 8AF
Tel 028-37510821
(Armagh, retired)

Murray, Tom PP
Ballinalee, Co Longford
Tel 043-3323110
(*Clonbroney*, Ardagh & Cl.)

Murtagh, Brian (CSSp)
Holy Spirit Missionary College,
Kimmage Manor,
Whitehall Road, Dublin 12
Tel 01-4064300

Murtagh, Colm, Very Rev, PE
Parochial House, Kildalkey,
Co Meath
Tel 046-9546488
(Meath, retired)

Murtagh, Michael (CSsR), PP
103 Cherry Orchard Avenue,
Cherry Orchard, Dublin 10
Tel 01-6267930
(*Cherry Orchard*, Dublin)

Murtagh, Michael, Co-PP
69 Anne Devlin,
Ballyroan, Dublin 14
Tel 01-4950444
(*Ballyroan*, Dublin)

Murtagh, G. Michael, Very Rev, PP
Parochial House,
Old Chapel Lane, Dunleer,
Co Louth
A92 W29X
Tel 041-6851278
(*Dunleer*, Armagh)

Murtagh, Liam, Very Rev
33 Grace Park Road,
Drumcondra, Dublin 9
(Dublin, retired)

Murtagh, Michael (CSsR)
Superior,
Clonard Monastery,
1 Clonard Gardens,
Belfast, BT13 2RL
Tel 028-90445950

Murtagh, Michael, CC
5 St Mary's Terrace,
Arklow, Co Wicklow
Tel 0402-41505
(*Arklow*, Dublin)

Murtagh, Ray (SPS)
St Patrick's, Kiltegan,
Co Wicklow
Tel 059-6473600

Murtala, Moses Daniel, TA
75 Ludford Road,
Ballinteer, Dublin 16
(*Meadowbrook*, Dublin)

Murtha, Kieran (SSCC)
Cootehill, Co Cavan
Tel 049-5552188

Mushawasha, Martin, PC
80 St Mary's Road,
East Wall, Dublin 3
Tel 01-8560980
(*East Wall-North Strand*, Dublin)

Mutunzi, Eladius Leonard, PC
Presbytery 2, 6 Old Hill,
Leixlip, Co Kildare
Tel 01-6243673
(*Leixlip*, Dublin)

Mwale, Hector, PC
The Presbytery,
St Martin de Porres Parish,
Firhouse Road West
Dublin 24 D24 K198
Tel 01-4510160
(*Bohernabreena*, Dublin)

Myers, David (IC)
Provincial, Clonturk House,
Ormond Road,
Drumcondra, Dublin 9
Tel 01-6877014

N

Nagle, Cathal
(Galway, retired)

Nagle, Joseph (OFMCap)
Capuchin Friary,
Holy Trinity,
Fr Mathew Quay,
Cork T12 PK24
Tel 021-4270827

Nallen, Michael, Very Rev, PP
Aughoose, Ballina,
Co Mayo
Tel 097-87990
(*Kilcommon-Erris*, Killala)

Nallukunnel, Antony (OFMConv)
Friary of the Visitation,
Fairview Strand, Dublin 3
Tel 01-8376000

Nally, Frank Rev (SSC)
St Columban's,
Dalgan Park,
Navan, Co Meath
Tel 046-9021525

Nally, John, Very Rev
Waterford
(Meath)

Nash, Ger, Most Rev, DD
Bishop's House
Summerhill, Wexford
Tel 053-9122177
(Ferns)

Nash, Tom (CSSp)
Blackrock College,
Blackrock, Co Dublin
Tel 01-2888681

Naughton, John, Very Rev
Clonfert Avenue,
Portumna,
Co Galway H53 WC82
(Clonfert, retired)

Naughton, Richard, Very Rev, PP, VF
Mountain Lodge,
132 Dublin Road, Newry,
Co Down BT35 8QT
Tel 028-30262174
(*Cloghogue (Killeavy Upper)*, Armagh)

Naughton, Ultan (SSCC)
Room RD-117,
Rathdown House,
TU Dublin, Grangegorman
Dublin D07 H6K8
(Dublin)

Nawrat, Lukasz (SDB)
Provicial Secretary,
Salesian College,
Maynooth Road,
Celbridge,
Co Kildare W23 W0XK

Neary, Donal (SJ)
35 Lower Leeson Street,
Dublin 2
Tel 01-6761248
(Editor, Sacred Heart Messenger)
Tel 01-6767491

Neary, Michael, Most Rev, DD
Retired Archbishop of Tuam,
Blackfort, Castlebar,
Co Mayo
(Tuam)

Nechikattil, Pius (SSP)
c/o Society of St Paul,
Moyglare Road,
Maynooth, Co Kildare
Tel 01-6285933

Ndugwa, Severinus, PC
No. 2 Presbytery,
St Canice's Parish,
Finglas, Dublin 11
Tel 087-8180097
(*Finglas*, Dublin)

Needham, Gerard, Very Rev
The Presbytery,
Bunowen Road,
Louisburgh,
Co Mayo F28 P635
(Tuam)

Neenan, Daniel, Rt Rev Mgr,
Holy Trinity Abbey Church,
Adare, Co Limerick
Tel 061-396172/
087-2208547
(*Pastoral Unit 11*, Limerick)

Neeson, Patrick, Very Rev,
Parochial House,
Drumardan Road,
Ballygalget BT22 1NE
(Down & C., retired)

LIST OF CLERGY IN IRELAND

Nejad, Damian, CC
Parochial House,
Letterkenny, Co Donegal
F92 CF88
Tel 074-9121021
(*Letterkenny*, Raphoe)

Nestor, Dermot, Very Rev, Co-PP
Parochial House,
Nutgrove Avenue,
Dublin 14
Tel 01-2985916
(*Churchtown*, Dublin)

Neville, Alan (MSC)
Western Road,
Cork T12 TN80
Tel 021-4804120

Neville, Anthony
Moycullen, Co Galway
Tel 095-44668
(*Tuam*, retired)

Nevin, John (MHM)
St Joseph's House,
50 Orwell Park,
Rathgar, Dublin D06 C535
Tel 01-4127700

Nevin, Michael G.
(priest in residence)
The Presbytery,
Harrington Street,
Dublin 8
Tel 01-4789093
(*Harrington Street*, Dublin)

Newell, Martin, Very Rev Canon, PE
Claran, Ower P.O.,
Co Galway H91 YR6A
Tel 093-35436
(*Tuam*, retired)

Newman, John, Very Rev, PP
Glanmire, Co Cork
Tel 021-4866307
(*Glanmire*, Cork & R.)

Neylon, Gerard Rev
Regional Vice-Director,
St Columban's,
Dalgan Park,
Navan, Co Meath
Tel 046-9021525

Neylon, Finbarr, CC
c/o Parish Office,
St John the Evangelist,
Greendale Road,
Kilbarrack, Dublin 5
Tel 01-8390433
(*Kilbarrack-Foxfield*, Dublin)

Neylon, Sean, Very Rev, PP
Taghmaconnell,
Ballinasloe,
Co Galway H53 RT28
Tel 090-9683929
(*Taghmaconnell*, Clonfert)

Ngalame, Bernard, CC
Forthill House,
The Batteries,
Athlone, Co Westmeath
Tel 0906-492171
(*Athlone*, Elphin)

Nguyen, Dan An, Very Rev, Co-PP
Parochial House,
Sperrin Road, Dublin 12
Tel 01-4550133
(*Mourne Road*, Dublin)

Nicholas, Michael (OFM)
23/25 Oudstrijderslaan,
1950 Kraainem, Belgium
Tel 0032-2-720-1970

Nilan, Colman (SMA)
SMA House, Cloonbigeen,
Claregalway,
Co Galway H91 YK64
Tel 091-798880

Niyoyita, Kizito (SJ)
Jesuit Community,
27 Leinster Road,
Rathmines, Dublin 6
Tel 01-4970250

Njarakattuvely, Joy, CC
Cathedral Presbytery,
O'Connell Street,
Ennis, Co Clare
Tel 065-6824043
(*Abbey Pastoral Area*, Killaloe)

Nkede, Evaristus, Very Rev, PP
Parochial House, Rooskey,
Carrick-on-Shannon,
Co Roscommon
(*Kilglass*, Elphin)

Nkem, Clinton, PC
St Maur's Parish Church,
Rush, Co Dublin
Tel 01-8949464
(*Rush*, Dublin)

Nohilly, Michael (SMA)
African Missions,
Blackrock Road,
Cork T12 TD54
Tel 021-4292871

Nohilly, Seamus (SMA)
Superior, SMA House,
Cloonbigeen, Claregalway,
Co Galway H91 YK64
Tel 091-798880

Nolan, Anthony (MSC)
Woodview House,
Mount Merrion Avenue,
Blackrock, Co Dublin
Tel 01-2881644

Nolan, Brendan, Very Rev, PP
Blackwater, Enniscorthy,
Co Wexford
Tel 053-9127118
(*Blackwater*, Ferns)

Nolan, Brian (CM)
41 Park View,
Dunard Road, Dublin 7

Nolan, Brian (CSsR)
Coordinator, Scala,
Castlemahon Road,
Castle Road, Blackrock,
Cork
Tel 021-4358800

Nolan, Damien, Co-PP
Director,
Ennis ACCORD Centre,
7 Carmody Street
Business Park,
Ennis, Co Clare
Tel 1850-585000
Parish: 1a Laghtagoona,
Corofin, Co Clare
Tel 065-6837178/
086-8396636
(*Imeall Boirne Pastoral Area*, Killaloe)

Nolan, Francis, PP
The Presbytery, Fenit,
Tralee, Co Kerry
Tel 066-7136145
Director, Accord,
St John's Pastoral Centre,
Castle Street, Tralee,
Co Kerry
Tel 066-7122280
(*Spa*, Kerry)

Nolan, J. Michael, Rt Rev Mgr
26 Harmony Avenue,
Donnybrook, Dublin 4
(Dublin, retired)

Nolan, James, Very Rev, PP
Davidstown, Enniscorthy,
Co Wexford
Tel 053-9238240
(*Davidstown and Courtnacuddy*, Ferns)

Nolan, John P., Very Rev, PP
Duncannon, New Ross,
Co Wexford
Tel 051-389118
(*Duncannon*, Ferns)

Nolan, Joseph
(Kerry, retired)

Nolan, Mark-Ephrem M. (OSB), Rt Rev Dom
Abbot,
Benedictine Monks,
Holy Cross Abbey,
119 Kilbroney Road,
Rostrevor,
Co Down BT34 3BN
Tel 028-41739979

Nolan, Martin (OSA)
St John's Priory,
Thomas Street, Dublin 8
Tel 01-6770393

Nolan, Robert, Very Rev, PP
Adamstown, Enniscorthy,
Co Wexford
Tel 053-9240512
(*Adamstown*, Ferns)

Nolan, Rory, Very Rev, PP
Borris, Co Carlow via Kilkenny
Tel 059-9773128
(*Borris*, Kildare & L.)

Nolan, Seán, Very Rev, PE
Parochial House,
Donaghmoyne,
Co Monaghan A81 WP63
Tel 042-9661586
(*Donaghmoyne*, Clogher)

Nolan, Simon (OCarm)
Prior, Carmelite Priory,
Whitefriar Street Church,
56 Aungier Street,
Dublin D02 R598
Tel 01-4758821

Nolan, Tod, Very Rev, PP
Newport, Co Mayo
Tel 098-41123
(*Newport (Burrishoole)*, Tuam)

Noonan, Bernard, Mgr, PP, VG
Moate, Co Westmeath
Tel 090-6481180
(*Moate and Mount Temple*, Ardagh & Cl.)

Noonan, James (OCD)
St Teresa's,
Clarendon Street
Dublin 2
Tel 01-6718466/6718127

Noonan, Joseph, Very Rev, PE
Adare, Limerick
(Limerick, retired)

Noonan, Mark (CM), Very Rev
Phibsboro,
St Peter's, Dublin 7
Tel 01-8389708/8389841

Noonan, Michael, Very Rev, PE
Portarlington, Co Laois
Tel 057-8623431
(Kildare & L., retired)

Noonan, Michael, Very Rev, PP
Parochial House, Ardagh,
Co Limerick
Tel 087-6796217
(*Pastoral Unit 15*, Limerick)

Noone, Cletus (OFM)
Franciscan Friary,
Ennis, Co Clare
Tel 065-6828751

Noone, Martin G., Very Rev, Co-PP, VF
7 Seabury Drive,
Malahide, Co Dublin
K36 YN67
Tel 01-8451902
(*Yellow Walls*, Dublin)

Noone, Sean
The Presbytery,
Pollathomas,
Co Mayo
(Dublin, retired)

Noone, Thomas, Very Rev, PP
69 Griffith Avenue,
Dublin 9
Tel 01-8332864
(*Marino*, Dublin)

Norman, James, PC
Dun Bhríd,
64 Orwell Park Rise,
Dublin 6W
Tel 01-8376027
(*Willington*, Dublin)

LIST OF CLERGY IN IRELAND

Norris, Thomas, Dr, CC
St Canice's Presbytery,
Kilkenny R95 VYOT
Tel 056-7752994/
083-3241438
(*St Canice's*, Ossory)

Norton, Gerard (OP)
Prior, St Mary's Priory,
Tallaght, Dublin 24
Tel 01-4048100

Ntambang, Roland, PC
St Luke the Evangelist Parish,
Kilbarron Road,
Kilmore West, Dublin 5
Tel 01-8488149
(*Kilmore Road West*, Dublin)

Nugent, Eugene M., Most Rev, DCL
Apostolic Nunciature,
Yarmouk,
Block 1, Street 2, Villa NI,
Kuwait City, Kuwait
Tel +965-25337767
(Killaloe)

Nugent, Pat, CC
Springhill,
Glanmire, Co Cork
Tel 021-4866306
(*Glanmire and Glounthaune*, Cork & R.)

Nulty, Denis, Most Rev, DD
Bishop of Kildare and Leighlin,
Bishop's House, Carlow
Tel 059-9142796/
059-9176725
Apostolic Administrator,
Diocese of Ossory
Ossory Diocesan Office,
James Street,
Kilkenny R95 NH60
Tel 056-7762448
(Kildare & L.)

Nunes, Jose (SSP)
Society of Saint Paul,
Moyglare Road,
Maynooth Co Kildare
Tel 01-6285933

Nunez Yepez, Eduardo (OMI), PP
The Presbytery, Darndale,
Dublin 17
Tel 086-7954706
(*Darndale-Belcamp*, Dublin)

Nwanko, Jonathan, PC
c/o 12 Coarsemoor Park,
Straffan, Co Kildare
Tel 01-6288827
(*Celbridge*, Dublin)

Nwaogwugwu, Cornelius (CM)
St Vincent's College,
Castleknock,
Dublin D15 PD95
Tel 01-8213051

Nwakuna, Hyacinth (CSSp), CC
The Presbytery,
Kilmacanogue,
Co Wicklow
Tel 01-2760030
(*Enniskerry/Kilmacanogue*, Dublin)

Nwigwe, Peter, PC
12 Coarsemoor Park,
Straffan, Co Kildare
Tel 01-6012303
(*Celbridge*, Dublin)

Nyameh, Charles, CC
The Presbytery,
Loughrea, Co Galway
Tel 091-841212
(*Loughrea, St Brendan's Cathedral*, Clonfert)

Nyhan, Charles, CC
Cork Road, Carrigaline,
Co Cork
Tel 021-4371860
(*Carrigaline*, Cork & R.)

O

Ó Baoighill, Padraig, PP
Derrybeg, Letterkenny,
Co Donegal
Tel 074-9531310
Séiplíneach,
Pobalscoil Ghaoth Dobhair, Derrybeg,
Letterkenny, Co Donegal
Tel 074-9531040
(*Gweedore*, Raphoe)

Ó Baoill, Donnchadh, CC
Fintown, Donegal Town,
Co Donegal
Tel 074-9546107
(*Glenties (Iniskeel)*, Raphoe)

Ó Bréartúin, Liam S. (OCD)
53/55 Marlborough Road,
Dublin 4
Tel 01-6601832

Ó Brolcháin, Cormac (CSSp)
Community Leader,
Blackrock College,
Blackrock, Co Dublin
Tel 01-2888681

Ó Cochláin, Pádraig, Very Rev Canon, PP
Parochial House,
Arklow, Co Wicklow
Tel 0402-32294
(*Arklow*, Dublin)

Ó Cochláin, Seosamh, SP
c/o Diocesan Office,
Redemption Road, Cork
(Cork & R., retired)

Ó Conaire, Máirtín, PP
Teach an tSagairt
Kilronan, Aran Islands,
Co Galway H91 H7YW
Tel 099-61221
(*Aran Islands*, Tuam)

Ó Conghaile, Eamon
Árd Thiar, Carna, Co na Gaillimhe
(Tuam, retired)

Ó Cuill, Pádraig (OFMCap)
Capuchin Friary,
Station Road,
Raheny, Dublin D05 T9E4
Tel 01-8313886

Ó Cuív, Liam, Very Rev, Adm
126 Furry Park Road,
Dublin 5
Tel 01-8333793
(*Killester*, Dublin)

Ó Dochartaigh, Michael
(Kerry, retired)

Ó Dochartaigh, Tadhg, Very Rev
(Kerry, retired)

Ó Domhnaill, Ruairí, Very Rev, PP
Chapel Lane,
Newbridge, Co Kildare
Tel 045-431741
(*Caragh, Droichead Nua/Newbridge*, Kildare & L.)

Ó Dúill, Séamus (SDS)
Ard Mhuire, Kilmoon,
Lisdoonvarna, Co Clare
Tel 086-1030261
(retired)

Ó Fatharta, Pádraig (SPS)
St Patrick's, Kiltegan,
Co Wicklow
Tel 059-6473600

Ó Fearghaill, Fergus, DSS
Carlow College,
College Street, Carlow
Tel 059-9153200
(Kildare & L.)

Ó Fearraí, Cathal, Very Rev, PP, VF
Kilbarron House,
College Street
Ballyshannon, Raphoe
Tel 071-9851295
(*Ballyshannon (Kilbarron), Ballintra (Drumholm)*, Raphoe)

Ó Galláchóir, Nigel, PP
Annagry, Co Donegal
Tel 074-9548902
(*Annagry*, Raphoe)

Ó Gallchóir, Colm, Very Rev, PP
Killybegs, Co Donegal
Tel 074-9731030
(*Killybegs*, Raphoe)

Ó Gallchóir, Seán, Very Rev, PP
Tory Island, Co Donegal
Tel 074-9135214
(*Gortahork*, Raphoe)

Ó Giolláin, Leon (SJ)
Loyola House,
Milltown Park,
Sandford Road, Dublin 6
Tel 01-2180276

Ó Griofa, Gearóid, Very Rev, PP
Lettermore, Co Galway
Tel 091-551169
(*Lettermore*, Galway)

Ó hÍcí, Liam, PP
Ovens, Co Cork
Tel 021-4871180
(*Ovens*, Cork & R.)

Ó hAodha, Donncha
Nullamore,
Richmond Avenue South,
Dublin 6
Tel 01-4971239
(Opus Dei)

Ó hÓbáin, Éanna (OCarm)
Prior and Bursar,
Principal Senior School,
Terenure College,
Terenure,
Dublin D6W DK72
Tel 01-4904621

Ó Huallacháin, Maelísa (OFM)
Franciscan House of Studies, Dún Mhuire,
Seafield Road, Killiney,
Co Dublin
Tel 01-2826760

Okereke, Christopher
St Mary's,
Lucan, Co Dublin
Tel 01-6217041
(*Lucan*, Dublin)

Okolo, Felix (OCD)
Avila, Bloomfield Avenue,
Morehampton Road,
Dublin 4
Tel 01-6430200

Ó Laoide, Caoimhín (OFM)
Franciscan Friary,
Killarney, Co Kerry
Tel 064-6631334/6631066

Ó Loingsigh, Micheál, Very Rev, PP
Grenagh, Co Cork
Tel 021-4886128
(*Grenagh*, Cloyne)

Ó Longaigh, Seán,
Askeaton, Co Limerick
Tel 061-392249
(*Pastoral Unit 12*, Limerick)

Ó Maoldhomhnaigh, Conn, MA
Vice-President and Chaplain,
Carlow College,
College Street, Carlow
Tel 059-9153200
(Kildare & L.)

Ó Mathúna, Tadhg, Very Rev Canon, AP
2 Parochial House,
Blackrock, Cork
Tel 021-4358025
(*Blackrock*, Cork & R.)

Ó Murchú, Ailbe (OFM)
Franciscan Friary,
Ennis, Co Clare V95 A4N2
Tel 065-6828751

Ó Murchú, Daithí
Chaplain,
Holy Cross Hospital,
Hindhead Road,
Haslemere,
Surrey GU27 1NQ, UK
(Galway)

Ó Murchú, Tomás, SP
Riverstick, Kinsale, Co Cork
Tel 021-4771332
(Clontead, Cork & R.)

Ó Murchú, Diarmuid (MSC)
Formation House,
56 Mulvey Park, Dundrum,
Dublin 16
Tel 01-2951856

Ó Riain, Diarmaid (OFM)
Franciscan Friary,
Multyfarnham,
Co Westmeath
Tel 044-9371114/9371137

Ó Ríordáin, John J. (CSsR)
Mount Saint Alphonsus,
Limerick
Tel 061-315099

Ó Ruairc, Caoimhín (SJ)
Irish Jesuit Provincialate
Milltown Park,
Sandford Road, Dublin 6
Tel 01-4987333

Ó Siochrú, Colm R.
Our Lady's Manor,
Bulloch Castle, Dalkey,
Co Dublin
(Dublin, retired)

Ó Tuathaigh, Antoin
c/o Diocesan Office,
Social Service Centre,
Henry Street, Limerick
(Limerick, retired)

O'Boyle, Aidan, Very Rev, VF
Cathedral Presbytery,
Ballina, Co Mayo
Tel 096-71365
(Ballina, Killala)

O'Boyle, Eugene
Parochial House,
Glenamaddy,
Co Galway F45 YD27
Tel 094-9659962
Administrator,
Williamstown
(Templetoher)
Parochial House,
Williamstown,
Co Galway
(Glenamaddy
(Boyounagh),
Williamstown
(Templetoher), Tuam)

O'Boyle, John, Rt Rev Mgr
Dalysfort Road,
Salthill, Co Galway
(Tuam, retired)

O'Boyle, Kevin, (SSC)
St Columban's, Dalgan
Park, Navan, Co Meath
Tel 046-9021525

O'Boyle, Paul, Very Rev, PP
Clane, Naas, Co Kildare
Tel 045-868249
(Clane, Kildare & L.)

O'Brien, Anthony, Rt Rev
Mgr, PP, VG, Adm
Mallow, Co Cork
Tel 022-20391
(Mallow/Mourne Abbey,
Cloyne)

O'Brien, Anthony (OCSO)
Mount Saint Joseph
Abbey, Roscrea,
Co Tipperary E53 D651
Tel 0505-25600

O'Brien, Anthony (SSC)
St Columban's,
Dalgan Park
Navan, Co Meath
Tel 046-9021525

O'Brien, Augustine (MSC)
'Croí Nua', Rosary Lane,
Taylor's Hill, Galway
Tel 091-520960

O'Brien, Ben (OSA)
Duckspool House
(Retirement Community),
Abbeyside, Dungarvan,
Co Waterford
Tel 058-23784

O'Brien, Daniel (MSC)
Parish House,
Leap, Skibbereen,
Co Cork P81 NN52
Tel 028-33177

O'Brien, Eamon, Very Rev
No. 5 Hopecroft,
Main Street,
Glenavy BT29 4LN
(Down & C., retired)

O'Brien, Eamonn
Church Road, Croom,
Co Limerick
Tel 061-397213/
087-0767521
(Limerick)

O'Brien, Eamonn, Very Rev, PE
Newbrook Nursing Home,
Mullingar, Co Westmeath
(Meath, retired)

O'Brien, Evin, CC
The Presbytery,
Skibbereen, Co Cork
Tel 028-22877
(St Patrick's Cathedral,
Skibbereen,
Rath and the Islands, Cork
& R.)

O'Brien, Francis, Very Rev, PP
Parochial House,
51 Victoria Road, Larne,
Co Antrim BT40 1LY
Tel 028-28273230/
28273053
(Larne, Down & C.)

O'Brien, George (SPS)
St Patrick's, 21 Leeson
Park,
Dublin 6 D06 DE76
Tel 01-4977897

O'Brien, Gerard, PP
Bornacoola,
Carrick-on-Shannon,
Co Leitrim
Tel 071-9638229
(Bornacoola, Ardagh & Cl.)

O'Brien, Gregory, Very Rev, PP
Parochial House,
Old Hill, Leixlip,
Co Kildare
Tel 01-6245597
(Confey, Leixlip, Dublin)

O'Brien, James, Rt Rev Mgr, PP
Ballyea, Co Cork
Tel 063-81470
(Ballyhea, Cloyne)

O'Brien, James, Very Rev, AP
Parochial House,
Feakle, Co Clare
Tel 061-924035/
087-2665793
(Inis Cealtra Pastoral Area,
Killaloe)

O'Brien, Jerry, AP
Bridgetown, Co Clare
Tel 061-376137
(Scáth na Sionnaine,
Killaloe)

O'Brien, John (CSSp)
Holy Spirit Missionary
College
Kimmage Manor,
Whitehall Road,
Dublin D12 P5YP
Tel 01-4064300

O'Brien, John (OFM)
Franciscan Abbey,
Multyfarnham,
Co Westmeath
Tel 044-9371114/9371137

O'Brien, John (SMA)
Vice-Superior, SMA House,
81 Ranelagh Road,
Ranelagh, Dublin 6
Tel 01-4968162/3

O'Brien, John, Very Rev, PP
Parochial House, Killinure,
Tullow, Co Carlow
Tel 059-9156344
(Clonmore, Kildare & L.)

O'Brien, John, Very Rev, PP
Parochial House, Oristown,
Kells, Co Meath
Tel 046-9054124
(Oristown, Meath)

O'Brien, John (SPS)
Kiltegan House,
11 Douglas Road, Cork
Tel 021-4969371

O'Brien, John, Very Rev, Adm
Parochial House,
211 Navan Road, Dublin 7
Tel 01-8681436
(Navan Road, Dublin)

O'Brien, Jordan (OP), Very Rev, PP
St Mary's Priory,
The Claddagh, Galway
Tel 091-582884

O'Brien, Joseph (OP)
Prior, Holy Cross,
Tralee, Co Kerry
Tel 066-7121135

O'Brien, Joseph, Very Rev
Canon, PP
Lackaghmore,
Turloughmore, Co Galway
(Tuam, retired)

O'Brien, Kieran, Very Rev, Adm, VF
Killarney, Co Kerry
Tel 064-6631014
Moderator,
Kilcummin Parish
(Killarney, Kilcummin,
Kerry)

O'Brien, Liam, Very Rev, PP
Sneem, Co Kerry
Tel 064-6645141
(Sneem, Kerry)

O'Brien, Lorcan, Rt Rev Mgr, Adm
Pro-Cathedral House,
83 Marlborough Street,
Dublin 1
Tel 01-8745441
(Pro-Cathedral, Dublin)

O'Brien, Martin, Very Rev, PP
1 Cuan an Chláir,
Cahercalla,
Ennis, Co Clare
Tel 087-2504075
(Killaloe)

O'Brien, Michael
St Anne's Presbytery,
Convent Hill, Waterford
Tel 051-855819
(Waterford & L., retired)

O'Brien, Michael (MHM)
St Joseph's House,
50 Orwell Park,
Rathgar, Dublin D06 C535
Tel 01-4127700

O'Brien, Rory (SPS)
St Patrick's, Kiltegan,
Co Wicklow
Tel 059-6473600

O'Brien, Ned (SAC)
(Residing elsewhere)

O'Brien, Pat (SPS), CC
Kiltegan, Co Wicklow
Tel 059-6473211
(Rathvilly, Kildare & L.)

LIST OF CLERGY IN IRELAND

O'Brien, Pat, Very Rev, PP
The Parochial House,
Cahreenard
Caherlistrane,
Co Galway H91 Y06D
Tel 093-55428
(*Caherlistrane*
(*Donaghpatrick and
Kilcoona*), Tuam)

O'Brien, Patrick, Very Rev
Canon
No 9 Bungalow,
Chambersland,
New Ross, Co Wexford
(*Ferns*)

O'Brien, Paul (OSA)
The Abbey, Fethard,
Co Tipperary
Tel 052-31273

O'Brien, Peter, Very Rev, PP
Kilfian, Killala, Co Mayo
Tel 096-32420
(*Killala, retired*)

O'Brien, Sean (MHM)
St Joseph's House,
50 Orwell Park, Rathgar,
Dublin 6
Tel 01-4127700

O'Brien, Terrence (MSC), PP
Parochial House,
Leap, Co Cork
Tel 028-33177
(*Kilmacabea*, Cork & R.)

O'Brien, Timothy, Very Rev,
AP
Carrigatoher, Nenagh,
Co Tipperary
Tel 067-31231/
087-6548331/087-2623922
(*Odhran Pastoral Area,*
Killaloe)

O'Byrne, Christopher, Rt Rev
Mgr, PE
3 Grange Court,
Magherafelt,
Co Derry BT45 5RU
Tel 028-79631791
(*Armagh, retired*)

O'Byrne, Gerard, Very Rev,
PE, CC
Rathangan, Co Kildare
Tel 045-524316
(*Rathangan*, Kildare & L.)

O'Byrne, John,
St Mary's,
Athlunkard Street,
Limerick
Tel 085-7491268
(*Pastoral Unit 4,* Limerick)

O'Byrne, Michael, Very Rev,
AP
Kilmeaden, Co Waterford
Tel 051-384117
(*Portlaw,* Waterford & L.)

O'Byrne, Paddy, CC
Presbytery No 2,
Church Grounds
Tel 01-2882257
(*Kilmacud-Stillorgan,*
Dublin)

O'Byrne, Patrick, Very Rev,
PE, CC
St Mary's, Daingean,
Co Offaly
Tel 057-9353064
(*Daingean*, Kildare & L.)

O'Byrne, Patrick, Co-PP
No. 2 The Presbytery,
Mountview,
Blanchardstown, Dublin 15
Tel 01-8216380
(*Mountview,* Dublin)

O'Byrne, Patrick J., CC
194 Navan Road,
Dublin 7
Tel 01-8383313
(*Navan Road,* Dublin)

O'Byrne, Thomas, Very Rev,
Adm
The Presbytery,
Old Dublin Road, Carlow,
Tel 059-9131227
(*Cathedral, Carlow*,
Kildare & L.)

O'Byrne, William, Very Rev,
PP
Kill, Naas, Co Kildare
Tel 045-878008
(*Kill,* Kildare & L.)

O'Callagahan, Flor (OSA)
St Augustine's Priory,
Dungarvan, Co Waterford
Tel 058-41136

O'Callaghan, Benedict
(OCarm),
Prior, Carmelite Priory,
Kinsale,
Co Cork P17 WR88
Tel 021-4772138

O'Callaghan, Ciarán (CSsR)
Vicar, Clonard Monastery,
1 Clonard Gardens,
Belfast BT13 2RL
Tel 028-90445950

O'Callaghan, Denis, Rt Rev
Mgr, PE
Mallow, Co Cork
Tel 022-21112
(*Cloyne, retired*)

O'Callaghan, Enda (SJ)
St Ignatius Community &
Church,
27 Raleigh Row, Salthill,
Galway
Tel 091-523707

O'Callaghan, Flor (OSA)
St Augstine's Priory
O'Connell Street,
Co Limerick

O'Callaghan, John (OSB)
Glenstal Abbey, Murroe,
Co Limerick
Tel 061-386103

O'Callaghan, Kevin, Rt Rev
Mgr, AP,
The Presbytery, Lissarda,
Co Cork
Tel 021-7336053
(*Kilmurry, Ovens,* Cork &
R.)

O'Callaghan, Peadar, Very
Rev, PE
Suimhneas, Charleville,
Co Cork
Tel 086-8054040
(*Cloyne, retired*)

O'Caoimh, Tomás
c/o Diocesan Office,
Killarney, Co Kerry
(*Kerry*)

O'Carroll, Ciaran, Very Rev
Mgr, PP, VG
Parochial House,
Stillorgan Road, Dublin 4
Tel 01-2693926
(*Donnybrook,* Dublin)

O'Carroll, Gerard (SPS)
St Patrick's, Main Street,
Knock, Co Mayo
Tel 094-9388661

O'Ciarain, Peadar
Sons of Divine Providence,
Orione House,
13 Lower Teddington
Road, Hampton, Wick,
Kinston-upon-Thames,
KT1 4EU
(*Dublin, retired*)

O'Connell, Anthony, Very
Rev
5 Parkside, Stoneybatter,
Wexford
(*Ferns, retired*)

O'Connell, Con (MSC)
Formation House,
56 Mulvey Park, Dundrum,
Dublin 16
Tel 01-2951856

O'Connell, Conal (SSC)
St Columban's,
Dalgan Park,
Navan, Co Meath
Tel 046-9021525

O'Connell, David, Very Rev,
PP
Lislevane, Bandon,
Co Cork
Tel 023-8846171
(*Barryroe,* Cork & R.)

O'Connell, Henry, CC
Westport, Co Mayo
Tel 098-28871
(*Westport (Aughaval),*
Tuam)

O'Connell, James (SM), Very
Rev, Adm
Cerdon, Marist Fathers,
St Mary's Road,
Dundalk, Co Louth
(*Dundalk,* Armagh)

O'Connell, James, Very Rev,
Adm
Parochial House,
Ballon, Co Carlow
Tel 059-9159329
(*Ballon,* Kildare & L.)

O'Connell, James (CSSp)
Holy Spirit Missionary
College
Kimmage Manor,
Whitehall Road,
Dublin D12 P5YP
Tel 01-4064300

O'Connell, Jim (MHM)
Editor of St Joseph's
Advocate,
St Joseph's House,
50 Orwell Park,
Rathgar, Dublin D06 C535
Tel 01-4127700

O'Connell, Jimmy (SM), Adm
Superior, Holy Family
Parish,
Parochial House, Dundalk,
Co Louth
Tel 042-9336301
(*Holy Family,* Armagh)

O'Connell, John, Very Rev,
PE
17 King Edwards Court
Bray, Co Wicklow
Tel 01-2867309
(*Dublin, retired*)

O'Connell, John, Very Rev,
PE
The Presbytery,
Two-Mile-House,
Naas, Co Kildare
Tel 045-876160
(*Kildare & L., retired*)

O'Connell, Liam (SJ)
St Ignatius (Residence),
27 Raleigh Row,
Galway H91 FTX8
Tel 091-523707

O'Connell, Matthew (SMA)
African Missions,
Blackrock Road,
Cork T12 TD54
Tel 021-4292871

O'Connell, Michael (MSC)
MSC Mission Support
Centre, PO Box 23,
Western Road,
Cork T12 WT72
Tel 021-4545704/4543988

O'Connell, Patrick (MHM)
St Joseph's House,
50 Orwell Park,
Rathgar, Dublin D06 C535
Tel 01-4127700

O'Connell, Philip, Very Rev,
PE
(*Kerry, retired*)

O'Connell, Raymond (OSM),
Very Rev
Servite Priory,
Benburb, Dungannon,
Co Tyrone, BT71 7JZ
Tel 028-37548241

O'Connell, Seamus, PEm
St Patrick's College,
Maynooth, Co Kildare
Tel 01-6285222
(*Derry, retired*)

O'Connell, Terence
142 Mayorstone Park,
Limerick
(Limerick, retired)

O'Connell, Tomás Very Rev, PP
Pallasgreen, Co Limerick
Tel 061-384114
(Pallasgreen, Cashel & E.)

O'Conor, Joseph, PEm
17 Ashbourne View,
Omagh,
Co Tyrone BT78 1HN
Tel 028-82244806
(Derry, retired)

O'Connor, Anthony, Very Rev, PP
Kilmacow, via Waterford,
Co Kilkenny
Tel 087-2517766
(Kilmacow, Ossory)

O'Connor, Benjamin
c/o Cloyne Diocesan Centre, Cobh, Co Cork
Tel 021-4811430
(Cloyne)

O'Connor, Brendan
Ely University Centre,
10 Hume Street, Dublin 2
Tel 01-6767420
(Opus Dei)

O'Connor, Charles (OMI)
170 Merrion Road,
Ballsbridge, Dublin 4
Tel 01-2693658

O'Connor, Christopher (MHM)
St Mary's Parish,
25 Marquis Street,
Belfast BT1 1JJ
Tel 028-90320482

O'Connor, Christopher, Very Rev Dean, PE
Kilkerrin, Ballinasloe,
Co Galway
(Galway, retired)

O'Connor, Columba (OSA)
Duckspool House
(Retirement Community),
Abbeyside, Dungarvan,
Co Waterford
Tel 058-23784

O'Connor, Daniel J., Very Rev Mgr, PC
St Mary's, Irishtown Road,
Dublin 4
Tel 01-6697429
(Ringsend, Dublin)

O'Connor, Daniel, Very Rev Canon, PE
The Presbytery,
Dungarvan, Co Waterford
Tel 058-42381
(Waterford & L., retired)

O'Connor, Donie (Daniel) (MHM)
6 Allen Park Road,
Stillorgan,
Co Dublin A94 X261
Tel 089-9796447
(Clonskeagh, Kilmacud-Stillorgan,
Mount Merrion, Dublin)

O'Connor, Declan, Moderator,
Duagh, Listowel, Co Kerry
Tel 068-45102
(Duagh, Kerry)

O'Connor, Denis, (CSsR) CC
Dún Mhuire,
461/463 Griffith Avenue,
Dublin D09 X651
Tel 01-5180196
(Dún Mhuire, Dublin)

O'Connor, Dermot (SJ)
Irish Jesuit Provincialate,
Milltown Park,
Sandford Road, Dublin 6
Tel 01-4987333

O'Connor, Dominic (OP)
Newbridge College,
Droichead Nua, Co Kildare
Tel 045-487200

O'Connor, Donal
Chaplain, Munster Technological University,
Tralee, Co Kerry
Tel 066-7145639/7135236
(Kerry)

O'Connor, Eamonn, Very Rev, PP
Strokestown,
Co Roscommon
Tel 071-9633027
(Strokestown (Kiltrustan, Lissonuffy and Cloonfinlough), Elphin)

O'Connor, Edward (SMA)
African Missions,
Blackrock Road,
Cork T12 TD54
Tel 021-4292871

O'Connor, Fergus (Opus Dei), Very Rev, PP, VF
31 Herbert Avenue,
Dublin 4
Tel 01-2692001
(Merrion Road, Dublin)

O'Connor, Frank,
Cathedral House,
Cathedral Place, Limerick
Tel 061-414624/
087-2642393
(Pastoral Unit 1, Limerick)

O'Connor, Gerard, PE
St John's Presbytery,
New Street, Waterford
Tel 051-874271
(Waterford & L., retired)

O'Connor, Gerard (CSsR)
Scala, Castlemahon House,
Castle Road,
Blackrock, Cork
Tel 021-4358800

O'Connor, John (SAC), Very Rev,
St Patrick's, Corduff,
Blanchardstown, Dublin 15
Tel 01-8213596/8215930
(Corduff, Dublin)

O'Connor, John C., Very Rev
c/o Lisbreen,
73 Somerton Road,
Belfast BT15 4DE
(Down & C., retired)

O'Connor, John (OSA)
Duckspool House
(Retirement Community),
Abbeyside, Dungarvan,
Co Waterford
Tel 058-23784

O'Connor, John, J. (OSA)
St John's Priory,
Thomas Street, Dublin 8
Tel 01-6770393

O'Connor, Kevin (OMI)
Oblate House of Retreat,
Inchicore, Dublin 8
Tel 01-4534408/4541805

O'Connor, Laurence, Very Rev, PP
Bunclody, Enniscorthy,
Co Wexford
Tel 053-9377319
(Bunclody, Ferns)

O'Connor, Liam (OCSO)
Mount Saint Joseph Abbey, Roscrea,
Co Tipperary
Tel 0505-25600

O'Connor, Martin, Very Rev Canon, PP, VF
The Parochial House,
Ballindine, Claremorris,
Co Mayo F12 EO96
Tel 094-9364423
Administration for Crossboyne and Taugheen
(Ballindine (Kilvine), Tuam)

O'Connor, Michael Very Rev, Adm
Presbytery No. 2,
Church Grounds,
Kill Avenue, Dun Laoghaire, Co Dublin
Tel 01-2140863
(Kill-O'-The-Grange, Dublin)

O'Connor, Michael, Very Rev
c/o St John's Pastoral Centre, John's Hill,
Waterford
(Waterford & L.)

O'Connor, Michael (OMI), CC
Superior, The Presbytery,
Darndale, Dublin 17
Tel 01-8474547
(Darndale-Belcamp, Dublin)

O'Connor, Michael G. (CSsR)
Mount Saint Alphonsus,
Limerick
Tel 061-315099

O'Connor, Muiris, Very Rev,
Pastoral Area Assignment,
Askeaton,
Co Limerick
(Limerick)

O'Connor, Pat (CSsR)
Clonard Monastery,
1 Clonard Gardens,
Belfast, BT13 2RL
Tel 028-90445950

O'Connor, Patrick, Very Rev, PP, VF
Parochial House,
Dunboyne, Co Meath
Tel 01-8255342
(Dunboyne, Meath)

O'Connor, Peter, Very Rev, Adm
24 Barclay Court,
Blackrock, Co Dublin
Tel 01-2832302
(Blackrock, Dublin)

O'Connor, Philip, Very Rev, PP
Parochial House,
Mountnugent, Co Cavan
Tel 049-8540123
(Mountnugent, Meath)

O'Connor, Richard
Villa Maria Assunta, Via Aurelia Antica 284,
00-165, Roma, Italia
(Kerry)

O'Connor, Sean, Very Rev, PP
Ballyhale,
Kilkenny R95 Y9F4
Tel 056-7756889/
086 3895911
(St John's, Ossory)

O'Connor, Thomas, DD
St Patrick's College,
Maynooth, Co Kildare
Tel 01-6285222
(Meath)

O'Connor, Tim
Abbeyville, Manister,
Croom, Co Limerick
Tel 087-7859028
(Pastoral Unit 8, Limerick)

O'Connor, Tom, CC
Dublin Road, Portlaoise,
Co Laois
Tel 057-8692153
(Portlaoise, Kildare & L.)

O'Connor, Tom (OSCam)
St Camillus,
South Hill Avenue,
Blackrock, Co Dublin

O'Connor, Tom (SPS)
District Leader for Ireland,
St Patrick's, Kiltegan,
Co Wicklow
Tel 059-6473600

O'Cuilleanáin, Fionnbarra (SMA)
African Missions,
Blackrock Road,
Cork T12 TD54
Tel 021-4292871

O'Cuiv, Shan
Team Assistant, c/o The Presbytery, Clonburris,
Clondalkin, Dublin 22
Tel 01-4573440
(*Clondalkin/Rowlagh/Neilstown/Deansrath/Bawnogue*, Dublin)

O'Dea, Francis,
Parochial House,
The Square,
Dromcollogher,
Co Limerick
Tel 063-83718/
087-2443106
(*Pastoral Unit 16*, Limerick)

O'Doherty, Bartie (SPS)
St Patrick's, Kiltegan,
Co Wicklow
Tel 059-6473600

O'Doherty, Colm, PP
6 Orchard Park,
Murlog, Lifford,
Co Donegal
Tel 074-9142022
(*Lifford (Clonleigh)*, Derry)

O'Doherty, Daniel, Very Rev, PE
St Eunan's Nursing Home,
Letterkenny,
Co Donegal
(Raphoe, retired)

O'Doherty, Donal, Very Rev Mgr, PE
Orwell Healthcare Home,
112 Orwell Road
Rathgar, Dublin 6
(Dublin, retired)

O'Doherty, Kieran, Very Rev,
159 Glen Road,
Maghera,
Co Derry BT46 5JN
Tel 028-79642496
(*Maghera*, Derry)

O'Doherty, Michael
(Kerry, retired)

O'Doherty, Seán, Very Rev Archdeacon
Durrow, Co Laois
Tel 057-8736156
(Ossory, retired)

O'Donnell, Chris, AP, EV
Jerpoint, Sheares Street,
Kilmallock,
Co Limerick
Tel 087 6323309
(*Pastoral Unit 9*, Limerick)

O'Donnell, Cornelius, Very Rev, PE
Rathcormac, Fermoy,
Co Cork
Tel 025-36286
(Cloyne, retired)

O'Donnell, Desmond (OMI)
Oblate House of Retreat,
Inchicore, Dublin 8
Tel 01-4534408/4541805

O'Donnell, Edward (SJ)
Gonzaga College,
Sandford Road, Dublin 6
Tel 01-4972943

O'Donnell, Edward, Very Rev, PP
42 Derryvolgie Avenue,
Belfast BT9 6FP
Tel 028-90665409
(*St Brigid's*, Down & C.)

O'Donnell, Gerard, Very Rev, PP
Kilfian, Killala
Co Mayo
Tel 096-32420
(*Kilfian*, Killala)

O'Donnell, Hugh (OFM)
Dún Mhuire,
Seafield Road,
Killiney, Co Dublin
Tel 01-2826760

O'Donnell, Hugh (SDB), CC
Vice-Rector, Rinaldi House,
72 Sean McDermott Street, Dublin 1
Tel 01-8363358
(*Sean McDermott Street*, Dublin)

O'Donnell, James, Very Rev, PP
Killenaule, Co Tipperary
Tel 052-9156244
(*Killenaule*, Cashel & E.)

O'Donnell, James, Rt Rev Mgr, AP
Macroom, Co Cork
Tel 026-41042
(*Macroom*, Cloyne)

O'Donnell, Louis (OSA), Most Rev
St John's Priory,
Thomas Street, Dublin 8
Tel 01-6770393

O'Donnell, Owen, Very Rev, PE
Parochial House,
Dunamore, Cookstown,
Co Tyrone
Tel 028-86751216
(Armagh, retired)

O'Donnell, Pat, Very Rev Canon, PP, VF
Rathmore, Co Kerry
Tel 064-7758026
(*Rathmore*, Kerry)

O'Donnell, Sean, CC
Parochial House,
32 Chapel Road,
Waterside, Derry BT47 2BB
Tel 028-71342303
(*Waterside (Glendermott)*, Derry)

O'Donnell, Terence (IC)
Clonturk House,
Ormond Road,
Drumcondra, Dublin 9
Tel 01-6877014

O'Donoghue, Brendan, Very Rev Canon, AP
12 Tullyglass Square,
Shannon, Co Clare
Tel 061-361257/
086-8308153
(*Tradaree Pastoral Area*, Killaloe)

O'Donoghue, Fergus (SJ), PC
Gonzaga College,
Sandford Road, Dublin 6
Tel 01-4972943
(*Clonskeagh*, Dublin)

O'Donoghue, James
Ballinahinch, Birdhill,
Limerick
Tel 061-781510
(*Ballinahinch*, Cashel & E.)

O'Donoghue, Neil Xavier
Theology Faculty,
St Patrick's College,
Maynooth, Co Kildare
Tel 087-7708819
(Newark, NJ, USA)

O'Donoghue, Neville (SM)
St Columba's,
Church Avenue,
Ballybrack, Co Dublin
Tel 01-2858301

O'Donoghue, Patrick
119 Grace Park Manor,
Drumcondra, Dublin 9
(Dublin)

O'Donoghue, Patrick, CC
Mitchelstown, Co Cork
Tel 025-84077
(*Mitchelstown*, Cloyne)

O'Donoghue, Patrick (SSC)
St Columban's,
Dalgan Park,
Navan, Co Meath
Tel 046-9021525

O'Donoghue, Paul, CC
Cathedral Presbytery, Cork
Tel 021-4304325
(*Cathedral of St Mary & St Anne*, Cork & R.)

O'Donohoe, Joseph (OPraem)
Holy Trinity House,
Lismacanican,
Mountnugent, Co Cavan

O'Donohoe, Seán (OFMCap)
Guardian, Capuchin Friary,
Station Road, Raheny,
Dublin 5 D05 T9E4
Tel 01-8313886

O'Donohue, Patrick
FSSP Chaplain,
Waterford & Lismore
2 John's Hill,
Waterford City X91 FWY1
(Galway)

O'Donoghue, Patrick (SSP)
St John's Parish,
Waterford
(*St John's*, Waterford & L.)

O'Donovan, Chris, AP
The Presbytery,
Turner's Cross, Cork
(Cork & R.)

O'Donovan, Colman, Very Rev Canon, PE
1 Youghal Road,
Midleton, Co Cork
Tel 021-4621617
(Cloyne, retired)

O'Donovan, Ignatius (OSA)
The Abbey,
Fethard, Co Tipperary

O'Donovan, James, Very Rev Canon, AP
St Finbarr's West,
The Lough, Co Cork
Tel 087-2553021
(*Ballyphehane*, *The Lough*, Cork & R.)

O'Donovan, John C., CC
The Presbytery,
Bandon, Co Cork
Tel 023-8865067
(*Bandon*, Cork & R.)

O'Donovan, John, Very Rev Canon, Adm
Tel 021-4501022
(*Cathedral of St Mary & St Anne, Blackpool/The Glen*, Cork & R.)

O'Donovan, Padraig (SSC)
House Superior,
St Columban's,
Dalgan Park,
Navan, Co Meath
Tel 046-9021525

O'Donovan, Pat, PP
Parochial House, Tirelton,
Macroom, Co Cork
Tel 026-46012/086-2578065
(*Kilmichael, Uibh Laoire*, Cork & R.)

O'Donovan, William, Very Rev, PP
Conna, Mallow, Co Cork
Tel 058-59138
(*Conna*, Cloyne)

O'Dowd, Sean (SPS), CC
Disciples of Divine Master,
8 Castle Streer, Athlone,
Co Westmeath
Tel 090 6490575
Chaplain to Sisters of Mercy
(*Athlone*, Elphin)

LIST OF CLERGY IN IRELAND

O'Driscoll, Aidan, Rt Rev Mgr, PP, VG
Parochial House,
Clonakilty, Co Cork
Tel 023-8833165
Adm, Ardfield and Rathbarry
(*Ardfield and Rathbarry, Clonakilty and Darrara,* Cork & R.)

O'Driscoll, Augustine (SMA), AP
Vice Superior,
SMA House, Wilton,
Cork T12 KR23
Tel 021-4541069/4541884

O'Driscoll, Eamonn (OFM)
Franciscan Friary,
Killarney, Co Kerry
Tel 064-6631334/6631066

O'Driscoll, Fintan (MSC), PP
Sacred Heart Parish,
Killinarden, Tallaght,
Dublin D24 R521
Tel 01-4522251
(*Killinarden*, Dublin)

O'Driscoll, Kieron, PP
The Presbytery,
Togher, Co Cork
Tel 021-4964986
(*Ballinhassig*, Cork & R.)

O'Driscoll, Martin, Very Rev Canon
The Presbytery,
Bantry, Co Cork
Tel 027-50096
Adm, Muintir Bháire
Tel 027-56398
(*Bantry, Muintir Bháire,* Cork & R.)

O'Driscoll, P. J., CF
The Welfare Office, MOD Stafford,
First Battalion Royal Regiment of Fusiliers,
Mooltan Barracks,
Tidworth,
Wiltshire, SP9 7EN
Tel 0044-1980651468
(Cloyne)

O'Driscoll, Paul, Very Rev, PP
5 New Cabra Road,
Phibsboro, Dublin 7
Tel 01-8388874/
087-2573857
(*Travelling People*, Dublin)

O'Duill, Seamus (SDS)
Ard Mhuire, Kilmoon,
Lisdoonvarna, Co Clare
Tel 086-1030261

O'Dúill, Fergal (LC)
Vocations Director,
Leopardstown Road,
Foxrock, Dublin 18
Tel 01-2955902
Chaplain, Clonlost Retreat and Youth Centre,
Killiney Road, Killiney,
Co Dublin
Tel 01-2350064

O'Dwyer, Christy, Rt Rev Mgr, AP, VG
Diocesan Archivist,
Moyne, Thurles,
Co Tipperary
Tel 0504 45129
(*Templetuohy*, Cashel & E.)

O'Dwyer, John, Very Rev Dean, PE
20 Cloonarkin Drive,
Oranmore, Co Galway
Tel 091-484501
(Galway, retired)

O'Dwyer, Michael (SAC), CC
9 Seaview Lawn, Shankill,
Co Dublin
Tel 01-2822277
(*Shankill*, Dublin)

O'Dwyer, Michael, Very Rev, PP
Parochial House,
31 Church Street,
Ballygawley,
Co Tyrone BT70 2HA
Tel 028-85567096
(*Ballygawley (Errigal Kieran)*, Armagh)

O'Dwyer, Richard (SJ), PP
The Presbytery,
Upper Gardiner Street,
Dublin 1
Tel 01-8363411
(*Gardiner Street*, Dublin)

O'Dwyer, Sean, Very Rev, PE
Clonmel Road, Cahir,
Co Tipperary
Tel 087-4184213
(Waterford & L., retired)

O'Farrell, Ambrose (OP)
St Mary's,
The Claddagh, Galway
Tel 091-582884

O'Farrell, Edward (CSSp)
Holy Spirit Missionary College,
Whitehall Road, Dublin 12
Tel 01-4064300

O'Farrell, Martin, Very Rev
Acorn Nursing Home,
Cashel, Co Tipperary
(Dublin, retired)

O'Farrell, Michael (SSC)
St Columban's Retirement Home
Dalgan Park,
Navan, Co Meath
Tel 046-9021525

O'Farrell, Patrick, Very Rev, PP
Lisdowney, Co Kilkenny
Tel 056-8833138/
087-2353520
(*Lisdowney*, Ossory)

O'Farrell, Peter, PP
Milford, Charleville,
Co Cork
Tel 063-80038
(*Milford*, Cloyne)

O'Fearraigh, Brian, CC
Derrybeg, Letterkenny
Tel 074-9531947
Séiplíneach, Pobalscoil Chloich Cheannfhaola,
Falcarragh, Letterkenny,
Co Donegal
Tel 074-9135424/9135231
(*Gweedore*, Raphoe)

O'Flaherty, Séan, Rt Rev Mgr, PE
St Mary's Nursing Home,
Shantalla, Galway
Tel 091-540500
(Galway, retired)

O'Flynn, Ciaran (SPS), CC
The Presbytery,
Strokestown,
Co Roscommon
Tel 071-9633041
(*Strokestown*, Elphin)

O'Flynn, Finbarr, CC
Dungourney, Co Cork
Tel 021-4668406
(*Imogeela (Castlemartyr)*, Cloyne)

O'Flynn, Michael (CSsR)
St Patrick's, Esker,
Athenry, Co Galway
Tel 091-844007

O'Flynn, Silvester (OFMCap)
Guardian, St Francis Capuchin Friary,
Rochestown, Co Cork T12 NH02
Tel 021-4896244

O'Flynn, Thomas (OP)
St Mary's Priory, Tallaght,
Dublin 24
Tel 01-4048100

O'Gara, Francis (OCarm)
Carmelite Community,
Gort Muire, Ballinteer,
Dublin D16 EI67
Tel 01-2984014

O'Gara, John (SM), PC
The Presbyerty,
78A Donore Avenue,
Dublin 8
Tel 01-4542425
(*Donore Avenue*, Dublin)

O'Gorman, Charles, CC
Killeshandra, Co Cavan
Tel 049-4334179
(*Killeshandra*, Kilmore)

O'Gorman, Daniel, Very Rev, PP
The Parochial House,
Mullinahone,
Co Tipperary
Tel 052-9153152
(*Mullinahone*, Cashel & E.)

O'Gorman, Daniel (SSC)
St Columban's Retirement Home,
Dalgan Park, Navan,
Co Meath
Tel 046-9021525

O'Gorman, Eamonn, Very Rev, PP
Ballyragget, Co Kilkenny
Tel 087-2236145
(*Ballyragget, Lisdowney,* Ossory)

O'Gorman, John, Very Rev, PP
Turloughmore, Co Galway
Tel 091-797114
(*Lackagh*, Tuam)

O'Gorman, Kevin (SMA)
SMA House, Wilton,
Cork, T12 KR23
Tel 021-4541069/4541884

O'Gorman, Maurice, Very Rev, PP
Clashmore, Co Waterford
Tel 024-96110
(*Clashmore*, Waterford & L.)

O'Gorman, Patrick, Very Rev, AP
Golden, Co Tipperary
Tel 087-6347773
(*Kilcommon*, Cashel & E.)

O'Gorman, Tom, Co-PP,
The Presbytery, Quin,
Co Clare
(*Abbey Pastoral Area,* Killaloe)

O'Grady, Desmond (SJ)
Gonzaga College,
Sandford Road, Dublin 6
Tel 01-4972943

O'Grady, James, Very Rev
120, Eallaigh Estate,
Galway Road, Headford,
Co Galway H91 R9F5
Tel 093-35448
(Tuam)

O'Grady, Michael, Very Rev, Co-PP
No 3 Presbytery,
Dunmanus Court,
Cabra West, Dublin 7
Tel 01-8384325
(*Cabra, Cabra West,* Dublin)

O'Grady, Peter (OFM)
Franciscan Friary,
Liberty Street,
Cork T12 D376
Tel 021-4270302/4275481

LIST OF CLERGY IN IRELAND

O'Grady, Vincent (CSSp)
Holy Spirit Missionary College
Kimmage Manor,
Whitehall Road,
Dublin D12 P5YP
Tel 01-4064300

O'Hagan, Eugene, Very Rev,
75 Somerton Road,
Belfast BT15 4DE
Tel 028-90776185
(Down & C.)

O'Hagan, Francis, PP
71 Duncrun Road,
Bellarena, Limavady,
Co Derry BT49 0JD
Tel 028-77750226
(Magilligan, Derry)

O'Hagan, Hugh J., Very Rev, PP
Parochial House,
31 Ballynafie Road,
Ahoghill BT42 1LF
Tel 028-25871351
(Ahoghill, Down & C.)

O'Hagan, Mark, Very Rev, PP, VF
Lourdes Pilgtimage (Director)
St Patrick's Presbytery,
Roden Place, Dundalk,
Co Louth
Tel 042-9334648
(Dundalk, St Patrick's, Armagh)

O'Hagan, Martin, Very Rev, PP
71 North Street,
Newtownards,
Co Down BT23 4JD
Tel 028-91812137
(Newtownards, Down & C.)

O'Hagan, Patrick, PP
Parochial House, Moyville,
Co Donegal
Tel 074-9382057
(Moville (Moville Lower), Derry)

O'Halloran, Giles (OSA)
Bursar and Sub-Prior,
St John's Priory,
Thomas Street, Dublin 8
Tel 01-6770393

O'Halloran, James (SDB)
St Catherine's Centre,
North Campus, Maynooth
Co Kildare

O'Halloran, John
Chaplain's Office,
University Hospital Galway,
Galway
Tel 091-524222
(Galway)

O'Halloran, Philip (MHM)
Regional Superior, Rector,
St Joseph's House,
50 Orwell Park,
Rathgar, Dublin D06 C535
Tel 01-4127773/4127735/
089-4385320

O'Halloran, Richard, PP
Portlaw, Co Waterford
Tel 051-387227
(Portlaw, Waterford & L.)

O'Halloran, Tom, Very Rev, Co-PP, VF
Parochial House,
Borrisokane, Co Tipperary
Tel 067-27105
(Cois Deirge Pastoral Area, Killaloe)

O'Hanlon, David, PP
Parochial House, Dysart,
Mullingar, Co Westmeath
Tel 044-9226122
(Dysart, Meath)

O'Hanlon, Denis, Very Rev, PP
Lisgoold
Tel 021-4642363
(Lisgoold, Cloyne)

O'Hanlon, Denis Luke (OCSO)
Mount Melleray Abbey,
Cappoquin,
Co Waterford P51 R8XW
Tel 058-54404

O'Hanlon, Donal (SSC)
St Columban's,
Dalgan Park,
Navan, Co Meath
Tel 046-9021525

O'Hanlon, Francis, PE
c/o Diocesan Office,
St Michael's, Longford
Tel 043-6672319
(Ardagh & Cl., retired)

O'Hanlon, Gerard (SJ)
25 Croftwood Park,
Cherry Orchard, Dublin 10
Tel 01-6267413

O'Hara, David (SDB)
Rinaldi House,
72 Sean McDermott Street, Dublin 1
Tel 01-8363358

O'Hara, Emmet (SAC)
Protem,
St Benin's, Dublin Road,
Shankill, Co Dublin
Tel 01-2824425
(Shankill, Dublin)

O'Hara, Jarlath (OCarm)
Gort Muire, Ballinteer,
Dublin 16
Tel 01-2984014

O'Hara, Vincent (OCD)
St Teresa's,
Clarendon Street, Dublin 2
Tel 01-6718466/6718127

O'Hare, Martin (SMA)
African Missions,
Blackrock Road,
Cork T12 TD54
Tel 021-4292871

O'Hare, Paddy (SM)
France

O'Hare, Peter, Very Rev, PP
St Anne's Parochial House,
Kingsway, Finaghy,
Belfast BT10 0NE
Tel 028-90610112
(St Anne's, Down & C.)

O'Hea, John (SMA)
African Missions,
Blackrock Road,
Cork T12 TD54
Tel 021-4292871

O'Higgins, Kevin (SJ)
c/o St Francis Xavier's,
Upper Gardiner Street,
Dublin 1

O'Hora, Gerard, Very Rev, PP, VF
Enniscrone, Ballina,
Co Mayo
Tel 096-36164
(Kilglass, Killala)

O'Horo, Michael, Very Rev
Templeboy, Co Sligo
(Killala, retired)

O'Kane, Aidan (CP)
Passionist Retreat Centre
Downpatrick Road,
Crossgar, Downpatrick
Co Down BT30 9EQ
Tel 028-44830242

O'Kane, David, PP
9 Church Street, Claudy,
Co Derry BT47 4AA
Tel 028-71337727
(Claudy (Cumber Upper & Learmount), Derry)

O'Kane, Hugh (SMA)
African Missions,
Dromantine, Newry,
Co Down BT34 1RH
Tel 028-30821224

O'Kane, James (SMA)
African Missions,
Dromantine, Newry
Co Down BT34 1 RH

O'Kane, James, Very Rev, PE, CC
21 Knocknacarry Avenue,
Cushenden,
Co Antrim BT44 0NX
Tel 028-21761269
(Cushendun, Down and C.)

O'Kane, Patrick, PP
1 Aileach Road,
Ballymagroarty,
Derry BT48 0AZ
Tel 028-71267070
(Holy Family, Ballymagroarty, Derry)

O'Kane, Peter, CC,
48 Brook Street, Omagh,
Co Tyrone, BT78 5HD
Tel 028-82242092
(Drumquin (Langfield), Omagh (Drumagh), Derry)

O'Kane, Peter (OP)
St Mary's Dominican Priory,
Pope's Quay, Cork
Tel 021-4502267
(Cork)

O'Kane, Peter, Very Rev, PP
16 Rossglas Road,
Killough,
Co Down BT30 7QQ
Tel 028-44841221
(Killough (Bright), Down & C.)

O'Kane, Peter (OP)
St Mary's Priory,
Tallaght, Dublin 24
Tel 01-4048189

O'Keeffe, Anthony (OFMCap)
Capuchin Friary,
Holy Trinity,
Fr Mathew Quay,
Cork T12 PK24
Tel 021-4270827
(Cork & R.)

O'Keeffe, Anthony,
Shanagolden, Co Limerick
Tel 069-60112/087-4163401
(Pastoral Unit 13, Limerick)

O'Keeffe, John, Very Rev, PP
Birdhill, Killaloe,
Co Tipperary
Tel 061-379172/
087-2421678
(Newport, Cashel & E.)

O'Keeffe, John (SJ)
Gonzaga Community,
Sandford Road,
Ranelagh,
Dublin D06 KF95
Tel 01-4972943

O'Keeffe, John (SMA)
SMA House, Wilton,
Cork T12 KR23
Tel 021-4541069/4541884

O'Keeffe, Joseph
42 Nessan Court,
Church Road, Raheen,
Limerick
Tel 061-309151/
086-3333539
(Limerick)

O'Keeffe, Joseph, Very Rev, PP
Main Street, Rathcormac,
Co Cork
Tel 025-37371
(Rathcormac, Cloyne)

O'Keeffe, Laurence, Very Rev,
The Presbytery,
Slieverue, Co Kilkenny
Tel 051-832773
(Ossory)

O'Keeffe, Martin (OMI)
Oblate House of Retreat,
Inchicore, Dublin 8
Tel 01-4534408/4541805

O'Keeffe, Patrick (CSsR)
St Patrick's, Esker,
Athenry, Co Galway
Tel 091-844007

O'Keeffe, Thomas, Very Rev Assistant,
20 Glen Avenue,
The Park, Cabinteely,
Dublin 18
Tel 01-2853643/
086-2646270
(Dublin, retired)

O'Keeffe, Martin (OMI)
Mazenod House,
Churchfield,
Knock, Co Mayo

O'Kelly, Francis (SSC)
St Columban's Retirement Home
Dalgan Park,
Navan, Co Meath
Tel 046-9021525

O'Kelly, Michael A., Very Rev,
(Moderator),
Cluain Mhuire,
Killarney Road,
Bray, Co Wicklow
(Bray Grouping, Dublin)

O'Leary, Aidan (OSA)
St Augustine's,
Taylor's Lane,
Ballyboden, Dublin 16
Tel 01-4241000

O'Leary, Alan, Very Rev, Adm
Parochial House,
Ballincollig, Co Cork
Tel 021-4871206
(Ballincollig, Cork & R.)

O'Leary, Anthony (CP)
St Gabriel's Retreat,
The Graan, Enniskillen,
Co Fermanagh
Tel 028-66322272

O'Leary, Brian (SJ)
Milltown Park,
Sandford Road, Dublin 6
Tel 01-2698411

O'Leary, Finbarr, Rt Rev Mgr
The Presbytery, Clogagh
Co Cork
Tel 023-8869682
(Timoleague and Clogagh, Cork & R.)

O'Leary, Gerald, Very Rev, PP
Horeswood, Campile,
Co Wexford
Tel 051-388129
(Horeswood and Ballykelly, Ferns)

O'Leary, Gerard
Kerry General Hospital,
Tralee, Co Kerry
Tel 066-7126222
(Kerry)

O'Leary, Gerard
Curates House,
Athlunkard, Limerick
Tel 087-9378685
(Pastoral Unit 4, Limerick)

O'Leary, John, Very Rev, PE, AP
4 Moorehall Retirement Village,
Hale Street, Ardee,
Co Louth A92 K6R9
Tel 041-9826106
(Ardee & Collon, Armagh)

O'Leary, Joseph
1-38-16 Ekoda, Nakanoku,
Tokyo, 16J0022 Japan
(Cork & R.)

O'Leary, Michael (SMA), Very Rev, PP
St Joseph's SMA Parish,
Wilton, Cork T12 E436
Tel 021-4341362
(St Joseph's, Cork & R.)

O'Leary, Noel (SMA),
Superior, SMA House,
Wilton, Cork
Tel 021-4541069/4541884

O'Leary, Oscar (OFM)
Franciscan Friary,
Liberty Street, Cork
Tel 021-4270302/4275481

O'Leary, Sean (White Fathers)
Cypress Grove,
Templeogue, Dublin 6W
Tel 01-4055263/4055264

O'Leary, Timothy, Very Rev
Mount Oliver,
Martinstown,
Kilmallock, Co Limerick
(Limerick, retired)

O'Leary, Oscar (OFM)
Franciscan Friary,
Liberty Street, Cork
Tel 021-4270302/4275481

O'Leary, Seán (White Fathers)
Provincial Delegate
Cypress Grove Road,
Templeogue,
Dublin D6W YV12
Tel 01-4063965

O'Loan, Fergus (OCarm)
Gort Muire, Ballinteer,
Dublin 16
Tel 01-2984014

O'Looney, Michael (CSSp)
Holy Spirit Missionary College
Kimmage Manor,
Whitehall Road,
Dublin D12 P5YP
Tel 01-4064300

O'Loughlin, Declan
Diocesan Advisor for Religious Education (Post-Primary),
Parochial House,
30 Newline, Killeavy,
Newry, Co Down BT35 8TA
Tel 028-30889609
(Armagh)

O'Loughlin, Michael (SSC)
43 Moyland, Shanballa,
Loughville, Lahinch Road,
Ennis, Co Clare
Tel 065-6845321

O'Loughlin, Peter, AP
Kilmihil, Co Clare
Tel 065-9050016/
086-8250016
(Inis Cathaigh Pastoral Area, Killaloe)

O'Mahony, Anthony, CC
Parochial House
Inchigeela, Macroom,
Co Cork
Tel 026-49838
(Uibh Laoire, Cork & R.)

O'Mahony, Bartholomew, Very Rev Canon, PP
Woodlawn,
Model Farm Road,
Ballineaspaig, Co Cork
Tel 021-4346818
(Ballineaspaig, Cork & R.)

O'Mahony, Colm (OSA)
Prior and Master of Pre-Novices,
St Augustine's Priory,
Shop Street,
Drogheda, Co Louth
Tel 041-9838409

O'Mahony, Damien, PP
Glounthaune, Co Cork
Tel 021-4232881
(Glounthaune, Cork & R.)

O'Mahony, Dan, Very Rev, PE
Magheraboy, Kilmovee,
Ballaghadereen, Co Mayo
Tel 087-2401625
(Achonry, retired)

O'Mahony, Dan Joe (OFMCap)
Capuchin Friary,
Station Road, Raheny,
Dublin 5 D05 T9E4
Tel 01-8313886

O'Mahony, Denis, Very Rev, PP, VF
Abbeydorney, Co Kerry
Tel 066-7135146
(Abbeydorney, Kerry)

O'Mahony, Donal, Very Rev Canon, PP
Charleville, Co Cork
Tel 063-81319
(Charleville, Cloyne)

O'Mahony, John K., Very Rev Canon, PE
Mount Desert
Lee Road, Cork
(Cork & R., retired)

O'Mahony, Joseph, Adm
Macroom, Co Cork
Tel 026-41092
(Cill na Martra, Macroom, Cloyne)

O'Mahony, Kieran (OSA), PC
Presbytery No. 2,
Stillorgan Road, Dublin 4
(Donnybrook, Dublin)

O'Mahony, Michael, PP
Ballinspittle, Co Cork
Tel 021-4778055
(Courceys, Cork & R.)

O'Mahony, Nicholas, Rt Rev Mgr, PP
Diocesan Administrator of Waterford and Lismore,
Parochial House, Tramore,
Co Waterford
Tel 051-381525
(Tramore, Waterford & L.)

O'Mahony, Pat (SMA), CC
St Patrick's Presbytery,
Rochestown Road, Cork
Tel 021-4892363
(Douglas, Cork & R.)

O'Mahony, Stephen, Very Rev, PP
Bohola, Claremorris,
Co Mayo
Tel 094-9384115
(Bohola, Achonry)

O'Mahony, Stephen, Very Rev, PE
Liscarroll, Mallow, Co Cork
Tel 022-48128
(Cloyne, retired)

O'Mahony, Thomas, Very Rev, PP
Parochial House, Skryne,
Tara, Co Meath
Tel 046-9025152
(Skryne, Meath)

O'Malley, Donough, Very Rev Canon,
19 School House Lane,
Rear of Barrington Street,
Limerick
Tel 086-2586908
(Limerick, retired)

O'Malley, Michael
c/o Archbishop's House,
Tuam
(Tuam, retired)

LIST OF CLERGY IN IRELAND

O'Meara, Donagh, Co-PP, VF
Parochial House,
Carhuligane,
Mullagh, Co Clare
Tel 065-7087012
(*Críocha Callan Pastoral Area*, Killaloe)

O'Meara, Michael, Very Rev, Co-PP
Kinnity, Birr, Co Offaly
Tel 057-9137021/
087-7735977
(*Brendan Pastoral Area*, Killaloe)

O'Meara, Noel (CSSp)
Holy Spirit Missionary College
Kimmage Manor,
Whitehall Road,
Dublin D12 P5YP
Tel 01-4064300

O'Melia, Joseph (OMI)
Oblate House of Retreat,
Inchicore, Dublin 8
Tel 01-4534408/4541805

O'Neill, Arthur, TA
1B Willow Court,
Druid Valley, Cabinteely,
Dublin 18
Tel 087-2597520
(*Cabinteely*, Dublin)

O'Neill, Charles
Colmanswell, Charleville,
Co Limerick
Tel 063-89459
(*Limerick*, retired)

O'Neill, Daniel (MSC)
(Resident elsewhere)

O'Neill, Eugene, Very Rev, PP
Parochial House,
31 Brackaville Road,
Coalisland,
Co Tyrone BT71 4NH
Tel 028-87740221
(*Coalisland*, Armagh)

O'Neill, Eugene, Very Rev, Adm
St Patrick's Presbytery,
199 Donegal Street,
Belfast BT1 2FL
Tel 028-90324597
(*St Patrick's*, Down & C.)

O'Neill, Francis, Very Rev, PP
Castlemartyr, Co Cork
Tel 021-4667133
(*Imogeela (Castlemartyr)*, Cloyne)

O'Neill, Ian, Very Rev Canon, PP
Parochial House,
Claregalway, Co Galway
Tel 091-798104
(*Claregalway*, Galway)

O'Neill, Joe, CC
Priest's House, Emo,
Portlaoise, Co Laois
Tel 089-4535533
(*Emo, Portarlington*, Kildare & L.)

O'Neill, John, Very Rev Canon, PP, VF
Lisvernane, Aherlow
Co Tipperary
Tel 062-56155
(*Galbally*, Cashel & E.)

O'Neill, Kevin, Rt Rev Mgr, BA, MSc Ed
President, Carlow College,
College Street, Carlow
Tel 059-9153200
(Kildare & L.)

O'Neill, Kevin (SSC)
No 3 and 4,
Ma Yau Tong Village,
Po Lam Road,
Tseung Kwan O,
Kowloon, Hong Kong, SAR

O'Neill, Larry (SPS)
St Patrick's, Kiltegan,
Co Wicklow
Tel 059-6473600

O'Neill, Míceál (OCarm)
Centro Internazionale S. Alberto,
Via Sforza Pallavicini 10,
00193 Roma, Italia

O'Neill, Michael (IC)
Clonturk House,
Ormond Road,
Drumcondra, Dublin 9
Tel 01-6877014

O'Neill, Niall (SJ)
Crescent College Comprehensive,
Dooradoyle, Limerick
Tel 061-480920

O'Neill, Patrick, Co-PP
Ruan, Co Clare
Tel 065-6827799/
086-2612124
(*Imeall Boirne Pastoral Area*, Killaloe)

O'Neill, Peter (SSC)
House Superior,
St Columban's,
Dalgan Park,
Navan, Co Meath
Tel 046-9021525

O'Neill, Roger, CC
St Michael's, Gorey,
Co Wexford
Tel 053-9421117
(*Gorey*, Ferns)

O'Neill, Seamus (SPS)
Bursar General,
St Patrick's, Kiltegan,
Co Wicklow
Tel 059-6473600

O'Neill, Seamus (SSC)
20 Tobermore Road,
Moykeenan, Draperstown,
Co Derry BT45 7HG
Tel 048-79627206

O'Neill, Sean, PP
Parochial House,
1 Rockstown Road,
Carrickmore, Omagh,
Co Tyrone BT79 9BE
Tel 028-80761207
(*Termonmaguirc (Carrickmore, Loughmacrory & Creggan)*, Armagh)

O'Neill, Shane, CC
Priest's Road, Tramore,
Co Waterford
Tel 051-391868
(*Tramore*, Waterford & L.)

O'Rahelly, Edmond V., Very Rev, AP
Main Street,
Ballina, Co Tipperary
Tel 087-2262636
(*Ballina*, Cashel & E.)

O'Regan, Kevin, Very Rev, PP
The Presbytery,
Frankfield, Cork
Tel 021-43061711
(*Frankfield-Grange*, Cork & R.)

O'Regan, Liam, Very Rev Canon, PE
Cramer's Court Nursing Home,
Ballindeenisk,
Kinsale, Co Cork
(Cork & R., retired)

O'Regan, Noel (SMA), Most Rev
(Retired Bishop)
SMA House, Wilton,
Cork, T12 KR23
Tel 021-4541069/4541884

O'Reilly, Anthony
Newry, Co Armagh
(Kerry)

O'Reilly, Arthur P.
(Derry, retired)

O'Reilly, Bernard (OCarm)
Gort Muire, Ballinteer,
Dublin D16 EI67
Tel 01-2984014

O'Reilly, Brian, Team Assistant,
83 The Rise,
Mount Merrion,
Co Dublin
Tel 01-2881271/
01-2783804
Team Assistant, Kilmacud-Stillorgan
Tel 087-7414857
(*Mount Merrion, Kilmacud-Stillorgan*, Dublin)

O'Reilly, Colm, Most Rev, DD
Retired Bishop of Ardagh and Clonmacnois,
Deanscurragh, Longford
Tel 043-3347831
(Ardagh & Cl.)

O'Reilly, Damian, Very Rev Canon,
83 Marlborough Street,
Dublin 1
Tel 01-8745441
Chaplain, St Vincent's University Hospital,
Elm Park, Dublin 4
Tel 01-2094325
(*Pro-Cathedral*, Dublin)

O'Reilly, Desmond
Our Lady of Lourdes, 1951 North Avenue,
Sacramento, CA 95838
USA
(Dublin)

O'Reilly, James (SPS)
Sally's Bridge,
Crettyard, Carlow

O'Reilly, James, Very Rev, CC
St Joseph's Presbytery,
56 Greystone Road,
Antrim BT41 1JZ
Tel 028-9429103
(*Antrim*, Down & C.)

O'Reilly, John
Drinagh, Rosslare,
Co Wexford
(Ferns, retired)

O'Reilly, Joseph (IC)
Provincial, Vocations Director,
Clonturk House,
Drumcondra,
Dublin D09 F821
Tel 01-6877014

O'Reilly, Kevin (OP)
Newbridge College,
Droichead Nua, Co Kildare
Tel 045-487200

O'Reilly, Kieran (SMA), Most Rev, DD
Archbishop of Cashel and Emly,
Archbishop's House,
Thurles,
Co Tipperary E41 NY92
Tel 0504-21512
(Cashel & E.)

O'Reilly, Leo, Most Rev, DD
Retired Bishop of Kilmore,
4 Carraig Beag,
Cootehill Road, Co Cavan
(Kilmore, retired)

O'Reilly, Marius
Chaplain,
Mercy University Hospital
Grenville Place, Co Cork
Tel 021-4271971
(Cork & R.)

O'Reilly, Myles (SJ)
35 Lower Leeson Street,
Dublin 2
Tel 01-6761248

O'Reilly, Oliver, Very Rev, PP, VF
Ballyconnell, Co Cavan
Tel 049-9526291
(*Kildallan and Tomregan*, Kilmore)

O'Reilly, Paddy (OSA), CC
Parochial House,
St Helena's Drive,
Dublin 11
Tel 01-8343444/
086-8279504
(*Rivermount*, Dublin)

O'Reilly, Peter, Rt Rev Mgr, PP, VG
1 Darling Street,
Enniskillen,
Co Fermanagh BT74 7DP
Tel 028-66322075
(*Enniskillen, Tempo (Pobal)*, Clogher)

O'Reilly, Peter, Very Rev, Adm
16 Brookwood Grove,
Artane, Dublin 5
(*Artane*, Dublin)

O'Reilly, Seamus, (SPS)
St Patrick's, Kiltegan,
Co Wicklow W91 YO22
Tel 0596473600

O'Reilly, Thomas, Very Rev, Adm
Clonaslee, Co Laois
Tel 057-8648030
(*Clonaslee*, Kildare & L.)

O'Reilly, Thomas (SSC)
St Columban's,
Dalgan Park,
Navan, Co Meath
Tel 046-9021525

O'Riordan, Anthony (SJ), Very Rev, PP
Irish Jesuit Provincialate,
Milltown Park,
Sandford Road,
Dublin 6
Tel 01-4987333

O'Riordan, Anthony (SVD)
Praeses,
133 North Circular Road,
Dublin 7
Tel 01-8386743

O'Riordan, Daniel, Rt Rev Mgr, PP
(Kerry, retired)

O'Riordan, David, Very Rev, PE
2 Connolly Street,
Midleton, Co Cork
Tel 086-3590047
(Cloyne, retired)

O'Riordan, Jeremiah, Very Rev, PP
Donoughmore, Co Cork
Tel 021-7337023
(*Donoughmore*, Cloyne)

O'Riordan, John P. (CSsR), CC
Mahon Parish,
2 The Presbytery,
Mahon, Cork
Tel 021-4515460
(*Mahon*, Cork & R.)

O'Riordáin, John J. (CSsR)
Mount St Alphonsus,
South Circular Road,
Limerick
Tel 061-315099

O'Rourke, Brendan
The Presbytery, Ballsgrove,
Drogheda, Co Louth
Tel 041-9831991
(*Drogheda, Holy Family*, Meath)

O'Rourke, Brendan (CSsR)
Dún Mhuire,
461/463 Griffith Avenue,
Dublin D09 X651
Tel 01-5180196

O'Rourke, Denis (SPS)
St Patrick's, Kiltegan,
Co Wicklow
Tel 059-6473600

O'Rourke, John (OP)
Holy Cross,
Tralee, Co Kerry
Tel 066-7121135/29185

O'Rourke, Kieran, Very Rev, PP
Looscaun, Woodford,
Co Galway H62 AK18
Tel 090-9749100
(*Woodford and looscaun*, Clonfert)

O'Rourke, Patrick (SMA)
Superior,
African Missions,
Blackrock Road,
Cork T12 TD54
Tel 021-4292871

O'Rourke, Patrick, CC
The Prebytery,
St Patrick's Road,
Wicklow Town,
Co Wicklow
(*Wicklow*, Dublin)

O'Rourke, Sean
15 Seaview Park, Shankill,
Co Dublin
(Dublin, retired)

O'Rourke, Seamus, CC
Curate's Residence,
Dublin Road,
Carrick-on-Shannon,
Co Leitrim
Tel 071-9620054
(*Carrick-on-Shannon (Kiltogher)*, Ardagh & Cl.)

O'Shaughnessy, Anthony,
Moderator
41 St Agnes' Road,
Crumlin, Dublin 12
Tel 01-5611500
(*Clogher Road, Crumlin, Mourne Road*, Dublin)

O'Shaughnessy, Sean (CSSp)
Holy Spirit Missionary College
Kimmage Manor,
Whitehall Road,
Dublin D12 P5YP
Tel 01-4064300

O'Shaughnessy, Thomas F.,
73 Annamoe Road,
Dublin 7
Tel 01-8385626
(*Cabra*, Dublin)

O'Shaughnessy, William, CC, VF
70 Maplewood Road
Tallaght, Dublin 24
Tel 01-4590746
(*Springfield*, Dublin)

O'Shea, A. B., Very Rev, PE
Rowantree Cottage,
Church Grounds,
Riverstown, Co Sligo
(*Riverstown*, Elphin)

O'Shea, Colum (SMA)
Vice-Superior, SMA House,
Wilton,
Cork, T12 KR23
Tel 021-4541069/4541884

O'Shea, Donagh (OP)
St Mary's Priory, Tallaght,
Dublin 24
Tel 01-4048100

O'Shea, Fintan (OFM)
96 Fr Scully House,
Middle Gardiner Street,
Dublin 1

O'Shea, Henry (OSB)
Glenstal Abbey, Murroe,
Co Limerick
Tel 061-386103

O'Shea, John, Canon
St Nessan's Presbytery,
Raheen, Co Limerick
Tel 061-301112/
087-9708282
(*Pastoral Unit 6,* Limerick)

O'Shea, Kieran, Very Rev PP
Ferrybank, Waterford
Tel 086-8272828
(*Slieverue*, Ossory)

O'Shea, Martin, Rt Rev Mgr, Co-PP
23 Clare Road,
Drumcondra, Dublin 9
Tel 01-8378552
(*Drumcondra*, Dublin)

O'Shea, Maurice, Very Rev, PE
64 White Oaks,
Clonskeagh, Dublin 14
(Dublin, retired)

O'Shea, Michael (IC)
Clonturk House,
Ormond Road,
Drumcondra,
Dublin D09 F821
Tel 01-6877014

O'Shea, Michael,
Parochial House,
Kilfinane, Co Limerick
Tel 063-91016/
087-9791432
(*Pastoral Unit 9,* Limerick)

O'Shea, Michael, Very Rev, PP
The Presbytery,
12 School Street, Wexford
Tel 053-9122055
(*Wexford*, Ferns)

O'Shea, Michael (SMA)
African Missions,
Blackrock Road,
Cork T12 TD54
Tel 021-4292871

O'Shea, Morty (SOLT), CC
Ardaghey, Co Donegal
Tel 074-9736007
(*Inver*, Raphoe)

O'Shea, Philip, Very Rev, PE
Clonagoose,
Borris, Co Carlow
(Kildare & L., retired)

O'Shea, Thomas, Very Rev, PE
Gowran Abbey Nursing Home,
Gowran, Co Kilkenny
(Kildare & L., retired)

O'Shea, Thomas (OMI)
Oblate House of Retreat,
Inchicore, Dublin 8
Tel 01-4534408/4541805

O'Siochru, Colm
Our Lady's Manor,
Bulloch Castle,
Dalkey, Co Dublin
(Dublin, retired)

Osthues, Gerhard (SVD), PC
c/o Parish Office,
Maynooth, Co Kildare
Tel 01-6286220
(*Maynooth*, Dublin)

O'Sullivan, Alan (OP)
St Saviour's,
Upper Dorset Street,
Dublin 1
Tel 01-8897610

O'Sullivan, Andrew, Adm
52 Lower Rathmines Road,
Dublin 6 D06 AK19
Tel 01-4969049
(*Rathgar, Rathmines*, Dublin)

O'Sullivan, Andrew (SMA)
African Missions,
Blackrock Road,
Cork T12 TD54
Tel 021-4292871

O'Sullivan, Anthony, Very Rev, PP
Irremore, Listowel,
Co Kerry
Tel 066-7132111
(*Lixnaw*, Kerry)

LIST OF CLERGY IN IRELAND

O'Sullivan, Billy, PP
The Presbytery,
Turner's Cross, Cork
Tel 021-4313103
(Turner's Cross, Cork & R.)

O'Sullivan, Brendan, PP
Ballinahown, Athlone,
Co Westmeath
Tel 090-6430124
(Ballinahown, Boher &
Pullough
(Lemanaghan), Ardagh &
Cl.)

O'Sullivan, Brian, PE
The Cottage,
Glengara Park,
Glenageary, Co Dublin
Tel 01-2360681
(Dublin, retired)

O'Sullivan, Brian (OSA)
St John's Priory,
Thomas Steet,
Dublin 8

O'Sullivan, Cian, CC
The Bungalow,
St Mary & St John,
Ballincollig, Co Cork
Tel 021-4877161
(Ballincollig, Cork & R.)

O'Sullivan, Denis (SMA)
SMA House, Wilton,
Cork T12 KR23
Tel 021-4541069/4541884

O'Sullivan, Denis, Very Rev, PE
c/o Bishop's House, Carlow
(Kildare & L., retired)

O'Sullivan, John (MSC)
Woodview House,
Mount Merrion Avenue,
Blackrock, Co Dublin
Tel 01-2881644

O'Sullivan, Kieran, Very Rev, PP
Glenbeigh, Co Kerry
Tel 066-9768209
(Glenbeigh, Kerry)

O'Sullivan, Louis
Our Lady's Manor,
Bullock Castle, Dalkey,
Co Dublin
(Dublin, retired)

O'Sullivan, Michael (SJ)
35 Lower Leeson Street,
Dublin 2
Tel 01-6761248

O'Sullivan, Michael P.
(White Fathers)
Community Superior,
Cypress Grove,
Templeogue, Dublin 6W
Tel 01-4055263/4055264

O'Sullivan, Noel, Very Rev
Dr
St Patrick's College,
Maynooth, Co Kildare
(Cork & R.)

O'Sullivan, Owen (OFMCap)
Capuchin Friary,
137-142 Church Street,
Dublin D07 HA22
Tel 01-8730599

O'Sullivan, Padraig, Co-PP
St Columba Parish House,
New Road, Clondalkin,
Dublin 22
Tel 01-4640441
(Bawnogue, Clondalkin,
Deansrath,
Neilstown, Rowlagh and
Quarryvale, Dublin)

O'Sullivan, Patrick, Very Rev
(MSC), Adm
Leap, Co Cork
Tel 028-33177
(Kilmacabea, Cork & R.)

O'Sullivan, Patrick
17 Alderwood Avenue,
Caherdavin Heights,
Limerick
Tel 061-421050/
087-2376032
(Pastoral Unit 5, Limerick)

O'Sullivan, Richard Rev (SSC)
St Columban's Retirement
Home, Dalgan Park,
Navan, Co Meath
Tel 046-9021525

O'Sullivan, Séan, Very Rev, PP
New Parochial House,
Monkstown, Co Cork
021-4863267
(Monkstown, Passage
West, Cork & R.)

O'Sullivan, Ted, Very Rev
Canon, PP
Parochial House, Douglas
Co Cork
Tel 021-4891265
(Douglas, Cork & R.)

O'Sullivan, Timothy, Very Rev
Villa Maria, Farnanes,
Co Cork
(Cork & R., retired)

O'Toole, Patrick (CSSp)
The Presbytery,
Ballintubber, Castlerea,
Co Roscommon
Tel 094-9655226

O'Toole, Sean
Ballintubber,
Claremorris, Co Mayo
F12 VY17
(Dublin, retired)

O'Toole, Thomas, Very Rev, PP
Glenmore,
Via New Ross,
Co Kilkenny
Tel 051-880080/
087-2240787
(Glenmore, Ossory)

Ogbonna, Magnus (MSP), PP
Parochial House,
Chapel Hill,
Carlingford,
Co Louth A91 FX76
Tel 042-9373111
(Carlingford and
Clogherny, Armagh)

Ohiemi, Luke, CC
Parochial House,
Tullamore, Co Offaly
Tel 057-9321587
(Tullamore, Meath)

Okpeh, Addison, PP
Kilmainhamwood,
Kells, Co Meath
Tel 046-9052129
(Kilmainhamwood and
Moybologue, Kilmore)

Okpetu, Peter, CC
The Presbytery,
Cavan
Tel 049-4331404/4332269
(Cavan (Urney and
Annagelliff), Kilmore)

Olin, Richard (CSSp)
St Mary's College,
Rathmines, Dublin 6
Tel 01-4995760

Ormonde, Noel (OMI)
170 Merrion Road,
Ballsbridge, Dublin 4
Tel 01-2693658

Orr, Thomas, CC,
New Ross, Co Wexford
(New Ross, Ferns)

Owen, John (SVD) PC
c/o St Philip the Apostle
Church,
No. 2 Presbtery,
Mountview,
Blanchardstown, Dublin 14
Tel 01-8249695
(Blakestown/Huntstown/Mountview, Dublin)

Owens, Finnian (OCSO)
Our Lady of Bethlehem
Abbey,
11 Ballymena Road,
Portglenone, Ballymena,
Co Antrim BT44 8BL
Tel 028-25821211

Owens, John (SVD)
The Presbytery,
Blakestown,
Clonsilla, Dublin 15
Tel 01-8210874
(Blakestown/Mountview,
Dublin)

Owens, Peter, Very Rev, PP
Parochial House,
8 Minorca Place,
Carrickfergus,
Co Antrim, BT38 8AU
Tel 028-93363269
(Carrickfergus, Down & C.)

Oxley, Brian (SSC)
St Columban's,
Dalgan Park, Navan,
Co Meath
Tel 046-9021525

Orzechowski, Arkadiusz
(SDB)
St Catherine's Centre,
North Campus, Maynooth

P

Pace, Paul (SJ)
Manresa House,
426 Clontarf Road,
Dollymount, Dublin 3
Tel 01-8331352

Padathiparambil, Clement,
CC
The Presbytery, Church
Grounds,
Kilmacud Co Dublin
Tel 01-2884009
(Kilmacud-Stillorgan,
Dublin)

Padilla Rocha, Rubén (MCCJ)
8 Clontarf Road, Clontarf,
Dublin 3
Tel 01-8330051

Paradiyil, Tomy (OSCam)
St Camillus,
11 St Vincent Street North,
Dublin 7
Tel 01-8300365

Parokkaran, Martin (OCarm)
Terenure College,
Terenure,
Dublin D6W DK72
Tel 01-4904621

Parys, Bart (SVD)
Donamon Castle,
Roscommon
Tel 090-6662222

Patton, Gerard, Very Rev
43 Head Road, Kilkeel,
Co Down BT34 4HX
(Down & C., retired)

Payne, Brendan (SPS)
St Patrick's, Kiltegan,
Co Wicklow
Tel 059-6473600

Pazhampilly, Rojan Peter
(OCarm)
Bursar,
Carmelite Priory,
White Abbey,
Co Kildare R51 X827
Tel 045-521391

Pecak Marek
(priest in residence)
Castlelyons, Fermoy,
Co Cork
Tel 087-1410470
(Castlelyons, Cloyne)

LIST OF CLERGY IN IRELAND

Peelo, Adrian (OFM)
The Abbey,
8 Francis Street,
Galway H91 C53K
Tel 091-562518

Peluchi, Alberto (MCCJ)
Provincial, Comboni Missionaries,
London Road, Sunningdal,
Berks Sl5 OJY, UK

Pender, Martin CC
Ballymitty,
Co Wexford
Tel 051-561128
(*Bannow*, Ferns)

Peoples, William, Very Rev, PP
Kilcar, Co Donegal
Tel 074-9738007
(*Kilcar*, Raphoe)

Pepper, Pierre, CC
Parochial House,
Boherquill,
Lismacaffrey, Mullingar,
Co Westmeath
Tel 043-6685847
(*Rathowen (Rathaspic, Russagh & Streete)*,
Ardagh & Cl.)

Perrotta, John (FDP)
Sarsfield House,
Sarsfield Road,
Ballyfermot, Dublin 10
Tel 01-6266193/6266233

Perry, Jim (SVD)
Maynooth, Co Kildare
Tel 01-6286391/2

Perumparambil, Thomas Devesia
Society of Saint Paul,
Moyglare Road,
Maynooth Co Kildare
Tel 01-6285933

Petrisor, Robert, CC
Sallins Road,
Naas, Co Kildare
Tel 045-897703
(*Naas*, Kildare & L.)

Peyton, Patrick, Very Rev Canon, PP
Parochial House,
Collooney, Co Sligo
Tel 071-9167235
(*Collooney (Kilvarnet)*,
Achonry)

Phair, John, Very Rev, PP
Kinlough, Co Leitrim
Tel 071-9841428
(*Kinlough and Glenade*,
Kilmore)

Philip, John (OSCam)
Chaplain to Waterford Hospital,
St Camillus,
11 St Vincent St North,
Dublin 7
Tel 01-8300365

Philomin, Leo, Very Rev (OMI), Moderator
Our Lady of the Wayside,
118 Naas Road,
Bluebell, Dublin 12
Tel 01-4501040
(*Inchicore, Mary Immaculate, Inchicore, St Michael's*, Dublin)

Pierce, Patrick (IC)
Doire na hAbhann,
Tickincar, Clonmel,
Co Tipperary E91 XY71
Tel 052-6126914

Piert, John, Very Rev Canon,
Team Assistant,
Our Lady's Manor,
Bulloch Harbour,
Glenageary,
Dalkey, Co Dublin
(Dublin)

Pinheiro da Salva Neto, Severino (OFMCap)
Capuchin Friary,
137-142 Church Street,
Dublin D07 HA22
Tel 01-8730599

Plasek, Dariusz, Co-PP
Polish Chaplain,
Bodyke, Co Clare
Tel 061-921060/
087-7036053
(*Inis Cealtra Pastoral Area*,
Killaloe)

Planell, Francis
Harvieston,
Cunningham Road,
Dalkey, Co Dublin
Tel 01-2859877
(Opus Dei)

Plower, Thomas (MSC)
'Croí Nua', Rosary Lane,
Taylor's Hill Road,
Galway H91 WY2A
Tel 091-520960

Plunkett, Oliver, AP
13 Castle Court,
Clancy Strand,
Limerick
Tel 087-6593176
(*Pastoral Unit 4*, Limerick)

Poland, James, Very Rev
Rostrevor, Co Down
(Dromore, retired)

Polly, Damian (OP)
St Mary's, Pope's Quay,
Cork
Tel 021-4502267

Poole, John (OMI)
Oblate House of Retreat,
Inchicore,
Dublin 8
Tel 01-4534408/4541805

Poole, Joseph (CSSp),
Holy Spirit Missionary College
Kimmage Manor,
Whitehall Road,
Dublin D12 P5YP
Tel 01-4064300

Porcellato, Antonio (SMA)
Superior General,
Missioni Africane,
Via della Nocetta 11
00164 Rome, Italy
Tel 06-6616841

Porter, Michael, PE
(Derry, retired)

Pound, Rufus (OSCO)
Mellifont Abbey,
Collon, Co Louth
Tel 041-9826103

Powell, Gerald, Very Rev, PP, VF
4 Holymount Road,
Gilford, Craigavon,
Co Armagh BT63 6AT
Tel 028-40624236
(*Tullylish*, Dromore)

Powell, Oliver
Gort Ard University Residence,
Rockbarton North, Galway
Tel 091-523846
(Opus Dei)

Power, Anthony, CC
35 Grange Park Avenue,
Raheny, Dublin 5
Tel 01-8480244/
086-3905205
(*Grange Park*, Dublin)

Power, Brian, Very Rev, PP
Parochial House,
Killea, Dunmore East,
Co Waterford
Tel 051-383127
(*Killea (Dunmore East)*,
Waterford & L.)

Power, Jackie (OSA)
St Augustine's,
Taylor's Lane,
Ballyboden, Dublin 16
Tel 01-4241000

Power, Joseph, Very Rev, PP
Kilrush, Bunclody,
Enniscorthy, Co Wexford
Tel 053-9377262
(*Kilrush and Askamore*,
Ferns)

Power, Liam, Very Rev, PP
Parish Office, SS Joseph and Benildus,
Newtown, Waterford
Tel 051-873073
(*St Joseph and Benildus*,
Waterford & L.)

Power, Patrick (OFM), PP
Provincial Delegate,
St Anthony's Parish
(English-Speaking Chaplaincy),
23/25 Oudstrijderslaan,
1950 Kraainem, Belgium
Tel 0032-2-7201970

Power, Robert, Very Rev, Adm
Parochial House,
Clogheen, Cahir,
Co Tipperary
Tel 052-7465268
Administrator,
Ballyporeen
(*Ballyporeen, Clogheen*,
Waterford & L.)

Power, Seamus, Very Rev, PE
19 Halcyon Place,
Park Village,
Castletroy, Limerick
(Limerick, retired)

Power, Thomas J., (MSC) PP
The Presbytery,
Killinarden, Tallaght,
Dublin 24
Tel 01-4522251
(*Killinarden*, Dublin)

Pozzerle, Iaccopo (OFM)
The Abbey,
8 Francis Street, Galway
H91 C53K
Tel 091-562518

Prendiville, James, CC
The Presbytery, Hollywood
(via Naas), Co Wicklow
Tel 045-864206
(*Ballymore Eustace*,
Dublin)

Price, Cathal
54 Foxfield St John,
Dublin 5
Tel 01-8323683
(Dublin, retired)

Prior, Dermot, Very Rev, PP, VF
Virginia, Co Cavan
Tel 049-8547063
(*Virginia (Lurgan)*,
Kilmore)

Prior, Paul
Mullagh, via Kells,
Co Meath
Tel 046-42208
(*Mullagh*, Kilmore)

Pudota, Anthaiah, Very Rev, Adm
Parochial House,
Letterfrack,
Connemara, Co Galway
Tel 095-41053
(*Inishbofin, Letterfrack (Ballinakill)*, Tuam)

Purba, Justinus (SVD)
Maynooth, Co Kildare
Tel 01-6286391/2

LIST OF CLERGY IN IRELAND

Purcell, Brendan
St Mary's Cathedral House,
St Mary's Road,
Sydney NSW 2000,
Australia
(Dublin)

Purcell, Denis
Mount Carmel, Callan,
Co Kilkenny
(Ossory)

Purcell, Eamon, Co-PP
Parteen, Co Clare
Tel 087-7635617
(*Pastoral Unit 4*, Limerick)

Purcell, Frank, Very Rev, VF
Inistioge, Co Kilkenny
Tel 051-423619/
086-6010001
(*Inistioge*, Ossory)

Purcell, James, Very Rev, PP
Cathedral Presbytery,
Thurles, Co Tipperary
Tel 0504 22229/22779/
087-8211045
(*Thurles, Cathedral*, Cashel & E.)

Purcell, Richard (OCSO) Rt Rev Dom, Abbot,
Mount Melleray Abbey,
Cappoquin, Co Waterford
Tel 058-54404

Purcell, William Very Rev
Director of Vocations,
St Kieran's College,
Kilkenny
Tel 056-7721086
St Mary's Cathedral,
Kilkenny
Tel 056-7721253/
087-6286858
(*St Mary's*, Ossory)

Puthiyaveettil, Antony, CC
The Presbytery,
John's Mall,
Birr, Co Offaly
Tel 057-9120098
(*Brendan Pastoral Area*, Killaloe)

Pyburn, Daniel, Very Rev Dr, PP
The Presbytery, Dromore,
Bantry, Co Cork
(*Caheragh*, Cork & R.)

Q

Quigley, Damien. Rev, CC
27 Woodhill,
Monaghan Row,
Newry,
Co Down BT35 8DP
(*Middle Killeavy (Newry)*,
Armagh)

Quigley, Sean
Tara Wintrop Nursing
Home,
Nevinstown Lane,
Pinnockhill, Swords,
Co Dublin
(Dublin, retired)

Quigley, Thomas, Very Rev, PE
Parochial House,
Latton, Castleblayney,
Co Monaghan
A75 E953
Tel 042-9742212
(*Latton (Aughnamullen West)*, Clogher)

Quinlan, Brendan, CC
Presbytery, Church
Grounds,
Laurel Lodge, Castleknock,
Dublin 15
Tel 01-8208144
(*Castleknock, Laurel Lodge-Carpenterstown*, Dublin)

Quinlan, John
(Kerry, retired)

Quinlan, Leo, Very Rev
42a Strand Street, Skerries,
Co Dublin
(Dublin, retired)

Quinlivan, Brendan, Very Rev, Co-PP, VF
Parochial House,
Newline, Tulla, Co Clare
Tel 065-6835117
(*Ceanntar na Lochanna Pastoral Area*, Killaloe)

Quinn, Brian, Very Rev, PP
Ballyraine, Letterkenny,
Co Donegal
Tel 074-9127600
(*Aughaninshin*, Raphoe)

Quinn, Denis, CC
The Presbytery,
Kimberley Road,
Greystones, Co Wicklow
Tel 01-2877025
(*Greystones*, Dublin)

Quinn, Denis, Very Rev, PP
Carrick, Co Donegal
Tel 074-9739008
(*Carrick (Glencolmcille)*, Raphoe)

Quinn, Edward (OMI)
The Presbytery,
Darndale, Dublin 17
Tel 01-8474547

Quinn, Frank (IC)
Mission Secretary,
Clonturk House,
Ormond Road,
Drumcondra,
Dublin D09 F821
Tel 01-6877014

Quinn, James, Very Rev Canon, AP, Adm
Taugheen, Claremorris,
Co Mayo
Administration Taugheen
Tel 094-9362500
(*Crossboyne and Taugheen*, Tuam)

Quinn, John (SDB)
Bursar, Rinaldi House,
72 Sean McDermott
Street, Dublin 1
Tel 01-8363358

Quinn, John, PP
Gortletteragh,
Carrick-on-Shannon,
Co Leitrim
Tel 071-9631074
(*Gortletteragh*, Ardagh & Cl.)

Quinn, Ken
Chaplain to Wexford
General Hospital,
Newton Road, Wexford
Tel 053-9142233
(Ferns)

Quinn, Michael, Very Rev, PP
Kiltimagh (Killedan),
Co Mayo
Tel 094-9381198
(*Kiltimagh (Killedan)*, Achonry)

Quinn, Richard (CSSp)
11 Silchester Court,
Glenageary, Co Dublin
Tel 01-2806375

Quinn, Séamus, Very Rev, PP
Parochial House,
Belcoo East, Belcoo
Co Fermanagh BT93 5FL
Tel 028-66386225
(*Arney (Cleenish)*, Clogher)

Quinn, Sean J., Very Rev, PE
Parochial House,
Dillonstown, Dunleer,
Co Louth
Tel 041-6863570
(Armagh, retired)

Quinn, Seán F., Very Rev, PE
Moorehall Lodge,
Hale Street, Ardee,
Co Louth
(Armagh, retired)

Quinn, Stephen (OCD)
Prior,
St Joseph's Carmelite
Retreat Centre
Termonbacca
Derry BT48 9XE
Tel 028-71262512

Quinn, Tadhg, Very Rev, Canon, PP
St John the Apostle,
Knocknacarra, Galway
Tel 091-590059
(*St John the Apostle*, Galway)

Quirke, Ciaran (SJ)
St Ignatius Community & Church,
27 Raleigh Row, Salthill,
Galway
Tel 091-523707

Quirke, Gerard
Priestly Society of St Peter
(Tuam, retired)

Quirke, Gerard, Very Rev, PP
Ballingarry, Thurles,
Co Tipperary
Tel 052-9154115
(*Ballingarry*, Cashel & E.)

R

Rabbitt, Joseph (SPS)
St Patrick's, Kiltegan,
Co Wicklow
Tel 059-6473600

Rabbitte, Peter, Very Rev Mgr, PP, VG
The Cathedral, Galway
Tel 091-563577
(*Cathedral*, Galway)

Radley, William, Very Rev, PP
(Kerry, retired)

Rafferty, James (CM)
99 Cliftonville Road,
Belfast BT14 6JQ
Tel 028-90751771

Rafferty, Terence, Very Rev
c/o Bishop's House
(Dromore)

Raftery, Eamon (SMA)
St Vincent's College,
Castleknock,
Dublin D15 PD95
Tel 01-8213051

Raftery, Gregory
Zum Holzfeld 25,
30880 Loatzen,
Germany
(Galway, retired)

Raftery, Thomas (CSSp)
Templeogue College,
Dublin 6W
Tel 01-4903909

Raleigh, Patrick (SSC)
St Columban's,
Dalgan Park,
Navan, Co Meath
Tel 046-9021525

Ralph, Joseph (OP)
St Catherine's,
Newry,
Co Down BT35 8BN
Tel 028-30262178

Ranahan, George Very Rev (SAC)
Pallottine College, Thurles,
Co Tipperary
Tel 0504-21202

Ratu, Nicodemus Lobo (SVD)
 Our Lady of Sorrows &
 St Bridget of Sweden
 112 Twickenham Road,
 Islworth TW7 6DL, UK
Reaume, Michael (SM)
 Marianist Community,
 13 Coundon Court,
 Killiney,
 Co Dublin A96 K0T9
 Tel 01-2858301
Rebamontan, Jonas, CC
 Parichial House, Boyle,
 Co Roscommon
 Tel 071-9662012
 (*Boyle*, Elphin)
Reburn, Frank, Co-PP
 137 Ballymun Road,
 Dublin 11
 Tel 01-8376341
 (*Ballymun Road*, Dublin)
Reche, Charles-Benoit (CFR)
 St Columba Friary,
 Fairview Road,
 Derry BT48 8NU
 Tel 028-71419980
Reddan, Michael (SVD),
 Seir Kieran,
 Clareen, Birr, Co Offaly
 Tel 0509-31080/
 087-4345898
 (*Seir Kieran*, Ossory)
Redmond, Noel (CSSp)
 Holy Spirit Missionary
 College
 Kimmage Manor,
 Whitehall Road,
 Dublin D12 P5YP
 Tel 01-4064300
Redmond, Richard, PP
 Ramsgrange, New Ross
 Co Wexford
 Tel 051-389148
 (*Ramsgrange*, Ferns)
Redmond, Tim (SPS)
 Editor, Africa,
 St Patrick's, Kiltegan,
 Co Wicklow
 Tel 059-6473600
Regan, Harry
 Presbytery 1,
 Church Grounds,
 Kill Avenue, Dun
 Laoghaire, Co Dublin
 Tel 01-2800901
 (Dublin, retired)
Regan, James (SPS)
 St Patrick's, Kiltegan,
 Co Wicklow
 Tel 059-6473600
Regan, John (SAC), CC
 The Presbytery, Corduff,
 Blanchardstown, Dublin 15
 Tel 01-8215930
 (*Corduff*, Dublin)
Regan, Michael, Very Rev,
 PP
 1B Riverside Grove,
 Riverstick, Co Cork
 (*Clontead*, Cork & R.)

Regan, Padraig (CM)
 St Peter's, Phibsboro,
 Dublin 7
 Tel 01-8389708/8389841
Regula, Robert (OP), CC
 St Mary's Priory, Tallaght,
 Dublin 24
 Tel 01-4048100
 (*Tallaght, St Mary's*,
 Dublin)
Reid, Desmond (CSSp)
 Holy Spirit Missionary
 College
 Kimmage Manor,
 Whitehall Road,
 Dublin D12 P5YP
 Tel 01-4064300
Reid, Norbert (SPS)
 St Patrick's, Kiltegan,
 Co Wicklow
 Tel 059-6473600
Reidy, Colm (CSSp)
 Community Leader,
 Holy Spirit Missionary
 College,
 Kimmage Manor,
 Whitehall Road, Dublin 12
 Tel 01-4064300
Reidy, Denis, Very Rev Mgr,
 PE
 4 Carrigdowns,
 Carrigtwohill, Co Cork
 (Cloyne, retired)
Reihill, Seamus (SPS)
 St Patrick's, Kiltegan,
 Co Wicklow
 Tel 059-6473600
Reilly, Anthony, Very Rev
 Canon, PP
 Parochial House,
 Palmerstown, Dublin 20
 Tel 01-6266254
 (*Palmerstown*, Dublin)
Reilly, John, Very Rev, PP
 Lahardane, Ballina,
 Co Mayo
 Tel 096-51007
 (*Lahardane*, Killala)
Reilly, Liam
 On Loan to Diocese of
 Reno, Nevada, USA
 (Killala)
Reilly, Michael,
 Park Place, Colehill,
 Co Longford
 (Ardagh & Cl., retired)
Reilly, Michael, Very Rev, PP
 Parochial House,
 Bunninadden, Ballymote,
 Co Sligo
 Tel 071-9183232
 (*Bunninadden (Kilshalvey,
 Kilturra and Cloonoghill)*,
 Achonry)
Reilly, Michael, Very Rev,
 PP, VF
 Belmullet, Co Mayo
 Tel 097-81426
 (*Belmullet*, Killala)

Reilly, Michael, Very Rev
 Canon
 Castlegar, Galway
 Tel 091-751548
 (Galway)
Reilly, Patrick (OPraem), PP
 13 Seaview Park, Portrane,
 Co Dublin
 Tel 01-8436099
 Chaplain, St Ita's, Portrane
 Tel 01-8436337
 (*Donabate*, Dublin)
Reilly, Peter J., Very Rev,
 Adm
 Presbytery 1,
 Ballycullen Avenue,
 Firhouse, Dublin 24
 Tel 01-4599855
 (*Firhouse*, Dublin)
Reilly, William
 Casilla 09-01-5825,
 Guayaquil, Ecuador
 (Killala)
Reji, Kurian
 Boher, Ballycumber,
 Co Offaly
 Tel 057-9336119
 (*Ballinahown, Boher and
 Pullough (Lemanaghan)*,
 Ardagh & Cl.)
Reyhart, Bernard, CC
 Curate's House,
 Prosperous, Co Kildare
 Tel 045-868187
 (*Prosperous*, Kildare & L.)
Reynolds, Daniel (LC)
 Community Secretary,
 Leopardstown Road,
 Dublin 18
 Tel 01-2955902
 Chaplain, Woodlands
 Academy,
 Wingfield House, Bray,
 Co Wicklow
 Tel 01-2866323
Reynolds, Kenneth
 (OFMCap)
 Capuchin Friary,
 Holy Trinity,
 Fr Mathew Quay,
 Cork T12 PK24
 Tel 021-4270827
 (Cork & R.)
Reynolds, Kevin (MHM), CC
 Presbytery, Patrick Street,
 Castlerea, Co Roscommon
 Tel 094-9620039
 (*Castlerea (Kilkeevan)*,
 Elphin)
Reynolds, Michael B. (CSSp)
 Holy Spirit Missionary
 College
 Kimmage Manor,
 Whitehall Road,
 Dublin D12 P5YP
 Tel 01-4064300

Reynolds, William (SJ)
 Rector, Manresa House,
 426 Clontarf Road,
 Dollymount, Dublin 3
 Tel 01-8331352
Rice, Patrick, Very Rev
 Canon, PE
 Little Sisters of the Poor,
 Holy Family Residence,
 Roebuck Road, Dundrum,
 Dublin 14
 (Dublin, retired)
Rice, Séamus, Very Rev, PE
 4 Ballymacnab Road,
 Armagh BT60 2QS
 Tel 028-37531620
 (Armagh, retired)
Rice, Tony (CSsR)
 St Joseph's, Dundalk,
 Co Louth
 Tel 042-9334042/9334762
Richardson, William
 c/o The Presbytery,
 Harrington Street,
 Dublin 8
 Tel 01-4789093
 (*Harrington Street*, Dublin)
Rigney, Liam, Very Rev
 Canon, PP, PhD
 Parochial House,
 1 Stanhope Place, Athy,
 Co Kildare
 Tel 059-8631781
 PP Moone Parish
 Tel 059-8624109
 Chaplain, St Vincent's
 Hospital,
 Athy, Co Kildare
 Tel 059-8646022
 (*Athy, Moone,
 Narraghmore*, Dublin)
Riordan, Michael, Very Rev
 Canon
 Mount Desert,
 Lee Road, Cork
 (Cork & R., retired)
Riordan, Patrick (SJ)
 Irish Jesuit Provincialate,
 Milltown Park,
 Sandford Road, Dublin 6
 Tel 01-4987333
Riordan, Raymond CC
 (Chaplain to Cork Prison)
 1 The Presbytery,
 Farranree, Co Cork
 Tel 021-2388000/
 086-1689292
 (Cork & R.)
Riordan, Tom, Very Rev
 Willow Lawn,
 Ballinlough, Cork
 (Cork & R., retired)
Roban, Myles (SSC)
 10 Belfield Springs,
 Enniscorthy, Co Wexford
 Tel 053-9237770

LIST OF CLERGY IN IRELAND

Roberts, Donal, Very Rev
Canon, PP, VF
Macroom, Co Cork
Tel 026-21068
Administrator,
Aghinagh Parish, Co Cork
(Cloyne)

Robinson, Denis, CC
The Presbytery,
Mourne Road, Dublin 12
Tel 01-4556199
(*Mourne Road*, Dublin)

Robinson, John, Very Rev, PP
Borris-in-Ossory,
Portlaoise, Co Laois
Tel 0505-41148/
087-2431412
(*Borris-in-Ossory*, Ossory)

Roche, Donal (OP), Adm
Prior, St Mary's Priory,
Tallaght, Dublin 24
Tel 01-4048100
(*Tallaght, St Mary's*, Dublin)

Roche, Donal, Very Rev, Adm, VG
The Abbey,
Wicklow, Co Wicklow
Tel 0404-67196
Administrator Kilbride and Barndarrig
(*Wicklow*, Dublin)

Roche, Eamon, CC
Monument Hil,
Fermoy, Co Cork
Tel 025-32963
(*Fermoy*, Cloyne)

Roche, Garrett (SVD)
Maynooth, Co Kildare
Tel 01-6286391/2

Roche, John (SPS)
Assistant House Leader,
St Patrick's, Kiltegan,
Co Wicklow W91 Y022
Tel 059-6473600

Roche, Joseph, Very Rev, PP
Parochial House, Labane,
Ardrahan, Co Galway
Tel 091-635164
Priest in charge, Kilchreest
(*Ardrahan, Kilchreest*, Galway)

Roche, Luke, Very Rev
(Kerry, retired)

Rochford, Seamus, Very Rev, AP
Emly, Co Tipperary
Tel 062-57103
(*Emly*, Cashel & E.)

Rodgers, Michael (SPS)
Tearmann Spirituality Centre, Brockagh,
Glendalough,
Co Wicklow
Tel 0404-45208

Rodgers, Peter (OFMCap)
Capuchin Friary,
137-142 Church Street,
Dublin D07 HA22
Tel 01-8730599

Rodrigues Da Silva, Edvaldo (CSSp), Very Rev, Co-PP
Parish of St Ronan's,
Deansrath,
Clondalkin, Dublin 22
Tel 01-4570380
(*Deansrath*, Dublin)

Rodriguez, Paulino (MSC)
(Peru) c/o Parish Office,
Herbert Road, Bray,
Co Wicklow
Tel 01-2868413
(*Bray, Holy Redeemer*, Dublin)

Rogan, Edward, Very Rev
On loan to Diocese of Chulucanas
(Killala)

Rogan, Sean, Very Rev
Canon, PE
546 Saintfeild Road,
Carryduff,
Belfast BT8 8EU
Tel 028-90812238
(*Drumbo & Carryduff*, Down & C.)

Rogers, Patrick (CP)
St Paul's Retreat,
Mount Argus, Dublin 6W
Tel 01-4992000

Rogers, Thomas, Very Rev, PP
2 Carmel, Priest's Road,
Tramore, Co Tipperary
Tel 051-511275
Administrator,
Ballybricken
(*St John's, Ballybricken*, Waterford & L.)

Rohan, Joseph, Very Rev, PP
Clondrohid, Macroom,
Co Cork
Tel 026-31915
(*Clondrohid*, Cloyne)

Ronayne, James, Very Rev, PP, VF
The Parochial House,
Clifden,
Co Galway H71 WF44
Tel 095-21251
(*Clifden (Omey and Ballindoon)*, Tuam)

Rooney, Joseph, Very Rev
(priest in residence)
45 Ballyholme Esplanade,
Bangor,
Co Down BT20 5NJ
Tel 028-91465425
(*Bangor*, Down & C.)

Rooney, Joseph, Very Rev, JCL
Parochial House,
69 Doagh Road,
Ballyclare,
Co Antrim BT39 9BG
Tel 028-93342226
(*Ballyclare & Ballygowan*, Down & C.)

Rooney, Noel, Very Rev, PP
279 Sunset Drive,
Cartron Point, Sligo
Tel 071-9142422
Chaplain,
Ballinode Vocational School, Sligo
Tel 071-9147111
(*Sligo, Calry St Joseph's*, Elphin)

Rosario, Ripon (SJ)
John Sullivan House
56/56A Mulvey Park,
Dundrum, Dublin 14
Tel 01-298397

Rosbotham, Gabriel, CC
Crossmolina, Chapel Road,
Co Mayo
Tel 096-31344
(*Crossmolina*, Killala)

Rosney, Arnold, Co-PP, VF
Ss John and Paul Presbytery,
4 Dún na Rí, Shannon,
Co Clare
Tel 061-471513/
087-8598710
(*Tradaree Pastoral Area*, Killaloe)

Ross, Jim (SM)
Fiji

Rothery, Colin, Very Rev, Co-PP
5 Lissenhall Park,
Seatown Road,
Swords, Co Dublin
Tel 01-8403378
(*Brackenstown, River Valley, Swords*, Dublin)

Router, Michael, Most Rev, DD
Titular Bishop of Lugmad and Auxiliary Bishop of Armagh
Annaskeagh, Ravensdale,
Dundalk, Co Louth
A91 KP64
(*Armagh*)

Rowan, Kevin, Co-PP
Parochial House,
Carrickbrennan Road,
Monkstown, Co Dublin
Tel 01-2802130
(*Monkstown*, Dublin)

Rudczenko, Sergiusz, PP
Lanesboro, Co Longford
Tel 043-3321166
(*Lanesboro*, Ardagh & Cl.)

Ruddy, Michael (SSCC), Very Rev
Sacred Heart,
St John's Drive,
Clondalkin,
Dublin D22 W1W6
Tel 01-4570032
(*Sruleen*, Dublin)

Rushe, Patrick, Very Rev, PP, VF
Parochial House,
Monasterboice,
Drogheda,
Co Louth A92 RT66
Tel 086-8807470
(*Monasterboice*, Armagh)

Russell, Thomas (OFM)
Franciscan Friary,
Clonmel,
Co Tipperary E91 X9T8
Tel 052-6121378

Russell, William,
Riddlestown,
Rathkeale, Co Limerick
Tel 087-2272825
(*Pastoral Unit 10*, Limerick)

Ryan, Aidan
Spiritua Director,
Pontifical Irish College,
Via Dei SS Quattro 1,
00184 Roma, Italy
(Ardagh & Cl.)

Ryan, Anthony, Rev, PP
Upperchurch, Thurles,
Co Tipperary
Tel 054-54492
(*Upperchurch*, Cashel & E.)

Ryan, Con (SPS)
St Patrick's, 21 Leeson Park,
Dublin 6 D06 DE76
Tel 01-4977897

Ryan, Conor, Very Rev
Canon, PP, VF
Castlefarm, Hospital,
Co Limerick
Tel 061-383108
(*Hospital*, Cashel & E.)

Ryan, Damian,
Manister, Croom,
Co Limerick
Tel 061-397335/
087-2274412
(*Pastoral Unit 7*, Limerick)

Ryan, Daniel J.
c/o Archbishop's House,
Thurles, Co Tipperary
(Cashel & E., retired)

Ryan, Denis J. (SMA)
African Missions,
Blackrock Road,
Cork T12 TD54
Tel 021-4292871

LIST OF CLERGY IN IRELAND

Ryan, Derek (CSsR), Very Rev Adm
Holy Family Parish,
Hoey's Lane,
Muirhevnamor,
Dundalk,
Co Louth A91 K761
Tel 042-9336301
(*Dundalk, Holy Family*, Armagh)

Ryan, Dermot, Rt Rev Dr
President,
St Kieran's College,
Kilkenny
Tel 056-7721086
Priest Secretary to Apostolic Administrator,
Diocesan Office,
James's Street, Kilkenny
Tel 056-7762448
(*Ossory*)

Ryan, Edmond (SPS)
St Patrick's, Kiltegan,
Co Wicklow
Tel 059-6473600

Ryan, Fergal, Very Rev, PP
The Presbytery,
Beaufort, Co Kerry
Tel 064-6644128
(*Beaufort (Tuogh)*, Kerry)

Ryan, Fergus (OP)
Convent of SS Xystus and Clement
Collegio San Clemente,
Via Labicana 95,
00184 Roma
Tel 0039-06-7740021

Ryan, James, Rt Rev Mgr, AP
Bohermore, Cashel,
Co Tipperary
Tel 062-61353
(*Cashel*, Cashel & E.)

Ryan, James, Very Rev
(priest in residence)
Cleariestown, Co Wexford
Tel 053-9139110
(Ferns, retired)

Ryan, John, Very Rev, PE, CC
Midleton, Co Cork
Tel 021-4631094
(*Midleton*, Cloyne)

Ryan, Joseph, Very Rev, Co-PP
41 Cremore Heights,
St Canice's Road,
Glasnevin, Dublin 11
Tel 01-8573776
(*Ballygall*, Dublin)

Ryan, Liam (OSA)
St Augustine's,
Taylor's Lane,
Balyboden, Dublin 16
Tel 01-4241000

Ryan, Martin (OCarm)
Gort Muire, Ballinteer,
Dublin 16 D16 EI67
Tel 01-2984014

Ryan, Michael
c/o Archbishop's House,
Thurles, Co Tipperary
Tel 0504-21512
(Cashel and E.)

Ryan, Michael (SSC)
112 The Sycamores,
Freshford Road, Kilkenny
Tel 086-8977569

Ryan, Michael, Rt Rev Dom (OCSO)
Abbot, Bolton Abbey,
Moone, Co Kildare
Tel 059-8624102

Ryan, Michael, Rt Rev Mgr, PP, VG
Castlecomer, Co Kilkenny
Tel 056-4441262/
086-3693863
(*Castlecomer*, Ossory)

Ryan, Patrick (OCSO)
Prior,
Mount Melleray Abbey,
Cappoquin,
Co Waterford P51 R8XW
Tel 058-54404

Ryan, Patrick J. (CSSp)
Holy Spirit Missionary College
Kimmage Manor,
Whitehall Road,
Dublin D12 P5YP
Tel 01-4064300

Ryan, Patrick, M. (CSSp)
Holy Spirit Missionary College
Kimmage Manor,
Whitehall Road,
Dublin D12 P5YP
Tel 01-4064300

Ryan, Seamus, Very Rev
Milbrea Nursing Home,
Newport, Co Tipperary
(Dublin, retired)

Ryan, Thomas, Very Rev, CC
Gleneden,
North Circular Road,
Limerick
Tel 087-2997733
(*Pastoral Unit 5*, Limerick)

Ryan, Thomas A.,
8 Merval Crescent,
Clareview, Limerick
Tel 085-1387001
(Limerick, retired)

Ryan, Thomas J., Very Rev Canon, AP, VF
Bohergar, Brittas,
Co Limerick
Tel 061-352223
(*Murroe and Boher*, Cashel & E.)

Ryan, Tom, Very Rev, Co-PP, VF
Director, Lourdes Pilgrimage,
Cathedral Presbytery,
O'Connell Street,
Ennis, Co Clare
Tel 065-6869097
(*Abbey Pastoral Area*, Killaloe)

Ryan, Tom (SPS)
St Patrick's, Kiltegan,
Co Wicklow W91 Y022
Tel 059-6473600

Ryan, William (OFMCap) PC
Capuchin Friary,
Clonshaugh Drive,
Priorswood,
Dublin D17 RP20
Tel 01-8474469
(*Priorswood*, Dublin)

Ryan, William, Very Rev Canon, PP, VF
Parochial House,
Dungarvan, Co Waterford
Tel 058-42374
Adm, Ring and Old Parish
(*Dungarvan, Kilgobnet, Ring and Old Parish*, Waterford & L.)

Ryder, Andrew (SCI)
Sacred Heart Fathers,
Fairfield,
66 Inchicore Road,
Dublin 8
Tel 01-4538655

Ryder, John, PEm
16 Whitehouse Park,
Buncrana Road, Derry
(Derry, retired)

Rynn, Sean (SPS)
St Patrick's, Kiltegan,
Co Wicklow W91 Y022

S

Sakwe, Willibrord, CC
St Mary's Temple Street,
Sligo
Tel 071-9162670
(*Sligo, St Mary's*, Elphin)

Salud Abila, Laurent M. (OSB)
119 Kilbroney Road,
Rostrevor,
Co Down BT34 3BN
Tel 028-41739979

Samugana, Victor (MSP), CC
St Mary's, Temple Street,
Sligo
071-9162670
(*Sligo, St Mary's*, Elphin)

Sammon, Frank (SJ)
Milltown Park,
Sandford Road,
Dublin D04 NX39

Samosir, Bavo (OCSO)
Mount Saint Joseph Abbey, Roscrea,
Co Tipperary E53 D651
Tel 0505-25600

Sanchez, Oscar (LC)
Director, Dublin Oak Academy,
Kilcroney, Bray,
Co Wicklow
Tel 01-2863290

Sandham, Denis (OSCam)
Superior, St Camillus,
South Hill Avenue,
Blackrock, Co Dublin
Tel 01-2882873

Saniuta, Ignacy, CC
Parochial House, St Eugene's Cathedral,
Derry BT48 9AP
(*Derry City*, Derry)

Savio, Dominic,
10 Castletroy Heights,
Castletroy, Co Limerick
Tel 089-2322418
(Limerick)

Scallon, Paschal (CM), Very Rev
Provincial,
Provincial Office,
St Paul's, Sybil Hill,
Raheny, Dublin D05 AE38
Tel 01-8510842
Superior,
St Vincent's College,
Castleknock,
Dublin D15 PD95
Tel 01-8213051

Scanlan, Charles
Ballinwillin, Lismore,
Co Waterford
Tel 058-54282
(Waterford & L., retired)

Scanlan, Liam V. (SPS)
St Patrick's, Kiltegan,
Co Wicklow
Tel 059-6473600

Scanlan, Patrick, Very Rev, PE
Castlemagner,
Mallow, Co Cork
(Cloyne, retired)

Scanlon, Michael, PE
Parochial House, Cloghan,
Co Offaly
(Ardagh & Cl., retired)

Scanlon, Thomas (CP)
Superior,
Passionist Retreat Centre
Downpatrick Road,
Crossgar, Downpatrick
Co Down BT30 9EQ

Scheifele, Claus (OFM)
Franciscan Friary,
Killarney, Co Kerry
Tel 064-6631334/6631066

LIST OF CLERGY IN IRELAND

Scott, Michael (SDB)
  Salesian House,
  45 St Teresa's Road,
  Crumlin, Dublin 12
  Tel 01-4555605
Scott, Philip (OCSO)
  Our Lady of Bethlehem Abbey,
  11 Ballymena Road,
  Portglenone, Ballymena,
  Co Antrim BT44 8BL
  Tel 028-25821211
Scott, Thomas (SPS)
  St Patrick's, Kiltegan,
  Co Wicklow W91 Y022
  Tel 059-6473600
Screene, Michael (MSC)
  Woodview House,
  Mount Merrion Avenue,
  Blackrock, Co Dublin
  Tel 01-2881644
Scriven, Richard, Very Rev, Adm
  St Mary's Cathedral,
  Kilkenny R95 CP46
  Tel 056-7721253/
  087-2420033
  (*St Mary's*, Ossory)
Scully, Anthony
  Dunmanus Road,
  Cabra, Dublin 7
  (Dublin, retired)
Scully, Brendan (OFM)
  Franciscan Friary,
  Liberty Street,
  Cork T12 D376
  Tel 021-4270302/4275481
Seaver, Patrick, CC
  4 Glenview Terrace,
  Farranshone, Limerick
  Tel 061-328838/
  086-0870297
  (*Pastoral Unit 4*, Limerick)
Sekongo, Alphonse (SMA), Very Rev, PP,
  St Joseph's SMA Parish,
  Blackrock Road,
  Cork T12 X281
  Tel 021-4293325
  (*St Joseph's (Blackrock Road)*, Cork & R.)
Serrage, Michael (MSC)
  Woodview House,
  Mount Merrion Avenue
  Blackrock,
  Co Dublin A94 DW95
  Tel 01-2881644
Sexton, Frank (OSA)
  St Augustine's,
  Taylor's Lane,
  Ballyboden, Dublin 16
  Tel 01-4241000
Sexton, John
  Rossinver, Co Leitrim
  Tel 071-9854022
  (*Ballaghameehan*, Kilmore)

Sexton, Pat, Very Rev
  5 Cottage Gardens,
  Station Road, Ennis,
  Co Clare
  Tel 065-6840828/
  087-2477814
  (Killaloe, retired)
Sexton, Peter (SJ)
  House 27, Trinity College,
  Dublin 2
  Tel 01-8961260
  (Dublin)
Sexton, Sean, Very Rev, AP
  Kilnamona, Ennis,
  Co Clare
  Tel 065-6829507/
  087-2621884
  (*Críocha Callan Pastoral Area*, Killaloe)
Sexton, Tom (OSA)
  St Augustine's Priory
  Washington Street, Cork
  Tel 021-4275398/4270410
Shanahan, John,
  (Kerry, retired)
Shanahan, Martin, Co-PP
  Parochial House,
  Inagh, Co Clare
  Tel 087-7486935
  (*Críocha Callan Pastoral Area*, Killaloe)
Shanahan, Tom (OCD)
  The Abbey, Loughrea,
  Co Galway
  Tel 091-841209
Shanet, Jacob
  Parish Chaplain,
  c/o 12 Coarsemoor Park,
  Straffan, Co Kildare
  Tel 01-6288827
  (*Celbridge*, Dublin)
Shannon, Declan CF
  Chaplain, Custume Barracks, Athlone,
  Co Westmeath
  Tel 090-6421277
  (*Ardagh & Cl.*)
Shannon, Richard, Adm
  Parochial House,
  78 St Mary's Road,
  East Wall, Dublin 3
  Tel 01-8742320
  (*East Wall-North Strand*, Dublin)
Sharkey, Liam (SPS)
  St Patrick's, Kiltegan,
  Co Wicklow
  Tel 059-6473600
Sharkey, Liam
  Ballyweelin, Rosses Point,
  Co Sligo
  (Elphin, retired)
Sharkey, Lorcan, Very Rev, PP
  Cloghan, Lifford,
  Co Donegal
  Tel 074-9133007
  (*Cloghan*, Raphoe)

Sharpe, Jackie
  Ogonnelloe, Co Clare
  Tel 086-8940556
  (*Inis Cealtra Pastoral Area*, Killaloe)
Sharpe, John M. (CSSp)
  Parish House,
  Ballybrohan, Ogonnelloe
  Co Clare
Shaughnessy, Bernard
  The Parochial House,
  Coolarne, Athenry,
  Co Galway H65 X796
  Tel 091-797626
  (Tuam)
Sheary, Patrick (SJ), CC
  Milltown Park,
  Sandford Road,
  Dublin D06 V9K7
  Tel 01-2693903
  (*Donnybrook*, Dublin)
Sheehan, Anthony, AP
  Love Lane,
  Charleville, Co Cork
  Tel 063-32320
  (*Charleville*, Cloyne)
Sheehan, Diarmuid, (White Fathers)
  Cypress Grove,
  Templeogue, Dublin 6W
  Tel 01-4055263/4055264
Sheehan, Edward CF
  Chapain, Collin's Barracks,
  Cork
  Tel 021-4502734
  (*Cork & R.*)
Sheehan, Martin, Very Rev, Adm
  Adrigole, Bantry,
  Co Cork
  Tel 027-60006
  (*Adrigole*, Kerry)
Sheehan, Michael, Adm
  Ard Eismuinn,
  Dundalk, Co Louth
  Tel 042-9334259
  (*Dundalk, Holy Redeemer*, Armagh)
Sheehan, Michael, Very Rev, PP
  546 Saintfeild Road,
  Carryduff,
  Belfast BT8 8EU
  Tel 028-90812238
  (*Drumbo & Carryduff*, Down & C.)
Sheehan, Niall
  Portadown, Co Armagh
  (Dromore, retired)
Sheehan, Patrick
  (Kerry, retired)

Sheehan, Patrick, Very Rev, PP
  Elmfield,
  165 Antrim Road,
  Glengormley
  Newtownabbey,
  Co Antrim BT36 7QR
  Tel 028-90832979
  (*St Mary's on the Hill*, Down & C.)
Sheehan, Rory, Very Rev, PP
  Netherley Lodge,
  130 Upper Dunmurry Lane,
  Belfast BT17 0EW
  Tel 028-90616300
  (*Our Lady Queen of Peace, Kilwee*, Down & C.)
Sheehy, James (SSC)
  Dungarvan, Co Waterford
  (retired)
Sheehy, Richard, Very Rev, VF
  (Moderator)
  50 Cremore Road,
  Glasnevin, Dublin 11
  Tel 01-5582697
  (*Ballygall, Ballymun Road, Glasnevin, Iona Road*, Dublin)
Sheerin, Michael, Very Rev
  Woodlands Nursing Home,
  Navan, Co Meath
  Tel 046-9053155
  (Meath, retired)
Sheerin, Tony (SPS)
  St Patrick's, Kiltegan,
  Co Wicklow
  Tel 059-6473600
Sheil, Michael (SJ)
  Rector,
  Clongowes Wood College,
  Clane,
  Co Kildare W91 DN40
  Tel 045-868663/868202
Shelley, Padraig, Very Rev, PP
  The Presbytery, Arles
  Tel 059-9147637
  (*Arles*, Kildare & L.)
Shen-yi Hssii, Matthew (SJ)
  John Sullivan House,
  56/56A Mulvey Park,
  Dundrum, Dublin 14
  Tel 01-2983978
Sheppard, Jim, Very Rev
  189 Carrigenagh Road,
  Ballymartin, Kilkeel,
  Co Down BT34 4GA
  (Down & C., retired)
Sheridan, Billy (SMA) CC
  St Patrick's Presbytery,
  Ballina, Co Mayo
  Tel 096-71360
  (*Ballina (Kilmoremoy)*, Killala)

Sheridan, Christopher CC
7 Bayside Square East,
Sutton, Dublin 13
Tel 01-8322964
(*Bayside*, Dublin)

Sheridan, James (CP)
St Paul's Retreat,
Mount Argus, Dublin 6W
Tel 01-4992000

Sheridan, John-Paul
Annacurra, Aughrim,
Co Wicklow
Tel 0402-36119
(*Ferns*)

Sheridan, Paddy, CC
Robeen, Hollymount,
Co Mayo
Tel 094-9540026
(*Robeen*, Tuam)

Sheridan, Patrick (CP)
St Paul's Retreat,
Mount Argus, Dublin 6W
Tel 01-4992000

Sherlock, Vincent, Very Rev, PP
Diocesan Communications Officer,
Parochial House,
Emmet Street,
Tubbercurry,
Co Sligo F91 NH34
Tel 071-9185049
(*Tubbercurry (Cloonacool)*, Achonry)

Shibanada, Julius
Church of the Sacred Heart, Donnybrook,
Dublin 4
(*Donnybrook*, Dublin)

Shiel, Patrick, Very Rev
Canon
74 Mount Drinan Avenue,
Kinsealy Downs,
Swords, Co Dublin
(Dublin, retired)

Shiels, Michael, CC
Presbytery 1,
St Canice's Parish,
Finglas, Dublin 11
Tel 01-8341051
(*Finglas*, Dublin)

Shine, Larry (CSSp)
Holy Spirit Missionary College, Kimmage Manor,
Whitehall Road,
Dublin D12 P5YP
Tel 01-4064300

Shire, Joseph, Very Rev
Canon,
Ballyagran, Kilmallock,
Co Limerick
Tel 087-6924563
(*Pastoral Unit 8*, Limerick)

Shortall, Bryan (OFMCap),
PP, VF
Clonshaugh Drive,
Priorswood,
Dublin 17 D17 RP20
Tel 01-8474469/8474358
(*Priorswood*, Dublin)

Shortall, Maurice (CSSp)
Holy Spirit Missionary College
Kimmage Manor,
Whitehall Road,
Dublin D12 P5YP
Tel 01-4064300

Shortall, Michael, PC
87 Beechwood Lawns,
Rathcoole, Co Dublin
Tel 01-4587187
(*Saggart*, Dublin)

Shorten, Kieran (OFMCap)
Vicar, Capuchin Friary,
Ard Mhuire,
Creeslough, Letterkenny,
Co Donegal
Tel 074-9138005

Shube Bawe, Philip (MHM)
St Joseph's House,
50 Orwell Park,
Rathgar, Dublin D06 C535
Tel 01-4127700

Sikora, Krzysztof (SVD), PP
Polish Chaplain,
Roundstone, Co Galway
Tel 095-37123
(*Roundstone*, Tuam)

Simpson, Michael, CC
St Kevin's Presbytery,
Pearse Street,
Sallynoggin, Co Dublin
Tel 01-2854667
(*Sallynoggin*, Dublin)

Sinnott, John, Very Rev, Co-PP
56 Auburn Road, Killiney,
Co Dublin
Tel 01-2856660
(*Johnstown-Killiney*, Dublin)

Sinnott, Patrick
Parkannesley,
Ballygarrett,
Gorey, Co Wexford
(Ferns, retired)

Sinnott, Peter J., CC
No. 3 Presbytery,
Castle Street, Dalkey,
Co Dublin
Tel 01-2859212
(*Dalkey*, Dublin)

Skelly, Oliver, Very Rev, PP
Parochial House, Coole,
Co Westmeath
Tel 044-9661191
(*Coole*, Meath)

Slater, Brian, CC, VF
Parochial House,
3 Convent Road,
Cookstown,
Co Tyrone BT80 8QA
Tel 028-86763490
(*Cookstown (Desertcreight and Derryloran)*, Armagh)

Slater, David (OSA)
St Augustine's,
Taylor's Lane,
Ballyboden, Dublin 16
Tel 01-4241000

Slattery, Sean, Very Rev
18 The Orchard,
Limerick V94 F97N
(Clonfert, retired)

Sleeman, Simon (OSB)
Glenstal Abbey, Murroe,
Co Limerick
Tel 061-621000

Sloan, Robert, CC
Royal Victoria Hospital
111 Queensway, Lambeg,
Lisburn, BT27 4QS
Tel 028-90606980
(Down & C.)

Slowey, Harry (CM)
St Paul's, Sybil Hill,
Raheny, Dublin D05 AE38
Tel 01-8318113

Small, Thomas
Okpetu, Peter, CC
The Presbytery,
Cavan
Tel 049-4331404/4332269
(*Cavan (Urney and Annagelliff)*, Kilmore)

Smith, Adrian (SM), Most Rev Archbishop
Nazareth House,
Malahide Road, Dublin 9

Smith, David (MSC)
Woodview House,
Mount Merrion Avenue,
Blackrock, Co Dublin
Tel 01-2881644

Smith, Declan, Very Rev, PP
Parochial House,
Taghmon,
Mullingar, Co Westmeath
Tel 044-9372140
(*Taghmon*, Meath)

Smith, Desmond (SMA)
Rathduff,
Ballina, Co Mayo
Tel 096-21596
(*Backs*, Killala)

Smith, Martin (SPS), CC
1 Green Road, Carlow
Tel 059-9142632
(*Cathedral, Carlow*, Kildare & L.)

Smith, Michael, Most Rev, DCL, DD
Bishop Emeritus of Meath,
St Oliver's, Beechfield
Dublin Road, Mullingar,
Co Westmeath
Tel 044-9340636
(Meath)

Smith, Philip, Very Rev, PP
Tir-ee, Harbourstown,
Stamullen, Co Meath
Tel 01-8020708
(Meath, retired)

Smith, Sean, Very Rev
Canon, CC
The Presbytery,
Newtownmountkennedy,
Co Wicklow
Tel 01-2819253
(*Kilquade*, Dublin)

Smith, Terence (CSSp)
Holy Spirit Missionary College
Kimmage Manor,
Whitehall Road,
Dublin D12 P5YP
Tel 01-4064300

Smyth, Brendan, Very Rev, PP
Parochial House,
10 Downpatrick Street,
Crossgar, Downpatrick,
Co Down BT30 9EA
Tel 028-44830229
(*Crossgar (Kilmore)*, Down & C.)

Smyth, Derek
No. 2 Kill Lane,
Foxrock, Dublin 18
Tel 01-2894734
(Dublin, retired)

Smyth, Edmund (OCD)
St Teresa's
Claredon Street, Dublin 2
Tel 01-6718466/6718127

Smyth, James (SJ)
Cherryfield Lodge,
Milltown Park, Ranelagh,
Dublin D06 V9K7
Tel 01-4985800

Smyth, Michael (MSC)
'Croí Nua', Rosary Lane,
Taylor's Hill, Galway
Tel 091-520960

Smyth, Michael (SDB)
Vice-Rector,
Salesian House,
Milford, Castletroy,
Limerick
Tel 061-330268

Smyth, Patrick (OCarm)
Carmelite Priory,
Whitefriar Street Church,
56 Aungier Street,
Dublin D02 R598
Tel 01-4758821

Smyth, Patrick (SSC)
St Columban's,
Dalgan Park,
Navan, Co Meath
Tel 046-9021525

Smyth, Robert, Very Rev, Adm
Presbytery, Montrose Park,
Beaumont, Dublin 5
Tel 01-8710013
(*Beaumont*, Dublin)

Smyth, Terry (OPraem)
Holy Trinity House,
Lismacanican,
Mountnugent, Co Cavan

Solomon, Ciprian
St Mary's Drogheda,
Co Louth
Tel 041-9834958
(*Drogheda, St Mary's*, Meath)

LIST OF CLERGY IN IRELAND

Somers, James (SDB)
Salesian House,
45 St Teresa's Road,
Crumlin, Dublin 12
Tel 01-4555605

Somers, P. J., Very Rev, PP
Chaplains House, Curragh
Camp, Co Kildare
Tel 045-441277
(*Curragh Camp*, Kildare & L.)

Soukup, Bernardino Maria Rev (CFR)
St Patrick Friary
64 Delmege Park,
Moyross,
Limerick V94 859Y
Tel 061-458071

Spain, Michael (OCD)
St Joseph's Carmelite Retreat Centre
Termonbacca
Derry BT48 9XE
Tel 028-71262512

Spence, Michael, Very Rev, CC
28 Willowbank Park,
Belfast BT6 0LL
Tel 028-90793023
(*St Bernadette's*, Down & C.)

Spencer, Paul Francis (CP), PP
St Paul's Retreat,
Mount Argus, Dublin 6W
Tel 01-4992000
(*Mount Argus*, Dublin)

Spillane, David (LC)
Dublin Oak Academy
Kilcroney, Bray,
Co Wicklow
Tel 01-2863290

Spillane, Martin, Very Rev, PP
Brosna, Co Kerry
Tel 068-44112
(*Brosna*, Kerry)

Spillane, Martin (SPS)
On temporary diocesan work

Spinharney, Isaac (CFR)
St Columba Friary,
Fairview Road,
Derry BT48 8NU
Tel 028-71419980

Spring, Finbarr (OSA)
St Augustine's Priory,
Dungarvan,
Co Waterford
Tel 058-41136

Spring, Noel, Very Rev Canon, PP
Castletownbere, Co Cork
Tel 027 70849
(*Castletownbere and Bere Island*, Kerry)

St John, Paul (SVD), Adm
4 Claremont Drive,
Ballygall, Dublin 11
Tel 01-8087553
(*Ballygall*, Dublin)

Stafford, Patrick, Very Rev,
Tomsollagh, Ferns,
Enniscorthy, Co Wexford
(Ferns, retired)

Standún, Padraic, Very Rev Canon, PE
Cill Chiaráin, Co Galway
(Tuam, retired)

Stanley, Cathal
Dominic Street, Portumna,
Co Galway H53 EC66
Tel 090-9759182
(Clonfert, retired)

Stanley, Gerard, Very Rev, PP
Parochial House,
Rathkenny, Co Meath
Tel 046-9054138
(*Rathkenny*, Meath)

Stanley, Paddy (SM), PC
The Presbytery,
Coolock Village, Dublin 5
Tel 01-8477133
(*Coolock*, Dublin)

Stanley, Thomas (SCJ)
Sacred Heart Fathers,
Fairfield,
66 Inchicore Road,
Dublin 8
Tel 01-4538655

Stansfield, Oliver, (IC), CC
Parochial House,
Kilcurry, Dundalk,
Co Louth A91 E8N8
Tel 042-9334410
(*Faughart*, Armagh)

Stapleton, Christy
St Michael's, Longford
(Ardagh & Cl.)

Stapleton, Jim (CSSp)
Holy Spirit Missionary College
Kimmage Manor,
Whitehall Road,
Dublin D12 P5YP
Tel 01-4064300

Stapleton, John, Very Rev, PP
Killeigh, Co Offaly
Tel 057-9344161
(*Killeigh*, Kildare & L.)

Stapor, Tomasz (SJ) (PME)
Jesuit Community,
27 Leinster Road,
Rathmines, Dublin 6
Tel 01-4970250

Starken, Brian (CSSp), Co-PP
The Prebystery,
Bawnogue,
Clondalkin, Dublin 22
Tel 01-4519810/4570380
(*Bawnogue, Deansrath*, Dublin)

Staunton, Brendan (SJ), PC
Pro-Cathedral House,
83 Marlborough Street,
Dublin 1
Tel 01-8745441
(*Pro-Cathedral*, Dublin)

Staunton, Ray (SM)
Chanel College, Coolock,
Dublin 5
Tel 01-8480655/8480896

Steblecki, Hilary (OFM)
Franciscan Friary,
Liberty Street, Cork
Tel 021-4270302/4275481

Steed, Bernard (SSC)
St Columban's,
Dalgan Park, Navan,
Co Meath
Tel 046-9021525

Stenson, Alex, Rt Rev
5 Calderwood Avenue,
Drumcondra,
Dublin 9
(Dublin, retired)

Stevenson, Liam, Very Rev Canon, PP,
70 North Street, Lurgan,
Co Armagh BT67 9AH
Tel 028-38323161
(*Shankill, St Paul's (Lurgan)*, Dromore)

Stevenson, Patrick, Very Rev, PP
The Presbytery,
Crosshaven, Co Cork
Tel 021-4831218
(*Crosshaven*, Cork & R.)

Stokes, John, Very Rev
Sacred Heart Residence,
Sybil Hill Road,
Raheny, Dublin 5
(Dublin, retired)

Stolnicu, Andrei
Cathedral House,
Mullingar,
Co Westmeath
Tel 044-9348338/9340126
(*Mullingar*, Meath)

Stone, Tom (OCD)
Avila, Bloomfield Avenue,
Morehampton Road,
Dublin 4
Tel 01-6430200

Stopa, Jerzy (OFMCap)
Capuchin Friary,
Friary Street,
Kilkenny R95 NX60
Tel 056-7721439

Strain, Paul, Very Rev, Adm
Holy Family Presbytery,
Newington Avenue,
Belfast BT15 2HP
Tel 028-90743119
(*Holy Family*, Down & C.)

Stritch, Denis, Very Rev, PP
Meelin, Newmarket,
Co Cork
Tel 029-68007
(*Rockchapel and Meelin*, Cloyne)

Stuart, Gerard, Very Rev, PP, VF
Parochial House, Ratoath,
Co Meath
Tel 01-8256207
Adm, Ardcath and Curaha
(*Ardcath, Curraha, Ratoath*, Meath)

Stuart, William (IC)
Clonturk House,
Ormond Road,
Drumcondra, Dublin 9
Tel 01-6877014

Stubbs, Jimmy (MSC)
Carrignavar, Co Cork
Tel 021-4884044

Sugrue, Patrick (CSsR)
2 The Presbytery,
Mahon, Cork
(*Mahon*, Cork & R.)

Sullivan, Kevin, Very Rev Canon, PP
The Presbytery, Killorglin,
Co Kerry
Tel 066-9761172
(*Killorglin*, Kerry)

Sullivan, Paul (OCD)
St Teresa's,
Clarendon Street, Dublin 2
Tel 01-6718466/6718127

Sullivan, Shane, CC
Carna, Co Galway
Tel 095-32232
(*Carna (Moyrus)*, Tuam)

Surlis, Tómas Very Rev, DD
St Patrick's College,
Maynooth, Co Kildare
Tel 01-784700
(Achonry)

Surungai Ruto, Amos, CC
St Brendan's,
Tralee, Co Kerry
Tel 066-7125932
(*Tralee, St Brendan's*, Kerry)

Susai, Jega (SVD)
Maynooth, Co Kildare
Tel 01-6286391/2

Suttle, Peter (CSSp), Very Rev, Adm,
Parochial House, Parke,
Castlebar, Co Mayo
Tel 094-9031314
(*Keelogues/Parke (Turlough)*, Tuam)

Swan, Colum, Very Rev, PE
c/o Bishop's House, Carlow
(Kildare & L., retired)

Swan, William, Very Rev, Adm
The Presbytery,
12 School Street, Wexford
Tel 053-9122055
(*Wexford*, Ferns)

Sweeney, Charles (MSC)
'Croí Nua', Rosary Lane,
Taylor's Hill, Galway
Tel 095-520960

Sweeney, Dennis (IC)
Clonturk House,
Ormond Road,
Drumcondra, Dublin 9
Tel 01-8374840

Sweeney, Desmond, Very Rev, PE
17 Meadowvale,
Ramelton
Tel 074-9151085
(Raphoe, retired)

Sweeney, Donal, (OP), Very Rev, PP
Prior, St Mary's Priory,
The Claddagh,
Galway
Tel 091-582884
(St Mary's, Galway)

Sweeney, Eugene, Very Rev, PP, VG
Parochial House,
9 Fair Street, Drogheda,
Co Louth
Tel 041-9838537
(Drogheda, Armagh)

Sweeney, Gerard (SMA)
SMA House, Cloonbigeen,
Claregalway,
Co Galway H91 YK64
Tel 091-798880

Sweeney, Gerard, PP
Parochial House, 447
Victoria Road,
Ballymagorry, Strabane,
Co Tyrone BT82 0AT
Tel 028-718802274
(Leckpatrick (Leckpatrick and part of Donagheady), Derry)

Sweeney, James, Very Rev, PP
Director of Fatima Pilgrimage,
Frosses, Co Donegal
Tel 074-9736006
(Inver, Raphoe)

Sweeney, James (CP)
Provincial,
St Paul's Retreat,
Mount Argus,
Dublin 6W
Tel 01-4992000/4992050

Sweeney, John (SAC)
Pallottine College, Thurles,
Co Tipperary
Tel 0504-21202

Sweeney, Liam (SAC)
Sacred Heart Residence,
Sybil Hill Road,
Raheny, Dublin 5

Sweeney, Michael, Very Rev, PE
Ballynabrockey, Fanad
Co Donegal
(Raphoe, retired)

Sweeney, Oliver, Very Rev,
24 The Willows,
Wellingtonbridge,
Co Wexford
(Ferns, retired)

Sweeney, Patrick,
Team Assistant,
13 Home Farm Road,
Drumcondra, Dublin 9
Tel 01-8377402
(Ballymun Road, Dublin)

Sweeney, Raymond, Very Rev, PP
Ballymacward,
Ballinasloe,
Co Galway H53 P2W0
Tel 090-9687614
(Ballymacward & Gurteen (Ballymacward & Clonkeenkerril), Clonfert)

Swinburne, Robbie (SDB),
Salesian House,
Milford, Castletroy,
Limerick
Tel 061-330268
(Pastoral Unit 1, Limerick)

Symonds, Paul
c/o Lisbreen,
73 Somerton Road,
Belfast BT15 4DE
(Down & C.)

Szalwa, Marian (SCJ), PC
Parochial House,
St John Vianney,
Ardlea Road, Dublin 5
Tel 01-8474123
(Ardlea, Dublin)

T

Taaffe, Eugene, Very Rev, Moderator
The Presbytery,
James Street, Dublin 8
Tel 01-4531143
(Francis Street, James's Street, Meath Street and Merchants Quay, Dublin)

Talbot, Denis, Very Rev, Canon, AP
Galbally, Co Tipperary
Tel 062-37929
(Galbally, Cashel & E.)

Talty, Robert (OP)
St Mary's, Pope's Quay, Cork
Tel 021-4502267

Tamas, Eugen Dragos, CC
Curate's House,
Chapel Lane,
Newbridge, Co Kildare
Tel 045-433979
(Droichead Nua/Newbridge, Kildare & L.)

Tanham, Gerard, Very Rev, PC,
Presbytery No 1,
Thormanby Road,
Howth, Co Dublin
Tel 01-8232193/8167599
(Baldoyle, Howth, Sutton, Dublin)

Tapley, Paul (OFMCap)
Capuchin Friary,
137-142 Church Street,
Dublin D07 HA22
Tel 01-8730599

Tarrant, Joseph, Very Rev, PP
Ballydesmond,
Mallow, Co Cork
Tel 064-7751104
(Ballydesmond, Kerry)

Taylor, Joe (SPS)
St Patrick's, Kiltegan,
Co Wicklow W91 Y022

Taylor, Leonard, Very Rev
Rathlee, Easkey, Co Sligo
(Killala, retired)

Taylor, Liam, Very Rev, PP
Ballycallan,
Co Kilkenny R95 E8N0
Tel 056-7769564/
086-8180954
Administrator, Tullaroan Parish
(Ballycallan, Tullaroan, Ossory)

Taylor, Paul, Adm, VF
49 Rathgar Road, Dublin 6
Tel 01-4971058
(Beechwood Avenue, Rathgar, Dublin)

Teehan, William, Very Rev, Co-PP, VF
Director of ACCORD,
Nenagh Centre,
Loreto House,
Kenyon Street, Nenagh,
Co Tipperary
Tel 067-31272
Parish
The Spa, Castleconnell,
Co Limerick
Tel 061-377170/
087-2347927
(Scáth na Sionnaine Pastoral Area, Killaloe)

Temgo, Michel Simo (SCJ), CC
Parochial House,
St John Vianney,
Ardlea Road, Dublin 5
Tel 01-8474173
(Ardlea, Dublin)

Terry, John, Very Rev Canon, PE
Terriville, Ballylanders,
Cloyne, Co Cork
Tel 021-4646779
(Cloyne, retired)

Thandiparambil Chacko, Antony (OCarm)
Prior,
Carmelite Priory,
White Abbey,
Co Kildare R51 X827
Tel 045-521391

Thankachan Njaliath, Paul
Chaplain for Pastoral Care of the Syro-Malabar Community in the Dublin Diocese, based in Tallaght
Tel 01-4510166
(Dublin)

Thazamhon, Cherian, CC
Chaplain to Syro Malankara Community
30 Wheatfield Close,
Clondalkin, Dublin 22
(Neilstown, Rowlagh and Quarryvale, Dublin)

Thennattil, Vinod Kurian (IC), Very Rev, PP
Parochial House, Kilcurry,
Dundalk, Co Louth
Tel 042-9334410/9333235
(Faughart, Armagh)

Thettayil, Polachan (IC)
Rector, Rosmini House,
Dunkereen,
Innishannon,
Co Cork T12 N9DH
Tel 021-4776268/4776923

Thomas, Jose, CC
Curate's House,
129 Túr Uisce,
Doughiska, Galway
Tel 091-756823
St Thomas Syro-Malabar Chaplaincy
(Good Shepherd, Galway)

Thomas, Robin, AP
42 Nessan Court,
Raheen, Co Limerick
Tel 089-4333124
(Pastoral Unit 6, Limerick)

Thompson, Declan (SPS), PP
St Mary's, Daingean,
Co Offaly
Tel 057-9362653
(Daingean, Kildare & L.)

Thorne, Bernard (OSM)
Prior, Servite Priory,
Benburb, Dungannon,
Co Tyrone, BT71 7JZ
Tel 028-37548241

Thornton, Gerard (MSC), PP
Parish House, Union Hall,
Skibbereen, Co Cork
Tel 028-34940
(Castlehaven, Cork & R.)

Thornton, Paul, Adm,
Episcopal Vicar
Parochial House,
Brackenstown Road,
Swords, Co Dublin
Tel 01-8401661
(Brackenstown, Dublin)

Thynne, Eoin, Rt Rev Mgr, Adm, VF
24 The Court,
Mulhuddart Wood,
Mulhuddart, Dublin 15
Tel 087-2401432
(Mulhuddart, Dublin)

LIST OF CLERGY IN IRELAND

Tiernan, Peter, PP
Cloone, Co Leitrim
Tel 071-9636016
(*Aughavas and Cloone*, Ardagh & Cl.)

Tierney, Celsus, PP
The Parchioal House,
Holy Cross, Thurles,
Co Tipperary
Tel 0504-43124
(*Holy Cross*, Cashel & E.)

Tierney, Philip (OSB)
Glenstal Abbey, Murroe,
Co Limerick
Tel 061-386103

Tighe, Paul, Rt Rev Mgr
Secretary of the Pontifical Council for Social Communications,
Vatican City
(Dublin)

Tillotson, Aelred (OSB)
Silverstream Priory,
Stamullen,
Co Meath K32 T189
Tel 01-8417142

Timmons, Declan (OFM)
Dún Mhuire,
Seafield Road,
Killiney, Co Dublin
Tel 01-2826760

Timoney, Charles (White Fathers)
Cypress Grove,
Templeogue, Dublin 6W
Tel 01-4055263/4055264

Timothy, Malcolm (OFM)
Franciscan Abbey,
Multyfarnham,
Co Westmeath
Tel 044-9371114/9371137

Timpu, Eugene
Sean McDermott Street,
Dublin 1
Tel 086-3266467
(*Sean McDermott Street*, Dublin)

Toal, Donal (SMA)
Apt 1, Parochial House,
Balbriggan, Co Dublin
Tel 01-8412116
(*Balbriggan*, Dublin)

Tobin, James
St Patrick's Presbytery,
Lower Road, Cork
(Cork & R., retired)

Tobin, Martin, Very Rev, PP
Mooncoin, Co Kilkenny
051-895123/086-2401278
(*Clogh*, Ossory)

Tobin, Richard (CSsR)
St Patrick's, Esker,
Athenry, Co Galway
Tel 091-844007

Tohill, David (OP)
Superior,
St Catherine's, Newry,
Co Down BT35 8BN
Tel 028-30262178

Toland, Liam, Very Rev, CC
29 Killough Road,
Downpatrick,
Co Down BT30 6PX
Tel 028-44612443
(*Downpatrick*, Down & C.)

Toman, Columba Mary (OP)
St Malachy's, Dundalk,
Co Louth
Tel 042-9334179/9333714

Tomasik, Daniel
'Elm View', Roxboro Road,
Limerick
Tel 061-410846/087-6092086
(*Pastoral Unit 3*, Limerick)

Tomasik, Teodor (SVD)
Maynooth, Co Kildare
Tel 01-6286391/2

Tomulesei, Marius (OFMConv)
Friary of the Visitation of the BVM,
Fairview Strand, Dublin 3
Tel 01-8376000
(*Fairview*, Dublin)

Toner, Michael C., Very Rev, PP
Chancellor of the Diocese,
Parochial House,
15 Moy Road,
Portadown,
Co Armagh BT62 1QL
Tel 028-38350610
(*Portadown (Drumcree)*, Armagh)

Toner, Terence, Very Rev, PP
Parochial House,
Kilmessan, Co Meath
Tel 046-9025172
(*Kilmessan*, Meath)

Toner, William (SJ)
25 Croftwood Park,
Cherry Orchard, Dublin 10
Tel 01-6267413

Tonge, Ivan, Very Rev, PP
St Patrick's,
2 Cambridge Road,
Dublin 4
Tel 087-2726868
(*Ringsend*, Dublin)

Toomey, Michael, Very Rev Adm
Newcastle, Clonmel,
Co Tipperary
Tel 052-6136387
(*Newcastle and Fourmilewater/Ardfinnan, Waterford* & L.)

Touhy, Séamus (OP)
St Mary's Priory, Tallaght,
Dublin 24
Tel 01-4048100

Towey, Thomas, Very Rev, PP
Ballisodare, Co Sligo
Tel 071-9167467
(*Ballisodare*, Achonry)

Townsend, Mark, Very Rev, PP
Parochial House,
Graignamanagh,
Co Kilkenny
Tel 059-9724238
(*Graignamanagh*, Kildare & L.)

Tracey, Finbarr (SVD)
Rector, Maynooth,
Co Kildare
Tel 01-6286391/2

Tracey, Liam (OSM), Very Rev, CC
Prior,
Church of the Divine Word,
Marley Grange,
25-27 Hermitage Downs,
Rathfarnham, Dublin 16
Tel 01-4944295/4941064
(*Marley Grange*, Dublin)

Tranter, Carl (MSC)
Provincial Leader,
65 Terenure Road West,
Dublin 6W
Tel 01-4906622

Travers, Charles, Rt Rev Mgr
1 Convent Court,
Roscommon
Tel 090-6628917
(Elphin, retired)

Travers, Vincent (OP)
St Mary's Priory,
Tallaght, Dublin 24
Tel 01-4048100

Treacy, Bernard (OP), Prior,
St Dominic's Retreat House,
Montenotte, Co Cork
Tel 021-4502520

Treacy, John, PP
SS Peter and Paul's,
Clonmel, Co Tipperary
Tel 052-6126292
(*Clonmel, SS Peter and Paul's*, Waterford & L.)

Treacy, Patrick, Co-PP
The Presbytery,
Convent Hill,
Roscrea, Co Tipperary
Tel 0505-21370/089-4967028
(*Cronan Pastoral Area*, Killaloe)

Treacy, Thomas (SMA)
African Missions,
Blackrock Road,
Cork T12 TD54
Tel 021-4292871

Treanor, Martin, Very Rev, PP
Inniskeen, Dundalk,
Co Louth A91 WN32
Tel 042-9378105
(*Inniskeen/Killanny*, Clogher)

Treanor, Noel, Most Rev, DD
Bishop of Down and Connor,
Lisbreen,
73 Somerton Road,
Belfast,
Co Antrim BT15 4DE
Tel 028-90776185
(Down & C.)

Treanor, Oliver
St Patrick's College,
Maynooth, Co Kildare
Tel 01-6285222
(Down & C.)

Tremer, Gerard, Very Rev, PP, VF
Parochial House,
Tullynaval Road,
Cullyhanna, Newry,
Co Down BT35 OPZ
Tel 028-30861235
(*Cullyhanna (Creggan Lower)* Armagh)

Trias, Francis (CP)
Holy Cross Retreat,
432 Crumlin Road,
Ardoyne, Belfast BT14 7GE
Tel 028-90748231

Troy, Michael (OCarm)
Provincial,
Gort Muire, Ballinteer,
Dublin 16 D16 EI67
Tel 01-2984014

Troy, Ulic (OFM)
Franciscan Friary,
Friary Lane,
Athlone, Co Westmeath
Tel 090-6472095

Trzcinski, Kazimierz (OFMConv)
The Friary,
St Francis' Street, Wexford
Tel 053-922758

Tulbure, Eusebius, CC
St Mary's Presbytery,
The Fairgreen, Navan,
Co Meath C15 X0A3
Tel 046-9027518
(*Navan*, Meath)

Tully, Andrew, Very Rev, PP
Lavey, Stradone,
Co Cavan
Tel 049-4330125
(*Lavey*, Kilmore)

Tumilty, Stephen (OP)
St Catherine's, Newry,
Co Down BT35 8BN
Tel 028-30262178

Tuohy, Fergus (SMA), CC
The Presbytery, Clonakilty,
Co Cork
Tel 023-8834441
(*Clonakilty and Darrara*, Cork & R.)

Tuohy, Thomas (SM)
Mount St Mary's,
Milltown, Dundrum Road,
Dublin 14
Tel 01-2697322

Turbitt, Hugh,
St Michael's, Longford
(Ardagh & Cl.)

Turley, Paul (CSsR)
Clonard Monastery,
1 Clonard Gardens,
Belfast BT13 2RL
Tel 028-90445950

Twohig, David (OCarm)
Assistant Provincial,
Gort Muire, Ballinteer,
Dublin D16 EI67
Tel 01-2984014

Twohig, Jamie (SAC) CC
St Benin's, Dublin Road,
Shankill, Co Dublin
Tel 01-2824425
(Shankill, Dublin)

Twohig, Pat (OSA)
St Augustine's Priory
Washington Street, Cork

Twomey, Bernard (OSA)
St Catherine's,
Meath Street, Dublin 8
Tel 01-4543356
(Meath Street and
Merchants' Quay, Dublin)

Twomey, Christopher (OFMCap)
Vicar, Capuchin Friary,
Friary Street,
Kilkenny R95 NX60
Tel 056-7721439

Twomey, Donal (SPS)
St Patrick's, Kiltegan,
Co Wicklow
Tel 059-6473600

Twomey, John (Jack) (OFMCap)
Capuchin Friary,
Holy Trinity,
Fr Mathew Quay,
Cork T12 PK24
Tel 021-4270827
(Cork & R.)

Twomey, Patrick, Very Rev
Canon, PE
Bellevue,
Mallow, Co Cork
Tel 022-55632
(Cloyne, retired)

Twomey, Vincent (SVD)
Donamon Castle,
Roscommon
Tel 090-6662222

Tyburowski, Krzystof,
134 Cosgrove Park,
Moyross, Limerick
Tel 087-4110997
(Pastoral Unit 1, Limerick)

Tynan, Joseph, PP, Adm
The Parochial House.
Kilteely, Co Limerick
Tel 061-384213
(Kilteely, Knocklong,
Cashel & E.)

Tyndall, David
c/o Archbishop's House,
Dublin 9
(Dublin)

Tyrrell, Gerard, CC
Presbytery, Blacklion,
Greystones, Co Wicklow
Tel 012860704
(Greystones, Dublin)

Tyrrell, Patrick (SJ)
St Ignatius (Residence),
27 Raleigh Row,
Galway H91 FTX8
Tel 091-523707

Tyrrell, Paul, Very Rev PP
St Michael's Parochial
House,
4 Eblana Avenue,
Dun Laoghaire, Co Dublin
Tel 01-28012100
(Crumlin, Dublin)

U

Udofia, Daniel (MSP), PP
Parochial House,
Ballyleague,
Co Roscommon
Tel 043-3321171
(Kilgefin (Ballagh,
Cloontuskert and
Curraghroe), Elphin)

Ugwu, Stephen (OCD)
Avila, Bloomfield Avenue,
Morehampton Road,
Dublin 4
Tel 01-6430200

Ukut, Joseph (MSP), CC
The Presbytery,
Longford
Tel 043-3346465
(Longford
(Templemichael,
Ballymacormack), Ardagh
& Cl.)

Uwah, Innocent
The Presbytery,
12 Coarse Moor Park,
Straffan, Co Kildare
Tel 01-6012197/
085-1404355
(Celbridge, Dublin)

V

Van Gucht, Koenraad (SDB),
Salesian House, Milford,
Castletroy,
Co Limerick V94 DK44
Tel 061-330268/
086-3814353
(Pastoral Unit 1, Limerick)

Vard, David, CC,
Annebrook,
Stradbally Road,
Portlaoise, Co Laois
Tel 057-8688440
(Portlaoise, Kildare & L.)

Varghese, Joseph, CC,
2 Station Road,
Dungiven,
Derry BT47 4LN
Tel 028-77741256
(Dungiven, Derry)

Varghese, Nideesh, CC
72 Nursery Avenue,
Coleraine,
Co Derry BT52 1LR
Tel 028-70343156
(Coleraine, Derry)

Varghese, Shoji, AP
42 Nessan Court
Lower Church Road,
Raheen, Co Limerick
Tel 089-4431922
(Pastoral Unit 6, Limerick)

Vasquez, Oscar (SM)
Provincial, Provincial
Headquaters,
4425 West Pine Boulevard,
St Louis, MO 6308-2301,
USA
Tel 001-314-533-1207

Vaughan, Aidan (OFMCap),
CC
Ascension Presbytery,
Gurranabraher, Cork
Tel 021-4303655
(Gurranabraher, Cork & R.)

Vaughan, Denis
45 The Oaks,
Maryborough Ridge,
Douglas, Cork
(Cloyne, retired)

Villarreal, Andres (LC)
Chaplain,
Dublin Oak Academy,
Kilcroney, Bray,
Co Wicklow
Tel 01-2863290

Vijaykumar, Francis Xavier,
CC
Sacred Heart Presbytery,
21 The Folly, Waterford
Tel 051-873759
(Sacred Heart, Waterford
& L.)

Vinduska, Aaron (LC) PC
The Presbytery, St Mary's
Sandyford, Dublin 18
Tel 01-2958933
(Sandyford, Dublin)

W

Wadding, George (CSsR)
Vicar-Superior,
Dún Mhuire,
461/463 Griffith Avenue,
Dublin D09 X651
Tel 01-5180196

Wade, Thomas (SMA)
African Missions,
Blackrock Road,
Cork T12 TD54
Tel 021-4292871

Waldron, Kieran, Very Rev
Canon, PE
Devlis, Ballyhaunis,
Co Mayo F35 AP62
Tel 094-9630246
(Tuam, retired)

Waldron, Paul, Very Rev, PP
Parochial House,
Chapel Street,
Carrick-on-suir,
Co Tipperary
Tel 051-640168
(Carrick-on-Suir,
Waterford & L.)

Walker, David (OP)
Provincial Bursar
Provincial Office,
St Mary's, Tallaght,
Dublin D24 X585
Tel 01-4048118

Wall, John, PP
Annaduff,
Carrick-on-Shannon,
Co Leitrim
Tel 071-9624093
(Annaduff, Ardagh & Cl.)

Wall, Michael
Chaplain,
Mary Immaculate College
of Education
Tel 061-204331
(Limerick)

Wall, Richard (SMA)
SMA House, Wilton,
Cork, T12 KR23
Tel 021-4541069/4541884

Wallace, Laurence, Very
Rev, PP, VF
Muckalee, Ballyfoyle,
Co Kilkenny
Tel 056-4441271/
087-2326807
(Muckalee, Ossory)

Walsh, Aidan (OFMConv)
Friary of the Visitation of
the BVM,
Fairview Strand,
Dublin 3
Tel 01-8376000
(Fairview, Dublin)

Walsh, Brendan, Very Rev,
PP
Causeway, Co Kerry
Tel 066-7131148
Moderator, Ballyheigue
Tel 0667133110
(Ballyheigue, Causeway,
Kerry)

Walsh Brendan (SAC)
Pallottine College,
Thurles, Co Tipperary
Tel 0504-21202

Walsh, David (SPS)
Director of Promotion,
St Patrick's, Kiltegan,
Co Wicklow
Tel 059-6473600

LIST OF CLERGY IN IRELAND

Walsh, Des, Very Rev Canon, PE
Claremorris, Co Mayo
(Tuam, retired)

Walsh, Donal, Very Rev
Tinnahinch,
Graiguenamanagh,
Co Kilkenny
Tel 059-9725550
(Ossory, retired)

Walsh, Eamonn, Most Rev, DD
Titular Bishop of Elmham
and Auxiliary Bishop
Emeritus of Dublin,
Head of the Office for
Clergy,
Naomh Brid,
Blessington Road,
Tallaght, Dublin 24
Tel 01-4598032
Chaplain, Blackrock Clinic
Blackrock, Co Dublin
Tel 01-2832222
(Dublin)

Walsh, Edward (SPS)
St Patrick's, Kiltegan,
Co Wicklow
Tel 059-6473600

Walsh, Gearóid, Very Rev
Canon, PP, VF
Ballymacellicyott,
Co Kerry,
Tel 066-7137118
(Ballymacellicyott, Kerry)

Walsh, James, Very Rev
Canon, AP
Parochial House,
Kilmeena, Westport,
Co Mayo F28 T628
Tel 098-41270
(Kilmeena, Tuam)

Walsh, Jarlath (SMA)
Provincial Bursar,
African Missions, Feltrim,
Blackrock Road,
Cork T12 N6C8
Tel 021-4292871

Walsh, John H. (OP), Very Rev,
St Saviour's Priory,
Upper Dorset Street,
Dublin 1
Tel 01-8897610

Walsh, John,
Mount David,
North Circular Road,
Limerick
Tel 087-4493228
(Pastoral Unit 2, Limerick)

Walsh, John, Very Rev, PP
The Presbytery,
Farranree, Cork
Tel 021-4393815/4210111
(Farranree, Cork & R.)

Walsh, John, Very Rev
Canon
Knock, Co Mayo
(Tuam, retired)

Walsh, John R., CC
Parochial House,
Buncrana, Co Donegal
Tel 074-9361393
(Buncrana, Derry)

Walsh, Joseph, CC
Cathedral Presbytery,
Thurles, Co Tipperary
Tel 0504-22229
(Thurles, Cathedral, Cashel & E.)

Walsh, Joseph (OFM)
Franciscan Abbey,
Multyfarnham,
Co Westmeath
Tel 044-9371114/9371137

Walsh, Kevin, CC
c/o Bishop's House,
Dublin Road, Carlow
(Kildare & L.)

Walsh, Laurence (OCSO)
Mount Saint Joseph
Abbey,
Roscrea, Co Tipperary
E53 D651
Tel 0505-25600

Walsh, Liam (OP)
St Saviour's Priory,
Upper Dorset Street,
Dublin 1
Tel 01-8897610

Walsh, Michael, Very Rev, PP
Parochial House,
Carnaross, Kells, Co Meath
Tel 046-9245904
(Carnaross, Meath)

Walsh, Michael F., Very Rev, PE
Ballinarrid, Bonmahon,
Co Waterford
Tel 051-292992
(Waterford & L., retired)

Walsh, Pádraig, Very Rev, PP
St Brendan's, Tralee,
Co Kerry
Tel 066-7125932
(Tralee, St Brendan's, Kerry)

Walsh, Pat
Priests House, Ahiohill,
Enniskeane, Co Cork
(Cork & R., retired)

Walsh, Patrick J., Most Rev, DD
Retired Bishop Emeritus of
Down and Connor,
Nazareth House Care
Village
516 Ravenhill Road,
Belfast BT15 OBW
Tel 0044-7732104366
(Down & C.)

Walsh, Paul (CSSp)
Holy Spirit Missionary
College
Kimmage Manor,
Whitehall Road,
Dublin D12 P5YP
Tel 01-4064300

Walsh, Paul (SM)
Communaté Mariste,
22 Rue Victor Clappier,
83000 Toulon, France

Walsh, Pearse, Adm
The Presbytery,
City Quay, Dublin 2
Tel 01-6773073
(City Quay, Dublin)

Walsh, Richard (OP)
Holy Cross, Sligo, Co Sligo
Tel 071-9142700

Walsh, Sean (IC)
Clonturk House,
Ormond Road,
Drumcondra, Dublin 9
Tel 01-6877014

Walsh, Stephen (CSSp), CC
St Anne's, Sligo
Tel 071-9145028
(Sligo, St Anne's, Elphin)

Walsh, Tomás (SMA), PP
Ascension Presbytery,
Gurranbraher, Cork
Tel 021-4303655
(Gurranbraher, Cork & R.)

Walsh, William, Most Rev, DD
Retired Bishop of Killaloe,
'Camblin',
College View,
Clare Road, Ennis,
Co Clare
Tel 065-6842540
(Killaloe, retired)

Walsh, William,
Cathedral House,
Cathedral Place, Limerick
Tel 061-414624/
086-8564673
(Pastoral Unit 1, Limerick)

Walshe, Adrian, Very Rev, PP
Teach na Sagart,
Beech Corner
Castleblayney,
Co Monaghan A75 KR96
Tel 042-9740027
(Castleblaney (Muckno),
Aughnamullen East,
Clontibret, Clogher)

Walshe, Philip Rev (CM)
St Paul's, Sybil Hill,
Raheny, Dublin D05 AE38
Tel 01-8318113

Walshe, Thomas, Very Rev, PP
Rosenallis, Portlaoise,
Co Laois
Tel 057-8628513
(Rosenallis, Kildare & L.)

Walshe, William (SPS)
St Patrick's, Kiltegan,
Co Wicklow
Tel 059-6473600

Walton, James, Very Rev, PP
Ballybricken,
Grange, Killmallock,
Co Limerick
Tel 061-351158
(Ballybricken, Cashel & E.)

Ward, Alan,
(On sabbatical)
18 Drumlin Heights,
Enniskillen,
Co Fermanagh BT74 7NR
(Clogher)

Ward, Brendan, CC
Carnamuggagh Lower,
Letterkenny, Co Donegal
(Aughaninshin, Raphoe)

Ward, John M., Very Rev, PE
1 Chestnut Grove,
Ballymount Road,
Kingswood Heights,
Dublin 24
Tel 01-4515824
(Dublin, retired)

Ward, Kevin (SAC)
Pallottine College,
Thurles, Co Tipperary
086-3103934

Ward, Pat, Very Rev, PP, VF
Burtonport, Co Donegal
Tel 074-9542006
(Burtonport, Raphoe)

Ward, Paul, Very Rev, Adm
St Mochta's, Porterstown,
Dublin 15
Tel 01-8213218
(Porterstown-Clonsilla, Dublin)

Warner, Freddy (SMA)
Church of Our Lady of the
Rosary and St Patrick,
61 Blackhorse Road,
Walthamstow,
London E17 7AS, UK

Warrack, Colin (SJ)
Gonzaga College,
Sandford Road, Dublin 6
Tel 01-4972943

Waters, Ignatius (CP)
St Paul's Retreat,
Mount Argus,
Dublin 6W
Tel 01-4992000

Waters, Michael (SMA)
African Missions,
Blackrock Road,
Cork T12 TD54
Tel 021-4292871

Watters, Brian, CC
St Peter's Cathedral
Presbytery,
St Peter's Square,
Belfast BT12 4BU
Tel 028-90327573
Assistant Priest,
St Mary's Parish
(The Cathedral (St Peter's),
St Mary's, Down & C.)

LIST OF CLERGY IN IRELAND

Watters, David (OSB)
Silverstream Priory,
Stamullen,
Co Meath K32 T189
Tel 01-8417142

Weakliam, David (OCarm),
Gort Muire, Ballinteer,
Dublin D16 EI67
Tel 01-2984014

Wehrmeier, Augustinus (OFM)
Franciscan Friary,
Killarney, Co Kerry
Tel 064-6631334/6631066

Weir, Noel, CC
St Mary's Presbytery,
The Fairgreen, Navan,
Co Meath C15 X0A3
Tel 046-9027518
(*Navan*, Meath)

Welsh, Oscar (SMA)
African Missions,
Blackrock Road,
Cork T12 TD54
Tel 021-4292871

Whearty, Roderick, Very Rev,
St Fiacre's Gardens,
Bohernatownish Road,
Loughboy,
Kilkenny R95 RF97
Tel 056-77701730/
086-8133661
(*St Patrick's*, Ossory)

Whelan, Brian, Adm
Craanford, Gorey,
Co Wexford
Tel 053-9428163
(*Craanford*, Ferns)

Whelan, Gerard (SJ)
(Temporarily outside Ireland)
Irish Jesuit Provincialate,
Milltown Park,
Sandford Road, Dublin 6
Tel 01-4987333

Whelan, John (OSA)
St Augustine's Priory,
St Augustine's Street,
Galway
Tel 091-562524

Whelan, Joseph, Very Rev,
Co-PP
Parochial House,
Our Lady Queen of Peace,
Putland Road, Bray,
Co Wicklow
Tel 01-2865723
(*Bray, Putland Road*, Dublin)

Whelan, Martin CC
Parochial House,
Maree, Oranmore,
Co Galway
Tel 091-794113
(*Galway*)

Whelan, Michael
c/o Archbishop's House,
Tuam
(*Tuam*)

Whelan, Patrick, Very Rev, PP
St Patrick's Presbytery,
Forster Street, Galway
Tel 091-567994
(*St Patrick's*, Galway)

Whelan, Seamus (SPS)
St Patrick's, Kiltegan,
Co Wicklow
Tel 059-6473600

Whelan, Tom (CSSp)
Holy Spirit Missionary College
Kimmage Manor,
Whitehall Road,
Dublin D12 P5YP
Tel 01-4064300

Whelan, Tom, Co-PP
The Spa, Castleconnell,
Co Limerick
Tel 061-377126/087-2730299
(*Scáth na Sionnaine*, Killaloe)

White, Brian, CC
Parochial House,
6 Circular Road,
Dungannon,
Co Tyrone BT71 6BE
Tel 028-87722631
(*Dungannon (Drumglass, Killyman and Tullyniskin)*, Armagh)

White, David, Very Rev, PP
Parochial House,
182 Garron Road,
Glenariffe,
Co Antrim BT44 0RA
Tel 028-21771249
(*Glenariffe*, Down & C.)

White, Jerry (SSCC), CC
Sacred Hearts Community,
Tanagh, Cootehill,
Co Cavan H16 CA22
Tel 049-5552188
(*Rockcorry (Ematris)*, Clogher)

White, Laurence, Very Rev, Co-PP
119 Stiles Road,
Clontarf, Dublin 3
Tel 01-8333394/
086-4143888
(*Clontarf, St Anthony's*, Dublin)

White, Morgan
Boolavogue, Ferns,
Wexford
Tel 053-9366282
(*Monageer*, Ferns)

White, Patrick
Training and Development Officer,
Youth Link Training Offices,
Farset Enterprise Park,
683 Springfield Road,
Belfast BT12 7DY
Tel 028-90323217
(*Down & C.*)

White, Séamus, Very Rev, PP, VF
Parochial House,
40 The Village,
Jonesboro, Newry,
Co Down BT35 8HP
Tel 028-30849345
(*Dromintee*, Armagh)

Whiteford, Kieran, Very Rev, PP
Parochial House,
28 Chapel Road,
Ballymena BT44 0RS
Tel 028-21771240
(*Cushendall, Cushendun, Down and C.*)

Whitney, Ciarán, Very Rev Canon
24 Kildallogue Heights,
Strokestown,
Co Roscommon
(*Elphin*, retired)

Whitney, Seamus (SPS)
St Patrick's, Kiltegan,
Co Wicklow
Tel 059-6476488

Whittaker, Michael, Very Rev, PP
The Presbytery, Enfield,
Co Meath
Tel 046-9541282
(*Enfield*, Meath)

Whooley, Eoin, Very Rev, PP, Adm
South Presbytery,
Dunbar Street, Cork
Tel 085-1471147
Adm, St Patrick's
Tel 021-4502696
(*St Finbarr's South, St Patrick's*, Cork & R.)

Whyte, Daniel, Very Rev
53 Marlo Park, Bangor,
Co Down BT19 6NL
Tel 078-12184624
(*Down & C.*, retired)

Wickham, Anthony, Very Rev, PP
Newtownshandrum,
Charleville, Co Cork
Tel 063-70836
(*Newtownshandrum*, Cloyne)

Williams, John (OSA)
St Augustine's,
Taylor's Lane,
Balyboden, Dublin 16
Tel 01-4241000

Wilson, John Rt Rev Mgr
St Mary's,
97 Ballymun Road,
Dublin 9
Tel 01-8375440
(*Dublin*, retired)

Winkle, Patrick, Very Rev, PP
Carrigtwohill, Co Cork
Tel 021-4882439
(*Carrigtwohill*, Cloyne)

Winter, William, Very Rev PP
Banteer, Co Cork
Tel 029-56010
(*Banteer (Clonmeen)*, Cloyne)

Woodruff, Peter (SSC)
PO Box 752, Niddrie,
VIC 3042 Australia

Woods, Daniel, Very Rev, PP
Kilcommon,
Co Tipperary
Tel 062-78103
(*Kilcommon*, Cashel & E.)

Woods, Michael, Very Rev, PP, VF
Parochial House,
10 Acton Road,
Poyntzpass, Newry,
Co Down BT35 6TB
Tel 028-38318471
(*Tandragee (Ballymore and Mullaghbrack)*, Armagh)

Woods, Thomas
Edenville, Kinlough,
Co Leitrim
(*Kilmore*, retired)

Woods, Thomas, Rt Rev Mgr, DD
Newbrook Nursing Home,
Mullingar, Co Westmeath
(*Meath*, retired)

Wozniak, Josef (SC), CC
68 North Street, Lurgan,
Co Armagh BT67 9AH
Tel 028-38323161
(*Shankill, St Paul's & St Peter's (Lurgan)*, Dromore)

Wrenn, Timothy (SDB)
Salesian College, Don Bosco Road
Pallaskenry, Co Limerick
V94 WP86
Tel 061-393105

Wright, Colum, Very Rev
Lisadell, 54 Francis Street,
Lurgan,
Co Armagh BT66 6DL
Tel 028-38327173
(*Shankill, St Paul's & St Peter's (Lurgan)*, Dromore)

LIST OF CLERGY IN IRELAND

X

Xianbin, Anthony Xiao
Chaplain to the Chinese Community,
The Presbytery,
51 Home Farm Road,
Dublin 9
Tel 085-7417168
(*Drumcondra*, Dublin)

Y

Yang, Paul
Priest's Road,
Tramore, Co Tipperary
(*Tramore*, Waterford & L.)
Yaqoob, Amer
Parochial House,
Ballivor, Co Meath
Tel 046-9546488
(*Ballivor/Kildalkey*, Meath)
Young, Callum,
Catherdal Presbytery,
38 Hill Street,
Newry BT34 1AT
Tel 028-30262586
(*Newry*, Dromore)
Young, Joseph
21 Marian Avenue,
Janesboro, Limerick
Tel 061-405835
(Limerick)
Young, Robert, Very Rev, PP
The Presbytery, Kinsale,
Co Cork
Tel 021-4774019
(*Kinsale*, Cork & R.)
Younge, Patrick (OFM)
Franciscan Friary,
Liberty Street,
Cork T12 D376
Tel 021-4270302/4275481

Z

Zacharek, Maciej, CC
St Patrick's Presbytery,
Roden Place, Dundalk
Co Louth A91 K2P4
Tel 042-9334648
(*Dundalk, St Patrick's*, Armagh)
Zacharis, Roni, CC
Parochial House,
32 Chapel Road,
Derry BT47 2BB
Tel 028-71342303
(*Waterside (Glendermott)*, Derry)
Zacrzewski, Patryk (OP)
St Saviour's,
Upper Dorset Street,
Dublin 1
Tel 01-8897610
Zaggi, Douglas, CC
Curate's Residence,
Abbey Street,
Roscommon
(*Roscommon*, Elphin)
Zielonka, Rafal, CC
The Presbytery,
Dunmanway, Co Cork
Tel 023-8845000
(*Dunmanway*, Cork & Ross)
Zong, Bernard, PC
Churh of the Assumption,
Howth, Dublin 13
Tel 01-8397398
(*Howth*, Dublin)
Zuribo, Aloysius, CC
Presbytery No. 1,
4 Old Hill, Leixlip,
Co Kildare
Tel 01-6243718
(*Leixlip*, Dublin)
Zwierzchowski, Dominick (OMI), Co-PP
Our Lady of the Wayside,
118 Naas Road,
Bluebell, Dublin 12
Tel 01-4501040
(*Inchicore, St Michael's*, Dublin)

PARISH INDEX

Where a parish has an alternative or historical name, both names are given e.g. Arney/Cleenish. In such cases the parish appears in the list in each form, i.e. Arney/Cleenish and Cleenish/Arney.

A

Parish	Diocese	Page
Abbeydorney	Kerry	189
Abbeyfeale	Limerick	233
Abbeygormican & Killoran/Mullagh & Killoran	Clonfert	116
Abbeyknockmoy	Tuam	93
Abbeylara	Ardagh	104
Abbeyleix	Kildare	201
Abbeyside	Waterford	261
Achill	Tuam	93
Achonry	Achonry	99
Adamstown	Ferns	176
Adare	Limerick	233
Addergole & Liskeevey/Milltown	Tuam	95
Addergoole/Lahardane	Killala	209
Adrigole	Kerry	189
Aghaboe	Ossory	249
Aghabullogue	Cloyne	120
Aghada	Cloyne	120
Aghaderg	Dromore	165
Aghagallon & Ballinderry	Down	152
Aghaloo/Aughnacloy	Armagh	28
Aghalurcher/Lisnaskea	Clogher	111
Aghamore	Tuam	93
Aghanagh/Ballinafad	Elphin	170
Aghavea-Aghintaine/Brookeboro	Clogher	110
Aghaviller	Ossory	249
Aghinagh	Cloyne	120
Aghyaran/Termonamongan	Derry	140
Aglish	Waterford	261
Aglish, Ballyheane & Breaghwy/Castlebar	Tuam	94
Ahamlish/Cliffoney	Elphin	170
Ahascragh/Ahascragh & Caltra	Elphin	170
Aghoghill	Down	152
Allen	Kildare	201
Allihies	Kerry	189
Anacarty	Cashel	83
Annaclone	Dromore	165
Annacurra	Ferns	176
Annaduff	Ardagh	104
Annagh/Ballyhaunis	Tuam	94
Annagh/Belturbet	Kilmore	221
Annaghdown/Corrandulla	Tuam	94
Annagry	Raphoe	256
Annascaul	Kerry	189
An Spidéal	Galway	183
Antrim	Down	152
Aran Islands	Tuam	93
Ardagh	Killala	208
Ardagh & Carrickerry	Limerick	233
Ardagh & Moydow	Ardagh	104
Ardara	Raphoe	256
Ardboe	Armagh	28
Ardcarne/Cootehall	Elphin	170
Ardcath	Meath	240
Ardee & Collon	Armagh	28
Ardfert	Kerry	189
Ardfield & Rathbarry	Cork & Ross	130
Ardfinnan	Waterford	261
Ardglass & Dunsford	Down	153
Ardkeen/Kircubbin	Down	154
Ardlea	Dublin	42
Ardmore	Derry	140
Ardmore	Waterford	261
Ardpatrick	Limerick	232
Ardrahan	Galway	182
Ardstraw East/Newtownstewart	Derry	142
Ardstraw West & Castlederg/Castlederg	Derry	140
Ardtrea/Moneymore	Armagh	30
Ardtrea North & Magherafelt	Armagh	30
Arklow	Dublin	42
Arles	Kildare	201
Armagh	Armagh	27
Armoy	Down	152
Arney/Cleenish	Clogher	110
Arran Quay & Halston Street	Dublin	48
Artane	Dublin	42
Ashbourne-Donaghmore	Meath	240
Ashford	Dublin	42
Ashford	Limerick	233
Askea	Kildare	201
Askeaton/Ballysteen	Limerick	233
Athboy	Meath	240
Athea	Limerick	233
Athenry	Tuam	93
Athleague/Athleague & Fuerty	Elphin	170
Athlone	Ardagh	104
Athlone, SS Peter & Paul's	Elphin	170
Athy	Dublin	42
Attymass	Achonry	99
Aughadown	Cork & Ross	130
Aughagower	Tuam	93
Aughaninshin	Raphoe	256
Aughaval/Westport	Tuam	93
Aughavas & Cloone	Ardagh	104
Aughnacloy/Aghaloo	Armagh	28
Aughnamullen East	Clogher	110
Aughnamullen West/Latton	Clogher	111
Aughnish/Ramelton	Raphoe	256
Aughrim	Dublin	42
Aughrim/Aughrim & Kilmore	Elphin	170
Aughrim & Kilconnell	Clonfert	115
Aughrim Street	Dublin	42
Avoca	Dublin	42
Ayrfield	Dublin	42

B

Parish	Diocese	Page
Backs	Killala	208
Badoney Lower/Gortin	Derry	141
Badoney Upper/Plumbridge	Derry	142
Bagenalstown/Muinebheag	Kildare	203
Bailieboro/Killann	Kilmore	221
Balally	Dublin	43
Balbriggan	Dublin	42
Baldoyle	Dublin	43
Balla & Manulla	Tuam	93
Ballagh/Cloontuskert, Kilgefin & Curraghroe	Elphin	170
Ballaghaderreen/Castlemore & Kilcolman	Achonry	99
Ballaghameehan	Kilmore	221
Ballina	Cashel	83
Ballina/Kilmoremoy	Killala	208
Ballinabrackey	Meath	240
Ballinafad/Aghanagh	Elphin	170
Ballinaglera	Kilmore	221
Ballinahinch	Cashel	83
Ballinahown, Boher & Pollough/Lemanaghan	Ardagh	104
Ballinakill	Clonfert	116
Ballinakill	Kildare	201
Ballinakill/Letterfrack	Tuam	95
Ballinameen/Kilnamanagh & Estersnow	Elphin	170
Ballinamore/Drumreilly Lower	Kilmore	221
Ballinascreen/Draperstown	Derry	140

PARISH INDEX

Parish	Diocese	Page
Ballinasloe, Creagh Kilclooney	Clonfert	115
Ballincollig	Cork & Ross	130
Ballindaggin	Ferns	176
Ballindereen	Galway	182
Ballinderry	Armagh	28
Ballindine/Kilvine	Tuam	94
Ballineaspaig	Cork & Ross	130
Ballingarry	Cashel	83
Ballingarry & Granagh	Limerick	232
Ballinhassig	Cork & Ross	130
Ballinlough	Cork & Ross	130
Ballinlough/Kiltullagh	Tuam	94
Ballinora	Cork & Ross	130
Ballinrobe	Tuam	94
Ballinskelligs/Prior	Kerry	189
Ballinteer	Dublin	43
Ballintemple	Kilmore	221
Ballintober & Ballymoe/Ballintubber	Elphin	170
Ballintoy	Down	152
Ballintra/Drumholm	Raphoe	256
Ballintubber/Ballintober & Ballymoe	Elphin	170
Ballisodare	Achonry	99
Ballivor	Meath	240
Ballon	Kildare	201
Ballyadams	Kildare	201
Ballyagran & Colmanswell	Limerick	232
Ballybane	Galway	182
Ballybay/Tullycorbet	Clogher	110
Ballyboden	Dublin	43
Ballybrack-Killiney	Dublin	43
Ballybricken	Cashel	83
Ballybricken	Waterford	261
Ballybrown/Patrickswell	Limerick	232
Ballybunion	Kerry	189
Ballycallan	Ossory	249
Ballycastle/Kilbride & Doonfeeny	Killala	208
Ballycastle/Ramoan	Down	152
Ballyclare & Ballygowan	Down	153
Ballyclough	Cloyne	120
Ballycroy	Killala	208
Ballycullane	Ferns	176
Ballydesmond	Kerry	189
Ballydonoghue	Kerry	189
Ballyduff	Waterford	261
Ballyfermot	Dublin	43
Ballyfermot Upper	Dublin	43
Ballyferriter	Kerry	189
Ballyfin	Kildare	201
Ballyforan/Dysart & Tisrara	Elphin	170
Ballygalget	Down	153
Ballygall	Dublin	43
Ballygar/Killian & Killeroran	Elphin	170
Ballygarrett	Ferns	176
Ballygawley/Errigal Kieran	Armagh	28
Ballyhahill/Loughill	Limerick	233
Ballyhale	Ossory	249
Ballyhaunis/Annagh	Tuam	94
Ballyhea	Cloyne	120
Ballyheigue	Kerry	189
Ballylanders	Cashel	83
Ballylongford	Kerry	189
Ballylooby	Waterford	261
Ballymacelligott	Kerry	189
Ballymacoda & Ladysbridge	Cloyne	120
Ballymacormack, Templemichael/Longford	Ardagh	104
Ballymascanlon & Lordship	Armagh	30
Ballymacward & Gurteen/Ballymacward & Clonkeenkerril	Clonfert	116
Ballymahon/Shrule	Ardagh	104
Ballymena/Kirkinriola	Down	153
Ballymoney & Derrykeighan	Down	153
Ballymore	Meath	240
Ballymore Eustace	Dublin	43
Ballymore & Mayglass	Ferns	176
Ballymore & Mullaghbrack/Tandragee	Armagh	31
Ballymote/Emlefad & Kilmorgan	Achonry	100
Ballymun, St Pappins	Dublin	43
Ballymun Road	Dublin	43
Ballynacally/Clondegad	Killaloe	213
Ballynacargy	Meath	240
Ballynahinch/Magheradroll	Dromore	165
Ballyneale & Grangemockler	Waterford	261
Ballyovey/Partry	Tuam	95
Ballyphehane	Cork & Ross	130
Ballyphilip/Portaferry	Down	154
Ballyporeen	Waterford	261
Ballyragget	Ossory	249
Ballyroan	Dublin	43
Ballyscullion/Bellaghy	Derry	140
Ballyshannon/Kilbarron	Raphoe	256
Ballysokeary	Killala	208
Ballyvaughan	Galway	182
Ballyvourney	Cloyne	120
Ballywaltrim/Bray	Dublin	44
Baltinglass	Kildare	201
Balyna	Kildare	201
Banagher	Derry	140
Banbridge/Seapatrick	Dromore	165
Bandon	Cork & Ross	131
Bangor	Down	153
Bannow	Ferns	176
Banogue	Limerick	232
Bansha & Kilmoyler	Cashel	83
Banteer/Clonmeen	Cloyne	120
Bantry	Cork & Ross	131
Barndarrig & Kilbride	Dublin	49
Barryroe	Cork & Ross	131
Bawnogue	Dublin	43
Bayside	Dublin	43
Beagh/Gort	Galway	183
Bearna	Galway	182
Beaufort/Tuogh	Kerry	189
Beaumont	Dublin	44
Beauparc	Meath	240
Beechwood Avenue	Dublin	44
Bekan	Tuam	94
Bellaghy/Ballyscullion	Derry	140
Belleek-Garrison/Inis Muighe Samh	Clogher	110
Belmullet	Killala	209
Belturbet/Annagh	Kilmore	221
Bennekerry	Kildare	201
Beragh	Armagh	28
Bere Island & Castletownbere	Kerry	190
Berkeley Road	Dublin	44
Bessbrook/Killeavy Lower	Armagh	28
Birr	Killaloe	216
Blackpool/The Glen	Cork & Ross	131
Blackrock	Cork & Ross	131
Blackrock	Dublin	44
Blackwater	Ferns	176
Blakestown	Dublin	44
Blanchardstown	Dublin	44
Blaris/Lisburn	Down	154
Blarney	Cloyne	120
Blessington	Dublin	44
Bluebell	Dublin	44
Bodyke & Ogonnelloe/Kilnoe & Tuamgraney	Killaloe	215
Boher & Murroe	Cashel	84
Boherbue/Kiskeam	Kerry	189
Boherlahan & Dualla	Cashel	83
Bohermeen	Meath	240
Bohernabreena	Dublin	44
Bohola	Achonry	100
Bonane/Glengarriff	Kerry	190
Bonniconlon/Kilgarvan	Achonry	100
Bonnybrook	Dublin	44
Booterstown	Dublin	44
Bornacoola	Ardagh	104
Borris	Kildare	201
Borris-in-Ossory	Ossory	249
Borrisokane	Killaloe	216
Borrisoleigh	Cashel	83
Botha/Derrygonnelly	Clogher	111
Bournea/Couraganeen	Killaloe	216
Boyle	Elphin	170
Boyounagh/Glenamaddy	Tuam	94
Brackenstown	Dublin	44
Braid	Down	153
Bray/Ballywaltrim	Dublin	44
Bray/Holy Redeemer	Dublin	44
Bray, Putland Road	Dublin	45
Bray, St Peter's	Dublin	45
Bree	Ferns	176
Bright/Killough	Down	154
Broadford	Killaloe	214
Broadford/Dromcollogher	Limerick	233
Brookeboro/Aghavea-Aghintaine	Clogher	110
Brookfield	Dublin	45
Brosna	Kerry	189
Bruckless/Killaghtee	Raphoe	256
Bruff/Meanus/Grange	Limerick	232
Bruree/Rockhill	Limerick	232
Bulgaden/Martinstown	Limerick	232
Bullaun, Grange & Killaan/New Inn & Bullaun	Clonfert	116
Bunclody	Ferns	176
Buncrana/Desertegney & Lower Fahan	Derry	140
Bundoran/Magh Ene	Clogher	110
Bunninadden/Kilshalvey, Kilturra & Cloonoghill	Achonry	100
Burgess and Youghal/Youghalarra	Killaloe	215

PARISH INDEX

Parish	Diocese	Page
Burren/St Mary's	Dromore	165
Burriscarra & Ballintubber	Tuam	94
Burrishoole/Newport	Tuam	95
Burt, Inch & Fahan/Fahan	Derry	141
Burtonport/Kincasslagh	Raphoe	256
Butlerstown	Waterford	261
Buttevant	Cloyne	120

C

Parish	Diocese	Page
Cabinteely	Dublin	45
Cabra	Dublin	45
Cabra West	Dublin	45
Caheragh	Cork & Ross	131
Caherconlish	Cashel	83
Caherlistrane/Donaghpatrick & Kilcoona	Tuam	94
Cahir	Waterford	262
Cahirciveen	Kerry	189
Cahirdaniel	Kerry	189
Callan	Ossory	249
Camolin	Ferns	176
Camross	Ossory	249
Camus/Strabane	Derry	142
Cappagh	Limerick	233
Cappagh/Killyclogher	Derry	141
Cappamore	Cashel	83
Cappatagle & Kilrickle/Killalaghtan & Kilrickile	Clonfert	115
Cappawhite	Cashel	83
Cappoquin	Waterford	262
Caragh	Kildare	201
Carbury	Kildare	201
Carlingford & Clogherny	Armagh	28
Carlow, Cathedral	Kildare	201
Carna/Moyrus	Tuam	94
Carnaross	Meath	240
Carndonagh/Donagh	Derry	140
Carnew	Ferns	176
Carnlough	Down	153
Carracastle	Achonry	100
Carraig na bhFear	Cork & Ross	131
Carraroe/Kileen	Tuam	94
Carrick/Glencolmcille	Raphoe	256
Carrick-Finea/Drumlumman South & Ballymachugh	Ardagh	104
Carrick-on-Shannon/Kiltoghert	Ardagh	104
Carrick-on-Suir	Waterford	261
Carrickbeg	Waterford	261
Carrickedmond & Abbeyshrule/Taghshiney, Taghshinod & Abbeyshrule	Ardagh	104
Carrickfergus	Down	153
Carrickmacross/Machaire Rois	Clogher	110
Carrickmore/Loughmacrory/Creggan/Termonmaguirc	Armagh	31
Carrigaholt & Cross/Kilballyowen	Killaloe	213
Carrigaline	Cork & Ross	131
Carrigallen	Kilmore	221
Carrigart/Meevagh	Raphoe	256
Carrigtwohill	Cloyne	120
Carron & New Quay	Galway	183
Cashel	Cashel	83
Cashel/Newtowncashel	Ardagh	105
Castlebar/Aglish, Ballyheane & Breaghwy	Tuam	94
Castleblayney/Muckno	Clogher	110
Castlebridge & Curracloe	Ferns	176
Castlecomer	Ossory	249
Castleconnell	Killaloe	215
Castleconnor	Killala	209
Castlederg/Ardstraw West & Castlederg	Derry	140
Castledermot	Dublin	45
Castledockrell & Marshallstown	Ferns	177
Castlegar	Galway	183
Castlegregory	Kerry	189
Castlehaven	Cork & Ross	131
Castleisland	Kerry	189
Castleknock	Dublin	45
Castlelyons	Cloyne	120
Castlemagner	Cloyne	120
Castlemaine	Kerry	190
Castlemartyr/Imogeela	Cloyne	121
Castlemore & Kilcolman/Ballaghadereen	Achonry	99
Castlepollard	Meath	240
Castlerahan & Munterconnaught	Kilmore	221
Castlerea/Kilkeevan	Elphin	170
Castletara	Kilmore	221
Castletown	Dublin	45
Castletown	Ossory	249
Castletown-Geoghegan	Meath	240
Castletown-Kilpatrick	Meath	240
Castletownbere & Bere Island	Kerry	190
Castletownroche	Cloyne	121
Castleview-Kilnamanagh	Dublin	49
Castlewellan/Kilmegan	Down	153
The Cathedral/St Peter's	Down	151
Cathedral	Galway	182
Cathedral, Carlow	Kildare	201
Cathedral of St Mary & St Anne	Cork & Ross	130
Cathedral of the Assumption/Tuam	Tuam	93
Causeway	Kerry	190
Cavan/Urney & Annagelliff	Kilmore	221
Celbridge	Dublin	45
Chapelizod	Dublin	45
Charlestown/Kilbeagh	Achonry	100
Charleville	Cloyne	121
Cherry Orchard	Dublin	45
Christ the Redeemer, Lagmore	Down	151
Christ the King	Limerick	232
Churchtown	Dublin	45
Churchtown/Liscarroll	Cloyne	121
Cill na Martra	Cloyne	121
City Quay	Dublin	42
Clane	Kildare	201
Clara	Meath	240
Clara	Ossory	249
Clare Abbey/Clarecastle	Killaloe	214
Clare Island/Inishturk	Tuam	94
Clarecastle/Clare Abbey	Killaloe	214
Claregalway	Galway	183
Claremorris/Kilcolman	Tuam	94
Clarinbridge	Galway	183
Clashmore	Waterford	262
Claudy/Cumber Upper & Learmount	Derry	140
Cleariestown and Rathangan	Ferns	177
Cleenish/Arney	Clogher	110
Clerihan	Cashel	83
Clifden/Omey & Ballindoon	Tuam	94
Cliffoney/Ahamlish	Elphin	170
Clogagh & Timoleague	Cork & Ross	132
Clogh	Ossory	249
Cloghan/Kilteevogue	Raphoe	256
Cloghan & Banagher/Gallen & Reynagh	Ardagh	104
Clogheen	Waterford	262
Cloghen/Kerry Pike	Cork & Ross	131
Clogher	Clogher	110
Clogher Road	Dublin	45
Clogherhead	Armagh	28
Cloghogue/Killeavy Upper	Armagh	28
Clonakilty & Darrara	Cork & Ross	131
Clonard	Ferns	176
Clonaslee	Kildare	202
Clonbroney	Ardagh	104
Clonbullogue	Kildare	202
Clonbur/Ross	Tuam	94
Clonburris (see Clondalkin)	Dublin	45
Clonca/Malin	Derry	142
Clondahorkey/Dunfanaghy	Raphoe	256
Clondalkin	Dublin	45
Clondavaddog/Tamney	Raphoe	257
Clondegad/Ballynacally	Killaloe	213
Clondrohid	Cloyne	121
Clonduff/Hilltown	Dromore	165
Clonegal	Kildare	202
Clones	Clogher	110
Clonfeacle/Moy	Armagh	30
Clonfert, Donanaghta & Meelick/Eyrecourt, Clonfert & Meelick	Clonfert	116
Clongeen	Ferns	176
Clonguish/Newtownforbes	Ardagh	105
Clonlara/Doonas & Truagh	Killaloe	215
Clonleigh/Lifford	Derry	142
Clonmacnois/Shannonbridge	Ardagh	105
Clonmany	Derry	140
Clonmeen/Banteer	Cloyne	120
Clonmel, St Mary's	Waterford	262
Clonmel, St Oliver Plunkett	Waterford	262
Clonmel, SS Peter & Paul's	Waterford	262
Clonmellon	Meath	240

PARISH INDEX

Parish	Diocese	Page
Clonmore	Kildare	202
Clonoe	Armagh	28
Clonoulty	Cashel	83
Clonrush/Mountshannon	Killaloe	215
Clonskeagh	Dublin	46
Clontarf, St Anthony's	Dublin	46
Clontarf, St John's	Dublin	46
Clontead	Cork & Ross	131
Clontibret	Clogher	111
Clontuskert	Clonfert	116
Cloonacool/Tubbercurry	Achonry	100
Clooncagh, Kiltullagh & Killimordaly	Clonfert	116
Cloonclare and Killasnett	Kilmore	221
Cloone/Cloone-Conmaicne	Ardagh	104
Cloontuskert, Kilgefin & Curraghroe/Ballagh	Elphin	170
Clostoken & Kilconieran (Kilconickny, Kilconieran & Lickerrig)	Clonfert	116
Cloughbawn & Poulpeasty	Ferns	176
Cloughjordan	Killaloe	215
Cloughprior & Monsea/Puckane	Killaloe	215
Cloverhill/Oran	Elphin	171
Cloyne	Cloyne	121
Coagh	Armagh	28
Coalisland	Armagh	28
Cobh, St Colman's Cathedral	Cloyne	120
Coleraine	Down	153
Coleraine/Dunboe, Macosquin & Aghadowey	Derry	140
Collinstown	Meath	241
Collon & Ardee	Armagh	28
Collooney/Kilvarnet	Achonry	100
Colmcille	Ardagh	104
Conahy	Ossory	249
Confey	Dublin	46
Cong & Neale	Tuam	94
Conna	Cloyne	121
Conwal & Leck/Letterkenny	Raphoe	256
Cookstown/Desertcreight & Derryloran	Armagh	28
Coolaney/Killoran	Achonry	100
Coolcappa	Limerick	233
Coole/Mayne	Meath	241
Cooleragh & Staplestown	Kildare	202
Cooley	Armagh	29
Coolmeen & Kildysart/Kilfidane	Killaloe	213
Coolock	Dublin	46
Cooraclare/Kilmacduane	Killaloe	213
Cootehall/Ardcarne	Elphin	170
Cootehill/Drumgoon	Kilmore	221
Corcaghan/Kilmore & Drumsnat	Clogher	111
Corduff	Dublin	46
Corlough/Templeport	Kilmore	221
Corofin	Killaloe	214
Corpus Christi	Down	151
Corpus Christi	Limerick	231
Corrandulla/Annaghdown	Tuam	94
Couraganeen/Bournea	Killaloe	216
Courceys	Cork & Ross	131
Craanford	Ferns	176
Craigavon/Moyraverty	Dromore	165
Cratloe	Limerick	232
Craughwell	Galway	183
Crecora/Mungret	Limerick	232
Creggan Lower/Cullyhanna	Armagh	29
Creggan Upper/Crossmaglen	Armagh	29
Creggs/Glinsk & Kilbegnet	Elphin	170
Croagh & Kilfinny	Limerick	233
Croghan/Killukin & Killummod	Elphin	170
Croom	Limerick	232
Crossabeg & Ballymurn	Ferns	176
Crossboyne & Taugheen	Tuam	94
Crosserlough	Kilmore	221
Crossgar/Kilmore	Down	153
Crosshaven	Cork & Ross	131
Crossmaglen/Creggan Upper	Armagh	29
Crossmolina	Killala	209
Crumlin	Dublin	46
Crusheen/Inchicronan	Killaloe	214
Cúl Máine/Ederney	Clogher	111
Culdaff	Derry	141
Culfeightrin	Down	153
Cullyhanna/Creggan Lower	Armagh	29
Culmore	Derry	141
Cumber Upper & Learmount/Claudy	Derry	140
Cummer/Kilmoylan & Cummer	Tuam	94
Curragh Camp	Kildare	202
Curraha	Meath	241
Curraheen Road	Cork & Ross	131
Currin, Killeevan & Aghabog/Killeevan	Clogher	111
Curry	Achonry	100
Cushendall	Down	153
Cushendun	Down	153
Cushinstown & Rathgarogue	Ferns	176

D

Parish	Diocese	Page
Daingean	Kildare	202
Dalkey	Dublin	46
Danesfort	Ossory	249
Darndale-Belcamp	Dublin	46
Darver & Dromiskin	Armagh	29
Davidstown & Courtnacuddy	Ferns	176
Deansrath	Dublin	46
Delvin	Meath	241
Denn	Kilmore	221
Derriaghy	Down	151
Derry City/Templemore St Eugene's & Templemore St Columba's	Derry	140
Derrygonnelly/Botha	Clogher	111
Derrylin/Knockninny	Kilmore	222
Derrymacash/Seagoe	Dromore	165
Derrynoose/Keady	Armagh	29
Desertcreight & Derryloran/Cookstown	Armagh	28
Desertegney & Lower Fahan/Buncrana	Derry	140
Desertmartin/Desertmartin & Kilcronaghan	Derry	141
Devenish/Irvinestown	Clogher	111
Dingle	Kerry	190
Dollymount	Dublin	46
Dolphin's Barn/Rialto	Dublin	46
Dominick Street	Dublin	46
Donabate	Dublin	46
Donacavey/Fintona	Clogher	111
Donagh	Clogher	111
Donagh/Carndonagh	Derry	140
Donagheady/Dunamanagh	Derry	141
Donaghmede-Clongriffin-Balgriffin	Dublin	46
Donaghmore	Armagh	29
Donaghmore	Dromore	165
Donaghmore/Knockea	Limerick	231
Donaghmore/Killygordon	Derry	141
Donaghmoyne	Clogher	111
Donaghpatrick & Kilcoona/Caherlistrane	Tuam	94
Donegal Town/Tawnawilly	Raphoe	256
Doneraile	Cloyne	121
Doneyloop/Urney & Castlefinn	Derry	141
Donnybrook	Dublin	47
Donnycarney	Dublin	47
Donore	Meath	241
Donore Avenue	Dublin	47
Donoughmore	Cloyne	121
Doon	Cashel	83
Doonane	Kildare	202
Doonas & Truagh/Clonlara	Killaloe	215
Doonbeg/Killard & Kilkee	Killaloe	213
Doora & Kilraghtis	Killaloe	214
Douglas	Cork & Ross	131
Downpatrick	Down	153
Drangan	Cashel	83
Draperstown/Ballinascreen	Derry	140
Drimoleague	Cork & Ross	131
Drogheda, Holy Family	Meath	241
Drogheda, St Mary's	Meath	241
Drogheda	Armagh	27
Droichead Nua/Newbridge	Kildare	202
Drom & Inch	Cashel	83
Dromara	Dromore	165
Dromard	Ardagh	104
Dromcollogher/Broadford	Limerick	233
Dromin & Athlacca	Limerick	232
Dromintee	Armagh	29
Dromod/Waterville	Kerry	191
Dromore	Clogher	111
Dromore	Dromore	165
Dromore-West/Kilmacshalgan	Killala	209
Dromtariffe	Kerry	190

PARISH INDEX

Parish	Diocese	Page
Drumachose, Tamlaght, Finlagan & part of Aghanloo/Limavady	Derry	142
Drumahaire & Killargue	Kilmore	222
Drumaroad & Clanvaraghan	Down	153
Drumbo	Down	153
Drumcliff/Maugherow	Elphin	170
Drumcondra	Dublin	47
Drumconrath	Meath	241
Drumcree/Portadown	Armagh	31
Drumgath/Rathfriland	Dromore	165
Drumglass, Killyman & Tullyniskin/Dungannon	Armagh	27
Drumgooland	Dromore	165
Drumgoon/Cootehill	Kilmore	221
Drumholm/Ballintra	Raphoe	256
Drumkeerin-Inishmagrath	Kilmore	222
Drumlane	Kilmore	222
Drumlish	Ardagh	104
Drumlumman North/Mullahoran & Loughduff	Ardagh	105
Drumlumman South & Ballymachugh/Carrick-Finea	Ardagh	104
Drumoghill/Raymochy	Raphoe	256
Drumquin/Langfield	Derry	141
Drumragh/Omagh	Derry	142
Drumraney	Meath	241
Drumrat/Keash	Achonry	100
Drumreilly Lower/Ballinamore	Kilmore	221
Drumshanbo/Murhaun	Ardagh	104
Duagh	Kerry	190
Dublin Airport (see Swords)	Dublin	54
Duleek	Meath	241
Dun Laoghaire	Dublin	47
Dunamaggan	Ossory	250
Dunamanagh/Donagheady	Derry	141
Dunboe, Macosquin & Aghadowey/Coleraine	Derry	140
Dunboyne	Meath	241
Duncannon	Ferns	176
Dundalk, Holy Family	Armagh	27
Dundalk, Holy Redeemer	Armagh	27
Dundalk, St Joseph's	Armagh	27
Dundalk, St Patrick's	Armagh	27
Dunderry	Meath	241
Dundrum	Dublin	47
Dundrum & Tyrella	Down	153
Duneane	Down	153
Dunfanaghy/Clondahorkey	Raphoe	256
Dungannon/Drumglass, Killyman & Tullyniskin	Armagh	27
Dungarvan	Waterford	262
Dungiven	Derry	141
Dungloe/Templecrone & Lettermacaward	Raphoe	256
Dunhill	Waterford	262
Duniry & Abbey/Duniry & Kilnelehan	Clonfert	116
Dunkerrin	Killaloe	215
Dunlavin	Dublin	47
Dunleer	Armagh	29
Dunloy & Cloughmills	Down	153
Dunmaggan	Ossory	250
Dunmanway	Cork & Ross	131
Dunmore	Tuam	94
Dunmore East/Killea	Waterford	262
Dunsford & Ardglass	Down	153
Dunshaughlin	Meath	241
Durrow	Ossory	250
Dysart	Meath	241
Dysart & Ruan	Killaloe	214
Dysart & Tisrara/Ballyforan	Elphin	170

E

Parish	Diocese	Page
Eadestown	Dublin	47
Easkey	Killala	209
East Wall-North Strand	Dublin	47
Edenderry	Kildare	202
Edenmore	Dublin	47
Ederney/Cúl Máine	Clogher	111
Edgeworthstown/Mostrim	Ardagh	104
Effin/Garrienderk	Limerick	232
Eglish	Armagh	29
Eglish	Meath	241
Elphin/Elphin & Creeve	Elphin	170
Ematris/Rockcorry	Clogher	112
Emlefad & Kilmorgan/Ballymote	Achonry	100
Emly	Cashel	83
Emo	Kildare	202
Enfield	Meath	241
Ennis, Cathedral	Killaloe	214
Ennis, Christ the King	Killaloe	214
Ennis, St Joseph's	Killaloe	214
Enniscorthy, Cathedral of St Aidan	Ferns	176
Enniskeane & Desertserges	Cork & Ross	131
Enniskerry/Kilmacanogue/part of Bray Grouping	Dublin	47
Enniskillen	Clogher	111
Ennistymon	Galway	183
Errigal/Garvagh	Derry	141
Errigal Kieran/Ballygawley	Armagh	28
Errigal Truagh	Clogher	111
Esker-Doddsboro-Adamstown	Dublin	47
Eskra	Clogher	111
Eyeries	Kerry	190
Eyrecourt, Clonfert & Meelick/Clonfert, Donanaghta & Meelick	Clonfert	116

F

Parish	Diocese	Page
Fahan/Burt, Inch & Fahan	Derry	141
Fahy & Quansboro/Fahy & Kilquain	Clonfert	116
Fairview	Dublin	47
Fairymount/Tibohine	Elphin	170
Falcarragh	Raphoe	256
Farranree	Cork & Ross	131
Faughanvale/Faughanvale & Lower Cumber	Derry	141
Faughart	Armagh	29
Feakle & Killanena-Flagmount	Killaloe	215
Fedamore	Limerick	232
Feenagh & Kilmeedy	Limerick	233
Fenagh	Ardagh	104
Ferbane High Street & Boora/Tisaran & Fuithre	Ardagh	104
Fermoy	Cloyne	120
Ferns	Ferns	176
Ferrybank	Ossory	250
Fethard	Cashel	83
Finglas	Dublin	47
Finglas West	Dublin	47
Fintona/Donacavey	Clogher	111
Firhouse	Dublin	47
Firies	Kerry	190
Fohenagh & Kilgerrill/Fohenagh & Killure	Clonfert	116
Forkhill/Mullaghbawn	Armagh	30
Fossa	Kerry	190
Fourmilehouse/Kilbride	Elphin	170
Foxford/Toomore	Achonry	100
Foxrock	Dublin	47
Foynes & Shanagolden	Limerick	233
Francis Street	Dublin	48
Frankfield-Grange	Cork & Ross	131
Frenchpark/Kilcorkey & Frenchpark	Elphin	170
Freshford	Ossory	250

G

Parish	Diocese	Page
Galbally	Cashel	83
Gallen & Reynagh/Cloghan & Banagher	Ardagh	104
Galloon/Newtownbutler	Clogher	112
Galmoy	Ossory	250
Gardiner Street	Dublin	48
Garrienderk/Effin	Limerick	232
Garristown	Dublin	48
Gartan & Termon/Termon	Raphoe	257
Garvagh/Errigal	Derry	141
Geevagh	Elphin	170
Glanmire	Cork & Ross	131
Glantane	Cloyne	121
Glanworth & Ballindangan	Cloyne	121
Glasnevin	Dublin	48
Glasson–Tubberclaire	Meath	241
Glasthule	Dublin	48
The Glen/Blackpool	Cork & Ross	131
Glenamaddy/Boyounagh	Tuam	94

PARISH INDEX

Glenariffe	Down	153	Holy Family	Limerick	231	Kilbarron &		
Glenarm/			Holy Rosary	Down	151	Terryglass	Killaloe	216
Tickmacreevan	Down	153	Holy Trinity	Down	151	Kilbeacanty/		
Glenavy & Killead	Down	153	Holy Trinity			Peterswell	Galway	183
Glenbeigh	Kerry	190	Cathedral/Trinity			Kilbeagh/		
Glenbrien & Oylegate	Ferns	177	Within &			Charlestown	Achonry	100
Glencolmcille/			St Patrick's	Waterford	261	Kilbeg	Meath	242
Carrick	Raphoe	256	Holywood	Down	153	Kilbeggan	Meath	242
Glendalough	Dublin	48	Horeswood &			Kilbegnet/		
Glendermott/			Ballykelly	Ferns	176	Creggs	Elphin	170
Waterside	Derry	142	Hospital	Cashel	84	Kilbehenny	Cashel	84
Glenfarne	Kilmore	222	Howth	Dublin	48	Kilbride/		
Glenflesk	Kerry	190	Huntstown	Dublin	48	Fourmilehouse	Elphin	170
Glengarriff/Bonane	Kerry	190				Kilbride/Leenane	Tuam	95
Glenmore	Ossory	250				Kilbride & Barndarrig	Dublin	49
Glenravel/Skerry	Down	153	**I**			Kilbride & Doonfeeny/		
Glenroe & Ballyorgan	Limerick	232				Ballycastle	Killala	208
Glenswilly/Glenswilly			Imogeela/			Kilbrittain	Cork & Ross	131
& Templedouglas	Raphoe	256	Castlemartyr	Cloyne	121	Kilbroney/Rostrevor	Dromore	165
Glenties/Iniskeel	Raphoe	256	Inagh/Kilnamona	Killaloe	213	Kilcar	Raphoe	256
Glin	Limerick	233	Inch & Kilmaley	Killaloe	213	Kilchreest	Galway	183
Glounthaune	Cork & Ross	131	Inchicore, Mary			Kilcleagh &		
Glynn	Ferns	176	Immaculate	Dublin	48	Ballyloughloe/Moate		
Golden	Cashel	84	Inchicore,			& Mount Temple	Ardagh	105
Goleen	Cork & Ross	131	St Michael's	Dublin	49	Kilclief & Strangford	Down	153
Good Shepherd	Galway	182	Inchicronan/			Kilcloon	Meath	242
Gorey	Ferns	176	Crusheen	Killaloe	214	Kilcock	Kildare	202
Gort/Beagh	Galway	183	Inis Muighe			Kilcolman	Killaloe	216
Gortahork/			Samh/Belleek-			Kilcolman	Limerick	233
Tory Island	Raphoe	256	Garrison	Clogher	110	Kilcolman/		
Gortin/Badoney			Inishbofin	Tuam	94	Claremorris	Tuam	94
Lower	Derry	141	Inishmagrath/			Kilcommoc/Kenagh	Ardagh	105
Gortletteragh	Ardagh	104	Drumkeerin	Kilmore	222	Kilcommon	Cashel	84
Gortnahoe	Cashel	84	Iniskeel/Glenties	Raphoe	256	Kilcommon/		
Gowran	Ossory	250	Inistioge	Ossory	250	Roundfort	Tuam	95
Graignamanagh	Kildare	202	Inniscarra	Cloyne	121	Kilcommon-Erris	Killala	209
Graiguecullen	Kildare	202	Innishannon	Cork & Ross	131	Kilconduff &		
Granard	Ardagh	104	Inniskeen	Clogher	111	Meelick/Swinford	Achonry	100
Grange/			Inver	Raphoe	256	Kilconly & Kilbannon	Tuam	94
Bruff/Meanus	Limerick	232	Iona Road	Dublin	49	Kilcoo	Down	153
Grange Park	Dublin	48	Irvinestown/			Kilcooley &		
Greencastle	Derry	141	Devenish	Clogher	111	Leitrim/Leitrim &		
Greenhills	Dublin	48	Iskaheen/Iskaheen &			Ballyduggan	Clonfert	116
Greenlough/Tamlaght			Upper Moville	Derry	141	Kilcorkey &		
O'Crilly	Derry	141	Islandeady	Tuam	94	Frenchpark/		
Grenagh	Cloyne	121				Frenchpark	Elphin	170
Greystones	Dublin	48				Kilcormac	Meath	242
Gurranabraher	Cork & Ross	131	**J**			Kilcornan	Limerick	233
Gurteen/Kilfree &						Kilcullen	Dublin	49
Killaraght	Achonry	100	James's Street	Dublin	49	Kilcummin	Kerry	190
Gweedore	Raphoe	256	Jobstown	Dublin	49	Kildalkey	Meath	242
			Johnstown-Killiney	Dublin	49	Kildallan & Tomregan	Kilmore	222
			Johnstown	Meath	241	Kildare	Kildare	202
H			Johnstown	Ossory	250	Kildimo & Pallaskenry	Limerick	233
						Kildorrery	Cloyne	121
Hacketstown	Kildare	202				Kildress	Armagh	29
Haddington Road	Dublin	48	**K**			Kildysart & Coolmeen/		
Haggardstown &						Kilfidane	Killaloe	213
Blackrock	Armagh	29	Kanturk	Cloyne	121	Kileen/Carraroe	Tuam	94
Halston Street &			Keadue, Arigna &			Kilfarboy/Miltown		
Arran Quay	Dublin	48	Ballyfarnon/			Malbay	Killaloe	213
Hannahstown	Down	153	Kilronan	Ardagh	105	Kilfenora	Galway	183
Harold's Cross	Dublin	48	Keady/Derrynoose	Armagh	29	Kilfian	Killala	209
Harrington Street	Dublin	48	Keash/Drumrat	Achonry	100	Kilfidane/Kildysart		
Hartstown	Dublin	48	Keelogues	Tuam	94	& Coolmeen	Killaloe	213
Headford/Killursa &			Kells	Meath	242	Kilfinane	Limerick	232
Killower	Tuam	94	Kenagh/Kilcommoc	Ardagh	105	Kilfree & Killaraght/		
Hilltown/Clonduff	Dromore	165	Kenmare	Kerry	190	Gurteen	Achonry	100
Hollyhill/			Kerry Pike/Clogheen	Cork & Ross	131	Kilgarvan	Kerry	190
Knocknaheeny	Cork & Ross	132	Kilanerin & Ballyfad	Ferns	177	Kilgarvan/		
Holy Cross	Cashel	84	Kilballyowen/			Bonniconlon	Achonry	100
Holy Cross	Down	151	Carrigaholt &			Kilgeever/Louisburgh	Tuam	95
Holy Family	Down	151	Cross	Killaloe	213	Kilglass	Killala	209
Holy Family	Waterford	261	Kilbarrack-Foxfield	Dublin	49	Kilglass/Kilglass &		
Holy Family,			Kilbarron/			Rooskey	Elphin	170
Ballymagroarty	Derry	140	Ballyshannon	Raphoe	256			

PARISH INDEX

Parish	Diocese	Page
Kilglass & Rathreagh/Legan & Ballycloghan	Ardagh	105
Kilglass & Rooskey/Kilglass	Elphin	170
Kilgobinet	Waterford	262
Kilkee & Doonbeg/Killard	Killaloe	213
Kilkeedy/Tubber	Killaloe	214
Kilkeel/Upper Mourne	Down	153
Kilkeevan/Castlerea	Elphin	170
Kilkerley	Armagh	29
Kilkerrin & Clonberne	Tuam	94
Kill	Kildare	202
Killaghtee/Bruckless	Raphoe	256
Killala	Killala	209
Killalaghtan & Kilrickle/Cappatagle & Kilrickle	Clonfert	116
Killaloe	Killaloe	215
Killanave & Templederry	Killaloe	215
Killanena-Flagmount & Feakle	Killaloe	215
Killanin/Rosscahill	Galway	183
Killann/Baileboro	Kilmore	221
Killanny	Clogher	111
Killard/Doonbeg & Kilkee	Killaloe	213
Killarney	Kerry	189
Killascobe/Menlough	Tuam	95
Killashee	Ardagh	105
Killasnett/Cloonclare	Kilmore	221
Killasser	Achonry	100
Killaveney & Crossbridge	Ferns	177
Killavullen	Cloyne	121
Killcluney	Armagh	29
Killea/Dunmore East	Waterford	262
Killeagh	Cloyne	121
Killeavy Lower/Bessbrook	Armagh	28
Killeavy Upper/Cloghogue	Armagh	28
Killedan/Kiltimagh	Achonry	100
Killeedy	Limerick	233
Killeentierna	Kerry	190
Killeeshil	Armagh	29
Killeevan/Currin, Killeevan & Aghabog	Clogher	111
Killeigh	Kildare	202
Killenaule	Cashel	84
Killenummery & Ballintogher/Killenummery & Killery	Ardagh	105
Killererin	Tuam	94
Killeshandra	Kilmore	222
Killesher/Kinawley	Kilmore	222
Killester	Dublin	49
Killian & Killeroran/Ballygar	Elphin	170
Killimer & Kilrush	Killaloe	213
Killimor & Tiranascragh/Killimorbologue & Tiranascragh	Clonfert	116
Killimordaly, Killtulagh & Clooncagh	Clonfert	116
Killinagh & Glangevlin	Kilmore	222
Killinarden	Dublin	49
Killiney-Ballybrack	Dublin	43
Killinkere	Kilmore	222
Kill-O'-The-Grange	Dublin	49
Killoe	Ardagh	105
Killoran/Coolaney	Achonry	100
Killorglin	Kerry	190
Killough/Bright	Down	154
Killucan	Meath	242
Killukin & Killummod/Croghan	Elphin	170
Killursa & Killower/Headford	Tuam	94
Killybegs	Raphoe	256
Killyclogher/Cappagh	Derry	141
Killygarvan & Tullyfern/Rathmullan	Raphoe	257
Killygordon/Donaghmore	Derry	141
Killyleagh	Down	154
Killymard	Raphoe	256
Kilmacanogue (see Enniskerry)	Dublin	47
Kilmacabea	Cork & Ross	131
Kilmacduane/Cooraclare	Killaloe	213
Kilmacow	Ossory	250
Kilmacrennan	Raphoe	256
Kilmacshalgan/Dromore-West	Killala	209
Kilmactigue/Tourlestrane	Achonry	100
Kilmacud-Stillorgan	Dublin	49
Kilmaine	Tuam	94
Kilmainhamwood & Moybologue	Kilmore	222
Kilmalinogue & Lickmolassey/Portumna	Clonfert	116
Kilmallock	Limerick	232
Kilmeen	Tuam	94
Kilmeen & Castleventry	Cork & Ross	131
Kilmeena	Tuam	94
Kilmegan/Castlewellan	Down	153
Kilmessan	Meath	242
Kilmichael	Cork & Ross	132
Kilmihil	Killaloe	213
Kilmore & Kilmore Quay	Ferns	177
Kilmore	Kilmore	222
Kilmore/Crossgar	Down	153
Kilmore	Armagh	30
Kilmore & Drumsnat/Corcaghan	Clogher	111
Kilmore Road West	Dublin	49
Kilmore-Erris	Killala	209
Kilmoremoy/Ballina	Killala	208
Kilmovee	Achonry	100
Kilmoylan & Cummer/Cummer	Tuam	94
Kilmuckridge/Litter & Monamolin	Ferns	177
Kilmurray-Ibrickane/Mullagh	Killaloe	213
Kilmurry	Cork & Ross	132
Kilmurry McMahon	Killaloe	213
Kilnadeema & Aille/Kilnadeema & Kilteskill	Clonfert	116
Kilnamanagh-Castleview	Dublin	49
Kilnamanagh & Estersnow/Ballinameen	Elphin	170
Kilnamartyra	Cloyne	121
Kilnamona/Inagh	Killaloe	213
Kilnoe & Tuamgraney/Ogonnelloe & Bodyke	Killaloe	215
Kilquade	Dublin	49
Kilrane & St Patrick's	Ferns	177
Kilrea & Desertoghill/Kilrea	Derry	141
Kilronan/Keadue, Arigna & Ballyfarnon	Ardagh	105
Kilrossanty	Waterford	262
Kilrush & Askamore	Ferns	177
Kilsaran	Armagh	30
Kilshalvey, Kilturra & Cloonoghill/Bunninadden	Achonry	100
Kilsheelan	Waterford	262
Kilsherdany & Drung	Kilmore	222
Kilskeery/Trillick	Clogher	112
Kilskyre	Meath	242
Kiltane	Killala	209
Kilteely	Cashel	84
Kilteevogue/Cloghan	Raphoe	256
Kiltimagh/Killedan	Achonry	100
Kiltoghert/Carrick-on-Shannon	Ardagh	104
Kiltoom/Kiltoom & Cam	Elphin	170
Kiltormer & Oghill/Lawrencetown & Kiltormer	Clonfert	116
Kiltrustan, Lissonuffy & Cloonfinlough/Strokestown	Elphin	171
Kiltubrid	Ardagh	105
Kiltulagh, Killtulagh, Killimordaly & Clooncagh	Clonfert	116
Kiltullagh/Ballinlough	Tuam	94
Kilvarnet/Collooney	Achonry	100
Kilvine/Ballindine	Tuam	94
Kilworth	Cloyne	121
Kimmage Manor	Dublin	49
Kinawley/Killesher	Kilmore	222
Kincasslagh/Burtonport	Raphoe	256
Kingscourt	Meath	242
Kinlough & Glenade	Kilmore	222
Kinnegad	Meath	242
Kinnitty	Killaloe	216
Kinsale	Cork & Ross	132
Kinsealy	Dublin	49
Kinvara	Galway	183
Kircubbin/Ardkeen	Down	154
Kirkinriola/Ballymena	Down	153
Kiskeam/Boherbue	Kerry	189
Knock	Tuam	95
Knock/Spiddal	Tuam	95
Knockaderry & Cloncagh	Limerick	232
Knockainey	Cashel	84
Knockanore	Waterford	262
Knockavilla	Cashel	84
Knockbride	Kilmore	222

PARISH INDEX

Parish	Diocese	Page
Knockbridge	Armagh	30
Knockcroghery/St John's	Elphin	170
Knocklong	Cashel	84
Knocklyon	Dublin	50
Knockmitten (see Clondalkin)	Dublin	45
Knocknagoshel	Kerry	190
Knocknaheeny/Hollyhill	Cork & Ross	132
Knockninny/Derrylin	Kilmore	222
Kyle & Knock	Killaloe	216

L

Parish	Diocese	Page
Lackagh	Tuam	95
Lacken	Killala	209
Ladysbridge & Ballymacoda	Cloyne	120
Lahardane/Addergoole	Killala	209
Lanesboro/Rathcline	Ardagh	105
Langfield/Drumquin	Derry	141
Laragh	Kilmore	222
Larkhill-Whitehall-Santry	Dublin	50
Larne	Down	154
Lattin & Cullen	Cashel	84
Latton/Aughnamullen West	Clogher	111
Laurel Lodge-Carpenterstown	Dublin	50
Lavey	Kilmore	222
Lavey/Termoneeny & part of Maghera	Derry	142
Lawrencetown & Kiltormer/Kiltormer & Oghill	Clonfert	116
Laytown-Mornington	Meath	242
Leckpatrick/Leckpatrick & part of Donagheady	Derry	142
Leenane/Kilbride	Tuam	95
Legan & Ballycloghan/Kilglass & Rathreagh	Ardagh	105
Leighlin	Kildare	203
Leitrim & Ballyduggan/Kilcooley & Leitrim	Clonfert	116
Leixlip	Dublin	50
Lemanaghan/Ballinahown, Boher & Pollough	Ardagh	104
Letterfrack/Ballinakill	Tuam	95
Letterkenny/Conwal & Leck	Raphoe	256
Lettermore	Galway	183
Lifford/Clonleigh	Derry	142
Limavady/Drumachose, Tamlaght, Finlagan & part of Aghanloo	Derry	142
Lisburn/Blaris	Down	154
Liscannor	Galway	183
Liscarroll/Churchtown	Cloyne	121
Lisdoonvarna & Kilshanny	Galway	183
Lisdowney	Ossory	250
Lisgoold	Cloyne	121
Lismore	Waterford	262
Lisnaskea/Aghalurcher	Clogher	111
Lissan	Armagh	30
Listowel	Kerry	190
Litter/Kilmuckridge & Monamolin	Ferns	177
Little Bray (see Bray, St Peter's)	Dublin	45
Lixnaw	Kerry	190
Lobinstown	Meath	242
Longford/Templemichael, Ballymacormack	Ardagh	104
Longwood	Meath	242
Lordship & Ballymascanlon	Armagh	30
Lorrha & Dorrha	Killaloe	216
The Lough	Cork & Ross	132
Lough Gowna & Mullinalaghta/Scrabby & Colmcille East	Ardagh	105
Loughall	Armagh	30
Loughglynn/Loughglynn & Lisacul	Elphin	170
Loughguile	Down	154
Loughill/Ballyhahill	Limerick	233
Loughilly/Whitecross	Armagh	31
Loughinisland	Down	154
Loughlinstown	Dublin	50
Loughmore	Cashel	84
Loughrea, St Brendan's Cathedral	Clonfert	115
Louisburgh/Kilgeever	Tuam	95
Louth	Armagh	30
Lower Mourne	Down	154
Lucan	Dublin	50
Lucan South	Dublin	50
Lurgan, St Paul's, Shankill	Dromore	165
Lurgan, St Peter's, Shankill	Dromore	166
Lurgan/Virginia	Kilmore	222
Lusk	Dublin	50
Lusmagh	Clonfert	116

M

Parish	Diocese	Page
Machaire Rois/Carrickmacross	Clogher	110
Macroom	Cloyne	121
Magh Ene/Bundoran	Clogher	110
Maghera	Derry	142
Maghera/Newcastle	Down	154
Magheracloone	Clogher	112
Magheradroll/Ballynahinch	Dromore	165
Magherafelt & Ardtrea North	Armagh	30
Magheralin	Dromore	165
Magilligan	Derry	142
Mahon	Cork & Ross	132
Mahoonagh	Limerick	233
Malahide	Dublin	50
Malin/Clonca	Derry	142
Mallow	Cloyne	121
Manister	Limerick	232
Marino	Dublin	50
Marley Grange	Dublin	50
Marshallstown and Castledockrell	Ferns	177
Martinstown/Bulgaden	Limerick	232
Maugherow/Drumcliff	Elphin	170
Mayfield/St Joseph's	Cork & Ross	132
Mayne/Coole	Meath	241
Maynooth	Dublin	50
Mayo Abbey/Mayo & Rosslea	Tuam	95
Mayobridge/St Patrick's	Dromore	165
Meadowbrook	Dublin	50
Meanus/Bruff/Grange	Limerick	232
Meath Street & Merchants Quay	Dublin	51
Meelick & Kilconduff/Swinford	Achonry	100
Meelick & Eyrecourt, Clonfert/Clonfert, Donanaghta & Meelick	Clonfert	116
Meelick/Parteen	Limerick	231
Meelin & Rockchapel	Cloyne	122
Meevagh/Carrigart	Raphoe	256
Mell	Armagh	30
Mellifont	Armagh	30
Melmount/Mourne	Derry	142
Menlough/Killascobe	Tuam	95
Merchants Quay & Meath Street	Dublin	51
Merrion Road	Dublin	51
Mervue	Galway	182
Middle Killeavy/Newry	Armagh	30
Middletown/Tynan	Armagh	30
Midleton	Cloyne	122
Milford	Cloyne	122
Millstreet	Kerry	190
Milltown	Dublin	51
Milltown	Kerry	190
Milltown	Meath	242
Milltown/Addergole & Liskeevey	Tuam	95
Miltown Malbay/Kilfarboy	Killaloe	213
Mitchelstown	Cloyne	122
Moate & Mount Temple/Kilcleagh & Ballyloughloe	Ardagh	105
Modeligo	Waterford	262
Mohill/Mohill-Manachain	Ardagh	105
Monagea	Limerick	233
Monageer	Ferns	177
Monaghan	Clogher	110
Monaleen	Limerick	231
Monamolin & Kilmuckridge/Litter	Ferns	177
Monasterboice	Armagh	30
Monasterevin	Kildare	203
Moneymore/Ardtrea	Armagh	30
Monkstown	Cork & Ross	132
Monkstown	Dublin	51
Mooncoin	Ossory	250
Moone	Dublin	51
Moore	Tuam	95
Mostrim/Edgeworthstown	Ardagh	104
Mount Argus	Dublin	51
Mount Merrion	Dublin	51
Mountbellew & Moylough	Tuam	95
Mountcollins/Tournafulla	Limerick	233
Mountmellick	Kildare	203
Mountnugent	Meath	242

PARISH INDEX

Parish	Diocese	Page
Mountrath	Kildare	203
Mountshannon/Clonrush	Killaloe	215
Mountview	Dublin	51
Mourne/Melmount	Derry	142
Mourne Abbey	Cloyne	122
Mourne Road	Dublin	51
Moville/Moville Lower	Derry	142
Moy/Clonfeacle	Armagh	30
Moycarkey	Cashel	84
Moycullen	Galway	183
Moygownagh	Killala	209
Moylough & Mountbellew	Tuam	95
Moynalty	Meath	242
Moynalvey	Meath	242
Moyraverty/Craigavon	Dromore	165
Moyrus/Carna	Tuam	94
Moyvane	Kerry	190
Muckalee	Ossory	250
Muckno/Castleblayney	Clogher	110
Muinebheag/Bagenalstown	Kildare	203
Muintir Bháire	Cork & Ross	132
Mulhuddart	Dublin	51
Mullagh	Kilmore	222
Mullagh/Kilmurray-Ibrickane	Killaloe	213
Mullagh & Killoran/Abbeygormican & Killoran	Clonfert	116
Mullaghbawn/Forkhill	Armagh	30
Mullahoran & Loughduff/Drumlumman North	Ardagh	105
Mullinahone	Cashel	84
Mullinavat	Ossory	250
Mullingar, Cathedral of Christ the King	Meath	240
Multyfarnham	Meath	242
Mungret/Crecora	Limerick	232
Murhaun/Drumshanbo	Ardagh	104
Murragh & Templemartin	Cork & Ross	132
Murroe & Boher	Cashel	84
Myshall	Kildare	203

N

Parish	Diocese	Page
Naas	Kildare	203
Narraghmore	Dublin	51
The Nativity	Down	152
Naul	Dublin	51
Navan	Meath	240
Navan Road	Dublin	51
Neilstown	Dublin	51
Nenagh	Killaloe	215
New Inn	Cashel	84
New Inn & Bullaun/Bullaun, Grange & Killaan	Clonfert	116
New Ross	Ferns	177
Newbawn & Raheen	Ferns	177
Newbridge	Armagh	30
Newbridge/Droichead Nua	Kildare	202
Newcastle	Dublin	52
Newcastle/Maghera	Down	154
Newcastle & Fourmilewater	Waterford	262
Newcastle West	Limerick	233
Newmarket	Cloyne	122
Newmarket-on-Fergus	Killaloe	214
Newport	Cashel	84
Newport/Burrishoole	Tuam	95
Newry	Dromore	165
Newry/Middle Killeavy	Armagh	30
Newtown	Waterford	262
Newtownards	Down	154
Newtownbutler/Galloon	Clogher	112
Newtowncashel/Cashel	Ardagh	105
Newtowncunningham/Killea	Raphoe	256
Newtownforbes/Clonguish	Ardagh	105
Newtownpark	Dublin	52
Newtownshandrum	Cloyne	122
Newtownstewart/Ardstraw East	Derry	142
Nobber	Meath	242
North Wall-Seville Place	Dublin	52
North William Street	Dublin	52

O

Parish	Diocese	Page
O'Callaghan's Mills	Killaloe	214
Ogonnelloe & Bodyke/Kilnoe & Tuamgraney	Killaloe	215
Ogulla & Baslic/Tulsk	Elphin	171
Oldcastle	Meath	243
Omagh/Drumragh	Derry	142
Omey & Ballindoon/Clifden	Tuam	94
Oran/Cloverhill	Elphin	171
Oranmore	Galway	183
Oristown	Meath	243
Oughterard	Galway	183
Oulart & Ballaghkeene	Ferns	177
Our Lady Help of Christians	Limerick	231
Our Lady of Lourdes	Limerick	231
Our Lady of Lourdes, Steelstown	Derry	140
Our Lady of the Rosary	Limerick	232
Our Lady Queen of Peace	Limerick	231
Our Lady Queen of Peace, Kilwee	Down	151
Our Lady's Island & Tacumshane	Ferns	177
Ovens	Cork & Ross	132
Oylegate & Glenbrien	Ferns	177

P

Parish	Diocese	Page
Pallasgreen	Cashel	84
Palmerstown	Dublin	52
Parke/Turlough	Tuam	95
Parteen/Meelick	Limerick	231
Partry/Ballyovey	Tuam	95
Passage West	Cork & Ross	132
Patrickswell/Ballybrown	Limerick	232
Paulstown	Kildare	203
Peterswell/Kilbeacanty	Galway	183
Pettigo	Clogher	112
Phibsborough	Dublin	52
Piercestown & Murrintown	Ferns	177
Plumbridge/Badoney Upper	Derry	142
Pobal/Tempo	Clogher	112
Pomeroy	Armagh	31
Portadown/Drumcree	Armagh	31
Portaferry/Ballyphilip	Down	154
Portarlington	Kildare	203
Porterstown-Clonsilla	Dublin	52
Portglenone	Down	154
Portlaoise	Kildare	203
Portlaw	Waterford	262
Portmarnock	Dublin	52
Portroe	Killaloe	215
Portrush	Down	154
Portstewart	Down	154
Portumna/Kilmalinogue & Lickmolassey	Clonfert	116
Poulpeasty & Cloughbawn	Ferns	176
Powerstown	Waterford	262
Prior/Ballinskelligs	Kerry	189
Priorswood	Dublin	52
Pro-Cathedral	Dublin	42
Prosperous	Kildare	203
Puckane/Cloughprior & Monsea	Killaloe	215

Q

Parish	Diocese	Page
Quin	Killaloe	214

R

Parish	Diocese	Page
Rahan	Meath	243
Raheen	Kildare	203
Raheen	Limerick	232
Raheny	Dublin	52
Ramelton/Aughnish	Raphoe	256
Ramoan/Ballycastle	Down	152
Ramsgrange	Ferns	177
Randalstown	Down	154
Ransboro/Strandhill	Elphin	171
Raphoe	Raphoe	257
Rasharkin	Down	154
Rath & the Islands	Cork & Ross	132
Rathangan & Cleariestown	Ferns	177
Rathangan	Kildare	203
Rathaspic, Russagh & Streete/Rathowen	Ardagh	105
Rathcline/Lanesboro	Ardagh	105
Rathcormac	Cloyne	122
Rathdowney	Ossory	250
Rathdrum	Dublin	52
Rathfarnham	Dublin	52
Rathfriland/Drumgath	Dromore	165
Rathgar	Dublin	52
Rathgormack	Waterford	262
Rathkeale	Limerick	232
Rathkenny	Meath	243
Rathmines	Dublin	52
Rathmore	Kerry	190

PARISH INDEX

Parish	Diocese	Page
Rathmullan/Killygarvan & Tullyfern	Raphoe	257
Rathnure & Templeudigan	Ferns	177
Rathowen/Rathaspic, Russagh & Streete	Ardagh	105
Rathowen & Streete	Ardagh	105
Rathvilly	Kildare	203
Ratoath	Meath	243
Raymochy/Drumoghill	Raphoe	256
Renmore	Galway	182
Rhode	Kildare	203
Rialto/Dolphin's Barn	Dublin	46
Ring & Old Parish	Waterford	262
Ringsend	Dublin	52
River Valley	Dublin	53
Riverchapel, Courtown Harbour	Ferns	177
Rivermount	Dublin	53
Riverstown	Elphin	171
Robeen	Tuam	95
Robertstown	Limerick	233
Rochfortbridge	Meath	243
Rockchapel & Meelin	Cloyne	122
Rockcorry/Ematris	Clogher	112
Rockhill/Bruree	Limerick	232
Rolestown-Oldtown	Dublin	53
Rosbercon	Ossory	250
Roscommon	Elphin	171
Roscrea	Killaloe	216
Rosenallis	Kildare	203
Roslea	Clogher	112
Rosmuc	Galway	183
Ross/Clonbur	Tuam	94
Rosscahill/Killanin	Galway	183
Rosscarbery & Lissavaird	Cork & Ross	132
Rosses Point	Elphin	171
Rostrevor/Kilbroney	Dromore	165
Roundfort/Kilcommon	Tuam	95
Roundstone	Tuam	95
Roundwood	Dublin	53
Rowlagh and Quarryvale	Dublin	53
Roxboro	Limerick	231
Rush	Dublin	53

S

Parish	Diocese	Page
Sacred Heart	Cork & Ross	132
Sacred Heart	Down	152
Sacred Heart	Waterford	261
Sacred Heart Church	Galway	182
Saggart/Rathcoole/Brittas	Dublin	53
Saintfield & Carrickmannon	Down	154
Sallins	Kildare	203
Sallynoggin	Dublin	53
Salthill	Galway	182
Sandyford	Dublin	53
Sandymount	Dublin	53
Saul & Ballee	Down	154
Saval	Dromore	165
Scariff/Moynoe	Killaloe	215
Schull	Cork & Ross	132
Scrabby & Colmcille East/Lough Gowna & Mullinalaghta	Ardagh	105
Seagoe/Derrymacash	Dromore	165
Sean McDermott Street	Dublin	42
Seapatrick/Banbridge	Dromore	165
Seir Kieran	Ossory	250
Seville Place-North Wall	Dublin	52
Shanagolden & Foynes	Limerick	233
Shankill/ St Paul's, Lurgan	Dromore	165
Shankill/St Peter's, Lurgan	Dromore	166
Shankill	Dublin	53
Shannon	Killaloe	214
Shannonbridge/Clonmacnois	Ardagh	105
Shinrone	Killaloe	216
Shrule	Galway	183
Shrule/Ballymahon	Ardagh	104
Silvermines	Killaloe	215
Sion Mills	Derry	142
Sixmilebridge	Killaloe	214
Sixmilebridge	Limerick	232
Skerries	Dublin	53
Skerry/Glenravel	Down	153
Skibbereen, St Patrick's Cathedral	Cork & Ross	130
Skreen & Dromard	Killala	209
Skryne	Meath	243
Slane	Meath	243
Slieverue	Ossory	250
Sligo, St Anne's	Elphin	170
Sligo, Calry St Joseph's	Elphin	170
Sligo, St Mary's	Elphin	170
Sneem	Kerry	190
Solohead	Cashel	84
Spa	Kerry	190
Spiddal/Knock	Tuam	95
Springfield	Dublin	53
Sruleen	Dublin	53
St Agnes'	Down	152
St Anne's	Down	152
St Anthony's	Down	152
St Augustine's	Galway	182
St Bernadette's	Down	152
St Brigid's	Down	152
St Canice's	Ossory	249
St Columba's & St Eugene's Cathedral/Templemore/Derry City	Derry	140
St Colmcille's	Down	151
St Finbarr's South	Cork & Ross	132
St Gerard's	Down	152
St James's/Whiteabbey	Down	152
St John's	Down	152
St John's	Ossory	249
St John's	Waterford	261
St John's/Knockcroghery/Rahara	Elphin	170
St John's Cathedral	Limerick	231
St John the Apostle	Galway	182
St Johnston/Taughboyne	Raphoe	257
St Joseph's	Galway	182
St Joseph's	Limerick	231
St Joseph's/Blackrock Road	Cork & Ross	132
St Joseph's/Mayfield	Cork & Ross	132
St Luke's	Down	152
St Malachy's	Down	152
St Mary's	Down	151
St Mary's	Galway	182
St Mary's	Limerick	232
St Mary's	Ossory	249
St Mary's/Burren	Dromore	165
St Mary's, Creggan	Derry	140
St Mary's on the Hill	Down	152
St Matthew's	Down	152
St Michael's	Down	152
St Michael's	Limerick	231
St Mullins	Kildare	203
St Munchin's & St Lelia's	Limerick	231
St Nicholas	Limerick	232
St Oliver Plunkett	Down	152
St Patrick's	Cork & Ross	132
St Patrick's Cathedral, Skibbereen	Cork & Ross	130
St Patrick's	Down	151
St Patrick's	Galway	182
St Patrick's	Limerick	231
St Patrick's	Ossory	249
St Patrick's/Mayobridge	Dromore	165
St Paul's	Down	152
St Paul's	Limerick	232
St Paul's	Waterford	261
St Peter's/The Cathedral	Down	151
St Peter's/Warrenpoint	Dromore	165
St Saviour's	Limerick	231
St Saviour's	Waterford	261
St Senan's, Enniscorthy	Ferns	177
St Teresa's	Down	152
St Vincent de Paul	Down	152
St Vincent's, Sunday's Well	Cork & Ross	132
Stamullen	Meath	243
Strabane/Camus	Derry	142
Stradbally	Kildare	203
Stradbally	Waterford	262
Straide/Templemore	Achonry	100
Strandhill/Ransboro	Elphin	171
Stranorlar	Raphoe	257
Strathfoyle/Strathfoyle, Enagh Lough	Derry	142
Streete & Rathowen	Ardagh	105
Strokestown/Kiltrustan, Lissonuffy & Cloonfinlough	Elphin	171
SS Joseph & Benildus	Waterford	261
SS Peter's & Paul's	Cork & Ross	132
Summerhill	Meath	243
Suncroft	Kildare	203
Sutton	Dublin	54
Swatragh	Derry	142
Swinford/Kilconduff & Meelick	Achonry	100
Swords	Dublin	53

T

Parish	Diocese	Page
Taghmaconnell	Clonfert	116
Taghmon	Ferns	177
Taghmon	Meath	243
Taghshiney, Taghshinod & Abbeyshrule/Carrickedmond & Abbeyshrule	Ardagh	104
Tagoat	Ferns	177
Tallaght, Dodder	Dublin	54

PARISH INDEX

Tallaght, Oldbawn	Dublin	54	Tickmacreevan/			**U**		
Tallaght, St Mary's	Dublin	54	Glenarm	Down	153			
Tallaght, Tymon North	Dublin	54	Timoleague & Clogagh	Cork & Ross	132	Uibh Laoire	Cork & Ross	132
Tallanstown	Armagh	31	Tinryland	Kildare	203	University Church	Dublin	54
Tallow	Waterford	262	Tipperary	Cashel	85	Upper Mayfield	Cork & Ross	132
Tamlaght O'Crilly/			Tirellan	Galway	182	Upper Mourne/Kilkeel	Down	154
Greenlough	Derry	141	Tisaran &			Upperchurch	Cashel	85
Tamney/			Fuithre/Ferbane			Urlingford	Ossory	250
Clondavaddog	Raphoe	257	High Street & Boora	Ardagh	104	Urney & Annagelliff/Cavan	Kilmore	221
Tandragee/ Ballymore &			Togher	Armagh	31	Urney & Castlefinn/		
Mullaghbrack	Armagh	31	Togher	Cork & Ross	132	Doneyloop	Derry	141
Tarbert	Kerry	191	Toomevara	Killaloe	215			
Tarmonbarry	Elphin	171	Toomore/Foxford	Achonry	100	**V**		
Taughboyne,			Tory Island/					
St Johnston	Raphoe	257	Gortahork	Raphoe	256	Valentia	Kerry	191
Tawnawilly/			Touraneena	Waterford	262	Valleymount	Dublin	54
Donegal Town	Raphoe	256	Tourlestrane/			Virginia/Lurgan	Kilmore	222
Templeboy	Killala	209	Kilmactigue	Achonry	100			
Templecrone & Lettermacaward/			Tournafulla/ Mountcollins	Limerick	233	**W**		
Dungloe	Raphoe	256	Tracton Abbey	Cork & Ross	132	Walkinstown	Dublin	54
Templeglantine	Limerick	233	Tralee, St Brendan's	Kerry	191	Warrenpoint/		
Templemartin & Murragh	Cork & Ross	132	Tralee, St John's	Kerry	191	St Peter's	Dromore	165
Templemichael,			Tramore	Waterford	262	Watergrasshill	Cork & Ross	132
Ballymacormack/			Travelling People	Dublin	54	Waterside/		
Longford	Ardagh	104	Trillick/Kilskeery	Clogher	112	Glendermott	Derry	142
Templemore	Cashel	84	Trim	Meath	243	Waterville/		
Templemore/Derry City, St Eugene's			Trinity Within & St Patrick's/			Dromod	Kerry	191
Cathedral &			Holy Trinity			Westland Row	Dublin	42
St Columba's	Derry	140	Cathedral	Waterford	261	Westport/Aughaval	Tuam	93
Templemore/Straide	Achonry	100	Tuam/Cathedral of			Wexford	Ferns	176
Templeogue	Dublin	54	the Assumption	Tuam	93	Whiteabbey/		
Templeorum	Ossory	250	Tuamgraney & Kilnoe/			St James's	Down	152
Templeport/Corlough	Kilmore	221	Ogonnelloe &			Whitecross/		
Templetoher/			Bodyke	Killaloe	215	Loughilly	Armagh	31
Williamstown	Tuam	95	Tubber	Meath	243	Whitefriar Street	Dublin	54
Templetown			Tubber/Kilkeedy	Killaloe	214	Whitehouse	Down	152
& Poulfur	Ferns	177	Tubbercurry/			Wicklow	Dublin	54
Templetuohy	Cashel	85	Cloonacool	Achonry	100	Williamstown/		
Tempo/Pobal	Clogher	112	Tulla	Killaloe	214	Templetoher	Tuam	95
Terenure	Dublin	54	Tullaherin	Ossory	250	Willington	Dublin	54
Termon/Gartan &			Tullamore	Meath	243	Wilton, St Joseph's	Cork & Ross	132
Termon	Raphoe	257	Tullaroan	Ossory	250	Windgap	Ossory	251
Termonamongan/			Tullow	Kildare	204	Woodford	Clonfert	116
Aghyaran	Derry	140	Tullycorbet/Ballybay	Clogher	110			
Termoneeny and part of Maghera/			Tullyfern & Killygarvan/			**Y**		
Lavey	Derry	142	Rathmullan	Raphoe	257	Yellow Walls,		
Termonfeckin	Armagh	31	Tullylish	Dromore	166	Malahide	Dublin	54
Termonmaguirc/			Tulsk/Ogulla & Baslic	Elphin	171	Youghal	Cloyne	122
Carrickmore, Loughmacrory			Tuogh/Beaufort	Kerry	189	Youghalarra/		
& Creggan	Armagh	31	Tuosist	Kerry	191	Burgess &		
The Three Patrons	Derry	140	Turlough/Parke	Tuam	95	Youghal	Killaloe	215
Thomastown	Ossory	250	Turner's Cross	Cork & Ross	132			
Thurles, SS Joseph and			Two-Mile-House	Kildare	204			
Brigid	Cashel	83	Tydavnet	Clogher	112			
Thurles, Cathedral			Tyholland	Clogher	112			
of the Assumption	Cashel	83	Tynagh	Clonfert	116			
Tibohine/			Tynan/Middletown	Armagh	30			
Fairymount	Elphin	170						

GENERAL INDEX

A

Abbots, Mitred, 17
ACCORD, 19
Achonry, Diocese of, 98-101
Adorers of the Sacred Heart of Jesus of Montmartre, 287
Aiken Barracks, Dundalk, 305
Aiséirí, Ferns, 179
Alexian Brothers (CFA), 286
America, Irish chaplaincy in, 307
Apostolic Nuncio, Britain, 321
Apostolic Nuncio, Ireland, 15
Ardagh and Clonmacnois, Diocese of, 102-7
Ardfert Retreat Centre, 301
Armagh, Archdiocese of, 25-34
 charitable and other societies, 34, educational institutions, 34, parishes, 27-31, religious orders and congregations, 32-4
Armagh Inter-Diocesan Marriage Tribunal, 304
Association of Patrons and Trustees of Catholic Schools (APTCS), 295
Augustinians (OSA), 267
Avila Carmelite Centre, Morehampton Road, Dublin, 300

B

Benedictines (OSB), 267, Sisters, 287
Benedictine Monks of Perpetual Adoration of the Most Holy Sacrament (OSB), 268
Bishops, of Ireland, 16-17
Blessed Sacrament Congregation (SSS), 268
Blessed Sacrament Sisters, 287
Bon Secours de Troyes, Sisters of, 287
Bon Secours Sisters (Paris), 287
Brigidine Sisters, 287
Britain, Archbishops and Bishops, 320-2
Britain, The Irish Chaplaincy in, 306
Brothers, Religious, 286-7
Brothers of Charity, 286

C

Camillians (OSCam), 268
Capuchins (OFMCap), 268-9
Caritas Christi, 293
Carlow College, 206
Carmelite Retreat Centre, Derry, 300
Carmelite Sisters, 287
Carmelite Sisters for the Aged and Infirm, 287
Carmelites (OCarm), 269
Carmelites (OCD), 269-70
Cashel, Archdiocese of, and Diocese of Emly, 81-6

Castlerea Prison, 171
Cathal Brugha Barracks, Dublin, 55, 305
Catholic Communications Office, 21
Catholic Education Services Committee, The (CESC), 294
Catholic Education Services Trust (CEST), 294
Catholic Education Partnership (CEP), 295
Catholic Primary School Management Association (CPSMA), 19, 295
CEIST, 296
Chaplains, 305-7 see also under individual institutions
Charity of Jesus and Mary Sisters, 288
Charity of Nevers Sisters, 288
Charity of St Paul the Apostle Sisters, 288
Charity of the Incarnate Word Sisters, 287
Christian Brothers (CFC), 286
Christian Education, Religious of, 292
Christian Renewal Centre, Newry, 300
Christian Retreat Sisters, 288
Church of Ireland, 312, Archbishops and Bishops, 313
Cistercian Order (OCSO), 270, Sisters, 288
Clarissan Missionary Sisters of the Blessed Sacrament, 288
Clogher, Diocese of, 108-13
Clonfert, Diocese of, 114-17
Cloyne, Diocese of, 118-24
Collins Barracks, Cork, 305
Columba Community, 139, 293, 302
Comboni Missionaries (MCCJ), 270
Congregation of the Most Holy Redeemer (CSsR), 280
Congregation of Our Lady of Charity of the Good Shepherd, 290
Congregation of the Passion (CP), 279
Congregation of the Sacred Hearts of Jesus and Mary (SSCC), 270-1
Congregation of the Sisters of Mercy, 288
Congregation of the Sisters of Nazareth, 291
Congregations, Rome, 13
Cork & Ross, Diocese of, 129-37
Cork Prison, 133
Cork Regional Marriage Tribunal, 304
Council for Clergy of the Irish Episcopal Conference, 23
Cross & Passion Congregation, 288
CROSSCARE, 41
Curia, Roman, The, 13-14
Curragh Camp, 305
Custume Barracks, Athlone, 305

D

Daughters of Charity of St Vincent de Paul, 288
Daughters of the Cross of Liège, 288
Daughters of the Heart of Mary, 288

Daughters of the Holy Spirit, 288
Daughters of Mary and Joseph, 289
Daughters of Our Lady of the Sacred Heart, 289
Daughters of Wisdom (La Sagesse), 289
De La Salle Brothers (FSC), 286
Defence Forces Chaplaincy Service, 305
Derry, Diocese of, 138-44
Disciples of Divine Master Sisters, 289
Divine Word Missionaries (SVD), 271
Dominican Contemplatives, 289
Dominican Order (OP), 271-2
Dominican House of Study, Dublin, 299
Dominican Pastoral Centre, Cork, 301
Dominican Retreat Centre, Tallaght, 300
Dominican Sisters, 289
Dominican Sisters of St Cecilia, 289
Dowdstown House, Meath, 302
Down and Connor, Diocese of, 149-58
Dromantine Retreat and Conference Centre, Newry, Co Down, 300
Dromore, Diocese of, 163-7
Drumalis Retreat Centre, Co Antrim, 300
Dublin, Archdiocese of, 39-76, parishes, 42-54, religious orders and congregations, 58-75
Dublin City University, 54
Dublin Inter-Diocesan Marriage Tribunal, 304

E

Ecclesiastical address, forms of, 323
Ecumenics, Irish School of, 299
Education, Special Institutes of, 299
Elphin, Diocese of, 168-73
Emly, Diocese of, see Cashel, Archdiocese of, 81-6
Emmanuel House of Providence, Co Galway, 301
Emmaus, Swords, Co Dublin, 300
England and Wales, Bishops' Conference of, 320-21
Episcopate, Irish, 16-23
ERST, 296
ERST NI, 296
Esker Retreat House, Co Galway, 301
Europe, Irish Chaplaincy in, 306

F

Family of Adoration Sisters, 289
Ferns, Diocese of, 174-9
Finner Army Camp, Ballyshannon, 112, 305
Franciscan Brothers (OSF), 286
Franciscan Friars of the Renewal (CFR), 274
Franciscan Missionaries of the Divine Motherhood, 289
Franciscan Missionaries of Mary, 289
Franciscan Missionaries of Our Lady, 289
Franciscan Missionaries of St Joseph, 289

429

GENERAL INDEX

Franciscan Missionary Sisters for Africa, 289
Franciscan Order (OFM), 272-3
Franciscan Order (OFMConv), 273-4
Franciscan Sisters of the Immaculate Conception, 289
Franciscan Sisters of Littlehampton, 289
Franciscan Sisters of the Renewal, 289
Franciscan Sisters, 289

G

Galway, Kilmacduagh and Kilfenora, Dioceses of, 180-6
Galway Regional Marriage Tribunal, 304
General Information, 308-27
Glenstal Abbey Monastic Guest House, Murroe, 302
Gormanston Camp, Co Meath, 305
Greek Orthodox Church in Ireland, 312, 314

H

Handmaids of the Sacred Heart of Jesus, 290
Hierarchy, Irish, 16-17
Holy Child Jesus, Society of the, 290
Holy Cross Abbey, 302
Holy Faith Sisters, 290
Holy Family of Bordeaux Sisters, 290
Holy Family of Saint Emilie de Rodat Sisters, 290
Holy Spirit Congregation (CSSp), 274-5
Houses of Study, 200
Hydebank Wood College and Women's Prison, 154

I

Infant Jesus Sisters, 290
Inter-Church Centre, Belfast, 312
Intercom, 21
International Military Pilgrimage to Lourdes, 305
Ireland's Cardinals, 316
Irish Chaplaincy in Britain, The, 306
Irish Council of Churches, 312-15
Irish Episcopal Council for Emigrants, 20
Irish Episcopal Council for Immigrants, 20
Irish Episcopal Council for Liturgy, 22
Irish Episcopal Conference, 17
Irish School of Ecumenics, 299
Irish School of Evangelisation (ISOE) 76

J

James Stephens Barracks, Kilkenny, 305
Jesuits (SJ), 275-6
Jesuit Communication Centre, 275
Jesus and Mary, Congregation of, 290
John Paul II Centre, Killarney, 301

K

Kerry, Diocese of, 187-94
Kildare and Leighlin, Diocese of, 199-206
Kilfenora, Diocese of, see under Galway

Killala, Diocese of, 207-10
Killaloe, Diocese of, 211-18
Kilmacduagh, Diocese of, see under Galway
Kilmore, Diocese of, 219-24

L

La Retraite Sisters, 290
La Sainte Union des Sacres Coeurs, 290
La Salle Pastoral Centre, Portlaoise, 301
La Verna, Drumshanbo, 302
Lay Secular Institutes, 293
Legionaries of Christ (LC), 60, 276-7
Limerick, Diocese of, 229-37
Limerick Prison, 234
Little Company of Mary, 290
Little Sisters of the Assumption, 290
Little Sisters of the Poor, 290
Liturgy, Irish Episcopal Council for, 22
Liturgy, National Centre for, 22
Loreto Sisters (IBVM), 290
Lough Derg, St Patrick's Purgatory, 113
Loughan House, Co Cavan, 223, 306
Lutheran Church in Ireland, 312

M

McKee Barracks, Dublin, 55, 305
Maghaberry Prison, Co Antrim, 154
Magilligan Prison, Co Derry, 143
Manresa House, Dublin, 300
Marianists (SM), 277
Marie Auxiliatrice Sisters, 290
Marie Reparatrice Sisters, 290
Marino Institute of Education, 76
Marist Brothers (FMS), 286
Marist Fathers (SM), 277, Sisters, 290
Marriage Tribunals, 304
Meath, Diocese of, 238-46
Medical Missionaries of Mary, 290
Methodist Church in Ireland, 312, 314
Mill Hill Missionaries (MHM), 277
Missions, Council for the Missions of the Irish Episcopal Conference, 22
Missionaries of Africa (White Fathers), 278
Missionaries of Charity, 291
Missionaries of the Sacred Heart (MSC), 278
Missionary Francisan Sisters of the Immaculate Conception, 291
Missionary Sisters of the Assumption, 291
Missionary Sisters of the Holy Cross, 291
Missionary Sisters Servants of the Holy Spirit, 291
Missionary Sisters of St Columban, 291
Missionary Sisters of St Peter Claver, 291
Missionary Sisters of the Gospel, 291
Missionary Sisters of the Holy Rosary, 291
Monastery of St Catherine of Siena, Louth, 301
Moravian Church, Irish District, 312
Mount St Anne's, Co Laois, 301

N

Nano Nagle Birthplace, 301
National Association of Post-Primary Diocesan Advisors (NAPPDA), 296
National Association of Primary Diocesan Advisors (NAPDA), 296
National Centre for Liturgy, 22
National Chaplaincy for Deaf People, 41
National Marriage Appeal Tribunal, 304
Naval Base, Haulbowline, Co Cork, 305
Non-Subscribing Presbyterian Church, 312
Norbertine Canons (OPraem), 278

O

Obituary List, 308-11
Oblates of Mary Immaculate (OMI), 278-9
Offices, Roman Curia, 13-14
Opus Dei, 266
Ordinations, 311
Ossory, Diocese of, 247-53
Our Lady of Apostles Sisters, 292
Our Lady of Bethlehem Abbey, Portglenone, 302
Our Lady of the Cenacle, 291
Our Lady's Choral Society, Dublin, 76

P

Pallottines (SAC), 279
Papal Nuncio, 15
Passionists (CP), 279
Passionist Retreat Centre, 300
Pastoral Centres, 301-2
Patrician Brothers (FSP), 286
Permanent Deacons, 303
Perpetual Adoration Sisters, 291
Pontifical Councils, Rome, 13-14
Pontifical Irish College, Rome, 298
Poor Clares, 291
Poor Servants of the Mother of God, 291
Prelatures, Personal, 266
Presbyterian Church in Ireland, 312, 314
Presentation Brothers (FPM), 286
Presentation of Mary Sisters, 292
Presentation Sisters, 291-2
Private Retreats, 302
Provinces, Diocesan, 24

Q

Queen's University, Belfast, 157

R

Raphoe, Diocese of, 254-58
Redemptoris Mater Archdiocesan Missionary House of Formation, 299
Redemptoristines, 292
Redemptorists (CSsR), 280
Regional Marriage Tribunals, 304
Regnum Christi, 276
Religious of Christian Education, 292
Religious of Sacred Heart of Mary, 292
Religious Brothers, Communities of, 286-7

Religious Orders and Congregations, 267-93, see also under individual dioceses
Religious Sisters, Communities of, 287-93
Religious Sisters of Charity, 292
Religious Society of Friends, 312
Renmore Barracks, Galway, 305
Retreat Houses, 300-1
Retreats, Private, 302
Review of Irish Episcopal Conference, 8-12
Roman Curia, 13-14
Roman Pontiffs, The, 324-7
Romanian Orthodox Church in Ireland, 312, 314-5
Rosminians (IC), 281
Russian Orthodox Church in Ireland, 312

S

Sacred Heart Fathers (SCJ), 281
Sacred Heart Society, 292
Sacred Hearts of Jesus and Mary, 292
Sacred Hearts of Jesus and Mary (Picpus), 292
St Aidan's Monastery of Adoration, Ferns, 302
St Anthony's Retreat Centre, Dundrean, 300
St Benedict's Priory Retreat House, The Mount, Cobh, 300
St Bricin's Military Hospital, Dublin, 56
St Catherine of Siena Monastery, Drogheda, 289
St Clare Sisters, 292
St Columban's Missionary Society (SSC), 281-2
St Francis of Philadelphia Sisters, 289
St John of God Brothers (OH), 286-7
St John of God Sisters, 292
St John's Pastoral Centre, Waterford, 265, 302
St Joseph of Annecy Sisters, 292
St Joseph of the Apparition Sisters, 292
St Joseph of Chambery Sisters, 292
St Joseph of Cluny Sisters, 292
St Joseph of the Sacred Heart Sisters, 292
St Kieran's College, Kilkenny, 248
St Louis Sisters, 292
St Macartan's College, Monaghan, 113
St Mary's University College, 157
St Mary Madeleine Postel Sisters, 293
St Patrick's College, Maynooth, 76, 298
St Patrick's Missionary Society (SPS), 282-3
St Patrick's Purgatory, Lough Derg, 113
St Paul, Society of (SSP), 285
St Paul de Chartres Sisters, 293
St Peter's Diocesan College, Wexford, 179
St Vincent de Paul Night Shelter, Dublin, 76
Salesian Sisters of St John Bosco, 292
Salesians (SDB), 283-4
Salvation Army, 312
Salvatorians (SDS), 284
Sarsfield Barracks, Limerick, 234
Scotland, Hierarchy of, 322
Secretariat of Secondary Schools (SSS), 295
Secretariat of State, Rome, 13
Seminaries, 298
Servant Sisters of the Home of the Mother, 292
Servite Priory, Benburb Centre, Co Tyrone, 301
Servitium Christi, 293
Servites (OSM), 284
Sisters, Religious, 287-93
Society of African Missions (SMA), 284-5
Society of Jesus (SJ), Jesuits, 275-6
Society of Mary (SM), Marianists, 277
Society of Mary (SM), Marist Fathers, 277
Society of St Paul (SSP), 285
Sons of Divine Providence (FDP), 285
Special Institutes of Education, 299
Statistics, 317-9
Syro-Malabar Eparchy, 321

T

Tallaght Rehabilitation Project, 300
Threshold, 76
Trócaire, 22
Tribunals, Rome, 13
Trinity College, Dublin, 55
Tuam, Archdiocese of, 91-7

U

Ukrainian Apostolic Eparchy, 321
United States of America, Irish Chaplaincy, 307
University College, Cork, 133
University College, Dublin, 55
Univertisy Hospital, Cork, 133
University Hospital, Galway, 184
Univertisy Hospital, Limerick, 234
Univertisy Hospital, Sligo 171
Univertisy Hospital, Waterford, 263
University of Ulster, Coleraine, 157
University of Ulster, Jordanstown, 157
Ursulines, 293
Ursulines of Jesus, 293

V

Veritas Communications, 21
Veritas Company DAC, 21
Veritas Publications, 21
Verna, La, Drumshanbo, 302
Vincentians (CM), 285-6

W

Waterford and Lismore, Diocese of, 259-65
Waterford and Lismore Diocesan Pastoral Centre (St John's), 265, 302
Whiteoaks Rehabilitation Centre, Donegal, 301
World Missions, Ireland, 22

Wherever the Church is, Missio is there